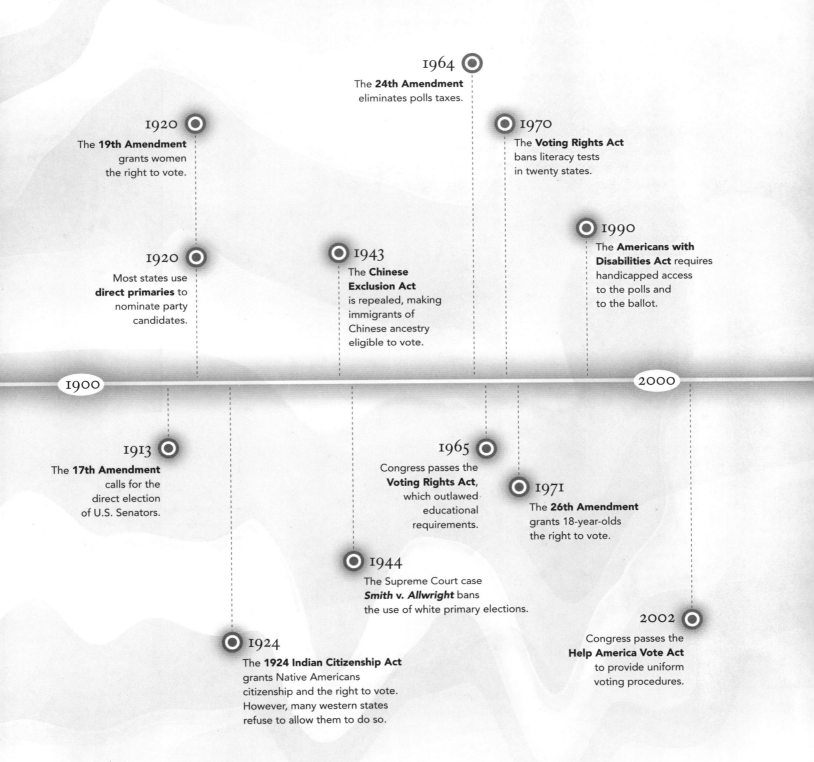

S0-CBR-787

1964
The **24th Amendment** eliminates polls taxes.

1920
The **19th Amendment** grants women the right to vote.

1970
The **Voting Rights Act** bans literacy tests in twenty states.

1920
Most states use **direct primaries** to nominate party candidates.

1943
The **Chinese Exclusion Act** is repealed, making immigrants of Chinese ancestry eligible to vote.

1990
The **Americans with Disabilities Act** requires handicapped access to the polls and to the ballot.

1900

2000

1913
The **17th Amendment** calls for the direct election of U.S. Senators.

1965
Congress passes the **Voting Rights Act**, which outlawed educational requirements.

1971
The **26th Amendment** grants 18-year-olds the right to vote.

1944
The Supreme Court case *Smith v. Allwright* bans the use of white primary elections.

1924
The **1924 Indian Citizenship Act** grants Native Americans citizenship and the right to vote. However, many western states refuse to allow them to do so.

2002
Congress passes the **Help America Vote Act** to provide uniform voting procedures.

* Register to vote now:
See **http://www.eac.gov** for instructions on how to use the voter registration form that appears on the first page of this text.

Voter Registration Application

Before completing this form, review the General, Application, and State specific instructions.

Are you a citizen of the United States of America? ☐ Yes ☐ No Will you be 18 years old on or before election day? ☐ Yes ☐ No **If you checked "No" in response to either of these questions, do not complete form.** (Please see state-specific instructions for rules regarding eligibility to register prior to age 18.)	This space for office use only.

1	(Circle one) Mr. Mrs. Miss Ms.	Last Name	First Name	Middle Name(s)	(Circle one) Jr Sr II III IV

2	Home Address		Apt. or Lot #	City/Town	State	Zip Code

3	Address Where You Get Your Mail If Different From Above	City/Town	State	Zip Code

4	Date of Birth ___/___/___ Month Day Year	**5**	Telephone Number (optional)	**6**	ID Number - (See Item 6 in the instructions for your state)

7	Choice of Party (see item 7 in the instructions for your State)	**8**	Race or Ethnic Group (see item 8 in the instructions for your State)	

9	I have reviewed my state's instructions and I swear/affirm that: ■ I am a United States citizen ■ I meet the eligibility requirements of my state and subscribe to any oath required. ■ The information I have provided is true to the best of my knowledge under penalty of perjury. If I have provided false information, I may be fined, imprisoned, or (if not a U.S. citizen) deported from or refused entry to the United States.	_____ Please sign full name (or put mark) ▲ Date: ___/___/___ Month Day Year

If you are registering to vote for the first time: please refer to the application instructions for information on submitting copies of valid identification documents with this form.

Please fill out the sections below if they apply to you.

If this application is for a **change of name,** what was your name before you changed it?

A	Mr. Mrs. Miss Ms.	Last Name	First Name	Middle Name(s)	(Circle one) Jr Sr II III IV

If you were **registered before but this is the first time you are registering from the address in Box 2**, what was your address where you were registered before?

B	Street (or route and box number)	Apt. or Lot #	City/Town/County	State	Zip Code

If you live in a rural area but do not have a street number, or if you have no address, please show on the map where you live.

C	■ Write in the names of the crossroads (or streets) nearest to where you live. ■ Draw an **X** to show where you live. ■ Use a dot to show any schools, churches, stores, or other landmarks near where you live, and write the name of the landmark. Example — Route #2 — ● Grocery Store — Woodchuck Road — Public School ● — X	NORTH ▲

If the applicant is unable to sign, who helped the applicant fill out this application? Give name, address and phone number (phone number optional).

D	

Mail this application to the address provided for your State.

Revised 10/29/2003

PLEASE HELP US CONTAIN COSTS FOR STUDENTS AND DO NOT SELL THIS INSTRUCTOR REVIEW COPY.

PLEASE HELP US CONTAIN COSTS FOR STUDENTS AND DO NOT SELL THIS INSTRUCTOR REVIEW COPY.

PLEASE HELP US CONTAIN COSTS FOR STUDENTS AND DO NOT SELL THIS INSTRUCTOR REVIEW COPY.

livingdemocracy

NATIONAL EDITION

DANIEL M. SHEA

Allegheny College

JOANNE CONNOR GREEN

Texas Christian University

CHRISTOPHER E. SMITH

Michigan State University

PEARSON

Prentice Hall

Upper Saddle River, New Jersey 07458

NOTICE:
This work is protected by U.S. copyright laws and is provided solely for the use of college instructors in reviewing course materials for classroom use. Dissemination or sale of this work, or any part (including on the World Wide Web) is not permitted. Complimentary examination copies of Pearson Education college textbooks that will not be adopted for course use can be returned to the publisher by using the pre-paid mailing label that is available on our website at www.prenhall.com/returnlabel.

VP, Editorial Director: Charlyce Jones-Owen
Executive Editor: Dickson Musslewhite
AVP, Director of Production and Manufacturing: Barbara Kittle
Director of Marketing: Brandy Dawson
Senior Marketing Managers: Kate Mitchell and Emily Cleary
Assistant Marketing Manager: Andrea Messineo
Regional Campaign Manager: Halee Dinsey
Prepress and Manufacturing Manager: Nick Sklitsis
Prepress and Manufacturing Buyer: Mary Ann Gloriande
Editor-in-Chief/Development: Rochelle Diogenes
Development Editor: Susanna Lesan
Copyeditor: Bruce Emmer
Proofreaders: Barbara DeVries and Susan Plog
Development Intern: Elyse Levesque
Associate Editor: Rob DeGeorge
Production Editor: Cheryl Keenan

Production Assistant: Marlene Gassler
Editorial Assistant: Jennifer Murphy
Marketing Assistant: Jennifer Lang
Creative Design Director: Leslie Osher
Art Directors: Anne Bonanno Nieglos/Kathy Mrozek
Interior and Cover Design: Anne DeMarinis
Line Art Illustration: Mirella Signoretto
Director, Image Resource Center: Melinda Lee Patelli
Manager, Rights and Permissions: Zina Arabia
Manager, Visual Research: Beth Brenzel
Manager, Cover Visual Research and Permissions: Karen Sanatar
Image Permissions Coordinators: Richard Rodrigues and Cynthia Vincenti
Photo Researcher: Carousel Research, Inc.
Media Editor: Shannon Gattens
Cover Art: Scott Bookman; Katvan Studios/Workbookstock

This book was set in 10/13 Adobe Caslon Regular by Pine Tree Composition, Inc. and was printed and bound by Courier/Kendalville. The cover was printed by The Lehigh Press.

For permission to use copyrighted material, grateful acknowledgment is made to the copyright holders listed on page C-1, which is considered an extension of this copyright page.

Copyright © 2007 by Pearson Education, Inc.,
Upper Saddle River, New Jersey 07458

Pearson Prentice Hall. All rights reserved. Printed in the United States of America. This publication is protected by Copyright and permission should be obtained from the publisher prior to any prohibited reproduction, storage in a retrieval system, or transmission in any form or by any means, electronic, mechanical, photocopying, recording, or likewise. For information regarding permission(s), write to: Rights and Permissions Department.

Pearson Prentice Hall™ is a trademark of Pearson Education, Inc.
Pearson® is a registered trademark of Pearson plc
Prentice Hall® is a registered trademark of Pearson Education, Inc.

Pearson Education LTD.
Pearson Education Singapore, Pte. Ltd
Pearson Education, Canada, Ltd
Pearson Education–Japan
Pearson Education Australia PTY, Limited

Pearson Education North Asia Ltd
Pearson Educación de Mexico, S.A. de C.V
Pearson Education Malaysia, Pte. Ltd
Pearson Education, Upper Saddle River, New Jersey

10 9 8 7 6 5 4 3 2 1

contents

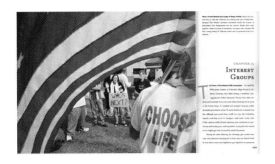

participate . . .

Living **Democracy** fulfills an important need in today's classroom: it inspires students to want to learn about American Government. Through a clear, engaging overview of the dynamics of the American political system—and a passionate emphasis on political participation—the text provides students with knowledge that they can use long after they leave the classroom.

Each chapter begins with an engaging anecdote that grabs the reader's attention. These chapter-opening stories provide tangible links between popular culture and the political process, helping students relate to the material.

CHAPTER 5

CIVIL LIBERTIES

Restrictions on Freedom of Speech   On May 3, 2003, a caravan of cars drove to Crawford, Texas, from Austin. The vehicles contained dozens of people who hoped to stage a protest against President George W. Bush during his visit to his ranch. Many of the protesters carried signs with such slogans as "Give Peace a Chance!" and "Impeach Bush!"[1] As they approached Crawford, the would-be protesters found the road blocked by thirty-five police officers, who ordered them to disperse and threatened them with arrest for failing to obey a city ordinance against staging demonstrations without a permit. Under the ordinance, anyone wishing to stage a "procession, parade, or demonstration" in Crawford, Texas, must give city officials fifteen days' advance notice, obtain permission from the sheriff, pay a $25 fee, and confine their activities to the high school football field. The only exceptions specified by the ordinance

153

. . . in learning

practicequiz

1. "Civil liberties" refer to freedoms and legal protections that the federal government can suspend or modify at any given time.
   a. true   **b.** false

2. The Supreme Court's role as guardian of civil liberties
   a. is spelled out in the Bill of Rights.
   b. is first mentioned in the Declaration of Independence.
   c. emerged in the middle of the twentieth century.
   d. emerged in the Court's formative decades, 1801–1835.

3. Before the incorporation process (which had the effect of nationalizing Americans' constitutional rights), all provisions of the Bill of Rights protected
   a. only against actions by the *federal* government.
   b. only against infringement of *white citizens'* rights.
   c. only against infringement of *men's* (not women's) rights.
   d. b and c.

4. The Fourteenth Amendment, preventing states from "abridg[ing] the privileges or immunities of citizens of the United States," was enacted
   a. during Thomas Jefferson's administration.
   b. soon after the Civil War.
   c. during Lyndon Johnson's administration.
   d. in the wake of the civil rights movement.

Answers: 1-b, 2-c, 3-a, 4-b.

Chapter Review

1. Civil liberties, drawn from the Bill of Rights and judicial decisions, provide legal protections for individuals and limit the authority of government.

2. The Supreme Court originally applied the Bill of Rights only to protect individuals against the federal government, but through its incorporation of decisions interpreting the Fourteenth Amendment's due process clause, it was by the end of the 1960s applying most of those protections to the actions of state and local officials as well.

3. Americans consider the civil liberties contain[ed in the] Amendment, which cover freedom of speech[...] bly, and religion, essential to the maintenance [...] and a free society.

4. The actual protections for freedom of sp[...] absolute than implied by the words of the Firs[...] because the Supreme Court has accepted ti[...] manner restrictions and other limitations that [...] interests for safety, order, and the protecti[...]

Self-assessment tools throughout each chapter help students review material as they work through the text. Practice Quizzes and Chapter Tests offer multiple-choice questions and answer keys so students can check their progress. Discussion Questions prompt students to synthesize ideas from different chapters.

▶ **How did the Supreme Court get involved in protecting individual rights?**

Barron v. Baltimore (1831)
early Supreme Court interpretation of the Fifth Amendment declaring that the Bill of Rights provided legal protections only against actions by the federal government

CIV[...]

must be respected by officials, and there must be judges who are willing to interpret and enforce the underlying meanings.

EARLY INTERPRETATION OF THE BILL OF RIGHTS

During the first years after the ratification of the U.S. Constitution and the Bill of Rights, the tiny federal court system handled relatively few cases. The U.S. Supreme Court was seen as a weak institution that did not have much influence over major issues of public affairs. For example, John Rutledge, one of the first justices, resigned from the Court after only two years in order to become chief justice of the South Carolina Supreme Court, a position he regarded as more prestigious and influential.[3] The U.S. Supreme Court's most important cases from this era involved decisions that defined the authority of the various institutions of American government and clarified the respective powers of state and federal governments. The Supreme Court played an important role in interpreting constitutional provisions in ways that created a workable distribution of power among branches of government and defined the relationships between state and federal governments.

▶ **How did the Supreme Court get involved in protecting individual rights?** The Supreme Court's role as a guardian of civil liberties did not emerge until the 1950s, when the Bill of Rights became a central focus of decisions by federal judges. One reason that the federal courts did not focus much attention on the Bill of Rights was because of the way the Supreme Court first interpreted the legal protections for individuals contained in the Constitution. In the early 1830s, a man named Barron filed a lawsuit against the city of Baltimore claiming that road construction by the city had ruined his wharf in the harbor. Barron claimed that the city's action [...]

The text features actual **student questions** in top margins that serve as a starting point for class discussion. These questions are then repeated in the text where students can find the related discussion.

participate . . .

Living **Democracy** was designed with input from students to ensure a visual presentation from which they will enjoy learning.

▶ The Fifteenth Amendment gave African Americans the right to vote in 1870, so why did we need the Voting Rights Act nearly a century later?

Civil Rights Act of 1964
federal statutes that prohibited racial discrimination in public accommodations (hotels, restaurants, theaters).

Voting Rights Act of 1965
Federal statute that effectively attacked literacy tests and other techniques used to prevent African Americans from voting.

The 1963 March on Washington showed a national television audience that tens of thousands of African Americans and whites were working together to advance the cause of civil rights. Martin Luther King Jr.'s "I Have a Dream" speech on the steps of the Lincoln Memorial is considered by many observers to be one of the most inspirational moments in American political history. How might such memorable events contribute to cultural change?

rarely did events and speeches that occurred in local communities get national news coverage.

In contemporary times, by contrast, the development of communications technology has enhanced the capabilities of interest groups, including those that attempt to mobilize supporters around issues concerning civil rights. National news telecasts create opportunities for groups to organize highly publicized marches and speeches that will be broadcast into living rooms throughout the country (and even the world). In addition, contemporary civil rights organizations can educate the public and communicate with their members via the Internet. Through their Web sites, civil rights organizations can attract new members, solicit donations, educate the public, and facilitate networking between members of different organizations. E-mail permits organizations to send messages instantly and use these messages to mobilize their members to lobby legislatures and organize meetings and demonstrations. For example, the Web site of the National Council of La Raza (http://www.nclr.org), an organization that seeks to reduce discrimination and poverty affecting Latinos, describes various programs and provides information relevant to its constituents. Web sites are important tools for different kinds of organizations, including private advocacy groups (for example, the Equal Justice Society, http://www.equaljusticesociety.org), government agencies (such as U.S. Civil Rights Commission, http://www.uscrc. gov), and university-based organizations (for example, the Harvard University Civil Rights Project, http://www.civilrightsproject. harvard.edu). Check out these Web sites and others that present information on civil rights issues of interest to you. ■

People came from around the country to participate in the 1963 March on Washington to express support for legislation to combat discrimination and enforce civil rights. The quarter of a million participants included tens of thousands of whites.[25] Among the many leaders who spoke to the crowd from the steps of the Lincoln Memorial was the keynote speaker, Martin Luther King Jr., who delivered what later came to be known as his "I Have a Dream Speech," one of the most famous public addresses in American history. News coverage showed a nationwide television audience, the huge throng of people, black and white, who peacefully rallied for the cause of civil rights. A few months after President Kennedy was assassinated, the new president, Lyndon Johnson, was able to use public sentiment aroused by the martyred president's death, as well as growing concerns about racial discrimination, to push the **Civil Rights Act of 1964**

through Congress, despite last-ditch resistance from conservative white southern politicians.

▶ **The Fifteenth Amendment gave African Americans the right to vote in 1870, so why did we need the Voting Rights Act nearly a century later?** In 1965, national attention was drawn to Selma, Alabama, where protests focused on registering African American voters. Many locales across the South used rigged literacy tests in which African Americans were asked to read and explain long, complicated words and phrases, only to be flunked by officials no matter how accurate their responses and thus denied the opportunity to vote. A protest march, planned to proceed from Selma to the state capital, Montgomery, was stopped by dozens of Alabama state police, who attacked the peaceful marchers and beat them with clubs. The brutality of the police attack received significant coverage in newspapers and on television. During the planning for another march, James Reeb, a white minister from Boston, was attacked and killed by a club-wielding mob of whites. The death of the white minister so shocked whites in the North that Selma was flooded with additional protesters, and civil rights advocates gained additional support.[26] Public reactions to the violence directed at civil rights protesters helped push Congress into enacting the **Voting Rights Act of 1965**, the long-sought federal legislation that finally facilitated the participation of African Americans through voting and campaigning for elective office.

CIVIL RIGHTS LEGISLATION

The grassroots mobilization of blacks and whites for African Americans' civil rights helped change public acceptance of racial discrimination, and it lent momentum to efforts to induce legislators to enact new laws intended to advance racial equality. Many of these new laws were directed at discrimination practiced by private individuals and businesses—discrimination that was beyond the reach of the equal protection clause. Title II of the Civil Rights Act of 1964, for example, forbids discrimination by race, color, religion, or national origin in "public accommodations," which includes hotels, restaurants, gas stations, movie theaters, and sports stadiums.

The Voting Rights Act of 1965 was not the first congressional legislation that sought to prevent the racial discrimination that limited African Americans' access to the ballot—discrimination that the Fifteenth Amendment had sought to outlaw back in 1870. The Civil Rights Acts of 1957, 1960, and 1964 all contained provisions aimed at barriers to voting. However, they all proved ineffective because they relied on litigation for enforcement, while

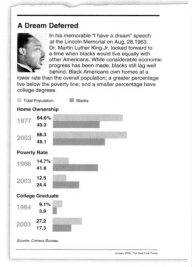

A Dream Deferred

In his memorable "I have a dream" speech at the Lincoln Memorial on Aug. 28, 1963, Dr. Martin Luther King Jr. looked forward to a time when blacks would live equally with other Americans. While considerable economic progress has been made, blacks still lag well behind. Black Americans own homes at a lower rate than the overall population; a greater percentage live below the poverty line; and a smaller percentage have college degrees.

☐ Total Population   ■ Blacks

Home Ownership
1977 64.6% / 43.3
2003 68.3 / 48.1

Poverty Rate
1966 14.7% / 41.8
2003 12.5 / 24.4

College Graduate
1964 9.1% / 3.9
2003 27.2 / 17.3

Source: Census Bureau

January 2005, The New York Times

FIGURE 6.2
A Dream Deferred

Although the measures displayed in this figure show progress, this progress occurred very slowly over the span of two decades and significant gaps still remain. Are there actions that the government can take to speed up the process of attaining equality in the measures? Should the government take such actions?

The text features numerous **compelling photos** that were selected by students to accompany important concepts in the text.

. . . in learning

306 CHAPTER EIGHT THE PRESIDENCY

FIGURE 8.1

Scandals Reach the White House

One of the concerns of the Anti-Federalists was that corruption would seep into the executive branch—and because presidents are vested with law enforcement powers, it would go unchecked. This *New York Times* figure highlights two scandals: the Iran Contra Affair and Watergate. Since then, special prosecutors have taken aim at people tied to the executive office more than 20 times. What do all of these scandals say about presidential powers, and the ability to check corruption in the White House?

The book presents many different types of **graphs and charts,** including more real-world graphics than other texts. The presentation of information in a variety of formats helps students grasp key concepts.

participate . . .

Living **Democracy** includes a variety of engaging features that foster in-class participation and discussion. Additionally, the book offers activities that encourage students to apply key concepts outside the classroom.

Conclusion

Civil liberties are an especially important part of the governing system in the United States. They reflect the high value that the U.S. Constitution accords to personal liberty, individualism, and limited government. The Bill of Rights, as well as other provisions in the federal Constitution and the state constitutions, defines legal protections for individuals and at the same time imposes limitations on what government can do to individuals. The specific civil liberties enjoyed by individuals are defined and changed through decisions by judges that interpret constitutional provisions. As you saw with respect to the right to privacy, judges may use flexible approaches to interpretation that enable them to recognize new rights and expand or shrink existing rights.

The Supreme Court and other courts will face new issues that arise from changing developments in society, such as post-9/11 questions concerning whether suspected terrorists in government custody are entitled to the protections of the Bill of Rights and how far the government can go in conducting warrantless wiretaps of people suspected of being in contact with terrorist organizations. The ever-changing world in which we live continually produces conflicts between individuals and government that lead to battles in the court pathway. Judges are therefore likely to remain highly influential in determining aspects of public policy related to civil liberties issues.

The changing nature of civil liberties issues highlights the importance of the court pathway for shaping law and changing public policy. Litigants present their arguments in court in the hope of persuading judges to issue new decisions that revise the meaning of constitutional rights and advance specific policy goals. Because many of the issues presented in the court pathway are extremely controversial, such as school prayer, abortion, pornogra-

who are disappointed by judges' decisions often raise questions about the extent of proper judicial authority and whether judges' decisions have "gone too far." These controversies have also made the process of nominating and confirming appointments to federal court positions, especially to the Supreme Court, a matter of high-stakes politics. Americans' lack of agreement about the meaning of the Bill of Rights guarantees that these debates will continue and that presidents will attempt to use their appointment powers in ways that seek to influence civil liberties cases through the selection of federal judges who share a particular president's values and beliefs.

YOUR turn!

The case mentioned in this chapter concerning student-led prayers at football games began with the actions of students. Students who are knowledgeable about First Amendment rights are well positioned to identify situations in which they believe that their rights or those of other students have been violated. Courts are passive institutions that do not actively jump into controversies. Thus civil liberties disputes are clarified in the court pathway only when knowledgeable citizens challenge laws through their actions or bring forward lawsuits that address important issues for society.

To learn about contemporary issues and viewpoints on civil liberties, examine the Web sites of two organizations that often use the court pathway to advance very different perspectives on civil liberties. Go to the Web site of the Pacific Justice Institute (**http://www.pacificjustice.org**) and compare its positions with those of the American Civil Liberties Union (**http://www.aclu.org**). What issues in your community or on your campus might be of interest to either of these organizations?

At the end of each chapter, YOUR turn! suggested activities challenge students to take on a project that requires them to apply the information they've learned to a real-world situation.

. . . in the classroom

discussion questions

1. What restrictions on speech are permissible under the Supreme Court's interpretations of the First Amendment? Do you agree with these restrictions?

2. Should people be prosecuted for expressing their views about politics and public affairs? If so, under what circumstances should this occur?

what YOU can do!

Find out what restrictions and regulations exist concerning public protests in your community or on your campus. Look in your college's student handbook for rules for behavior. See if your community's municipal ordinances are available online. Are these regulations too restrictive? If you wanted to organize a public protest, would the regulations prevent you from doing so?

board had violated Tinker's First Amendment rights (*Tinker* v. *Des Moines Independent Community School District,* 1969).

Tinker later became a nurse at a Veterans Administration hospital. Although she opposed the Vietnam War, she considered it "a privilege to work with our veterans who have sacrificed part of their lives."[6]

How far has the Supreme Court moved in broadening the concept of freedom of speech? In 1989, the Court considered the case of Gregory Johnson, a protester at the 1984 Republican National Convention, who burned an American flag during a political demonstration. He was convicted under a Texas law prohibiting flag desecration. However, a five-justice majority on the U.S. Supreme Court overturned his conviction by declaring that burning the flag is symbolic speech, a protected form of political expression that falls within the coverage of the First Amendment (***Texas v. Johnson,*** 1989). In the words of Justice William Brennan, who wrote the majority opinion, "If there is a bedrock principle underlying the First Amendment, it is that the Government may not prohibit the expression of an idea simply because society finds the idea itself offensive or disagreeable." The Court's decision aroused anger in many segments of American society and spurred members of Congress to propose

The Ku Klux Klan is an organization founded after the Civil War to use violence to terrorize African Americans. As shown in the photo of a 1998 Klan demonstration in Texas, when the

what YOU can do! features prompt students to explore politics on a local level— on campus and in their local governments. Included throughout each chapter, **discussion questions** prompt students to consider course material in a more conceptual way and provide opportunities for class discussion.

participate . . .

Living Democracy provides students with the means—and the inspiration—to participate directly in the political process. Recurring *Pathways* features help students understand the dynamic nature of the American political system—and their ability to make a difference.

Pathways appear within the narrative—rather than set off in boxes—making it more likely that students will read these enriching passages.

pathways past and present

pathways profile

pathways of action

pathways of action
CRUEL AND UNUSUAL PUNISHMENTS

At first, the Eighth Amendment's prohibition of "cruel and unusual punishments" merely meant that the *federal* government could not impose torturous punishments on offenders who committed *federal* crimes. As individuals pursued their cases through the court pathway, the Supreme Court eventually broadened its conception of this Eighth Amendment right. In 1910, the Court expanded the definition to include punishments that are disproportionate to the crime, as well as punishments that are similar to torture (*Weems v. United States*). The 1910 case concerned a man sentenced to fifteen years at hard labor in ankle chains, plus the loss of citizenship rights, for stealing a small amount of money. Later, another individual's case led to the incorporation of the Eighth Amendment into the Fourteenth Amendment due process clause for application against the states (*Robinson v. California*, 1962). Eventually, additional cases led the Supreme Court to include limited rights for prisoners to receive medical care and food, as well as issues concerning the administration of the death penalty. In 2005, for example, an appeal on behalf of Christopher Simmons, who confessed to a vicious kidnapping and murder at the age of 17, convinced the Supreme Court to declare that the prohibition on "cruel and unusual punishments" bars the imposition of the death penalty for crimes committed by offenders under the age of 18 (*Roper v. Simmons*). Through the use of the court pathway, individual provisions of the Bill of Rights may be interpreted and reinterpreted by judges to either expand or reduce the legal protections provided by the Constitution. During the twentieth century, such interpretations led to an expansion of the protections provided by the Eighth Amendment. The words *cruel and unusual punishments* did not change, but the interpretation and application of those words did as judges applied them to a wider array of actions undertaken by officials at all levels of government.

pathways profile
MARY BETH TINKER

In 1965, Mary Beth Tinker, a 13-year-old student at Harding Junior High School in Des Moines, Iowa, wore a black armband to school to express her opposition to the Vietnam War. She was suspended from school. Subsequently, her brother and several other students in Des Moines schools were also suspended for the same reason. Despite receiving numerous death threats, Tinker and the others continued to assert their right to peacefully express their views about a matter of public concern through the use of "symbolic speech" (wearing a black armband). **Symbolic speech** occurs when people take an action designed to communicate an idea. With the help of lawyers from the American Civil Liberties Union, Tinker's case eventually reached the U.S. Supreme Court. In a 7–2 ruling, the Court decided that the Des Moines school board had violated Tinker's First Amendment rights (*Tinker v. Des Moines Independent Community School District*, 1969).

Tinker later became a nurse at a Veterans Administration hospital. Although she opposed the Vietnam War, she considered it "a privilege to work with our veterans who have sacrificed part of their lives."[6]

How far has the Supreme Court moved in broadening the concept of freedom of speech? In 1989, the Court considered the case of Gregory Johnson, a protester at the 1984 Republican National Convention, who burned an American flag during a political demonstration. He was convicted under a Texas law prohibiting flag desecration. However, a five-justice majority on the U.S. Supreme Court overturned his conviction by declaring that burning the flag is symbolic speech, a protected form of political expression that falls within the coverage of the First Amendment (*Texas v. Johnson*, 1989). In the words of Justice William Brennan, who wrote the majority opinion, "If there is a

pathways past and present
SUPREME COURT WORKLOAD

As we saw in LINK *Chapter 4, p. 000–000*, the justices on the U.S. Supreme Court control the number of cases that they accept for argument. Few of the cases submitted to them are accepted. During the 1990s, the justices appeared to make a conscious effort to decide fewer cases, even though the number of cases presented to them continued to rise (see Table 5.1). Many observers believe that some of the justices want the court pathway to be less influential and are intentionally limiting the number of issues in which they will use their judicial power.[7]

TABLE 5.1
Supreme Court Workload

YEAR	TOTAL CASES ON DOCKET	CASES ACCEPTED FOR ORAL ARGUMENT
1980	5,144	154
1990	6,316	125
1995	7,565	90
2000	8,965	86
2004	8,588	87

SOURCES: U.S. Census Bureau, *Statistical Abstract of the United States, 2006* (Washington, DC: U.S. Government Printing Office, 2006), tab. 324; Administrative Office of the U.S. Courts, *Judicial Business of the United States Courts, 2005* (Washington, DC: U.S. Government Printing Office, 2006), tab. A-1.

The interests of the press can clash with governmental priorities when reporters have information sought by the government and refuse to share it with prosecutors and other officials. Reporters claim that a free press can survive only if they can protect the identities of their sources of inside information. Otherwise people would not be willing to provide reporters with controver-

Pathways of Action

explain how an individual or a group has influenced government. These stories help students understand how average citizens have affected change, and how they might too.

Pathways Profiles

provide detailed information on individuals who have made a difference in American politics.

Pathways Past and Present help

students understand how historical events have shaped contemporary politics.

. . . in change

Visual Pathways offer in-depth, photographic presentations of core policy issues.

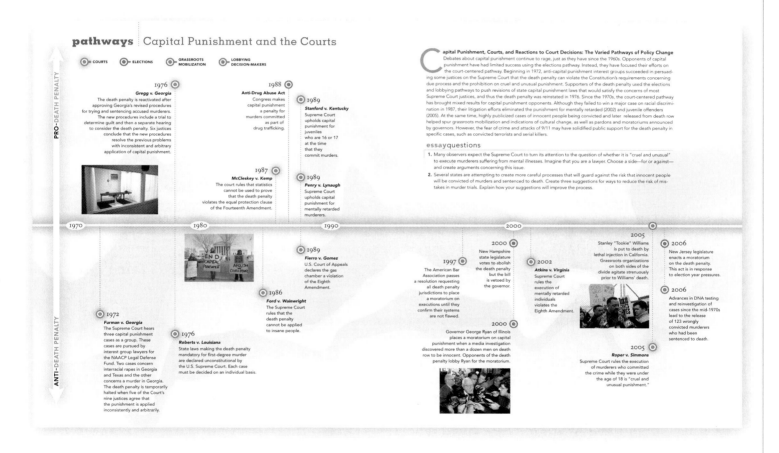

pathways Capital Punishment and the Courts

COURTS   ELECTIONS   GRASSROOTS MOBILIZATION   LOBBYING DECISION-MAKERS

PRO-DEATH PENALTY

1976
Gregg v. Georgia
The death penalty is reactivated after approving Georgia's revised procedures for trying and sentencing accused murderers. The new procedures include a trial to determine guilt and then a separate hearing to consider the death penalty. Six justices conclude that the new procedures resolve the previous problems with inconsistent and arbitrary application of capital punishment.

1988
Anti-Drug Abuse Act
Congress makes capital punishment a penalty for murders committed as part of drug trafficking.

1989
Stanford v. Kentucky
Supreme Court upholds capital punishment for juveniles who are 16 or 17 at the time that they commit murders.

1987
McCleskey v. Kemp
The court rules that statistics cannot be used to prove that the death penalty violates the equal protection clause of the Fourteenth Amendment.

1989
Penry v. Lynaugh
Supreme Court upholds capital punishment for mentally retarded murderers.

Capital Punishment, Courts, and Reactions to Court Decisions: The Varied Pathways of Policy Change
Debates about capital punishment continue to rage, just as they have since the 1960s. Opponents of capital punishment have had limited success using the elections pathway. Instead, they have focused their efforts on the court-centered pathway. Beginning in 1972, anti-capital punishment interest groups succeeded in persuading some justices on the Supreme Court that the death penalty can violate the Constitution's requirements concerning due process and the prohibition on cruel and unusual punishment. Supporters of the death penalty used the elections and lobbying pathways to push revisions of state capital punishment laws that would satisfy the concerns of most Supreme Court justices, and thus the death penalty was reinstated in 1976. Since the 1970s, the court-centered pathway has brought mixed results for capital punishment opponents. Although they failed to win a major case on racial discrimination in 1987, their litigation efforts eliminated the punishment for mentally retarded (2002) and juvenile offenders (2005). At the same time, highly publicized cases of innocent people being convicted and later released from death row helped spur grassroots mobilization and indications of cultural change, as well as pardons and moratoriums announced by governors. However, the fear of crime and attacks of 9/11 may have solidified public support for the death penalty in specific cases, such as convicted terrorists and serial killers.

essayquestions

1. Many observers expect the Supreme Court to turn its attention to the question of whether it is "cruel and unusual" to execute murderers suffering from mental illnesses. Imagine that you are a lawyer. Choose a side—for or against— and create arguments concerning this issue.

2. Several states are attempting to create more careful processes that will guard against the risk that innocent people will be convicted of murders and sentenced to death. Create three suggestions for ways to reduce the risk of mistakes in murder trials. Explain how your suggestions will improve the process.

1970   1980   1990   2000   2005

2000
New Hampshire state legislature votes to abolish the death penalty but the bill is vetoed by the governor.

1997
The American Bar Association passes a resolution requesting all death penalty jurisdictions to place a moratorium on executions until they confirm their systems are not flawed.

2002
Atkins v. Virginia
Supreme Court rules the execution of mentally retarded individuals violates the Eighth Amendment.

2005
Stanley "Tookie" Williams is put to death by lethal injection in California. Grassroots organizations on both sides of the divide agitate strenuously prior to Williams' death.

2006
New Jersey legislature enacts a moratorium on the death penalty. This act is in response to election year pressures.

2006
Advances in DNA testing and reinvestigation of cases since the mid-1970s lead to the release of 123 wrongly convicted murderers who had been sentenced to death.

1989
Fierro v. Gomez
U.S. Court of Appeals declares the gas chamber a violation of the Eighth Amendment.

1986
Ford v. Wainwright
The Supreme Court rules that the death penalty cannot be applied to insane people.

1972
Furman v. Georgia
The Supreme Court hears three capital punishment cases as a group. These cases are pursued by interest group lawyers for the NAACP Legal Defense Fund. Two cases concern interracial rapes in Georgia and Texas and the other concerns a murder in Georgia. The death penalty is temporarily halted when five of the Court's nine justices agree that the punishment is applied inconsistently and arbitrarily.

1976
Roberts v. Louisiana
State laws making the death penalty mandatory for first-degree murder are declared unconstitutional by the U.S. Supreme Court. Each case must be decided on an individual basis.

2000
Governor George Ryan of Illinois places a moratorium on capital punishment when a media investigation discovered more than a dozen men on death row to be innocent. Opponents of the death penalty lobby Ryan for the moratorium.

2005
Roper v. Simmons
Supreme Court rules the execution of murderers who committed the crime while they were under the age of 18 is "cruel and unusual punishment."

ANTI-DEATH PENALTY

Pathways combine photographs and text to present a visually rich treatment of a specific core policy issue. These features conclude with provocative essay questions that prompt students to consider the interrelated forces that affect the democratic process.

your instructor resources . . .

Living Democracy is accompanied by an extensive supplements package that delivers classroom support in a variety of media.

A comprehensive
Instructor's Resource Manual

offers recent news and pop culture examples, discussion topics, activities, assignments, and a list of related Internet activities for students, all correlated content in each chapter. **ISBN: 978-0-13-612930-1**

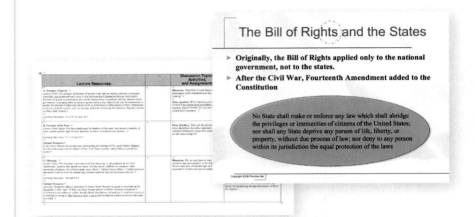

The Faculty Resource CD-ROM contains PowerPoint presentations, including a Lecture presentation that covers each chapter in detail, a Special Topic presentation for each chapter, and a Graphics presentation that includes all of the chapter's graphs, charts, and illustrations. It also includes the Test Item File and Instructor's Manual. **ISBN: 0-13-240831-7**

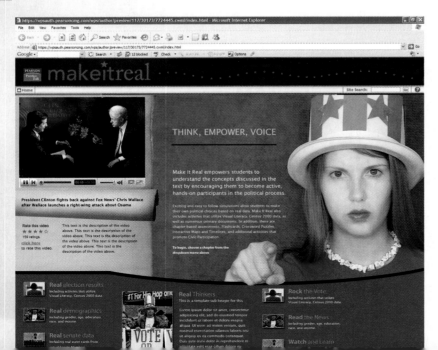

MakeItReal is an online resource that offers provocative activities and simulations that bring core concepts of American government to life. An updated version is now available for use with *Living Democracy*. URL:
www.prenhall.com/makeitreal

. . . in print, on CD, and on the web

MyPoliSciLab is an easy-to-use online resource that allows instructors to assess student progress and adapt course material to meet the specific needs of the class. **MyPoliSciLab** enables students to diagnose their progress by completing an online self-assessment test. Each student is provided with a customized study plan, including a variety of tools to help each fully master the material. **MyPoliSciLab** offers the major resources for *Living Democracy*—including Faculty Resource PowerPoint presentations, Make It Real online resources, and ABC News video clips—in one convenient location. URL: www.mypoliscilab.com

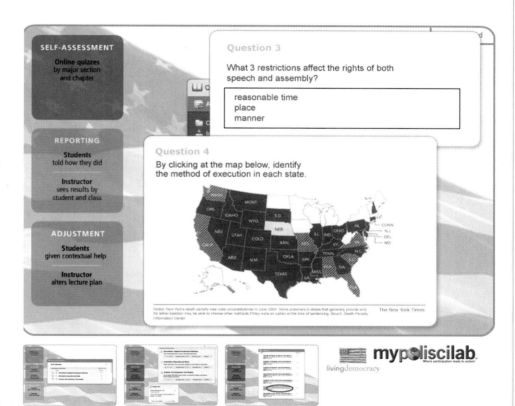

Custom Solutions

It's your course. Why not teach from your book? The Pearson Custom Publishing program allows you to tailor the content and organization of *Living Democracy* to the specific needs of your course, including the addition of your own course notes and original content. Pearson custom editions are available in groundbreaking full color. Visit **www.pearsoncustom.com** to begin building your ideal text.

DEVELOPING
livingdemocracy

Living Democracy is the result of an extensive development process involving the contributions of hundreds of instructors and students. More than 250 manuscript reviewers provided invaluable feedback. More than two-dozen focus group participants contributed to decisions about text organization, content coverage, and pedagogical innovation. Over 750 students class-tested the manuscript prior to publication. Student reviewers evaluated the writing style and visual design, helped select the text's photos, and provided feedback on the in-text assessment tools. We are grateful to all who participated in shaping the manuscript and design of this text.

Adam Newmark, *Appalachian State University*
Adam Schiffer, *TX. Christian*
Adam Warber, *Clemson University*
Agber Dimah, *Chicago State University*
Alana S. Jeydel, *Oregon State University*
Alesha Doan, *University of Kansas*
Alison Howard, *Dominican University of California*
Allyn Cigler, *University of Kansas*
Amy Black, *Wheaton College*
Amy Jasperson, *University of Texas at San Antonio*
Angela Halfacre-Hitchcock, *College of Charleston*
Anne Hildreth, *SUNY Albany*
Anthony Giarino, *Tarrant CC*
Asher J Matathias, *St John's University*
Ashlyn Kuersten, *Western Michigan University*
Baogang Guo, *Dalton State College*
Beat Kernen, *SW Missouri State University*
Bernard Rowan, *Chicago State University*
Brad Lockerbie, *University of Georgia*
Brett Sharp, *University of Central Oklahoma*
Brian Dille, *Mesa Community College*
Brian Frederick, *Northern Illinois University*
Brian Harward, *Southern Illinois University Edwardsville*
Brian Smith, *St. Edward*
Bruce Altschuler, *SUNY Oswego*
Calvin Scheidt, *Tidewater Community College*
Carlos Cunha, *Dowling College*
Carol Botsch, *USC Aiken*
Carolyn Taylor, *Rogers State University*
Catherine Bottrell, *Tarrant CC*
Charles Gossett, *California State Polytechnic University, Pomona*

Charles Jacobs, *Kent State University*
Charles Turner, *California State University, Chico*
Cherie Strachan J., *Eastern MI*
Chris Cooper, *Western Carolina University*
Chris Saladino, *Virginia Commonwealth University*
Chris Turner, *Laredo Community College*
Christopher Latimer, *SUNY at Albany*
Christopher Reaves, *School of Social and Behavioral Sciences*
Chunmei Yoe, *Southeastern Oklahoma State University*
Clarissa Peterson, *DePauw University*
Dana Glencross, *OK City CC*
Daniel Aseltine, *Chaffey College*
Daniel Ponder, *Drury University*
Danny Adkison, *OK State University*
Dave Dulio, *Oakland University*
David Birch, *Tomball college*
David Keefe, *SUNY Brockport*
David Mann, *College of Charleston*
David Penna, *Gallaudet University*
David Uranga, *Community College*
Demetrius Bereolos, *Tulsa Community College*
Denise DeGarmo, *SIUE*
Dennis Goldford, *Drake University*
Derek Maxfield, *Capital Community College*
Diane Heith, *St. Johns University*
Diane Schmidt, *California State University*
Dina Krois, *Lansing Community College*
Donald Dahlin, *The University of South Dakota*
Donald Roy, *Ferris State University*
Donna Hooper, *N. Central TX College*
Dwight Vick, *University of South Dakota*

Eddie Washington, *Rio Hondo College*
Eric Miller, *Blinn College*
Erich Saphir, *Pima Community College*
Evelyn Ballard, *Houston Community College*
Fran Goldman, *Binghamton University*
Frank Hernandez, *Glendale Community College*
Frank Jones, *Del Mar College*
Fred R. Hertrich, *Middlesex County College*
Gay Lyons, *Pellissippi state Technical Community College*
Geoffrey Peterson, *UW-Eau Claire*
Greg Rabb, *Jamestown Community College*
Greg Schaller, *Villanova University*
Hamed Madani, *Tarrent Community College*
Hans Hacker, *Stephen F. Austin State University*
Heather Frederick, *Slippery Rock University*
Heather Wyatt-Nichol, *Stephen F. Austin State University*
J. Cherie Strachan, *Central Michigan University*
J. Eddy, *Monroe Community College*
J. Philip Rogers, *San Antonio College*
James Chalmers, *Wayne State University*
James Corey, *High Point University*
James F. Sheffield, Jr., *University of Oklahoma*
James Newman, *Idaho State University*
James Rhodes, *Luther College*
James Van Arsdall, *Metropolitan Community College*
James Wilson, *Southern Methodist University*
Jan Rabin, *Roanoke College*
Jason Mycoff, *University of Deleware*
Jennifer Hora, *Valparaiso University*
Jeremy Teigen, *Ramapo College*

Jim Startin, *University of Texas at San Antonio*

Jodi Balma, *Fullerton College*

John Ambacher, *Framingham State College*

John Arnold, *Itawamba Community College*

John C. Green, *University of Akron*

John Fielding, *Mount Wachusett Community College*

John Fliter, *Kansas State University*

John H. Culver, *CA Polytechnic State University*

John Linantud, *University of Houston Downtown*

John Roche, *Palomar College*

John Speer, *Houston Community College, Southwest*

Joseph A. Barder, *Robert Morris College*

Joseph Jozwiak, *Texas A&M Corpus Christi*

Joseph Scrocca, *West Point*

Joyce Gelb, *City College of New York*

Judy Tobler, *Northwest Arkansas Community College*

Karen Smith, *Columbia Southern University*

Katherine Nelson-Born, *Columbia Southern University*

Keith Eakins, *University of Central Oklahoma*

Ken Moffett, *Southern Illinois University, Edwardsville*

Ken Robbins, *United States Military Academy*

Kenneth Hicks, *Rogers State University*

Kevin Davis, *North Central Texas College*

Kirk Randazzo, *University of KY*

Kwame Antwi-Boasiako, *Stephen F. Austin State University*

Kwame Dankwa, *Albany State University*

Laura Olson, *Clemson University*

Laurie Rice, *Southern Illinois University Edwardsville*

Lee Rademacher, *Purdue University Calumet*

Lisa Langenbach, *Middle Tennessee State*

Lydia Andrade, *University of the Incarnate Word*

Madhavi McCall, *San Diego State University*

Marian Currinder, *College of Charleston*

Marjorie Hershey, *Indiana University*

Mark Cichock, *University of Texas at Arlington*

Mark Daniels, *Slippery Rock University*

Mark Joslyn, *University of Kansas*

Mark Milewicz, *Gordon College*

Mark Shomaker, *Blinn College/Bryan Campus*

Martha Burns, *Tidewater CC*

Martha Musgrove, *Tarrant County College — SE Campus*

Martin Gruberg, *University of Wisconsin-Oshkosh*

Matthew Eshbaugh-Soha, *University of North Texas*

Matthew Morgan, *Bentley College*

Maurice Mangum, *Southern Illinois University Edwardsville*

Mel Hailey, *Abilene Christian University*

Melanie J. Blumberg, *California University of Pennsylvania*

Michael Bordelon, *Houston Baptist University*

Michael Deaver, *Sierra College*

Michael Harkins, *Harper College*

Michael Kryzanek, *Bridgewater State College*

Michael Margolis, *University of Cincinnati*

Mike Lee Western, *Texas College*

Mitzi Ramos, *University of Illinois at Chicago*

Nancy Marion, *University of Akron*

Napp Nazworth, *Texas A&M University - Corpus Christi*

Nathan Griffith, *Belmont University*

Nikki Isemann, *SE CC*

Pamela Stricker, *Ohio University*

Pat O'Connor, *Oakland CC/Auburn Hills*

Paul Benson, *Tarrant County*

Paul Cooke, *Cy-Fair College*

Paul Davis, *Truckee Meadows Community College*

Paul Hathaway, *Idaho State University*

Paul Labedz, *Valencia Community College*

Paul Rozycki, *Mott Community College*

Paul Weizer, *Fitchburg State College*

Peter Doas, *South Texas College*

Peter Ngwafu, *Albany State University*

Peter Yacobucci, *Walsh University*

Phil Branyon, *Gainesville State College*

Prosper Bernard, *Baruch College*

Randy Nobles, *North East TX CC*

Rebecca Harris, *Washington and LeeUniversity*

Richard Glenn, *Millersville University*

Richard Kiefer, *Waubonsee Community College*

Richard M. Pearlstein, *Southeastern Oklahoma State University*

Richard Medlar, *Dickinson State University*

Richard Pacelle, *Georgia Southern University*

Richard Unruh, *Fresno Pacific University*

Rick Donohoe, *Napa Valley College*

Robert Ballinger, *South Texas College*

Robert C Lowry, *University of Texas at Dallas*

Robert Dewhirst, *North East Missouri State University*

Robert Locander, *North Harris College*

Robert Sterken, *The University of Texas at Tyler*

Rodd Freitag, *University of Wisconsin—Eau Claire*

Roger Handberg, *University of Central Florida*

Ronald Brecke, *Park University*

Ronald Kuykendall, *Greenville Technical College*

Ronald Vardy, *Wharton County Community College*

Ronnee Schreiber, *San Diego State University*

Russell Farnen, *University Of Connecticut*

Ruth Ann Watry, *Northern Michigan University*

Scott Comparato, *Southern Illinois University*

Scott Frisch, *California State University Channel Islands*

Scott Johnson, *Frostburg State University*

Sean Wilson, *Penn State*

Shannon Jenkins, *University of Massachusetts Dartmouth*

Stacia Munroe, *Lincoln Land Community College*

Stephen Kerbow, *SWTJC*

Steve Marin, *Victor Valley College*

Steve Shupe, *Sonoma State Univesity*

Steven Reti, *College of the Canyons*

Susan Johnson, *University of Wisconsin-Whitewater*

Susan M. Behuniak, *Le Moyne College*

Susan Macfarland, *Gainesville College*

T.M. Sell, *Highline College*

Terri Fine, *University of Central Florida*

Terri Johnson, *University of Wisconsin-Green Bay*

Theresia Stewart, *Elizabethtown Community and Technical College*

Tom Simpson, *Missouri Southern State University*

Trey Hood, *University of Georgia*

Victor Aikhionbare, *Palm Beach CC*

Wendy Watson, *University of North Texas*

William Adler, *Hunter College*

William Cunion, *Mount Union College*

William Downs, *Georgia State University*

William Kelly, *Auburn University*

William Murin, *University of Wisconsin-Parkside*

Willie Hamilton, *Mt. San Jacinto College*

Wilson Dr. Ugwu, *Concordia University*

Yan Bai, *Grand Rapids Community College*

acknowledgments

We are extremely grateful to the people at Prentice Hall for sharing and supporting our vision of a new approach for teaching American government. Although it required the work of numerous people to make this book possible, several deserve special recognition. We are grateful for the support of Yolanda de Rooy, President, Humanities and Social Science Division, Charlyce Jones-Owen, Vice President and Editorial Director, and Editor-in-Chief of Development Rochelle Diogenes. Developmental editor James Miller provided wonderful suggestions in an early phase of the project. Production Editor Cheryl Keenan and Senior Managing Editor Lisa Iarkowski deserve thanks for playing essential roles in keeping the authors on track, solving numerous problems, and ensuring the quality and consistency of our presentation. The innovative design ideas that make this book distinctive are due to the creative efforts of Leslie Osher, Anne Nieglos, Anne DeMarinis, Kathy Mrozek, Mirella Signoretto, Scott Bookman, Zina Arabia, Beth Brenzel, Melinda Lee Patelli, and Karen Sanatar. We enjoyed unprecedented enthusiasm and support from the marketing and sales force at Prentice Hall, especially Brandy Dawson, Emily Cleary, Halee Dinsey, and Jennifer Lang. Several people guided the development of the ancillary material, and we are grateful to Shannon Gattens, Jennifer Murphy and Rob DeGeorge.

A special thanks goes to Susanna Lesan, who has a very keen talent of transforming academic prose into material that undergraduates can comprehend. Finally, Executive Editor for Political Science, Dickson Musslewhite, was instrumental in shaping the final book in innumerable ways and he deserves our enduring gratitude for his energy and vision.

Three scholars were kind enough to make significant contributions to the content of the policy chapters: Richard Barberio of the State University of New York at Oneonta, Paul Benson of Tarrant County Community College, and James Hastedt of James Madison University.

Joanne would like to thank her student Haley Swedlund for her assistance and her Political Science colleagues at Texas Christian University. A special thanks goes to her dear family, Craig, Emma and Connor. Chris thanks his wife Charlotte and children, Alicia and Eric, for their support and encouragement. Finally, Dan wishes to thank students C. Dan Myers, Jenna Wolf, Iam McMeans and Kaylin Lowmaster, and his colleagues at the Department of Political Science and at the Center for Political Participation at Allegheny College. And of course a social thanks for the ceaseless support from his dear family, Abigail, Danny, Brian and Christine.

To **Dennis M. Shea** and in the memory of **Rosemary Bowers Shea,** whose ideas and suggestions served as a critical catalyst for this book and whose careers, respectively as a professor of political science and a local county political party chairperson, embody the two groups—American government instructors and engaged participants in the American democracy—whose efforts inspired our work.

about the authors

Daniel M. Shea is a Professor of Political Science and Director of the Center for Political Participation at Allegheny College. He earned his Bachelor of Arts degree in Political Science and American Studies from the State University of New York at Oswego, his Master of Arts degree in Campaign Management from the University of West Florida, and his Ph.D. in Political Science from the State University of New York at Albany. Dan has received numerous awards for his teaching and scholarship and has authored or co-authored several books on the American political process. In the fall of 2002, he founded the Center for Political Participation (CPP) to foster a greater appreciation for political engagement and to develop hands-on programs that bring young people into the civic realm. The CPP develops programs for Allegheny students, for community partners, and for scholars nationwide, and several of their recent initiatives have garnered national media attention. ■

Joanne Connor Green is an Associate Professor of Political Science and the Director of Women's Studies at Texas Christian University. She earned her Bachelor's degree in Political Science from the University of Buffalo in 1990 and her Ph.D. in American Politics from the University of Florida in 1994. Joanne's research and teaching interests include the role of gender in congressional elections and interest group politics. She has published a number of articles in scholarly journals, including *Women & Politics*, as well as other academic outlets. ■

Christopher E. Smith is a Professor of Criminal Justice at Michigan State University. He previously taught at the University of Akron and the University of Connecticut at Hartford. He earned his Ph.D. in Political Science at the University of Connecticut at Storrs and also holds degrees from Harvard University, the University of Bristol (U.K.), and the University of Tennessee College of Law. As a specialist on courts and constitutional law, he has written more than 20 books as well as 90 scholarly articles that have appeared in a variety of journals. ■

Your words can carry great weight. Even in the quiet setting of hearings on the terror attacks of September 11, 2001, the mother of a victim lets government officials know where she stands. In the American governing system, our democracy provides many opportunities for you to express yourself and shape the direction of our nation.

CHAPTER I

AMERICAN GOVERNMENT: DEMOCRACY IN ACTION

American Democracy and the Individual Citizen   Everyone knows that government affects our lives. We must obey laws created by government. We pay taxes to support the government. We make use of government services, ranging from police protection to student loans. It is easy, however, to see government as a distant entity that imposes its will on us. It provides benefits and protections, such as schools, roads, and fire departments. But it also limits our choices by telling us how fast we can drive and how old we must be to get married, purchase alcoholic beverages, and vote.

Would your view of government and your sense of distance from this source of power change if a new law dramatically affected your choices, plans, or expectations? Imagine that you and your four best friends decide to rent a house together for the next academic year. You find a five-bedroom furnished house near campus

For young people, enrollment in college is a giant step into adulthood. As adults, students can participate in our democracy as voters, campaign workers, and even elected officials. Our country needs your participation. Today's students are tomorrow's generation of leaders whose decisions will determine public policy. What do you see as the challenges in participating in this way?

that is owned by a friendly landlord. You sign a lease, put down your deposit, and look forward to the fun that you will have when fall semester begins. During the summer, however, the landlord sends you a letter informing you that two of your friends will need to find someplace else to live. The city council has passed a new ordinance—the kind of law produced by local governments—declaring that not more than three unrelated people may live in a house together. The council copied the *ordinance* from identical laws used in other college towns, such as West Lafayette, Indiana, home of Purdue University, and Springfield, Missouri, home of Missouri State University. These laws are intended to prevent overcrowding in rental housing and to limit the number of college students in residential neighborhoods.

Now what would you think about government? Your planned living situation and social life for the upcoming year might change dramatically. Moreover, you would be faced with the issue of whether only three people can afford the large house. After your initial feelings of anger about the new ordinance, you might resign yourself to the disappointment of moving back into a dormitory or finding a less expensive small apartment. You might also ask yourself an important question: Is there anything that you can do about this new ordinance? A distinguishing feature of democracy, the form of government in the United States, is that people have opportunities to influence the decisions of government. A single individual cannot realistically expect to

control the government's choice of priorities or the laws that are produced. In fact, individuals may fail in their attempts to change laws. In some circumstances, however, a single individual may make plans and participate in activities that ultimately change government and lead to the creation of new laws.

As a college senior, Wendy Kopp proposed Teach For America's creation in her undergraduate thesis. She was convinced that many in her generation were searching for a way to assume a significant responsibility that would make a real difference in the world and that top college students would choose teaching over more lucrative opportunities if a prominent teacher corps existed. During Teach For America's first year in 1990, 500 men and women began teaching in six low-income communities across the country. Since then, some 17,000 individuals have joined, Teach For America has become the nation's largest provider of teachers for low-income communities, and it has been recognized for building a pipeline of leaders committed to educational equity and excellence. ▨

▶ **I vote in every election.**
What else can I do to
influence government?

litigation
act of carrying on a lawsuit

politics
the process by which the character, membership, and actions of a government are defined. It is the means by which the will of a community is determined and implemented.

public policy
what government decides to do or not do; governmental laws, rules, or expenditures that express the government's goals.

▶ **I vote in every election. What else can I do to influence government?**

In the United States, voting is not the only form of participation available to people seeking to influence American government. Let's take the example of the housing ordinance and consider what you might do to attempt to change a law:

- You could encourage students to register to vote and help with political campaigns for city council candidates who promise to listen to students' concerns and get rid of the housing ordinance. In some college towns, individual students have become so energized by specific political issues that they have actually run for and been elected to the city council. These activities, *voting and elections*, are the most familiar forms of citizen participation in a democracy.

- You could organize your friends to write letters and make phone calls to members of the city council asking them to change the restrictive new law. You could also go to city council meetings and voice your opposition to the law. We often characterize these activities as *lobbying* lawmakers in order to pressure them or persuade them to make specific decisions.

- You could talk to the local landlords' association about whether it might file a lawsuit challenging the ordinance on the grounds that it improperly interferes with the landlords' right to decide how to use their private property. You might talk to an attorney yourself about whether, under the laws of your state, a new ordinance can override the rental lease agreement that you and your friends had already signed. If the new ordinance violates other existing laws, then taking the issue to court by filing lawsuits—a process known as **litigation**—may provide the means for an individual's lawyer to persuade a judge to invalidate the city council's action.

- You could write articles in the college newspaper to inform other students about the new ordinance and the effect of the law on their off-campus housing choices. You could publicize and sponsor meetings in order to organize *grassroots activities* such as marches, sit-ins, or other forms of nonviolent protests. All this will draw news media attention and put pressure on city officials to reconsider their decision.

There is no guarantee that any of these approaches will produce the change that you desire. But each of these courses of action, depending on the circumstances in the community and the number of people who provide support, presents the possibility that the government's decision may be changed.

All these approaches are part of **politics.** A more complete discussion of this topic is provided in ⓁⓁⓃⓀ *Chapter 2, pages 36–38,* but for now you should understand that politics concerns the activities and interactions that seek to affect the composition, power, and actions of government.

As indicated by this example, American government should *not* be viewed as "distant," "all-powerful," or "unchangeable." It might be easy to see the government in these terms. When you see a courthouse, a state capitol building, or one of the massive stone buildings that house government agencies in Washington, D.C., it's easy to see these impressive structures as monuments to be revered and admired. Government buildings are often designed to instill a feeling of respect and convey permanence, stability, and power. In reality, these buildings are much more than awe-inspiring works of architecture. They are *arenas of activity* that determine **public policy**—the rules of society and the priorities for government resources and action. In this book, we will treat the institutions of government as much more than powerful entities that make rules for society. We will describe and analyze them as components of a democratic governing system that can be influenced and changed through the actions of citizens. Laws and policies produced by government affect the lives of everyone in the United States. But these laws and policies are themselves influenced by the actions of individuals and organized groups both within and outside of the institutions of government (Table 1.1).

At the beginning of each chapter, you will find "Key Questions" meant to guide your consideration of the material the chapter presents. Some of the terms may be unfamiliar, but don't worry, the chapter will explain them. As you examine the following questions, think about your views on American government. Can you imagine a role for yourself in influencing the decisions of government?

Key Questions

As you read this chapter, please keep the following questions in mind:

1. What are totalitarian forms of government, and how do they differ from the government of the United States?
2. Why is citizen participation important for American government?
3. What are pathways of action for citizen participation?
4. Why is diversity an important factor in American society and government?

what YOU can do!

To see an example of a local housing law, go to the ordinances of West Lafayette, Indiana, at **http://www.city.west-lafayette.in.us/ government/ordinances.html** You may also be able to use an Internet search to find the housing ordinances for your community.

TABLE 1.1
Government Is All Around Us

Doubt government plays a role in your daily life? Consider the following timeline of a typical day in the life of an average college student, and the number of times governmental control comes into play. Keep in mind that this is only the tip of the iceberg.

TIME	EVENT	GOVERNMENT AGENCY
6:22 a.m.	You are awakened by the sounds of a garbage truck outside. Annoyed, you realize that you have forgotten to bring the recyclables to the street last night.	Local department of sanitation; local recycling program
6:49 a.m.	Unable to get back to sleep, you take a shower, thinking about the cost of rent for your apartment and wondering if your next place will have a decent shower.	Local water filtration plant; federal Department of Housing and Urban Development
7:22 a.m.	You read the newspaper, noting that interest rates are going up and the war in the Middle East is going badly.	Federal Reserve Board; Selective Service; Department of Defense
8:34 a.m.	Driving to class, you notice the airbag—and you don't notice dirty car exhaust. You also note that your inspection sticker is about to expire.	Federal Environmental Protection Agency, state and local environmental agencies; state Motor Vehicle Bureau
8:43 a.m.	You stop at a gas station and wonder why fuel prices continue to shoot upward.	Federal government investments in oil exploration and alternative fuels; presidential oversight of the Strategic Oil Reserves; federal trade agreements
9:05 a.m.	You arrive on campus, find a parking space, and walk to class.	State and federal support for higher education; state and federal tuition support and student loan programs
11:00 a.m.	In accounting class, you discuss the CPA exam	State professional licensing program
12:09 p.m.	At lunch, you discuss the upcoming elections. Your best friend realizes that she won't be able to vote because she missed the registration deadline.	State election commission
3:00 p.m.	You receive a paycheck for your part-time restaurant job. In spite of the low hourly wage you receive, a great deal of money has been deducted for taxes.	Federal and state minimum wage laws; local, state, and federal income tax regulations; federal unemployment program; federal Social Security program
4:15 p.m.	You figure out a customer's bill, carefully adding the sales tax to the total.	Local and state sales taxes
9:47 p.m.	You settle in for some television after studying and are surprised at how much profanity cable stations allow.	Federal Communications Commission
11:49 p.m.	You collapse into bed and slip into a peaceful sleep, taking for granted that you are safe.	Local police department; state militia; U.S. military

▶ **What is unique about**
the way Americans
practice democracy?

COUNTRY	RATING	CLASSIFICATION
Canada	1	Free
France	1	
Netherlands	1	
South Africa	1	
United States	1	
India	2	
Jamaica	2	
Mexico	2	
Bolivia	3	
Kenya	3	
Nigeria	4	Partly Free
Afghanistan	5	
Jordan	5	
Egypt	6	Not Free
Russia	6	
China	7	
North Korea	7	
Saudi Arabia	7	

MAP OF FREEDOM, 2005

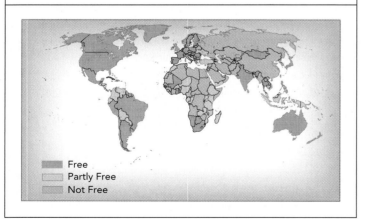

- Free
- Partly Free
- Not Free

FIGURE 1.1
Global Ratings on Political Rights

Do you find anything in this figure surprising,
or are the ratings as you expected?
SOURCE: Reprinted by permission of Freedom House,
Inc. www.freedomhouse.org

5. Which pathways of action have been used to shape policy concerning abortion?

6. What factors are necessary for the existence of stable democracy in the United States?

The Unique Democracy of the United States

The government of the United States is different from other governments in the world; it developed as a result of the specific social conditions, social values, and historical events that shaped this country. Our government and laws reflect the country's history as a group of former British colonies that fought a war for independence, expanded westward across a wilderness through the efforts of pioneers, and that survived a bloody civil war, in large part over the issue of race-based slavery.

▶ **What is unique about the way Americans practice democracy?** Many aspects of American government, such as elections and the right to a fair trial before being convicted of a crime, can be found in other countries, but the organization of American elections and the rights possessed by criminal defendants in American courts differ from those elsewhere in the world. There are other aspects of American politics and government that are unique to the United States. Because democracy creates opportunities for citizens to influence government, people can seek to adjust the design and operation of government as well as to affect the laws and policies produced by government.

If we look at countries around the world, we can discover a variety of forms of government. By classifying forms of government according to two factors, citizen participation in governmental decisions and freedom for individuals, a number of different types of governments emerge. (We'll also say more about this in (L)(I)(N)(K) *Chapter 2, pages 38–40.*) Freedom House, a non-profit, non-partisan organization, makes just such an assessment. Every year it issues a rating of countries according to the extent of political rights (for example, voting) and individual liberties (for example, freedom of speech) that their citizens have. Countries are rated on a scale from 1-7, with 1 meaning the highest level of political rights. Political rights are evaluated based on voters presented with genuine choices, selection of candidates without government approval, a lack of military involvement in elections and government, and related factors. Representative findings are shown in Figure 1.1.

At the top end of the scale are democracies, including the United States, in which citizens enjoy a large measure of personal freedom and have meaningful opportunities to participate in government through voting, organizing protests against government

what YOU can do!

If you want to see state laws concerning crimes, traffic regulation, and other matters that concern you where you live or are attending college, look up statutes by state on the Internet at **http://www.findlaw.com**

policies, and other forms of free speech and political action. All democracies are not identical, however. As we will see later in the book, compared to judges in other democracies, American judges possess significant power to invalidate laws and policies created by other government decision makers. Thus Americans have unique opportunities to use litigation as a means to influence government. Democracies also differ in the organization and rules for their governments.

As a knowledgeable student of American government and, more importantly, as a citizen whose actions can help shape decisions in a democracy, you should seize the opportunity to think critically about the design and operation of the governing system. Unlike the residents of many other countries throughout the world, you can actually use your knowledge and critical analysis to improve your country's laws and policies. Your efforts might be aimed at decisions by local government, as in the example of the controversial housing ordinance. You can also seek to affect government at the state and national levels. The chapters of this book will help you to see how you can actively participate in processes that influence the decisions and actions of your government.

Themes of This Book

American government is complex. The functions of government are divided among different institutions and people. Courts handle certain kinds of decisions that are presented to government in the form of lawsuits. Congress and other lawmaking bodies handle other kinds of matters. And the President bears responsibility for additional matters, such as military affairs. In some countries, a national government creates law and public policy to handle all issues and priorities for its people. In the United States, by contrast, there are multiple governments. In addition to the familiar institutions of national government, including the President, Congress, and the United States Supreme Court, there are parallel institutions and actors in all fifty states, plus additional agencies and actors in cities, counties, and townships within each state. Although this book primarily focuses on the national government that affects the lives of people throughout the country, you must remain aware of the importance of laws and policies produced by other levels of government. The city housing ordinance described in the opening of the chapter is just as much a law that people are required to obey as is any law initiated by the President and enacted by Congress. But the ordinance applies only to people within the city's boundaries.

To show you how government works and how you can affect the way it works, this text first shows the opportunities for *citizen participation in democratic government*. This does not mean that all

Americans are well positioned to participate or equally able to influence the government. Differences in knowledge, education, self-assurance, social connections, wealth, and other resources can affect people's involvement in democratic processes. Second, the text will identify and analyze the *pathways of action* through which individuals and groups can seek to influence law and public policy in American government. This chapter's opening example of the housing ordinance has already provided a glimpse of several pathways, such as elections, lobbying, litigation through the courts, and mobilizing citizen action. These pathways, as well as others, will be discussed throughout the text. Later in this chapter you will see why these pathways are important elements in the stability of the American governing system. Third, the text will emphasize the importance of American society's *diversity and the effect that has on government and our participation in it*. Let's take a moment to consider these three themes in greater detail.

CITIZEN PARTICIPATION IN DEMOCRATIC GOVERNMENT

As we noted earlier, opportunities for citizens to participate in their government are a distinguishing feature of democracy. In nondemocratic governing systems, people have few ways, if any, to shape law and policy. For example, totalitarian governments swiftly arrest and even kill people who express opposition to the central authority, whether that authority is an individual dictator, a royal family, or the central committee of a ruling political party. But the near absence of opportunities for citizen participation and input does not mean that citizens can never do anything to influence the government. The only option available to citizens in some countries is an armed revolt, using violence to change the system of government. In today's world, given the firepower that all governments (and especially dictatorial ones) command, such revolts rarely succeed. And when they occur, violent revolts typically impose significant destruction and human suffering, especially on innocent civilians who are caught in the crossfire of combat or who are targeted for retribution by the government if they are suspected of assisting the rebels. When violence is the sole mechanism available to citizens who seek to influence their government, the results of that violence can lead to very unpredictable and tragic results. Countries may collapse into years of civil war with thousands of deaths. Usually, however, the citizens must endure violent crackdowns by totalitarian governments that will stop at nothing to maintain their grip on power.

In contrast, people in the United States have opportunities to express their viewpoints and take actions to influence the government without resorting to violence. Opportunities for citi-

▶ **What happens if some** groups don't have the money or interest to participate in government? How does that affect the types of policy decisions made?

RIGHT: **Political activists used jarring slogans** in an effort to spur young voters to cast their ballots in the 2004 election. Although voter participation rose in 2004, it is unclear whether young voters will become increasingly involved. What strategy would you use to get Americans to participate more actively in elections?

LEFT: **In 1989, a lone student, whose ultimate fate was unknown,** faced down tanks during pro-democracy demonstrations in China. Because democracy in the United States provides several pathways for seeking to change government policy, many Americans cannot imagine risking their lives in order to seek political rights. Are students at your college actively engaged in the American political system? If not, why do you think that is?

zen participation can help create and maintain a stable society. The chapters of this book will provide many examples of such opportunities. These opportunities for citizen participation will not be fully effective, however, unless people actually become engaged in public affairs. If large numbers of people in a democracy neglect to vote, fail to keep themselves informed about the government's actions, or passively accept all decisions by lawmakers, governing power may come to rest in the hands of a small number of individuals and groups.

▶ **What happens if some groups don't have the money or interest to participate in government? How does that affect the types of policy decisions made?** The quality and effectiveness of laws and policies may suffer if there is inadequate input from the full range of people who will be affected by them. Without knowledge about the lives of the poor, for example, well-intentioned decisions to

what **YOU** can do!

Read about voter turnout issues as described by International IDEA **http://www.idea.int** or the Center for Voting and Democracy **http://www.fairvote.org/turnout** Think about arguments to make to your friends or ideas to suggest to government leaders about how to increase voter turnout in the United States.

address poverty by Congress and the president may be misdirected and fail to get at the actual source of problems in affected neighborhoods. In the same way, lawmakers might make more effective laws concerning financial aid programs for college students if students are involved in providing information and expressing viewpoints about the best course of action. As indicated by these examples, the laws and policies of a democracy can reflect the preferences and viewpoints of a diverse country only if citizens from all segments of society actively make their voices heard by decision makers in government. Look at the comparison of voting rates in Figure 1.2; does this raise any concerns about whether Americans are active enough in shaping their government's decisions? Note that some of the countries with the highest voting rates impose fines on citizens who fail to register to vote and cast their ballots. Would such a law violate Americans' notions of freedom?

Not only is election turnout in the United States lower than in other democracies, it has also been declining since the 1960s, although the presidential elections of 2000 and 2004 showed a slight increase. Even so, Americans seem less and less interested in political processes. Voting participation is just one way to judge involvement, but it is one of the easiest to measure and monitor. It is ironic that the legal opportunities to participate, especially to vote, have expanded greatly during the past fifty years, but at the same time a shrinking percentage of us seem willing to do so.

FIGURE 1.2

(a) A Comparative Look at Voting Rates Since 1992; (b) Voter Turnout in Six Democracies

(a) **Americans clearly vote less often** than citizens in other countries. Why do you suppose this is true? (b) Not only do Americans vote less often than citizens of other nations, the general trend since the 1960s has been toward less participation.

*Percentage of total voting-age population participating in election for highest-level office (president of the United States, for example.)

SOURCE: Reprinted by permission of CIRCLE, School of Public Affairs, University of Maryland. www.idea.int; www.civicyouth.org and Electionworld.org

	Average Voter Turnout*	**Compulsory Voting**
Australia	82.4%	Yes
Austria	72.2	No
Belgium	83.2	Yes
Canada	58.9	No
Denmark	82.4	No
Finland	79.1	No
France	72.3	No
Germany	73.9	No
Greece	86.2	Yes
Ireland	47.7	No
Israel	84.6	No
Italy	88.8	Yes
Japan	57.5	No
Netherlands	72.6	No
New Zealand	77.8	No
Norway	74.8	No
Spain	77.3	No
Sweden	80.7	No
Switzerland	35.3	No
United Kingdom	67.5	No
United States	51.2	No (a)

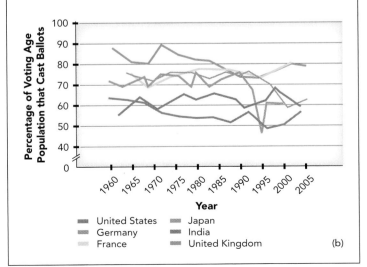

(b)

▶ **Besides voting, in what** other ways can Americans influence government decision-making?

pathways of action
the various activities, institutions, and decision points in American politics and government that affect the creation, alteration, and preservation of laws and public policies.

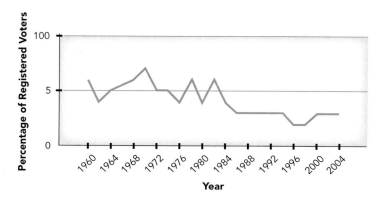

FIGURE 1.3

Americans Who Say They Worked for a Political Party or Candidate, 1960-2004

This figure suggests that since the 1960s, fewer Americans have been willing to spend time volunteering in elections, particularly in more recent decades. Why would this be the case, given that we seem to have such faith in the electoral process? What do you suppose will be the ramifications of this growing disinterest in politics?

SOURCE: The American National Election Studies at www.electionstudies.org

▶ **Besides voting, in what other ways can Americans influence government decision-making?** There are other election-related activities besides voting. Figure 1.3 charts the percentage of Americans who helped a party or candidate in elections since 1960. Again, we seem less and less interested in participating in the election process.

Active citizen participation is necessary in order for a democracy's laws and policies to reflect what people want. Yet there will always be disagreements and conflicts among an active citizenry. Democracy can seem inefficient because debates and competing groups' political strategies can prolong the process of making decisions. As a result, laws and policies in a democracy often represent compromises between the viewpoints and interests of individuals and groups. Active citizen participation does not produce smooth policymaking. Instead, it simply makes sure that a range of viewpoints and interests are presented before compromises are produced.

As you will see throughout this book, getting what you want out of government requires patience and perseverance. Citizens' actions don't always produce desired results. Some people can work

for many years seeking to change a specific law yet never succeed, but that's not a reason to be discouraged. History provides too many lessons about the value of patience and perseverance for us to give up on efforts that seem unlikely to succeed in the near future.

PATHWAYS OF ACTION

Pathways of action are the various activities, institutions, and decision points in American politics and government that affect the creation, alteration, and preservation of laws and public policies. Certain pathways are open to individual citizens who can cast their votes, initiate lawsuits, and organize public demonstrations as a means to influence government. The effectiveness of activities within these pathways may depend on the resources, organizational skills, and knowledge possessed by the people making use of them. For example, people who have a lot of money may be able to use litigation more effectively because they can hire experienced lawyers and carry their lawsuits through all levels of the court system. Resources and organizational skills can also affect people's efforts to conduct petition drives, advertise community meetings, and stage public rallies. Because resources, knowledge, and skill can enhance the effectiveness of citizen participation, powerful organized groups, such as the National Rifle Association, and the Chamber of Commerce, and AARP, are often better positioned than single individuals to achieve their public policy goals through specific pathways.

As you will see, not all pathways of action are equally open to all people. For example, effective lobbying and the use of personal contacts to influence decisions by Congress may require resources and skills possessed only by organized groups and experienced, well-connected individuals. However, because personal freedom in the United States includes opportunities to publicize ideas and form political organizations, highly motivated individuals may be able to gain the resources and contacts necessary for active participation in these less accessible pathways of action. For example, Mothers Against Drunk Driving (MADD) was started in 1980 by a small group of ordinary people with friends or family members who had been killed by drunken drivers. Two decades later, MADD had three million members and exerted substantial influence over national, state, and local policies concerning alcohol consumption and traffic enforcement.

The existence of several pathways of action to influence American government does not mean that the United States is always able to resolve conflicts peaceably. The bloody Civil War of 1861–1865, which cost more American lives than any other war, reflected the nation's inability to use democratic processes to

▶ What is lobbying?
Can anyone be a lobbyist?

resolve the controversial issues of race-based slavery and federal versus state control of public policy. These conflicts ran so deep that they were probably not susceptible to compromise solutions. Timothy McVeigh's politically motivated bombing of a federal office building in Oklahoma City in 1995, which killed 168 people, shows that some individuals and groups reject the give-and-take interactions and compromise results of nonviolent pathways of action in a democratic society. If people have fundamental objections to the nature and existence of the democratic governing system of the United States, they may resort to terrorism. Brief episodes of public disorder and violence also erupt periodically in urban neighborhoods, often triggered by police officers shooting a suspected criminal. These episodes are often attributed to frustration felt by poor people who perceive their opportunities for effective political participation and economic success to be blocked by racial, ethnic, or social-class discrimination. Some participants in these events may simply join a frenzy of theft and property destruction. Others may participate, in part, because they do not believe that pathways of action, such as voting, lobbying, and organized protests, provide realistic opportunities for them to have their viewpoints heard and understood by decision makers in government. Throughout American history, we can identify instances in which people, in seeking to express themselves and influence government, used violence instead of the pathways of peaceful action presented in this book. However, the relative stability of American society and the longevity of its governing system are attributable to the existence of nonviolent pathways that provide opportunities for meaningful participation in democratic government.

The chapters of this book are organized to highlight important pathways of action that provide opportunities for citizens' participation in and influence over American government. Let's introduce these pathways of action. As you consider these opportunities for citizen action, think about how you might contribute to or participate in activities within each pathway. Figure 1.4, on pp. 14–15, shows the ten steps to choosing a pathway of action.

ELECTIONS PATHWAY   American government is based on representative democracy, in which voters elect leaders and then hold those leaders accountable for the decisions they make about law and public policy. If the voters disagree with the decisions leaders make, the voters can elect different leaders in the next election. Because government leaders in a democracy are usually concerned about maintaining public support in order to gain reelection, they feel pressured to listen to the public and to please a majority of the

voters with their actions. Even officials who do not plan to run for reelection or who have served the maximum number of terms the law permits, such as a president who has been elected to a second four-year term, demonstrate their concern for voters' preferences because they want to help the election chances of other members of their political party.

A variety of activities, actors, and institutions are involved in the elections pathway. For example, political parties are important actors in this pathway. By organizing like-minded individuals into a group that can plan strategies for winning elections, political parties can raise money and provide public information in ways that will help put into office leaders who share the party's specific values and policy preferences. Activities in the elections pathway include voter registration drives, fundraising, political campaigning, and each individual voter's action in casting a ballot.

LOBBYING DECISION-MAKERS PATHWAY   Legislatures are the central lawmaking bodies at the national, state, and local levels of government. At the national level, the federal legislature is Congress. States also have their own legislatures, and local legislatures include city councils, county commissions, and village boards. Legislatures are made up of elected representatives who must regularly face the voters in elections. Unlike the elections pathway (the mechanisms by which candidates are chosen to fill offices), the lobbying pathway involves attempting to influence the activities, actors, and institutions of government by supplying information, persuasion, or political pressure. Lobbying activities target legislatures and executive officials, such as presidents and governors, as well as the bureaucrats who staff government agencies.

▶ **What is lobbying? Can anyone be a lobbyist?** In the lobbying pathway, individuals and organized groups present information and persuasive arguments to government officials, aiming to convince these decision makers either to support specific proposed laws or to oppose proposed changes in existing laws and policies. Lobbying occurs in the context of the decision-making processes used by each institution. In the legislature, individuals and organized groups can testify before committee hearings attended by legislators. With the president or a governor, the individual or group representative seeks a direct appointment with the decision maker or else presents information and arguments to the executive's top aides. Lobbyists also seek meetings with legislators, often buying them meals or taking them on trips that will supposedly educate them about issues. Information and persuasion may well be accompanied by financial contributions to the reelection campaigns of legislators or elected executives. Lobbying, in the form

Step 1	Historical Context	It is essential that the activist understand the legal context, the history surrounding the issue, past governmental and political developments, and previous actors. It is especially important to understand the successes and failures of similar movements and the pathways that were used.	Drunk driving and related injuries and deaths are rampant in the United States. In 1980, some 25,000 are killed by drunk drivers.
Step 2	The Trigger	What is it that made you become concerned about the issue? Was it a steady development, where eventually a straw was added to break the camel's back, was there an immediate disturbance—a shock that forced you to become active? In short, what drew your attention to the issue and what fuels your motivation to act?	13-year old Cari Lightner is killed by a drunk driver as she walks down a quiet street. Her grieving mother, Candy, sets her sights on tougher drunk driving laws and in 1980 forms Mothers Against Drunk Driving (MADD).
Step 3	Actors that Will Help	Who might you reasonably expect to help your efforts and what are their motivations? Much related, who are your *potential* supporters and what would trigger their action?	Other grieving parents, those in communities that have seen horrific drunk driving accidents, youth advocacy groups such as Students Against Destructive Decisions (SADD)
Step 4	Actors with the Opposition	Who is likely to oppose your efforts and why? How motivated will they be?	Tavern and restaurant owners, liquor industry, civil libertarian groups such as the Center for Consumer Freedom
Step 5	Timing	When might you best proceed with your efforts? Will there be particular stages to your efforts or a singular bold stroke? How long will things take?	As new data is revealed on drunk driving accidents, after a high-profile event stirs public emotions

FIGURE 1.4

The Ten Steps in Choosing a Pathway of Action *An Illustration: Toughening Drunk Driving Regulations*

In this case, the pathway selected was Grassroots Mobilization. MADD began with a massive letter-writing campaign, attracted media attention, and changed public opinion. In the end, decision makers had little choice but to respond.
*Note: It is critical that the activist understand that the selection of a pathway is not fixed, but rather is dependent upon new developments, successes and failures, and the adjustments of the opposition. Yet, all political action begins with a step down a pathway of action. Also, remember that several pathways often exist to pursue your objectives—if you are not successful using one pathway, look to another. History has proven that diligence is often the key to success.

| Step 6 | **Your Resources** | What resources will you bring to the cause? A partial list includes your time, intelligence, passion, financial resources, networks of like-minded activists, ability to garner sympathetic media attention, expertise and experience in similar endeavors, and much else. | Passion, time, media attention, public sympathy |

| Step 7 | **Your Opposition's Resources** | What will your opposition bring to the table? Will their resources be similar or different? If they are similar, how can you take best advantage of your resources and minimize the effectiveness of your opponents' resources? | Lobbyists, money, long-standing access to decision-makers, campaign resources |

| Step 8 | **Pathway Access** | Even though your resources might suggest a particular course of action, not all issues fit for each of the pathways. For example, there might be no way to pursue a legal course of action. Along similar lines, decision makers might be more receptive to efforts directed down certain pathways. For instance, judges often express indifference to rallies and protests surrounding an issue. | No clear court pathway point of access, yet the cause is ideal for attracting public attention. Graphic stories and visuals are available. |

| Step 9 | **Pathway Selected by the Opposition** | What pathway has your opposition used, and has it proven successful? If your efforts are successful, which pathway will the opposition likely take? | Lobbying decision-makers; elections |

| Step 10 | **How to Measure Success** | How will you measure success? How will you sustain your efforts until success is reached? Be thoughtful in establishing your goals—often success is marked with incremental accomplishments rather than grand victories. Establishing incremental goals can allow for celebration as they are achieved to create and sustain momentum. | New laws passed, data shows a shrinking number drive while intoxicated, fewer are injured and killed by drunk drivers |

boycott
a coordinated action by many people who agree not to buy a specific product, use a specific service, or shop at a specific store until a policy is changed.

of information and persuasion, can also be directed at permanent employees in government agencies who have the authority to create government regulations, such as rules concerning the environment, business practices, and consumer products. Because agency officials do not run for election, any money offered to them by lobbyists would be an illegal bribe. Instead, individuals and organized groups seek to persuade these officials while at the same time lobbying legislators and elected executives to put pressure on the government agencies to advance or block specific policy goals.

Effective lobbying typically requires money and time, as well as other resources such as a large organizational membership to flood officials' offices with letters and e-mails, or personal relationships between lobbyists and government officials, as when interest groups hire former members of Congress to represent them in presenting information and arguments. Under the right circumstances, people who lack resources may effectively influence government by getting the attention of key officials. For example, research has shown that letters and phone calls from ordinary citizens are an important source of ideas for new laws and policies.[1]

pathways of action
ACTIVE STUDENTS AND LOCAL AIR POLLUTION LAWS

When budget cuts in 2002 forced the city of Cincinnati to eliminate its Office of Environmental Management, many people believed that the city no longer had any way to address issues of pollution. At the same time, air pollution in the Cincinnati area violated federal health standards. However, Nithin Akuthota, a 23-year-old law student at the University of Cincinnati, along with another student, Mike Cappel, began talking to environmental groups and city council members to find a way to pass a new ordinance to address air pollution. Council member John Cranley was persuaded by environmental groups and the students that it would be possible to enforce pollution laws without additional costs in the city budget. Without any city environmental agency in existence, the county investigates pollution complaints and refers its findings to Ohio's Environmental Protection Agency. However, the state agency often failed to follow through with any enforcement action against polluters.

Akuthota and Cappel developed a plan for city prosecutors to use the findings from county investigations to prosecute its own cases in municipal court. Thus Cincinnati could combat pollution problems without the expense of creating and maintaining a municipal agency responsible for pollution investigations.

After the new plan was developed, the city council voted 8–1 to create a new Cincinnati clean air ordinance that included the option of pressing criminal charges against repeat offenders. Akuthota sought to make such strong penalties available because companies sometimes find it cheaper just to pay fines while continuing to pollute. Akuthota's efforts demonstrated that students can make use of the lobbying pathway if they gather accurate information about a problem, develop a viable solution, and educate government leaders about how to solve a problem.[2] ■

COURT PATHWAY In the United States, judges have broader authority than in other countries to order the government to take specific actions. Because people in the United States are granted specific legal rights, they can use those rights as a basis for filing lawsuits against the government. For example, if a man was charged under an old state law for the crime of shouting profanity in front of women and children, his lawyer could challenge the validity of the law by asking a judge to declare that it violated the man's legal right to freedom of speech. Such a case actually occurred in Michigan in 1998, where judges eventually ruled that the law violated the man's free speech rights because it was too vague to give him guidance about what words were illegal.[3] Individuals can also file lawsuits asking judges to order the government to follow its own laws. This often happens in cases concerning environmental issues or consumer products, when people believe that government officials are failing to enforce the law properly.

▶ **Can I use the court pathway if I don't have much money to pay for legal costs?** Litigation is expensive. People who use this pathway must hire an attorney and pay for gathering and presenting evidence to a court. Organized groups interested in the issue may use their resources to help people carry their cases through the courts. For example, the National Rifle Association (NRA) may provide assistance to individuals who sue to invalidate firearms regulations, or the American Civil Liberties Union (ACLU) may supply attorneys to represent people who believe that their rights to freedom of speech have been violated by the government. Many important policies have been shaped by the actions of individuals and groups who successfully used the court-centered pathway. The U.S. Supreme Court's decision in *Brown* v. *Board of Education of Topeka* (1954), which prohibited state and local governments from engaging in racial discrimination in public schools, is one of the most famous examples of this pathway in action. The origins of the case can be traced to a lawsuit filed by the father of Linda Brown, an African American girl in Topeka, Kansas, who was not permitted to attend an all-white public school near her home. The Brown family was represented in court by lawyers from an interest group, the National Association for the Advancement of Colored People (NAACP).

GRASSROOTS MOBILIZATION PATHWAY   Highly motivated individuals can seek to attract the attention of government officials and influence the direction of law and policy by mobilizing others to join them in strategic actions. Historically, when members of certain groups in society feel that the government is unresponsive to their concerns (as expressed through lobbying and elections activity), they seek other means to educate the public and pressure those officials. Martin Luther King Jr. became a nationally known civil rights figure in the 1950s as a result of his role in organizing and leading a boycott of the public transit system in Montgomery, Alabama, to protest racial segregation on buses. A **boycott** is a coordinated action by many people who agree not to buy a specific product, use a specific service, or shop at a specific store until a policy is changed. Boycotts were a powerful vehicle of colonial protest against British laws in the period leading up to the American Revolution and have been used many times since then. Boycotts can place financial pressure on businesses and governments that rely on daily revenue, such as bus fares or the sale of products, in order to stay in business. Advocates of racial equality, opponents of the Vietnam War, individuals concerned about restrictive immigration policies, and others organized protest marches as a means to attract public attention and pressure the government to change laws and policies. These actions are seldom instantly successful, but over time they may draw more and more supporters until elected officials begin to reconsider their prior decisions. Successful grassroots mobilization requires organizational skill, publicity, careful planning, and a solid core of committed activists who are willing to take public actions in support of their cause.

CULTURAL CHANGE PATHWAY   The cultural change pathway is a more indirect approach to influencing government. It is a long-term strategy that requires persistence and patience. Through this approach, individuals and organized groups attempt to change the hearts and minds of their fellow citizens. By educating the public about issues and publicizing important events, the dominant values of society may change over time. This can lead to changes in law and policy as newly elected officials bring the new values into government with them.

Until the twentieth century, for example, many Americans—men and women alike—believed that women should occupy a secondary role in society by devoting themselves to the roles of wife and mother. Federal, state, and local laws reflected this belief, and women were generally not permitted to vote in elections and were formally barred from certain occupations. Over a period of several decades, beginning before the Civil War, activist women and their male supporters used newspaper articles, speeches, and demonstrations to educate the public about women's capabilities and the need to grant them opportunities to live and work as citizens equal to men.

In the late nineteenth and early twentieth centuries, women finally gained the right to vote, first on a state-by-state basis but eventually through passage of the Nineteenth Amendment (1920), which guaranteed the vote to women nationwide. But discriminatory attitudes toward women remained prevalent through the 1960s, requiring decades of continued educational work. Gradually, laws and policies changed to protect women against gender discrimination. Eventually, most Americans accepted the idea of women becoming doctors, lawyers, police officers, and elected officials at all levels of government. By 2006, public opinion polls indicated that a majority of Americans would consider voting for a woman for president of the United States. Law and policy changed through the long-term effort to change the culture and values of American society.

The cultural change pathway can be used for a variety of issues, including abortion, the death penalty, environmental protection, and even privatizing Social Security. For people who seek to change society's values, the ultimate outcome of the cultural change pathway can be quite uncertain. Indeed, for some issues, change may occur only long after the passing of the people who initiated the efforts to alter public opinion and social values. And sometimes change never comes.

One aim of this book is to present American politics as a process of continuity and change. There are important structural and institutional components that shape the nature and outcome of participation, and there are numerous actors vying for control, players who operate within the rules specified by government. Yet the heart of the democratic process is the *way* in which individuals and groups seek to affect government.

ABOVE: **Labor union leader A. Philip Randolph** used the lobbying and grassroots mobilization pathways to push the federal government to act against racial discrimination. He took these actions during an era when many African Americans were blocked from participating in the elections pathway. Can you think of any emerging leaders today who seek to use the grassroots mobilization pathway?

BELOW: **The Ditmas Park area in Brooklyn, New York**, is home to a melting-pot of ethnic and racial groups. As in other communities throughout the United States, people must work with, listen to, and accept those who come from different backgrounds. Could a democracy survive if people's sole loyalty were to their own ethnic, racial, or religious group?
Photo: Tyler Hicks/The New York Times

▶ **Who is a good** example of someone who used the pathways to right some wrongs?

pathways profile

A. PHILIP RANDOLPH

▶ **Who is a good example of someone who used the pathways to right some wrongs?**

In 1925, Asa Philip Randolph organized a labor union, the Brotherhood of Sleeping Car Porters, made up of African American workers at a time in history when racial discrimination led most labor unions to limit their membership to whites. Before this, he had founded a magazine, *The Messenger,* that published articles and essays advocating equal rights and an end to racial discrimination. These experiences provided the foundation for Randolph's contributions to both cultural change and grassroots mobilization pathways. Randolph organized protest marches against discrimination as early as the 1940s. His most famous march was the 1963 March on Washington, during which Martin Luther King Jr. delivered his famous "I Have a Dream" speech. The march helped pressure Congress to pass new laws to prohibit racial discrimination in employment, public services, and voting. Randolph also lobbied government officials, and his efforts helped persuade President Franklin Roosevelt to issue executive orders in 1940 that barred racial discrimination in federal government employment and also in companies that held government defense contracts. Randolph made use of several pathways of action to influence government policies concerning racial equality. Table 1.2 describes other individuals who have made effective use of pathways arenas. ■

DIVERSITY IN AMERICAN SOCIETY

This book's third theme is the impact of diversity on American government and on the laws and policies that government produces. Many of the issues facing American government are products of the country's history, and many policy issues that are debated today have their roots in America's history of race-based slavery. Slavery and its consequences, including blatant discrimination against African Americans, which persisted until the 1970s, are at the heart of such difficult contemporary problems as chronic poverty, decaying urban neighborhoods, disproportionate minority unemployment rates, and lingering racial and ethnic hostility and mistrust. Cultural change eventually created a widespread consensus in American society that it was imperative to eliminate overt racial discrimination. Laws and policies, such as the Civil Rights Act of 1964 and the Voting Rights Act of 1965, were enacted in the second half of the twentieth century to prohibit many forms of discrimination that had been endorsed and enforced by various levels of government. However, there is no consensus on how to address

TABLE 1.2
A Sampling of the Political Activists Profiled in This Text

	AREAS OF CONTRIBUTION
Thomas Paine 1737–1809	Political theorist and writer; author of *Common Sense,* which helped define the rationale for the American Revolution. (Ch. 2)
John Marshall 1755–1835	Chief Justice of the Supreme Court whose decisions established the central role of the courts in the political system and supremacy of the national government. (Ch. 3)
Ruth Bader Ginsburg 1933–	Second woman to serve on the Supreme Court; strong advocate of broadening the interpretation of the Fourteenth Amendment's Equal Protection Clause to prohibit discrimination by gender. (Ch. 4)
Mary Beth Tinker 1952–	As a 13-year-old student at Harding Junior High School in Des Moines, Iowa who wore a black armband to school to express her opposition to the Vietnam War. She was suspended from school but later won a Supreme Court case that helped broaden freedom of expression rights. (Ch. 5)
Fred Korematsu 1919–2005	An American of Japanese ancestry who filed a legal challenge asserting that the internment of Japanese Americans in World War II was racial discrimination. The U.S. Supreme Court ruled against him. (Ch. 6.)
Barbara Jordan 1936–1996	The first black representative from Texas; a 1994 recipient of the Medal of Freedom, the nation's highest civilian honor. (Ch. 7.)
Nancy Pelosi 1940–	A congresswoman from San Francisco, the first woman to ever serve as the leader of a party caucus in Congress; outspoken advocate of progressive causes. (Ch. 7.)
Joan Claybrook 1937–	An aggressive, outspoken consumer advocate; head of the National Highway Traffic Safety Administration under Jimmy Carter. (Ch. 9.)
George Gallup 1901–1984	A pioneer in the field of public opinion polling. (Ch. 10.)
Dorothea Lange 1895–1965	One of America's first women photojournalists; perhaps best known for documenting the terrible distress of migratory workers in California during the Depression. (Ch. 11.)
Alice Stokes Paul 1885–1977	An instrumental actor in the fight for equal rights for women; founder of the National Woman's Party in 1913. (Ch. 12.)
Ralph Nader 1934–	Consumer advocate and author of *Unsafe at Any Speed,* about the American auto industry; presidential candidate in 2000 and 2004. (Ch. 13.)
Russ Feingold 1953–	Senator from Wisconsin; architect of campaign finance reform legislation. (Ch. 14.)
George Washington Plunkett 1842–1924	Democratic local party operative in New York City; outspoken advocate for party politics. (Ch. 15.)
Rachel Carson 1907–1964	A leading voice in the male-dominated scientific community of the 1950s and 1960s; author of *Silent Spring* in 1962, which documented the growing dangers of pesticide use in America. (Ch. 16.)
Alan Greenspan 1926–	Former chairman of the Federal Reserve Board of Governors. (Ch. 17.)
Madeline Albright 1937–	Served under Clinton as the first female Secretary of State; former U.S. Ambassador to the United Nations. (Ch. 18.)

SOURCE: www.idea.int

▶ **Which pathways have been useful in addressing diversity?**

other problems arising out of the legacy of slavery and racial discrimination. There have been attempts to apply specific remedies, such as court-ordered busing to achieve public school desegregation, affirmative action programs to increase minority enrollment in colleges and universities, and programs to diversify government employment and contract opportunities. But they have all caused bitter debate and political conflict.

Other challenging policy controversies also relate to the nation's diversity. Contemporary debates about immigration often focus on undocumented workers arriving from Mexico and other countries in violation of American law. While some Americans want stronger measures to prevent illegal immigration, many businesses hire these undocumented workers because they work more cheaply than most American citizens. At the same time, Latinos in the United States have grown in numbers, in 2004 becoming the nation's largest minority group. As noted in Table 1.3, the Hispanic population in the United States is expected to double in the next few decades. Hispanics have also expanded their political power by becoming a significant voting presence in many cities and winning an increasing number of important offices, including mayor of Los Angeles. Many native-born and naturalized Latino citizens are wary of certain anti-immigration proposals, fearing that they may contribute to ethnic discrimination against U.S. citizens while treating noncitizens unduly harshly.

▶ **Which pathways have been useful in addressing diversity?** The example of contemporary immigration policy debates shows how the United States' diverse ethnic and racial composition contributes to the nation's political controversies at the same time that it adds complexity to the mix of actors seeking to use the action pathways that our political system provides. All these pathways—elections, lobbying, courts, grassroots mobilization, and cultural change—have been used by a diverse array of Americans, including women, the disabled, and people of color, who have felt excluded from meaningful participation in American government.

Now that we have highlighted the book's important themes, we'll consider an example that illustrates how citizen participation and pathways for action affect the operations of American government.

practicequiz

1. This section suggests that our democratic system of government is nearly identical to other democracies across the globe.
   a. true   **b.** false

2. Which of the following was *not* noted as a core theme of this book?
   a. Average citizens should become involved in the political process.
   b. Diversity has always been and will continue to be an important aspect of American politics.
   c. There are numerous ways for average citizens to change the course of government.
   d. To be politically effective in our system, personal wealth is essential.

TABLE 1.3
The Face of a Changing Nation

| | PERCENTAGE OF TOTAL POPULATION | | | | | |
	2000	2010	2020	2030	2040	2050
Total	100.0%	100.0%	100.0%	100.0%	100.0%	100.0%
White not Hispanic	69.4	65.1	61.3	57.5	53.7	50.1
Black not Hispanic	12.7	13.1	13.5	13.9	14.3	14.6
Asian	3.8	4.6	5.4	6.2	7.1	8.0
All other races[1]	2.5	3.0	3.5	4.1	4.7	5.3
Hispanic (of any race)	12.6	15.5	17.8	20.1	22.3	24.4

[1]Includes American Indians and Alaska Natives, Native Hawaiians, other Pacific Islanders, and people who belong to two or more racial designations.

SOURCE: U.S. Census Bureau, International Database, Table 094 http://www.census.gov

discussionquestions

1. Why is active citizen participation important in a democracy?
2. What are the various pathways of action citizens can use to influence government?

3. Which of the following was *not* noted as a "pathway of action" in our political system?
   a. The violent disruption of commerce in order to draw the attention of political leaders
   b. Using the courts to redirect public policy
   c. Changing the way citizens think about big questions in society
   d. Bringing like-minded citizens together to protest a governmental decision

4. Even though Americans vote less than citizens in some countries, the good news is that we are more and more interested in other forms of political participation activities, such as helping a political party or a candidate.
   a. true   b. false

Answers: 1-b, 2-d, 3-a, 4-b

Citizen Participation and Pathways: The Example of Abortion

We began this chapter by considering the example of a local housing ordinance and what actions you might take if you sought to change it. We've also provided brief examples of several pathways of action that you could apply in that situation. But citizen participation and pathways of action are important—and available—when dealing with the national government as well as with state and local governments. Abortion is a divisive, wrenching issue that continues to generate controversy among Americans nationwide. Several major institutional components of American government, including Congress, the president, the U.S. Supreme Court, and state governments, have been involved in defining and changing abortion laws and policies. Thus the abortion issue helps show how American government operates and how citizens can use pathways of action to influence the results of those operations.

Abortion and birth control became *political* issues by the end of the nineteenth century as reproductive freedom became linked to the women's rights movement. Some Americans wanted government to maintain policies that forbade abortion; others, wishing to permit individuals to make their personal choices, wanted government to avoid enacting such laws.

Although women gained the right to vote nationwide in the early twentieth century, advocates using the *lobbying pathway* failed to persuade state legislatures to enact abortion choice laws until the 1960s, and then only in a few states. In the early 1970s, however, two

ABOVE: **The U.S. Supreme Court building is reflected** in a protester's sunglasses during a demonstration against abortion rights. Americans are free to use many methods of expressing their views to public officials. Have you ever made your views known to decision makers in government? What were the results?
Photo: Carol T. Powers/New York Times

BELOW: **Planned Parenthood, an interest group** that advocates a right of choice for abortion, prepared signs to mobilize people in opposition to a 2006 South Dakota law intended to drastically limit abortions in that state. Why do activists use various pathways for an issue that was originally defined in the court pathway?
Photo: Carmel Zucker/New York Times

▶ **What other pathways were**
used after *Roe* v. *Wade* was
passed?

young lawyers in Texas volunteered to help a woman who unsuccessfully sought an abortion after she claimed that she had been raped. The lawyers began a legal case to challenge the Texas law that made it a crime to obtain or perform an abortion. The case worked its way through the levels of the court system until it reached the U.S. Supreme Court. In a landmark decision in *Roe* v. *Wade* (1973), the justices of the Supreme Court voted 7–2 to strike down the Texas law as a violation of women's right to privacy in making personal choices about reproduction. Much more will be said about this case in subsequent chapters. But for now, you should understand that the *court pathway* was used to change the law for the entire nation.

▶ **What other pathways were used after *Roe* v. *Wade* was passed?** Of course, opponents of abortion were anxious to move government in a different direction. In the aftermath of *Roe* v. *Wade*, opponents of abortion mobilized supporters and organized political action groups. They used several pathways in their efforts to reimpose legal prohibitions on abortion. In the *elections pathway*, they sought to recruit and elect candidates who pledged to fight abortion. They used the *lobbying pathway* to pressure and persuade elected officials to pass new laws that would place restrictions on abortion that would be acceptable to the courts. They also used the *grassroots mobilization pathway* to organize protest marches and, especially, demonstrations at abortion clinics intended to discourage women from entering the clinics to seek abortions. A few opponents of abortion even rejected democratic processes as a means to seek change, instead engaging in such violent acts as firebombing abortion clinics and assaulting or even killing doctors who performed abortions.

Abortion opponents who worked within the governing system achieved partial success in many state legislatures and in Congress. New laws were adopted imposing restrictions that could discourage or hinder women's efforts to obtain abortions—for example, blocking the use of government funds to pay for poor women's abortions. Laws also limited the ability of teenagers to obtain abortions without informing their parents or obtaining the permission of a judge. States imposed new requirements for counseling women about abortion procedures and, after the counseling session, making them wait twenty-four hours before making a second trip to the clinic to have the abortion procedure performed by a doctor.

Throughout the three decades in which abortion opponents used these pathways to seek restrictions on abortion, they also focused on the *elections pathways* in an effort to elect Republican presidents who might appoint new Supreme Court justices willing to overturn *Roe* v. *Wade* and to elect senators who would confirm these justices. As a result, the process of obtaining the U.S. Senate's

approval of the president's nominees for the Supreme Court became part of the political battles over abortion. Both opponents and supporters of women's right of choice used the *lobbying pathway* to pressure senators to either endorse or oppose judicial nominees on the basis of their perceived stance on abortion. By 2005, the U.S. Supreme Court was closely divided on the issue of abortion rights, with Justice Sandra Day O'Connor casting decisive votes to uphold *Roe* v. *Wade* in a number of close cases. President George W. Bush's nomination of Judge Samuel Alito to replace Justice O'Connor upon her retirement mobilized both supporters and opponents of abortion rights for what both sides realized might be a crucial battle over the issue. After Senate approval of the nomination in 2006, his earlier role as a government lawyer seeking to limit abortion rights raised expectations that Justice Alito might tip the balance on the divided Supreme Court and thereby severely restrict or eliminate a woman's right to choose to terminate a pregnancy.

The struggle between opponents and defenders of abortion choice moved between different pathways. With each legislative success that abortion foes won, advocates of choice returned to the *court pathway* to challenge the new state and federal laws on the grounds that they improperly clashed with the Supreme Court's declaration in *Roe* v. *Wade* that women had a constitutionally protected right to choose to have an abortion. Although the Supreme Court and lower federal courts struck down some state laws as conflicting with *Roe* v. *Wade*, the courts also upheld many laws that imposed regulations while not depriving women of the opportunity to make choices.

In March 2006, when Justice Alito began to hear his first cases as a member of the Supreme Court, state legislators in South Dakota acted quickly to enact a statute that would virtually abolish abortion in their state. Under the law, abortion would be permitted only to save the life of a pregnant woman. Doctors faced criminal prosecution and prison sentences for performing other abortions, including those performed in the aftermath of rape or incest. The purpose of the statute, in large part, was to generate a legal challenge that might ultimately lead the newly constituted Supreme Court to overturn *Roe* v. *Wade*.

If changes in the makeup of the Supreme Court lead to a new decision that *Roe* v. *Wade* must be overturned, supporters of abortion rights will spring into action. They will try other pathways, especially the *elections pathway* and the *cultural change pathway*, in an effort to promote legislative action to keep abortion legal in specific states. Political groups that are strongly committed to a particular public policy do not surrender in the face of adverse

discussionquestions

1. Why are opportunities for citizen participation important for a democracy's stability?

2. What shared values contribute to the stability of the American governing system?

what YOU can do!

Depending on your views on the issue of abortion, you can learn about and provide support for one of the competing organizations involved in the issue, either the National Right to Life Committee **http://www.nrlc.org** or NARAL Pro-Choice America **http://www.naral.org**

decisions by government authorities. They pursue new strategies through the use of the other available pathways of action.

The opposing sides in the abortion debate have attempted to shape public opinion through the *cultural change pathway.* Supporters of choice seek to persuade the public that control over "reproductive freedom" is a key component of women's equality in American society. They also raise warnings about the risks to women's health if abortion is banned, referring to the time when abortion was illegal and women turned to abortionists who were not doctors, causing many desperate women to die from bleeding and infections. Opponents insist that abortion is murder and make use of graphic pictures of both developing and aborted fetuses in their publicity campaigns.

This brief snapshot of the abortion issue illustrates how law and policy develop and change through the complex interaction of the pathways of action and the American government's various institutions. Throughout this continuing battle over abortion, both sides rely on the participation of individual citizens for lobbying, contributing money, campaigning, voting, engaging in public protests, and carrying out the specific activities of each pathway of action.

practicequiz

1. While those in favor of protecting a right to abortion have used the courts to change public policy, abortion opponents have focused nearly exclusively on changing our political culture.
   a. true   b. false

2. Which of the following shapes which pathway of action will be chosen by a political actor or group of political actors?
   a. The nature of the issue of concern
   b. The resources available to the individual or group
   c. The course of action taken by people or groups on the other side of the issue
   d. All of the above

3. Which events in 2006 were regarded as contributing to potential future changes in government policy regarding a woman's right to make choices about abortion?
   a. President Bush's declaration that abortion would no longer be permitted
   b. The appointment of Samuel Alito as a new justice to the U.S. Supreme Court and the South Dakota legislature's action in passing a law that sought to impose strict limits on abortion within that state
   c. Medical research leading to the discovery and development of a pill that permits women to induce their own abortions at home without the knowledge of the government
   d. The Supreme Court's decision overturning *Roe v. Wade.*

4. We argue that the pathways of action have been a critical part of our system for over two centuries because
   a. they have allowed different groups of citizens, at different times in our history, to move government in new directions.
   b. they promote involvement among all citizens, not just wealthy citizens.
   c. democracy necessitates an active citizenry, and these routes help make that happen.
   d. All of the above

Answers: 1-b, 2-d, 3-b, 4-d

Change and Stability in American Government

As we have seen, the pathways of action provide opportunities for citizens to take nonviolent actions to make their voices heard by decision makers in American government. The existence of these pathways is also important for the preservation of the American governing system. No form of government is automatically stable. No form of government automatically functions smoothly. If disagreements within the population are great enough or if a segment of the population does not accept the design and operation of the governing system, then even democracies will experience violence, disorder, instability, and collapse. The American Civil War vividly reminds us of what can happen when pathways fail to resolve controversies. In that example, the divisive issues of slavery and state governments' authority were inflamed rather than resolved through actions in the elections pathway (the election of Lincoln as the antislavery president) and the court-centered pathway (a Supreme Court decision that helped the spread of slavery to western territories—*Dred Scott* v. *Sanford,* 1857). To understand American government and its ability to endure, we must examine the factors that contribute to stability as well as those that help Americans change what their government is doing. This book focuses on pathways of action as a key element for understanding how American government operates. These pathways help explain why the American system of government continues to exist, even after two centuries that included significant social changes and a bloody civil war.

Every nation experiences periods of transformation. These are eras in which new issues, fundamental changes in social and economic conditions, or major events spur adjustments in society and in the priorities and actions of government decision makers. These transformations can also produce changes in a country's system of

▶ **What do you mean** by 'stability' in government?

checks and balances
a principle of the American governmental system whereby each branch of government (legislative, executive, and judicial) has the power to limit the actions of the others. For example, Congress can pass laws, but the president can veto these measures.

capitalism
an economic system in which the means of production and distribution are privately owned and there is little governmental interference.

government. In the 1990s, the world witnessed the emergence of new governing systems in places such as South Africa and the formerly communist countries of Eastern Europe and Russia. South Africa ended its official policies of racial discrimination, known as *apartheid,* and wrote a new constitution that established equal political rights for people of all races, including black and mixed-race people, who had previously been excluded from voting and other forms of political participation. As communism ended in the Soviet states and Eastern Europe, these countries wrote new constitutions in an effort to move toward democratic government and economies based on free enterprise. In the United States, we have maintained the same Constitution and general blueprint for government through more than two hundred years of significant changes in society, politics, and the economy. However, aspects of American governing institutions and processes have undergone adjustments in response to specific developments in society. For example:

1. A flowering of broad-based political participation occurred during and after Andrew Jackson's presidency in the 1830s.

2. Seemingly irreconcilable conflicts over slavery and states' rights culminated in the Civil War of 1861–1865.

3. When the North won the Civil War and thus ensured the continuation of the federal union, it also imposed constitutional changes that abolished slavery and granted citizenship and legal equality to former slaves.

4. The adoption of the Nineteenth Amendment in 1920 granted women the right to vote nationally and helped the United States fulfill the ideals of equality set forth in the Declaration of Independence.

5. In the 1930s, governmental responses to the Great Depression, which included the creation of new federal agencies and programs regulating the economy, combating unemployment, and relieving agricultural distress, put additional policy issues onto the national agenda.

6. Since the 1950s, the political landscape has changed as a result of political battles for equality and rights by ethnic and racial minorities, women, homosexual men and women, people with disabilities, and members of other groups who had felt excluded from social acceptance, political participation, and governmental benefits.

Over the course of history, the number and nature of the pathways of action have changed, as have the identities of participants in politics and government and the issues of public controversy.

SOURCES OF STABILITY

▶ **What do you mean by 'stability' in government?** Stability in American government and in the governing systems of other countries cannot be taken for granted. We cannot automatically assume that governing systems will be stable or remain stable for any predictable period. Stability in any political system is the result of three closely related elements:

- A broadly accepted political and economic framework
- A stable, powerful political culture
- A variety of ways for citizens to seek and achieve policy changes

We will discuss each of these elements in turn.

BROADLY ACCEPTED FRAMEWORK: REVERENCE FOR THE CONSTITUTION AND CAPITALISM   Early in his political career, Abraham Lincoln delivered a speech in which he urged that our Constitution be the "political religion of the nation."[4] We have taken his advice to heart. Indeed, one of the interesting and somewhat unique aspects of American politics is our reverence for the structure of our governing system. Some would say that we treat the Constitution as our nonreligious "bible"—the written document that Americans deeply respect and obey.

This would be a bit surprising to the authors of the Constitution. They planned to compel the sharing of powers among three branches of government. They designed a form of government that divided powers between the national government and the states. They also initiated an elaborate system of **checks and balances** between branches of government. In their view, however, the Constitution was a collection of compromises, ambiguities, and generalized grants of authority to the national government. They wrote the Constitution to replace an earlier governmental blueprint, the Articles of Confederation. If the Constitution had been rejected by the American public or had failed to work well, they might have been forced to go back to the drawing board to write a third version. In other words, to the originators of the country, the Constitution was a practical plan for creating a government, not a set of sacred principles. Yet today Americans express a shared belief in the special wisdom of the Constitution's authors for creating a system of government that would both endure and embody important principles of democracy.

▶ **What is capitalism? Why is it so important to Americans?** Modern Americans' reverence for the institutional framework of

▶ What is capitalism? Why is it so important to Americans?

socialism
an economic system in which the government owns and controls most factories and much or all of the nation's land.

their country's political system extends to their economic system as well. Indeed, the "American dream" rests mostly on the notion that intelligence, ingenuity, and hard work are sufficient for economic success—and for most Americans, economic success is an important goal. Faith in **capitalism** is deeply ingrained in Americans' values and beliefs. Capitalism is the economic system based on free enterprise in which individuals compete with each other for jobs, operate privately owned businesses that may succeed or fail, and focus their efforts on accumulating wealth for themselves and their families. In an alternative economic system, **socialism**, the government owns and controls key factories and sometimes also the land and may even use that control to assign individuals to specific jobs. Socialist systems may focus on the ideal of individuals working for the good of society rather than pursuing self-interest. In the United States, by contrast, most people have always believed that society as a whole benefits through the continuous creation of new businesses, new jobs, and increased wealth when all individuals pursue their own interests and have opportunities to use their own private property and businesses to create jobs and generate income.

The American idea that people have ample opportunities to become economically successful through their own hard work is not always fulfilled in practice. Historically, racial and gender discrimination have limited opportunities for many Americans to find good jobs or start their own businesses. The ability of rich people to provide superior education for their children and pass on their wealth to family members provides and perpetuates advantages that most Americans do not share. The significant power wielded by corporations in the United States and vast disparities of individual wealth—today, 70 percent of the nation's wealth is owned by the top 10 percent of the population, while the bottom 40 percent of the population owns less than 1 percent of the wealth—have led to occasional calls for a change in the American economic system. For critics, the gap between the promise and realities of the free enterprise system is unacceptable. Various plans for a redistribution of wealth to assist poor people have been proposed, for example, through higher taxes on the rich to fund antipoverty programs. For the most part, however, criticisms are focused on specific aspects of the capitalist system, and in recent decades people have rarely suggested that the United States switch to a different system. Support for free enterprise and capitalism remains strong even when critics point out that the United States falls short of its ideals of equal economic opportunities for all Americans.

Americans believe strongly in the core elements of our political and economic system. Lincoln's hope that Americans would

One of the best illustrations of our nation's reverence for the Constitution *and* capitalism is our currency. On one side to the dollar bill we pay tribute to the hero of the Revolution and the first president, and on the other side we find the Great Seal of the United States (front and back). The pyramid symbolizes strength and its 13 steps represent the original 13 colonies. The unfinished summit on the pyramid implies a "work in progress." Do you think the larger message is that our government's fate is linked to the future of free enterprise in America? Or, as capitalism goes, so goes our system of government?

political culture
the norms, customs, and beliefs that help citizens understand appropriate ways to act in a political system; also, the shared attitudes about how government should operate.

Alexis de Tocqueville
a French scholar who traveled throughout the United States in the early 1830s. He published his notes on the trip as *Democracy in America*, that is still widely read.

▶ What is our political culture?

protect their system through an almost religious reverence has come to pass. James Madison and the other founders of the United States would presumably be pleased—and perhaps surprised—to know that the experimental governing system they designed has survived for more than two centuries. They would be doubly surprised to see how Americans cherish the Constitution—the experimental document full of compromises—as the crown jewel of democracy.

POLITICAL CULTURE: THE "AMERICAN CREED" ▶ **What is our political culture?** Scholars have long recognized the powerful influence of a nation's **political culture.** Much more will be said of this concept in ⓁⒾⓃⓀ *Chapter 10, pages 380–382*, but for now simply note that the term refers to the fundamental values and dominant beliefs that are shared throughout society and that shape political behavior and government policies. It is the umbrella under which political activities take place, and it defines the arena where political questions are resolved. Political culture incorporates both citizens' personal values—that is, their ideas about what is right and wrong—and their shared ideas about how they should be governed.[5]

One nation's political culture may be more open and obvious than another's. It springs from a number of sources, including the origins of the nation (sometimes called the nation's "creation myth"), historical struggles in the nation's history, the deeds and thoughts of past leaders, important documents and texts, economic conditions, and distinct subcultures. Religion may also play a role, depending on a nation's history and culture. To some extent, a nation's popular culture, including its entertainment, fashions, and media, also contribute to its political culture. For instance, the counterculture movement in the 1960s (hippie culture) had a direct impact on the political process. And many observers suggest that the portrayal of gay men and women in film and on television in recent years has raised levels of tolerance toward homosexuals throughout society. When some or all of these pieces are missing or are not clearly defined, the nation's political identity becomes less clear. Nations with a strong, clearly defined political culture are generally more stable.[6]

pathways profile

THE POLITICAL CULTURE OF OUR NEIGHBOR TO THE NORTH

Canada has faced a number of difficulties in the past few decades. On several occasions, voters came close to deciding that Quebec, the country's second populous province, should become a separate nation. Quebec is the only province where the majority of its inhabitants speak French as their first language rather than English, the language spoken elsewhere in the country. There are many forces driving Quebec's separatist movement, but even so, the peaceful breakup of an industrialized democracy has been a rare occurrence in world history—it would be like voters in the United States agreeing that Texas or Florida should become a separate nation.

How could Canadians contemplate such a move? Again, there are many forces at work, but aspects of Canada's political culture and history stand out as factors, especially when compared to the United States. When and why did Canada become a nation? Were the circumstances surrounding its national independence dramatic, the stuff of folklore? Canada celebrates its independence day on July 1— the anniversary of the British Parliament's passage of a law that granted the country authority over its domestic affairs. However, many people recognize that Canada's independence actually evolved gradually. The country's authority over its own foreign affairs was not established until the early decades of the twentieth century, and Britain's full, legal recognition of Canada's authority to make all of its own laws did not come until passage of the Canada Act of 1982.

Because Canada's Independence evolved over time, Canadians cannot as easily focus on, revere, and mythologize a founding generation and a set of foundational documents from a specific historic era. Whereas Americans use the eighteenth-century Declaration of Independence and Constitution as symbols from a glorified, revolutionary age, Canada's Charter of Rights and Freedoms (1982) is little more than two decades old, a document that succeeded and strengthened a bill of rights that dates only to 1960. Indeed, some commentators question whether Canadians possess a national identity in the same sense as other countries that have longer histories as nations and distinctive political cultures. These commentators ask whether there is anything distinctive about being Canadian.

In fairness, Canada is a dynamic, progressive, diverse nation. It is a country that consistently ranks near the top of nearly all "quality of life" indexes with respect to literacy, availability of health care, and average life expectancy. In fact, it ranks higher than the United States. But it is also fair to say that our neighbor's political identity is less well defined, and this reality may contribute to a greater risk of political instability. ■

Alexis de Tocqueville (uh-lek-see duh TOKE-vil), a French scholar who traveled throughout the United States in the early

what YOU can do!

To succeed at influencing government, active citizens must often demonstrate that their ideas and suggestions represent the viewpoints of broad segments of society. Can you make a list of goals, values, and beliefs that you believe are shared broadly in American society? Check your list against the results of public opinion polls, such as the Gallup Poll at **http://www.gallup.com**

After the death of former President Ronald Reagan in 2004, people silently filed past his coffin in the rotunda of the Capitol in Washington, D.C. Why do public ceremonies and rituals help to make Americans feel united despite their many disagreements?
Photo: Doug Mills/New York Times

1830s, found our nation's emerging political culture to be distinctive and powerful. In *Democracy in America,* he wrote:

> How does it happen that in the United States, where the inhabitants have only recently immigrated to the land which they now occupy, and brought neither customs nor traditions with them there; where they met one another for the first time with no previous acquaintance; where, in short, the instinctive love of country can scarcely exist; how does it happen that everyone takes as zealous an interest in the affairs of his township, his country, and the whole state as if they were his own? It is because everyone, in his sphere, takes an active part in the government of society.[7]

This American notion of active citizenship arises from a powerful political culture. The essence of American politics, Tocqueville suggests, lies not in the complex maze of political institutions crafted by the framers but rather in the shared values of American citizens. In fact, Tocqueville suggested, along with this powerful political identity comes a downside: "I know of no country in which there is such little independence of mind and real freedom of discussion as in America."[8] The widespread nature of shared values and beliefs among Americans, which was observed by Tocqueville and continues through today, has tended to limit the range of discussions about government and public policy. As with the economic system, people tend to focus on fixing specific problems within the current system rather than suggesting that the system itself should be changed.

American political culture, noted the Swedish social scientist Gunnar Myrdal (GUN-er MEER-dahl) in 1944, is "the most explicitly expressed system of general ideals" of any country in the West[9]—so much so that he saw fit to call our belief system the "American Creed." At least in the abstract, Americans embrace the concepts of "freedom," "equality," "liberty," "majority will," "religious freedom," and "due process under the law." According to Myrdal, "Schools teach the principles of the Creed; the churches preach them; the courts hand down judgment in their terms."[10] According to one commentator, "Myrdal saw the Creed as the bond that links all Americans, including nonwhite minorities, and as the spur forever goading Americans to live up to their principles."[11] Yale University political scientist Robert Dahl echoed this idea a few decades later when he called our set of beliefs the "democratic creed." He writes, "The common view seems to be that our system is not only democratic but is perhaps the most perfect expression of democracy that exists anywhere . . . . To reject the democratic creed is in effect to refuse to be an American."[12]

There are many sources of the creed, stemming back to the very rationale for colonizing the new land and creating a new nation. The deeds and accomplishments of early settlers and those involved in the Revolution are key elements. The nation's founding heroes are celebrated. Their portraits are hung in every schoolhouse and printed on our currency and postage stamps. We also have our esteemed documents. When Lincoln's Gettysburg Address so eloquently reminded us that the birth of the nation was "four score and seven years ago," he was referring not to the ratification of the Constitution in 1789 but rather to the signing of the Declaration of Independence in 1776. Lincoln's Gettysburg statement of government "of the people, by the people, and for the people" defines American values and norms; it shapes the connection of citizens to government and to one another.

There are many things that define the American creed, many of which will be discussed in later chapters. The important point here is to understand that the United States possesses a powerful political culture that is clearly defined and long-lasting. The historical national consensus on political values and democratic institutions helped create stability during times of profound social change. As waves of change transformed the workplace, home life, leisure patterns, and intellectual fabric of the nation, Americans found strength in the stability of their political system.

NUMEROUS AVENUES OF CHANGE Two necessary conditions for any country's political stability are broad popular acceptance of its government and economic system and a clearly defined political culture. If either element is missing, the likelihood of upheaval and collapse increases. These are necessary components for stability, but they do not guarantee stability. For a democratic system to remain stable, its citizens must believe that they can influence the outcome of government activity. The design and operation of government must permit popular participation. In addition, the political culture and laws must encourage civic involvement and protect activists from being silenced either by the government or by majority opinion. There must also be a variety of ways to achieve desired ends. Severe limitations on citizen participation and influence can lead to frustration, cynicism, and, in the end, conflict and potential upheaval if people feel forced to use means outside the governing system, such as violence, to make their voices heard. Stated a bit differently, stability in a democratic regime springs from a system that allows participation, a culture that promotes involvement, and a set of options to help redirect public policy.

Conclusion

A key feature of all democracies is the opportunity for citizens to participate in public affairs in order to influence the decisions of government. The design and operation of American government provide a variety of opportunities for citizens to make their voices heard at the national, state, and local levels. In the United States, citizens can use the different pathways for action to influence government and public policies. These pathways include opportunities to participate in campaigns and elections, to file lawsuits in the courts, to lobby government officials, and to mobilize large groups of citizens to either pressure officials or seek to change the culture and values of society.

Citizen participation should not be viewed as just a hobby. It is an essential element for maintaining stability in a democratic society. In the United States, stability also depends on shared beliefs in the political and economic systems, as well as the shared values that make up what has been called the American creed. In many other countries, ethnic conflict and social transformations can lead to profound changes in the form of government or public policies. By contrast, despite significant social changes in our diverse society, the United States has maintained a high degree of stability under a founding document, the Constitution, which was written in the eighteenth century. At one point, profound disagreements in society led to the bloody four-year Civil War.

However, after the North's victory resolved regional disagreements over slavery and states' rights, the United States again became a stable democracy thanks to the opportunities it granted to all citizens to participate and share in political and economic values.

In the next chapter, we will examine the design of American government, beginning with the blueprint developed in the United States Constitution. Subsequent chapters will discuss key elements in government and politics, such as the news media and public opinion, as well as the specific institutions of government, such as Congress and the U.S. Supreme Court. As you learn about these key elements and institutions, think about which pathways of action are most important for each aspect of American government. You should also consider how you can participate as an engaged citizen when you want to assert influence over the decisions and priorities of your government.

YOUR turn!

As you think about your daily life, are there laws or government policies that you regard as unfair or misguided? Listen to the people around you. Are they debating issues that affect their lives? Many people disagree about whether motorcyclists should be required to wear helmets. Other people feel deeply about issues such as abortion or American military actions overseas. Some of your classmates may believe that public universities have raised their tuition and fees to a level that is too high for the average citizen to afford. Yet others may feel most strongly about the availability of health insurance for students and other individuals with limited incomes. Throughout the country, Americans debate such issues as gun control and affirmative action. Do you worry about whether Social Security funds will be available for your support when you retire? Unfortunately, many people, including students, appear to feel helpless, and they act as if there is no point in getting involved in contemporary issues. This may in part explain why voter participation rates in the United States are low compared to those in many other democracies. As you evaluate your views about government and society, ask yourself: As a college-educated person, do you really want all laws and policies that affect your life and determine what happens in your country to be decided by other people?

How can you start to see yourself as an engaged citizen?

1. Identify issues that are important to you. Perhaps they are issues that directly affect your daily life. Perhaps they are issues that arouse your passions about what happens elsewhere in the country or the world.

2. Investigate the issues you have identified. Read newspapers and magazines, and seek information on the Internet. Look

up laws at **http://www.findlaw.com** and other Web sites for your city or state. There may be organized interest groups that share your views, and their publications and Web sites may provide a wealth of information.

3. Find out which government decision makers influence these issues. Do you know who represents you on your city council? In the state legislature? In Congress? Do you have ideas, information, or complaints that should be directed to specific officials?

4. As you proceed through the chapters of this book, think seriously about the pathways of action. Try to think about which pathway might be most effective for advancing your goals.

The example of the rental housing ordinance at the start of this chapter was a hypothetical situation based on actual laws that exist in many college towns. The possibility of students working to change such laws, however, is very real. Remember the example in Pathways of Action of the University of Cincinnati students who created and successfully lobbied for a new air pollution law. American government presents opportunities for you to make your voice heard by government officials and make a difference in the world. ◼

Chapter Review

1. American government is based on democracy and provides opportunities for citizens to participate in shaping the decisions and priorities of government leaders.

2. Citizens throughout the United States, including college students, can take actions to make their voices heard by government officials at the local, state, and national levels.

3. All democracies are not alike. They vary in many structural details and in their underlying political culture. American government has its own design and rests on a unique political culture, and it presents opportunities for citizen participation that are different from those available in other countries.

4. One major theme of this book focuses on the importance of citizen participation for making the American governing system fulfill the ideals of a democracy.

5. Another major theme is the need to understand the *pathways of action* available for citizens who wish to influence government. These pathways include the *elections pathway, lobbying*

pathway, court pathway, grassroots mobilization pathway, and *cultural change pathway.*

6. The diversity of American society has shaped the policy issues that it faces, as well as the political involvement of different groups and the evolving ethnic composition of the government's decision makers.

7. The issue of abortion provides a good illustration of the pathways of action because competing groups have used various pathways to influence government policies.

8. Except for the disruption caused by the Civil War, the American governing system has enjoyed significant stability despite immense social and economic changes that have occurred since the late eighteenth century.

9. Stability in the American democracy depends on several essential factors: consensus about the political and economic systems; shared values in the political culture as embodied in the "American creed;" and a variety of pathways for political participation and government influence by citizens.

CHAPTER REVIEW TEST

1. For the purposes of this book, *politics* means
   a. the exercise of power at all levels of society.
   b. competition among people within any group or in society at large.
   c. activities of governmental officials and citizens that intend to affect the makeup, authority, and actions of the government.
   d. propaganda.

2. Historically, voter turnout in different democracies is dictated by whether voting is legally required in that country.
   a. true   **b.** false

3. Historically, all American citizens have been equally able to participate in or influence American politics.
   a. true   **b.** false

4. Democracies are inefficient because
   a. it takes a long time to hear from every citizen.
   b. there is a lot of red tape in the bureaucracies of Washington, D.C.
   c. competition among contesting views and political strategies slow down decision making in the government.
   d. politicians love to talk.

5. Which of the following would be an example of political activism within an accepted "pathway of action" in this country's political process?
   a. circulating a petition for a third-party candidate
   b. stockpiling guns and ammunition to use against federal agents
   c. refusing to sit in the back of a municipal bus even though a city ordinance requires that you do so
   d. a and c

6. Which of the following resources help citizens use pathways of action?
   a. money
   b. social influence and personal connections
   c. organizational skills
   d. a, b, and c

7. Successful lobbying requires money.
   a. true   b. false

8. The example of two students working to make the city of Cincinnati comply with federal health standards for air quality illustrates that
   a. well-informed and motivated young people can successfully lobby local government officials to affect government policies.
   b. knowing powerful officials is crucial to effective lobbying.
   c. the office of environmental manager is not important in any city.
   d. a, b, and c

9. The prohibition against racial discrimination in U.S. public schools was initiated through which pathway?
   a. lobbying
   b. court-centered activism
   c. elections
   d. grassroots mobilization

10. Which of the following is an example of grassroots mobilization?
    a. boycotts
    b. calling your senators to persuade them to vote no on upcoming legislation
    c. writing a book about the dangers of Social Security privatization
    d. speaking to passersby on a street corner

11. Who was A. Philip Randolph?
    a. a union organizer for African Americans
    b. founder of the magazine *Messenger*
    c. organizer of the 1963 march on Washington
    d. a, b, and c

12. Why is diversity a theme in this book?
    a. It is politically correct to include this subject.
    b. The world contains a diversity of political systems.
    c. America's human diversity has had a strong influence on the evolution of its government and its laws and policies.
    d. The framers of the Constitution did not anticipate how diverse the U.S. population would become.

13. Pathways of action have allowed various disempowered groups, such as women, racial minorities, and the disabled, genuine influence over the policies and laws of the United States government.
    a. true   b. false

14. In the United States, a woman's right to obtain an abortion was secured with the passing of the Nineteenth Amendment.
    a. true   b. false

15. *Roe* v. *Wade* defended a woman's right to obtain an abortion in the United States by invoking what constitutional principle?
    a. the right to privacy
    b. freedom of expression
    c. life, liberty, and the pursuit of happiness
    d. the separation of church and state

16. Whereas most countries experience periods of transformation, the United States does not.
    a. true   b. false

17. Which of these factors has helped make American government as stable as it has been over the last 200 years?
    a. Americans' loyalty to the flag and national rituals such as the singing of the national anthem
    b. fluctuations in voter turnout over the years
    c. the different ways in which ordinary citizens can affect governmental policies
    d. the existence of powerful families in positions of power

18. The free-enterprise system, though based on the principle of private ownership and personal economic success, has had the effect of securing the financial security of almost everyone in American society.
    a. true   b. false

19. Critics of capitalism complain about
    a. the wide gap between the rich and the poor.
    b. the principles of capitalism being at odds with the U.S. Constitution.
    c. capitalism's supplanting of religion.
    d. a, b, and c.

20. Compared to the framers' original intentions in writing the Constitution, our current view of the document is surprising because

    a. we revere the document, whereas for them it was just a rough draft.

    b. We revere the document, yet it was the result of a series of pragmatic compromises at the time.

    c. we revere the document, yet it was supposed to be superseded by the Articles of Confederation.

    d. we regard the document with much more skepticism than the framers themselves.

Answers: 1: c; 2: b; 3: b; 4: c; 5: d; 6: d; 7: b; 8: a; 9: b; 10: a; 11: d; 12: c; 13: a; 14: b; 15: a; 16: b; 17: c; 18: b; 19: a; 20: b.

DISCUSSION QUESTIONS

1. How might a college student attempt to influence local government decisions about a specific law or policy?

2. How is American government different from both democratic and nondemocratic governments elsewhere in the world?

3. How does the United States compare to other countries with respect to political freedom ratings and rates of voter turnout?

4. Why is citizen participation important for American government?

5. What are the pathways of action available to Americans?

6. How is diversity important for understanding American government?

7. What pathways of action have been important for shaping policies concerning the issue of abortion?

8. What elements are essential for maintaining stability in American government?

9. What is the "American creed"?

INTERNET RESOURCES

To see comparisons of the United States and other countries in political rights and individual freedom, visit the Freedom House Web site at **http://www.freedomhouse.org**

To see comparisons of the United States and other countries in voter turnout, see the Web site of International IDEA at **http://www.idea.int**

To read about one organization's strategies for using various pathways to affect government policy concerning firearms, see the Web site of the National Rifle Association at **http://www.nra.org**

To learn about proposals for improving voter participation and the effectiveness of elections, see the Web site of the Center for Voting and Democracy at **http://www.fairvote.org**

ADDITIONAL READING

Halperin, Morton, Joseph T. Siegle, and Michael M. Weinstein. *The Democracy Advantage: How Democracies Promote Prosperity and Peace.* New York: Routledge, 2004.

Hull, N.E.H., and Peter Charles Hoffer. Roe *v.* Wade: *The Abortion Rights Controversy in American History.* Lawrence: University Press of Kansas, 2001.

Pintor, Rafael Lopez, and Maria Gratschew. *Voter Turnout since 1945: A Global Report.* Stockholm, Sweden: International Institute for Democracy and Electoral Assistance, 2002.

Tocqueville, Alexis de. *Democracy in America.* New York: Signet Books, 2001. (Originally published 1835–1840)

KEY TERMS

de Tocqueville, Alexis   26

boycott   16

capitalism   24

checks and balances   24

litigation   6

pathways of action   12

political culture   26

politics   6

public policy   6

socialism   25

A Declaration by the Representatives of the U[nited States]

OF AMERICA, in General Congress assembl[ed]

When in the course of human events it becom[es]
dissolve the political bands which have connected them w[ith]
~~[struck out line]~~
sume among the powers of the earth the separate and e[qual]
which the laws of nature & of nature's god entitle
to the opinions of mankind requires that they sho[uld]
which impel them to ~~[struck]~~ the separation.

We hold these truths to be self-evident;
created equal ~~& independent~~ that ~~from~~ they are endow[ed]
~~[struck]~~ certain inherent & inalienable rights; that among ~~which~~
life, liberty, & the pursuit of happiness; that
-vernments are instituted among men, deriving
the consent of the governed; that whenever any
~~[struck]~~ becomes destructive of these ends, it is the r[ight]
or to abolish it, & to institute new government, l[aying]
such principles & organising it's powers in suc[h]

A work in progress. Did you know that Thomas Jefferson's "original Rough draft" of the Declaration of Independence included criticisms of slavery? The tragic irony is that while the final version is a powerful rationale for democratic governance, the system sanctioned slavery and discriminated against groups for centuries. Perhaps, however, our government should be seen as a work in progress—where each generation adds its own edits, its own corrections.

CHAPTER 2

EARLY GOVERNANCE AND THE CONSTITUTIONAL FRAMEWORK

The Cry for Liberty, Equality, . . . and Slavery? One of the great riddles of our nation's early years—a question you should wrestle with as you read along—is how a nation born of democratic principles could also suppress groups of people. What could possibly explain such a glaring hypocrisy as slavery in a democracy? One way to explain this, called cultural relativism, suggests that we see the question through an eighteenth-century lens. That is, the acceptance of slavery in a democracy may seem hypocritical to us, but to people of the eighteenth century, the double standard was less obvious. Thomas Jefferson seemed philosophically opposed to slavery even though he owned hundreds of human beings and probably had several children with one of his slaves, Sally Hemings. Perhaps Jefferson's own beliefs collided with the cultural norms of his times. Cultural relativism holds that people's views are shaped by the culture in which

(Photo: North Wind Picture Archives)

33

Bill and Hillary Rodham Clinton standing in Door of No Return, Goree Island, Senegal, in 1998. This was a portal where slaves were put on ships for transport to America. Our nation's legacy of racial discrimination is unpleasant to consider—and some see little point in rehashing the past. Yet, remembering the tragic parts of our history can help future generations better advance the goals of freedom, liberty, and equality. Why should we pay close attention to our blemishes—as well as all our successes?

they live; culture gives meanings to objects and events. We might say, then, that slavery seemed necessary and thus reasonable in the eighteenth century even as the nation embraced the ideals of liberty and freedom.

Yet many of the strongest advocates of breaking from English rule pointed out the inhumanity of slavery. Abigail Adams, for example, wrote to her husband, John, while he was at the Second Continental Congress in 1776, of the smallpox outbreak that devastated their town of Braintree, Massachusetts. "Heartsick, searching for an answer as to why such an evil should 'befall such a city and people,' Abigail had pondered whether it could be God's punishment for the sin of slavery."[1] And within a year after the ratification of the Constitution, two Quaker delegations petitioned the House of Representatives to put an immediate end to the slave trade.[2] Cultural relativism alone cannot explain slavery in a new democracy: Not all contemporaries were blind to the evils of slavery.

The thinking of those at the time regarding *when* and *why* our nation was born shaped perspectives on slavery. One perspective is that our nation was created in 1776, with the signing of the Declaration of Independence. This was when we decided to give self-governance and democracy a try. The rationale for revolution was greater equality; many Americans came to believe that they should break from England because, under British rule, citizens did not have liberty and did not have a say in their government.

The Declaration of Independence stated that just public policy springs from citizens and that all humans are created equal, with rights given only by God. When in 1863 Abraham Lincoln said in his Gettysburg Address that our nation had been born "four score and seven years ago" (that is, eighty-seven years earlier), he was reaching back to 1776, to the Declaration of Independence.

A second perspective holds that our nation was forged in 1788, when the Constitution was finally ratified. Before this point, each state operated virtually independently, establishing its own currency and commercial system and conducting its own foreign affairs. The American experiment seemed to be on the verge of collapse when in 1787 delegates came to Philadelphia and decided to draw up a better system. After the Constitution was drafted, it was sent to the states for ratification; when at least two-thirds of the states (nine of the thirteen) agreed, our nation was born.

Most people who felt that the new nation was based on egalitarian principles believed there was no room for slavery. From this vantage point, one historian, Bernard Bailyn, has written, "The American Revolution was both a triumphant and transformative moment in world history, when all laws and human relationships dependent on coercion would be swept away forever." Jefferson's Declaration "gave lyrical expression to a widespread belief that a general emancipation of slaves was both imminent and inevitable."[3]

Most people who traced the birth of the nation to the adoption of the U.S. Constitution had a much different take on the slavery issue. According to James Madison, the central figure at the Constitutional Convention, slavery haunted its sessions, all of which were conducted behind closed doors and nailed-down windows. Most outsiders assumed that the delegates forged alliances based upon the size of the state, but Madison saw it differently: "The States were divided into different interests not by their difference of size, but principally from their having or not having slaves."[4] On numerous occasions, the Convention came close to collapse, but negotiation and compromise held things together. It seems very clear that several states would have left the proceedings had a constitution that outlawed slavery been proposed. Southerners considered slavery indispensable to their region's economy. One southern delegate bluntly asserted, "The people of those States would never be such fools as to give up so important an interest."[5]

In the end, neither side got what it wanted. Slavery was neither sanctioned nor outlawed by the Constitution. In fact, the words *slave* and *slavery* never even appeared in the Constitution until the Thirteenth Amendment, which abolished slavery at the end of the Civil War. "The distinguishing feature of the document when it came to slavery was its evasiveness," writes historian Joseph Ellis.[6] The issue was put on hold. ■

▶ **So did the Constitution** guarantee equality and freedom?

ideology
the core beliefs that guide an individual's thinking.

pragmatism
the consideration of practical issues when assessing situations and solving problems.

government
the formal structures and institutions through which binding decisions are made for citizens of a particular area.

civil law
a body of law that applies to private rights, such as the ownership of property or the ability to enter into contracts.

What does this quick look at the slavery question tell us about the foundations of our system of government? One lesson might be that while our nation was forged on egalitarian concepts, such as liberty and freedom, hard-won compromises were used to keep us together. Both components—ideology and pragmatism—were clearly evident in the work of the Constitutional Convention, and both continue to play an important role in American governance, as we will see throughout this book. **Ideology** refers to core beliefs that guide thinking about the proper role of government and the citizens, and **pragmatism** refers to the nuts-and-bolts matters of actual governance.

▶ **So did the Constitution guarantee equality and freedom?** A second and perhaps more important point is that equality did not arrive with the Revolution, ratification of the Constitution, or any other single event in our nation's history. Our political system is still unfolding. Democracy in America is not a state of being but rather a process of growth. Put a bit differently, the story of liberty and freedom in America has been the movement toward the realization of an ideal. The Preamble to the Constitution, with its statement that the people are seeking a "more perfect union," implies that perfection is not possible, that the ideal is not achievable. But it also suggests that the challenge is to *strive* toward an open, free, and just system. America is clearly, if somewhat slowly, moving in that direction.

Key Questions

1. What is the difference between *government* and *politics* and between *power, authority,* and *legitimacy*?

2. What developments led to the American Revolution?

3. Why is the Declaration of Independence heralded as one of the great documents of governance, and what are the various elements of Jefferson's bold statement?

4. What are the basic components of the Constitution, and in what ways are several of these elements unique?

5. What made "pathways of change" relevant at particular points in our nation's formative years?

The Nature of Government and Politics

Before looking further into the foundations of the American political system and the various avenues of change that it presents, it's important to understand several important concepts. First and perhaps most elemental is the word **government.** We all use this word frequently but rarely consider what it actually implies.

In real ways, government is all around us. Government is the formal structures and institutions through which binding decisions are made for citizens of a particular area. We might also say that it is the organization that has formal jurisdiction over a group of people who live in a certain place. Government is *not* the process by which things take place in a political system; rather, it is the "rules of the game" and the structures (the institutions) that make and enforce these rules. In the United States, such institutions include legislatures (city councils, state legislatures, Congress), executives (mayors, governors, the president), the courts, the bureaucracy, and a few independent agencies such as the Federal Reserve System. It would not include political parties, interest groups, and public opinion, for example; they are key elements of our political system but not formal parts of the governmental structure.

This definition also helps clarify the different types and layers of government. The rules and formal structures of a city government apply to the people living in that city. A school or club government applies only to the students in that school or the members of that particular club. Occasionally, some people may question their loyalty and obedience to a particular government or feel compelled to change their allegiance from one government to another. On the eve of the Civil War, for example, many Southern-born officers, such as General Robert E. Lee of Virginia, felt a sense of duty to the United States, for they had served in the United States military and were trained at West Point. (Lee had been a commandant at West Point, and President Lincoln offered him command of the United States Army.) But they felt an even greater responsibility to their home state. Lee considered this loyalty to

▶ Power, authority, legitimacy . . . all these terms seem similar. What's the difference?

criminal law
a body of law that applies to violations against rules and regulations defined by the government.

power
the ability to exercise control over others and get individuals, groups, or institutions to comply.

authority
the recognized right of a particular individual, group, or institution to make binding decisions, and compel others to obey them.

Virginia more important than his duty to the United States. Indeed, before the Civil War, many Americans felt that they had dual citizenship: first in their state and second in the federal union. Today, most Americans would consider choosing "state citizenship" above federal citizenship rather odd.

What does it mean to be "under the rule of the government?" At the most basic level, this suggests that government has the power to enforce its regulations and collect the resources it needs to operate. Rules can be enforced in many ways. One way is for citizens to be required to pay money as a penalty for breaking a rule. In the American setting, this is referred to as **civil law.** A person who loses a civil court case is not sent to prison but rather is required to pay a fine. **Criminal law,** by contrast, prescribes that citizens who do not follow regulations must pay a monetary penalty (a fine) or may be removed from society for a period or even permanently (through a sentence of death or of life imprisonment without parole). Taxation is the most common way to collect revenue to make the government run. Another example of the government's enforcing its regulations is the draft. If you are male, you are required to register with the Selective Service at age 18, and Congress and the president can activate the draft in the event of a national emergency.

The words *power* and *authority* are related to government's ability to enforce its rules and to collect resources. **Power,** in the political context, is the ability to get individuals, groups, or institutions to do something. Power determines the outcome of conflicts over governmental decisions; it charts the course of public policy. When the ranks of an interest group grow to the point that governmental decision makers are forced to listen, that group is said to have power. If a handful of corporate elites can persuade public officials to steer public policy their way, they too have power. The media would be considered powerful if they were to shift public opinion in favor of one candidate over another or persuade Congress and the president to adopt or to change a certain policy. We might also note that if a Middle Eastern country manipulates its sale of oil to the United States, it too has power.

▶ **Power, authority, legitimacy . . . all these terms seem similar. What's the difference? Authority** is defined as the

recognized right for a particular individual, group, or institution to make binding decisions. Most Americans believe that Congress has the authority to make laws, impose taxes, or draft people into service in the military. We may not like the decisions made in Washington, in our state capital, or at city hall, but we recognize that in our system of government, elected officials have the authority to make those decisions. However, many people balk at the idea of *appointed* bureaucrats making regulations, given that they are not elected, which means that they don't have to answer to the people but only to those who appointed them. Thus bureaucrats have *power* but lack *authority.* We often also hear criticisms of judges' "legislating from the bench," meaning that when they make decisions that affect policy matters, they overstep their bounds—that is to say that they lack authority to make such decisions because they were not elected by the people and do not have to answer to them.

Some individuals, groups, and institutions have both power and authority. Again, most Americans believe that Congress has the authority to make laws and that federal law enforcement units have the power to enforce those laws. Most people dread getting a letter from the Internal Revenue Service requiring them to submit to an audit of their tax returns. But we have pointed out, power and authority are not the same. Perhaps the best contemporary example of when power and authority collide might be education reform. As you'll see in ⓁⒾⓃⓀ *Chapter 3, pages 79–81,* a few years ago, the federal government wrote into law a dramatic effort to improve public education, the No Child Left Behind Act. There is little question that the federal government has the power to enforce this sweeping law. Yet for all of our nation's history, state and local governments have controlled education policy. Many people get angry at the notion of "legislators off in Washington telling us how to run our schools." Many therefore believe that the federal government lacks the authority to regulate education policy.

A final term to consider is *politics.* As noted in ⓁⒾⓃⓀ *Chapter 1, page 6, politics* is the *process* by which the character, membership, and actions of a government are arrived at. It is also the struggle to move government to a preferred course of action. All citizens might agree that a change is needed, but how to reach

monarchy
a system of hereditary rule in which one person, a king or queen, has absolute authority over the government.

constitutional monarchy
a political system in which the king or queen performs ceremonial duties but plays little or no role in actually governing the country.

dictator
the sole ruler of a political system with the power to control most or all actions of government.

oligarchy
a government run by a small group of people.

pluralism
a system of government in which multiple competing and responsive groups vie for power.

democracy
a political system in which all citizens have a right to play a role in shaping government action and are afforded basic rights and liberties.

Baseball

Official Rules (Government)	How the Game is Played (Politics)
1. Pitchers can start from either the windup or the stretch position.	Pitchers grip the ball in different ways to throw fastballs, curveballs, or knuckleballs. Also, pitchers release the ball at different points to change the batter's view of the ball.
2. Batters must keep both feet in the batter's box while hitting.	Batters can "crowd the plate" by standing close to the inside edge of the box.
3. A batter will run to first base after hitting a ball in fair territory.	Batters do not always make a full swing with the bat (for example, bunting).
4. All fielders must be in fair territory when that team's pitcher delivers the ball.	Defense can shift to accommodate for a batter who tends to hit in a certain direction.

American Government

Official Rules (Government)	How the Game is Played (Politics)
Article 1, Section 2 The House of Representatives shall choose their speaker and other officers	The majority party uses their power to elect a speaker and other officers from their party, thus enabling them to push their legislative agenda.
First Amendment Freedom of the Press	Corporate conglomerates own media outlets.
Article 1, Section 7 Presidential Veto	Presidents can threaten to veto a bill before it passes through Congress in order to influence the legislation.
Article1, Section 3 each Senator shall have one vote	Lobbyists can provide information on issues and influence the way a Senator or Representative votes.
Article 1, Section 2 The House of Representatives shall be composed of members chosen every second year by the people of the several States	Candidates raise money and campaign before election day to influence the opinions of the voters.

FIGURE 2.1
Government and Politics: What's the Difference?

It is important that you understand the difference between government and politics. We suggest government is analogous to the official rules of baseball, and politics is similar to how the game is actually played. What is another analogy that might help you and your classmates better understand the difference between governmental institutions and the political process?

SOURCE: www.usconstitution.net

the desired goal can be hotly disputed. Given that governmental decisions create winners and losers—that is, acts by the government rarely please everyone—politics is a process that causes many to be left frustrated and at times angry. Moreover, politics can prove to be a slow process. The famous German sociologist Max Weber once suggested that politics is the "strong and slow boring of hard boards," and this makes good sense.[7]

The key difference you should keep in mind is that politics is the *process*, whereas government involves the *rules* of the game. An analogy might be helpful: The baseball rulebook is long and complex. It states how runners can arrive at first base safely, how outs are made, and how a team wins. Most rules are clear and have remained the same for generations. But the actual *conduct* of the game is another matter. The rulebook says nothing about split-finger fastballs, change-ups, bunts, intentional walks, double steals, pitching rotations, closers, stoppers, lineup strategy, and many other aspects of how the game is played. The rulebook represents government; the way the game is played is politics (Figure 2.1).

TYPES OF GOVERNMENTS

Governments come in many forms and modes of operation. Perhaps the best way to think about these differences is to focus on two critical questions: Who is allowed to govern? And how are governmental decisions reached?[8] With regard to *who* is allowed to

liberty
freedom from government interference in private actions.

republic
a system of government in which members of the general public select agents to represent them in political decision making.

representative democracy
a republic in which the selection of elected officials is conducted through a free and open process.

totalitarian regime
a system of government in which the ruling elite holds all power and controls all aspects of society.

authoritarian regime
a system of government in which leaders face few formal legal restrictions but are checked by noninstitutional forces such as political parties, religious groups, and business leaders.

constitutional government
a political system in which leaders are subject to both procedural checks and institutional limits. The United States has a constitutional government.

set the rules and regulations and to enforce them, there are several broad possibilities. **Monarchy** is a system of rule in which one person, such as a king or queen, possesses absolute authority over the government by virtue of being born into a royal family and inheriting the position. Monarchies have been the most common form of rule in world history, and they are still in place in some nations around the globe. For example, Saudi Arabia still relies on a royal family for ultimate authority. (In history, few monarchies were truly "absolute"; kings were normally limited by custom and by the need to consult powerful groups. But in theory, the monarch's authority was unlimited.) Almost all kings and queens today head **constitutional monarchies** in which they perform ceremonial duties but play little or no role in actually governing their country. Examples include the United Kingdom, Spain, Belgium, the Netherlands, and Japan. A **dictator** is also a sole ruler, but often this person arrives at the position of power through a violent overthrow of the previous government. (Sometimes contemporary dictators, such as North Korea's Kim Jong Il or Syria's Bashar Assad, succeed to power like a king or queen on the death of a parent.) Like an absolute king, a dictator theoretically has unlimited control of the government, though again this power is often limited by the bureaucracy, the military, the ruling party, or even members of the dictator's family.

In some forms of government, a small group, such as military leaders or the economic elite, hold the reins of power. This is known as elitism or **oligarchy** (rule by a few). Decisions in such systems are often made through a council. An example today would be Pakistan, where a small group of military leaders rules the nation. **Pluralism** occurs when a number of groups in a system struggle for power. In other words, in a pluralist system, there are multiple centers of power.

Finally, **democracy** is a political system in which all citizens have a right to play a role in shaping government action—a mechanism often referred to as popular sovereignty. Citizens in a democracy are afforded basic rights and liberties, as well as freedom from government interference with private actions (that is, **liberty**). In a direct or pure democracy, all citizens make all decisions. Some tiny Swiss cantons (states) operate in this way, and a small number of communities in the United States are governed through town hall meetings where everyone in the community has

a say in making town policy. A **republic** is governed by a small group of elected representatives acting on behalf of the many. If these representatives closely follow the wishes of their constituents (the people they are sent to represent), and if they are elected through a fair and open process in which everyone has the same opportunity to participate, the system is considered a **representative democracy.** The United States is a republic—as are most of the industrialized nations of the world (though some are constitutional monarchies). Whether or not we are a true representative democracy, however, is a point of dispute. Perhaps by the end of the semester, you will be able to make your own assessment on this issue.

The second important question to consider is *how* decisions are reached in a government. In a **totalitarian regime,** leaders have no real limits on how they proceed or what they do. (Formal constitutions might exist in such regimes, seemingly full of formal limits on power, but in practice such limits are meaningless.) Totalitarian governments control—or at least try to control—almost every aspect of society.[9] The term *totalitarian* was invented in the 1920s by Benito Mussolini in Italy, although in practice his government exercised less than total control. Nazi Germany, the Soviet Union under Joseph Stalin, China under Mao Zedong, and present-day North Korea are the clearest examples of truly totalitarian dictatorships. Under a dictatorship, there may be an individual ruler, a small group, or even a number of groups, but none of these acknowledges any formal limitations.

In an **authoritarian regime,** government policies are kept in check by informal limits, such as by other political forces (maybe political parties), the military, and social institutions (for example, religious groups). Leaders face real limits, but there are no formal or legal restrictions. A good example here would be the president of Egypt, Hosni Mubarak. The Egyptian constitution grants the president exceptional powers, and parliament generally agrees to all of Mubarak's wishes. Yet he does face limits from business leaders and religious groups in his country. For instance, Mubarak himself has seemed inclined to maintain a close relationship with the United States but has been forced to demonstrate greater independence due to these influences. When there are both informal and legal limits, the system is a **constitutional government.** In the United States, for example, government action is controlled by strong social and political forces (including religions, interest

▶ **If the royal governors** were responsive to the concerns of the assemblies, why did the colonists revolt?

communism
an economic system in which all property is owned by the community and each person contributes and receives according to his or her ability and needs.

capitalist system
an economic system in which the means of production and distribution are privately owned and there is little governmental interference. Also known as an *open-market* or *free-market system.*

TABLE 2.1
Types of Government and Economic Systems

GOVERNMENT SYSTEMS	DEFINITION	EXAMPLES
WHO IS ALLOWED TO PARTICIPATE?		
Monarchy	Individual ruler with hereditary authority holds absolute governmental power	Bhutan, Saudi Arabia, Swaziland
Constitutional Monarchy	Monarch figurehead with limited power, actual governing authority belongs to another body	Denmark, Japan, United Kingdom
Dictatorship	Individual ruler with absolute authority, often comes to power through violent uprising	Hussein's Iraq, North Korea
Oligarchy	A small group of the rich or powerful controls most of the governing decisions	Tunisia, 20th century South Africa, Pakistan
Pluralism	Multiple centers of power vying for authority	Canada, Great Britain, United States
HOW ARE DECISIONS REACHED?		
Pure Democracy	Citizens make all governmental decisions	Some Swiss states, some towns in New England
Representative Democracy	Citizens elect representatives to carry out government functions	United States, Germany, France
Totalitarian Regime	Leaders have no limits on authority	Nazi Germany, 1920s Italy
Authoritarian System	Leaders have no formal legal restraints on authority, but are limited by informal forces (i.e. the military, religious forces)	South Korea, Singapore, Taiwan
Constitutional System	Government has both informal and legal restraints on the exercise of power	United States, Germany, France, Mexico
ECONOMIC SYSTEMS		
Communism	All citizens share in the production and distribution of goods; no private property; usually brought about by revolution	People's Republic of China, Republic of Cuba, Socialist Republic of Vietnam
Socialism	Government controls key economic functions; usually brought about democratically	Chile, Brazil, Uruguay
Capitalism	Individual citizens control the production and distribution of goods	United States, Hong Kong

groups, political parties, and the media) and by what the laws, the courts, and the Constitution allow (see Table 2.1).

ECONOMIC SYSTEMS

It is worth briefly stepping away from our discussion of types of government to touch on economic systems. There is more to the matter, but under **communism,** everyone shares in the production and distribution of goods. There are no owners and no private property; rather, all members of the society are regarded as workers *and* owners. Communism has never been completely realized in practice, but it was the stated goal of the former Soviet Union. *Socialism* is an economic system in which key elements of the economy, such as transportation, health care, and heavy industry, are controlled by the government. The fact that not all means of production are under government control and that individuals retain certain rights and liberties distinguishes socialism from communism. Also, socialist governments are often established through democratic mechanisms, whereas communist systems are usually imposed through violent revolution. Under a free-market or **capitalist system,** individuals rather than the government own both the means of production and the distribution of goods. In

discussionquestions

1. Define "government" and "politics." How might the differences between these concepts help in people's quest to be more active citizens?

2. What are some of the key differences between types of governments?

what YOU can do!

The World Wide Web has revolutionized the research process allowing an endless number of topics to be investigated. Explore how other nations structure their government. To get started, try World Wide Governments at **http://www.gksoft.com/govt/en/world.html**

---

true open-market systems, there are no limits to how much capital or wealth an individual might acquire, and there are no governmental regulations of the economy whatsoever. The United States in the nineteenth century approached this model. Our present-day economic system is based on capitalism, but it is no longer a pure open-market system; there are a number of regulations, ranging from ones that protect workers to ones that govern industry's effects on the environment.

practicequiz

1. Which of the following is a governmental institution?
   a. the legislature
   b. the constitution
   c. political parties
   d. both a and b.

2. Which of the following describes "politics"?
   a. the struggle to alter government outputs—what we call public policy
   b. the process by which political actors seek to arrive at a preferred outcome
   c. the process by which the character and actions of government are arrived at
   d. a, b, and c.

3. The United States is a direct democracy because we elect leaders to speak and act on our behalf.
   a. true   b. false

4. The United States is considered to have a "constitutional" government because
   a. not everyone can play a role in the decision-making process.
   b. there are both substantive and procedural restrictions on what government officials can do.
   c. the federal government is just one piece of the overall structure, which includes state and local governments as well.
   d. we limit the role of government in the affairs of business—that is, we have a pure capitalist system.

Answers: 1-d, 2-d, 3-b, 4-b.

Early Governance in America

To see how Americans have governed themselves, let's go back to 1620. In that year, a tiny group of English people (forty-one men and an unknown number of women and children) sailed across the Atlantic to what was called at the time the New World. They were crammed into a leaky old ship called the *Mayflower*. Some members of this band would later be dubbed the Pilgrims because they were coming to America in hopes of finding religious freedom. (Some of the other passengers were not part of this religiously motivated group.) All the *Mayflower* passengers were bound for Virginia, where they expected to join an English colony that had been founded a few years earlier, in 1607. Unfortunately, the place where they landed—New England—was outside the recognized boundaries of Virginia, and the captain of the ship refused to go any farther. Winter was coming, and he did not want to risk any more voyaging. He let the passengers stay on board during the winter, but in spite of this half of them died. When spring arrived, the captain took his ship back to England, leaving the passengers high and dry on the coast of New England.

Recognizing that they were stuck in this bleak place, the Pilgrim leaders insisted that everyone, Pilgrim and non-Pilgrim alike, sign the Mayflower Compact, a document legalizing their position as a "civil body politic" under the sovereignty of King James I. Most important for our concerns is that these people, finding themselves in a place outside the jurisdiction of English rule, sought a system where laws, not a small group or a single person, would rule their society.

From the Mayflower Compact until the American Revolution, a mixed system characterized colonial governance. On the one hand, most of the colonies were established though charters from England. There was no question that these settlements would be governed under English rule. Governors were appointed by the Crown to oversee different colonies and were responsible only to the king. On the other hand, the New World was an ocean away. Settling an untamed wilderness created its own set of problems, and ideas favoring self-governance grew in intellectual circles both in America and in Mother England. The compromise came in the form of colonial assemblies. (The first of them was the House of Burgesses, at Jamestown.) Here colonists elected representatives to speak on their behalf and to counsel the governors on the best courses of action. Every colony had an assembly. These bodies had little legal authority, but they carried substantive powers. The royal governors were eager to receive good advice and to win the esteem of the citizens. They did not have to listen to this advice, but very often it made sense to do so. This mix of appointed rule and self-governance seemed to work at first.

▶ **If the royal governors were responsive to the concerns of the assemblies, why did the colonists revolt?** Two developments upset this balance. First, many colonists brought with them

▶ **What did the Sons** of Liberty *do* to protest against Parliament?

French and Indian War
the nine-year conflict (1754–1763) in North America that pitted Great Britain and its North American colonies against France. France lost, and the British maintained control of much of North America.

Great Squeeze
the British Parliament's passage of a series of measures to raise additional revenue from colonists in order to recoup some of the costs of the French and Indian War.

Imagine you have arrived with your family, friends, and a bunch of strangers in a land without any formal rules or regulations. How would you establish order, create rules, enforce regulations? Given the system that the Pilgrims were accustomed to, one might think that they would have ordained a single person, or a small group of men, to rule as they saw fit. Instead, they bound themselves to a system where laws would be established. Thus, the Mayflower Compact will go down in history as an important step in the evolution of democracy in America.

the political customs and traditions from their homeland, meaning that the debate over the extent of royal authority in the conduct of government came along as well. As in England, those supporting the Crown were often the wealthiest, having received immense land grants and special privileges from the king. (In eighteenth-century Britain, this group, which dominated Parliament, was often referred to as the Court Party.) Those who were not part of the political in-group were deeply suspicious of the favored elite. Their cynicism ran deep, and their numbers swelled as the years passed. On top of this, if a local governing authority proved oppressive, colonists had the option of simply packing up and moving. This made opposition to royal and elite control easier.

Second, and more significantly, new financial pressures were thrust on the colonists in the mid-1750s. The **French and Indian War** in North America, which began in 1754 and ended nine years later, pitted Great Britain against France. (The war was part of a larger Anglo-French struggle for global power.) The French and Indian War began over control of the upper Ohio River valley, but the larger issue was which nation would eventually control the continent. Most of the (relatively few) settlers in this area were British, but the French had entered into trade agreements (and later a military alliance) with many Indian tribes. Through a series of spectacular military engagements over the course of several years, the British defeated the French and took control of North America. Britain won this war with relatively little colonial assistance.

All wars are expensive, but given that this one had been waged an ocean away, the price of protecting Britain's New World empire proved to be very high. Facing massive debt and grumbling taxpayers, Parliament, with the king's blessing, looked for new ways of raising revenue. It seemed logical, because the war had been fought to protect the colonists, that they should bear much of the responsibility for paying the bill. Thus began a period known as the **Great Squeeze** in which Parliament passed one measure after another, including the Sugar Act (1764), the Stamp Act (1765), the Townshend Acts (1767), and the Tea Tax (1773), all designed to wring as much revenue from the colonists as possible. To make matters worse, the Great Squeeze came after more than a generation of what was called "salutary neglect," a policy of casual, loose enforcement of trade laws in the colonies. Parliament had hoped that this freedom would stimulate greater commercial growth, leading to greater profits for British investors. Parliament's decision to raise revenue through a number of taxes after a century of trade freedom proved a bitter pill for the Americans to swallow.

In truth, the new taxes were not severe, and colonial Americans were probably among the least taxed people in the

Euro-American world at the time. But the colonists were in constant fear of the corruption that in their eyes a faraway and arbitrary government could impose on them. ("Corruption" to eighteenth-century Americans meant more than bribery and embezzlement; it also included the distribution of government favors to what we would today call "special interests.") These taxes and other presumed abuses were seen as the opening wedges of creeping corruption and tyranny. It seems, then, that the colonists' obsession about corruption and tyranny and their insistence on guaranteeing limited, accountable government became fundamental to Americans' ideas of just governance. The relationship between the royal governors and the colonial assemblies soured. Because it was the duty of the governors to enforce these unpopular revenue-raising acts, they became the targets of colonial outrage.

pathways of action
THE SONS OF LIBERTY

During the uneasy and turbulent times of pre-Revolutionary America, various resistance groups began to organize, often in secret. In 1765, in opposition to the Stamp Act imposed by Parliament to pay off the debts resulting from the French and Indian War, several of these early interest groups became collectively known as the Sons of Liberty, a name closely linked with protests against Parliamentary rule over the colonies. Led by powerful, important figures such as John and Samuel Adams, but also enlisting the support of artisans, shopkeepers, and other working people who could be depended on to rebel against abuses like the Tea Tax, the Sons of Liberty organized in one community after another.

▶ **What did the Sons of Liberty *do* to protest against Parliament?** They held rallies, sponsored "committees of correspondence" (letter-writing campaigns) to spread their views, and recruited community leaders to their cause. They protested the Townshend Acts, the Tea Tax, and every other move by Parliament seen as oppressive to colonists. They understood the importance of building organizations, rallying individuals in every community, and shaping public opinion. In the end, the Sons of Liberty proved to be one of our nation's first and most influential interest groups, helping set the stage for a revolution and for the creation of a democratic system of government. And of course the groups also demonstrated the power of civic involvement. ■

Americans are fortunate to have many symbols that underscore a commitment to democratic principles. Here a building to house the Liberty Bell is constructed in front of Independence Hall in Philadelphia, the site where the Declaration of Independence was signed. We are not a perfect democracy, as you will read in subsequent chapters, but we stand apart from most other nations in our long commitment to a government "by the people." The question you should consider throughout the semester is whether we are indeed headed toward a "more perfect union," as suggested in the Preamble of the Constitution.
Photo: Salvatore C. DiMarco Jr./New York Times

Acts for Trade
a series of moves by Parliament to channel money from the American colonies back to the commercial class in Great Britain during the mid-1700s.

Coercive Acts/Intolerable Acts
passed by the British Parliament in 1774 in response to growing unrest in the American colonies. Enforcement of these laws played a major role in the outbreak of the American Revolutionary War. The colonists called them the **Intolerable Acts.**

John Locke (1632–1704)
an English political theorist who introduced the notion of a "social contract" under which all just governments derive their powers from the consent of the governed. Locke's writings provided the theoretical framework of Thomas Jefferson's Declaration of Independence and the entire Revolutionary movement in America.

► **What about the famous Boston Tea Party . . . wasn't that about taxes?**

THE BOSTONIANS PAYING THE EXCISE-MAN OR TARRING & FEATHERING

Many students assume that all colonists were true believers in the revolutionary cause. Some were, of course, but many were anxious to remain loyal to the Crown and "Mother England." Animosity between the Patriots and the Loyalists burst into violence in many communities, and tar and feathering, as depicted above, was not uncommon. Why do you suppose passions ran so high?

practicequiz

1. In the pre-Revolutionary period, a "mixed system" characterized colonial governance. This meant that
   a. some colonies were considered democratic while others were more elitist.
   b. some colonies rejected British rule while others seemed content with the system.
   c. the British Crown appointed royal governors to oversee colonies, but at the same time most colonies had a locally elected assembly.
   d. the colonies were open to economic development but closed when it came to religious freedoms.

2. The Great Squeeze was a period in American history when
   a. Parliament sought to recoup the money spent during the French and Indian War by levying new taxes on the colonists.
   b. colonists were no longer able to sell their products to British merchants.
   c. there was an effort to merge southern colonies into a separate nation distinct from northern colonies.
   d. royal governors were asked to surrender their lands to colonial assemblies.

3. The taxes imposed on the colonists in the pre-Revolution period had a crippling effect on livelihoods, leading to mass starvation.
   a. true   b. false

4. "Salutary neglect" referred to
   a. the way Parliament abandoned the colonists to fight French forces on the frontier.
   b. British policies that led to the casual enforcement of trade laws, with the hopes of great economic gain.
   c. the abandonment of colonial merchants during the French and Indian War.
   d. Parliament's general disinterest in the affairs of the New World.

Answers: 1-c, 2-a, 3-b, 4-b.

The American Revolution

The causes and meanings of the American Revolution are best broken into two broad categories: financial and ideological. With regard to the financial concerns—what you might call Americans'

Adam Smith (1723–1790)
a Scottish political and economic philosopher whose views on free trade and capitalism were admired in colonial America.

John Adams (1735–1826)
one of the founders of the American political system. He later served as vice president under George Washington and as president from 1797 to 1801.

discussionquestions

1. How would you describe the early relationship between colonial assemblies and the royal governors? Was it always confrontational?

2. In what ways do the colonial forms of government continue to shape the political and economic systems we have today?

pragmatic issues—the Great Squeeze made life in the colonies harder and the prospects of a profitable future dimmer for most colonists, not only for those in the business class but also for working people in port cities like Boston and Philadelphia. The Stamp and Sugar Acts were oppressive, and the backlash against them was fierce. Parliament also passed many measures that placed lands in the western regions under British control. Because land represented profits—from sales of acreage, lumber, or farm products—many colonists saw this move as unbearable. The **Acts for Trade** were an additional series of moves by Parliament to channel money back to the commercial class in Great Britain. King George III (along with Parliament) sought to save money by demanding that each colony pay for the upkeep of the British soldiers occupying their territory. On a practical level, the Revolution was about the money.

▶ **What about the famous Boston Tea Party . . . wasn't that about taxes?** At a deeper level was a desire growing among Americans to create a system in which all citizens (at least all white, male, propertied citizens) would have a say in the conduct of government and in which basic freedoms of life and liberty would be protected. Echoing this idea, one of the rallying cries during this period was "No taxation without representation." The essence of self-governance, Americans argued, was the ability to control taxes. After Parliament imposed yet another revenue-raising measure, this time giving the bankrupt but politically powerful East India Company a monopoly on importing tea into the colonies, a band of enraged colonists, disguised as Indians, stormed a merchant ship in Boston harbor in the dark of night and threw the company's tea overboard. For many colonists, the so-called Boston Tea Party was a galvanizing event that rallied patriotic sentiment. It was a public expression of deep and growing animosities between an aristocratic government thousands of miles away and a public yearning for freedom and self-rule. For Parliament and George III, the event reflected growing unrest in the colonies—it was an act of insolence that had to be punished and suppressed. Parliament quickly passed five new measures, which the British called the **Coercive Acts** and the colonists referred to as the **Intolerable Acts** (see Table 2.2). Of course, these new measures only stoked the flames of rebellion.

But taxation without representation was not the only ideological issue. The old splits over parliamentary prerogatives were transformed into a debate on the exact nature of self-governance. The colonists had grown accustomed to an unprecedented level of freedom. In Great Britain and throughout Europe, laws and customs limited access to trades and professions, controlled land usage, and compelled people to belong to established churches. The Pilgrims had come to the New World in search of religious freedom, and in large measure they had found it. The following generations began to consider and demand what they saw as their "rights."

During this period, a good deal of attention was paid to the writings of great philosophers on the rights of citizens and the proper conduct of government (see Table 2.3, on page 46). The English political theorist **John Locke** (1632–1704), in particular, had written a number of widely read essays on the subject, most notably *Two Treatises of Government,* which first appeared in 1690. Locke argued that all legitimate governing authority is based on the consent of the governed and that all individuals have "natural rights." Later in the eighteenth century, the Scottish economist **Adam Smith** (1723–1790) wrote about the importance of limiting government as a protection of the economic rights of citizens.

In the colonies, a number of people started to write on liberty, including a young Massachusetts lawyer named **John Adams**

TABLE 2.2 **The Intolerable Acts, 1774**	
Boston Port Bill	Closed Boston harbor
Massachusetts Government Act	Annulled the Massachusetts colonial charter
Administration of Justice Act	Protected British officials from colonial courts by sending them home for trial if arrested
Quartering Act	Legalized the housing of British troops in private homes
Quebec Act	Created a highly centralized government for Canada

SOURCE: www.u_s_history.com

▶ What is the "common sense" of democracy?

TABLE 2.3
Foundational Philosophers of the Revolution

Philosopher's Name	Philosopher's Dates	Country of Origin	Core Ideas to the Revolution	Key Quote
John Locke	1632–1704	England	Just governments are directed by the will of its citizens; that is, just governments are limited. Also, revolutions are not only a right, but an obligation under certain circumstances.	"And reason . . . teaches all mankind who will but consult it, that being all equal and independent, no one ought to harm another in his life, health, liberty or possessions."
Adam Smith	1723–1790	Scotland	Free markets can help ensure the success of a nation and the success of limited governments.	"Every man, as long as he does not violate the laws of justice, is left perfectly free to pursue his own interest his own way, and to bring both his industry and capital into competition with those of any other man or order of men."
John Adams	1735–1826	United States	Freedom is an inalienable right of all people.	"The way to secure liberty is to place it in the people's hands, that is, to give them the power at all times to defend it in the legislature and in the courts of justice."
Thomas Paine	1737–1809	England	Average citizens can be responsible for creating their own laws.	"That government is best which governs least."
Thomas Jefferson	1743–1826	United States	When government fails, it is the right of citizens to cast that system aside and start something new.	"I would rather be exposed to the inconveniences attending too much liberty than those attending too small a degree of it."
Thomas Hobbes	1588–1679	England	People create governments to enhance their own security.	In the state of nature, life was "solitary, poor, nasty, brutish, and short." "The right of nature . . . is the liberty each man hath to use his own power, as he will himself, for the preservation of his own nature; that is to say, of his own life."

There were practical forces that pushed colonists to the revolutionary cause, but there were also emerging theoretical notions about "just" governments and the freedoms of average citizens. This table provides information on several important political theorists. You should also know that their perspectives continue to shape debate about the proper role of government and citizens.

Stamp Act Congress
a meeting in October 1765 of delegates from Britain's American colonies to discuss the recently passed Stamp Act. The Congress adopted a declaration of rights and wrote letters to the king and both houses of Parliament. Many historians view this gathering as a precursor of the American Revolution.

Thomas Paine (1737–1809)
an American Revolutionary writer and democratic philosopher whose pamphlet *Common Sense* (1776) argued for complete independence from Britain. Later pamphlets inspired colonists to join the Patriot cause.

(1735–1826). In 1765, he began publishing a series of essays in which he offered a fervent defense of patriotism. "Liberty must at all hazards be supported," he argued.[10] The writings struck an immediate chord, noted one historian.[11] That same year, a group of delegates from the colonies gathered to discuss the new Stamp Act and to consider responses to it. The **Stamp Act Congress** produced the Declaration of Rights and Grievances, a powerful statement on the rights of citizens that was widely circulated. A decade later, when Americans found themselves debating the fateful step of seeking independence, **Thomas Paine** (1737–1809) wrote a highly influential and persuasive tract promising freedom, equality, and the prospect of democracy.

pathways profile

THOMAS PAINE AND THE "COMMON SENSE" OF DEMOCRACY

▶ **What is the "common sense" of democracy?**

Immigrating to America in 1775 on the advice of Benjamin Franklin, the English journalist Thomas Paine became known as the "common sense" writer of Revolutionary America. Paine was among the first writers of political pamphlets, his most famous of which, *Common Sense,* strengthened the colonists' will to achieve independence and to demand their rights as citizens. Though not as widely lauded today as George Washington, Thomas Jefferson, and John Adams, Paine was a spirited patriot and a pioneer of grassroots political activism. Perhaps more than anyone else in his day, Paine understood the power of public opinion and how to stir the passions of common men and women. "It is Paine who speaks not only for his own time, the time of change, but for our own, in a language that spans two centuries," wrote a modern scholar.[12] After the American Revolution, Paine returned to England with the intention of building a bridge that he had designed, but with the outbreak of the French Revolution in 1789, he took up the cause of ordinary people in France by writing his equally strong work *The Rights of Man.* Paine had the bad luck to back the wrong French Revolutionary faction and barely escaped the guillotine. Returning to the United States, he lived the rest of his life in poverty; he was no longer popular among Americans because he had become, like so many of the French revolutionaries, a vocal critic of Christianity. ▪

A statue of Thomas Paine in his hometown, Thetford, England, February 2006. You might be surprised to hear that our former mother country is dotted with both large and small tributes to American history and culture.

Photo: The New York Times

▶ **What was the Continental Congress—did it have real powers?**

Edmund Burke (1729–1797) a British writer and politician who was a member of Great Britain's House of Commons during America's pre-Revolutionary period.

The very nature of life in the New World created a yearning for basic rights, equality, and freedom. All settlers faced the same realities: an untamed wilderness, the approach of winter, and the prospects of disease, starvation, and often hostile natives. In a very real sense, there was simply less opportunity for a rigid class system to emerge in the New World because all the settlers had to roll up their sleeves and work together. And if colonists felt the yoke of oppression, they could simply move to the next colony. America was not a truly egalitarian society, but realities of life in the New World encouraged thinking about rights, freedoms, and egalitarian societies. And at the very least, the prospects of moving up from the laboring class were somewhat more real here than in Europe, and it was on the mind of every laborer who toiled to make a better life. As John Adams would write, "Let us recollect it was liberty, the hope of liberty, for themselves and us and ours, which conquered all discouragements, dangers, and trials."[13]

Together, financial issues and concerns over the rights of citizens fueled a revolt against British rule. The issue had started to boil over by the mid-1770s. **Edmund Burke,** a member of Great Britain's House of Commons, noted at the time that "the state of America has been kept in continual agitation. Everything administered as remedy to the public complaint, if it did not produce, was at least followed by, an heightening of the distemper." Burke observed that the colonists "owe little or nothing to any care of ours" thanks to "a wise and salutary neglect" from their British overlords.[14] In other words, the stage was set for a dramatic event.

THE DECLARATION OF INDEPENDENCE

▶ **What was the Continental Congress—did it have real powers?** By September 1774, in the aftermath of the Coercive Acts and the Boston Tea Party, events seemed to be spinning out of control. Every colony except Georgia sent delegates to the First Continental Congress in Philadelphia. At this point, few openly spoke of breaking ties with Great Britain; most still hoped to find a compromise that would protect the rights of Americans and pull back the harshest tax measures. Still, in the absence of dramatic changes by George III and Parliament, the delegates called on the colonists to boycott all British goods.

Matters did not improve. Within a year, the royal governor of Massachusetts, Thomas Gage, ordered his troops to seize what was believed to be a growing supply of arms from the colonists at Concord. Before the 700 red-coated British troops sent from Boston reached Concord, 77 militia, called "Minutemen," met them at the small town of Lexington. Shots were fired, and the Minutemen retreated. The Redcoats pressed forward, but by the time they arrived at Concord the Patriot forces had swelled to more than 300. After another battle, the royal troops had to retreat and were attacked repeatedly as they marched back to Boston. In the end, some 270 British soldiers and 95 colonists were killed. The event sent shockwaves throughout the colonies and across the Atlantic Ocean. The wheels of war had been set in motion.

Although there was still strong sentiment in America for reconciliation with Great Britain, many of the delegates who attended the Second Continental Congress in 1775 considered compromise impossible. They understood that war had in fact begun. But they still had to convince others throughout the colonies that armed rebellion was their only remaining chance. Not all Americans were convinced. British oppression had been real, but a war for independence was an altogether different matter. Many of those who had protested British abuses still remained loyal to England, and others were quite unsure of open rebellion. At the very same time that delegates were arriving at Philadelphia, petitions were circulating in towns and villages throughout the colonies calling for reconciliation with Great Britain. Something needed to be done to convince more colonists to rebel, to move with force toward a system of self-governance. Perhaps a statement, a clearly written rationale, would do the trick. A committee of five was formed, and the task of writing a draft was given to a young, rather shy delegate from Virginia by the name of Thomas Jefferson. He was considered a thoughtful young man and an excellent writer.

Jefferson's Declaration of Independence is today regarded as one of the most lucid statements ever written on the rights of citizens and the proper role of government in a free society. It is one of the world's great democratic documents and has been the inspiration of people yearning for freedom around the globe. As one recent writer noted, even today, "you can still get a rush from those opening paragraphs. 'We hold these truths to be self evident.' The

▶ **Just that first sentence** of the Declaration of Independence says a lot, doesn't it?

natural rights
basic rights that no government can deny.

social contract theory
a political theory that holds that individuals give up certain rights in return for securing certain freedoms. If the government breaks the social contract, grounds for revolution exist. This notion was at the core of the Declaration of Independence.

Thomas Hobbes (1588–1679)
an English philosopher who argued that humans are selfish by nature and live lives that are "nasty, brutish, and short." For safety, people form governments, but give up certain rights. His most influential book was *Leviathan*, published in 1651.

This famous picture depicts one of the greatest moments in the history of democratic governance—the signing of the Declaration of Independence. Did you know that these men all feared they were signing their own death warrants? Indeed if the British had won the war, it is highly likely that these men would have been hanged as traitors. Would you have put your life on the line for the "cause of liberty?"

audacity!"[15] The core of the statement can be found in just eighty-three words:

> We hold these truths to be self-evident, that all men are created equal, that they are endowed by their Creator with certain unalienable Rights, that among these are Life, Liberty and the pursuit of Happiness. That to secure these rights Governments are instituted among Men, deriving their just power from the consent of the governed, That whenever any Form of Government becomes destructive of these ends, it is the Right of the People to alter or abolish it, and to institute new Government. . . .

Rarely has more been said in so few words. Let us examine this passage in detail. (You might also wish to examine the annotated version of the Declaration in Appendix 1, page A-1.)

▶ **Just that first sentence of the Declaration of Independence says a lot, doesn't it?** First, Jefferson presents a notion of **natural rights.** That is, individuals possess certain privileges—certain guarantees by virtue of being human. Second, these rights are *not* granted by government but instead by God, whom Jefferson calls the Creator. They cannot be given, nor can they be taken away. Third, Jefferson introduces the **social contract theory,** drawn in large measure from the writings of John Locke. Humans have the option of living alone in what Locke called "the state of nature." According to this theory, humans originally lived without government or laws, enjoying complete personal freedom. Yet the state of nature meant "a war of all against all," in which—in the words of another philosopher, **Thomas Hobbes**—life was "solitary, poor, nasty, brutish, and short." To end this perpetual conflict and insecurity, people created governments, thereby giving up some of their freedoms in order to protect their lives and their property. Fourth, Jefferson agreed with Locke that governments, having been created by the people to protect their rights, are limited; they get their powers from the will of the people and no one else. (In arguing this, Locke was attacking the traditional claim

ABOVE: **Patriots pulling down a statue of King George III** in New York, after hearing the news of the signing of the Declaration of Independence.

BELOW: **Saddam Hussein** being pulled down in Bagdad on April 9, 2003. Many assumed that with the toppling of Hussein's regime, a democracy could be created in Iraq. But this goal has proven illusive, and the occupation of Iraq has been vastly more difficult than most had expected. Can you think of some reasons why this is so?

that kings ruled by the will of God.) Finally, said Jefferson (again following Locke), when a government fails to respect the will of the people—that is, when it appears no longer to be limited—it becomes the right, indeed the obligation, of citizens to change the government. This passage is Jefferson's call for revolution.

It should be restated that Jefferson's assignment was not to create a grand, original statement on the rights of citizens or the proper nature of government. His task was to craft a document that would sum up his fellow patriots' thinking and would provide a justification for colonists as they took up arms against British rule. His job was to write a persuasive statement, aimed at public opinion in America, in Britain, and in continental Europe. In fact, he did far more.

But was the Declaration of Independence effective in rallying support behind the Revolutionary cause? We do know that many New Yorkers were so inspired upon hearing these words that they toppled a statute of King George and had it melted down to make 42,000 bullets for war.[16] Still, this is a difficult question to answer, because there was no accurate way to measure public opinion in those days. Many did take up arms and rally to the Patriot cause, but many balked at joining the Revolution and even enlisted in the British Army. We also know that public support for the Continental Army, headed by George Washington, lagged considerably throughout the Revolution. Most Americans were deeply suspicious of professional armies, fearing them as a threat to liberty. There were no mechanisms to collect funds to support the Continental Army; state contributions were very stingy (which helps explain the terrible conditions that the troops suffered at Valley Forge in the winter of 1777–1778); and many citizens remained cautious about joining in the bold gamble for independence.

Either way, war had begun between the most powerful nation in the world—Great Britain—and the American colonies. At first, things looked grim for the Patriot cause, and many Americans feared that all would be lost within a matter of weeks. By December 1776, the end seemed near. But three startling developments seemed to turn the tide.

First, with bold leadership from Washington, the Continental Army was able to gain a few high-profile victories, which served to assure Patriots and foreign governments that the war could in fact be won and that their financial contributions to the war effort would not be wasted.

Second, from 1776 to 1783, Thomas Paine espoused the virtues of democracy in his sixteen famous "Crisis" papers. Their tone is apparent in the famous opening of "The American Crisis,

Number 1," published on December 19, 1776, when Washington's army was on the verge of disintegration:

> These are the times that try men's souls. The summer soldier and the sunshine patriot will, in this crisis, shrink from the service of their country; but he that stands it now, deserves the love and thanks of man and woman. Tyranny, like hell, is not easily conquered; yet we have this consolation with us, that the harder the conflict, the more glorious the triumph.

This was powerful stuff. Washington ordered the pamphlet read to all his troops.[17]

Third, the French government decided to support the Revolutionary forces. This decision came, after a prolonged diplomatic effort spearheaded in Paris by Benjamin Franklin, upon news that the Americans had inflicted a serious defeat on the British Army at Saratoga in October 1777. Financial support, arms and ammunition, and military assistance from the French government proved immensely helpful—particularly on occasions when the prospects for victory still seemed bleak.

THE COLONIAL EXPERIENCE AND THE PATHWAYS OF CHANGE

Having some gripes with your government is one thing; deciding to break away and form a new government is quite another. A move of this sort would seem especially momentous given that in 1776 Britain had the world's most powerful army and navy. It has been said that the signers of the Declaration of Independence assumed that they were signing their own death warrants. Barbara Ehrenreich writes, "If the rebel American militias were beaten on the battlefield, their ringleaders could expect to be hanged as traitors."[18]

How did things come to this? Ideas of liberty, equality, and self-governance—captured so well by Jefferson's pen—had simmered throughout the colonies for decades. Jefferson's prose captured a sentiment, but he did not bring the idea of democracy to life. Like flowers bursting from the ground after a long winter, liberty and equality were destined to blossom in the American soil. Also, as we noted in (L I N K) *Chapter 1, pages 23–28,* governments whose citizens yearn for liberty are stable only if these citizens have avenues of change—the means to move public policy in new directions as times and circumstances change. What pathways of change had been available to the colonists? Could they elect a

new government or petition the courts for redress? Might average citizens effectively lobby members of Parliament, an ocean away? Protests were tried, such as the Boston Tea Party, but they were met with additional acts of repression. There seemed no option for change. The only recourse was to declare independence and prepare for war. In a very real way, the American Revolution underscores the importance of our pathways concept.

Another interesting issue to ponder is what might be the right course for those who *perceive* no viable pathways of change. If you think that your government is no longer listening to your concerns—the concerns of average citizens—and that there is no way to bring the system back in line, must revolution follow? Is not Jefferson clear that under such circumstances, revolution is justified? In 1787, Jefferson claimed that "the tree of liberty must be refreshed from time to time with the blood of patriots and tyrants."[19] And have we seen this process played out in American history since the Revolution? Indeed we have.

pathways past and present
TIMOTHY MCVEIGH'S REVOLUTION?

To some when thinking about Jefferson's notion of refreshing the tree of liberty, the bombing of the Alfred P. Murrah Federal Building by Timothy McVeigh in April 1995 comes to mind. This was one of the most horrific crimes in American history—the worst terrorist attack on American soil before the twenty-first century. Tragically, 169 men, women, and children were killed.

Was this act in any way similar to what occurred shortly after the Second Continental Congress proclaimed colonial independence? Revolutions are usually bloody affairs, and they have to begin in some way, so were McVeigh's actions different from Jefferson's? McVeigh felt profoundly frustrated by the direction of government and society and by his inability to change things. He was a white separatist who believed that the federal government had become oppressive, particularly through its restrictions on gun ownership. Philosophically speaking, was his "revolution" all that different from Jefferson's?

Yes. There are many important differences between McVeigh's act and what Jefferson set in motion—not the least of which was McVeigh's killing of civilians, including children. ("Collateral damage," he callously called these deaths.) Moral dimensions surely matter. We might also underscore two additional differences. First, the colonists possessed few, if any, avenues

ABOVE: **Timothy McVeigh's bombing** of the Alfred P. Murrah Federal Building in April of 1995 was one of the most horrific crimes in American history. Some 169 men, women, and children were killed.

BELOW: **McVeigh targeted a federal government building** because he considered the act part of a war against the government. Might this horrendous act be considered a "revolution" in any way similar to what Jefferson envisioned when he penned the Declaration of Independence? What were some of the peaceful pathways for change that McVeigh might have used—that the patriots were denied?

discussionquestions

1. The Declaration of Independence is hailed as one of the greatest statements in the history of self-governance. What makes it so special?

2. It has been said that oppressed groups will not rebel until they perceive a gap between the way things are and the way they should be. That is, rebellions are spurred on by rising expectations. How does this help explain the American Revolution?

for change. McVeigh had many other options for expressing his protest and working toward his goals. Although change often comes slowly, American history has shown that determined individuals and groups *can* move governmental policy in a new direction. The pathways of change available to McVeigh were vast compared to what the colonists confronted, but he never tried those other routes. Second, Jefferson seemed to anticipate the question of "frequent revolutions" and went to great lengths to list the long train of abuses by the British government. Roughly nine-tenths of the Declaration of Independence is a list of grievances. Quoting almost verbatim from his intellectual mentor John Locke, Jefferson reminds us that "prudence . . . will dictate that governments long established should not be changed for light and transient causes." Revolution, the violent overthrow of one's government, is serious business, not to be undertaken lightly. Horrific acts of violence cannot be justified by calling them "revolutionary." ■

practicequiz

1. The call for "no taxation without representation"
   a. suggested that taxes were simply too high in the colonies and that a new system of government was needed to bring them down.
   b. told of a growing ideological movement to create a system in which all citizens (at least all white, male, propertied citizens) would have a say in the affairs of government.
   c. did very little to bring colonists to the Patriot cause.
   d. a and c.

2. Which of the following men spoke of "limited governments"?
   a. Thomas Paine
   b. John Locke
   c. Adam Smith
   d. Benjamin Franklin

3. The nature of life in the New World promoted a more democratic system because
   a. there were few leaders to promote their own narrow interests.
   b. everyone had to work together to overcome the difficulties of frontier life.
   c. when colonists felt the yoke of oppression, they simply moved to another village or state.
   d. b and c.

▶ **What kind of government**
did the colonies adopt
during the revolution?

what **YOU** can do!

By 1765, Patrick Henry, a lawyer from Hanover County, Virginia, had emerged as a leader in protests against British tyranny. His speech to the Virginia Assembly—demanding "Give me liberty or give me death"—was repeated in taverns, homes, and courtyards throughout the colonies. It is a powerful discourse on the duty of every citizen in a democracy to join the political fray, even when there are risks. You can hear his speech at **http://www.history.org/Almanack/people/bios/biohen.cfm**

---

4. Thomas Jefferson suggested in the Declaration of Independence that just governments are "limited." This means that governments must
   a. have no more than three branches.
   b. derive their powers from the consent of the governed.
   c. tax people only if they have a voice in the process.
   d. be renewed by the people through revolutions now and again.

Answers: 1-b, 2-a, b, c, d, 3-b, 4-b.

Raquel Reburn, of California, (left) and Chuck Sciens of Dayton Ohio argue over the case of Oklahoma City Bomber Timothy McVeigh outside the federal prison in Terre Haute, Indiana, June 10, 2001. Sciens, who said that McVeigh was a patriot, argued with Reburn, whose husband works in the prison system. McVeigh was executed just after dawn by lethal injection, June 11, 2001.

The Articles of Confederation

▶ **What kind of government did the colonies adopt during the revolution?** Less than a week after the signing of the Declaration of Independence, the Continental Congress set to work drawing up a system of government for the self-declared independent American states. After a year's effort, the model that emerged was called the Articles of Confederation. The idea was to draw the thirteen states together but at the same time to allow each state to remain independent. In this system, the central government could coordinate and recommend policies, but it had no ability to enforce these policies if the states refused. Even so, it took three years for all the states to approve the plan, meaning that during much of the war, no central government existed (although Congress continued to function). The Articles of Confederation were formally adopted on March 1, 1781.

The Articles provided for a one-house Congress, in which each state had one vote. The delegates to the Congress were just messengers of the states, appointed to their posts by their state legislature. They were paid by the states and could be removed by their state legislature at any time. (An analogy would be today's United Nations, where each nation has one delegate and one vote and where this person serves at the discretion of the home government.) On paper, at least, this Congress had power to conduct

▶ Why did the Articles of Confederation fail?

foreign affairs, wage war, create a postal service, appoint military officers, control Indian affairs, borrow money, and determine the value of the coinage.[20] But the Articles did not give the national government the power to force its policies on the states, nor did it allow for the levying of taxes to support the federal government (see Table 2.4). It was up to the states to contribute to the federal government's support as they saw fit (just as each member nation of the United Nations contributes what it wishes to the UN budget). And the Articles said nothing about judicial matters.

The fact that the Articles guarded state sovereignty is really not surprising. Given the hardships that the colonists had endured under the government of King George III, one can surely understand the desire for something different. In a very real way, our first system of national government was designed to be the opposite of what colonists had experienced under authoritarian, centralizing British rule. It was also widely believed at the time that democracy was possible only when government is local. The "will of the people," thought most Americans, is best expressed on a local scale. Would it really make sense to merge the interests of northeastern manufacturing states and those of southern agricultural states? Moreover, if the government were to be a republic, in which representatives speak and act for constituents, then smaller governments would also make better sense because their representatives would more likely know the interests of their constituents. We should also not be surprised to learn that under the Articles the governing authority, although weak, rested in the legislature.

TABLE 2.4
Powers of Congress under the Articles of Confederation

What Congress Could Do	What Congress Could Not Do
Borrow money	Regulate commerce
Request money from states	Collect taxes from citizens
	Prohibit states from conducting foreign affairs
Conduct foreign affairs	Establish a national commercial system
Maintain army and navy	Force states to comply with laws
Appoint military officers	Establish a draft
Establish courts	Collect money from states for services
Establish a postal system	
Control Indian affairs	

The Articles did not create an executive office (such as a president). Once again, Americans' fear of creating a system similar to the British model led them in a different direction. Why would they consider crafting a new system of government with a powerful executive, given their recent experience with George III?

LIMITATIONS OF THE ARTICLES OF CONFEDERATION

▶ **Why did the Articles of Confederation fail?** The Articles failed for several reasons. First, the national government had no way to collect revenue from the states or from the states' citizens. No government can survive without some means of obtaining the resources it needs to operate. Second, the national government had no way of regulating commerce. For example, each state could tax the goods imported from other states or coin or print its own money. Imagine the problems that would result today if each of the fifty states issued its own currency! Third, the national government was unable to conduct foreign affairs—that is, to speak to other nations with a unified voice. Fourth, the mechanism to alter the Articles proved too difficult, as any change required the unanimous consent of all thirteen states. (In other words, just one state could veto any change.) So even if adjustments could improve matters, such as giving the national government the power to collect taxes, the chances of achieving unanimous agreement to do so were slim.

Yet another shortcoming of the Articles was the lack of leadership and accountability within the federal government. There was no one in charge. This was intentional, of course, reflecting the fear that any person or group placed in a position of authority would have the power to abuse the position and become corrupt. This issue of accountability came to a head in 1786 with an event that rocked western Massachusetts. During the mid-1780s, the nation had experienced an economic depression. Particularly hard hit were farmers, who were receiving much less for their crops than in previous years due to a flood of imports. Desperate for relief, a group of farmers, led by Daniel Shays, a veteran Patriot militia captain who had fought against the British at Bunker Hill in 1775, gathered to demand changes. Frustrated that their calls for help seemed to fall on deaf ears at the state legislature, Shays's forces grew to nearly 2,500. Soon violence broke out as the group clashed with state militia forces. Shays's men even turned their anger at the national government, threatening to storm an arsenal in Springfield, Massachusetts. The governor and state legislature appealed for assistance in putting down the protest, which, they argued, had deteriorated into a full-blown riot. Surely this was a

▶ What happened
to the rebels?

Shays's Rebellion
an armed uprising in Western Massachusetts in 1786 and 1787 by small farmers
angered by high debt and tax burdens.

Constitutional Convention
a meeting in Philadelphia in 1787 where
delegates from the colonies drew up a
new system of government. The finished
product was the Constitution of the
United States.

matter for the central government to deal with. But there was no
person or group outside Massachusetts to take the call for assistance, and no help was available.

▶ **What happened to the rebels?** Many of the rebels were
captured and sentenced to death for treason, but all were later
pardoned. Yet **Shays's Rebellion** had a profound impact on the
future of our nation because it suggested that liberty and freedom—that is, an open democratic society—carried risks. Many
people believed that a truly open system was fertile soil for violence and anarchy. George Washington commented, "There are
combustibles in every state which a spark might set fire to. . . .
If government cannot check these disorders, what security has
a man for life, liberty, or property?"[21] Washington's young
wartime aide Alexander Hamilton agreed, noting that the rebellion prompted "the question, whether societies of men are really
capable or not of establishing good government from reflection
and choice, or whether they are forever destined to depend
for their political constitutions on accident and force."[22] Many
people feared that the answer was the latter. At the very least,
the event suggested that the national government was woefully
inept.

A few months after the uprising in Massachusetts, a meeting
was organized to revise the Articles. This was the **Constitutional
Convention.**

SHAYS'S REBELLION:
AN ALTERNATIVE LOOK

The traditional view of the forces that led to the Constitutional
Convention emphasizes the shortcomings of the Articles, which
we've summarized. The national government was just too weak,
says the traditional perspective; it was not able to regulate commerce or conduct foreign policy, and there was no mechanism to
deal with emergencies. Shays's Rebellion was simply the straw that
broke the camel's back, a focusing event that set the wheels of
change in motion.

But there is another way to look at this related to how you
interpret Shays's uprising. Why would Shays and his 2,500 followers turn to violent protest? Were there no other pathways for
change?

Money, especially specie or "hard money" (silver and gold
coin), became very scarce throughout the United States in the
1780s, resulting in a severe depression that lasted nearly a decade.
But not everyone was affected the same. Hardest hit were working-class citizens and small farmers. Because these people had

Shays's Rebellion in 1786 is shown. We often
hear that this event shocked the nation and
led to the Constitutional Convention a year
later. But what did the event signify?
What caused Shays and his followers to vent
their frustration at the government in
Springfield, Massachusetts? Does
the answer say anything about the nature
of government in Massachusetts in the 1880s?

▶ **Why did the delegates**
from large and small states
favor different plans at the
Contitutional Convention?

discussionquestions

1. Where did governmental power rest under the Articles of Confederation? Why?

2. Would it be fair to say that our experience with the Articles of Confederation was a complete failure?

little or no hard money with which to pay their debts, bank fore-closures skyrocketed. By the mid-1780s, demands for action grew louder. Very much in keeping with the structure of government during this period, people's cries for assistance were directed to the state legislatures. That often worked, and the state legislatures responded with many changes. "Stay laws" were passed to post-pone foreclosures, and "tender laws" allowed farmers to use agri-cultural products (rather than hard money) to help pay loans. Partly as a result, inflation surged, and as paper money became more widespread, it became easier to use this inflated currency to pay off debts, such as the mortgage on a farm. In a very real sense, democracy seemed to be working. There was a call for help, and *most* state legislatures responded.[23]

In one state, however, the legislature dragged its feet: Massachusetts. What made this state different? For one thing, business interests dominated the state legislature. Instead of help-ing small farmers, the legislature saw fit to levy heavy taxes in an attempt to pay off the state's wartime debts, with most of the money going to wealthy business owners in Boston. From this vantage point, Shays's Rebellion broke out because the channels of the democratic process were *not* working in Massachusetts. There seemed no other viable pathway for change, and violence erupted.

This perspective also allows us to reconsider the motiva-tions of the delegates to the Constitutional Convention. Today, many historians believe that the aim of that meeting was to fine-tune the democratic process and to create a stronger national government. In some ways this is true. But the policies of the state governments designed to protect farmers and laborers dur-ing the depression of the 1780s created hardship for a different group—the economic elite. As noted earlier, there are always winners and losers in politics, and during this period much that was given to the farmers was taken from business owners and bankers. There were many more farmers and laborers, so you might conclude that the "will of the people" was dictating public policy, a very democratic notion. Perhaps, then, some of the rationale for calling delegates to Philadelphia was to revise the Articles in order to make sure that state governments could not limit the "liberty" of the economic elite. Even James Madison gave a hint at this when, in The *Federalist Papers* (described later in this chapter), he called the "rage for paper money" (inflation) as an "improper" and "wicked" project.[24] Would Captain Shays and his followers have thought of inflation and other policies designed to help them keep their homes and livelihoods as

wicked? Certainly not. At the very least, perhaps the conven-tion's goal was to check the "democratic spirit" of the public in the name of stability. This is a controversial perspective but something you might consider.

practicequiz

1. As you now know, the Articles of Confederation provided for a weak national government. This was done because
   a. the people who put the plan together made a series of mistakes.
   b. there was an ongoing fear of a strong centralized govern-ment.
   c. there was a belief that democracy was possible only when government is small and localized.
   d. b and c.

2. Under the Articles of Confederation, each state could
   a. conduct its own foreign affairs.
   b. print its own money.
   c. regulate its own commercial system.
   d. a, b, and c.

3. Shays's Rebellion led to the Constitutional Convention because
   a. it suggested that even one individual could bring down the federal government.
   b. the federal government was too weak to respond to a crisis.
   c. state governments were willing to crush the liberties of individuals if given the opportunity.
   d. Shays was a powerful reformer who carried a lot of weight with other elites in the system.

4. The alternative view of Shays's Rebellion suggests that one of the motivations of the constitutional framers was to pro-tect the economic interests of business owners.
   a. true   b. false

Answers: 1-d, 2-d, 3-b, 4-a

The Constitutional Convention

In late May 1787, some fifty-five delegates from every state except Rhode Island came together at the Pennsylvania State House in Philadelphia for the purpose of proposing changes to the Articles of Confederation. Congress itself had authorized the meeting, but

> ► **What was really at stake** in this compromise, and why was it so hard to reach agreement?

Virginia Plan
a plan made by delegates to the Constitutional Convention from several of the larger states, calling for a strong national government bicameral legislature, a national executive, a national judiciary, and legislative representation based on population. Much of this plan found its way into the Constitution.

New Jersey Plan
a scheme for government advanced at the Constitutional Convention that was supported by delegates from smaller states. It called for equal representation of states in a one-house legislature.

it did not expect that the Articles would be completely replaced by a new system of government. The delegates were not "average" men but rather included many of America's leading political, economic, and social figures of the time. (Thomas Jefferson, then serving as U.S. minister to France, was not present.) George Washington was selected as the convention's presiding officer, and on May 29, the delegates set to work. Interestingly, and perhaps contrary to what you might think, the convention deliberated in total secrecy—even to the extent of nailing the windows shut!

Opening the convention, Governor Edmund Randolph of Virginia offered a series of resolutions that amounted to an assault on the Articles. Rather than attempting to modify them, Randolph argued, the Articles should be dumped altogether. The delegates agreed; something new and vastly different was needed. Small groups were formed, charged with drawing up plans for a new government. In the end, five plans were submitted for consideration, but the delegates quickly narrowed their consideration to two.

The first was the **Virginia Plan,** named for the home state of its principal author, James Madison. The delegates from the more populous states favored it. Table 2.5 provides an overview of what the new government would look like under this plan.

► **Why did the delegates from large and small states favor different plans at the Constitutional Convention?** Most delegates agreed with the core idea of the Virginia Plan—that the central government should be strengthened. Yet big differences in population between the states seemed a problem. The most populous states were Virginia, Pennsylvania, North Carolina, Massachusetts, and New York; the smallest states included (besides absent Rhode Island) Georgia, Delaware, Connecticut, and New Jersey. Delegates from the smaller states realized that this scheme would put them at a real disadvantage in the national government—their state's interests would be overwhelmed by those of the larger states. Opposition to the Virginia Plan grew. William Paterson of New Jersey offered an alternative approach. His **New Jersey Plan** was designed to stick closer to the Articles of Confederation and would create a system of equal representation among the states: Each state would have the same number of national legislators. Table 2.6 on page 58 is an overview of this plan.

Although it might seem that both models are similar when it comes to the supremacy of the national government, this was really not the case. A national legislature was at the core of both plans, but under the New Jersey Plan each state would have equal say in the making of public policy. Since a majority of state governors

TABLE 2.5
The Virginia Plan

- Three branches of government—a national legislature, an executive, and a judiciary.
- Force each of the branches to rely on the others.
- Grant each branch the ability to keep an eye on the other two so that no one segment of the government would become too powerful.
- Have a legislature with an upper and lower house, with members of the lower house chosen by the people in the various states and the upper chamber made up of legislators chosen by the lower house from a list of nominees put forward by the state legislatures.
- Allow each state a number of seats in the national legislature based on its population (thus the larger states would have more delegates and the smaller states fewer).
- Have an executive, selected by the legislature and serving a single term.
- Have judges who would be appointed to the bench by the legislature for life terms.
- Establish a "council of revision," with members from both the executive branch and the judiciary, which would review all national and state laws; this body would have some control over national legislation and an absolute veto over state legislation.
- Be supreme over the state governments—that is, acts of the new national government would override state law.

could change the makeup of the executive council, this plan was clearly more state-centered. It was much more in keeping with the "confederation model" that underlay the Articles. In contrast, the Virginia Plan clearly laid out what was called at the time a "consolidated government," one that all but absorbed the states.

THE GREAT COMPROMISE

► **What was really at stake in this compromise, and why was it so hard to reach agreement?** All the delegates at the convention knew that the legislative branch was critical, but the argument over the allocation of seats in the legislature nearly ended the

**Great Compromise/
Connecticut Compromise**
an agreement at the Constitutional Convention that the new national government would have a House, in which the number of members would be based on each state's population, and a Senate, in which each state would have the same number of representatives. This was a compromise between two competing proposals, the Virginia Plan and the New Jersey Plan. Also known as the **Connecticut Compromise.**

census
a precise count of the population.

TABLE 2.6
The New Jersey Plan

- Have three parts of government—a national legislature, an executive council, and a judiciary.
- Have a legislature consisting of one body, in which each state would have one vote.
- Have a multiperson executive council, chosen by the legislature, with the responsibility of executing national laws; its members could be removed by a vote of a majority of state governors.
- Have a judiciary appointed by the executive council.
- Have a national legislature with the ability to tax the states, proportional to their population.
- Be supreme over the state governments, with the national legislature having the right to override state law.

---

proceedings. "Delegates conferred, factions maneuvered, and tempers flared."[25] The dispute was serious because the delegates believed that if the new national government had real powers (as they all hoped), control of the legislative branch was critical. The stakes were high.

The issue also boiled down to different views of representation: a *state-based approach* versus an *individual-based approach*. It should be remembered that at this time most Americans considered loyalty to their state first over any sort of national allegiance. At the time, even Thomas Jefferson considered Virginia, not the United States, "my country." As noted earlier, a widespread sense of national citizenship did not emerge until after the Civil War, some eighty years later. So the argument over representation came down to which states would have more sway in the new system, and delegates of the smaller states were not about to join a union that would put their own people at a disadvantage. They argued that states were on an equal par, of course, so all should have the same weight in the new national government. *States* were the units to be represented, not the

citizens within each state. But the large states relied on an individual-based notion of representation. The new national government should speak on behalf of *citizens*, not states. If one state had significantly more citizens than another, it was self-evident that the bigger state would have more national representatives.

On June 30, 1787, Roger Sherman of Connecticut presented a compromise plan: The national legislature would have a House of Representatives, based on proportional representation (as under the Virginia Plan), but a second branch, the Senate, would contain an equal number of representatives from each state (as the New Jersey Plan proposed). This **Great Compromise,** sometimes called the **Connecticut Compromise,** settled the matter (see Table 2.7). Few of the delegates were completely satisfied; indeed, some walked out of the proceedings, but most agreed that it was the best possible solution. Several of the states had tried this in their own legislatures, with much success. The plan was accepted, and the convention continued.

THE THREE-FIFTHS COMPROMISE

If one of the chambers of the national legislature was to be based on population (the House of Representatives) and if taxation was to be fixed around each state's population, how would the inhabitants of each state be counted? The delegates quickly agreed that a **census** (a complete count) would be conducted every ten years, and this was written into the Constitution. But *who* might be counted as an inhabitant was a vastly more difficult matter. Here we find one of the most distressing parts of the Constitutional Convention. The issue boiled down to slavery. Over 90 percent of the slaves in North America at that time lived in five American states: Georgia, Maryland, North Carolina, South Carolina, and Virginia.[26] The delegates from these states argued that for the purposes of allocating House seats, slaves should be counted. This was quite a twist, given that slaves were considered property and were not given any rights of citizenship in these states—and the delegates from the northern states retorted as much. Yet given the huge slave populations in the southern states (40 percent or more in some states), not counting them would prove significant. If slaves were not counted, the southern states would have just 41 percent of the seats in the House; if slaves were counted, the South would have 50 percent.

Mourners gather to view the casket of civil rights icon Rosa Parks, whose remains lie in honor in the U.S. Capitol rotunda, October 30, 2005. One of the tragic ironies of our nation's formative period is that while notions of freedom and equality warmed the hearts of patriots and provided a theoretical foundation for the new system of government, slavery was not eliminated in the Constitution.

Once again the Convention came to a standstill, again delegates threatened to bolt, and again a compromise was reached. Population would be used to determine each state's delegation to the House of Representatives, and slaves would be counted as three-fifths of a white person. Put a bit differently, five slaves would equal three white persons in the census. Precisely how the formulation was determined is a bit unclear. We know that a three-fifths figure was used under the Confederation and was thus ready to hand. Perhaps different offers were sent back and forth until a final figure was accepted. Slaves would not be allowed to vote or to have any of the rights that Jefferson had written about in his Declaration of Independence, but they would be counted as inhabitants, or rather three-fifths of an inhabitant, in order to get both sides to agree to the Constitution. Our history is filled with such tragic ironies.

THE SECTIONAL COMPROMISE

There was still another deal, what some historians have called the most important compromise reached at the Constitutional Convention.[27] Even Madison considered this agreement the most important of all deals at the Convention. It dealt with slavery and commerce.

TABLE 2.7
Differences Between the Virginia Plan, the New Jersey Plan, and the Great Compromise

ISSUE	VIRGINIA PLAN	NEW JERSEY PLAN	COMPROMISE
Source of Legislative Power	Derived from the people and based on popular representation	Derived from the states and based on equal votes for each state	A mix; from the people for one house, from the states for the other
Legislative Structure	Bicameral	Unicameral	Bicameral; one house of equal representation, and another based on population
Executive	Size undetermined; elected and removable by Congress	More than one person; removable by state majority	Single executive; removed by impeachment
Judiciary	Life tenure, able to veto legislation in council of revision	No power over states	Life tenure, judicial review ambiguous
State Laws	Legislature can override	Government can compel obedience to national laws	National supremacy
Ratification	By the people	By the states	Ratification conventions in each state, thus allowing both the people and the states to be involved

▶ **How did the Constitution** provide enough power for the government to act decisively, while preventing it from becoming too powerful?

discussionquestions

1. Discuss the motivations of the constitutional framers. What were they trying to accomplish?

2. Why were so many compromises necessary? What do these compromises say about the theory and practice of governance in the United States?

Many northerners hated slavery and pointed out the irony of celebrating the American Revolution and creating a free nation while at the same time preserving the institution of slavery. Southern delegates were not about to join a government that stripped them of their slaves, and even northerners realized that abolishing slavery would shatter the South's economic base. According to one observer, "The subject haunted the closed-door debates."[28]

Most delegates agreed that the new Congress would have the power to regulate commerce, but many also worried about the potential for abuse. This was a very important power. Southern delegates, in particular, worried that because the House would be based on proportional representation and because the power to regulate commerce would reside in the new national government, their states' economic future was at risk. They argued that Congress should require a supermajority (a two-thirds vote, rather than a simple majority) whenever it attempted to regulate commerce. The northern delegates said no, once again worried about giving too much power to less populous states.

This led to another compromise: The Atlantic slave trade would be protected for at least twenty years. Article 1, Section 9, Clause 1 of the Constitution prohibited Congress from stopping the importation of slaves from overseas until 1808. (Slave trading within and among states was not mentioned.) In exchange, it was agreed that a simple majority of both houses of Congress would be needed to regulate commerce. Once again, the convention was able to continue.

practicequiz

1. Which of the following was an element of the Virginia Plan?
   a. a plural executive (an executive with several members)
   b. allotting seats in the legislature in proportion to each state's population
   c. having judges appointed for life
   d. both b and c

2. The Great Compromise created
   a. three branches of government.
   b. a bicameral legislature.
   c. a branch of the legislature directly elected by the people.
   d. both b and c.

3. The sectional compromise dealt with
   a. slavery.
   b. the control of commerce by the national government.
   c. the counting of slaves as part of each state's official population.
   d. both a and b.

4. What best describes the relation between the Constitution and its precursor, the Articles of Confederation?
   a. The Constitution revised a few of the principles of the Articles of Confederation.
   b. The Constitution replaced the Articles of Confederation with something quite different.
   c. The Constitution granted more power to the states and less power to the federal government than did the Articles of Confederation.
   d. Both a and c.

Answers: 1-d, 2-d, 3-d, 4-b

The U.S. Constitution

On September 17, 1787, after five hot, argumentative months, the delegates to the Constitutional Convention finished their work. After hearing the clerk read the entire document, Ben Franklin rose to the floor to remark that although the form of government they had drafted was not perfect, it was the best that could have been achieved under the circumstances. He then made a motion that each delegate sign the final version. Thirty-nine of the original fifty-five who had begun the convention did so.

Most Americans believe that our Constitution is one of the greatest schemes of government ever devised—due in no small measure to the overarching structural framework that created a vibrant yet controlled government, a system that is both rigid and flexible. Much more will be said of provisions in the Constitution in subsequent chapters, but some key points are outlined here. (You might also wish to review the annotated Constitution in the Appendix.)

The Constitution breaks down into seven articles.

Article I: The Legislative Branch (Congress)

Article II: The Executive Branch (President)

Article III: The Judicial Branch (Courts)

Article IV: Guidelines for Relations between States

Article V: The Amendment Process

Article VI: Federal-State Relations (Supremacy Clause); Oath for Officers

Article VII: How the Constitution Will Be Ratified

Let us consider several core principles embodied in the Constitution.

sharing of powers
the U.S. Constitution's granting of specific powers to each branch of government while making each branch partly dependent on the others for carrying out its duties.

horizontal powers
the powers distributed among the three branches of the U.S. national government, as outlined in the Constitution. See also *sharing of powers*.

- **Three Branches of Government.** Understanding both the complexity of governance and the potential for corruption, the framers saw fit to create a system with different branches of government—legislative, executive, and judicial. Simply stated, the legislature would *make* the laws, the president would *enforce* the legislature's will, and the judicial branch would *interpret* the laws and *resolve* disputes according to the law.

  ▶ **How did the Constitution provide enough power for the government to act decisively, while preventing it from becoming too powerful?**

- **Separate Institutions Sharing Powers.** One of the greatest challenges the framers faced was creating a system that was neither too weak nor too strong. A weak government would suffer the fate of the Articles of Confederation, but too strong a government might lead to corruption and an excessive concentration of power, minimize the role of the states, infringe on individual rights, and perhaps collapse in civil war. The framers believed that they had found a middle ground through the granting of specific powers for each branch while at the same time making sure that each branch is partly dependent on the others for carrying out its powers. This is called the **sharing of powers.**

  We will have a lot to say about the powers and duties of each branch, as well as about the connections between the branches, in the chapters that follow, but a few examples might be helpful here. Although Congress passes laws and appropriates funds, the executive branch enforces these laws and spends the money. The judicial branch can pass judgment on disputes that arise, but it must rely on the executive branch to enforce its rulings. The judiciary is "independent," but its members are appointed to the bench by the president with the "advice and consent" (vote of approval) of a majority in the Senate. Congress can also create different layers of the federal court system. The president can negotiate treaties with other nations, but the Senate must ratify these agreements before they take effect. Likewise, the president can nominate ambassadors and cabinet officers, but the Senate must confirm these nominations. The powers between the different branches of the national government are sometimes referred to as the **horizontal powers.**

- **Checks and Balances.** Just as each branch shares powers with the others, each branch is limited ("checked") by the other two. That is to say, each branch can review, and in some ways restrict, the acts of the other branches. For instance, Congress passes laws, but the president can veto proposed legislation—and if both houses can put together a two-thirds vote, they can override a presidential veto. The president can be impeached by the House and, if convicted by a two-thirds vote in the Senate, be removed from office. Federal judges can likewise be removed by impeachment and conviction. The judiciary can invalidate acts of Congress or the president when they are considered "unconstitutional," but Congress and the states can enact amendments to the Constitution that get around judicial decisions (see Figure 2.2, on page 62).

- **Representative Republicanism.** The framers were anxious to create a republican system, in which leaders speak on behalf of constituents, but they also feared a "runaway" democracy. They wanted to create a limited government, a government "by the people," but they worried that the whims of public opinion would lead to an unstable government and perhaps mob rule or "anarchy." The government, as Madison would later remark, should "enlarge and refine" the public's will. Representative republicanism proved the solution. The system would not be a direct democracy, where each person has a say on all public matters, but rather a representative republic in which a small group of elected leaders speak and act on behalf of the many. Members of the House of Representatives are elected directly by the voters; under the original Constitution, senators were to be selected by the state legislatures (a provision that changed to direct popular election when the Seventeenth Amendment was adopted in 1913); and the president would be chosen by an electoral college—envisioned in 1787 as a gathering of a small group of notable leaders in each state to select the federal chief executive. The Constitution rests firmly on the representative republican principle.

- **Federalism.** None of the framers intended to create a centralized government; instead, they all envisioned a system in which a viable national government would undertake certain responsibilities and state governments would handle others. This is known as *federalism*—a system of government in which powers and functions are divided among different layers of the system. The Constitution clearly defines many of

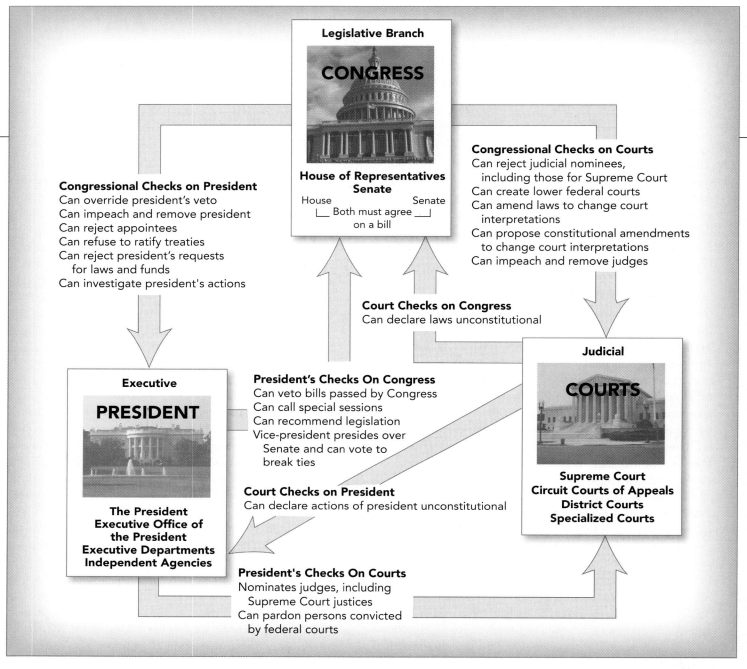

Legislative Branch

CONGRESS

**House of Representatives
Senate**

House   Senate
└─ Both must agree ─┘
on a bill

Congressional Checks on President
Can override president's veto
Can impeach and remove president
Can reject appointees
Can refuse to ratify treaties
Can reject president's requests
   for laws and funds
Can investigate president's actions

Congressional Checks on Courts
Can reject judicial nominees,
   including those for Supreme Court
Can create lower federal courts
Can amend laws to change court
   interpretations
Can propose constitutional amendments
   to change court interpretations
Can impeach and remove judges

Court Checks on Congress
Can declare laws unconstitutional

Executive

PRESIDENT

**The President
Executive Office of
the President
Executive Departments
Independent Agencies**

President's Checks On Congress
Can veto bills passed by Congress
Can call special sessions
Can recommend legislation
Vice-president presides over
   Senate and can vote to
   break ties

Court Checks on President
Can declare actions of president unconstitutional

Judicial

COURTS

**Supreme Court
Circuit Courts of Appeals
District Courts
Specialized Courts**

President's Checks On Courts
Nominates judges, including
   Supreme Court justices
Can pardon persons convicted
   by federal courts

FIGURE 2.2
Shared Powers, Checks and Balances

Many applaud this unique system of government in which each branch is somewhat dependent on the others, and each branch is in some ways checked by the others. Our system's longevity would suggest this model works, but others argue that this model makes change difficult—especially when different political parties control other branches of the government. What do you think? Does this system favor pathways for change, or does it stifle the will of the people?

▶ **Has the Constitution changed** much since it was first written? How are changes made?

expressed powers
the powers explicitly granted to the national government in the U.S. Constitution.

police powers
the powers reserved to state governments related to the health, safety, and well-being of citizens.

Bill of Rights
the first ten amendments to the U.S. Constitution, ratified in 1791, protecting civil liberties.

the powers of the national government, which are referred to as the **expressed powers.**

In 1787, states' governments were considered closest to the people and thus best able to look after their health, safety, and well-being. These powers were called **police powers.** The national government, for its part, would focus on commercial matters, foreign affairs, and national security.

- **Reciprocity among the states.** Although the Constitution permitted each state a degree of independence, delegates to the convention were concerned that citizens should be treated equally in every state. The framers had in mind, for example, that a marriage in one state would be recognized in other states. Two "comity" clauses accomplished this goal. The full faith and credit clause (Article IV, Section 1) said that each state must accept the legal proceedings of the other states, and the privileges and immunities clause (Article IV, Section 2) mandated that out-of-state citizens have the same legal rights as citizens of that state. While on vacation in New York, for instance, you have the same rights as people living there.

    ▶ **Has the Constitution changed much since it was first written? How are changes made?**

- **A Fixed System Open to Change.** The framers had in mind a rather fixed scheme of government, something that would not change with the winds of public opinion or the shifting personnel of government. What good would a constitution be if it could be changed every time new issues emerged or when new people took office? At the same time, they recognized that their document was not perfect and that new pressures would arise as the nation grew and as society changed. The outcome was to create a difficult but navigable route for change. The Constitution can be amended by a total of four procedures, as noted in Figure 2.3 on page 64.

    Since the Constitution's ratification, there have been thousands of proposals for constitutional amendments, but only twenty-seven have made it through the journey to formal amendment. The first ten amendments, which make up the **Bill of Rights** (see Table 2.8), were enacted during the very first session of Congress, in large part as a response to criticisms of the original Constitution by its opponents during the ratification process. It would seem that the framers accomplished their goal of creating a fixed structure but also one that could be changed at critical times. The Bill of Rights

TABLE 2.8
The First Ten Amendments to the Constitution (The Bill of Rights)

Safeguards of Personal and Political Freedoms
1. Freedom of speech, press, and religion, and right to assemble peaceably and to petition government to redress grievances
2. Right to keep and bear arms

Outmoded Protection Against British Occupation
3. Protection against quartering troops in private homes

Safeguards in the Judicial Process and Against Arbitrary Government Action
4. Protection against "unreasonable" searches and seizures by the government
5. Guarantees of a grand jury for capital crimes, against double jeopardy, against being forced to testify against oneself, against being deprived of life or property without "due process of law," and against the taking of property without just compensation
6. Guarantees of rights in criminal trials including right to speedy and public trial, to be informed of the nature of the charges, to confront witnesses, to compel witnesses to appear in one's defense, and to the assistance of counsel
7. Guarantee of right of trial by a jury of one's peers
8. Guarantees against excessive bail and the imposition of cruel and unusual punishment

Description of Unenumerated Rights and Reserved Powers
9. Assurance that rights not listed for protection against the power of the central government in the Constitution are still retained by the people
10. Assurance that the powers not delegated to the central government are reserved by the states, or to the people

► How did the Constitution get ratified by the states?

discussionquestions

1. What are the strengths and limitations of our system of "checks and balances"?

2. Where might we see the issue of reciprocity being played out in contemporary politics?

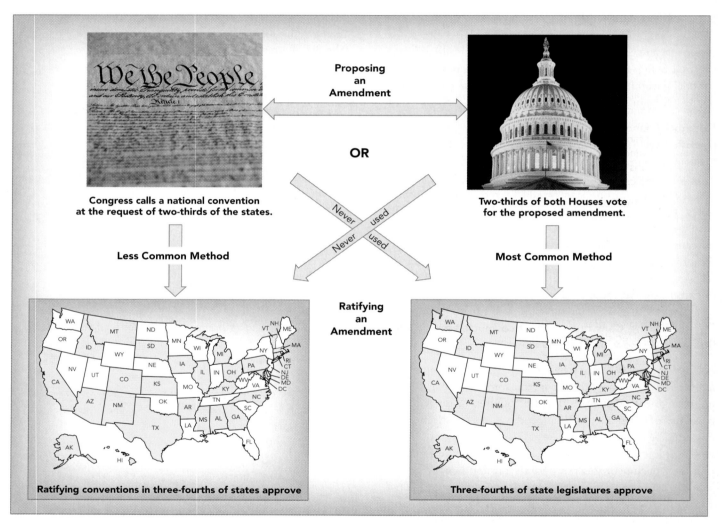

Proposing an Amendment

OR

Never used

Never used

Congress calls a national convention at the request of two-thirds of the states.

Two-thirds of both Houses vote for the proposed amendment.

Less Common Method

Most Common Method

Ratifying an Amendment

Ratifying conventions in three-fourths of states approve

Three-fourths of state legislatures approve

FIGURE 2.3

How the Constitution Can be Amended

The framers of the Constitution wanted a system that would remain both permanent and flexible to change. The process outlined above shows how the Constitution can be changed—and indeed it has been amended some 27 times. Yet, given there have been thousands of proposed amendments, do you think the process is too cumbersome? Did the framers put too much emphasis on stability?

SOURCE: Reprinted by permission of Online Highways. www.u_s_history.com

▶ **Who were the Federalists
and the Anti-Federalists?
Why did they disagree?**

what YOU can do!
Everyone makes reference to the Constitution, often by suggesting that a public policy or proposal is "unconstitutional." But few people have actually read the document. Turn to the U.S. Constitution at the beginning of this chapter, and spend some time looking it over. You may not grasp the complexity of our system simply by reading the Constitution, but at least you will be familiar with the rules!

is discussed in greater detail in subsequent chapters. Table 2.9 on page 66 lists Amendments 11 through 27.

practicequiz

1. Which of the following is a core principle of the Constitution?
   a. that each state has equal representation in the federal government
   b. that one branch of the government can check the acts of another branch.
   c. that power is divided among the layers of government.
   d. both b and c.

2. The framers of the Constitution wanted both a government by the people but also a system that checked the "passions of the public."
   a. true   b. false

3. Reciprocity among the states implies that
   a. citizens must be treated equally in every state.
   b. each state must accept the legal proceedings of the other states.
   c. states with larger populations should have more say in the national legislature.
   d. a and b.

4. What are the basic obligations of the three branches of government?
   a. The executive will create the laws, the legislature will enforce them, and the courts will punish people who do not follow these laws.
   b. The legislature will make laws, the executive will execute these laws, and the courts will resolve disputes according to the laws.
   c. The legislature will pass laws, the president will OK these laws, and the courts will enforce them.
   d. The national government will create laws, the states will enforce them, and the courts will resolve disputes according to the law.

Answers: 1-d, 2-a, 3-d, 4-b.

The Struggle over Ratification

Reaching agreement at the Constitutional Convention on the framework of government was the first step. But the Constitution said that for it to become the law of the land (replacing the Articles of Confederation), it would have to be ratified by nine of the thirteen states. Most contemporaries also understood that if larger states, such as Virginia, Pennsylvania, and Massachusetts, failed to ratify the document, the chances for the long-term success of the new government were slim. The framers said that nine states were needed, but most hoped that ratification would be unanimous. The document was sent to the states, where special ratification conventions would be held.

▶ **How did the Constitution get ratified by the states?** It says a lot that state legislatures were bypassed in the ratification process. Most of the framers understood that state governments, fearing the loss of their autonomy, would balk at the formation of the proposed national government. Smaller states also worried about being overpowered by the larger states, and even the larger states were bothered by the supremacy of the national government. The Constitution, with its invocation of "We the people" and the means it prescribed for ratification, implied a system of divided citizenship. A government might be created that included both individual states for local affairs and a federal union for national concerns such as commerce, foreign affairs, and security. That concept was unknown to the makers of the Articles of Confederation and was a great innovation compared to earlier notions that sovereignty must never be divided. The new Constitution was a radical change—and marked a necessary one for the creation of a true "United States." But this improvement would also lead to difficulties down the road as states sought to exert their sovereignty over federal law. Even today, as you will see in (L I N K) *Chapter 3, pages 96–106,* the battle arising out of divided sovereignty is a key part of American politics—and a critical one for you to understand.

As soon as the ratification process began, two sides emerged. The Constitution's supporters became known as **Federalists,** and opponents were called **Anti-Federalists.** They took their dispute to state capitals, to city halls, to taverns, and to kitchen tables across the nation. It was a critically important issue and it was taken very seriously; much was at stake. But the matter was settled peacefully, through logic, persuasion, eloquence, and deliberation. It was the first test of our new take on democracy—and we passed.

▶ **Who were the Federalists and the Anti-Federalists? Why did they disagree?** The Federalists believed that a representative republic was possible and desirable—especially if populated by citizens "who possess [the] most wisdom to discern, and [the] most

Federalists
supporters of the ratification of the U.S. Constitution.

Anti-Federalists
opponents of the ratification of the U.S. Constitution in 1787 and 1788.

The *Federalist Papers*
a series of eighty-five essays in support of the ratification of the U.S. Constitution, written by James Madison, Alexander Hamilton, and John Jay and published under the byline "Publius" in New York City newspapers between October 27, 1787, and May 28, 1788.

TABLE 2.9
Constitutional Amendments after the Bill of Rights

Number	Proposed	Ratified	Subject	Purpose
11	1794	1795	To sue a state in federal court, individuals need state consent	Overruled a Supreme Court decision
12	1803	1804	Requires separate electoral college votes for president and vice president	Corrected a government plan flaw
13	1865	1865	Prohibits slavery	Expanded rights
14	1866	1868	Gives citizenship to freed slaves, guarantees them due process and equal protection of the laws, and protects their privileges and immunities	Expanded rights
15	1869	1870	Grants freed slaves the right to vote	Expanded voting rights
16	1909	1913	Grants Congress power to collect income tax	Overruled a Supreme Court decision
17	1912	1913	Provides for direct election of the Senate (formerly elected by state legislatures)	Expanded voting rights
18	1917	1919	Prohibited the manufacture, sale, and transportation of intoxicating liquor	Public policy
19	1919	1920	Grants women the right to vote	Expanded voting rights
20	1932	1933	Changes presidential inauguration date from March 4 to January 20, and opening date of Congress to January 3	Revised a government plan
21	1933	1933	Repeals the Eighteenth Amendment	Public policy
22	1947	1951	Limits the president to two terms in office	Revised a government plan
23	1960	1961	Grants citizens of Washington, D.C., status in electoral college to vote for president	Expanded voting rights
24	1962	1964	Prohibits charging a poll tax to vote	Expanded voting rights
25	1965	1967	Provides for succession of president or vice president in the event of death, removal from office, incapacity, or resignation	Revised a government plan
26	1971	1971	Grants the right to vote to eighteen- to twenty-year olds	Expanded voting rights
27	1789	1992	Prohibits a pay raise voted by Congress from going into effect until the following session	Public policy

virtue to pursue, the common good of society."[29] Anti-Federalists countered with the argument that representatives in any government must truly reflect the people, possessing an intimate knowledge of their circumstances and their needs. This could be achieved, they argued, only through small, relatively homogeneous republics, such as the existing states. A prominent Anti-Federalist put it this way: "Is it practicable for a country so large and so numerous [as the whole United States] . . . to elect a representative that will speak their sentiments? . . . It certainly is not."[30]

THE *FEDERALIST PAPERS*

Persuading citizens that the Constitution should be approved was no simple matter. Today the battle for public opinion would be fought on cable news programs, through television and radio advertisements, in direct mail, and over the Internet. In the late 1780s, the battle raged in interpersonal settings, such as formal meetings or casual tavern conversations, and in newspapers and pamphlets, which were often read aloud in group settings or passed from hand to hand. Three leading Federalists—James Madison, Alexander Hamilton, and John Jay—teamed up to write a series of essays, known collectively as the ***Federalist Papers,*** on the virtues of the Constitution. The essays—eighty-five in all—were published in a New York City newspaper, for New York State, where Anti-Federalist sentiment ran high, was a key battleground in the campaign for ratification. The three authors adopted the *nom de plume* Publius, Latin for "public man."

Step by step, the *Federalist Papers* worked their way though the most fought-over provisions in the Constitution, laying out in clear logic and powerful prose why each element was necessary. The essays also explained what the framers had been thinking in Philadelphia while hammering out the document. Indeed, in many places, the Constitution is vague, and if you are interested in understanding what the framers had in mind, the *Federalist Papers* are the best place to look. Constitutional lawyers and Supreme Court justices still cite them.

Some of the essays are particularly important. *Federalist No. 10,* written by James Madison, is at the top of the list (reprinted in the Appendix). The exact purpose of the essay is a bit unclear at first. Madison begins with a detailed discussion of the dangers of "factions," groups that form to pursue the interests of their members at the expense of the national interest. "The friend of popular governments never finds himself so much alarmed for their character and fate, as when he contemplates their propensity to this dangerous vice." In other words, interest groups and political parties have been a problem for all democratic governments—and they all failed sooner or later. "Measures," Madison notes, "are too often decided, not according to the rules of justice and the rights of the minor party, but by the superior force of an interested and overbearing majority." What can be done about factions? Madison takes the reader through different alternatives, suggesting that suppressing them would be a huge mistake: "Liberty is to faction what air is to fire." Instead, he presents a two-part solution. First, if the faction is less than a majority, then the "republican principle" will solve things, meaning that elected officials, representing the wishes of a majority of constituents, will do the right thing. But if the faction constitutes a majority, which often happens in a community or a state, things are a bit tougher. Here Madison reveals the true purpose of the essay: Extended republics (that is, large countries) make the formation of majority factions less likely. He writes:

> Extend the sphere, and you take in a greater variety of parties and interests; you make it less probable that a majority

of the whole will have a common motive to invade the rights of other citizens; or if such a common motive exists, it will be more difficult for all who feel it to discover their own strength, and to act in unison with each other.

Using powerful, direct reasoning, Madison explains why one large nation is preferable to many smaller ones—thus challenging the logic of many political theorists who argued that only small democracies could survive. *Federalist No. 10* is a lucid justification for forming the United States of America, and Madison's insistence on this seeming paradox makes him one of the greatest political philosophers of all time.

Another important essay is *Federalist No. 51,* also written by Madison (and also reprinted in the Appendix). Here he explains the logic behind the sharing of powers and the essence of checks and balances. It is an awkward scheme of government, he admits, but also the best way to give the new government power but not *too much* power. "If men were angels no government would be necessary," he writes. And "if angels were to govern men, neither external nor internal controls on government would be necessary." Since neither condition prevails, other precautions are needed. Madison proposes that "ambition must be made to counteract ambition"—a truly innovative idea, since all republican thought for two thousand years had focused on schemes to make citizens more virtuous. In brief, a system of shared powers and of checks and balances would secure the democratic character of the government. Madison also introduces a "double security": Not only will each branch of the national government be dependent on the others, but the federal system itself, in which powers are divided between national and state governments, will help secure the rights of the people. Madison's argument is incredibly innovative when viewed from the standpoint of classical political theory. It had always been assumed that virtue (truly good citizens) could ensure the survival of a republic—a view that stretched back to Plato in ancient Greece. Madison, by arguing that ambition can be harnessed and checked by other ambitions through a layered system of governments, was turning political theory on its head.

THE ANTI-FEDERALISTS' RESPONSE

The Anti-Federalists offered clear and thought-provoking counterarguments, many of which also appeared in newspapers. Some of these essays, published under the byline Brutus (the name of the ancient Roman republican leader who had assassinated Julius

▶ **What happened to resolve**
this issue of individual rights?

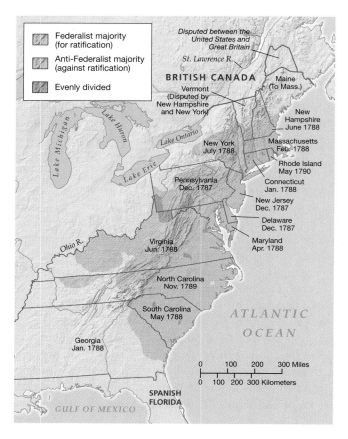

FIGURE 2.4
The Ratification of the Constitution, 1787–90

Clearly, support for ratification of the Constitution was more robust in some parts of the country than others. Why was this true? Do you think commercial interests might have been an important factor?

SOURCE: Faragher, John Mack; Czitrom, Daniel; Buhle, Mari Jo; Armitage, Susan H. *OUT OF MANY*, combined ed., 5th, © 2006. Electronically reproduced by permission of Pearson Education, Inc. Upper Saddle River, NJ.

Caesar to stop him from establishing a monarchy), called attention to the very nature of democracy. Brutus, echoing traditional republican ideology, insisted that large governments could not heed the wishes of average citizens. If we want legislators to speak on behalf of citizens, as democracy demands, these leaders must know the interests of their constituents. When districts are large, as they would have to be in the proposed government, the number of constituents per legislator would be excessive. How could a legislature actually know the wishes of 30,000 residents, the number proposed for House districts? (Today there are more than 650,000 residents per House district!) The Anti-Federalists further argued that the president would inevitably build up too much power and dominate the other branches. Indeed, much of their concern centered on Article II of the Constitution, the office of president. Their worries were slightly eased by the realization that if the Constitution were ratified, George Washington, with his spotless reputation for honesty and patriotism, would be chosen as the first president. (As you will see throughout this book, many of the arguments against ratification of the Constitution continue to be used today against the current political system—including what appears to be the expanding scope of presidential powers.)

Finally, the Anti-Federalists argued that the Constitution did not contain provisions to protect individuals. There were checks on each branch of government but none against the government's infringement on individual rights and liberties. This omission would seem glaring, yet Madison took exception to the criticism, arguing that the national government would be limited exclusively to the powers outlined in the document. It could not infringe on the rights of citizens because it did not have the power to do so. The absence of such provisions, argued Madison, would be a clear check. But many people found this "protection by omission" worrisome. "Where is the barrier drawn between the government and the rights of citizens?" asked George Mason, a prominent Virginian who had participated in the Convention but refused to sign the Constitution?[31] Concerns over the perceived lack of protection of individual rights threatened to doom ratification efforts.

▶ **What happened to resolve this issue of individual rights?**
In response to these objections, the Federalists gave in: If the states would ratify the Constitution, they agreed that the first matter of business for the new government would be to amend the Constitution to include a list of individual safeguards—a list of individual protections, which became known as the Bill of Rights. With

discussionquestions

1. What was the central argument made by the Anti-Federalists against ratification of the Constitution? Do they make any sense today?

2. Why might we still feel pride in the overall ratification process? Do any aspects of the ratification process strike you as questionable?

what YOU can do!

It's been said that many countries around the world have fashioned their systems of government after ours—that our Constitution has become a model. But is this really true? Check for yourself at the Findlaw.com Web site **http://findlaw.com/01topics/06constitutional/03forconst/** which boasts over 125 national constitutions from around the world, from Albania to Zimbabwe. Contrast one or two of the other constitutions with ours. What similarities and differences do you notice?

---

this guarantee, the tide of public opinion shifted, and by June 1788, the necessary nine states had ratified the Constitution (see Figure 2.4). In the end, all the states did so. (North Carolina at first rejected the Constitution but then hastily reconvened a ratification convention after the other states had accepted the document. Rhode Island also at first rejected the Constitution and then waited until 1790, when its convention finally voted to join the Union.) The vote in many of the state conventions was quite close. In New York, the margin was 30 to 27; in Massachusetts, 187 to 168; in New Hampshire, 57 to 47; in Virginia, 89 to 79; and (eventually) in Rhode Island, 34 to 32.

The Federalists kept their word and moved to amend the Constitution with the goals of protecting individuals from government infringements. Numerous changes were offered, and eventually twelve were voted on. Ten of these amendments were successful, all passed in 1791. (One additional draft amendment did not receive ratification by three-fourths of all the states until 1992, whereupon it finally became the Twenty-Seventh Amendment. It delays any increase in compensation for members of Congress by at least one election cycle.)

practicequiz

1. The struggle over ratification of the Constitution was
   a. one of the low points in U.S. history because of the wide-spread violence that broke out.
   b. not very heated because the Federalists were so popular and so trusted.
   c. especially heated because it pitted southern slave states against northern abolitionist states.
   d. a high point in our nation's history because a very important question was settled through logic and deliberation and through peaceful means.

2. The Anti-Federalists opposed ratification of the Constitution primarily because
   a. they believed that too much power would be given to the national government.
   b. they feared that too much power would be given to one person, the president.
   c. they feared that members of Congress would not know the interests of the citizens in their districts because these districts would be so large.
   d. a, b, and c.

3. James Madison's logic in *Federalists No. 10* is about the virtues of a large national government as opposed to a set of smaller republics.
   a. true   b. false

4. Madison's "double security," discussed in *Federalist No. 51*, refers to
   a. checks and balances.
   b. the powers of both the federal courts and the state courts.
   c. checks and balances and the division of powers between the national government and the states.
   d. shared powers between branches of government and the president's power to veto unconstitutional legislation.

Answers: 1-d, 2-d, 3-a, 4-c.

Other Challenges Faced by the New Nation

Most introductory books on American government conclude their discussion of the nation's formative period with the ratification of the Constitution. This makes sense, given that the system we still live under was set in motion back then, in the late 1780s. Yet on closer inspection, we find that a few other early events also helped build the foundation of our system, especially with respect to the political process. Knowledge of these challenges might be especially informative for young Americans interested in getting involved and making a difference.

A SECOND REVOLUTION

We often assume that the war against the British had a singular focus, even though two names for the conflict are often used interchangeably: the War for Independence and the Revolutionary War. These names suggest different ways of interpreting the same event. To some observers, the war was about breaking away from British control. A distant government had imposed laws and taxes on Americans without the input of Americans. British citizens had rights and liberties that were for some reason not extended to those living in the new lands. After repeated appeals, it seemed only proper that a new nation be established, the better to protect these liberties. The war was about independence. After victory had been won, there would be a return to the established order, much as before. A writer during this period suggested that

▶ **You often hear about**
Jacksonian democracy—
what was it?

THE PROVIDENTIAL DETECTION

In this cartoon, Thomas Jefferson kneels before the altar of Gallic despotism as God and an American eagle attempt to prevent him from destroying the United States Constitution. He is depicted as about to fling a document labeled "Constitution & Independence U.S.A." into a fire fed by the flames of radical writings. Many believe that the character of our democratic system was settled with the ratification of the Constitution, but historians and political scientists understand the importance of the election of 1800. Why was this "second revolution" so significant?

the demagogues, who infest you, know how to trace the history of your liberty; they confound it with the history of your independence . . . The truth is . . . your revolution was undertaken not to acquire, but to maintain liberty, not settle and determine your rights, but to repel an attack on them.[32]

The true meaning of this perspective, however, was about the proper rule of common folks. Liberty and equality were wonderful theoretical constructs, but day-to-day rule should be entrusted to enlightened gentlemen, to whom ordinary people should accord great deference. Those holding this perspective argued that "once the state and national constitutions secured the election of rulers, they warranted obedience, rather than suspicion, from the people."[33]

To others—likely a majority of Americans—the war was not only about independence but also about a dramatic change in the nature of governance. It was about shifting control from a small group of elites to *all* citizens. It was a revolution in governance and a revolution in thinking about the proper nature of government and politics. The "Spirit of '76" was about liberty, equality, and the creation of a limited government. "The Revolution had been a social upheaval," this side argued, "a transformation that had won equal rights, liberties, and opportunities for common men by defying domestic aristocrats as well as British rule."[34]

The distinction between these perspectives was very important during the early years, as we began the difficult process of taking our first steps as a sovereign nation. The matter came to a head in the late 1790s as big issues—namely, a series of economic and foreign policy questions—pulled Americans into a debate about the role of average citizens in governance. Alexander Hamilton, Washington's secretary of the treasury, proposed a series of measures that he believed would secure the nation's long-term economic future. But these policies, discussed in greater detail in (L I N K) *Chapter 15, pages 594–595,* seemed to help the business class at the expense of the poor. As for foreign policy, our allegiance in the war between England and France was fiercely debated. Should we help England, our principal trading partner, or France, our ally in the Revolution? The group in power during this period, led by the second president, John Adams, had adopted the name Federalists (inspired by the leaders who had worked to get the Constitution ratified a few years earlier). The other group, led by Thomas Jefferson and James Madison, had begun referring to itself as the Republicans or the Democratic-Republicans, the distant precursor of today's Democratic Party.

The ferocity of the debate and the depth of feelings on each side seemed to threaten the nation in its infancy. Republicans believed that the economic policies of the Federalists and their moves to stifle criticism were an assault on free government. For many people, the

Era of Good Feelings
the period in American history from about 1815 to 1824 when the ruling political party, the Democratic-Republicans, faced no opposition.

issue boiled down to the role of average citizens in society and in the conduct of government. Things came to a head in the election of 1800, which pitted John Adams against Thomas Jefferson (See Figure 2.5). Jefferson narrowly defeated his former friend. Republicans were swept into the Congress and state legislatures across the nation.

Beyond policy changes, the election of 1800 marked three critically important events. First, one administration (led by the Federalists) was removed from power peacefully, replaced by its political rival. A "Second Revolution" had occurred without violence—a rarity in history. This in itself was a stunning success for the new government. Second, efforts to stifle criticism of government leaders backfired. Finally, the election of 1800 seemed to signify that there should be no privileged class in American politics. The process set in motion by the Declaration of Independence was indeed a revolution, not simply a war for independence.

JACKSONIAN DEMOCRACY

▶ **You often hear about Jacksonian democracy—what was it?** After the tumultuous period of the late 1700s, most Americans seemed eager for political calm and tranquility. The Federalists never regained their political dominance after Jefferson's election, and the party collapsed after the successful end of the War of 1812 (which the dwindling Federalist Party had opposed). With the Federalists gone, the Republicans were the only remaining party functioning at the national level. The nation entered the period that people of the time called, somewhat misleadingly, the **Era of Good Feelings,** from about 1815 until 1824. The Federalist Party faded into the history books; many members retired to private life, and others actually joined the Democratic-Republican Party, including John Quincy Adams, the son of the second (Federalist) president.

Without opposing parties to channel political rivalries, the battle for the presidency became chaotic as the end of James Monroe's second term loomed in 1824. Four candidates, all Republicans, entered the contest. Andrew Jackson from Tennessee, the hero of the Battle of New Orleans (which had brought the War of 1812 to a glorious conclusion), won more votes than any other candidate, as well as more votes in the electoral college. But he did not win a *majority* in the electoral college. So, as stipulated in the Constitution, the matter was settled in the House of Representatives. The speaker of the House at this time was Henry Clay, who had also run for the presidency that year but was eliminated from consideration because he had finished fourth. The second-place finisher was John Quincy Adams. Most representatives assumed that the House would name Jackson president, given that he had won more popular and electoral college votes than any other candidate. But it seems

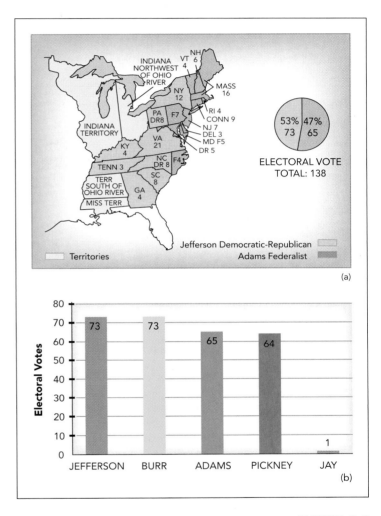

(a)

(b)

FIGURE 2.5

The Electoral College Vote Totals in 1800

The election of 1800, which pitted John Adams and his Federalist followers against Thomas Jefferson and his Democratic-Republican team, was extremely close. One of the greatest things about this election is that the transition from control of government of one party to the next was done peacefully. (Burr and Pickney were vice presidential candidates. It was not until the Twelfth Amendment that separate votes were cast for a President and Vice President.)

SOURCE: Reprinted by permission of Online Highways. Used by permission of MultiEducator. www.multied.com

Jacksonian democracy
a political and social egalitarian movement that rejected political aristocracy and emphasized the role of the average citizen in public life. It began in 1828 with the election of Andrew Jackson to the presidency and lasted several decades.

discussionquestions

1. Why is the election of 1800 sometimes called the "Second Revolution"? What was so special about it?

2. What was the Corrupt Bargain, and how did it lead to higher levels of political participation?

TABLE 2.10
The Presidential Vote of 1824

CANDIDATE	ELECTORAL VOTE	POPULAR VOTE
PRESIDENTIAL		
John Quincy Adams (MA)	84	115,696
Henry Clay (KY)	37	47,136
Andrew Jackson (TN)	99	152,933
William H. Crawford (GA)	41	46,979
VICE PRESIDENTIAL		
John C. Calhoun (SC)	182	
Nathan Sanford (NY)	30	
Nathaniel Mcaon (NC)	24	
Andrew Jackson (TN)	13	
Martin Van Buren (NY)	9	
Henry Clay (KY)	2	
Votes not cast	1	

Even though Andrew Jackson won more Electoral College and more popular votes than any other candidate, he was denied the presidency in 1824 through a deal between Henry Clay and John Quincy Adams. This election marked the birth of Jacksonian Democracy, the idea that average citizens should play a major role in the electoral process and in government.

that Clay made a deal with Adams: Clay would use his power in the House to throw the election in Adams's favor in exchange for being appointed the secretary of state, which was generally believed to be the second most important position in government and traditionally a stepping-stone to the presidency. Adams seems to have agreed, and thus occurred the Corrupt Bargain of 1824 (see Table 2.10).

As rumors of the deal spread, resentment and anger swelled. Once again, elitism had reared its ugly head; the will of the people had been trumped by a backroom deal. Jackson, along with a team of skilled operatives, decided to take back the presidency. They would do so in the next election by pulling average citizens into the political process and thus would simply overwhelm the ruling elite. Sure enough, turnout in the 1828 election doubled from four years earlier, and Jackson was swept into the White House.

Historians point to this period as the birth of popular democracy, what has also been dubbed **Jacksonian democracy.** Indeed, the heyday of electoral participation in America—a time when voting rates were highest and when politics was at the center of daily life of most Americans—was the mid-1800s. We often marvel at the passion of politics during this period and wonder how anyone could listen to political debates for hours. Property requirements for voting were removed, and the turnout of eligible voters during this period often exceeded 80 percent in presidential elections. (Today it rarely exceeds 55 percent.) Of course, it should be noted that "eligible voters" consisted exclusively of white men, a point that we'll take up in greater detail in ⓁⒾⓃⓀ *Chapter 14, pages 562–570.*

practicequiz

1. Which of the following was *not* an important development arising from the election of 1800?
   a. Even though passions ran high and the stakes were large, one group of elected officials was replaced by another through peaceful means.
   b. Americans came to accept that criticism of people in positions of power was acceptable and perhaps even beneficial in a democratic system.
   c. Notions of a privileged class of politicians were rejected.
   d. Partisanship and party politics would eventually corrupt the political process.

2. Which of the following issues seemed to divide the country in the election of 1800?
   a. Alexander Hamilton's economic policy plans, which seemed to favor the business class
   b. our allegiance in the war between England and France
   c. leadership style; Adams versus Jefferson
   d. a and b

3. The Corrupt Bargain of 1824 centered around
   a. a deal to bring John Quincy Adams to the presidency through a provision in the electoral college even though he lost the election among voters.
   b. the use of national government funds to support the election of John Quincy Adams.
   c. the ability of one president to appoint his successor—in this case, John Adams's selection of his son as the new president.
   d. control of the election process by local political parties.

4. Jacksonian democracy is best described as
   a. the birth of widespread participation in electoral politics in America.
   b. a period when politics became integral to the daily lives of average citizens.
   c. property restrictions on voting were removed.
   d. a, b, and c.

Conclusion

One of the themes of this textbook is that the nature and spirit of democracy in America has shifted and changed with the times; it is an evolving *process,* not a state of being. The early period began the journey of liberty and equality in our country, but most observers would agree that we have not yet arrived at a final destination. We might also underscore the interplay of political power, authority, and legitimacy. As noted, even though a government might have the power to compel action by citizens, it may not have the authority; the cry of "no taxation without representation" clearly echoed this notion. But after independence was secured, the tables were turned. On paper, the Articles of Confederation seemed to give Congress an avenue for collecting funds, but the scheme contained few provisions to impose the will of the national government on the states. The central government simply lacked power. And of course, the true challenge of the constitutional framers was to find a balance between power and legitimacy.

Another theme springing from these pages is the importance of political participation. Citizens stood up, demanded liberty and freedom, and forged their own system of government. We often hear that the constitutional framers were an atypical lot—much wealthier and better educated than average citizens. Although this may be true, we still need to remember the role played by average men and women during this period, not the least of which were the patriots who helped fill the ranks of the Continental Army and the local militias. Our democracy would have stumbled—indeed, it would not have taken its first step—were it not for the hard work of citizens fighting for a better life and a better system of government. Widespread political and civic engagement has been one of the many things that has distinguished the American system of government.

Finally, this chapter is also about the importance of pathways of change. As colonists came to believe in individual liberties and their right to participate in the conduct of government, the greater their frustration became over British rule. The Revolution was about creating a limited government—a government that would reflect the concerns of the people. Yet the framers had to fashion a system that was *both* responsive to popular will *and* stable. In some very real ways, the Constitution limits the democratic process and harnesses the will of the people, with the goal of creating a powerful, secure system of government. On its face, you might be hard pressed to label the original Constitution (before the amendments) a plan to enhance democratic principles. But thanks to changes to the original framework (the Bill of Rights in particular) and the toil and sacrifice of countless citizens, numerous pathways have emerged to make the system more democratic.

YOUR turn!

In the chapters that follow, we will provide concrete suggestions for involvement—ways average citizens can get involved in the political process. The topic of this chapter is historical, so going back to the formative period is clearly out of the question. But there are things that you can do now. Understanding the foundation of our government is a crucial part of being an activist in the twenty-first century. It may seem like "ancient history," but many of the themes discussed in this chapter continue to shape American politics. Understanding how the Constitution diffuses power between the national and state levels, for example, might help focus efforts to change policy *at the appropriate level.* An important group of conservative legal experts today insists that the Supreme Court should be guided by the "original intent" of the Constitution's framers—but what was their original intent? How can we know for sure? Knowing the correct role of citizens in a democracy might inspire you to become more involved. We suggest, then, that you spend more time investigating these topics and thinking about how they are relevant today. What did John Locke mean by limited government, and how is that applied in the American setting? What were the arguments the framers used to support elements of the Constitution, and did the Anti-Federalists have any good points? How does our framework of government create opportunities and limitations for average citizens?

One suggestion for tackling some of these issues is to invite a few colleagues, friends, or fellow students to do a little reading and investigation on these topics and then to hold a roundtable discussion. Why not tempt them with some pizza and soda? Reading and background information will be helpful, but a robust discussion on the foundations of American politics will likely prove especially valuable. ■

Chapter Review

1. There are many different forms of government. It was suggested that grouping these different forms can be made easier by considering two dimensions: Who is allowed to govern, and how much governmental control is permitted?

2. During the early years of our nation's history, colonial assemblies worked closely with royal governors. This relationship soured, however, when the British government tried to recoup some of its expenses from the French and Indian War by squeezing as much tax revenue as possible from the colonists.

3. Both financial and ideological forces brought about the American Revolution. Many colonists believed that the measures imposed by Parliament made the prospects of future prosperity more difficult. The ideological concerns centered on the growing beliefs that just governments spring from the will of citizens and that each citizen has unalienable rights.

4. The Articles of Confederation failed because that national government had little power to impose its will and to draw the states into unified action. This was especially problematic in foreign affairs and in the regulation of commerce.

5. Delegates to the Constitutional Convention came with a unified purpose—to construct a more viable national government—but when it came to the details of how that system would work, opinions diverged, and a number of significant compromises became necessary.

6. The debate over ratification of the Constitution was serious and heated but peaceful. The Federalists won the day, due in part to the many *Federalist* essays that were written in support of the new system.

7. Two additional critical periods in the early history of American politics were the election of 1800, often dubbed the "Second Revolution," and the advent of Jacksonian democracy.

8. Numerous themes have emerged from this chapter, including the evolving nature of democracy, the key role played by average citizens, and the necessity of pathways of change in a democracy.

CHAPTER REVIEW TEST

1. The institution of slavery is utterly at odds with the principles of democracy. Why, then, wasn't slavery abolished during the formation of the United States' democratic government?
   a. Because the framers of the Constitution simply never thought about slavery.
   b. Because some of the framers of the Constitution were a product of their eighteenth-century culture.
   c. Because compromises were necessary for the inclusion of the southern states in the newly-formed nation.
   d. Both b and c.

2. Before the revolution, what helped sour relations between colonial governors and colonists?
   a. Colonists' suspicions about the monarchy in England.
   b. The "Big Squeeze."
   c. A century of "salutary neglect" by England which made the Big Squeeze all the more painful.
   d. All of the above.

3. John Locke was important to the revolutionary cause because
   a. He argued persuasively, at the end of the seventeenth-century, that legitimate governments must be based on the consent of the governed.

   b. He argued persuasively, at the end of the seventeenth-century, that government should be limited in order to protect citizens' economic rights.
   c. He was one of the Sons of Liberty.
   d. All of the above.

4. When Thomas Paine wrote in 1776 that "These are the times that try men's souls," he was
   a. Consoling the British royalty because General Washington's army was defeating the British army.
   b. Referring to the unfair practices of the Federalists.
   c. Complaining about the Articles of Confederation.
   d. None of the above.

5. What document contains the following sentence: "We hold these truths to be self-evident, that all men are created equal, that they are endowed by their Creator with certain inalienable Rights, that among these are Life, Liberty and the pursuit of Happiness"?
   a. The Declaration of Independence
   b. The United States Constitution
   c. The Gettysburg Address
   d. The *Federalist Papers*

6. Thomas Jefferson's Declaration of Independence produced an immediate and overwhelming groundswell of support in the colonies for the revolutionary cause.
   a. true   b. false

7. Timothy McVeigh, the Oklahoma City terrorist, was acting out against what he saw as an oppressive United States federal government. How were his actions different from the promotion of revolution in the Declaration of Independence?
   a. McVeigh had many more pathways of change available to him than did Thomas Jefferson and his peers, making McVeigh's violent actions less justifiable.
   b. The Declaration of Independence did not condone violence under any circumstances.
   c. The Declaration did not condone fomenting revolution against a government based inside one's own country.
   d. Both a and b.

8. What gathering, authorized by Congress, produced the Constitution of the United States of America?
   a. The First Continental Congress
   b. The Second Continental Congress
   c. The Constitutional Convention
   d. The Articles of Confederation

9. The "Great Compromise" during the formation of the Constitution refers to the decision to
   a. Count a slave as equivalent to three-fifths of an inhabitant in determining the number of representations accorded each state in the House of Representatives.
   b. Make congressional representation both reflect state population levels (in the House of Representatives) and represent each state equally, no matter its size (through the United States Senate).
   c. Protect the Atlantic slave trade for at least twenty more years but grant Congress the ability to regulate commerce through a simple majority.
   d. Grant the Presidency strong executive powers but limit his tenure in office to two terms.

10. Among other effects, the ratification of the Constitution created an immediate and widespread sense of citizenship in the country.
    a. true   b. false

11. Why does it make sense to describe our governmental system as both rigid and flexible?
    a. Through the amendment process, it's possible to alter the Constitution, but it's not easy and rarely happens.
    b. Because of the power-sharing and checks and balances built into the government's structure, it's very unlikely that one branch of government could seize control and change our system of government, the way a dictator might in an authoritarian regime.

c. Our governmental system is rigid because it is now quite old; it is flexible because a revolution could still happen at any time.
    d. Both a and b.

12. Which branch of the government is in charge of enforcing legislation?
    a. The police branch
    b. The executive branch
    c. The judicial branch
    d. The legislative branch

13. The Constitution refers to "expressed powers" and "police powers." What is the difference between these two kinds of powers?
    a. Expressed powers are powers that politicians claim through writing and speaking; police powers are the powers that law enforcers physically exert.
    b. Expressed powers belong to the national government; police powers belong to the states.
    c. Expressed powers concern commercial matters, foreign affairs, and national security; police powers concern the health, safety, and well-being of individuals.
    d. Both b and c.

14. Why do constitutional lawyers and Supreme Court justices still refer to the Federalist Papers in formulating their own assertions?
    a. Because the Federalist Papers are particularly relevant to the issue of federal (versus state) power.
    b. Because citing the Federalist Papers is required of the judicial branch by the Constitution.
    c. Because the Federalist Papers explain more fully than does the Constitution itself the principles and intentions behind the Constitution.
    d. None of the above.

15. In the Federalist Papers James Madison recognized the dangers of factions in democratic governments. He did not recommend suppressing them, though, because
    a. If a faction constitutes less than a majority, then its representatives will be outvoted or overruled by government officials representing the wishes of the majority of constituents.
    b. All factions would naturally wither over time—"no living thing endures over the long course of human affairs."
    c. In the "extended republic" of the whole nation, factions would usually not constitute a majority and thus would not direct governmental policy.
    d. Both a and c.

16. Madison also asserted that a layered system of government, with checks and balances, would ensure the endurance of our republic because
    a. Such a system cultivated the virtue of every citizen
    b. In such a system the ambitions of participants in government counteracted the ambitions of others, and vice versa.

c. Both a and b.

d. None of the above.

17. It's reasonable to argue that, while the Anti-Federalists lost in their attempt to prevent the formation of a strong, centralized national government, their own arguments bore fruit in the creation of the Bill of Rights.

a. true   **b.** false

18. The Bill of Rights is

a. A list of individual protections for American citizens.

b. Amendments to the U.S. Constitution passed in the late eighteenth century.

c. One of the key negotiation points that enabled the unanimous ratification of the Constitution.

d. All of the above.

19. The election of 1800 was significant because

a. One administration was peacefully replaced by another, effecting a "Second Revolution."

b. Efforts to suppress criticism of the government succeeded.

c. It suggested that there was now a seasoned and privileged class in American politics.

d. Both a and c.

20. Voting rates in national elections, which began to surge during Andrew Jackson's first campaign for President in 1824, have increased steadily ever since.

a. true   **b.** false

Review Test Answers: 1: d; 2: d; 3: a; 4: d; 5: a; 6: b; 7: a; 8: c; 9: b; 10: b; 11: d; 12: b; 13: d; 14: c; 15: d; 16: c; 17: a; 18: d; 19: a; 20: b.

DISCUSSION QUESTIONS

1. What are the two dimensions used to describe types of governments across the globe?

2. How would you describe the colonial governing system—that is, the model that existed prior to the Articles of Confederation?

3. What were some of the forces that seemed to fuel the democratic movement in America prior to the Revolution?

4. What was the foremost weakness of the Articles of Confederation?

5. What are the core elements of the Declaration of Independence? What makes this statement so powerful and enduring?

6. Did the compromises reached at the Constitutional Convention weaken or strengthen the democratic character of the nation?

7. Describe the principal features of the U.S. Constitution. Which of these components would you say is the most important? Would you say any are especially cumbersome given politics in the twenty-first century?

8. What does this chapter suggest about the role of individuals in shaping the outcome of politics in a democracy?

INTERNET RESOURCES

To learn more about the formative years in American history, visit the Library of Congress's America's Story Web site at **http://www.americaslibrary.gov/cgi-bin/page.cgi**

Learn about the period before, during, and after the Constitutional Convention at the History Place Web site: **http://www.historyplace.com**

For an online, searchable copy of the *Federalists Papers,* see **http://www.law.ou.edu/hist/federalist**

To better understand some of the developments from the first hundred years of our nation's history, visit From Revolution to Reconstruction at **http://odur.let.rug.nl/~usa**

Visit the Annenberg Learning Center: A Biography of America at **http://www.learner.org/biographyofamerica**

For general information on numerous early American documents, try the Avalon Project at Yale University at **www.yale.edu/lawweb/avalon/avalon.htm**

If you are interested in the writings of some of the leading figures of the formation period, the following may be helpful:

For George Washington: **http://gwpapers.virginia.edu**

For Thomas Jefferson: **http://memory.loc.gov/ammem/mtjhtml/ mtjhome.html**

For James Madison: **http://www.virginia.edu/pjm/home.html**

For John Adams: **http://odur.let.rug.nl/~usa/P/ja2/about/bio/ adamsxx.htm**

For Abigail Adams: **http://www.whitehouse.gov/history/firstladies/ aa2.html**

For Thomas Paine: **http://www.ushistory.org/paine**

ADDITIONAL READING

Bailyn, Bernard. *The Ideological Origins of the American Revolution.* Cambridge MA: Harvard University Press, 1967.

Burns, James MacGregor. *The Vineyard of Liberty.* New York: Knopf, 1982.

Butler, Jon. *Becoming America: The Revolution before 1776.* Cambridge, MA: Harvard University Press, 2000.

Ellis, Joseph. *Founding Brothers: The Revolutionary Generation.* New York: Vintage Books, 2002.

McCullough, David. *John Adams.* New York: Simon & Schuster, 2001.

Morgan, Edmund S. *The Meaning of Independence: John Adams, Thomas Jefferson, George Washington.* New York: Norton, 1978.

Smith, Page. *The Shaping of America: A People's History of the Young Republic.* New York: McGraw-Hill, 1979.

Wills, Garry. *Inventing America: Jefferson's Declaration of Independence.* New York: Random House, 1978.

Wood, Gordon S. *The Radicalism of the American Revolution.* New York: Vintage Books, 1993.

KEY TERMS

When devastating events rock our country, we turn to the federal government for relief. For most of our history local communities were largely required to help their own residents, but throughout the twentieth century the role of the federal government has expanded dramatically. At left, Eddie Mae Smith (then 75) sits in dire need of help in her mold-infested home in the days following Hurricane Katrina in the fall of 2005.

CHAPTER 3

FEDERALISM

No Child Left Behind and the Ongoing Debate Over Authority   One of George W. Bush's most significant accomplishments in his first term was the passage of the No Child Left Behind Act (NCLB), which requires states and local school systems to meet or exceed federal standards in reading and mathematics. School districts must produce annual "report cards" that inform parents and communities about their progress, and those that do not make improvements must provide supplemental services to students, such as free tutoring or after-school assistance. If they are still not making adequate yearly progress after five years, dramatic changes must be made, including paying for students to enroll in nonpublic schools.

Bush ran for the White House in 2000 as a "compassionate conservative," and he talked at length about students from under-privileged backgrounds being trapped by what he called "the soft

President Bush's signature educational law,
No Child Left Behind, emphasizes increasing
student proficiencies in reading, math and
spelling. Success is measured largely by
standardized tests. Some schools have raised
test scores primarily by spending more time
on these classes, limiting time spent on other
subjects like music and fine arts. Some are
concerned that too much emphasis is placed
on test performance, harming the ability of
schools to make students better rounded
individuals. But if performance is not measured
by standardized tests, how else can it be
evaluated?

Photo: Max Whittaker/The New York Times

bigotry of low expectations." He considered education reform one of his greatest achievements as governor of Texas, and he wanted to show he could lead on a social-policy area traditionally thought of as Democratic "turf." He began his efforts by inviting twenty members of both parties to his Texas ranch to discuss education policy more generally and then moved ahead with a detailed blueprint of a bill. Next, Bush sought partnerships with key legislators, including Senator Edward Kennedy of Massachusetts, a leading Democrat. Finally, the president compromised on certain elements of the bill, making it more acceptable to hard-line conservatives. "The result," noted one observer, "was a three-way coalition among conservative Republicans, New Democrats, and the Democratic regulars."[1] The measure passed, and Bush signed it into law on January 8, 2002. It was a significant accomplishment.

While most Americans would agree that keeping track of a school's math and reading scores is a good idea, the measure has proved to be quite controversial. For one thing, extending the role of the federal government into the affairs of local school districts seems a rather odd move for a Republican president. For decades, the GOP has sought to reduce the role of the federal government in the affairs of state and local governments. Many conservatives also believe that this law crosses one of the most time-honored boundaries of our political system: Since colonial times, education was considered the province of the states and local communities and not the business of any central government. The NCLB

shifts the federal government from being a rather modest source of funding (about 10 cents of every public school dollar) and makes it a major actor in shaping the substance of K–12 instruction. One analyst noted, "The federalism debate has been increasing in intensity since the passage of the law. Nearly half the states are considering resolutions or similar actions to get more flexibility." Moreover, "the role of the federal government in local schools brings up critical issues in both constitutional and case law."[2]

On top of this, many critics see this measure as yet another "unfunded mandate," a recurring tale in the relationship between states and the federal government during recent decades. Setting higher requirements and raising standards are excellent goals, but they require significant financial resources. As has happened frequently before, the new federal law included some added money, but not enough to meet the new requirements that it laid on state governments. Notes one critic, "The public schools are mandated to do something which is virtually impossible, and the teachers and children have been condemned to failure."[3]

It seems, then, that one of George Bush's greatest accomplishments in his first term has also proved to be a problem even within his own party. By the fall of 2005, forty-seven states had challenged NCLB in some way. Utah—a state that overwhelmingly backed Bush in 2000 and 2004—simply refused to follow several of the law's mandates. "Only three states have not challenged in some way NCLB's extension of federal supervision over education K through grade 12, wrote one columnist in November 2005, but no state has done so with as much brio as Utah."[4] Starting with Connecticut, by the spring of the following year, several states had filed suits against the Department of Education over the law's requirements. Education policy surely is—and always has been—within the scope of a governor, a state legislature, and a local school board, but should the president also have a hand in what goes on in America's classrooms? What's wrong with the federal government's stepping in at the local level? ▪

▶ **What's the difference**
between a unitary system
and a federal system?

unitary system
a system of government in which political power and authority is located in one central government that runs the country and may or may not share power with regional sub-units.

sovereignty
the exclusive right of an independent state to reign supreme and have absolute power over a geographic region and its people.

Governmental authority in the United States has been a source of conflict for more than two centuries. Unlike countries like the United Kingdom and France, which are governed under a **unitary system** (that is, a system where all ruling authority rests in a single national government), in the American model, powers and responsibilities are divided between layers of governments.

▶ **What's the difference between a unitary system and a federal system?** There seemed good reasons for dividing power and responsibility when the Constitution was framed: Federalism would create yet another check against the potential abuses of state and local governments, for instance. Yet this unique system has created much uncertainty and many practical management problems and at times in our history has even led to violence. Indeed, the greatest crisis in our history, the Civil War, was very much about "states' rights" versus the authority of the national government. We can imagine why foreign policy would fall under the scope of the national government, but what about the general welfare of American citizens? Is crime a problem for a local government, a state government, or the national government? Should the national government be able to control the conduct of doctors and regulate what services they can or cannot provide? How about lawyers, electricians, or hairdressers? And certainly the abortion question is very much entangled with the issue of federalism. So are others: If a state considers the medical use of marijuana permissible, should the federal government be able to step in and ban it? Can the federal government bar gay couples from getting married under one state's laws or force other states to recognize that marriage?

Then there is the issue of transportation. Just because the Constitution says that Congress shall regulate commerce, does that mean that the federal government is responsible for fixing all roads and bridges? Would we want the federal government telling us how many stop signs to put up on a stretch of road? That may seem an extreme example, yet the issue of speed limits has been controversial for decades. In the mid-1970s, when the nation faced a fuel shortage, one of the measures used to save energy was to fix the national speed limit at 55 miles per hour. Many states, especially those in the West, refused to abide by the federal law. In response, Congress threatened to cut off federal highway aid to any state that did not enforce the law. Some states rejected the money and set the speed limits they wanted, and others simply lowered the fines for speeding tickets. The federally mandated 55-mph limit has since been dropped, but some states still abide by it while others allow up to 75 mph. If you exceed the 75 mph limit in Montana, you might get a $40 fine, and in Wyoming, it would be just $25, but in many other states, it could cost you more than $300.

▶ **It sounds as if the national government has taken over more and more control from state and local governments. Is that the case?** In education, law, medicine, transportation, crime, and many other areas of American life, the line between federal and state control has been controversial and fluid. For example, in the not too distant past, cleanup from a natural disaster, such as a flood or a hurricane, was entirely the responsibility of state and local governments; today everyone expects the federal government to take the lead. Indeed, one of the low points in George W. Bush's administration was the federal government's inept response following Hurricane Katrina in the summer of 2005. Ironically, many of these critics are the same people who argue that the federal government is getting too big and that it should stay out of the affairs of local governments. You might be tempted to draw a conclusion that things have moved toward more federal control, but even if this is true in some policy areas, in other spheres the states are now being given more control and greater responsibility. Politicians eager to promote local control often suggest that state governments are the "laboratories of democracy," a concept first enunciated by Supreme Court Justice Louis Brandeis in 1932, meaning that difficult challenges are more likely to be resolved when fifty entities are working to find innovative solutions rather than just the federal government. One area where states are being given more authority is welfare reform. During Bill Clinton's administration (1993–2001), oversight and control of social welfare programs was shifted from the federal government to the states. In short, the pendulum of governmental authority swings both ways.

This chapter will explore the complex, important issue of levels of governmental authority in the United States. As with many elements in our political system, many changes have occurred over the years. Today the relationship between the states and the federal government is vastly different from what it was at the dawn of our nation's history. Rather than being simply a unique, interesting aspect of our government, the debate over governmental authority has been at the center of most of the trying events in our history. This issue also says a great deal about the future directions of American government.

The goal of the chapter is to help you understand that public policy does not spring simply from "government" but rather from

▶ **It sounds as if the national** government has taken over more and more control from state and local governments. Is that the case?

different *layers* of government. It would make little sense, for example, to lobby members of Congress to change the zoning in a particular municipality or to ask a city council to help lower the cost of prescription drugs. Different governments are responsible for different policies in the United States. This chapter explains why we have such a unique system, examines its advantages and disadvantages, and explores changes over the past two hundred years. Politics is not simply about pushing government in a given direction but instead knowing *which* government to push and how.

Key Questions

1. What are the theoretical advantages and disadvantages of dividing authority between layers of government?

2. How does the Constitution define federalism? That is, what are some of the key provisions for allocating appropriate governmental authority? Have certain amendments been important in reshaping federalism?

3. What role have the courts played in defining governmental authority in the United States?

4. Why was Franklin Roosevelt's New Deal so important for shaping the modern relationship between the national and state levels of American government?

5. How did Lyndon Johnson's Great Society change the federal-state relationship?

6. How do issues of federalism shape our perspective regarding the pathways of change? That is, what does this chapter suggest about the ability of average Americans to shift governmental policy?

Why Divide Authority in the First Place?

The federal structure of the United States is not unique: Several other democracies also have federal systems of government, including Canada, Australia, Germany, Switzerland, and India. But most countries, whether or not they are democratic, have **unitary systems** (see Table 3.1 on page 84). In those countries, there may be viable and active local authorities, but the national government has **sovereignty.** This means that the national government has the ultimate governing authority (and the final say). In the United Kingdom, for example, Parliament can change city and town government boundaries at any time. It may allow certain regions to create their own government, as has been the case with Scotland and Northern Ireland, but at any point Parliament can abolish these structures and override any of their policies.[5]

President Clinton addresses the National Governor's Association in Washington in 1993. He promised the governors he would allow states to use federal money for welfare reform experiments, provided they "have the courage to quit" if the initiatives fail. How have the states responded to Clinton's challenge?

► **Why did the framers choose** a federal system over a unitary one? Wouldn't it be simpler and more efficient to have just one level of government?

federal system
a system of government in which power and authority is divided between a central government and regional sub-units.

Montesquieu, Charles-Louis de Secondat (1689–1755)
a French political thinker who was famous for his writings on the importance of separation of power, with a balance of power and authority.

TABLE 3.1
Each type of governmental system uses a different means to enact policies. Looking at this table carefully, which system do you think works best? Why?

FEDERAL	UNITARY	CONFEDERATION
Governmental authority is divided between a national government and state governments. United States under the Constitution (1789–present), Australia, Brazil, Germany, Mexico, Nigeria	Ultimate governmental authority comes from the national government. France, Spain, Tanzania	Ultimate authority comes from the states. United States under Articles of Confederation (1781–1789), Confederate States of America (1861–1865), Confederation of Independent States (States of the former Soviet Union)

► **Why did the framers choose a federal system over a unitary one? Wouldn't it be simpler and more efficient to have just one level of government?** Why, then, would the United States choose to create a **federal system,** where sovereignty is divided among different levels of government? One explanation is rooted in the history of government in North America. During the period of exploration and discovery, set into motion by Christopher Columbus's voyage in 1492, a number of nations, including England, France, Spain, Portugal, and the Netherlands, sought to establish colonies in the New World. Believing that these lands represented immense economic potential, the race was on to claim different territories. Spain quickly colonized Mexico, Central America, and much of South America (except for Portuguese Brazil), as well as what are now Florida and the southwestern parts of the United States. France, spurred on by the rich fur trade, set its sights on what is now Canada, and the Dutch colonized what is now New York State. England eventually planted more than thirteen colonies on the North American mainland.[6] As settlers eventually moved to these colonies, they set up their own governments. As we noted in (LINK) *Chapter 2, pages 41–42,* before setting foot on American soil in 1620, the Pilgrims drew up the Mayflower Compact, essentially an agreement to form a government. In the Virginia colony, a legislative body called the House of Burgesses was established just twelve years after Jamestown, the first permanent British town in the Americas, was settled. Eventually, each colony established its own governing structure.

These governments were not sovereign, of course, given that the English Parliament and king could dissolve them at any time (and did so on various occasions), but it is important to understand that as our nation began to take shape, there were many distinct governing entities. Moreover, it is worth noting that there existed a great deal of suspicion and rivalry between the colonies and, after independence, between the early states. One of the greatest hurdles confronted by those anxious to break ties with Great Britain on the eve of the American Revolution was to get people to consider themselves citizens of an American nation, rather than just citizens of their individual colonies. Throughout the Revolutionary War, there was no national government, for the Articles of Confederation were designed to protect state sovereignty while loosely binding the states in ways that might better ensure security and prosperity. After independence had been won, the central point of dispute over the ratification of the Constitution in 1787 and 1788 was the extent to which the new national government might, at some future time, take over the role of state governments. Many Americans agreed that a stronger national government was needed to regulate commerce and deal with foreign nations, but few envisioned that the national government would be fully sovereign.

One explanation for our federal system lies, then, in the historical roots of the United States. Our nation was born through the fusing of independent states—states that would never have agreed to a merger if giving up their independence was part of the

▶ **Isn't federalism similar to the separation of powers we read about in Chapter 2?**

discussionquestions

1. What might the early years of governance in North America suggest about the rationale for our current federated system?

2. What is Madison's "double security"?

deal. Federalism was a compromise. We might also point to the writings of philosophers who guided the thinking of the framers of our system. As discussed in (L I N K) *Chapter 2, pages 45–46,* the framers relied heavily on the writings of John Locke, Adam Smith, and Thomas Hobbes. Another very influential philosopher was the Frenchman Baron **Montesquieu,** who in the early eighteenth century had written of the virtues of dividing power and authority between different parts of the government. This might be done, he argued, by having different branches of government *and* by creating layers of governmental authority. James Madison echoes Montesquieu's idea in *Federalist No. 51:*

> In the compound republic of America, the power surrendered by the people is first divided between two distinct governments, and then the portion allotted to each subdivided among distinct and separate departments. Hence a double security arises to the right of the people.

▶ **Isn't federalism similar to the separation of powers we read about in** (L I N K) *Chapter 2, pages 61–63?* In other words, federalism, coupled with the checks and balances and sharing of powers at the national level, would help guarantee a republican government. Montesquieu also argued that republican institutions were more likely to flourish in a small-scale political system, such as a Swiss canton (state), yet such small states were incapable of defending themselves against attack. The problem could be solved by the creation of a system that would permit a consensus with regard to the domestic affairs among the separate governing units but provide unified action for the common defense.[7]

Still another significant factor behind federalism is the geographic, cultural, and economic diversity of the United States. The distinctiveness of different American regions has been eroding dramatically in recent decades, due in large measure to changes in transportation, entertainment, and the economy. A Wal-Mart in Boise, Idaho, looks exactly the same as a Wal-Mart in Bath, Maine. Kids in Albany, Georgia, watch the same Saturday morning cartoons as kids in Albany, New York. Throughout most of our history, however, culture, language, demographics, economic conditions, and many other aspects of life varied from region to region, from state to state, and even from community to community. The United States remains one of the most diverse nations in the world, and this diversity has contributed to a sense of a localized citizenship.

Finally, federalism has made sense in the American setting for practical reasons. Historians agree that if in 1787 the separate states had not been permitted to have significant powers, the Constitution would never have been ratified. The federal system was also helpful in adding new states to the Union, and it has aided the nation's economic growth. Our system is unique and has some disadvantages, but in many ways, creating a system of layers of governmental authority has made good sense. But that is not to say that things have remained the same since the Constitution was framed.

practicequiz

1. The controversy over the No Child Left Behind Act illustrates that
   a. the federal government now has very little say over how local school districts go about their business.
   b. local and state governments sometimes resist federal initiatives in education.
   c. unfunded (or underfunded) mandates can frustrate local governments and school boards.
   d. b and c.

2. The United States is the only country in the world that divides authority between the national government and subunit governments.
   a. true   b. false

3. In the formation of our governmental structure, it is fair to say that federalism was a compromise because
   a. it preserved some of the independence states enjoyed under the Articles of Confederation while granting the national government enough authority to regulate commerce and interact with other countries.
   b. although it made inroads into state sovereignty, it preserved enough independence for each state that each agreed to merge into one unified nation.
   c. it made the country a unitary system.
   d. a and b.

4. The preservation of local authority in American federalism reflects the fact that
   a. most Americans are unwilling to think of themselves in national terms.
   b. most American communities are much like one another, so each needs to make itself distinctive.
   c. most American communities were originally very different from one another; local governance was a practical expression of those distinctions.
   d. a and c.

Answers: 1-d, 2-b, 3-d, 4-c.

▶ **How did the Constitution**
divide power between national
and state governments?

Chief Justice John Marshall, administering
the oath of office to Andrew Jackson in 1829,
played a major role in Supreme Court
decisions that helped define the power of the
federal government in the early nineteenth
century. How would history have been different
if Marshall had not led the Supreme Court to
issue decisions strengthening the federal
government's authority?

The Evolution of Federalism in the United States

▶ **How did the Constitution divide power between national
and state governments?** During the first few decades after the
ratification of the U.S. Constitution, there was great uncertainty
about where the lines lay dividing authority and power between
the national government and the states. While there seemed
strong arguments for such a division of authority and power, the
people who wrote and ratified the Constitution did not share a
consistent, clear vision of the meaning of American federalism.
Fairly broad agreement about the need for a stronger national
government had led to the end of the Articles of Confederation
and the drafting of the Constitution, but there remained strong
disagreements about exactly how much power the states kept
under the new governing document. As a result, arguments about
federalism played a central role in shaping the country's political
system.

BEFORE THE CIVIL WAR

In the United States, disputes are often resolved through lawsuits
that call on federal judges to interpret constitutional provisions
defining the extent of federal authority. The judiciary's role in
shaping American federalism is not a modern development.
Judges have issued rulings on federalism since the first decades
after the Constitution's ratification.

pathways profile

JOHN MARSHALL

John Marshall served as chief justice of the United States for
thirty-four years (1801–1835). These were crucial formative
years, when important first decisions had to be made about the
powers of national governing institutions. Before his appointment to the Supreme Court by President John Adams, Marshall
had served as secretary of state and as a member of Congress and
of Virginia's state legislature. As chief justice, Marshall was the
leader on the Court, and he wrote many of its most important
decisions, defining various aspects of federalism. As we will see in
Ⓛ Ⓘ Ⓝ Ⓚ *Chapter 4, pages 126–127,* Marshall's most famous
opinion, *Marbury* v. *Madison* (1803), helped establish the power
of federal judges to examine and invalidate actions by other
branches of government. In general, Marshall advanced a vision
of a strong national government. By leading the Court in interpreting the Constitution to enhance the powers of Congress and
the federal courts, Marshall's opinions necessarily diminished the
power of states, which would otherwise exercise any authority
not granted by the Constitution to the federal government.
According to the historian Charles Hobson, Marshall's "constitutional jurisprudence and his political views were decidedly hostile
to the doctrine of states' rights."[8] If a different chief justice had
led the Supreme Court during the nation's first decades, federalism might have developed in a very different way. ■

In 1816, Congress enacted legislation to charter the Second
Bank of the United States. Two years later, the Maryland legislature imposed a tax on all banks within the state that were not
chartered by the state legislature. James McCulloch, an official at
the Baltimore branch of the federally chartered Bank of the
United States, refused to pay the tax. The dispute arrived before
the U.S. Supreme Court as the case of *McCulloch* v. *Maryland*
(1819), and it presented Chief Justice John Marshall with the

► **What is "dual federalism"?**

dual federalism
the powers of the federal and state governments are strictly separate, with interaction often marked by tension rather than cooperation.

opportunity to define the respective powers of the state and federal governments.

Marshall's opinion in the case first examined whether the U.S. Constitution granted to Congress the power to charter a bank. Such a power is not explicitly stated anywhere in Article I of the Constitution, which defines the authority of the national legislature. But Marshall focused on the constitutional provision that grants Congress the power to make "all laws which shall be necessary and proper, for carrying into execution the foregoing powers, and all other powers vested by this constitution, in the government of the United States, or in any department thereof." This phrase in the Constitution, known as the *necessary and proper clause,* does not specify what powers, if any, flow from its words. Nevertheless, Marshall relied on the necessary and proper clause to conclude that Congress possessed the power to charter a national bank. The chief justice concluded that the creation of the Bank of the United States was "necessary and proper" as a means to carry out other powers that Article I explicitly granted to Congress, such as the powers to collect taxes, coin money, and regulate commerce. Marshall's opinion rejected Maryland's claim that the word *necessary* granted only powers that were absolutely essential. In reaching this conclusion, Marshall demonstrated the power of judges to give meaning to vague phrases in the Constitution. In this case, Marshall interpreted the Constitution in a way that enhanced the powers of the federal government and empowered Congress to make choices about how it would develop public policy.

After establishing that Congress had properly chartered the bank, Marshall's opinion went on to invalidate Maryland's efforts to impose taxes on the federal government's agencies. "The power to tax," wrote Marshall in a memorable phrase, "is the power to destroy." Realizing that states could use taxation to weaken or destroy federal institutions, the chief justice asserted that the federal government necessarily retained the power to preserve its creations. According to Marshall, the people of the United States grant powers "to a government whose laws, made in pursuance of the constitution, are declared to be supreme. Consequently, the people of a single state cannot confer a sovereignty" on their own government that would extend beyond the borders of the state. By invalidating Maryland's tax on the bank chartered by Congress, Marshall made a strong initial statement about the superior position of the national government in the evolving system of federalism.

Chief Justice Marshall also led the Supreme Court in making other decisions that shaped the law affecting federalism. In *Cohens*

v. *Virginia* (1821), for example, brothers who had been convicted under a Virginia law for selling tickets in a lottery approved by Congress appealed to the U.S. Supreme Court. Virginia claimed that the Court had no authority to review decisions by its state courts. Marshall wrote an opinion rejecting that argument and asserting that the U.S. Supreme Court had ultimate authority over judicial matters concerning federal law, whether or not earlier decisions on the matter had been issued by state courts or by lower federal courts. In *Gibbons* v. *Ogden* (1824), Marshall's Court considered a challenge to a New York law that granted specific steamboat operators the exclusive privilege of providing service between New York and New Jersey. The chief justice announced a broad definition of the power granted to Congress by the Constitution to regulate commerce "among the several states." His opinion concluded that Congress possessed exclusive authority over the regulation of interstate commerce, including navigation, and that therefore New York and other states had no power to grant such exclusive licenses to steamboat operators. In short, by these and other key decisions, the early U.S. Supreme Court, under Marshall's leadership, shaped federalism by interpreting the Constitution to give the federal government superior powers in certain matters of public policy, thereby imposing limits on the power of the states.

► **What is "dual federalism"?** However, these decisions did not solve all issues or clearly define the respective powers of state and federal governments. The wording of the Constitution raised many questions about the powers of states and the national government. For example, the Tenth Amendment states that "the powers not delegated to the United States by the Constitution, nor prohibited by it to the States, are reserved to the States respectively, or to the people." Many Americans viewed this amendment as embodying a fundamental premise of the Constitution: Governmental powers not explicitly granted to the federal government continue to reside with the states. This viewpoint supported a theory of federal-state relations known as **dual federalism.** Under dual federalism, state governments and the national government were equally authoritative. The federal government was not superior; it had merely been granted authority over a specific, limited set of responsibilities. In other words, this theory rested on the idea that the national government possessed authority over its powers listed in the Constitution, such as coining money and establishing post offices and military forces, while the Tenth Amendment specifically reserved to the states all other governmental powers not discussed in the Constitution.

▶ **I thought the Civil**
War was about slavery.
What does federalism have
to do with the Civil War?

doctrine of nullification
theory that state governments had a right to rule any federal law unconstitutional and therefore null and void in that state. The doctrine was ruled unconstitutional but served as a source of southern rebellion, contributing to the secession of southern states from the Union and ultimately the Civil War.

doctrine of secession
theory that state governments had a right to declare their independence and create their own form of government. Eleven southern states seceded from the Union in 1860–61, created their own government (the Confederate States of America) and thereby precipitated the Civil War.

In practice, in early-nineteenth-century America, dual federalism faced criticism from two directions. Advocates of a strong national government believed that where their spheres of activity overlapped, the powers of the federal government must be superior to those of the states. For example, both the states and the federal government sought to regulate certain aspects of business and commerce, and the Marshall Court had ruled in *Gibbons* v. *Ogden* (1824) that Congress has exclusive authority over "interstate commerce." Others saw the states as the central, sovereign governmental entities in the American governing system. These advocates of "states' rights" asserted that the states possessed specific powers superior to those of the national government.

Before the Civil War, southern leaders' **doctrine of nullification** stated that each state had retained its sovereignty upon joining the United States. Therefore, a state could declare any laws or actions of the national government "null and void" if they clashed with that state's interests and goals. The nullification doctrine was stated most forcefully by John C. Calhoun (1782–1850), a U.S. senator from South Carolina who also served as vice president and secretary of state. In the 1830s, the South Carolina legislature voted to nullify federal tariffs that were believed to help northern manufacturing businesses while hurting southern planters and slave owners. The state later cancelled its action, and no other states acted on the nullification doctrine, although the idea was advocated by many who wanted to protect southern agricultural interests and to prevent Congress from interfering with slavery.

The most extreme expression of dual federalism before the Civil War was the **doctrine of secession.** By asserting that states retained sovereignty and were not subordinate to the national government, advocates of secession claimed that states could choose to withdraw from the United States if they had profound disagreements with laws and policies produced by the national government. When in 1861 eleven states acted on this theory by leaving the United States and forming the Confederate States of America, a bloody four-year civil war erupted between North and South. The Confederacy's defeat in 1865 ended—presumably forever—the idea that dual sovereignty could be carried to the point of justifying secession.

▶ **I thought the Civil War was about slavery. What does federalism have to do with the Civil War?** Competing conceptions of federalism still color historical references to that war because of differences in what Americans learned in school, depending on their home region. Until the second half of the twentieth century, students in many southern states were taught to call the conflict of 1861–1865 the "War between the States." This label was based on an understanding of the war as reflecting profound disagreements about the rights of states to manage their own affairs without interference from the federal government, and it coincided with efforts by southern whites to defend state-mandated racial segregation. By contrast, elsewhere in the United States, students learned to call the bloody event the "Civil War" and to interpret it as having been fought over North-South disagreements about the institution of slavery and the southern states' unlawful assertion of a right to secede. The very name *Civil War* reflects a conception of federalism, advanced by Abraham Lincoln, characterizing the United States, embodied in its national government, as a sovereign entity that could not be dismantled by its constituent parts, the individual states. This is not to say that the Civil War was caused solely by a dispute about federalism. As the historian James W. Loewen has noted, "History textbooks now admit that slavery was the primary cause of the Civil War."[9] However, the policy issue of slavery was intertwined with disputes about federalism because the slave states resisted any move by the federal government to outlaw slavery in new territories and states.

pathways of action

THE CIVIL WAR AND THE FAILURE OF AMERICAN POLITICS

Throughout this book, we describe the pathways of American politics that produce public policies and shift the balance of power between different political actors and governing institutions. One or more of the pathways can almost always be used to describe and explain activities that shape and change policies. However, the Civil War represents the best example of a policy dispute that was *not* controlled by one of the pathways of American politics. The operation of the pathways depends on the American people's shared democratic values, commitment to the preservation of the constitutional governing system, and willingness to accept individual policy outcomes that are contrary to their personal preferences. In the case of slavery, however, no workable compromise balanced the interests of those who sought to abolish

▶ **So was the result of the** Civil War to weaken the power of the states relative to the national government?

or at least prevent the territorial expansion of slavery and those who wanted to preserve and spread race-based slavery. As a result, people turned to violence to advance their interests. It took many battles and a half-million deaths to settle American policy on slavery and secession. In this instance, the forces that shaped American policy change resembled the forces that even today use armed conflict to determine policies in unstable countries.

In the post–Civil War American political system, intractable disagreements about public policies need not lead to violent conflicts. Today, for example, there are bitter disagreements over abortion, and some advocates on opposing sides cannot see any workable compromise. However, except for a few extremists who in isolated instances have committed violent acts against abortion clinics or individual abortion providers, activists on both sides of the issue remain committed to the governing system and devote their policy-shaping energies to lobbying, voter mobilization, the courts, and the other strategies that use the pathways described in this book. The Civil War demonstrates that not all policy issues have been settled using the pathways of American politics, yet that war stands as such an unusual example of internal military conflict that it also reminds us of the importance of the pathways for nearly all other policy disputes in American history. ▪

The doctrines of nullification and secession were put to rest with the Union victory in the Civil War. The war's outcome did not, however, end all attempts to preserve a "states' rights" conception of federalism. Such arguments remained common, for example, by those southern whites who during the 1950s and 1960s resisted passing and enforcing federal voting rights legislation and other antidiscrimination laws seeking to prevent the victimization of African Americans. The term *states' rights* is seldom used today because of its discredited association with efforts to preserve slavery and, later, to deny civil rights to African Americans.

FEDERALISM AFTER THE CIVIL WAR

▶ **So was the result of the Civil War to weaken the power of the states relative to the national government?** In the aftermath of the Civil War, the Constitution was amended to prevent specific assertions of state authority, particularly with respect to the treatment of newly freed African Americans. The Thirteenth

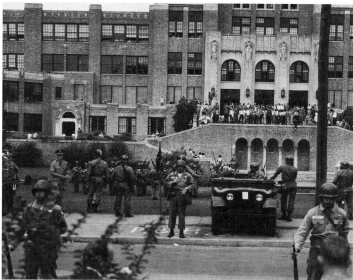

ABOVE: **The bloody Civil War** reflected the failure of the pathways of political action to solve disagreements about slavery and federalism. The usual democratic mechanisms of lobbying, elections, and litigation could not forge a compromise resolution. Are there reasons that make another Civil War highly improbable in today's United States? What are they?

BELOW: **Although the Civil War** put to rest the most extreme arguments advocating states' rights, states' rights claims lingered for decades afterward, often as a means to justify discrimination against African Americans. In the 1950s, for example, President Dwight Eisenhower sent federal troops to Little Rock, Arkansas, to protect nine brave African American students who were attempting to desegregate Central High School. State and local officials in Arkansas were opposed to desegregation. What circumstances today might require the president to use the military in order to force state and local officials to comply with the law?

▶ **Why did the Supreme Court** reverse directions and stop the federal government from regulating business? Did they want to give that power back to the states?

monopoly
exclusive control by one group or individual over specified services or commodities.

In the 1980s, President Ronald Reagan sought to reduce the influence of the federal government and increase the power and authority of states to manage their own affairs. What might be some public issues that should be removed from the authority of the federal government and placed under the control of state and local officials?

Amendment (1865) banned slavery, thereby eliminating that issue as a source of conflict between states and the national government. The Fourteenth Amendment (1868) sought directly to limit states' authority to interfere with certain rights of individuals. "No State," the Fourteenth Amendment declares, shall deny "due process of law" or "the equal protection of the laws." According to the Fifteenth Amendment (1870), the right to vote shall not be denied "by the United States or by any State on account of race, color, or previous condition of servitude" (that is, slavery). In addition, each of the three post–Civil War amendments contained a statement specifically empowering Congress to enact legislation to enforce them. These amendments specifically limited state authority and enlarged that of the federal government. Unfortunately, for nearly a century, federal institutions—courts, Congress, and presidents alike—did not vigorously apply the powers granted by these amendments to protect African Americans from discrimination at the hands of state and local authorities. However, in what was called "nationalizing the Bill of Rights," federal courts, beginning slowly in the 1920s and 1930s and later accelerating the process in the 1960s, often used the Fourteenth Amendment to strike down state laws and state-sanctioned policies that violated the Bill of Rights in such areas as criminal justice, freedom of speech, and the separation of church and state. In the 1960s, the Supreme Court revived nineteenth-century federal antidiscrimination statutes affecting contracts, housing, and other matters by declaring that they were appropriate exercises of congressional power under the Thirteenth Amendment. Congress meanwhile relied on the Fifteenth Amendment to enact important voting rights legislation aimed at preventing discrimination in state elections. And as early as the 1940s, presidents issued executive orders designed to ensure the equal treatment of racial minorities, as well as vigorously enforced antidiscriminatory court decisions and congressional legislation.

In the decades following the Civil War, American society was transformed enormously. Many new technologies were developed and refined that helped reshape the economy. The expanded use of railroads, telegraph, and industrial machinery shifted the country's economy from one based primarily on agriculture to one deriving most of its wealth from urban industry. Cities grew with the spread of factories. Industrial demands for energy expanded employment opportunities in coal mines, in shipyards, and on railroads. People left farms and small towns to seek jobs in factories,

Through the first decades of the twentieth century, it was common for American children to work long hours under harsh and dangerous conditions in textile mills, mines, and other industrial settings. Until the late 1930s, the U.S. Supreme Court blocked legislative efforts to enact laws that would protect workers, including children, from danger and exploitation in the workplace. What would labor laws be like today if all regulation was controlled by state governments?

Photo: Lewis Hine (American, 1874–1940) "A Carolina Spinner" 1908. Gelatin Silver Print 4¾ × 7 in. Milwaukee Art Museum, Gift of the Sheldon M. Barnett Family 1973.83

urban offices, and retail businesses. Increasing numbers of job-seeking immigrants arrived from Europe and East Asia in search of new lives in American cities. In addition, large corporations grew, attempting to consolidate control over entire industries. The changes brought by urbanization and industrialization presented the country with new kinds of economic and social problems. Many government officials believed that new policies were needed to foster economic growth, prevent predatory business practices, protect the interests of workers, and address the growing problems of urban poverty.

Late-nineteenth-century Americans looked first to their states to deal with the effects of industrialization and urbanization. But in most states, corporate interests had significant influence on the state legislatures, which therefore did relatively little to address these issues. Because industries (such as mining companies in West Virginia) could use their substantial resources to influence politics and policy, in only a few states did the legislatures enact economic regulation and social welfare legislation. At the federal level, Congress enacted statutes intended to address specific concerns that affected the entire nation. For example, the Interstate Commerce Act (1887) established the Interstate Commerce Commission, a regulatory agency responsible for implementing rules for transporting goods by rail and ship. The Sherman Antitrust Act (1890) sought to prevent individual companies from controlling entire industries and to stop companies from working together to rig prices at artificially high levels. If companies became **monopolies** by gaining control over most or all of a particular industry, those companies could harm the national economy and consumers by raising prices in unjustified ways because there would be no competing companies to which consumers could turn to obtain similar products. Congress wanted to encourage the existence of a variety of companies in each industry so that market forces, in the form of competition between companies, would keep prices at economically justifiable levels. But such federal legislation did relatively little to curb the excesses of big business. Only in the early twentieth century did some state legislatures and Congress enact additional legislation addressing such issues as working conditions and wages. In 1916, for example, Congress prohibited the transportation across state lines of goods produced using child labor.

Many laws passed in response to changing social conditions and problems were tested through the court pathway. But unlike Marshall's Supreme Court a century earlier, which had consis-

tently sought to strengthen and expand the powers of the federal government, the justices of the Supreme Court of the late nineteenth and early twentieth centuries handed down decisions that generally limited government authority to regulate commerce and address social welfare issues. For example, in 1895, the Supreme Court rejected the government's charge that the American Sugar Refining Company had become an illegal monopoly in violation of the Sherman Antitrust Act, even though the company, by buying up competing sugar businesses, had gained control over 98 percent of the country's sugar refining capacity (*United States v. E. C. Knight Company*). The Court concluded that although the Constitution empowered Congress to regulate interstate commerce, "manufacturing," such as sugar refining, was a separate activity from "commerce." Therefore, the federal government could not regulate the company and other manufacturing enterprises. In *Hammer v. Dagenhart* (1918), the Supreme Court struck down the 1916 federal statute barring the interstate transport of goods produced by child labor. The Court said that because the goods themselves were not harmful, the statute had improperly sought to regulate child labor. It ruled that Congress, in exercising its power over "interstate commerce," possessed only the authority to regulate the *transportation* of goods. Decisions like these temporarily limited the expansion of federal governmental authority during decades when Congress sought to become more active in regulating the economy and advancing social welfare goals.

▶ **Why did the Supreme Court reverse directions and stop the federal government from regulating business? Did they want to give that power back to the states?** The Supreme Court's

New Deal
programs designed by Franklin D. Roosevelt to bring economic recovery from the Great Depression by expanding the role of the federal government in providing employment opportunities and social services; advancd social reforms to serve the needs of the people, greatly expanding the budget and activity of the federal government.

court-packing plan
proposal by Franklin D. Roosevelt in 1937 to appoint an additional Supreme Court Justice for every sitting justice over age 70 in hopes of changing the composition of the court to make it more supportive of his New Deal proposals.

actions in limiting federal power did not necessarily mean that the justices intended to shift federalism's balance of power in favor of the states. The Court also struck down similar laws enacted by state legislatures. In 1905, for example, in *Lochner* v. *New York,* the Supreme Court invalidated a New York State statute that sought to limit the working hours of bakery employees to not more than ten hours per day or sixty hours per week. Although the New York legislature intended to protect the health and well-being of bakers, the Court found that the statute interfered with the workers' liberty to work as many hours as they wished to work. (Of course, workers typically did not toil such long hours because they enjoyed it; they did it because hourly wages were so low that they had to.) In effect, the Supreme Court's decisions were not aimed specifically at federalism. Scholars argue that the decisions reflected the justices' views on the limits of legislative power generally, both state and federal.[10] Still, the judicial decisions of this era had the primary effect of preventing the federal government from expanding its authority.

FEDERAL POWER: THE SUPREME COURT AND THE NEW DEAL

The stock market crash of 1929 signaled the beginning of the Great Depression, which would last through the 1930s. Manufacturing dropped, banks failed, and by early 1933, nearly one-quarter of the American workforce was unemployed. Elected president in 1932, Franklin D. Roosevelt was inaugurated in early 1933 at the depth of the economic crisis, and he immediately sought to use the federal government's power to spur economic recovery and revive employment. Roosevelt's domestic policy, known as the **New Deal,** included programs to regulate farm and industrial production; to provide government jobs in construction, environmental conservation, and other public sector projects; and to give relief to people suffering from economic hardships (see also LINK *Chapter 8, pages 311–312*). It also established Social Security. Many of the New Deal programs that Congress enacted collided with the Supreme Court justices' conservative views on the limits of government authority, and the Court initially struck down several important laws that Roosevelt had sponsored. In 1936, for example, the Court decided that Congress lacked the power to impose minimum wage

and maximum work hour regulations on coal mines (*Carter* v. *Carter Coal Co.*).

President Roosevelt criticized the Supreme Court for blocking New Deal economic and social welfare laws. In 1937, after he had been elected to a second term, Roosevelt proposed changing the Supreme Court so that the president could appoint a new justice whenever a sitting justice reached the age of 70. The Constitution does not state the size of the Supreme Court, so Congress has the authority to change the number of justices who make up the Court. At the time Roosevelt made his proposal, six justices were older than 70, so under the proposed law, the president would have been able immediately to alter the balance of power on the Court by appointing a half-dozen new justices who would support his New Deal program. This proposal became known as Roosevelt's **court-packing plan.** Even though Roosevelt had won reelection by an overwhelming popular margin, the public saw in the court-packing plan an attempt to overturn the constitutional system of checks and balances. Reflecting this negative public reaction, Congress rejected the proposal. But many historians believe that the proposal itself may have pushed at least one justice to reconsider his opposition to expanded federal power. The episode is sometimes referred to in jest as "the switch in time that saved nine" (the nine justices on the Court). As the constitutional law scholar Gerald Gunther observed, "While the controversy was raging, the Court handed down a number of decisions sustaining regulatory statutes, and [one justice] retired."[11]

In the late 1930s, after several elderly conservative justices left the bench, Roosevelt was finally able to reshape the Supreme Court by appointing new justices, whom the Senate confirmed. Their views on congressional commerce power and federalism led them to uphold the constitutionality of the New Deal's expansion of federal power. For decades thereafter, the Court permitted Congress to justify nearly any kind of social, economic, and civil rights legislation as an exercise of power under its constitutional authority to regulate interstate commerce. Congress used this power to enact a variety of laws, some which clearly had primary goals other than the regulation of commerce. In the 1960s, for example, people active in several pathways of American politics, including the elections, lobbying, grassroots mobilization, and courts, sought to create laws that would guarantee voting rights and other protections to African Americans against racial discrimination. Other political actors, especially members of Congress from southern states, opposed these initiatives. In 1964, Congress enacted Title II of the Civil Rights Acts of 1964, barring racial discrimination in restaurants, hotels, movie theaters, and other "public accommodations" provided by private businesses. Although it was widely recognized that the statute was created to advance civil rights and combat discrimination, the Supreme Court rejected challenges to the law and accepted the federal government's argument that Title II regulated commerce by attacking a major barrier to interstate travel by African Americans. Before the law's enactment, African Americans often could not find restaurants and motels that would serve them when they traveled. The Court also permitted the law to be applied to businesses that had relatively little contact with interstate commerce because they sold local products and services to local people (*Heart of Atlanta Motel* v. *United States,* 1964; *Katzenbach* v. *McClung,* 1964). The Court's decisions in these and other cases seemed to indicate that Congress had nearly unlimited authority to make laws under the premise of regulating interstate commerce.

According to the supremacy clause in Article VI of the Constitution, federal laws "shall be the supreme law of the land." Acts of Congress were thus to take precedence over state laws. As a result, the expansion of federal lawmaking affected federalism by simultaneously limiting the scope of the states' authority to control their own affairs. State laws still controlled most matters affecting criminal justice, education, property, and many other areas of public policy. Over time, however, the federal government became more active in additional realms of law and policy. In the 1960s and thereafter, Congress defined certain crimes as federal offenses, many of which overlapped with existing state statutes. The federal government became involved in funding, and therefore regulating, various aspects of education. Congress also began to create environmental protection laws that took precedence over state laws and affected individuals' ability to make their own decisions about how to use their property. As the federal government expanded its involvement in public policy, the Supreme Court generally accepted the expansion of federal power at the expense of state authority (see Figure 3.1 on pages 94–95).

A boy uses a drinking fountain on the county courthouse lawn in Halifax, North Carolina. The Civil Rights Act of 1964 barred racial discrimination in "public accommodations." What examples of discrimination have you observed in recent years?

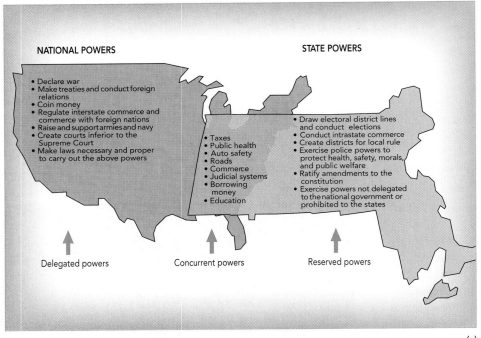

NATIONAL POWERS

- Declare war
- Make treaties and conduct foreign relations
- Coin money
- Regulate interstate commerce and commerce with foreign nations
- Raise and support armies and navy
- Create courts inferior to the Supreme Court
- Make laws necessary and proper to carry out the above powers

- Taxes
- Public health
- Auto safety
- Roads
- Commerce
- Judicial systems
- Borrowing money
- Education

STATE POWERS

- Draw electoral district lines and conduct elections
- Conduct intrastate commerce
- Create districts for local rule
- Exercise police powers to protect health, safety, morals, and public welfare
- Ratify amendments to the constitution
- Exercise powers not delegated to the national government or prohibited to the states

Delegated powers   Concurrent powers   Reserved powers

(a)

FIGURE 3.1
Governmental Powers and Control of Policy Issues

(a) **Distribution of Powers Between National and State Governments.** The founders of our government created a system that divided power, authority, and responsibility between the federal and state governments. Some powers are exclusive to one entity, but many are shared. Throughout our history, the power of the federal government has grown, but states remain important actors in our political system. Unfortunately many in our country are overwhelmed with the size of our government and do not correctly understand which level of government is responsible for different issues. How do you think we can better explain to individuals how power is divided and shared?

(b) **The Changing Functions of National Grants to States and Localities.** Over the past half-century, the federal government has significantly expanded its involvement in policy issues. As indicated by changes in the percentage of funds devoted to various programs, the federal government now affects a variety of policies that were entirely under the control of states in 1960. A key element of federal involvement for many of these programs has been in providing funding for cities and states. Is the federal government involved in too many policy issues or is its involvement necessary to address the country's problems?

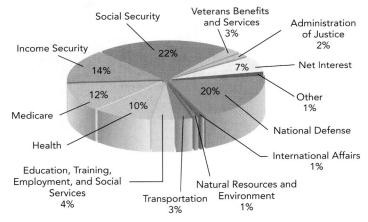

2005 Fiscal Year

1960 Fiscal Year

2001 Fiscal Year

(b)

(c) **Ready or Not.** Most states are ready or nearly ready to manage a catastrophic event. However, a number of states are not prepared. Why do you think that states on or near the southern border of our country are more likely to be prepared than those near the northern border? What do you think should be done, and by whom, to ensure that all states are ready for a catastrophic event?

(d) **Medicaid's Growing Share of State Budgets.** State governments, on average, increased the percent of their budget spent on Medicaid by nearly ten percent from 1990 to 2003. If this trend continues, costs for health care will become increasingly difficult for many states to meet. As you can see in this figure, some states are better able to absorb the costs than are other states. Tennessee, for example, spent $966 million more than they had allocated for Medicaid in 2003, while nearly one half of the states did not have to overspend to pay for Medicaid claims. If a state can't afford to pay for health care for their residents,

Ready or Not

Results of a survey by the Department of Homeland Security on the readiness of states to manage a catastrophic event .

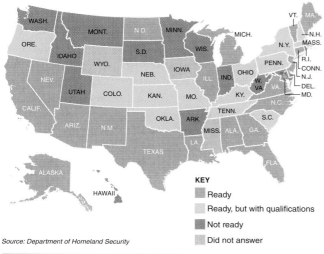

KEY
- Ready
- Ready, but with qualifications
- Not ready
- Did not answer

Source: Department of Homeland Security

February 2006, The New York Times

(c)

Medicaid's Growing Share of State Budgets

Dramatic increases in costs are causing many states to spend substantial and increasing portions of their budgets on Medicaid ...

MEDICAID SPENDING AS PERCENT OF STATE'S TOTAL EXPENDITURES, 2003

10% 20 24 28 34

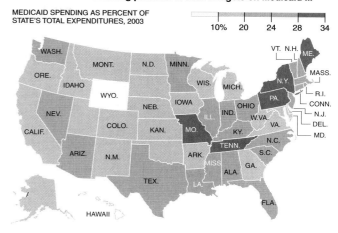

TOTAL STATE EXPENDITURES BY CATEGORY

Medicaid	K-12 Education	Higher education	Transportation	Corrections and public assistance	All other	
						1990
12%	23%	12%	10%	8%	35%	
						2003
21%	22%	11%	8%	6%	32%	

... but in many states, it's still not enough.

PERCENTAGE AND AMOUNT BY WHICH STATES EXCEEDED THEIR MEDICAID BUDGET, 2003

State	Percentage	Amount
Tennessee	16.4%	$966 million
New Mexico	14.8	49
New Jersey	10	236
Nevada	8.5	67
California	7.3	723
Mississippi	7.0	50
Missouri	5.5	238
New York	5.3	1,775
Texas	5.0	286
Idaho	4.8	41
Wyoming	3.8	12
Connecticut	3.7	97
Rhode Island	2.9	38
Washington	2.6	71
Maryland	2.4	77
Colorado	2.0	47
Pennsylvania	1.8	189
Vermont	1.7	13
Arizona	1.4	50
Alaska	1.0	6
Florida	0.9	104
Illinois	0.8	54
South Dakota	0.3	15

Source: National Association of State Budget Officers

January 2005, The New York Times

(d)

► **Why is cooperative federalism like a marble cake?**

cooperative federalism
the powers of the federal and state government are intertwined and shared. Each level of government shares overlapping power, authority and responsibility.

practicequiz

1. In general, Chief Justice John Marshall's many rulings addressing the relative powers of national and state governments had the effect of
   a. strengthening the national government.
   b. strengthening state governments.
   c. compromising the influence the courts had over federalism issues.
   d. b and c.

2. The doctrine of nullification
   a. was never fully exercised by any state in the Union.
   b. was a natural extension of John Marshall's federalist philosophy.
   c. is explained in the Tenth Amendment to the Constitution.
   d. was an idea promoted by southern states before the Civil War and is now endorsed by almost all states.

3. The Civil War constituted a policy dispute that was controlled by
   a. the court pathway of American politics.
   b. the cultural pathway of American politics.
   c. the grassroots activism pathway of American politics.
   d. neither a, b, nor c.

4. The New Deal
   a. referred to a collection of antitrust regulations instituted by the Theodore Roosevelt administration.
   b. referred to a collection of domestic policies instituted by the Franklin Roosevelt administration to counteract the effects of the Great Depression.
   c. represented the imposition of federal programs at the state and local level.
   d. b and c.

Answers: 1-a, 2-a, 3-d, 4-d.

Recent Trends in Federalism

THE NEW DEAL AND COOPERATIVE FEDERALISM

► **Why is cooperative federalism like a marble cake?** Franklin Roosevelt's New Deal programs marked a dramatic shift in our federal system of government. Before the New Deal, many Americans believed that the power of the federal government

should be severely limited. However, the Great Depression made it vividly clear that the economic crisis was far too large to be effectively addressed by individual state or local governments or by private charities. As the way in which Americans viewed the responsibilities of the federal government changed, a shift occurred in the nature of federalism itself. FDR used the power of the presidency and his remarkable personal skills to sell his new vision of federalism to the American people. Under his vision, the power and influence of the federal government changed dramatically, as did the relationship between the national and state governments. Many of FDR's programs involved cooperation between the states and the national government to deal with the complex economic situation. Unprecedented interaction between the different levels of government resulted. Political scientists refer to this changing relationship as **cooperative federalism**—the belief that state and national governments should work together to solve problems. Programs that involved joint involvement were far-ranging, including public works projects, welfare programs, and unemployment assistance. Many observers believe this marked the beginning of an era of national supremacy, shown in the dramatic growth of the power, budget, and scope of the federal government. Morton Grozdins, a historian of federalism, aptly contrasted a layer cake and a marble cake in describing the shift from the older dual federalism to the new cooperative federalism, with its high levels of national-state interaction.[12] As you know, in a marble cake, the two colors are separate, like state and federal governments, but they exist next to each other throughout the cake rather than resting exclusively in separate layers of the cake. The marble cake analogy symbolically portrays state and federal government as coexisting and cooperating in a variety of policy areas. Since the New Deal, the division of power in the federal system has become less relevant, just as the relationship between the different layers of governments has grown increasingly important. The New Deal era was critical in reshaping federalism in the United States. State and national governments had cooperated before, but the extent of the nation-state interaction clearly made the marble cake the most appropriate metaphor for American federalism. Perhaps the most significant change resulting from the New Deal has been in the way Americans thought about their problems and the role of the

discussionquestions

1. What did the Supreme Court decide in *McCulloch* v. *Maryland,* and why was this decision so important?

2. What role did the U.S. Supreme Court play in shaping federalism in the decades following the Civil War? In the New Deal era and thereafter?

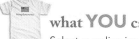

what YOU can do!

Select a policy issue of particular interest to you. Which level of government, state or federal, should be responsible for that policy issue? Is your answer to that question determined by an objective view or a different strategy depending on the level of government that you seek to influence?

---

national government in solving them. Issues and problems that at one time had been seen as personal or local are now often seen as national problems needing national solutions. Today Americans take it for granted that issues concerning morality, values, and social policy will be debated at the national level and that Congress and the president will feel pressured to take action. For many years, this has been true of the issue of abortion, but in recent years, it has expanded to other issues traditionally under state control, such as debates about civil unions and legal marriages for gays and lesbians.

THE GREAT SOCIETY AND CREATIVE FEDERALISM

The nature and role of the federal government and of federalism itself continued to change throughout the twentieth century. The presidency of Lyndon B. Johnson (1963–1969) marked a critical point in the evolution of federalism. Johnson proposed many new social programs to achieve what he called the Great Society. Of crucial importance in his vision was the War on Poverty, which channeled federal money to states, local governments, and even citizen groups to combat poverty and racial discrimination. Funds were allocated to a variety of social programs for urban renewal, education, and improving the lives of underprivileged children (an example is Head Start). The money was used to advance the agenda of Johnson and liberal Democrats in Congress, the direct result of which was to bypass governors, state legislatures, and local officials. As we see in Figure 3.2, such federal departments as Agriculture and Commerce, which Democratic leaders did not target, saw only limited growth in the 1960s, while agencies with responsibility for health care, education, and community development saw dramatic growth during Johnson's presidency. These patterns reflected the domestic priorities of Johnson and the liberal wing of the Democratic Party. These priorities are very clear when we examine one aspect of Johnson's Great Society plan, urban development. Figure 3.3 on page 98 shows the remarkable increases in federal grants for subsidized housing and in urban renewal grants, from $212 million in 1964 to $1.049 billion in 1970.

Under Johnson, the federal government funneled record amounts of money to states to combat discrimination and to fight poverty. Many states (especially in the South) were blamed

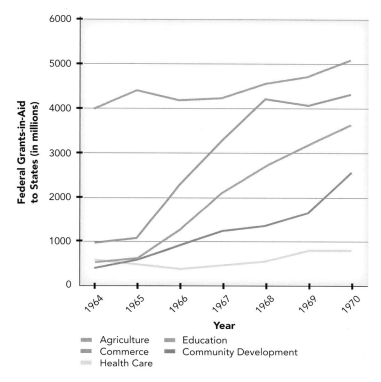

FIGURE 3.2

Grants-in-Aid from the Federal Government to States (1964–1970)

The pattern of distributions of federal grants-in-aid is a good indicator of the priorities of our government and its leaders. During the 1960s, we saw enormous growth in grants for commerce, education, and community development. While there was an increase in grants for agriculture and health care, the rate of growth was substantially less than the other categories, reflecting the policy priorities of Lyndon Johnson and the Democratic leadership in Congress.

for dragging their feet in carrying out social reforms to promote equal rights. If the federal authorities decided that states and local communities were not cooperating, they withheld funds. By using a reward and punishment system to allocate resources, the federal government was very successful in getting the states and localities to do its bidding. Liberal members of Congress intentionally bypassed conservative governors, state legislatures, and

▶ **418 billion dollars!**
For what kinds of projects are these grants used?

grants-in-aid
funds given from one governmental unit to another governmental unit for specific purposes.

categorical grants
grants of money from the federal government to state or local governments for very specific purposes. The grants often require that funds be matched by the receiving entity.

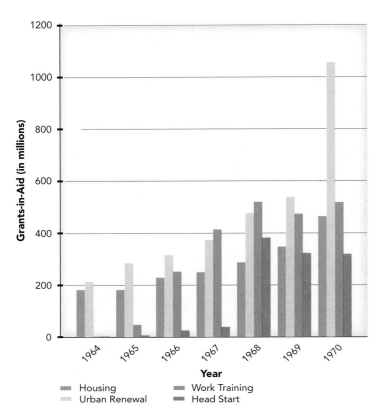

FIGURE 3.3
Grants-in-Aid Selected Programs 1964–1970

Spending on urban renewal increased from around $200 million in 1964 to over $1 billion in 1970. Spending for Head Start and work training increased dramatically over the same time period. During that decade we saw greater demands for minority voting rights and protection from racial and ethnic discrimination. As a larger number of less affluent people got involved in politics, using the grassroots mobilization and elections pathways, the manner in which we allocated federal grants changed. Figures 3.2 and 3.3 provide evidence that our officials respond to our demands for change.

mayors, giving urban renewal and social welfare grants directly to citizen groups. This put local activists in direct competition with local elected officials, often causing tension. Because Chicago Mayor Richard Daley, for example, failed to promote policies aimed at helping the poor and minorities of his city, federal money went directly to local citizen groups, circumventing the city government.

Before the Great Society, states had asked the federal government for money for specific purposes. Under Johnson, Congress increasingly began to use monetary grants to advance specific agendas—for example, helping the urban poor, combating crime, and protecting the environment. Often these issues had been low priorities for state and local governments, but given the availability of federal funds to develop new programs, local governments began to restructure their priorities to conform to Washington's wishes. Consequently, as federal aid increased, so did state and local dependence on it.

THE CHANGING NATURE OF FEDERAL GRANTS

Grants-in-aid are federal funds given to state and local governments on the condition that the money be spent for specified purposes, defined by officials in Washington. They are a means for redistributing income. Under this system, money collected from all citizens by the national government in the form of taxes is then allocated by the federal government for the benefit of certain citizens in specific cities and states. These grants often work to reduce notable inequalities among states, as many are based on economic need. It is important to note, however, that whatever its form, grant money comes with strings attached. Many stipulations are imposed to ensure that the money is used for the purpose for which it was given; other conditions are designed to evaluate how well the grant is working. Both give rise to complex reporting and accounting requirements.

Grants-in-aid go back to our earliest days. The national government gave money to the states to help them pay debts from the Revolutionary War. One of the most important early examples of grants-in-aid was the decision of the national government in the mid-nineteenth century to give the states land grants for educational institutions and to build railroads that promoted westward expansion. (Many of today's leading public universities were founded with the proceeds of these grants.) Cash grants-in-aid were distributed by the federal government early in the nation's history, for example to pay for state militias, but they did not become common until the twentieth century. Today, however, they

formula grants
specific type of categorical grant in which money is allocated and distributed based upon a prescribed formula.

project grants
a type of categorical grant in which a competitive application process is required for a specific project (often scientific or technical research or social services).

block grants (sometimes called revenue sharing grants)
grants of money to states, which are given substantial discretion to spend the money with minimal federal restrictions.

President Lyndon Johnson used various forms of grants from the federal government in order to spur state and local action against such social problems as poverty and racial discrimination. What might be some problems caused by the federal government's use of financial incentives in this way?

are enormously important. It is estimated that in 2004, the federal government spent more than $418 billion in grants-in-aid to state and local governments, benefiting millions of Americans.[13]

▶ **418 billion dollars! For what kinds of projects are these grants used? Categorical grants** are targeted for specific purposes. Typically they have strict restrictions, often leaving little room for discretionary spending. Two types of categorical grants exist: formula grants and project grants. Let's consider each in turn.

Formula grants are distributed according to a particular formula, which specifies who is eligible and for how much. For example, the number of school-age children living in families below the poverty line is used to allocate federal funds to each state to subsidize school breakfasts and lunches. The states must spend this money on school meals, according to a very specific formula allowing no flexibility. The money at stake under grants of this type is one reason why the state population figures and other demographic data revealed each decade by the national census are so important—and so controversial. Consider what happens when it is proposed to allocate money to states for homeless shelters based on the number of homeless people in each state. States that are better at finding and counting the homeless would receive more money than other states that are less successful or less diligent in accounting for their homeless population—a problem compounded by the irregular lives of many homeless people, who often migrate for a variety of reasons (including the weather).

The second type of categorical federal grants, **project grants,** are awarded on the basis of competitive applications rather than a specified formula. Consider homeless shelters. A community could apply for a project grant to develop a new model of a shelter, one that not only houses the homeless but also involves the efforts of other community organizations to provide education, job training, and substance abuse counseling. The community could receive federal grant money based on the strength of its application and its prospect for innovation.

As noted, categorical grants are for purposes specified by federal law that are often used to advance the vision of lawmakers and federal executives in Washington. Typically, state governments must contribute some money of their own, but often the federal funds support the primary cost of the program. State and local officials have often found these grants frustrating, as they are defined so narrowly and may not fit the needs of the locality. For example, money might be available to hire more public school teachers, but a local school district may actually need money to purchase new textbooks and build new schools. Under most categorical grants, school districts lack discretion: They must either follow Washington's requirements (hire new teachers, for example) or forgo the funds. The lack of flexibility has often meant that local needs are not well served and that money is wasted.

Block grants (sometimes called *revenue-sharing grants*) were developed in 1966 as a response to these problems. Block grants are still earmarked for specific programs, but they are far more flexible. To continue our earlier example, a categorical grant for education might specify that the money be used for teacher salaries, even if that isn't the greatest need in the school district. A block grant would still be available to improve education, but the school district could decide (within specified parameters) how to spend the money—it might choose to buy textbooks rather than hire more teachers. Because block grants allow greater spending flexibility, many observers feel they are a more efficient and more effective form of federal grant.

▶ **What's "new" about**
New Federalism?

mandates
an authoritative instruction that is
required.

Prison conditions in many states were found
to violate the Eighth Amendment's prohibition
on cruel and unusual punishments. Federal
judges ordered prison officials to undertake
expensive construction and renovations to
improve facilities and living conditions. Should
federal judges be able to order state officials
to take action?

pathways of action
MANDATES TO PROMPT CHANGE

Mandates are a means for the federal government to require states to do its bidding, typically in areas relating to civil rights and environmental protection. Mandates often accompany federal aid, forcing states to comply with Washington's rules as a condition for receiving its grants. From the beginning, most categorical grants were matching grants with strings attached. Although the number of categorical grants has decreased, the federal government has been able to continue enforcing its will by enacting laws that mandate certain behavior by state and local governments. State and local leaders often resent these mandates, as many are unfunded. For example, a federal law demands new standards for clean air. Localities that violate the standards can be subject to lawsuits and fines or can lose highway funds because the federal authorities link pollution control to carpooling. In effect, the federal government says to the states, "Do as we say—even if we do not provide enough money to fund your compliance—or else

you will lose money that we have given you for various other purposes." As you can easily imagine, such "unfunded mandates" are attractive to many in Washington as a means for extending their influence without accepting financial responsibility. However, conservatives' concerns about the far-reaching role of the federal government at the state and local levels produced the Unfunded Mandates Reform Act of 1995. The law requires Congress to estimate the costs of proposals that may cost more than $50 million. Congress must then vote to pass the program, publicly taking responsibility for the cost. The law attempts to shift power to the states and to limit Congress's ability to pass unfunded mandates, but in reality it simply makes members of Congress vote twice to enact such mandates. But they have to do it publicly.

Federal courts generate mandates too. Citizens often seek federal court mandates as a pathway to challenge many local practices, from the hiring of firefighters to the quality of public housing, often with great success. Desegregation and prison reform have been important examples. For prisons, in response to lawsuits initiated by prisoners and by advocates of prison reform, federal judges have imposed rules for state prison construction and management, as well as rules for prisoner treatment—rules that can be costly to fulfill. For example, it can be quite expensive for a state to comply with a court order to replace deteriorating buildings, upgrade plumbing and heating in prisons, and hire and train additional personnel. Perhaps the best-known federal mandates that have originated with the courts grew out of the civil rights movement and have resulted in such actions as school desegregation, busing, and affirmative action. ■

NEW FEDERALISM

The power and influence of the federal government expanded dramatically in the twentieth century. Every president since Richard Nixon (1969–1974) has voiced concern over the size and influence of the federal government. In 1976, Georgia governor Jimmy Carter successfully ran for the White House as an outsider who opposed federal mandates, with which as governor he had disagreed for a variety of reasons. Although as president Carter did cut back federal grant expenditures, his cuts paled in comparison to those of his successor, Ronald Reagan.

▶ **What's "new" about New Federalism?** Winning election over Carter in 1980, Reagan pledged to promote a new form of federalism in which more power and responsibility would be returned to the states, including financial responsibility. Reagan and other conservatives strongly disagreed with the diminishing role of state

Dillon's Rule
Iowa state court decision in 1868 that narrowly defined the power of local governments and established the supremacy of state governments when conflict exists with localities. Subsequently upheld by the Supreme Court.

home rule
in contrast to Dillon's Rule, this view asserts that local governments should be granted greater authority. According to this view, local government may exercise all authority not specifically denied to it by state constitution or state law.

governments in our federal system, which had developed over the previous decades. He saw states as vital instruments in our governmental apparatus and vowed to increase their presence. His goals were reflected not only in his rhetoric but also in his budgetary policies. In addition to large income tax cuts, Reagan proposed massive cuts in domestic spending that would roll back and even eliminate many programs created by the Democratic administrations from the New Deal to the Great Society. He declared that "government is not the solution; it's the problem." Reagan successfully pressed Congress not only to reduce the amount of federal grant money that it disbursed but also to shift more money into flexible block grants, which fell into four broad categories—income guarantees, education, transportation, and health. He argued that the states knew best how to serve their citizens and that mandates from Washington were wasteful, failing to meet the needs of the people and also taking away legitimate authority from state and local governments. As you know, this idea of state authority is not new, going back to a view of states as laboratories for public policy experiments. However, this view of states' independence and control over their own affairs diminished over the course of the twentieth century. By the 1980s, with the power and the budget of the federal government reaching record levels, the idea of strengthening states and curbing the federal government struck a chord with the American public. As is evident in Figure 3.4, Reagan was quite successful in fulfilling his pledge to reduce the role of the federal government in funding state and local government budgets.

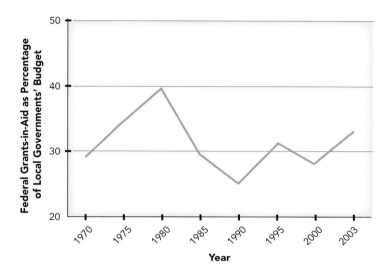

FIGURE 3.4
Federal Grants-in-Aid as a Percentage of State and Local Government Budget

In 1980, 40 percent of local government budgets came from the federal government in the form of grants-in-aid. Ronald Reagan campaigned on a platform that argued that the size, scope, and budget of the federal government needed to be limited. As this graph indicates, he was successful in diminishing the reliance of local governments on federal grants. During Bill Clinton's first term in office, federal grants-in-aid increased, but they began to decrease in the mid-1990s. Why might it be a mistake for local governments to rely on federal grants?

pathways past and present
DILLON'S RULE VERSUS HOME RULE

▶ **Is there some kind of "federalism" between state and local governments?** There is a long-standing tradition in the United States of active and powerful local governments. In the earliest days of colonial America, many colonies were actually federations of local governments. In fact, newly independent states often included stipulations in their first constitutions to guarantee that local governments would retain influence over their own affairs. These new arrangements were in striking contrast to English common law, under which local governments had only the powers explicitly assigned to them by the state and hence were very limited in power and influence.

However, some states did hold to the English tradition of weak local governments. A ruling in 1868 by Judge John Dillon of the Iowa Supreme Court held that local governments could rule only in areas explicitly permitted by the state government, providing a legal framework for this view of state-local relationships. His decision became known as **Dillon's rule.** Legally, state governments create and control local governments. Because of this, state governments have great influence on the nature and character of local municipalities. States that follow Dillon's rule give local governments very narrow and explicit power to fulfill their responsibilities. Consequently, these state governments are very powerful and have a great deal of influence over municipalities within the state. In contrast are states that follow the theory of **home rule,** which holds that city governments can do anything to serve the needs of their residents that is not prohibited by state law. Although city ordinances must comply with state laws and state legislatures can preempt local laws, home rule states give far more authority to the local governments. Local governments are very important for the administration of many governmental services. As

special governments
local governmental units established for
very specific purposes such as the regulation of water and school districts, airports
and transportation services.

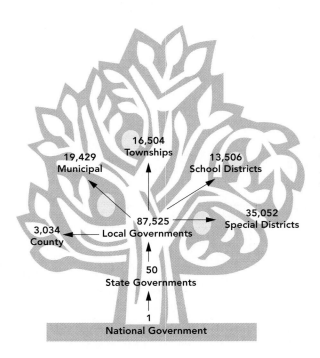

FIGURE 3.5
Forms of Local and Special Governments

There are over 175,000 types of governments in the United
States. At the center is the national government, and the branches
of government stretch far and wide, giving residents many points
of access to governmental officials and leaders. Thus there are
numerous pathways that can be used to initiate change or
promote the status quo.

you can see in Figure 3.5, there were 87,525 local governments in
2002, the largest of which were special governments. **Special gov-**
ernments include a wide variety of entities, the most numerous of
which are natural resource, fire, housing, and community development districts. It is difficult to imagine life without our local
governments. ■

DEVOLUTION

Concerns about the power and influence of the national government continued to be voiced after Reagan left the White House.
Federal grants-in-aid increased through 1995, leading many advocates of states' authority to be upset with the nature of the federal

system in the United States. Republicans once again began to
object to the national government asserting such a large role in our
federal system. In 1994, the Republican congressional leadership
announced an agenda it called its "Contract with America," which
called for reducing the size of the federal government and for
returning money, responsibility, and power to the states—what has
come to be known as **devolution,** or the transfer of power to political subunits. With Republican majorities elected in the House
and Senate in 1994, interest in minimizing the role of the federal
government increased. The Republican initiative focused, in part,
on returning power to the states, having states complete what had
been federal tasks. One prominent example is welfare. Congress
passed reforms that returned management of welfare programs to
the states. With the aim of moving welfare mothers into the working world, new rules were enacted that limited the number of years
women with dependent children could continue receiving public
assistance.

▶ **What factors led to the call for devolution in the 1990s?**
Devolution is motivated by a number of factors. One important
factor is deeply held ideological beliefs that the federal government is less effective in delivering services and solving problems
than the states and localities. Many supporters of devolution
believe that the state governments are best equipped to solve their
own problems and that they only need the power and flexibility to
do so. Worry over increasing federal deficits also fuels devolution,
with the aim of transferring not only power but also fiscal responsibility to the states. However, many policy advocates are opposed
to devolution, fearing a return to the days of great inequality
between states and between citizens within states. The weak
economies of some states prevent them from keeping pace with
other states in education funding, highway construction, and other
vital services unless they have financial support from the federal
government. In economic hard times, the number of people in
need grows dramatically, while the tax revenues required to satisfy
these needs shrinks. Thus at a time of great hardship, states often
have little ability to meet their citizens' needs adequately.
Moreover, most state and local governments are legally prohibited
by their own state constitutions from incurring budget deficits,
whereas the federal government can freely cover whatever deficits
it incurs by selling bonds. So when their tax revenues fall, states
have to make the difficult choice between raising taxes and cutting
services. Devolution has complicated state and local politics by
forcing states to compete for fewer and fewer federal grants.

what YOU can do!
Invite some of your classmates or friends to share coffee and discuss the proper role of the federal government in funding local projects such as the ones under way in your area. Should the federal government be paying for local projects, and if so, should it have a say in how the funds are spent and the desired outcomes? What are the benefits of the federal government's role in local policy development? What are the disadvantages?

devolution
transfer of jurisdiction and fiscal responsibility for particular programs from the federal government to state or local governments.

Moreover, during the recession of the early 1990s, many states and cities found themselves in difficult situations because of reduced revenue. In 2003, for instance, New York City had to lay off 3,400 city employees, close eight firehouses, and cut 3,200 jobs in the Department of Education. In Oregon, police stations often sat vacant at night to save money. Schools had to cut programs, and some districts even had to shave days off the school year. State after state closed schools, faced prison overcrowding, cut Medicaid spending, and raised tuition in public universities.[14] Interestingly, despite these severe experiences, the public generally supports the idea of cutting back on the federal government; thus devolution seems likely to continue in the immediate future.

Although the idea of having more powerful and more independent state governments is popular under today's theory of a new federalism, we have yet to see it reach fruition. Many observers doubt that this vision will ever become a reality. The very issues that brought about a more active federal government—poverty, economic instability, complex relationships at home and with other global powers—still exist. It is therefore difficult to imagine that the federal government might become substantially less active and less involved in the wide array of policy issues. Consider what would happen if one state did not maintain high educational standards. The economy of the entire region could be harmed as the quality of the workforce deteriorated, encouraging employers to relocate their businesses. If the health care system of one state became significantly substandard, neighboring states would experience a crisis as people flocked in seeking better services. Population shifts can create new burdens for states. When thousands of people left New Orleans and moved to Texas in the aftermath of Hurricane Katrina in 2005, they stretched Texas's resources for education, health care, and housing assistance. With increased globalization and the resultant international competition for scarce resources, the days of big national government are not likely to end.

pathways of action
INTERGOVERNMENTAL LOBBYISTS

As federal grants-in-aid become ever more competitive, one important consequence is that states now must compete with one another for them. Many states and cities (and even public universities) have hired lobbyists to represent them in Washington, helping make them more competitive. These lobbyists

Congressman Newt Gingrich led the Republicans' 1994 takeover of Congress by effectively publicizing the promised "Contract with America" that included a commitment to reduce the influence of the federal government. Although states gained added authority over some policy issues, many states also experienced increased financial burdens in trying to provide programs and services that previously received more funding from the federal government. What potential problems can occur if states are completely responsible for their own health care, welfare, and education programs?

▶ In what direction is federalism
headed today?

discussionquestions

1. How did the New Deal shape federalism in the United States? How and why were the programs of the Great Society significant in shaping and redefining federalism?

2. What is devolution? What are some of its consequences?

When Hurricane Katrina devastated New Orleans and the Gulf coast in 2005, the federal government's emergency response agencies were initially slow and ineffective. However, because the federal government possesses many more resources than state and local governments, observers believe that the federal government must maintain a role in responding to major disasters. How can the federal government be more effective and provide better support and coordination with state and local officials when natural disasters occur?

collectively make up the intergovernmental lobby. Intergovernmental groups are not new—many formed during the New Deal era—but in the current budget-cutting environment, the number of intergovernmental lobbying groups is at record levels. One of the earliest and most prominent groups is the National Governors' Association (formed in 1908). The NGA meets twice a year; has a year-round, full-time staff; and gets a good deal of press and public attention. The United States Conference of Mayors (established in 1933) organizes the mayors of cities with more than 30,000 residents. Recent trends in population and economic growth from the industrial Northeast to the South, Southwest, and West have prompted a fresh round of debate over how the federal government distributes aid. Since most federal block grants are based on formulas, which often take population into account, even slight shifts in the formula can result in changes of millions

of dollars. Great attention is paid to how money is distributed, as many people believe that aid can help one state or region while hurting others. As a consequence, the census has become increasingly important and controversial, because population shifts mean significant shifts in aid. Urban areas, for instance, that lose population risk losing millions of dollars in federal aid for some important projects. Given today's budgetary realities, competition between states and cities is likely to increase, making governing all the more difficult.

pathways of action

STATES' RIGHTS—FOR LIBERALS?

Nobody would ever confuse the Massachusetts liberal Congressman Barney Frank (D-MA) with the South Carolina conservative Senator Strom Thurmond (R-SC). But when the tart-tongued Frank appeared on *Fox News Sunday* in 2005, it sounded as if an aide had accidentally slipped him some of Thurmond's talking points from the 1950s, when Thurmond was a states' rights segregationist. "Should the federal government say no state can make this decision for itself?" Frank asked. He had ventured onto Fox to assert each state's right to marry gay couples.

Frank isn't the only supporter of gay marriage to sing the praises of federalism. Last December, Andrew Sullivan argued in *The New Republic*, "The whole point of federalism is that different states can have different policies on matters of burning controversy—and that this is OK." That same month, Paul Glastris, the editor of the *Washington Monthly*, posed the question, "Why shouldn't the Democrats become the party of federalism?"

In some respects, they already have. Liberal energies once devoted to expanding the national government are being redirected toward the states. New York's then attorney general Eliot Spitzer, declaring himself a "fervent federalist," used state regulations to prosecute corporate abuses that George W. Bush's Department of Justice wouldn't touch. While the federal minimum wage hasn't budged since the middle of the Clinton era, 13 states and the District of Columbia have hiked their local wage floors in the intervening years. After Bush severely restricted federal stem cell research, California's voters passed an initiative pouring $3 billion into laboratories for that very purpose, and such initiatives are under way in at least a dozen other states.

SOURCE: Excerpted from Frank Foer, "The Joy of Federalism," *New York Times*, March 6, 2005. Used with permission.

what YOU can do!

After major natural disasters, victims often look to the government—federal, state, or local—for aid and assistance. Following Hurricane Katrina in the fall of 2005, residents of the Gulf Coast looked to the Federal Emergency Management Agency (FEMA) for help—but were disappointed with what they got. The agency's director, Michael Brown, was soon "reassigned." Yet after earlier disasters, FEMA had received high marks.

Conduct a Web search to learn more about this increasingly important and often controversial federal agency starting with the agency's own page, at **http://www.fema.gov/** To read criticisms of FEMA's performance, go to **http://govexec.com** and search on "Katrina." You could also look at the government Web site in your own state.

THE SUPREME COURT'S SHIFT IN PERSPECTIVE

▶ **In what direction is federalism headed today?** During the 1970s, 1980s, and 1990s, Republican presidents selected nine of the eleven new justices who served on the Court during these decades. In their judicial opinions, several of these justices expressed concern about a steady lessening of states' authority to manage their own affairs. One of them, Sandra Day O'Connor, had once been a state legislator and seemed especially interested in requiring Congress and federal judges to show greater respect and deference to state governmental authority. By the mid-1990s, the justices concerned about striking a new balance of power in American federalism gained a slim five-to-four majority. Beginning in 1995, for the first time since the late 1930s, the Supreme Court issued decisions limiting the power of the federal government and consequently opened the way for states to control a greater number of policy issues. In *United States* v. *Lopez* (1995), the Supreme Court struck down the Gun-Free School Zones Act of 1990, which made it a crime to possess a firearm near a school. The Court's majority concluded that congressional power to regulate interstate commerce did not include the authority to create this particular law. The Court made a similar decision in striking down portions of the Violence against Women Act of 1994, in which Congress had permitted victims of sexual violence and gender-based attacks to file federal lawsuits against their attackers (*United States* v. *Morrison*, 2000).

The Court also revived the Tenth Amendment, a provision of the Constitution that was generally treated as a powerless slogan by justices from the late 1930s through the mid-1990s. In *Printz* v. *United States* (1997), the Court declared that Congress cannot require state and local officials to conduct background checks on people who seek to buy firearms. The Court's decisions on the Tenth Amendment's protection of state authority and the limits of congressional power to regulate interstate commerce indicated that the Supreme Court would no longer automatically endorse assertions of federal power at the expense of state authority.

By the first years of the twenty-first century, the Court had not fundamentally changed the relationship between the federal government and the states. The federal government remains actively involved in a wide array of public policies, including many that do not seem intimately connected to the congressional power to regulate interstate commerce. However, recent decisions indicate that the Supreme Court stands ready to selectively reject specific assertions of federal power that it considers excessive under its new vision of the Constitution's framework for federalism.

practicequiz

1. As one form of federal grants, grants-in-aid
  a. are a twentieth-century phenomenon.
  b. created many of our state universities.
  c. allowed President Reagan to subsidize state and local authority thanks to the flexible spending options associated with such grants.
  d. a and c.

2. Congress is the only branch of the federal government that generates mandates.
  a. true   **b.** false

3. What best describes the difference between Dillon's rule and home rule?
  a. Dillon's rule asserts the supremacy of the federal government over state and local government, while home rule asserts the opposite.
  b. Dillon's rule grants state governments significant influence over how municipalities operate, while home rule asserts that local governments can do anything for local residents not prohibited by state law.
  c. Dillon's rule reflects an attitude toward states' rights consistent with the current Republican Party view, while home rule treats states' rights in a way that's consistent with the current Democratic Party view.
  d. a and c.

4. Some people have raised objections to devolution, the transfer of power and resources from the federal government to state and local governments. Why?
  a. The relatively weak economies of some states make the quality of life for residents in those states inferior to that in states with strong economies.
  b. Some states cannot weather tough economic times as well as the federal government because their constitutions prohibit their running a deficit.
  c. In an economic downturn, just when the needs of state residents rise, states become less able to collect sufficient revenues to meet those needs.
  d. a, b, and c.

Answers: 1-b, 2-b, 3-b, 4-d.

Conclusion

We have outlined some practical and theoretical reasons for a federated system—why a democracy such as ours might have layers of governmental authority. The foremost original explanation for federalism in the American setting was the need for compromise. Most Americans understood the necessity of a stronger national government, given the failures of the Articles of Confederation, but many also worried about a distant, unresponsive, and potentially tyrannical national government. Why not look to one level of government to regulate commerce, conduct foreign policy, and safeguard national security while another level provided basic services and looked after law and order? Dual federalism seemed natural, even logical, during the early years of our republic. Yet determining precisely which layer of government is responsible for certain functions—and when push came to shove, which layer would be superior—has never been simple. The struggle over appropriate governmental authority has been at the heart of many of the most trying events in our nation's history. One might even say that federalism has been at the core of nearly all critical periods in American history.

Given that there is no clear or universally agreed upon way to allocate responsibilities between layers of our government, the nature of federalism has been shaped by the individuals who happened to be in charge of government, as either elected officials or judges, during critical periods of our history. In effect, the course of federalism can be like a pendulum that swings between different approaches to allocating national and state authority, depending on the problems faced by the nation and the viewpoints of the individuals in positions of political and judicial power. From FDR's New Deal until the 1980s, for example, the Democrats controlled the federal government most of the time, and with this control came an increase in the power and prerogatives of the national government. Democrats argued that government offers the best means of helping citizens reach their potential and ridding society of its ills. Their approach called for merging each layer of government into unified action to attack these problems. The use of categorical grants under Lyndon Johnson's Great Society program is a clear example of how officials in Washington have used federal monies to advance their priorities at the state and local levels. The election of Ronald Reagan in 1980 and of a Republican Congress in 1994 produced a shift to less federal intervention—and hence less federal money—at the state level. George W. Bush's recent budget proposals clearly reflect a more constrained view of the federal government's role in many domestic policy areas.

Make no mistake, state and local governments will remain vital in the United States no matter which party controls Congress, the White House, or the federal judiciary. But exactly how much federal help (or interference) states and communities will receive is an open question. One thing is certain: Anyone who is interested in playing a role in politics, in shifting policy to confront areas of concern, should pay close attention to the federalism debate. The pathways of change are not simply about pushing government in a certain direction but rather about pushing the *correct level* of government in a new direction.

YOUR turn!

When most young Americans think about government, the federal system comes to mind—that is, the president, Congress, and often the Supreme Court. But there are different layers in our system, and it is quite reasonable to suggest that local government has the greatest impact on the day-to-day lives of average Americans. States, counties, cities, and towns regulate transportation; they set sales, property, and income tax rates; they zone areas for development or housing; they maintain community parks; they support and run social programs; and they oversee public education. So if local government is that important, why not become involved at this level? Call your local city or town hall and find out when the next council meeting will take place. Attend the meeting, perhaps with a few friends, and learn more about some of the controversial issues. If some of these matters are of interest to you, consider ways of becoming a player in the process. Far too few Americans take part in local governance. The good news, however, is that individuals and small groups can have a dramatic impact on the policy process. You can make a difference at every level of government, and especially at your own city hall. ▮

Chapter Review

1. Unlike most democracies in the world, which have unitary systems of governance, the United States has a federal system. In this country, power and authority are divided among layers of government.

2. There are many explanations—historical, theoretical, cultural, and pragmatic—for why the United States relies on a federal system. Probably the best explanation is that dividing power between the national government and state govern-

ments was a compromise that kept the Constitutional Convention on track.

3. During the early years of our republic, there was much confusion over the division of authority, and this controversy produced crucial Supreme Court cases, such as *McCulloch* v. *Maryland* (1819).

4. Until the Civil War, dual federalism existed, meaning that neither the state nor the federal government was superior, and each had specific duties and obligations.

5. To a large extent, the Civil War was fought over the issue of supremacy—determining which level of government, state or national, should be supreme.

6. Numerous changes, including amendments to the Constitution and the Industrial Revolution, further confused issues of governmental authority.

7. The nature of federalism in the United States changed irrevocably during the Great Depression as Franklin Roosevelt's New Deal thrust the federal government into nearly every realm of domestic governance.

8. Different ways of providing state and local governments with federal money have shaped the federalism debate since the New Deal.

9. Although it seems that there are fewer and fewer policy areas where the reach of the national government does not extend, a growing concern, especially among conservative politicians, has been to revive local governing authority. *Devolution* is the term used to describe the return of authority from the federal to the state level.

10. Rather than conceptualize federalism as a static condition, this chapter suggests a "pendulum model," where power and authority continually shift, reflecting the perspective of the people in power, social and economic conditions, and the outlook of the courts.

CHAPTER REVIEW TEST

1. This chapter frequently refers to the layers of government when discussing federalism. What do these layers consist of?
   a. the executive, legislative, and judicial branches of the federal government.
   b. federal governmental officials—the president, members of Congress, judges—and all the people who work beneath them and for them.
   c. the federal, state, and local governments.
   d. the different federal administrations that have succeeded each other over time.

2. States' responses to federally mandated speed limits in the 1970s illustrate that
   a. when and where federal authority supersedes state authority are still contested questions.
   b. states have the constitutional right to set aside federal mandates when they think their independence is being threatened.
   c. federal control over state and local affairs has continually expanded since the New Deal.
   d. a, b, and c.

3. "Laboratories of democracy" refers to
   a. the countries in which different kinds of democratic-style governments have been initiated.
   b. states tackling social challenges through their own measures, a better path to policy innovation, proponents assert, than having the federal government impose one policy.
   c. town hall meetings in which local citizens rediscover what it means to live in a democratic country.
   d. early meetings among the framers of the Constitution.

4. The federal structure of the United States is unique among the nations of the world.
   a. true   b. false

5. The Articles of Confederation reflected a clear consensus on how much authority individual states should retain.
   a. true   b. false

6. In the Supreme Court case of *McCulloch* v. *Maryland*, John Marshall's opinion
   a. made use of the Bill of Rights.
   b. found it "necessary and proper" that Maryland tax banks in the state, even a branch of the Second Bank of the United States.
   c. found that the federal government's power to charter a national bank was consistent with the "necessary and proper" clause in the Constitution.
   d. a and c.

7. Dual federalism
   a. was a theory of federal-state relations promoted during the 1950s.
   b. asserted that neither the federal government nor state governments were superior to the other but had separate areas of responsibility.

c. asserted that the federal government had two areas of responsibility, one pertaining to national concerns, such as defense, and one pertaining to interstate concerns, like commerce.

d. a and c.

8. For a very long time, students from southern states were taught that the Civil War should be known as "the War between the States." What does this fact signify?

a. the endurance of a states' rights point of view in the South.

b. resistance in the South to the idea that the Civil War was fought over the issue of slavery.

c. a conception of federalism at odds with Abraham Lincoln's.

d. a, b, and c.

9. "States' rights" is, to this day, an idea promoted proudly by a large percentage of politicians.

a. true   b. false

10. What statement best summarizes the thrust of the intent of the Thirteenth, Fourteenth, and Fifteenth Amendments to the Constitution?

a. Racism, in all its forms, is a blot against American democracy.

b. No state has the authority to deny African American men the rights of full citizenship, including voting rights.

c. Dual federalism will apply to all states in the Union.

d. a, b, and c.

11. How many decades did it take for the Fourteenth and Fifteenth Amendments to become important sources of federal authority and to matter genuinely to the political lives of African Americans?

a. one   b. three
c. five   d. nine

12. Students of U.S. federalism should know about the Sherman Antitrust Act of 1890 because

a. it represents a step backward in the expansion of federal authority.

b. it represents a step forward in the expansion of federal authority.

c. it is an early example of Congress enacting a statute that addresses a national concern, in this case industrial monopolies.

d. b and c.

13. Congress's intervention against monopolies in the late nineteenth century is an example of the federal government making sure capitalism runs its natural course.

a. true   b. false

14. For the most part, judicial decisions in the late nineteenth and early twentieth centuries, such as *United States* v. *E. C. Knight Company* (1895) and *Hammer* v. *Dagenhart* (1918), had the effect of slowing the expansion of federal authority.

a. true   b. false

15. Decisions by the Supreme Court after Franklin Roosevelt's appointments of new justices

a. tended to preserve states' rights when they came into conflict with federal authority.

b. upheld the constitutionality of most of the New Deal initiatives.

c. constituted a check against FDR's executive authority.

d. a and c.

16. What specific authority granted by the Constitution was crucial to Congress's ability to legislate in the area of civil rights in the 1960s?

a. the First Amendment.

b. the Tenth Amendment.

c. the authority to regulate interstate commerce.

d. Article IV of the Constitution.

17. Why does the issue of federal funding matter to our understanding of federalism in contemporary America?

a. because in many cases, such as those involving the environment, federal funding acts as another form of interstate commerce.

b. because in many cases, such as those involving public education, federal funding establishes and enforces federal regulation at the state and local levels—that is, federal money comes with strings attached.

c. because such funding means that the federal government has more money and the states less.

d. a, b, and c.

18. Why is marble cake a better metaphor than layer cake for federalism in the New Deal era?

a. because it better describes the cooperative national-state interaction that characterized that period.

b. because it better describes the permanence of federal authority, as established in that period.

c. because people in that era began to assume that problems affecting them at the local level were also national problems, to be addressed, in part, by the national government.

d. a and c.

19. Lyndon Johnson's Great Society initiatives

a. allocated federal money to state and local governments to counteract poverty and racial discrimination.

b. advanced the agenda of southern Democrats in Congress.

c. are good examples of devolution.

d. a and c.

20. Welfare reform in the 1990s illustrated

a. the country's increased comfort with having social programs handled at the state level.

b. the validity of the "laboratories of democracy" idea.

c. the country's waning support for Johnson's War on Poverty initiatives.

d. a, b, and c.

DISCUSSION QUESTIONS

1. Why did the framers of our political system settle upon a federated system, as opposed to the unitary model? Do you think this system is still appropriate today? Why or why not?

2. What does the concept dual federalism imply, and how was this notion transformed by the Civil War?

3. How might the ways in which the federal government gives states and local government money impact the "federalism question"?

4. How would you describe recent trends in federalism in the United States?

5. What is the Tenth Amendment, and why is it relevant to federalism? How does the Tenth Amendment relate to the concepts of dual and cooperative federalism?

6. What changes in American society have created new issues for governments to address?

7. How has the Supreme Court changed with regard to its view of federalism?

INTERNET RESOURCES

Center for the Study of Federalism at Temple University: **http://www.temple.edu/federalism**

National Governors' Association: **http://www.nga.org**

United States Conference of Mayors: **http://www.usmayors.org**

United States Census Bureau: **http://www.census.gov**

ADDITIONAL READING

Barbour, Christine, Gerald C. Wright; with Matthew J. Streb, Michael R. Wolf. *Keeping the Republic: Power and Citizenship in American Politics.* Washington, D.C.: CQ Press, 3rd edition, 2006.

Burgess, Michael. *Comparative Federalism: Theory and Practice.* New York: Routledge, 2006.

Nagel, Robert F. *The Implosion of American Federalism.* New York: Oxford University Press, 2001.

O'Connor, James. *The Fiscal Crisis of the State.* New Brunswick, NJ: Transaction, 2002.

Osborne, David, and Peter Hutchinson. *The Price of Government.* New York: Basic Books, 2004.

Rodden, Jonathan A. *Hamilton's Paradox: The Promise and Peril of Fiscal Federalism.* New York: Cambridge University Press, 2005.

KEY TERMS

block grants   99

categorical grants   98

cooperative federalism   96

court-packing plan   92

devolution   103

Dillon's rule   101

doctrine of nullification   88

doctrine of secession   88

dual federalism   87

federal system   84

formula grants   99

grants-in-aid   98

home rule   101

mandates   100

monopoly   90

Montesquieu, Charles-Louis de Secondat   84

New Deal   92

project grants   99

sovereignty   82

special governments   102

unitary system   82

The Supreme Court is the center of attention. Samuel Alito, President Bush's nominee for the Supreme Court, pays a courtesy call on Senator Patrick Leahy prior to Alito's 2006 confirmation hearings. Because the Supreme Court is such an important policy-making institution, every nominee receives scrutiny from the news media as Democrats and Republicans battle to influence the composition of the Court.

CHAPTER 4

THE
JUDICIARY

ontroversy over Same-Sex Marriage   Three same-sex couples in three different towns in Vermont applied for marriage licenses from town clerks in 1997. The couples had lived together in committed relationships for periods ranging from four to twenty-five years. Two of the couples had raised children together. But the town clerks refused to issue marriage licenses. The couples responded by filing a lawsuit against their towns and against the state of Vermont for denying them the opportunity to marry. Clearly, these litigants sought to affect law and public policy through a judicial decision that would support the right of same-sex couples to have marriages recognized by the government and sanctioned by law.

On the first round, the couples lost. The trial judge dismissed the lawsuit by declaring that Vermont's marriage statute could not be interpreted to include recognition of same-sex relationships.

The issue of gay marriage generates strong disagreements and heated debate. Although Americans lack consensus on this issue, judges in a few states have declared that gays and lesbians may marry or enjoy the benefits of civil unions. Some argue that these judges are imposing their ideas on society, while others claim that they are upholding the concept of equal rights for minority groups. What do you think, and why?

Moreover, the judge ruled, Vermont's marriage statute did not violate the state constitution. The judge endorsed the state policy of defining marriage strictly in a manner that advanced human reproduction and the raising of children in families headed by heterosexual couples.

The couples did not give up. Because the court systems of the United States allow the losing side in a lawsuit to have the case reviewed by a higher court, they filed an appeal in the Vermont Supreme Court. (Vermont is one of twelve small states that do not have intermediate appellate courts. Therefore, all appeals go directly to the state's highest court.) After hearing oral arguments in the case, the Vermont Supreme Court examined whether the state's policies toward same-sex couples violated the state constitution and concluded that the state was indeed doing just that. According to the court's opinion, Chapter 1, Article 7 of the Vermont constitution guarantees equal treatment by the state (*Baker* v. *State*, 1999). The Vermont Supreme Court concluded that same-sex couples "may not be deprived of the statutory benefits and protections afforded persons of the opposite sex who choose to marry."

The Vermont Supreme Court very carefully emphasized that its decision was based solely on the Vermont constitution and not on the equal protection clause of the U.S. Constitution's Fourteenth Amendment. By basing its interpretation and conclusion wholly on the state constitution, the Vermont court was trying to

ensure that the U.S. Supreme Court would not later overturn its decision. The U.S. Supreme Court can rule only on matters of federal law. State supreme courts are the ultimate authorities on the meaning of their own state constitutions, but they must take care that their decisions do not violate the U.S. Constitution or federal law.

The decision of the Vermont Supreme Court forced the state legislature to create a legally recognized status, called "civil unions," that permits same-sex couples to enjoy protections and benefits comparable to those provided by law for married couples. Civil unions provide legal benefits that may be recognized in that state only. However, the concept raises great concern among critics of same-sex unions because of the "full faith and credit clause" in Article VI of the U.S. Constitution, which requires states to recognize the "public acts, records, and judicial proceedings" of other states, although scholars disagree about whether this would require that a same-sex marriage sanctioned in one state be recognized by other states.[1]

A similar scenario played out in Massachusetts, where seven same-sex couples initiated a legal action when they were denied marriage licenses in 2001. Like the Vermont Supreme Court, the Supreme Judicial Court of Massachusetts decided that these denials violated the state's constitution (*Goodridge* v. *Department of Public Health,* 2003). The Massachusetts justices went even further, however. When asked for an advisory opinion by the state legislature about whether the creation of civil unions for same-sex couples would satisfy the requirements of the state constitution, the Supreme Judicial Court set off a national uproar by ruling that same-sex couples were entitled to marry in the same manner as heterosexual couples.[2]

These examples illustrate how litigants can use the court-centered pathway to shape law and public policy. But in thinking about this pathway, you should also remember that controversial court decisions generate debates about whether it is proper for judges to make decisions that shape important public policy issues. Filing a lawsuit does not guarantee that you will prevail in the court pathway. Indeed, people frequently lose when they try to use the court pathway. And if you win a court victory, your success may trigger activity in other pathways and institutions that ultimately overrides or changes the policies that the courts may prescribe. For example, the Vermont and Massachusetts court decisions favorable to same-sex couples spurred opponents' efforts to amend many other states' constitutions to *prohibit* such couples from marrying. ■

▶ **It sounds as though** the adversarial system is more about winning the case than making sure justice prevails. Is that really how our legal system works?

adversarial system
legal system used by the United States and other countries that draw their legal traditions from England in which a judge plays a relatively passive role as attorneys provide zealous advocacy to protect each side's interests.

inquisitorial system
legal system in most of Europe in which a judge takes an active role in questioning witnesses and seeking to discover the truth.

dual court system
separate systems of state and federal courts throughout the United States, each with responsibilities for its own laws and constitutions.

Courts are important institutions for American society. They are responsible for processing disputes when people sue one another over contracts, personal injuries, and other such civil matters. They also provide the arenas where decision makers pass judgment on people who are accused of violating society's rules by committing crimes. In the United States, courts have a third function as well, serving as policymaking institutions deciding issues of great importance in such controversial areas as discrimination, the environment, affirmative action, abortion, and criminal justice. As a result, under our system of government, individuals and interest groups have long sought to use the court pathway to shape public policy.

In this chapter, you will examine the organization and operation of the judicial branch of American government. You will also analyze the actors in the court pathway who shape law and policy.

Both the existence and the operation of the judicial branch raise significant questions about the nature of American democratic government. How, for example, can a democracy permit unelected federal judges to make decisions that will affect people throughout the country? To understand how individuals and interest groups make use of the court pathway to affect public policy, you must also recognize why this pathway is consistent with and essential to constitutional democracy in the United States.

Key Questions

1. How are American court systems organized?
2. What makes American judges more powerful than those in other countries?
3. What political processes determine the selection of judges?
4. What is the image of the courts in the United States?
5. What litigation strategies are employed in the court pathway?
6. Is it appropriate for judges to shape public policy in a democracy?

Court Structure and Processes

The judicial branch is made up of courts that have different responsibilities. As you consider the elements of the judicial branch, remember that there are two types of courts—trial and appellate—and both types of courts operate in two parallel court systems—state and federal. If you watch television shows such as *Boston Legal* and *Law and Order,* you can become familiar with trial court processes. However, these programs typically emphasize one type of proceeding (trials) in one type of court (trial courts). They do not adequately convey the idea that most cases in trial courts end in plea bargains or negotiated settlements rather than trials. These television portrayals also won't educate you about the U.S. Supreme Court and other appellate courts that consider whether errors occurred when a case was decided by a judge or jury in a trial court.

THE ADVERSARIAL SYSTEM

A distinguishing feature of American court processes, as well as the processes used in other democracies with roots in English law (Canada and Australia, for example), is the **adversarial system.** Here, opposing attorneys zealously represent the interests of their clients. The adversarial system places a high priority on ensuring that each side in a case has its interests forcefully represented, including those of defendants in criminal cases. Thus the adversarial system serves as a vehicle for protecting the rights of individuals whose fates are placed in the hands of judges and jurors.[3]

▶ **It sounds as though the adversarial system is more about winning the case than making sure justice prevails. Is that really how our legal system works?** In the adversarial system, the judge usually serves as a relatively passive and detached referee whose job it is to make sure that the rules of procedure and evidence are followed. The judge does not argue with the attorneys or openly challenge the evidence that they present. In contrast, many democratic countries (those of Continental Europe, for example) use an **inquisitorial system** that requires judges to take an active role in discovering and evaluating evidence. The judge in an inquisitorial process will question witnesses during trial, ask questions about the evidence, and—if one side's attorney is not performing adequately—intervene to uncover important arguments and evidence.[4] In contrast to the adversarial system, the inquisitorial system is designed to seek the truth while placing less emphasis on zealous advocacy intended to advance one side's interests and protect individuals' rights.

The adversarial system presumes that the attorneys for each opposing side are equally knowledgeable and skilled. In reality, however, there are significant differences in expertise, experience,

criminal prosecutions
legal processes in which the government seeks to prove that an individual is guilty of a crime and deserving of punishment for it.

civil lawsuits
legal actions filed by individuals, corporations, or governments seeking remedies from private parties for contract violations, personal injuries, or other noncriminal matters.

what YOU can do!
Visit your local courthouse to see firsthand how lawyers present their cases in court. Courts are open to the public. Even if there are no trials occurring, there are usually preliminary hearings and other types of proceedings under way.

skill, and effectiveness among the nearly 1 million licensed attorneys in the United States. In some cases, brilliant lawyering appears to produce victories in lawsuits and help apparently guilty people avoid criminal punishment. In other cases, by contrast, defendants have been convicted of murder and sentenced to death after trials during which their attorney fell asleep or failed to follow the most elementary procedures designed to protect their rights. Moreover, in an American courtroom, the unequal resources that the opposing sides in an adversarial case can bring to bear may affect the outcome of a case. One side may be able to hire expert witnesses, jury consultants, and technology professionals who can produce impressive computer simulations that appear to re-create the events of a crime or an automobile collision. These resource advantages can help win cases that might have been decided for the opposition if both sides had been in a position to present their evidence with equal access to experts and technology.

TRIAL COURTS

The United States has a **dual court system.** In other words, two court systems, state and federal, exist and operate at the same time in the same geographic areas (see Table 4.1, on page 116). If you go to any large American city, you will find state trial courts operating within blocks of a federal trial court. Sometimes the two courts are right next door to each other in a downtown district. In small cities and towns, a courthouse may be run by a single judge. In larger cities, a dozen or more judges may hear cases separately in their own courtrooms within a single courthouse. Both court systems handle **criminal prosecutions,** involving accusations that one or more individuals violated criminal statutes and therefore should be punished. In addition, in both systems, **civil lawsuits** are presented, in which people or corporations seek compensation from those whom they accuse of violating contracts or causing personal injuries or property damage. Civil lawsuits can also seek orders from judges requiring the government, corporations, or individuals to take specific actions or to refrain from behavior that violates the law.

The existence of two court systems within each state reflects American federalism, under which state governments and the federal government both exercise authority over law and public policy. States are free to design their own court systems and to name the different courts within the state. Thus in some states, trial

The trial of Saddam Hussein in Iraq for crimes committed against the people of his country includes many features that are familiar in American trials, including arguments by attorneys and rulings by a judge. There are also differences in the Iraqi trial, such as the absence of a jury. Why is so much time and money spent on a lengthy trial when everyone agrees that an individual has committed horrible acts?

courts are called "superior courts," while in others they are known as "district courts," "circuit courts," or "courts of common pleas."

Federal trial courts are called U.S. district courts. The country is divided into ninety-four districts. Each state has at least one district court, and larger states are divided into multiple districts. Within each district, there may be multiple judges and courthouses. For example, Ohio is divided into the Northern District of Ohio, with federal courthouses in Toledo, Cleveland, Akron, and

TABLE 4.1

Structure of American Court System

FEDERAL COURT SYSTEM			STATE COURT SYSTEM
ORIGINAL JURISDICTION	*APPELLATE JURISDICTION*		
U.S. Supreme Court Limited categories of cases that rarely arise. Lawsuits involving: Two or more states The United States and a state Ambassadors and diplomats A state against a citizen of another state	Cases previously decided in U.S. courts of appeals or state supreme courts or Court of Military Appeals	courts of last resort	**52 State Supreme Courts*** Two states—Texas and Oklahoma—have separate highest courts for civil and criminal cases
13 U.S. Courts of Appeals No original jurisdiction	Appeals from decisions by U.S. district courts or government regulatory commissions or special courts with responsibility for specific topics (international trade, patents, veterans benefits, government contracts)	intermediate appellate courts	**40 State Courts of Appeals*** 10 states do not have intermediate appellate courts
94 U.S. District Courts Cases involve: Federal criminal and civil law Federal government Lawsuits between citizens of different states for amounts over $75,000 Bankruptcy Admiralty (shipping at sea)	No appellate jurisdiction	trial courts of general jurisdiction	**State Trial Courts (50 states)** Usually called superior courts, district courts, circuit courts, or courts of common pleas
(no federal limited jurisdiction trial court)		trial court of limited jurisdiction	**Lower-level State Trial Courts** Minor criminal and civil cases

Paths to the U.S. Supreme Court for Criminal and Civil Cases in State and Federal Court Systems

FEDERAL CRIMINAL CASE	FEDERAL CIVIL CASE	STATE CRIMINAL CASE	STATE CIVIL CASE
U.S. Supreme Court *U.S.* v. *Gonzalez-Lopez* (2006) Decision: 6th Amendment violation when defendant not allowed to hire attorney of his choice (defendant wins)	**U.S. Supreme Court** *Burlington Northern* v. *White* (2006) Decision: Job reassignment can be improper retaliation under federal employment law (claimant wins)	**U.S. Supreme Court** *Illinois* v. *Cabelles* (2005) Decision: Use of drug-sniffing dog was not an unreasonable search and seizure (defendant loses)	**U.S. Supreme Court** *Kelo* v. *New London* (2005) Decision: No constitutional violation when city used its power to force homeowners to sell home so that a private developer could use the property (claimant loses)
U.S. Court of Appeals Defendant wins	**U.S. Court of Appeals** Claimant wins	**Illinois Supreme Court** Defendant wins	**Connecticut Supreme Court** Claimant loses
U.S. District Court Defendant loses	**U.S. District Court** Claimant wins	**Illinois Appellate Court** Defendant loses	**Connecticut Superior Court** Claimant wins
		Illinois Circuit Court Defendant loses	

*A few states use different names for their courts of last resort (e.g., Court of Appeals [NY, MD], Supreme Judicial Court [ME, MA]).

original jurisdiction
a court's authority to hear a case in the first instance; authority typically possessed by trial courts but also to a limited extent by the U.S. Supreme Court in certain cases, primarily lawsuits filed by one state against another.

jury trials
trials in which factual determinations, decisions about guilt (criminal cases), and imposition of liability (civil cases) are made by a body of citizens drawn from the community.

settlements
negotiated resolutions of civil lawsuits prior to trial.

plea bargain
negotiated resolution of a criminal case in which the defendant enters a guilty plea in exchange for a reduction in the nature or number of charges or for a less-than-maximum sentence.

intermediate appellate courts
courts that examine allegations concerning uncorrected errors that occurred during trials; such courts exist in the federal court system (circuit courts of appeals) and in most state court systems (usually called courts of appeals).

courts of last resort
the highest courts in each American court system, typically called supreme courts, that hear selected appeals from the lower courts.

Youngstown, and the Southern District of Ohio, which has federal courthouses in Dayton, Columbus, and Cincinnati. Each courthouse can have many judges and courtrooms. Most cases filed in these courts concern federal law, with issues concerning the U.S. Constitution, statutes enacted by Congress, or regulations produced by federal government agencies.

Trial courts, whether state or federal, use specific rules and processes to arrive at decisions or otherwise resolve cases. Trial courts are courts of **original jurisdiction,** and it is here that cases are first filed and heard. The U.S. Supreme Court has original jurisdiction in only a small number of specific cases, mainly lawsuits pitting one state government against another. Trial courts tend to fit the image of courts you see portrayed on television. A single judge presides, and in some trials there is also a jury of citizens, who make the ultimate decision about guilt in criminal cases or liability in civil cases. Before a trial, preliminary hearings are held by the trial court, in which lawyers debate and seek rulings on pretrial disputes, such as whether criminal charges will be dropped or whether specific kinds of evidence will be admissible at trial. Proceedings in trial courts focus on the presentation of evidence and arguments concerning criminal guilt or civil liability. In bench trials, the opposing attorneys attempt to persuade the judge about the proper outcome of the case. By contrast, in **jury trials** the judge acts as a "referee", who seeks to ensure that rules of procedure and evidence are followed properly and that the citizens who are selected to serve as jurors understand the rules of law that will guide their ultimate decision.

Although the trial is the final possible stage for these lower-level courts, most cases do not get that far. Early in the process, the judge may dismiss a case if he or she finds that the lawsuit does not present a claim that is recognizable under law. A second reason that most cases never make it to trial is that trial courts actually process most cases through negotiated **settlements** rather than through trials. The negotiations may be adversarial, so the interactions between the attorneys may reflect the benefits and limitations of the adversarial process. But the ultimate resolution is not determined through the courtroom drama of trial as portrayed in television shows.

Only about 10 percent of criminal cases are decided at trial. If criminal cases are not dismissed for lack of evidence early in the process, they are typically resolved through a **plea bargain,** which in criminal cases is the familiar term for a negotiated settlement. Most civil lawsuits are also resolved through negotiated settlements. Negotiated settlements, including criminal case plea bargains, save time and money for lawyers and courts. They benefit the individuals involved because they provide an agreed outcome and, in criminal cases, a less-than-maximum sentence. This is often preferable, because when cases go to trial, all parties involved may face great uncertainty and risk, since no one can reliably predict what a jury or judge will decide.

APPELLATE COURTS

Most states, as well as the federal court system, have **intermediate appellate courts.** These courts, which are typically called "courts of appeals," hear appeals from judicial decisions and jury verdicts in the trial courts. In the federal system, the U.S. courts of appeals are divided into eleven numbered circuits, and there is also the District of Columbia circuit and a specialized federal circuit for patent and trade cases. The numbered circuits each handle the appeals from districts in specific states (see Figure 4.1 on page 118). For example, the U.S. Court of Appeals for the Fifth Circuit handles appeals from U.S. district courts in Texas, Louisiana, and Mississippi.[5]

The highest appellate courts in the state and federal systems are **courts of last resort.** In the federal system, the U.S. Supreme Court is the court of last resort. It can also be the court of last resort when federal law issues, such as questions about civil liberties under the Bill of Rights, arise in cases decided by state supreme courts. State supreme courts are courts of last resort for state law issues in their own judicial systems. State law issues are those that arise from disputes about the meaning of laws created by a state's legislature or about provisions of a state's constitution.

Appellate courts use different processes than trial courts do. Appeals are heard in multijudge courts. Typically, three judges hear cases in a state or federal intermediate appellate court. State supreme courts generally have five or seven members, while the U.S. Supreme Court is made up of nine justices. There are never

▶ How do I get my case
to the Supreme Court?

appellate briefs
written arguments submitted by lawyers in
appellate court cases.

majority opinion
appellate court opinion that explains the
reasons for the case outcome as determined by a majority of judges and that
establishes any rules of law produced by
that judicial decision.

FIGURE 4.1

Geographic Jurisdiction of Federal Courts

The U.S. Courts of Appeals are divided into
regional circuits throughout the country. Each
numbered circuit handles appeals from federal
cases in a specific set of states. In which circuit
do you live?

SOURCE: www.uscourts.gov/courtlinks.cfm

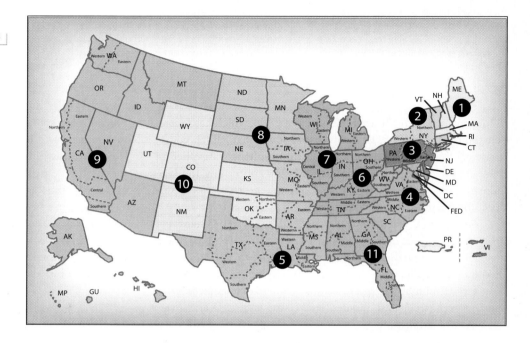

juries in appellate courts. These courts do not make decisions
about criminal guilt or issue verdicts in civil cases. Instead, they
consider narrow issues concerning alleged errors in the investigation and trial process that were not corrected by the trial judge.
Instead of listening to witnesses or examining other evidence,
appellate courts consider only elaborate written arguments, called
appellate briefs, submitted by each side's attorneys as well as oral
arguments.

The appellate process encourages judges to discuss arguments and reasoning with colleagues before making a decision.
Appellate judges issue detailed written opinions to explain their
decisions. The outcome of the case and any announcement of a
legal rule are expressed in the **majority opinion.** This opinion
represents the views of the majority of judges who heard the case.
The majority opinion can create law by announcing or refining
rules. There are many examples of judge-made legal rules, such as
"police officers must inform suspects of their right to remain
silent and be represented by an attorney during questioning"
(*Miranda* v. *Arizona,* 1966) or other authoritative statements
about individuals' rights, government officials' responsibilities,
and other matters governed by law.

Concurring opinions are written by judges who agree with
the outcome favored by the majority but wish to present their own

reasons for agreeing with the decision. Appellate decisions are not
always unanimous, and so judges who disagree with the outcome
may write **dissenting opinions** to express their points of disagreement with the views expressed in the majority opinion.[6]
Sometimes concurring and dissenting opinions develop ideas that
will take hold in later generations and help shape law after new
judges are selected for service on appellate courts.

THE UNITED STATES SUPREME COURT

At the top of the American judicial system stands the U.S.
Supreme Court. It does not have authority over all cases, because
state supreme courts are the final interpreters of their own state
constitutions and statutes. However, the U.S. Supreme Court has
authority over any decision by a state court (including those of a
state supreme court) that concerns the U.S. Constitution or federal
law. In particular, the U.S. Supreme Court is regularly called on to
decide whether state statutes violate the U.S. Constitution or
whether decisions and actions by state and local officials collide
with federal constitutional principles.

The U.S. Supreme Court is especially important for the court
pathway, and is a special target for the interest groups that use this

concurring opinion
appellate court opinion by judge who
endorses the outcome decided by the
majority of judges, but wants to express
different reasons to justify that outcome.

dissenting opinion
appellate court opinion explaining the
views of one or more judges who disagree
with the outcome of the case as decided
by the majority of judges.

writ of certiorari
a legal action that asks a higher court to
call up a case from a lower court; the legal
action used to ask the U.S. Supreme
Court to accept a case for hearing.

pathway, because unlike other American courts with limited geographic jurisdictions, the highest court's decisions affect the entire country. As a result, the U.S. Supreme Court is often asked to address many of the nation's most controversial policy disputes. On a single day in December 2002, for example, the Supreme Court agreed to hear an affirmative action case pressed by political conservatives that challenged the use of race as one criterion in university admissions and a privacy case that sought to invalidate state laws criminalizing sexual relations between homosexuals behind the closed doors of their own bedrooms. The Court's decisions in such cases shape law and public policy for the entire country and often either advance or block long-sought objectives of policy advocates who may have been unsuccessful in seeking favorable action by authoritative decision makers in other branches of government.

By contrast, state supreme courts' decisions, such as in the same-sex marriage controversy in Massachusetts, apply only within the boundaries of the specific state. In the two cases just mentioned that applied nationally, a majority of justices decided that universities can use race as a consideration in admissions but cannot automatically give an applicant a specific number of points in the admissions process just for being a member of an underrepresented racial group (*Grutter* v. *Bollinger*, 2003). They also decided that states cannot make it a crime for homosexual adults to have consensual sex in the privacy of their own homes (*Lawrence* v. *Texas*, 2003). Such laws violate the constitutional right to privacy. Table 4.2 on page 120–121 gives the names and backgrounds of the Supreme Court justices who currently make these decisions.

▶ **How do I get my case to the Supreme Court?** As the nation's court of last resort, the U.S. Supreme Court enjoys significant discretionary jurisdiction, meaning that it can pick and choose its own cases from among those submitted for consideration. Nearly all cases are presented to the Court through a petition for a **writ of certiorari,** a traditional legal order that commands a lower court to send a case forward. The Court receives more than 7,000 certiorari petitions each year, but it grants complete hearings and produces full written opinions in only seventy-five to eighty-five cases each year. The petitions are reviewed by the Court's law clerks, recent graduates of top law schools who spend one year working as an assistant to a specific justice. The law clerks write "cert memos," brief descriptions and analyses of each submitted case, which are distributed to each justice. In their private weekly meetings, the justices vote on which cases to accept for hearing. Cases are selected for hearing through the Court's "rule of four," meaning that four justices must vote to hear a specific case in order for it to be scheduled for oral

argument. The justices often choose to hear cases that will settle disagreements between different federal courts of appeals about how the Constitution or a specific federal statute should be interpreted. Several dozen additional cases may receive decisions based on written filings but without oral arguments. These latter cases typically do not establish any new legal rules but merely reinforce prior decisions by the Supreme Court.

Overall, the Supreme Court dismisses the vast majority of certiorari petitions. In those cases, the preceding judgment in the case made by a federal court of appeals or a state supreme court stands as the final decision. During the Supreme Court's 2003–2004 term, the Court received 7,814 petitions but granted oral arguments for only ninety-one cases. Because some of these cases were later combined or sent back to the lower courts, it produced only seventy-three full opinions. People who angrily announce that "I'm going to take my case all the way to the Supreme Court!" are engaging in wishful thinking. Thousands of people and corporations ask the Court to hear their cases each year, but very few are accepted for hearing.

The Supreme Court's selectivity in evaluating cases has two important implications for the court pathway. First, many policy-shaping decisions come from courts other than the U.S. Supreme Court. The federal courts of appeals and the fifty state supreme courts provide the final judicial decisions for many more cases each year than those finalized with decisions from the U.S. Supreme Court. Second, because of the relatively small number of cases selected for decision by the Supreme Court, the court pathway is not easily available for people who wish to use it in order to have a nationwide impact on public policy.

The Supreme Court's annual term runs from October through June. Oral arguments for accepted cases are scheduled from October through April. The Court usually reserves the months of May and June exclusively for writing opinions. Each side in the case is given thirty minutes to present its oral arguments. The justices read each side's detailed written arguments, submitted as appellate briefs, before listening to the attorneys' arguments. Although the attorneys prepare to speak for thirty minutes, the justices typically interrupt to ask questions. The attorneys must be good at thinking quickly on their feet in order to respond to the justices' questions. The justices sometimes exchange argumentative comments with each other during oral arguments, too.

After oral arguments, the justices meet in their weekly conference to present their views on the case. No one other than the justices is allowed into the room to hear the discussion. The chief

TABLE 4.2
Supreme Court Justices

Name:	John Roberts	John Paul Stevens	Antonin Scalia	Anthony M. Kennedy
Voting Record:	Conservative	Liberal	Conservative	Moderate
Nominated by:	George W. Bush	Gerald Ford	Ronald Reagan	Ronald Reagan
Date Confirmed:	September 29, 2005	December 19, 1975	September 26, 1986	February 18, 1988
Confirmation Vote Numbers:	78–22	98–0	98–0	97–0
Previous Experience:	Federal Judge, Government Lawyer	Federal Judge, Private Attorney	Federal Judge, Law Professor	Federal Judge, Law Professor

justice speaks first, and the other justices follow in order of seniority. When all of the justices have stated a position, the chief justice announces the preliminary vote based on the viewpoints expressed. If the chief justice is in the majority, he designates which justice will write the majority opinion for the Court. If the chief justice is in the minority, then the senior justice in the majority assigns the opinion for the Court. The chief justice (or senior justice in the majority) also has the option of assigning the majority opinion to himself or herself. Other justices can decide for themselves whether to write a concurring or dissenting opinion. With the assistance of their law clerks, justices draft preliminary opinions as well as comments on other justices' draft opinions. These draft opinions and comments are circulated to all of the justices. They help shape the ultimate reasoning of the final opinions issued in the case. In addition, these draft opinions and comments can sometimes persuade wavering justices to change sides. In some cases, a justice will reconsider his or her original vote after spending weeks reading draft opinions and comments from colleagues with opposing viewpoints. In a case with a preliminary vote of 5–4, one justice switching from the majority will change the out-

come of the case entirely and cause the opinion originally being drafted to represent the majority's viewpoint to become a dissent instead.

When the decision of the Court is publicly announced and the opinions for that case are published, the decision becomes final. The legal rule announced in the decision, however, is not necessarily permanent. Sometimes justices come to regret their votes in an announced decision, but the decision cannot be changed at that point. In such situations, the justices must wait for a new case to raise similar issues in order to revise a decision they previously made. If at least five justices agree that the prior decision was wrongly decided, they can use the new case to overrule the Court's earlier opinion and establish a new rule of law on the subject in question. Presidents often focus on this goal when they select new appointees for the Supreme Court with the hope that the new justices will vote to overrule decisions with which the president disagrees. President George W. Bush, for example, appeared to select new justices with the hope that the newcomers would eventually form the core of a five-member majority to overturn *Roe* v. *Wade* (1973), the Supreme Court's decision that

David Hackett Souter	Clarence Thomas	Ruth Bader Ginsburg	Stephen G. Breyer	Samuel Anthony Alito, Jr
Liberal	Conservative	Liberal	Liberal	Conservative
George H.W. Bush	George H.W. Bush	Bill Clinton	Bill Clinton	George W. Bush
October 9, 1990	October 23, 1991	August 10, 1993	August 3, 1994	January 31, 2005
90–9	52–48	96–3	87–9	58–42
Federal Judge, State Judge	Federal Judge, Government Administrator	Federal Judge, Law Professor	Federal Judge, Law Professor	Federal Judge, Government Lawyer

established a constitutional right for women to make choices about abortion.

pathways profile
RUTH BADER GINSBURG

The second woman to serve on the United States Supreme Court—Sandra Day O'Connor was the first—Ruth Bader Ginsburg was born in 1933, graduated from Columbia University's law school, and went on to become a law professor at Rutgers University and Columbia University. Throughout the 1970s, she directed the Women's Rights Project at the American Civil Liberties Union (ACLU). In that capacity, she presented arguments before the Supreme Court in the gender discrimination cases that first successfully turned the high court's attention to such issues. These cases were not just about discrimination against women. She also presented arguments on behalf of men, such as a case challenging Oklahoma's authority to set a higher minimum drinking age for men than for women (*Craig* v. *Boren*,

1976). As a result of Ginsburg's arguments and successful litigation efforts, the Supreme Court broadened its interpretation of the Fourteenth Amendment's equal protection clause to prohibit certain kinds of governmental discrimination by gender. Previously, the clause was used almost exclusively to prevent governmental discrimination based on race. In 1980, Ginsburg was appointed by President Jimmy Carter to serve on the U.S. Court of Appeals for the District of Columbia Circuit. President Bill Clinton appointed her to serve as an associate justice on the U.S. Supreme Court in 1993.

During her years as a lawyer, Ginsburg earned a reputation as a strong advocate for equal rights. As a judge, however, she claimed that her job was very different. Rather than advocate for a particular vision of law and policy, she saw herself as carefully interpreting and applying the Constitution and federal statutes. Because her performance on the U.S. Court of Appeals showed her to be a thoughtful judge, the Senate easily confirmed her appointment by a 96–3 vote. As a Supreme Court justice, Ginsburg has supported individuals' claims concerning violations of constitutional rights more frequently than most of her colleagues. ■

discussionquestions

1. What is the adversarial system?

2. How do trial courts differ from appellate courts? How does the U.S. Supreme Court affect law and policy?

Alexander Hamilton believed that the judiciary would be the least powerful branch of American government under the U.S. Constitution. Although the judiciary became more powerful than Hamilton predicted, is it more or less powerful than the other branches of government?

practicequiz

1. In the United States, courts function as institutions that make public policy on many controversial issues.
   a. true   b. false

2. What are the characteristic features of an adversarial system that are employed in court cases?
   a. Attorneys argue zealously for opposing sides as a judge passively listens, enforces court rules, and instructs the jury on how to apply the law.
   b. The judge aggressively questions witnesses and investigates the case to make absolutely certain that all information is brought forward for consideration.
   c. Attorneys work together cooperatively to make sure that all information is brought forward for consideration.
   d. The government provides attorneys to argue for one of the sides in every criminal and civil case, thus ensuring that the people's views are represented.

3. Approximately how many criminal cases are decided at trial?
   a. 50 percent   b. 75 percent
   c. 10 percent   d. 1 percent

4. How do certain cases make it to the U.S. Supreme Court?
   a. Each federal court of appeals sends a small percentage of its cases to the Supreme Court.
   b. The Supreme Court chooses which cases to hear, receiving most of them through a petition for a *writ of certiorari*.
   c. Each justice is allowed to choose up to fifteen cases a year for the Court to hear, filing a *writ of certiorari* with the chief justice.
   d. The chief justice chooses up to one hundred cases each year, following his or her own discretion.

Answers: 1-a, 2-a, 3-c, 4-b.

The Power of American Judges

The eighteenth-century authors of the United States Constitution did not expect the judicial branch to be as powerful as the executive and legislative branches. Although some of the framers wanted to permit judges to evaluate the constitutionality of statutes, they did not generally believe that the courts would be influential policymaking institutions. In *Federalist No. 78*, Alexander Hamilton called the judiciary the "least dangerous" branch of government because it lacked the power of "purse or sword" that the other branches could use to shape policy and spur people to follow policy decisions. Congress could use its "power of the purse" to levy taxes or provide government funds in order to encourage or induce people to comply with government policies. The president, as the nation's commander in chief, could use the "sword" of military action to force people to obey laws. But judges produced only words written on paper and thus appeared to lack the power to force people to obey their decisions.

Hamilton was not wrong to highlight the inherent weakness of the judiciary's structure and authority. The courts controlled no army and possessed no authority to levy taxes or dispense money. Hamilton merely failed to see how the Supreme Court and other courts would assert their power, gain acceptance as legitimate policymaking institutions, and become the forums in which many of the nation's most controversial issues are debated and decided.

To maintain the public's confidence in their fairness, courts portray themselves as the "nonpolitical" institutions of American government. Judges wear black robes and sit on benches elevated above other seats in the courtroom. People are required to rise when judges enter the courtroom and remain standing until given permission to sit down. Judges are verbally addressed as "Your Honor," a special form of address that is not typically enjoyed by other American public officials. Such requirements reinforce the status of judges and convey a message that other citizens are subordinate to judicial officers. Many courts operate in majestic buildings with marble columns, purple velvet curtains, fancy woodwork, and other physical embellishments designed to elicit respect for the importance and seriousness of these institutions. The atmosphere of court buildings often makes them seem more like religious temples than institutions of democratic government.

The physical imagery of courts, as well as the dress and language associated with judges, helps convey the message that the judicial branch is different from the other branches of government. In the executive and legislative branches, political battles are open and obvious. Elected officials maneuver for advantage in partisan contests that will determine who gains or keeps public office and thereby remains positioned to shape public policy. Democrats and Republicans criticize one another and portray their opponents' arguments as harmful to the nation's best interests.

Judicial proceedings, however, are relatively quiet. Competing attorneys take turns making arguments that must follow detailed rules of evidence and procedure. Both in trials of criminal cases and in lawsuits between individuals, judges explain the law in order to instruct citizen-jurors on how to decide properly which side should prevail. In many cases that shape public policy, an individual judge or panel of judges issues a decision that may define the nature of citizens' rights or impose limits on the powers of the other branches of government. It is assumed that judges make decisions by following established legal rules—and often this is true. Lower-court judges follow the decisions that higher courts made in similar cases. In so doing, judges convey the impression that they are neutral decision makers merely following the law and, unlike their "political" counterparts in the legislative and executive branches, are not creating rules and policies on their own. In the words of the late U.S. Supreme Court Justice Harry Blackmun, "The legitimacy of the Judicial Branch ultimately depends on its reputation for impartiality and nonpartisanship."[7] Thus Americans can accept the legitimacy of court decisions because they appear to be based on law, rather than politics, and because they come from respected decision makers in the solemnity of impressive courtrooms rather than by partisan politicians in the mud-slinging turmoil of legislative and executive battles.[8]

The judiciary's cultivation of a nonpolitical image does not, in fact, mean that politics has no role in judicial decision making. To begin with, political battles determine who will be selected to serve as judges, and judges' personal political values and beliefs can affect their decisions. In addition, the process of interpreting the Constitution and statutes gives judges the opportunities to steer many decisions toward their own policy preferences. But despite the reality of political influences within courts, the imagery of courts and law contributes to public acceptance of judicial decisions.

There are structural elements and traditions in the American judicial system that make judges in the United States more powerful than their counterparts in many other countries. Let's examine several of these factors. In particular, we will see the importance, first, of judges' authority over constitutional and statutory interpretation; second, of judicial review; and third, in the federal court system, of judges' protected tenure in office.

CONSTITUTIONAL AND STATUTORY INTERPRETATION

In the United States, although participants in constitutional conventions write constitutions and elected legislators draft statutes, these forms of law still require judges to interpret them. Inevitably, the wording of constitutions and statutes contains ambiguities. Whenever there are disputes about the meaning of the words and phrases in constitutions and statutes, those disputes come to courts in the form of lawsuits, and judges are asked to provide interpretations that will settle the disputes. Therefore, judges can provide meaning for law produced by *other* governmental institutions, as well as for case law developed by judges.

For example, the Eighth Amendment to the United States Constitution forbids the government to impose "cruel and unusual

▶ **Where did the power** of judicial review come from if it's not mentioned in the Constitution?

statutes
laws written by state legislatures and by Congress.

judicial review
the power possessed by American judges to nullify decisions and actions by other branches of government if the judges decide that those actions violate the U.S. Constitution or the state constitution.

punishments." Clearly, the provision intends to limit the nature of punishments applied to people who violate criminal laws. However, the words themselves provide no specific guidance about what kinds of punishments are not allowed. Thus judges have been asked to decide which punishments are "cruel and unusual." When these words were added to the Constitution in 1791, the American public was accustomed to the death penalty for a variety of offenses, as well as the use of physical punishments such as whipping. Many decades later, however, federal judges decided that it is "cruel and unusual" for the government to undertake such actions as whipping prison inmates (*Jackson* v. *Bishop*, 1968) or imposing death sentences on mentally retarded murderers (*Atkins* v. *Virginia*, 2002). On the other hand, judges have found no violation of the cruel and unusual punishments clause when teachers paddle and injure public school students with wooden boards (*Ingraham* v. *Wright*, 1978) or when a prisoner was mistakenly shot by corrections officers who were seeking to stop other prisoners involved in a disturbance (*Whitley* v. *Albers*, 1986). None of these results were clearly determined by the words of the Eighth Amendment. Instead, they were determined by the interpretations of judges who hear and decide individual cases. When interpreting the Eighth Amendment, judges' interpretations are typically based on their assessments about whether specific punishments are consistent with the values of contemporary society.

Judges may emphasize different aspects of analysis when addressing other parts of the Constitution. For example, judges often balance the interests of individuals against the needs of society when deciding whether police have violated the Fourth Amendment prohibition on "unreasonable searches." As we will see in ⓁⒾⓃⓚ *Chapter 5, page 167* and *Chapter 6, page 225*, American judges also use their interpretive authority to define the law for the other provisions of the Constitution, including those that concern freedom of speech, rights for criminal defendants, and the powers of the president.[9]

Statutes provide similar opportunities for judges to shape the law. Statutes are laws written by the people's elected representatives in legislatures. Statutes for the entire country are produced by Congress, the national legislature. Each state also has its own legislature to write laws that apply only within its borders. When they interpret statutes, judges are supposed to advance the underlying purposes of the legislature that made the statutes—but those purposes are not always clear. Many kinds of questions can arise concerning the statutes' meaning. For example, if workers' compensation statutes provide for payments to workers injured "in the course of employment," does that include coverage for a disability resulting from a gunshot wound suffered in a lunch-hour robbery in a

restaurant near the place of business? Are prisons required to provide special accommodations and services for prisoners who claim an entitlement to such privileges under the Americans with Disabilities Act? Inevitably, judges must answer such questions, because legislatures cannot anticipate every possible situation in which issues about a statute's meaning might arise. Thus statutory interpretation provides judges with additional power over the content of American laws and the policies that result from those laws.

As you will see in the later discussion of methods for selecting judges, political battles in state judicial election campaigns and in the nomination processes for federal judges largely arise from the interpretive authority that American judges possess. Because there is no clear set of words or agreed upon principle that tells judges how to interpret constitutions and statutes correctly, judges inevitably apply their own attitudes, values, and policy preferences in shaping the meaning of law. Thus political parties, interest groups, and politicians seek to secure judgeships for people who share their values and policy preferences.

JUDICIAL REVIEW

One of the most significant powers of American judges is that of **judicial review.** Judicial review permits judges to invalidate actions by other governmental actors, including striking down statutes enacted by Congress, by declaring that these actions violate the Constitution. Judges can also invalidate actions by the president or other executive branch officials by declaring that those actions violate the Constitution (see Table 4.3). Indeed, a primary reason that individuals and interest groups seek to use the court pathway for shaping law and public policy is to ask judges to invalidate actions by states, Congress, or the president that block the advancement of their interests and policy preferences. Very few countries permit their judges to wield such awesome power over other branches of government.[10] A leading constitutional law expert describes judicial review as "certainly the most controversial and at the same time the most fascinating role of the courts of the United States."[11]

The institutions and officials of the federal government draw their authority from the provisions of the U.S. Constitution. Congress, for example, looks to Article I, Section 8, of the Constitution for a detailed list of the national legislature's powers. These topics include regulating interstate commerce, coining money, establishing post offices, and organizing military forces. By contrast, as you can see from examining Article III of the Constitution, ⓁⒾⓃⓚ to *Chapter 2, page 59*, there is no mention of the judiciary's power of judicial review.

TABLE 4.3
Judicial Review Cases

Case Name	Date	Vote	Affected Institution	Overview of Case
Granholm, Governor of Michigan v. Heald	May 16, 2005	5–4	State legislatures in Michigan and New York	State laws in Michigan and New York prohibited direct sales of wine to consumers by out-of-state wineries—thus preventing Internet sales and other orders. The U.S. Supreme Court struck down these state laws as violating the Commerce Clause of the U.S. Constitution.
United States v. Booker	January 12, 2005	5–4	Congress	Portion of the Sentencing Reform Act of 1984 that makes Federal Sentencing Guidelines mandatory in federal criminal cases found to be unconstitutional as a violation of the Sixth Amendment right to jury trial, because it permits judges to make factual determinations that should be the responsibility of the jury.
Hamdi v. Rumsfeld	June 28, 2004	8–1 on the issue in question	President	American citizens detained as terrorism suspects are entitled to appear in court and contest the basis for their detention. The U.S. Supreme Court rejected arguments about the president's power to hold suspects indefinitely without any rights, any contact with attorneys, or any access to the courts.
Ashcroft v. Free Speech Coalition	April 16, 2002	6–3	Congress	U.S. Supreme Court invalidated portions of the Child Pornography Prevention Act of 1996 as overly broad and in violation of the First Amendment. Congress cannot ban movies and pictures in which adults portray teenagers engaged in sexual activity.

The Constitution declares that there will be "one supreme Court" in Article III, Section 3, but leaves it to Congress to design and establish the other courts of the federal court system. The tenure of federal judges is described as service "during good Behaviour." To protect judges against political pressure, Section 1 declares that their salaries "shall not be diminished" during their service on the bench. Section 2 describes the kinds of cases that fall under the authority of federal courts, including cases concerning federal law, disputes between states, and matters involving foreign countries. Section 3 defines the crime of "treason" and specifies the evidence necessary for conviction. As indicated by this brief description, nothing in Article III directly addresses the power of judicial review.

As Hamilton noted in *Federalist No. 22*, a viable national government would be impossible if each state had the authority to make laws that were inconsistent with the legal rules laid down by the U.S. Constitution and established by national governing institutions. Federal courts therefore needed the authority to oversee state governmental actions. If judicial review were applied to actions by Congress and the president, however, there would be risks that this potentially awesome power would permit the unelected judges in the federal judiciary to become more powerful than the people's elected representatives in Congress or the elected president. Would we still have a democracy if federal judges appointed to office by the president can overrule decision makers in other branches who were selected by the nation's voters? On the other hand, do we need a mechanism, such as judicial review, to prevent elected officials from violating the principles of the Constitution?

▶ **Where did the power of judicial review come from if it's not mentioned in the Constitution?** The framers of the Constitution were aware of the concept of judicial review, yet they

▶ **Why did the framers** decide to allow federal judges to serve for life?

Marbury v. Madison (1803) case in which the U.S. Supreme Court asserted the power of judicial review, despite the fact that this is not explicitly mentioned in the U.S. Constitution.

Judiciary Act of 1789 early statute in which Congress provided the initial design of the federal court system.

writ of mandamus a legal action that asks a judge to order a government official to take a specific action.

made no mention of it in the founding document. Did this mean that the idea had been considered and rejected by the Constitution's authors? Apparently not—at least not in the eyes of everyone debating the drafting and ratification of the Constitution. In *Federalist No. 78,* Hamilton argued in favor of judicial review, asserting not only that legislative acts that violate the Constitution must be invalid but also that federal judges must be the ones who decide whether statutes are unconstitutional. According to Hamilton, limitations on congressional actions "can be preserved in practice no other way than through the medium of the courts of justice, whose duty it must be to declare all acts contrary to the manifest tenor of the constitution void." But notwithstanding the certainty of Hamilton's convictions about the necessity of judicial review, other founders worried that it would elevate the power of the judiciary above that of other governmental branches.

At the beginning of the nineteenth century, the Supreme Court did not rely on any specific provision of the Constitution to justify its exercise of the power of judicial review. Instead, under the leadership of Chief Justice John Marshall, it simply asserted its authority to review the actions of other governmental branches in the case of *Marbury* **v.** *Madison* (1803). William Marbury was one of many officials in the administration of Federalist President John Adams who received last-minute judicial appointments as Adams was leaving office. The appointment of these "midnight judges" was an effort by Adams to place his supporters in positions of judicial influence to counteract changes in government that would inevitably occur under the administration of the incoming president, Thomas Jefferson. However, in the rush of final activities, the outgoing secretary of state in the Adams administration, John Marshall, never managed to seal and deliver to Marbury his commission as a justice of the peace for the District of Columbia. When Jefferson took office, the incoming secretary of state, James Madison, refused to deliver these commissions to Marbury and several other judicial appointees. Marbury sought his commission by filing a legal action. He followed the requirements of the **Judiciary Act of 1789** by seeking a **writ of mandamus** from the U.S. Supreme Court. A writ of mandamus is a traditional legal order through which a court directs a government official to take a specific action required by law.

Marbury's legal action presented the Supreme Court with a difficult dilemma. Coincidentally, the Court's new chief justice was also a last-minute Adams appointee, just confirmed by the lame-duck Federalist-dominated Senate. This was John Marshall,

the very man whose failure, as Adams's outgoing secretary of state, to seal and deliver Marbury's commission on time had created the legal dispute in the first place. If Marshall and the other justices decided that Marbury was entitled to his commission, it seemed very likely that President Jefferson and Secretary Madison would simply disobey the Court by refusing to deliver the commission. Were that to happen, the Court had no practical means to force the president to act. Thus a decision in Marbury's favor carried the risk of the Supreme Court's image and legitimacy being tarnished by revealing that the judiciary has little practical power in the face of resistance by the president and other political actors. Ultimately, the Supreme Court issued a decision that asserted the power of the judiciary without risking any appearance of weakness.

In a unanimous decision written by Chief Justice Marshall, the Court declared that Marbury was indeed entitled to his commission and that the Court possessed the authority to order President Jefferson to have the commission delivered to him. However, the Court declined to issue such an order to the president because—so it declared—a portion of the Judiciary Act of 1789 was unconstitutional. Therefore, it ruled, Marbury had relied on an unconstitutional statute in seeking a writ of mandamus directly from the Supreme Court without first proceeding through the lower courts. According to the Court, statutes, such as the Judiciary Act, cannot define the kinds of cases that may be filed directly in the U.S. Supreme Court without being heard first in lower courts. Article III of the Constitution specifically lists the kinds of cases in which the Supreme Court has original jurisdiction. Any effort by Congress to expand that list amounts to an improper effort to alter the Constitution by statute rather than through the constitutional amendment process. In general, the Supreme Court has **appellate jurisdiction** over cases decided in lower courts that are later brought to the highest court through appeals and other posttrial processes. The Constitution specifies that the Supreme Court will make the first or original decision only in cases concerning states and those involving high officials, such as ambassadors. Marbury's action seeking a writ of mandamus did not fit within these narrow categories of cases specified by the Constitution.

The decision in *Marbury* v. *Madison*—one of the most important Supreme Court decisions in American history—asserted the authority and importance of the Supreme Court without actually testing the Court's power in a confrontation with the president. President Jefferson was able to regard the decision

appellate jurisdiction
authority of specific courts to hear appeals concerning allegations of specific errors in cases previously decided in trial courts.

impeachment
process in Congress for removal of the president, federal judges, and other high officials.

as a victory for his position. Yet the long-term impact of the case actually strengthened the power of the judiciary in future confrontations with the executive and legislative branches. The Court simply asserted the power of judicial review in striking down a portion of the Judiciary Act without providing any elaborate discussion in its opinion that would raise questions about whether such a power even existed under the Constitution.

The Court did not immediately begin to pass judgment on the propriety of executive and legislative actions. Instead, it waited more than fifty years before again asserting its power of judicial review. In 1857, in its highly controversial decision in *Dred Scott* v. *Sandford,* the Court invalidated the Missouri Compromise—a series of decisions by Congress in 1820 and 1821 that had put limits on the spread of slavery into western territories. The *Dred Scott* decision was one of the triggering events that led to the Civil War. Although critics of the *Dred Scott* decision, including President Abraham Lincoln, vowed to make enough replacement appointments to the Court so that the offensive decision would ultimately be reversed, they did not attack the process of judicial review itself. Instead, the federal judiciary's power to review actions by other governmental branches had come to be accepted as part of the American governing system.[12]

By 1900, the power of judicial review came to be used more frequently, and it was often used throughout the twentieth century. Eventually, federal courts struck down hundreds of state statutes and more than one hundred acts of Congress. Today, judicial review is well entrenched in American governing processes and provides a primary source of judicial power.

FEDERAL JUDGES' PROTECTED TENURE

▶ **Why did the framers decide to allow federal judges to serve for life?** As described earlier, Article III of the Constitution specifies that federal judges will serve "during good Behaviour." Effectively that means lifetime tenure, since these judges typically are removed through **impeachment** by Congress only if they commit a crime. The tenure granted to federal judges underscores the emphasis that the Constitution places on ensuring the independence of judicial decision makers. If judges are not afraid of losing their jobs by making unpopular decisions, then presumably they will possess enough protection against political attacks to enable them to do the right thing (see Figure 4.2, p. 128). This protection may be especially important when judges make decisions that

Chief Justice John Marshall's opinion in *Marbury* v. *Madison* helped to establish the concept of judicial review, an important power for American judges. This power was not specifically granted to judges by the U.S. Constitution. Do you think it was implied in that document, or did Marshall act improperly in announcing his opinion?
Photo: John Marshall by Chester Harding (1792–1886), Oil on canvas, 1830. U.R. 106.1830. Collection of the Boston Athenaeum.

A Persistence of Vision

Recent Supreme Court justices have tended to remain on the bench longer, and later in life, than their predecessors. Here are the justices whose terms ended after 1940. *

	A recent short-timer...		...and the record-holder:
Arthur J. Goldberg 2 years, 9 months, 24 days			**William O. Douglas** 36 years, 6 months, 25 days

	COURT TENURE	AGE OF JUSTICES
Charles E. Hughes	1910–16, 1930–41	
James C. McReynolds	1914–41	
James F. Byrnes	1941–42	
Owen J. Roberts	1930–45	
Harlan F. Stone	1925–46	
Frank Murphy	1940–49	
Wiley B. Rutledge	1943–49	
Fred M. Vinson	1946–53	
Robert H. Jackson	1941–54	
Sherman Minton	1949–56	
Stanley F. Reed	1938–57	
Harold H. Burton	1945–58	
Felix Frankfurter	1939–62	
Charles E. Whittaker	1957–62	
Arthur J. Goldberg	1962–65	
Thomas C. Clark	1949–67	
Earl Warren	1953–69	
Abe Fortas	1965–69	
Hugo Black	1937–71	
John M. Harlan	1955–71	
William O. Douglas	1939–75	
Potter Stewart	1958–81	
Warren E. Burger	1969–86	
Lewis F. Powell Jr.	1971–87	
William J. Brennan Jr.	1956–90	
Thurgood Marshall	1967–91	
Byron R. White	1962–93	
Harry A. Blackmun	1970–94	
CURRENT JUSTICES:		
William H. Rehnquist	1971–	
John Paul Stevens	1975–	
Sandra Day O'Connor	1981–	
Antonin Scalia	1986–	
Anthony M. Kennedy	1988–	
David H. Souter	1990–	
Clarence Thomas	1991–	
Ruth Bader Ginsburg	1993–	
Stephen G. Breyer	1994–	

Listed in order of the end of court terms.

* Current Supreme Court as of June 2005
Sources: the Columbia Encyclopedia, the Oyez Project, the Supreme Court Historical Society

Photographs by Associated Press (left) and George Tames Supreme Court Justices' Length of Service January 2005, The New York Times

FIGURE 4.2

Length of Service of Modern Supreme Court Justices

Some justices have served for several decades and continued to decide cases even after they reached the age of 80. What would be a reason *not* to limit the term in office for Supreme Court justices?

protect the rights of minorities whom large segments of society view unfavorably. For example, many controversial judicial decisions in the mid-twentieth century advancing the equality of African Americans were vigorously criticized because racial prejudice was widespread among whites. Decisions that identify and expand the rights of criminal defendants and convicted offenders are also frequently denounced by citizens who see judges as "coddling criminals." Although legal protections against excessive actions by police and corrections officials will benefit everyone, innocent or guilty, who becomes enmeshed in the criminal justice system, critics often claim that judges have gone too far in defining the extent of protections provided by constitutional rights. At other times, unpopular court decisions have protected the interests of corporations and the wealthy. For example, in 2005, the U.S. Supreme Court outraged critics by ruling that local governments can force individuals to sell their homes in order to turn the property over to developers who want to advance local economic progress by building office buildings and hotels (*Kelo* v. *City of New London*, 2005).

Because federal judges are exempted from democracy's traditional accountability mechanism—the need to face periodic elections—which often keeps other public officials from making unpopular decisions, judges are better positioned to make decisions that go against society's dominant values and policy preferences (see Figure 4.2). This lack of accountability also creates risks that judges' decisions will go "too far" in shaping law and policy in ways that are unpopular and detrimental to society, as well as risk a backlash against the entire court system.

A famous example of backlash against the Supreme Court arose in the late 1930s. In 1937, President Franklin D. Roosevelt was frustrated that the life-tenured justices on the Supreme Court were using their power of judicial review to invalidate New Deal legislation that he believed to be necessary to fight the Great Depression. As a result, he proposed restructuring the Supreme Court to permit the president to appoint an additional justice for each serving justice who reached the age of 70. His "court-packing plan," as the press and congressional opponents immediately branded it, would have enabled him to select six new justices immediately and thereby alter the Court's dynamics. Political and public opposition blocked Roosevelt's plan, and he set it aside when elderly justices began to retire, thus permitting him to name replacements who supported his New Deal legislation. Although the structure of the nine-member Court was preserved, Roosevelt's actions demonstrated that decisions by life-tenured judges can stir controversy, especially when those decisions clash with policies preferred by the public and their elected representatives in government. The reaction against packing the Court also

discussionquestions

discussionquestions

1. What factors make American judges unusually powerful?

2. Why is *Marbury* v. *Madison* considered such an important Supreme Court decision?

demonstrated how much the American public had come to value the judiciary's independence.

practicequiz

1. As originally conceived by the framers of the Constitution, the judicial branch of the government was supposed to be
   a. as powerful as the other two branches.
   b. more powerful than the legislative branch but less powerful than the executive branch.
   c. more powerful than the executive branch but less powerful than the legislative branch.
   d. less powerful than the other two branches.

2. The power of judicial review is defined in Article III of the U.S. Constitution.
   a. true   **b.** false

3. Why do judges need to interpret constitutions and statutes?
   a. Because the legislators who draft these documents are not trained to do this interpretation themselves.
   b. Because judges establish and maintain their authority through such interpretations.
   c. Because constitutions and statutes frequently contain ambiguities that need to be resolved.
   d. Because constitutions and statutes were often misinterpreted in earlier court cases.

4. Why does judicial review make U.S. judges enormously powerful?
   a. because it grants them the authority to invalidate as unconstitutional statutes enacted by Congress and actions taken by the president
   b. because it comes with the trappings of authority: the black robe, the seat on high, the requirement that all in the court must rise when the judge enters
   c. because it means that they are appointed for life
   d. because it means that they can intervene in any case, ask witnesses and litigants their own questions, and reach verdicts entirely on their own

Answers: 1-d, 2-b, 3-c, 4-a.

President Franklin D. Roosevelt caused controversy when he proposed changing the size of the Supreme Court and giving himself the authority to appoint additional justices. Why did he think it necessary to propose changes in the structure of other branches of government?

Judicial Selection and Judges' Decision Making

Because it is widely recognized today that judges have significant influence on public policy through the court pathway, the selection of judges increasingly involves major political battles. In fact, political parties and interest groups now regard the judicial selection process as an important means to influence the court pathway. By securing judgeships for individuals who share their political values, these groups can enhance their prospects for victory when they subsequently use the court pathway in seeking policy formulation and change. Judges' important influence over public policy has led scholars to declare that "of all the difficult choices confronting societies when they go about designing legal systems, among the most controversial are those pertaining to judicial selection."[13]

In the American political system, judges are placed on the bench in a process that in theory emphasizes the qualifications of thoughtfulness and experience. In reality, American lawyers do not

▶ **What is senatorial courtesy?**

senatorial courtesy
traditional deference by U.S. senators to the wishes of their colleagues representing a state concerning the appointment of specific individuals to federal judgeships in that state.

filibuster
process in the United States Senate used to block or delay voting on proposed legislation or on the appointment of a judge or other official by talking continuously. Sixty senators must vote to end a filibuster.

become judges because they are the wisest, most experienced, or fairest members of the legal profession. Instead, they are selected through political processes that emphasize their affiliations with political parties, their personal relationships with high-ranking officials, and often their ability to raise money for political campaigns. The fact that judges are selected through political processes does not necessarily mean that they are unqualified or incapable of making fair decisions. Individuals who are deeply involved in partisan politics or who seem to fit the dominant party's ideological preferences may, upon appointment, prove quite capable of abandoning overt partisanship and aspiring to fulfill a judge's duty to be neutral and open-minded. Other judges, however, appear to make decisions that are driven by their preexisting values and policy preferences. After examining methods for selecting judges, you will learn how judges make decisions. Then you can consider how the results of judicial selection may help shape the law.

JUDICIAL SELECTION IN THE FEDERAL SYSTEM

The Constitution specifies that federal judges, like ambassadors and cabinet secretaries, must be appointed by the president and confirmed by a majority vote of the U.S. Senate. Thus both the White House and one chamber of Congress are intimately involved in judicial selection.

The process begins with the president's selection of appointees. Because there are more than 800 judgeships in the federal district courts and courts of appeals, the president is never personally knowledgeable about all the pending vacancies. The president does, however, become personally involved in the selection of appointees for the U.S. Supreme Court because that body, standing at the top of the court pathway, is so important and influential in shaping national law and policy. For lower federal court judgeships, the president relies heavily on advice from White House aides, senators, and other officials from his own political party.

▶ **What is senatorial courtesy?** Traditionally, senators from the president's political party have effectively controlled the selection of appointees for district court judgeships in their own states. Through a practice known as **senatorial courtesy,** senators from the president's party have virtual veto power over potential nominees for their home state's district courts. They are also consulted on nominations for the federal court of appeals that covers their state. Because senators are so influential in the selection of federal district court judges, the judges who ultimately get selected are usually acquainted personally with the senators, active in the political campaigns of the senators and other party members, or accomplished in raising campaign funds for the party.

pathways past and present

DIVERSITY IN THE JUDICIARY

Many people believe that a diverse judiciary is necessary to maintain the courts' legitimacy, as well as to have decision makers who are knowledgeable about and sensitive to issues that affect all segments of society. One of the most significant changes affecting the judiciary in recent decades has been the expansion of opportunities for women and members of minority groups to serve as judges. Before the presidency of Jimmy Carter (1977–1981), nearly all federal judges were white men. The Carter administration made a concerted effort to identify qualified female and minority candidates for district and court of appeals judgeships through merit selection nominating committees. President Bill Clinton made a similar effort to stress diversity in the 1990s. Although they did not match Carter's or Clinton's emphasis on diversity, presidents George H. W. Bush and George W. Bush exceeded most of their predecessors in seeking to identify women for judicial appointments. Over time, federal judges have increasingly reflected the diversity of the American population (see Figure 4.3).

For vacancies on U.S. courts of appeals, which are important law- and policy-shaping bodies just one step below the Supreme Court, senators are influential in making recommendations, but the president's staff is sometimes more active in sifting through possible candidates. In particular, the president's advisers may want to feel confident that the appointee shares the administration's values and is likely to decide cases in a manner that would meet with the president's approval. Once a federal judge takes office, no president can control the judge's decisions, especially because, as you've already seen, federal judges cannot be removed from office unless impeached for serious misconduct and cannot have their salaries reduced. Thus the president's advisers will look closely at the appointee's record of political activity in order to make a prediction about the political values and judicial philosophy that the person

what YOU can do!
Follow news reports about new nominations for federal judgeships, especially in your home state. Go online to find articles about the nominee and that individual's viewpoints and professional experience. Write a letter to your state's senators or to all of the members of the Senate Judiciary Committee expressing your views on the nomination. Consider organizing a letter-writing campaign if you feel strongly about the nominee's experience or lack thereof.

▶ **What happens if the Senate objects to the president's nominee?**

will bring to the bench. Such scrutiny has become especially intense in recent decades. As a result, it is rare for a president to select a judge from outside his own political party.

For vacancies on the U.S. Supreme Court, presidents also take account of the demographic characteristics of the justices. In prior decades, presidents sought political support by claiming to keep various religions and regions of the country represented among the justices. In recent years, the emphasis has shifted to issues of race and gender. In 1991, upon the retirement of Thurgood Marshall, the Court's first African American justice, President George H. W. Bush appeared to feel obligated to select an African American, Clarence Thomas, as his replacement, lest Bush be responsible for making the nation's highest court all-white once again. President George W. Bush avoided this pressure when Justice Sandra O'Connor, the Court's first female justice, retired in 2006 because a second woman, Ruth Bader Ginsburg, remained on the Court at that time. Bush appointed a man, Samuel Alito, to replace O'Connor.

The process begins with the submission of an appointee's name to the Senate Judiciary Committee. The committee typically receives letters of support from individuals and interest groups that endorse the nomination, as well as similar communications from people and groups opposed to giving the appointee a life-tenured federal judgeship. There are always letters of support for a nominee, but many face little or no opposition. A few nominees do encounter organized opposition and negative publicity campaigns, but this typically happens primarily with nominations to the Supreme Court or the federal courts of appeals. Interest group representatives may be invited to provide testimony supporting or opposing a nomination during the Judiciary Committee's hearings on a specific candidate.

▶ **What happens if the Senate objects to the president's nominee?** After the Judiciary Committee completes its hearings, its members vote on a recommendation to the full Senate. Typically, when a nomination reaches the full Senate, that body votes quickly, based on the Judiciary Committee's report and vote. But in controversial cases or when asked to confirm appointments to the Supreme Court, the Senate may spend time debating the nomination. A majority of senators must vote for a candidate in order for that person to be sworn in as a federal judge. However, members of the minority political party in the Senate may block a vote through a **filibuster** (see ⓛⓘⓝⓚ *Chapter 7, page 275*),

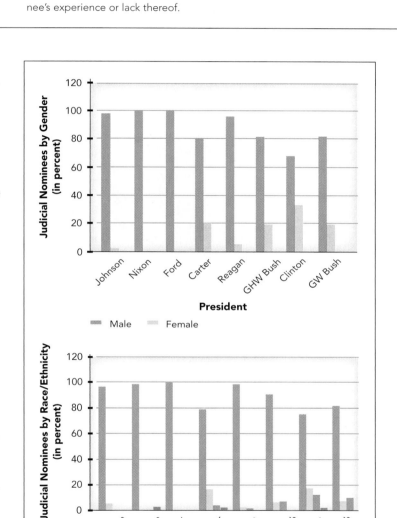

FIGURE 4.3

Diversity Within the Federal Courts

Although the percentage of women and minority judges increased in the federal courts over the past three decades, their numbers still do not reflect their composition of American society. How could the credibility or image of the court system be harmed if important decision-making positions remain dominated by white males in an increasingly diverse society?

SOURCE: www.albany.edu

▶ **What are the advantages**
of each type of state judicial
selection process?

Samuel Alito, shown here at his Senate confirmation hearings, replaced Sandra O'Connor
on the U.S. Supreme Court in 2006. Because it
was widely believed that Alito would tilt the
Supreme Court in a more conservative direction, 42 senators opposed his confirmation.
How do you think the increased role of partisan
politics in the selection and confirmation of
Supreme Court nominees affects the quality
of the individuals selected?
Photo: Doug Mills/The New York Times

keeping discussion going indefinitely unless three-fifths of the
Senate's members—sixty senators—vote to end it. Democrats
used a filibuster to block several judicial nominations during the
first term of President George W. Bush. Eventually, however, senators from both parties negotiated a resolution that permitted
Bush's nominees to gain approval.

As in state systems, judicial selection at the federal level is a
political process. Judges are not necessarily chosen for their experience and qualifications. Presidents seek to please favored constituencies and to advance their policy preferences in choosing
appointees. Interest groups find avenues through which they seek to
influence the president's choices, as well as the confirmation votes of
senators. These activities by interest groups are one of the strategies

that they use to shape the court pathway. Judicial selection processes
are a primary reason that American courts are political institutions
despite their efforts to appear "nonpolitical."

Let's illustrate the politics of judicial selection, using the
recent, highly publicized maneuvering after Justice Sandra Day
O'Connor announced her retirement from the U.S. Supreme
Court in 2005. O'Connor's retirement was to take effect as soon as
a nominee was confirmed by the U.S. Senate to replace her. Justice
O'Connor, the first woman ever appointed to the Supreme Court
(by President Ronald Reagan in 1981), was a decisive "swing" vote
between the Court's liberal and conservative wings on several key
issues. President Bush and his political supporters saw O'Connor's
retirement as an opportunity to turn the Court in a new direction
on issues that closely divided the justices, especially abortion and
affirmative action. Liberal and conservative interest groups mobilized their members and prepared significant advertising and lobbying campaigns for the battle over O'Connor's replacement. If
she were to be replaced by a more conservative appointee, new
decisions by the Supreme Court could potentially rewrite several
aspects of constitutional law.

Unexpectedly, President Bush first nominated his longtime
personal lawyer, Harriet Miers. Because he was personally
acquainted with her, Bush may have felt confident that Miers
would make decisions in a manner that would advance his preferred policies. However, she aroused intense public opposition
from conservative journalists and interest group leaders, as well as
some Republican senators, who perceived her as neither profes-
sionally distinguished nor sufficiently conservative. Under heavy
political pressure, Miers withdrew her name and Bush nominated
Judge Samuel Alito in her place. No one questioned Alito's outstanding educational credentials and professional experience as an
attorney and a judge. But it was widely anticipated that Alito would
be more consistently conservative than O'Connor and that his
votes could move the Court to the right. A group of Democratic
senators attempted to block Alito's confirmation by raising concerns about his judicial decisions involving constitutional rights and
questions about his attitudes regarding gender discrimination and
other issues. However, he was confirmed in January 2006, following a largely party-line vote of 58–42, with only one Republican
voting against him and only four Democrats supporting him.

JUDICIAL SELECTION IN THE STATES

Compare the federal judicial selection process with the various
processes used to select judges for state court systems. In general,
there are four primary methods that states use for judicial selec-

tion: partisan elections, nonpartisan elections, merit selection, and gubernatorial or legislative appointment. Table 4.4 shows how judges are selected in each state. Although each of these methods seeks to emphasize different values, they are all closely linked to political processes.

▶ **What are the advantages of each type of state judicial selection process?** Partisan elections emphasize the importance of popular accountability in a democratic governing system. When judges are elected and must subsequently run for reelection, the voters can hold them accountable if they make decisions that are inconsistent with community values. In selecting candidates to run for judgeships, political parties typically seek individuals with name recognition and the ability to raise campaign funds rather than the lawyer with the most experience. The involvement of political parties in partisan judicial elections helps voters identify which candidates share their particular party affiliation and, presumably, their values. Voters frequently know very little about judicial candidates, so the party label next to the person's name on

TABLE 4.4
Methods of Judicial Selection for State Judges

PARTISAN ELECTION	NONPARTISAN ELECTION	MERIT SELECTION	LEGISLATIVE (L) OR GUBERNATORIAL (G) APPOINTMENT
Alabama	Arkansas	Alaska	California (appellate) G
Illinois	Arizona (trial)	Arizona (appellate)	Maine G
Indiana (trial)	California (trial)	Colorado	New Hampshire G
Louisiana	Florida (trial)	Connecticut	New Jersey G
New York (trial)	Georgia	Delaware	South Carolina L
Pennsylvania	Idaho	Florida (appellate)	Virginia L
Tennessee (trial)	Kentucky	Hawaii	
Texas	Michigan	Indiana (appellate)	
West Virginia	Minnesota	Iowa	
	Mississippi	Kansas	
	Montana	Maryland	
	Nevada (appellate)	Massachusetts	
	North Carolina	Missouri	
	North Dakota	Nebraska	
	Ohio	Nevada (trial)	
	Oklahoma (trial)	New Mexico	
	Oregon	New York (appellate)	
	South Dakota (trial)	Oklahoma (appellate)	
	Washington	Rhode Island	
	Wisconsin	South Dakota (appellate)	
		Tennessee (appellate)	
		Utah	
		Vermont	
		Wyoming	

SOURCE: American Judicature Society, *Judicial Selection in the States: Appellate and General Jurisdiction Courts*, Des Moines, IA: American Judicature Society, 2004, pp. 1–4. Available at www.ajs.org

merit selection
a method for selecting judges used in some states that seek to reduce the role of politics by having the governor select new judges from lists of candidates presented by a selection committee.

retention elections
elections held in merit selection systems in which voters choose whether to keep a particular judge on the bench after that judge has completed a term in office.

the ballot can provide important information that distinguishes the candidates in the eyes of the voter. Partisan elections are used to select judges for at least some levels of courts in eleven states. Some states use one selection method for trial judges and a different method for appellate judges.

In an effort to reduce the impact of partisan politics, several states began to use nonpartisan elections in the first decades of the twentieth century. In such elections, judicial candidates' campaign literature does not specify political party affiliation, nor is such affiliation indicated on the ballot. Ideally, voters will simply choose the best judge rather than be influenced by political party labels. In reality, however, political parties remain deeply involved in "nonpartisan" elections. Although technically nonpartisan, in these elections political parties often choose the candidates and provide organizational and financial support for their campaigns.

Many voters know little, if anything, about judicial candidates in nonpartisan elections. Incumbency can be a powerful influence in such elections because voters often cast their ballots for the candidate designated as the sitting judge or because the incumbent is the only one whose name sounds familiar. Political parties often seek to inform their members about their endorsed candidates. Other voters may cast ballots based on the gender or perceived ethnicity of the judicial candidates, or they may simply skip voting for any judicial offices on the ballot.

As you can see, politics is unavoidable in partisan and "nonpartisan" election systems for selecting judges. Political parties do get involved, and judicial campaigns can produce intense competition, especially for appellate courts, which political parties and interest groups consider especially influential on law and policy.

More than twenty states have sought to reduce the influence of politics and to give greater attention to candidates' qualifications when selecting judges. These states have adopted various forms of **merit selection** systems. The first merit selection process for choosing judges was developed in Missouri in 1949, and many states have used Missouri as a model for developing similar processes. Under the "Missouri plan," the governor appoints a committee to review potential candidates for judgeships. It is presumed that the committee will focus on the individuals' personal qualities and professional qualifications rather than on political party affiliations. The committee provides the governor with a short list of recommended candidates, from which he or she chooses one candidate and appoints that individual to be the judge. Periodically after that, the judge must face the voters in **retention elections.** In a retention election, the judge's name is on the ballot and voters simply decide whether or not to give the

judge an additional term in office; they don't have a choice of judicial candidates.

Merit selection systems do not remove politics from the selection of judges. The opportunity for political attacks against judges in retention elections is the most obvious example of politics and partisanship in the process. Partisanship and political considerations are less visible but equally important in the merit selection system. In particular, behind the scenes, interest groups may battle one another to get a place on the selection committee that makes recommendations to the governor. In addition, because the governor makes the ultimate appointments, it is easy to favor candidates from a specific political party while using the merit selection process to disguise the partisanship that underlies it. Fundamentally, because judges in the United States have an important role in shaping law and public policy, political parties and interest groups will always work to ensure that judges are selected who share their political values and policy preferences. The merit selection process by no means avoids politics; it merely shifts the form and visibility of political activity involved in judicial selection.

In a handful of states, judges are appointed directly by the governor or the legislature. Obviously, those selected are likely to be from the same political party as those holding the appointment power. Some governors in these states have appointed commissions to advise them on the qualifications of judicial candidates.

JUDGES' DECISION MAKING

▶ **How much do a judge's political beliefs and ideology affect his or her judicial decisions?** The political battles over Supreme Court nominations, as well as over judges at other levels of state and federal court systems, reflect the widespread recognition that judges do not merely "follow the law" in making their decisions. When judges interpret the U.S. Constitution, state constitutions, and statutes, they rely on their own values and judgments. These values and judgments ultimately have a significant effect on public policy affecting many aspects of American life. Hence in appointing federal judges, the president seeks to name men and women with a politically compatible outlook. Similarly, the involvement of political parties and interest groups in supporting or opposing judicial candidates reflects their interests in securing judgeships for those whom they believe will make decisions that advance their policy preferences. Research by social

case precedent
a legal rule established by a judicial decision that guides subsequent judicial decisions. The use of case precedent is drawn from the common law system brought from Great Britain to the United States.

what YOU can do!

Learn how judges are selected in your state by going to the Web site of the American Judicature Society, **http://www.ajs.org** and see how the method of selection could have an impact on how the court pathway influences law and policy in your state?

scientists reinforces this assessment of judges. Studies show, for example, that decisions favoring individuals' claims of rights are more frequently associated with Democratic judges and that decisions favoring business and favoring the prosecution in criminal cases are more frequently associated with Republican judges.

Although judges can apply their values in making many kinds of decisions, they do not enjoy complete freedom to decide cases as they wish. Lower-court judges, in particular, must be concerned that their decisions will be overturned on appeal to higher courts if they make decisions that conflict with the judgments of justices on courts of last resort. What guides judges to reach conclusions that are not likely to be overturned? They rely on **case precedent.** Case precedent is the body of prior judicial opinions, especially those from the U.S. Supreme Court and state supreme courts, that establishes the judge-made law that develops from interpretations of the U.S. Constitution, state constitutions, and statutes. When lower-court judges face a particular issue in a case, they do research to determine whether similar issues have already been decided by higher courts. Typically, they will follow the legal principles established by prior cases, no matter what their own personal views on the issue. However, if they believe that the precise issue in their case is distinguishable from the issues in prior cases, or if they have new ideas about how such issues should be handled, they can issue an opinion that clashes with established case precedent. Judges make such decisions in the hope that the reasons explained in their opinions persuade the judges above them to change the prevailing precedent. The law changes through the development of new perspectives and ideas by lawyers and judges that ultimately persuade courts of last resort to move the law in new directions.

For example, when the U.S. Supreme Court decided in 2005 (in *Roper* v. *Simmons*) that the cruel and unusual punishments clause in the Eighth Amendment prohibits the execution of murderers who committed their crimes before the age of 18, it established a new precedent, overturning its previously established precedent permitting execution for murders committed at the ages of 16 and 17 (*Stanford* v. *Kentucky*, 1989). In reaching its conclusion, the nation's highest court upheld a decision by the Missouri Supreme Court that advocated a new interpretation of the Eighth Amendment (*State ex. rel. Simmons* v. *Roper*, 2003).

The U.S. Supreme Court often seeks to follow and preserve its precedents in order to maintain stability in the law. However, it is not bound by its own precedents, and no higher court can overturn the Supreme Court's interpretations of the U.S. Constitution. Thus the justices enjoy significant freedom to shape the law by advancing their own theories of constitutional interpretation and by applying their own attitudes and values concerning appropriate policy outcomes from judicial decisions. State supreme courts enjoy similar freedom when interpreting the constitutions and statutes of their own states. Lower-court judges can also apply their own approaches to constitutional and statutory interpretation, especially when facing issues that have not been addressed by any court. Their new approaches may be overturned on appeal, but they may also help establish new law if higher courts agree.

Judicial selection battles in the federal courts, especially those over the nomination of Supreme Court justices, often focus on nominees' approaches to constitutional interpretation. Among the members of the Supreme Court, Justices Clarence Thomas and Antonin Scalia are known for advocating an original intent approach to constitutional interpretation. These justices and their admirers argue that the Constitution must be interpreted in strict accordance with the original meanings intended by the people who wrote and ratified the document. According to Thomas and Scalia, constitutional interpretation must follow original intent in order to avoid "judicial activism," in which judges allegedly exceed their proper sphere of authority by injecting their own viewpoints into constitutional interpretation. That is why the followers of the original intent approach are also known as advocates of "judicial restraint," in which judges defer to the policy judgments of elected officials in the legislative and executive branches of government. Despite their use of "judicial restraint," judges who follow original intent still affect public policy with their decisions. They merely disagree with others about which policies should be influenced by judges.

Critics of original intent argue that there is no way to know exactly what the Constitution's authors intended with respect to each individual word and phrase or even whether one specific meaning was intended by all of the authors and ratifiers. Moreover, these critics typically argue that the ambiguous nature of many constitutional phrases, such as "cruel and unusual punishments" and "unreasonable searches and seizures," represents one of the document's strengths, because it permits judges to interpret and reinterpret the document in light of the nation's changing social circumstances and technological advances. What would James Madison and the other eighteenth-century founders of the nation have thought about whether the use of wiretaps and other forms of electronic surveillance violates the Fourth Amendment prohibition on "unreasonable searches"? Critics of original intent argue that contemporary judges must give meaning to those words in light of *current* values and policy problems. Hence the critics of original intent typically want a

▶ **What do we know** about how Supreme Court justices really make decisions?

flexible interpretation
approach to interpreting the U.S. Constitution that permits the meaning of the document to change with evolving values, social conditions, and problems.

legal model
an approach to analyzing judicial decision making that focuses on the analysis of case precedent and theories of interpretation.

attitudinal model
an approach to analyzing judicial decision making that looks at individual judges' decision patterns to identify the values and attitudes that guide their decisions.

rational choice model
an approach to analyzing judicial decision making that identifies strategic decisions made by judges in order to advance their preferred case outcomes.

flexible interpretation that enables judges to draw from the Constitution's underlying principles in addressing contemporary legal issues. Nearly all of the Supreme Court's justices in the past fifty years have used flexible interpretation, including John Paul Stevens, Ruth Bader Ginsburg, and Anthony Kennedy among the justices serving in 2006. The justices who use flexible interpretation frequently disagree with one another about how much flexibility should apply to various provisions in the Constitution.

As you can see, debates about the proper approach to interpreting the Constitution can be central elements in the political battles over the selection of judges. The successful confirmations of Bush appointees John Roberts and Samuel Alito may indicate that Justices Thomas and Scalia have gained new allies in their advocacy of judicial restraint and interpretation by original intent. Only time will tell whether Chief Justice Roberts and Justice Alito share these views.

President George W. Bush clearly hoped that his appointees would decide cases in the manner of Thomas and Scalia, but presidents are sometimes disappointed. Presidents cannot accurately predict how a nominee will decide every kind of case, especially because new and unexpected issues emerge each year. Moreover, some Supreme Court justices, as well as judges on lower courts, *do* change their views over the course of their careers. The views that led the president to select the nominee are not always the views held by nominees at the end of their careers. Justice Harry Blackmun, for example, an appointee of Republican President Richard Nixon, served on the Supreme Court from 1970 to 1994 and became increasingly protective of individuals' rights over the course of his career. He was regarded as one of the Court's most liberal justices at the time of his retirement, despite the fact that Nixon envisioned him as a conservative decision maker.

POLITICAL SCIENCE AND JUDICIAL DECISION MAKING

▶ **What do we know about how Supreme Court justices really make decisions?** Supreme Court justices present themselves as using particular approaches to constitutional interpretation in making their decisions, and they may honestly believe that these interpretive approaches guide their decisions. Political scientists, however, question whether the justices' decisions can be explained in this way. Through systematic examination of case decisions and close analysis of justices' opinions, researchers identify patterns and inconsistencies. These examinations of Supreme Court decisions have led to alternative explanations for the primary factors that shape the justices' decisions.

The idea that justices follow specific theories of constitutional interpretation and carefully consider precedents in making decisions is often labeled the **legal model.** Critics argue, however, that the justices regularly ignore, mischaracterize, or change precedents when those case decisions seem to impede the desire of the majority of justices to have a case come out a certain way. As you will see in the discussion of freedom of religion in Ⓛ Ⓘ Ⓝ Ⓚ *Chapter 5, page 177,* the justices seem to decide cases on the separation of church and state according to a specific test of whether government actions advance a particular religion. In specific cases, however, they ignore the test if it leads to a result that they do not desire. For example, they permitted the Nebraska state senate to hire a minister to lead prayers at the start of each legislative session (*Marsh* v. *Chambers,* 1984). If they had applied the usual test, however, they would presumably have been required to prohibit the entanglement of church and state through the use of a Christian minister to deliver prayers in this context.

An alternative theory of judicial decision making, known as the **attitudinal model,** states that Supreme Court justices' opinions are driven by their attitudes and values. Advocates of this model see the justices' discussion of interpretive theories and precedent as merely a means to obscure the actual basis for decisions and to persuade the public that the decisions are based on law. Researchers who endorse the attitudinal model do systematic analyses of judicial decisions to identify patterns that indicate the attitudes and values possessed and advanced by individual justices. Put more simply, the attitudinal theorists argue that some justices decide cases as they do because they are conservative and others decide cases differently because they are liberal.[14]

Other political scientists see judicial decision making as influenced by a **rational choice model.** According to this theory, Supreme Court justices vote strategically in order to advance their preferred goals, even if it means voting contrary to their actual attitudes and values in some cases. For example, a justice may be keenly interested in a specific issue raised by a case presented to the Court. Yet the justice could vote against hearing the case if he or she fears that there would not ultimately be enough support among the justices to advance a preferred outcome. By declining to hear the case,

new institutionalism
an approach to understanding judicial decision making that emphasizes the importance of courts' structures and processes as well as courts' roles within the governing system.

1. How does politics influence each method of judicial selection?

2. What competing approaches are advocated for constitutional interpretation?

the justice helps avoid setting an adverse precedent and can wait for a similar issue to arise again after the Court's composition has changed in a favorable direction. Justices may also vote strategically in order to build relationships with allies in less important cases with the hope that these relationships will increase the likelihood of persuading these allies to support specific decisions in other cases. These are just two examples of a variety of ways that rational choice strategies may influence Supreme Court decisions.[15]

In recent years, some political scientists have broadened their studies of courts, including judicial decision making, through an approach commonly labeled **new institutionalism.** New institutionalism emphasizes understanding courts as institutions and seeing the role of courts in the larger political system.[16] The adherents of new institutionalism do not necessarily agree with one another about the causes and implications of judicial action. They do, however, seek to move beyond analyzing judicial decisions solely by looking at the choices of individual Supreme Court justices. They may focus instead on the Supreme Court's processes, its reactions to statutes enacted to undercut particular judicial decisions, or decisions that minimize direct confrontations with other branches of government. Alternatively, the focus could be on judicial inaction, as when the Supreme Court refused to consider lawsuits against President Richard Nixon in the early 1970s for conducting an allegedly "illegal war" in Cambodia during the Vietnam War. In this example, the Supreme Court avoided involvement in presidential war powers issues that would generate conflicts among the country's governing institutions.

Political scientists continue to debate which model provides the best explanation for judicial decisions. New models are likely to be developed in the future. For students of American government, these models serve as a reminder that you should not automatically accept government officials' explanations for their decisions and behavior. Systematic examination and close analysis of decisions may reveal influences that the government decision makers themselves do not fully recognize.

practicequiz

1. As dictated by the Constitution, federal judges are appointed by the president and confirmed by
   a. a majority vote in Congress.
   b. a two-thirds vote in the House of Representatives.
   c. a majority vote in the Senate.
   d. a two-thirds vote in the Senate.

2. Why are the characters and political philosophies of nominees for the federal bench so carefully scrutinized?
   a. When judges interpret constitutions and statutes, they inevitably rely on their own values—and their decisions can significantly affect the lives of millions of Americans.
   b. No president wants to be blamed for nominating a lackluster judge; nor does the Senate want to be blamed for confirming such a figure.
   c. The Judiciary Act of 1789 requires such scrutiny.
   d. Article II of the Constitution requires such scrutiny, without which judges are subject to impeachment.

3. Usually, the decisions of lower-court judges rely on case precedent, even if their personal views on the issue suggest a different decision.
   a. true   b. false

4. In *Roper* v. *Simmons* (2005), the Supreme Court reinterpreted the Eighth Amendment, concluding that
   a. same-sex marriage was protected under the "right to privacy."
   b. executing murderers who committed their crimes before the age of 18 constituted "cruel and unusual punishment."
   c. Installing a 6-foot crucifix in a government building violated the separation of church and state.
   d. Internet filters on public library computers constituted a violation of free speech.

Answers: 1-c, 2-a, 3-a, 4-b.

Action in the Court Pathway

In theory, any individual in the United States can make use of the resources of the judicial branch merely by filing a legal action. Such actions may be directed at small issues, such as suing a landlord to recover a security deposit. They may also be directed at significant national issues, including actions aimed at Congress or the president in battles over major public policy issues.

In reality, filing a lawsuit at any level above small-claims courts (where landlord-tenant cases are typically argued) is

▶ **Is the court pathway**
more effective for certain
types of groups or issues
than for others?

pro bono
short for the Latin phrase *pro bono publico*, meaning "for the public good" and describing lawyers representing clients without compensation as a service to society.

expensive and requires professional legal assistance. As a result, the courts are not easily accessible to the average American, and it can be difficult to use the court pathway. Typically, this policy-shaping process falls to legal professionals who have technical expertise and financial resources. Nor will courts accept every kind of claim: Claims must be presented in the form of legal cases that embody disputes about rights and obligations under the law. Thus organized interests and wealthy individuals are often best positioned to gain access to the judicial branch.

pathways profile

JOHN G. ROBERTS JR.

John Roberts was educated at Harvard College and Harvard Law School. After graduation from law school, he served as a law clerk for a judge on the U.S. Court of Appeals in New York City and then spent a year as a law clerk for U.S. Supreme Court Associate Justice (and future Chief Justice) William Rehnquist. Later, during the presidency of Ronald Reagan, Roberts served as an assistant first to the U.S. attorney general and then to the White House counsel. He then entered private practice with a major Washington, D.C., law firm. During the presidency of George H. W. Bush (1989–1993), Roberts served as the deputy solicitor general and in that role argued cases in front of the U.S. Supreme Court on behalf of the federal government. President Bush nominated him for a judgeship, but the Senate never voted on his nomination—usually a sign that a judicial nomination has become part of a political battle between Democrats and Republicans. Roberts then returned to his law firm during Bill Clinton's presidency (1993–2001).

During the first term of President George W. Bush, Roberts was appointed—and this time confirmed by the Senate—to a seat on the U.S. Court of Appeals for the District of Columbia. Later, upon the death of Chief Justice William Rehnquist in 2005, President Bush nominated him to become chief justice of the United States.

Despite being a newcomer to the Court as well as its youngest member, Roberts assumed leadership duties as chief justice. This means leading the discussion of cases and designating the specific justices who write opinions on behalf of the Court in cases in which the chief justice has voted with the majority. In

major cases, the chief justice often assigns the majority opinion to himself.

Bush selected Roberts for the Supreme Court in the apparent belief that Roberts would move the high court in a conservative direction on such issues as expanded presidential power during the war on terrorism, abortion, affirmative action, and diminished rights for criminal defendants. It remains to be seen whether Roberts' performance on the Supreme Court will fulfill the hopes and expectations of President Bush and his political supporters. ■

INTEREST GROUP LITIGATION

Many organized groups seek to use the court pathway to advance their policies, and some specialize in it. For others, the court pathway is just one among several approaches for shaping law and policy. The American Civil Liberties Union (ACLU), a group that advocates clear and expansive applications of the Bill of Rights, has become especially well known for pursuing litigation to advance its goals.[17] In many states, ACLU chapters began to devote significant attention to legislative lobbying and similar activities directed at other pathways when they perceived that the political composition of the judiciary had shifted. By contrast, business organizations and other groups, such as the National Association of Manufacturers (NAM), which are best known for their legislative lobbying, expanded their activities into the court pathway when they recognized that they needed to advance their policy objectives in every governmental arena in which those policies might be affected. Despite its traditional emphasis on lobbying decision makers in legislatures and the executive branch, NAM's lawyers also use the court pathway by filing legal arguments to support litigants in cases challenging environmental regulations or seeking to protect specific industries from liability in citizens' lawsuits.

▶ **Is the court pathway more effective for certain types of groups or issues than for others?** The court pathway is often attractive to small interest groups because it is possible to succeed with fewer resources than those required for effective action in other pathways. To be effective in legislatures, for example, groups need lots of money and large numbers of aroused and vocal members. Lobbyists need to spend money by donating to politicians' campaign funds, wining and dining public officials, and mounting public relations campaigns to sway public opinion. They also need to mobilize their membership to flood legislators' offices with

discovery
pretrial stage in the litigation process in which the lawyers for each side gather information, interview potential witnesses, and request documents and information from their opponents.

what YOU can do!
Learn about an interest group that uses the courts to advocate policy positions with which you agree. Depending on your views, examples might include the Washington Legal Foundation, the Pacific Legal Foundation, the ACLU, or the Southern Poverty Law Center. Study the group's Web site. How does the group seek involvement or support from members of the public?

telegrams, phone calls, and e-mail messages to provide political pressure—as well as to vote on election day. By contrast, a small group with few members and limited resources may have little opportunity to compete in the legislative arena. However, that small group may be successful in the court pathway if it has an effective attorney and enough resources to sustain a case through the litigation process. The most important resources for effective litigation are expertise, resources for litigation expenses, and patience.[18]

EXPERTISE   For effective advocacy in litigation, expertise is essential. This includes thorough knowledge in the areas of law relevant to the case, as well as experience in trial preparation or appellate advocacy, depending on which level of the court system is involved in a particular case. Attorneys who have previously dealt with the issues in those cases will know the intricate details of the relevant prior court decisions and are better able to formulate effective arguments that use those precedents to advance a particular litigant's cause. In addition, attorneys affiliated with large, resource-rich law firms or interest groups have at their disposal teams of attorneys who can handle research and other aspects of investigation and preparation.

LITIGATION RESOURCES   Interest groups and individuals who use the court process must have the resources to handle various expenses in addition to the cost of attorneys' fees, which are generally very high unless the lawyers have volunteered to work for little or nothing on a **pro bono** basis. (*Pro bono publico* is a Latin phrase that translates as "for the public good." It means that attorneys and other professionals are waiving their usual fees to work for a cause in which they believe. Some interest groups rely heavily on securing pro bono professional support.)

Just to file the papers that will start litigation requires litigants to pay filing fees, running as high as $200. Then litigants must pay for "service of process," the cost of delivering papers to the opposition providing notification about the lawsuit. Additional expenses are incurred as trial-level cases proceed through the **discovery** process, the pretrial stage in which the opposing sides interview witnesses and request documents and other information from each other. Discovery typically entails travel costs to meet with witnesses and track down documents, not to mention such associated costs as photocopying, long-distance phone calls, and hiring research assistants. (Photocopying may not sound very expensive, but charges can mount rapidly if each side must copy thousands of pages of documents.) Trials may incur additional significant costs, such as hiring experts to provide favorable testimony.

PATIENCE   Frequently, organized interest groups can take a long-term view of their policy objectives and patiently pursue selected cases in the court system. But an injured person may need immediate financial compensation for physical or psychological injuries or property damage. The desire for compensation may make such people accept negotiated settlements that short-circuit the processes of the court pathway. If these individuals had fought their cases all the way through the system, they might have won favorable judicial decisions that shape law and policy in ways that are beneficial to others. But because it can take years for a case to work its way through the court system, many people are not well positioned to use the court pathway.

pathways of action
THE NAACP AND RACIAL SEGREGATION

Beginning in the 1930s, the National Association for the Advancement of Colored People (NAACP), an important civil rights interest group founded in 1910, filed lawsuits to challenge state laws that segregated African Americans into separate, inferior educational institutions. These lawsuits tested the 1896 U.S. Supreme Court decision (*Plessy* v. *Ferguson*) that had ruled that no constitutional violation exists when government gives people from different races "separate but equal" facilities and treatment. Unfortunately, many states used that court decision to justify their existing practice of providing separate and grossly inferior schools and services to African Americans. Rigid racial segregation was imposed, especially in the South, after the end of the post–Civil War Reconstruction period, and it was vigorously enforced for decades afterward.

Led by Thurgood Marshall, an attorney who later became the first African American to serve on the U.S. Supreme Court (1967–1991), the NAACP argued that the separate facilities that *Plessy* sanctioned were *not* equal and therefore violated the equal protection clause of the Constitution's Fourteenth Amendment. As we will examine in greater detail in LINK *Chapter 6, page 222,* from the 1930s to the 1950s, the NAACP sued such states as Maryland, Missouri, Texas, and Oklahoma for excluding African American students from state universities' law schools and graduate programs. By 1950, the U.S. Supreme Court had issued several

test case
a case sponsored or presented by an interest group in the court pathway with the intention of influencing public policy.

The new Chief Justice John Roberts poses for photographs outside the Supreme Court after his swearing-in ceremony in 2005 as his young son rushes to greet him. It has been argued that someone who is barely over 50 years of age lacks the experience and knowledge to lead one of the nation's most powerful policymaking institutions. Do you agree with this argument? Why or why not?

Photo: Stephen Crowley/The New York Times

decisions that rejected states' false claims that they provided "separate but equal" facilities for African Americans in colleges and universities. It was at that point that litigation began, backed by the NAACP, that would lead to declaring public school racial segregation unconstitutional.

After Earl Warren, the governor of California, was appointed chief justice in 1953, the nation's highest court made one of its most famous and important decisions. The nine justices unanimously declared that school segregation laws are unconstitutional because they violate the equal protection clause. That decision, *Brown* v. *Board of Education of Topeka* (1954), was based on a lawsuit filed by the NAACP on behalf of African American parents and school children in Topeka, Kansas. The *Brown* decision established the foundation for subsequent NAACP lawsuits in the 1960s and 1970s seeking to desegregate public school systems throughout the United States. ■

ELEMENTS OF STRATEGY

All litigants engage in certain types of strategies, for example, in presenting evidence and formulating arguments. Interest groups may benefit from additional opportunities to use specific strategies by choosing which case to pursue or by choosing the court in which a case may be filed. For example, whereas individual litigants can only pursue their own cases, even if those cases are not supported by the strongest possible evidence, interest groups can hunt for strong cases and offer their lawyers' services to the individuals involved in those cases.

SELECTION OF CASES Interest groups choose carefully among potential cases for the pursuit of their objectives. They seek to find an appropriate **test case** that will serve as the vehicle to persuade judges to change law and policy. Sometimes they can recruit plaintiffs and then provide legal representation and litigation expenses to carry the case through the court system. In challenging laws that restrict choices about abortions, an interest group would rather bring the case on behalf of a teenage rape victim than pursue the case for a married woman who became pregnant after being insufficiently careful with a method of birth control. The interest group is likely to believe that the rape victim's case will provide more compelling arguments that can generate sympathy from many judges. It is easier to argue that a restrictive abortion law, such as one that requires a waiting period or parental consent, is unduly harsh in a case that affects the young victim of a violent crime who became pregnant through no fault of her own.

Interest groups cannot always choose precisely which case would best serve their interests. They may adopt a particular case that happens to come along and raises an issue of importance to them. In such circumstances, they simply cannot afford to watch passively and risk seeing a court issue a decision that is contrary to their policy preferences.

CHOICE OF JURISDICTION One important factor in litigation strategies is the choice of courts in which to pursue a legal action. Because of the country's dual court system, there is often a choice to be made about whether state or federal courts are more likely to produce outcomes favorable to a group's interests. In addition to considering whether state or federal law may be more likely to produce a favorable result, litigators may consider whether a spe-

amicus briefs
written arguments submitted to an appellate court by lawyers who are interested in the issue being examined in a case but are not representing either party in the case; often submitted by interest groups' lawyers to advance a specific policy position.

1. What advantages do interest groups possess in using the court pathway?

2. How and why do participants in the court pathway seek to select which cases to pursue?

cific federal or state judge would be sympathetic to their values and policy preferences.

FRAMING THE ARGUMENTS Litigants must make strategic decisions about how to frame the legal issues and arguments that they present in court. In some cases, they must decide which legal issues to raise. A challenge to a Georgia statute regulating the private sexual behavior of adults in their own bedrooms may have been lost because the litigants argued that it violated the right to privacy. The challenge lost by a 5–4 vote in the Supreme Court, but Justice Lewis Powell's opinion concurring with the majority indicated that his decisive vote upholding the Georgia law might have gone the other way had the litigants argued that the long prison sentences mandated by the statute for breaking the law violated the Eighth Amendment's prohibition of cruel and unusual punishments (*Bowers* v. *Hardwick*, 1986, a decision that was overturned seventeen years later in *Lawrence* v. *Texas*, 2003). This example shows how lawyers must assess the judges before whom the case will be presented and must make strategic decisions about which arguments will appeal to the particular decision makers who will consider the case.

When an interest group is not itself involved in a case, it may still seek permission to present written arguments as *amicus curiae*, Latin for "a friend of the court." For example, it is very common for multiple interest groups to submit **amicus briefs,** detailed written arguments that seek to persuade the U.S. Supreme Court to endorse a specific outcome or to adopt reasoning that is favorable to the groups' policy preferences. Amicus briefs can be influential because justices' opinions sometimes draw from these briefs rather than from the arguments presented by the two parties in the case. Participants in a Supreme Court case typically welcome the submission of amicus briefs on behalf of their side. Indeed, one strategy is to gain the endorsement of as many interest groups as possible to impress the Supreme Court with the broad support that exists for a particular position. Over the course of Supreme Court history, individuals and interest groups have increasingly sought to influence the Court's decisions through amicus briefs. From 1946 through 1955, amicus briefs were filed in only 23 percent of Supreme Court cases, but they were filed in 85 percent of the cases considered between 1986 and 1995.[19]

PUBLIC RELATIONS AND THE POLITICAL ENVIRONMENT Interest groups have a strong incentive to receive sympathetic coverage from the news media about cases that they are pursuing through the court pathway. Attorneys often develop relationships with reporters in hopes that sympathetic stories will be written about

policy-oriented legal cases. Such stories help educate the public and perhaps shape public opinion about an issue. They may also influence judges, because, just like other people, they read the newspapers or watch television news every day.

practicequiz

1. One advantage in using the court pathway to shape public policy is that
  a. it takes less time than the other pathways.
  b. nearly anyone can do it.
  c. it may require fewer resources than those needed in most other pathways.
  d. it almost always works.

2. When interest groups submit amicus briefs in appellate case, they are
  a. objecting to the appellate court's decision to accept the case for hearing.
  b. presenting elaborate written arguments on behalf of one side in a case, even though they are not directly involved in the case.
  c. informing the judges that they will provide financial campaign contributions and volunteer workers to help the judges win reelection.
  d. announcing that they will monitor the actions of the legislature and executive.

3. What is one drawback to an individual's accepting a negotiated settlement in a personal injury trial?
  a. Such a settlement sometimes short-circuits a process—fighting a case all the way through the system—that would result in a change in law or policy benefiting others besides the original litigant.
  b. Such a settlement usually wins the litigant less money than he or she would win seeing the case to its conclusion.
  c. Such a settlement usually means that it will be more difficult to effect a law or policy change in that area through other pathways.
  d. Such a settlement can end up costing more money in legal fees and other related expenses than letting the legal process play out.

4. Which of the following is an accepted strategy used by interest groups to make their work in the court pathway as successful as possible?
  a. Keeping their participation in a case difficult to detect.
  b. Running advertisements in the area where the case is being tried.
  c. Lobbying the judge or, in the case of an appellate court, the judges, predisposing them to hear the case favorably.
  d. Choosing cases, jurisdictions, and arguments best suited for the policy outcomes they desire.

Answers: 1-c, 2-b, 3-a, 4-d.

▶ **Does the executive branch**
ever refuse to enforce the
courts' decisions?

Thurgood Marshall and other attorneys for
the NAACP stand outside the Supreme Court
after presenting arguments seeking to end
racial segregation. Their success inspired
other interest groups to use the court pathway
for additional policy issues. What would have
happened in American society if the NAACP
had been unsuccessful in its litigation efforts
in the 1950s?

Implementation and Impact

▶ **Does the executive branch ever refuse to enforce the courts'
decisions?** Court decisions are not automatically implemented or
obeyed. Judges have the authority to issue important pronouncements that dictate law and policy, but they have limited ability to
ensure that their orders are carried out. To see their declarations of
law translated into actual public policy, judges must typically rely
on public obedience and on enforcement by the executive branch
of government. As you saw earlier in this chapter, this is a primary
reason that judges are concerned about preserving the courts' nonpolitical image. If the public came to believe that the courts were
no different from branches of government in which partisanship
dictates operations and outcomes, the public might be less likely to
obey court decisions.

During the Watergate scandal of the 1970s, in which
President Richard Nixon conspired to cover up information about
a burglary at Democratic Party offices committed by people working for his reelection campaign, the Supreme Court handed down
a decision ordering Nixon to provide a special prosecutor with
recordings of secretly taped White House conversations. Years
later, Supreme Court Justice Lewis Powell observed that had
Nixon refused to comply with the Court's order, "there was no way
that we could have enforced it. We had [only] 50 police officers [at
the Supreme Court], but Nixon had the [U.S. military at his dis-
posal]."[20] But Nixon handed over the tapes and shortly thereafter
resigned from office, presumably realizing that public support for
his impeachment, already strong, would lead to his conviction by
the Senate if he disobeyed a unanimous Court decision that citizens and members of Congress viewed as legitimate.

The weakness of courts has been revealed in a number of cases
over the course of American history. In the 1830s, the Cherokee
Nation successfully litigated a case against laws that ordered the
removal of Cherokees from their lands. The state of Georgia supported removal on behalf of whites who invaded Cherokee lands to
search for gold. The U.S. Supreme Court, still led by the aged Chief
Justice John Marshall, supported the Cherokees' property rights,
but President Andrew Jackson refused to enforce the ruling. ("John
Marshall has made his decision," Jackson is supposed to have said,
"now let him enforce it.") Thus despite using the court pathway in
an appropriate manner to protect their property rights, these
Native Americans were eventually forced off their land. A few years
later, they were marched at gunpoint all the way to an Oklahoma
reservation, an estimated 4,000 dying along the way. The
Cherokees' infamous Trail of Tears forced march and loss of land
demonstrated that courts cannot automatically ensure that their

decisions are enforced and obeyed. Unlike the situation in the 1970s in which President Nixon felt strong public pressure to obey the Supreme Court or face impeachment, the Cherokees and the Supreme Court of the 1830s did not benefit from public acceptance and political support.

In modern times, analysts have questioned the effectiveness of courts in advancing school desegregation. Although the Supreme Court has earned praise for courageously standing up for equal protection by declaring racial segregation in public schools unconstitutional in *Brown,* the 1954 decision did not desegregate schools. Racial separation continued in public schools throughout the country for years after the Court's decision. In two highly publicized incidents, military force was necessary to enroll African American students in all-white institutions. In 1957, President Dwight D. Eisenhower sent troops to force Little Rock Central High School to admit a half-dozen black students, and in 1962, President John F. Kennedy dispatched the Army to the University of Mississippi so that one African American student could enroll. In both situations, there had been violent resistance to court orders, but the presidents effectively backed up the judicial decisions with a show of force. In other cities, desegregation was achieved piecemeal over the course of two decades as individual lawsuits in separate courthouses enforced the *Brown* mandate.

According to Professor Gerald Rosenberg, the actual desegregation of public schools came only after the president and Congress had acted in the 1960s to push policy change, using financial incentives and the threat of enforcement actions to overcome segregation. In Rosenberg's view, courts receive too much credit for policy changes that actually only occur when other actors become involved. Courts receive this credit, in part, because of the symbolism attached to their publicized pronouncements. He concludes that the United States has "flypaper courts" that attract the attention of policy advocates and get them stuck in the court pathway as they squander their resources in a process that does not produce effective policy change.[21]

Similar arguments can be made about other policy issues. For example, the Supreme Court's decision recognizing a woman's right to make choices about abortion (*Roe* v. *Wade,* 1973) does not ensure that doctors and medical facilities will perform such procedures in all locations or that people have the resources to make use of this right.

Other analysts see the courts differently, as important and effective policymaking institutions. They argue that *Brown* v. *Board of Education* and other judicial decisions about segregation were essential elements of social change. Without these judicial decisions initiating, guiding, and providing legitimacy for change,

Early in the nation's history, the Cherokee Nation used the court pathway to protect their ancestral lands in Georgia. They won a victory in the Supreme Court. However, President Andrew Jackson refused to enforce the court decision. The many deaths that resulted from their forced march to a reservation in Oklahoma stand as a stark reminder of a fundamental weakness in the court pathway. In light of this tragic episode in American history, why do so many individuals and interest groups continue to use the court pathway?
Photo: Robert Lindneux, American. *Trail of Tears.* Woolaroc Museum, Bartlesville, Oklahoma.

the changes might not have occurred. For example, until the mid-1960s, southern members of Congress who supported segregation were able to block corrective legislation because the seniority system gave them disproportionate power on congressional committees. They also used the Senate filibuster to prevent consideration of civil rights legislation. Thus they could make sure that proposed bills died in committee or never came to a vote in Congress. In addition, elected officials at all levels of government and in all parts of the country were often too afraid of backlash from white voters to take strong stands in support of equal protection for African Americans. Analysts point to other court decisions, such as those requiring police officers to inform suspects of their *Miranda* rights in 1966 and recognizing abortion rights in 1973, to argue that the court pathway has been an important source of policy change.[22] Unelected judges were arguably the only actors positioned to push the country into change.

▶ **Do the Supreme Court** justices follow the wishes of the majority? And should they?

After the death of Chief Justice William Rehnquist in 2005, Justice John Paul Stevens leads the other justices down the steps of the Supreme Court building following a ceremony to honor the late chief justice. This small group of unelected officials has significant power to create new law and policy. How do you think this has affected the "separation of powers" set forth in the Constitution?

Photo: Doug Mills/The New York Times

Judicial Policymaking and Democracy

Notwithstanding the framers' expectation that the judiciary would be the weakest branch of government, the court pathway presents an avenue for pursuing public policy objectives because American judges possess important powers. But these powers often stir up debates about the role of courts in the constitutional governing system. These controversies are most intense when focused on the actions of federal judges who are appointed to office and serve for life, unless, in rare cases, they are removed from office for serious misconduct through the impeachment process.[23] In a democratic system, how can unelected, life-tenured officials be permitted to make decisions that shape the lives of all citizens? This is an important question for Americans and their government.

The power of the judicial branch and the effectiveness of the court pathway for policy change pose significant potential risks for American society. What if life-tenured judges make decisions that create bad public policy? What if they make decisions that nullify popular policy choices made by the people's elected representatives or that force those elected representatives to impose taxes needed to implement those decisions? Because of these risks, some critics call judicial policymaking undemocratic. They argue that judges should limit their activities to narrow decisions that address disputes between two parties in litigation and avoid any cases that might lead unelected officials in black robes to supersede the preferences of the voters' accountable, elected representatives in the legislative and executive branches. These critics want to avoid the risk that a small number of judicial elites, such as the nine justices on the U.S. Supreme Court, will be able to impose their policy choices on the nation's millions of citizens.

Although judicial policymaking by unelected federal judges does not fit conceptions of democracy based on citizens' direct control over policy through the election of decision makers, advocates of judicial policymaking see it as appropriate. According to their view, the design of the governing system in the U.S. Constitution rests on a vision of democracy that requires active participation and policy influence by federal judges. The conception of democracy underlying the U.S. Constitution does not permit the majority of citizens to dictate every policy decision. The Constitution facilitates citizen participation and accountability through elections, but the need to protect the rights of individuals under the Bill of Rights demonstrates that the majority should not necessarily control every decision and policy. In 1954, for example, racial segregation was

discussionquestions

1. What problems do courts face in implementing their decisions?

2. Is it proper for unelected judges to make decisions that shape public policy? What are the competing arguments on this issue?

strongly supported by southern whites, who were the majority of the population in every state in the region. Should majority rule have dictated that rigid racial segregation continue in those states? In essence, the American conception of constitutional democracy relies on citizen participation and majority rule *plus* the protection of rights for individuals, including members of unpopular political, religious, racial, and other minorities.

For example, in the aftermath of the September 11, 2001, terrorist attacks on the World Trade Center and the Pentagon, public opinion polls indicated that a majority of Americans favored "requiring Arabs, including those who are U.S. citizens, to undergo special, more intensive security checks before boarding airplanes in the U.S."[24] Imagine that Congress responded by enacting a law that imposed these requirements based on ancestry without regard to its detrimental impact on U.S. citizens of Arab extraction. Such a policy, if supported by a majority of citizens, would meet many of the requirements for democratic policymaking. However, it would collide with the Fourteenth Amendment's requirement of "equal protection of the laws" for Americans from all races and ethnic groups.

▶ **Do the Supreme Court justices follow the wishes of the majority? And should they?** To ensure that majority interests do not trample the rights of minorities, the Constitution positions federal judges as the decision makers to protect constitutional rights. In this position, because they are appointed, life-tenured officials, federal judges are supposed to have the independence and the insulation from politics necessary to make courageous decisions on behalf of minority group members, no matter how unpopular those minorities may be. In practice, federal judges do not always go against the wishes of the majority, even when the rights of minority group members are threatened or diminished. Such was the case when the Supreme Court endorsed the detention of innocent Japanese Americans in internment camps during World War II (*Korematsu* v. *United States,* 1944). But in other cases, the Supreme Court and other courts can provide a check against the excesses of majority policy preferences. There is broad agreement that judges must uphold the U.S. Constitution, state constitutions, and laws enacted by legislatures through the use of their power of interpretation. Disagreements exist, however, about whether judges have acted properly in interpreting the law, especially when judicial decisions shape public policy. Was it improper for the Supreme Court to recognize a constitutional right of privacy that grants women the opportunity to make choices about abortions (*Roe* v. *Wade,* 1973)? Should the Fifth Amendment's privilege against compelled self-incrimination include a require-

ment that police officers inform suspects about their rights (*Miranda* v. *Arizona,* 1966)? Should the U.S. Supreme Court have prevented the Florida courts from ordering recounts of votes during the closely contested presidential election of 2000 (*Bush* v. *Gore,* 2000)? These and other questions will continue to be debated for decades to come for three primary reasons. First, courts are authoritative institutions that shape law and policy in ways that cannot be directly controlled by the public and other institutions of government. Second, court decisions often address controversial issues that reflect Americans' most significant disagreements about social values and public policies. And third, elected officials may choose to avoid taking action on controversial issues, thereby leaving the court pathway as the sole avenue for government action.

practicequiz

1. A court decision is a declaration of law; once it is formulated by a court, it automatically operates as effective public policy.
   a. true   b. false

2. It's fair to say that the desegregation of public schools in this country resulted from
   a. the Supreme Court's decision in *Plessy* v. *Ferguson.*
   b. a series of legislative decisions starting with *Brown* v. *Board of Education.*
   c. the Court's reversal of *Plessy* v. *Ferguson,* lower-level courts' complementary decisions, and enforcing actions by Presidents Eisenhower and Kennedy.
   d. cultural change that inspired most people in segregated school districts to embrace desegregation.

3. Why might it be appropriate in a democracy that federal judges help formulate public policy?
   a. Federal judges are the elected representatives of the people.
   b. Federal judges can be fired if their decisions too often run contrary to the sentiments of the majority.
   c. Some democratic principles (such as individual rights) can conflict with majority sentiments. Federal judges, appointed for life and insulated from the pressures of popular sentiment, are well positioned to preserve such principles.
   d. Federal judges are appointed by governmental officials who are themselves elected. The votes that elected officials receive represent a level of citizen trust that transcends the changeable sentiments of a majority, making judges appointed by these officials a purer expression of democracy than elected judges would be.

Answers: 1-b, 2-c, 3-c.

Conclusion

The judicial branch serves important functions under the constitutional governing system of the United States. Judges and juries resolve disputes, determine whether criminal defendants are guilty, impose punishment on those convicted of crimes, and provide individuals with a means to challenge actions by government. These functions are carried out in multilevel court systems made up of trial courts and appellate courts that exist in each state, as well as a national system under the federal government. Each system is responsible for its own set of laws, though all must be in accord with the U.S. Constitution, "the supreme law of the land."

The judicial branch provides opportunities for individuals and interest groups to seek to shape law and public policy. Through the litigation process in the court pathway, they can frame arguments to persuade judges as to the best approaches for interpreting the law. Judicial opinions shape many significant public policies for society, including those affecting education, abortion, the environment, and criminal justice. These opinions interpreting constitutions and statutes are written by judges who are selected through political processes, including elections in many states and presidential appointment in the federal system. American judges are exceptionally powerful because of their authority to interpret the U.S. Constitution and their ability to block actions by the other branches of government through the power of judicial review. The important impact of federal judges on major public policy issues raises difficult questions about the proper role of unelected officials in shaping the course of a democracy.

The courts are not easily accessible to citizens because their effective use depends on expensive resources, including the patience to sustain extended litigation and the funds to hire expert attorneys and pay for litigation expenses. Because of their resources and expertise, organized interest groups are often better positioned than individual citizens to use the court pathway in pursuing their own policy objectives or in blocking competing interests' policy goals. However, judges' limited ability to implement their own decisions is one factor that leads some observers to debate whether the court pathway provides processes that can consistently and properly develop public policies that are useful and effective.

YOUR turn!

Many people participate in the court pathway for policy-making by making financial contributions to interest groups that engage in litigation strategies on behalf of policy issues that they support. Such groups exist for all kinds of issues and represent a range of political perspectives—conservative, libertarian, liberal, and radical. As a starting point for thinking about how you might contribute to the court pathway, do an Internet search to identify interest groups in your state or nationwide that advocate issues that are important to you. As you check out these groups' Web sites, ask yourself whether they emphasize litigation as one of the primary pathways they use. If you are interested in issues concerning education, property rights, the environment, abortion, education, or civil rights, you will probably find groups that use the courts as one of their arenas of action. If you can envision a possible career as a lawyer making arguments in court, perhaps you can take the additional step of seeking an internship with one of these organizations. After graduation, be aware that these groups often hire college graduates as investigators, researchers, and paralegals even if they have not attended law school.

As you learn about the use of the court pathway, remember that issues affecting specific individuals, including students, often provide the basis for court decisions affecting law and policy. Individuals can use the pathway by standing up for their beliefs and using their individual circumstances as the basis for legal action. Lindsay Earls, a student in Tecumseh, Oklahoma, filed a lawsuit challenging her high school's policy of requiring random drug testing for all students involved in extracurricular activities. An honors student involved in choir and marching band, she eventually enrolled at an Ivy League college. Although she had nothing to hide, she objected to the school's intrusion on her right to privacy and her Fourth Amendment protection against unreasonable searches, even when there was no reason to suspect her of wrongdoing. When individuals such as Lindsay Earls become involved in controversial litigation, they often expose themselves to significant financial expenses as well as ridicule and rejection from others in the community who disagree with the lawsuit. Thus the use of the court pathway may require enough courage to endure media attention and the possibility of being the center of public debate. Ultimately, in a closely divided 5–4 decision, the U.S. Supreme Court ruled against Lindsay Earls (*Board of Education* v. *Earls*, 2002). Despite her loss, she had performed a valuable service by raising an important issue of concern so that it could receive careful consideration and clarification by judges in the court pathway. ▪

Chapter Review

1. The United States has a "dual court system" in which each state, as well as the federal government, operates its own multilevel system with trial and appellate courts.

2. The U.S. Supreme Court carefully selects a limited number of cases each year and then decides important issues of law and policy.

3. Despite the close connections between the judicial branch and the political system, judges seek to preserve the courts' image as the "nonpolitical" branch of government.

4. In contrast with judicial officers in other countries, American judges are especially powerful because of their authority to interpret constitutions and statutes, their power of judicial review, and, in the federal system, their protected tenure in office.

5. Many states use election systems or merit selection to choose judges, while federal judges must be appointed by the president and confirmed by the Senate.

6. Debates exist about the proper way to interpret the Constitution and statutes, and these debates affect choices about who will be selected to serve as judges.

7. Individuals and interest groups use many strategies in the court pathway, and their likelihood of success will be enhanced if they have expertise, resources, and patience.

8. Judges cannot always ensure that their decisions are implemented. As a result, their ability to shape public policy may vary from issue to issue.

9. Vigorous debates continue to occur about whether it is appropriate for life-tenured federal judges to create law and public policy in a democracy.

CHAPTER REVIEW TEST

1. The judicial branch of the federal government consists of
   a. the Supreme Court and all state superior courts.
   b. U.S. district courts, U.S. circuit courts, and the U.S. Supreme Court.
   c. trial and appellate courts at the state and federal levels.
   d. all trial courts at the municipal, state, and federal levels.

2. Unlike some other countries' courts, courts in the United States proceed by
   a. an adversarial system.
   b. a confrontational system.
   c. an inquisitorial system.
   d. an interrogatory system.

3. One advantage of the U.S. legal system is that success in the courtroom is not affected by the wealth or poverty of any of the participants.
   a. true   b. false

4. One difference between criminal and civil law cases is that
   a. criminal cases are tried before a jury and civil cases are not.
   b. criminal cases can go all the way to the Supreme Court and civil cases cannot.
   c. judgments in criminal cases can produce monetary compensation for the litigant and judgments in civil cases cannot.
   d. judgments in criminal cases determine whether someone is guilty of a crime and deserving of punishment.

5. What is a bench trial?
   a. a trial in which multiple lawyers for both sides represent their clients and plead their case.
   b. a criminal trial in which lawyers plead their case before a jury.
   c. any trial in which lawyers plead their case before a judge.
   d. any trial in which a lawyer represents the U.S. government.

6. What are appellate courts?

  a. courts at the federal level.

  b. courts at either the federal or state level that hear appeals of prior trial decisions.

  c. courts in a different jurisdiction from the original trial to which the trial is moved by a judge's orders.

  d. another name for district courts.

7. Each state has its own supreme court.

  a. true   **b.** false

8. Why does the American public by and large remain confident of U.S. courts' fairness, even when judges are appointed, not elected?

  a. Because courts effectively portray themselves as nonpolitical institutions of impressive authority.

  b. Because lawyers are as committed to serving justice as judges are.

  c. Because nearly every court decision is, in retrospect, proved to be correct.

  d. Because the public is not informed of cases that are over-turned through appeal or cases in which convicted defen-dants are later exonerated.

9. What are statutes?

  a. Bylaws that guide court protocols and proceedings.

  b. Legal principles stated or implied in the Constitution.

  c. Laws formulated by federal or state legislatures.

  d. Rules governing the interactions among the three branches of government.

10. Article III of the Constitution establishes some dimensions of the U.S. court system, including

  a. the judiciary's power of judicial review.

  b. the establishment of a Supreme Court.

  c. the fact that Supreme Court justices will be elected.

  d. the nature and interrelation of state and municipal courts.

11. *Marbury* v. *Madison* is such an important case in U.S. judicial his-tory because it in effect established

  a. that the Supreme Court has a largely appellate jurisdiction, so cases should not originate there.

  b. the use of a writ of mandamus.

  c. the right of the president to nullify executive orders from prior presidents

  d. the judiciary's power of judicial review.

12. Federal appellate judges can be removed from office if they

  a. are not reelected.

  b. are criticized by the American Bar Association.

  c. too often interpret legislation to be unconstitutional.

  d. are impeached.

13. Regarding diversity in the judiciary, it is fair to say that

  a. the percentage of women and minorities presiding over fed-eral courts now matches their percentage of the national population?

  b. women and minorities are radically overrepresented on the federal bench?

  c. the percentage of women and minorities on the federal bench has increased dramatically over the past couple of decades, although it still does not match their percentage of the national population?

  d. the number of women and minorities on the federal bench is not really a matter of concern, since it does not affect the legitimacy of the judiciary's work?

14. To be confirmed as a federal judge, nominees must

  a. receive a majority vote of approval from the U.S. Senate.

  b. receive a two-thirds vote of approval from Congress.

  c. endure a filibuster in the House of Representatives.

  d. receive a majority vote of approval from the Senate and the House of Representatives.

15. States that use a merit selection system to choose their judges avoid

  a. bringing politics into the process of selecting judges.

  b. having the voters deeply influence judicial selection .

  c. having a judge's selection determined by a state's gover-nor.

  d. racial homogeneity in their judgeships.

16. Federal judges who exercise judicial restraint

  a. tend to hand down lighter sentences than those who do not.

  b. interpret the Constitution flexibly.

  c. recognize that the Constitution could not anticipate and address many of today's legal questions.

  d. defer most policy decisions to the authority of the other two branches of the government.

17. Some political scientists argue that Supreme Court justices do not actually reach decisions the way they profess to—through a careful consideration of legal precedents and a consistently applied theory of constitutional interpretation—but that they instead operate by

  a. a "derivative model," in which the research of their clerks largely dictates their own conclusions.

  b. a "jurisdictional model," in which the prevailing political sentiments of their home region largely dictate their own conclusions.

  c. a "rational choice model," in which they think strategically, voting on cases in order to advance their longer-range goals.

d. an "affective model," in which the combination of moods, psychological stimuli, and the justice's relation to authority deeply influence voting patterns.

18. One of the virtues of the court pathway in our democracy is that it is a practical means of addressing nearly every sort of claim or grievance that matters to the lives of most Americans.
a. true   **b.** false

19. The infamous Trail of Tears and the Cherokee Nation's loss of property rights that preceded it remind us that
a. the Supreme Court has not always made its decisions fairly or in a way that is consistent with the Constitution.

b. the Supreme Court did not always choose to hear cases it should have.
c. there is sometimes a wide gap between what is legal and what is just.
d. the Supreme Court cannot on its own ensure that its decisions will be obeyed.

20. Through the litigation process, interest groups and individuals can make arguments that persuade judges of the best approaches to interpreting the law, and that process can result in significant changes in public policy that affect society as a whole.
a. true   **b.** false

Answers: 1: b; 2: a; 3: b; 4: d; 5: c; 6: b; 7: a; 8: a; 9: c; 10: b; 11: d; 12: d; 13: c; 14: a; 15: b; 16: b; 17: c; 18: b; 19: d; 20: a.

DISCUSSION QUESTIONS

1. What is the adversarial system?

2. What courts operate at the various levels of the American court system? How do courts at different levels differ in their responsibilities and processes?

3. What processes do Supreme Court justices use to decide cases and make opinion writing assignments?

4. How and why do judges and courts seek to maintain a certain image in the eyes of the public?

5. What elements make American judges especially powerful?

6. What is the importance of *Marbury* v. *Madison?*

7. How do states select judges?

8. What is the process for the selection of federal judges, and why are the political stakes sometimes high?

9. Why are organized interests often better situated than individual litigants to make use of the court pathway?

10. What strategies do interest groups use when they plan litigation?

11. Can judges effectively implement their decisions? What other forces are sometimes necessary to ensure that judicial decisions get implemented?

12. Why would critics argue that judicial review is improper in a democracy? What do you think?

INTERNET RESOURCES

Read judicial opinions from the U.S. Supreme Court and other courts: **http://www.law.cornell.edu** and **http://www.findlaw.com**
Explore the federal court system: **http://www.uscourts.gov**
Explore state court systems: **http://www.uscourts.gov** and **http://www.courts.state.tx.us**

Discover interest groups that use the court pathway: Washington Legal Foundation, **http://www.wlf.org**; Pacific Legal Foundation, **http://www.pacificlegal.org**; American Civil Liberties Union, **http://www.aclu.org**; NAACP Legal Defense Fund, **http://www.naacpldf.org**

Examine competing perspectives on judicial selection: **http://www.ajs.org** (advocates for merit selection of judges); **http://www.judicialselection.org** (advocates the appointment of politically conservative federal judges); **http://www.allianceforjustice.org** (advocates the appointment of politically liberal justices)

Learn about upcoming law and policy controversies that will be addressed by the U.S. Supreme Court: Northwestern University's "On the Docket" Web site, **http://journalism.medill.northwestern .edu/docket**

ADDITIONAL READING

Epstein, Lee, and Joseph F. Kobylka. *The Supreme Court and Legal Change: Abortion and the Death Penalty.* Chapel Hill: University of North Carolina Press, 1992.

Goldman, Sheldon. *Picking Federal Judges: Lower Court Selection from Roosevelt through Reagan.* New Haven, CT: Yale University Press, 1997.

Lazarus, Edward. *Closed Chambers: The First Eyewitness Account of the Epic Struggles inside the Supreme Court.* New York: Times Books, 1998.

O'Brien, David. *Storm Center: The Supreme Court in American Politics,* 6th ed. New York: Norton, 2002.

Smith, Christopher E. *Courts, Politics, and the Judicial Process,* 2nd ed. Chicago: Nelson-Hall, 1997.

Yalof, David Alistair. *Pursuit of Justices.* Chicago: University of Chicago Press, 2001.

KEY TERMS

They are taking liberty with Liberty. This photo was taken from the torch of the statue in September 1938 while it was being renovated for the World's Fair. The Statue of Liberty was a gift of international friendship from the people of France to the people of the United States, and has become a universal symbol of political freedom and democracy.

CHAPTER 5

CIVIL LIBERTIES

Restrictions on Freedom of Speech   On May 3, 2003, a caravan of cars drove to Crawford, Texas, from Austin. The vehicles contained dozens of people who hoped to stage a protest against President George W. Bush during his visit to his ranch. Many of the protesters carried signs with such slogans as "Give Peace a Chance!" and "Impeach Bush!"[1] As they approached Crawford, the would-be protesters found the road blocked by thirty-five police officers, who ordered them to disperse and threatened them with arrest for failing to obey a city ordinance against staging demonstrations without a permit. Under the ordinance, anyone wishing to stage a "procession, parade, or demonstration" in Crawford, Texas, must give city officials fifteen days' advance notice, obtain permission from the sheriff, pay a $25 fee, and confine their activities to the high school football field. The only exceptions specified by the ordinance

A deputy guards protesters as the motorcade of President George Bush passes by in Crawford, Texas. Cindy Sheehan (L), the organizer of the protest, lost her son, U.S. Army Specialist Casey Austin Sheehan, when he was serving in Iraq. She holds up a cross bearing her son's name. How effective do you think such protests are in influencing public officials?

were for funerals, schools, police and fire department activities, and military parades. Five of the anti-Bush protesters were arrested for violating the ordinance when instead of returning to their vehicles and leaving the area, they argued with the police about whether the ordinance violated their constitutional rights to freedom of speech and assembly. They were taken to the McLennan County Jail.

The protesters filed a lawsuit in September 2003 seeking to have a federal judge declare that the ordinance should be invalidated as an unconstitutional violation of people's rights. However, because the litigation process typically proceeds over the course of many months, the protesters faced prosecution in the local court for violating the ordinance while they waited for their federal lawsuit to move forward.

The protesters' criminal cases came to trial in the local state court in February 2004. They argued that they were arrested despite the fact that they never actually staged the type of "procession, parade, or demonstration" mentioned in the ordinance. More important, they argued that the city's ordinance violated the U.S. Constitution because it prevented people from exercising their First Amendment rights to freedom of speech and freedom of assembly. The Crawford police chief testified that people could be arrested under the ordinance for merely wearing a Peace button or handing out leaflets. The defendants' attorney argued that the city ordinance was "overbroad and arbitrarily enforced." After

HUMAN BEINGS UNDERSTAND REASON, COMPASSION, DIGNITY

PREDATORS UNDERSTAND STRENGTH

the two-day trial, the jury, all of whom were local residents, convicted the protesters of violating the ordinance. The judge ordered them to pay fines ranging from $200 to $500.

Several months later, a county judge dismissed the charges after ruling that the Crawford ordinance violates freedom of speech rights under the First Amendment. The protesters, who had spent a night in jail after being arrested, filed a civil rights lawsuit in 2005 seeking compensation from criminal justice officials for violating their rights.

The case of the Crawford protesters shows the kinds of conflicts that arise between government policies and rights of individuals. It also shows how individuals and interest groups can use the *court pathway* to identify and protect constitutional rights. Representing the protesters was an attorney from the Texas Civil Rights Project, an organization dedicated to seeking judicial decisions to advance its vision of constitutional rights. [2]

Does the Crawford ordinance violate the constitutional right to freedom of speech? Certainly, the ordinance and the manner in which it was enforced prevented individuals from publicly asserting their opinions in a location where they hoped to capture the attention of the president of the United States and of the national press, which follows the president everywhere. It seems clear that requiring demonstrations to be confined to the high school football field would have the effect of sparing President Bush from ever coming face to face with unfriendly signs and slogans while visiting his Texas ranch. On the other hand, confining protests to the football field and requiring fifteen days' notice also helps local officials protect the president's personal security and prevents traffic jams, littering, and other potential problems. Does the ordinance advance important societal interests in an appropriate manner? Or is the right to free speech so important and so absolute that the government should not be able to control the expression of citizens' opinions in this way? These kinds of important questions—and visible public conflicts—confront judges who must make decisions about the protection of the civil liberties guaranteed by the Bill of Rights. Civil liberties are individuals' freedoms and legal protections that cannot be denied or hindered by the actions of government. In Chapter 5, you will learn about civil rights, legal protections concerning equality and citizens' participation in the country's democratic governing processes. In making decisions about civil liberties, judges often try to balance the interests of society. For example, they may weigh the need for police to undertake searches in a specific situation against the individual's entitlement to protection against unreasonable searches. ▮

▶ **What are civil liberties?**
Are they like civil rights?

civil liberties
individual freedoms and legal protections guaranteed by the Bill of Rights that cannot be denied or hindered by government.

civil rights
public policies and legal protections concerning equal status and treatment in American society to advance the goals of equal opportunity, fair and open political participation, and equal treatment under the law, without regard to race, gender, disability status, and other demographic characteristics.

▶ **What are civil liberties? Are they like civil rights?**

Civil liberties are individuals' freedoms and legal protections that cannot be denied or hindered by the actions of government. In (L)(I)(N)(K) *Chapter 6, pages 208–213,* you will learn about **civil rights,** legal protections concerning equality and citizens' participation in the country's democratic governing processes. In making decisions about civil liberties, judges often try to balance the interests of society. For example, they may weigh the need for police to undertake searches in a specific situation against the individual's entitlement to protection against unreasonable searches.

In this chapter, we will examine civil liberties protected by the U.S. Constitution through decisions of the courts. Civil liberties are an important part of Americans' beliefs in individualism and the need to limit the power of government. Americans place a high value on individual liberty, including their ability to criticize the government and to be protected against arbitrary and unfair governmental actions. Court decisions that define the protections enjoyed by individuals tell government officials what they can and cannot do. When, for example, a judge decides that the Crawford, Texas, ordinance violates the First Amendment, that decision limits the kinds of laws that Crawford can enact and the police can enforce. It also sends a message to officials in other cities about the limits of their lawmaking authority.

Sometimes these court decisions are very controversial, especially when they define protections for individuals who are despised by others in society, such as criminal defendants or con-

victed offenders serving sentences in prison. Such controversies reflect the fact that Americans do not always agree on the meaning and coverage of the protections provided by the Bill of Rights. They also reflect the fact that American judges have consistently stated that all individuals, no matter who they are or what they have done, enjoy certain legal protections under the Constitution.

Key Questions

1. How "free" is free speech in the United States?
2. What are the two dimensions of freedom of religion under the First Amendment?
3. What protections does the Bill of Rights provide for criminal defendants?
4. Why is the right to privacy controversial?
5. Have judges gone too far in defining civil liberties protections through the processes of the court pathway?

The Bill of Rights in History

As you've seen in earlier chapters, the ten constitutional amendments that make up the Bill of Rights were added to the United States Constitution in 1791. These amendments were enacted in response to fears that the Constitution had failed to provide enough legal protections for individuals. Eighteenth-century Americans' experiences with British rule gave the founders reason to be concerned that a government might become too powerful and thereby fail to respect individuals' liberty and property. The Bill of Rights spelled out the legal protections that individuals could expect from the federal government. However, mere words on paper do not, by themselves, provide protection against actions by government officials. Those words must be respected by officials, and there must be judges who are willing to interpret and enforce the underlying meanings.

Anti-war protesters camp outside President George W. Bush's ranch in Crawford, Texas, to express their opposition to the American invasion of Iraq. Those who were arrested used the court pathway to challenge city ordinances that limited their ability to assemble and speak out in a manner of their own choosing. What policy issues do you feel strongly enough about to take part in a public protest?

▶ How did the Supreme Court get involved in protecting individual rights?

Barron v. Baltimore (1833) early Supreme Court interpretation of the Fifth Amendment declaring that the Bill of Rights provided legal protections only against actions by the federal government.

John Marshall (1755–1835) important chief justice of the early U.S. Supreme Court (1801–1835) who wrote many opinions establishing the power of the federal government and the authority of the Court.

EARLY INTERPRETATION OF THE BILL OF RIGHTS

During the first years after the ratification of the U.S. Constitution and the Bill of Rights, the tiny federal court system handled relatively few cases. The U.S. Supreme Court was seen as a weak institution that did not have much influence over major issues of public affairs. For example, John Rutledge, one of the first justices, resigned from the Court after only two years in order to become chief justice of the South Carolina Supreme Court, a position he regarded as more prestigious and influential.[3] The U.S. Supreme Court's most important cases from this era involved decisions that defined the authority of the various institutions of American government and clarified the respective powers of state and federal governments. The Supreme Court played an important role in interpreting constitutional provisions in ways that created a workable distribution of power among branches of government and defined the relationships between state and federal governments.

▶ **How did the Supreme Court get involved in protecting individual rights?** The Supreme Court's role as a guardian of civil liberties did not emerge until the 1950s, when the Bill of Rights became a central focus of decisions by federal judges. One reason that the federal courts did not focus much attention on the Bill of Rights was because of the way the Supreme Court first interpreted the legal protections for individuals contained in the Constitution. In the early 1830s, a man named Barron filed a lawsuit against the city of Baltimore claiming that road construction by the city had ruined his wharf in the harbor. Barron claimed that the city's action had violated his protections under the Fifth Amendment. Under that amendment, people cannot be "deprived of . . . property, without due process of law; nor shall private property be taken for public use, without just compensation." Barron's lawsuit sought "just compensation" for the loss of his property's value that had occurred because of the city's road-building activities.

The Supreme Court's opinion in **Barron v. Baltimore** (1833) was written by Chief Justice **John Marshall,** the crucial figure who, as you saw in ⓛⓘⓝⓚ *Chapter 4, pages 126–127,* shaped the Supreme Court's role in the nation during the federal judiciary's formative decades, 1801–1835. After examining the arguments in the case, Marshall concluded:

> We are of the opinion that the provision in the Fifth Amendment to the Constitution . . . is intended solely as a limitation

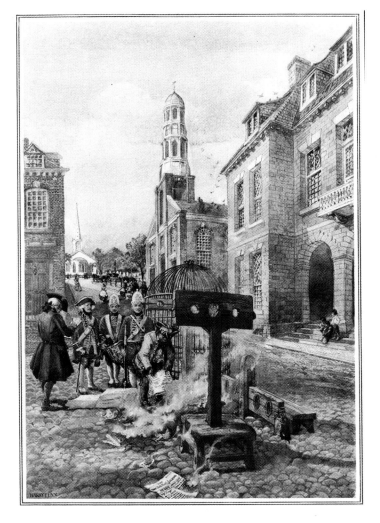

In 1734, British authorities burned copies of John Peter Zenger's *Weekly Journal* in order to stop Zenger from criticizing the colonial governor of New York. Memories of such actions by British authorities remained in the minds of Americans when they later wrote the provisions of the Bill of Rights to protect freedom of the press. How would the United States be different today without the protections for free expression contained in the Bill of Rights?

Photo: Copyright © North Wind/North Wind Picture Archives. All rights reserved.

▶ **Then how did we** get our civil liberties protected in the states?

due process clause
a statement of rights in the Fifth Amendment (aimed at the federal government) and the Fourteenth Amendment (aimed at state and local governments) that protects against arbitrary deprivations of life, liberty, or property. The Fourteenth Amendment phrase is also interpreted flexibly by the Supreme Court to expand a variety of rights.

Gitlow v. New York (1925)
the case in which the U.S. Supreme Court applied the First Amendment right of free speech against the states. It was the first case to incorporate a personal right from the Bill of Rights into the due process clause of the Fourteenth Amendment.

Susette Kelo's house (visible behind the fence) was the last building left in her neighborhood after the city of New London, Connecticut, used its power of eminent domain, the government power to force individuals to sell their land to the city. Kelo tried to use the court pathway to stop the city's efforts. In 2005, the Supreme Court ruled against her. The case demonstrated that issues about Fifth Amendment property rights still arise regularly. What is the purpose of allowing the government to force landowners to sell their land?

on the exercise of power by the Government of the United States, and is not applicable to the legislation of the States.

Marshall's decision reflected the original intent of the Bill of Rights, as well as the literal words at the start of the First Amendment, which refer to the federal government: "Congress shall make no law . . .". The effect of Marshall's decision went beyond merely limiting the Fifth Amendment's protections; it also established the fact that all of the provisions of the Bill of Rights protected *only* against actions by the *federal* government, not against actions by state and local officials.

Think about the implications of the Court's decision. Although Americans take justifiable pride in the Bill of Rights as an important statement about civil liberties, in reality, during most of American history, those protections applied only against actions by the federal government. State constitutions provided protections for individuals within the boundaries of individual states, but the rights listed in these documents varied from state to state and were defined and implemented in varying ways. Many state courts did not rigorously interpret and enforce individual rights. The actual civil liberties enjoyed by citizens could differ dramatically, depending on which state a person happened to inhabit or be visiting. As a result, many states had laws restricting speech, press, assembly, and other aspects of civil liberties, and these laws were unaffected by the existence of the idealistic language of the Bill of Rights.

THE INCORPORATION PROCESS AND THE NATIONALIZATION OF CONSTITUTIONAL RIGHTS

As you will study in greater detail in (L I N K) *Chapter 6, pages 215–216,* three amendments were added to the Constitution after the Civil War (1861–1865). Members of Congress proposed the amendments primarily to provide protections for African Americans who were newly freed from slavery. One of the amendments, the Fourteenth, did not merely protect African Americans. The ratification of the Fourteenth Amendment (1868) gave the Constitution language granting legal protections for all individuals against actions by state and local officials. The key language in the first section of the Fourteenth Amendment says:

No State shall make or enforce any law which shall abridge the privileges or immunities of citizens of the United States; nor shall any State deprive any person of life, liberty, or property, without due process of law; nor deny to any person within its jurisdiction the equal protection of the laws.

The words of the amendment specified that these constitutional protections were aimed against actions by states, but the precise protections were not clear. It would require interpretations by judges to determine what specific protections, if any, would be provided by the phrases "privileges or immunities of citizens," "due process of law," and "equal protection of the laws." One scholar has called the Fourteenth Amendment "probably the most controversial and certainly the most litigated of all amendments adopted since the birth of the Republic."[4]

▶ **Then how did we get our civil liberties protected in the states?** Lawyers used the court pathway to present arguments to the U.S. Supreme Court and other courts about specific legal protections that they believed the Fourteenth Amendment should provide for their clients. In particular, they asked the Court to interpret the **due process clause** of the amendment as providing specific civil liberties to protect individuals against actions by state and local officials.

For several decades, except for one case recognizing property rights protected by the concept of due process (*Chicago, Burlington & Quincy Railroad* v. *Chicago,* 1897), the Supreme Court generally refused to specify the protections provided by the phrase "due process." In 1925, however, the Court began to move in a new direction by declaring that the First Amendment right to free speech is included in the protections of the Fourteenth Amendment due process clause. According to the Court's decision that year in ***Gitlow* v. *New York,*** individuals enjoy the right to freedom of speech against actions and laws by state and local governments. New York prosecuted Gitlow, a member of the Socialist Party, for distributing publications that advocated overthrowing the U.S. government. Although the Supreme Court said that individuals enjoy the protections of free speech against actions by state governments, Gitlow's conviction was upheld because the Court did not regard his advocacy of socialism as protected by the First Amendment. Today the Supreme Court takes a broader view of

Benjamin Gitlow (RIGHT), shown speaking to a rally of the Workers Party in New York City in 1928, used the court pathway to challenge his criminal conviction for expressing ideas about dramatically altering the American system of government. The U.S. Supreme Court used Gitlow's case in 1925 to begin the incorporation process by declaring that First Amendment protections for freedom of speech also apply against state governments. Are there any statements or ideas that are so dangerous that the government should be able to place people in prison for expressing them? If so, what might they be?

▶ **So now the states** have to protect all the civil liberties found in the Bill of Rights?

Near v. Minnesota (1931)
U.S. Supreme Court decision that incorporated the First Amendment right to freedom of the press and applied that right against the states.

incorporation
process used by the Supreme Court to protect individuals from actions by state and local government by interpreting the due process clause of the Fourteenth Amendment as containing selected provisions of the Bill of Rights.

Duncan v. Louisiana (1968)
the case in which the U.S. Supreme Court incorporated the Sixth Amendment right to trial by jury and applied it to the states under the due process clause of the Fourteenth Amendment.

In the 1930s, President Franklin D. Roosevelt clashed with the Supreme Court as it struck down many of the federal government's economic and social welfare programs. The cartoon depicts the Court as holding up progress. As the Court's composition later changed, the court pathway was used increasingly for civil liberties issues and the incorporation of the Bill of Rights. Do you view today's Supreme Court as advancing or hindering democracy and public policy in the United States?

free speech, and Gitlow could not be prosecuted for criticizing the government or advocating change.

In subsequent years, the Court began to bring other specific civil liberties under the protection of the Fourteenth Amendment's due process clause. For example, in **Near v. Minnesota** (1931), the Court included freedom of the press under the Fourteenth Amendment. The Court added the First Amendment's right to free exercise of religion under the due process clause in 1934 (*Hamilton* v. *Regents of the University of California*) and firmly repeated that conclusion in 1940 (*Cantwell* v. *Connecticut*).

The process through which the Supreme Court examined individual provisions of the Bill of Rights and applied them against state and local officials is called **incorporation.** The Court *incorporated* specific civil liberties from the Bill of Rights into the meaning of the due process clause of the Fourteenth Amendment. Incorporation gave individuals throughout the nation the same civil liberties protections against actions by state and local governments. This incorporation occurred slowly, over the course of a half-century.

As the makeup of the Court changed in the late 1930s with the appointment of new justices by President Franklin D. Roosevelt, it eventually shifted its focus to cases concerning the various civil liberties described in the Bill of Rights. On a case-by-case basis through the 1960s, the Court ultimately expanded the meaning of "due process" under the Fourteenth Amendment by selectively incorporating individual civil liberties from the Bill of Rights. By the time of the Supreme Court's decision to apply the right to trial by jury in state courts in 1968 (**Duncan v. Louisiana**), most of the provisions in the first eight amendments had been included under the protections of the Fourteenth Amendment's due process clause.

pathways of action
CRUEL AND UNUSUAL PUNISHMENTS

At first, the Eighth Amendment's prohibition of "cruel and unusual punishments" merely meant that the *federal* government could not impose torturous punishments on offenders who committed *federal* crimes. As individuals pursued their cases through the levels of the court pathway, the Supreme Court justices broadened the definition of this Eighth Amendment right. In 1910, the Court expanded the definition to include punishments that are

preferred freedoms
the rights contained in the First Amendment that judges have viewed as especially important in the eyes of the country's founders and essential for a society based on personal liberty and a democratic governing system.

1. In what ways was passage of the Fourteenth Amendment essential to the expansion of constitutional rights for individuals?

2. How has the definition of the Eighth Amendment's cruel and unusual punishments clause evolved? Have judges interpreted the clause properly?

disproportionate to the crime, as well as punishments that are similar to torture (*Weems* v. *United States*). The 1910 case concerned a man sentenced to fifteen years at hard labor in ankle chains, plus the loss of citizenship rights, for stealing a small amount of money. Later, another individual's case led to the incorporation of the Eighth Amendment into the Fourteenth Amendment due process clause for application against the states (*Robinson* v. *California*, 1962). Eventually, additional cases led the Supreme Court to include limited rights for prisoners to receive medical care and food, as well as issues concerning the administration of the death penalty. In 2005, for example, an appeal on behalf of Christopher Simmons, who confessed to a vicious kidnapping and murder at the age of 17, convinced the Supreme Court to declare that the prohibition on "cruel and unusual punishments" bars the imposition of the death penalty for crimes committed by offenders under the age of 18 (*Roper* v. *Simmons*). By pursuing cases through the court pathway, individual provisions of the Bill of Rights may be interpreted and reinterpreted by judges to either expand or reduce the legal protections provided by the Constitution. During the twentieth century, such interpretations led to an expansion of the protections provided by the Eighth Amendment. The words *cruel and unusual punishments* did not change, but the interpretation and application of those words did as judges applied them to a wider array of actions undertaken by officials at all levels of government. ◼

▶ **So now the states have to protect all the civil liberties found in the Bill of Rights?** Total incorporation of the Bill of Rights did not occur. A few provisions of the Bill of Rights have never been incorporated and thus still provide protections solely against actions by the federal government. Most notably, these include the Second Amendment's provision linking "a well-regulated Militia" and the right to bear arms; the Third Amendment's provision against housing troops in private homes; the Fifth Amendment's right to a grand jury; the Seventh Amendment's requirement of jury trials in civil cases contesting any amount over $20; and the Eighth Amendment's prohibition of excessive bail (see Figure 5.1a,b on pages 162–165). It seems unlikely that the Supreme Court would ever incorporate the provisions concerning grand juries and jury trials in civil cases concerning small amounts of money. Imposing these requirements on the states would place significant financial burdens on state and local courts.

The incorporation process served the important function of nationalizing the Bill of Rights (see Figure 5.1b on page 164–165). As a result, most of its provisions apply everywhere within the borders of the United States to protect individuals against actions by all levels of government. Thus the process of incorporation is also referred to as the "nationalization" of the Bill of Rights.

1. "Civil liberties" refer to freedoms and legal protections that the federal government can suspend or modify at any given time.
   a. true b. false

2. The Supreme Court's role as guardian of civil liberties
   a. is spelled out in the Bill of Rights.
   b. is first mentioned in the Declaration of Independence.
   c. emerged in the middle of the twentieth century.
   d. emerged in the Court's formative decades, 1801–1835.

3. Before the incorporation process (which had the effect of nationalizing Americans' constitutional rights), all provisions of the Bill of Rights protected
   a. only against actions by the *federal* government.
   b. only against infringement of *wealthy citizens'* rights.
   c. only against infringement of *men's* (not women's) rights.
   d. b and c.

4. The Fourteenth Amendment, preventing states from "abridg[ing] the privileges or immunities of citizens of the United States," was enacted
   a. during Thomas Jefferson's administration.
   b. soon after the Civil War.
   c. during Lyndon Johnson's administration.
   d. in the wake of the civil rights movement.

Answers: 1-b, 2-c, 3-a, 4-b.

First Amendment Rights

Many political scientists believe that the drafters of the Bill of Rights placed special importance on the rights that they chose to list first. Indeed, several Supreme Court justices have argued that First Amendment rights should be regarded as **preferred freedoms** that should receive extra attention from judges.[5] The very

1925
Gitlow v. *New York*
1st Amendment freedom of speech protection applies against the states through 14th Amendment due process clause

1791
Ratification of the Bill of Rights

1943
West Virginia v. *Barnette*
1st Amendment protection for free exercise of religion permits members of religious minorities to decline to recite the Pledge of Allegiance in public schools

1919
Schenck v. *United States*
1st Amendment right of free speech is subject to a "clear and present danger" test

1868
Ratification of the 14th Amendment, including due process clause

1931
Near v. *Minnesota*
1st Amendment freedom of the press applies against states through the 14th Amendment

1963
Gideon v. *Wainwright*
6th Amendment right to counsel for non-petty offenses applies to the states through 14th Amendment

1833
Barron v. *Baltimore*
Bill of Rights apply only against federal government

1897
Chicago, Burlington & Quincy Railroad v. *Chicago*
5th Amendment right to just compensation applied against states (property right, not personal civil liberties protection for individuals)

1961
Mapp v. *Ohio*
Exclusionary rule protection of the 4th Amendment applies against states through the 14th Amendment

FIGURE 5.1a

Key Decisions on Civil Liberties

The Bill of Rights initially protected individuals' civil liberties only against actions by the federal government. The Fourteenth Amendment (1868) added language to the Constitution to prohibit state and local officials from violating the right to "due process." Over the course of several decades, the U.S. Supreme Court interpreted the phrase "due process" in ways that required state and local officials to respect specific civil liberties protections in the Bill of Rights. The Supreme Court also interpreted specific provisions in the Bill of Rights to expand the legal protections enjoyed by individuals.

1971

Tinker v. Des Moines Independent School District

1st Amendment protects the symbolic speech rights of students who wish to wear black armbands in school in order to protest the Vietnam War

New York Times v. United States

1st Amendment protection for freedom of the press prevented the government from stopping newspapers' publication of a report on the Vietnam War

Lemon v. Kurtzman

1st Amendment test for Establishment Clause violations focuses on the intent of government policies and the entanglement of government with religion

1969

Brandenburg v. Ohio

1st Amendment protection for freedom of speech is broadened to forbid government restraint unless there is a danger of "imminent lawless action" such as a riot or other violence.

1968

Duncan v. Louisiana

6th Amendment right to trial by jury applies against the states through the 14th Amendment

1989

Texas v. Johnson

Burning a flag as part of political protest is a protected form of symbolic speech under the 1st Amendment

2003

Lawrence v. Texas

The right to privacy prevents states from punishing adults' private, noncommercial sexual conduct, including conduct by gays and lesbians

1966

Miranda v. Arizona

5th Amendment protection against compelled self-incrimination requires officers to inform suspects about rights prior to questioning while in custody

1973

Roe v. Wade

Right to privacy includes women's right to make choices about abortion in the first six months of pregnancy

Miller v. California

1st Amendment test for obscene materials focuses on contemporary community standards and patently offensive sexual content

Photo: Carol T. Powers/The New York Times

FIGURE 5.1b

The Selective Incorporation of the Bill of Rights

Amendment	Right	Date Incorporated	Case	The Right in the News
First Amendment	Speech	1925	*Gitlow* v. *New York*	Howard Stern claims that his recent move to Sirius Radio Network was a matter of protecting his First Amendment rights. 
	Press	1931	*Near* v. *Minnesota*	*New York Times* reporter Judith Miller was jailed for 12 weeks in 2005 for refusing to reveal her source of information concerning an investigation to discover who revealed the identity of a CIA agent.
	Assembly and Petition	1937	*Dejonge* v. *Oregon*	In response to protesters gathered at military funerals, Congress enacted the for Fallen Heroes Act in 2006 to bar protests within 300 feet of national cemeteries during funerals.
	Religion– Exercise	initial 1934	*Hamilton* v. *University of California*	No current issue
	Religion– Exercise	confirmed 1940	*Cantwell* v. *Connecticut*	The U.S. Supreme Court rules in 2006 that the federal government cannot prevent a small religious sect from using a South American tea containing a regulated hallucinogenic drug as part of its ceremonies.
	Religion– Establishment	1947	*Everson* v. *Board of Education*	In 2005, a federal judge in Pennsylvania ruled that intelligent design theory cannot be taught as an alternative to evolution in public schools, because intelligent design represents a religious viewpoint that the government (local school board) is imposing on students. 
Second Amendment	Bear Arms	Not Incorporated		In June 2006, a California state judge relied on state law to strike down a voter-approved law that banned the sales of firearms and the possession of handguns in the City of San Francisco. 
Third Amendment	Quartering Troops	Not Incorporated		No current issue
Fourth Amendment	Search & Seizure	1949	*Wolf* v. *Colorado*	The U.S. Supreme Court announced in 2006 that police cannot enter and conduct a warrantless search of a home with the consent of an occupant when another occupant of the home objects to the search.
	Exclusionary Rule	1961	*Mapp* v. *Ohio*	The U.S. Supreme Court decided in 2006 that evidence obtained from a search need not be excluded from use in court when officers using a search warrant violate the traditional legal rule requiring them to knock and announce their presence before entering the home to be searched. 
Fifth Amendment	Takings and Compensation	1897	*Chicago, B & Q Railroad* v. *Chicago*	The U.S. Supreme Court ruled in 2005 that a city does not violate the Fifth Amendment provision about taking property for public use when it takes people's homes in order to turn the land over to private developers. 
	Self Incrimination	1964	*Malloy* v. *Hogan*	The Supreme Court of Georgia concluded that Spanish-speaking suspects did not need to be given Miranda warnings by a certified translator (2006).
	Grand jury	Not Incorporated		No current issue

Amendment	Right	Date Incorporated	Case	The Right in the News
	Double jeopardy	1969	*Benton* v. *Maryland*	In 2005, a Salt Lake City man decided to clear his conscience by admitting that he had murdered a toddler in 1991—however, he could not be prosecuted, because he had been tried and found not guilty of the charge fourteen years earlier.
Sixth Amendment	Public trial	1948	*In re Oliver*	A federal appeals court overturned the conviction of a man after the trial judge closed the courtroom and removed spectators while rape victims testified against the defendant (2006).
	Right to counsel	1963	*Gideon* v. *Wainwright*	In 2006, the U.S. Supreme Court considered the question of whether a violation of the right to counsel occurs when the trial judge does not permit the defendant to choose which attorney will represent him.
	Confrontation	1965	*Pointer* v. *Texas*	The U.S. Supreme Court found a violation of the right to confrontation when the prosecution played a tape recording of statements by the defendant's wife, but the wife, never testified at the trial (2004).
	Impartial jury	1966	*Parker* v. *Gladden*	In 2006, the murder trial of a college student accused of killing his father was moved from Albany to a different city in New York, because a judge concluded that extensive publicity about the case in Albany would make it impossible to have an impartial jury in that city's court.
	Speedy trial	1967	*Klopfer* v. *North Carolina*	A federal judge found a violation of the right to a speedy trial for a robbery defendant and dismissed all charges after the defendant endured three aborted trials (mistrials) over a seventeen-month period; however, a court of appeals reversed that decision and ordered yet another trial for the defendant (2006).
	Compulsory process	1967	*Washington* v. *Texas*	A Wisconsin court of appeals rejected a claim that the right to compulsory process was violated when a defendant was not allowed to call his friend as a witness. The court concluded that the friend's testimony would not have been relevant to the defendant's self-defense claim (2006).
	Jury trial (criminal)	1968	*Duncan* v. *Louisiana*	The U.S. Supreme Court has struck down sentencing laws that permit judges to enhance sentences based on facts that were never decided upon by the jury (2004).
Seventh Amendment	Jury trial (civil)	Not Incorporated		Availability of jury trials in civil cases is determined by each state's individual laws.
Eighth Amendment	Cruel punishment	1962	*Robinson* v. *California*	The U.S. Supreme Court permitted death row inmates to file lawsuits alleging that execution by lethal injection constitutes cruel and unusual punishment in violation of the Eighth Amendment (2006).
	Excessive bail	Not Incorporated		After being convicted in 2006 of conspiracy and fraud charges, former Enron Corporation CEO Kenneth Lay was released on $5 million bail after the trial, but died before he was sentenced. Photo: Michael Stravata/The New York Times
	Excessive fines	Not Incorporated		In 2006, a Belgian chemical company was sentenced by a federal court in California to pay a criminal fine of $40.9 million after admitting guilt to violating laws against price fixing.

▶ **How does the court** balance the individual's rights and society's rights?

clear and present danger test
a test for permissible speech articulated by Justice Oliver Wendell Holmes in *Schenck* v. *United States* (1919) that allows government regulation of some expressions.

ABOVE: **Richard Ceballos**, a prosecutor in Los Angeles, claimed that he was transferred for criticizing police officers, yet the Supreme Court declared in 2006 that his free speech rights were not violated. RIGHT: **Freedom of speech issues** continue to arouse controversy. In 2006, the U.S. Senate came within one vote of initiating a proposed constitutional amendment intended to prohibit flag burning as a form of political expression. BELOW: **The Rev. Fred Phelps** leads loud protests at the funerals of American military personnel killed in Iraq and Afghanistan by claiming that the deaths came from God's decision to punish the United States for being too tolerant of gays and lesbians. Should the First Amendment right to freedom of speech protect the actions of any of the individuals in these pictures? If so, which actions and why?

first rights listed in the First Amendment concern freedom of religion, speech, and press:

> Congress shall make no law respecting an establishment of religion, or prohibiting the free exercise thereof; or abridging the freedom of speech, or of the press; or the right of the people peaceably to assemble, and to petition the Government for redress of grievances.

The importance of these rights to the founders of the United States is quite understandable. Many colonists came to North America from Europe because their membership in minority religious groups led them to seek a land where they could worship as they pleased without interference by the government. Thus the central place of religious freedom in the First Amendment appears to reflect the history of the North American colonies. This protection was fundamental to their desire to create a new society.

In the same way, freedom of speech and of the press were considered fundamental in the eighteenth century. A central grievance against the British authorities who administered the American colonies was the British effort to punish people for making statements critical of King George III and Parliament. Indeed, many scholars of government regard freedom of expression as an essential element for any democratic system. If people cannot freely criticize government officials, there is little opportunity to share information and opinions that will shape the voting processes that keep government officials accountable to their constituents. As we look around the world and see countries where rulers keep their citizens from voting in free elections and otherwise participating in democratic processes, we typically see severe restrictions on the expression of ideas in speech and the press.

FREEDOM OF SPEECH

The First Amendment protections for speech and press are expressed in absolute terms: "Congress shall make no law . . . abridging the freedom of speech, or of the press; or the right of the people peaceably to assemble, and to petition the Government for redress of grievances." Although the words of the amendment seem to say that the government cannot impose *any* limitations on your ability to speak, write, or participate in peaceful public demonstrations, you can probably think of several kinds of expressions that are actually limited under American law—for example:

> Claiming that you were merely exercising your right to freedom of speech if you telephoned the leaders of North Korea and told them how to build nuclear weapons

> Claiming that you were merely using free speech and free press if you filled bottles with tap water and sold them through advertisements that called them "The Amazing Liquid Cure for Cancer"

> Writing a novel about the life of a college student by copying sections, word for word, from other novels about college life

▶ **How does the court balance the individual's rights and society's rights?** These examples raise questions about whether freedom of speech is absolute or whether the government can impose limitations. Judges interpret the First Amendment in ways that seek to strike a balance between individual liberty and important societal interests. In the first example, national security interests may outweigh an individual's desire to transmit a specific communication. The second example shows that the government can regulate product advertisements and medicines in ways that protect society from harm, even when they limit an individual's speech and written expression. And the third example concerns the protection of intellectual property such as books, songs, and poems that are an individual's or a group's creative expressions, protected through copyright laws. Freedom of expression is important for democracy and liberty in the United States, but these and other limitations are regarded as essential for protecting individuals and society against specific harms. This does not say that governments have unlimited authority to place limitations on freedom of expression that they claim will protect society. Judges typically demand that governmental regulations concerning speech and press be supported by strong, persuasive justifications before they can be applied to limit individuals' opportunities to express themselves.

A police officer broke up a public demonstration in 1917 by New York City women who opposed drafting young men into the Army to fight in World War I. At that time cities and states could prohibit protests and arrest people who spoke out against government policies. In subsequent decades, the U.S. Supreme Court broadened the application of the First Amendment to cities and states. If new threats to the United States led to the resumption of the military draft, would you expect to see public protests? How would the government respond to such protests?

During American involvement in World War I (1917–1918) and the years immediately after, the federal government prosecuted people for publishing pamphlets that were critical of the military draft and the war or called for a socialist form of government in the United States. The Supreme Court took a narrow view of the right to free speech and upheld these criminal convictions. In a famous majority opinion, however, Justice Oliver Wendell Holmes argued for a **clear and present danger test** that would permit prosecution only for speeches and publications that actually posed a tangible, immediate threat to American society (*Schenck* v. *United States*, 1919). Holmes illustrated his point with an especially famous descriptive example: "The most stringent protection of free speech would not protect a man in falsely shouting fire in a theater, and causing a panic."

Brandenburg v. Ohio (1969)
U.S. Supreme Court decision that articulated a test for permissible speech by allowing the government to regulate expressions that incite a danger of imminent lawless action, such as a riot or other violent event.

political speech
expressions concerning politics, government, public figures, and issues of public concern—the form of expression that contemporary commentators view as most deserving of First Amendment protection.

commercial speech
texts such as advertising, promoting business ventures. Such speech is subject to government regulation to ensure truthfulness and to protect the public from unsafe products.

symbolic speech
the expression of an idea or viewpoint through an action, such as wearing an armband or burning an object. Symbolic speech can enjoy First Amendment protection.

Texas v. Johnson (1989)
controversial U.S. Supreme Court decision providing First Amendment protection for flag burning as symbolic speech.

reasonable time, place, and manner restrictions
permissible government regulations on freedom of speech that seek to prevent disruptions or threats to public safety in the manner in which expressions are presented. Such regulations cannot be used to control the content of political speech.

Mary Beth Tinker used the court pathway to gain the Supreme Court's endorsement of her right to express her views on the Vietnam War by wearing a black armband in school. Controversies continue to arise in American schools about clothing containing symbols, including the Confederate flag, gang signs, and profanity. Should the First Amendment be interpreted to protect symbolic speech, even when those symbols do not concern public policy issues? Why or why not?

Throughout the twentieth century, advocates of free speech pursued cases in the court pathway to challenge laws that limited people's ability to express their beliefs and viewpoints. By the 1960s, the Supreme Court had adopted, expanded, and refined Holmes' suggested test so that political protests, whether by civil rights advocates, antiwar activists, or communists, could express critical viewpoints, as long as the nature and context of those expressions did not pose an immediate threat. As expressed by the Supreme Court's decision in *Brandenburg* v. *Ohio* (1969):

> The constitutional guarantees of free speech and free press do not permit a State to forbid or proscribe advocacy of the use of force or of law violation except where such advocacy is directed to inciting or producing imminent lawless action and is likely to incite or produce such action.

Nowadays, it is difficult for people to be prosecuted for **political speech** that expresses their viewpoints about government and public affairs. By contrast, **commercial speech** may be subject to greater regulation because of concerns about protecting the public from misleading advertisements and other harms.

pathways profile
MARY BETH TINKER

In 1965, Mary Beth Tinker, a 13-year-old student at Harding Junior High School in Des Moines, Iowa, wore a black armband to school to express her opposition to the Vietnam War. She was suspended from school. Subsequently, her brother and several other students in Des Moines schools were also suspended for the same reason. Despite receiving numerous death threats, Tinker and the others continued to assert their right to peacefully express their views about a matter of public concern through the use of "symbolic speech" (wearing a black armband). **Symbolic speech** occurs when people take an action designed to communicate an idea. With the help of lawyers from the American Civil Liberties Union, Tinker's case eventually reached the U.S. Supreme Court. In a 7–2 ruling, the Court decided that the Des Moines school

discussion questions

1. What restrictions on speech are permissible under the Supreme Court's interpretations of the First Amendment? Do you agree with these restrictions?

2. Should people be prosecuted for expressing their views about politics and public affairs? If so, under what circumstances should this occur?

what YOU can do!

Find out what restrictions and regulations exist concerning public protests in your community or on your campus. Look in your college's student handbook for rules for behavior. See if your community's municipal ordinances are available online. Are these regulations too restrictive? If you wanted to organize a public protest, would the regulations prevent you from doing so?

board had violated Tinker's First Amendment rights (*Tinker* v. *Des Moines Independent Community School District*, 1969).

Tinker later became a nurse at a Veterans Administration hospital. Although she opposed the Vietnam War, she considered it "a privilege to work with our veterans who have sacrificed part of their lives."[6] ■

How far has the Supreme Court moved in broadening the concept of freedom of speech? In 1989, the Court considered the case of Gregory Johnson, a protester at the 1984 Republican National Convention, who burned an American flag during a political demonstration. He was convicted under a Texas law prohibiting flag desecration. However, a five-justice majority on the U.S. Supreme Court overturned his conviction by declaring that burning the flag is symbolic speech, a protected form of political expression that falls within the coverage of the First Amendment (***Texas v. Johnson,*** 1989). In the words of Justice William Brennan, who wrote the majority opinion, "If there is a bedrock principle underlying the First Amendment, it is that the Government may not prohibit the expression of an idea simply because society finds the idea itself offensive or disagreeable." The Court's decision aroused anger in many segments of American society and spurred members of Congress to propose constitutional amendments to protect the flag. Despite the outcry, the Court's decision remains in place and demonstrates that protected speech has been defined broadly, even when it offends or angers many people.

There are several contexts in which the Supreme Court is more willing to permit government-imposed limitations on First Amendment rights. The Court accepts **reasonable time, place, and manner restrictions** on political assemblies—restrictions that affect the rights of both speech and assembly. Such restrictions were at issue in the legal challenge to the Crawford, Texas, ordinance discussed at the start of this chapter. Judges recognize that chaos and disruption could harm society if protesters could freely block roadways, jail entrances, hospital parking lots, and other locations in a community. However, this recognition does not give government officials the power to prohibit protests because they

The Ku Klux Klan is an organization founded after the Civil War to use violence to terrorize African Americans. As shown in the photo of a 1998 Klan demonstration in Texas, when the Klan holds protests today, the police must often protect their right to free speech by guarding them against attacks by counter-protesters who object to their philosophy of racial hatred. Do Klan members have the right to express their ideas, or should they be prohibited from using hate speech? What reasons would you give for prohibiting the use of hate speech?

▶ What about speech that offends or scares people—is that protected by the First Amendment?

hate speech
expressions that direct animosity toward individuals based on their race, gender, national origin, religion, sexual orientation, or other characteristic. Certain forms of hate speech may be regulated through the use of criminal laws.

fighting words doctrine
the U.S. Supreme Court's formulation of a justification for government regulation of expressions, such as personal insults, that are likely to provoke a fistfight or other immediate breach of the peace.

do not support the ideas being expressed. Instead, the government must demonstrate that important societal interests justify any regulations and that these restrictions strike an appropriate balance between protecting those interests and permitting people to express their views.

▶ **What about speech that offends or scares people—is that protected by the First Amendment?** A contemporary controversy concerns **hate speech,** the expression of ideas that cause hostility toward people because of their skin color, ethnicity, gender, religion, or other characteristic. Advocates of restrictions on hate speech argue that certain words and phrases serve to degrade, insult, and injure people in especially harmful ways because they perpetuate historic prejudices, harassment, and discrimination. These advocates have characterized hate speech as falling under the Supreme Court's **fighting words doctrine.** According to this doctrine, government can prohibit and prosecute expressions that constitute insults likely to provoke a fistfight or some other immediate breach of the peace. Courts have examined hate speech laws, as well as related forms of regulations such as public universities' conduct codes (which may include restrictions on students' expressions of hatred or prejudice). Although judges' decisions often support free speech, even when it is offensive, people may be convicted of violating such laws, especially if they do not possess sufficient resources to hire an attorney who will challenge the government through the entire course of the court pathway. In 2003, a Michigan State University student was convicted of misdemeanor harassment for posting a racially offensive flyer that portrayed stereotyped images of African Americans on a dormitory bulletin board.[7]

A U.S. Supreme Court decision on the issue concerned Virginia's law against the symbolic hate speech underlying the burning of crosses, a traditional form of intimidation used by the Ku Klux Klan and other groups that voice racial hatred (*Virginia v. Black*, 2003). The Court concluded that "the First Amendment permits Virginia to outlaw cross burnings done with the intent to intimidate." Thus certain forms and contexts of hate speech may be limited by government regulation.

practicequiz

1. Free speech and a free press, guaranteed by the First Amendment, are crucial to the healthy operation of any democracy.
   a. true   b. false

2. In 1919, Supreme Court Justice Oliver Wendell Holmes asserted that freedom of speech should be protected unless
   a. such speech represented a violation of a community's moral standards.
   b. such speech represented a clear and present danger to the public.
   c. such speech expressed deep disloyalty to the commander in chief.
   d. a and b.

3. Currently, regarding freedom of speech, the Supreme Court
   a. distinguishes between political speech and commercial speech.
   b. interprets the First Amendment as protecting symbolic speech, like flag burning.
   c. has been less inclined to protect commercial speech than political speech.
   d. a, b, and c.

4. To regulate free speech, the government must
   a. demonstrate that such regulation serves important societal interests.
   b. follow language used in the First Amendment.
   c. demonstrate that such regulation fairly balances societal interests and individuals' desires to express their views freely.
   d. a and c.

Answers: 1-a, 2-b, 3-d, 4-d.

FREEDOM OF THE PRESS

Like free speech, freedom of the press is guaranteed by the First Amendment's absolutist language, and Americans regard this freedom as an essential element of democracy. Voters need free-flowing, accurate information in order to evaluate their elected

prior restraint
government prohibition or prevention of the publication of information or viewpoints. Since its decision in *Near* v. *Minnesota* (1931), the U.S. Supreme Court has generally forbidden prior restraint as a violation of the First Amendment freedom of the press.

New York Times Company v. United States (1971)
U.S. Supreme Court decision prohibiting prior restraint of the Pentagon Papers, thus permitting major newspapers to publish information on the Vietnam War that the government had sought to keep secret.

leaders. They have little hope of using democratic processes to hold their leaders accountable or to elect new legislators and executive officials unless they have access to information about what is happening in the world. In countries where national leaders closely control the news media, the people seldom have opportunities to use democratic processes to select new leaders.

The Supreme Court issued a strong statement against **prior restraint** of publications that criticize public officials in *Near* v. *Minnesota* (1931). Prior restraint is the government's attempt to prevent certain information or viewpoints from being published. In the *Near* case, the Supreme Court struck down a state law intended to prevent the publication of articles or editorials that used inflammatory language to criticize government officials. As a result, the government generally cannot prevent articles from being published. However, the principle of no prior restraint does *not* prevent authors and publishers from later being sued for the publication of false or misleading information that harms people's reputations. The Court's decision established the basic presumption that the government will not censor the news media, except perhaps in the most extreme circumstances.

In 1971, the Supreme Court faced a case that raised the issue of prior restraint when the federal government claimed that the publication by newspapers of a top-secret internal Defense Department study concerning the Vietnam War would seriously damage national security. The so-called Pentagon Papers had been given to the *New York Times* and the *Washington Post* by Daniel Ellsberg, a Defense Department analyst who had concluded that the public needed more information about what was really happening in the war, even though he was legally forbidden to make the information available. When the newspapers began to publish this book-length document, under the title *History of the U.S. Decision-Making Process on Vietnam Policy,* the government sought a court order to stop the newspapers. The two newspapers in question, arguably the nation's most prominent at that time, had the money and legal expertise to battle the government on equal terms in the court pathway. The Supreme Court heard the case on an accelerated basis and issued a quick decision in which the majority declared that the

newspapers could continue to publish the report (***New York Times Company* v. *United States*,** 1971). Three justices adopted the absolutist position that the First Amendment bars *all* prior restraint by the government, and three additional justices decided that the government had not adequately proved that publication of the report would actually harm national security.[8] The decision reaffirmed the prevailing presumption against prior restraint of news publications and demonstrated that many judges would require exceptionally compelling proof of harm to society before permitting government censorship of publications about public affairs.

pathways past and present

SUPREME COURT WORKLOAD

As we saw in LINK *Chapter 4, pages 119–120,* the justices on the U.S. Supreme Court control the number of cases that they accept for argument. Few of the cases submitted to them are accepted. During the 1990s, the justices appeared to make a conscious effort to decide fewer cases, even though the number of cases presented to them continued to rise (see Table 5.1). Many observers believe that some of the justices want the court pathway

TABLE 5.1
Supreme Court Workload

Year	Total Cases on Docket	Cases Accepted for Oral Argument
1980	5,144	154
1990	6,316	125
1995	7,565	90
2000	8,965	86
2004	8,588	87

SOURCES: U.S. Census Bureau, *Statistical Abstract of the United States, 2006* (Washington, DC: U.S. Government Printing Office, 2006), tab. 324; Administrative Office of the U.S. Courts, *Judicial Business of the United States Courts, 2005* (Washington, DC: U.S. Government Printing Office, 2006), tab. A-1.

▶ **How do judges** decide whether something is obscene?

reporter's privilege
the asserted right of news reporters to promise confidentiality to their sources and to keep information obtained from sources, including evidence of criminal activity, secret. The U.S. Supreme Court has held that reporter's privilege does *not* fall within the First Amendment right to freedom of the press.

press shield law
statute establishing reporter's privilege. Such statutes exist in some states and have been proposed in Congress.

contempt of court
a finding made by a judge concerning an individual's disobedience of court rules or a judicial order. This can be a basis for sending individuals to jail without trial, as in the case of news reporters who refuse to provide information about criminal investigations.

Miller v. California (1973)
U.S. Supreme Court decision that provided the primary test for obscenity to determine what materials, especially pornography, can be regulated as outside of the protection of the First Amendment.

to be less influential and are intentionally limiting the number of issues in which they will use their judicial power.[9] ■

The interests of the press can clash with governmental priorities when reporters have information sought by the government and refuse to share it with prosecutors and other officials. Reporters claim that a free press can survive only if they can protect the identities of their sources of inside information. Otherwise people would not be willing to provide reporters with controversial and even potentially incriminating information about governmental activities and issues of public interest. Government officials argue in response that reporters, like other citizens, should be required to cooperate with criminal investigations to ensure that criminal enterprises are thwarted and that guilty people receive appropriate punishment.

Advocates for the news media feel that the First Amendment should be interpreted to recognize a **reporter's privilege,** which authorizes news agencies to decline to provide information requested by the government. Although some states have enacted **press shield laws** to protect reporters in state justice processes, the federal courts have refused to recognize a constitutional privilege to protect reporters nationwide. Thus reporters are occasionally jailed for **contempt of court** if they refuse to cooperate with criminal investigations. For example, in 2001, Vanessa Leggett, a freelance writer in Houston who was conducting research for a book on a controversial murder case, spent 168 days in jail for refusing to testify before a federal grand jury about her interviews with criminal suspects. She was released only when the grand jury ended its investigation.[10]

OBSCENITY

Judges face challenges in determining if expressions that offend the sensibilities of some community members fall under the protection of the First Amendment. In particular, legislators have regularly sought to prohibit or regulate material with sexual content,

such as books, magazines, live performances, films, and Web sites. The Supreme Court has said that anything that is "obscene" falls outside of the First Amendment and is not considered part of free expression. It has been very difficult, however, for the Court to provide a clear definition of the word *obscene.* This issue can cause major conflicts because images and performances that some people consider artistic expression can be regarded by others as harmful to the morals of society.

In the early twentieth century, people were regularly prosecuted in various communities for possessing or selling written materials or pictures with sexual content. James Joyce's novel *Ulysses,* published in France in 1922 and today regarded as one of the greatest works of modern literature, could not legally be printed, imported, or sold in the United States because it contained four-letter words and certain sexual allusions. Only in 1933 did a federal judge lift the ban after a leading American publisher brought a lawsuit challenging it.

In the 1950s, the Supreme Court developed a test for obscenity. Its initial efforts focused on whether the work in question was "utterly without redeeming social importance" (*Roth* v. *United States,* 1957). This test was refined as the Court's composition changed over the next two decades.

▶ **How do judges decide whether something is obscene?** In an important case challenging the prosecution of a man who mailed brochures that advertised sexually explicit books, the Supreme Court articulated a new test for obscenity. According to Chief Justice Warren Burger's opinion, materials that met the three-part test for obscenity could be prohibited by legislation and lead to prosecutions. The Court's test was stated as follows in ***Miller*** v. ***California*** (1973):

The basic guidelines for the trier of fact must be:
(a) whether the "average person, applying contemporary community standards" would find that the work, taken as a whole, appeals to the prurient interest; (b) whether the work depicts or describes, in a patently offensive way, sexual

discussion questions

1. What is prior restraint? Under what conditions, if any, do you believe it is appropriate?

2. What is obscenity? What kinds of images and other materials should be regulated for being obscene?

what YOU can do!

Go to the Web site of the Reporters Committee for Freedom of the Press, **http://www.rcfp.org** Read about the organization's efforts to encourage Congress to enact a law to create a reporter's privilege. Can you come up with counterarguments opposing the organization's position? Do you believe that protection for reporters is essential to the existence of a free press?

conduct specifically defined by the applicable state law; and (c) whether the work, taken as whole, lacks serious literary, artistic, political, or scientific value.

The test for obscenity is thus based on "community standards," and those standards change over time. For example, in the 1960s, actors portraying married couples in movies and on television were often shown sleeping in separate single beds, so as not to convey any sexual implications by having a double bed on the set. By contrast, today, scantily clad performers in sexy embraces and dance routines are everyday fare for music videos shown around the clock on cable channels. It seems clear that "community standards" regarding acceptable entertainment have changed over the years. Does this mean that "anything goes" in American entertainment media? No. The Federal Communications Commission (FCC) continues to regulate television and radio broadcasts, and it imposes fines for profanity and sexual content that it believes have gone too far. Broadcasting is subject to stricter government control than newspapers because the government has the power to regulate use of the public airwaves. The uproar over the momentary exposure of singer Janet Jackson's bare breast on television during the half-time show for the 2004 Super Bowl served as a reminder that there are still limits to expression, especially when that expression is broadcast to the televisions and radios of unwitting consumers who assume that certain standards are in place.

Obviously, a different situation exists for consumers who intentionally seek sexually explicit material in specific magazines or in the back room of their local DVD rental store. Generally, pornographic films and magazines that once would have led to prosecution in most communities are now widely available in the United States, without legal repercussions as long as the sellers and distributors of such materials take steps to keep such items away from children.

Indeed, except for content standards for broadcasts regulated by the FCC, most regulation of obscenity today focuses on the exposure of children to obscene material or their exploitation in its production. Laws impose prison sentences for the creation, dissemination, and possession of child pornography.

Howard Stern moved his show to satellite radio in 2006 in order to avoid government-imposed fines for broadcasting graphic sexual discussions. By moving his show to satellite radio, Stern now entertains only voluntary, paying customers and thereby moved himself outside the Federal Communication Commission's mandate to protect unsuspecting consumers. The Supreme Court has ruled that obscene material is not protected by the First Amendment and thus can be regulated by the government. What kinds of verbal expression do you think are outside the protections of the First Amendment?

LEFT: **Thomas Jefferson first used the words** "separation of church and state" in a letter he wrote in 1802, and this phrase has been argued about ever since. Controversies about the place of religion in American society and government regularly occur in the court pathway.

RIGHT: **A group of demonstrators protested in 2003** outside the Federal Court Building in Montgomery, Alabama, over a federal court order mandating the removal of the Ten Commandments monument from the State Judicial Building. If a city displayed quotations from the Bible on a large mural in city hall, do you think this should be regarded as violating the First Amendment? What if the quotations were from the religious books of another religion, such as Islam, or Judaism? Explain your answer.

practicequiz

1. The First Amendment addresses freedom of the press
   a. in broad and vague terms.
   b. in absolutist language.
   c. as a civil liberty that is much less important than freedom of religion.
   d. in ways that do not apply to today's society.

2. The Supreme Court's ruling that the *New York Times* acted within its legal rights in publishing the Pentagon Papers
   a. reinforced the traditional view that the First Amendment prohibits all prior restraint by the government.
   b. revealed the conservative bias of the Court.
   c. suggested that judges needed little proof of harm to society before allowing government censorship of publications about public affairs.
   d. a and c.

3. What are press shield laws?
   a. laws that shield judges from the scrutiny of the press
   b. state laws that protect journalists from governmental censorship
   c. state laws that protect journalists from having to provide confidential information requested by the government
   d. a and c

establishment clause
clause in the First Amendment guarantee-ing freedom from religion by providing the basis for Supreme Court decisions limiting government support for and endorsement of particular religions.

free exercise clause
clause in the First Amendment guarantee-ing freedom to practice one's religion without government interference as long as those practices do not harm other indi-viduals or society.

LEFT: **Some Christians believe that judges** and other public officials discriminate against their religion by banning nativity scenes in pub-lic areas and by preventing teacher-led prayers in public schools.

RIGHT: **Protesters against the removal of a** Ten Commandments monument in Texas hold a prayer vigil in front of the Supreme Court. How has the Supreme Court been inconsistent in its decisions on this subject?

4. The Supreme Court uses the community standards of the time as one of the measures by which public material can be deemed "obscene" and its purveyors legally prosecuted. This means that legal standards for obscenity have changed markedly over time.
   a. true   **b.** false

Answers: 1-b, 2-a, 3-c, 4-a.

FREEDOM OF RELIGION

Religious liberty is the very first right protected by the Constitution's First Amendment: "Congress shall make no law respecting an establishment of religion, or prohibiting the free exercise thereof." The amendment's first section, called the **establishment clause,** concerns the connections between govern-ment and religion. The establishment clause can be characterized as providing "freedom *from* religion." The second section, the **free exercise clause,** focuses on people's ability to practice their reli-gion without governmental interference. This clause provides "freedom *of* religion." Both aspects of religious freedom have been the subject of significant litigation because individuals and

► **How does the Supreme Court decide cases that involve religion?**

separationist
interpretive approach to the establishment clause of the First Amendment, which requires the clause a "wall of separation" between church and state.

accommodationist
interpretive approach to the establishment clause of the First Amendment that would permit the government to provide financial support for certain religious institutions and programs or sponsor specific religious practices, such as prayer in public schools.

In 1962, the Supreme Court decided that teachers could not lead public school students in prayer because such actions violate the First Amendment as an improper "establishment of religion" by government. As a result of the Supreme Court's decision, students in public schools can bow their heads individually in prayer or meet before school for a student-led prayer. However, school officials are not supposed to be involved. Why did this Supreme Court decision generate so much controversy?

interest groups have used the court pathway to challenge governmental actions as violating the First Amendment.

Agreement is widespread that the establishment clause forbids the designation or sponsorship by government of a national religion. Many people describe this clause as mandating "the separation of church and state." However, significant disagreements exist about what connections between religion and government are permitted by the First Amendment. Under a strict **separationist** view, government must avoid contacts with religion, especially those that lead to government support or endorsement of religious activities. This perspective argues that the government cannot provide financial support for religious schools, display religious documents in public buildings, or permit Christian displays in public parks or public schools during the Christmas season. Advocates of this viewpoint see such actions as implying governmental favoritism or endorsement of one religion over others—or of religion itself. Because conflict between religious groups is often a source of division in religiously diverse societies, a democratic government that seeks to represent the interests of all people should avoid any affiliation with particular religions.

By contrast, the **accommodationist** view would permit the government to provide support for religion and associated activities. Advocates of this perspective argue that the government can give financial support to religious schools for the nonreligious aspects of education (for example, reading, math, and science) that are provided in those schools. Some—but not all—accommodationists also support the practice of teachers leading prayers in public schools, although they would usually accept an opportunity for nonbelievers or members of minority religions to leave the room during such activities.

During the 1960s, the Supreme Court issued two controversial decisions that tilted toward the strict separationist perspective. In *Engel* v. *Vitale* (1962), the Court found a violation of the establishment clause in the common public school practice of beginning the day with a prayer—in this case, a generic prayer that had been jointly developed by Protestants, Catholics, and Jews on a statewide school board: "Almighty God, we acknowledge our dependence upon Thee, and we beg Thy blessings upon us, our parents, our teachers, and our country."[11] Although the prayer was designed to avoid offending any religion, several parents used the court pathway to challenge the constitutionality of the practice. The parents included people who represented various religious and philosophical perspectives, including atheists. According to

Lemon test
a three-part test for establishment clause violations deriving from the U.S. Supreme Court's decision in *Lemon v. Kurtzman* (1971) that examines whether government policies or practices provide support for religion or cause an excessive entanglement between government and religion.

what YOU can do!

Find out if there are any restrictions that might hinder a small or unpopular religious group from holding meetings at your college. What if the group wanted to practice animal sacrifice or ingest hallucinogenic substances as part of a religious ceremony on your campus?

Justice Hugo Black's majority opinion, "When the power, prestige, and financial support of government is placed behind a particular religious belief, the indirect coercive pressure upon religious minorities to conform to the prevailing officially approved religion is plain."[12] By declaring that a long-standing practice provided improper government endorsement and pressure on behalf of religious belief, the Supreme Court generated a storm of controversy that still continues.

A second decision that barred public schools from reading the Lord's Prayer and Bible verses over its public address system reinforced accommodationists' unhappiness with the Supreme Court (*School District of Abington Township, Pennsylvania v. Schempp*, 1963). Although many Americans wonder whether such governmental practices actually cause any harm, the Supreme Court has been sensitive to the concern that nonbelievers or members of minority religions, especially children, will feel pressured to participate or will be ostracized by others if they decline to participate.

In the years following these decisions, critics complained that the Supreme Court had "improperly removed God from the schools" and thereby reduced morality and social order in society. Some state legislatures responded by enacting statutes that challenged the Court's decision through various means, such as mandating the public display of the Ten Commandments in schools, the teaching of Bible-based creationism in public school science classes, and student-led school prayers or moments of silence. Some of these practices were also initiated by local school officials who objected to the Supreme Court's decisions. Such practices were challenged in the court pathway by parents who viewed gov-

ernment-sponsored religious activities as inconsistent with civil liberties under the establishment clause.

▶ **How does the Supreme Court decide cases that involve religion?** In deciding cases concerning establishment clause issues, the Supreme Court has usually instructed judges to follow the so-called *Lemon* **test,** a standard developed in a case in 1971 (*Lemon* v. *Kurtzman*). Under this test, a court is to ask three questions about any governmental practice challenged through the court pathway as a violation of the establishment clause (see Table 5.2):

1. Does the law or practice have a secular (nonreligious) purpose?
2. Does the primary intent or effect of the law either advance or inhibit religion?
3. Does the law or practice create an excessive entanglement of government and religion?

If a law or government practice flunks any of the three questions, the law or practice violates the establishment clause and is unconstitutional. The Supreme Court has used the test to invalidate programs that provided public support for religious schools (*Grand Rapids* v. *Ball*, 1985), school-sponsored benediction prayers at public school graduation ceremonies (*Lee* v. *Weisman*, 1992), and mandatory instruction in "creation science" as an alternative to evolutionary theory in high school science classes (*Edwards* v. *Aguillard*, 1987).

Although the *Lemon* test has provided the primary guidance for judges in these cases since 1971, several justices on the Supreme Court have harshly criticized the test and sought to replace it with an accommodationist perspective. These critics, including the late Chief Justice William Rehnquist and Justices Antonin Scalia and Clarence Thomas, may have come close to eliminating the test in the case

TABLE 5.2
Two Pillars of Religious Freedom

"Congress shall make no law respecting an establishment of religion, or prohibiting the free exercise thereof."

ESTABLISHMENT CLAUSE	FREE EXERCISE CLAUSE
Prohibits:	Protects:
1) the establishment of a national religion by Congress	1) the freedom to believe
2) government support for or preference of one religion over another or of religion over non-religious philosophies in general	2) the freedom to worship and otherwise act in accordance with religious beliefs
Everson v. Board of Education, 1947	*Hamilton v. University of California*, 1934
	Cantwell v. Connecticut, 1940

West Virginia v. Barnette (1943)
U.S. Supreme Court decision protecting First Amendment free exercise rights by prohibiting schools from punishing children who, for religious reasons, decline to recite the Pledge of Allegiance.

compelling government interest
the demonstration of necessity that the government must provide to justify interference with fundamental rights—the central element of a strict scrutiny standard for examining the existence of rights violations.

Jose Luiz DeOliveira of Brazil and fellow church members stand before the Supreme Court in 2005 to discuss his group's claim in the court pathway that the federal government violates the First Amendment by preventing them from drinking hallucinogenic tea from South America as part of their religious practices. In 2006, the U.S. Supreme Court declared that it agreed with the group's arguments. Should people be allowed to endanger themselves during religious services by, for example, handling poisonous snakes or injecting themselves with heroin? When should government regulation of religious practices be regarded as violating the First Amendment?

concerning school graduation prayers (*Lee* v. *Weisman,* 1992). The justices originally voted 5–4 to permit such prayers, but during the process of drafting opinions, Justice Anthony Kennedy changed his mind and provided the decisive fifth vote for the justices who declared that the practice was unconstitutional.[13] Justice Kennedy's opinion echoed the logic of the *Engel* school prayer case thirty years earlier:

> [There is] public pressure, as well as peer pressure, on attending students to stand as a group or, at least maintain respectful silence during the Invocation and Benediction. . . . But for the dissenter of high school age, who has a reasonable perception that she is being forced by the State to pray in a manner her conscience will not allow, the injury is no less real.

On a single day in 2005, the Court issued two establishment clause decisions that highlighted the difficulties experienced by the justices in attempting to interpret the First Amendment in a clear, consistent manner. In *McCreary County* v. *ACLU* (2005), a majority of justices applied the *Lemon* test to rule that copies of the Ten Commandments could not be posted in Kentucky courthouses. However, a different combination of justices declared that the *Lemon* test need not apply when they formed a majority in *Van Orden* v. *Perry* (2005) to permit Texas to keep a Ten Commandments monument on the state capitol grounds amid a variety of other monuments. The justices regarded the two situations as distinctively different because the courthouses displayed only the religious documents, whereas Texas mixed the religious monument with other cultural and patriotic symbols. These decisions create uncertainty about how the Court will decide individual cases in the future and whether the *Lemon* test will eventually be abandoned. The appointment of new justices, including Chief Justice John Roberts and Justice Samuel Alito in 2005, could eventually change the Court's decisions if new justices do not endorse and apply the *Lemon* test in the same manner as their predecessors.

The free exercise clause concerns individuals' right to engage in religious practices and follow their beliefs without governmental interference. Several of the important cases that expanded civil liberties in this area were pursued through the court pathway by Jehovah's Witnesses. Just prior to World War II, the Supreme Court ruled that public schools could punish Jehovah's Witness students for refusing to salute the flag and recite the Pledge of Allegiance, even though the students claimed that it violated their religious beliefs if they were required to salute anything other than God (*Minersville School District* v. *Gobitis,* 1940). Shortly afterward, several justices had second thoughts about the issue, and the

strict scrutiny
an exacting test for violations of fundamental rights by requiring the government to demonstrate a compelling interest when policies and practices clash with certain constitutional rights.

Court reversed itself in ***West Virginia v. Barnette*** (1943). The appointment of several new justices after the *Gobitis* decision also contributed to the 8–1 decision in *Barnette*. Justice Robert Jackson's opinion contained a lofty statement about the importance of freedom of thought and religious belief:

> If there is any fixed star in our constitutional constellation, it is that no official, high or petty, can prescribe what shall be orthodox in politics, nationalism, religion, or other matters of opinion or force citizens to confess by word or act their faith therein.

This does not mean, however, that the free exercise clause provides an absolute right to do anything in the name of religion. For example, if a person believed that his religion demanded that he engage in human sacrifice or cannibalism, the Supreme Court would permit legislation to outlaw such practices. In 1990, an opinion written by Justice Antonin Scalia declared that the "right to free exercise of religion does not relieve an individual of the obligation to comply with a 'valid and neutral law of general applicability'" (*Employment Division of Oregon v. Smith*). In that case, Native American counselors lost their jobs and were denied unemployment compensation after ingesting peyote, a natural hallucinogenic drug, as a part of their culture's traditional religious ceremonies. Many members of Congress, however, want judges to look carefully at which laws will be permitted to override religious practices so that religion does not yield to every law passed by a legislature. They have passed statutes seeking to require that the free exercise of religion take precedence over all laws except those supported by a **compelling government interest.** In effect, these legislators want judges to apply a kind of analysis called **strict scrutiny** to free exercise of religion cases. This analysis places the burden on the government to demonstrate the necessity of a specific law in order to outweigh an individual's desire to engage in a religious practice. The most recent statute mandating this test is the Religious Land Use and Institutionalized Persons Act (2000), which requires the compelling government interest test for two kinds of free exercise situations: churches' efforts to avoid zoning and other property restrictions and access to worship materials and services for institutionalized convicted offenders and mental patients. A related law, the Religious Freedom Restoration Act, which applies only to actions by the federal government, was used by the Supreme Court in 2006 when it found government objections to be insufficiently compelling and thereby permitted a small religious sect to follow its traditional religious practices by ingesting tea containing a hallucinogenic, controlled substance from South America (*Gonzales v. O Centro Espirita Benficiente Unaio do Vegetal*, 2006).

ABOVE: **Football players at Odessa High School,** a public school in Texas, pray before a game. Even when such prayer sessions comply with Supreme Court rulings by being student-led and not involving coaches or teachers, critics complain that young people feel pressured to participate for fear of being rejected by teammates and coaches. What arguments can be made for prohibiting all prayers at public schools? Would such a prohibition violate students' right to free exercise of religion?

BELOW: **Prison officials in some states** permit churches to run programs that use religion to help prisoners rehabilitate themselves. Because prisons are government institutions, these programs raise concerns about whether prisoners are being pressured to follow the religious practices of a specific church. If you were a judge, how could you be sure that prisoners were voluntarily participating in religious programs and not responding to pressure from prison officials?

There are often apparent conflicts between civil liberties protected under the establishment clause and those protected by the free exercise clause. For example, some critics argue that the Court's establishment clause decisions barring sponsored prayers in public schools effectively violate the free exercise rights of students who wish to pray. However, the apparent clash with free exercise of religion is less substantial than it may appear because the Court has never barred individual students from bowing their heads in prayer in public schools. The prohibition concerns prayers sponsored by school officials that are thought to risk coercing or isolating members of minority religions and nonbelievers. In some schools, students acted on their opposition to the Court's decisions by organizing their own prayers every morning around the school flagpole or in a hallway. The Court has not ruled against student-organized and student-led prayers in public schools, except when those prayers are conducted in a manner that implies sponsorship by school officials, such as a student reading a prayer over the stadium public address system prior to high school football games (*Santa Fe Independent School District* v. *Doe*, 2000).

practicequiz

1. The establishment clause in the First Amendment
   a. gives citizens freedom *from* religion.
   b. is relevant to some school prayer cases.
   c. means that we can practice any religion we want without governmental interference.
   d. a and b.

2. The teaching of creationism in public schools can be viewed as a violation of the establishment clause because
   a. creationism isn't accepted as non-religious science.
   b. creationism implicitly promotes a Judeo-Christian worldview.
   c. creationism contradicts the worldview of the framers of the Constitution.
   d. a and b.

3. As currently interpreted by the Supreme Court, the First Amendment's free exercise clause grants citizens the right to practice any sort of religion they want,
   a. provided that such practices do not "offend the community standards" of the time.
   b. provided that the participants can prove these practices to be a "long-standing component of a genuine religious ceremony."
   c. provided that such practices do not violate "a valid and neutral law of general applicability," such as the laws forbidding murder or the use of illegal drugs.
   d. a, b, and c.

4. Arguing that the prohibition against prayer in public school violates an individual's constitutional rights
   a. is unconvincing because school prayer violates the establishment clause only when such prayer is being endorsed by the school (by having a teacher lead the prayers, for instance).
   b. suggests the inconsistencies of the First Amendment.
   c. shows how easily different civil liberties can come into conflict.
   d. a, b, and c.

Answers: 1-d, 2-b, 3-c, 4-a.

Civil Liberties and Criminal Justice

Several amendments in the Bill of Rights describe protections afforded people who are subject to police investigations, prosecutions, sentencing, and criminal punishment. The protections described in these amendments do not merely safeguard civil liberties for people who have committed crimes. These amendments are designed to protect everyone in the United States, including innocent people, from excessive actions by overzealous law enforcement officials who are seeking to prevent and solve crimes.

THE RIGHT TO BEAR ARMS

The Second Amendment contains words about "the right of the people to keep and bear arms." Although this amendment is not always regarded as concerning criminal justice, many Americans see a connection between firearm ownership and criminal justice, in two ways. First, people can be prosecuted and sentenced to prison for possessing, carrying, or selling firearms in violation of local, state, or federal laws. And second, advocates of a right to bear arms argue that strong Second Amendment rights are necessary for citizens to protect themselves against criminals.

The Second Amendment is a source of controversy. People interpret its words in quite different ways, and the contemporary U.S. Supreme Court has avoided making a definitive statement about the amendment's precise meaning. The words of the amendment are

discussionquestions

1. What are the strict separationist and accommodationist perspectives? Which approach is closest to your viewpoint?

2. Why has the Supreme Court barred sponsored prayers in public schools? Do you think that this ban is justified? Why or why not?

problematic because in one single sentence, without separable, freestanding clauses, the Second Amendment mentions "a well-regulated Militia" and "the right of the people to keep and bear arms." The amendment says, "*A well-regulated Militia, being necessary for the security of a free State, the right of the people to keep and bear Arms, shall not be infringed.*" Most scholars interpret the amendment as guaranteeing states' ability to arm their state militias, known today as the National Guard. Scholars point to the U.S. Supreme Court's decision in *United States* v. *Miller* (1939), which makes reference to the amendment's focus on the militia. The Supreme Court has never treated the final part of the amendment as a separate clause that provides individual citizens with a right to own guns. In recent years, one U.S. Court of Appeals in Louisiana interpreted the Second Amendment as providing a personal right for individuals (*United States* v. *Emerson,* 5th Circuit, 2001), but a U.S. Court of Appeals in California reached a different conclusion and said that the amendment only concerns maintaining an armed state militia (*Silviera* v. *Lockyer,* 9th Circuit, 2002). Many gun rights advocates wish the Supreme Court would settle these differing interpretations by declaring once and for all that the Second Amendment creates an entitlement for individual citizens to own guns. However, only one justice, Clarence Thomas, has expressed an interest in having the Supreme Court become involved in the heated controversy over the Second Amendment's meaning.

It should be noted that because the Supreme Court has never incorporated the Second Amendment, the amendment does not prevent cities and states from enacting their own gun control laws (see Figure 5.2 on page 182). States' ability to regulate firearms may be limited by provisions similar to the Second Amendment that exist in their own state constitutions. In light of current understandings of the meaning of this amendment, Congress can also enact gun control legislation that limits individuals' ability to sell or transport firearms. Because of effective activity in the lobbying pathway by interest groups, especially the National Rifle Association, the ability of adults without criminal records to own firearms appears to be a secure political privilege even if the U.S. Supreme Court never declares it to be a constitutional right.

SEARCH AND SEIZURE

The Fourth Amendment is focused on protecting people against improper searches and seizures. In the words of the amendment:

> The right of the people to be secure in their persons,
> houses, papers, and effects, against unreasonable searches

HUMAN BEINGS UNDERSTAND REASON, COMPASSION, DIGNITY

PREDATORS UNDERSTAND STRENGTH

Interest groups use advertising to persuade the public to support their interpretations of the Second Amendment. Those who see the Amendment as guaranteeing a right for individuals to own firearms design advertisements to emphasize that good citizens are vulnerable to victimization by criminals. The opposing side emphasizes the risks from freely available guns falling into the wrong hands. If you were on the Supreme Court, how would you interpret the words of the Second Amendment?

▶ **It sounds as if** all these protections make it harder for police to do their job—so why do we have them?

exclusionary rule
general principle that evidence obtained illegally, including through the violation of Fourth Amendment rights, cannot be used against a defendant in a criminal prosecution. The Supreme Court has allowed certain exceptions to the rule that permit the use of improperly obtained evidence in particular circumstances.

Mapp v. Ohio (1961)
U.S. Supreme Court decision that applied the exclusionary rule to state criminal justice cases.

FIGURE 5.2
Gun Laws in the United States

The Second Amendment is about "the right of the people to keep and bear arms." But because the Supreme Court has never incorporated the Second Amendment, the amendment does not prevent cities and states from enacting their own gun laws. The result can be seen on this map, which shows the many different restrictions and requirements set by states for the purchase, ownership, and right to carry guns, rifles, and shotguns.

SOURCE: www.nra.com

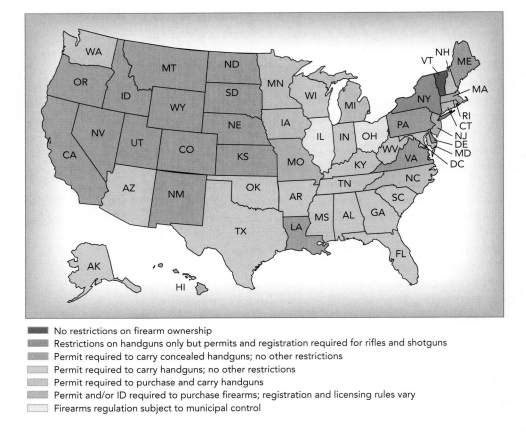

■ No restrictions on firearm ownership
■ Restrictions on handguns only but permits and registration required for rifles and shotguns
■ Permit required to carry concealed handguns; no other restrictions
■ Permit required to carry handguns; no other restrictions
■ Permit required to purchase and carry handguns
■ Permit and/or ID required to purchase firearms; registration and licensing rules vary
□ Firearms regulation subject to municipal control

and seizures, shall not be violated, and no Warrants shall issue, but upon probable cause, supported by Oath or affirmation, and particularly describing the place to be searched, and the persons or things to be seized.

The two key parts of the amendment are the prohibition on "unreasonable searches and seizures" and the requirements for obtaining search and arrest warrants. Like other provisions of the Constitution, the Fourth Amendment contains inherently ambiguous language that must be interpreted by judges. The word *seizure,* for example, includes arrests when people are taken into police custody (that is, seizures of people), as well as situations in which officers seize property that may be evidence of criminal

wrongdoing. But how do you know whether a search or seizure is "unreasonable"? Clearly, such a determination is a matter of judgment, and all people will not agree about whether specific actions are "searches" or whether they are "unreasonable."

▶ **It sounds as if all these protections make it harder for police to do their job—so why do we have them?** The U.S. Supreme Court endorsed the application of the **exclusionary rule** in *Weeks* v. *United States* (1914). Under this rule, evidence that is obtained improperly by the police cannot be used to prosecute someone accused of a crime. The intent of the rule is to stop police from undertaking illegal searches or improperly questioning suspects and to remedy the violation of suspects' civil liberties. At first, the rule applied only against federal law enforcement officials, such as FBI

agents, but the Supreme Court, in the famous case of *Mapp* v. *Ohio* (1961), subsequently applied it to all police officers throughout the country. The *Mapp* decision provoked a storm of controversy and has led to decades of debate about whether the exclusionary rule reflects an appropriate interpretation of the Constitution. Critics claim that the rule improperly "ties the hands of the police" and lets guilty people go free due to honest errors by law enforcement officials. Social science research shows that the rule does benefit some guilty people, but it affects the outcomes of only a small percentage of cases.[14]

As Republican presidents appointed new justices in the 1970s and 1980s who interpreted civil liberties under the Bill of Rights in a narrower manner, Chief Justice Warren Burger (1969–1986) was able to lead the changing Court toward creating limitations on and exceptions to the exclusionary rule. The rule went from being a broad, clear restriction on police after *Mapp* v. *Ohio* to one with many situational exceptions. The limitations on the exclusionary rule now in effect include the following:

- The prosecution may use evidence obtained through certain kinds of improper questioning if the questioning was conducted in the midst of a situation that threatened "public safety" (*New York* v. *Quarles*, 1984).

- The prosecution may use improperly obtained evidence if it would have been "inevitably discovered" by the police later through the use of a legal search (*Nix* v. *Williams*, 1984).

- The prosecution may use evidence obtained through the use of an improper search warrant if a judge made an error in issuing the warrant and the police honestly, albeit mistakenly, believed that they had sufficient evidence to justify a warrant (*United States* v. *Leon*, 1984).

- Improperly obtained evidence may be used in nontrial proceedings, such as grand jury hearings that determine whether someone will be charged with a crime and parole revocation hearings that determine whether an offender who has been released should be returned to prison for misconduct. (*Pennsylvania Board of Pardons and Parole* v. *Scott*, 1998)

Chief Justice Burger never succeeded in eliminating the exclusionary rule. The rule still applies in many situations, but law enforcement officers now have greater leeway to make errors in

ABOVE: **In 2005, the New York City police** increasingly searched the bags and packages of subway riders in order to reduce the threat of a terrorist attack. In the court pathway, the Supreme Court has interpreted the Fourth Amendment to require a balance between protecting the individual's right against unreasonable searches and the need for government officials to maintain safety and security. When your bag is searched at an airport, concert, or stadium, do you feel that your privacy rights under the Fourth Amendment have been violated?

BELOW: **News reports in 2006** revealed that the federal government undertook secret monitoring of Americans' telephone calls and financial transactions without judicial authorization as part of its anti-terrorism efforts. At Senate hearings on the issue, senators grilled Attorney General Alberto Gonzales on the legality of such actions. The hearings showed that the elections and lobbying pathways can also provide a basis for action in response to civil liberties controversies. In what ways might the government's war against terrorism be leading to an erosion of Americans' civil liberties?

▶ **Do the police have** the power to stop and search you or your car if they don't have a warrant?

warrant
a judicial order authorizing a search or arrest. Under the Fourth Amendment, police and prosecutors must present sufficient evidence to constitute "probable cause" in order to obtain a warrant from a judge.

double jeopardy
being tried twice for the same crime, a practice prohibited by the Fifth Amendment.

compelled self-incrimination
being forced through physical abuse or other coercion to provide testimony against oneself in a criminal case, a practice that is prohibited by the Fifth Amendment.

Miranda v. Arizona (1966)
U.S. Supreme Court decision that requires police officers, before questioning a suspect in custody, to inform that suspect about the right to remain silent and the right to have a lawyer present during custodial questioning.

conducting searches and questioning suspects without automatically facing the exclusion of evidence.

▶ **Do the police have the power to stop and search you or your car if they don't have a warrant?** With respect to a **warrant,** which is an order from judges authorizing a search or an arrest, the Fourth Amendment specifically requires the police and prosecutor to show the judge sufficient reliable information to establish "probable cause" about the location of evidence or a person's criminal behavior. Other searches conducted without warrants are governed only by the prohibition on "unreasonable searches and seizures." The Supreme Court has identified specific situations in which warrants are not required because these searches are reasonable. Permissible warrantless searches include the following:

- "Stop and frisk" searches of a suspect's outer clothing on the streets when officers have a reasonable basis to suspect that a person is involved in criminal behavior and potentially poses a danger to the public (*Terry* v. *Ohio,* 1968)

- "Exigent circumstances" in which an immediate warrantless search must be undertaken because of danger to the public or the possible loss of evidence (*Cupp* v. *Murphy,* 1973)

- Searches of a suspect at the scene of the suspect's arrest in order to make sure that the suspect does not have a weapon and that no evidence will be lost (*Chimel* v. *California,* 1969)

- Automobile searches done without warrants so that the vehicles do not drive away with the evidence, although the officer must have a justification for searching each portion of the automobile and its contents (for example, *California* v. *Acevedo,* 1991)

- Searches based on "special needs" beyond the normal purposes of law enforcement, such as luggage searches at airports, searches at national border-crossing points, drug tests of high school student athletes and certain government employees, and police roadblocks serving as sobriety checkpoints to identify drunk drivers (for example, *Michigan Department of State Police* v. *Sitz,* 1990)

The creation of these categories of warrantless searches demonstrates how judges' decisions in the court pathway define rights and clarify the authority of law enforcement officials. As the United States develops homeland security policies in response to the terrorist attacks of September 11, 2001, new cases will arise that test the government's authority to conduct searches and surveillance, including warrantless monitoring of telephone calls, a practice expanded under the administration of President George W. Bush.

SELF-INCRIMINATION

The Fifth Amendment describes several rights related to criminal justice, including the concept of **double jeopardy,** which refers to the protection against being tried twice for the same crime. Many controversial cases arise concerning another protection: the privilege against **compelled self-incrimination.** In the words of the amendment, no person may be "compelled in any criminal case to be a witness against himself." This does not mean that people cannot provide evidence against themselves. During questioning, criminal suspects can fully confess or provide police with partial details about their involvement in crimes. However, they cannot be *compelled* to provide statements that will be used against them. For their incriminating statements to be used by the prosecution, the statements must be made *voluntarily.* The police cannot use threats of violence or actual violence to obtain confessions.

If the individual is not free to walk away from police questioning, the police must make it clear that the person has a right to remain silent and to have an attorney present during questioning. The latter requirement emerged from the Supreme Court's famous and controversial decision in *Miranda* **v.** *Arizona* (1966). Television programs with crime themes regularly show police officers reading people their "*Miranda* rights":

> You have the right to remain silent. Anything that you say can be used against you in a court of law. You have the right to have an attorney present during questioning. If you cannot afford an attorney, one will be appointed to represent you.

Recognize that police are required to inform people of their *Miranda* rights only if they are in police custody and are not free to walk away, such as people who have been arrested. When police question people on the streets or people come to the police station voluntarily, the police do not have to inform them of their rights. The primary exception to this rule concerns motorists stopped for traffic violations who are not free to drive away; the

discussionquestions

1. What is the exclusionary rule? Is it essential to the preservation of rights, or does it unnecessarily interfere with police officers' work?

2. When can police undertake searches without a warrant? Is the search authority possessed by police too broad, or do search rules provide sufficient protection for people's rights?

police can ask them questions without informing them about their *Miranda* rights.

When the Supreme Court announced its decision in the *Miranda* case, many critics complained that the Court had extended Fifth Amendment rights too far. They believed that many guilty people would go free by simply exercising the right to remain silent. Over time, the Court's decision became less controversial because police developed techniques to follow the *Miranda* rules while still eliciting incriminating information. These techniques include asking questions before making an arrest and pretending to befriend the suspect during questioning.[15] In addition, many suspects make incriminating statements despite being given *Miranda* warnings because they are seeking a favorable plea bargain, wish to pin the crime on an accomplice, feel frightened or overwhelmed with guilt, or simply do not listen closely to and think about the implications of the warnings.

practicequiz

1. The amendments in the Bill of Rights concerning criminal justice grant individuals protection from the potential excesses of law enforcement officials; they are meant to protect both people accused of a crime and people who are not.
   a. true   **b.** false

2. Today most legal scholars assert that the Second Amendment
   a. grants all citizens of the United States the right to own arms.
   b. guarantees each state the ability to arm its National Guard units.
   c. is one of the least important amendments in the Bill of Rights.
   d. a and b.

3. Why is the right to bear arms now a secure political privilege in this country?
   a. because of the Supreme Court's interpretation of the Second Amendment
   b. because the Second Amendment explicitly says as much
   c. because of intense and effective activity in the lobbying pathway
   d. a, b, and c.

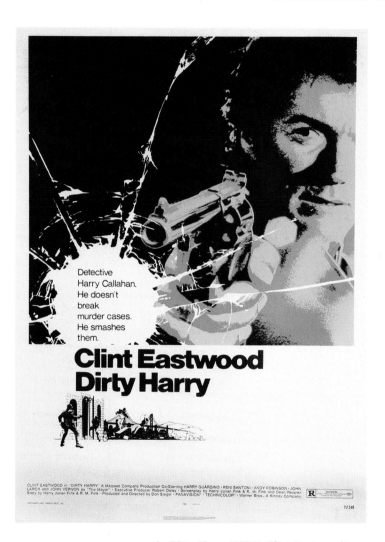

Detective Harry Callahan. He doesn't break murder cases. He smashes them.

Clint Eastwood Dirty Harry

CLINT EASTWOOD in "DIRTY HARRY" A Malpaso Company Production Co-Starring HARRY GUARDINO · RENI SANTONI · ANDY ROBINSON · JOHN LARCH and JOHN VERNON as "The Mayor" · Executive Producer Robert Daley · Screenplay by Harry Julian Fink & R. M. Fink and Dean Riesner · Story by Harry Julian Fink & R. M. Fink · Produced and Directed by Don Siegel · PANAVISION® · TECHNICOLOR® · Warner Bros., A Kinney Company.

In *Dirty Harry* (1971), Clint Eastwood portrayed a cop who throws away the rule book and uses raw violence to fight crime. The classic film is regarded as a criticism of the Supreme Court's expansion of rights for criminal suspects in *Miranda v. Arizona* (1966) and other cases from the court pathway. Do you believe that the Supreme Court's decisions have given criminal suspects too many rights? If so, which rights are too broad?

▶ Aren't there ways to
avoid a trial?

confrontation
right contained in the Sixth Amendment for criminal defendants to see their accusers in court and hear at first hand the accusations and evidence being presented against them.

compulsory process
a right contained in the Sixth Amendment to enable criminal defendants to use court orders to require witnesses to appear and to require the production of documents and other evidence.

speedy and public trial
a right contained in the Sixth Amendment to prevent indefinite pretrial detention and secret trials.

trial by jury
a right contained in the Sixth Amendment to have criminal guilt decided by a body of citizens drawn from the community.

4. Warrants, an extension of the Fourth Amendment's aim of protecting people against improper searches and seizures,
   a. are granted to law enforcement officials if they can demonstrate to a judge "probable cause" about a person's criminal behavior or the location of evidence.
   b. are not required in circumstances in which a delay in such a search or seizure would clearly jeopardize public safety.
   c. are required less often than they used to be.
   d. a, b, and c.

Answers: 1-a, 2-b, 3-c, 4-d.

TRIAL RIGHTS

▶ **Aren't there ways to avoid a trial?** The Sixth Amendment contains a variety of legal protections for people who face a criminal trial:

> In all criminal prosecutions, the accused shall enjoy the right to a speedy and public trial, by an impartial jury of the State and district wherein the crime shall have been committed, which district shall have been previously ascertained by law, and to be informed of the nature and cause of the accusation; to be confronted with the witnesses against him; to have compulsory process for obtaining witnesses in his favor; and to have the Assistance of Counsel for his defence.

The rights to **confrontation** and **compulsory process** are considered essential to providing fair trials for criminal defendants. The right to confrontation permits the defendant to be present in the courtroom when the victim and other witnesses provide testimony about the defendant's alleged guilt. The entitlement to compulsory process permits the defendant to use the power of the court to require witnesses to appear at court and to obtain needed documents that might be relevant to the case. If defendants had no ability to compel others to appear and present testimony, they might have little hope of counteracting the evidence being presented against them by the prosecution.

The right to a **speedy and public trial** provides important protections for criminal defendants. Without a right to a public trial, it would be possible for the government to hold secret proceedings that prevent citizens from knowing whether evidence actually existed to prove a defendant's guilt. Under a system that permits secret trials, people can be convicted and sentenced without the government demonstrating that it is properly exercising its awesome powers to deprive people of their liberty through incarceration.

The right to a speedy trial prevents the government from ruining a person's life by holding charges over his or her head for an indefinite period of time. When people have been charged with a crime, they may lose their jobs or see their families disintegrate if they sit in jail awaiting trial. Even if they gain release on bail, they may be ostracized by the community and find it difficult to obtain employment. Thus the Sixth Amendment obligates the government to move forward in presenting its evidence of criminal activity. The Supreme Court has not provided a clear time limit for prosecutions; instead, judges must examine each case to make an individual determination about whether the speedy trial right has been violated. This determination must consider the length of the delay before trial and the reason for the delay. For example, was the delay caused by the prosecutor or by the defendant? It is not unusual for defendants to wait more than a year to go to trial on serious charges.

The right to **trial by jury** evolved in England more than seven centuries ago as there came to be less reliance on trial by combat and trial by ordeal as the means to determine criminal guilt. Before this, it was presumed that God would indicate an accused person's innocence by allowing him to win in a hand-to-hand combat with his accuser. Today, jury trials can be seen as the democratic component of the judicial process by permitting citizens to be involved in important decisions. Initially, the right to trial by jury applied only to federal cases, but the Supreme Court incorporated the right in 1968 and applied it to state proceedings (*Duncan* v. *Louisiana*).

Although dramatic scenes from jury trials are a central feature of television shows like *Law and Order,* in reality only about 10 percent of criminal convictions result from trials, and only half of those are the result of jury trials.[16] The other trials are **bench trials,** in which the verdict is determined by a judge without a jury. Defendants may request bench trials because they are afraid that jurors may be biased and emotional, especially if there are controversial charges involving sex offenses, guns, or drugs. The other 90 percent of criminal convictions are obtained through plea bargaining, a process approved by the Supreme Court in which prosecutors and defense attorneys negotiate a guilty plea in exchange for a less-than-maximum number of charges or a less severe sentence. Plea bargaining has become an essential way of disposing of the

what **YOU** can do!

Visit a local courthouse to observe the processing of criminal cases. As you watch preliminary hearings, pleas, trials, or sentencing, can you see evidence that rights contained in the Bill of Rights affect how cases are processed in court? And the next time you watch a TV show in which the police and prosecutors try to bring criminals to justice, keep an eye out for how the Bill of Rights guarantees of due process are being observed—or not observed.

bench trials
trials in which a judge presides and makes determinations of fact and law, including decisions about guilt, without a jury.

vast number of cases that would otherwise overwhelm the resources of the criminal justice system if they all proceeded to trial

The Sixth Amendment's exact words, "In all criminal prosecutions, the accused shall enjoy a right to . . . an impartial jury," have not been enforced by the Supreme Court. According to the Court, the right to a trial by jury applies only in cases concerning "serious offenses" that are punishable by six months or more in jail or prison (*Lewis* v. *United States,* 1996). For lesser crimes, the accused can be forced to accept a bench trial. Because jury trials are expensive and time-consuming, it appears that the Court's interpretation is designed to reduce the costs and administrative burdens that courts would otherwise face.

The right to counsel is an especially important part of the Sixth Amendment. As early as 1932, the Supreme Court recognized the value of this legal protection by requiring Alabama to provide attorneys for nine African American youths who had previously been convicted and sentenced to death. Their brief, attorneyless proceeding was based on rape accusations from two white women, one of whom later admitted that her charges were false (*Powell* v. *Alabama*). Many people in the North had regarded these death sentences as a reflection of extensive racial discrimination in the courts of southern states. Interest group lawyers volunteered to assist the youths, and large protest marches occurred in Washington, D.C., and elsewhere. Many observers see the Supreme Court's decision in this case as influenced by pressure from both the court pathway and the grassroots mobilization pathway.

After this, the Supreme Court required that the government provide attorneys for all indigent defendants facing serious criminal charges in federal court (*Johnson* v. *Zerbst,* 1938) and state courts (*Gideon* v. *Wainwright,* 1963). Indigent defendants are people who do not have enough money to hire their own attorneys. If people have sufficient funds, they are expected to hire an attorney, and the Sixth Amendment right merely means that the government cannot prevent them from seeking legal advice.

pathways profile

CLARENCE EARL GIDEON

Clarence Earl Gideon (1910–1972) was a convicted burglar and thief who spent much of his life in and out of jails and prisons. Despite being a grade school dropout, Gideon initiated the

Michael Jackson enters the courtroom during his 2005 trial on child molestation charges. Because of his wealth, Jackson was able to make full use of his Sixth Amendment trial rights. He had the resources to hire an expensive legal team that could fully challenge the prosecution's case. Ultimately, the jury found Jackson not guilty of the charges. If you were charged with a crime and faced a criminal trial, would you prefer to trust your fate to the decision of a jury, or a judge? Why?

▶ **Is the electric chair** cruel and unusual punishment for a murderer?

capital punishment
a criminal punishment, otherwise known as the *death penalty,* in which a person is subject to execution after conviction. Reserved for the most serious offenses.

bifurcated proceedings
the division of capital punishment trials into two separate parts: an initial trial to determine guilt, followed by a separate hearing focused entirely on the question of whether the convicted individual will be sent to prison or executed.

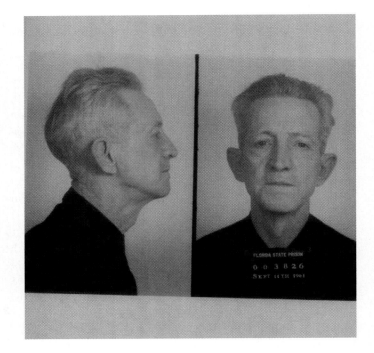

LEFT: **Hurricane Katrina** wrecked the courthouses in New Orleans in 2005. Here evidence for pending criminal cases was severely damaged by flood waters that reached the courthouse. Poor defendants who could not afford to obtain release on bail were trapped in flooded jail cells for several days. They remained in jail for extended time periods because their cases were delayed due to a lack of available attorneys and courtrooms. How could we reform our justice system to ensure that poor defendants receive proper representation by defense attorneys and the complete benefits of constitutional rights?

RIGHT: **Despite a lack of formal education,** Clarence Earl Gideon earned a place in the history of American civil liberties by doggedly pursuing his case through the court pathway. Today thousands of prisoners with little education continue to file cases concerning constitutional rights, but very few of them are able to effectively present proper issues that will be considered by the Supreme Court. If you were in prison, how would you initiate a case in the court pathway?

court case that led the Supreme Court to incorporate the Sixth Amendment right to counsel. After being denied his request for appointed counsel, Gideon defended himself in court—unsuccessfully—against charges of breaking into a Panama City, Florida, pool hall. While sitting in his prison cell, Gideon carefully wrote out a petition to the U.S. Supreme Court asserting the claim that the right to counsel should apply to the states. The Supreme Court accepted the case and appointed a prominent attorney and future Supreme Court justice, Abe Fortas, to present arguments on Gideon's behalf. Although most states already provided attorneys for indigent defendants when Gideon's case was decided in 1963, his effort helped ensure nationwide coverage for the Sixth Amendment right. Gideon's case also showed that it is possible, in some cases, for penniless people to initiate change through the court pathway—provided that judges and attorneys are prepared to consider the case at the moment that it is brought to their attention.

Gideon's success in the Supreme Court did not automatically set him free. However, he was granted a new trial, this time represented by an attorney. In the second trial, Gideon was acquitted

For nearly all executions in the United States, the condemned prisoner is strapped down and a lethal series of chemicals are injected into the offender's veins as news reporters and family members watch through a glass window. Interest groups opposed to the death penalty use the court pathway to claim that lethal injection violates the Eighth Amendment prohibition on cruel and unusual punishments. The U.S. Supreme Court has yet to rule on the issue. Will an adverse judicial decision end capital punishment? Why or why not?

because the lawyer's preparation and questioning of witnesses revealed evidence pointing to the man who had testified against Gideon at the original trial as the actual perpetrator of the offense. After his acquittal, Gideon apparently stayed out of trouble, remarried, and lived quietly until his death in 1972. ■

The right to counsel for indigents was expanded to all cases in which the potential punishment involves incarceration, even a short stay in jail (*Argersinger* v. *Hamlin,* 1972), as well as initial appeals (*Ross* v. *Moffitt,* 1974). There are many kinds of cases, however, for which indigent people are not automatically entitled to have an attorney provided by the government: appeals to state supreme courts, petitions to the U.S. Supreme Court, civil lawsuits between private individuals, and civil rights lawsuits by people against the government.

CAPITAL PUNISHMENT

▶ **Is the electric chair cruel and unusual punishment for a murderer?** The Constitution also provides rights for people who have been convicted of crimes, including those who have committed the very worst crimes, such as multiple murders. The Constitution does not require people to forfeit all of their rights if they violate society's rules. The words of the Eighth Amendment include a prohibition of "cruel and unusual punishments." This clearly implies that there is some limitation on the government's ability to punish. Criminal sanctions must not violate this provision, either by being

similar to torture or by being disproportionate to the underlying crime. To illustrate the point, burning an offender at the stake, in the manner that offenders were punished in Europe centuries ago, would today be found to be torture. Sentencing someone to death for having a parking ticket would certainly be disproportionate for the offense. In its practical application, the Eighth Amendment applies to a variety of contemporary contexts, such as the denial of medical care for prisoners or the administration of beatings to people serving short sentences in jail. The Supreme Court has said that the phrase "cruel and unusual punishments" must be defined according to society's contemporary standards, and thus the meaning of the phrase changes as society's values change (*Trop* v. *Dulles,* 1958).

An important battleground for the meaning of the Eighth Amendment has been cases concerning **capital punishment** that are appealed through the court pathway.[17] In 1972, the Supreme Court ruled that the death penalty was unconstitutional as it was then being administered (*Furman* v. *Georgia*). Some justices thought that the death penalty is unconstitutional because it should be regarded as "cruel and unusual" according to the values of contemporary civilization. Other justices believed that the punishment was applied too inconsistently and unfairly, and thus they saw it as violating the Fourteenth Amendment right to due process. The death penalty was reinstated in 1976 after the latter group of justices became persuaded that states had adopted fairer procedures for administering capital punishment cases (*Gregg* v. *Georgia*) (see Figure 5.3 on page 190). The special procedures for death penalty cases include **bifurcated proceedings** (separate

▶ **Where in the Constitution**
do you find the right
to privacy?

FIGURE 5.3
Executions by State

The number of executions carried out in a state does not depend on the number of people murdered or the murder rate in the state. The frequency of executions is determined by the political culture in that state and the values and beliefs of politicians and the public. Thus the cultural change pathway may ultimately play an important role in determining whether the use of captial punishment expands or shrinks. How might political values explain the relatively large number of executions in Southern states and the small number of executions in California, a large state with many murders?

SOURCE: www.deathpenaltyinfo.org

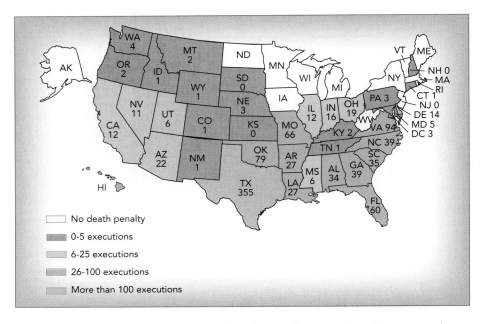

No death penalty
0-5 executions
6-25 executions
26-100 executions
More than 100 executions

trials to determine guilt and to decide on the appropriate sentence). In addition, judges and juries look specifically for "aggravating factors" that make a particular crime or offender worse than others, such as a murder by a repeat offender or a killing in the course of committing another felony. They also weigh "mitigating factors," such as the offender's age or mental problems, which might make an offender less deserving of the death penalty.

The death penalty raises important policy issues concerning the appropriate punishments for people who commit murders, acts of terrorism, and other crimes that society considers the most harmful. The weight of scholarly evidence suggests that the death penalty does not deter crime.[18] The prospect of possible execution does not scare people away from committing serious criminal acts, in part because many people are not thinking rationally when they commit murders and also because murderers usually do not believe that they will be caught. Advocates of the death penalty argue that only the ultimate punishment can satisfy victims and survivors and show how strongly society disapproves of the worst crimes. Yet many states have discovered significant problems with the accuracy of their legal proceedings. Between 1973 and 2006, a total of 123 people condemned to death in the United States were later released from prison when it was discovered that they were actually innocent.[19] Some of these people were exonerated through the use of DNA testing that showed that physical evidence related to the crime had not been adequately analyzed. Most innocent people were convicted because they had incompetent defense attorneys, because jailhouse informants provided false testimony, or for other reasons that cannot always be accurately identified and corrected. We do not know how many other innocent people may be on death row, and debates therefore continue about whether the American legal system is capable of imposing capital punishment accurately and fairly.

Because the Supreme Court has addressed so many issues concerning capital punishment, the court pathway has significantly shaped public policy (see Pathways figure on pages 196–197). For example, the justices have forbidden states from executing mentally retarded murderers (*Atkins* v. *Virginia*, 2002) and individuals who committed serious crimes before having reached the age of 18 (*Roper* v. *Simmons*, 2005). A majority of justices on the Court views such executions as violating the prohibition on cruel and unusual punishments by being out of step with contemporary values.

The Court refused, however, to recognize statistical evidence showing that racial discrimination affects decisions about which offenders will be sentenced to death (*McCleskey* v. *Kemp*, 1987). Social scientists found, through studying more than 2,000 cases in Georgia, that people accused of killing whites are much more likely to be sentenced to death than people accused of killing members of minority groups, especially if the accused killers are African Americans. Had it accepted the statistical evidence, the Court might have found that capital punishment violates the Fourteenth Amendment's equal protection clause. Instead, the justices said that proof of discrimination must stem from officials' actions in a specific case and not from statistical analyses of an entire state's legal system.

right to privacy
a constitutional right created and expanded in U.S. Supreme Court decisions concerning access to contraceptives, abortion, private sexual behavior, and other matters, although the word *privacy* itself does not appear in the Constitution.

discussionquestions

1. In what cases is an indigent defendant entitled to have an attorney provided by the government? Why might this right provide insufficient protection for defendants?

2. Has the Supreme Court imposed too many limitations on capital punishment? Explain your answer.

practicequiz

1. The rights to confrontation and compulsory process, as spelled out in the Sixth Amendment, refer, respectively, to
   a. a defendant's right to be present in a court of law when someone testifies against him or her and a defendant's right to require witnesses and documents to appear in court if they are relevant to the case.
   b. a defendant's right to a speedy trial and a defendant's right to a trial by jury.
   c. a defendant's right to a public trial and a defendant's right to plea bargain.
   d. a and c.

2. According to the Supreme Court's interpretation of the Sixth Amendment, a "speedy trial," to which all defendants are entitled, means
   a. a trial within one month of the arrest or indictment.
   b. a trial within one year of the arrest or indictment.
   c. a trial without too many long speeches or long recesses.
   d. a trial within an unspecified amount of time.

3. The Supreme Court has enforced the Sixth Amendment's statement, "In all criminal prosecutions, the accused shall enjoy a right to . . . an impartial jury."
   a. true   b. false

4. The Eighth Amendment protects all criminals against "cruel and unusual punishments." This means that prisoners
   a. cannot be tortured.
   b. must receive punishment in proportion to their crime.
   c. must receive punishment that, in its intensity, meets society's contemporary moral standards.
   d. a, b, and c.

Answers: 1-a, 2-d, 3-b, 4-d.

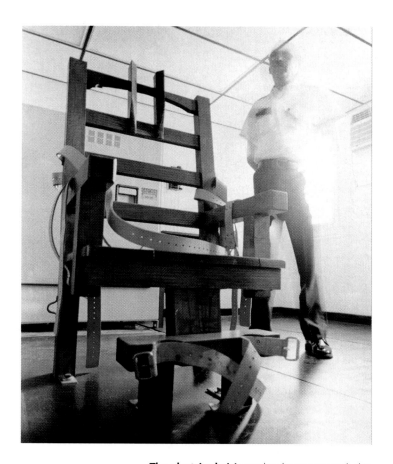

The electric chair's use has been suspended in Florida since March of 1997. Governor Chiles announced Friday, Oct. 31, 1997, that he would continue suspension of its use until lawmakers have an opportunity to act on legislation that creates an alternative form of execution, a proposal suggested by the state's supreme court to avoid further legal challenges. The state now uses lethal injection for execution. Do you think execution itself is a form of cruel and unusual punishment?

Privacy

▶ **Where in the Constitution do you find the right to privacy?**
The word *privacy* does not appear in the Constitution. The Supreme Court has nevertheless used its interpretive powers to recognize a **right to privacy** that protects people from government interference in a number of contexts. The justices first explicitly recognized a right to privacy in 1965. In this case, Connecticut had a statute that made it a crime to sell, possess, use, or counsel the use of contraceptives. A doctor was convicted for providing information about contraceptives to a married couple. After the law was challenged in the court pathway, the Supreme Court struck it down (*Griswold* v. *Connecticut*, 1965). The majority opinion by Justice William O. Douglas concluded that a right to

▶ **Why is it, when someone is nominated for the Supreme Court, everyone talks about their stand on abortion?**

Roe v. Wade (1973) controversial U.S. Supreme Court decision, which declared that women have a constitutional right to choose to terminate a pregnancy in the first six months following conception.

Justice William O. Douglas (1898-1980) served on the U.S. Supreme Court for thirty-six years (1939-1975), a longer period than any other justice in history. His most ontroversial opinion came in *Griswold v. Connecticut* (1965), in which he explained the Supreme Court's recognition of a constitutional right to privacy, even though the word "privacy" does not appear in the Bill of Rights. The Supreme Court still faces privacy issues in the court pathway. Should a right of choice concerning abortion be considered as a part of a constitutional right to privacy? Why or why not?

privacy exists as an unstated element of several rights in the Bill of Rights: the First Amendment right to freedom of association, the Third Amendment protection against the government housing troops in private homes, the Fourth Amendment protection against unreasonable searches, and the Fifth Amendment privilege against compelled self-incrimination. Douglas wrote:

> The present case . . . concerns a relationship lying within the zone of privacy created by several fundamental constitutional guarantees. . . . Would we allow the police to search the sacred precincts of marital bedrooms for telltale signs of the use of contraceptives? The very idea is repulsive to the notions of privacy surrounding the marriage relationship.

Critics complained that the Court's decision created a new constitutional right that was not grounded in the Bill of Rights. In the words of Justice Hugo Black's dissenting opinion, "I like my privacy as well as the next [person], but I am nevertheless compelled to admit that government has a right to invade it unless prohibited by some specific constitutional provision." Critics feared from this that a five-member majority on the Supreme Court could invent any new rights that the justices wanted to impose on society, whether or not those rights were intended by the words or history of the Constitution. By contrast, defenders of the flexible approach to constitutional interpretation claimed that the Court is obligated to adjust the Constitution's meaning to make sure that it remains consistent with the changing problems, values, and needs of American society. In subsequent cases, the Court's flexible approach to constitutional interpretation led to the application of a right to privacy to new situations.

ABORTION

In Ⓛ Ⓘ Ⓝ Ⓚ *Chapter 1, pages 21–23*, we noted that the issue of abortion has generated activity in several pathway of politics. The recognition of a right to privacy in the court-centered pathway helped trigger later activity in other pathways. In 1969, two young lawyers in Texas, Linda Coffee and Sarah Weddington, met a woman who claimed that she had become pregnant as the result of being raped. Because Texas, like other states, made abortion a crime, the woman could not legally terminate the pregnancy (see Figure 5.4). Although the woman gave birth to the baby, she wanted to use her case to challenge the Texas statute through the court pathway. The lawyers took the case, ***Roe v. Wade,*** all the way to the U.S. Supreme Court. ("Jane Roe" was not the woman's real name, but it was used in the case to protect her privacy.) Her lawyers argued that the Texas statute violated the woman's right to make choices about abortion.

FIGURE 5.4

Data on Abortion

Some aspects of abortion have changed since *Roe* v. *Wade* in 1973, but public opinion on the question has held steady for 30 years.

In 1973, after the Supreme Court heard arguments from lawyers on both sides of the issue, the justices voted 7–2 to declare that the Texas statute violated the Constitution. According to Justice Harry Blackmun's majority opinion:

> The Court has recognized that a right of personal privacy, or a guarantee of certain areas or zones of privacy, does exist under the Constitution. . . . This right of privacy, whether it be founded in the Fourteenth Amendment's concept of personal liberty and restrictions upon state action, as we feel it is, or as the District Court determined, in the Ninth Amendment's reservation of rights to the people, is broad enough to encompass a woman's decision whether or not to terminate her pregnancy.

Several state legislatures sought to counteract the Court's decision by enacting statutes that make it more difficult to obtain abortions by specifying expensive medical procedures and other matters during the second trimester. In addition, abortion opponents in Congress fought against the Court's decision by using their authority to limit public funding for abortion. Initially, the Court struck down several of these restrictive state laws. Later, however, as new justices were appointed, the Court became more flexible about accepting regulations.

▶ **Why is it, when someone is nominated for the Supreme Court, everyone talks about their stand on abortion?** Abortion became a central consideration in the appointment of newcomers to the Supreme Court as justices retired from the bench. Interest groups representing abortion opponents lobbied presidents and senators and sought to arouse public opinion in support of their position; so did pro-choice groups. Advocates on both sides sought to influence the composition of the nation's highest court. Presidents Ronald Reagan (1981–1989) and George H. W. Bush (1989–1993) vowed to use their appointment powers to put new justices on the Court who would work to overturn the right of choice established in *Roe* v. *Wade*. Thus the stage seemed set for a reconsideration of *Roe* v. *Wade* when the case known as *Planned Parenthood* v. *Casey* (1992) reached the Court.

Pennsylvania had enacted statutes requiring that doctors provide women seeking abortions with detailed information about fetal development, mandating a twenty-four hour waiting period before a woman could proceed with an abortion, and specifying that minors obtain parental consent and that married women notify their spouses before obtaining an abortion. These regulations were challenged in the court pathway as interfering with women's right to make choices about their own health care. In 1992, only one member of *Roe*'s

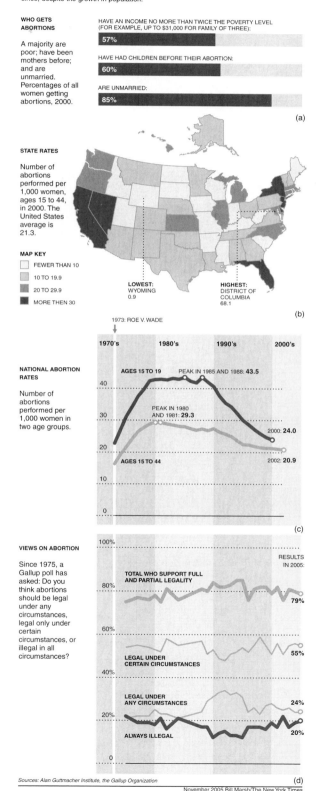

ABOVE: **Thousands of anti-abortion protesters** gathered in Washington, D.C. in 2006 to mark the thirty-third anniversary of *Roe v. Wade* (1973), the Supreme Court's decision that established a constitutional right of choice for abortion. They displayed piles of plastic fetuses to graphically convey their view that abortion kills people.

BELOW: **Both opponents and supporters** of abortion rights use the grassroots mobilization, elections, and lobbying decision-makers pathways as well as the court pathway. If you chose to become involved in actions to influence the abortion issue, which pathway would you recommend for your allies to use?

seven-member majority, Justice Blackmun, remained on the Court to defend that decision. However, in a ruling that surprised observers, three appointees of Presidents Reagan and Bush joined in writing an opinion that preserved the right of choice originally created by *Roe*. Justices Sandra Day O'Connor, Anthony Kennedy, and David Souter believed that a decision to overturn *Roe* after nearly twenty years would cause "profound and unnecessary damage to the Court's legitimacy, and to the Nation's commitment to the rule of law" by making it appear as if the right of choice disappeared merely because the Court's composition changed. Justice Blackmun, a Nixon appointee, and Justice John Paul Stevens, an appointee of President Gerald Ford, also voted to keep the *Roe* precedent. The four other justices, including Rehnquist and White, opposed the *Roe* decision. Thus by a 5–4 vote, the Court approved most of Pennsylvania's regulations but preserved the essence of the right of choice by declining to overturn *Roe*. The majority supporting the preservation of *Roe* later increased to six justices when President Bill Clinton appointed Justice Ruth Bader Ginsburg upon the retirement of Justice Byron White in 1993.

Modest changes in the Court's composition could eventually eliminate the 1973 precedent. Chief Justice John Roberts's appointment in 2005 upon the death of Chief Justice William Rehnquist was expected to preserve one of the existing votes against *Roe*. The announcement in 2005 of Justice O'Connor's planned retirement raised the possibility that her replacement might eventually provide an additional vote against *Roe v. Wade*. Indeed, President George W. Bush's chosen successor for O'Connor, Justice Samuel Alito, had previously developed antiabortion arguments as a government attorney. If, as predicted, Alito opposes *Roe*, then one more retirement from among the *Roe* supporters could set the stage for the elimination of the controversial precedent.

Although some people erroneously hope—or fear—that legal abortion will disappear if *Roe* is eliminated, in reality the Court's decision merely tells states what laws they *cannot* create. Overturning *Roe* would permit states to prohibit or severely restrict abortion. Some will choose to do so, but other states are likely to preserve the opportunity for women to terminate their pregnancies legally. Thus abortion is likely to remain legal in some places in the United States even if it is no longer recognized by the Supreme Court as a constitutional right. As a result, the debates and political battles about abortion may ultimately have direct effects on only two groups of women: those who are either too poor or too young to travel to a state where abortion is legal, safe, and available.[20]

Lawrence v. Texas (2003)
U.S. Supreme Court decision invalidating state laws regulating consenting, noncommercial, private sexual conduct between adults as violations of the constitutional right to privacy. Many such laws had been enforced against gays and lesbians.

discussionquestions

1. How did the Supreme Court derive the right to privacy from the words of the Constitution? Do you agree with the Court's decision recognizing a right to privacy?

2. How did the Supreme Court majority's perspective on the right to privacy change from *Bowers v. Hardwick* (1986) to *Lawrence v. Texas* (2003)? Do you think this change was appropriate, or has the Court extended the right of privacy too far?

PRIVATE SEXUAL CONDUCT

Griswold v. *Connecticut* (1965), the case that produced the Supreme Court's first explicit recognition of a constitutional right to privacy, concerned married couples' personal lives. The public did not generally object to recognizing a right to privacy in this context. By contrast, the private sexual conduct of nonmarried adults can produce controversy because the American public does not share a consensus about all aspects of morality.

In *Bowers v. Hardwick* (1986), a homosexual man in Georgia was charged with violating the state's sodomy law—which mandated sentences of up to twenty years in prison for sexual conduct other than intercourse between a man and a woman—when a police officer entered his home and found him in a bedroom having sex with another man. The Supreme Court was deeply divided on the question of whether the right to privacy should protect the private sexual behavior of homosexuals. The five-member majority of the Court treated the case as if it only concerned, in Justice Byron White's words, "whether the Federal Constitution confers a fundamental right upon homosexuals to engage in sodomy." To that question, the majority answered no. By contrast, the four dissenters, who argued that the law was unconstitutional, viewed the Georgia law as making a general attack on privacy. According to Justice Harry Blackmun's dissenting opinion:

> This case is about "the most comprehensive of rights and the right most valued by civilized men," namely "the right to be let alone." The statute at issue denies individuals the right to decide for themselves whether to engage in particular forms of private, consensual sexual activity.

Seventeen years later, the Supreme Court revisited the issue in **Lawrence v. Texas** (2003), a case challenging the constitutionality of a Texas statute that criminalized sexual conduct between persons of the same gender. This time, however, the majority on the Supreme Court overruled *Bowers* v. *Hardwick* and declared that the right to privacy protects the private, noncommercial sexual conduct of adults, including homosexuals. In the words of Justice Anthony Kennedy's majority opinion:

> The petitioners are entitled to respect for their private lives. The State cannot demean their existence or control their destiny by making their private sexual conduct a crime. Their right to liberty under the Due Process Clause gives

them the full right to engage in their conduct without intervention by the government.

As you learned in (LINK) *Chapter 4, pages 144–145,* there are vigorous debates about how far judges should go in shaping public policy by using their interpretive authority to recognize new rights and expand existing rights. Do you believe that the Supreme Court has gone too far in identifying and defining the right to privacy? Some people are concerned that judges will do whatever they want to do in creating new rights and affecting public policy. Because of new technology as well as increased governmental surveillance efforts related to computer crime, Internet child pornography, and the war on terrorism, additional privacy issues are likely to emerge concerning government intrusion into e-mail, computer systems, and wireless communications. It remains to be seen whether or how the Court will define privacy protections in these contexts.

practicequiz

1. Although the Supreme Court has clearly established that all Americans have a right to privacy, no such right is spelled out in the Constitution.
   a. true
   b. false

2. In *Roe v. Wade,* the Supreme Court majority opinion
   a. cited the Fourteenth Amendment's "concept of personal liberty and restrictions upon state action" in its decision to decriminalize abortion.
   b. found abortion to be "a criminal act in its violation of society's contemporary moral standards."
   c. asserted that the right of privacy was "broad enough to encompass a woman's decision whether or not to terminate her pregnancy."
   d. a and c.

3. The case of *Griswold* v. *Connecticut*
   a. concerned the personal lives of a gay couple.
   b. generated the Supreme Court's first explicit recognition of a constitutional right to privacy.
   c. outraged many Americans.
   d. a, b, and c.

4. The history of U.S. court decisions shows that how judges interpret laws, including the Constitution, can have the effect of
   a. shaping public policy.
   b. undermining basic democratic principles.
   c. legislating from the bench.
   d. a, b, and c.

Answers: 1-a, 2-d, 3-b, 4-a.

pathways | Capital Punishment and the Courts

 COURTS   ELECTIONS  GRASSROOTS MOBILIZATION  LOBBYING DECISION-MAKERS

PRO-DEATH PENALTY

1976
Gregg v. Georgia
The death penalty is reactivated after approving Georgia's revised procedures for trying and sentencing accused murderers. The new procedures include a trial to determine guilt and then a separate hearing to consider the death penalty. Six justices conclude that the new procedures resolve the previous problems with inconsistent and arbitrary application of capital punishment.

1988
Anti-Drug Abuse Act
Congress makes capital punishment a penalty for murders committed as part of drug trafficking.

1989
Stanford v. Kentucky
Supreme Court upholds capital punishment for juveniles who are 16 or 17 at the time that they commit murders.

1987
McCleskey v. Kemp
The court rules that statistics cannot be used to prove that the death penalty violates the equal protection clause of the Fourteenth Amendment.

1989
Penry v. Lynaugh
Supreme Court upholds capital punishment for mentally retarded murderers.

1970   1980   1990

ANTI-DEATH PENALTY

1989
Fierro v. Gomez
U.S. Court of Appeals declares the gas chamber a violation of the Eighth Amendment.

1986
Ford v. Wainwright
The Supreme Court rules that the death penalty cannot be applied to insane people.

1972
Furman v. Georgia
The Supreme Court hears three capital punishment cases as a group. These cases are pursued by interest group lawyers for the NAACP Legal Defense Fund. Two cases concern interracial rapes in Georgia and Texas and the other concerns a murder in Georgia. The death penalty is temporarily halted when five of the Court's nine justices agree that the punishment is applied inconsistently and arbitrarily.

1976
Roberts v. Louisiana
State laws making the death penalty mandatory for first-degree murder are declared unconstitutional by the U.S. Supreme Court. Each case must be decided on an individual basis.

Capital Punishment, Courts, and Reactions to Court Decisions: The Varied Pathways of Policy Change

Debates about capital punishment continue to rage, just as they have since the 1960s. Opponents of capital punishment have had limited success using the election pathway. Instead, they have focused their efforts on the court pathway. Beginning in 1972, anti-capital punishment interest groups succeeded in persuading some justices on the Supreme Court that the death penalty can violate the Constitution's requirements concerning due process and the prohibition on cruel and unusual punishment. Supporters of the death penalty used the elections and lobbying pathways to push revisions of state capital punishment laws that would satisfy the concerns of most Supreme Court justices, and thus the death penalty was reinstated in 1976. Since the 1970s, the court pathway has brought mixed results for capital punishment opponents. Although they failed to win a major case on racial discrimination in 1987, their litigation efforts eliminated the punishment for mentally retarded (2002) and juvenile offenders (2005). At the same time, highly publicized cases of innocent people being convicted and later released from death row helped spur grassroots mobilization and indications of cultural change, as well as pardons and moratoriums announced by governors. However, the fear of crime and attacks of 9/11 may have solidified public support for the death penalty in specific cases, such as convicted terrorists and serial killers.

essayquestions

1. Many observers expect the Supreme Court to turn its attention to the question of whether it is "cruel and unusual" to execute murderers suffering from mental illnesses. Imagine that you are a lawyer. Choose a side—for or against—and create arguments concerning this issue.

2. Several states are attempting to create more careful processes that will guard against the risk that innocent people will be convicted of murders and sentenced to death. Create three suggestions for ways to reduce the risk of mistakes in murder trials. Explain how your suggestions will improve the process.

2000

2000

New Hampshire state legislature votes to abolish the death penalty but the bill is vetoed by the governor.

1997

The American Bar Association passes a resolution requesting all death penalty jurisdictions to place a moratorium on executions until they confirm their systems are not flawed.

2002

Atkins v. Virginia

Supreme Court rules the execution of mentally retarded individuals violates the Eighth Amendment.

2005

Stanley "Tookie" Williams is put to death by lethal injection in California. Grassroots organizations on both sides of the divide agitate strenuously prior to Williams' death.

2006

New Jersey legislature enacts a moratorium on the death penalty. This act is in response to election year pressures.

2006

Advances in DNA testing and reinvestigation of cases since the mid-1970s lead to the release of 123 wrongly convicted murderers who had been sentenced to death.

2000

Governor George Ryan of Illinois places a moratorium on capital punishment when a media investigation discovered more than a dozen men on death row to be innocent. Opponents of the death penalty lobby Ryan for the moratorium.

2005

Roper v. Simmons

Supreme Court rules the execution of murderers who committed the crime while they were under the age of 18 is "cruel and unusual punishment."

Photo: Jim Wilson/The New York Times

Conclusion

Civil liberties are an especially important part of the governing system in the United States. They reflect the high value that the U.S. Constitution accords to personal liberty, individualism, and limited government. The Bill of Rights, as well as other provisions in the federal Constitution and the state constitutions, defines legal protections for individuals and at the same time imposes limitations on what government can do to individuals. The specific civil liberties enjoyed by individuals are defined and changed through decisions by judges that interpret constitutional provisions. As you saw with respect to the right to privacy, judges may use flexible approaches to interpretation that enable them to recognize new rights and expand or shrink existing rights.

The Supreme Court and other courts will face new issues that arise from changing developments in society, such as post-9/11 questions concerning whether suspected terrorists in government custody are entitled to the protections of the Bill of Rights and how far the government can go in conducting warrantless wiretaps of people suspected of being in contact with terrorist organizations. The ever-changing world in which we live continually produces conflicts between individuals and government that lead to intense battles in the court pathway. Judges are therefore likely to remain highly influential in determining aspects of public policy related to civil liberties issues.

The changing nature of civil liberties issues highlights the importance of the court pathway for shaping law and changing public policy. Litigants present their arguments in court in the hope of persuading judges to issue new decisions that revise the meaning of constitutional rights and advance specific policy goals. Because many of the issues carried forth in the court pathway are extremely controversial, such as school prayer, abortion, pornography, and the rights of gays and lesbians, individuals and groups who are disappointed by judges' decisions often raise questions about the extent of proper judicial authority and whether judges' decisions have "gone too far." These controversies have also made the process of nominating and confirming appointments to federal court positions, especially to the Supreme Court, a matter of high-stakes politics. Americans' lack of agreement about the meaning of the Bill of Rights guarantees that these debates will continue and that presidents will attempt to use their appointment powers in ways that seek to influence civil liberties cases through the selection of federal judges who share a particular president's values and beliefs.

YOUR turn!

The case mentioned in this chapter concerning student-led prayers at football games began with the actions of students. Students who are knowledgeable about First Amendment rights are well positioned to identify situations in which they believe that their rights or those of other students have been violated. Courts are passive institutions that do not actively jump into controversies. Thus civil liberties disputes receive attention in the court pathway only when knowledgeable citizens challenge laws through their actions or bring forward lawsuits that address important issues for society.

To learn about contemporary issues and viewpoints on civil liberties, examine the Web sites of two organizations that often use the court pathway to advance very different perspectives on civil liberties. Go to the Web site of the Pacific Justice Institute (**http://www.pacificjustice.org**) and compare its positions with those of the American Civil Liberties Union (**http://www.aclu.org**). What issues in your community or on your campus might be of interest to either of these organizations?

Chapter Review

1. Civil liberties, drawn from the Bill of Rights and judicial decisions, provide legal protections for individuals and limit the authority of government.

2. The Supreme Court originally applied the Bill of Rights only to protect individuals against the federal government, but through its incorporation of decisions interpreting the Fourteenth Amendment's due process clause, it was by the end of the 1960s applying most of those protections to the actions of state and local officials as well.

3. Americans consider the civil liberties contained in the First Amendment, which cover freedom of speech, press, assembly, and religion, essential to the maintenance of a democracy and a free society.

4. The actual protections for freedom of speech are less absolute than implied by the words of the First Amendment because the Supreme Court has accepted time, place, and manner restrictions and other limitations that serve society's interests for safety, order, and the protection of national

security, intellectual property, and personal reputations. Courts generally rule against government efforts to impose prior restraints on the press.

5. Freedom of the press claims by reporters can clash with other priorities, such as the government's need to gather evidence about witnesses and suspects in criminal cases.

6. The First Amendment does not protect obscenity, but the Supreme Court has struggled to develop a workable definition of what materials are "obscene." As a result, governmental prosecution of obscene material focuses primarily on child pornography, a subject on which a broader consensus about the harm from published materials exists.

7. Freedom of religion in the First Amendment consists of two components: the establishment clause and the free exercise clause. Judicial decisions concerning the establishment clause have forbidden sponsored prayers in public schools and other activities that are judged to provide excessive government support for or entanglement with religion.

8. Congress has sought to protect the free exercise of religion by requiring courts to apply a strict scrutiny test to such cases. This test forces the government to show a compelling reason for laws and politics that clash with the free exercise of religion.

9. The Fourth Amendment protection against unreasonable searches and seizures requires significant interpretation by courts, especially because so many different situations arise in which the government examines people and their property for evidence of crimes.

10. The Supreme Court has approved a list of situations in which no warrant is required for searches because such searches are regarded as "reasonable." Individuals subjected

to unreasonable searches may gain protection from prosecution through the exclusionary rule, but the Supreme Court has created exceptions to the rule that permit the use of improperly obtained evidence in some situations.

11. The Supreme Court's requirement of *Miranda* warnings prior to the questioning of suspects in custody serves as a central component of the Fifth Amendment privilege against compelled self-incrimination.

12. The Sixth Amendment contains trial rights, including the right to confrontation, the right to compulsory process, and the right to trial by jury. The right to trial by jury applies only for "serious" charges, and the right to counsel applies only for specific stages of the criminal process, from custodial questioning through criminal trials and the first appeal.

13. Capital punishment is a controversial issue that has divided the Supreme Court's justices over questions about whether it is "cruel and unusual" in violation of the Eighth Amendment. The Supreme Court's decisions have created rules and restrictions for the use of capital punishment.

14. The Supreme Court used its interpretive powers to identify and develop a right to privacy that has been applied to give individuals rights related to choices about abortion, contraceptives, and adults' private, noncommercial sexual conduct.

15. Flexible approaches to constitutional interpretation have triggered debates about whether judges have gone too far in shaping law and public policy and led to a general politicization of the process of appointing and confirming members of the federal judiciary, especially with respect to the Supreme Court.

CHAPTER REVIEW TEST

1. When reaching decisions about civil liberties, judges often need to
   a. think first about what would be the most practical outcome for society as a whole.
   b. remember that the Bill of Rights was written so long ago that its details are mostly not applicable to contemporary cases.
   c. balance the rights of individuals with the interests of society.
   d. b and c.

2. When court decisions define the protections of an individual's civil liberties—for example, when a judge decides that a Craw-

ford, Texas, ordinance limiting public demonstrations violates the First Amendment—those decisions
   a. cannot affect the authority that officials in other communities can wield.
   b. can affect the authority that officials in other communities can wield.
   c. almost always meet with public approval, since they reflect our society's tradition of embracing, with one mind, the ideals of the Bill of Rights.
   d. b and c.

3. Today, unlike a century ago, if you made a speech advocating a complete change in our form of government,
   a. you could not be prosecuted because such speech is protected under a broad interpretation of the First Amendment.
   b. your right to free speech, protected under the due process clause in the Fourteenth Amendment, would shield you from prosecution.
   c. you could be prosecuted for treasonous speech.
   d. a and b.

4. The Eighth Amendment's prohibition of "cruel and unusual punishments"
   a. has had no bearing on how the death penalty is applied in this country.
   b. has helped lawyers and death penalty opponents limit the forms and applications of capital punishment in this country.
   c. has remained a clear, unchanging standard by which judges handle the penalty phase in criminal trails.
   d. a and c.

5. "Preferred freedoms" refers to
   a. freedom of religion, speech, and press.
   b. freedom of religion and the right to bear arms.
   c. the rights listed first in the First Amendment.
   d. a and c.

6. The Supreme Court's rulings against the government's exercise of prior restraint means that
   a. the government typically cannot prevent even subversive or slanderous articles from being published.
   b. authors and publishers cannot be sued for publishing slanderous or inaccurate articles.
   c. citizens may say or do whatever they want but must be prepared to face the consequences.
   d. a and b.

7. What does the case that involved Vanessa Leggett illustrate?
   a. that shield laws protecting the confidentiality of journalists' sources do not exist at the federal level
   b. that it is against the law to reveal the identity of undercover CIA officers
   c. that reporters are sometimes jailed for contempt of court
   d. a and c

8. Strict separationists interpret the establishment clause as saying that the government cannot financially support or endorse any religion, even indirectly. This means that the government cannot offer aid to parochial schools, even for the teaching of nonreligious subject matter, nor can it permit religious displays in public parks or public schools.
   a. true   b. false

9. An accommodationist approach to the establishment clause
   a. has become more prevalent in recent years in the courts, including in the Supreme Court.

b. is at odds with the so-called *Lemon* test for governmental practices challenged for their violation of the establishment clause.
   c. approves of some forms of governmental support for religiously affiliated schools.
   d. a, b, and c.

10. Triggered by the rise of gun control legislation, the Supreme Court has since the 1990s issued several rulings regarding the meaning of the Second Amendment.
    a. true   b. false

11. The Supreme Court's exclusionary rule, an extension of the Fourth Amendment's prohibition of "unreasonable searches and seizures,"
    a. means that federal prosecutors cannot exclude evidence from a trial's proceedings, even if such evidence undermines their case.
    b. means that evidence improperly obtained by police cannot always be used to prosecute someone accused of a crime.
    c. has had the effect of benefiting some guilty people but not very many.
    d. b and c.

12. Law enforcement officials now
    a. have less latitude in how and when they conduct searches and question suspects than they did in the 1970s.
    b. have more latitude in how and when they conduct searches and question suspects than they did in the 1970s.
    c. enjoy immunity from the exclusionary rule.
    d. need warrants for only the most politically sensitive searches and seizures.

13. "*Miranda* rights"
    a. must be recited to suspects who appear voluntarily for questioning at a police station.
    b. have deeply compromised efforts to convict criminals apprehended through police action.
    c. help prevent suspects from feeling compelled to say anything that might incriminate them.
    d. are likely to be declared unconstitutional under the due process clause.

14. About half the criminal convictions in this country never reach a courtroom but are resolved through plea bargaining.
    a. true   b. false

15. The Supreme Court case of *Gideon* v. *Wainright*
    a. incorporated the Sixth Amendment right to counsel.
    b. demonstrated that a person with no money could genuinely change society through the court pathway.
    c. involved a convicted burglar with a long history of petty crime.
    d. a, b, and c.

16. The death penalty, reinstated in the United States in 1976, still strikes some people as unconstitutional because

   a. death penalty cases involve bifurcated proceedings

   b. convicts on death row are disproportionately racial minorities, a possible violation of the equal protection clause of the Fourteenth Amendment.

   c. mitigating factors, such the age or mental capacity of the accused, are not taken into consideration by the courts, making execution a cruel and unusual punishment.

   d. a, b, and c.

17. More than one hundred death row inmates have been exonerated through DNA testing and other sources of new evidence.

   a. true   **b.** false

18. The decision in *Roe* v. *Wade* and many other controversial Supreme Court decisions reflect a philosophy in the Court that it should

   a. ignore the wording of the Constitution and legislate from the bench, creating precedents that fit the needs of contemporary society.

   b. follow the literal meaning of the Constitution, irrespective of the emerging problems, values, and needs of contemporary American society.

   c. exercise a flexible approach to constitutional interpretation, adjusting the Constitution's meaning to fit the emerging problems, values, and needs of American society.

   d. a and b.

19. The process of nominating and confirming appointments for federal court positions, including those of the Supreme Court, has become a matter of high-stakes politics because

   a. everything in Washington these days boils down to the news media creating fictional controversies.

   b. many of the issues at play in the court pathway are controversial.

   c. federal judges have gained considerable authority over morally sensitive social issues by interpreting the Constitution more loosely than in the past.

   d. b and c.

20. With the appointment to the Supreme Court of George W. Bush's nominees John Roberts and Samuel Alito, we know for sure that

   a. the Court's decisions will reflect the president's conservative position on social issues.

   b. the Court's decisions will become predictably conservative, making the court pathway less inviting as an avenue for social change.

   c. the Court's decisions will continue to stir up controversy since no consensus exists in the country about how to interpret the Constitution's definition of civil liberties.

   d. a and c.

Review Test Answers: 1: c; 2: b; 3: d; 4: b; 5: d; 6: a; 7: d; 8: a; 9: d; 10: b; 11: d; 12: b; 13: c; 14: b; 15: d; 16: b; 17: a; 18: c; 19: d; 20: c.

DISCUSSION QUESTIONS

1. Why has the protection of civil liberties been important in the American system of government ever since the framing of the Constitution?

2. What is the process of incorporation, and how did it expand the coverage of civil liberties?

3. How "free" is freedom of speech in the United States?

4. What issues have courts examined concerning freedom of the press?

5. How has the Supreme Court defined rights under the establishment clause?

6. How has Congress sought to influence the Supreme Court's approach to the free exercise clause?

7. How has the Supreme Court defined obscenity?

8. What words in the Fourth Amendment require frequent interpretation as various situations arise, and how have these interpretations shaped Americans' rights?

9. What is the exclusionary rule, and how has it been shaped by Supreme Court decisions?

10. When can police officers conduct a search without a warrant?

11. What are *Miranda* warnings, and when do they apply? When do they *not* apply?

12. What rights does the Sixth Amendment protect?

13. What is the right to privacy, and how did the constitutionally protected right to privacy develop?

14. How has the Supreme Court applied the right to privacy?

15. Do you believe that the Supreme Court has exceeded its proper authority in defining and applying the right to privacy? Why or why not?

INTERNET RESOURCES

Read about the history of the Bill of Rights at **http://www.archives.gov/ national_archives_experience/bill_of_rights.html**

For up-to-date reports on current First Amendment issues, see **http://www.firstamendmentcenter.org**

A professor's Web site provides comprehensive information about religious freedom in the United States and elsewhere in the world: **http://religiousfreedom.lib.virginia.edu**

To read perspectives from an interest group advocating broader interpretations of the Bill of Rights, go to **http://www.aclu.org**

To read perspectives from an interest group advocating narrow interpretations of the Bill of Rights with respect to criminal justice issues, see **http://www.cjlf.org**

The U.S. Department of Justice's Child Exploitation and Obscenity Section provides information about a law enforcement perspective on obscenity: **http://www.usdoj.gov/criminal/ceos**

The national organization for criminal defense attorneys describes the right to counsel on its Web site: **http://www.nlada.org**

A Web site sponsored by abortion opponents presents their views about *Roe* v. *Wade:* **http://www.roevwade.org**

An interest group presents a pro-choice perspective at **http://www.naral.org**

ADDITIONAL READING

Abraham, Henry J., and Barbara Perry. *Freedom and the Court: Civil Rights and Liberties in the United States* (8th ed.). Lawrence: University Press of Kansas, 2003. Detailed history of the U.S. Supreme Court's decisions concerning civil liberties.

Bodenhamer, David J. *Fair Trial: Rights of the Accused in American History.* New York: Oxford University Press, 1992. A historical analysis of constitutional rights affecting criminal cases.

Curtis, Michael Kent. *No State Shall Abridge: The Fourteenth Amendment and the Bill of Rights.* Durham, NC: Duke University Press, 1986. An examination of debates concerning the incorporation process and the application of the Bill of Rights to the states.

Irons, Peter H. *The Courage of Their Convictions: Sixteen Americans Who Fought Their Way to the Supreme Court.* New York: Free Press,

1988. The individual stories of people who used the court pathway to bring civil liberties issues before the Supreme Court, including cases about the First Amendment and the right to privacy.

Lewis, Anthony. *Gideon's Trumpet.* New York: Random House, 1964. The detailed inside story of Clarence Earl Gideon's claim that he was entitled to be represented by counsel, the case that led the Supreme Court to incorporate the right to counsel.

Walker, Samuel. *In Defense of American Liberties: A History of the ACLU.* New York: Oxford University Press, 1990. A review of many important civil liberties issues and cases through a historical examination of an interest group that actively pursues its objectives through the court pathway.

KEY TERMS

accommodationist   176

Barron v. *Baltimore*   157

bench trials   187

bifurcated proceedings   188

Brandenburg v. *Ohio*   168

capital punishment   188

civil liberties   156

civil rights   156

clear and present danger test   166

commercial speech   168

compelled self-incrimination   184

compelling government interest   178

compulsory process   186

confrontation   186

contempt of court   172

double jeopardy   184

due process clause   158

Duncan v. *Louisiana*   160

establishment clause   175

exclusionary rule   182

fighting words doctrine   170

free exercise clause   175

Gitlow v. *New York*   158

hate speech   170

incorporation   160

Lawrence v. *Texas*   195

Lemon **test**   177

Mapp v. *Ohio*   182

Marshall, John   157

Miller v. *California*   172

Courage can be required to make democracy work. This nation's struggle for racial equality moved forward through people's willingness to face violent opposition. Any effort to push the government to advance principles of fairness and justice may require courage—the courage to speak up, the courage to be unpopular, the courage to work persistently despite unfavorable odds.

CHAPTER 6

CIVIL RIGHTS

The Controversy over Affirmative Action During the 1990s, the University of Michigan's Law School gave a general preference to members of underrepresented minority groups in order to build a more diverse student body. In pursuit of the same goal, the undergraduate admissions office at the University of Michigan took a slightly different approach. In deciding whom to admit as an undergraduate, the university used a point system. Each applicant was given a specific number of points based on various factors, such as grade point average and scores on nationally standardized tests. Minority applicants automatically received 20 extra points as part of the university's effort to build a diverse undergraduate student body. Similar bonus points were also awarded to white students in other categories, such as recruited athletes, offspring of university alumni,

Americans live in a diverse society that has been shaped by a history of racial discrimination. Contemporary Americans agree that racism is wrong, but they disagree about what, if anything, should be done to address the issue of inequality. Affirmative action is a controversial tool for increasing diversity and reducing inequality in education and employment. How do such policies advance or hinder civil rights and equality?

and residents of Michigan's Upper Peninsula, an underrepresented group composed almost exclusively of white applicants.

University admissions programs that give race-based preferences, such as those at the University of Michigan, are governed by a controversial 1978 U.S. Supreme Court decision. That decision said that the creation of a diverse student body was so beneficial to students' educational experiences that it justified considering an applicant's race as one factor in the admissions decisions at public universities (*Regents of the University of California* v. *Bakke*). Race-based preferences in university admissions, employment, and government contracts are commonly known as affirmative action. The *Bakke* case justified affirmative action at universities by focusing on the value of diversity. Other affirmative action programs in employment and government contracts are sometimes justified as a way to remedy past discrimination against women, racial minority groups, and the disabled. There are great disagreements, however, about whether universities, government, and other institutions in American society should use preferential treatment as a way to promote diversity or make up for past discrimination.

The *Bakke* decision prohibited the use of strict numerical quotas in determining the number of students from each racial or ethnic group who would be admitted but permitted university admissions offices to consider an applicant's race as one consideration. As the University of Michigan's admissions offices for both the law school and the undergraduate student body looked at

each applicant's grades, test scores, essays, letters of recommendation, extracurricular activities, work experiences, and family connections to the university, admissions officials also considered whether a student's racial group was underrepresented in its student body. Thus it was possible that a white applicant might be rejected, while a minority applicant with lower grades and test scores was admitted.

Two white applicants who were rejected for admission filed lawsuits against the University of Michigan. One challenged the admissions practices at the law school, and the other sought to invalidate affirmative action in undergraduate admissions. They did not attack preferences given to athletes, children of alumni, and other groups that included white beneficiaries. Their lawsuit sought to use the court-centered pathway to convince judges that the use of race in admissions decisions violated the equal protection clause of the Fourteenth Amendment to the U.S. Constitution. The university defended its policies, supported by additional arguments from other universities, civil rights advocacy organizations, corporate executives, and retired military commanders, by emphasizing the value of diversity and the need to open doors for individuals from groups that historically have been victimized by discrimination in American society.

The U.S. Supreme Court in 2003 narrowly approved the continued use of racial preferences. The justices struck down the University of Michigan's undergraduate admissions program by declaring that applicants could not receive a fixed number of bonus points by virtue of their racial classification. However, the justices upheld the law school's practices by endorsing the idea that race can be considered as a factor among the many others used in making admissions decisions (*Grutter* v. *Bollinger*, 2003). Thus the undergraduate admissions office could also use race as one consideration as long as it switched away from a point system and simply gave a general preference to members of underrepresented racial groups.

Because Americans are deeply divided about the use of racial preferences for university admissions, the Supreme Court's decision did not settle the issue. It merely guaranteed that battles over affirmative action would continue in various pathways, including statewide petition drives to place the issue directly before voters and legislative proposals to limit affirmative action. ◼

▶ **When the framers said,** "All *men* are created equal," did they mean all *men and women?*

political equality
fundamental value underlying the governing system of the United States that emphasizes all citizens' opportunities to vote, run for public office, own property, and enjoy civil liberties protections under the Constitution.

These fists raised in protest before the Lincoln Memorial, in Washington, D.C. symbolize the aspiration—and demand—for equality asserted by members of minority groups in the second half of the twentieth century. Over the course of history, many people have become increasingly frustrated by what they see as the gap between the ideal of equality presented in American law and the reality of widespread inequalities in American society. Have you ever experienced discrimination or had other reasons to feel angry about inequality?
Doug Mills/The New York Times

The debates over affirmative action highlight continuing disagreements about civil rights and equality in the United States. Unlike the civil liberties issues that we discussed in LINK *Chapter 5, page 156,* which typically focus on the freedoms and due process that the Bill of Rights protects for individuals, civil rights issues concern equal status and treatment. Of particular importance are equal opportunities for political participation in voting and running for office, as well as the elimination of discriminatory practices that prevent equal access to jobs, housing, and other essential aspects of life. People's membership in groups, including those based on race, gender, religion, nationality, and other such attributes, has been an important aspect of civil rights. The importance of group membership is rooted in this country's history of discrimination against individuals based on physical appearance, "ethnic" names, and generalized, stereotyped perceptions of personal characteristics. In contemporary society, the news media's attention often focuses on discrimination based on race or gender. But it is important to remember that other bases for unequal treatment have existed in different historical eras. In the mid-nineteenth century and continuing in various forms through the twentieth century, there was discrimination against immigrants. Sometimes the discrimination has been nationality-based, as when people from Ireland, Italy, and other countries were mistreated. Other forms of discrimination are based on religion, such as housing discrimination and unfair hiring practices during various historical eras aimed at Catholics, Jews, and Muslims. People of Asian and Hispanic ancestry have also been victims of significant levels of generalized discrimination based on race, culture, religion, and ethnicity.

Struggles to acquire civil rights and equal treatment vary by group, depending largely on whether discriminatory practices aimed at them are intense, entrenched, and widespread. For some groups, such as immigrants from Europe, civil rights and a measure of equality came as they gained acceptance from and intermarried with other whites who had already settled in the United States. For other groups, the struggle was more difficult, both because their physical characteristics, such as skin color, made them stand out and because whites—or in the case of women, males—often held strong negative beliefs about their social habits, intelligence, and capabilities. In this chapter, we will examine the actions of governmental institutions, interest groups, and other actors that shape laws and policies affecting issues of equality.

In both World Wars, American military units were segregated and African American troops were often commanded by white officers. President Harry Truman's Executive Order in 1948 desegregated the armed forces, but other segments of society remained thoroughly segregated at this time. Could Truman have ordered desegregation throughout American society? What would have happened if he had attempted such a bold move?

Several pathways of policy change have been important for civil rights. In an example of influential decision making by a political leader who was the target of lobbying by interest groups, President Harry Truman issued an executive order in 1948 that required "equality of treatment and opportunity for persons in the armed forces without regard to race, color, religion, or national origin." This led to the elimination of the practice of separating white and African American military personnel into segregated units.[1] Later in the chapter, we will see that Congress and many state legislatures also wrote laws in the 1960s and subsequent decades intended to prevent various forms of discrimination in employment, housing, and other aspects of American life. Of particular importance are two other pathways. The example of the challenge to the University of Michigan's admissions practices demonstrates the role of the court pathway in shaping civil rights law and policy. In addition, the grassroots mobilization pathway has been especially important for civil rights as people have mobilized protest campaigns and voter registration drives to advance equal rights for African Americans, Latinos, women, the disabled, and others. Over time, these campaigns have helped change values in American society. Discrimination against African Americans, Latinos, and women was once widely accepted and given support in the decisions of judges, legislators, and other policymakers. Now many forms of race and gender discrimination are universally condemned by mainstream opinion, with resulting impacts for the kinds of laws created by legislatures and endorsed by courts.

Key Questions

1. How do Americans define the nature of equality that underlies their conception of civil rights?

2. What kinds of discrimination and inequality in the United States have created the problems that people seek to redress through litigation and grassroots civil rights movements?

3. How did the NAACP use the court pathway to pursue civil rights for African Americans?

4. How did women, African Americans, and Latinos seek civil rights through grassroots mobilization?

5. What kinds of laws have been enacted by Congress to stop discrimination and advance civil rights?

6. How have contemporary civil rights issues become more complex than those that served as the focus of political and legal activity in the early twentieth century?

The Ideal of Equality

As we've discussed in earlier chapters, the founders of the United States wanted to enjoy **political equality,** which would allow them to express their views, own property, and participate in what they called a "republican" governing system. The most famous expression of the founders' emphasis on equality lies in the words of the Declaration of Independence: "All men are created equal." The founders believed that political equality was an essential element of the natural world and a fundamental principle of human life, and they considered that principle violated when a social system or government grants extra status and power to favored individuals.

▶ **When the framers said, "All *men* are created equal," did they mean all *men and women*?** As indicated by the Declaration of Independence, the political leaders of the new nation focused on equality for *men*. The nation's founders simply took it for granted that women need not participate as important decision makers in economic and political affairs. Women were viewed as needing protection and as being destined for such roles in society as cooks, maids, wives, and mothers. In addition, the founders intended equality to apply in practice only to certain men of European ancestry. Many of the founders of the United States were slave owners, and even some who did not own slaves viewed African Americans as less-than-equal beings who neither had nor deserved freedom, let alone the benefits of law and an opportunity to participate in politics. Nor did the founders view Native Americans as equal to whites. Native Americans were pushed from their lands from the mid-seventeenth century through the late nineteenth century, often through military force and other violence. Those who survived were often forced to live on isolated reservations, sometimes hundreds of miles from their traditional homelands.

equality of condition
conception of equality that exists in some countries that value equal economic status as well as equal access to housing, health care, education, and government services

equality of opportunity
conception of equality that seeks to provide all citizens with opportunities for participation in the economic system and public life but accepts unequal results in income, political power, and property ownership

Civil rights protesters use graphic examples to remind the American public of our country's history of violence and unequal treatment aimed at members of racial minority groups. Are such reminders just an attempt to generate guilt or does this history still have relevance for the problems that we face today?

In practice, the founders did not even view all white men as completely equal for purposes of political participation and influence over public policy. Thus many laws at first restricted voting rights to white men who owned land. John Adams, for example, rejected arguments that favored voting rights for all free adult males; he thought that decisions should be made by men with personal "independence," as evidenced by ownership of land.[2] Men without property, it was feared, would be too easily controlled by their employers or creditors to act independently.

Much has changed over the course of the twenty-three decades since the nation's founders gave original expression of the ideal of equality in the Declaration of Independence. The Declaration's statement that "all men are created equal" served as a beacon of inspiration for Americans in all segments of society. Instead of accepting the founders' original limited conception of equality, people have focused on the underlying ideal and asked themselves and their fellow Americans, "Shouldn't I be included in that statement?" Women, African Americans, Latinos, the disabled, and homosexuals, among others, have worked through various pathways to change law and policy to reflect broader applications of the original ideal of equality. These groups have not always been successful in redefining equality and civil rights to fit their own visions. Over the course of American history, several factors contributed to widespread acceptance of a redefinition of political equality that extends beyond white males. These factors include grassroots mobilization, legislative action, legal cases, and even the bloody Civil War of the 1860s. Political activity and social changes over many decades produced new and now widely accepted conceptions of equality that embrace women and members of racial and other minority groups (see Table 6.1 on pages 212–213).

The founders' ideal of equality focused on political participation and civil liberties. By contrast, it would be possible to have a governing system that emphasizes **equality of condition.** Some governing systems use policy decisions rather than constitutional rights as the means to advance equality of condition. For example, the system of taxation and government benefits in Sweden and some other European countries seeks to redistribute wealth by heavily taxing the affluent and providing generous medical, housing, education, and other benefits for the less well off. The purpose and effect of such a system is to lift low-income people into the middle class while pushing the wealthy down closer toward the

discussionquestions

1. Does political equality exist for citizens of the United States? If not, what would need to be done to achieve political equality for all citizens?

2. Should the United States seek equality of condition instead of equality of opportunity? How would the country be different if we had that goal?

what YOU can do!

Do men still dominate or benefit from favoritism in any aspects of your community? Look at Web sites for country clubs or social organizations with local chapters (such as religious, fraternal, or community service clubs) to see if there are membership restrictions. If restrictions exist, do the membership policies of these kinds of organizations have an equal opportunity in American society?

middle class. A fundamental objective of governing systems that pursue such policies is to reduce economic disparities between citizens and thus to ensure that everyone has access to important goods and services, such as education, medical care, housing, and at least a modest income.

The American system seeks to advance **equality of opportunity.** This goal has expanded beyond the founders' original concept of political equality to include also the elimination of *some* discriminatory barriers to education, employment, and public accommodation. As we will see, some forms of discrimination are perfectly legal in the United States, while the law bans others. The system does not claim to seek the *elimination* of all differences and disparities or to provide goods and services to everyone. The American political ideology and our free-enterprise economic system emphasize individual achievement and the acquisition of wealth through hard work. People are expected to be self-reliant and to earn enough money to buy their own goods and services. If the government chooses to provide a service, such as public schools or health care for the elderly, it cannot discriminate by race, gender, or ethnicity in serving members of the public. However, the U.S. Constitution does not require the government to provide those services.

The drive for civil rights in the twentieth century focused on two areas: equal access to voting and the prohibition of certain forms of "categorical discrimination," which meant exclusion, by reason of race, gender, or disability, from public education, employment, housing, and public accommodations (restaurants, hotels, and stores). The advancement of these opportunities does not, however, mean that the American governing system is committed to complete equality of opportunity for all people. Belief in the values of individualism and self-reliance in American ideology leads people to benefit from social networks, contacts, and the achievements of their friends and relatives. Many people, for example, get jobs through referrals from family members and friends. (As a college student, you may very well have seen such preferences in action.) Some people inherit money from wealthy relatives and use that money to start businesses or attend expensive private universities. People with wealth and social contacts typically have many more educational and employment opportunities than poor people. This disparity is an accepted aspect of the American free-enterprise system and its emphasis on individual-

ism. As a result, it is clear that the equality of opportunity advanced by civil rights is limited to specific contexts and does not reflect a comprehensive goal that is vigorously pursued by the American governing system.

practicequiz

1. Unlike civil liberties, civil rights concern
   a. the individual freedoms that the Bill of Rights protects.
   b. guaranteed education and health care.
   c. equal status and treatment for different groups of people.
   d. social issues addressed exclusively at the federal level.

2. Which two pathways have been particularly important for the advancement of civil rights in this country?
   a. The lobbying and cultural change pathways.
   b. The court and grassroots mobilization pathways.
   c. The court and legislative pathways.
   d. The grassroots mobilization and cultural change pathways.

3. Even today, some forms of discrimination are legal in this country.
   a. true   b. false

4. Categorical discrimination refers to unfair treatment of people because of their
   a. race, gender, or disability.
   b. ideas.
   c. home state.
   d. consumer practices.

Answers: 1-c, 2-b, 3-a, 4-a.

Equal Protection of the Law

From the 1600s, people who were abducted and brought by force from Africa, and their descendants, worked as slaves in North America. Slavery existed in all northern colonies as well as in the South. It was merely less extensive and abolished years earlier— within several decades of the American Revolution—in the North. State laws mandating the gradual emancipation of slaves in New York and Connecticut, for example, meant that there were still small numbers of slaves in those states as late as 1827. Slavery

Table 6.1. Various groups used specific pathways in order to seek the promise of equality outlined in the Declaration of Independence and the equal protection clause of the Fourteenth Amendment. Multiple pathways were employed, and each group did not use the same strategies.

TABLE 6.1
Rights, Pathways, and Results in Advancing Equality of Opportunity

GROUP	MINORITY RIGHT	PATHWAY	OUTCOME	
African Americans	Basic Civil Rights, Prohibit Discrimination, Voting Rights	Equal Access to Education: Court pathway Prohibit Discrimination: Grassroots Mobilization Elections and Court pathways Voting Rights: Grassroots Mobilization pathway	*Brown v. Board of Education* (1954) [school desegregation]; Civil Rights Act of 1964 [no discrimination in employment and public accommodations]; Voting Rights Act of 1965	
Women	Voting Rights, Prohibit Discrimination	Voting Rights: Grassroots Mobilization and Elections pathways; Prohibit Discrimination: Elections, Court, and Cultural Change pathways	Nineteenth Amendment (1920) [women's right to vote]; Equal Pay Act of 1963; *Reed v. Reed* (1971) [no discrimination in inheritance laws]	
Japanese Americans	Compensation for deprivation of rights during World War II	Compensation for Rights' Deprivation: Elections pathways	American Japanese Claims Act of 1948; Civil Liberties Act of 1988	
Disabled	Prohibit Discrimination	Prohibit Discrimination: Elections and Grassroots Mobilization pathways	Section 504 of the Rehabilitation Act of 1973 [no discrimination in federally-funded programs]; Americans with Disabilities Act of 1990 [no discrimination in employment and public accommodations]	

what YOU can do!

Use the Internet to read about laws and social policies in Sweden. Can you identify laws and policies that seem to advance equality of condition? Are there any laws and policies that you would consider suggesting to your representative in Congress or the state legislature?

TABLE 6.1 (continued)
Rights, Pathways, and Results in Advancing Equality of Opportunity

GROUP	MINORITY RIGHT	PATHWAY	OUTCOME	
Older Workers	Prohibit Discrimination in Employment	Prohibit Discrimination Employment: Elections pathway	Age Discrimination in Employment Act of 1967 [no discrimination against workers age 40 and over]	
Latinos	Basic Civil Rights, Prohibit Discrimination	Basic Civil Rights and Prohibit Discrimination: Grassroots Mobilization and Elections pathways	Agricultural Labor Relations Act of 1975 (California state law) [right of farmworkers to unionize]; Voting Rights Act of 1975 [no discrimination against language minority groups]	
Gays and Lesbians	Basic Civil Rights, Prohibit Discrimination	Basic Civil Rights and Prohibit Discrimination: Court and Elections pathways	State court decisions on civil unions and marriage; *Romer* v. *Evans* (1996) [protection against legislation targeted at gays and lesbians]; state and local antidiscrimination laws	
Native Americans	Basic Civil Rights, Prohibit Discrimination, Economic Development	Basic Civil Rights, Prohibit Discrimination, Economic Development: Elections pathway	Covered by federal antidiscrimination laws concerning race and ethnicity that were primarily spurred by African Americans; economic development, including gambling enterprises, through state laws	

▶ **How does our history** of slavery affect the current debate on inequality in the United States?

In 1986, Dolly Green stands outside the South Carolina plantation where her grandparents had worked as slaves more than 120 years earlier. Slavery ended many decades ago, yet its legacy, including the century of harsh racial discrimination that followed, has contributed to continuing inequality in American society. What suggestions would you make for reducing the continuing issue of racial inequality?

was a brutal life with dehumanizing effects for the African Americans subjected to violence and oppressive controls, as well as for the whites who absorbed an ideology of racial superiority and animosity to justify their mistreatment of dark-skinned people. Slaves worked from sunup to sundown under harsh conditions. They were forced to live in circumstances of limited nutrition, housing, medical care, and clothing, and they had few opportunities to use their creativity, intelligence, and effort to improve the quality of their lives. Slaves could be beaten and whipped at the whim of their owners. Families were forcibly divided, as husbands, wives, and children were separated from their loved ones to be sold at auction and never seen again.[3] Race-based slavery and the years of racial discrimination that followed laid the foundation for today's racial gaps in wealth, education, housing patterns, and employment opportunities.[4] These enduring disadvantages for Americans of African ancestry have often proven extremely difficult to undo or overcome (see Table 6.2).

▶ **How does our history of slavery affect the current debate on inequality in the United States?** The descendants of whites could enjoy the benefits of education, business contacts, and employment opportunities through social networks. Throughout the United States, freed slaves and their descendants faced the problem of starting from scratch without accumulated or inherited assets. To succeed in the economic system, they needed to seek access to education, employment, political participation, bank loans, land leases, and business contracts—all sectors of society dominated by whites until the late twentieth century. Yet the visibility of their skin color made African Americans easy to exclude from employment, housing, and services by whites who wished to use discrimination to preserve for themselves superior status and to monopolize educational, political, and business opportunities. To varying degrees, women, Latinos, and members of other minority groups faced parallel problems of exclusion and discrimination.

One central question continues to be debated by individuals and groups who seek to shape American civil rights law and policy: How much should government—federal, state, or local—do to make up for the nation's history of discrimination and its continuing effects? As we've seen in tracing the battle over affirmative action, there are significant disagreements about which governmental actions appropriately advance Americans' limited concept of equality of opportunity.

what YOU can do!
Learn about the continuing existence of slavery in various countries. See, for example, the Web site of Anti-Slavery International at **http://www.antislavery.org** and **http://www.freetheslaves.net** What actions could be taken today to eliminate modern slavery and advance civil rights for victimized people around the world? What role should the United States play?

TABLE 6.2
Educational Attainment and Poverty Status by Race, 2004 (percentage of adults)

Ethnic Group	HIGH SCHOOL OR HIGHER	FOUR OR MORE YEARS OF COLLEGE	BELOW 50 PERCENT OF POVERTY LEVEL[a]
White, not Hispanic	90.0	30.6	3.8
African American	80.6	17.6	12.6
Hispanic	58.4	12.1	8.6

[a] For example, the poverty level for a family of three (two parents and one child under age 18) was $14,974 in 2004.

SOURCES: U.S. Census Bureau, "College Degree Nearly Doubles Annual Earnings," March 28, 2005, http://www.census.gov/Press-Release/www/releases/archives/education/004214.html; Peter Fronczek, *Income, Earnings, and Poverty from the 2004 American Community Survey* (Washington, DC: U.S. Census Bureau, 2005), p. 19.

Differences in educational attainment and poverty rates are evident among major ethnic groups in the United States. Over time, some of these disparities have become less stark than in the past. However, these issues that affect millions of Americans have not changed easily or swiftly.

THE FOURTEENTH AMENDMENT AND RECONSTRUCTION

Immediately after the Civil War, between 1865 and early 1867, President Andrew Johnson—who had succeeded Abraham Lincoln after his assassination—permitted southern whites to determine how the South would reconstruct itself. Not surprisingly, they created laws that sought to maintain white superiority and power. As described by the historian Eric Foner:

> Southern state governments enforced [their] view of black freedom by enacting the notorious Black Codes, which denied blacks equality before the law and political rights, and imposed on them mandatory year-long labor contracts, coercive apprenticeship regulations, and criminal penalties for breach of contract. Through these laws, the South's white leadership sought to ensure that plantation agriculture survived emancipation.[5]

Northerners in Congress reacted by passing the Reconstruction Act of 1867, which required the southern states to establish new state governments based on the granting of voting rights to all men, both white and African American.[6] With the southern states still under Union occupation in the years following the Civil War, military commanders repealed many elements of the Black Codes, and African Americans enjoyed their first opportunities to vote and to run for political office. African Americans were elected to high political offices, and eighteen served as members of Congress.[7] But events in the late 1870s ended this brief period of political participation by African Americans and eventually led to the reintroduction of severe forms of racial discrimination.

Members of Congress from the North also led the effort to create three constitutional amendments after the Civil War to provide important protections for African Americans. However, they could not transform society and create equality merely by adding new words to the Constitution. According to the historian David Kyvig:

> Each of the three Civil War amendments represented an effort to define the rights of free slaves and to give those rights constitutional protection. Each provided less protection than intended, whether as a result of sloppy draftsmanship, deliberate compromises that produced ambiguous perceptions, or determined resistance.[8]

The Thirteenth Amendment (1865) abolished slavery. The Fourteenth Amendment (1868) extended to former slaves the rights of full citizenship, including the equal protection of the laws and the right to due process under the law. The Fifteenth Amendment (1870) sought to guarantee that men would not be denied the right to vote because of their race. Women had not yet gained the right to vote and were deliberately excluded from the purview of the Fifteenth Amendment, over the bitter opposition of women's rights crusaders, who had also been abolitionists.

▶ **With those amendments** passed after the Civil War, how did the southern states get away with denying African Americans their civil rights?

Jim Crow laws
Laws enacted by southern state legislatures immediately after the Civil War that mandated rigid racial segregation. The laws were named after a minstrel song that ridiculed African Americans.

RADICAL MEMBERS OF THE S⁰. C⁴. LEGISLATURE.

As indicated by this nineteenth century poster concerning state government in South Carolina, for a brief period in the aftermath of the Civil War, African Americans were elected to Congress and state legislatures. The end of Reconstruction led to many decades in which racial minorities were seldom elected to high offices. In 2006, we saw the first African American elected as governor of Massachusetts and both Republicans and Democrats putting forward African Americans as U.S. Senate and gubernatorial candidates in Maryland, Tennessee, Ohio, and Pennsylvania. Do these recent developments indicate that we are reaching a time when people of all races have an equal opportunity to win elections?

The language and intended meaning of the Thirteenth and Fifteenth Amendments were relatively straightforward, although, as we will discuss later in this chapter, it took additional legislation and court decisions to fulfill the Fifteenth Amendment's goal of ensuring voting rights without racial discrimination. In contrast, the words of the Fourteenth Amendment were ambiguous and required extensive judicial interpretation as its meaning was refined and adjusted over many decades. These interpretations had a great impact on the definition of civil rights for all Americans because the Fourteenth Amendment contains the equal protection clause that victims of discrimination rely on when they go to court to seek judicial protection against unequal treatment by government. Unlike the Bill of Rights—which, as we saw in LINK *Chapter 5, page 158*, was originally intended to protect individuals against actions by the federal government and only during the twentieth century came to be applied against state and local governments—the Fourteenth Amendment is aimed directly at actions by state governments. The amendment says that "no State shall" deprive people of specific rights. According to one historian, "It was the Fourteenth Amendment, approved by Congress in 1866 and ratified two years later, that for the first time enshrined in the Constitution the ideas of birthright citizenship and equal rights for all Americans."[9]

THE RISE AND PERSISTENCE OF RACIAL OPPRESSION

The disputed outcome of the presidential election of 1876 between Republican Rutherford B. Hayes and Democrat Samuel Tilden affected the fates of African Americans. Election returns from several southern states were in dispute, preventing either Hayes or Tilden from claiming an electoral college victory. After a special commission (consisting of members of Congress and the Supreme Court) awarded Hayes all of the disputed electoral votes, Hayes became president and promptly withdrew the federal occupation troops from the South. Ending federal occupation permitted those states greater freedom in developing their own laws and policies.[10]

▶ **With those amendments passed after the Civil War, how did the southern states get away with denying African Americans their civil rights?** The absence of federal troops gave further encouragement to the Ku Klux Klan and other violent secret societies that had the stated intention of terrorizing African

Americans—by beatings, house burnings, and murders—to prevent them from voting, running for political office, or otherwise asserting political and social equality. After 1876, in one southern state after another, self-styled "conservative" white-dominated governments came to power and did everything possible to raise legal barriers to black political participation. These laws could not simply say "black people cannot vote," because such wording would clash with the Fifteenth Amendment's prohibition on racial discrimination in voting. Instead, the new laws did such things as impose literacy tests and "government knowledge" tests as a condition of voter registration. These could also be used to exclude poor whites from voting. In some places, white county clerks administered the tests in a discriminatory fashion to fail all African American applicants but applied the tests less rigorously to whites. Intimidation and violence were also used to discourage African Americans from voting. If they appeared at the courthouse to register to vote, they risked being arrested by the county sheriff for some imaginary criminal offense or could be beaten—or worse—by the Klan. As a result, between the 1870s and the 1890s, the numbers of African American men who were registered to vote in southern states dropped from tens of thousands to only a handful.

The white-dominated conservative state governments also began enacting **Jim Crow laws,** labeled after a minstrel song that ridiculed African Americans. These laws mandated rigid racial segregation throughout southern society. State and local governments required that African Americans and whites attend separate schools and use separate public facilities. By the early twentieth century, this policy evolved into designating separate waiting areas in bus stations, separate public restrooms, and even separate public drinking fountains. Often no attempt at all was made to provide separate public facilities; public swimming pools and parks, for example, were set aside for the use of whites only.

With the end of Reconstruction and the rise of government-enforced racial discrimination, life for many African Americans was little better than slavery. They had no opportunities for economic success and were generally stuck in slavelike positions as poorly paid agricultural workers and other laborers. As described by the historian Leon Litwack, African Americans were told "to embrace self-help and the work ethic, [but] whites consciously withheld from blacks the tools and opportunities available to other Americans to lift themselves up economically."[11] They were virtually unprotected by the law. If whites committed crimes against African Americans, including such horrific acts as rape and

From the introduction of slavery through the first five decades of the twentieth century, African Americans were victimized by horrific violence and enjoyed little protection from the legal system. White mobs lynched African Americans—hanged and often mutilated innocent people—based on rumors of criminal acts or even for violating white people's expectations that they show deference and obedience. Which pathway had the greatest impact in moving the United States from these gut-wrenching scenes to where we are today: court pathway, elections pathway, grassroots mobilization pathway, decision-makers pathway or cultural change pathway?

ABOVE: **The "separate or equal" doctrine** led to strict racial separation in many aspects of American life, especially in southern states. Although some whites argued that separation affected both races equally, the inferiority of services and facilities provided for African Americans made it very clear that the policy targeted one particular group for victimization. Did your parents or other relatives observe or experience aspects of racial segregation? If so, what effect did those experiences have on them?

BELOW: **The ideology of white superiority** developed as a justification for slavery and then was taught to generations of white children by their parents. Such beliefs motivated individuals to threaten and attack civil rights activists in the 1950s and 1960s. News coverage of such attacks helped to make northern whites sympathetic to African Americans' struggle for equality. How have your views about equality been shaped by news stories, books, or historical events?

▶ What did the Court mean by "separate but equal?"

murder, there was little likelihood that any arrest would be made and still less that a conviction would follow.

▶ **What did the Court mean by "separate but equal?"** In the 1890s, a light-skinned African American man named Homer Plessy, described in court papers as "7/8ths white," worked with lawyers from the North in planning a legal challenge to the rigid segregation of Jim Crow laws. Plessy illegally sat in a "whites only" railroad car and refused to move when asked. As he and his lawyers had planned, Plessy was arrested for violating the law when he disobeyed the racial separation mandated by Louisiana's state law. When the case reached the Supreme Court, Plessy's lawyers argued that racial segregation laws violated the equal protection clause of the Fourteenth Amendment. However, in an 8–1 decision, the Supreme Court decided that there was no violation of the constitutional right to equal protection when states had "separate but equal" facilities and services for people of different races (***Plessy* v. *Ferguson***, 1896). The Court's decision effectively endorsed racial discrimination by government, because the separate facilities provided to African Americans, including railroad cars, public restrooms, and schools, were always inferior to those provided for whites. The majority of the justices did not examine whether the separate facilities were ever equal; it was merely assumed that they were, and the Court turned aside African Americans' hopes for civil rights protection under the Fourteenth Amendment.

The lone dissenter in the *Plessy* case, Justice John Marshall Harlan, who grew up in a Kentucky family that had previously owned slaves, wrote one of the Court's most famous opinions. "Our Constitution is color-blind," he wrote. As if looking in a crystal ball, he accurately predicted that "the destinies of the two races in this country [whites and African Americans] are indissolubly linked together." The Court's decision endorsing the infliction of harm on one race would, he foresaw, lead to long-term consequences that would adversely affect the entire nation. In Harlan's words, "The common government of all [should] not permit the seeds of race hate to be planted under the sanction of law."

In the southern states, rigid segregation and exclusion of African Americans from political participation continued through the 1960s. Black people continued to be intimidated by violence, including lynching, and remained unprotected by the law. Southern whites maintained their superior status and economic benefits. African Americans in the region had little chance to

Plessy v. Ferguson (1896)
U.S. Supreme Court decision that endorsed the legality of racial segregation laws by permitting "separate but equal" services and facilities for African Americans, even though the services and facilities were actually inferior. This case was later overturned by the Supreme Court's decision in *Brown v. Board of Education of Topeka* (1954).

de jure segregation
racial segregation mandated by laws and policies created by government officials.

de facto segregation
racial segregation in housing and schools that was presumed to occur through people's voluntary choices about where they wanted to live but was actually facilitated by the discriminatory actions of landlords, real estate agents, and banks.

succeed in life outside the narrow areas that white prejudice allowed. After 1900, many African Americans began leaving the South and seeking employment in the industrial centers of the North, where they also faced racial discrimination. The South practiced **de jure segregation,** in which state and local laws mandated discrimination and separation. Northern cities also victimized African Americans, but they used less formal means, often labeled **de facto segregation.** Patterns of segregated housing in the North were usually justified by a presumption that African Americans preferred to live together in the poorest section of each city. In reality, with the help of government home-financing programs, many private decision makers, especially real estate agents and mortgage bankers, steered African Americans into ghettos by refusing to show them houses or to finance their attempts to purchase homes in white neighborhoods. In turn, northern school boards used these discriminatory housing patterns as a way to keep African Americans segregated into a school district's worst, most crowded schools. Other school boards redrew school boundaries and transported students to new locations in order to keep African Americans from attending schools with white students. In the same way, African Americans were victimized by other decision makers' racial discrimination, including employers' hiring decisions and police officers' discretionary decisions about whom to stop, search, and arrest.

Other groups also faced discrimination during this era. For example, immigrants from China began to come to the United States before the Civil War, but they were invariably forced into difficult, low-paying jobs with little opportunity for advancement. At various times, Congress actually banned further immigration from China. Chinese who lived in the United States always faced severe prejudice and discrimination.[12] In 1927, the U.S. Supreme Court upheld a Mississippi law that barred Chinese American children from white schools and required them to attend inferior segregated schools for African Americans (*Gong Lum* v. *Rice*). People of Japanese ethnic heritage were victimized by similar treatment in California and other West Coast states where most of them settled. In short, unequal treatment and racial discrimination were pervasive aspects of American life throughout the United States for most of the century, in spite of the post–Civil War amendments that prohibited slavery and promised "equal protection of the laws."

White students at southern universities mounted their own protests against integration in the 1960s. They had been taught to support the idea of white superiority and the policy of racial segregation. As these individuals look back at their actions in the 1960s in light of what has happened since that time, how do you suppose they feel about what they did?

In 1998, President Bill Clinton honored Fred Korematsu with the Presidential Medal of Freedom, the nation's highest honor for civilians. What does it say about cultural change in the United States when a former wartime detainee who broke the law is later given a high honor at a White House ceremony?

pathways profile

FRED KOREMATSU

In the aftermath of Japan's surprise attack on the U.S. naval base at Pearl Harbor, Hawaii, on December 7, 1941, government officials were worried about the loyalty of Japanese Americans in the United States. There were fears that they might seek ways to help Japan in the war. In early 1942, Fred Korematsu, an American of Japanese ancestry who had been born in California, was a 22-year-old welder working in the San Francisco shipyard when President Franklin D. Roosevelt issued an executive order requiring that West Coast Japanese Americans be placed in detention camps. Among the many local officials who had favored this action was California's attorney general and later governor, Earl Warren, who would subsequently serve on the U.S. Supreme Court as chief justice. Without any proof or even hint of wrongdoing, Japanese Americans were forced to give up their homes and businesses and submit to detention at desert camps in places such as Utah and Arizona merely because the government feared that they might spy or provide other assistance for Japan.

Korematsu refused to report for detention. He was arrested and charged with a crime. With the assistance of the American Civil Liberties Union of Northern California, the civil liberties interest group discussed in **LINK** *Chapter 4, pages 138–139*, he filed a legal challenge to the president's order by asserting that it was a form of racial discrimination. Ultimately, the U.S. Supreme Court ruled against him in 1944. Many historians regard that decision as one of the most obvious errors made by the Court in the twentieth century. One group of people lost their liberty without any charges or hearings merely because they or their ancestors came from an enemy country many years before the war started. Japanese Americans were held in detention for several years, sometimes with children separated from their parents. Nearly forty years later, Congress enacted a law apologizing for the mass detentions based only on the detainees' ethnicity and authorizing financial compensation for surviving detainees. In 1998, President Bill Clinton bestowed on Korematsu the Presidential Medal of Freedom to honor his courageous stand. Through the use of the court pathway, Korematsu challenged an instance of severe national-origin discrimination. In so doing, he eventually increased awareness of equal protection of the laws.

After the terrorist attacks on the World Trade Center and the Pentagon on September 11, 2001, Korematsu spoke out again when

practice quiz

1. During Reconstruction, the political experience for African Americans in the South can best be described as
   a. Equally oppressive as it was during slave times.
   b. Very promising, with some African Americans getting elected to high offices.
   c. Without promise because of the rise of the KKK.
   d. Better than the political experience of African Americans today.

2. The equal protection clause, so important to the civil rights activism in the court pathway, can be found in which amendment of the Constitution?
   a. Thirteenth
   b. Fourteenth
   c. Fifteenth
   d. First

3. The notorious "separate but equal" idea endorsing segregation nationally was the result of what Supreme Court case?
   a. *Marbury* v. *Madison*
   b. *Murray* v. *Maryland*
   c. *Plessy* v. *Ferguson*
   d. *Hamdi* v. *Rumsfeld*

4. De facto segregation of African Americans was routine in the North, even in the twentieth century.
   a. true
   b. false

Answers: 1-b, 2-b, 3-c, 4-a.

National Association for the Advancement of Colored People (NAACP) Civil rights advocacy group founded by African Americans and their white supporters in 1909 that used the court pathway to fight racial discrimination in the 1930s through the 1950s and later emphasized the elections and lobbying pathways.

discussionquestions

1. Why did racial discrimination continue to exist after the Civil War?

2. What is the importance of the U.S. Supreme Court's decision in *Plessy* v. *Ferguson*?

the U.S. government made hundreds of arrests of people of Middle Eastern ancestry. Many of these people were held for weeks without being charged with crimes. Some were deported for immigration violations, but others were eventually released without charges. Korematsu also spoke out against the harassment of Muslims that occurred in several communities. In 2003, an appellate brief was filed on his behalf in the U.S. Supreme Court arguing that the federal government does not have the authority to detain suspected terrorists without giving them the opportunity to consult with an attorney and challenge their detentions in court proceedings. "It may be that it is essential in some circumstances to compromise civil liberties in order to meet the necessities of wartime," read the brief, "but history teaches that we tend too quickly to sacrifice those liberties in the face of overbroad claims of military necessity."[13] In June 2004, the Supreme Court agreed with Korematsu's argument that Americans are entitled to basic rights when they are detained by their own government (*Hamdi* v. *Rumsfeld*). Fred Korematsu continued his civil rights activism even at the age of 85.

SOURCE: "Of Civil Wrongs and Rights: The Fred Korematsu Story." July 2003. http://www.pbs.gov/pov; Nat Hentoff, "Fred Korematsu v. George W. Bush." *The Village Voice*, February 19, 2004. http://www.villagevoice.com. ▧

LITIGATION STRATEGIES AND SCHOOL SEGREGATION

The **National Association for the Advancement of Colored People (NAACP),** a civil rights advocacy group founded by African Americans and their white supporters in 1909, sought to use the court pathway as the means to attack the forms of segregation and discrimination endorsed by the Supreme Court's decision in *Plessy* v. *Ferguson*. The group originated during a period that historians regard as one of the worst for African Americans. In the first three decades of the twentieth century, the Ku Klux Klan grew to more than a million members (many of them outside the South) and was so accepted that President Warren G. Harding reportedly was inducted into membership in a White House ceremony.[14] Racial attacks on African Americans, often called "race riots," broke out in dozens of northern and southern cities, sometimes over nothing more than an African American crossing an invisible dividing line at a segregated beach. In these riots, whites typically roamed the streets assaulting and murdering African Americans and destroying homes and busi-

During World War II, Japanese Americans were removed from the West Coast and held in detention camps without any proof of wrongdoing. The detainees lost homes and businesses as a result of the government's actions. Forty years later, the government paid several thousand dollars to each surviving detainee. If you had been among those detainees, how would you have reacted to this payment?

nesses. Modern historians' research has publicized the large-scale racial assaults on African American communities in Chicago (1919) and Tulsa (1921), and there were similar attacks in many other places. Lynchings continued in the South as well as the North, in which individual African Americans who had been accused of some crime or other transgression were brutally mutilated and murdered by white mobs, who didn't have to fear that

▶ **How "equal" were the** separate facilities and services for whites and African Americans?

Brown v. Board of Education of Topeka (1954)
U.S. Supreme Court decision that overturned *Plessy* v. *Ferguson* (1896) and declared that government-mandated racial segregation in schools and other facilities and programs violates the equal protection clause of the Fourteenth Amendment.

authorities would punish them.[15] Thus the NAACP began its strategic actions for civil rights at a moment when African Americans faced their greatest hostility from American society.

▶ **How "equal" were the separate facilities and services for whites and African Americans?** Instead of directly attacking the "separate but equal" *Plessy* rule, the NAACP's lawyers initiated a series of cases that helped to demonstrate that in practice, the rule had plenty of "separate" but virtually no "equal." In the 1930s, the organization represented an African American resident of Maryland who was denied admission to the law school at the University of Maryland, despite being an outstanding graduate of prestigious Amherst College in Massachusetts. Although the state of Maryland sought to defend against the lawsuit by saying that the state would create a law school just for African Americans or pay for the man to attend an out-of-state school, Maryland's supreme court ruled that the admissions policy violated the right to equal protection and ordered that the man be admitted. The court recognized that the alternatives offered by Maryland would not be equal for the purposes of someone who planned to practice law in Maryland (*Murray* v. *Maryland,* 1936). Over the years, the NAACP pursued similar lawsuits and eventually won cases in the U.S. Supreme Court that banned specific discriminatory graduate school admissions practices at universities in Missouri, Texas, and Oklahoma.

During the 1940s and early 1950s, it became clear that the Supreme Court recognized that segregation in law schools and graduate schools did not fulfill the "separate but equal" requirement. This was especially clear when states undertook such tricks as setting up a one-room law school without a library or other necessary facilities simply to claim that a law school existed for African Americans that was equal to the one provided for whites at the state's main university.

Having won a series of court victories in cases demonstrating lack of equality caused by racial segregation in law schools and graduate schools, the NAACP took the next step: pursuing a similar claim with respect to the public education provided for school-age children. This step was very risky. It was widely—and correctly—assumed that whites would have an easier time accepting the presence of small numbers of college-educated African Americans in graduate schools than they would accepting the prospect of their children attending grade school and high school with large numbers of students of a race that many of them feared and despised.

In 1953, the Supreme Court heard the case **Brown v. Board of Education of Topeka,** concerning racial segregation in the pub-

lic schools of Topeka, Kansas. NAACP attorney Thurgood Marshall, who later became the first African American appointed to serve as a Supreme Court justice, presented the case and argued that the *Plessy* rule of "separate but equal" was inherently unequal. Several justices were reluctant to endorse Marshall's arguments, fearing that a decision striking down racial segregation would lead to violence against African Americans in the South. Other justices believed that the Court needed to be unanimous in such an important decision in order to show the nation that the high court was united in its conclusion. The Court's new chief justice, former California governor **Earl Warren,** felt strongly that racial segregation violated the equal protection clause. Using his leadership skills and effective persuasion, he convinced his reluctant colleagues to join a strong opinion condemning racial segregation and overturning the "separate but equal" doctrine of *Plessy* v. *Ferguson.*[16] When the Court finally announced its ruling in *Brown* v. *Board of Education* (1954), the decision was a controversial blockbuster. Suddenly, it was made clear that an important branch of government, the federal judiciary, had endorsed a new concept of equality in which state and local governments were forbidden to provide separate services and facilities for people of different races.

▶ **Why did it take so long to end school segregation after the *Brown* decision?** The *Brown* decision did not immediately end racial segregation. A second Supreme Court decision concerning the *Brown* case (*Brown* v. *Board of Education,* 1955—known as "*Brown* II") left it to individual lower court judges and school districts to design and implement desegregation plans "with all deliberate speed." Ultimately, it took two decades of individual lawsuits against school systems and other government institutions throughout the country, both in the South and in the North, to produce the hundreds of court orders that chipped away at racial segregation. Some observers contend that the Supreme Court has been given too much credit for advancing civil rights through its famous first decision in *Brown* because it was actually the long, slow process of many lawsuits and court decisions after *Brown* II that finally broke down the barriers of official segregation. Still, there is broad agreement that the Supreme Court's first *Brown* ruling was a bold and necessary step in the process of increasing civil rights protections for African Americans by withdrawing the judiciary's earlier endorsement of racial segregation.

Additional lawsuits also challenged racial restrictions imposed by government in other aspects of American life. One of

▶ **Why did it take** so long to end school segregation after the *Brown* decision?

Earl Warren (1891–1974) chief justice of the Supreme Court (1953–1969) who led the Court to its unanimous decision in *Brown v. Board of Education of Topeka* (1954) and also took a leading role in many decisions expanding civil liberties and promoting civil rights.

the final breakthroughs occurred in 1967, when the Supreme Court struck down state laws that prohibited people from marrying individuals of a different race (*Loving* v. *Virginia*). Today, many people are surprised to realize that only four decades ago, it was a crime in several American states for people of different races to marry.

Why did the NAACP use the court pathway instead of other pathways? Official, legal racial segregation was firmly entrenched in the states of the South, where the majority of African Americans lived. An ideology of white superiority and racial separation was widespread among whites, who controlled dominant institutions, including government. Because African Americans were blocked from voting in southern states, they could not elect their own candidates for public office who would seek to eliminate discriminatory laws through the legislative process. When members of Congress from northern states proposed federal legislation to counteract racial discrimination, congressional committees dominated by seniority-protected southern senators and representatives blocked these proposals, which could seldom reach the point of even being considered for a vote. Delaying tactics by southern senators had the same effect.

Presidents and others in the executive branch of the federal government had little authority over the local and state laws that required segregation and other forms of discrimination. As noted earlier, President Truman issued an executive order that led to the desegregation of the armed forces. President Dwight Eisenhower sent troops to help enforce a judicial order to desegregate Little Rock Central High School in 1957, and President John Kennedy took similar actions in 1962 and 1963 to help enroll the first African American students at the University of Mississippi and the University of Alabama. In addition, presidents could propose and endorse federal civil rights legislation. But they could not make sure that Congress passed such laws, nor could they do anything to change the laws and policies set by state legislatures, city councils, and school districts. State and local laws and policies are not under the control of the federal government. As a result of the unresponsiveness and lack of effectiveness of elected officials, the NAACP saw courts as the only institutions through which to advance the principles of equal protection.

Although judicial action barred governments from continuing the practice of formal racial segregation, the courts did not make sure that schools were integrated and equal in quality. The Supreme Court limited the ability of lower courts to issue deseg-

President Dwight D. Eisenhower sent U.S. Army troops to protect nine African American students who faced violence and harassment when they enrolled at the previously all-white Little Rock Central High School in Arkansas. The effectiveness of pathways of change also depends on the actions of individuals who carry out new laws and policies. This may include physical courage, as illustrated by the Little Rock Nine, and the political courage of leaders such as Eisenhower. Can you think of other examples of courage—physical or political— that helped carry out changes in public policy?

regation orders by requiring that all orders only affect students within the boundaries of a single school system (*Milliken* v. *Bradley,* 1974). Racial separation remains very common when the composition of city schools is compared to the composition of suburban schools that may be only a few blocks away. Today racial separation is created by housing patterns reflecting boundaries of cities and suburbs and the inability of poorer people to afford housing in affluent school districts. Judicial decisions prevent

► **What about civil rights**
for women: They had to be
fought for too, didn't they?

discussionquestions

1. Why did the NAACP focus its attention on the court pathway prior to the 1960s?

2. What was the racial composition of the student body at your high school? Why did that composition exist at your school? If someone wanted to create more diversity at your high school, what would effective strategy that could be used to advance that goal?

---

racial segregation created by law, but they do not prevent the sort of racial separation that exists in many metropolitan areas.

The foregoing discussion does not mean that the court process was the only pathway of action on civil rights. As we shall see later in this chapter, the grassroots mobilization pathway was important, too, as ordinary people sought to expand civil rights through protest marches, voter registration drives, and other forms of citizen activism.

practicequiz

1. The detention of Japanese Americans during World War II
   a. was deemed a violation of the equal protection clause by the Supreme Court in 1944.
   b. was never examined by the Supreme Court.
   c. did not prompt any protests at the time.
   d. triggered Fred Korematsu's long-lived activism on behalf detainees' rights in the United States.

2. The NAACP began its civil rights work in the court pathway by directly seeking to overturn the "separate but equal" ruling of 1896.
   a. true   b. false

3. The Supreme Court's decision in *Brown* v. *Board of Education* was so important for the advancement of civil rights in this country because
   a. it signaled the federal judiciary's condemnation of racial discrimination and made state-mandated segregation illegal.
   b. it brought an end to segregation nationwide.
   c. it confirmed that racial segregation could not be examined by courts.
   d. it ushered in a dramatic surge in racial harmony in both the North and the South.

4. In many areas of this country, public schools still reflect racial separation and unequal conditions because
   a. the Supreme Court's decision in *Brown* v. *Board of Education* has not been enforced.
   b. subsequent court cases have reversed parts of the *Brown* decision.
   c. a disproportionate number of African Americans are still too poor to live in school districts with top-notch facilities and programs.
   d. some areas care more about education than others.

Answers: 1-d, 2-b, 3-a, 4-c.

CLARIFYING THE COVERAGE OF THE EQUAL PROTECTION CLAUSE

► **What about civil rights for women: They had to be fought for too, didn't they?** On several occasions, advocates of gender equality pursued cases with the hope that the Supreme Court would interpret the equal protection clause to prohibit discrimination against women. But the Supreme Court's 1873 decision in *Bradwell* v. *Illinois* had established a long-standing precedent that provided judicial endorsement of laws that discriminated against women because of their gender—much as the 1896 *Plessy* case did with respect to African Americans. In *Bradwell*, the Court upheld an Illinois statute that prohibited women from becoming licensed attorneys in that state. Justice Joseph P. Bradley's now-discredited opinion relied on prevailing social values and nineteenth-century assumptions about women's "natural destiny" to work solely in the roles of wives and mothers:

> The natural and proper timidity and delicacy which belongs to the female sex evidently unfits it for many of the occupations of civil life. The constitution of the family organization, which is founded in the divine ordinance, as well as in the nature of things, indicates the domestic sphere as that which properly belongs to the domain and functions of womanhood.

The attitudes evident in the *Bradwell* opinion continued for many decades and help explain why women did not obtain the right to vote nationally until the ratification of the Nineteenth Amendment in 1920. In later decades, additional cases tested whether the Court would alter its interpretation of the equal protection clause to advance civil rights for women. In *Goesaert* v. *Cleary* (1948), for example, the Court upheld a Michigan statute that prohibited women from working in establishments that served alcoholic beverages unless they were the wives or daughters of the owner. Like many other statutes that mandated unequal treatment by gender, this law was justified by the state's stated desire to protect women. Such attitudes still dominated the thinking of legislatures and courts in the 1960s, as shown by the Supreme Court's endorsement of a Florida law that automatically excluded women from jury duty unless they asked to serve. This law led to an overrepresentation of men on juries and even to many all-male juries, yet the justices endorsed the law by noting that

▶ **How does the Supreme** Court decide whether a specific law or policy violates the equal protection clause?

what YOU can do!

Identify issues of discrimination and inequality that are of concern to you. Use the Internet to find Web sites of organizations that share your concerns. For example, look at **http://www.dredf.org** (Disability Rights, Education, and Defense Fund) or **http://www.narf.org** (Native American Rights Fund). Do these organizations provide opportunities for citizens to contribute to or participate in their activities?

"woman is still considered as the center of home and family life." The Court concluded that states could enact protective laws that sought to avoid interfering with women's "special responsibilities" as wives and mothers (*Hoyt* v. *Florida*, 1961).

During the 1970s, the Women's Rights Project of the American Civil Liberties Union (ACLU) tried to copy the approach of the NAACP by using the court pathway to argue for the application of the equal protection clause to gender discrimination. The Supreme Court first struck down a gender-based law as discriminatory in *Reed* v. *Reed* (1971), a case concerning Idaho's inheritance statute that mandated preferences for men. Led by law professor Ruth Bader Ginsburg, who in 1993 would be appointed as the second woman justice on the U.S. Supreme Court, the ACLU hoped to persuade the justices in other cases that the equal protection clause should protect against gender discrimination in the same manner that the courts used the clause to prohibit racial discrimination by government (see Table 6.3). As part of the ACLU's litigation strategy, Ginsburg sought to illuminate the issue of gender discrimination for the then all-male Supreme Court by demonstrating that many discriminatory laws treated men in an unequal fashion. Ginsburg wanted to show that gender discrimination was not merely a "women's rights" issue. In a 1976 case concerning Oklahoma's law imposing a higher drinking age for males than females, a majority of justices struck down the law that discriminated against men (*Craig* v. *Boren*). In making this decision, the Court clarified how lower-court judges should apply the equal protection clause to gender discrimination claims.

▶ **How does the Supreme Court decide whether a specific law or policy violates the equal protection clause?** The Supreme Court analyzes equal protection cases through three different tests, depending on the nature of the discrimination alleged in the case. In cases alleging discrimination by race or national origin, the Court directs judges to provide the greatest level of protection for individuals. In such cases, the courts apply *strict scrutiny*, a concept discussed in Ⓛ Ⓘ Ⓝ Ⓚ *Chapter 5, pages 178–179*, with respect to alleged violations of fundamental rights. For these cases, the courts require the government to show a compelling justification for any laws, policies, or practices that result in racial discrimination (or the denial of fundamental rights).

By contrast, the Supreme Court applies *intermediate scrutiny* to claims of gender discrimination. In such cases, the government need only show a substantial justification, rather than a compelling

reason, to explain the different treatment of men and women. This lower level of protection against gender discrimination explains, for example, why the courts accept differential treatment of men and women in military matters, such as the requirement that only men must register with Selective Service (for draft eligibility) when they reach the age of 18.

A third level of scrutiny, called the *rational basis test*, applies for other kinds of equal protection claims. In these cases, the government can justify different treatment by merely providing a rational reason for using a particular policy or practice that advances legitimate governmental goals. For example, the government can have policies and programs that adversely affect the poor. The Supreme Court made this point clear in approving methods of financing public schools, such a property tax systems, that give advantages to residents in wealthy school districts (*San Antonio Independent School District* v. *Rodriguez*, 1973). Similar issues would arise if people sought to use the equal protection clause to raise claims in court concerning discrimination based on age, disability, and other characteristics.

The Supreme Court's decisions have made it clear that the equal protection clause is available only to prohibit specific kinds

TABLE 6.3

Median Earnings of Workers in Selected Occupational Groups by Sex, 2004

Occupational Group	MEN	WOMEN
Full-time, year-round civilian workers, —age 16 and over	$41,353	$31,476
Management occupations	$65,393	$48,118
Business and financial occupations	$57,922	$42,256
Computer- and mathematics-related —occupations	$66,130	$56,585
Architectural and engineering —occupations	$64,496	$51,581
Sales and related occupations	$43,483	$27,862
Production occupations	$34,126	$22,845

SOURCE: Data from Peter Fronczek, *Income, Earnings, and Poverty from the 2004 American Community Survey* (Washington, DC: U.S. Census Bureau, 2005), p. 11.

TABLE 6.4
Three Tests for the Equal Protection Clause

Types of Rights and Discrimination Claims	Types of Tests: Strict Scrutiny Test	Continuing Controversies
Fundamental freedoms: religion, assembly, press, privacy. Discrimination based on race, alienage (foreign citizenship), ethnicity: called "suspect classifications" (i.e., such bases for discrimination are especially suspicious in the eyes of judges)	Does the government have a compelling reason for the law, policy, or program that clashes with a fundamental freedom or treats people differently by "suspect" demographic characteristics (i.e., race, alienage, ethnicity)? If there is a compelling justification for the government's objective, is this the least restrictive way to attain that objective? *Example: Loving* v. *Virginia* (1967) Virginia has no compelling justification for prohibiting marriages between whites and people from other races	*Grutter* v. *Bollinger* (2003). A slim five-member majority of the Supreme Court approved race-conscious affirmative action programs in admissions decisions at public universities by concluding that the advancement of diversity is a compelling government interest.
	Intermediate Scrutiny Test	
Gender discrimination	Is gender discrimination from a law, policy, or government practice substantially related to the advancement of an important government interest? *Example: Mississippi University for Women* v. *Hogan* (1982) The preservation of a public university as a single-sex institution is not an important government interest that can justify excluding men from a graduate nursing program.	*Rostker* v. *Goldberg* (1981). Despite the service of and casualties suffered by female military personnel in the war zone of Iraq, the Supreme Court has said that the government is advancing an important interest in military preparedness by limiting mandatory Selective Service registration to males, because women are theoretically not eligible for combat roles.
	Rational Basis Test	
Other bases of discrimination, including age, wealth, and other classifications not covered by strict scrutiny or heightened scrutiny	Is the government's law, policy, or practice a rational way to advance a legitimate government interest? *Example: San Antonio Independent School District* v. *Rodriguez* (1973) Despite the extra money generated for children in wealthy school districts and the reduced funding for children in poor districts, the use of a property tax system for financing public schools was rational and acceptable.	In *Bush* v. *Gore* (2000), the Supreme Court terminated the Florida vote recount that might have affected the outcome of the contested presidential election by asserting that the recount procedures would violate the equal protection rights of individual voters. The Court's decision did not directly answer whether this case signaled the Court's willingness to thereafter look at voters as claimants deserving of higher levels of scrutiny for equal protection claims.

restrictive covenant
a clause added to a deed restricting real estate sales for a reason.

discussionquestions

1. What kinds of discrimination claims can be pursued successfully in the courts by invoking the equal protection clause?

2. Should the strict scrutiny test be applied to all allegations of discrimination? What effect would such an application of the test have on government and society?

of discrimination by government, especially race and gender discrimination. It does *not* require the government to treat all people in an equal fashion. As a result, the court pathway does not provide all groups with an equally promising means of advancing civil rights issues by relying on the equal protection clause. The disabled, the elderly, and other groups can use the court pathway to enforce legislatively created *statutes*, such as the Age Discrimination in Employment Act, that protect them from specific kinds of discrimination. It is much more difficult for them to use the equal protection clause, because nearly all government policies and practices can be justified under the rational basis test, even if they adversely affect the disabled, the elderly, children, or members of other groups not protected by the strict scrutiny (race and national origin) or intermediate scrutiny (gender) test (see Table 6.4).

pathways of action
RESTRICTIVE COVENANTS

The Shelley family, African Americans who had moved from Mississippi to St. Louis, Missouri, saved their money to buy a home outside of the poor, predominantly African American neighborhood in which they first lived. After they purchased a house in 1945, their white neighbors filed a legal action against them based on a **restrictive covenant** that was included in the deed to each house, forbidding the sale of any house in the neighborhood to African Americans. Such restrictive covenants were a common technique used in real estate to force minority group members to live in ghetto neighborhoods. In some parts of the country, these restrictive covenants also prevented real estate sales to Jews, Asian Americans, and other religious or ethnic minorities. With assistance from the NAACP, the Shelleys' attorney fought the case all the way to the U.S. Supreme Court, where legal briefs supporting the Shelleys were submitted by a variety of civil rights groups representing Asian Americans, Native Americans, Jews, and labor organizations.[17]

The legal issue was a potential problem because this form of discrimination involved a contract between private property owners and therefore appeared to fall outside the coverage of the equal protection clause, which is aimed at "state action" (discrimination by government). In an important victory for the civil rights of minority group members, the Supreme Court struck down the enforcement of such restrictive covenants. Even though covenants were a form of private discrimination, the Court ruled that any enforcement of these provisions by government institutions, including courts, constituted state action and therefore violated the equal pro-

tection clause. The decision prohibited people from using race-based restrictive covenants to prevent their neighbors from selling homes to members of minority groups. However, it did not prevent homeowners from racially discriminating when selling their own property. This form of private discrimination was not barred by legislation until the 1960s. The case of *Shelley* v. *Kraemer* (1948) thus demonstrated how individuals can use the court process to advance equality and civil rights. But it also showed that court decisions alone cannot block all forms of discrimination. ■

practicequiz

1. The Supreme Court's 1873 decision in *Bradwell* v. *Illinois*
   a. marked the beginning of successful women's rights activism in the courts.
   b. reinforced culturally dominant views of women as naturally domestic and unfit for professional lives.
   c. delayed progress in women's rights but helped later activists connect women's rights to the equal protection clause.
   d. helped usher in the enfranchisement of women in the United States.

2. Many years before she became the second woman on the Supreme Court, Ruth Bader Ginsburg
   a. was a legal secretary with a law degree.
   b. was a Freedom Rider in the South.
   c. led the ACLU's attempts to persuade the Court that the equal protection clause protects against gender discrimination by the government.
   d. argued, on behalf of the ACLU, that gender discrimination was worse for men than for women.

3. In cases involving alleged gender discrimination, the Supreme Court uses which test to guide its thinking?
   a. Strict scrutiny.
   b. Moderate scrutiny.
   c. Rational basis.
   d. Conditional basis.

4. What are restrictive covenants?
   a. Clauses in deeds that prohibit owners from selling their property to racial or ethnic minorities.
   b. Legal agreements established by communities that make racial integration mandatory.
   c. State laws that allow politicians to redraw the boundaries of congressional districts every ten years.
   d. Clauses in the charters of private clubs that make it legal for them to discriminate in their admission policies.

Answers: 1-b, 2-c, 3-b, 4-a.

ABOVE: **An all-white, all-male jury** listened to testimony in the trial of two white men accused of murdering Emmett Till, the African American teenager who was abducted and killed after he allegedly whistled at a white woman in Mississippi.

BELOW: **In the 1955 trial, Mose Wright** risked his life by testifying against the defendants at a time when African Americans could be killed for speaking out against whites. Ultimately, as happened in so many cases in the segregated South in which African Americans were victims of violence, the all-white jury acquitted the defendants. What does this example show about the role of law in controversies over discrimination and inequality?

▶ **Why was the Montgomery** bus boycott so important?

Grassroots Mobilization and Civil Rights

Judicial interpretations of the U.S. Constitution had important but limited effects on the advancement of equality and civil rights. Judicial decisions, as we've seen, primarily limit what governments can do to enforce certain kinds of discrimination based on race and gender. However, the Constitution did not cover many forms of discrimination practiced by private individuals in making decisions about hiring people for jobs, selling or renting houses, providing goods and services, and generally treating other people in the course of everyday life. Thus judicial decisions based on the Constitution could not, by themselves, transform the daily lives of discrimination victims. The changes in American society that have affected these other aspects of discrimination developed as a result of grassroots mobilization and evolving social values that eventually produced both new legislation and new attitudes about equality.

AFRICAN AMERICANS AND CIVIL RIGHTS

Protest marches and other forms of grassroots mobilization were used by various groups before the civil rights movement of the 1950s. In the quest to achieve their policy goals, American labor unions, veterans' groups, and other organizations had long attempted to mobilize support. African Americans and their sympathizers, however, became famous for their courage, their visibility, and their success in changing both laws and societal attitudes.

Several events in the mid-1950s led the African American civil rights issue to capture the attention of the American public. In 1954, the Supreme Court's monumental *Brown* decision got significant attention—including outrage and vows of resistance by southern whites. One year later, a 14-year-old African American youth from Chicago named Emmett Till, visiting relatives in Mississippi and probably unaware of local ways, was brutally murdered and mutilated after he allegedly whistled at a passing white woman. Charles Diggs, a black Congressman from Michigan at the time of the murder, observed that a photograph in *Jet* magazine, an African-American publication, showing Emmett Till's mutilation "was probably the greatest media product in the last forty or fifty years, because that picture stimulated a lot of interest and anger on the part of blacks all over the country."[18] The trial of the white men who abducted and murdered Till was covered by news media throughout the country. Despite the defendants' being

Martin Luther King Jr. (1929–1968)
civil rights leader who emerged from the
Montgomery bus boycott to become a
national leader of the civil rights movement and a recipient of the Nobel Peace
Prize.

identified by eyewitnesses, the all-white jury quickly returned a
"not guilty" verdict. Reaction was swift. African Americans held
protest rallies in major cities throughout the country, and editorials in major newspapers condemned the verdict. As one commentator noted, the Till case had a powerful mobilizing effect on
Americans, both African Americans and whites:

> Through the extensive press coverage, all America saw the
> injustice that had taken place. But black Americans, partic-
> ularly in the South, saw something else as well. . . . They
> saw black people stand in a court of law and testify against
> white people.[19]

A major problem for the mobilization of African Americans,
especially in the South, was the fact that whites controlled the
region's entire criminal justice system, including the police and the
prosecutors.[20] Any African American who challenged the status
quo by complaining about discrimination and inequality ran the
risk of being arrested on phony charges, beaten by the police, or
even killed by whites who knew that they would not be convicted
for their crimes. Thus the grassroots mobilization of African
Americans required great courage in the face of violent responses
by whites dedicated to the preservation of the privileges a segregated society gave them.

▶ **Why was the Montgomery bus boycott so important?** In
December 1955, African Americans in Montgomery, Alabama,
began a boycott of the city bus system in protest against a Jim Crow
ordinance that forced them to either sit in the back of the bus or to
stand whenever a white person needed a seat. The local chapter of
the NAACP had been thinking about initiating a boycott like the
ones that had been attempted in other cities. Around that time, one
of the organization's active members, a 43-year-old seamstress
named Rosa Parks, refused to surrender her seat to a white man who
boarded the bus after she did. The bus driver had her arrested, and
she was convicted of violating segregation laws. In response, the
NAACP and ministers of local African American churches organized a boycott.[21] In selecting a leader for the boycott organization,
the Montgomery Improvement Association (MIA), the civil rights
advocates turned to **Martin Luther King Jr.,** a 26-year-old minister
who had only recently arrived in town to lead a local Baptist church.
King proved to be a thoughtful and charismatic leader whose powerful speeches and advocacy of nonviolent methods of protest carried him to the forefront of the national civil rights movement.

The Montgomery bus boycott lasted thirteen months. The
MIA purchased station wagons to carry African Americans to
work, and blacks who owned cars, as well as sympathetic whites,

The Rev. Dr. Martin Luther King, Jr., sat
in a jail cell after one of his many arrests
for leading non-violent civil rights protests.
What would have happened in the African
Americans' struggle for equality if no one
had organized mass mobilization, or if civil
rights advocates had emphasized the use of
violence as a means to seek social change?

▶ **Why did President Eisenhower** send troops to a high school in Little Rock, Arkansas?

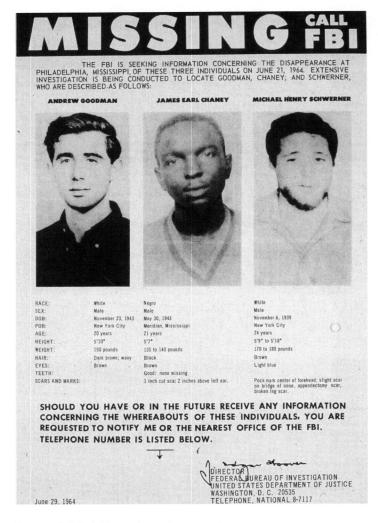

Poster of civil rights workers who were missing for more than a month before Ku Klux Klan informers helped the FBI solve the case and locate their buried bodies. These murders, carried out by local law enforcement officers and members of the Klan, outraged whites in the North and helped to shift public opinion in favor of African Americans' efforts to gain voting rights and political equality. How do shifts in public opinion help to change public policy?

volunteered to drive the boycotters to work. Many people walked rather than ride the bus. The bus company lost significant revenue, but the white leaders of Montgomery refused to compromise by changing the Jim Crow ordinance. They fought back against the boycott by pressuring insurance agencies to deny coverage to the MIA's vehicles. They prosecuted African Americans for congregating on corners while waiting for rides. Other whites firebombed the homes of King and other boycott leaders, and snipers fired at African Americans. Eventually, the prosecutor in Montgomery charged King and dozens of other leaders with violating a state law against boycotts. King's trial and conviction brought national news media attention to the boycott, and he was invited to give speeches throughout the country about racial discrimination and civil rights.[22] King's prominence as a civil rights leader enabled him to advocate the benefits of nonviolent, mass mobilization as a means for policy change. In the following excerpt from King's writings, you can see why he chose grassroots mobilization as an effective pathway for action.

> You may well ask, Why direct action? Why sit-ins, marches, and so forth? Isn't negotiation a better path? You are quite right in calling for negotiations. Indeed, this is the very purpose of direct action. Nonviolent direct action seeks to create such a crisis and foster such a tension that a community which has constantly refused to negotiate is forced to confront the issue. It seeks so to dramatize the issue that it can no longer be ignored. . . . My friends, I must say to you that we have not made a single gain in civil rights without determined legal and nonviolent pressure. Lamentably, it is a historical fact that privileged groups seldom give up their privileges voluntarily. . . . We know from painful experience that freedom is never voluntarily given by the oppressor; it must be demanded by the oppressed. . . . We have waited for more than 340 years for our constitutional and God-given rights. The nations of Asia and Africa are moving with jetlike speed toward gaining independence, but we still creep at horse-and-buggy pace toward gaining a cup of coffee at a lunch counter. . . .

Excerpt from Martin Luther King Jr.'s "Letter from Birmingham Jail," addressed to fellow ministers and written in April 1963 while King was jailed during protests in Alabama.

Source: "Letter from Birmingham Jail" in *Why We Can't Wait* by Martin Luther King Jr. Copyright © by Martin Luther King Jr. Reprinted 1991 by Coretta Scott King. Reprinted by arrangement with The Heirs to the Estate of Martin Luther King Jr. c/o Writers House as agents for the proprietor.

The boycott ended after the MIA used the court pathway by filing a successful lawsuit asserting that in accordance with the recently developed principles of *Brown*, enforced racial segregation on the buses was illegal. The actions in Montgomery inspired African Americans in other southern cities to launch their own bus boycotts against segregation. The boycott also inspired the formation of new grassroots organizations, such as the Southern Christian Leadership Conference.

▶ **Why did President Eisenhower send troops to a high school in Little Rock, Arkansas?** As grassroots protests against racial discrimination continued in many cities, other events contributed to move public opinion as well as the federal government's political power away from acceptance of segregation. For example, the national news media gave great attention to the Little Rock Nine, a group of African American students who attempted to enroll at all-white Little Rock Central High School in Arkansas after a successful court case in 1957. President Dwight D. Eisenhower sent hundreds of troops from the U.S. Army's 101st Airborne Division to escort the students into the school and provide protection for them after they were barred from the school and subjected to harassment, threats, and violence.[23]

Some white Americans got involved in the civil rights movement. Later instances of violence against African Americans and white civil rights activists continued to capture headlines and produced gripping television footage. Whites rioted at the University of Mississippi in 1962, leading to two deaths and hundreds of injuries, as they attempted to prevent one man, Air Force veteran James Meredith, from enrolling as the university's first African American student. After dozens of federal marshals were injured, including several with gunshot wounds, President John F. Kennedy sent soldiers to restore order. Television showed the vicious use by city police of fire hoses, tear gas, and attack dogs to subdue peaceful protesters in Birmingham, Alabama, in 1963. The bombing of a Birmingham church that year, which took the lives of four young African American girls attending a Bible study class, shocked the nation. "Revulsion at the church bombing," wrote one historian, "spread swiftly around the world."[24]

In 1964, two young white men from the North, Michael Schwerner and Andrew Goodman, and an African American civil rights worker from Mississippi, James Chaney, were abducted and murdered in Philadelphia, Mississippi, as they sought to register African American voters. The vehemence and violence of white resistance to desegregation helped move national public opinion in favor of the African Americans' cause, and it pushed the federal government to take long-overdue action in support of civil rights.

Edgar Ray Killen is led away from the courthouse in Philadelphia, Mississippi, in 2005 after being convicted of manslaughter for the 1964 killings of civil rights workers James Chaney, Michael Schwerner, and Andrew Goodman. At his original trial in 1964, the jury had been unable to reach a verdict, although seven other conspirators were convicted of federal charges at that time. Four decades later, prosecutors retried Killen successfully. Why was it so important to pursue this case forty years after the murders occurred?
Lori Waselchuk/The New York Times

pathways past and present

TECHNOLOGY AND GRASSROOTS MOBILIZATION

For most of American history, grassroots mobilization relied on personal contact as speakers traveled from town to town and their supporters tried to attract a crowd by posting and distributing printed notices. Literate Americans could also read newspaper accounts of speeches given in their community. Only

▶ **The Fifteenth Amendment**
gave African Americans the
right to vote in 1870, so why
did we need the Voting Rights
Act nearly a century later?

Civil Rights Act of 1964
federal statutes that prohibited racial discrimination in public accommodations
(hotels, restaurants, theaters).

Voting Rights Act of 1965
federal statute that effectively attacked literacy tests and other techniques used to
prevent African Americans from voting.

The 1963 March on Washington showed a
national television audience that tens of thousands of African Americans and whites were
working together to advance the cause of civil
rights. Martin Luther King Jr.'s "I Have a Dream"
speech on the steps of the Lincoln Memorial is
considered by many observers to be one of the
most inspirational moments in American political history. How might such memorable events
contribute to cultural change?

rarely did events and speeches that occurred in local communities
get national news coverage.

In contemporary times, by contrast, the development of communications technology has enhanced the capabilities of interest
groups, including those that attempt to mobilize supporters around
issues concerning civil rights. National news telecasts create opportunities for groups to organize highly publicized marches and speeches
that will be broadcast into living rooms throughout the country (and
even the world). In addition, contemporary civil rights organizations
can educate the public and communicate with their members via the
Internet. Through their Web sites, civil rights organizations can
attract new members, solicit donations, educate the public, and facilitate networking between members of different organizations. E-mail
permits organizations to send messages instantly and use these messages to mobilize their members to lobby legislatures and organize
meetings and demonstrations. For example, the Web site of the
National Council of La Raza (http://www.nclr.org), an organization
that seeks to reduce discrimination and poverty affecting Latinos,
describes various programs and provides information relevant to its
constituents. Web sites are important tools for different kinds of organizations, including private advocacy groups (for example, the Equal
Justice Society, http://www.equaljusticesociety.org), government
agencies (such as U.S. Civil Rights Commission, http://www.uscrc.
gov), and university-based organizations (for example, the Harvard
University Civil Rights Project, http://www.civilrightsproject.
harvard.edu). Check out these Web sites and others that present
information on civil rights issues of interest to you. ▪

People came from around the country to participate in the
1963 March on Washington to express support for legislation to
combat discrimination and enforce civil rights. The quarter of a
million participants included tens of thousands of whites.[25]
Among the many leaders who spoke to the crowd from the steps
of the Lincoln Memorial was the keynote speaker, Martin Luther
King Jr., who delivered what later came to be known as his "I Have
a Dream Speech," one of the most famous public addresses in
American history (see Figure 6.1). News coverage showed a
nationwide television audience, the huge throng of people, black
and white, who peacefully rallied for the cause of civil rights. A few
months after President Kennedy was assassinated, the new president, Lyndon Johnson, was able to use public sentiment aroused by
the martyred president's death, as well as growing concerns about
racial discrimination, to push the **Civil Rights Act of 1964**

through Congress, despite last-ditch resistance from conservative white southern politicians.

▶ **The Fifteenth Amendment gave African Americans the right to vote in 1870, so why did we need the Voting Rights Act nearly a century later?** In 1965, national attention was drawn to Selma, Alabama, where protests focused on registering African American voters. Many locales across the South used rigged literacy tests in which African Americans were asked to read and explain long, complicated words and phrases, only to be flunked by officials no matter how accurate their responses and thus denied the opportunity to vote. A protest march, planned to proceed from Selma to the state capital, Montgomery, was stopped by dozens of Alabama state police, who attacked the peaceful marchers and beat them with clubs. The brutality of the police attack received significant coverage in newspapers and on television. During the planning for another march, James Reeb, a white minister from Boston, was attacked and killed by a club-wielding mob of whites. The death of the white minister so shocked whites in the North that Selma was flooded with additional protesters, and civil rights advocates gained additional support.[26] Public reactions to the violence directed at civil rights protesters helped push Congress into enacting the **Voting Rights Act of 1965,** the long-sought federal legislation that finally facilitated the participation of African Americans through voting and campaigning for elective office.

CIVIL RIGHTS LEGISLATION

The grassroots mobilization of blacks and whites for African Americans' civil rights helped change public acceptance of racial discrimination, and it lent momentum to efforts to induce legislators to enact new laws intended to advance racial equality. Many of these new laws were directed at discrimination practiced by private individuals and businesses—discrimination that was beyond the reach of the equal protection clause. Title II of the Civil Rights Act of 1964, for example, forbids discrimination by race, color, religion, or national origin in "public accommodations," which includes hotels, restaurants, gas stations, movie theaters, and sports stadiums.

The Voting Rights Act of 1965 was not the first congressional legislation that sought to prevent the racial discrimination that limited African Americans' access to the ballot—discrimination that the Fifteenth Amendment had sought to outlaw back in 1870. The Civil Rights Acts of 1957, 1960, and 1964 all contained provisions aimed at barriers to voting. However, they all proved ineffective because they relied on litigation for enforcement, while

---

A Dream Deferred

In his memorable "I have a dream" speech at the Lincoln Memorial on Aug. 28,1963, Dr. Martin Luther King Jr. looked forward to a time when blacks would live equally with other Americans. While considerable economic progress has been made, blacks still lag well behind. Black Americans own homes at a lower rate than the overall population; a greater percentage live below the poverty line; and a smaller percentage have college degrees.

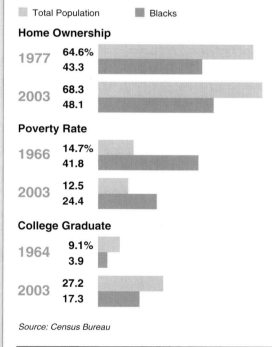

■ Total Population   ■ Blacks

Home Ownership

1977   64.6%
       43.3

2003   68.3
       48.1

Poverty Rate

1966   14.7%
       41.8

2003   12.5
       24.4

College Graduate

1964   9.1%
       3.9

2003   27.2
       17.3

Source: Census Bureau

January 2005, The New York Times

FIGURE 6.1

A Dream Deferred

Although the measures displayed in this figure show progress, this progress occurred very slowly over the span of two decades, and significant gaps still remain. What actions can the government take to speed up the process of attaining equality in these measures? Should the government take such actions?

▶ **When were women first allowed to vote in the United States?**

U.S. Commission on Civil Rights
federal commission created in 1957 to study issues of discrimination and inequality in order for the federal government to consider whether additional laws and policies are needed to address civil rights matters.

U.S. Equal Employment Opportunity Commission
federal commission created in 1964 to handle complaints about employment discrimination and file lawsuits on behalf of employment discrimination victims.

universal suffrage
the right to vote for all adult citizens.

Voter registration rates for African Americans in southern states increased dramatically after the Voting Rights Act of 1965 helped to eliminate discriminatory barriers.

TABLE 6.5
Percentage of Eligible Citizens Registered to Vote

	MARCH 1965			NOVEMBER 1988		
	AFRICAN AMERICAN	WHITE	GAP	AFRICAN AMERICAN	WHITE	GAP
State						
Alabama	19.3	69.2	49.9	68.4	75	6.6
Georgia	27.4	62.6	35.2	56.8	63.9	7.1
Louisiana	31.6	80.5	48.9	77.1	75.1	–2.0
Mississippi	6.7	69.9	63.2	74.2	80.5	6.3
North Carolina	46.8	96.8	50.0	58.2	65.6	7.4
South Carolina	37.3	75.7	38.4	56.7	61.8	5.1
Virginia	38.3	61.1	22.8	63.8	68.5	4.7

SOURCE: Data from Bernard Grofman, Lisa Handley, and Richard G. Niemi, *Minority Representation and the Quest for Voting Equality* (New York: Cambridge University Press, 1992), pp. 23–24.

states frequently found new ways to discriminate.[27] The Voting Rights Act of 1965 (and its subsequent extensions in 1970 and later years) barred the use of the literacy tests that had been used to keep African Americans away from the polls. Table 6.5 shows the impact of the Voting Rights Act in increasing the registration of African American voters. The act was also more powerful and effective because of its "preclearance" provision, which required officials in designated districts, primarily in southern states, to obtain the permission of the attorney general before making any changes in elections and voting procedures. The lawsuits filed under the Voting Rights Act provided the basis for judges to stop efforts in several states to create new voting districts that would dilute the voting power of black voters and thereby reduce the potential for African Americans to be elected to public office or to elect candidates favorable to their interests.

Another result of the civil rights movement was the creation of new government agencies to monitor compliance with and enforcement of antidiscrimination laws. The **U.S. Commission on Civil Rights,** created in 1957, was given the task of investigating and reporting to Congress about discrimination and the deprivation of civil rights. The **U.S. Equal Employment Opportunity Commission** was created in 1964 and charged with investigating

complaints about illegal employment discrimination. If the commission cannot negotiate compliance agreements with employers, it can initiate lawsuits on behalf of discrimination victims. Within each major federal government department there is now an Office for Civil Rights, with responsibility to guard against discrimination in the programs that the department funds and oversees. Subsequently, states and cities created their own agencies to investigate and enforce their own civil rights laws. These agencies are typically called "civil rights commissions" (for example, the Iowa Civil Rights Commission), "human rights commissions" (for example, the San Francisco Human Rights Commission), or "equal opportunity commissions" (for example, the Nebraska Equal Opportunity Commission).

practicequiz

1. For the most part, court decisions in the area of civil rights
   a. address the legality of behavior of individual U.S. citizens.
   b. authorize the government to take certain actions to advance the civil rights of minorities.
   c. limit what the government can do to enforce certain forms of discrimination.
   d. generate new ways of relating civil rights to the Constitution.

discussionquestions

1. Why was nonviolence ultimately a successful strategy for African Americans in their struggle for civil rights?

2. In addition to the Civil Rights Act of 1964, the Voting Rights Act of 1965, and the creation of various civil rights commissions, are there other kinds of laws that Congress should enact in order to protect civil rights?

what YOU can do!

States have their own laws to protect civil rights. Often these laws include protections different from those in federal laws. Find out what civil rights laws exist in your state. You can use Internet sources, such as **http://www.findlaw.com**

---

2. Who was the African American 14-year-old murdered in Mississippi in 1955 for supposedly whistling at a white woman?
   a. James Meredith
   b. Andrew Goodman
   c. James Chaney
   d. Emmett Till

3. What was the first effect of the Montgomery bus boycott?
   a. the prosecution of local African Americans and physical attacks on Martin Luther King Jr. and other black leaders
   b. a revision of the city's Jim Crow bus policy, allowing African Americans to sit "in any open seats"
   c. the celebrity of Rosa Parks
   d. the demise of the Montgomery Improvement Association

4. The March on Washington, the Civil Rights Act, the Voting Rights Act, and the Montgomery bus boycott came in what order chronologically?
   a. march, boycott, Voting Rights Act, Civil Rights Act
   b. boycott, march, Civil Rights Act, Voting Rights Act
   c. Civil Rights Act, boycott, march, Voting Rights Act
   d. Voting Rights Act, boycott, Civil Rights Act, march

Answers: 1-c, 2-d, 3-a, 4-b.

WOMEN AND CIVIL RIGHTS

Beginning with public meetings and speeches in the first half of the nineteenth century, grassroots mobilization played a crucial role in obtaining the right to vote for women. After the Civil War, the Fifteenth Amendment sought to give African American men the right to vote. Although advocates for women's civil rights were disappointed that the amendment did not help women get the vote, they took action to mobilize supporters in favor of **universal suffrage**—the right to vote for all adult citizens. One of the most prominent organizations, the National Woman Suffrage Association, was founded and led by Susan B. Anthony and Elizabeth Cady Stanton. These organizations did not agree on all issues. Some focused solely on gaining women the right to vote, while others also sought a wider range of laws that would help women attain equality in American society.[28]

▶ **When were women first allowed to vote in the United States?** Women were able to vote in several northeastern states

Advocates of voting rights for women went to great lengths over the course of many decades to educate the public about the need for universal suffrage. The ratification of the Nineteenth Amendment, which established women's right to vote, represented a major change in the American political system. How would politics and public policy in the United States be different if women were not permitted to participate in the elections pathway?

after the Declaration of Independence in 1776. By 1807, however, all of these states had revoked women's right to vote. It was not until the late nineteenth century that women in various states gradually began to return to polling places as voters.

The first American jurisdiction to grant women the permanent right to vote was the Territory of Wyoming in 1869, followed by the Territory of Utah in 1870. When Wyoming became a state in 1890, its admission effectively permitted its female residents to be the first women in the country to vote in presidential and congressional elections. Colorado and Idaho followed later in the decade. As the rest of the country observed women participating successfully in elections in these sparsely settled states, activists continued to press for suffrage throughout the rest of the country. Over the years, in addition to lobbying legislators and educating the public through publications and speeches, advocates of suffrage organized protest marches and other public demonstrations. Anthony and other activists intentionally faced arrest and prosecution by attempting to vote on election day. Court cases involving the casting of illegal ballots by women attracted additional public attention to the cause of women's suffrage. In later years, other women went to jail for picketing at the White House, and while incarcerated, they went on hunger strikes to draw public attention to their harsh treatment and to their cause.[29]

Another important strategy was seeking to place the question of women's suffrage on statewide ballots as often as possible. As described by one historian, "From 1870 to 1910, there were 480 campaigns in thirty-three states, just to get the issue submitted to the voters, of which only seventeen resulted in actual referendum votes."[30] In the early twentieth century, the suffrage movement

gained momentum after winning successful ballot-issue campaigns in Washington (1910), California (1911), Arizona (1912), Kansas (1912), and Oregon (1912). In 1917, several state legislatures gave women the right to vote for specific elections, such as the presidential election or primary elections.[31] Finally, in 1918, the women's suffrage amendment received sufficient support to pass through Congress and be sent to the states for approval. It was ratified as the Nineteenth Amendment and added to the Constitution in 1920.

The right to vote came through organized political action over the course of eight decades. Figure 6.2 illustrates the universal struggle for women's suffrage in the U.S. and other countries. The mobilization of supporters alone did not lead to women's suffrage. At the same time, American society gradually changed as women gained opportunities to enter the workforce, obtain education, and enter professions that had previously excluded them. All this contributed to the societal changes necessary for women to be viewed as legitimate participants in political processes.

The ratification of the Nineteenth Amendment was extraordinarily important, but it did not ensure that women would enjoy equal rights. Large segments of the public continued to see women as properly destined for subservient roles as wives and housekeepers or for roles in a few "helping professions," such as nursing, teaching, and secretarial services. Women frequently could not gain consideration for other jobs. Even Sandra Day O'Connor, who eventually became the first woman appointed to the U.S. Supreme Court, after graduating near the top of her class in Stanford Law School in the 1950s, received offers to work only as a legal secretary, not as a lawyer. It took decades for women to be elected to public office in appreciable numbers. Even in the twenty-first

FIGURE 6.2
Women Gain Votes

Women's suffrage has been entwined with other struggles. Canadian women won the right to vote in 1917—except for native Americans. They (and native men) were denied the vote until 1960. Likewise, Australia gave most women the vote in 1902, but its aboriginal population had to wait six more decades. New Zealand led the way with universal suffrage in 1893. Here is a timeline showing when some countries—from democracies to dictatorships—granted women the vote, and some others that have yet to do so.

Women Gain Votes

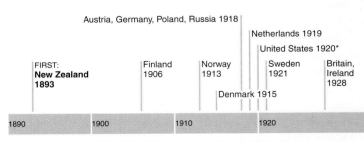

Sources: Interparliamentary Union, United Nations Development Program, CIA World Factbook
*Voting rights for all Americans were not fully guaranteed until passage of the Voting Rights Act in 1965.

century, despite the increasing frequency with which women win elections for Congress, governorships, and state judgeships, they remain underrepresented.

Legislatures took little action to initiate laws that would protect women from discrimination until a new grassroots women's movement emerged in the 1960s and 1970s. By then, larger numbers of women were attending college, entering the workforce, participating in campaigns and elections, and challenging traditional expectations about women's subordinate status in society.

By contrast, men and women between the ages of 18 and 21 gained the right to vote during the Vietnam War era through a relatively quick process driven by political elites, especially in Congress, rather than through grassroots mobilization. Previously, the voting age was 21. However, as men younger than 21 were sent to fight and die for their country, the issue of lowering the voting age arose. According to the historian David Kyvig, young people's grassroots activism in antiwar protests and African Americans' civil rights movement of the 1960s actually led older voters to oppose lowering the voting age:

> Resentment against several years of campus demonstrations, sporadic urban rioting, and antiwar protests undoubtedly did more to persuade older citizens not to lower the voting age than it did to convince them that younger people possessed the requisite political maturity.[32]

However, the Twenty-Sixth Amendment was ratified by the necessary thirty-eight states just three and a half months after it was approved by Congress in 1971. This speed can be explained in part because members of Congress and state legislators sought to

Author and political activist Betty Friedan, who kept a bust of Abraham Lincoln, another champion of equality, in her home, helped to inspire the women's rights movement of the 1960s and 1970s with her book, *The Feminist Mystique.* She was also a founder of the activist interest group NOW (National Organization for Women). When authors are regarded as influencing policy change, which pathway or pathways are affected by their work?

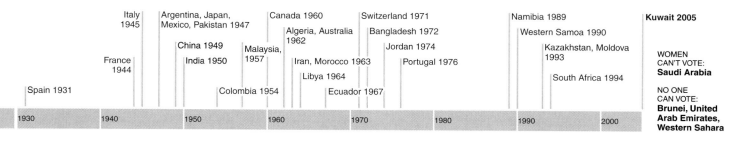

Spain 1931 | France 1944 | Italy 1945 | Argentina, Japan, Mexico, Pakistan 1947 | China 1949 | India 1950 | Colombia 1954 | Malaysia, 1957 | Canada 1960 | Algeria, Australia 1962 | Iran, Morocco 1963 | Libya 1964 | Ecuador 1967 | Switzerland 1971 | Bangladesh 1972 | Jordan 1974 | Portugal 1976 | Namibia 1989 | Western Samoa 1990 | Kazakhstan, Moldova 1993 | South Africa 1994 | Kuwait 2005

WOMEN CAN'T VOTE: **Saudi Arabia**

NO ONE CAN VOTE: **Brunei, United Arab Emirates, Western Sahara**

BILL MARSH

May 2005, The New York Times

▶ **What are the main** civil rights issues affecting Latinos in the United States?

César Chávez (1927–1993)
Latino civil rights leader who founded the United Farm Workers and used grassroots mobilization to seek civil rights for Latinos and improved working conditions for agricultural workers.

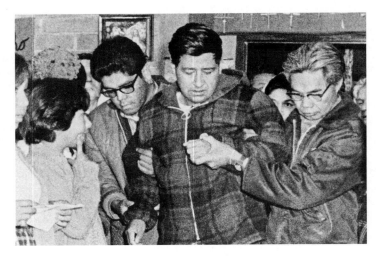

ABOVE: **César Chávez, the farmworkers' leader** who led Latinos' civil rights struggle, used hunger strikes as a means to gain public attention for his cause. Although he was physically weakened while on hunger strikes, his willingness to risk his own health in order to advance equality helped to make him a revered civil rights leader. Why might Chávez have chosen to use this technique instead of other pathways of action?

BELOW: **Thousands of Latino protesters** and their supporters held marches in cities throughout the United States in 2006 to express their objections to restrictive immigration legislation proposed in Congress. Do such protests intend to influence legislators, public opinion, or both? How did you react to news reports about these protests? Monica Almeida/The New York Times

establish one national voting age through the constitutional amendment process. They wanted to prevent the risk of an inconsistent policy of individual states creating their own separate voting ages.

LATINOS AND CIVIL RIGHTS

Latinos, who are frequently also referred to as Hispanics, share a Spanish-speaking heritage but ethnically and racially are highly diverse. Their ancestors may have come from Mexico, Puerto Rico, Cuba, El Salvador, or some other part of Central or South America. They have long faced discrimination in the United States. Some Americans perceive Latinos to be recent arrivals who may have entered the country without proper permission from immigration authorities. In reality, many Latinos are descended from people who lived in the territory that became the United States even before whites became the numerically dominant group. For centuries, Latino people lived in parts of what are today California, Texas, New Mexico, and Arizona—all states whose territory originally belonged to Mexico, which the United States annexed in the 1840s after the Mexican War. Latinos from Puerto Rico and Cuba began moving to New York and Florida in the late 1800s. The United States gained control of both islands after the Spanish-American War (1898). Cuba became an independent country, but Puerto Rico remains under American sovereignty, as an "associated commonwealth," and its people can travel freely to the mainland to live and work. When the Mexican Revolution broke out in the early twentieth century, thousands of Mexicans came north in search of safety and employment. Many American businesses actively recruited workers from Mexico and elsewhere in Latin America.[33] The recruitment and hiring of these workers, including undocumented workers who entered the United States in violation of immigration laws, continued throughout the twentieth century.

▶ **What are the main civil rights issues affecting Latinos in the United States?** Latinos in the United States often received less pay than white workers while being assigned the most difficult and burdensome tasks. Migrant farm workers, who are typically of Mexican or Central American origin, traveled throughout the country harvesting crops, receiving very low pay and facing difficult living conditions. Latinos suffered discrimination and segregation in housing, employment, public accommodations, and education and often faced harsh treatment from police officers and other government officials.[34]

Latinos formed labor unions and civil rights organizations in the early twentieth century at the same time that others in the

United States were forming such groups. Other civil rights organizations emerged when Latinos mobilized in conjunction with the highly publicized civil rights movement of African Americans. Many organizations continue to exist today that focus their work on the advancement of civil rights and equality for Latinos. The Mexican-American Legal Defense and Education Fund (MALDEF), headquartered in Los Angeles and with regional offices elsewhere in the country, dates from 1968. MALDEF uses litigation, legislative lobbying, and public education strategies to advance its civil rights goals. The Puerto Rican Legal Defense and Education Fund was founded in 1972 in New York City. It uses similar strategies and often works in a coordinated fashion with other civil rights groups.

The best-known grassroots movement was led by **César Chávez,** who founded the National Farm Workers Association, later renamed the United Farm Workers (UFW). As you will see in LINK *Chapter 13, page 512,* the discussion of effective, charismatic interest group leaders, Chávez led protest marches and organized a national boycott of grapes harvested by nonunion workers during the 1960s. He also went on hunger strikes to protest poor pay and working conditions for farm workers as well as other issues, such as their exposure to dangerous pesticides.[35] He worked on voter registration drives to encourage more Latinos to vote (see Figure 6.3). Although his union's work focused primarily on California agriculture, he inspired Latino activists and their supporters to join his boycotts and organize efforts elsewhere in the country to advance equality for Latinos. Chávez was not always successful in seeking to gain better contracts for poorly paid farm workers. However, his efforts brought public attention to the issues of poor working conditions for agricultural workers as well as discrimination against Latinos. As a result, his struggle contributed to the enactment of new statutes to provide protection for farm workers. Chávez was a charismatic leader who advocated nonviolent methods of direct political action and protest. For Latinos striving for civil rights and equality, his stature as an inspirational leader is comparable to African Americans' reverential view of Martin Luther King Jr.

Chávez's struggle was not completed by the time he passed away in 1993. The issue of civil rights and equal treatment for Latinos continues in the twenty-first century, especially because Latinos are now the largest minority group in the United States, surpassing the number of African Americans in 2003 and continuing to grow at a faster rate than most other demographic groups. Latino activists continue to be concerned about such issues as unequal treatment in employment, housing, and the criminal justice system.

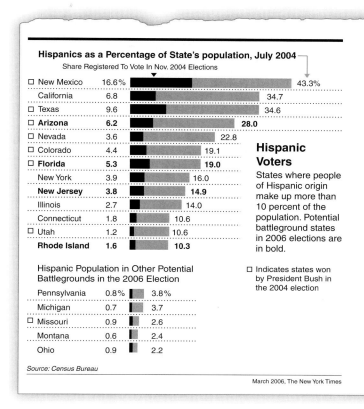

Hispanics as a Percentage of State's population, July 2004

Share Registered To Vote In Nov. 2004 Elections

☐ New Mexico	16.6%	43.3%
California	6.8	34.7
☐ Texas	9.6	34.6
☐ **Arizona**	**6.2**	**28.0**
☐ Nevada	3.6	22.8
☐ Colorado	4.4	19.1
☐ **Florida**	**5.3**	**19.0**
New York	3.9	16.0
New Jersey	**3.8**	**14.9**
Illinois	2.7	14.0
Connecticut	1.8	10.6
☐ Utah	1.2	10.6
Rhode Island	**1.6**	**10.3**

Hispanic Voters

States where people of Hispanic origin make up more than 10 percent of the population. Potential battleground states in 2006 elections are in bold.

Hispanic Population in Other Potential Battlegrounds in the 2006 Election

Pennsylvania	0.8%	3.8%
Michigan	0.7	3.7
☐ Missouri	0.9	2.6
Montana	0.6	2.4
Ohio	0.9	2.2

☐ Indicates states won by President Bush in the 2004 election

Source: Census Bureau

March 2006, The New York Times

FIGURE 6.3

Hispanics' voting power

Because of trends in population growth, Hispanics will become an increasingly important segment of the American electorate. Political strategists from both the Republican and Democratic parties are already hard at work on plans for persuading Hispanic voters to favor their political party.

▶ **With so many legal** efforts to end discrimination in the United States, why is it still such a problem?

In 2006, Congress considered legislation to address immigration issues. Latinos, including U.S. citizens, permanent legal residents, and workers who entered the country illegally, turned out for demonstrations in many cities to support proposed laws to create opportunities to gain citizenship for people who have resided here without authorization for several years. The demonstrators opposed other proposed bills, such as those that sought to impose harsher criminal penalties on people who entered the country illegally and people who provide assistance to them. President Bush supported a program to permit foreigners to stay in the United States as "guest workers" for a limited number of years. Critics of President Bush's proposal fear that a "guest worker" program would create a permanent underclass of low-paid workers handling difficult, undesirable jobs who will never have an opportunity to earn citizenship and participate in the government processes that rule their lives through laws enacted by legislatures. In the eyes of some observers, debates about the status and treatment of longtime residents of the United States who entered the country in violation of immigration laws constitute the country's newest civil rights issue.

practicequiz

1. What's the definition of universal suffrage, for which women's rights activists advocated after the Civil War?
   a. It refers simply to the right of all adult citizens to vote.
   b. Suffrage refers to other legal entitlements, such as property rights, along with the right to vote.
   c. Suffrage refers to social entitlements, such as education, along with the right to vote.
   d. Suffrage means the right to vote in a representational democracy; it does not mean the right to vote in a pure democracy.

2. What amendment to the Constitution granted women the right to vote, and when was the amendment ratified?
   a. Eighteenth Amendment, ratified in 1919
   b. Nineteenth Amendment, ratified in 1920
   c. Seventeenth Amendment, ratified in 1918
   d. Nineteenth Amendment, ratified in 1919

3. Today, thanks to the grassroots mobilization work of Susan B. Anthony, Elizabeth Cady Stanton, and thousands of their political descendants, women are guaranteed equal treatment in all aspects of American life.
   a. true   b. false

4. César Chávez brought national attention to the plight of Latinos by
   a. organizing lawsuits that exposed the infringement of Latinos' civil rights.
   b. organizing protests against restrictive covenants.
   c. becoming the first Hispanic to run for public office.
   d. exposing the exploitation of and dangerous conditions for migrant workers.

Answers: 1-a, 2-b, 3-b, 4-d.

Contemporary Civil Rights Issues

Much of the twentieth-century American civil rights movement centered on efforts to prohibit overt discrimination mandated by government laws and practiced by private businesses. As we have now seen, women, African Americans, and Latinos all used both grassroots mobilization and court processes to gain the right to vote and to produce laws against discrimination in employment, education, and other contexts. After laws were changed in the 1960s to forbid rather than mandate open discrimination, unequal treatment and inequality still remained. Some forms of discrimination became more subtle, such as police officers using their discretion to stop African American and Latino drivers by alleging a minor traffic violation when they really want to search a vehicle for drugs. Studies of police actions on some highways have shown that members of minority groups are significantly overrepresented among those stopped and searched by the police, despite evidence that their rate of violating traffic laws does not exceed that of more numerous white drivers.[36]

▶ **With so many legal efforts to end discrimination in the United States, why is it still such a problem?** Discrimination laws typically require strong, clear proof of improper treatment to justify orders for remedies. However, many kinds of discrimination, especially those based on discretionary decisions, are very difficult to prove. Why, for example, are women and members of minority groups seldom chosen by boards of directors to lead large corporations? Why are women's salaries on average lower than men's for the same occupations? Why are murderers who kill white people often given more severe sentences than those inflicted on murderers who kill African Americans?[37] These and other outcomes are the products of discretionary choices by decision makers. How can one know, let alone prove, whether any intent to

► **What other groups in** the United States have sought civil rights protection?

discussionquestions

1. Are there still issues concerning the equality of women that require the creation of new laws and public policies? If so, name some of the issues.

2. Should the status of illegal immigrants be considered a civil rights issue? Why or why not?

discriminate underlies the decisions that produce these results? Unequal outcomes continue to exist that are not remedied by laws, which merely prohibit the open forms of discrimination.

Inequality can be perpetuated by social conditions that are a legacy of past discrimination, such as disadvantages endured by poor minority group members whose parents, due to past discrimination, could not afford to accumulate sufficient assets to move within the boundaries of the top public school systems or save enough money to send their children to college. Discrimination also continues to result from less visible decisions by employers, police officers, and others whose discretionary authority affects their fellow citizens.

Further efforts to address continuing issues of inequality and discrimination may depend on the evolution of societal values and politics through the cultural change pathway, rather than through judicial decisions in the court pathway. In the future, the elections pathway may also be a source of policy change regarding civil rights as immigration and differential birthrates among ethnic groups make whites less numerically dominant among the voting-age population.

COMPLEXITY OF ISSUES

The role of discretionary decisions in the continuation of discrimination and unequal outcomes for members of different demographic groups has made contemporary civil rights issues more complex. Although society's values and laws have changed to reflect general agreement that people should not be excluded from government programs and jobs because of their race or gender, deep disagreements remain about what additional policies are necessary to provide full civil rights and full equality for all Americans. Some people believe that equality of opportunity has been created through the enactment of laws that forbid discrimination by race and gender. But others believe that more policy actions are necessary to achieve equality for members of groups that have been held back by discrimination.

This chapter's opening discussion of the U.S. Supreme Court's examination of the University of Michigan's admissions policies illustrated the continuing debate about affirmative action. This debate demonstrates that there are disagreements about whether racial preferences are a necessary element of equal opportunity in a society in which discretionary decisions and other factors continue to provide evidence of unequal treatment and outcomes.

Legal disputes persist over the creation of legislative districts, at both the federal and the state level. As you will see in **LINK** *Chapter 7, pages 259–263,* legislative districts are drawn in varying geographic sizes and shapes. They are required to have equivalent populations, but they do not have to be drawn as rectangular entities with straight boundary lines. Usually, districts are designed to advance the prospects of either Republican or Democratic candidates, depending on which party controls the state's legislature. Issues of race and ethnicity can arise when districts are redrawn, which occurs after every ten-year census and sometimes more frequently. Should lines be drawn to facilitate the election of African American and Latino legislators by concentrating voters from those groups in specific districts? The creation of these so-called majority-minority districts has generated much controversy. White voters in some states have challenged the creation of such districts, while some civil rights advocates see the existence of such districts as important for increasing the likelihood of minority representation in legislatures. But other critics contend that creating a few majority-minority districts actually helps white conservatives, who thereby gain a larger number of "safe" seats in areas where fewer liberal-leaning minority voters live.

EMERGING GROUPS

► **What other groups in the United States have sought civil rights protection?** The visibility and success of litigation strategies by African Americans and women and grassroots mobilization strategies of those groups and Latinos provided examples for plans and action by other individuals who see themselves as victims of discrimination. For example, beginning in the 1970s, people with disabilities lobbied legislators and held public demonstrations protesting discrimination in employment and public accommodations. People who use wheelchairs, for example, often found themselves rejected for jobs merely because an employer assumed that they were incapable of working. Similarly, they often could not be served as customers at restaurants, entertainment facilities, and other public accommodations that lacked wheelchair access. In the Rehabilitation Act of 1973, Congress prohibited discrimination against people with disabilities who work in government or who seek services from federally funded programs. The Americans with Disabilities Act, passed in 1990, provided protection against discrimination in employment and public accommodations.

Advocates of civil rights protections for gays and lesbians use legislative lobbying, litigation, and grassroots mobilization to

Disabled protesters crawled up the steps of the U.S. Supreme Court in 2004 as the Court prepared to hear a case about the accessibility of courthouses for people who must use wheelchairs. Which pathways of action seem most likely to advance disabled people's goals for new laws and policies to advance their interests?
Stephen Crowley/The New York Times

seek legal protections comparable to those provided for African Americans and women. As you saw in ⓁⒾⓃⓀ *Chapter 4, page 112,* gay and lesbian couples used the court pathway in Vermont and Massachusetts to gain legal recognition of their committed relationships in civil unions and marriages. Although no federal law prevents employment discrimination based on a worker's sexual orientation, some states and cities have enacted statutes and ordinances to prohibit such discrimination in housing and public accommodations.

Americans are divided over whether new civil rights laws should address discrimination against gays and lesbians. The U.S. Supreme Court has considered two important cases concerning this issue. In *Romer* v. *Evans* (1996), the Court declared that cities such as Aspen, Boulder, and Denver could pass antidiscrimination laws to protect gays and lesbians. The Court relied on the equal protection clause in striking down a statewide referendum approved by Colorado voters that had banned the passage of such antidiscrimination laws. But in *Boy Scouts of America* v. *Dale* (2000), the Court found that New Jersey's law against sexual orientation discrimination in public accommodations could not be used to require the Boy Scouts to accept a gay man as a troop leader. According to the Court, such an application of the state law would violate the Boy Scouts organization's First Amendment right of expressive association, which means that a private group cannot be forced to accept a member it does not want.

Although the Court blocked Colorado from creating a law that would single out homosexuals for adverse treatment, it has not made any decisions granting specific civil rights for gays and lesbians. As gays and lesbians lobby, litigate, and demonstrate for the right to marry and for legal protections against discrimination, it appears that any success they achieve may initially come on a state-by-state basis. Wider success for these goals will occur only if American society moves closer to a consensus about the need to protect the civil rights of gays and lesbians.

Issues of equal treatment under the law have long been a matter of concern for Native Americans. They suffered from overt discrimination, nonexistent economic opportunities, and widespread poverty. Because of their relatively small numbers and isolated locations, Native Americans have not enjoyed success through the grassroots mobilization strategies. In recent years, however, they have advanced their cause through the court pathway, especially the case of *Cobell* v. *Norton,* originally filed in 1996 and still ongoing a decade later. In the case, federal courts found that over the years, the U.S. Department of Interior's Bureau of Indian Affairs had mismanaged and lost billions of dollars owed to Native Americans for oil and gas revenues and other leases on their lands administered by the federal government. Eventually, the government stopped contesting the claim and began haggling over how much money it should be required to pay. Senator John McCain (R-Arizona) and other members of Congress became concerned about the delay and litigation costs in the case, so they promised to propose legislation to help settle it.[38] The slow-moving court process did not solve the problem, but it eventually provided political pressure to spur decision makers to take notice.

At the end of the twentieth century, some Native American groups became more capable of exerting pressure through the lobbying pathway. Several Native American groups used their reservations' status as self-governing, sovereign territories as a means to open casinos that would otherwise not be permitted in the states in which the reservations were located. They used revenue from the casinos to increase their efforts to hire lobbyists and make campaign contributions as a means to gain favorable influence and support among members of Congress. These efforts have not gained equality and decent living conditions for all Native Americans. They have, however, influenced decision makers to pay more attention to issues affecting some Native American groups.

practicequiz

1. Contemporary kinds of discrimination based on discretionary decisions are
   a. very rare.
   b. very hard to prove.
   c. nearly nullified through the court pathway.
   d. a problem mostly in the South.

1. What emerging issues will continue to provide the basis for debates, litigation, and grassroots action concerning civil rights?

2. Are today's civil rights issues more complex than those in the past? If so, how does this make it more difficult to create effective laws and policies to address these issues?

---

2. The redrawing of district lines to create majority-minority legislative districts is usually intended as a way to
   a. enhance the possibility of minority representation in legislatures.
   b. ensure bipartisan legislatures.
   c. ensure greater participation of the electorate.
   d. enhance federal legislative power at the local and state levels.

3. There is now a federal law prohibiting employment discrimination based on a worker's sexual orientation.
   a. true   b. false

4. Through which pathway are Native American activists succeeding in their attempts to recoup some of the debt owed them by the United States government?
   a. Election pathway.
   b. Grassroots mobilization pathway.
   c. Cultural change pathway.
   d. Court pathway.

Answers: 1-b, 2-a, 3-b, 4-d.

Conclusion

The United States has a long history of unequal treatment of women and members of various minorities within its society. Although the founders of the United States did not advocate equality for all people, their lofty ideal of equality for most white men provided inspiration for others in American society to share in the benefits of that vision. Hence there have been efforts throughout American history to gain political equality for women, African Americans, various immigrant groups, and others who were initially excluded from full acceptance and participation in the nation's governing and economic systems.

The court and grassroots mobilization pathways have been especially important for the advancement of civil rights. In the twentieth century, the NAACP's litigation strategy, which gradually succeeded in gaining the Supreme Court's rejection of racial segregation, helped make the Fourteenth Amendment's equal protection clause a viable tool for challenging governmental laws and policies that foster discrimination. Advocates of civil rights for members of other victimized groups could copy the NAACP's strategies in using the court pathway to advance their own causes. Beginning in the 1960s, when Congress and state legislatures began enacting

additional civil rights laws, opportunities opened to use the court pathway as a means to gain judicial enforcement of statutes intended to prevent discrimination by employers, landlords, and other private actors. Judicial enforcement of these statutes has facilitated significant changes in American society and created opportunities for upward mobility and respectful treatment that would have been nearly unimaginable to African Americans and women a generation earlier.

Grassroots mobilization is a long-standing method of seeking changes in public policy, going all the way back to the origins of the United States. Over the years, various groups in our society, including labor union organizers and veterans seeking government benefits, have used this pathway. Civil rights advocates did not invent grassroots action, but they have employed it in an especially successful manner. Ever since the mid-nineteenth century, women's rights advocates have used meetings and protests to educate the public in their struggle to gain the right to vote. The African American civil rights movement of the 1950s and 1960s had an exceptionally powerful impact on the attitudes of ordinary citizens and eventually convinced the government to create and enforce antidiscrimination laws. Seeing the effectiveness of African Americans' protests, other groups emulated these tactics, although these protesters rarely faced the kinds of violent opposition inflicted on African Americans.

Political equality is an important component of democracy. If voting rights are restricted and certain groups are excluded from full participation in society, the governing system will represent only the interests of those who have status and wield power. The efforts to obtain civil rights for excluded groups in the United States constitute an important chapter in this country's history. Without these efforts, the American governing system would fall well short of its professed aspiration to be a democracy that sets an example for other countries around the world.

YOUR turn!

Grassroots mobilization for civil rights can begin with strategic plans for meetings and protests. Mobilization can also begin through actions of individuals who take a courageous stand and then join with like-minded individuals to win over public opinion and to prod public officials into taking action. For example, Arab Americans have expressed concern that they are presented as stereotyped characters in many films, television shows, and video games. Increasingly, they see Arabs and Muslims presented as the enemies of the United States and as people prone to violence. The Walt Disney film *Aladdin* was criticized for images and song lyrics that portrayed Arabs as barbaric. In one Illinois community, a 10-year-old girl educated and persuaded her music teacher to change choral music in order to avoid using an *Aladdin* song with offensive lyrics.[39] When an Oklahoma school district enforced its dress code against hats by forbidding a Muslim girl from wearing a head scarf required by her religion, she refused to surrender her religious beliefs. By standing her ground, she ended up gaining the support of the U.S. Department of Justice in a legal action to support her religious rights.[40]

In another example, college and high school students around the country hold an annual Day of Silence protest as a means of calling attention to the harassment and violence frequently directed at gay and lesbian students. According to one study, teachers and administrators often ignore bullying directed at gays and lesbians. By remaining silent throughout the Day of Silence, college and high school students call attention to and help educate people about an issue that affects the equal treatment of one group within society.[41] In 2004, an Alhambra, California, high school girl filed a complaint under Title IX, the federal law forbidding gender discrimination in education, because the girls' softball team had to change uniforms in a tin shed with no bathroom facilities, while the boys' baseball team played at a plush facility in which the city had invested $900,000 for renovations.[42] Grassroots actions—as well as court challenges—start with individuals who recognize unequal treatment when they see it and take a stand in order to educate others and improve society. Do you have enough awareness and courage to speak out when you experience improper unequal treatment or, even more important, when you see such treatment being applied to others? ■

Chapter Review

1. Civil rights concern issues of equality and involve the development of laws and policies that prevent discrimination, especially forms of discrimination that exclude members of selected groups from full participation in the economic and governing systems.

2. The court process and grassroots mobilization have been two especially important pathways for political action affecting civil rights issues.

3. The founders of the United States advocated an ideal of equality for white men that became a source of inspiration for women, African Americans, Latinos, and others who sought full inclusion in society.

4. Equality in the United States and laws that advance the American vision of equality focus on equality of opportunity, not equality of condition.

5. The United States has a long history of discrimination against women, African Americans, Latinos, and others that inspired the development of civil rights action.

6. The Fourteenth Amendment's equal protection clause has been an especially important focus of litigation to combat discrimination by government.

7. Formal racial segregation and discrimination, often enforced by violence against African Americans, became entrenched in American society for nearly a century after the Civil War.

8. The U.S. Supreme Court originally endorsed racial segregation in *Plessy* v. *Ferguson* (1896), but after a three-decade court litigation strategy practiced by Thurgood Marshall and the NAACP, the Court became the first major governing institution to firmly reject segregation laws as violating the equal protection clause (*Brown* v. *Board of Education of Topeka*, 1954).

9. The Supreme Court's interpretation of the equal protection clause provides protection against racial and gender discrimination by government but little protection against wealth discrimination and some other forms of unequal treatment by government.

10. African Americans' civil rights movement, led by Martin Luther King Jr., emerged in the 1950s and 1960s. Whites' violent response to African Americans' nonviolent demonstrations helped dramatize the need for civil rights protections by changing public opinion and spurring the federal government to take action.

11. The civil rights movement pushed Congress and state legislatures to enact a variety of statutes aimed at preventing discrimination by private actors as well as government entities.

12. Women organized meetings and protests as early as the mid-nineteenth century in a grassroots effort to obtain the right to vote, a goal finally achieved in 1920.

13. Latinos have used grassroots mobilization to seek civil rights and equal treatment, especially through the farm workers' movement led by César Chávez.

14. Additional groups emerged to seek civil rights protection through the court pathway process and grassroots

mobilization. These groups include the disabled as well as gays and lesbians. Although disabled people have been successful in pushing for laws to guard against discrimination in employment and public accommodations, gays and lesbians have been successful in just a few states.

CHAPTER REVIEW TEST

1. Why is political equality crucial to a democratic society?
   a. Citizens who have no voice in how political decisions are made will always revolt.
   b. Discrimination is essentially unfair.
   c. The government will represent the interests of only some of the people if others have their voting rights or other forms of political input restricted.
   d. Our Constitution guarantees political equality to all citizens because the founders understood the need for the government to represent property owners.

2. The American system of government advances equality of opportunity for all, meaning that it
   a. helps guarantee access to important goods and services to all Americans.
   b. expects people to be self-reliant and helps ensure that self-reliance by outlawing *some* discriminatory barriers to education, employment, and public accommodation.
   c. works to reduce economic disadvantages for the poor so that they too can have access to important goods and services, such as education, health insurance, and public housing.
   d. assumes that everyone can live the American dream no matter what barriers exist.

3. Why did the disadvantages of slavery continue to burden the descendants of slaves a century after emancipation?
   a. Because economic disadvantage, like economic advantage, accumulates: poor people cannot afford expensive college educations for their children, which makes those children less likely to get high-paying jobs, which makes them less likely to send their children to expensive colleges, and so on.
   b. Because people can inherit a "slave mentality" for many generations, meaning that they will not think they are capable of success.
   c. Because there have been no leaders to inspire change in our laws and culture that would knock down obstacles to success for the descendants of slaves.
   d. Because after the Civil War, Andrew Johnson stacked the Supreme Court with white southern sympathizers.

4. The equal protection clause protects people from being deprived of their rights if those rights are being infringed on by
   a. other individuals.
   b. the federal government.
   c. a state government.
   d. local clubs or associations.

5. In the two decades following Reconstruction, the number of African American men registered to vote in southern states dropped from tens of thousands to a small number.
   a. true   b. false

6. Why should any student of American civil rights history know about the Supreme Court case *Plessy* v. *Ferguson?*
   a. It was the first time the Court applied the equal protection clause to individual acts of discrimination.
   b. It started to turn the tide against Jim Crow legislation at the state level.
   c. It changed how interstate train lines conducted business.
   d. It justified segregation nationally, a backward step in civil rights law that would not be remedied until the middle of the twentieth century.

7. In the twentieth century, presidents were able to play what kind of role in civil rights reform?
   a. No role at all.
   b. A modest but occasionally significant role.
   c. A significant role.
   d. The sole dicision maker.

8. What are strict scrutiny, moderate scrutiny, and rational basis?
   a. Levels of citizen participation in national politics, as theorized in *The Federalist Papers.*
   b. The three tests by which the Supreme Court analyzes cases having to do with the limitations of states' rights.
   c. The three tests the Supreme Court chooses from when analyzing cases involving the equal protection clause.
   d. The three levels of discrimination that prosecutors can claim before the Supreme Court.

9. According to decades of Supreme Court interpretation, the equal protection clause provides general protection for civil rights by requiring the government to treat all people in an equal fashion.
   a. true   b. false

10. Because restrictive covenants are a form of private discrimination, the Supreme Court initially ruled that enforcement of these covenants by government bodies was permissible.
    a. true   b. false

11. What best characterizes the relation between grassroots mobilization and civil rights legislation in the early 1960s?
    a. Grassroots activism helped pave the way for the enactment of progressive legislation.
    b. Dramatic civil rights legislation emboldened activists to mobilize at the grassroots level.
    c. Legislators and activists worked hand in hand, sometimes even collaborating, so that their efforts toward civil rights reform would coincide.
    d. The two activities operated in isolation; neither had any effect on the other.

12. By working to ensure equal access to the ballot for all voters irrespective of race, the Voting Rights Act of 1965 accomplished what lawmakers had first tried to accomplish in
   a. the Civil Rights Act of 1947.
   b. the Civil Rights Act of 1920.
   c. New Deal legislation of the 1930s.
   d. the Fifteenth Amendment of 1870.

13. The Nineteenth Amendment, granting women the right to vote,
   a. was the product, almost exclusively, of early-twentieth-century grassroots mobilization.
   b. catapulted women into positions of authority equal to men.
   c. resulted in part from a positive shift in cultural assumptions about women's capabilities.
   d. spelled out what the Fifteenth Amendment implied.

14. In the early 1950s, after graduating from Stanford Law School near the top of her class, Sandra Day O'Connor's best job offer in the legal field was
   a. a clerkship under Chief Justice Earl Warren.
   b. a faculty position at the Columbia University School of Law.
   c. a position as a legal secretary.
   d. a circuit judgeship in California.

15. The Twenty-Sixth Amendment, which lowered the national voting age to 18, was swiftly ratified because
   a. young people had forcefully demonstrated their commitment to the political process through protests against the Vietnam War.
   b. political elites wanted it that way for practical reasons.
   c. young political activists worked for ratification through intensive grassroots mobilization.
   d. the ACLU successfully lobbied for this result.

16. Antidiscrimination activism on behalf of Latinos will probably continue in the years to come because
   a. Latinos are now the largest minority group in the country.
   b. César Chávez would insist that such activism continue.

   c. current immigration law prohibits such discrimination.
   d. President George W. Bush has made the country more sensitive to such discrimination.

17. We know that intentional discrimination based on discretionary decisions is very hard to prove and thus very hard to prohibit legally. But what *are* discretionary decisions?
   a. decisions that are guided by legal conventions, such as strict scrutiny
   b. decisions that are guided by preestablished rules of governance
   c. decisions that are made on the order of judges.
   d. decisions that are based on an individual's own, sometimes subjective reasoning

18. Our society is full of examples of unequal outcomes; some people have been treated less fairly by the world than others. Yet our antidiscrimination laws cannot do much to remedy this situation because
   a. people with political power want to be in charge of helping disadvantaged citizens.
   b. the law only prohibits open forms of discrimination (where the intention to discriminate is discernible to others).
   c. inequality is required by the Constitution.
   d. measures that are meant to help, such as affirmative action policies, never have any impact.

19. The Americans with Disabilities Act of 1990 requires that all private homes be made accessible fot the disabled.
   a. true   b. false

20. What pathways have been especially crucial to civil rights progress?
   a. elections and court pathways
   b. court and lobbying pathways
   c. grassroots mobilization and lobbying pathways
   d. grassroots mobilization and court pathways

Answers: 1: c; 2: b; 3: a; 4: c; 5: a; 6: d; 7: b; 8: c; 9: b; 10: b; 11: a; 12: d; 13: c; 14: c; 15: b; 16: a; 17: d; 18: b; 19: b; 20: d.

DISCUSSION QUESTIONS

1. What was the founders' vision of equality?

2. What is the difference between civil rights and civil liberties?

3. What were the post–Civil War amendments to the U.S. Constitution, and why are they important in understanding civil rights and civil liberties?

4. What treatment did African Americans experience in the century after the Civil War?

5. How did the U.S. Supreme Court interpret the equal protection clause in the nineteenth century?

6. What was the NAACP's litigation strategy? What did it achieve?

7. How has the Supreme Court interpreted the equal protection clause in the twentieth century?

8. How and when did the African American civil rights movement emerge? What were the most important milestones in the movement?

9. How did many whites in the South respond to the civil rights movement?

10. What did the civil rights movement achieve?

11. How did women obtain the right to vote?

12. How have Latinos worked to advance their civil rights and seek equal treatment?

13. What major federal statutes have been enacted to protect civil rights?

14. What other groups have used the court pathway process or grassroots mobilization to seek equality?

15. How have civil rights issues become more complex in recent decades?

INTERNET RESOURCES

Read about the NAACP, an important interest group for African Americans' struggle for civil rights, at **http://www.naacp.org**

Read about the United Farm Workers, an important interest group for Latinos' struggle for civil rights, at **http://www.ufw.org**

Read about Martin Luther King Jr., one of the most important civil rights leaders, at **http://www.stanford.edu/group/King**

Read about the National Organization for Women, an active group working for equality for women, at **http://www.now.org**

The U.S. Civil Rights Commission is an important federal agency that studies and makes recommendations about civil rights issues: **http://www.usccr.gov**

The Disability Rights Education and Defense Fund seeks legal protections for the disabled: **http://www.dredf.org**

The National Asian Pacific American Legal Consortium coordinates civil rights efforts for Asian Americans: **http://www.napalc.org**

ADDITIONAL READING

Flexner, Eleanor and Ellen Fitzpatrick. *Century of Struggle: The Women's Rights Movement in the United States,* 3rd ed. Cambridge, MA: Belknap Press, 1996.

Foner, Eric. *The Story of American Freedom.* New York: Norton, 1998.

Kyvig, David. *Authentic and Explicit Acts: Amending the U.S. Constitution, 1776–1995.* Lawrence: University Press of Kansas, 1996.

Loewen, James W. *Sundown Towns: A Hidden Dimension of American Racism.* New York: The New Press, 2005.

Takaki, Ronald. *A Different Mirror: A History of Multicultural America.* Boston: Little, Brown, 1993.

KEY TERMS

The legislative process is at the center of our political world. In many ways it defines the nature and spirit of our government—and who we are as a nation. More than any other branch of government, the struggle of popular governance is played out in Congress—the "people's branch." In this photo Democratic and Republican members of Congress stand shoulder to shoulder to sing "The Star-Spangled Banner" on the steps of the Capitol in Washington on Monday evening, Sept. 11, 2006.

CHAPTER 7

CONGRESS

Health, Human Services, . . . and Less Restrictive Gun Laws? After months of negotiations, the massive 2004 Health and Human Services appropriations bill was ready for approval. At the very last minute, however, a small but significant item unrelated to spending federal money was inserted into the bill: a measure that would require federal officials to destroy the records of gun purchases within twenty-four hours, instead of waiting ninety days as stipulated previously.

The issue of background checks and gun purchase records had been simmering for years in Congress. In spite of fierce opposition from gun rights activists, Congress passed the Brady Gun Control Law in 1998. Under the law, gun dealers must fax a form containing information about each prospective buyer to either the F.B.I. or a state law enforcement agency. A computerized search is

Photo: Jamie Rose/The New York Times

One of the most successful interest groups in Washington
is the gun lobby—namely, the National Rifle Association. As
you read along you will see that they were able to work with
sympathetic members of Congress to achieve a behind-the-
scenes victory in 2004. There is an old saying that knowledge
is power, and it is especially true when it comes to the
lobbying decision-makers pathway. Do you think this sort
of knowledge will help engage you in the political process?

conducted to make sure that this person does not fall into one of
several categories of people barred from buying a gun. As to what
would become of these background check records, known as *audit
logs,* the law was vague. Many gun-rights advocates contended
that they create, in essence, a national gun registry—a program
not within the scope of the law. They argued that these records
must be destroyed after the checks are complete.

The issue took on greater importance shortly after the terrorist attacks on September 11, 2001. The Federal Bureau of
Investigation requested from the Department of Justice the
opportunity to match audit log information with a list of 1,200
people they had detained as possible suspects in the terror attacks.
Had any of these people purchased guns in recent months? This
seemed like a simple request, especially given the nature of the
crisis. But in a surprise move the Attorney General, John
Ashcroft, ruled that his agency would not allow the FBI access to
the records. Doing so, he argued, would allow the FBI to step
beyond the law.

A former senator from Missouri, Ashcroft was a strong supporter of gun ownership rights, so many saw his decision to deny
the FBI access to the data as more reflective of his personal positions than a objective interpretation of the law. In fact, as a senator Ashcroft voted for an amendment to the Brady Bill that mandated the quick destruction of gun purchase records after the
background checks—but the amendment was defeated. Many
were simply shocked that an administration so focused on finding

those responsible for the attacks would chose to disregard this important source of information. According to one commentator during the dispute, "The Justice Department's action has frustrated some F.B.I. and other law enforcement officials who say it puts the department at odds with its own priorities. Even as the department is instituting tough new measures to detain individuals suspected of links to terrorism, they say, it is being unusually solicitous of foreigners' gun rights." [Fox Butterfield, "A Nation Challenged: Background Checks; Justice Department Bars Use of Gun Checks in Terror Inquiry," *New York Times,* December 6, 2001, p. A1.]

The issue remained unsettled, and by 2004 the National Rifle Association and many Republican legislators had set their sights on mandating the destruction of these audit logs. Rather than introducing the measure as a separate bill and going through the normal process, it was quietly inserted at the last minute into the appropriations bill. Democrats and pro–gun control Republicans, having negotiated for months on the thousands of other spending measures in the bill, had little choice but to back the entire bill. Had they chosen to stop the bill with a filibuster in the Senate, they would have run the risk of being blamed for delaying the spending bill and perhaps even shutting down the federal government. They had no choice but to vote in favor of the whole spending measure.

As news of the gun-licensing change emerged in the media, Republicans argued that it was simply good public policy. "For us law-abiding citizens," said Kansas Republican Representative Todd Tiahrt, who introduced the measure, "there is no need to have this debate. It is a freedom issue. It is a privacy issue."[1] Republicans also argued that last-minute changes to appropriations bills had been common when the Democrats controlled the legislature; such maneuvers are simply one of the many advantages of majority-party control in the legislative process. Many Democrats and gun control advocates were enraged not only by the change in law but by the last-minute trick. Sarah Brady, the wife of Ronald Reagan's press secretary, James Brady, who was permanently brain-injured in the 1981 attempted assassination of the president, has become one of the nation's most outspoken advocates of gun control. She argued that the measure was a "shameful step backward."[2] The *New York Times,* which favors strict gun control, editorialized about the power of the NRA: "Buried in the print of the government appropriations bill now headed for passage is a potent measure of the gun lobby's muscle in the Republican-controlled Congress."[3] But it was too late. President George W. Bush signed the measure into law as part of the appropriations bill.

Records of gun purchases are now destroyed after twenty-four hours, greatly complicating the work of law enforcement agencies in tracking down weapons used to commit violent crimes. ▪

▶ **When representatives** disagree with their constituents, should they do what constituents want, or what they think is best?

delegate model of representation legislators should adhere to the will of their constituents.

trustee model of representation legislators should consider the will of the people but act in ways that they believe are best for the long-term interests of the nation.

politico model of representation legislators should follow their own judgment (that is, act like a trustee) until the public becomes vocal about a particular matter, at which point they should follow the dictates of constituents.

This incident from the politics of 2004 hints at many key elements of the legislative process, ranging from the role of lobby groups, party control, and individual legislators to the weight of committees, media, public opinion, and constituencies. Much has changed in the American political process since we began our journey well over 200 years ago. For all this change, the role of the legislature has remained central. Just as the serial robber Willy Sutton hit the nail on the head when he responded to the question of why he robbed banks ("That's where the money is!"), so too might we suggest our rationale for studying Congress: That's where policy is made! Indeed, those interested in choosing the pathway for change would do well to keep a sharp eye on lobbying decision-makers and the legislative process. Precisely how the legislature goes about creating public policy in the twenty-first century is different from every other moment in our history. It is here, in the legislative process, where we begin our discussion of the lobbying decision-makers pathway. You will find that appealing directly to members of Congress (or any legislature) is a viable means of changing government, but it takes a precise, detailed understanding of how the process works. In 2004, the gun lobby won its battle to change gun purchase records, not because the public demanded such a change or because the president stepped into the process or because the media ran related stories, but because the gun lobby knew how to use this pathway.

Key Questions

1. What are the various approaches to representation, and which one seems to be in favor these days?

2. How did the framers of our constitutional system think Congress would operate internally?

3. Which provisions in Article I of the Constitution enhance the "democratic character" of the legislative branch, and which provisions move things in the other direction?

4. What are the most important organizational components of the modern-day legislature?

5. Do these organizational components allow average citizens greater access to the legislative process, or do they make things more difficult?

6. Who serves as a legislator these days—and who served in the past? Does this matter when it comes to the "democratic character" of Congress?

7. Describe the various points of access for citizens who wish to influence the outcome of the legislative process.

The Nature and Style of Representation

▶ **When representatives disagree with their constituents, should they do what constituents want, or what they think is best?** There are a number of important questions that we can ask about the precise job of members of Congress. Whom do they represent, and what do they seek to accomplish? At the core, the job of any representative is to speak and act on behalf of others. As we saw in ⓛⒾⓝⓚ *Chapter 2, page 39*, except in the smallest of settings—such as a small New England town or a tiny Swiss canton—direct democracy is either impossible or impractical. And even if direct democracy became possible—say, if a tamperproof computer system were installed in our homes to allow every citizen to vote directly on every proposed law—would we really want such a system? A republic is a democracy in which representatives speak and act on behalf of the citizens. This concept implies a direct extension of popular will. Thomas Paine, the revolutionary propagandist and political thinker, suggested in his famous 1776 pamphlet *Common Sense* that legislators must "act in the same manner as the whole body would act, were they present." This perspective has been called the **delegate model of representation** (see Figure 7.1, p. 254). Here the legislator does his or her best to discern the will of the people and then acts accordingly.

A very different approach is called the **trustee model of representation.** This was the outlook favored by most of the delegates at the Constitutional Convention. It holds that the legislator should consider the will of the people but then should do what he or she thinks is best for the nation as a whole and in the long term. Edmund Burke, a famous eighteenth-century British politician and political theorist who was very sympathetic to the American colonists' protests, forcefully articulated this perspective. Legislators, he reasoned, should focus their efforts on protecting the "general whole," rather than simply obeying the wishes of local interests. They are to think of the entire nation and of future generations, not just of a particular district here and now. Burke further argued that legislators owe their constituents their reason, expertise, and knowledge; simply following the whims of public opinion is a disservice to their nation and a sin in the eyes of God.

Which model is correct? This is a difficult question, and there is no right or wrong answer. It does seem clear, however, that

▶ **What kinds of issues** should legislators focus on, big topics or constituent needs?

conscience model of representation
legislators should follow the will of the people (that is, act like a delegate) until they truly believe that it is in the best interests of the nation to act differently.

representational style
a legislator's priorities—for example, the ratio of time devoted to constituent issues versus time spent on the development of public policy.

constituent service
a legislator's responsiveness to the questions and concerns of the people he or she represents.

one or other of the models has held more sway at different points in our history. As noted, in the early years of the Republic, most legislators held tight to the trustee perspective. Many observers suggest that several changes in the past few decades have made the delegate model more popular today. For example, the number of people wishing to be a legislator for a career has shot up in recent decades. Losing an election often short-circuits such plans, so legislators seem eager to appease the public. "Public opinion" is also much easier to discern these days, given the accuracy and frequency of polls. And finally, a growing number of citizens seem concerned that members of Congress do not seem to listen to average citizens, thus making the trustee model a dangerous position. Few legislators these days seem willing to vote against their "informed judgment." (Burke got into trouble with *his* constituents by trying to do this!) "The core dictate of this new breed of politician, as we might expect, is to win reelection each year," conclude two contemporary American political scientists. "This means keeping your votes in line with the wishes of those in the district."[4]

Occasionally, we can see the struggle between these models of representation being played out in the legislature. During Bill Clinton's impeachment trial in 1999, for example, Senator Paul Wellstone, a Democrat from Minnesota (and once a Carleton College political science professor), argued that public opinion should guide the outcome of the trial. He offered polling data indicating that some 80 percent of Americans believed that Clinton should not be removed from office and that the trial should end. Old Tom Paine would doubtless have agreed. Responding to Wellstone for the Republicans was Representative Henry Hyde of Illinois. Using true Burkean logic, Hyde argued, "We are not delegates who are sent here to weigh our mail every day and to vote accordingly. We are elected to bring our judgment, our experience, and our consciences with us."[5] In the end, Clinton remained in office; the vote was fifty-five senators saying "not guilty" and forty-five saying "guilty."

Of course, there are middle-ground perspectives, too. The **politico model of representation** holds that legislators should feel free to follow their own judgment on matters where the public remains silent. In other words, legislators should be trustees and vote how they see fit until the public gets involved, at which point they should return to the delegate mode. Another perspective is called the **conscience model of representation,** or what we might call the "pillow test." On most matters, representatives heed the wishes of constituents, but if this position really disturbs representatives to the point that they can't sleep at night, they vote the other way. They are delegates most of the time, but if an issue keeps their head off the pillow at night, they turn into trustees.

▶ **What kinds of issues should legislators focus on, big topics or constituent needs?** There's also the issue of whether legislators should spend their time working on broad-based policy initiatives or on direct constituency needs. We might call this a question of **representational style.** Some legislators focus on major policy matters, such as health care reform, foreign policy, national defense, international trade, and immigration; others concentrate on helping constituents get their share from the federal government. Former New York Republican Senator Alfonse D'Amato got the nickname "Senator Pothole" because of his unending attention to constituent needs. (Fixing potholes, you ask? Yes, federal monies are often used for transportation projects, including the repair of roadways.) **Constituent service** (also called *casework*) makes up a great deal of what legislators and their staff do on a daily basis. Letters, telephone calls, e-mails, faxes, and walk-ins every day bring pleas for assistance. These requests are on a variety of issues, including information about pending legislation, finding government jobs, obtaining veterans' benefits, getting help with Social Security, inquiring into military matters, and much else. Although some legislators tackle constituent service with more gusto than others, all agree that it is an important part of representation.

Finally, there is the issue of shared attributes. There is a story about President Calvin Coolidge and his response to criticism that he had appointed a less-than-able businessman to one of his cabinet posts: "But Mr. President," an aide objected, "that fellow is an idiot." "Well," responded Coolidge in his usual dry way, "don't you think they ought to be represented, too?"[6] Humorous as this might seem, many analysts have argued that an important facet of legislators' job is to speak on behalf of the groups they belong to—especially their demographic group. Regardless of party affiliation, district, or state, many theorists suggest that female legislators should look after the interests of women throughout America. The same might be said about Latino or African American legislators. Some observers have argued that

► **Why did the framers** create a bicameral legislature (and what is it)?

symbolic representation
the assumption that a legislator will represent or favor only his or her own ethnic group or gender among the constituency, as opposed to the entire population; also known as *descriptive representation*.

bicameral legislature
a legislature composed of two houses.

"To say the sovereignty rests in the people, and that they have not a right to instruct and control their representatives, is absurd to the last degree."—
Representative **Eldridge Gerry** (1744–1814) of Massachusetts during a debate over the ratification of the First Amendment

Delegate Model

The job of a legislator is to stick to the will of the people

"In the case of presidential impeachment, it's especially important to consult public opinion, because one's being asked, in effect, to overturn a popular election."
Senator Paul Wellstone (1944–2002) of Minnesota during the debate on President Bill Clinton's impeachment in 1999

"The average legislator early in his career discovers that there are certain interests or prejudices of his constituents which are dangerous to trifle with." –
Senator J. Willian Fulbright, (1905–1995) of Arkansas

Politico Model

A legislator might follow his or her own sense of what is right until the public becomes involved in the issue, at which point he or she should heed their wishes

Former House member **Sherwood Boehlert** (1936–) of New York called this the "pillow test." He argued that the job of a legislator is to follow the will of constituents until doing so keeps the legislator awake at night.

Conscience Model

A legislator follows the will of the people in most instances until conscience pulls him or her in a different direction

"Have the people of this country snatched the power of deliberation from this body? Are we a body of agents and not a deliberate one? **John C. Calhoun** (1782–1850) of South Carolina, Vice President and member of the House and Senate during a debate over a bill fixing compensation for members of Congress

The job of a legislator is to use information and the powers of deliberation to arrive at his or her own assessment; to "enlarge and refine the public's will"

Trustee Model

"We're not delegates who are sent here to weigh our mail every day and then to vote accordingly. We are elected to bring our judgment, our experience, and our consciences with us here."
Representative Henry Hyde (1924–) of Illinois during the Clinton impeachment proceedings

FIGURE 7.1

Representing the Will of the People

There are different approaches to representation, as this figure suggests. Should legislators act as their constituents would if they were present, or should they work to "enlarge and refine" the public will? Are there acceptable intermediate positions? Does it depend on the issue at hand? Which perspective would you hold if you were an elected official? Also, are there contemporary forces pushing legislators toward one perspective?

symbolic representation—the notion that a group of citizens is best represented by a legislator who belongs to that group—is so important that changes in the law, and perhaps even the Constitution, are needed to guarantee it. Representative Bella Abzug of New York was an outspoken advocate of a constitutional amendment that would change the composition of the Senate to fifty women and fifty men (one of each from every state). Although this suggestion never made much headway, the idea that representative bodies should look more like the citizens they represent is picking up steam. As a prominent scholar of the legislative process recently noted, "When a member of an ethnic or racial group goes to Congress, it is a badge of legitimacy for the entire grouping. . . . Moreover, there can be tangible gains in the quality

what YOU can do!

Is symbolic representation important? Invite three or four of your friends or classmates for some coffee or a lunch to talk over this important issue. Can men speak to women's issues? Do white Americans understand issues that confront people of color? Can older folks appreciate what the younger generation deems important? Of course, the exercise will be most useful if you have a diverse set of participants.

discussionquestions

1. Does a legislator's approach to the job have an impact on the role of average citizens in the lawmaking process?

2. What forces push legislators toward the delegate model of representation? What are some of the consequences?

of representation."[7] More will be said of symbolic representation when we discuss redistricting.

practicequiz

1. At the most basic level, the job of a member of Congress is to
   a. interpret the Constitution.
   b. uphold the laws of the land.
   c. speak and act on behalf of others.
   d. formulate new policies.

2. What's the difference between the delegate and trustee models of representation?
   a. Representatives following the delegate model find out the will of their constituents and act on their behalf; representatives following the trustee model simply do what they think is best for the nation.
   b. Representatives following the delegate model delegate their responsibilities to staff members; representatives following the trustee model carry out those responsibilities themselves.
   c. Representatives following the delegate model simply do what they think is best for the nation; representatives following the trustee model find out the will of their constituents and act on their behalf.
   d. Representatives following the delegate model find out the will of their constituents and act on their behalf; representatives following the trustee model consider the will of their constituents but then do what they think is best for the nation in the long run.

3. If a legislator supported a measure letting factories be built on a river in her home district but then reversed her position when local environmental activists protested the measure, what model of representation would she be following?
   a. hypocritical model
   b. politico model
   c. trustee model
   d. conscience model

4. Which of the following would be an example of constituent service performed by a representative?
   a. drafting a bill that would bring federal assistance to the representative's home district
   b. helping parents in the home district find out where their son is stationed overseas
   c. voting to raise veterans' benefits and announcing that vote to people in the home district
   d. campaigning for reelection by marching in a local parade

Answers: 1-c, 2-d, 3-b, 4-b.

Congress and the Constitution

Although the passion for democracy in Revolutionary Era America remained vibrant after independence was assured, there was also a growing realization in some quarters that the system of governance under the Articles of Confederation, which allowed the state legislatures unchallenged supremacy, was flawed. Critics pointed out that the system was not merely responsive to citizens' needs but in fact *hyperresponsive* and hence unstable in the long run. The will of the people should be respected, argued the critics, but there were other ways to structure government so that the democratic process would be a bit slower, a bit more deliberate. Representatives should "enlarge and refine the public's will," suggested James Madison in *Federalist No. 10.* Setting up such a system would be no small chore, especially given the diverse interests represented by the framers.

In L I N K *Chapter 2, pages 57–60*, we discussed three compromises that in 1787 kept the Philadelphia Constitutional Convention on track: The Great Compromise, which created a bicameral legislature; the Three-Fifths Compromise, which settled how slaves would be counted for purposes of representation; and the Sectional Compromise, which gave Congress the power to regulate commerce with a simple majority vote in exchange for permitting the Atlantic slave trade for at least twenty more years. In this section, we will take the additional step of outlining the numerous provisions in the Constitution that define the powers, duties, and obligations of Congress.

It is no accident that the framers decided to fill Article I with many details about the legislative branch. They were trying to send the message that Congress would be the heart of the new government, the most important element of the complex new system. (The Constitution, with numerous annotations, is found in Appendix 2.) Let's look more closely at a few of the most significant elements in this article.

▶ **Why did the framers create a bicameral legislature (and what is it)?** Article I, Section 1 established a two-chamber or **bicameral legislature** (see Table 7.1 on page 256). The House of Representatives, with its legislators directly elected by the people to relatively short terms of office, seemed to stick closely to the spirit of 1776. That is to say, the House reflected the idea that average citizens should select leaders who would follow their wishes rather closely. Yet the other chamber of the legislature, the Senate, seemed at first glance to move in another direction. By allowing state legislatures to pick senators and by granting them six-year terms, the Constitution seemed to check the democratic impulses of the day.

▶ **What are the qualifications to serve in Congress?**

Seventeenth Amendment
change to the U.S. Constitution, ratified in 1913, that provides for the direct election of senators.

rotation
the staggering of senatorial terms such that one-third of the Senate comes up for election every two years.

TABLE 7.1
Key Differences between the House and the Senate

HOUSE OF REPRESENTATIVES	SENATE
435 members (apportionment based on state population)	100 members (2 from each state)
2-year terms	6-year terms
Less flexible rules	More flexible rules
Limited debate	Virtually unlimited debate
Policy specialists with an emphasis on taxes and revenues	Policy generalists with an emphasis on foreign policy
Less media coverage	More media coverage
Centralized power (with committee leaders)	Equal distribution of power
More partisan	Less partisan
High turnover rate	Moderate turnover rate

How do these differences shape the way members of each chamber approach their job of representing the "will of the people?"

But on closer inspection we see that by giving each state equal representation, the Senate also reflects the spirit of 1776. The Continental Congress gave each state equal weight—a principle that the Articles of Confederation had continued. We might say, then, that the battle of the Virginia Plan against the New Jersey Plan in the Philadelphia Convention had involved two conflicting Revolutionary Era visions of representation: sovereign people versus sovereign states. This balancing act would be revisited throughout much of our history. Before the Civil War, for example, John C. Calhoun, a representative and later a senator from South Carolina, as well as vice president under Andrew Jackson, advocated a theory of "nullification." Calhoun's idea was that within their own borders, states had the right to nullify—to declare null and void—acts of Congress. Roughly one hundred years later, southern lawmakers again argued that "states' rights" and "state sovereignty" granted them the right to ignore desegregation mandates from the federal courts. More recently, similar battles may be heating up over controversial issues such as doctor-assisted suicide, medical marijuana, and same-sex marriage.

▶ **What are the qualifications to serve in Congress?** Article I, Section 2, sets the length of terms for House members (two years) and specifies the basic qualifications for service. House members must be 25 years of age, a citizen of the United States for at least seven years, and a resident of the state where they are elected. Notice, however, that the Constitution does *not* say that House members must reside in the district they represent. Throughout our history, on a number of occasions, politicians have been elected to represent districts in which they did not live. Nor does the Constitution put any limit on the number of terms a representative may serve. In the early 1990s, a number of states tried to limit the terms of members of Congress—both the House and the Senate. The Supreme Court, however, in *Term Limits, Inc. v. Thornton* (1995), found such restrictions unconstitutional. It seems, then, that the only way to limit the number of terms for members of Congress would be a constitutional amendment.

Section 3, dealing with the Senate, begins with how a senator is selected. Originally, the Constitution stated that each state legislature would select its two U.S. senators. But this changed with ratification of the **Seventeenth Amendment** in 1913, and senators are now elected directly by the voters of their state. The next clause deals with the length of senatorial terms (six years) and makes a special provision called **rotation.** Rather than have all senators come up for election every six years, the Constitution divides the Senate into three "classes," each of which must stand for election every two years. Put a bit differently, one-third of the Senate must face the voters every two years, and elections for the two Senate seats in the same state are always held in different years. While at first this might seem unimportant, the idea was to ensure that the Senate's membership could never be changed all at once just because the public had become outraged over some issue. To radically change the Senate, two or three elections are needed. That gives the Senate greater stability than the House—exactly what the framers intended.

A senator must be 30 years old, a citizen of the United States for at least nine years, and a resident of the state he or she represents. But it does not stipulate *how long* the person has to be a resident of that state before serving in the Senate. Occasionally, politicians are elected to represent a state where they had not previously lived. The most recent example was the election to the Senate in 2000 of Hillary Rodham Clinton, a native of Illinois and a resident of Arkansas (where her husband had been governor before becoming president), to represent the state of New York.

Section 4 outlines the congressional election process. Each state can decide the time, place, and manner of elections to the national legislature, so long as Congress remains silent in the

pocket veto
the president's killing of a bill that has been passed by both houses of Congress simply by not signing it; occurs only if Congress has adjourned within ten days of the bill's passage.

matter. For the most part, Congress has left the regulation of congressional elections to the states, but it has stepped in at important and controversial times. Poll taxes, literacy tests, and excessive residency requirements were used, particularly in many southern states, to keep African Americans from voting (in defiance of the Fifteenth Amendment). Congress responded with the Voting Rights Act of 1965. Later, in 1993, hoping to get more Americans to the polls, Congress passed the National Voter Registration Act (also know as the "Motor Voter Law"), which mandates that all states allow citizens to register to vote at certain frequently used public facilities, including motor vehicle offices. Recently, Congress moved to standardize the manner of voting after the Florida presidential election recount fiasco in 2000. As you may recall, the election remained undecided for several weeks because the outcome in Florida was extremely close and election officials were forced to manually count millions of ballots in key counties. This painstaking process dragged on and on, and the public became aware of the many problems of paper and punch card ballots and the dangers of idiosyncratic voting methods. The Help America Vote Act of 2002 mandates election machinery updates (mostly to get rid of fault-prone punch cards, which had caused so much trouble in Florida) and provided some funds to pay for these changes.

Section 5 deals with a number of procedural matters, such as that each house may determine its own rules and set forth what constitutes a quorum. It stipulates that each chamber keep a journal of its proceedings. Section 6 spells out how members of Congress will be paid (out of the U.S Treasury, not from state governments), and it stipulates that members cannot be arrested while they are attending a session of Congress—except for "Treason, Felony, and Breach of Peace." It further notes that members of the national legislature cannot hold any other federal position.

Section 7 addresses how a bill becomes law and also specifies the checks and balances between the two houses of the legislature and between the other branches of the government. The same piece of legislation must be approved by a majority of each house of the legislature before it goes to the president for signature into law. If the president signs the bill, it becomes law. Should the president fail to act on the bill for ten days (not counting Sundays), it becomes law anyway—unless Congress has adjourned in the meantime. But if the president vetoes the bill, a two-thirds vote in both houses is necessary to override the veto. A **pocket veto** can also be used. This is when the president withholds approval of a bill after Congress has adjourned, thereby killing the bill without a formal veto. Much more will be said later in the chapter about how a bill becomes a law. (See also ⓁⒾⓃⓀ *Chapter 8, page 320*.)

TABLE 7.2
Powers of Congress under the U.S. Constitution

CLAUSE	POWER GRANTED IN ARTICLE I, SECTION 8
1	Lay and collect taxes and duties and provide for the common defense
2	Borrow money on credit
3	Regulate commerce with foreign nations and between the states
4	Establish rules on naturalization and bankruptcy
5	Coin money
6	Create punishments for counterfeiting
7	Establish post offices
8	Promote the progress of science and the arts
9	Constitute tribunals below the Supreme Court
10	Punish crimes on the high seas
11	Declare war
12	Raise and support the army
13	Provide and maintain a navy
14	Make rules for the use of armed forces
15	Call out the militia
16	Organize, arm, and discipline the militia
17	Exercise exclusive legislation over the district of the seat of the federal government
18	Make all laws deemed "necessary and proper" for implementing these powers

One of the dangers of listing an organization's powers is that all circumstances may not be covered. The framers of the Constitution understood this and added the final element to deal with unforseen circumstances. Yet, the "elastic clause" has proven controversial because the Supreme Court has interpreted it in broad terms, thus granting Congress sweeping powers. Do you think the national legislature should have these expansive powers?

Section 8 is very important. It lists the powers of the legislative branch—including the power to collect taxes, to regulate commerce, to coin money, to declare war, and to raise and support armies and the navy (see Table 7.2). This list was controversial for two reasons: First, although the framers thought it important to define Congress's powers, there was still widespread public resistance to giving

▶ **What are implied powers?**
How do we know what they
include?

elastic clause/necessary and proper clause
a statement in Article I, Section 8, of the U.S. Constitution that grants Congress the power to pass all laws "necessary and proper" for carrying out the list of expressed powers.

at-large districts
districts encompassing an entire state or large parts of a state in which House members are elected to represent the entire state.

geographic representation
the idea that a legislator should represent the interests of the people living in a specific geographic location.

excessive power to the national government. After all, Americans had only recently rid themselves of a very strong central government—that of King George III. Second, even though the framers were willing to give the national government broad powers, listing them carried a risk of leaving something out, something that might later prove significant. Inclusion of the last clause of Section 8 seemed to provide a solution. This provision, often called the **elastic clause** or the **necessary and proper clause,** states that Congress has the power to make all laws "necessary and proper" to implement any of the other powers mentioned in the section. This clause suggested that many of Congress' powers were *implied* rather than spelled out in detail.

▶ **What are implied powers? How do we know what they include?** The issue of implied versus spelled-out powers came up early in the new republic, when in 1790 Secretary of the Treasury Alexander Hamilton pushed through Congress a bill to charter a national bank, the Bank of the United States. Nowhere did the Constitution directly state that Congress had the power to do this, and Thomas Jefferson and James Madison insisted that Hamilton's proposal went too far. They asked President Washington to veto the bill. Hamilton fought back by citing the "necessary and proper" clause: A national bank, he said, was necessary to ensure that the nation's credit and currency were sound. Washington considered both sides' arguments before accepting Hamilton's position and signing the bill, thus setting an important precedent for interpreting the Constitution's grant of powers broadly rather than narrowly.

By 1819, the Supreme Court had put the argument for implied powers on a stronger foundation. In his majority opinion in the very important case of *McCulloch* v. *Maryland,* Chief Justice John Marshall made it clear that Congress did indeed have "implied powers." The case concerned a branch of the federally chartered Bank of the United States located in the state of Maryland. Banks being profitable institutions, the state of Maryland had chartered its own bank, but it was losing money because of competition with the national bank. To recover some of these losses, the Maryland legislature decided to levy a tax on the Bank of the United States. But can a state government tax an institution created by the national government? And—resurrecting the question that Jefferson and Madison had asked back in 1790—where does the Constitution give Congress the power to create a national bank?

As to the first question, Marshall wrote, "The power to tax involves the power to destroy." That would suggest some sort of supremacy. Yet the Constitution is clear that the national government is supreme, so the tax (which could, if heavy enough, put the national bank out of business) was unconstitutional.

As to the broader question, the power to charter a bank, Marshall used the same argument Hamilton had advanced:

> Let the end be legitimate, let it be within the scope of the constitution, and all means which are appropriate, which are plainly adapted to that end, which are not prohibited, but consistent with the letter and spirit of the constitution, are constitutional.

In one clean sweep, Marshall's ruling greatly expanded the scope of the national government's power.

practicequiz

1. The framers of the Constitution thought that members of Congress should not merely represent the will of their constituents but should "enlarge and refine the public's will."
   a. true   **b.** false

2. What is the primary difference between the Senate as it was designed by the Constitutional Convention and how it operates now?
   a. Senators were originally limited to two four-year terms.
   b. Senators could serve an unlimited number of terms, but each was two years long.
   c. Each state was granted a number of senators proportional to its population.
   d. Each state legislature picked its U.S. senators; they were not chosen through popular election.

3. Article I, Section 8, of the Constitution
   a. explains who qualifies to run for legislative office.
   b. explains the relationships of the three branches of government.
   c. lists the powers of the legislative branch.
   d. explains how the House of Representatives differs from England's houses of Parliament.

4. What provision in the Constitution says that Congress has the power to make all the laws it needs to carry out the other powers specified in the Constitution?
   a. the sufficient and provisional clause
   b. the necessary and proper clause
   c. the *McCulloch* v. *Maryland* clause
   d. the congressional sovereignty clause

Answers: 1-a, 2-d, 3-c, 4-b.

redistricting
the process of redrawing legislative district boundaries within a state to reflect population changes.

gerrymandering
drawing legislative district boundaries in such a way as to gain political advantage.

discussionquestions

1. Which elements of Article I of the Constitution could you point to as enhancing the role of citizens in the government? Which elements inhibit the citizens' role?

2. What does *McCulloch* v. *Maryland* say, and why is it regarded as such an important Supreme Court decision?

Redistricting

The Great Compromise stipulated that Congress be divided into two houses, one with an identical number of legislators from each state (the Senate) and the other based on population (the House of Representatives). But how would we know the number of citizens in each state? The Constitution also stipulates that a census be conducted every ten years and that seats be allocated to each state based on this count. But if a state gets more than one seat (and most states do), who then is responsible for drawing the boundaries of legislative districts—or should there even *be* legislative districts? Why not elect all the state's representatives on an at-large basis? These questions the Constitution left to the states to decide, and they have caused considerable controversy ever since.

In the earliest days of the Republic, some states did use **at-large districts.** If they were granted three seats in the House, they would simply elect three members from the entire state. Those states had no districts. But most states chose to divide their territory into a number of congressional districts equal to the number of seats they were allocated in the House of Representatives. A state with five seats would create five congressional districts. The idea of changing legislative districts in response to population shifts stems from the American idea of **geographic representation.** That is, our representatives should be directly responsible to a group of people living in a specific geographic location. This comes from Americans' early experience with the "rotten boroughs" in the British Parliament. Eighteenth-century British parliamentary districts, called *boroughs,* never regularly changed their lines to reflect population shifts. As a result, some places, including major cities, were not represented at all in the House of Commons, while others were vastly overrepresented. Until 1832, some rotten boroughs had *no* residents at all—everyone had moved away or the area had sunk under the sea. The aristocrat who owned that patch of land—or water—got to name whoever he wanted to represent it in Parliament.

Today, drawing the boundaries for congressional districts has become a tricky and controversial process. In all states except the very small ones that have only a single representative, the process must be undertaken every ten years to reflect changes in the state's overall population relative to the rest of the country, as well as responding to population shifts within the state. This process of redrawing the boundaries of legislative districts is called **redistricting.** The Constitution gives state legislatures the redistricting power. Because these bodies have nearly always been partisan (controlled by a majority of members from one party), you probably won't be surprised to hear that the process causes a lot of partisan wrangling.

Gerrymandering is the drawing of legislative districts for partisan advantage. The word immortalizes one Elbridge Gerry, who as governor of Massachusetts around 1800 persuaded his followers in the state legislature to draw an odd-shaped district wiggling across the state, designed to elect a political ally. Looking at the map, someone said that the new district looked like a salamander, to which someone else replied that it wasn't a salamander but "a gerrymander" (see Figure 7.2 on page 260).[8] The name stuck. Gerrymandering means to carve the state up into oddly shaped districts that will elect the most candidates from the majority party. This has been done in a number of ways, but mostly through either *packing* or *cracking.* Packing is lumping as many opposition voters as possible into one district. For instance, if the state has five districts, the idea is to fill one of these districts overwhelmingly with supporters of the other party. The party in power—the politicians drawing the lines—would give up that one seat, but the other four districts would be shaped to nearly guarantee that candidates of their party would win. Cracking involves splitting up groups of voters thought favorable to the opposition so that they do not make up a majority in any district and thus cannot win in any district.

As you might guess, the redistricting process has also been used to minimize the representation of African Americans and other minority groups. Thirty percent of a state's population, for example, might be black, but through cracking it could be fixed so that these voters would never be able to elect an African American legislator without the help of white voters. Or through packing, most of the black population might be concentrated in one virtually all-black district, enabling whites to elect representatives from the other districts. The tendency of African American voters to support Democratic candidates could therefore be exploited by a Republican-majority state legislature to minimize the election of Democrats and of African Americans to represent the state in the House.

▶ **These tactics for redistricting** don't seem very democratic. Are they legal?

quorum
the minimum number of members that must be present at a meeting to make proceedings valid.

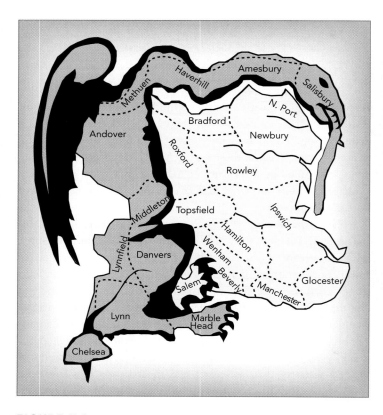

FIGURE 7.2
That's not a salamander, its a Gerrymander!

As Governor of Massachusetts in 1812, Elbridge Gerry prompted his fellow Republicans in the state legislature to draw congressional district lines that favored their party. As the story goes, a reporter looked at one of these new districts and commented that it looked like a salamander. Another noted, "That's not a salamander, that's a Gerrymander!" Partisan-based redistricting is an age-old problem. Should legislatures allow nonpartisan groups to draw new district lines?

Democratic Congressman Charlie Stenholm at a senior center in Hereford, Texas on October 11, 2004. After serving nearly three decades in the House, Stenholm lost his reelection bid. Was Stenholm a victim of partisan gerrymandering or changing demographics and population shifts, as argued by Republicans in the Texas State Legislature?
Photo: Rick Scibelli Jr./The New York Times

pathways of action

THE TEXAS REDISTRICTING BATTLE

The quarrelsome nature of redistricting is evident after every census is announced—and it has repercussions in most state legislatures. In 2003, all eyes turned to the struggle over a plan to redraw congressional district lines in Texas. In a somewhat unprecedented move, the Republican Texas congressman and House majority leader, Tom DeLay, inserted himself into the process. The outcome of his efforts with state legislative leaders, also Republican, was a redistricting plan that many Democrats saw as overwhelmingly partisan. According to the Democrats, the scheme would make at least twenty-two of the state's thirty-two congressional districts unshakably Republican, up from the current fifteen "safe" Republican seats. Moreover, Democrats argued that the plan would deprive millions of minority people of their voting rights. Republicans responded by arguing that previous redistricting plans had given the Democrats an artificial advantage and that their plan better matched demographic shifts throughout the state.

▶ **Does every district have**
the same number of residents?

majority-minority districts
voting districts in which members of a
minority group make up the majority of
the population.

To stop the state legislature from adopting the plan, many Democrats in both the state house and senate refused to attend legislative sessions to vote on the measure, denying the Republicans a **quorum** (the minimum number of members who by law must be present in order to transact official business). Fearing that the Republican governor would send state troopers to bring them by force to the legislature and compel a vote, fifty-three Democrats left the state and holed up in a hotel in Ardmore, Oklahoma, in May 2003. Without a quorum in the state legislature, the plan stalled. But how long could these legislators stay away from their homes and families? The nation watched and waited. By midsummer, two Democrats broke ranks and, returning to Austin, gave the Republicans a quorum. Then the others returned and the measure passed during a special legislative session. The scheme seemed to work. In 2002, there had been fifteen Republicans in the Texas delegation to the U.S. House. After November 2004, there were twenty-one.[9]

The question of whether the Texas redistricting was legal went to the Supreme Court in the spring of 2006. Rather than directly deciding the constitutionality of the new lines, the Court provided Democrats a partial victory by saying that when excessive political considerations are used to redraw congressional district lines, the result may be unconstitutional. But as to whether that was the case with the new lines in Texas, the Court ordered a three-judge Circuit Court panel to investigate the issue in detail. The findings of the panel were not expected until the following year, well after the 2006 election. In a way, the issue was put on hold. ■

▶ **These tactics for redistricting don't seem very democratic. Are they legal?** Some states are moving toward using nonpartisan organizations to draw district lines. Iowa has taken this trend furthest, using a complex computer program administered by a nonpartisan commission to draw geographically compact and equal districts. The state legislature then votes these districts up or down, but it cannot amend them. This process has spared Iowa from court challenges and has produced competitive congressional races. For example, in the 2004 election, three out of five of Iowa's U.S. House races were considered competitive, compared to one out of ten in the rest of the nation.[10]

For the most part, redistricting has been a tricky issue for the courts. On a number of occasions, they have refused to get involved in the controversy, arguing that the issue was a "political question" and therefore "not justiciable."[11] In other words, the courts have concluded that the issue is inappropriate for them to resolve and that another branch of the government must decide. The court has signaled a greater willingness to hear such cases in

recent decades, but the complexity of the reapportionment process makes judicial intervention difficult. Some public anger about uncompetitive elections is now brewing. But perhaps it is noteworthy that in 2005, voters in both Ohio and California rejected referendum proposals to reform the system—in both states, after the party that benefits from congressional gerrymandering (Republicans in the former and Democrats in the latter) argued that the proposed reforms would hurt them! The whole issue remains tangled up in partisanship and is far from settled.

POSITIVE GERRYMANDERING Amendments to the Voting Rights Act of 1965, which were passed in 1982, approached the racial gerrymandering issue from an entirely different direction. If the redistricting process has been used in the past to limit minority representation, could it not be used to *increase* minority representation? Perhaps census data could be used to construct districts that would better ensure the election of minority legislators. Following the 1990 census, twenty-four **majority-minority districts** were created in different states—districts in which a minority group made up a majority of the population. Fifteen of these districts had majorities of African American voters and nine a majority of Hispanic voters. The scheme seemed to work: In each of these districts, the voters chose a minority legislator. Nevertheless, two issues came up. First, the resulting districts were often exceptionally oddly shaped. In North Carolina's Twelfth Congressional District, for example, a roughly 100-mile strip of Interstate 85, on which almost no one lived, connected black communities in Durham and Charlotte. Second, the overt consideration of race in drawing highly irregular districts was challenged in the courts as an affront to the equal protection clause of the Fourteenth Amendment. Although the U.S. Supreme Court had tended to stay out of redistricting disputes, this time it did not. In a series of decisions, the Court generally supported plans that improved the likelihood of minority representation, but it also seemed reluctant to allow highly irregular shaped districts (*Shaw* v. *Reno*, 1993) or to approve schemes that use race as the primary criterion for drawing district lines (*Miller* v. *Johnson*, 1995).

▶ **Does every district have the same number of residents?**
NUMBER OF RESIDENTS PER DISTRICT Related to the difficult issue of drawing district lines is the question of the number of residents per district. Oddly enough, the Constitution is silent on this matter, and for most of our history, many states did not try to ensure the same number of constituents in every district. Questionable motivations were at work in some instances. On

Baker v. Carr (1961)
Supreme Court case that set the standard that House districts must contain equal numbers of constituents, thus establishing the principle of "one person, one vote."

FIGURE 7.3
Distribution of Congressional Power

The framers understood that our nation would grow. They were wise enough to mandate that a census be taken every ten years, and that the allocation of House seats to each state be reapportioned accordingly. This map shows the changes after the most recent Census (in 2000). What are some of the patterns that emerge? What might be the root of these changes? Also, what will be some of the political implications of population changes in the decades to come?
SOURCE: U.S. Census Bureau.

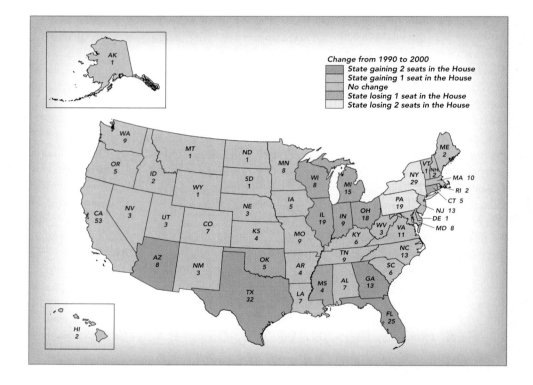

Change from 1990 to 2000
- State gaining 2 seats in the House
- State gaining 1 seat in the House
- No change
- State losing 1 seat in the House
- State losing 2 seats in the House

the other hand, precise equality between districts often did not seem logical. Imagine, for example, a state that was allotted three representatives. There were two urban areas, in opposite corners of the state, and one agricultural region in the middle. Wouldn't it seem logical to group constituents with similar interests, producing two urban districts and one rural one, even if they weren't quite equal in numerical size? But because most Americans believe that each voter should have the same political weight—that all men and women are politically equal—such badly apportioned districts appear to violate this ideal, and others also suggest that it violates the spirit of the Constitution. (Interestingly, few people seem interested in challenging the legitimacy of the U.S. Senate, where the least populous state, Wyoming, and the most populous state, California, each have the same number of seats: two.)

The issue of malapportionment came to a head in the mid-twentieth century when a group of Tennessee residents claimed that the state legislature had denied them equal protection under

the law by refusing to draw districts with the same size population. In 1961, the Supreme Court decided that the Tennessee districts were so out of proportion that they did violate the plaintiffs' constitutional rights. This case, **Baker v. Carr,** wrote the "one person, one vote" principle into federal law.[12] It sparked a revolution in the way legislative districts were drawn. In the post-*Baker* era, geographic concerns took a back seat to ensuring equal population in all districts. These cases also mandated that redistricting happen every ten years even if the size of the state's congressional delegation remained unchanged, since the new census meant the old districts likely no longer had equal populations, given population shifts over a decade. Perhaps most important, *Baker* v. *Carr* inserted the federal courts into the redistricting process, thereby leaving any plan open to a court challenge. Along with the mandate under the 1965 Voting Rights Act to prevent racial discrimination in voting, *Baker* v. *Carr* has made redistricting a tedious process of moving district lines block by block until the population balance is correct, while

reapportionment
the process by which seats in the House of Representatives are reassigned among the states to reflect population changes following the census (every 10 years).

discussionquestions

1. What tactics have been used to minimize the electoral relevance of minority groups through legislative redistricting? Which groups have suffered from these tactics?

2. Are there any arguments to be made against the idea that our system requires the same number of residents in every congressional district? Is it possible that representation can be enhanced when districts are *not* equally apportioned?

constantly under the threat that a federal court would find the entire scheme unconstitutional.[13]

REAPPORTIONMENT Finally, the redistricting process has been argued about because the allotment of seats per state shifts with each new census (see Figure 7.3). The process of shifting the number of seats allotted to each state is called **reapportionment.** Originally, the Constitution set the ratio of residents per House member at 1 to 30,000, meaning there were 65 House members in the First Congress. As the nation's population grew, so did the number of representatives in the House. The membership of the House jumped from 141 in 1800 to 240 in 1830. By 1910, the House had grown to 435 members. That seemed large enough, so its membership was capped by Congress. Since then, the ratio has gotten smaller and smaller. Today, there are roughly 670,000 residents for each House district. (If today's House districts still had the 30,000 residents that the Constitution prescribed for the First Congress, there would be 22,333 representatives in the House!)

Reapportionment implies that the fastest-growing states gain seats after each census and that seats are taken from the slower-growing states. (Only North Dakota today is actually losing population.) After the 2000 census, for example, New York and Pennsylvania each lost two House seats. The winners are southern and southwestern states. These trends, of course, reflect the shift of the United States population toward the Sunbelt and away from the old industrial and farming states.

Losing seats in the national legislature can be devastating for a state because much of federal government's domestic spending is proportionate to a state's population. Having fewer residents means getting fewer federal dollars. And of course, when states lose seats, it often forces some of the state's incumbent representatives to run against one another for the seats that remain. There is nothing an incumbent hates more than to run against a fellow incumbent!

An interesting argument has also emerged over the actual population of each state. Some, mostly Democrats, charge that many citizens are missed in the counting process of the census. They argue that statistical models for estimating populations would actually yield more accurate results than trying to physically count everyone. Others, mostly Republicans, point out that the Constitution stipulates a full *person-by-person* count; until the Constitution

is changed, they say, there is no alternative. It is a partisan battle because most analysts agree that the chance of citizens' being missed is greatest in the northeastern urban states, which lean Democratic. The argument is likely to simmer for a long time and to climax every ten years, when a new census is conducted. But for now, the Republicans seem to have the courts on their side.

practicequiz

1. In the early years of the Republic, a minority of states chose their congressmen for the House of Representatives through at-large elections, not through elections by congressional district.
  a. true   **b.** false

2. What would be an example of "cracking" in the gerrymandering of districts?
  a. redistricting so that in a predominantly Democratic state that used to have multiple districts with a Republican majority, now only one Republican district existed with a much greater concentration of Republicans
  b. redistricting so that there were more majority-minority districts than there used to be
  c. redistricting so that in a predominantly Republican state, districts that had held a slim Democratic majority were redrawn so that some of them became Republican-majority districts
  d. redistricting so that in a predominantly Republican state, more districts became Democratic, but only by very slim majorities

3. What compelled the desire to reapportion districts so that each U.S. representative represents roughly the same number of constituents?
  a. the desire to have each state get as much federal money as any other
  b. the democratic principle of all voters' being granted the same political weight in Congress
  c. the idea that no state or district should be paying higher taxes than any other
  d. the recognition that "separate" is never "equal"

4. What Supreme Court case wrote the "one person, one vote" principle into federal law?
  a. *McCulloch* v. *Maryland*
  b. *Plessy* v. *Ferguson*
  c. *Marbury* v. *Madison*
  d. *Baker* v. *Carr*

Answers: 1-a, 2-c, 3-b, 4-d.

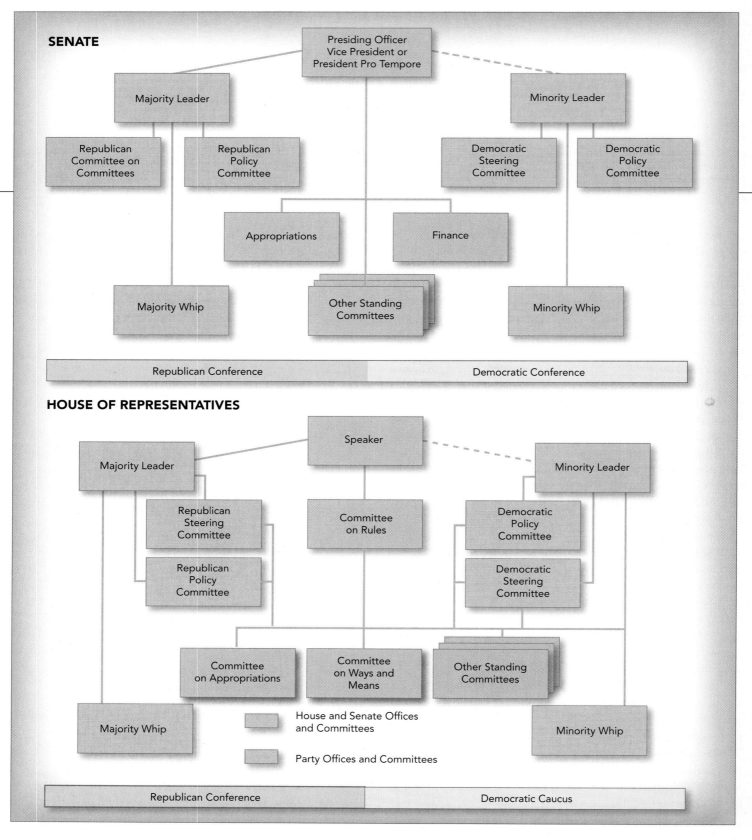

FIGURE 7.4

Leadership in Congress Prior to the Election

In the early years of Congress all members were treated equally; there were no "leaders." By the 1830s, however, there was a realization that party leaders could help organize the process and advance the goals of their party. Indeed, the legislature is more efficient with aggressive leaders. But at what cost? Can an organization be internally democratic when some members are more powerful, more influential than others?

SOURCE: Dye, Thomas R. *Politics in America*, Basic version, 6th, 2005. Electronically reproduced by permission of Pearson Education, Inc. Upper Saddle River, NJ.

what YOU can do!

Do you know what your own congressional district looks like? Do you know which counties, cities, towns, and neighborhoods are located in the district? Go to the Web or a nearby library and get this information. You might first try *Almanac of American Politics* or *Politics in America*, two congressional reference books. Would you say that the interests of most constituents in that district would be similar, or do you think there is a great deal of diversity?

Organizing the Legislative Process

The Constitution says very little about how the two legislative chambers should be structured. This might seem especially odd, given the pains that the framers took to lay out the legislative powers, and it was a pressing matter nearly from the beginning. Today, how the legislature is organized is as important as its precise powers and responsibilities. Further, this issue is very important when considering how change might be accomplished through the legislative process and how individual citizens might make a difference. Each of the organizing elements that we will discuss here gives citizens points of access into the policy development process. For instance, understanding the importance of committees allows an activist to focus attention on this stage of the process, where real decisions are made. You can no more learn your potential to change the course of government by reading only Article I of the Constitution than you could learn how to succeed as a major league football coach just by reading the NFL rule book. This section looks at the key organizing forces within the legislative process, the nonconstitutional components that help hundreds of individual legislators merge into a lawmaking, appropriating, oversight body.

STANDING COMMITTEES: THE WORKHORSES OF THE LEGISLATURE

Standing committees are the permanent structures that perform the detailed work of a legislature, such as drafting bills for consideration. There are many advantages to the standing committee system, which was first set up in the House in 1810 and in the Senate shortly thereafter. First, members of each committee become experts in that policy area, so they can better determine the importance and implications of proposals. To accomplish this, each committee acquires a staff of experts who help legislators make informed decisions. As issues become more and more complex, the "expertise function" becomes even more important. Second, by dividing the legislature's work between dozens of committees, or "minilegislatures," a vast number of measures can be considered simultaneously. As two leading congressional

scholars have noted, "Without committees, a legislative body consisting of 100 senators and 440 House members could not handle roughly 10,000 bills and nearly 100,000 nominations biennially, a national budget over $2 trillion, and a limitless array of controversial issues."[14]

A third advantage is that this system enhances the representation process by allowing legislators to sit on committees that deal with issues of interest to their constituents. For example, many legislators from the midwestern farm belt might best serve their constituents by serving on an agriculture committee. Most often, however, constituent interests are varied, making the fit with a particular committee impossible. Even so, many legislators seek committee assignments that allow them to serve their constituents better. Fourth, committees have taken on a "safety valve" function by becoming the forum for public debate and controversy. They give average citizens a place to vent concerns and frustrations, and they can absorb conflict and resolve the strains of a democratic system. (Of course, by blocking action on measures that some citizens and interest groups ardently support, legislative committees can also promote conflict and increase tensions.)

Finally, and much related to the pathways of change, committees offer citizens many points of access into the legislative process. Though it might be too much to expect a citizen or a small group of like-minded citizens to persuade an entire chamber, shifting the course of committee decisions may be more manageable. Given that very few measures are considered by the full legislature without first being passed at the committee level, and given also that committee votes are often won or lost by a few votes, swinging a couple of legislators to your point of view can sometimes change the fate of a piece of legislation. This heightens the power of citizens in the policy process. The number of standing committees has varied over the years. Different subject areas have been more important in some periods than in others. Today there are nineteen standing committees in the House and sixteen in the Senate (see Table 7.3 on page 266). The size of each committee varies as well, but generally speaking, House committees consist of about fifty members and Senate standing committees have roughly twenty. As we'll see later in this chapter, the balance of power between the parties in each chamber is reflected in each committee.

Although standing committees are clearly the most important, there are three other types of legislative committees. Nearly

▶ **How are bills assigned to committees, and who does it?**

subcommittees
specialized groups within standing committees.

seniority system
giving leadership positions to the legislators who have served in Congress the longest.

select committee
a temporary committee created to deal with a specific issue.

TABLE 7.3
Standing Committees of the 109th Congress

COMMITTEES OF THE SENATE	COMMITTEES OF THE HOUSE
Agriculture, Nutrition, and Forestry (20 members)	**Agriculture** (46 members)
Appropriations (28 members)	**Appropriations** (66 members)
Armed Services (24 members)	**Armed Services** (66 members)
Banking, Housing, and Urban Affairs (20 members)	**Budget** (39 members)
Budget (22 members)	**Education and the Workforce** (49 members)
Commerce, Science, and Transportation (22 members)	**Energy and Commerce** (58 members)
Energy and Natural Resources (22 members)	**Financial Services** (72 members)
Environment and Public Works (18 members)	**Government Reform** (41 members)
Finance (20 members)	**Homeland Security** (34 members)
Foreign Relations (18 members)	**House Administration** (9 members)
Health, Education, Labor, and Pensions (20 members)	**International Relations** (49 members)
Homeland Security and Governmental Affairs (16 members)	**Judiciary** (40 members)
Judiciary (18 members)	**Resources** (52 members)
Rules and Administration (18 members)	**Rules** (13 members)
Small Business (18 members)	**Science** (44 members)
Veterans' Affairs (14 members)	**Small Business** (36 members)
Senate Special or Select Committees:	**Standards of Official Conduct** (10 members)
Aging (19 members)	**Transportation and Infrastructure** (75 members)
Ethics (6 members)	**Veterans' Affairs** (28 members)
Indian Affairs (14 members)	**Ways and Means** (41 members)
Intelligence (15 members)	

all standing committees have one or more **subcommittees** under their jurisdiction. Much the same rationale for apportioning legislative work to committees also applies to subcommittees, whose members and staffers specialize, thus breaking down a broad policy area into more manageable parts. Today, usually any piece of legislation that comes before a committee is quickly referred to the appropriate subcommittee. Most of the day-to-day lawmaking and oversight of Congress now occurs at the subcommittee level.[15]

Subcommittees have not always been a key feature of the legislative process, however. During most of our nation's history, the full committee, and its all-powerful chairman, ran the show. But this was a closed system in which initiatives lived or died at the pleasure of the committee and its chairman. (In those days, there

were few women in Congress and none with the seniority to chair the important committees.) By the early 1970s, though, a great many of the rank-and-file legislators—the average legislators—had grown frustrated with the committee system, especially with regard to civil rights legislation. Many of the full committee chairs had risen to their post through the **seniority system,** whereby the longest-serving majority party member automatically assumed the chair. These senior party members were most often conservative southern Democrats. The proliferation of subcommittees, as well as the growth of their power, resulted from an internal revolt of previously marginalized members. The idea was to spread power so that there would be many power centers. There were moves to reduce the number of subcommittees in 1995 when the Republicans took over the House. Today there are roughly ninety in the

joint committee
units that conduct oversight or issue research, but do not have legislative powers.

multiple referrals
the forwarding of a piece of legislation to more than one committee for consideration.

conference committee
a committee of members of the House and Senate that irons out differences in similar measures that have passed both houses to create a single bill.

hearings
committee sessions for taking testimony from witnesses and for collecting information on legislation under consideration or for the development of new legislation.

House and seventy in the Senate, making control of the legislative process more decentralized than in the past.

Congress also uses three other kinds of committee. Today, both chambers establish **select committees** to deal with a particular issue or problem. They are temporary, so they disappear either when the problem is resolved or, more likely, when the congressional session ends. They serve primarily in an investigative role and cannot approve legislation or move it forward. Of much more significance is the **conference committee.** For legislation to become law, both branches of the legislature must first pass exactly the same bill. When each chamber passes similar but not identical legislation, a conference committee is assembled to work out the differences and reach a compromise. Some conference committees are small, consisting of the chairs of corresponding House and Senate committees and a few members; others, dealing with higher-profile matters, can have hundreds of members. In some ways, these conference committees actually write legislation—as suggested in the opening of this chapter, the version that emerges from conference often contains vital details that differ from what either house originally passed and may deal with entirely unrelated matters. So important are conference committees that some have dubbed them "the third house of Congress." Finally, **joint committees** are composed of members selected from each chamber. The work of these committees generally involves investigation, research, and oversight of agencies closely related to Congress. Permanent joint committees, created by statute, are sometimes called standing joint committees.

WHAT COMMITTEES DO

Committees are critical to the lawmaking process, and while they do present a few drawbacks, it is impossible to imagine a modern legislature functioning without committees. But what, exactly, do committees do? Let's take a closer look.

▶ **How are bills assigned to committees, and who does it?**
REFERRAL AND JURISDICTION The 1946 Legislative Authorization Act stated that every piece of legislation introduced for consideration must first be referred to a committee. This may seem rather mechanical, simply matching the topic of the bill with an appropriate committee. But the process is much more complex and, at times, quite contentious. For one thing, often the topic of the proposed legislation could fall within the jurisdiction or policy area of several committees. In the House, for instance, proposed legislation dealing with an energy issue might be referred to the Energy and Commerce Committee, but it could also go to the Resources, Science, or Transportation Committee.

The job of referral is given to the speaker of the House or, in the Senate, to the majority leader. During most of our nation's history, bills were referred to just one committee, which caused much turf warfare. Sometimes which committee a bill got referred to depended less on jurisdictional fit than on the impact, positive or negative, that the chair of that committee might have on its fate. Referral to one particular committee over another would often either seal a proposed measure's doom or give it a good chance of enactment. This helped ensure that the committee process was closed and undemocratic. By the early 1970s, as a consequence of the revolt mentioned earlier, the House adopted a process of **multiple referrals.** Now instead of assigning a new bill to just one committee, it is possible to send the measure to several committees at the same time. Although the process has changed somewhat over the years, it has become customary to designate a "primary committee" that considers a bill but also to assign it to other committees as well.

On the positive side, multiple referrals promote what some scholars laud as "integrated policy-making, broader public discussion of issues, wide access to the legislative process, and consideration of alternative approaches."[16] But some suggest that multiple referrals make the legislative process even more complex and yield even less accountability. A committee may stall on a measure while suggesting that one of the other committees move the measure forward if it thinks it important. Opportunities for foot-dragging and buck-passing are therefore widespread.

HEARINGS The vast majority of bills that are introduced in the House or Senate and are then assigned to a committee and then often to a subcommittee wind up being never acted on. That is, most bills are deemed unworthy of consideration and are killed. If a measure is not moved out of the committee considering it, it dies at the end of the legislative term. Roughly 90 percent of all measures stall in committee and thus die a slow death.

For measures that have a modest chance of committee approval, **hearings** are often the first step. These are fact-finding, informational events that usually first take place in a subcommittee. Experts are asked to testify at hearings, including the sponsor of the bill, state and federal officials, interest group leaders, private officials, and (if arranged for by the bill's sponsor, by its

▶ **Why is the House Rules**
Committee considered so
powerful?

markup
the section-by-section review and revision of a bill by committee members; the actual writing of a piece of legislation.

prime sponsor
the member of Congress responsible for the language of legislation.

open process
allowing a bill to be amended on the floor of the House of Representatives.

closed process
prohibiting a bill from being amended on the floor of the House of Representatives.

opponents, or by advocacy groups) even ordinary citizens making highly emotional pleas, largely for the benefit of the media. Occasionally, on high-visibility issues, celebrities get to testify, too. Although a celebrity might not be an expert in the area, the main reason for allowing him or her to speak is publicity. "Quite candidly, when Hollywood speaks, the world listens," Pennsylvania Senator Arlen Specter once commented. "Sometimes when Washington speaks, the world snoozes."[17]

MARKUP   If the measure is still considered important after hearings have been held, the next step in the process is called **markup.** Here the actual language of the bill is hammered out. The member responsible for crafting the language is called the **prime sponsor.** Often the prime sponsor is the subcommittee chair, but not always. Markup can be a critical step in the process: The language of the bill must address the concerns of the sponsor, but it also must win the approval of the committee and then the full chamber. Many a good idea has languished in the legislature because its language failed to gather enough support. And sometimes the language becomes so complex that no one is quite sure what it means.

After the hearings and markup, the subcommittee may take no action, thus killing the bill, or they may vote on the measure, which generally leads to approval. Once approved in subcommittee, the bill is sent to the full committee, which may conduct its own hearings, change the language through a second markup process, take no action, or send it back to the subcommittee for more information. Again, this is a stage at which much proposed legislation dies.

REPORTS   For the fraction of measures that win committee approval, the next step is to send the bill to the floor for consideration. At this point, the staff of the committee prepares a report on the legislation. This report summarizes the bill's provisions and the rationale behind it. It is, in essence, a summary of the committee's deliberations and an argument for why the full chamber should approve the measure. This too is a critical step in the process.

▶ **Why is the House Rules Committee considered so powerful?**
THE RULES REPORT   There is another stop—a critically important one—before a bill is sent to the floor. Every bill in the House and Senate must past through a Rules Committee. On the surface, the rationale behind this committee seems logical: to establish rules regarding the consideration of the legislation, which helps streamline the process and makes things fair. How long might the House deliberate on a particular bill? Should amendments be allowed? If amendments are permitted, in what order should they be voted on? Among much else, the House Rules Committee states whether the process of consideration will be **open** (meaning that it may be amended), **closed** (so that changes to the bill are prohibited), or **modified** (making certain amendments possible). A related matter is the **time-structured rule,** which allows amendments but only within a predetermined time frame.[18] An entire set of rules governs the overall length of debate for each measure and how much time each member has to comment on it.

On closer inspection, though, we find that the ability to structure the rules for deliberation of a bill can be a weighty factor in deciding that bill's fate. To be sure, the Rules Committee is a critically important element in the majority party's arsenal of mechanisms to help control the chamber and thus the creation of public policy. One of the best examples of the strategic use of the Rules Committee was in late 1950s and early 1960s, when Howard W. "Judge" Smith of Virginia was the chair. Smith was a Democrat, but also an ultraconservative and an unyielding foe of civil rights legislation. In 1957, for example, while the House was considering a civil rights bill, Smith used an endless set of delaying tactics to stall floor consideration of these bills. At one point, he simply left Washington when the committee was scheduled to meet, thus preventing the bill's consideration on the floor. Later, in the early 1960s, Smith was able to bottle up most of President John F. Kennedy's liberal legislative proposals. And it was not until the majority leadership added new members to the committee that Smith finally lost control.

BUREAUCRATIC OVERSIGHT   Our discussion of committee action thus far has centered on policymaking, the process of creating or changing federal law. This is a key aspect of committee work but not the only aspect. Another critical committee function is **oversight**—Congress's responsibility to keep a close eye on the federal bureaucracy's implementation of federal law. The Constitution does not spell out a congressional oversight role, but neither does it prohibit such work, and congressional oversight has become increasingly important. Senator Trent Lott, a Republican from Mississippi and a former Senate majority leader, has said, "I have always felt that one-third of the role of Congress should be oversight."[19] Oversight is especially time-consuming and contentious in times of divided government—that is, when the president is of one party and the opposition party controls at least one house of Congress.

modified process
allowing certain amendments to a bill on the floor of the House of Representatives.

time-structured rule
allowing amendments to a bill being discussed in the House of Representatives only within a certain time frame.

oversight
Congress's responsibility to keep an eye on agencies in the federal bureaucracy to ensure that their behavior conforms to its wishes.

INVESTIGATIONS Similar to the hearing process, both the House and the Senate often investigate dramatic issues or ongoing matters of great concern. Many times a special committee will be assembled to deal with a specific issue. A notorious example was the House Committee on Un-American Activities (usually called HUAC), first put together in 1938—amid great fanfare—to investigate alleged threats to national security and potential subversion, mostly by communists and (more often) by people falsely accused of being communists. Joseph McCarthy, the anticommunist Wisconsin demagogue, did much the same thing at the helm of a special Senate committee before the Senate finally censured him in 1954, effectively ending his career. At other times, preexisting committees are called on to investigate high-profile issues. For instance, the Senate Judiciary Committee regularly holds hearings on nominees to fill openings on the federal bench. In the fall and winter of 2005, the committee held a series of public hearings on George W. Bush's nominees to the Supreme Court, John Roberts and Samuel Alito. Supreme Court nomination hearings are always exciting and a bit contentious, but given that the death of Chief Justice William Rehnquist and the retirement of Justice Sandra Day O'Connor seemed about to change the ideological balance of the Court, the hearings in late 2005 were dramatic and closely watched.

THE IMPORTANCE OF COMMITTEE STAFF Finally, you cannot accurately understand the process and powers of congressional committees without sharply focusing on staff. Given the hectic schedules of members of Congress and the ever-growing complexity of policy alternatives, it should come as no surprise to learn that staffers do most of the committees' work. "Committee staff spend a lot of their time on policymaking activities," the political scientist David Vogler has noted. "They research issues and generate information relevant to administrative oversight; draft bills; prepare speeches, statements, and reports; organize and help run committee hearings; and sometimes engage directly in legislative bargaining."[20] Furthermore, the size of the committee staff—what some observers have termed the "unelected representatives"[21]—grew tremendously in the late twentieth century. In 1967, there were roughly 600 committee staffers at work on Capitol Hill, but by 1994, their number had jumped to more than 3,000.[22] As the Republicans took control in 1995, moves were made to reduce the overall number of staffers. But the concern remains: A good deal of policymaking is done by staff, without much involvement of the elected representatives.

Scene in the Caucus Room of the House Office Building as the House Un-American Activities Committee opened its investigation into alleged Communist activities in the movie industry. Jack L. Warner, VP of Warner Brothers, is the first witness on the stand. Do you recognize the congressman sitting second from the right? (Hint: he took up residence at 1600 Pennsylvania Avenue NW in Washington, D.C. two decades later.)

▶ **So the image we have** of Congress debating the great issues of the day is all wrong? All the real decisions are made in committees?

orientation function
the job of familiarizing a new member of Congress with the procedures, norms, and customs of the chamber.

agenda
list of issues that legislative leaders wish to address during a session of Congress.

voting cues
summaries encapsulating the informed judgment of others in the legislature on which members of Congress rely to streamline the decision-making process.

party unity
voting along party lines, often used as a measure of legislators' loyalty.

▶ **So the image we have of Congress debating the great issues of the day is all wrong? All the real decisions are made in committees?** Let's summarize. Much of the work of the legislature gets done in congressional committees. Ordinary citizens often believe that floor debates are dramatic events, where opinions are formed through lively discourse, point and counterpoint. Some people think that decisions about tough policy choices are made on the floor and that if you want to influence the policy process, you should focus on this final step. That's wrong. Although occasionally the outcome of a floor vote may be uncertain down to the last minute, the great majority of congressional decisions are made far earlier—usually at the committee level. It's here that information gets collected through hearings and investigations, that the actual writing of bills is done, that negotiations are carried on, and that members are persuaded to support or oppose a measure. Once again, understanding how committees work and grasping their importance is critical for anyone interested in shaping government outputs through an internal, mostly behind-the-scenes lobbying approach. For individuals and interest groups with a stake in the outcome, it is essential to get involved at those early stages. Committees are not only a hub of activity; they are also the principal decision-making structure of the legislative process.

POLITICAL PARTIES AND THE LEGISLATURE

As we will see in Chapter 15, for more than two centuries, political parties have been a fact of life in the United States Congress. But how do parties organize the legislative process? In several ways.

For one thing, parties in the legislature serve an **orientation function.** The job of legislating has always been difficult, but during the past few decades, it has become exceedingly complex. Being a good legislator requires a great deal of time and effort, and no prior experience can prepare anyone for a job as a member of Congress. Running for the national legislature is one thing; serving is quite another. Both parties conduct extensive orientation sessions for incoming members of Congress. These events often last several days and cover a range of topics. "Beyond the briefings on everything from setting up the office, ethics, legislative customs, and rules," note two scholars of the legislative process, "these orientations help break new representatives into the social fabric of the capital. Scores of receptions and dinners help newcomers feel welcome and at the same time socialize the new representative to the ways of the legislative world."[23] You might assume that orientations are a minor issue, something like your own freshman orientation when you first came to campus. But you can imagine how difficult things would be if thirty or forty new members each term were simply given the keys to their offices and told, "Get to work!"

Second, the congressional leaders of the parties set the **agenda** for the coming session and establish priorities. Each legislator comes to Washington with an agenda, a list of issues that he or she would like to address and in some way resolve. These issues originate with constituents, interest groups, and other elected officials, as well as reflect the convictions of the legislators themselves. Combined, this would make a long, dizzying array of topics. Parties allow rank-and-file members to express their concerns to the leadership, where they are prioritized into an agenda for the session. This process not only narrows the list but also focuses members' efforts on priority items. No longer, for example, are there 200 different members of the same party independently fighting for some type of prescription drug program but rather (or so the party leaders hope) 200 legislators working in a unified, synchronized effort toward a common goal.

Third, parties give their members an important time-saving tool when it comes to committee service and floor voting. Thousands of complex measures are introduced and considered each term. Expecting legislators to be fully informed on all, or even most, of these measures is simply impossible. Parties help legislators cut though the complex maze of initiatives by providing briefs and, more important, **voting cues.** Party leaders will often take positions on issues, thereby "suggesting" to other members of their party that they do the same. Members of Congress do not have to follow this cue from leadership, and occasionally they do not—but quite often they do. (This makes the position of American legislators quite different from that of members of Parliament in Great Britain, who ignore their party leadership only at great peril.) Legislators can make a rational decision by knowing little more than what position their party's leaders have taken on the matter. We might expect that each legislator would study every matter in great detail, but this is unrealistic. Today, party cue-taking helps make the legislative process more efficient than the chaos that might occur in a leaderless Congress—a Congress of the sort that the framers of the Constitution envisioned.

The degree of **party unity** that legislators show in their voting patterns can be measured statistically. In many parliamentary

committee appointment process
party leaders' assignment of party members to committees.

speaker
the presiding officer of the House of Representatives, who is also the leader of the majority party in the House.

majority leader
the head of the majority party in the Senate; the second-highest-ranking member of the majority party in the House.

systems, most votes are strictly along party lines. In these democracies, it is expected that a member of the party will vote with party leadership on all votes, or at the very least on all controversial matters. If a legislator cannot vote with his or her party at tough times, the person is told to leave the party. In the United States Congress, the tradition is that legislators expect and get more leeway when it comes to sticking with the party. Members generally vote with their party when it suits them, but if the party seems to be falling in public favor and members think that they are in for a tough race for reelection, they will follow self-interest and not toe the party line. Rarely would American party elites suggest, either privately or publicly, that a dissident member consider leaving the party. And only occasionally does a member switch parties voluntarily—although the last time this happened, in 2001, it had a major impact. On that occasion, liberal Republican Senator James Jeffords of Vermont declared himself an independent. His defection ended Republican control of the closely divided chamber and put the Democrats in charge. The tradition has been to tolerate independent-minded partisans and to try, over time, to bring them into the party fold. (For a more complete discussion of party unity, see (L)(I)(N)(K) *Chapter 15, pages 586–588*.)

Finally, parties organize the **committee appointment process.** We noted earlier that legislators try to sit on committees that cover topics of most importance to their constituents. This does not mean, however, that every committee assignment is equally desirable. Some committees, such as those dealing with the raising and distribution of money (Budget, Appropriations, Finance, and Ways and Means) are in more demand than others. There is an important pecking order. Party leaders handle the difficult and sometimes contentious chore of committee appointments—and being a "regular" who goes along with the leadership certainly helps a member get a choice assignment.

THE IMPORTANCE OF MAJORITY STATUS   Beyond these organizing functions, another issue to consider when thinking about the importance of parties in the legislative process is status. In each branch, there is a majority party and a minority party, determined by the number of legislators in each party. The majority party has many significant advantages. For one, as you've already seen, on all committees, the majority of members belong to the majority party. The majority party sets the ratio of party representation on each committee (which reflects the size of the majority it enjoys in that chamber), and it names the chair of each committee and subcom-

Jim Jeffords' decision to leave the Republican Party and become an independent meant that Democrats would take control of the Senate. This switch led to a great deal of anger against Jeffords. What makes majority party control so important?

mittee. And as we have discussed, the majority also manages the critically important Rules Committee in the House, thus controlling the flow of legislation to the floor.

Given the importance of this stage of the process, this advantage alone underscores how crucial it is whether a party is in the majority or the minority. The majority party selects the leaders in each chamber. The House elects a **speaker,** who has a number of advantages, including, as noted, the power of referral. These votes to "organize" the House, which are conducted as soon as each session of Congress convenes, are always along party lines, inevitably leading to the victory of someone from the majority party. Similarly, the Senate chooses a **majority leader,** who has many of the same advantages. (Not quite as many, for Senate tradition dictates that individual members have more leeway to do what they please than House members have.) Finally, given the advantages of majority status, external players—interest groups and the media, for example—are much more interested in their interactions with the majority party's members.

Thus you can appreciate what a virtual earthquake Senator Jeffords caused in 2001 with his "treason" (in Republican eyes) of leaving GOP ranks and voting, as an independent, with the Democrats to "organize" the Senate. Now backed by a one-vote margin, South Dakota Senator Tom Daschle suddenly went from

whips
assistants to House and Senate leaders, responsible for drumming up support for legislation and for keeping count of how members plan to vote on different pieces of legislation.

being Senate minority leader to being Senate majority leader; every committee immediately switched from a Republican to a Democratic chair; and new committee assignments were made to ensure that Democrats were in the majority on every one. This remained the way the Senate was organized until January 2003, when Republicans regained leadership of the Senate after the voters had given them back a majority of senatorial seats.

LEGISLATIVE PARTIES AND CHANGE Obviously, then, when you consider the possible ways of bringing about change using the congressional pathway, another factor to remember is the far-reaching role of political parties in Congress. Political parties are very much alive and well in Congress. Other things being equal, an activist would surely find it more profitable to lobby and work with members of the majority party than with minority-party legislators. In fact, most seasoned political activists consider it so important whether a party with which they are dealing is the majority or minority party that the first step of their lobbying strategy is to focus on elections. If, as an activist, your concerns match one of the party's platforms or philosophy better than the other, then helping that party either win or retain control of the legislature is critical to everything you want to accomplish. Hence the enormous amounts of money and member effort that organizations such as the National Rifle Association (NRA), the National Organization for Women (NOW), the NAACP, the labor unions, and the Christian Coalition give to the benefit of one party or the other.

LEGISLATIVE LEADERSHIP

As noted, the constitutional framers believed that giving one legislator or a group of legislators more power in the system would upset what should be an enlightened, deliberative process. The Constitution states that each chamber will have "leaders": in the House, a speaker (the title *speaker* was used in the British House of Commons and in the colonial assemblies), and in the Senate, a president. But these posts were, in the framers' minds, meant to aid organization; each was to be a mere parliamentarian who structured debate, made sure that rules of order were followed, guaranteed equal access, and so forth. Leaders were to be impartial. This is precisely what occurred for the first few decades; legislative leaders simply helped create an orderly process. It was rare, in fact, for leaders of either chamber to even cast a vote.

All that changed in the 1820s. First, the election of 1824, leading to the so-called corrupt bargain, reinvigorated party spirit in the United States, and partisanship soon intensified in both houses of Congress. Any advantage was thought important, and many politicians realized that leadership posts might provide an edge. Second, Henry Clay of Kentucky had been elected speaker in 1823. An affable, whiskey-drinking, card-playing master of politicking in the Washington boarding houses where members lived during sessions of Congress, Clay was also aggressive, outspoken, ambitious, and highly partisan. And he was not about to use his position merely to aid debate. As speaker, he cast votes on nearly every measure, began the practice of referral, and used his office to fill the majority of committee posts with his supporters. Speaker of the House Clay in fact contributed enormously to building what eventually became the Whig Party. The role of speaker as moderator faded into the history books.[24] In the Senate, the move to aggressive leadership was a bit slower, given the smaller size of the chamber and most senators' insistence on their greater political independence, but within two decades, it too developed aggressive, partisan leadership. (Clay eventually moved from the House to the Senate, and there too he was always one of the top Whig leaders.)

The Constitution does not mandate that the speaker actually be a member of the House, but in fact he always has been. At the beginning of each legislative term—that is, at each two-year interval—every member of the House casts a vote for a speaker. Since the 1820s, the winner of these internal elections has always been a member of the majority party. It has become customary for the members of each party to decide on their choice for speaker in advance and to expect every member to vote for that person. Because deviations from this party line vote never occur, the majority party's candidate always prevails.

Rather than having one leader, a hierarchy of leadership now exists for both parties in both chambers. In the House, the most powerful person after the speaker is the majority leader, followed by the majority **whips.** In brief, majority leaders work with the speaker to coordinate strategy and to advance the party's policy goals. Whips are responsible for garnering support for the party's agenda and for making sure that the party leadership has an accurate count of the votes for and against different pieces of legislation. If members of the party are inclined to vote against a measure deemed important to the leadership, it is the whips' job to help those legislators think otherwise—that is, to "whip" them into

president pro tempore
the chief presiding officer of the Senate in the absence of the vice president.

minority leader
the leading spokesperson and legislative strategist for the minority party in either the House or the Senate.

what YOU can do!

Take a look at the biographies of the leaders of both parties in both chambers of Congress. Are there any surprises, or are these the types of people you would expect to find? The Congressional Institute maintains a good Web site for this kind of information: **http://www.conginst.org/ congressleaders/senate-dem.html**

Nancy Pelosi hands Rep. Dennis Hastert the gavel after his election to Speaker of the 108th Congress, on Jan. 7, 2003. Pelosi (D-CA), won applause from Republicans and Democrats alike when she told them she was the first woman to have her name placed in nomination for speaker. It was a ritual election that she lost in the GOP-controlled House to Hastert, from Illinois, who was sworn in as speaker for a third term. By 2007, after the Democrats won back control of the House, Peolsi would again make history by becoming the first woman speaker. Stephen Crowley/The New York Times

line. All members become part of the leadership team, working to help the speaker and to promote the party's agenda. The whips have the added responsibility of passing information along to other members and of working to ensure that members of their party show up for important floor votes and stick to the party line when thought important. This person's principal responsibility is to help the leadership team develop a legislative agenda.

The Constitution stipulates that the vice president of the United States shall be president of the Senate. Under the Constitution, however, the vice president can vote only to break a tie. The first vice president, John Adams, came into office expecting that he would also be able to take a leading role in Senate deliberations, even if he did not vote—and he was bitterly disappointed and offended when the senators told him that all he could do was preside, in silence. "The most insignificant office that the mind of man ever devised" was Adams's sour verdict on the vice presidency.

When the vice president is not present—which is usually the case except on solemn occasions or when a tie vote is expected—the Senate is formally led by its elected **president pro tempore** (*pro tempore* is a Latin phrase meaning "for the time being" and is usually abbreviated to *pro tem*). Through tradition, this position has become purely ceremonial and is always bestowed on the most senior member of the majority party. The real job of moderating

debate in the Senate usually falls to a junior member of the majority party, chosen for that assignment on a rotating basis. The job confers little real power. Much more power in the Senate rests with the majority leader. In some ways similar to the speaker in the House, the majority leader of the Senate is elected and is the head of his or her party. Correspondingly, the Senate **minority leader** is the top dog of the minority party. Each has an assistant leader and network of whips, charged with much the same responsibilities as those in the House. There are also conference chairs for both parties in the Senate. Recall that Figure 7.4, on page 264, shows the various leadership positions in both chambers.

pathways profile

CONGRESSWOMAN NANCY PELOSI MAKES HISTORY

Few people would be surprised to hear that the number of women who have served in Congress has been small. But it may be dismaying for some to hear that no woman ever led a party in either branch of Congress until the fall of 2002. Nancy Pelosi, a Democrat from San Francisco, waited until her children were grown to begin her political career—though she comes from a

▶ **Why is the Speaker** of the House considered the most powerful person in Congress?

unanimous consent
agreement of all senators on the terms of debate, required before a bill goes to the floor.

political family: Both her grandfather and her father, who had the same name, Thomas D'Alessandro, had been mayors of Baltimore, Maryland. She was first elected to the House of Representatives in 1986 and has been reelected easily ever since. Known as a smart, aggressive, congenial legislator, Pelosi quickly gained the respect of colleagues in both parties. She also worked hard to raise funds for Democratic congressional and presidential candidates. So when the sitting House minority leader stepped down in the summer of 2002, it seemed only natural that her caucus would turn to Pelosi. She was overwhelmingly elected, in November 2006 becoming the first woman speaker of the House of Representatives. A seasoned observer of Washington politics suggests that Pelosi "is one of the most savvy political figures around,"[25] and one of the leading national magazines writes, "Prodded by their relentless new leader, Nancy Pelosi, House Democrats say that they have a newfound energy in confronting President Bush and the Republicans."[26] ■

▶ **Why is the Speaker of the House considered the most powerful person in Congress?** What makes legislative leaders so powerful? The answer is a mix of formal and informal powers. Let's begin with the formal powers: Speakers of the House refer legislation to committee, preside over floor proceedings, appoint members to conference and other joint committees, and set the rules of how legislation will be debated and how long such debates might last. They establish the floor agenda, meaning that they decide which bills will be scheduled for consideration on the floor and which will not. These are weighty formal advantages, but they are just the beginning. The speaker can also use the force of personality and prestige to persuade other members of the legislature to go along with his or her wishes. Great speakers have been able to merge their formal and informal powers. The ability of the speaker to attract national press attention has become another powerful tool. Few speakers were more adept at seizing national press coverage, and thus enhancing their power base, than Georgia Republican Newt Gingrich in his first term (1995–1997).

But great as the powers of the speaker may be, they are not absolute. On a number of occasions, a speaker has seemed to go too far and was humbled by his fellow legislators. Joseph Cannon, for example, presided over the House with an iron fist in the early part of the twentieth century. Members of his own party, as well as in the opposition party, revolted against "Uncle Joe" in 1910. He was stripped of his post, and a number of changes, many dealing with the control of the Rules Committee, reduced the powers that all subsequent speakers wield. Although Gingrich was clearly a powerful speaker at first, many members of his own party soon thought him too heavy-handed. He also lost favor with the public because of his confrontational ways and his advocacy of heavy cuts in popular government programs. When challenged for the post after the 1998 midterm election, in which the Republicans lost seats, Gingrich resigned from the House.

In the Senate, the majority leader's powers are broad but clearly not as extensive as the speaker's. Majority leaders have great influence on committee assignments, on the schedule of floor debate, on the selection of conference committee members, and in picking their own conference's leaders. Yet majority leaders have less sway in the Senate, for several reasons: first, because of that institution's somewhat different internal rules; second, because of the long-standing notion that the Senate is the "upper chamber," filled with more experienced and higher-status politicians; and third, because Senate norms dictate a more egalitarian process. Writing about some of these differences, congressional scholar Steven S. Smith suggests:

> Senate rules protect individuals' and the minority right to participate far more than do House rules. The rights to filibuster and to offer non-germane amendments on the Senate floor give senators leverage with committees and party leaders that representatives in the House do not have. . . . Agenda setting in the Senate is a process of negotiation, compromise, and mediation, to a degree that would seem exotic in the House.[27]

LEGISLATIVE RULES AND NORMS

The final organizing elements in any legislative body are its formal and informal rules of behavior. Let's begin with the formal regulations. The Constitution states that each house establishes its own rules. Not surprisingly, given the different sizes of the two chambers, the House has a longer set of rules than the Senate. It is difficult to list all the regulations that structure proceedings in the House, but a few of the most significant deal with how measures proceed from committee to floor consideration and with the actions that might be taken to modify that measure once it reaches the floor. Scheduling refers to floor (full-house) consideration of committee-approved measures. All bills approved at the committee level must be scheduled for consideration on the floor. This might seem a straightforward matter, but many issues come into play with this process, including when—if ever—the bill will be considered (see Table 7.4). If a measure is able to find itself on a floor calendar, rules regarding amendments become important, as noted earlier.

▶ **Can a senator really** defeat legislation by talking a bill to death?

cloture
rule declaring the end of a debate in the Senate.

hold
rule that allows a senator to announce the intention to use delaying tactics if a particular piece of legislation moves to a vote.

TABLE 7.4
Creative Congressional Rules

Queen of the Hill rule	A special rule providing that for any proposal, a number of substitute amendments can be put forward. The original proposal is then made to compete against the substitutes. The legislation receiving the most votes is adopted.
Self-executing rule	A sometimes controversial rule dictating that when the House adopts one rule, it simultaneously agrees to pass another measure. The policy implemented by this "two for one" vote varies.
Restrictive rule	A special rule limiting members' ability to put forth amendments to proposed measures. This rule tends to be unpopular among minority party and rank-and-file members.
Multiple-step rule	A rule with numerous variations designed to maintain order throughout the amendment process by granting the Rules Committee the right to continuously regulate debate on a measure.
Anticipatory rule	A rule allowing the Rules Committee to approve a rule before the issue to which it would apply has been reported. Formerly called "buying a pig in a poke," this measure is designed to speed up the decision-making process.

Reprinted by permission from Roger H. Davidson and Walter J. Oleszek, "Congress and Its Members" Congressional Quarterly, 10th ed., Washington, DC p. 252 www.cqpress.com

---

▶ **Can a senator really defeat legislation by talking a bill to death?** The Senate is somewhat less bound by formal rules than the House, but this does not mean that anything goes. Three formal rules stand out as most significant. First, quite often leaders of both parties in the Senate will informally negotiate the terms for debate and amendment of a bill scheduled to be sent to the floor. This is called **unanimous consent** because all senators must be in agreement. The idea is to try to establish some limits and control in order to expedite floor actions and to impose some predictability. To block legislation or confirmation votes, Senate minorities may resort to use of the filibuster, or unlimited debate—one senator or a group of senators keeps talking without interruption unless three-fifths of the chamber (sixty senators) votes to end the discussion.

Conservative southern Democrats were particularly known for filibustering civil rights bills. The longest filibustering speech in American history occurred in 1957, when Senator Strom Thurmond of South Carolina (a Democrat who later became a Republican) held the floor for more than twenty-four hours in an effort to block a vote on what became the Civil Rights Act of 1957. More recently, Republicans have used filibusters in an attempt to derail campaign finance legislation, and Democrats have threatened to use them to block the appointment of several of George W. Bush's judicial nominations.

To some observers, use of the filibuster is a clear violation of majority rule. However, where you stand on the strategic use of the filibuster is most likely a function of the issue under consideration. Recently, liberal Democrats argued that it was a fair and common procedural move to block "extreme" conservatives from joining the courts, but in the past, as when it was used to block civil rights legislation, they argued that filibusters thwarted the majority will.

Without a unanimous-consent agreement, extended debates can become a problem. A filibuster can be used, but another delay variant is to switch control of floor discussion from one member to another, thereby postponing a vote. The goal is to tie things up until the other side backs down or decides to compromise. The tool used to cut off these debates is called **cloture.** Here, three-fifths of the senators must vote to end the discussion of a bill—that is, "to invoke cloture." This rule can be used for general floor debate or to end a filibuster. Still another variation, often used these days, is called a **hold:** A senator signals to the rest of the chamber that it would be pointless to bring a piece of legislation to the floor because he or she intends to use delaying tactics to stave off a final vote. A hold can be trumped, of course, with sixty votes for cloture.

Frustrated by what they perceived to be unreasonable delay tactics by the Democrats in the Senate, particularly in regard to the confirmation of court nominees, Republicans responded by threatening the "nuclear option" in 2005. The plan was for the Senate president to rule that the United States Constitution

▶ Are there unwritten rules
in the Senate? What are they?

seniority
length of time served in a chamber of the legislature. Members with greater seniority have traditionally been granted greater power.

specialization
extensive knowledge in a particular policy area.

prohibits filibusters against judicial nominations, and then a vote would then be held on an appeal. When this happens, only fifty-one votes are needed to uphold the ruling. Thus the Republicans would end the practice. Thus far, the Republicans have only threatened this change, but Democrats have taken notice. (Of course, some Republican senators worried that if they ended the right to filibuster, the tactic would be denied to them next time they were in the minority—which happened two years later.)

▶ **Are there unwritten rules in the Senate? What are they?** You might think that informal rules or legislative norms and customs are less significant than the formal regulations. In fact, informal rules likely do *more* to structure the day-to-day legislative process than any other organizing mechanism. More than forty years, ago a distinguished political scientist, Don Matthews, noted the power and importance of "folkways" in the legislature.[28] Much of what Matthews suggested still applies today.

Seniority stipulates that the longer a member of either chamber has served, the greater deference and the more power he or she should have. Such senior members usually deserve respect because of their long service and accumulated wisdom, but Senate traditions normally also grant them more power in the chamber. It is no longer a hard-and-fast rule that the longest-serving member of a committee becomes its chair (or, if in the minority party, its ranking minority member), but it still does occur. Senior members are often given a greater share of their appropriation requests than a novice, and they are more likely to have their bills at least considered by a committee. In recent years, junior members perceived to be vulnerable to an election defeat are helped by the party leadership, but generally speaking, seniority still matters.

Along with seniority, there is a powerful apprenticeship norm. In the past, green (novice) legislators were expected to work hard, get along, be deferential and polite, keep their mouths shut most of the time, and study the legislative process. They were to be "workhorses" instead of "show horses." This was true even when House members moved to the Senate; junior senators were expected to be seen and not heard. In recent years, this norm, like that of seniority, has been observed less and less. In fact, in some instances, party leaders have advised first-term senators to speak up and make a name for themselves. But the norm is not gone completely. Hillary Rodham Clinton, for example, who came to the Senate after being first lady, was careful to observe this tradition.

Civility is another powerful norm in both chambers. Regardless of party, ideology, or position on issues, it is expected that members accord each other respect and a high, even exaggerated level of courtesy. Even when tempers rise, politeness is to remain. "Political disagreements should not influence personal feelings,"[29] suggests Matthews. By tradition, a senator or a representative refers even to his or her bitter political rivals and personal enemies as "the distinguished gentleman [or lady] from . . ." whatever the state might be. When members publicly lapse from this norm of civility, they are expected to apologize, which very often they do. It was not always so. Before the Civil War, members of Congress, including Henry Clay, sometimes fought duels with each other (always in some secluded spot!). Perhaps the worst breakdown of civility in the halls of Congress occurred in 1856, when Massachusetts Senator Charles Sumner was nearly beaten to death with a cane by a congressman.

Although violence rarely erupts these days, the civility norm also seems to be on the decline. In 2004, for instance, Vice President Dick Cheney, who as president of the Senate was in the chamber for "picture day," turned to Vermont Democratic Senator Patrick Leahy and admonished him over the senator's criticism of the vice president. In response to Cheney, Leahy reminded Cheney that the vice president had once accused him of being a bad Catholic, to which Cheney replied with a vulgarity. "I think he was just having a bad day," said Leahy, "and I was kind of shocked to hear that kind of language on the floor."

pathways past and present

THE CANING OF SENATOR CHARLES SUMNER

One of the most violent episodes in the history of the U.S. Congress took place on May 22, 1856. The Senate was not in session when South Carolina Representative Preston S. Brooks entered the chamber to avenge the insults that Senator Charles Sumner of Massachusetts had leveled at his elderly cousin, Senator Andrew P. Butler. Sumner's "Crime against Kansas" speech of May 19–20 was vehemently critical, descending to personal insults, of Butler and several other senators who had supported the "popular sovereignty" provisions of the 1854 Kansas-Nebraska Act. Sumner was working at his desk when Brooks began his attack, striking the senator repeatedly with a walking

reciprocity/logrolling
supporting a lesislator's bill in exchange
for support of one's own bill.

earmarks (pork-barrell legislation)
legislation that benefits one state or district, also called *particularized* legislation.

cane, which splintered with the force of the blows. Although two friendly House members eventually intervened to end the assault (while some Democratic senators stood by approvingly), Sumner, who had ripped his desk loose from the bolts holding it to the floor in his effort to escape, was knocked unconscious. He regained consciousness shortly after the attack, but it would be three years before he felt able to resume his senatorial duties. Brooks meanwhile was applauded everywhere he went in the South, and admirers repeatedly presented him with gold-headed replacement canes.

The caning of Senator Sumner was part of the collapse of all attempts at compromise and sectional accommodation in the Senate, and indeed throughout the United States, foreshadowing the violence that would erupt in the Civil War after eleven southern states seceded from the Union during the winter and spring of 1860–1861.

Source: U.S. Senate, http://www.senate.gov/vtour/sumner.htm.

Specialization is a norm that suggests that members of both chambers are expected to become well versed in a small number of policy areas. Specialization allows members to defer to their colleagues on some policy matters rather than try to bone up on every issue that might come before the legislature. In this there is an expectation of **reciprocity.** That is, members are expected to support each other's initiatives on a "you scratch my back and I'll scratch yours" basis. Wrote Don Matthews, "Every senator, at one time or another, is in the position to help out a colleague. The folkways of the Senate hold that a senator should provide this assistance and that he [or she] be repaid in kind."[30] This is often called **logrolling,** which means that members reciprocally exchange support, often on **earmarks,** or what is sometimes termed **pork-barrel legislation.** *Pork* is slang for particularized assistance: federal money and programs that largely or wholly benefit just one state or congressional district. Every member wants to "bring home the bacon" to his or her district, and their constituents expect it; and one way to get it is through logrolling (see Figure 7.5). For instance, a House member from Tennessee might agree to support a New York City member's appropriation to build a commuter rail station in her district for support for a new stretch of interstate through his part of Tennessee.

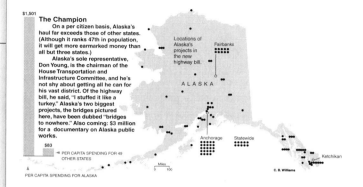

Fresh Pork, Coming to a District Near You

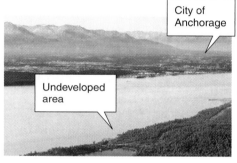

$231 MILLION
Site of Knik Arm Bridge, which has been named "Don Young's Way" after Alaska's sole representative.

City of Anchorage

Undeveloped area

$223 MILLION
Rendering of Gravina Island Bridge.

Gravina Island, population 50

Ketchikan, population 8,002

Knik Arm Bridge below and Toll Authority (above);

July 2005, The New York Times

FIGURE 7.5

Fresh Pork, Coming to a District Near You

In the summer of 2006, the House and Senate approved the transportation bill, and government watchdogs tried to figure out exactly what was in it. About 8 percent of the $286.4 billion bill is set aside for more than 6,000 special projects inserted by lawmakers. Many of them were added by senators to an already bulging House version of the bill that passed in March of that year. Are earmarks a corruption of the legislative process, or are they simply ways to bring needed federal dollars to certain districts?

▶ **Can anyone introduce a bill in Congress?**

bill sponsor
the member of Congress who introduces a bill.

pathways of action

BRIDGES TO NOWHERE?

Some of the highest-profile and most controversial earmarks in recent years have been for the state of Alaska. In 2005, the federal budget included funding for two massive bridges. One, longer than the Golden Gate Bridge and higher than the Brooklyn Bridge, would connect Gravina Island (population 50) with Ketchikan (population 8,000). The price tag for its construction is $223 million. The second, also a massive structure, would stretch from Anchorage, the state's largest city, to a rural port that has one tenant and a handful of homes. Its price tag is upward of $200 million. The budget included several other massive federally funded construction projects. According to Taxpayers for Common Sense, a nonpartisan watchdog group in Washington, it broke down to $1,150 for every Alaskan, twenty-five times what the average American gets for his or her home state. This occurred at a time when most Americans, as well as members of Congress from both parties, had grown increasingly worried about the federal budget deficit. And it also took place at the same time residents of the Gulf Coast were struggling to rebuild after Hurricane Katrina.

So why would federal funds flow to Alaska and not, say, to Louisiana or Mississippi? Why the exceptional treatment for the forty-ninth state? The explanation lies in the clout of the Alaskan congressional delegation. At the time, Alaska's Republican Senator Ted Stevens was the powerful chair of the Appropriations Committee, the committee in charge of overseeing federal spending. And the state's lone member of the House is Republican Don Young, formerly chair of the House Transportation Committee, the committee that oversees all federally funded construction projects across the nation. When Democrats and Republicans in both chambers voiced their opposition to the Alaskan earmarks, Stevens and Young let it be known that they would not take kindly to serious challenges. Few members of Congress wanted to get on the wrong side of these powerful chairs, and so the measures were passed by Congress and signed into law by President Bush.

But there has been grumbling from outside the walls of Congress. The national media gave the whole transaction very negative publicity. The conservative Heritage Foundation circulated a paper saying the bridges are a "national embarrassment." Even an Alaskan wrote to his local paper that "Alaskans owe an apology to the people of New Orleans, to Alaskan Native People and to the Nation for their selfish shortsightedness."

SOURCES: Rebecca Clarren, "A Bridge to Nowhere," Salon.com, http://www.salon.com/news/feature/2005/08/09/bridges/index_np.html, August 9, 2005;

Heritage Foundation, "The Bridge to Nowhere: A National Embarrassment," http://www.heritage.org/Research/Budget/wm889.cfm, October 20, 2005; USA Today Online, "Alaska Thanks You," http://www.usatoday.com/news/opinion/editorials/2005-05-17-alaska-edit_x.htm, May 17, 2005. ■

So what might we conclude about the many mechanisms used to organize our national legislature? Many critics suggest that efforts to bring more efficiency into the legislative process have come at the expense of democracy. Not every member of the legislature is allowed the same input. Committee and subcommittee chairs preside over their policy domains, and little happens or is approved in their committees without their approval. Majority party members clearly have a leg up over minority party legislators, and of course, leaders on both sides of the aisle carry more weight than rank-and-file members. Finally, there are a great many rules that stack the deck against certain members.

As a budding political activist, you must understand the importance of these organizing elements. Just as legislators must be strategic in negotiating the legislative maze, so too must citizen travelers carefully wend their way down any pathway that leads to trying to persuade legislators to act.

practicequiz

1. The structure of Congress's standing committees is spelled out in Article I of the Constitution.
   a. true   **b.** false

2. Most of the work of lawmaking and oversight in Congress happens
   a. on the House floor.
   b. at the committee level.
   c. at the subcommittee level.
   d. in congressional staff meetings.

3. When the vice president is not present, the Senate is presided over by
   a. the senate majority leader.
   b. the majority whip.
   c. the president pro tempore.
   d. the speaker of the House.

4. A senator who for strategic reasons would like to halt discussion of a bill on the Senate floor can
   a. move that the Senate vote to "invoke cloture."
   b. organize a filibuster.
   c. "call the question" and have the Senate vote on returning the bill to committee.
   d. introduce another bill that has "preemptive status" over the first bill.

Answers: 1-b, 2-c, 3-c, 4-a.

discussionquestions

1. In the U.S. Congress, which of the organizing elements is most important, and why?

2. Efficiency generally comes at a cost. What might be the downsides of an efficient legislative process, particularly in Congress?

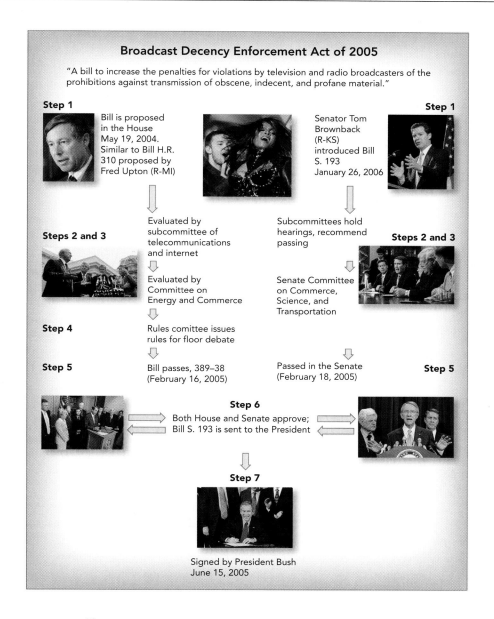

Broadcast Decency Enforcement Act of 2005

"A bill to increase the penalties for violations by television and radio broadcasters of the prohibitions against transmission of obscene, indecent, and profane material."

Step 1
Bill is proposed in the House May 19, 2004. Similar to Bill H.R. 310 proposed by Fred Upton (R-MI)

Step 1
Senator Tom Brownback (R-KS) introduced Bill S. 193 January 26, 2006

Evaluated by subcommittee of telecommunications and internet

Subcommittees hold hearings, recommend passing

Steps 2 and 3

Evaluated by Committee on Energy and Commerce

Senate Committee on Commerce, Science, and Transportation

Steps 2 and 3

Step 4
Rules comittee issues rules for floor debate

Step 5
Bill passes, 389–38 (February 16, 2005)

Passed in the Senate (February 18, 2005)

Step 5

Step 6
Both House and Senate approve; Bill S. 193 is sent to the President

Step 7
Signed by President Bush June 15, 2005

FIGURE 7.6

How a Bill Becomes a Law

The scheme to make each branch of government somewhat dependent on the others to perform their duties, and to be in certain ways checked by the other branches is well exemplified in "how a bill becomes a law." Goodness, what a complex process! Some would say that the numerous steps and hurdles weed out unnecessary measures, but others argue that the system is too cumbersome and that it makes change too difficult. And when we add political parties to the mix, something that the framers did not envision, the process can become even more intricate. What's your take on this important issue: Does this complex process serve the nation well, or does it inhibit needed change?

How a Bill Becomes Law

Once you begin to think about the many ways potential chaos gets channeled into constructive deliberation in Congress, you can begin to understand some of the many hurdles that bills must cross in order to become law. Here, we'll walk through this process in greater detail. Please keep in mind that this outline is a theoretical model and that in practice things are rarely this neat. Also, the process is similar in both chambers, but not exactly the same. What follows is a general pattern (see Figure 7.6).

▶ **Can anyone introduce a bill in Congress?**

Step 1. Introduction of a Bill. The idea (and frequently the language) of a bill can originate from many sources. Often an administrative agency will draw up a bill. Interest groups often have a hand, both in the broad outlines of a measure and in its exact wording. Yet to begin the actual process of legislating, a member of Congress must always introduce a bill in one chamber of that body. This person becomes the **bill sponsor,** the official "parent" of

one-house bill
a bill that is passed in only one house of Congress.

the legislation. With the exception of tax bills, which under the Constitution can only be introduced in the House of Representatives, any member of the national legislature can introduce any measure he or she sees fit.

Step 2. Referral. Soon after a bill is introduced, it is referred to a committee, and from there it is usually sent to the appropriate subcommittee.

Step 3. Committee Consideration. Most measures go no further than the subcommittee level. As we've seen, hearings are held, the language is sometimes modified (in the markup process), and if a bill is approved at this level, it is reported to the full committee. Additional changes are sometimes made at the full-committee level, but often the committee will simply accept or reject the measure offered by the subcommittee. On most occasions, the committee will then move the bill forward; after all, the same party always controls both the full committees and all the subcommittees.

Step 4. Rules for Floor Action. Any bill approved by a full committee is sent to the floor for full-chamber consideration. In the House of Representatives, however, a required stop is the Rules Committee. As already noted, here many procedural issues are set, such as the length of time the bill will be debated and the types of amendments, if any, that can be accepted. Once again, the majority party controls the Rules Committee. There is no similar procedure in the Senate.

Step 5. Floor Consideration. This is where every member of the chamber has an opportunity to express his or her support (or lack of support) for the bill. Most measures do not entail lengthy floor debate. Indeed, robust, meaningful floor debate is rare even in the Senate, where rules allow each member more opportunity to speak up. The reason for this is that most measures are low-profile, highly technical matters (such as adjustments to complex statutes) that draw little public interest. When the public becomes involved, however, floor debate can be intense. But few legislators are persuaded by floor debate; the fireworks are geared more to the constituents back home or to the national media than to persuading fellow legislators. By this time, just about every legislator's own mind will have been made up (whether or not the person says so in public).

Step 6. Conference Committee. For a bill to become a law, an identical version must be approved in both houses. Quite a few measures passed in one house will not have a counterpart in the other house. These are called **one-house bills.** If the other chamber has also passed an identical version of the bill, it is moved along to the president for signature—or to face a veto (see step 7). Many times a similar (but not identical) bill is passed in the other chamber. To reconcile differences, a conference committee, created for that measure, sets to work. Three outcomes from conference deliberations are possible. First, one of the versions of the bills might be accepted as the final agreement. When this occurs, the chamber accepting changes has to vote on the measure again (for, as we have seen, each chamber must approve exactly the same wording). Second, some sort of compromise or middle-of-the-road position might be crafted, making it necessary for both houses to vote again on the compromise version. Finally, compromise might not be possible (this often happens when Congress is about to adjourn), and each measure remains a failed one-house bill.

Step 7. Presidential Action. Modern presidents and their staffs are involved in the goings-on in Congress and work closely with legislators. When the president is of the same party as the majority in both houses, it is rare that important measures are approved without the president's blessing. (If they are, it is a sure sign that the president is in deep political trouble.) Even when there is a divided government, most bills approved by Congress do wind up winning presidential support. A bill becomes a law when the president signs it. If ten days pass without the president having signed the bill—a rare occurrence that generally indicates that the president does not like the bill but chooses not to cause an uproar by vetoing it—the bill becomes law. Or the president can veto the bill, sending it back to the Congress. As we'll discuss in LINK *Chapter 8 page 320,* vetoes have recently become quite rare, especially compared to the number of measures that win presidential approval. Given a president's grave concern about having his veto overridden, when the president does reject an important bill, it certainly makes news.

discussionquestions

1. There are many hurdles for any piece of legislation on its way through Congress. Which do you suspect is the most difficult?

2. If you wanted to stop a piece of legislation, where would you focus your efforts, and why?

what YOU can do!

To truly understand the complexity of the lawmaking process—the myriad twists and turns, special procedures, and factors that decide a bill's fate—check out Barbara Sinclair's book *Unorthodox Lawmaking*. Most libraries will have a copy, and you can also buy one online.

Step 8. Overriding a Presidential Veto. Presidential vetoes are always accompanied by a written message—a statement to Congress that says why the measure was rejected. The measure can still become a law if two-thirds of each house of Congress votes to override the veto. This rarely occurs, for two reasons: First, if at least two-thirds of both houses of Congress approve of the bill, it is very likely that the president would also be behind it—unless it is a period of sharply divided government in which the White House and the party that dominates Congress are bitterly at odds. (Modern instances have included much of President Harry S Truman's two terms, from 1945 to 1953, and the mid-1970s presidency of Gerald Ford, who took over after Richard Nixon was forced to resign in disgrace.) Second, presidents are usually unwilling to have their prestige damaged by seeing their veto overridden.

MAKING LAWS: A SUMMARY

The number varies somewhat from year to year, but roughly speaking, in the two years that any Congress sits, more than 10,000 measures are introduced. Of these, roughly 400 become law.[31] Most of these are low-profile, technical adjustments to existing laws; only a handful of truly significant measures gets passed each session. The road from introduction to presidential signature is long and difficult—deliberately so. Some measures are introduced in the full realization that they will not make the full journey. This is done for many reasons, including attempts to satisfy special-interest groups or to draw attention to an issue for future political exploitation. But even proposals that seem popular in the legislature and are supported by most Americans can get bogged down. On the one hand, we might suggest that the difficulty of the process implies a shortcoming in the legislative process: The will of the people should be more easily and more quickly expressed through the national legislature. But on the other hand, many people would agree that the process *should* be difficult, that there *should* be many potholes, roadblocks, and detours along the pathway. They would argue that the federal government must act cautiously when deciding the laws citizens must obey. That, after all, was the intent of the framers of our Constitution.

practicequiz

1. One likely sequence for a bill that becomes law could include the following steps:
   a. It is drafted by a congressional staffer and an interest group, introduced by a member of Congress, signed by the president, polished in the appropriate subcommittee, and approved by a vote on the House floor.
   b. It is drafted by a congressional staffer with input from an interest group, introduced on the House floor by a sponsoring representative, referred to a standing committee, sent to the appropriate subcommittee where hearings about the measure are held and the markup is done, and sent back to the full committee and is approved; rules for its discussion on the House floor are set by the Rules Committee; it passes by a majority vote in the House; meanwhile, a nearly identical bill follows a nearly identical path in the Senate; a conference committee realizes there are no real differences between the two bills; and the president signs it into law.
   c. It is drafted in a Senate committee, discussed on the Senate floor, and passed by a majority vote; it is then referred to the House, where it goes into another committee and then to the appropriate subcommittee within that committee; hearings are held, and language is agreed on; it is sponsored on the House floor, passed by a majority vote there, and then goes into a conference committee, where differences between the House and Senate versions of the bill are ironed out; then the president signs it into law.
   d. It is drafted by a group of staffers in the president's office; a conference committee consisting of powerful senators and members of Congress deliberates over the bill, drafting compromise language; it is then approved in subcommittees in both chambers; next the bill is voted for constitutionality by clerks for the Supreme Court and, if necessary, by the justices themselves; it is then signed into law by the president.

2. Floor debate in the Senate and House rarely influences legislators' votes; it is usually performed for the benefit of voters at home.
   a. true   b. false

3. What is one procedural difference between the Senate and the House?
   a. The Senate needs a quorum (an established minimum number of senators present) to conduct the day's business, but the House does not.
   b. Discussion on the floor of the House allows for spontaneous interruption from other representatives, whereas Senate discussion does not.

▶ Is Congress still mostly rich, white, and male?

c. Discussion on a bill in the House is governed by rules created by a Rules Committee, whereas Senate discussion is not.

d. Discussion on a bill in the Senate is governed by parliamentary procedure, whereas House discussion is not.

4. What is one reason bills are introduced in Congress even though the sponsor knows they stand little chance of success?

a. because Article I of the Constitution obliges every member of Congress to sponsor at least one bill every six years

b. because most members of Congress have hired and are paying staffers for the primary purpose of drafting legislation

c. because representatives are then able to say, during a reelection campaign at home, that they are working hard to accomplish whatever the proposed bill suggests

d. because sponsoring such legislation takes a lot less work than sponsoring successful bills, yet it makes the representative look equally hardworking

Answers: 1-b, 2-a, 3-c, 4-c.

Who Sits in Congress?

As we have emphasized in discussing representative democracy, representation means that someone speaks and works on behalf of others. Perhaps this process can be enhanced when the representative understands the issues and concerns that confront a district, and perhaps this is more likely to happen when he or she reflects the demographic makeup of the constituency of the district. Many people feel that at the very least, a legislative body should look like the nation as a whole. Race, ethnicity, gender, sexual orientation, occupation, age, and other demographics all matter, according to this viewpoint. This preference for *symbolic* or *descriptive representation* is the logic behind the drive, discussed earlier in this chapter, to create majority-minority districts.

▶ **Is Congress still mostly rich, white, and male?** Let's survey the range of types of Americans who have been members of Congress.

GENDER

Start with the number of women in Congress. The first woman elected to the House of Representatives was Jeannette Rankin of Montana, in 1916. She was elected even before women nationally got the right to vote under the Nineteenth Amendment. A peace activist, Rankin voted against declaring World War I. She was also in the House in 1941, where she cast the only vote against declaring war after Pearl Harbor. The first woman to serve in the Senate was Rebecca Felton from Georgia in 1922, who was appointed to fill a vacant seat. There were very few female members of either chamber during the following decades—about a dozen in the House and just two in the Senate. By the 1950s, there were seventeen female national legislators (in House and Senate combined), and that number actually dipped during the 1960s and 1970s. But as Table 7.5 demonstrates, there has been a steady increase since the 1980s, with a big jump in number and salary coming after the 1992 election (called by journalists the "Year of the Woman" because of the large number of women who ran for office that year). In the 110th Congress, sixteen women served in the U.S. Senate—equal to the total number of women who had served in *all* the years before 1978. In the House of Representatives, there are seventy-two women in the 110th Congress. Most people would agree that things are moving in the right direction, with the change in the Senate being especially significant. Yet it would seem that parity between the genders is still a long way off. Recall that there are 435 members in the House and 100 members in the Senate. Women today therefore make up about 16 percent of the federal legislature, compared to 51 percent of the U.S. population and to nearly 54 percent of the electorate.

RACE AND ETHNICITY

The picture for African Americans in Congress in some ways resembles that for women and in other ways is even more vexing. The first black elected to the House of Representatives was Joseph Hayne Rainey of South Carolina in 1870. Rainey was a slave as a child and was requisitioned for labor by the Confederacy during the Civil War. He escaped on a blockade-runner ship and made his way to Bermuda, a British colony where slavery had been abolished. After the war, he returned to South Carolina and began working with the Republican Party. He was sent to the House after a special election in 1870, where he served for eight years.[32] The first African American was also elected to the Senate in 1870: Hiram Rhodes Revels, representing Mississippi. Interestingly, he was elected by the "reconstructed" state legislature to complete Jefferson Davis's unfinished term. (Davis had left his place in the U.S. Senate to become president of the Confederacy.) After serv-

what YOU can do!

Thousands of bills are introduced in the House and Senate each year. One of the best online tracking sites is called Thomas, sponsored by the Library of Congress. It is a powerful search engine that lets you look up legislation by key word or phrase. Check it out and explore legislation that may be of interest to you. It's at **http://thomas.loc.gov**.

TABLE 7.5
Top Twenty Richest Members of 109th Congress

Legislator (State)	Party	Estimated Net Worth
Sen. John Kerry (MA)	D	$750 million
Former Sen. Jon Corzine (NJ)	D	$262 million
Sen. Jay Rockefeller (WV)	D	$200 million
Sen. Herb Kohl (WI)	D	$136 million
Rep. Jane Harman (CA)	D	$128 million
Rep. Darrell Issa (CA)	R	$121 million
Rep. Robin Hayes (NC)	R	$60 million
Rep. Charles Taylor (NC)	R	$55.3 million
Sen. Dianne Feinstein (CA)	D	$40 million
Sen. Lincoln Chafee (RI)	R	$39 million
Rep. Rodney Frelinghuysen (NJ)	R	$21 million
Rep. Gary Miller (CA)	R	$19.2 million
Rep. Nancy Pelosi (CA)	D	$16 million
Sen. Bill Frist (TN)	R	$14.2 million
Sen. Elizabeth Dole (NC)	R	$14 million
Rep. Nita Lowey (NY)	D	$13.9 million
Sen. Hillary Rodham Clinton (NY)	D	$13.5 million
Rep. Randy Marchant (TX)	R	$12.4 million
Sen. John McCain (AZ)	R	$12 million
Rep. Mike McCaul (TX)	R	$12 million

ing only one year, Revels left the Senate to become president of Alcorn State College.[33]

In all, only five African Americans have ever been elected to the Senate, including the currently serving Barack Obama, a Democrat from Illinois. In the House, just over one hundred African Americans have served. These are discouraging statistics, especially in the Senate. But as with women, the numbers seem to be improving since the 1980s. In recent years, about thirty-seven members of the House have been black, roughly 8.5 percent of the chamber. Given that African Americans make up about 13 percent of the national population, we might say that the situation is improving, especially compared to that of women.

pathways profile

CONGRESSWOMAN BARBARA JORDAN OF TEXAS

Barbara Jordan, the first black representative from Texas, was born in Houston on February 21, 1936. She was educated in the public schools of Houston and graduated from Phillis Wheatley High School in 1952. After receiving a B.A. in political science and history from Texas Southern University in 1956, she attended law school. In 1959, she was admitted to the Massachusetts and Texas bars, and she commenced practice in Houston in 1960.

In 1972, Jordan defeated Republican Paul Merritt to represent Texas's Eighteenth District in the U.S. House of Representatives. She was a member of the Judiciary Committee in the Ninety-Third Congress and also joined the Committee on Government Operations during the Ninety-Fourth and Ninety-Fifth Congresses.

Shortly after the Ninety-Third Congress convened in 1973, it began struggling with the Nixon administration over budgetary reform, a troubled economy, the war in Indochina, and other very serious issues. Jordan and other freshman representatives met with Speaker Carl Albert and arranged a meeting on the House floor in April to provide newly elected Democrats an opportunity to vent their frustration over the difficult relations between Congress and the executive branch. Jordan herself praised the House's capacity for self-reform. During the same Congress, she attached civil rights amendments to legislation authorizing cities to receive direct Law Enforcement Assistance Administration grants, rather than apply to state governments for the money. Jordan questioned the civil rights record of House Republican leader Gerald Ford when Nixon nominated him for the vice presidency. (This occurred after the previous vice president, Spiro Agnew, was forced to resign in a plea bargain after he pleaded no contest to charges of having taken bribes.) Jordan joined seven other Judiciary Committee members in voting against Ford's confirmation.

Jordan won national acclaim during the Judiciary Committee's hearings into Nixon's possible impeachment in the summer of 1974. In a deep, resonant, and dignified voice that few who watched the televised proceedings could ever forget, she eloquently reaffirmed her faith in the Constitution while voting for all five articles of impeachment.

In December 1977, Jordan announced that she would not be a candidate for reelection. In 1979, she became a professor at the Lyndon B. Johnson School of Public Affairs at the University of

▶ **Why are there still** so few women and minorities in Congress?

The late Congresswoman Barbara Jordan during Watergate House Judiciary Committee meetings in 1974. What forces have played a role in limiting the number of minorities and women in Congress?

Texas in Austin. In August 1994, President Bill Clinton awarded Jordan the Medal of Freedom, the nation's highest civilian honor. After suffering for years from a chronic illness, Jordan died on January 17, 1996, in Austin, Texas.

Source: "Black Americans in Congress, 1870–1989," http://www.house.gov/jacksonlee/AllAboutHouston/barbara_charline_jordan.htm, March 2004. ▪

Hispanic Americans (Latinos) are the fastest-growing demographic group in America and have recently succeeded African Americans as the nation's largest minority group. By 2006, there were roughly 40 million Hispanic Americans, making up some 14 percent of the population. (The U.S. Census Bureau estimates that Hispanics have accounted for 40 percent of the nation's population growth since 1990.) But their representation in Congress has lagged far behind. In recent years, however, things have improved for Hispanics as well; today about twenty-five members of the national legislature, or about 5 percent, are of Hispanic descent.

▶ **Why are there still so few women and minorities in Congress?** Why are few women and minority citizens elected to Congress? One reason is that historically, fewer women and minorities have sought office, likely due to a wide range of factors that included biases in the campaign process, discriminatory voter attitudes, and lags in the number of these groups who entered professions—especially the law—that have typically led to a political career. For whatever reason, some Americans still find it difficult to vote for minority and female candidates. One prominent elections scholar has observed that one way "to achieve fairer and more equal representation for minorities is to eliminate the allegiances and attitudes (some consider them biases and prejudices) that favor the majority."[34] A related explanation lies in the nature of our electoral system and specifically our reliance on single-member districts. There is no requirement in the Constitution that specific districts be drawn within each state, only (as noted earlier) that states receive an overall number of representatives relative to that state's population. The practice of creating individual districts was embraced in early days of the Republic, and it stuck. Another possibility, however, would be to substitute an at-large system, under which states that have two or more representatives would have no distinct districts: Voters would vote for at-large candidates, and they would get into the House in descending order according to the number of votes they won. (Alternatively, large states like California and New York could be divided into a number of large districts, each of which would elect a group of at-large representatives.) Under such a system, if a minority group makes up one-fifth of a state's population, which is often the case, and that state has been allotted ten seats in the House of Representatives chosen at large, we might expect that more minority candidates would be elected—perhaps two. But when one candidate is selected from a single district, that same 20 percent minority group is simply drowned out by the majority. And if attitudes about supporting minority candidates do not change, the prospects of that group's gaining a voice in the legislature will be small.

INCOME AND OCCUPATION

What about income and occupation? Once again, we find that the national legislature does not reflect America very well. Members of Congress are far better educated and far wealthier than the average

▶ **Can a legislature made**
up of elites really represent
the average citizen?

American. (And that is what the framers of the Constitution—themselves drawn from the elite—expected.) The Senate is often called the "millionaires' club." According to a study conducted by CNN, about forty of the one hundred senators in the 108th Congress were millionaires.[35] During this same time, the average American household brought in $42,400, and only about 5 percent of Americans earned over $150,000 per year. Less than 1 percent of Americans are worth a million dollars or more.[36]

And there have always been lawyers in Congress—lots and lots of lawyers. Roughly 40 percent of members of Congress serving at any given time are attorneys. Bankers and business professionals make up about the same percentage, and educators (schoolteachers and professors) account for roughly 15 percent.[37] (Dennis Hastert, former speaker of the House, was once a high school wrestling coach.) All other occupational backgrounds, including clergy, farmers, and retired military personnel, have been represented by only 5 percent of the members. Laborers, small farmers, ordinary housewives, service employees, and other blue-collar workers, who make up a vast majority of the American workforce, have never accounted for more than a tiny fraction of the members of Congress (see Figure 7.7).

▶ **Can a legislature made up of elites really represent the average citizen?** Perhaps it makes sense that some occupations are overrepresented in Congress. Lawyers, after all, are trained to understand the nuances of the law; it is natural that they would take the lead in writing laws. We might hope that the best and the brightest would serve in the national legislature—perhaps the same kinds of individuals who have earned advanced degrees and succeeded at their profession (that is, made lots of money). This is precisely what the framers of our system hoped for Congress, especially the Senate. Of course, it is possible that such representatives can understand the concerns of diverse groups of people and work on their behalf. Some of the greatest legislative champions of women's rights have been male legislators, and some of

FIGURE 7.7
**Education, Party Profile,
and Gender Composition of the 110th Congress**

What conclusions can you draw about the occupations, education and gender of Congress? How can it become more diversified and representative of the average citizen?

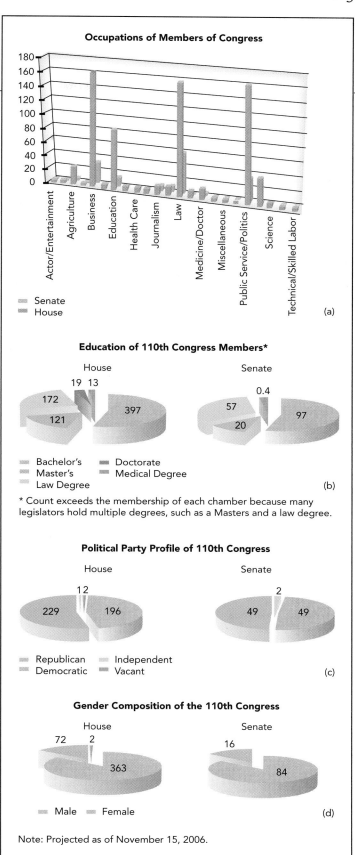

Occupations of Members of Congress

- Senate
- House

(a)

Education of 110th Congress Members*

House — 172, 19, 13, 121, 397
Senate — 57, 0.4, 20, 97

- Bachelor's
- Master's
- Law Degree
- Doctorate
- Medical Degree

(b)

*Count exceeds the membership of each chamber because many legislators hold multiple degrees, such as a Masters and a law degree.

Political Party Profile of 110th Congress

House — 229, 12, 196
Senate — 49, 2, 49

- Republican
- Democratic
- Independent
- Vacant

(c)

Gender Composition of the 110th Congress

House — 72, 2, 363
Senate — 16, 84

- Male
- Female

(d)

Note: Projected as of November 15, 2006.

▶ **There have been so** many scandals in Congress recently. Are things getting worse?

their concerns would get more attention if more members of their group were players on the field, rather than simply spectators from the sidelines or the bleachers.

TABLE 7.6
Public Opinion Poll on Congressional Ethics

"Would you rate the level of ethics and honesty of members of Congress as excellent, good, not so good, or poor?" (5/26–30/06)

Excellent	1%
Good	26%
Not so Good	36%
Poor	30%
Unsure	7%

"And would you rate the level of ethics and honesty of your own representative to the U.S. House of Representatives in Congress as excellent, good, not so good, or poor?" (5/26–30/06)

Excellent	9%
Good	45%
Not so Good	23%
Poor	13%
Unsure	10%

"When it comes to the level of ethics and honesty among politicians, do you think the Democrats are generally better than the Republicans, the Republicans are generally better than the Democrats, or isn't there much difference between them when it comes to ethics and honesty? (5/26–30/06)

Democrats Better	16%
Republicans Better	9%
Isn't Much Difference	72%
Unsure	3%

N = 1,044 adults nationwide. Margin of Error plus or minus 3. Fieldwork by ICR

SOURCE: ABC News Poll. May 26–30, 2006.

practicequiz

1. Regarding gender representation in Congress, it's fair to say that
   a. since the 1920s, the number of women in both chambers has steadily increased.
   b. the percentage of women in Congress is finally close to the percentage in the general population.
   c. the number of women in the federal legislature is higher now than in the 1920s but still not close to reflecting the percentage of women in the general population.
   d. women today make up about 5 percent of the federal legislature.

2. Joseph Hayne Rainey was the first African American elected to the U.S. House of Representatives. When did that happen?
   a. 1864   b. 1870
   c. 1921   d. 1946

3. Barbara Jordan first claimed national attention
   a. during her legislative work on civil rights in 1972.
   b. by participating in nonviolent demonstrations in the South in the 1950s.
   c. by taking *Brown v. Board of Education* before the Supreme Court in 1955.
   d. by her participation in the Judiciary Committee's hearings on Nixon's impeachment in 1974.

4. Working-class Americans, service employees, small farmers, and ordinary housewives have only ever constituted a tiny fraction of the members of Congress.
   a. true   b. false

Answers: 1-c, 2-b, 3-d, 4-a.

Congress's most aggressive advocates for the poor have been rich. Many white legislators fought valiant battles against slavery and segregation. Moreover, given that all Americans have the right to vote and that most legislators do everything they can to stay in office, we can imagine that members of Congress would be very attentive to *all* their constituents—especially to large blocs of voters, many of whom are far from affluent. Yet those who feel underrepresented in the halls of Congress—women, African Americans, Asian Americans, Hispanics, blue-collar workers, farmers, gays and lesbians, persons with disabilities, and the poor—feel that

Congressional Ethics

▶ **There have been so many scandals in Congress recently. Are things getting worse?** One of the central players in Congress in the past decade was Tom DeLay, a Republican from Texas, first elected in 1984. (Before he came to Congress, he ran an exterminating business.) When the Republicans captured control of the

discussionquestions

1. What factors explain why there have been so few women and minority members in Congress and why these groups are still underrepresented relative to their place in the general population?

2. How much difference does it really make that a disproportionate number of federal legislators are well-to-do or wealthy?

House in 1994, DeLay quickly emerged as a powerful player and was elected majority whip. He had a passion for politics and was bright, articulate, shrewd—and ruthless. His nickname, "The Hammer," seemed apt. He quickly rose in the Republican conference, and in 2002, he was elected majority leader and was one of the most powerful men in Washington.

By the spring of 2005, however, DeLay's fortunes had taken a dramatic downward turn: A grand jury in Austin, Texas, indicted him on criminal charges of conspiracy to violate election laws in 2002. In the spring of 2006, he was forced to relinquish his post as majority leader. Even though DeLay would stay in office while he fought the charges, everyone in Washington understood that the star had fallen. By summer, DeLay had withdrawn his name from the November ballot; he had decided to leave the House altogether.

About the same time that DeLay was stepping down from his leadership position, shivers were running through official Washington. An influential lobbyist named Jack Abramoff had been under investigation by federal law enforcement officials for some time, and they finally hit him with a string of indictments. Abramoff quickly agreed to cooperate with the prosecutors in exchange for a lighter sentence. In other words, Abramoff was ready to talk about the lobbying practices in Congress and to "name names." The case, replete with luxury skyboxes, politicians shilling for gambling interests, and lobbyists stealing from Indian tribes, seemed to symbolize Washington's extreme cash-for-policy culture.

The Abramoff scandal probably did not come as a surprise to most Americans. Ethical transgressions have periodically seemed an integral part of Congress. Mark Twain's oft-cited line that Congress is the only "distinctly native American criminal class" still seems accurate to most Americans. And there have certainly been enough high-profile scandals to buttress this cynical judgment. In 1875, during the corrupt administration of President Ulysses S. Grant, Americans were shocked by the bribes and kickbacks of the so-called Whisky Ring involving various prominent congressional crooks. In the 1920s, the Teapot Dome scandal implicated several prominent members of the Senate (as well as some of President Warren G. Harding's cabinet). More recently, the Abscam scandal of 1980 ensnared nearly thirty public officials, including a prominent senator (they were caught when federal law enforcement officers disguised as Arabian potentates proffered bribes). In 1989, five members of the Senate were implicated in the Keating scandal, involving corrupt banking practices. In 1992, no fewer than 430 sitting and former

members of the House were exposed in a scandal centered on the bank that the House maintains for the convenience of its members. And this dismal list does not include dozens of individual ethics violations that have occurred, many of them turning on money but others involving sex, alcohol, and drugs. In November 2005, Randall "Duke" Cunningham resigned from the House and was sentenced to six years in prison after pleading guilty to federal charges of conspiracy to commit bribery, mail fraud, and tax evasion. He admitted receiving at least $2.4 million in bribes. Cunningham's tearful apology was touching, but few Americans were surprised to see another member of Congress led off in handcuffs. Finally, Congressman Mark Foley resigned in disgrace in Ocbober of 2006 after it was revealed that he had sent sexually explicit emails to male pages. In one national survey, just 20 percent of Americans rate the ethics of members of Congess as "high" or "very high" (see Table 7.6).[38]

Close observers of the legislative branch argue that in the past few decades, members of Congress have become more ethical and more upstanding than at any point in our nation's history. According to Fred Harris, a political scientist and former liberal Democratic senator from Oklahoma, members of the national legislature are a good deal cleaner than the average American.[39] Another observer put it this way: "Most observers would suggest that real corruption on the Hill has in fact declined significantly over the past 20 or 30 years, whether the misbehavior is licentiousness or bribery or financial chicanery."[40]

What, then, might explain the gap between perceptions and reality? There are a number of plausible explanations. For one, there is simply much more reporting of ethical transgressions than in the past. Particularly after the Watergate scandal in the early 1970s, aggressive investigative journalism has become an omnipotent force in American politics. Reporters, thirsting—and driven by their media bosses—to find the next big scoop, scour public and private information for dirt. Second, this intense competition pushes news outlets to relentlessly pursue stories on what might once have been dismissed as minor infractions. Noted scholar Larry Sabato has called it "a spectacle without equal in modern American politics: the news media, print and broadcast, go after a wounded politician like sharks in a feeding frenzy."[41] Finally, due to a series of reforms, especially since the 1970s, members of Congress are subject to tougher rules and proceedures and to far more public scrutiny than in the past.

But in very important ways, it is the preception of the public that really matters. Within weeks after the Abramoff scandal

pathways | The Stem Cell Research Battle

 COURTS   **CULTURAL CHANGE**   **ELECTIONS**    **GRASSROOTS MOBILIZATION**    **LOBBYING DECISION-MAKERS**

PRO-STEM CELL RESEARCH

2004

November 2
California voters pass Proposition 71, a ballot measure to allocate $3 billion over 10 years to stem cell research, becoming the first state to fund stem cell research.

2005

January 11
Due to behind the scenes efforts by interest groups and mounting public pressure, New Jersey's governor announces the state will fund a $150 million stem cell research center and promises to champion a ballot initiative to allocate another $230 million.

March 26
A letter from University Presidents (including Yale, Stanford, Harvard and Princeton) and three higher education associations is sent to President Bush lobbying him to continue federal funding of embryonic stem cell research.

May 2
The Christopher and Dana Reeve Paralysis Research Center opens. Much of their work is focused on advocating additional funding for stem cell research.

February 22
Eighty Nobel Prize winners sign a letter to President Bush lobbying him to allow government funded researchers to experiment with stem cells.

October 10
Christopher Reeve dies. In many of the news reports of his death this president's opposition to federal funding is discussed. Public opinion in favor of greater funding seems to be mounting

2001   2002   2004

2001   2002   2004   2005

ANTI-STEM CELL RESEARCH

2001

February
The month after taking office, and after much lobbying from conservative religious organizations, President George W. Bush requests a review of the NIH funding guidelines and puts a hold on federal funds for stem-cell research.

2001

July 29
Due, in part, to pressure from their conservative base, Senate and House Republican leaders come out in opposition to federal funding for research even though public opinion polls suggest most Americans disagree.

2001

August 9
The pressure from religious groups continues and President Bush announces his decision to limit funding to a few dozen lines of embryonic stem cells in existence at that date.

2006

July 18
Public pressure and direct lobbying Congress to pass the Stem Cell Enhancement Act; many Republicans break ranks and support the measure.

2005

May 24
Public pressure, patient advocacy groups, and medical research advocates push the House of Representatives to reverse course. It approves H.R. 810 to loosen Bush's restrictions on federal funding for stem cell research. In voting in favor of the bill, 50 Republicans break with Bush.

January 31
Michael J. Fox foundation for Parkinson's Research announced that it awarded nearly one million dollars in grants to four stem cell researchers. This move draws public attention to need for additional research funding.

2005

2005

May 31
Biotech industry leaders and voters push Connecticut lawmakers to earmark $100 million for stem cell research over 10 years in an effort to compete with California and New Jersey.

July 13
Responding to lobbying efforts and public opinion polls, Illinois Gov. Rod Blagojevich circumvents the legislature using an executive order to dedicate $10 million for stem cell studies after bills allocating funds for the research were voted down or shelved without a vote.

2005

August 9
Coalition for the Advancement of Medical Research held "Call the White House" Day, urging President Bush to support the bi-partisan bill.

2006

March 21
The First Annual Stem Cell Summit held in Chicago with much attention to increase federal funding.

May 5
Poll results say 72% of Americans support stem-cell research. The public is now solidly behind more federal funding.

2006

Federal Funding for Stem Cell Research and the Lobbying Process   Who could have imagined a few decades ago that medical researchers would unlock the life-saving potential of the human embryo? Medical researchers now hold that embryonic stem cell research has the possibility of transforming the very nature of medicine. But this work is controversial because it often entails the destruction of a human embryo, leading some to view it immoral.

The public policy question in recent years has been over the federal funding of stem cell research. The government spends a great deal of resources on all kinds of medical research, generally through the National Institute of Health. But is stem cell research something with which the Federal government should be involved? This pathways figure illustrates the importance of pressure groups, high profile individuals, and the lobbying decision-makers pathway—especially when it comes to narrow policy questions such as funding for a particular type of research.

essayquestions

1. Pennsylvania Senator Arlen Specter once remarked, "Quite candidly, when Hollywood speaks, the world listens. Sometimes when Washington speaks, the world snoozes." How might this apply to the story of federal funding for stem cell research, noted above. Also, what does this figure (and Specter's comment) suggest about the relationship between direct lobbying and public opinion?

2. In many respects, the story of federal funding for stem cell research speaks to the complexities federalism. Although the national government might limit its support for a project or policy, state governments can often move forward on their own. Write an essay on how you believe state governments can influence whether or not the federal government will increase funding for embryonic stem cell research.

July 19
Sticking to his guns and responding to pressure from Christian conservative groups, George W. Bush vetoes the Stem Cell Enhancement Act.

2006

▶ **How can I get** Congress
to act on my interest?

broke, numerous measures were introduced to tighten ethical conduct, especially as it affects the relationship between legislators (and their staffers) and lobbyists. And of course, each party in Congress has attempted to portray itself as more ethical than the other party. Because the Abramoff scandal centered mostly on Republicans' transgressions, Democrats fought hard to portray members of the opposition as "ethically challenged."

Corruption is almost inevitably entangled with power—especially *entrenched* power. The irony is that Republicans were implicated in the Abramoff scandal because they were the majority party and therefore the key decision makers—precisely the position that the Democrats covet. (And that was precisely where, during the 1970s and 1980s, certain prominent members of the Democratic congressional majority were caught with their hands in the till.) By 2007, the tables had turned and the Democrats were in the majority—the very position in which lobbyists want to shower them with favors.

Conclusion

Representation is the linchpin of our democracy. It is true that in some tiny communities, all citizens can participate directly in governmental decisions, but direct democracy is rare, is impracticable in all but the smallest settings, and presumes that all citizens *should* be involved in every decision. Our system relies on a small group to speak and act on behalf of the many. Ours is a representative republic, and few Americans would have it any other way.

Congress was established as the "first branch" because the framers believed it would be the part of our government closest to the people. As James Madison wrote in *Federalist No. 10,* legislators will be "more immediately and confidential guardians of the rights and liberties of the people." Today, the real issues surrounding Congress have little to do with the value or legitimacy of legislative bodies or whether they should be seen as first among equals; rather, what we worry about is how to make the system more efficient or more egalitarian. No one could realistically imagine getting rid of standing committees, leadership roles, or party structures, for instance. But at the same time, most people agree that these components do modify the character of the institution. Not every initiative that comes before Congress gets treated the same, and not every legislator has the same input in the process. What's more, for many Americans who are critical of Congress, the *kind* of person who gets to serve in our legislature raises deep questions about the breadth and quality of representation.

What does all this mean for individuals who want to change public policy by lobbying their representative or senator? For one thing, it means that many of Congress's organizational components create points of access. Focusing your efforts at the committee level or on the leadership is vastly more efficient than trying to persuade 51 percent of the entire chamber to see things your way. This also implies that the actors must be well versed in the nuances of legislative procedure—the precise route that measures travel from introduction to law, as well as the numerous pitfalls along the way. It also suggests access. The legislative process has become more efficient in recent decades, but it has also become more intricate and less obvious. Insiders familiar with the complexity of the legislative process and with access to decision makers are in high demand. It is little wonder that former members of Congress are sought as lobbyists and are very well paid.

We might revel in the idea of a well-meaning, good-hearted "Mr. Smith" who goes to Washington, learns a few tricks, takes some bruises, and carries the day though grit and faith in the democratic process. (In 1939, the great actor James Stewart played this role in a famous film titled *Mr. Smith Goes to Washington* that you can watch on DVD or videotape. But you will probably find the film rather naive and simplistic by today's standards.) We now know that Congress is a far more complex place than Mr. Smith could ever imagine. Still, average citizens *can* change the outcome of federal policy by lobbying members of Congress; it is a viable pathway of change today and will remain so in the future (see Pathways on pages 288–289). A clear understanding of how legislatures work and where real power resides is critical, however. Without this knowledge, the lobbying decision-makers pathway will give you no way out of the thick forest of legislative politics.

YOUR turn!

One of the most effective consumer advocates in American history has been Ralph Nader (who also ran for president as the Green Party nominee in 2000 and as an independent 2004). Nader has spent his whole career working to persuade legislators. Whether or not you agree with his outlook about politics, few people would dispute that he knows a great deal about lobbying. *Ralph Nader's Practicing Democracy: A Guide to Student Action* offers several pointers to help Americans play a bigger role in the legislative process.[42] These tips can be applied not only to Congress but also to state legislatures, county boards, city councils, and even college governing bodies. Perhaps there is an issue that has drawn your interest, a policy that you would like to initiate or change.

▶ **How can I get Congress to act on my interest?** Here are four concrete suggestions that should help turn your concerns into a plan of action.

- **Identify Key Players.** It is always wise to chart the important players in the legislature and those who might directly deal with your legislation. For example, why not determine the members of a relevant committee and how each tends to vote on legislation? Which members of both parties would be most sympathetic to your measure? Moreover, who are the committee staffers who work on similar legislation?

- **Write a Bill and Find a Sponsor.** Believe it or not, anyone can write a bill. Of course, it takes a member of the legislature to introduce the measure, but starting the ball rolling can make a big difference. The trick is to take great care to understand where the bill would fit into existing law, to craft the precise language, and to find a potential sponsor who would be most receptive. To get some pointers, you might want to contact groups with similar interests who have drafted legislation.

- **Recruit Experts for Hearings.** As noted, the first step for legislation is often committee hearings. Testimony at hearings is an important way to educate legislators and to set the tone of the debate on the issue. The trick is to find and recruit experts who can talk about the virtues of your proposal in simple English. Also, gimmicks or dramatic testimony from people affected personally by the issue often are successful in stressing a point and capture the attention of the public and the media.

- **Go Face to Face.** Visiting a legislator's office can often provide an opportunity to explain the importance of a proposal and to demonstrate the depth of support. Although it may be difficult to arrange a meeting with some legislators, such as committee chairs and party leaders, most do make themselves available for short chats with constituents. Be prepared, get right to the point, provide details, and send follow-up material. ■

Chapter Review

1. Legislatures have been an important part of our system of government since colonial times, well before the creation of Congress.

2. The Constitution specifies numerous powers granted Congress and the federal government, most of which are set forth in Article I, Section 8. The last element in this section, known as the necessary and proper clause, has been used throughout our history to expand congressional prerogatives.

3. Redistricting and the reapportionment of House districts have been controversial issues in our legislative process. Very often, the outcome of this process—undertaken every ten years, after each census—has discriminated against minority groups and the party out of power in the state.

4. The framers of our political system envisioned a legislative process in which each member would play an equal role and where slow, careful deliberation would take place.

5. Although the slow, deliberative process was democratic, by the early part of the nineteenth century, most legislators realized that greater efficiency was needed. Several organizing elements were introduced, including standing committees, political parties, legislative leadership, and rules and norms of behavior.

6. Committees play a central role in the legislative process.

7. A bill's journey from introduction to final passage is long and filled with hurdles. Only a fraction of the measures that get introduced eventually wind up as laws.

8. The demographic makeup of Congress does not accurately reflect the American population, nor has it ever done so. Congress has generally been filled with well-to-do, white, male lawyers, although this is slowly changing.

9. Owing to the complexity of our country's legislative process, ethical problems can arise. People who want to change things in this country can find it effective to work directly with key decision makers, but this pathway is effective only for those who understand the subtleties of the process and can get access to the key players.

CHAPTER REVIEW TEST

1. In recent years, Congress's mode of representation has shifted from a trustee to a delegate model. This has happened in part because
   a. people less often grow up with a set of strong political ideals, and so when they become legislators, they are inclined to turn to the public for guidance.
   b. it is a lot easier to discern public opinion these days.
   c. the public has become a much better informed source of legislative guidance and hence more worthy of the delegate model of representation.
   d. legislators care less about winning reelection than they used to, so they are more willing to risk being perceived as being obligated to their voters than they used to be.

2. Regarding representational style, members of Congress often decide to focus on either
   a. national policy issues or the needs of their constituents.
   b. the interests of lobbyists from the home district or the interests of their constituents.
   c. the agenda of their own political party or a bipartisan agenda.
   d. the dictates of their own conscience or the agenda of their senior colleagues.

3. How did the battle between the Virginia Plan and the New Jersey Plan in the Constitutional Convention of 1787 reflect two conflicting views of representation?
   a. The former held states sovereign, and the latter held individuals sovereign.
   b. The former held individuals sovereign, and the latter held states sovereign.
   c. The former required legislators to be trustees of their constituents, and the latter required them to be delegates of their constituents.
   d. The former required legislators to be delegates of their constituents, and the latter required them to be trustees of their constituents.

4. Legislative branch powers include
   a. the power to veto legislation.
   b. the power to declare legislation unconstitutional.
   c. the power to regulate commerce.
   d. the power to invoke executive privilege on behalf of the president.

5. What are majority-minority districts?
   a. districts in which most minorities vote for a majority (usually Caucasian) candidate
   b. districts in which most majority voters (usually Caucasians) vote for a minority candidate (usually African American or Latino)
   c. districts designated by the Voting Rights Act as likely to produce the majority of the Congress's minority representatives

   d. districts created through redistricting so that the majority of the voters in the district are minorities (African American, Latino, or Asian American, for example).

6. Reapportionment is the process whereby
   a. members of Congress are made to represent more constituents because of population growth.
   b. the number of seats granted each state is increased or decreased, depending on that state's population growth.
   c. the total number of seats in the House is changed, depending on the national population growth.
   d. districts within a state shift, depending on where most of the majority party's voters live.

7. One of the advantages of the standing committee system in Congress is that
   a. in a committee, seniority does not practically matter—it is a very democratic forum.
   b. committee membership changes frequently, so no small group of representatives possesses entrenched power over the issues in that committee.
   c. committee deliberations slow the legislative process, which is what the framers of the Constitution would have wanted.
   d. a very large number of measures that come to Congress can be considered simultaneously—that is, the process is quite efficient.

8. Generally speaking, most standing committees in the House and Senate have how many members?
   a. 20 and 10, respectively
   b. 10 and 8, respectively
   c. 50 and 20, respectively
   d. 75 and 30, respectively

9. The conference committee has been called
   a. a "mini-legislature."
   b. "the house of executive privilege."
   c. "Congress's Congress."
   d. "the third house of Congress."

10. About 90 percent of all proposed legislation stalls in committee and then dies, never reaching the chamber floor for a full vote.
    a. true   b. false

11. Markup happens in subcommittees, but what is it exactly?
    a. a bill's sponsor's determination of the cost of enacting the legislature
    b. the prime sponsor's working out of the language of the bill
    c. adding amendments to a bill to make it more likely to pass the House or Senate
    d. deciding which subcommittee considering the legislation will serve as the primary committee

12. Along with policymaking, congressional committees have what other crucial responsibility?
  a. caucusing for partisan decision making
  b. adjusting a bill's language so that it is consistent with the bill in the other chamber
  c. making sure that legislation gets properly implemented as federal law; that is, exercising congressional oversight
  d. assessing the influence of special-interest groups on the committee's decision-making process.

13. To investigate an issue or a matter of serious concern, the Senate or the House
  a. creates a committee for that particular investigation.
  b. uses the existing committee that best suits the circumstances.
  c. creates a joint Senate-House committee specifically for that investigation.
  d. either creates a special committee or uses an existing one that is appropriate for the circumstances.

14. Why should a student of congressional committees learn about Joseph McCarthy?
  a. He helped streamline committee work; the current efficiency of standing committees is due largely to his work.
  b. His anti-Communist crusade demonstrated, in a negative way, the high profile committee investigations can attain.
  c. In 1924, he was the first senator on a judiciary committee to call into question the competence of a Supreme Court nominee.
  d. He was a Supreme Court nominee whose nomination notoriously failed in judiciary committee hearings.

15. Congressional committees are the principal decision-making structure of the legislative process.
  a. true   **b.** false

16. When members of Congress need to vote on a measure in conference or on the chamber floor but have not had time to study the legislation in much depth,
  a. they invariably vote the way other representatives from their state vote.
  b. they often request a delay in the vote so that they can bone up on the details.
  c. they vote the way they are told to vote by a memo from the national chairman of their party.
  d. they often infer and follow voting cues from the positions senior members in their party have already staked out.

17. Rules in the Senate have the effect of giving individual senators, even when they are in the minority on an issue, much more leverage and freedom to express themselves than House rules grant individual representatives in the House.
  a. true   **b.** false

18. What's an example of a significant "folkway" in Congress?
  a. filibuster   **b.** floor debate
  c. logrolling   **d.** cloture

19. Because women's rights have been championed by male legislators and white legislators worked tirelessly against slavery and segregation,
  a. we can safely assume that Congress will always gradually move forward on civil rights issues.
  b. we should not automatically assume that the underrepresentation of women and minorities in Congress is a political problem for women and minorities nationwide.
  c. there's no reason for activists to try to improve the representation of women and minorities in Congress.
  d. no real progress is now needed in the area of civil rights.

20. On the whole, Congress is filled with well-to-do white male lawyers.
  a. true   **b.** false

Answers: 1: b; 2: a; 3: a; 4: c; 5: d; 6: b; 7: d; 8: c; 9: d; 10: a; 11: b; 12: c; 13: d; 14: b; 15: a; 16: d; 17: a; 18: c; 19: b; 20: a.

DISCUSSION QUESTIONS

1. Which model of representation do you think is most appropriate—delegate or trustee? Which of the compromise positions makes more sense?

2. Do you suppose the framers of Article I of the Constitution would have regretted any of the provisions? If so, which ones?

3. What might be the advantages and disadvantages of turning redistricting over to nonpartisan commissions?

4. Which of the organizing elements most drastically limit the egalitarian nature of the national legislature?

5. Most people would agree that Congress does not "look like the rest of America." But is this a serious problem? If so, what might be done about it?

6. As we noted in the conclusion of the chapter, former members of Congress are highly sought as lobbyists. Why? In

other words, what special qualifications do they seem to have—qualifications that enhance the potential of the direct lobbying pathway as a means to achieve change?

7. Are direct appeals to decision makers—in this case, to members of Congress—a viable option to change government?

What types of citizens or groups of citizens would find this approach most profitable? What types of issues are best suited for this pathway?

8. Why do we hear so much about the corruption of Congress, and what does—and should—Congress do to police itself?

INTERNET RESOURCES

To learn more about the history of the U.S. Congress: **http://clerk.house.gov/histHigh/index.php**

To read the specifics of Article I and to search for related court cases: **http://caselaw.lp.findlaw.com/data/constitution/article01**

To learn more about committees, specific pieces of legislation, roll call votes, and much more: **http://thomas.loc.gov**

To learn more about leadership in both chambers, as well as party unity scores over time: **http://clerk.house.gov/histHigh/Congressional_History/index.php**

For an online directory of members of Congress and details of how to contact them: **http://www.visi.com/juan/congress**

To explore the Census Bureau's redistricting data: **http://www.census.gov/clo/www/redistricting.html**

For an up-to-date look at what is happening on Capitol Hill: **http://www.rollcall.com**

ADDITIONAL READING

Davidson, Roger H., Susan Webb Hammond, and Raymond W. Smock, eds. *Masters of the House.* Boulder, CO: Westview Press, 1998.

Davidson, Roger H., and Walter J. Oleszek. *Congress and Its Members* (10th ed.). Washington, DC: Congressional Quarterly Press, 2005.

Fenno, Richard. *Homestyle: House Members in Their Districts.* Glenview, IL: Scott, Foresman, 1978.

Mayhew, David R. *Congress: The Electoral Connection.* New Haven, CT: Yale University Press, 1974.

Schroeder, Pat. *24 Years of House Work . . . and the Place Is Still a Mess: My Life in Politics.* Kansas City, MO: McMeel, 1998.

Sinclair, Barbara. *Unorthodox Lawmaking: New Legislative Processes in the United States Congress.* Washington, DC: Congressional Quarterly Press, 2000.

KEY TERMS

The framers of our government worried about too much power in the executive branch. Yet, during the last two centuries the American public has not only accepted strong presidents, we have grown to expect these leaders to steer the course of government and lead us though difficult times. Some presidents have risen to the challenge, while others have failed. Here President Bush speaks at the base of Mount Rushmore National Memorial on August 15, 2002, in South Dakota.

CHAPTER 8

THE PRESIDENCY

From Storyteller to Commander in Chief—in Seven Minutes! It is not unusual for presidents to step outside the White House for public events. Activities of this sort are very important for morale building during times of crisis, but they are also used to promote presidential policies or simply to remind citizens that the president is out there working for them. These media events, also called preplanned photo opportunities (or "photo ops"), are sometimes designed to capture the public's attention in order to sway policymakers, such as members of Congress. Presidents will head to a shipyard to announce a new defense measure, appear at a construction site to talk about a new home ownership initiative, tour a factory to talk about tax cuts for businesses, or stroll though a grocery story to discuss what's being done to battle inflation. It is an important part of a president's job. It is also not coincidence that presidents arrange

One of the themes of this chapter is that we expect a great deal from our presidents. We ask them to understand local concerns and to guide world affairs. Here George W. Bush first learns that a second jet has flown into the World Trade Center on September 11, 2001 while he sits with elementary school students in Florida. In a very real sense his presidency was defined at this very instant. Many believe he has risen to the challenge and provided decisive leadership for the nation, while others say Mr. Bush has failed. What is your view? How can a president forge a national consensus in our turbulent world?

for more photo ops in states that they narrowly won or lost in the previous election.

So it was not out of the ordinary when President George W. Bush decided to promote his education reform agenda by visiting the Emma E. Booker Elementary School in Sarasota, Florida—the state he had won by a handful of hotly disputed votes in 2000, giving him his electoral college victory. The presidential plan was to talk to teachers and administrators and then to sit with the children at a reading appreciation workshop. It was not an important or significant event, more or less all in a day's work for the president of the United States.

The book that the president was asked to read to the children was *My Pet Goat*. It is the tale of an undisciplined pet that goes from place to place eating anything within its reach, including cans and caps. As the preschoolers listened to the story, they were attentive, inquisitive, and of course oblivious to what was going on in the outside world.

But this was September 11, 2001. Shortly before President Bush sat down with the preschoolers, his staff informed him that a plane had just crashed into the North Tower of the World Trade Center in lower Manhattan. Everyone, including the president, assumed that a horrible accident had occurred; perhaps, Bush said to one of his aides, the pilot had a stroke or a heart attack. But not wanting to disturb the children and break his schedule, the president when through with his meeting with teachers and adminis-

trators and then sat down with the children to read *My Pet Goat.* There was cause for concern, but the photo op would proceed as scheduled.

Within a few minutes, the "horrible accident" became recognized as one of the most infamous events in America's history. At exactly 9:03 A.M. a second plane crashed into the South Tower of the World Trade Center. Clearly, this was no random mishap but a strategic strike. The planes had been hijacked, and the United States had come under attack. Within seconds, the pagers of the president's aides began to sound, and tension mounted in the room. The president's chief of staff, Andrew Card, interrupted the reading of the book to whisper in Bush's ear, "A second plane hit the towers. America is under attack."

The president's expression soured and grew intense, and he remained seated with the children for seven additional minutes before the Secret Service swept him away. Later recalling that moment, the president stated: "I'm trying to absorb that knowledge. I have nobody to talk to. I'm sitting in the midst of a classroom with little kids, listening to a children's story, and I realize I'm the commander in chief and the country has just come under attack."[1]

The story of President Bush and *My Pet Goat* tells us that within a blink of an eye, the role of the American president can be transformed from an actor at a public relations event to the most important person in the world. As commander in chief of the largest military in history, the American president is at the center of world affairs. As the events on September 11 unfolded, all thoughts turned to the victims of the horrific event—and to the whereabouts, safety, and actions of George W. Bush. ■

what YOU can do!

Watch a video clip of George W. Bush's recollection of that infamous day at the CBS News Web site,
http://cbsnews.com/stories/2002/09/11/60II/main521718.shtml

▶ Why were the founders
worried about having a
strong president?

prerogative power
extraordinary powers that the president
may use under certain conditions.

As you will see in this chapter, the framers of our Constitution were uncertain about the executive branch. They knew it was necessary and would prove indispensable in creating a viable national government, but they also worried that this part of the government might overwhelm the other branches, perhaps even lead the nation down the path of tyranny. Their solution was to keep things vague and to allow the men who would hold the position to define the duties, responsibilities, and powers of the office as time went on. Because they all knew that George Washington, whom they all trusted, would be the first to fill this role, their reluctance about creating a presidency melted somewhat. But in allowing presidents to define their office, they opened the door for a slow but steady expansion of presidential powers. George Washington or John Adams would find it rather odd that a successor would take time to read storybooks to preschool children, only seconds later to be rushed off to chart the response of the greatest military power on earth.

The steady expansion of presidential powers creates many new opportunities and challenges for our government—a system originally designed with the legislature at the center. For the men and women who will some day hold the position of president, this transformation comes as a double-edged sword. We expect more from presidents, but the realities of our world and the structure of our government make presidential failure and citizen disappointment all too frequent. At times they are the heroes, but far too often they are, shall we say, the goats.

This chapter stresses the expanding powers of the presidency (see Table 8.1). As you can imagine, persuading the president to support your policy objectives can be crucial. Directly lobbying the president is difficult and rare today. But this chapter will underscore the massive increase, in recent years, of the White House staff, many of whom influence the shaping of public policy and can be reached by lobbyists. On top of this, the enormous growth in the federal bureaucracy, coupled with Congress's growing willingness to provide broad, ambiguous directives, has created new opportunities for direct lobbying of the executive branch.

Key Questions

1. What role should the chief executive play in a democratic system?
2. Why did the framers of our Constitution fear executive power while at the same time considering it necessary?
3. What are the different models of presidential power? Which was predominant during the nineteenth century, and which applies to more recent presidents?
4. What are some of the informal powers that presidents can use to shape the outcome of government?
5. What are the different roles that presidents are expected to play in our political system today? Are some of these roles more important than others, or do you think they are all equally important?
6. What are some of the characteristics that scholars have used to explain "presidential greatness"? Are some of these characteristics more important than others?
7. What does the term *personal president* mean, and what does it suggest about the relationship between voters and chief executives?

Early Concerns about Executive Power

If we could bring the framers of our system back from the grave to see what had become of our experiment in democratic governance, they would probably recognize much of their handiwork. The structure of our system—the sharing of powers, the checks and balances, and the coexistence of the national and the state governments—has remained more or less the same through the centuries. Yet the workings of each branch of government and the interactions among them have changed considerably. One of these changes is the pivotal role of the president that has now emerged.

The framers were ambivalent about the exact role that the executive branch would have under the Constitution.[1] The history of strong executives with whom the framers were familiar was unsettling. From the very beginning of history, whenever human beings came together to form governments, the result was either autocracy (rule by one) or oligarchy (rule by a few).[2] Yet governing systems without executive power seemed inept, ripe for discord and anarchy. The framers were well versed in the philosophies of Hobbes, Montesquieu, and other theorists of the seventeenth and eighteenth centuries. These thinkers agreed that although we might wish for a political system without a powerful executive, governments that had none had proved ineffectual and short-lived. The English political philosopher John Locke, who was the thinker most admired by the framers of our Constitution, argued that legislative politics should be at the heart of a limited government—but also that it was necessary to give executives the powers to do "several things of their own free choice, where the law is silent, and sometimes, too, against the direct letter of the law, for the public good."[3] Locke called such action **prerogative power.**

▶ **Why were the founders worried about having a strong president?** For many Revolutionary era Americans, the royal governors seemed to represent the dangers of strong executives, and several of the new state constitutions drawn up after independence

TABLE 8.1
Growing Executive Powers under George W. Bush

EXECUTIVE ACTION	DESCRIPTION AND EXAMPLE	RESULTS FROM COURTS OR CONGRESS
Private deals with companies	Bush threatened his first presidential veto to protect a deal for a Dubai-owned company to take over some U.S. port operations.	Congressional Republicans and Democrats upended the deal, forcing the firm to promise to transfer the operations to a "U.S. entity."
Restricted access	The administration bypassed Congressional intelligence committees to inform only eight congressional leaders about such sensitive programs as the National Security Agency's warrantless-surveillance operation.	The Senate Intelligence Committee voted 9–6 to demand that the administration notify all members of the committees about intelligence operations.
Ignoring laws and treaties	Bush signed legislation banning torture in December 2005 but issued a "signing statement" in which he reserved the right to waive the ban, which he suggested violated his constitutional authority as commander in chief.	Senate Armed Services Chairman John Warner of Virginia and Arizona Sen. John McCain of Arizona, both Republicans, issued a joint statement in reply to Bush's "signing statement" vowing "strict oversight to monitor" implementation of the law.
Interpreting and curtailing new laws	Bush issued more than 750 "signing statements" that state his interpretation of new laws and sometimes declare that they infringe on his presidential powers.	The American Bar Association's board of governors voted to establish a bipartisan task force to investigate whether Bush had gone beyond his constitutional authority in asserting a right to ignore provisions of new laws.
First time a search warrant executed on a House member's office	FBI search in May 2006 of Rep. William Jefferson's (D-LA) congressional office.	General Michael Hayden, CIA Director, comments on the search powers of the executive branches of government.
Restrictions on judicial intervention	Lawyers for Salim Ahmed Hamdan, Osama bin Laden's former driver, challenged the administration's plan to put prisoners at Guantanamo Bay in Cuba on trial for war crimes in special military tribunals.	Case of *Hamdan* v. *Rumsfeld* was heard before the Supreme Court. On June 29, 2006, the Supreme Court ruled that Bush had overstepped his authority.

SOURCES: http://www.usatoday.com/news/washington/2006-06-05-power-play_x.htm

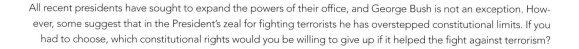

All recent presidents have sought to expand the powers of their office, and George Bush is not an exception. However, some suggest that in the President's zeal for fighting terrorists he has overstepped constitutional limits. If you had to choose, which constitutional rights would you be willing to give up if it helped the fight against terrorism?

This picture by H. Brueckner is called "The Prayer at Valley Forge." It is not possible to overstate the public's esteem for George Washington. In fact, much of the ambiguity in the Constitution regarding presidential powers springs from the near blind faith the framers had in Washington. What was it about Washington that brought him this kind of trust?

was declared either eliminated governors entirely or stripped them of almost all power. But other Americans insisted that for more than a century, executives had been essential to governing the colonies. In the face of strong popular faith in the supremacy of legislatures, critics of the "excessively" democratic Revolutionary state governments advocated having a vigorous executive power to counterbalance perceived legislative supremacy.[4] Liberty, these critics reasoned, was best protected when governmental power is divided among separate departments. Two successful state governments, New York and Massachusetts, both had relatively strong executives. The experience under the Articles of Confederation further suggested the need for a strong executive, for under the Articles, the national government lacked the power and the ability to respond quickly to emergencies. And advocates of an effective executive had an ideal republican leader readily at hand: George Washington, the hero of the Revolution.[5] Writes one historian:

> Babies were being christened after him as early as 1775. . . . To his admirers he was "godlike Washington," and his detractors complained to one another that he was looked upon as a "demigod" who it was treasonous to criticize. "Oh Washington," declared Ezra Stiles of Yale (in a sermon in 1783), "How I love your name! How have I often adored and blessed thy God, for creating and forming thee into the great ornament of humankind!"[6]

practicequiz

1. The executive branch was first imagined by the framers of the Constitution to be
   a. the center of governmental authority.
   b. necessary but potentially tyrannical.
   c. the weakest of the three branches.
   d. a reward for George Washington's noble efforts as general.

2. Although he asserted that legislative authority should be central to a limited government, John Locke also believed that an executive figure should be able to
   a. exercise prerogative power in some circumstances, even if it runs counter to the law of the land.
   b. execute the laws of the legislature when he believes them to be appropriate.
   c. declare martial law if the country slips into chaos.
   d. dissolve the legislature if it can no longer function effectively.

3. During the formation of the Constitution, one strong argument for granting substantial authority to the executive branch was
   a. the geographic breadth of the United States.
   b. the precedent of strong monarchical rule in England.
   c. George Washington's effective campaigning for such a position.
   d. George Washington himself.

4. The experience under the Articles of Confederation mattered to the framers' discussion of the presidency because
   a. that experience made it clear that the national government needed a decisive commanding figure.
   b. Washington, the acting president during that experience, had executed his duties very effectively.
   c. that experience demonstrated how ineffective the new state governors were.
   d. Washington, the nominal president during that experience, was not allowed to be an effective president.

Answers: 1-b, 2-a, 3-d, 4-a

The President and the Constitution

THE CONSTITUTIONAL CONVENTION

At the Philadelphia Constitutional Convention in 1787 (see LINK *Chapter 2, pages 56–60*), the first scheme for a new government that the delegates discussed, the Virginia Plan, was vague

discussionquestions

1. How did the history of executive power seem antagonistic to democracy?

2. What advantages might there be to strong executive power? What might be some of the disadvantages?

about the executive branch. The plan was unclear on the basic questions of whether one person or a group of people would hold executive power, how long the term of office would be, whether the president could be reelected, and even the precise powers of the presidency. The Virginia Plan's principal author, James Madison, was unsure about all these questions. The second scheme to emerge at the convention, the New Jersey Plan, was advanced by William Paterson (of that state). This scheme was clearly more state-centered, and although many of its provisions regarding the executive branch were also vague, it clearly envisioned a relatively weak office. As months passed and few key questions about the executive were resolved, the weak model gained support. But then, concerned that the executive branch would be overwhelmed by the power of the legislature, some of the most prominent and most talented delegates pushed for a stronger model. James Wilson and Gouverneur Morris, both representing Pennsylvania, worked hard in the Convention's sessions and in private meetings with other delegates to strengthen the executive office's constitutional powers. The "pro-executive" group grew and won victory after victory.[7]

In the end, ten key questions concerning the executive office were resolved.

1. **Shall the executive office consist of one person or several?** This issue took up a great deal of the convention's time. Vesting executive power in a small group would better ensure that no one individual would emerge as all-powerful, but many delegates countered that such a group would lack responsiveness. It was decided that the presidency would consist of one person.

2. **Shall the president be selected by Congress?** In a parliamentary model (Britain is an example), the chief executive typically comes from the majority party in the legislature and remains a member of the parliament. But Americans—having successfully rebelled against Parliament's rule over the colonies—did not want to establish a parliamentary system of government. The framers, wishing to guarantee the executive's independence from the legislature and to ensure a system of checks and balances, decided that under normal circumstances, Congress would play no role in selecting the president. (We will mention the exception shortly.)

3. **Shall all citizens select the president?** Not exactly. Once again we see an interesting compromise. Small states worried that if popular elections were used to pick the president, leaders from the larger states would dominate the national government. At the same time, however, most agreed that the voters should have some say in selecting the president. The compromise, the

electoral college, calls on the state legislatures—elected by average citizens—to pick a slate of electors who would then select the president. But if no candidate receives a majority of electoral college votes, the matter is decided in the House of Representatives—and there, each state casts one vote. Because there were no political parties at the time, and because the framers of the Constitution believed that several candidates would be considered for the presidency in each election, they thought that there was a rather high likelihood that the House would often wind up picking presidents, so that would not give any advantage to the big states with large congressional delegations. Because in this event the smallest states would have the same say in the House as the largest states, the plan seemed a neat compromise.

Interestingly, the Constitution does *not* require states to poll their citizens in the selection of electors. That is to say, the state legislature can simply select electors (there need not be elections). At first, that was the way electors were chosen. Most states moved to the direct election process that we now use only in the late 1820s. South Carolina was the last to change, in 1860.

4. **Shall the president have any role in legislative matters?** In keeping with the notion of shared powers, the framers thought it wise to give presidents a modest role in enacting laws. Presidents can, for example, recommend measures for legislative consideration, must periodically inform Congress about "the state of the union," and can veto proposed legislation. Of course, the president's veto can be overridden by a two-thirds vote in each house of the legislature. The first two presidents gave "state of the union" speeches, but between 1801 and the early twentieth century, presidents merely sent Congress a written message once a year.

5. **Who shall conduct foreign policy—Congress or the president?** Here the framers were clear: The president has the responsibility to conduct foreign policy. But once again a check was thought necessary: The president negotiates treaties, but the Senate ratifies them. The president appoints ambassadors to foreign nations, but the Senate must confirm their appointment.

6. **Shall the president be responsible for making war?** Once again, the Constitution reveals the framers' worries about the office of chief executive. War powers were to be split: The president is commander in chief of the armed forces, but Congress has the power to declare war and to raise and

▶ **Did people really think** they would end up with a monarch, after all they'd been through in the Revolution?

Alexander Hamilton (1755–1804) one of the framers of the Constitution and secretary of the treasury in George Washington's administration.

support the military. As we will see, this ambiguity has led to a good bit of controversy.

7. **How long shall the president serve? That is, how long should terms be, and should there be a limit on the number of terms a president may serve?** There should be enough time for presidents to accomplish something (in some states at the time, governors served for only one year, which was clearly not long enough), but the length of office should not be so long that presidents could become entrenched in power. In other words, if presidents were allowed to stay too long, they might grow accustomed to power and privilege and not want to leave. The compromise was four-year terms, with the chance of being reelected repeatedly. There was no limit on the number of terms. (The Twenty-Second Amendment, ratified in 1951 after Franklin D. Roosevelt had been elected four times, has since limited the number of terms to two.)

8. **Should a president be removable between elections?** Under normal circumstances, neither Congress nor the judiciary nor any other institution can remove a president. Yet the Constitution did give Congress the power to remove the president through impeachment and conviction for "treason, bribery, or other high crimes and misdemeanors." ("High crimes and misdemeanors" was added to the Constitution because many of the framers worried that the reasons given for impeachment—treason and bribery—were not enough. This was a well-known phrase in English common law, which essentially meant "great offenses." The definition of such offenses is a subjective assessment made by Congress.) No president has ever been removed from office using this process, but the possibility of being ejected from office is real, as Andrew Johnson, Richard Nixon, and Bill Clinton know all too well.

9. **Shall the president alone be responsible for carrying out the will of Congress, that is, for executing laws and spending money?** Here things seemed straightforward: The president shall be the head of the executive branch, with the power to appoint the officers (with the advice and consent of the Senate) who carry out national government policy. More will be said of this in the pages to follow.

10. **Finally, in a broader sense, shall the president have real powers—that is, shall presidents be authentic players in the system or merely administrators of what Congress decides?** The Constitutional Convention aimed to create a national government with real power. Therefore, argued the framers, the powers of the presidency should be real and significant. There would be no blank checks, writes one scholar, and nearly all the presidential powers would be shared with Congress. But presidents were meant to be significant players in the system.[8] The principal powers granted by the Constitution to presidents allowed them to influence the judiciary by appointing judges to the bench, to have a modest say in making legislation, and to conduct foreign policy. As we'll see in this chapter, these formal powers have proved to be merely the foundation of presidential authority.

ARTICLE II AND RATIFICATION OF THE CONSTITUTION

Previous chapters have noted that many of the fears about the new system were calmed by the central place that the legislature would have. But if Article I (the legislative branch) calmed citizens' fears, Article II raised their alarm. What was this "presidency," and what sorts of power would its occupants have? How long would this person serve? What would stop this person from gaining too much power and becoming another tyrant? Moreover, the scheme laid out in Article II was unfamiliar. As noted by a leading presidential scholar, "Not only was the presidency the most obvious innovation in the proposed plan of government, but its unitary nature and strong powers roused fears of the most horrifying political specter that most Americans could imagine: a powerful monarchy."[9]

Both proponents and opponents of the Constitution presented their arguments in the form of essays published in newspapers. Several essays in opposition were published under the pseudonym Cato in the *New York Journal*. One piece, appearing on September 27, 1787, only ten days after conclusion of the Constitutional Convention, was a powerful assault on the executive branch:

> It is remarked by Montesquieu, in treating of republics, that *in all magistracies, the greatness of the power must be compensated by the brevity of the duration; and that a longer time than a year, would be dangerous.* It is therefore obvious to the least intelligent mind, to account why, great power in the hands of a magistrate, and that power connected, with a considerable duration, may be dangerous to the liberties of a republic—the deposit of vast trusts in the hands of a single magistrate, enables him in their exercise, to create a numerous train of dependents—this tempts his *ambition*, which in a republican

discussionquestions

1. Which of the ten questions about the executive branch resolved at the Constitutional Convention do you think were most significant?

2. As you now know, the presidency was worrisome to many Americans during the ratification period. What set some of these fears to rest?

▶ **So how did we end up with a strong presidency?**

magistrate is also remarked, *to be pernicious* and the duration of his office for any considerable time favors his views, gives him the means and time to perfect and execute his designs—*he therefore fancies that he may be great and glorious by oppressing his fellow citizens, and raising himself to permanent grandeur on the ruins of his country.* [Emphasis in the original.]

Cato seemed to hit the nail on the head: The scheme outlined by the framers would allow the president to use his long term of office to take such a firm hold of the reins of power that it would ruin the democratic experiment.

▶ **Did people really think they would end up with a monarch, after all they'd been through in the Revolution?** **Alexander Hamilton** had the difficult chore of countering Cato's argument. Simply put, he had to ease fears about the presidency, and he undertook that task in *The Federalist Papers,* particularly *Federalist No. 69.* There, Hamilton sought to "place in a strong light the unfairness of such representations" of the proposed executive branch. He notes that while the king gains his post through heredity and holds it throughout his life, the president is elected for four years. The president can be impeached for treason, bribery, and other high crimes or misdemeanors (see Figure 8.1), but the king can be subjected to no punishment; he is "sacred and inviolable." A president may be able to veto legislation, but this decision can be overridden by the legislature. A king's judgment, on the other hand, is absolute. Repeatedly, Hamilton works to underscore the differences between a king and a president, with much effect. But once again, it was not persuasive arguments that carried the day but rather public sentiment toward one political leader. Everyone knew that George Washington would be the first president. He had not abused his authority as the commanding officer of the Continental Army, and many simply could not imagine such a great man amassing power and making himself a king. Faith in Washington allowed citizens to overcome their fears (for the moment) about a powerful executive.

practicequiz

1. The first efforts to define presidential power and responsibility were vague.
   a. true
   b. false

2. What sort of role in legislative matters did the framers of the Constitution grant the president?
   a. none at all, because of worries about a president's tyrannical powers
   b. a substantial role, as a check on and balance to Congress's power
   c. a modest role, with veto power that Congress can in turn override with a two-thirds majority vote
   d. a modest role, with veto power that Congress can easily override with a simply majority vote

3. We know that the framers of the Constitution thought that the legislative branch should be a check on presidential power in foreign affairs because
   a. they granted Congress the power to negotiate treaties.
   b. they granted Congress oversight of all foreign policy initiatives.
   c. they granted Congress the power to appoint ambassadors to foreign nations.
   d. they granted Congress the power to ratify treaties and confirm ambassador appointments.

4. What was Alexander Hamilton's role in the establishment of the presidency?
   a. He was the real author of the "Cato" argument against granting the president a four-year term.
   b. He worked behind the scenes at the Constitutional Convention to be named the first president.
   c. He countered "Cato's" arguments by explaining in *The Federalist Papers* the differences between the U.S. presidency and a monarchy.
   d. He explained in *The Federalist Papers* why a limited executive branch was crucial to the endurance of democracy in this country.

Answers: 1-a, 2-c, 3-d, 4-c

The Evolution of the Presidency

▶ **So how did we end up with a strong presidency?** The fact that the Constitution *allows for* a powerful president is not the same as *mandating* a powerful executive. Article II is less clear than other parts of the Constitution. Two forces have therefore shaped the nature of the presidency.

First, the breadth of presidential powers has been a function of the men who have served in the position and used those powers. Aggressive leaders have been able to use the vagueness of the Constitution to their advantage. Second, the overall evolution of the presidency has been toward ever-greater powers, so much so that today few of us can imagine a time when the president was not the center of the federal government. But indeed, there have been such times in our history.

When Criminal Charges Reach the White House

The CIA leak case could bedevil the Bush administration for months. So far, however, it has not nearly approached the scale of an earlier White House scandal, Iran-contra, and its 11 convictions.

The sweep of the Watergate scandal is in a class by itself. Since then, special prosecutors have taken aim at people tied to government's highest offices more than 20 times. Some inquiries, months or years long and costing millions, have found nothing to prosecute. Ronald Reagan's labor secretary, Raymond J. Donovan, was investigated for allegations of mob ties; Reagan's attorney general, Edwin Meese III was accused of financial improprieties. Neither was indicted. After six years, prosecutors could not prove that Bill and Hillary Clinton's Whitewater real estate venture involved any criminal behavior or attempt to conceal evidence.

Here is a who's who of the convicted and the pardoned.

BILL MARSH

Iran-Contra

Jose R. Lopez/The New York Times

The Reagan administration sold arms to Iran in secret, using proceeds to finance Nicaraguan rebels; 14 were charged and 11 convicted of crimes like fraud and obstruction, including John M. Poindexter, above. Only Thomas G. Clines was imprisoned. Shortly before leaving office, President George H. W. Bush pardoned six of those involved.

GUILTY

John M. Poindexter	National Security Adviser
Oliver L. North	National Security Council staff

Poindexter and North charges thrown out on appeal.

Richard V. Secord	Air Force major general
Thomas G. Clines	C.I.A. agent, businessman
Carl R. Channell	Businessman
Albert Hakim	Businessman
Richard R. Miller	Businessman

GUILTY AND PARDONED

Elliott Abrams	Assistant Secretary of State
Robert C. McFarlane	National Security Adviser
Clair E. George	Head of C.I.A. clandestine services
Alan D. Fiers Jr.	Head of C.I.A. Central American Task Force

PRE-TRIAL PARDONS

Caspar W. Weinberger	Defense Secretary
Duane R. Clarridge	C.I.A. chief of European operations

Lt. Col. Oliver L. North, left, and Brendan V. Sullivan Jr., his attorney.

Lana Harris/Associated Press

Ray Stubblebine/Associated Press

Former Attorney General John N. Mitchell, on trial for criminal conspiracy, reads about more Watergate indictments on March 7, 1973.

Watergate

A bungled 1972 burglary at the Democratic National Committee's office in the Watergate complex exposed a White House apparatus of dirty tricks, law-breaking and cover-up. Two years later, President Richard M. Nixon, facing impeachment, resigned. President Gerald R. Ford pardoned him of any wrongdoing a month later.

A total of 69 people were charged with crimes; 48 people and 20 corporations pleaded guilty.

SOME OF THOSE GUILTY IN COVER-UP

John N. Mitchell	Attorney general, Nixon re-election committee head
John W. Dean	White House counsel
John D. Ehrlichman	Domestic adviser
H. R. Haldeman	White House chief of staff
Fred C. LaRue	Nixon re-election committee deputy
Jeb S. Magruder	Nixon re-election committee official
Robert C. Mardian	Nixon re-election committee lawyer, former deputy attorney general

SOME OF THOSE GUILTY IN BREAK-INS

Charles W. Colson	White House aide
G. Gordon Liddy	White House aide, counsel to Nixon re-election committee
E. Howard Hunt	White House aide
Bernard L. Barker	D.N.C. burglar
Virgilio Gonzales	D.N.C. burglar
Eugenio Martinez	D.N.C. burglar
James W. McCord Jr.	D.N.C. burglar
Frank Sturgis	D.N.C. burglar

All of the above were imprisoned except for Mardian, whose conviction was overturned on appeal.

John D. Ehrlichman testifies and far right H. R. Haldeman faces the press.

Photographs by Associated Press

Sources: New York Times archives; Associated Press; Final Report of the Independent Counsel for Iran-contra Matters

October 2005, The New York Times

FIGURE 8.1

Scandals Reach the White House

One of the concerns of the Anti-Federalists was that corruption would seep into the executive branch—and because presidents are vested with law enforcement powers, it would go unchecked. This *New York Times* figure highlights two scandals: the Iran Contra Affair and Watergate. Since then, special prosecutors have taken aim at people tied to the executive office more than 20 times. What do all of these scandals say about presidential powers, and the ability to check corruption in the White House?

Teddy Roosevelt believed that presidents should use their position to articulate values, offer policy alternatives, and challenge accepted wisdom. That is to say, presidents should lead public opinion, rather than simply follow it. But what if this "bullish" advocacy leads to a divided public? Should presidents be responsible for finding compromises and common ground?

MODELS OF PRESIDENTIAL POWER

As we saw in ⬤L⬤I⬤N⬤K *Chapter 2, pages 60–65*, the framers of our system believed that Congress would be the primary branch of government. And that was precisely what occurred during the first century of our nation's history. Presidents did not dominate the federal government for most of the nineteenth century; they seemed quite willing to follow Congress. There were, of course, strong presidents, such as George Washington, Thomas Jefferson, Andrew Jackson, and Abraham Lincoln, but they were exceptions to the rule, and their powers sprang from extraordinary circumstances.

There were a number of reasons why it made sense that the presidency was not at the center of nineteenth-century American government.

First, the national economy still centered on agriculture; aggressive supervision and guidance of economic matters was not as important during this time as it would be after industrialization and urbanization took hold, as they did by the 1890s.

Second, the United States was not a central player in world affairs. It was not until the twentieth century that the United States became a world power, involved in military, diplomatic, and economic activities across the globe.

Finally, nineteenth-century political campaigning was party-centered, with less emphasis on presidential candidates and more attention to party platforms and the entire "ticket"—the slate of party candidates, most of whom were running for legislative seats.

On top of this was the general belief among presidents themselves that they should not be at the center of government. Most nineteenth-century presidents—and a few twentieth-century ones too—held closely to the idea that presidents are limited to the powers *explicitly* stated in the Constitution. Presidents should not go beyond those constitutional powers or the additional powers explicitly granted to the executive branch by Congress in the years since the Constitution was written. This attitude ensured that presidents would take a passive approach to presidential powers, and it placed the executive branch in a more acquiescent position.

This view of executive power, however, had begun to erode by the end of the nineteenth century. This was due in part to changing economic and geopolitical conditions. The nation's economy was shifting from farm-based to industrial, and our position in global affairs was expanding. Moreover—and perhaps most significant—some the men who occupied the White House after 1901 transformed the job of the president.

Most historians agree that the first truly assertive president who did not confront extraordinary circumstances was Theodore Roosevelt (1901–1909). Before becoming president, Roosevelt had been a vigorous reform-minded governor of New York. There he learned the power of shaping public opinion and using the support of the public to push his reform agenda through the state legislature. As president, he took the same route, transforming the office into a unique opportunity to preach to and inspire a "national congregation." It was becoming clear that by speaking out on controversial issues, the president could shape public opinion and direct the policy process. And TR, as the press called Roosevelt, was exceedingly good at it. According to one historian, "As a master of political theater with an instinctive understanding of how to dramatize himself and the policies he favored, TR was our first modern media president, and a brilliant huckster."[10]

pathways past and present

THEODORE ROOSEVELT AND THE BULLY PULPIT

Theodore Roosevelt (1858–1919), the twenty-sixth president, has gone down in history as one of our nation's greatest leaders. He was known for many things, not the least of which was his fame for having the teddy bear named after him. (By the way, he hated being called Teddy.) But Roosevelt has also been known as a

▶ **How did FDR get**
people to accept his idea
of a strong president?

bully pulpit
the public platform from which the president can urge people to support certain causes and "preach to the national congregation."

modern presidency
a political system in which the president is the central figure and participates actively in both foreign and domestic policy.

progressive, a pragmatist, a modernizer, the organizer of the cavalry unit called the Rough Riders, and a rousing orator. During his time in office (1901–1909), Roosevelt reformed the presidency, setting a precedent by traveling more extensively throughout the United States than any other previous chief executive, giving speeches everywhere he went. For Roosevelt, the presidency was a place from which he could influence the minds of the American people. He used what he called this **bully pulpit** to create a community, to articulate what he thought should be society's values, to offer policy alternatives, and to challenge the accepted wisdom of the day.[11] Roosevelt was one of the first presidents to understand that the pathway to shape policy begins with shaping public opinion. ◼

Roosevelt held firmly to a new view of presidential powers, one with no restrictions on presidential authority except those that are strictly *forbidden* in the Constitution. This perspective reversed the earlier model: Instead of using only the powers expressly granted, Roosevelt believed that *all* was possible *except* what was prohibited. This was especially true, he argued, when the good of the nation was at stake. Looking back on his presidency, TR boasted, "I did not usurp power, but I did greatly broaden the use of executive power. . . . I acted for the common well-being of our people . . . in whatever manner was necessary, unless prevented by direct constitutional or legislative prohibition."[12]

Not all the presidents who came after Roosevelt shared his activist views of presidential power. For example, his successor, William Howard Taft (1909–1913), took a more passive view of the presidency. But activism returned to the White House with Woodrow Wilson, the twenty-eighth president (1913–1921). Wilson was very much a stewardship-model president. He believed that the president should lead not only in national politics but also in international relations. Following World War I, Wilson set his sights on creating an international body to settle disputes between nations, which he called the League of Nations and which he unsuccessfully tried to have the United States join. (The League was the predecessor of the United Nations, which the United States would help form at the end of World War II.) Wilson's efforts have not been lost on historians such as Robert Dallek, who wrote, "No vision in twentieth-century presidential politics has inspired greater hope of human advance or has done more to secure a president's reputation as a great leader than Wilson's peace program of 1918–1919."[13] But like Theodore Roosevelt, Wilson was followed in office by successors who followed the Whig model by deferring to congressional leadership: Warren G. Harding (1921–1923), Calvin Coolidge (1923–1929), and to a lesser extent, Herbert Hoover (1929–1933).

▶ **How did FDR get people to accept his idea of a strong president?** The election to the presidency in 1932 of Franklin Delano Roosevelt shattered the restrained approach to the presidency and ushered in what many historians would describe as the **modern presidency.** Roosevelt—a distant cousin of TR and like him a former governor of New York—ran for the White House at the depths of the Great Depression. He swept into the presidency on a wave of public anger, frustration, fear, and perceived weakness of his predecessor, Herbert Hoover. Within a day of being sworn in, FDR took charge of the federal government. With panicked depositors withdrawing their savings from bank accounts (which at the time were not insured) and thus threatening the country's banking system with collapse, his first move was to declare a national bank holiday—something that most people doubted he had the legal authority to do. Legally or not, Roosevelt ordered every bank in the country temporarily closed until federal inspectors could go through its books and declare it sound, thus reassuring depositors. Then, with equally dubious legality, he banned the buying and selling of gold and halted the practice of linking the value of the dollar to the price of gold. Next, he sent Congress an emergency banking reform bill, which the House passed in thirty-eight minutes and the Senate accepted with very little debate that same night. This was just the beginning of a comprehensive package of measures designed to pull the nation out of the economic crisis. During the Hundred Days, as it was called, Roosevelt submitted to Congress a stream of proposed reform measures, all of which were quickly enacted into law. Roosevelt demanded "action—and action now." The New Deal, the name he gave to his series of programs and initiatives that transformed the national government, gave birth to the welfare state and shaped the modern presidency.[14]

Today, there no longer seems to be any question regarding the proactive role of the executive branch. Presidents are expected to lead the nation. They must come up with innovative solutions to our problems, give aid and comfort to American citizens in times of need, maintain a healthy and growing economy, and protect our nation from foreign and domestic threats. In times of peace and prosperity, we congratulate the president (who expects to be rewarded in the polls and at the ballot box), and in bad times, we place the blame squarely on the White House. Thus this transformation has presented presidents with a double-edged sword, but there is little question that the stewardship model, first articulated by Theodore Roosevelt, guides the contemporary presidency. Presidents have no choice but to lead—or else stand condemned as failures.

▶ **The Constitution didn't even mention a Cabinet, did it?**

cabinet
a group of presidential advisers, primarily the secretaries of federal departments.

TABLE 8.2
Departments of the United States Cabinet

DEPARTMENT	CREATED	RESPONSIBILITIES
State	1789	Create foreign policies and treaties
Treasury	1789	Coin money, regulate national banks, and collect income taxes
Defense	1789, 1947	Security and defense
Interior	1849	Maintain national parks and natural resources
Agriculture	1862	Protect farmland, nature, and wildlife; provide resources to rural and low-income families; ensure agricultural products are safe for consumers
Justice	1789	Ensure justice and public safety by enforcing the law
Commerce	1903	Promote economic stability, growth, and international trade
Labor	1913	Protect the rights of working citizens and retirees; monitor changes in employment and economic settings
Health and Human Services	1953	Promote research; provide immunizations and health care to low-income families; assure safety of food and drugs
Housing and Urban Development	1965	Guarantee everyone a right to affordable housing; enhance communities and increase the number of homeowners
Transportation	1966	Provide an efficient and safe transportation system that meets the needs of the American people
Energy	1977	Provide reliable energy and promote science while protecting the environment and national and economic securities
Education	1979	Ensure that all citizens can obtain a quality education
Veterans Affairs	1989	Provide support for the nation's veterans
Homeland Security	2002	Protect the United States from threats

SOURCE: www.whitehouse.gov, Cabinet websites

Presidents have always surrounded themselves with policy advisers, especially as the powers and duties of the executive branch broadened with FDR's administration. One source of support comes from the cabinet. Why have the number of cabinet positions increased over time?

INSTITUTIONAL CHANGES

Along with changes regarding the role of the chief executive in the federal government have come changes within the institution of the presidency. We refer here to the support staff and various offices and agencies designed to help the president succeed, as well as the changing role of the vice president.

▶ **The Constitution didn't even mention a Cabinet, did it?**
THE CABINET   Since the very beginning, presidents have relied on their staff. The framers of the Constitution rejected the idea of creating any type of council of presidential advisers, but once in office, Washington immediately realized that specific executive departments should handle the responsibilities of the federal gov-

ernment. The people who took charge of these departments became the president's **cabinet** (see Table 8.2). The cabinet consists of the secretaries of the major departments of the bureaucracy on whom the president relies heavily to carry out public policy. These officials are appointed by the president and are confirmed by the Senate. They can be removed at the president's will without the consent of the Senate. Unlike in parliamentary systems, members of the cabinet cannot also be members of Congress: The Constitution dictates that no one can hold more than one post in the federal government at the same time.

In Washington's administration, there were originally three executive agencies and hence three cabinet members: secretary of state (Thomas Jefferson), to handle foreign affairs; secretary of the

▶ **So many offices and boards!**
Are they all necessary?

inner cabinet
the advisers considered most important to the president—usually the secretaries of the departments of State, Defense, Treasury, and Justice.

Executive Office of the President (EOP)
a group of presidential staff agencies that provides the president with help and advice.

National Security Council (NSC)
an organization within the EOP to advise the president on foreign and domestic military policies related to national security.

national security adviser
the chief adviser to the president on national security matters; a lead member of the National Security Council.

TABLE 8.3
Executive Office of the President in 2006

Council of Economic Advisers
Council of Environmental Quality
Domestic Policy Council
National Economic Council
National Security Council
Office of Administration
Office of Faith-Based and Community Initiatives
Office of Management and Budget
Office of National AIDS Policy
Office of National Drug Control Policy
Office of Science & Technology Policy
Office of the United States Trade Representative
President's Critical Infrastructure Protection Board
President's Foreign Intelligence Advisory Board
USA Freedom Corps
White House Military Office

---

treasury (Alexander Hamilton); attorney general (John Marshall); and secretary of war (Henry Knox), in charge of the U.S. Army. In later administrations, a secretary of the navy was added, and after that, secretaries of the interior, commerce, agriculture, labor, and other departments. Some recent presidents expanded their cabinet without creating new departments. Jimmy Carter pushed Congress to create the Department of Education. Following the terrorist attacks of September 11, 2001, George W. Bush and Congress created a new cabinet-level agency, the Office of Homeland Security, soon transformed into the Department of Homeland Security under its first secretary, former Pennsylvania governor Tom Ridge (see LINK *Chapter 9, pages 345–346*). After the intelligence reform initiative was passed in the fall of 2004, Bush also added to his cabinet the director of intelligence.

Different presidents have used their cabinet in different ways. Some, such as Andrew Jackson, Dwight D. Eisenhower, Gerald Ford, and Jimmy Carter, staffed their cabinets with their closest advisers and allies. Other presidents have kept their cabinet at arm's length, consulting with members only for routine matters or for policy concerns within their particular area. John Kennedy once commented, "Cabinet meetings are simply useless. . . . Why should the Postmaster General sit there and listen to a discussion of the problems of Laos?"[15] Bill Clinton rarely spoke directly with many of his cabinet officers, and Ronald Reagan once mistook his secretary of urban affairs for another official when they were later introduced. Furthermore, most presidents informally establish an "inner" and "outer" cabinet, the former being the most important secretaries, usually those representing the departments of State, Defense, Treasury, and Justice. Members of the **inner cabinet** have more access to the president and are considered closer advisers.

Richard M. Nixon, who in his personal style relished secrecy and intrigue, is a classic example of a president pushing a key cabinet member into the shadow. Nixon formulated his foreign policy—including his conduct of the Vietnam War, his peace negotiations with North Vietnam, and his decision to seek normalized relations with the communist government of mainland China—in consultation with Henry Kissinger, his national security adviser, while keeping his secretary of state, William Rogers, completely in the dark. Kissinger even flew to Beijing in secret to begin negotiations with China's leader Mao Zedong. Only in his second term did Nixon actually appoint Kissinger as secretary of state.

EXECUTIVE OFFICE OF THE PRESIDENT Before Franklin Roosevelt, all presidents had a handful of clerks and personal assistants. A few nineteenth-century presidents also relied on informal input from a trusted circle of advisers—for example, the political cronies whom Andrew Jackson named his "kitchen cabinet," who were not part of his official cabinet. But as the role of the president in developing and carrying out federal programs expanded, so did the number of his personal advisers. FDR needed lots of experts, a great deal of information, and more staff—and pushed hard for institutional changes. The greatest single leap in this direction was the creation of the **Executive Office of the President (EOP)** in 1939. An act of Congress established a number of groups of advisers under the broad heading of the EOP, including the White House staff, the Bureau of the Budget, and the Office of Personnel Management. Through the years, new divisions were created, including the National Security Council, the Council of Economic Advisers, and the Office of Management and Budget. In George W. Bush's administration, the EOP consists of many offices, each with a group of members and a large support staff (see Table 8.3).

Office of Management and Budget (OMB)
the office that presidents use to better understand and control policies related to the financial operation of the government.

Council of Economic Advisers (CEA)
a group of economists within the EOP appointed by the president to provide advice on economic policy.

what **YOU** can do!

Why not learn about the backgrounds of some of the members of George Bush's cabinet? Go to the White House home page and spend a few minutes reading. It's at **http://www.whitehouse.gov/government/cabinet.html**

▶ **So many offices and boards! Are they all necessary?** Each component of the EOP is important, but some have proved more significant than others. The **National Security Council (NSC)** was established in 1947, and although its membership varies from administration to administration, it always includes the vice president and the secretaries of defense and state. The job of the NSC is to provide the president with information and advice on all matters concerning national security, including foreign and domestic threats. One of the key players of this group is the **national security adviser.** This person is appointed by the president without confirmation and is not officially connected with the Department of State or Department of Defense. As such, he or she is expected to give the president independent, unbiased advice on important national security matters. The **Office of Management and Budget (OMB)** has a number of sweeping responsibilities, including preparing the president's annual national budget proposal, monitoring the performance of federal agencies, and overseeing regulatory proposals. The **Council of Economic Advisers (CEA),** established in 1946, is led by three members—usually eminent economists—who are appointed by the president and confirmed by the Senate. Its duties include assisting the president in preparing an annual economic report to Congress, gathering timely information concerning economic developments and trends, evaluating the economic impact of various federal programs and activities, developing and recommending economic policies that boost the nation's economy, and making recommendations on economy-related policies and legislation.

One of the best known national security advisors, and one who still advises presidents from time to time, is Henry Kissinger. Kissinger advised President Nixon during the Vietnam War, from 1969 until its end, in 1974. To what extent do you think presidents should depend on advisers like Kissinger, who aren't elected and don't answer to the people?

pathways of action

FDR TAKES CHARGE!

When Franklin D. Roosevelt began his presidency in 1933, voters were looking for bold leadership and dramatic changes. Understanding his mandate, Roosevelt rolled up his sleeves and took the lead in redirecting the federal government. In doing so, he forever transformed the nature of the presidency. Many of the ideas for his New Deal programs came from a group of advisers whom he called his "Brain Trust," some of them college professors or other intellectuals. Roosevelt's advisers and cabinet members did not always agree with one another—sometimes, in

One of FDR's first acts in 1938 was the Energy Conservation Work (ECW) Act, more commonly known as the Civilian Conservation Corps. As he said, with this act he brought together two wasted resources, unemployed young men and the land, in an effort to save both. The Corps planted 3 billion trees in its 10 years of existence. If similar conditions existed today, what kinds of programs might help reduce unemployment?

fact, their ideas were flatly contradictory—but in the crisis, FDR was willing to try anything that seemed as if it might work. In fact, his leadership style included always listening to advice from different viewpoints, always making the final decision himself, and always keeping his options open to try something else.

A partial list of Roosevelt's policy achievements included the Federal Deposit Insurance Corporation (FDIC), which insured savings deposits to prevent future banking crises; the Securities and Exchange Commission (SEC), which protects investors from fraudulent stock market practices; the Wagner Act of 1935, which strengthened the organizing power of labor unions; and several measures designed to help homeowners finance mortgages and keep their homes. Maximum work hours and minimum wages were also set in certain industries in 1938. The most far-reaching of all the New Deal programs was **Social Security,** enacted in 1935 and expanded in 1939, which provided old-age and widows' benefits, unemployment compensation, disability insurance, and welfare programs for mothers with dependent children. (Medicare and Medicaid were added to Social Security in 1964.) ▧

Along with the expansion of presidential responsibilities has come a rapid growth in the president's personal staff. Today, the White House staff is a critical part of the Executive Office of the President. As you might expect, FDR expanded his personal staff significantly, to an average of 47. This number grew to 200 under Harry Truman and to 555 under Nixon. When Ronald Reagan left office, some 600 full-time employees had been working for him. These days, the number of White House staffers hovers around

500. The most important of the president's personal staff assistants is the **chief of staff.** Presidents have used their chiefs of staff differently; some have been granted more control and autonomy than others. Generally speaking, the chief of staff is especially close to the president and oversees all that the president might do on a typical workday, including who is allowed to meet the chief executive, what documents the president reads, and even what issues take up the president's time. Needless to say, this gatekeeping role makes the chief of staff one of the most important figures not only in the executive branch but also in the entire federal government.

RAMIFICATIONS OF STAFFING CHANGES   Many observers of the American presidency have noted that the nature of the office has been transformed by the dramatic expansion of the presidential staff. The modern presidency is no longer what it originally was—a one-person job. Today it is a massive network of offices, staff, and advisers, requiring a complex organizational chart to keep track of duties and responsibilities. This change broadened presidential powers because this massive network of staff has allowed presidents to be central to the policy process. Scholars now use the term **institutional presidency** to describe the burgeoning responsibilities and scope of presidential powers. Some suggest that the massive expansion of support staff has tipped the balance of power between the branches. It is little wonder, some would argue, that the president is now at the center of the federal government and that Congress has, in some respects, taken a back seat. The expansion of staff coincided with the changing perspective of presidential powers; some observers argue that this expansion played a key role in this change. It is true that over the years, congressional staffs have also increased, but not nearly at the pace of those in the executive branch. Others also point out that the duties and responsibilities of modern presidents have greatly expanded, making all this support necessary. And as you will see when we discuss the many jobs of the president, the list is indeed quite long. So perhaps, given these new obligations, the scales of power between the two branches have not been thrown drastically off balance.

A second ramification has been growing internal conflict—that is, the balance of power *within* the executive branch seems to be shifting. It is true, as we've seen, that some recent presidents have relied on their cabinet officers more than others. But in the past, cabinet secretaries and other policy experts played a key role in the executive branch. The president could always reject their advice, but it was taken for granted that they would have the president's ear—that they would provide counsel on important issues. This has been changing

Social Security
a federal program started in 1935 that taxes wages and salaries to pay for retirement benefits, disability insurance, and hospital insurance.

chief of staff
the highest-ranking member of the EOP and hence the most important of the president's advisers.

institutional presidency
a massive network of staff, analysts, and advisers with the president as its head.

in recent decades. As presidents surrounded themselves with White House staff, who were essentially *political* experts—with the goal of helping their boss win reelection, boost his poll ratings, and build his historical legacy—policy advisers have been pushed to the side.

The battle for the president's ear has become intense, and most analysts agree that the political experts are winning over the "policy wonks." President George W. Bush's right-hand adviser, Karl Rove, is known not for his policy prowess but for his *political* genius. Of course, politics and policy merge on any given issue, but some observers speculate that as political considerations rise to the top, policy initiatives will get little attention. Moreover, this will narrow the president's perspective on policy choices (sometimes the "right" policies are often unpopular) and will inhibit effective and responsive bureaucratic performance.[16] Criticism of George W. Bush's White House on just such grounds mounted after his administration's bungled response when Hurricane Katrina devastated New Orleans and the Gulf Coast in 2005.

Finally, when it comes to shaping the outcome of government, the explosion of executive branch staff has made the direct lobbying pathway more complex. On the one hand, we might say that the number of people to talk to has increased, quite similar to what we saw in ⓛⓘⓝⓚ *Chapter 7, pages 265–270*, in the case of Congress. Persuading a staffer close to the president can often be an effective means of shaping public policy. On the other hand, direct access to the president has become quite difficult. In an effort to protect their boss, White House aides may well be transforming the connection between the president and the people.

pathways profile

CONDOLEEZZA RICE, SECRETARY OF STATE AND POLITICAL SCIENTIST

Born in segregated Birmingham, Alabama, in 1954, Condoleezza Rice is the daughter of John Wesley Rice, who was a school guidance counselor and Presbyterian minister, and Angelena Rice, a schoolteacher. She excelled in her studies and became an outstanding pianist at an early age. She received a bachelor of arts degree in political science from the University of Denver in 1974 and within a year had received a master of arts degree from the University of Notre Dame. Rice then attended the University of Denver, where she received a Ph.D. in international studies in 1981—the same year she became a faculty member in

Two of George Bush's closest advisors are Karl Rove (above) and Secretary of State Condoleezza Rice (below). Rove is known as a brilliant political strategist, while Rice is an expert in foreign policy. One of the growing conflicts in the White House is access to the president. In which situations might the interests of policy conflict with those of political advisors?

▶ **What does the Vice President do? Does he just wait and see if the President gets sick or dies?**

Dick Cheney has emerged as one of the most influential vice presidents in American history. Does it make sense to have a powerful vice president? Has the job of president perhaps gotten too difficult for one person? What would you suggest as a solution?

Photo: Stephen Crowley/The New York Times

the Political Science Department at Stanford University and then provost at the stunningly young age of 39.

Having worked briefly in George H. W. Bush's administration, Rice in 1999 became a key foreign policy adviser to his son, George W. Bush, as he prepared for his run for the White House. After his election, she was named national security adviser, a key adviser to the president, and became a central figure in shaping the nation's foreign policy after the terrorist attacks on September 11, 2001. This included, among other things, helping to craft the Iraqi war plan. On January 26, 2005, Rice was named secretary of state, becoming the second woman and the first African American woman in U.S. history to hold that post.

Rice's future is bright. Although she has suggested that she will return to academia after leaving the White House, there has been much speculation about her as a candidate for the presidency. Although she is a controversial figure due to her steadfast support of George W. Bush's decision to invade Iraq, few people question Rice's qualifications or her intelligence. ▪

THE CHANGING ROLE OF THE VICE PRESIDENT

▶ **What does the Vice President do? Does he just wait and see if the President gets sick or dies?** Throughout most of American history, the vice presidency was considered an insignificant office. Benjamin Franklin once quipped that the vice president should be addressed as "your Superfluous Excellency."[17] Thomas Marshall, the vice president under Woodrow Wilson, once told a story of two brothers: "One ran away to sea; the other was elected vice president. And nothing was heard of either of them again."[18] In 1848, Senator Daniel Webster—who as one of his party's most influential figures had long hoped to gain the presidency—declined the vice presidential place on the Whig Party ticket. "I do not propose to be buried until I am dead," he snorted.[19] John Nance Garner, FDR's first vice president and a former speaker of the House, is quoted as saying that the vice presidency is "not worth a pitcher of warm spit."[20]

When Lyndon Johnson was asked by John Kennedy to be his running mate, the powerful Texas senator was reluctant to accept. Like Webster, LBJ worried about his political future. The job of vice president was mostly ceremonial—attending the funerals of

Presidents have learned that charisma can be used to advance their policy agenda, and one of the very best at this was John F. Kennedy. It is probably not a coincidence that Kennedy was also one of the first presidents to understand the power of television. Are leaders who lack charisma destined to fail? Do you think a politician's television persona really matters?

dignitaries, dedicating bridges and parks, and sitting in the Senate on special occasions—and as majority leader of the Senate, Johnson stood at the hub of the federal government. But he was convinced by friends and colleagues to take the place on the ticket because he would be a "heartbeat away from the presidency." And as fate would have it, Johnson did become president on November 22, 1963, upon the assassination of JFK. Indeed, the job of vice president has always been, first and foremost, to stand ready. Nine times in American history, a vice president has assumed the presidency: Those VPs were John Tyler, Millard Fillmore, Andrew Johnson, Chester Arthur, Theodore Roosevelt, Calvin Coolidge, Harry Truman, Lyndon Johnson, and Gerald Ford.

With the advent of the Cold War after 1945 and the proliferation of nuclear weapons, concerns grew about the vice president's readiness to take the helm at a moment's notice, fully abreast of world and military developments.[21] Truman, who became president on FDR's sudden death in April 1945, had been kept in the dark about the American project to build an atomic bomb, nor had he been fully apprised of the rapidly mounting tension between the United States and its ally, the Soviet Union, as World War II drew to its close. Truman had to learn everything "on the job"; fortunately for him and the nation, he was a man of intelligence and strong character who ranks as one of the country's near-great presidents. But it was a close call. Put a bit differently, by the 1950s, many Americans believed that there should be no learning curve for new presidents in an age of intercontinental ballistic nuclear missiles. Dwight Eisenhower remarked, "Even if Mr. Nixon (his vice president) and I were not good friends, I would still have him in every important conference of government, so that if the Grim Reaper [death] would find it time to remove me from the scene, he is ready to slip in without any interruption."[22] Thus began a move toward bringing vice presidents into the inner circle.

Consequently, in recent decades, the job of vice president has changed. Walter Mondale had full access to President Carter and became a trusted adviser on all important matters. Al Gore, Bill Clinton's vice president for eight years, was given numerous important responsibilities and also had full access to the president, including weekly one-on-one lunch meetings. Gore was very much in the inner circle, "one of three or four people whose advice Clinton sought on virtually every important matter."[23] And Dick Cheney has played so powerful a role in the Bush administration

that Democrats often suggest that he actually runs the show. Along with this changing role of vice presidents has come an equally significant growth of personal staff and resources.

Ultimately, of course, the power of the vice president is only what the president chooses to allow the occupant of that office to have. But the role of the vice president has come a long way in recent years.

INFORMAL POWERS OF THE PRESIDENT

In 1960, the political scientist Richard Neustadt published an important book called *Presidential Power*. It suggested that the formal powers of the presidency, as outlined in the Constitution, were rather minor: They amounted to little more than a clerkship, by which the occupant of the White House is in the position to provide services to others in the federal government.[24] Yet if we look beyond the formal powers to the *informal* powers, there is a great deal at the president's disposal. Presidential power, Neustadt argued, is the power to persuade. The real powers of any president are to use a combination of personality and political skills to lobby members of Congress. A president who feels strongly about a program or a policy initiative can tap into the many informal tools that the office makes possible, including the office's prestige,

▶ **What are the roles** of first ladies?

going public
appealing directly to the people to garner support for presidential initiatives.

First Lady Laura Bush pays a visit to U.S. military troops inside the Dragon Chow Hall at Bagram Air Base in Kabul, Afghanistan, March 30, 2005. The first lady is on a five-hour surprise visit to Afghanistan and will return home after sharing dinner with the troops. What message does her presence in Iraq carry to the troops?

charm, the fear of retribution, the need of a special favor, and bargaining skills. Neustadt's book was very much a prescription—a guide for presidents to understand the true breadth of their powers. Many took heed. Both John Kennedy and Bill Clinton, for example, were said to have kept *Presidential Power* next to his bed and to have read from it each night.

The ability (and necessity) to persuade has more or less always been central to a successful president. As president, Thomas Jefferson was a master of this tactic, holding dinner parties at which matters of state were informally discussed and decided by his cabinet and key members of Congress. A new route to persuasion opened up in the twentieth century and was used skillfully by Theodore Roosevelt, much to the benefit of presidential power. Instead of persuading lawmakers face to face, presidents can now use the bully pulpit to sway public opinion. With the successive development of radio and television, presidents have had widening opportunities to use modern communications to speak directly to the public. The process is called **going public.** Presidents have always been keenly aware of public opinion and promoted themselves and their policies in a number of ways, including giving speeches, doing interviews with members of the press, writing articles, and distributing pamphlets. But by the dawn of mass communications technology, especially the advent of television, presidents began to realize the weight of personal appeals. Winning the public's hearts and minds was found to be even more potent than persuading a few members of Congress. Franklin D. Roosevelt, who broadcast "fireside chats" on the radio, first showed how a president could establish a deep personal bond with the American people. John F. Kennedy used television to build an image that was both glamorous and admired. Ronald Reagan, dubbed "The Great Communicator" by the press, was especially skillful at connecting with the public on television, due in no small measure to his years of training as an actor—and also to his admiration for FDR. Going public is clearly important, as it helps presidents advance their policy goals. As suggested by Figure 8.2, some presidents have been more successful gathering support than others. Also, just because the president is supported by the public does not mean it will stay that way, as events can make ratings drop quickly. Moreover, going public can be risky: Members of Congress often feel neglected when presidents ignore them and appeal directly to the public.

what YOU can do!

New technologies also allow students of the presidency to see and hear some of the earlier occupants of the White House. Would you like to listen to Franklin D. Roosevelt's inaugural address or hear John Kennedy tell us why we needed to go to the moon? How do these two speeches differ from what you hear today? Many great presidential speeches are only a click away. Try logging on to the American Presidency Project (**http://www.presidency.ucsb.edu**) History and Politics Out Loud (**http://www.hpol.org**) or Great American Speeches (**http://www.pbs. org/greatspeeches**)

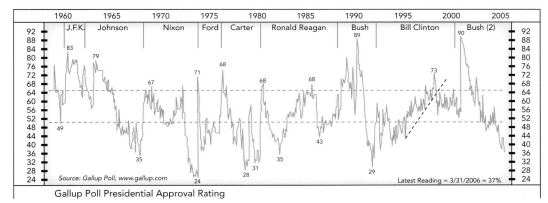

Gallup Poll Presidential Approval Rating

Source: Gallup Poll, www.gallup.com

Copyright © 1960–2005 The Gallup Organization.

FIGURE 8.2

The Ups and Downs of Presidential Approval Ratings

Presidents may benefit or suffer from the fickle winds of public opinion. But on closer inspection we see a pattern where most presidents begin their term of office with high approval ratings, and end their stay with lagging support. Are presidents bound to fail in the eyes of the public? What made Gerald Ford and Bill Clinton the exceptions?

FIRST LADIES

▶ **What are the roles of first ladies?** Another critically important source of presidential power has been first ladies. From Martha Washington to Laura Bush, these women have provided informal advice, advocated significant policy reform, undertaken a host of symbolic functions (such as attending public events), and lobbied lawmakers and foreign dignitaries to help promote their own agendas as well as those of their husbands.

During most of our nation's history, first ladies limited their political work to informal, behind-the-scenes activities. For instance, the profound role played by Abigail Adams in helping her husband John maintain a cool head during his entire political career—and especially his presidency—is well documented. Among much else, Abigail Adams was an early feminist who reminded her husband to "remember the ladies." She was a central political figure during these early days of our republic, even though much of her work was never known to the larger public. Another critically important behind-the-scenes first lady was Edith Bolling Galt Wilson. Her husband, Woodrow, suffered a stroke and was left partly paralyzed in 1919. He was incapacitated for several months, during which time Edith spoke and acted on his behalf. She also hand-picked the very few people who would have access to the ailing President Wilson. Her critics called her the "first lady president."

The activities of first ladies became much more public with Eleanor Roosevelt, the wife of Franklin D. Roosevelt. She traveled extensively and spoke on behalf of her husband's New Deal policies, as well as her own concerns (centering mostly on the condition of poor children in America). She also wrote a newspaper column and worked tirelessly for Democratic candidates across the country. After her husband's death, Eleanor Roosevelt became a U.S. delegate to the United Nations, taking a lead on issues related to human rights and world poverty.

Perhaps the most dramatic change to the role of first ladies came about with Hillary Clinton. As a Yale-trained lawyer, Clinton had been a key policy adviser in her husband's administration when he was governor of Arkansas. Among much else, she spearheaded a successful education reform task force and in the process drew a good bit of national media attention. As she and her husband took up residence in the White House, her role as a powerful aide to her husband continued, in a very public way. Upon leaving the White House in 2000, Hillary Clinton was elected U.S. senator from the state of New York. The most recent first lady, Laura Bush, has also been a key player in her husband's administration. Unlike Clinton, however, much of her work has been behind the scenes.

Few people doubt that the role of presidential spouses will evolve in the coming years. As more and more women lead high-profile professional lives, the restricted role of merely providing behind-the-scenes advice and undertaking public ceremonial functions is probably a thing of the past. The real question is, what role will the "first gentleman" perform in the future?

▶ **What happens when a president vetoes a bill?**

1. What were some of the most important institutional changes in expanding presidential powers?

2. In what way is the power to persuade related to the scope of presidential authority?

practicequiz

1. In the nineteenth century, the presidency was not a central force in American government in part because
   a. the men who were presidents at that time were passive and easily forgotten.
   b. there was no mass media to speak of, so presidents had no effective way of getting their agenda out to the broader public.
   c. issues that most compel presidential action, such as the national economy and America's responsibilities in world affairs, had not developed very fully yet.
   d. the Twenty-First Amendment, granting presidents executive privilege, had not yet been ratified.

2. The first president to become a national force through the routine conduct of presidential business was
   a. Theodore Roosevelt.
   b. Calvin Coolidge.
   c. Andrew Jackson.
   d. Woodrow Wilson.

3. Why is the claim that Franklin D. Roosevelt shaped the modern presidency an accurate one?
   a. because he was elected four times
   b. because his approach to the presidency was aggressively proactive
   c. because he was "the great communicator," taking advantage of the latest advance in communication technology, television
   d. because the programs he created as part of the New Deal have never been questioned since

4. The president's cabinet is an expanded form of what is specified in Article II of the Constitution.
   a. true   b. false

Answers: 1-c, 2-a, 3-b, 4-b

The Many Roles of Modern Presidents

Contemporary presidents are called on to perform a staggering number of duties and to play a dizzying variety of roles—and considering the awesome weaponry in the American military arsenal, it is not a mere figure of speech to say that the world's fate is at the president's fingertip. It has been said that no job can prepare you for the presidency and no job is similar. Still, we can break down a modern president's task into several categories or functional roles.

THE PRESIDENT AS CHIEF OF STATE

When George Washington took the helm of the federal government in April 1789, his role in ceremonial events was unclear. On the one hand, everyone understood the importance of ritual and formal events. There would be occasions when the nation would need a leader to perform such functions—addressing Congress, greeting foreign dignitaries, speaking on the nation's behalf during times of celebration and grief, or even meeting ordinary citizens. If the president would not perform these functions, who would? In most political systems throughout the world, both then and now, a monarch or dictator undertakes chief-of-state functions. Would George Washington be kinglike in this regard?

Washington rejected all titles. Vice President John Adams proposed to the Senate that the president be addressed with a dignified title, such as "His High Mightiness," but neither the senators nor Washington himself accepted such an idea, which would have been hated by most Americans of the time. Nor did Washington wear any sort of robe, crown, or military uniform. It was Washington who established two acceptable titles for all future chief executives: "Mr. President" or "Mr. [last name]." In many ways, presidents would be regular citizens.

Still, all presidents perform ceremonial functions. Washington held formal gatherings, called *levees,* at which citizens would line up and be greeted one by one with a grave presidential bow. That, in the late eighteenth century, was expected as a way of investing the presidency with dignity. (But even that seemed too kingly to many Americans, and beginning with President Jefferson, a more informal tone permeated the presidency.) Today we expect presidents to make a telephone call to the winning Super Bowl team, to throw out a baseball at the start of the World Series, and to pardon the White House turkey on Thanksgiving. We also look to presidents for stability, wisdom, and composure during times of crisis. When in 1995 the Murrah Federal Office Building in Oklahoma was bombed, killing 168 people, it was President Clinton who expressed the grief of all Americans at the memorial service. When the nation was shattered and shaken to its core by the terrorist attacks on September 11, 2001, we all turned to George W. Bush to steady the ship, to bring us together, and to help us move on.

Some critics look down on the chief-of-state role, suggesting that these sorts of activities are all fluff. But they are wrong. Any nation our size, and surely any nation as diverse as ours, must come together in good times and in bad. Who else would perform such functions—the speaker of the House or the chief justice of the United States? Whether we live on a dairy farm in Vermont, in the

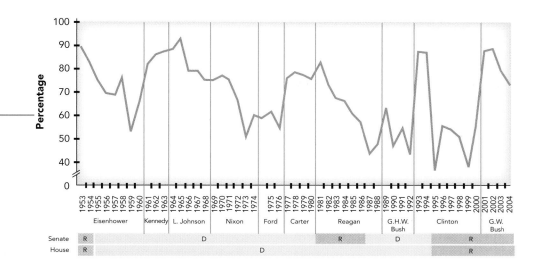

FIGURE 8.3
Congressional Support
for Presidential Initiatives

This figure charts the percentage of presidential initiatives that are approved by Congress. Clearly, some presidents are more successful with the legislature than others. What makes this figure especially interesting is that presidents *can* be successful even when the other party controls Congress. What force do you suppose leads to greater success with Congress, even when the president faces a "hostile" legislature?

SOURCE: Reprinted by permission from Harold Stanley and Richard Niemi, *Vital Statistics on American Politics, 2005–2006* (Washington DC: CQ Press, 2006) www.cqpress.com

suburbs of Los Angeles, or on a beach in North Carolina, we are all Americans. Ceremonial dinners and occasions to toss a baseball out at a special game might seem extraneous, but it is through these and many other unimportant events that our diverse nation becomes one. Moreover, when a president slips in his head-of-state role, the public reacts. When Hurricane Katrina slammed into New Orleans in September 2005, George W. Bush was finishing the last days of his vacation on his ranch. It was only as the breadth of the disaster became obvious, two days later, that Bush traveled to the scene. Bush could have done little to ease the pain of the disaster in the early days, but the fact that he seemed aloof, indifferent to the plight of millions in the Gulf region, took many Americans aback. Where was our leader? Why did it take him days to address the nation? Bush's approval rating dropped sharply within a week.[25]

THE PRESIDENT AS CHIEF LEGISLATOR

The Constitution's Article I states that Congress will undertake legislative functions—the passing of laws and the collecting and distributing of funds. Article II makes the executive branch responsible for implementing the will of the legislative branch. At the same time, in keeping with the design of shared power, presidents are given some legislative authority: the power to veto bills, the ability to recommend measures for consideration, and the duty from time to time to inform Congress as to the "state of the union."

Consistent with the restrained view of presidential powers, occupants of the White House were reluctant to dig deeply into legislative matters during the first 140 years of our nation's history. Presidents believed it their role to wait for Congress to act. In the eight years of his presidency, George Washington expressed an opinion on only five pieces of legislation.[26] Some presidents during this period—especially Andrew Jackson, Abraham Lincoln,

Theodore Roosevelt, and Woodrow Wilson—were deeply immersed in legislative matters, but they were exceptions to the rule. A good estimate is that during this period, only about one-quarter of all significant policy initiatives originated with the executive branch.

This changed in 1933 with the inauguration of Franklin D. Roosevelt. Amid the crisis of the Great Depression, not only did FDR send a stream of measures to Congress for consideration, but he and his aides also plunged into the legislative process with gusto, writing bills and twisting congressional arms to make sure that they passed. No one doubted that he was in charge of making policy during his first two terms, that he was very much the chief legislator.

All presidents since FDR have sought to lead the policy-making process, but some of them have been better at legislative matters than others. Lyndon Johnson was particularly good at "working the legislature." As a former member of the House and especially as the Senate's majority leader, Johnson understood how the system worked, including the incentives that might be most effective with a legislative leader or a rank-and-file member. He was aggressive about getting his way, routinely giving reluctant members of Congress the "Johnson treatment." Jimmy Carter's story was altogether different. Having never worked in Washington or served as a state or local legislator before moving into the White House—his only prior office was one term as governor of Georgia—Carter was simply unfamiliar with how things worked in the national legislature, and in the end, Carter got only modest support from Congress even though his own party (Democratic) controlled both chambers (see Figure 8.3).

▶ **What happens when a president vetoes a bill?**
LEGISLATIVE TOOLS   Presidents have at their disposal a number tools and resources to aid their efforts with the legislature. The

TABLE 8.4
Presidential Vetoes, 1789–2006

	REGULAR VETOES	POCKET VETOES	TOTAL VETOES	VETOES OVERRIDDEN
Washington	2	—	2	—
Madison	5	2	7	—
Monroe	1	—	1	—
Jackson	5	7	12	—
Tyler	6	3	9	1
Polk	2	1	3	—
Pierce	9	—	9	5
Buchanan	4	3	7	—
Lincoln	2	4	6	—
A. Johnson	21	8	29	15
Grant	45	49	94	4
Hayes	12	1	13	1
Arthur	4	8	12	1
Cleveland	304	109	413	2
Harrison	19	25	44	1
Cleveland	43	127	170	5
McKinley	6	36	42	—
T. Roosevelt	42	40	82	1
Taft	30	9	39	1
Wilson	33	11	44	6
Harding	5	1	6	—
Coolidge	20	30	50	4
Hoover	21	16	37	3
F. Roosevelt	372	263	635	9
Truman	180	70	250	12
Eisenhower	73	108	181	2
Kennedy	12	9	21	—
L. Johnson	16	14	30	—
Nixon	26	17	43	7
Ford	48	18	66	12
Carter	13	18	31	2
Reagan	39	39	78	9
G. H. W. Bush	29	17	46	1
Clinton	36	0	36	2
G. W. Bush	1	0	1	0

SOURCES: *Statistical Abstract of the United States, 1986*, p. 235; Senate Library, *Presidential Vetoes* (Washington D.C.: Government Printing Office, 1960), p. 199; From *The Paradoxes of the American Presidency* by Thomas Cronin and Michael A. Genovese. Copyright © 1998 by Oxford University Press, Inc. Used by permission of Oxford University Press, Inc.; updated by authors.

veto
disapproval of a bill or resolution by the president.

veto is critical. Presidents can shape legislation by rejecting measures passed by Congress. Sometimes presidents veto measures on principle, because they strongly disagree with the proposal (such as when George W. Bush vetoed a measure to increase funding for stem cell research) or think it unconstitutional; at other times they may consider the goals laudable but the details wrong. There are two types of vetoes. One approach is to simply send the legislation back to Congress with a message as to why the president disapproves—this is called a **veto message.** The legislation can still become law if two-thirds of both houses of Congress vote to override it. Overrides are very rare; only about 3 percent of all vetoes have been overridden. This makes sense, given that the president's political party is often the majority party in Congress and that presidents are very reluctant to lose face by vetoing bills that are likely to be overridden. If a president fails to act on a piece of legislation within ten days, it becomes law. But if Congress adjourns within the ten days, the president can let the measure die though a pocket veto. Here there is neither a signature nor a veto message. Pocket vetoes have been quite rare, especially on major legislation.

Some modern presidents have been more willing to veto bills than have others, as Table 8.4 suggests. One of the most interesting things about the table is that presidents with a Congress controlled by the same party are not necessarily less prone to using their veto pen than those that confront a hostile legislature controlled by the opposing party.

Table 8.4 is also misleading in a very important way: Actual vetoes are less significant in the legislative process than the *threat* of their use. That is, presidents will often send word to the legislature that if a piece of legislation comes before him, it will be vetoed. Not wanting to be embarrassed by the president or to waste everybody's time, the legislature responds either by not moving on the measure or by crafting a version of the bill that is acceptable to the president. Sometimes the threat is quite public. When Bill Clinton sought to reform the nation's health care system, he picked up a pen during a State of the Union address, waved it back and forth, and declared that if Congress did not send him a bill that covered all children, he would gladly use the pen to veto the bill. Many veto threats are delivered in private, either directly by the president or by presidential aides. It is difficult to know how often the threat of a veto is used, but observers of congressional and presidential dynamics agree on its significance.

The presidential duty to inform Congress of the state of the union each year has become another powerful legislative tool. Rather than regarding this as a chore, presidents now understand

veto message
a document appended to a veto that outlines the rationale for the president's
rejection of the measure.

it as a rare opportunity to set the legislative agenda for the coming year. It is an opportunity to lay out broad principles and to offer concrete measures. Even more important, it is an opportunity not only to speak to the legislature but also—ever since the invention of radio and television—to reach directly into people's living rooms. Most Americans watch the State of the Union address, and presidents use this rare occasion to shape public opinion, which of course goes a long way in persuading legislators (see Figure 8.4 on page 322).

All State of the Union addresses today are important, but some seem more crucial than others. By January 2002, for example, the nation had started to come to grips with the horror of the 9/11 tragedy. But our response to the attack was still unclear. George Bush used the occasion to outline his war on terror and to warn Congress and the nation that it would be a long, expensive endeavor. "Steadfast in our purpose," the president declared, "we now press on. We have known freedom's price. We have shown freedom's power. And in this great conflict, my fellow Americans, we will see freedom's victory." We all understood Bush's intentions and resolve after that important speech. Indeed, the 2002 State of the Union address proved to be the blueprint for the rest of Bush's presidency.

THE PRESIDENT AS CHIEF DIPLOMAT

Although presidential powers might be a bit cloudy in some areas of governance, when it comes to conducting foreign policy, the matter seems clear and long settled. Presidents are in charge of foreign affairs. This is what the framers had in mind, it is strengthened by 200 years of precedent, and it has been confirmed by several Supreme Court decisions. The president is the "sole organ" in conducting foreign affairs, stated the Court in *United States* v. *Curtiss-Wright* (1936), and his powers are "exclusive." Indeed, the president enjoys a freedom from congressional restrictions that "would not be admissible where domestic affairs alone are involved."[27] In other words, Congress should stay out of foreign affairs. Often, however, it refuses to do so.

There are a number of ways in which presidents can conduct foreign policy. Obviously, they can travel around the world, meeting with the leaders of other nations, forging ties and formal alliances. The Constitution states that they can appoint and receive ambassadors. In appointing ambassadors, which the Constitution requires them to do with the advice and consent of the Senate, presidents can choose officials who share their outlook toward a given nation or to foreign affairs more generally. Accepting

This is a caricature of Andrew Jackson as a despotic monarch, probably issued during the fall of 1833. Prior to Jackson, each president issued only a few vetoes, but Jackson issued a whopping 12 vetoes, including a contentious and popular bill to recharter the National Bank. Why did the framers make it possible for one individual to thwart the will of a popularly elected legislature?

The Words That Were Used

Number of times President Bush used the following words or phrases in State of the Union addresses.

	2001 FEB. 27*	2002 JAN. 29	2003 JAN. 28	2004 JAN. 20	2005 FEB. 2
DOMESTIC AFFAIRS					
Compassion(ate)	3	3	4	4	1
Health care	9	1	6	9	3
Medicare	12	1	5	8	
Ownership	1	1		2	1
Retirement	5	3	1	1	11
Social Security	15	2	2	2	18
TAXES AND THE ECONOMY					
Balanced budget	1		1		
Deficit(s)	1	1	1	1	1
Economy	3	4	10	14	11
Jobs	2	11	2	6	4
Surplus(es)	7				
Tax(es)	27	7	11	19	10
TERRORISM AND FOREIGN AFFAIRS					
Afghanistan		13	3	5	3
Al Qaeda		1	8	3	2
Osama bin Laden					
Democracy			1	4	8
Freedom	8	14	5	8	20
Saddam (Hussein)			19	5	2
Iraq/Iraqi(s)		2	22	24	27
Sept. 11		5	3	3	1
Terror/terrorist(s)	1	33	19	19	26
Weapons of mass destruction	1	4	4	3	1

* As a newly-elected president, Bush did not deliver a formal State of the Union address in 2001. His Feb. 27 speech to a joint session of Congress was analogous to the State of the Union, but without the title.

February 2005, Matthew Ericson/The New York Times

FIGURE 8.4

The Words that Bush Used

The Constitution dictates that presidents periodically confer with Congress as to the "state of the Union." Modern presidents have learned that this opportunity to speak directly to the American people can be a powerful tool in shaping the outcome of their policy agenda. What does this figure suggest about George W. Bush's agenda since 9/11?

treaty
a formal agreement between governments.

ambassadors might seem a less significant act, but it can be used as a powerful tool. When presidents "accept" the emissary of another nation, it signifies that the United States recognizes that nation's existence and that its leaders hold power legitimately. For instance, neither Bill Clinton nor George W. Bush recognized the Taliban as the legitimate government of Afghanistan.

Another critically important foreign policy tool is the **treaty,** a formal agreement between the United States and one or more other sovereign nations. The intent of the framers was that the Senate would work closely with the executive branch to negotiate and ratify treaties. This approach did not last long, as George Washington became frustrated with the slow pace of the Senate and the difficulties of arriving at a consensus. From that point onward, presidents have negotiated treaties independently and then asked the Senate to ratify them by the two-thirds margin that the Constitution requires. Given that presidents have usually been of the same party as the majority in the Senate, it should come as no surprise that the Senate has rejected very few treaties. A good many, roughly 150, have been withdrawn because they seemed to lack support. But of the approximately 1,500 that have been sent to the Senate, only 15 have been voted down.

Sometimes more important than treaties are **executive agreements.** The line between executive agreements and treaties is sometimes rather thin, but in general these are less formal agreements, sometimes called "arrangements," between the United States and other nations. Whereas treaties are generally high-profile matters, usually attracting a great deal of media attention, executive agreements are often arranged in secret. They do not require Senate approval, which makes them especially appealing to presidents—particularly if the president confronts a hostile Congress—but the Case Act of 1972 requires the president to inform Congress of executive agreements within sixty days. Presidents may make executive agreements only in areas where they have the power to act, and often they deal with relatively minor concerns, such as tariffs, customs regulations, or postal matters. Yet some presidents have used executive agreements in very important ways. In 1973, President Nixon used an executive agreement to end the American conflict (never a declared war) with North Vietnam and to exchange prisoners of war. Such an agreement was also used in 1981 to form a strategic alliance with Israel. Perhaps not surprisingly given the growing importance and complexity of world affairs, as well as the potential roadblocks to winning Senate approval of treaties, the number of executive agreements made by presidents has increased greatly in the past few decades. Some observers speculate that such agreements, rather than formal treaties, have become the foreign policy tool of choice.

executive agreements
binding commitments between the
United States and other countries agreed
to by the president but, unlike treaties,
not requiring approval by the Senate.

fast-track trade authority
the right of the president to negotiate trade
agreements with other nations, which are
then submitted to Congress for approval or
rejection within a specified time.

The Cold War with the Soviet Union and other communist powers was the primary focus of American foreign policy for all presidents between 1945 and the late 1980s, but that has now changed. Beginning in the 1980s, one of the most important transformations of the modern world has been the growth of global economic interdependence. Since the collapse of communism in the Soviet Union and Eastern Europe in 1989, and paralleling the rapid expansion of Asian economies (especially those of China and India), the management of America's trade relationships has been an expanding aspect of presidential foreign policy responsibilities. This change has created unique challenges for presidents. Opening foreign markets for American goods requires lowering or removing trade restrictions and tariffs on goods imported into the United States. Many imported products are cheaper because they are made by low-wage labor. Consumers want low-priced goods, but labor unions and manufacturers protest the importation of low-cost products, which threaten to close American factories and put Americans out of work.

Viewed from this perspective, China poses a special problem for American policymakers. That huge nation of 1.3 billion people boasts the world's fastest-growing economy and represents a massive new market for American goods. But low-cost imports from China threaten American manufacturing jobs, and many Americans are concerned about human rights violations in China. Moreover, China's rapid economic development complicates the serious global problems of climate change and resource depletion, and as its economy strengthens, China may also become a long-range political and military competitor to the United States.

To manage U.S. economic foreign policy, recent presidents have requested that Congress give them **fast-track trade authority.** First used in 1974, fast-track authority allows presidents to negotiate new trade agreements with other nations, which they then submit to Congress for either approval or rejection. No amendments are allowed, and Congress has ninety legislative days to approve or reject the measure. President George W. Bush signed the most recent measure, the Trade Promotion Authority (TPA), into law in 2002. The State Department strongly endorses this measure on the following grounds:

> TPA will promote freer trade by giving other countries confidence that the agreements they negotiate with the United States will not be subject to subsequent renegotiation. TPA will bring important economic benefits to the United States and its trading partners. This authority will be used to implement trade agreements that will encourage trade and investment, including in environmental goods and services.[28]

Most observers agree that fast-track trade authority, which gives presidents the power to move quickly, is a vital new presidential foreign policy power. But it is not without its critics. Some argue that it is yet another usurpation of legislative power—in other words, another example of how the executive branch has overstepped bounds.

THE PRESIDENT AS COMMANDER IN CHIEF

Article II, Section 2 of the Constitution appoints the president commander in chief of all American military forces. When they take the oath of office, presidents swear that they will "preserve, protect, and defend" our nation. The framers of our system believed it essential that one person be responsible for decisive action during times of crisis—in the event of an invasion, for example, which was a real threat in the late eighteenth century. But as for the oversight of an ongoing conflict or for direction of prolonged military engagements, the Constitution is a bit ambiguous. At the very least, this too is a shared power. That is, the president is commander in chief of the armed forces, but Congress is charged with declaring wars (in Article I, Section 8). Also, Congress has the responsibility to raise and support armies (that is, to raise and allocate funds for military matters).

During the first few decades, the decision to go to war was clearly shared with Congress. In 1803, for example, Thomas Jefferson sent the U.S. Navy to fight the Barbary pirates—North African rulers who were seizing American merchant vessels in the Mediterranean Sea and enslaving their crews unless the United States paid them tribute. But Congress had authorized this attack in advance.[29] Following the War of 1812 (which had been declared by Congress), presidential war powers began to expand. They took a leap forward during the Civil War. Congress was in recess when the southern states seceded at the end of 1860 and in early 1861, as well as when fighting began at Fort Sumter in April 1861, only a few weeks after Lincoln's inauguration. Without congressional authorization, Lincoln called up the state militias, suspended the writ of habeas corpus, and slapped a naval blockade on the rebellious southern states. Critics claimed that Lincoln's acts were dictatorial, but he argued that they were necessary to preserve the Union. His defense of his "doctrine of necessary" is rather compelling:

> [My] oath to preserve the Constitution to the best of my ability imposed upon me the duty of preserving, by every indispensable means, that government. . . . Was it possible to lose the nation and yet preserve the Constitution? By

ABOVE: **All presidents receive high levels of support** from the public and members of the military when hostile actions begin. But history has shown that this support often fades as wars drag on. George W. Bush has vowed to "stay the course" in Iraq, but election results in 2006 showed that the public was against staying in Iraq.

BELOW: **Some 58,000 American lives were lost** in Vietnam. While public support for our military efforts there was high in the early years, as the atrocities of the war and the number of casualties grew, Americans lost faith in Lyndon Johnson. How does Congress have the right (and obligation) to step in and change the course of military engagements after a period of time? At what point should it take such action?

general law, the limb must be protected, yet often a limb must be amputated to save a life; but a life is never wisely given to save a limb. I felt the measures otherwise unconstitutional might become lawful by becoming indispensable to the preservation of the Constitution through the preservation of the nation.[30]

Essentially, Lincoln acted and left it to Congress either to accept or cancel his action later. Presidents since Lincoln have taken this

▶ What happens if Congress disagrees with the President on a military engagement?

"presidential prerogative" to heart, arguing that they are uniquely situated to protect the nation and should be given a free hand in all military emergencies.

In 1950, Harry Truman ordered troops to defend South Korea against a North Korean attack without requesting congressional authority (he said that the United States was engaging in a "police action" in support of a United Nations act). In the 1960s and early 1970s, both Lyndon Johnson and Richard Nixon waged the Vietnam War without a formal congressional declaration. Indeed, many observers think that the day of Congress actually declaring war—which last happened right after Japan's 1941 attack on Pearl Harbor—may now be over.

▶ **What happens if Congress disagrees with the President on a military engagement?** In 1973, after the United States and North Vietnam signed a peace agreement, Congress attempted to rein in presidential warmaking by passing the **War Powers Resolution,** overriding President Nixon's veto of it. This act requires that the president consult with Congress in "every possible instance" before sending troops to combat, that the president report to Congress in writing within forty-eight hours after ordering troops into harm's way, and that any military engagement must end within sixty days unless Congress either declares war or otherwise authorizes the use of force (provisions allowed for ninety days under certain circumstances). Since 1973, every president, Democratic or Republican, has claimed that the War Powers Resolution is unconstitutional. In fact, many members of Congress also believe it is unconstitutional, given that it seems to usurp explicit and implied presidential powers granted in the Constitution. Nevertheless, rather than defy the act and test its constitutionality in the federal courts, and also in an effort to build broad public support (a critically important factor in waging successful long-term wars), all presidents who have sent American forces into battle have first sought congressional support for their action. For example, President George H. W. Bush asked for and received congressional authorization before launching the Persian Gulf War of 1991. So did President Clinton before leading NATO's military intervention in Kosovo in 1999, and so did President George W. Bush before invading Afghanistan in 2001 and Iraq in 2003. But all these presidents have also made it clear that if Congress refused authorization, they would go ahead anyway. Again, an important part of the calculation to seek congressional approval is to get widespread public support. It is also likely that congressional acts can give the president more authority to control the armed forces, especially if the war lingers for years.

It might seem, then, that modern presidents have unlimited foreign policy powers. But this is not exactly true. Congress still

War Powers Resolution
a measure passed by Congress in 1973 designed to limit presidential deployment of troops unless Congress grants approval for a longer period.

Iran-Contra affair
the Reagan administration's unauthorized diversion of funds from the sale of arms to Iran to support the Contras, rebels fighting to overthrow the leftist government of Nicaragua.

has the power to allocate or deny funds for military engagements. In 1974, Congress cut off further funding for the war in Vietnam. What if a situation arises in which the president sees military action as in our nation's interest but Congress disagrees and fails to appropriate the necessary resources? This issue came to a head in the 1980s in the **Iran-Contra affair.** Briefly stated, President Ronald Reagan was anxious to support a group of rebels, called the Contras, who were fighting the leftist government of Nicaragua. Many members of Congress, especially the Democrats who controlled the House of Representatives, saw too many parallels between this engagement and the early years of our involvement in Vietnam, waging a war that eventually cost more than 55,000 American lives. They therefore passed a measure known as the Boland Amendment that prohibited the federal government from providing military aid to the rebels. Members of the Reagan White House staff circumvented these restrictions by securing covert military aid to the Contras. (Much of these funds came from the profits of a secret sale of arms to Iran, despite a U.S. trade and arms embargo.) The story emerged late in Reagan's administration, drawing massive media attention, congressional ire, and an investigation by the Justice Department. To many people, this was a clear violation of the law: Congress had spoken through the Boland Amendment, and Reagan, the executive, had thwarted its will. Supporters of the president answered that Reagan and his deputies were simply fulfilling their duty to protect the United States. The Justice Department moved forward and eventually secured a number of felony convictions. As for Reagan himself, the president claimed that he was unaware of these activities, and because his second term was ending, there was little enthusiasm for impeachment proceedings. Moreover, once George H. W. Bush lost reelection in 1992, he pardoned everyone who had been convicted, and the scandal faded into the history books. The point of the Iran-Contra affair is that although presidents see their commander-in-chief authority as sweeping, Congress still has one crucial power—the power of the purse.

Another contentious issue related to presidential powers during times of war concerns treatment of people detained by the United States government. A firestorm of controversy arose in the spring of 2004, when photographs were published of Iraqi prisoners being humiliated and tortured by American military personnel at Abu Ghraib prison in Iraq. Other news reports focused on alleged abuses occurring at American bases in Afghanistan and at secret overseas prisons where President George W. Bush acknowledged sending particularly important terrorism suspects. The abuses at Abu Ghraib led to the prosecution and punishment of American soldiers.

President Bush, while stating that the United States does not use torture, argued that American intelligence agents need the flexibility to use harsh methods to obtain needed information from detainees. His administration established a detention facility at a U.S. Navy base in Guantanamo Bay, Cuba, as a place to hold foreign suspects beyond the authority of American judges, who might wish to declare that such suspects possess legal rights requiring lawyers and other protections that would be available to American citizens arrested within the United States. In 2004, however, the U.S. Supreme Court ruled in the case of *Rasul* v. *Bush* that the foreign detainees held at the navy base are entitled to have their cases heard by American courts. The Bush administration responded by developing special military courts in Guantanamo Bay to handle the cases of these terrorism suspects. These courts, usually referred to as tribunals, were controversial because the usual rules of evidence did not apply, suspects did not have attorneys during certain preliminary proceedings, and suspects were not entitled to know the evidence against them.

The U.S. Supreme Court invalidated the use of such military tribunals for trials of terrorism suspects in *Hamden* v. *Rumsfeld* (2006) by saying that Congress had never granted the president the power to create such proceedings. After heated debate, Congress passed the Military Commissions Act in September 2006 to authorize such proceedings and to bar terrorism suspects held overseas from filing legal claims in American courts. Thus the new law broadened presidential authority and simultaneously sought to reduce the judiciary's power to oversee the treatment of foreign detainees. President Bush and his supporters claimed that the law gave the U.S. government the needed flexibility to detain, interrogate, place on trial, and punish terrorists. In contrast, critics claimed that the law improperly sacrificed Americans' traditional emphasis on legal rights and gave too much unchecked power to the president.

THE PRESIDENT AS CHIEF EXECUTIVE

We have already discussed several important elements of the president's chief executive function, including the assembling of staff and the cabinet. We know that the president is charged with carrying out the will of Congress: enforcing laws and spending the funds that are allocated and appropriated. The president is in many ways the nation's chief administrator and head bureaucrat. This role might suggest that the president's hands are tied by the will of Congress—that this function affords little leeway to shape policy. But this is only partially correct. At times, Congress makes its will clear with exact instructions to the executive branch. At other times, only vague outlines are provided, thereby leaving a

▶ **So presidents don't have to depend on Congress to make policy?**

discussionquestions

1. What would you say is the foremost tool for presidents in shaping legislation?

2. How do executive agreements differ from treaties, and why would presidents be ever more willing to use them?

great deal of ambiguity and leeway. This gives presidents and the federal bureaucracy (see LINK *Chapter 9, pages 346–349*) a chance to shape public policy.

Second, many authorities believe that nowadays, the very size of the federal bureaucracy has shifted the balance of power toward the executive branch. During the first few decades, our government had only about 1,000 federal employees (most of whom staffed local post offices). Even so, President Jefferson thought that there were too many officials and carried out a severe staff reduction! In recent years, the number of federal employees has climbed to roughly 2.6 million (excluding active-duty members of the military). Although the vast majority of federal employees are civil service workers, the power to appoint certain high officials who lead the massive agencies and set their policies is an important executive function.

▶ **So presidents don't have to depend on Congress to make policy?** On top of this, presidents can issue **executive orders,** which are essentially rules or regulations that have the effect of law. At times, executive orders are used to clarify existing legislation, but at other times, they have the effect of making new policy. There are three types of executive orders: proclamations, which serve the ceremonial purpose of declaring holidays and celebrations, and national security directives and presidential decision directives, both of which deal with national security and defense matters. Three of the most famous executive orders were used to ease some of the barriers to black men and women caused by generations of racial discrimination. Abraham Lincoln issued the Emancipation Proclamation freeing the slaves of the South in 1863, Harry Truman issued an executive order in 1948 ending segregation in the armed forces, and Lyndon Johnson issued an executive order in 1966 making affirmative action a federal policy. More recently, George W. Bush used an executive order to create the White House Office of Faith-Based and Community Initiatives in 2001. The goal of the new office is to help religious organizations compete for federal dollars to help fund social service programs.

Another tool that presidents can use to shape public policy is called **signing statements.** Here, when a president signs a bill into law, he also issues a written proclamation of how the executive branch will interpret the measure, which is often different from what Congress intended. Controversy has arisen over the constitutionality of signing statements—especially the large number of statements issued by George W. Bush in recent years (see Table 8.1).

Given the growing importance of the federal bureaucracy and the opportunity that bureaucratic regulations present to shape policy, interest groups have come to see the executive branch as an important pathway for change (see LINK *Chapter 13, pages 527–528*). A great deal of lobbying is directed at agency heads and other bureaucratic decision makers. Indeed, much can change in American government without the input of a single elected official. Even if an issue is taken up by the legislature, it is common for a federal agency to be brought into the mix. Political scientists have described a cozy, often secretive relationship in policymaking among interest groups (often representing a corporation, business, trade association, or labor union), legislative committees, and bureaucratic agencies. Scholars debate the extent to which these "policy communities" exist these days, but the overarching point is that political actors can make a difference by directly lobbying nonelected bureaucrats.

practicequiz

1. In the long period from George Washington's presidency to Woodrow Wilson's, approximately how much significant legislation was initiated in the executive branch?
   a. 75 percent
   b. 50 percent
   c. 25 percent
   d. 5 percent

2. What twentieth-century president was best known for his ability to cleverly and aggressively work his legislative agenda through Congress?
   a. Lyndon Johnson
   b. Jimmy Carter
   c. Gerald Ford
   d. Franklin Roosevelt

3. Why are presidential vetoes rarely overridden by Congress?
   a. because senators frequently filibuster to thwart such an action
   b. because presidents rarely exercise a veto that they think will be overridden
   c. because most legislators rarely object to presidential vetoes
   d. because the authority of the executive branch has become nearly overwhelming in the past eighty years

4. The president's status as commander in chief means in part that
   a. the president can declare wars.
   b. the president is responsible for raising money for military matters.
   c. the president can send U.S. military forces into battle with congressional authorization.
   d. the president can control the size and nature of the country's military forces.

Answers: 1-c, 2-a, 3-b, 4-c

executive order
a regulation by the president that has the effect of law.

signing statements
written proclamations issued by presidents regarding how they intend to interpret a new law

Many Americans deemed Jimmy Carter inept because he couldn't do anything to secure the release of the 66 Americans held hostage for 444 days in Iran. Perhaps we expect too much from presidents? What other actions may have obtained the hostages release?

Presidential Greatness

Many political scientists believe that an important development has occurred in the past few decades in the relationship between the president and the public. The term personal presidency describes the mounting expectations that the public places on the president—"expectations that have grown faster than the capacity of presidential government to meet them."[31] In short, we Americans have developed a personal connection, an emotional bond with our president. A number of changes have led to this development, including the growing size and importance of the federal bureaucracy, the expansion of presidential powers, and the heavy use of television advertising during campaigns, which forces candidates to promise things they cannot deliver once in office. Americans put more and more faith in their presidents to solve their problems and meet all challenges, both foreign and domestic. An aide to Richard Nixon put it this way:

> People identify with a president in a way they do with no other public figure. Potential presidents are measured against an ideal that's a combination of leading man, God, father, hero, pope, king, with maybe just a touch of the avenging Furies thrown in. They want him to be larger than life, a living legend, and yet quintessentially human; someone to be held up to their children as a model; someone to be cherished by themselves as a revered member of the family, in somewhat the same way in which peasant families pray to the icon in the corner. Reverence goes where power is.[32]

The problem, however, is that the executive branch is only one piece of the federal government and only one element of the world's economy. "For most Americans the president is the focal point of public life," write two experts on the presidency. "This person appears to be in charge, [which is] reassuring. But the reality of the presidency rests on a very different truth: Presidents are seldom in command and usually must negotiate with others to achieve their goals."[33] The outcome is dissatisfaction; presidents often fail to meet our expectations, and we are left feeling disappointed and cynical. Some people would argue that this explains a string of "failed" presidencies. Of the ten presidents who have served since 1945, only three have finished two full terms—Eisenhower, Reagan, and Clinton. (Assuming that George W. Bush completes his second term, he will join this short list in 2009). Harry Truman and Lyndon Johnson—both of them vice presidents who entered the White House upon their predecessors' deaths—were rejected by their own party

after leading the nation into controversial military entanglements. John F. Kennedy grew enormously popular after narrowly winning election in 1960, and he probably would have been elected to a second term had he not been assassinated in 1963, but of course we will never know (see Table 8.5). Having won reelection in a landslide in 1972, Richard Nixon just two years later resigned in disgrace, facing impeachment and likely conviction, after his criminal misconduct in the Watergate affair was exposed. Jimmy Carter was perceived as bungling the nation's economy and being indecisive during the Iranian hostage crisis (which lasted for more than twelve months in 1979–1981), and the voters ejected him from office after just four years. George H. W. Bush was riding high early in his presidency and drew record high approval ratings after victory was won in the first Gulf War—but one year later, Bill Clinton defeated him, largely because the economy turned bad. Clinton did serve for two full terms, but in some respects, he too had a failed presidency. Being just the second president in U.S. history to be impeached—on grounds of personal conduct and despite acquittal by the Senate—was certainly no badge of honor. What is more, Reagan also faced a congressional inquiry into the Iran-Contra affair and may have escaped impeachment only because he was on the verge of retirement. One might conclude that modern executives are destined to fail, that "presidential greatness" is a thing of the past.

What is presidential greatness, anyway? What is it that makes one chief executive better than another? Are there ingredients that can be combined to create a successful, distinguished presidency? Perhaps it is only when our nation confronts adversity that greatness can emerge. The three presidents who top nearly all scholarly lists of great chief executives—Washington, Lincoln, and Franklin D. Roosevelt—each confronted a major national crisis.

▶ What determines a great president?

Washington led the nation in its founding years, when the very success of the federal experiment hung in the balance; Lincoln had to preserve the Union and chose to abolish slavery during a civil war that cost 600,000 lives; and Roosevelt faced the gravest economic crisis in the nation's history and then fought World War II. No other presidents, even those who rank relatively high, had to surmount crises as dangerous as these.

George W. Bush has said that his presidency was shaped by the events of September 11, 2001. He may be judged a great president because he met the challenge of our new realities—or a failure because in invading Iraq, he took the United States into the wrong war at the wrong time and with the wrong enemy. It is too early to say.

Perhaps simple luck has much to do with successful or failed presidencies. But bad luck can only explain so much. Herbert Hoover—a man superbly qualified by education and early experience for the presidency—claimed to be the unluckiest president in history, given the stock market's collapse on his watch in 1929. Yet Hoover was crippled by his rigid attempts to apply orthodox economic theories to a situation that required innovative thinking. He also projected a hardhearted and uncaring image while millions of Americans lost their money, jobs, homes, and hope—an unfair judgment but also understandable given Hoover's dour personality. Lyndon Johnson inherited the probably unwinnable conflict in Vietnam from his White House predecessors, and despite his noble championing of the civil rights movement and his policies aimed at eradicating poverty, his presidency was plagued by riots in the black ghettos and by massive antiwar demonstrations on college campuses. Johnson's public image was also negative: After the glamorous and eloquent Kennedy, LBJ seemed an uncouth, untrustworthy, and ruthless wheeler-dealer who spoke with a widely mocked Texas drawl. Jimmy Carter's hands were tied when the Iranian militants who had seized the U.S. embassy in Tehran threatened to kill the American diplomats whom they had taken hostage. Like his predecessor Gerald Ford (who similarly rates as an unimpressive president), Carter also faced skyrocketing oil prices and a stagnating economy.

▶ **What determines a great president?** It is worth remembering the words of the man always ranked as one of the greatest presidents, Abraham Lincoln, responding in 1864 to a newspaperman's question: "I claim not to have controlled events, but confess plainly that events have controlled me." How Lincoln *did* act when confronted with those events, however, is the measure of his greatness.

TABLE 8.5
Rankings of American Presidents

WALL STREET JOURNAL RANKING		C-SPAN RANKING	
RANK	NAME	RANK	NAME
1	George Washington	1	Abraham Lincoln
2	Abraham Lincoln	2	Franklin D. Roosevelt
3	Franklin D. Roosevelt	3	George Washington
4	Thomas Jefferson	4	Theodore Roosevelt
5	Theodore Roosevelt	5	Harry S Truman
6	Andrew Jackson	6	Woodrow Wilson
7	Harry S Truman	7	Thomas Jefferson
8	Ronald Reagan	8	John F. Kennedy
9	Dwight D. Eisenhower	9	Dwight D. Eisenhower
10	James K. Polk	10	Lyndon B. Johnson
11	Woodrow Wilson	11	Ronald Reagan
12	Grover Cleveland	12	James K. Polk
13	John Adams	13	Andrew Jackson
14	William McKinley	14	James Monroe
15	James Madison	15	William McKinley
16	James Monroe	16	John Adams
17	Lyndon B. Johnson	17	Grover Cleveland
18	John F. Kennedy	18	James Madison
19	William Howard Taft	19	John Quincy Adams
20	John Quincy Adams	20	George H. W. Bush
21	George H. W. Bush	21	Bill Clinton
22	Rutherford B. Hayes	22	Jimmy Carter
23	Martin Van Buren	23	Gerald R. Ford
24	Bill Clinton	24	William Howard Taft
25	Calvin Coolidge	25	Richard M. Nixon
26	Chester A. Arthur	26	Rutherford B. Hayes
27	Benjamin Harrison	27	Calvin Coolidge
28	Gerald R. Ford	28	Zachary Taylor
29	Herbert Hoover	29	James A. Garfield
30	Jimmy Carter	30	Martin Van Buren
31	Zachary Taylor	31	Benjamin Harrison
32	Ulysses S. Grant	32	Chester A. Arthur
33	Richard M. Nixon	33	Ulysses S. Grant
34	John Tyler	34	Herbert Hoover
35	Millard Fillmore	35	Millard Fillmore
36	Andrew Johnson	36	John Tyler
37	Franklin Pierce	37	William Henry Harrison
38	Warren G. Harding	38	Warren G. Harding
39	James Buchanan	39	Franklin Pierce
		40	Andrew Johnson
		41	James Buchanan

Note: William Henry Harrison, who died after just thirty days in office, and Garfield, who was mortally wounded four months after his inauguration and died two months later, are omitted from the *Wall Street Journal*'s ranking.

1. Which characteristics do you believe define successful presidents?

2. Do you think presidential rankings like the ones in Table 8.5 are worthwhile tools for understanding the American presidency? Why or why not?

Circumstances matter. Yet even unlucky events can turn into triumphs of leadership if the president has the necessary character. And what defines great character in a political leader? Scholars and biographers have wrestled with this question for thousands of years, and there is no shortage of lists. The historian and presidential scholar Robert Dallek suggests that five qualities have been constants in the men who have most effectively fulfilled the presidential oath of office:[34]

Vision. All great presidents have had a clear understanding of where they wanted to lead the nation in its quest for a better future.

Pragmatism. All great presidents have been realists, leaders who understood that politics is the art of the possible and that flexible responses to changing conditions at home and abroad are essential.

Consensus building. Great presidents understood that their success depended on the consent of the governed. Moving government in a new direction, often down a difficult path, requires building a national consensus first.

Charisma. The personality of the president, along with his ability to capture and retain the affection and admiration of average citizens, has been a key ingredient of presidential greatness.

Trustworthiness. All truly successful presidents have credibility and have been able to earn the faith of their fellow citizens.

Many groups have attempted to measure presidential greatness. The conservative Federalist Society, joining forces with the *Wall Street Journal* in November 2000, undertook one such effort. The study involved seventy-eight randomly selected presidency scholars: historians, political scientists, and law professors. Another, conducted by C-SPAN, also surveyed scholars, whose responses seem to have been slightly weighted in favor of the more liberal or "progressive" presidents. Table 8.5 shows the results from both polls.

Although we might argue over the precise order of these rankings—whether one president should be ranked higher than another, whether Washington was better than Lincoln, or whether Harding, Buchanan, or Andrew Johnson was the worst of all—nearly all assessments of past presidents suggest similar groupings. Lincoln, Washington, both Roosevelts, and Jefferson were great leaders, and those at the bottom of this list, the presidents whose names seem the most obscure to us, are generally considered failures. The interesting

part of this exercise is not the precise order but rather a consideration of the personal qualities and historical events that contributed to the success or failure of a given president. Why are James Madison and John Quincy Adams, who made enormous contributions to this country, not ranked among the greatest presidents? Why was Ulysses S. Grant at best only mediocre (as a president, not as a general), and why did Gerald Ford, such a fine American, fail as a president? What was it about Theodore Roosevelt that brings him near the top? And why is James K. Polk listed in the top tier in some rankings? Who *was* James K. Polk, anyway?

1. Which of the following acts best illustrates the notion of a "personal presidency"?
   a. Ronald Reagan telling the president of the Soviet Union, "Mr. Gorbachev, tear down this wall!"
   b. Bill Clinton telling the American people, "I feel your pain"
   c. John F. Kennedy telling the country in his inaugural address, "Ask not what your country can do for you; ask what you can do for your country"
   d. Abraham Lincoln's Emancipation Proclamation, outlawing slavery in 1863 by executive order

2. U.S. presidents are less in charge of governmental actions than most Americans assume because
   a. presidents are trained to sound more sure of themselves than they really are.
   b. no one can predict how circumstances will change after presidents have decided the course of governmental action.
   c. the legislative branch in the American system is much stronger than the executive branch.
   d. presidents must negotiate with other people to accomplish their goals.

3. Which of the following is generally considered a thoroughly successful president?
   a. James Madison
   b. Lyndon Johnson
   c. Ulysses Grant
   d. Harry Truman

4. According to presidential scholar Robert Dallek, what is one of the qualities that effective presidents must possess?
   a. great intelligence
   b. eloquence
   c. charisma
   d. consistency

Answers: 1-b, 2-d, 3-d, 4-c

Conclusion

The framers of our system of government might not have comprehended jet planes, skyscrapers, or suicide bombers. And they surely could not have imagined jets being flown into buildings, killing thousands of innocent people. They also could not have appreciated the speed at which the events of September 11, 2001, could be transmitted around the globe. Ours is a very different world than Franklin, Washington, Adams, Jefferson, and Madison could possibly have imagined.

If anything, however, the events of 9/11 have proved that the framers were visionaries and that they were right about the presidency. They anticipated grievous attacks against the United States and the necessity for an immediate response. They understood that after tragic events, citizens would look to a leader to calm, resolve, and console. They held that the heart of their new republic would be found in the legislature, but they also understood that a strong executive would keep the nation together during times of crisis. It is hard to imagine how our nation would have responded to any of the great challenges without the leadership of the president. Our first years under the Constitution were uncertain and turbulent, but to some extent, the steady hand and vision of George Washington helped keep the peace and ensure that the Union survived. Congress or state governments did not save the Union in 1861–1865, but the will, intellect, and political skill of Abraham Lincoln helped it survive and be reborn. Congress and the Hoover White House were paralyzed by the strife and anguish of the Great Depression, so not until Franklin D. Roosevelt took the helm did the federal government respond. From his first inaugural address, he calmed the waters by reminding us that "the only thing we have to fear is fear itself," and he rallied a nation horrified by the Japanese attack on December 7, 1941—"a date" he said, "which will live in infamy." After the humiliations of the 1970s, Ronald Reagan made Americans once again feel proud of their nation, and it was through his unwavering mixture of determination and moderation that the Cold War was brought to a peaceful end. The will of the American people is best expressed through representatives, but our resolve, our spirit, our sense of united purpose rests in the hands of the president. This is especially true during times of crisis.

However much we may praise the advantages of a single leader, endowing this person with too much prerogative distorts the balance of power that the framers so carefully built into the constitutional system. Our nation has grown from fewer than 4 million people in 1790 to more than 300 million today, requiring the federal government to step into all aspects of American life—and the power of the chief executive has mushroomed along with that explosive growth. Dramatically different from what was envisioned by Madison and his colleagues in Philadelphia in 1787, modern presidents have three main tasks: first, to develop a legislative program and work to persuade Congress to enact it; second, to engage in direct policymaking through bureaucratic actions that do not require congressional approval; and third, to lead a massive network of staff with the singular goal of helping the occupant of the White House succeed in achieving these first two goals.[35] Presidents do not act in a vacuum. They must constantly respond to public opinion, interest groups, party activists, and the media. Many pathways of change run through the White House. Even so, when one person holds so much power in a political system, it is only sensible to wonder about the democratic character of that nation. The "imperial presidency," as scholars have branded what emerged under Richard Nixon,[36] which shows signs of revival today, is surely not what the framers had in mind.

YOUR turn!

One of the key themes of this chapter has been the growth of the executive branch and the extent to which policy is created by the federal bureaucracy. This diffusion of power would seem to make the job of persuading the executive branch more difficult, and of course, bureaucrats are not elected officials. Yet paralleling the growth of committees and subcommittees in Congress, the expansion of the executive branch has also broadened the points of access for citizens needing help from the federal government or for those wishing to bring about change. Put a bit differently, you need not sit down with the president if you want to play a meaningful role in lobbying the executive branch. There are no easy tricks to working with the executive branch, but experts agree that the first step is to understand the real players—to know which person, in which office, to approach for different concerns.

Go to the Federal Citizen Information Center (http://www.info.gov), for example, and explore the many different ways citizens can become more informed about policy matters and the executive branch. You will note telephone numbers for different federal offices, a list of agency publications, and an opportunity to send inquiries by e-mail. Another critically important resource is the *Federal Directory*, which is a list of all national government agencies and offices. You may be interested in laws and policies related to housing issues in your community, for instance. If so, you would go to the *Federal Directory*, move to the section on the Department of Housing and Urban Development, and look up the section on the Office of Fair Housing and Equal Opportunity. Or perhaps you are concerned about protecting wetlands in your area. You would start with the Department of the Interior, move on to the Office of Policies and Management, and finally find the National Wildlife Refuge System. Federal directories can be found in hard copy at most libraries and online at **http://www. federaldirectory.com**. The advantage of using the online directory is that links are provided to each of the offices, which makes it easy to fine-tune your search.

Sticking with the wetlands example, once you reach the National Wildlife Refuge System Web page (**http://www.fws.gov/ refuges**), you might then explore scores of online brochures, learn how to volunteer, or find out the name of someone to contact with a concern or questions. Yes, the president is at the center of the executive branch, and you're not likely to get through the White House switchboard to let him know what to do about your local wetlands. But astute activists also understand that the executive branch is massive, and narrowing your efforts along the right pathway can make an important difference. ▪

Chapter Review

1. Executive power was uncertain in the early years of our republic. Many people understood the necessity of having a single person in charge, someone who could respond quickly in time of crisis, but they also understood that too much power in the hands of one individual could lead to tyranny.

2. This ambivalence about executive power found its way into the proceedings of the Constitutional Convention. Two plans emerged, and the strong-executive model won out.

3. There was much concern about Article II during the ratification period, but fears were in large measure set to rest by the recognition that George Washington would be the first president.

4. During the nineteenth century, most presidents saw fit to follow the lead of Congress. Although there were activist presidents, including Jefferson, Jackson, and Lincoln, the Whig model generally prevailed, under which presidents regarded themselves as strictly limited by narrowly defined powers outlined in the Constitution.

5. Since Franklin D. Roosevelt, all presidents have held to a different model, according to which presidents may take any actions except those specifically forbidden by the Constitution. This has cleared the way for presidents to move to the center of our political system.

6. Along with this change in perspective, a massive network of support staff and agencies now buttresses presidents—so much so that scholars often use terms such as *imperial presidency* or *institutional presidency* to described the scope of the executive branch.

7. Presidents are expected to fulfill a number of diverse, important roles.

8. As chief of state, the president seeks to unify the nation, to pull us together in times of celebration and in times of grief.

9. Presidents have now become chief lawmakers, using both formal and informal tools to push their proposals through Congress.

10. Presidents are expected to lead the nation's foreign policy efforts and are the sole foreign policy organ for the United States.

11. The balance between Congress's responsibility to declare war and the president's role as commander in chief has always been precarious. Most presidents believe that national security issues fall within their purview and therefore acknowledge few, if any, constraints when it comes to directing the military.

12. As chief executive, the president oversees a vast federal bureaucracy and can influence public policy through bureaucratic regulations and the selection of leaders to head different agencies.

13. What determines presidential success or greatness is difficult to pin down. Some historians have suggested that luck has much to do with it. Others contend that presidents' actions in office shape their destiny.

14. Along with the profound expansion of presidential powers have come irrational expectations. Many Americans place so much faith in presidents that they will almost inevitably be let down.

CHAPTER REVIEW TEST

1. The responsibilities of the executive branch are spelled out in which article of the Constitution?

a. Article I

b. Article II

c. Article III

d. Article IV

2. One of the central tasks of a modern president is

a. developing a legislative agenda and persuading Congress to enact it.

b. declaring wars and ratifying peace treaties with foreign powers.

c. controlling the revenues and expenditures of the federal government.

d. interpreting and applying the laws of the land, as described in the Constitution.

3. All citizens of the United States select the president.

a. true

b. false

4. During the nineteenth century, U.S. presidents informed Congress of "the state of the union" by

a. making a speech in the Capitol building once a year.

b. discussing the subject in the Oval Office with the speaker of the House and the Senate majority and minority leaders.

c. having a presidential aide read a proclamation on the subject, written by the president, every other year.

d. sending the joint Congress a written message on the subject once a year.

5. The Constitution originally set the duration of a president's term at

a. one year with unlimited eligibility for reelection.

b. four years with a one-term limit.

c. four years with a two-term limit.

d. four years with unlimited eligibility for reelection.

6. Over the centuries, the breadth of presidential authority has fluctuated in part because

a. many amendments have been added to the Constitution that have widened and narrowed that authority.

b. some presidents have used the vagueness of the Constitution aggressively, and some have not.

c. the American people's attitude toward presidential power has fluctuated as well.

d. modern society has experienced cultural and technological change at an increasingly rapid rate.

7. As the presidency has evolved, presidential authority has

a. remained steady.

b. steadily declined.

c. been ever-increasing.

d. been cyclical, with periods of increase followed by periods of decline.

8. What is the "bully pulpit"?

a. the president's unique position to shape public opinion on important national issues

b. the lectern from which Franklin Roosevelt delivered his famous fireside chats

c. a position presidents adopt when they use their own religious convictions to address moral issues in American society

d. a metaphor for America's military superiority to other countries in the world

9. What president proudly claimed that he "did not usurp power but . . . acted for the common well-being of our people . . . in whatever manner was necessary, unless prevented by direct constitutional or legislative prohibition"?

a. Richard Nixon

b. George Washington

c. Theodore Roosevelt

d. Herbert Hoover

10. Members of a president's cabinet cannot also serve in the Senate or House of Representatives at the same time.

a. true

b. false

11. Typically, a president's inner cabinet includes the heads of which departments?

a. Health, Education, and Labor

b. Transportation, Interior, and Homeland Security

c. Energy, Commerce, and Agriculture

d. Justice, Treasury, and Defense

12. The executive office of the president expanded most rapidly under which administration?

a. Gerald Ford's

b. James Polk's

c. Bill Clinton's

d. Franklin Roosevelt's

13. The expansion of the president's staff into an enormous network of individuals and offices has meant that

a. presidents themselves have become less significant politically.

b. presidents have had to make many fewer decisions themselves.

c. presidents have been able to play a central role in the policy process.

d. fewer people have access to the executive branch.

14. Why have recent presidencies experienced conflict between policy and political advisers within the executive branch?

a. because presidents now retain advisers whose job is to make sure their boss remains politically popular, even if that means setting aside policy commitments

b. because presidents have become much more involved with the policy process, making conflict with the political agenda inevitable

c. because political and policy advisers are by definition contentious

d. because presidents must now respond to the needs of many different political camps that are frequently in conflict

15. In the 1950s, what changed in the nature of the vice presidency, and why?

a. Vice presidents no longer attended cabinet meetings because the president's expanded staff could handle those responsibilities.

b. Vice presidents began to be routinely included in important presidential meetings so that they could quickly and competently assume the complex role of president if necessary.

c. The vice presidency became much more lucrative because television gave the office a much higher profile than it had before.

d. The vice president presided over the U.S. Senate much more often because the president, with his expanded policy duties, needed an active representative in that forum.

16. What book touting the informal powers of the presidency did Presidents Kennedy and Clinton keep at hand throughout their time in the White House?

a. *The Imperial Presidency*

b. *Profiles in Courage*

c. *Presidential Power*

d. *Banging the Bully Pulpit*

17. What woman first demonstrated how substantial and public the role of first lady could be?

a. Edith Bolling Galt Wilson

b. Abigail Adams

c. Hillary Clinton

d. Eleanor Roosevelt

18. Modern presidents use the State of the Union address to set the legislative agenda for the coming year and shape public opinion in support of that agenda.

a. true   **b.** false

19. Despite their expanded authority, modern presidents still cannot initiate the deployment of American forces in foreign lands without the prior approval of Congress.

a. true   **b.** false

20. Given the substantial numbers and authority of bureaucratic decision makers now working in the executive branch, it is safe to say that

a. there is not much an outsider can do to affect policy formation in the White House.

b. a lot can change in American government without the input of an elected official.

c. the President has little control over the policy direction of his own administration.

d. the executive branch is not a promising pathway for change.

Answers: 1: b; 2: a; 3: b; 4: d; 5: d; 6: b; 7: c; 8: a; 9: c; 10: a; 11: d; 12: d; 13: c; 14: a; 15: b; 16: c; 17: d; 18: a; 19: b; 20: b.

DISCUSSION QUESTIONS

1. Knowing what you now know about the presidency, where did the framers of our system really get things right, and where did they get things wrong? If you were able to go back to the Constitutional Convention to provide advice to the delegates on the presidency, what would you suggest?

2. Why have the powers of the presidency expanded so much? What are some of the ramifications? Can you think of any ways to rein in these expanding powers? *Should* they be limited?

3. As you now know, presidents are called on to undertake an immense list of duties. Which are most important? Would you want presidential staffers to take over some of these functions to ease the burden on the president?

4. How might the expansion of presidential staff change the democratic nature of the office? Might the organization of the staff also matter?

5. It's been argued that Americans are increasingly disappointed with their presidents. Why might this be the case? Are there any changes you can think of that might ease some of our disappointment?

6. Do you suppose the United States will ever elect a woman president? A person of color? What difference might the election of a woman or a minority make?

7. How can presidents shape the outcome of policy battles?

8. Can average citizens use presidents and their staff to shape the outcomes of the policy process? Put another way, does the pathway of change run through the White House?

INTERNET RESOURCES

To explore a range of topics on the presidency, especially presidential elections, go to the American Presidency Web site at **http://ap.grolier.com**

You can view some 52,000 documents at the American Presidency Project at **http://www.presidency.ucsb.edu/index.php**. This site also provides a number of important links.

Doing a research project on a president or a related topic? Check out the National Archives at **http://www.archives.gov/research_room/getting_started/research_presidential_materials.html** You might also take a look at one of the presidential libraries. For links to

them, try **http://www.archives.gov/research_room/getting_started/research_presidential_materials.html#faids**

The American Presidents Web site at **http://www.americanpresidents.org** contains a complete video archive of the C-SPAN television series *American Presidents: Life Portraits,* plus biographical facts, key events of each presidency, presidential places, and reference materials.

The White House Web site at **http://www.whitehouse.gov** provides a wealth of information about the current presidency.

ADDITIONAL READING

Neustadt, Richard E. *Presidential Power: The Politics of Leadership.* New York: Free Press, 1991.

Greenstein, Fred I. *The Presidential Difference: Leadership Style from FDR to George W. Bush.* Princeton, NJ: Princeton University Press, 2004.

Schlesinger, Arthur M. Jr. *The Imperial Presidency.* Buena Vista, VA: Mariner Books, Reprint Ed., 2004.

Ellis, Joseph J. *His Excellency: George Washington.* New York: Knopf, 2004.

KEY TERMS

Americans depend on government agencies. Police and other emergency personnel must train in realistic scenarios in order to respond to a variety of possible disasters. Americans do not always think of emergency workers as part of the government bureaucracy. Yet, like others who work in government agencies, these public employees perform important tasks for society. Here Seattle Police Department officers train a simulation of a terrorist attack in Seattle, Washington, on May 12, 2003.

CHAPTER 9

BUREAUCRACY

Government and Natural Disasters   When Hurricane Katrina roared across New Orleans and the Gulf Coast at the end of August 2005, all Americans became much more keenly aware of the role of government agencies in providing services to the public. Wind, rain, and storm surges from the hurricane caused an estimated 1,300 deaths; billions of dollars in damage to crops, homes, and businesses; and the displacement of a million people whose homes and neighborhoods suffered complete destruction.

Devastating events bringing destruction and human misery—though rarely on this scale—strike periodically throughout the United States in the form of earthquakes, tornadoes, floods, and wildfires. Human-made disasters, such as urban riots and the 2001 terrorist attacks on the World Trade Center and the Pentagon, can cause comparable (or even worse) damage and upheaval. These disasters

Hurricane Katrina brought death and despair to New Orleans in 2005. Most observers believe that much of the human suffering in the hurricane's aftermath could have been reduced if the federal government had been better organized and motivated to take action. Should we expect government agencies to be effective in undertaking their responsibilities? Alternatively, is that too much to ask of the government bureaucracy?

exact a huge toll on the lives and property of people in the affected areas and touch the lives of Americans everywhere.

Government provides a variety of services in the United States, from education to medical research to highway construction. Disaster relief is one of the services that Americans view as an essential responsibility of government. Obviously, citizens cannot expect the president or members of Congress personally to bring food and to pound nails into damaged roofs. These elected officials are the leaders of the national government, but they cannot carry out all of the expected functions of government. These functions are primarily carried out by the various agencies of government, each with a specified area of responsibility.

When disasters hit the United States, citizens expect that their needs will be addressed by a variety of agencies at all levels of government. In the aftermath of hurricanes, local police and fire departments conduct safety operations to pull people from collapsed buildings and reroute traffic away from flooded highways. State agencies, under the direction of the governor, assist in these operations and also try to organize aid programs for people in immediate need of clean water, shelter, and food. In addition, one federal agency, the Federal Emergency Management Agency (FEMA), bears responsibility for many aspects of disaster relief.

Because FEMA responded slowly and ineffectually to the initial human crisis in Hurricane Katrina's wake (see Fig. 9.1), many people questioned the adequacy of the agency's organization, leadership, and planning. Moreover, FEMA director Michael Brown's

apparent lack of experience and expertise in emergency management highlighted for the public the issue of whether presidents place sufficient emphasis on qualifications when appointing the leaders of federal agencies. Brown had been a lawyer for the International Arabian Horse Association. He had little, if any, training and experience in emergency management.[1] Bush appointed him deputy director of FEMA in 2001 and director in 2003.

Hurricane Katrina did not necessarily demonstrate that all agencies are incapable of performing their assigned missions effectively. The National Weather Service and its National Hurricane Service accurately predicted Katrina's path and intensity. The U.S. Coast Guard's performance in assisting hurricane victims was so impressive that a Coast Guard admiral was appointed to head the federal government's posthurricane relief efforts after public complaints and political pressure forced Brown to resign as the director of FEMA.

When catastrophic events occur, mayors and governors can ask the president to designate specific cities and counties disaster areas, which makes them eligible for federal assistance. After Katrina, many counties in the Gulf states were given that designation, and federal officials came to the scene to provide assistance. In addition to providing relief supplies and resources for emergency housing, FEMA experts are supposed to handle specialized tasks such as surveillance flights to survey damage over wide areas. FEMA is not the only federal agency to provide assistance after a hurricane. The Coast Guard provides search-and-rescue opera-

tions, most notably in Katrina's aftermath by using helicopters to lift stranded people off the rooftops of homes in flooded neighborhoods. The Small Business Administration provides low-interest loans to hurricane-struck business owners, and the Department of Agriculture's Farm Service Agency supplies financial assistance to farmers whose crops are devastated by a disaster.

Assistance provided to disaster victims by FEMA and other federal agencies is in accordance with laws enacted by Congress. These laws list the kinds of assistance to be provided by the federal government and authorize the spending of federal funds for disaster relief in specific locations. FEMA and other agencies do not simply decide for themselves when and where they will help. They must act within the guidelines set by Congress and the president. These guidelines typically leave room for agency officials to make specific decisions, but they cannot act beyond the scope of their authority as defined by law. For example, FEMA officials may decide that certain disaster area counties need more money or other specific kinds of assistance than other disaster-affected counties. In essence, Congress and the president write laws to define public policy; the officials who work in federal agencies then act to carry out those laws and policies.

In making their decisions, however, agency officials may be influenced by lobbying from legislators, state and local officials, and interest groups. Thus the bureaucracy becomes another arena of action for the pathway that relies on the lobbying of decision makers. ■

▶ What do we mean by "bureaucracy"? Is it a separate branch of government?

bureaucracy
an organization with a hierarchical structure and specific responsibilities that operates on management principles intended to enhance efficiency and effectiveness. In government, it refers to departments and agencies in the executive branch.

department
any of the fifteen major government agencies responsible for specific policy areas whose heads are usually called secretaries and serve in the president's cabinet.

Many Americans may take for granted that their drinking water is safe and clean, yet it is government agencies that set standards and inspections to ensure the safety of our water. Do you trust government agencies to make sure that Americans enjoy a healthy, safe environment?

▶ What do we mean by "bureaucracy"? Is it a separate branch of government?

In this chapter, we'll examine the agencies of the executive branch of the federal government that are collectively known as "the bureaucracy." The word **bureaucracy** refers to an organization with a hierarchical structure and specific responsibilities that operates on management principles intended to enhance efficiency and effectiveness. Bureaucracies exist in businesses, universities, and other organizational contexts. However, the general term *bureaucracy* is most frequently used to refer to government agencies. Action or inaction by these agencies determines whether and how policies are implemented and how these policies will affect the lives of Americans.

Agency officials can shape public policy through their authority to create rules for administering programs and for enforcing laws enacted by Congress and the president. They are also the source of information and ideas for members of Congress who wish to propose new statutes about various policy issues. The policy preferences of individual agency officials affect the day-to-day actions that these bureaucracies undertake. So do those officials' interactions with representatives from outside interest groups. And because the bureaucracy is part of the executive branch, and thus under the president's authority, policymaking decisions within government agencies can also be affected by partisan political considerations. Moreover, the president's political appointees assume the top positions in each agency.

Although the news media typically pay less attention to the bureaucracy than they do to the president, Congress, political parties, and interest groups, the agencies of the federal government are influential and important in determining the nature and impact of public policies. When an agency mishandles a situation for which it has responsibility, as FEMA did in the case of Hurricane Katrina, the repercussions may reverberate all the way to the White House.

pathways of action

ARSENIC STANDARDS FOR DRINKING WATER

The Safe Drinking Water Act was passed by Congress in 1974 to protect the quality of drinking water in the United States. The act authorizes the Environmental Protection Agency (EPA)

independent agencies
federal agencies with narrow responsibilities for a specific policy issue, such as the environment, not covered by one of the fifteen federal departments.

independent regulatory commissions
organizational entities in the federal government that are not under the control of the president or a department.

to create regulations that establish purity standards for drinking water systems. But exactly what those purity standards will be can present a thorny issue affecting the safety and welfare of every person in the country. It's a good illustration of the politics of the federal bureaucracy.

A 1999 report by the National Academy of Sciences said that arsenic in drinking water can cause various kinds of cancer. In 2000, an environmentalist interest group, the Natural Resources Defense Council, sued the EPA over arsenic standards, seeking to have the regulations changed to mandate arsenic levels at only 3 parts per billion (ppb) rather than the existing standard of 50 ppb. As a result of the lawsuit, EPA officials in President Bill Clinton's administration proposed a new standard of 5 ppb.

Objections poured in from the mining and wood-preservative industries that use and produce arsenic. Local water systems also raised concerns about the costs of meeting the proposed standard. As a result, the EPA adopted a standard of 10 ppb. This was in the waning days of the Clinton administration—but when President George W. Bush came into office in early 2001, its officials postponed the effective date of the new rule for one year. Critics complained that the Bush administration, which was perceived to be less concerned than the Clinton administration about water pollution and other environmental issues, was sacrificing public health in favor of the interests and profits of manufacturing and mining industries.

Several months later, at the Bush administration's request, a committee of the National Academy of Sciences produced a new report that reconfirmed the health risks from arsenic in drinking water. So the Bush administration moved forward on the regulation limiting arsenic in drinking water to 10 ppb or less. The new rule angered the National Rural Water Association, an interest group representing small communities. It argued that the new standard would impose excessive costs on small towns that must upgrade their water systems. Nor did the rule satisfy the Natural Resources Defense Council and other environmentalist groups. They awaited new studies with the hope of convincing the EPA to amend the regulation and require an even lower level of arsenic. And there matters rest, with no party truly satisfied with the outcome.

This story is typical of today's regulatory politics. Officials in the bureaucracy make decisions about a policy rule that affects water systems throughout the country—but their rule is shaped by the officials' interactions with and responses to other actors involved with the issue of water quality. Scientists provide influential information for the bureaucracy, and interests groups apply pressure through lobbying and litigation.[2]

Key Questions

1. In what ways is the bureaucracy different from other institutions in government, such as courts and legislatures?
2. What are the potential advantages of having a bureaucracy?
3. What are the problems that arise from government bureaucracy?
4. How is the executive branch of the federal government organized?
5. What is the role of presidential appointees?
6. How does the bureaucracy influence legislation?
7. In what other ways does the bureaucracy affect public policy?

Organization of the Federal Bureaucracy

The origins of the federal bureaucracy can be traced to the design of government presented in the United States Constitution of 1787. The federal bureaucracy changed over time in response to the changing problems facing the United States, moving toward greater governmental involvement in social issues and economic regulation. In addition, the bureaucracy experienced significant growth during the mid-twentieth century.

Today, the federal bureaucracy consists of four types of organizational entities: departments, independent agencies, independent regulatory commissions, and government corporations (see Table 9.1 on page 342). **Departments** are typically large organizations responsible for a broad policy realm, such as education, national defense, or transportation. **Independent agencies** have narrow responsibilities for a specific policy issue, such as the environment. They are independent in the sense that they are not subunits of a larger department, but like departments, their leaders are appointed by and under the control of the president. By contrast, **independent regulatory commissions** are not under the control of the president or a department. They have a focused policy mission governing a specific issue area, but they are run by a body of officials drawn from both

▶ **Are all the bureaucratic** agencies listed in the Constitution?

government corporations
agencies with independent boards and the means to generate revenue through sales of products and services, fees, or insurance premiums that are intended to run like private corporations.

TABLE 9.1
Cabinet Departments and Examples of Other Agencies

Departments	Independent Agencies
Agriculture	Environmental Protection Agency
Commerce	Peace Corps
Defense	Social Security Administration
Education	
Energy	**Independent Regulatory Commissions**
Health and Human Services	Federal Communications Commission
Homeland Security	Federal Trade Commission
Housing and Urban Development	Nuclear Regulatory Commission
Interior	
Justice	**Government Corporations**
Labor	National Railroad Passenger Corporation (Amtrak)
State	Overseas Private Investment Corporation
Transportation	United States Postal Service
Treasury	
Veterans Affairs	

SOURCE: LSU Libraries Federal Agencies Directory, www.lib.lsu.edu/gov/fedgov.html

political parties and appointed in staggered terms over the course of more than one presidential administration. **Government corporations** have independent boards and are intended to run like private corporations. They handle a specific needed function, such as the postal system or the passenger railroad, that Congress believes would not be handled effectively by private businesses because of the huge scope of the operation or issues of profitability. As you consider the role and operation of each of these components of the federal bureaucracy, ask yourself whether there might be a better way to organize the government. Alternatively, consider whether some of the bureaucracy's functions could be handled effectively and appropriately by private businesses without the expenditure of taxpayers' money.

DEVELOPMENT OF THE FEDERAL BUREAUCRACY

▶ **Are all the bureaucratic agencies listed in the Constitution?**
The roots of the federal bureaucracy go back to the original United States Constitution of 1787. Article I, Section 8, gives Congress the power to enact laws for specified purposes. These

include matters such as to "lay and collect taxes," to "coin Money," to "establish Post Offices," and to "provide and maintain a Navy." The president, as the head of the executive branch, is responsible for carrying out the nation's laws. But it soon becomes apparent that people working for the president must implement these laws and that agencies must be created to administer specific policies and programs. Post offices, tax agencies, and mints (where money is coined) handle tasks that require specialized personnel and facilities. They cannot be carried out inside the president's office in the White House. Indeed, Article I makes reference to congressional authority to "make all laws necessary and proper for carrying into Execution . . . all other Powers vested by this Constitution in the Government of the United States, or in any Department or Officer thereof." Thus the founding document explicitly acknowledged that government agencies, called "departments," would be established to carry out laws and programs.

Article II of the Constitution, which discusses the president and executive power, provides further acknowledgment of the need to create governmental departments that will execute the laws under the president's supervision and control. For example,

▶ **So as the federal government** became involved in more diverse policy areas, were more departments created?

what YOU can do!

Using government websites, compare the number and kinds of agencies in the federal government with those in your state's government. Do you have suggestions about additional agencies that should be created or those that can be eliminated?

Article II says that the president "may require the Opinion, in writing, of the principal Officer in each of the executive Departments, upon any subject relating to the Duties of their respective Offices."

Although the Constitution thus clearly anticipated the existence of executive departments, the actual development and organization of those departments over the course of American history were shaped by social developments and the country's response to emerging policy issues and priorities.

During the nation's first century, the federal government was involved in only a limited range of policy areas. The original departments of the federal government focused on policy matters related to specific powers granted by the Constitution to Congress and the president. Most policy issues came under the authority of state governments. This explains why the federal government after 1789 had only four departments:

Department of State—responsible for diplomacy and foreign affairs

Department of War (in 1947 consolidated, along with the Department of the Navy, a later creation, into the Department of Defense)—responsible for military matters and national defense

Department of Justice—responsible for legal matters under federal law

Department of the Treasury—responsible for tax revenues and government expenditures

These departments had very limited responsibilities because there were few federal laws to carry out and the country was relatively small, in terms of geography and population. They were also tiny compared to the gigantic departments that handle these same duties today.

Note how many of these agencies focused on matters that had motivated the Constitutional Convention to replace the Articles of Confederation with the new U.S. Constitution. Under the Articles, the national government lacked authority to handle taxation, the military, and interstate commerce; agencies to deal with these matters were clearly needed. Although the Department of Commerce was not created until the early twentieth century, the Constitution gave Congress the authority to enact laws regulating interstate commerce, and the Department of Justice could seek to enforce these laws.

▶ **So as the federal government became involved in more diverse policy areas, were more departments created?** As Con-

gress and the president expanded the scope of federal activities in law and policy, departments were created to operate in new areas. First came the Department of the Navy. In the mid-nineteenth century, Congress created the Department of the Interior to manage federal lands and the Department of Agriculture to assist the nation's most important industry.

During the last decades of the nineteenth century, the United States began to undergo significant changes. Industrialization, urbanization, and immigration shaped a new economy in which people moved to cities to work in factories and service occupations. The corporations that dominated the nation's finance, transportation, energy, and manufacturing became national entities of vast wealth and size, acquiring and developing property, factories, and facilities across state borders. Issues arose about the corporations' influence over the economy and about the working conditions of employees in factories, railroads, coal mines, and other industrial settings. Congress became increasingly assertive in using its constitutional authority to enact laws regulating interstate commerce to prevent business monopolies, control the exploitation of child labor, improve dangerous working conditions, and deal with other problems created by the new industrial economy. In the first decade of the twentieth century, Congress created the Departments of Commerce and Labor to address these emerging issues.

The Great Depression, which began with the stock market crash of 1929, brought years of record high unemployment and economic problems. At the depth of the Depression in 1932, Franklin D. Roosevelt was elected to the presidency. He strongly believed that the federal government had to take a active role in the economic and social welfare arenas in order to overcome the economic stagnation and correct the underlying causes of the Depression. He called his program the New Deal. The Roosevelt administration (1933–1945) contributed enormously to the growth in the federal bureaucracy, first by initiating various governmental programs in response to the Great Depression and later to wage World War II.

For example, in 1935, Congress created Social Security to provide income for senior citizens and dependents of deceased workers. It later added coverage for disabled workers and their dependents. Other New Deal programs created jobs for the unemployed, such as the Works Progress Administration (WPA) and Civilian Conservation Corps (CCC), and regulated economic activity, such as the price supports and crop production limits introduced by the 1933 Agricultural Adjustment Act. The size and complexity of the federal government increased tremendously

▶ How does an agency become a Cabinet department?

FIGURE 9.1

Growth in the Size of the Federal Bureaucracy

The Roosevelt administration's programs to address the Depression and World War II dramatically increased the size of the federal bureaucracy. After these crises had passed, why didn't the government shrink back to its size in the early years of the twentieth century?

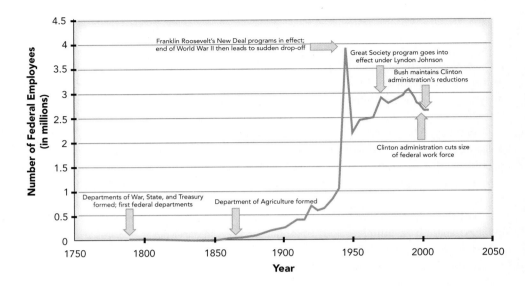

during the Roosevelt administration (see Figure 9.1). By the end of FDR's presidency in 1945, not only had the public accepted the federal government's involvement in a variety of policy issues, but many Americans had come to *expect* federal action on important matters, eventually including such areas as education and criminal justice that had traditionally been the exclusive preserve of state and local governments. Moreover, World War II had demonstrated the necessity of combining the War and Navy Departments (as well as the newly created Air Force Department) within a single structure, the Department of Defense.

In the 1950s, expanded public expectations of the federal government and the consequently broader range of legislative activity undertaken by Congress led to the creation of the Department of Health, Education and Welfare (HEW). The establishment of this department signaled the expansion of the federal bureaucracy's responsibilities into policy issues that the authors of the U.S. Constitution would never have envisioned as spheres of federal action. (In the 1970s, HEW was split into two agencies, the Department of Education and the Department of Health and Human Services.)

Heightened public awareness of urban decay, racial conflict, and poverty during the 1960s produced a new social welfare federal bureaucracy, the Department of Housing and Urban Development (HUD). Similarly, the Department of Transportation, created during the same decade, reflected concerns about urban mass transit, as well as a recognition that air travel was expanding and that continuing federal policy issues concerning ports and highways could be located in the new department.

In 1973, the energy crisis struck. In that year, the nation's ever-growing thirst for oil, natural gas, and other fossil fuels col-

lided with the determination of the oil-producing countries comprising the Organization of Petroleum Exporting Countries (OPEC) to increase their profits. Many Americans found themselves waiting in long lines at gas stations and paying skyrocketing prices to fill up their gas-guzzling cars and heat their energy-inefficient homes. Responding to the crisis atmosphere, Congress created the Department of Energy to implement new laws and develop policies designed to encourage fuel efficiency, develop new sources of energy, and relieve the nation's dependence on foreign oil producers.

▶ **How does an agency become a Cabinet department?** At the end of the 1980s, the Veterans Administration (created in 1930) was elevated to the status of a separate department called the Department of Veterans Affairs. Paying pensions and disability benefits to veterans had long been a federal responsibility in the aftermath of the Civil War, World Wars I and II, and the Korean and Vietnam Wars. By the 1980s, a huge cohort of World War II veterans had become senior citizens, and they looked to the federal government for health care and other benefits. Closely behind followed a cohort of Korean War veterans, and the middle-aged Vietnam era veterans were increasingly in need of benefits and services. It was widely felt that veterans deserved greater attention from government and improved benefits and services. When an agency gets the status of an executive department, its head becomes a member of the president's cabinet and is literally "at the table" when the president's top executive appointees discuss policies and budgets. Creation of the Department of Veterans Affairs implied a promise that veterans' interests would be taken into account in those negotiations. By elevating to cabinet status the agency responsible for veterans, Congress symbolically demon-

▶ **Which Cabinet department**
was created most recently?

strated its concern about veterans and simultaneously sought the political benefits of granting increased attention and stature to an important constituency.

▶ **Which Cabinet department was created most recently?** After terrorists attacked the World Trade Center and the Pentagon on September 11, 2001, public shock and congressional demands for action resulted in the creation of the federal government's newest department: the Department of Homeland Security (DHS). Like other departments, the DHS represented a response to a policy issue that had moved to the top of the nation's priorities. It consists of newly created agencies, such as the Transportation Safety Administration (TSA), as well as a consolidation of existing agencies moved from other departments.

pathways past and present
REORGANIZATION OF THE BUREAUCRACY

The creation of the Department of Homeland Security involved the development of a new agency by pulling together various existing agencies in order to seek better coordination of government actions related to domestic security issues. President Bush initially resisted creating a new department. The principles of his Republican Party usually advocate efforts to reduce the size of government. Moreover, many observers recognized that creating a new department that includes agencies from elsewhere in government would inevitably pose a variety of problems. Would agencies engage in "turf wars" over who should be in charge of specific tasks? Would employees resist a move to an unfamiliar department with unproven leadership and a still-developing mission? Could a new set of administrators provide guidance, supervision, and control over a gigantic and swiftly created department containing many employees who were accustomed to operating guidelines from a different department? Under pressure from Democrats and Republicans to take action in defense of national security, President Bush eventually moved forward with the creation of DHS, and inevitably, some of the feared problems materialized.

To give you an idea of the scope of the reorganization, this short list identifies a few of the agencies absorbed into the new department, as well as their previous homes within the bureaucracy.

Federal Emergency Management Agency (FEMA)—
previously an independent agency

Immigration and Naturalization Service (INS)—previously
in the Department of Justice

During the 1960s, President Lyndon B. Johnson tried to expand the activity and influence of federal government agencies in order to address poverty and racial discrimination. The Department of Housing and Urban Development (HUD) was created during his presidency. Has expanded action by the federal government actually helped to solve social problems?

▶ **How many people work**
for the federal government?

discussion questions

1. Based on the U.S. Constitution and the nature of the early federal government, what kind of bureaucracy did the nation's founders foresee?

2. What societal changes and historic events led to the creation of new departments?

Lyndon B. Johnson visiting with youth at a Philadelphia job opportunity center. As part of his "War on Poverty," Johnson created job training programs in partnership with industry.

from diminished focus on their domestic mission in light of the department's broader concerns about preventing attacks by international terrorists. Calls were heard to consider whether some of these agencies—including FEMA—could better serve the public as freestanding entities. ■

practice quiz

1. The first departments of the federal bureaucracy were created as a result of
   a. the words of the Declaration of Independence.
   b. the design of the government in the U.S. Constitution.
   c. the Civil War.
   d. President Franklin Roosevelt's New Deal program.

2. What kind of organizational entity in the federal bureaucracy is specifically mentioned in the U.S. Constitution?
   a. government corporations
   b. independent regulatory commissions
   c. departments
   d. independent agencies

3. What department was created in the 1980s in response to growing needs for medical care among a specific segment of the U.S. population?
   a. Department of Disease Control and Prevention
   b. Department of Health and Human Services
   c. Department of Medicare
   d. Department of Veterans Affairs

4. What department was created in response to the events of September 11, 2001?
   a. Department of Homeland Security
   b. Department of Defense
   c. Department of Air Traffic Security
   d. Department of Foreign Relations

Answers: 1-b, 2-c, 3-d, 4-a.

Coast Guard—previously in the Department of Transportation

Secret Service—previously in the Department of the Treasury

The fact that these agencies had historical roots in very different departments despite their need to coordinate homeland security efforts raises questions about whether there might be other related agencies scattered throughout the bureaucracy that could be brought together to seek greater efficiency on issues such as commerce and the environment. However, the slow response and general ineffectiveness of FEMA during and after Hurricane Katrina led many critics to complain that the Department of Homeland Security was too big. They claimed that individual agencies within the department had lost resources and suffered

DEPARTMENTS

During every presidential administration, the president's cabinet consists of the heads of the executive departments. These department heads typically have the title of secretary, such as secretary of defense for the head of the Department of Defense. However, the head of the Department of Justice is the attorney general of the United States. As new departments have been created, the cabinet

> ▶ **What does the president look**
> for in making appointments to
> federal offices?

has grown to include fifteen departments as well as the administrators of three agencies within the Executive Office of the President: the Office of Management and Budget (OMB), the Office of National Drug Control Policy, and Office of the U.S. Trade Representative. The head of one independent agency, the Environmental Protection Agency (EPA), also has cabinet rank. At earlier points in American history, the members of the cabinet would advise the president, debate policy options, and develop ideas to determine the president's agenda. In recent administrations, presidents have relied most heavily on their staffs and key cabinet members for advice. Cabinet meetings now serve the function of reporting to the president on the activities of each department. Cabinet members are expected to be loyal to the president and avoid any indication that they question the president's agenda or actions.

The various departments are divided according to areas of policy responsibility. Within each department, various agencies are assigned to implement laws, keep detailed records, and make consistent decisions in accordance with established rules. Table 9.2 lists the fifteen cabinet-level departments and some of the agencies housed in each. You'll notice many familiar agency names on the list, but you may be surprised within which department each agency operates. For example, many people don't realize that the National Weather Service is in the Department of Commerce and that the Financial Crimes Enforcement Network belongs to the Department of the Treasury rather than to the primary law enforcement department, the Department of Justice. The location of some agencies is a product of history and politics as much as of topical focus. For example, some people may believe that the Federal Bureau of Investigation (FBI) belongs in the new Department of Homeland Security, but it remains in its traditional home, the Department of Justice.

▶ **How many people work for the federal government?** Table 9.2 on page 348 also indicates the number of people employed in each executive department. The Office of Personnel Management reported in March 2004 that 2,640,212 civilians were employed in the executive branch of government. Nearly 1.7 million of these work in the executive departments, and an additional 956,000 are employed in independent agencies that we'll discuss later in this chapter. Although people's perceptions of impersonal, impenetrable bureaucracies often lead them to believe that all federal government agencies are huge, the departments actually vary significantly in size. They range in size from the Department of Education, which has under 4,500 employees, to

the Department of Defense, which has nearly 670,000 civilian employees in addition to 1.4 million active-duty military personnel and 1.2 million who serve in various reserve units.

There are also approximately 1,700 people who work directly for the president in the Executive Office of the President and its constituent agencies. Because they come under the direct control of the White House, these employees and agencies are typically considered an arm of the presidency rather than agencies within the federal bureaucracy.

The varying sizes of the bureaucracy's departments depend, in part, on whether they provide services at installations in far-flung locations and employ agents who work in the field or, on the other hand, primarily oversee the distribution of federal funds to state and local governments from a central office in Washington, D.C. For example, the Department of Housing and Urban Development, with only 10,000 employees, oversees the distribution of money, while the Department of Veterans Affairs, which runs veterans' hospitals and maintains other service offices, has 233,000 employees. Obviously, the large size of the Department of Defense is related to the number of bases and other facilities on which American military personnel serve throughout the United States and the world.

▶ **What does the president look for in making appointments to federal offices?** Presidential appointees who run federal executive departments are expected to be loyal members of the president's team. That means that they will defend the administration's policies and avoid public disagreements with the president. After being appointed by the president, they must be confirmed by the U.S. Senate. They are usually not regarded as working within the bureaucracy; instead, they work directly for the president and try to guide and push the bureaucracy to act in accordance with the president's policy preferences. Secretaries and assistant secretaries who are appointed by the president do not necessarily possess expertise on the policy issues and laws administered by their departments. For example, a former member of Congress or former governor from the president's political party may be chosen to run an agency as a reward for political loyalty or because the president thinks this person will be an effective spokesperson or good administrator in a particular policy area. Other high-level appointments in the departments, such as assistant secretaries and inspector generals, may go to people with policy experience, but they may also go to party loyalists or to the children of prominent political figures. Critics have cited Michael Brown's position as the director of FEMA as an example of an

► What are "independent agencies"?

TABLE 9.2

Departments in the Executive Branch of the Federal Government with Selected Subunits and Total Number of Employees, March 2004

Department of Agriculture (98,803 employees)
Agricultural Research Service
Animal and Plant Health Inspection Service
Cooperative State Research, Education and Extension Service
Economic Research Service
Farm Service Agency
Forest Service
Natural Resources Conservation Service
Department of Commerce (37,126 employees)
Bureau of the Census
Bureau of Export Administration
International Trade Administration
National Institute of Standards and Technology
National Oceanic and Atmospheric Administration
National Weather Service
Patent and Trademark Office Database
Department of Defense (667,192 civilian employees)
Air Force
Army
Defense Contract and Audit Agency
Defense Intelligence Agency
Marine Corps
National Guard
National Security Agency
Navy
Department of Education (4,448 employees)
Educational Resources and Information Center
National Library of Education
Department of Energy (15,140 employees)
Federal Energy Regulatory Commission
Los Alamos Laboratory
Southwestern Power Administration
Department of Health and Human Services (60,632 employees)
Centers for Disease Control and Prevention
Food and Drug Administration
National Institutes of Health

Department of Homeland Security (149,059 employees)
Customs and Border Protection
Coast Guard
Federal Emergency Management Agency
Secret Service
Department of Housing and Urban Development (10,330 employees)
Government National Mortgage Association (Ginnie Mae)
Office of Healthy Homes and Lead Hazard Control
Public and Indian Housing Agencies
Department of the Interior (70,240 employees)
Bureau of Indian Affairs
Bureau of Land Management
Fish and Wildlife Service
Geological Survey
National Parks Service
Office of Surface Mining
Department of Justice (103,318 employees)
Bureau of Alcohol, Tobacco, Firearms, and Explosives
Drug Enforcement Agency
Federal Bureau of Investigation
Federal Bureau of Prisons
United States Marshals Service
Department of Labor (16,009 employees)
Mine Safety and Health Administration
Occupational Safety and Health Administration
Department of State (32,977 employees)
Department of Transportation (57,668 employees)
Federal Aviation Administration
Department of the Treasury (126,408 employees)
Bureau of Engraving and Printing
Bureau of Public Debt
Internal Revenue Service
Office of the Comptroller of the Currency
United States Mint
Department of Veterans Affairs (232,818 employees)

SOURCE: Office of Personnel Management, http://www.opm.gov, March 2004.

President George W. Bush meets regularly with his cabinet in a private room at the White House. The news media can enter the room only for scheduled photo opportunities. Should the president's cabinet meetings be televised so that all Americans can see the discussions among the leaders of the executive branch?
Photo: Doug Mills/The New York Times

appointment based on political connections and loyalty rather than qualifications and experience.

In the confirmation process, senators may expect that the secretaries and other appointed officials in specific departments possess relevant experience and expertise. This is most likely to be true for the departments of State, Defense, and the Treasury, owing to the overriding importance of foreign affairs, national security, and the economy. Because of the publicity and widespread perceptions about deficiencies in Michael Brown's performance as FEMA's director during Hurricane Katrina, the list of appointed positions that receive close senatorial scrutiny may expand. For other positions, senators look less closely at the nominees' qualifications because they believe that presidents should generally be permitted to choose their own representatives to lead government agencies. Even the president's political opponents in the Senate may vote to confirm nominees simply because they would like other senators to show the same deference for appointments by future presidents from a different political party.

Presidents do not merely reward loyalists in their appointments. They also use the upper-level appointed positions to place above the bureaucracy knowledgeable political figures who will vigorously enforce the laws and regulations with which the president agrees—or alternatively, will fail to enforce, enforce weakly, or attempt to change laws and regulations with which the president disagrees. These elite actors influence the use of the bureaucracy's power and resources in shaping public policy.

In the final decades of the twentieth century, presidents increasingly used their appointment power to demonstrate a commitment to diversity as a means of pleasing their constituencies and attracting more voters. Women and members of minority groups increasingly receive appointments to highly visible positions at the top of executive departments. Presidents also seek geographic diversity so that the cabinet can be regarded as representing the nation. The composition of President George W. Bush's cabinet in 2004 illustrates this aspiration for diversity. Among the cabinet members were five former governors and members of Congress. There were three women, including Labor Secretary Elaine Chao, the first Asian American woman to sit in a presidential cabinet. One Asian American man was in the cabinet, Transportation Secretary Norman Mineta. The cabinet also included three African American men: Colin Powell, secretary of state; Rod Paige, secretary of education; and Alphonso Jackson, secretary of housing and urban development. Powell was later replaced by Condoleezza Rice, the first African American woman

to serve as secretary of state. Just as Democratic President Bill Clinton had attempted to demonstrate bipartisanship through his appointment of former Republican Senator William Cohen as defense secretary, Republican President Bush sought to make the same point through the appointment of Transportation Secretary Mineta, a former Democratic congressman.

Only a half-dozen cabinet-level nominees have ever been rejected in the confirmation process by the U.S. Senate. The most recent instance was the Senate's vote against John Tower, President George H. W. Bush's nominee for defense secretary in the late 1980s, after allegations surfaced of Tower's excessive drinking and other aspects of his personal life. Generally, senators believe that the president ought to be able to choose the heads of government agencies. However, senators may oppose someone who is viewed as patently unqualified for a specific position or someone whose political views are regarded as too extreme.

INDEPENDENT AGENCIES, INDEPENDENT REGULATORY COMMISSIONS, AND GOVERNMENT CORPORATIONS

▶ **What are "independent agencies"?** The executive branch includes nearly a hundred independent agencies, independent regulatory commissions, and government corporations that operate outside the fifteen executive departments. Table 9.3 on page 350, provides examples of some of the independent organizational entities in the federal government.

These agencies do not have identical functions. Some of them provide government grants or administer a specific government facility, such as a museum. Others are regulatory agencies that exert significant influence over public policy because Congress has delegated to them broad authority to interpret statutes,

Joan Claybrook testifies at congressional hearings and uses press conferences to publicize issues of automotive safety and to educate government officials about health and safety problems. Is it improper for such a policy advocate to be appointed to a leadership position in the federal bureaucracy?

create regulations, investigate violations of law, and impose sanctions on violators. The regulatory agencies are typically called commissions or boards, and, as such names imply, they are led by a group of officials. The heads of these agencies often serve staggered terms so that no new president can replace the entire commission or board upon taking office. For example, the members of the Board of Governors of the Federal Reserve Board serve fourteen-year terms, with one new member appointed to the seven-member board every two years. The Federal Reserve Board acts independently to shape monetary policy by, for example, setting certain interest rates that affect the cost of borrowing money.

For some other commissions, the authorizing legislation requires that the appointees contain a mix of Republicans and Democrats. For example, the Federal Communications Commission (FCC) and the Federal Trade Commission (FTC) each have five members, but the law requires that no more than three members can be from one political party. The FCC regulates television, radio, cell phones, and other aspects of communications. It also investigates and imposes sanctions for violations of law and policy. For example, it slapped a $550,000 fine on Viacom, the parent company of CBS Television, for the "wardrobe malfunction" that led singer Janet Jackson's bare breast to be momentarily visible to a national audience during the halftime show at the 2004 Super Bowl. The FTC enforces consumer protection laws, such as fining companies that do not comply with rules concerning the fair treatment of applicants for credit or loans.

pathways profile
JOAN CLAYBROOK

Joan Claybrook has spent her entire career advocating action by Congress and federal agencies to create and enforce regulations to protect the health and safety of consumers. After graduating from Goucher College and Georgetown University's Law School, Claybrook went to work for the National Traffic Safety Bureau. In 1966, she helped draft legislation to improve automobile safety

---

TABLE 9.3

Examples of Independent Agencies, Independent Regulatory Commissions, and Government Corporations, by Type

INDEPENDENT AGENCIES: FACILITY OR PROGRAM ADMINISTRATION

General Services Administration

National Archives and Records Administration

National Aeronautics and Space Administration

Peace Corps

Selective Service System

Smithsonian Institution

Social Security Administration

INDEPENDENT AGENCIES: GRANTS OF FUNDS

Harry S. Truman Scholarship Foundation

National Endowment for the Arts

National Endowment for the Humanities

National Science Foundation

INDEPENDENT REGULATORY COMMISSIONS

Consumer Product Safety Commission (toys, appliances, other products)

Federal Communications Commission (radio, television, cell phones)

Federal Elections Commission (campaign contributions, campaign advertising)

Federal Trade Commission (consumer credit, deceptive advertising)

National Labor Relations Board (labor unions, union voting, unfair practices)

National Transportation Safety Board (collisions involving aircraft, trains, trucks, other vehicles)

Nuclear Regulatory Commission (nuclear materials)

Securities and Exchange Commission (stock market, financial investments)

GOVERNMENT CORPORATIONS

Federal Deposit Insurance Corporation

National Railroad Passenger Corporation (Amtrak)

Pension Benefit Guaranty Corporation

Overseas Private Investment Corporation

United States Postal Service

discussionquestions

1. What kinds of people are selected to be members of the president's cabinet? Would the country be better served by selecting people with backgrounds different from those possessed by the kinds of people who currently head departments of the federal government?

2. Would the bureaucracy serve the public better if all departments were independent agencies?

Scientists at NASA's Jet Propulsion Laboratory in Pasadena, California, show their excitement on seeing the first photos sent back from the Mars Rover. Many people believe that space exploration must be handled by government because it is too expensive and too important to be developed by private businesses. What other activities and functions must be handled by government rather than by other kinds of organizations?

and then left government service to work with Ralph Nader and others on automobile safety and other consumer issues. During the administration of President Jimmy Carter (1977–1981), she was appointed to serve as administrator of the National Highway Traffic Safety Administration, the successor agency to the one where she began her career. She later returned to Public Citizen, an advocacy organization that she had helped form in the 1970s, becoming its president and continuing her advocacy of government regulations concerning automobiles, the safety of medicines, fraudulent business practices, and other issues of concern to American consumers. Much of her career has been spent lobbying government agencies to create and enforce new kinds of safety regulations. ■

Some independent agencies are government corporations with their own boards of directors. For example, the National Railroad Passenger Corporation manages Amtrak, the nation's national system of passenger trains. These agencies generate their own revenue through the sale of products or services, fees, or insurance premiums. They need to convince Congress to provide them with whatever operating funds they need beyond what they can raise from customers. Some members of Congress see Amtrak, the U.S. Postal Service, and similar agencies as providing services that could be provided more efficiently by private businesses, which explains why arguments for cutting off government funding for such enterprises are often raised. Defenders of these agencies argue that these essential services must be maintained and that private businesses may cut back or eliminate unprofitable enterprises, such as national rail service, or charge unreasonable prices, as might occur under a completely private postal system. Thus they defend government control and subsidies for these agencies.

Independent agencies are responsible for government facilities, such as the national museums in Washington, D.C., administered by the Smithsonian Institution, or specific programs, such as the Peace Corps, which sends American volunteers to teach and provide community service around the world. Such facilities and programs are likely to be considered too unique and important to ever be subjected to privatization. Similarly, special agencies, such as the National Aeronautics and Space Administration (NASA), the space exploration agency, may do things that are so expensive and important that private organizations cannot match the federal government's ability to pursue the agency's goals.

practicequiz

1. Most members of the president's cabinet are heads of what kinds of organizational entities in the bureaucracy?
   a. departments
   b. independent agencies
   c. independent regulatory commissions
   d. government corporations

2. Members of the cabinet are
   a. elected by voters.
   b. appointed by the president and confirmed by Congress.
   c. appointed by the president and confirmed by the Senate.
   d. selected through civil service tests and interviews.

3. Amtrak, the agency that handles railroad passenger service, is currently a
   a. department
   b. independent agency
   c. independent regulatory commission
   d. government corporation

4. The Federal Communications Commission is
   a. a department
   b. an independent agency
   c. an independent regulatory commission
   d. a government corporation

Answers: 1-a, 2-c, 3-d, 4-c.

▶ **Why do Americans have** such a negative image of bureaucracy?

People wait in line to mail income tax forms on the last day for filing taxes. U.S. Post Offices expect long lines as the midnight deadline approaches. Have you had positive or negative experiences in dealing with government agencies?

The Nature of Bureaucracy

Bureaucracies can be public entities, such as a state treasury department that collects taxes and enforces tax laws, or private entities, such as a bank with different departments for mortgages, commercial loans, and checking accounts. As you know very well, colleges and universities are also bureaucracies, with myriad offices responsible for admissions, financial aid, residential life, parking, and security. In a bureaucracy, workers typically have specific task responsibilities, and there are clear lines of authority in the organization's pyramid of supervision and leadership. One person is responsible for leading and supervising the organization, and beneath the leader lie different levels of responsibility and supervisory authority. In a private organization, such as a business corporation, the leader might be called the president or the chief executive officer. In a government agency, the title of the head person may depend on the nature of the agency and the definition of positions under relevant constitutional provisions or statutes. Departments are generally headed by a secretary, while independent regulatory commissions typically have a chairman.

THE IMAGE OF BUREAUCRACY

In the minds of most Americans, the word *bureaucracy* does not conjure up idealistic notions of efficient organizations that carry out specialized responsibilities for the public's benefit. Instead, *bureaucracy* can convey an image of gargantuan organizations filled with employees who push paper around on their desks all day and worry only about collecting their paychecks and earning their pensions. In government service, because these employees have secure jobs, they may be perceived to feel no pressure to work industriously or efficiently. Americans may visualize them as mindlessly enforcing "red tape" rules that keep aggrieved citizens from receiving expected benefits and services.

▶ **Why do Americans have such a negative image of bureaucracy?** Evidence of negative perceptions of government bureaucracy regularly emerges in public opinion polls. A poll concerning the performance of five federal agencies conducted by the Pew Research Center for the People and the Press found that "the agencies get generally poor ratings for how well they carry out their administrative tasks." The groups that were polled "criticize the agencies for working too slowly and making their rules and

▶ **Even though we dislike** bureaucracy, don't we need some sort of system to get things done in government?

what YOU can do!

If you needed to file a complaint with a government agency or apply for a specific benefit or service, would you know how to do it? Make a list of all of the government agencies with which you come into contact. Select two of these agencies, and study their Web sites to learn how to file a complaint or request a specific service.

forms too complicated."[3] Similarly, a 2006 nationwide poll for the Council for Excellence in Government found that only 31 percent of Americans had "a great deal or quite a lot of confidence" in civil servants or people who work for government, a figure that was below the confidence levels expressed for the military, the U.S. Supreme Court, mayors, and governors.[4]

The negative image of the bureaucracy may be enhanced by Americans' expectations that the government ought to operate for the benefit of the people in accordance with Abraham Lincoln's familiar words describing a "government of the people, by the people, and for the people." When people's anticipated Social Security checks are late or Medicare benefits are denied, citizens often feel frustrated and resentful about their treatment at the hands of bureaucrats who are paid by taxpayers yet do not seem responsive and obedient to the public. Perhaps you have felt such frustration in dealing with student loan applications or waiting for a tax refund.

This negative image of bureaucracies obviously includes generalizations about large organizations and the frustrations that individuals may face in dealing with the officials who work there. What is your image of a bureaucracy? When we talk about the bureaucracy in terms of government agencies, rather than banks, corporations, and universities, does your image of bureaucracy depend on which government officials come to mind? When a firefighter rushes into a blazing house and saves a child's life, few of us would associate this hero with the negative image of a bureaucracy. Yet the firefighter belongs to a bureaucracy: The fire department is a government agency, hierarchically organized and with specialized responsibilities for each rank, from the chief down through the captain and the individual firefighters.

As this example shows, our perceptions of government agencies may depend on actual experiences. When government officials respond quickly and provide expected services directly to us, there's no reason to associate these officials and their agency with the negative image of a bureaucracy. On the other hand, when responses to our requests are slow and we can't understand why we must fill out complicated forms or meet detailed requirements, the negative images come galloping back.

Because of their size and distance from many citizens, federal agencies may be especially susceptible to generating negative images. When citizens go to their local Social Security Administration office to apply for retirement or disability benefits, the office staff may need to seek approval from other officials back

at Social Security headquarters. Meanwhile, we may have to fill out many forms and provide copies of various documents—and then wait weeks for an answer. "Red tape!" we mutter. Direct services from a local firefighter or police officer put a human face on much appreciated and immediate government services. But federal officials are often distant, faceless decision makers whose contacts with citizens are based on slow and frequently disappointing correspondence in response to questions and requests.

Millions of Americans have annual contacts with such federal agencies as the Internal Revenue Service, the Social Security Administration, or the Veterans Administration, yet they may not associate any individual name or face with the communications that they receive. Look at the example (Table 9.4 on page 354) of the steps in applying for and appealing decisions about Social Security disability benefits. Think about how many different decision makers can affect what happens without the applicant actually knowing who these individuals might be. Unlike the equally faceless customer service representatives for online merchants and credit card companies, who nevertheless seem eager to respond to our phone calls and questions, the government officials with whom we communicate may appear detached and unresponsive—and (it seems), all too often agents at the IRS, Social Security, or the VA either insist that we pay more or tell us that we can't get some benefit. This does not necessarily mean that low-level government officials are by nature coldhearted. They may need to fill out many forms and gain approvals from superiors before they can address our claims and questions in a slow-moving process. Whether or not individual government officials are uncaring, it is easy to understand why the bureaucracy often has a negative image in the minds of Americans.

According to Charles Goodsell, people expect too much from the bureaucracy. Says Goodsell, we have negative images in part because "we expect bureaucracies not merely to expend maximum possible effort in solving societal problems but to dispose of them entirely, whether solvable or not."[5] Do you agree that government agencies receive blame unfairly for falling short of perfection?

THE ADVANTAGES OF BUREAUCRACY

▶ **Even though we dislike bureaucracy, don't we need some sort of system to get things done in government?** Officialdom does not exist by accident. Bureaucracies are created and evolve as a

patronage system
successful political candidates' and parties' rewarding their supporters with government jobs and firing supporters of the opposing party. Also known as the **spoils system.**

TABLE 9.4
Applying for Social Security Disability Benefits

APPLICANT	DECISION MAKERS
Step 1. *Submit application forms.* Records needed to demonstrate that applicant meets the criteria for 1) enough total years worked contributing money to the social security system to become eligible for consideration; 2) worked at least half the time in years preceding claimed disability; 3) contact information for doctors. *If disability claim is denied, then:*	<u>Decision makers:</u> After officials in Social Security Administration determine if applicant's work history makes individual qualified for benefits, medical personnel in state agency receive referral from Social Security Administration to obtain medical records and evaluate applicant's capacity to work.
Step 2. *Request reconsideration* *If disability claim is denied, then:*	<u>Decision makers:</u> Entire file reviewed by officials in Social Security Administration who did not take part in the original decision.
Step 3. *Appeal decision to quasi-judicial process in Social Security Administration* *If disability claim is denied, then:*	<u>Decision makers:</u> Administrative Law Judge (ALJ) within Social Security Administration will conduct a hearing at which the applicant and the applicant's attorney (if represented by counsel) can present evidence and witnesses before ALJ decides whether or not the original denial of benefits was improper.
Step 4. *Appeal decision to the Appeals Council within the Social Security Administration* *If disability claim is denied, then:*	<u>Decision makers:</u> Members of the Appeals Council within the Social Security Administration will review records and either deny the claim or refer the case back to the ALJ for further review.
Step 5. *File lawsuit in U.S. District Court.*	<u>Decision makers:</u> U.S. District Court judge considers evidence and determines whether the denial of benefits by the Social Security Administration was improper.

SOURCE: U.S. Social Security Administration, www.ssa.gov

---

means to undertake the purposes and responsibilities of organizations. The German sociologist Max Weber (1864–1920) is known for describing an ideal bureaucracy involving competent, trained personnel with clearly defined job responsibilities under a central authority who keeps detailed records and makes consistent decisions in accordance with established rules. In theory, these are beneficial elements for running an organization efficiently. If you were in charge of distributing retirement benefits throughout the United States, how would you organize your system of distribution? Would you simply appoint one individual in each state to be the coordinator in charge of the retirees in that state and then send that individual all of the money each month for that state's retirees? This approach appears to eliminate the current centralized bureaucracy of the Social Security Administration, but it also may create many problems. How would you know whether each state coordinator was using the same criteria and rules for determining eligibility for retirement funds? How would you know whether the coordinators were sending out the appropriate amounts of money on time? How would you know whether the coordinators were pocketing the money and shortchanging the retirees? This small example illus-

discussionquestions

1. How can the bureaucracy improve its image?

2. Are there ways to make the advantages of bureaucracy more widely recognized?

trates the advantages of government bureaucracies. When agencies are organized in a hierarchical fashion with specialized responsibilities, the federal government can try to diminish the risks from these problems. In fact, bureaucracies, despite their flaws and problems, may provide a number of advantages for implementing laws and public policies.

- **Standardization.** By having a centralized administration and a common set of rules, benefits and services can be provided in a standard fashion that avoids treating similarly situated citizens differently. A retiree in Idaho can receive the same federal benefits and services as a retiree of the same age and employment history in Maine.

- **Expertise and competence.** When people who work in an agency focus on specific areas of law and policy throughout their careers, they can develop expertise on those issues. This expertise will help them effectively carry out laws and policies and, moreover, permit them to advise Congress and the president on ways to improve law and policy. Presumably, their expertise will make them more competent than people who know little about the subject. Thus people who work for the Environmental Protection Agency are typically hired because of their education and interest in environmental issues, and they develop greater expertise on this subject as they spend years working in this area. The same is true of people in other agencies, such as the Department of Health and Human Services, the Department of Transportation, and the Federal Bureau of Investigation. Imagine how much less efficient government might be if workers were told, "This week you'll handle matters relating to veterans, next week you must enforce regulations concerning agriculture, and the following week you'll be working on space flights for NASA."

- **Accountability.** Congress can authorize a specific budget for particular programs and then monitor results for the targeted policy area. If $50 million is earmarked to combat air pollution, the existence of an agency dedicated to environmental issues—the EPA—permits those funds to be directed to the targeted issues and not mixed together with funds destined for education, transportation, and defense, all of which are handled by separate agencies in the bureaucracy. After the money is spent, air pollution can be evaluated, and Congress and the president can assess whether the EPA spent the money effectively and whether their intended policies were carried out correctly.

- **Coordination.** Efforts of different agencies can be more effectively coordinated when each has clearly defined responsibilities and a hierarchical structure. Hierarchy enables the leaders in each agency to direct subordinates to work in cooperation with other agencies. For example, if officials in the Department of Education and the Department of Health and Human Services are instructed to cooperate in implementing an antidrug program or an education program aimed at preventing teen pregnancy, the leaders of the respective agencies can work together to delegate shared responsibilities. When individual officials throughout the country act independently on issues, it is much more difficult to coordinate efforts effectively.

In general, these advantages may be helpful in both government and business organizations. One additional advantage has special importance for government bureaucracy: merit systems for hiring. But merit has not always been the criterion for hiring government workers.

Until a little over a century ago, government employees were hired and fired on the basis of their support for particular political parties and candidates for elective office. This was called the **patronage system** or **spoils system.** Political parties rewarded their supporters by giving them government jobs. At the same time, supporters of the opposing party were fired as soon as an election placed new leaders in office. "To the victor belongs the spoils," said a prominent Jacksonian era politician early in the nineteenth century, giving political patronage its alternative name, the *spoils system.* (By "spoils," he was referring to the practice of an army sacking a conquered city and soldiers carrying off whatever they could grab.) President Jackson justified such "rotation in office" after elections as democratic. Anyway, he said, most government posts were so easy that the average (white male) citizen could readily fill them, so why allow federal jobs to be monopolized by the elite that his predecessor, John Quincy Adams, had installed? And perhaps he did have a point, as many patronage jobs at the time involved collecting customs duties or running post offices.

Of course, the spoils system had many problems. There was an abrupt turnover after every election, particularly when the party or faction in power lost out to a rival. Unqualified people got government jobs despite lacking the knowledge and interest to carry out their tasks properly. Government workers steered benefits and services to fellow partisans and sought to deprive their political opponents of government services. Officials spent too much time

► **How does the civil** service make bureaucracy less "political"?

civil service system
government employment system in which employees are hired on the basis of their qualifications and cannot be fired merely for belonging to the wrong political party; originated with the federal Pendleton Act in 1883 and expanded at other levels of government in the half-century that followed.

Hatch Act
federal law that limits the participation of federal government employees in political campaigns to protect them from feeling obligated to donate money or work for political candidates.

TABLE 9.5
The Hatch Act

PERMITTED/PROHIBITED ACTIVITIES FOR EMPLOYEES WHO MAY NOT PARTICIPATE IN PARTISAN POLITICAL ACTIVITY

These federal employees may-

- register and vote as they choose
- assist in voter registration drives
- express opinions about candidates and issues
- participate in campaigns where none of the candidates represent a political party
- contribute money to political organizations or attend political fund raising functions
- attend political rallies and meetings
- join political clubs or parties
- sign nominating petitions
- campaign for or against referendum questions, constitutional amendments, municipal ordinances

These federal employees may not-

- be candidates for public office in partisan elections
- campaign for or against a candidate or slate of candidates in partisan elections
- make campaign speeches
- collect contributions or sell tickets to political fund raising functions
- distribute campaign material in partisan elections
- organize or manage political rallies or meetings
- hold office in political clubs or parties
- circulate nominating petitions
- work to register voters for one party only
- wear political buttons at work

SOURCE: www.osc.gov/ha_fed.htm#regulations

doing things that would help keep their party in power and themselves in their job. New roads, government contracts, and other benefits went to citizens who supported the elected officials who had hired the government workers. With self-interest unchecked, there were grave risks of corruption, as government workers and political leaders alike traded bribes for favoritism in distributing government services and benefits.

All these problems came to a head in the early 1880s. In the summer of 1881, a man claiming to be a disappointed office-seeker (he was probably insane) shot President James Garfield. Garfield's assassination made him a martyr for the cause of "good government." This event helped push forward previous proposals to reform the employment system within the federal government. Congress and President Chester A. Arthur found themselves under irresistible public pressure to enact legislation establishing a **civil service system** based on merit.

► **How does the civil service make bureaucracy less "political"?** In 1883, Congress passed and Arthur signed the Pendleton Act, creating the first federal civil service system. Under this act, applicants for specified federal government jobs were supposed to be tested, demonstrate their qualifications, and keep their jobs based on competent performance rather than political affiliation. The new system reduced, but did not entirely eliminate, such problems as unqualified employees and bribery. Over time, more federal jobs were brought under civil service rules, and civil service systems eventually developed as well in state and local governments, especially during the Progressive Era in the first decades of the twentieth century.

The civil service system is still the framework for the federal bureaucracy. Today, the president can appoint the top officials who oversee most federal government agencies. In doing so, the president seeks to steer the bureaucracy in policy directions that reflect the voters' presidential choice in the most recent election. However, except for these high officials and the staff in the Executive Office of the President, the vast majority of other federal workers are civil service employees who remain at their jobs as presidential administrations come and go. Standardization, expertise, and competence would all be endangered—indeed, under today's conditions, they would collapse—if federal agencies experienced the kind of massive turnovers in personnel after each election that were typical of mid-nineteenth-century America.

Civil service rules protect federal employees from being fired for failing to support a specific political party. And federal

▶ **Why is it so hard** to make changes in a bureaucracy?

what YOU can do!
Read about the history of civil service at the Web site of the U.S. Office of Personnel Management at **http://www.opm.gov/ BiographyofAnIdeal/SubMain1789-1883.asp** How would the bureaucracy be different today if these reforms had not taken place?

employees are further protected by the **Hatch Act,** a law that limits the participation of federal employees in political campaigns (see Table 9.5). They can vote and attend political rallies, but they cannot work on campaigns or endorse candidates. Although this law limits federal workers' political participation, it is intended to prevent them from being pressured by elected officials to donate their money and time to political campaigns. Prior to the implementation of civil service systems, it was very common for government employees to be required to work on political campaigns in order to keep their jobs. The current system spares them from fearing that they will lose promotions, raises, and other benefits for failing to support the party in power.

Although civil service systems are firmly established at the federal and state levels of government, vestiges of the old spoils system still exist in some cities and counties. This may be especially true in certain local court systems, where elected judges appoint a variety of clerks and bailiffs. For example, in the municipal court of Akron, Ohio, the elected clerk reportedly controls fifty-three patronage jobs.[6] Legislators, whose branch of government is separate from the executive branch that is covered by civil service, also typically hire and fire their own staff based on political loyalty.

THE PROBLEMS OF GOVERNMENT BUREAUCRACY

The advantages of a merit system do not mean, however, that government agencies necessarily fulfill their responsibilities efficiently and satisfy the expectations of citizens, the president, and Congress. Many practical problems tarnish the idealistic vision of civil service bureaucracies as effective, efficient organizations. For example, as organizations grow in size, decision-making layers proliferate between the employee whom the average citizen encounters and the policy-setting upper-level managers with final authority. Higher-level decision makers may be far removed from the practical policy problems affecting citizens. When decisions must move through a chain of command, there are obvious risks of delay, including the chance that documents will be misplaced or lost so that new forms must be completed to start a decision-making process all over again.

▶ **Why is it so hard to make changes in a bureaucracy?** Civil service protections can make it difficult for top officials to motivate government employees and spur them to take actions, especially when those actions require changing an agency's priorities or operating methods. Almost by nature, large organizations are resistant to change. People who have become accustomed to doing their jobs in a specific way may be reluctant to adopt new priorities and directives. Bureaucracies are not typically associated with innovation and bold ideas. They change slowly and usually in incremental fashion. When the president or Congress wants law and policy to move in a new direction, getting the bureaucracy to reorder its priorities and operate in different ways can be akin to the familiar image of "turning a battleship at sea"—a slow, gradual, laborious process. If executive agencies are slow to implement new laws, they can hinder or even undermine the achievement of a president's policy goals.

For policy change to be effective, laws and programs must be designed by taking account of the resources, characteristics, experience, and organizational structure of the agencies that must implement those laws and programs. President George W. Bush, for example, touted his No Child Left Behind (NCLB) law, passed in 2002, as the key to improving education throughout the country. The NCLB law required the testing of all students and provided for punishing schools whose students perform poorly. Two years later, however, the federal government's own watchdog agency, the Government Accountability Office (GAO, formerly known as the Government Accounting Office), reported that the law had been poorly implemented because data about schools and students were not collected consistently and systematically throughout the nation. States, moreover, complained that the Department of Education had failed to provide appropriate guidelines on how to gain full approval for their plans to fulfill NCLB's requirements. By October 2004, twenty-two states and the District of Columbia had gained only conditional approval for their plans.[7]

Implementation problems can be even more significant when, rather than just providing guidance and supervision for state and local governments, an agency bears responsibility for hiring staff, training personnel, and carrying out new tasks. When agencies are large bureaucracies, it can be exceptionally difficult to organize, implement, and monitor programs effectively. The federal bureaucracy bears responsibility for organizing initiatives nationwide, relying on thousands of individuals spread throughout the country at hundreds of locations. Under such conditions, supervisors in Washington, D.C., cannot monitor the daily activities and performance of far-flung operations.

▶ **Maybe private agencies** would do a better job—aren't they more efficient?

decentralization
proposed reform for government agencies intended to increase efficiency in administration and create closer contacts with the local public; permits regional and local offices to manage their own performances without close supervision from headquarters.

privatization
turning portions of government bureaucracy responsibilities over to private organizations on the assumption that they can administer and deliver services more effectively and inexpensively.

Let's take an example: the Transportation Security Administration, which was created in November 2001 in the aftermath of the 9/11 terrorist attacks. It is now part of the Department of Homeland Security. Among other responsibilities, the TSA screens passengers and their baggage for weapons and explosives before they board commercial airliners. In its first few years, the new agency was plagued with problems. Eighteen thousand screeners were hired and initially put to work without required background checks. Among the 1,200 screeners eventually fired after background checks revealed that they had lied on their applications or had criminal records, several with criminal records were permitted to remain on the job for weeks or months before termination.[8] The federal government paid hundreds of thousands of dollars in claims after screeners were caught stealing from passengers' luggage while searching for weapons and explosives. Morale problems developed as screeners complained of being required to work overtime without adequate compensation and of being assigned to use baggage-scanning equipment without receiving any training.[9] If the TSA had been given more time for planning, more opportunities to screen and train workers, and more resources to ensure adequate personnel and equipment at each airport, the implementation of the policy might have gone more smoothly. However, the bureaucracy must work in a constrained environment in which there are limits on time, resources, and expertise that result in implementation problems.

REFORM OF THE BUREAUCRACY

The gigantic size and nationwide responsibilities of modern federal agencies make it extremely difficult for the bureaucracy to live up to the ideals of efficient performance based on management principles in an organizational hierarchy. Some critics argue that alternative approaches to implementation could reduce the problems of government bureaucracy. One suggestion is to try **decentralization.** The federal government could give greater independence to regional offices that would be more closely connected to local issues and client populations. Alternatively, states could be given greater authority to handle their own affairs. For example, state inspection agencies could receive federal funds to enforce national air pollution or workplace safety laws. The argument for decentralization rests on a belief that smaller agencies, presumably more closely connected to

local problems, can be more efficient and effective. There are risks, however, that decentralization would lead to inconsistent standards and treatment for people in different parts of the country. Officials in one state may vigorously enforce pollution laws while those in another state may turn a blind eye to such problems because of the economic and political power of polluting industries.

▶ **Maybe private agencies would do a better job—aren't they more efficient? Privatization** has also been suggested as a cure for the problems of government bureaucracy. Critics argue that private businesses working under government contracts could deliver services and benefits to citizens with greater efficiency and less expense than when the bureaucracy handles such matters. All levels of government use private contracts in an effort to save money. Indeed, states have sent convicted offenders to prisons built and operated by private corporations, governments pay private contractors to repair highways and build bridges, states such as Florida and Kansas have privatized aspects of child welfare services, and the Department of Defense and the Central Intelligence Agency even used private contractors to interrogate prisoners during the war in Iraq.

In theory, businesses and nonprofit agencies are better than the government bureaucracy at finding ways to save money, developing innovations, and responding to feedback from client populations. One way that they save money is through compensation for low-level workers that is less generous than government pay and through flexible personnel policies that allow them to lay off or fire employees whose counterparts in government would have civil service job security protection. Privatization is controversial. In some circumstances, private contractors do not save money and do not deliver services more effectively than government agencies. In addition, it can be difficult to hold private companies accountable for their actions because they are not necessarily subject to the same oversight laws that govern public agencies. Moreover, there are risks of favoritism and corruption as private companies use campaign contributions, personal contacts with government officials, and lobbying to encourage expenditures of government funds that add to their profits but do not necessarily address the public's needs.

Periodically, efforts are made to reform the bureaucracy in order to improve its effectiveness. For example, Congress established the **Senior Executive Service (SES)** in 1978. The SES consists of senior administrators with outstanding leadership and

Senior Executive Service (SES)
program within the federal executive branch, established by Congress in 1978 to enable senior administrators with outstanding leadership and management skills to be moved between jobs in different agencies to enhance the performance of the bureaucracy.

discussionquestions

1. What problems arise in the federal government bureaucracy?

2. What challenges does the bureaucracy face in implementing laws?

management skills who can be moved between jobs in different agencies in order to enhance the performance of the bureaucracy. According to the description of the SES on the Web site of the Office of Personnel Management, "This concept holds that the Government needs executives who can provide strategic leadership and whose commitment to public policy and administration transcends their commitment to a specific agency mission or an individual profession." The development of the SES was intended to add flexibility in shifting personnel resources within the federal bureaucracy.

practicequiz

1. Which of the following is *not* assumed to be a beneficial aspect of bureaucracy?
   a. employees' expertise on policy issues
   b. citizens' direct access to high-level decision makers
   c. vertical lines of authority for supervision and control
   d. standardization of procedures and equal treatment of citizens

2. Civil service systems were developed in response to
   a. the Great Depression.
   b. Franklin Roosevelt's New Deal programs.
   c. the spoils system.
   d. the creation of independent regulatory commissions.

3. Decentralization of the federal government bureaucracy would
   a. give more authority to decision makers in regional and local offices.
   b. eliminate the need for any government officials to work in Washington, D.C.
   c. make the judiciary the most powerful branch of government.
   d. permit the president to issue direct orders to the nation's governors.

4. Proposals for reform of the bureaucracy through privatization assume that
   a. investors want to purchase the U.S. Capitol building.
   b. government agencies should grow larger than they are today.
   c. cabinet officers will be more highly motivated if they receive bonuses.
   d. private businesses operate more efficiently than government agencies.

Answers: 1-b, 2-c, 3-a, 4-d.

The Lobbying Pathway and Policymaking

From what you've read so far, you can see the bureaucracy's influence over policy through its responsibilities for implementation of laws enacted by Congress. As the examples of transportation safety and education have indicated, the effectiveness of agencies' implementation efforts can depend on their resources, information, and expertise.

The bureaucracy can affect policymaking in other ways, too. Its impact on the formulation of public policy comes primarily through the decisions and actions of elites, people with political connections, status, or expertise. This impact comes especially from the political appointees and policy experts at the upper levels of federal agencies. For example, officials in the bureaucracy formulate specific rules that provide precise details for how statutes should be implemented. In this section, we'll focus on these officials who influence the formulation of policies.

Lower-level personnel in the bureaucracy also affect policy outcomes through their influence over the day-to-day implementation of laws and regulations. These government employees include FBI agents, forest rangers, postal workers, water quality inspectors, and many others who have direct contact with the public. If an FBI agent does not follow mandated procedures when investigating a case or arresting a suspect, the laws of Congress and the regulations of the Department of Justice have not been implemented properly. Full and proper implementation of many laws and policies can rest in the hands of relatively low-level officials who make discretionary decisions about how they will treat individuals and businesses when conducting investigations or administering the distribution of government services and benefits.

THE BUREAUCRACY AND LEGISLATION

The ideal of the bureaucracy envisions employees with competence and expertise who work in a pyramid-shaped organizational structure with clear lines of authority and supervision. The lines of authority in a bureaucracy's organizational chart are meant to indicate that the downward flow of instructions guides the actions of personnel at each level of the agency. In reality, the decisions and actions of personnel within the bureaucracy are more complicated than that, because of the influence of informal networks and

▶ **How does an iron triangle work?**

iron triangle
the tight relationships between employees in government agencies, interest groups, and legislators and their staff members, all of whom share an interest in specific policy issues and work together behind the scenes to shape laws and public policy.

issue networks
interest groups, scholars, and other experts that communicate about, debate, and interact regarding issues of interest and thus influence public policy when the legislature acts on those issues; also known as **policy communities.**

relationships with organizations and actors outside the bureaucracy. In prior decades, political scientists often described the influence of these networks and relationships by focusing on the concept of the **iron triangle.**

▶ **How does an iron triangle work?** The concept of the iron triangle described the tight relationship and power over policy issues possessed by three entities sharing joint interests concerning specific policy goals. These three entities were (1) interest groups concerned with a particular policy issue, (2) the key committee members in Congress and their staff with authority over that issue, and (3) the bureaucracy's leaders and the experts on that particular issue within a given department or subagency. Within their sphere of expertise and interest, these iron triangles could, through discussion, communication, and consensus among members, control the writing of laws and the development of policies. The linkages and power of the iron triangle were enhanced as interest groups provided campaign contributions to legislators on relevant congressional committees and rallied their own members to support or oppose legislative proposals emanating from the iron triangle. The key committee members could draft legislation, block unwanted bills, and facilitate the passage of desired statutes through the legislative process. The bureaucracy's interested experts could provide needed information, help plan and facilitate implementation, and provide strategic opposition to counterproposals generated by those outside of the iron triangle. The concept of the iron triangle helped encourage recognition of the bureaucracy's role in shaping legislation through informal networks.

Contemporary scholars view the iron triangle concept as limited and outdated. The governing system has changed. There are growing numbers of interest groups active in lobbying, and individual members of Congress today have less absolute power over committee processes. In the iron triangle process, legislation might have been controlled by lobbyists from a few interested corporations or advocacy groups, along with friendly members of Congress on the relevant committee and the top officials from a federal agency. With respect to some policy issues, many more interest groups have now become involved, and their strategies include advertising campaigns to arouse the public and calling the news media's attention to issues that previously may have been decided largely behind the closed doors of a congressional committee room.

Realizing the inadequacies of the iron triangle framework for all policy issues, scholars now focus on concepts characterized as either **issue networks** or **policy communities.** Guy Peters describes these as "involving large numbers of interested parties,

each with substantial expertise in the policy area. . . . They may contain competing ideas and types of interests to be served through public policy."[10] Both terms describe ongoing relationships and contacts between individuals interested in specific policy issues and areas. These individuals have expertise and remain in contact over time as their particular public policy concerns rise and fall on the nation's policy agenda. At government conferences presenting research on environmental issues, conference attendees who interact with each other are likely to include a variety of individuals representing different perspectives: scholars who study the environment, officials from the Environmental Protection Agency, staff members from relevant congressional committees, representatives from interest groups concerned with such issues, and officials from businesses involved in waste disposal, manufacturing processes, and the cleanup of industrial sites.

Some of these individuals may change jobs over the years and move from universities and businesses into appointed positions in government or from congressional committees to interest groups. In 2004, it was reported that more than ninety former members of Congress were employed as lobbyists by businesses and interest groups, often with an emphasis on issue areas for which they were previously responsible on congressional committees.[11] High officials in the bureaucracy also move in and out of government. For example, Gale Norton, the secretary of the interior under George W. Bush, had previously worked as an attorney for the Mountain States Legal Foundation, an interest group that challenged environmentalist groups in court by arguing against government land use restrictions and by advocating the use of federal lands by ranchers, recreational vehicles, and oil exploration companies. She had moved in and out of government, holding positions in the departments of the Interior and Agriculture, as well as working as a private attorney on related issues.

Sounds like a revolving door! Is that good? Even as these actors move between jobs, their interests and expertise keep them in contact with each other through conferences and through individual communications as they develop working relationships. When bills are formally proposed, individuals from throughout the network are likely to use their contacts in seeking to amend the bill's wording, lobbying for its passage, or attempting to block its progress through the legislative process. The "revolving door" of employees moving between federal government service and interest groups or lobbying firms raises concerns that an agency may be "captured" or controlled by officials who have long alliances with and commitments to specific interest groups.

what **YOU** can do!

Check the backgrounds of several appointed officials who head federal agencies. Is there evidence of connections to interest groups? How could this be avoided?

Gale Norton's confirmation as interior secretary in 2001 was a disappointment to many environmentalists, who felt that the secretary of the interior should be someone known for trying to protect the environment. Norton's career before this had taken her in and out of government, and she had worked for or had connections with many industries (for example, as a lawyer she had lobbied for NL Industries, which was defending itself in lawsuits over children's exposure to lead paint). Under her watch and, some argue, at the urging of those industries, the Interior Department stripped protection from areas previously managed as wilderness, opened forests to increased logging, reopened Yellowstone National park to snowmobiles, and urged federal land managers to speed up drilling for gas on public land.

Photo: Omni-Photo Communications, Inc.

Except for a few members of the cabinet who are prominent politicians, the influential individuals in federal agencies, whether they are presidential appointees or longtime civil servants, are not well known. Less visible than other policymakers, they quietly influence laws and policies through interactions with members of Congress, congressional committee staff, interest groups, and others inside their particular issue networks.

pathways profile

JEFFREY N. SHANE

Let's see how the career paths of government personnel can give them expertise about issues and permit them to develop useful contacts within the sphere of their policy interests.

Jeffrey N. Shane, the undersecretary for transportation policy in the Department of Transportation during the administration of George W. Bush, earned his undergraduate degree from Princeton University and a law degree from Columbia University. His career path took him in and out of government and through positions in private law practice and with interest groups focused on transportation issues. Under President Ronald Reagan, he served in the Department of Transportation as deputy assistant secretary for policy and international affairs before being promoted to assistant secretary in the same division. When George H. W. Bush became president, Shane took his expertise on transportation issues to the Department of State, where he served as deputy assistant secretary of state for transportation affairs.

When the Republicans lost the White House in 1992, Shane went to work on transportation issues outside the government. Throughout the Clinton years, he chaired transportation committees for two important interest groups, the International Chamber of Commerce and the National Defense Transportation Association. He also practiced law with a major Washington, D.C. law firm. There, according to Shane's official government biography, "he had a domestic and international transportation practice, with a major emphasis on regulatory, legislative, and transactional issues."[12] During his career, he had also chaired an American Bar Association committee on air and space law and taught transportation law at Georgetown University.

Shane returned to an appointed position in the Department of Transportation during the next Republican administration, that of President George W. Bush. ■

THE BUREAUCRACY AND INFORMATION

Officials appointed by the president to head executive agencies invariably advocate laws that reflect the president's policy agenda, at least in public. This is especially true of the political appointees in each department, who were put in office precisely to create, revise, and implement laws that are consistent with the president's policy preferences. In looking at the backgrounds of officials like Jeffrey Shane, it is easy to see how they would have the necessary expertise and contacts to help guide, persuade, and pressure members of Congress and staff members on congressional committees. Over the course of many years, their participation in issue

▶ **Suppose people disagree** with a policy they have to work with—what can they do to try to change it?

whistleblower
an employee who reports or reveals misconduct by government officials or others.

Whistleblower Protection Act
a federal law intended to prevent employees in the bureaucracy from being punished for reporting or revealing governmental misconduct.

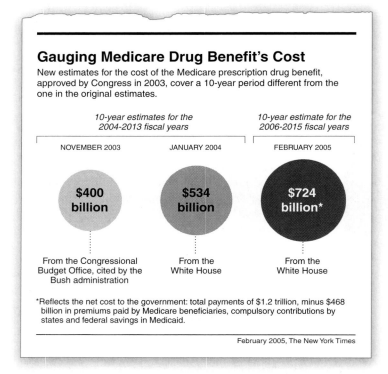

Gauging Medicare Drug Benefit's Cost

New estimates for the cost of the Medicare prescription drug benefit, approved by Congress in 2003, cover a 10-year period different from the one in the original estimates.

10-year estimates for the 2004-2013 fiscal years		10-year estimate for the 2006-2015 fiscal years
NOVEMBER 2003	JANUARY 2004	FEBRUARY 2005
$400 billion	$534 billion	$724 billion*
From the Congressional Budget Office, cited by the Bush administration	From the White House	From the White House

*Reflects the net cost to the government: total payments of $1.2 trillion, minus $468 billion in premiums paid by Medicare beneficiaries, compulsory contributions by states and federal savings in Medicaid.

February 2005, The New York Times

FIGURE 9.2
The Cost of Medicare Drug Benefits

In seeking to gain congressional approval for its Medicare prescription drug plan, the Bush administration reportedly pressured an expert in the bureaucracy to keep quiet about cost projections that it knew would make the plan unacceptable to many Republican members of Congress. The figures released showing significantly higher expected costs were only revealed after the program had been enacted into law. Does the president have too much influence over the bureaucracy?
SOURCE: The New York Times

networks and the relationships they develop there position them to identify and become acquainted with key decision makers in the legislature.

▶ **Suppose people disagree with a policy they have to work with—what can they do to try to change it?** Occasionally, long-time officials within the bureaucracy with experience and expertise may disagree with laws and policies sought by the president and presidential appointees. They may also disagree with new interpretations of existing laws or with presidential efforts to change current policies. These officials may get in touch with their contacts among personnel who work for congressional committees, thereby alerting sympathetic members of Congress to initiate investigations, publicize the president's actions, and oppose efforts to shape law and policy. They may also leak information to the news media in order to bring public attention to issues of concern to them.

An additional role played by officials in the bureaucracy is to provide information for Congress to use in crafting and approving statutes. They provide this information both formally and informally. Formally, some federal agencies, such as the U.S. Census Bureau, regularly send out a steady stream of information to all kinds of congressional committees that are interested in trends in the nation's population, as well as in such demographic issues as home ownership, poverty, and education. Other agencies gather, analyze, and provide information about very specific policy issues, usually working only with those congressional committees that are specifically concerned with these issues. Informal communication between the bureaucracy and Congress occurs when legislative staffers or individual members of Congress contact agency officials with questions about policy issues and government programs. These informal contacts can help build relationships within issue networks that lead to cooperative working relationships as members of Congress rely on agency officials for advice when crafting new legislative proposals.

Formal communications typically occur through committee proceedings or requests for reports and documents to be supplied by government agencies. Congressional committees often summon these officials to provide public testimony about policy problems, the effectiveness of current government programs, or ideas for creating new responses to emerging issues. Sometimes the officials face friendly questioning from members of Congress and their staffs because the legislative officials are genuinely interested in learning about policy issues. At other times, the give-and-take may be tense because members of Congress want to blame officials in the bureaucracy for failing to gather adequate information or providing ineffective implementation of programs.

regulations
legal rules created by government agencies based on authority delegated by the legislature.

Congressional reliance on officials in the bureaucracy for information can create problems if presidential appointees use their authority to direct subordinates to withhold or distort information as a means of advancing the president's policy agenda. For example, in 2004, several conservative Republicans threatened to oppose President Bush's Medicare bill if it would cost more than $400 billion, but had been reassured by the White House that it would not. The chief actuary for the Centers for Medicare and Medicaid Services conducted an analysis that indicated that the legislation would cost at least $100 billion more, but his superior, the director of the Medicare office, threatened to fire him if he revealed this to members of Congress. Two months after Congress approved the legislation, the White House budget director revealed that the new law would actually cost more than $530 billion (see Figure 9.2).[13]

This risk of distorted information is one reason that Congress also seeks to gather its own information through legislative committees and through the Congressional Budget Office and the Government Accountability Office, an investigative agency that reports to Congress. However, the range of policy issues is so vast that Congress must inevitably rely on officials in the bureaucracy for important information about many public policies. Even though most employees in the federal bureaucracy are civil servants who are not formally affiliated with a political party, they may face pressure from presidential appointees to take actions that violate their own ideals of performing their jobs with neutrality and competence. If they disobey superiors, they may be passed over for promotion, transferred to undesirable positions or offices, or threatened with dismissal based on phony charges of incompetence.

Some employees within the bureaucracy stand up against actions by executive branch superiors by providing information about misconduct by government officials. Individuals who are willing to provide such information are known as **whistleblowers,** and they often risk workplace retaliation in the form of dismissal, demotions, and other sanctions intended to punish them for their actions and to deter others from revealing politically damaging information. In 2004, for example, an issue emerged in the presidential campaign when a senior civilian contracting official in the Army Corps of Engineers claimed that Halliburton Corporation, the business previously chaired by Vice President Richard Cheney, had received preferential treatment in the awarding of lucrative no-bid contracts for reconstruction projects in Iraq.[14] Because the disclosure triggered investigative actions in Congress, the official's supporters feared that she would suffer retaliation. Her lawyer asserted that she should be shielded by the **Whistleblower Pro-**

tection Act, a federal law intended to prevent officials in the bureaucracy from being punished for their efforts to protect the country from governmental misconduct. As described by one agency's Web site, the act seeks to encourage useful revelations and protect whistleblowers:

> A federal agency violates the Whistleblower Protection Act if it takes or fails to take (threatens to take or fails to take) a personnel action with respect to any employee or applicant because of any disclosure of information by the employee or applicant that he or she reasonably believes evidences a violation of a law, rule or regulation; gross mismanagement; gross waste of funds; an abuse of authority; or a substantial and specific danger to public health or safety.[15]

In theory, this statute should protect whistleblowers, but in individual cases, it may be difficult for affected individuals to refute their superiors' claims that they are being punished for poor performance rather than for providing well-intentioned, revealing information. For example, just as her attorney feared, the civilian whistleblower from the Army Corps of Engineers was removed from her position and demoted, with a reduction in salary, after she testified before a congressional committee about alleged improprieties in awarding no-bid contracts.[16]

REGULATIONS

Depending on their responsibilities, federal agencies may receive rule-making authority from the statutes that Congress enacts. The rule-making process gives officials in the bureaucracy power over the development of public policy. In some cases, the legislation creating an agency will use general language to describe its mission. For example, as the political scientist Robert Katzmann concluded from his study of the FTC, "In the absence of clearly defined statutory objectives, the Federal Trade Commission apparently has wide discretion in determining the goal (or goals) that it should pursue."[17] General statutory language can become the basis for the bureaucracy's development of its own precise rules, agency-created laws called **regulations,** which govern the topics under a particular agency's jurisdiction. Commentators often describe regulations as filling in the precise details of rules for society, based on the broader directives set forth in statutes. In other cases, Congress may enact statutes that specifically delegate to agencies the authority to formulate the precise rules to govern a particular subject. For example, Chapter VII of the Federal Food,

▶ **Who writes the actual rules? Congress or the federal agencies?**

administrative law judge (ALJ)
official who presides over quasi-judicial proceedings within government agencies and renders decisions about disputes governed by statutes, such as appeals from denials of Social Security disability benefits.

Drug and Cosmetic Act, a statute intended to ensure the safety and effectiveness of these products, says that "the authority to promulgate regulations for the efficient enforcement of this Act . . . is vested in the Secretary [of Health and Human Services]."

▶ **Who writes the actual rules? Congress or the federal agencies?** Statutes written by Congress also specify the procedures that agencies must use in developing regulations. Normally these procedures include publication of proposed regulations, a period during which the public may comment on the proposals, and a process for hearings about the proposed regulations' desirability and potential effects. These procedures give interest groups the opportunity to encourage agencies to adopt new proposals, to work for change in proposals that originated with the government or other groups, or to block (if they can) proposed regulations adverse to their interests. For example, in 2004, food safety advocates pressed the government to issue regulations that would prevent the development and spread of mad cow disease in the United States. The National Cattleman's Beef Association sought to halt the development of rules that would impose expensive new requirements on ranchers and meat processors.[18] The government ultimately issued more restrictive rules, but consumer advocates claimed that many slaughterhouses did not obey the regulations.

The rule-making process creates opportunities for influencing the results. Interested individuals' relationships with bureaucracy officials come into play through issue networks. Interest groups that give campaign contributions and endorsements to the president's political party can also lobby overtly. Because some regulations are controversial, during election campaigns agencies are often instructed to slow down the processes by which rules are changed and created so that the political party opposing the president cannot use pending regulations as a political campaign issue.[19]

Let's look at an example of the rule-making processes that exist throughout the federal bureaucracy—in this case, examining procedures outlined in the Federal Food, Drug and Cosmetic Act of 1938. The act prescribes what can be done to create, amend, or repeal regulations. The first step is the publication of a proposal developed by the Food and Drug Administration (FDA) or given to the FDA by "any interested person showing reasonable grounds therefor." This means that interest groups and individuals can begin the initiation process but that the officials in the bureaucracy can use their judgment in determining whether there are "reasonable grounds" for outsiders' proposals. This is one element of elite influence over policymaking: Government officials can use their

discretion in making judgments about the worthiness of proposals emanating from the public or from interest groups. If "reasonable grounds" are found for proceeding, or if the proposed regulatory change emanates from the FDA, the proposal is then made available to the public through publication in the *Federal Register*, a government document available in libraries across the nation as well as on the Internet. The publication notice must include the date on which the new regulation or repeal will take effect. But prior to taking effect, there must be at least a thirty-day period during which "any person who will be adversely affected by such order may file objections." Individuals or interest groups that file objections must make specific criticisms of the proposed regulation and request a hearing on the matter. At the public hearing over the issues raised in the objections, "any interested person may be heard in person or by representative." Based on the evidence, the government official to whom the secretary of health and human services has delegated responsibility for the matter must issue an order specifying whether and when the regulation will take effect. Individuals or interest groups who object to this order can file an appeal with the United States Court of Appeals, where federal judges will examine the matter. However, judges typically defer to the decisions of the officials in the bureaucracy unless the decision was not supported by evidence or the rule-making procedures were not followed properly.

Clearly, this rule-making process gives officials in the bureaucracy significant influence over the development of regulations affecting a wide range of policy issues, ranging from air pollution rules to workplace safety regulations to the approval of new drugs and medical treatments.

Although judgments about the desirability of specific regulatory changes always depend on the values of a particular observer, it is generally agreed that presidents have opportunities to exploit the rule-making process to advance their own policy agendas. All administrations use their power to develop or change regulations to shape public policy behind the scenes when there may be insufficient support for such changes in Congress or when certain changes in policy, if publicized, might touch off an outcry and stir up political battles. George W. Bush's administration has tended to favor business interests, whereas other presidents have been more responsive to environmentalist interest groups or labor unions.

For example, critics accused the Bush administration of using these tactics to advance policy goals that, if widely publicized, would be unpopular. Significant regulatory changes during Bush's first term included lengthening the hours that long-haul truckers

what YOU can do!

Go to the *Federal Register* online and see whether there are any new or proposed regulations affecting issues of interest to you at **http://www.gpoaccess.gov/fr**

can drive in one shift, despite evidence about the risk of car–truck collisions when drivers are tired; approving logging in federal forests without the usual environmental reviews; diluting rules intended to protect coal miners from blacklung disease (see Figure 9.3); and relaxing air pollution regulations for factories and power plants.[20] The Bush administration and its supporters responded to criticisms by claiming that the government hampers business productivity with too many needless regulations. The administration, it said, was merely making "common-sense" refinements in the rules.

QUASI-JUDICIAL PROCESSES

The bureaucracy affects policy in some agencies through hearing processes that look similar to courts' duties in examining evidence and issuing decisions. In the course of making these decisions, officials in the bureaucracy interpret statutes and regulations and thereby shape policy through their application of the law. Depending on the agency and the purpose of the adjudicative procedures, these processes can be formal or informal. There are also differences in the extent to which these processes are adversarial and thereby permit two sides to argue against each other in front of decision makers within the bureaucracy.

Officials in government agencies may use these processes in investigating whether individuals and corporations are obeying laws and regulations. For example, when the Federal Communications Commission receives a complaint about matters such as obscenity and profanity in radio or television broadcasts, its Enforcement Bureau investigates. When the Fox Network's reality show *Married by America* allegedly presented overtly sexual behavior and dialogue in a televised bachelor party, the Enforcement Bureau asked the network to provide information and respond to the charges. After the bureau concluded that the broadcast material had been indecent, it presented its findings to the five-member FCC, whose members, upon examining the evidence, voted to levy a $1.2 million fine against the network and its affiliates.[21] Much like judges in a court, the commissioners made their decision based on an examination of evidence and an interpretation of the law related to broadcast standards. Moreover, their interpretation of the law and their imposition of a strong sanction helped shape policy and provide guidance for other broadcasters about permissible program content.

Adjudicative processes also exist when citizens are denied requested benefits from the government. For example, if people believe that their physical or mental disabilities prevent them from

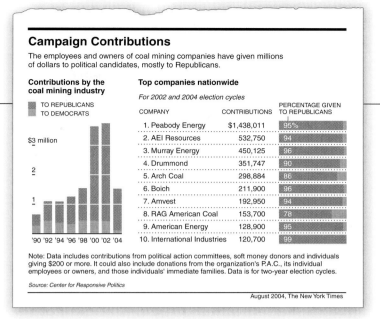

Campaign Contributions

The employees and owners of coal mining companies have given millions of dollars to political candidates, mostly to Republicans.

Contributions by the coal mining industry

■ TO REPUBLICANS
■ TO DEMOCRATS

$3 million

2

1

'90 '92 '94 '96 '98 '00 '02 '04

Top companies nationwide

For 2002 and 2004 election cycles

COMPANY	CONTRIBUTIONS	PERCENTAGE GIVEN TO REPUBLICANS
1. Peabody Energy	$1,438,011	95%
2. AEI Resources	532,750	94
3. Murray Energy	450,125	96
4. Drummond	351,747	90
5. Arch Coal	298,884	86
6. Boich	211,900	96
7. Amvest	192,950	94
8. RAG American Coal	153,700	78
9. American Energy	128,900	95
10. International Industries	120,700	99

Note: Data includes contributions from political action committees, soft money donors and individuals giving $200 or more. It could also include donations from the organization's P.A.C., its individual employees or owners, and those individuals' immediate families. Data is for two-year election cycles.

Source: Center for Responsive Politics

August 2004, The New York Times

FIGURE 9.3
Coal Industry Campaign Contributions 1990–2004

The Mine Safety and Health Administration's efforts to rewrite coal regulations is part of a broader push by the Bush administration to help an industry that had been out of favor in Washington. Safety and environmental regulations often shift with control of the White House, but the Bush administration's approach to coal mining has been a particularly potent example of the blend of politics and policy.

SOURCE: The New York Times

working and that they qualify for disability payments from the Social Security Administration, they must file an application with their local Social Security office and provide medical evidence about their disability. If their local office deems them ineligible, they can appeal to an **administrative law judge (ALJ)** within the Social Security Administration. The ALJ holds a formal hearing, in which the claimant may be represented by an attorney, and medical evidence is presented to document the claimed disability[22] (see Table 9.4). Similar ALJ hearings and quasi-judicial decisions are made in other agencies.

In other settings, the officials in the bureaucracy can appear even more like judges in court as they listen to adversarial parties present arguments and evidence. For example, the National Labor Relations Board handles disputes between unions, unionized workers (or would-be unionized workers), and employers. In

▶ Who holds bureaucrats accountable?

discussionquestions

1. What is a regulation, and what is the process for creating regulations?
2. What quasi-judicial processes exist in the bureaucracy?

disputes about unionization campaigns and labor practices under union contracts, one side may file claims of unfair labor practices against the other, and NLRB officials must examine the arguments and evidence to determine whether the parties are in compliance with federal labor laws.

OVERSIGHT AND ACCOUNTABILITY

As you've seen in the various ways by which agency officials shape policy, these bureaucrats can have significant influence. Yet their actions are typically not noticed by the public or the news media. Without public attention to the decisions of agency officials, it is difficult to know what they are doing and to make sure that they do not exceed their authority or otherwise make improper decisions. However, oversight mechanisms do exist.

▶ **Who holds bureaucrats accountable?** All three branches of government have the power to subject the bureaucracy to oversight and accountability. The president attempts to oversee, guide, and control the bureaucracy through the supervisory authority of political appointees at the top levels of each agency. These appointees are supposed to monitor the work of subordinates and ensure that officials in each agency are working to advance the president's preferred interpretations of laws as they produce regulations and implement statutes. But because there are so few political appointees and they are typically located in the central headquarters of each agency in Washington, D.C., it can be very difficult for these executive branch officials to know what is going on throughout their agencies. Even when they are troubled by what they learn, they cannot always immediately control what subordinate officials do. The threat of sanctions exists because even though it may be difficult to dismiss civil service employees for most of their actions, the superiors in each agency can affect promotions, bonuses, and job assignments through the performance evaluations that they conduct annually on each employee.

There is also legislative oversight. Christopher Foreman describes this as "two interlocking congressional processes: the efforts to *gather information* about what agencies are doing and to *dictate or signal to* agencies regarding the preferred behavior or policy."[23] Oversight by the legislative branch arises when congressional committees summon officials to testify. By pressing these bureaucrats with questions in a public hearing, members of Congress can attempt to discover whether laws are being implemented effectively and justly. If members are unhappy with the performance

of officials in specific agencies, they can publicize these problems and thereby cast political blame on the president. This tactic puts pressure on the president and top appointees to ensure that agencies perform properly. Moreover, Congress controls each agency's budget. If agencies disappoint or clash with Congress, they risk losing needed resources. Congressional control over funding therefore creates incentives for cooperation and compliance by officials in the bureaucracy.[24]

Judicial oversight comes into play when individuals and interest groups file lawsuits claiming that agencies are not implementing laws properly or are not following proper procedures in creating regulations. The many quasi-judicial processes within the bureaucracy are also subject to oversight through appeals to the federal courts from adverse judgments by ALJs, agency commissions and boards, and other bureaucratic decision makers.

practicequiz

1. What governmental entity creates regulations?
   a. Congress
   b. the president
   c. the Supreme Court
   d. an agency in the bureaucracy

2. Someone inside the bureaucracy who reveals to Congress that an agency has violated its own rules or misused funds is generally called a
   a. spotlighter
   b. whistleblower
   c. administrative law judge
   d. patron

3. What term has replaced *iron triangle* with reference to key factors affecting the development of policy by the bureaucracy?
   a. regulatory process
   b. *Federal Register*
   c. issue network
   d. Senior Executive Service

4. How many branches of the government possess the power to provide oversight and impose accountability on the bureaucracy?
   a. three (Congress, president, judiciary)
   b. two (Congress, president)
   c. one (Congress)
   d. none; the bureaucracy is independent

Answers: 1-d, 2-b, 3-c, 4-a.

A U.S. government whistleblower and two British business-men testify about waste and mismanagement by American companies that receive multi-million dollar government contracts to provide services for military operations and reconstruction projects in Iraq. Who should be held accountable for problems that occur when private contractors do not adequately fulfill their obligations to the federal government?

Conclusion

The size of the federal bureaucracy reflects the policy ambitions of the national government. If the government of the United States focused only on national defense, foreign relations, and taxation, as it did in the founding era and for most of the nineteenth century, the federal bureaucracy would be both smaller and narrowly focused on those limited areas. Today, however, Congress writes laws establishing rules and programs covering a host of policy issues, from agriculture to energy to health care. To implement these complex programs, create relevant regulations, and enforce the laws enacted by Congress, the bureaucracy needs sufficient resources and trained personnel. Despite the negative images the word *bureaucracy* calls to mind, the federal government needs large agencies to gather information, maintain records, educate the public, provide services, and enforce laws. As the national government enters new policy arenas or emphasizes new policy goals, such as homeland security in the aftermath of the terrorist attacks of September 11, 2001, the bureaucracy changes through reorganization and reallocations of money and personnel.

The bureaucracy plays a major role in public policy through a form of the lobbying decision makers pathway. Government agencies influence policy in several ways, none of which are clearly visible to the public or well covered by the media. Personnel in government agencies must implement the laws enacted by Congress and the policy initiatives developed by the president. If officials in the bureaucracy lack resources, knowledge, motivation, or supervision, the impact (or lack thereof) of policies on citizens' lives may differ from the outcomes intended by legislative policymakers and the executive branch.

Congress and the president rely on the bureaucracy for information and expertise about many policy issues. Officials in the bureaucracy may influence legislation through formal testimony to congressional committees, as well as through informal contacts in the issue networks with committee staffers and interest groups. Officials in the bureaucracy also create law and policy through rule-making processes for developing, changing, and eliminating regulations. Modern presidents see the rule-making process as a means to advance their policy agendas without seeking the approval of Congress—and often without announcing to the public the precise implications of the changes that have been made. In light of the bureaucracy's daily involvement in the complete range of policy issues affecting the United States, this component of national government will remain extremely important and

influential, despite the fact that the American public does not recognize or understand its actions and impact.

YOUR turn!

Because the decisions and actions in the bureaucracy that influence public policy are undertaken by elites, often in behind-closed-door interactions with other elites, it is difficult for individuals to see how they can affect these processes. There are, however, several concrete actions that you can undertake to make your voice heard.

First, become knowledgeable about the jurisdiction and authority of individual agencies in the policy areas that interest you. Find out which agency is in charge and what the agency can do about an issue, for not all agencies have the same powers or follow the same processes. Then if questions and controversies arise about specific policy issues of particular concern to you, you'll be much better positioned to communicate your concerns.

Second, with respect to the issues of greatest importance to you, pay attention to news reports about pending regulations or read the *Federal Register* yourself. Individuals can make their views known during the comment period on proposed regulations. If enough people speak up, it may catch the attention of the agency—and maybe even the media.

Third, communicate with other actors that have influence over the bureaucracy. Make sure that the news media pay attention to pending regulations and other actions in the bureaucracy. Give your time and money to interest groups that follow the rule-making process and actively participate in shaping regulations for the issues of greatest importance to you. You, and interest groups that you support, *can* make a difference. ▪

Chapter Review

1. The bureaucracy in the executive branch of the federal government is comprised of departments, independent agencies, independent regulatory commissions, and government corporations that have authority over specific topics across the vast array of policy issues facing the United States.

2. The executive branch is organized into departments, such as those of the Treasury, Education, Defense, and Commerce. The president appoints a secretary to head each department, as well as the attorney general to lead the Department of Justice, and these appointees (plus the heads of a few other designated agencies) constitute the president's cabinet.

3. Political appointees may be politicians who support the president or individuals with policy expertise who share the president's values and policy goals.

4. Political appointees also have leadership positions in subcabinet positions, such as assistant secretaries, as well as in independent agencies such as the Equal Employment Opportunity Commission and the Federal Communications Commission. However, the vast majority of personnel in the bureaucracy are civil service employees who remain on the job as presidential administrations come and go.

5. In late-nineteenth-century America, the introduction of federal and state civil service systems emphasized the hiring of government employees based on qualifications. Civil service systems displaced the older patronage or spoils system, under which partisanship and corruption flourished.

6. The image of the bureaucracy frequently calls to mind large, impersonal organizations that are inefficient and slow to respond to individuals. These images may be enhanced if a person has a disappointing encounter with a particular government employee or agency. But that is not all there is to the bureaucracy.

7. The advantages of a bureaucracy stem from providing organizations with clear lines of authority in which each employee has specific responsibilities, thus fostering an environment of expertise, competence, and efficiency. Bureaucracies are useful for standardization and consistency in providing government services and programs. Bureaucracies are also designed for coordination and accountability. However, they do not always work in accordance with idealized models.

8. The bureaucracy plays an essential role in implementing statutes and regulations, but its ability to implement effectively will be affected by limitations on its resources, information, and expertise, as well as by other factors.

9. Officials in the bureaucracy influence legislation through their informal communications with congressional committee staff and with interest groups in their issue networks, as well as through formal testimony that provides information and advice to Congress.

10. Whistleblowers are employees in the bureaucracy who provide information to Congress and law enforcement authorities about misconduct within agencies. They are supposed to be protected by the Whistleblower Protection Act, but they may be vulnerable to retaliation from higher-level officials.

11. Presidents seek to use the rule-making process to advance policy agendas through the creation, change, or elimination of regulations that provide many of the precise details of rules and policy for the federal government.

12. The rule-making process involves publication of proposed rules, a period for comments, and hearings on issues of debate. This process provides opportunities for interest groups to influence regulations, especially if those groups are political supporters of the president and viewed favorably by presidential appointees.

13. The bureaucracy also influences public policy through quasi-judicial processes that interpret and enforce statutes and regulations through hearings and appeals.

14. All three branches of government exert supervisory authority over aspects of the bureaucracy's actions, but no branch can completely control decisions made by personnel within government agencies.

CHAPTER REVIEW TEST

1. Why do bureaucracies exist?
   a. to grant greater authority to the organizations they represent
   b. to make sure the organizations they represent can cover a large geographic area
   c. to carry out the work of that organization in an efficient and effective way
   d. to act as a buffer between the executive decision makers of the organizations and the customers or constituents interacting with that organization

2. The size of the federal bureaucracy reflects the policy ambitions of the national government.
   a. true   b. false

3. How does the bureaucracy share the creation and implementation of public policy with other governmental entities?
   a. The president shapes laws that help define public policy; then Congress directs bureaucratic agencies to carry out those laws.
   b. Congress and the president write laws to define public policy; then officials working in federal agencies act to carry out those laws and policies.
   c. Experts in bureaucratic agencies recommend changes in laws and regulations; then Congress transforms these recommendations into legislation, which the president signs into law and orders Congress to carry out.
   d. Working up through a vertical hierarchy of authority, bureaucratic experts inform the president of needed laws that conform to his political views; then the president urges Congress to write the appropriate legislation, which he signs into law.

4. How many federal agencies can respond to natural disaster relief needs?
   a. one (FEMA)
   b. two (FEMA and Coast Guard)
   c. three (FEMA, Coast Guard, and U.S. Small Business Administration)
   d. many (FEMA, Coast Guard, U.S. Small Business Administration, the U.S. Department of Agriculture's Farm Service Agency, etc.)

5. As is suggested by the recent case of the EPA and water purity standards, officials in the bureaucracy make decisions about a policy rule with as little interference from other parties as possible.
   a. true   b. false

6. How many different organizational entities are in the federal bureaucracy?
   a. one (departments)
   b. two (departments and independent agencies)

   c. three (departments, independent agencies, and independent regulatory commissions)
   d. four (departments, independent agencies, independent regulatory commissions, and government corporations)

7. The creation of the Department of Health, Education, and Welfare (HEW) in the 1950s
   a. marked the expansion of the bureaucracy into policy areas that the Constitution did not foresee.
   b. was a natural extension of what the Constitution described for the reach of the bureaucracy.
   c. required a constitutional amendment since it so fully departed from the policy focus described in the Constitution.
   d. shifted federal authority in policy matters from the legislative to the executive branch.

8. Approximately how many people work in departments in the executive branch?
   a. 300,000   b. 850,000
   c. 1 million   d. 2.6 million

9. What do the heads of federal executive departments do?
   a. work within their departments to make sure the officials and employees beneath them are happy
   b. act as a liaison between the department and the economy
   c. work directly for the president, trying to make their department act in accordance with the president's policy preferences
   d. act as a buffer between their own department and the foreign governments

10. Regulatory agencies are usually called
    a. councils
    b. commissions or boards
    c. agencies
    d. caucuses

11. NASA is
    a. a governmental corporation.
    b. an independent agency.
    c. a department.
    d. an independent regulatory commission.

12. NASA's astronauts are part of the federal bureaucracy.
    a. true   b. false

13. Why are people's negative associations with federal bureaucracy sometimes unfair?
    a. because federal employees are always working hard and in the best interests of all Americans
    b. because federal employees do not get good wages or benefits

c. because people often do not realize the challenges of administering government programs

d. because "red tape" is a myth

14. Why was the civil service system enacted?
a. to make federal employees more courteous on the job
b. so allow federal employees would get and retain their jobs based on their competence, not their political affiliation or personal connections
c. so that federal employees could be legally bound to carry out their responsibilities effectively and could not receive benefits
d. so that federal employees could be held to consistent performance standards and could be fired if their superiors dislike them

15. What is one practical problem with the federal bureaucracy?
a. Standards of competence are so high that it becomes difficult to find and retain suitable employees.
b. It contains so many departments that presidents often have a difficult time knowing which department should carry out a particular policy.
c. Its size makes it slow to change or respond to policy shifts signaled from the president or Congress.
d. People working in it always become lazy, knowing that they can never be fired.

16. In order to save money, all levels of government use private contracts.
a. true   b. false

17. Why are critics worried about the pattern of officials leaving the federal bureaucracy to join interest groups or lobbying firms in the same topical area, and sometimes later still returning to the government in that same field?
a. because they can often get "burned out" in their field
b. because this pattern prevents a particular issue network from including a diverse group of participants
c. because such individuals might lack sufficient expertise
d. because the agencies such individuals return to might in effect be controlled by that person's alliances in the private sector

18. Why do the Congressional Budget Office and the Government Accountability Office exist?
a. to gather and communicate to Congress information available only to foreign governments
b. to communicate the results of Congressional hearings to the public
c. to gather and provide to Congress information undistorted by political agendas of the president or agencies
d. to monitor, in a nonpartisan way, the budgetary and policy actions of the Supreme Court

19. What has been President George W. Bush's typical approach to government regulation?
a. to add regulations or make them more stringent
b. to eliminate regulations or make them less stringent
c. to leave regulations unchanged
d. to defer to Congress most issues related to regulation

20. When government agencies influence policy—as so often happens—the public
a. usually finds out about it from the news media.
b. usually finds out about it from governmental publications.
c. almost never finds out about it.
d. really does not need to know about it.

Answers: 1: c; 2: a; 3: b; 4: d; 5: b; 6: d; 7: a; 8: d; 9: c; 10: b; 11: b; 12: b; 13: a; 14: c; 15: b; 16: a; 17: d; 18: c; 19: b; 20: c.

DISCUSSION QUESTIONS

1. What is the bureaucracy in the federal government?

2. How is the executive branch organized, and what is the president's cabinet?

3. What kinds of people become the president's political appointees in the bureaucracy?

4. What types of policy issues are handled by independent agencies?

5. What are the advantages and practical problems of having a bureaucracy?

6. What problems existed with the patronage or spoils system?

7. What are issue networks, and how do they operate?

8. How does the bureaucracy influence legislation, formally and informally?

9. What is the Whistleblower Protection Act, and how effective is it?

10. What is a regulation, and how does the rule-making process operate?

11. How and why do presidents seek to use the rule-making process to shape policy?

12. What kinds of quasi-judicial processes operate within the bureaucracy?

INTERNET RESOURCES

Read about the individual appointees in the president's cabinet and find links to the departments of the executive branch at **http://www.whitehouse.gov/government/cabinet.htm**

Independent agencies have their own Web sites, such as the Federal Communications Commission at **http://www.fcc.gov**, the Federal Trade Commission at **http://www.ftc.gov**, and the National Labor Relations Board at **http://www.nlrb.gov**

Learn about job opportunities and employment policies in the federal civil service at the Web site for the Office of Personnel Management at **http://www.opm.gov**

A quasi-judicial process is described in the materials concerning hearings and appeals for Social Security disability claims at **http://www.ssa.gov/oha**

Read published proposed regulations awaiting public comments at **http://www.regulations.gov**

ADDITIONAL READING

Foreman, Christopher H., Jr. *Signals from the Hill: Congressional Oversight and the Challenge of Social Regulation.* New Haven, CT: Yale University Press, 1988. An analysis of the challenges and dynamics of congressional oversight of the bureaucracy.

Fritschler, A. Lee. *Smoking and Politics: Policymaking and the Federal Bureaucracy* (3d. ed.). Englewood Cliffs, NJ: Prentice Hall, 1983. A brief, readable case study of the steps in the process of developing regulations related to cigarettes in the Federal Trade Commission.

Goodsell, Charles T. *The Case for the Bureaucracy* (4th ed.). Washington, DC: CQ Press, 2003. A defense of the bureaucracy through the examination of the public's expectations and the actual capacity of government agencies to perform their missions.

Katzmann, Robert A. *Regulatory Bureaucracy.* Cambridge, MA: MIT Press, 1979. A brief study of the Federal Trade Commission, its rule-making processes, and its influence over the public.

Kettl, Donald F. *The Politics of the Administrative Process,* (3rd ed.). Washington, D.C.: CQ Press, 2005. A leading scholar's description and analysis of policy-making processes in the government bureaucracy.

KEY TERMS

administrative law judge (ALJ) 364	**Hatch Act** 356	**privatization** 358
bureaucracy 340	**independent agencies** 341	**regulations** 363
civil service system 356	**independent regulatory commissions** 341	**Senior Executive Service** 359
decentralization 358	**iron triangle** 360	**spoils system** 354
department 340	**issue networks** 360	**whistleblower** 362
government corporations 342	**patronage system** 354	**Whistleblower Protection Act** 362

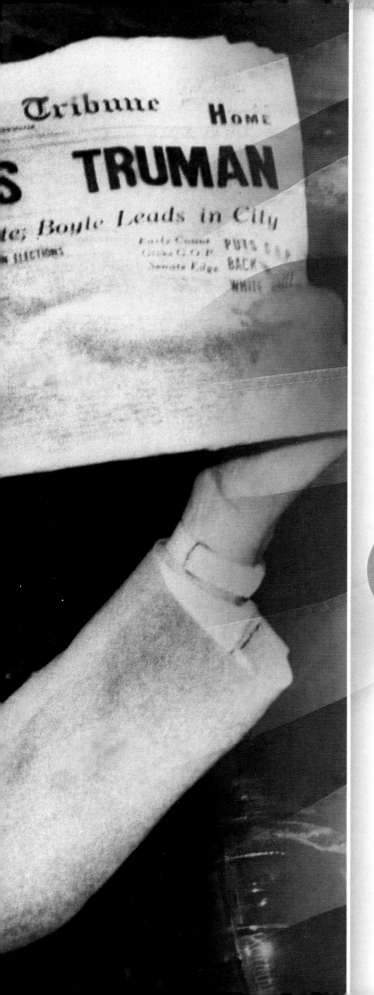

Delighted President Harry Truman exhibits the erroneous newspaper headline declaring his defeat to Thomas Dewey in the 1948 presidential election. If one were to fast forward fifty-two years, George W. Bush could have been pictured holding similarly incorrect newspaper headlines declaring Al Gore president in 2000. Techniques to measure public opinion have improved dramatically in the last 50 years, but they are not infallible.

CHAPTER 10

POLITICAL SOCIALIZATION AND PUBLIC OPINION

Change in Action: Views of Homosexuality   In 1981, NBC produced a TV sitcom titled *Love, Sydney*, starring the well-known actor Tony Randall portraying a gay man. It would have been the first major network television series in which the lead character was gay, but during development of the series, NBC faced complaints and pressures from interest groups, viewers, and advertisers, all opposed to what many people perceived as an endorsement of homosexuality. As a result, the network instructed the show's producers to make the main character a man of undefined sexual orientation, and after just one season *Love, Sydney* was cancelled.

Fast-forward to 1998: The very same network, NBC, introduced a TV series called *Will and Grace* with two openly gay men among the four lead characters. *Will and Grace* proved enormously popular; it lasted for eight seasons, earned Emmy awards for all of

Brokeback Mountain, directed by Ang Lee, won a number of prestigious honors, including three Academy Awards in 2006. The film challenged a number of stereotypes about homosexuals and stimulated a great number of conversations (and jokes). Do you think the movie helped break stereotypes and signaled attitudinal changes toward homosexuality or do you think that the movie was simply entertaining? Why or why not?

its lead actors, and attracted an audience averaging more than 17 million viewers per episode during its peak season, 2001–2002.

The comparison between public reactions to these two NBC situation comedies raises an important question: How did we get from a time when public reactions forced a major television network to avoid portraying a gay character to a time when the same network could proudly promote gay characters in leading roles? The answer comes from examining how public opinion both reflects and influences cultural change. By analyzing public opinion with respect to homosexuality, we can see how American society, including its political values and policy debates, changes over time. Public opinion on homosexuality is a useful starting point for discussion of cultural change, because various aspects of this issue, including marriage and adoption rights for gay couples, remain controversial. This issue demonstrates that cultural change is an ongoing process that does not necessarily ever reach a point of complete consensus in society.

To put these recent changes in popular culture and public opinion in context, let's go back a generation or two. In the mid-twentieth century, straight people viewed homosexuality as "perversion," and both male and female homosexuals usually did their best to stay "in the closet." The chief professional organization of American psychiatrists, the American Psychiatric Association (APA), classified homosexuality as a mental disorder. But in 1948, Indiana University biologist Alfred Kinsey published a

research study titled *Sexual Behavior in the Human Male,* which thrust the issue of sexual orientation onto the national stage. Kinsey's research showed that at least 10 percent of men and 50 percent of women had had a homosexual encounter sometime in their lifetime—a finding that shocked the American public and generated an enormous amount of discussion.

As people learned more about human behavior, things began to change. In 1973, the APA removed homosexuality from its list of mental disorders. The AIDS epidemic, first diagnosed in the United States among gay men in the early 1980s, had a powerful and chilling impact on television's portrayal of homosexuals. Then celebrities began to mobilize and organize to fight AIDS, and straight people started to view gays with more sympathy and acceptance.

By the late 1990s, progress was being made toward developing drugs to treat AIDS, and a growing public tolerance toward homosexuality became noticeable. It was at that point that NBC launched *Will and Grace.* Just one month later, a gay college student at the University of Wyoming, Matthew Shepard, was lured by two thugs from a bar near the campus, taken into the countryside, tied to a fence, tortured, beaten, pistol-whipped, and left to die in near-freezing temperatures. He died on October 12, 1998. At his funeral, a small but vocal group protested, brandishing signs inscribed "God Hates Gays" and "Get Back in the Closet."

The murder of Matthew Shepard and the ugly antigay demonstration at his funeral outraged the vast majority of Americans. Public sentiment condemning hate crimes and homophobia continued to evolve, and decisions and actions by governing institutions and cultural organizations signaled that gays and lesbians had gained significant acceptance by many Americans.

In *Lawrence* v. *Texas* (2003), the U.S. Supreme Court declared that states could no longer enforce laws that criminalized the private sexual behavior of adult homosexuals. States and cities increasingly enacted laws to define as "hate crimes" any violent acts directed at people because of their sexual orientations. *Queer Eye for the Straight Guy,* a cable network personal makeover program starring gay men, won the 2004 Emmy award for Outstanding Reality Program. In 2006, the movie *Brokeback Mountain,* a love story about two cowboys, led all films with eight Academy Award nominations.

Despite these changes, the topics of same-sex unions, homosexual adoption rights, and national laws to prohibit workplace discrimination still generate enormous controversy and opposition. In the 2004 elections, voters in eleven states passed referendums declaring that marriage could exist only between one man and one woman.

As you can see from this brief survey of changing attitudes toward homosexuality over the past half-century, popular culture both shapes and reflects our political reality.[1]

▶ **Do political decision makers** pay attention to public opinion?

public opinion
the attitudes of individuals regarding their political leaders and institutions as well as political and social issues.

elitism
the theory that a select few—better educated, more informed, and more interested—should have more influence than others in our governmental process.

In this chapter you will examine ways for individuals and groups to influence their communities and their governments by working to change cultural values and opinions. Although our culture and political values are relatively stable, change does occur—often gradually, but sometimes with dramatic speed. When our culture changes, our government responds. In this chapter you will examine the many factors that influence public opinion on the key issues that form our political culture. The factors that lead to cultural change will also be examined so that you can consider how cultural change affects our society, our expectations, and our government. In the chapters that follow, you will examine the power of opinion and culture to bring about change and influence our world.

Key Questions

1. How influential should public opinion be in swaying policymakers and individuals in our society? How and when does public opinion promote social and cultural change?

2. On the whole, how stable is public opinion? What factors promote stability, and why and how does public opinion change?

3. What is political ideology? How do liberals and conservatives differ?

4. What is political socialization? What factors influence how people acquire political values?

5. What factors affect the quality of poll data? Why do you need to understand the advantages and disadvantages of poll data?

Public Opinion

Our government, Abraham Lincoln reminded us in his Gettysburg Address, is "of the people, by the people, and for the people"—in short, a product and a reflection of the American public. So when you think about public opinion, the concept may at first seem quite straightforward—it's the opinion of the general public. However, in a society as large and diverse as ours, it is no easy job to determine *the* opinion of "the public." It is therefore helpful to think of **public opinion** as a mechanism that quantifies the various opinions held by the population or by subgroups of the population at a particular point in time. A complete picture of the opinions of more than 300 million Americans is difficult to estimate but nevertheless insightful.

Public opinion is grounded in political values, but it can be influenced by a number of sources and life experiences. Many people base their opinions on personal reflection, although most Americans have low levels of political knowledge. Despite the fact that we are a highly educated society, this advanced level of edu-

cation has not directly translated into a more politically informed citizenry. Seventy percent of Americans cannot name their senators or their members of Congress. However, those who are politically knowledgeable tend to have more stable political opinions. Many experts and political commentators believe that since most people don't base their opinions on specific knowledge, their opinions are neither rational nor reasonable.[2]

Other scholars have argued that a general sense of political understanding is enough to cast an informed ballot and to form reasonable political opinions.[3] Therefore, even though most citizens can't name the chief justice of U.S. Supreme Court, they can nevertheless form rational and coherent opinions on issues of public policy and political preferences. It is important to note that most research on public opinion often focuses on the voting population rather than the general population. This is an important distinction, because the voting population is generally more educated and more politically knowledgeable than the general population.

To what extent should public opinion drive public policy? There are many views on this, and they reflect assorted takes on the nature of democracy itself. Of central importance is the role of the public in the governing process. How influential should public opinion be? How much attention should our political leaders pay to our positions and attitudes? Some authorities believe (though they may not say this publicly) that public opinion should have little influence on the behavior and decision making of our leaders. They argue that democracies need to limit the influence of the people, allowing the better-informed and more educated leaders to chart our path. Others argue that the views of the people should be given great weight, as a representative democracy needs to pay attention to the will of the people.

Those who believe that democracies need to limit the ability of the public to influence events argue that information must be controlled and narrowly shared. Leaders should do the thinking and the planning, and the masses should step up occasionally to select their leaders in periodic elections and spend the rest of their time as spectators.[4] Many analysts are concerned that public opinion can change easily and is too unstable, with little solid grounding, to be given much regard. In many ways, this line of thought makes sense, as most people are too busy to pay much attention to politics. They aren't lacking in intelligence, but they certainly lack interest. This fact is behind the argument that the public should defer to the few who have the skill, knowledge, and power to make wise decisions. Some researchers have found evidence to support the notion that it might be best for leaders to minimize the impact of public opinion and to allow citizens to influence policymakers primarily through elections.[5] This **elitism** was forthrightly expressed in the early days of our republic but is not widely acknowledged among political leaders and commentators today.

The founders, on the whole, thought that too much influence was given to the preferences of the people under the Articles of Confederation. As you've seen, the Articles created a system that was very responsive to the broad public but not receptive to the elite. In the new constitutional system they created, the founders reacted by diminishing the relationship between the government and public opinion. The new system was designed to impose a sort of waiting period on the masses, reflecting the thought that officials should shape public opinion, not respond to it. For example, *Federalist No. 63* asserts that a "select and stable" Senate would serve as "an anchor against popular fluctuations," which would protect the people from their "temporary errors." In *Federalist No. 49,* Madison warns of the "danger of disturbing the public tranquility by interesting too strongly the public passions." Hamilton in *Federalist No. 68* argues for the indirect election of the president by a council of wise men (the electoral college) who must not react too quickly to the passion of the people, and in *No. 71* he further warns against following the "sudden breeze of passion" or listening to every "transient impulse" of the public. The founders saw the government as our guardian, protecting us from ourselves. They did believe that long-held views, those that lasted over the presidential term and the staggered Senate elections, should affect the course of government. They were more concerned with curbing *transient* ("here today, gone tomorrow") opinions, which they viewed as "common." Today, as we have become more educated and have adopted a political system with universal adult suffrage, people have come to expect their government to be open and responsive.

In direct opposition to this elitist theory, and by far the more commonly held view of contemporary political leaders and political scientists, has been a position based on pluralism. Whereas elitists have argued that complex decisions need to be made free from public pressure, pluralists believe that citizens should be informed and should participate in democratic decision making to ensure the health and vitality of the system. They argue that participation by the public gives legitimacy to the political process and governing officials. Pluralists urge that officials pay close attention to the desire of the people in charting their actions, for active participation is an essential part of a healthy democracy. Rational decision making will occur when many active groups get informed about the issues and discuss the many arguments. This line of reasoning goes back to the ancient Greek philosopher Aris-

totle, who believed that collective judgments were more likely to be wise and sound than the judgments of a few.

Political scientist Sidney Verba makes a strong case that public opinion should be heeded because polls are a more egalitarian form of political expression than other forms of participation, which tend to benefit the more educated and affluent. Since each citizen has an equal (but tiny) chance of being selected in a poll, there is a greater chance that the opinion of the broad public will be accurately determined—that the data will not be skewed. Some theorists insist that other forms of political expression are better gauges of public opinion because they require more effort from people, but Verba presents a strong argument that economic differences between the affluent and the less affluent make it difficult for the views of the general population to be heard, as the wealthy are better able to articulate and present their points of view. Hence, he says, it is a bit utopian to think that the concerns of all demographic groups could be fairly and accurately portrayed without public opinion polls.[6]

▶ **Do political decision makers pay attention to public opinion?** The reality of the situation probably lies somewhere between these two theories. There are times when officials respond to the views of the people—especially when the opinion is fairly popular and when an issue is presented that offers a chance to gain a political advantage. If the voting population is very interested in an issue and a dominant viewpoint seems to emerge, elected officials will be under great pressure to pay attention to the opinions and to act accordingly. Even unelected officials, including judges, are often influenced by public opinion.

At other times, officials pay less attention to the views of the public, including the views of voters. This is likely to happen when the public has focused relatively little attention on an issue. Officials may also choose not to be responsive when their convictions come into conflict with the views of the people. Elected officials may take unpopular positions that they nevertheless believe in, risking their public support for their convictions. Knowing when to follow public opinion and when to resist it is one of the marks of a truly great political leader.

One example of public opinion *not* swaying government policy is in the area of gun control. Imposing some form of gun control is popular among a large segment of the citizenry, but significant federal gun control legislation is rare. The Brady Bill, (which mandated waiting periods when purchasing handguns) passed in 1993, was the first major federal gun control law since 1968—and it was allowed to quietly die in 2004 despite its popularity among a large majority of Americans. Many critics cite this example to argue that public opinion is not influential in American politics.

discussion questions

1. How do the elitist and pluralistic theories of the importance of public opinion in American politics differ? Why do people support each?

2. Are there times when political leaders need to oppose public opinion? What are some examples of instances in which leaders may need to act in a manner that is opposed by the majority?

▶ **What are the values that** Americans hold in common?

Consider, however, a different example: drug policy. Following the highly publicized deaths of a few famous athletes, and with increased media coverage of drug abuse and the widespread availability of illicit drugs in the mid-1980s, the public became very concerned with drug abuse, citing it as the nation's most important problem. Congress and the White House struggled to catch up with public concern, each quickly presenting initiatives to address the country's "drug crisis." **LINK** *Chapter 8 page 317,* Significant legislation was passed, increasing the role of the federal government in a problem that had historically been regarded as primarily the responsibility of state governments. A major public service campaign was launched to persuade Americans to "just say no to drugs." A federal "drug czar" was appointed, and a "war on drugs" was declared.[7] Unlike gun control, this example demonstrates the power of the public in influencing government to respond to a problem—even though the "war on drugs" accomplished relatively little.

Why did the government respond to public concerns over drugs but fail to respond to the support for additional gun control provisions? **LINK** *Chapter 13 pages 499–501,* will offer one explanation: Organized and powerful interest groups vehemently oppose gun control, whereas no organized interest groups opposed the war on drugs. This, however, is the simple answer. The complete answer is far more complex. One reason why officials responded to the concern over drugs but not over guns is that people were more worried about the drug crisis than they were about assault weapons. In social science jargon, the drug crisis was simply more "salient" to the population. Moreover, the media reinforced the concern many felt about drug problems, but they did not focus much attention on concerns over the ready availability of military-style assault weapons. When public officials discuss issues and keep them in the limelight (as they did with drugs), public opinion appears to be influential. Given the lack of attention devoted to drug abuse and crimes at the national level today, you might think that we won the war on drugs. Did we? No. Drugs are still a major problem in our country, accounting for a great deal of crime, corruption, violence, and personal tragedy.

Why did the drug problem fade from the national agenda? Public officials and the media began to devote less time and attention to the issue, allowing it to disappear gradually from the public radar. This example demonstrates that our officials can and do respond to public opinion—but they also exert a good amount of influence over the shaping of public opinion as well.

practice quiz

1. Growing public tolerance toward homosexuality suggests that
   a. in the near future, the U.S. public will be completely accepting of homosexuality.
   b. such public opinion is shaped by cultural change.
   c. such public opinion shapes cultural change.
   d. b and c.

2. The *Federalist Papers* warned about granting too much political authority to the unstable opinions of the general public.
   a. true   b. false

3. Contemporary political leaders and political scientists view the participation of citizens in governmental decision making
   a. in an elitist way.
   b. as a force that legitimizes our political process.
   c. as a problem, given how transient public opinion can be.
   d. b and c.

4. The government's 1980s "war on drugs" illustrates that
   a. public opinion can influence governmental policy.
   b. public opinion can itself be influenced by the news media.
   c. such policies are doomed to failure.
   d. a and b.

Answers: 1-d, 2-a, 3-b, 4-d.

Fundamental Values

▶ **What are the values that Americans hold in common?** Most Americans are alike in many important ways and agree on a number of key political values. Most citizens can speak English and are proud to live in this country, and even though many see problems, they would rather live here than anywhere else. Most of us dream of a better future for our children and support our political institutions.

But while we share many common values, we often disagree over their meaning and differ on specific policies related to these

individualism
a social theory that stresses the importance of guaranteeing freedoms, rights, self-expression, and independent actions of human beings.

equality of outcome
egalitarian belief that government must work to diminish differences between individuals in society so that everyone is equal in status and value.

values. For example, one area of broad agreement is support for personal liberty. Our country was founded on the idea of protecting individual liberties and freedoms. As you saw in Chapters 5 and 6, our Constitution and Bill of Rights were written to protect individual freedoms "from" and "to." We are protected *from* unreasonable searches, *from* cruel and unjust punishments, and (with the Fourteenth Amendment) *from* discrimination. We are protected against infringement on our freedom *to* practice our religion freely, *to* express our minds, and *to* join with others in forming organizations. Most of us cherish these liberties. But the specific meaning of these freedoms can cause disagreement. Should hate groups have no limits on speech? Can the speech of the wealthy drown out the speech of the poor? When we move from the abstract to specific policies, there is often disagreement.

In addition to freedom, Americans highly value the idea of **individualism,** a belief that goes back to the earliest days of our republic. A reverence for individualism and individual rights is central to our democracy, as the government is expected to protect individuals and design policies that enhance the chances of reaching self-fulfillment. It is also central to our economic system: At the heart of capitalism lies a belief in individualism that in many cases permits individual interests to win out over community interests. (Socialism, by contrast, values community needs over individual wants.) The spirit of individualism also stresses the right of citizens to own property and to control their earnings (hence the conflict over tax policies). Comparing the general sense of individualism in the United States to that in Europe provides a vivid example of how varied opinions can be. Europeans generally have higher expectations of their government in addressing individual concerns, such as providing health care and alleviating poverty, than Americans do. Certainly we Americans would like for all to have health insurance, but for the most part we do not believe it is the government's role to fund universal health insurance programs. Europeans believe that such programs are valuable and should be funded. The root of this markedly different set of attitudes is the difference of opinion between individual and community responsibility.

Americans also have high levels of support for their democratic government. We believe in majority rule, coupled with the need to protect minority rights. We see fair, free, and competitive elections as essential to our democracy. The country has strong

Nancy Reagan throws out the first pitch in the 1988 World Series, drawing attention to her "Just Say No" anti-drug campaign. First Ladies today often participate in politics through initiatives to promote reading, fight drugs, and combat discrimination. Some believe that First Ladies should not engage in political activities, remaining involved only in traditional activities and keeping a low political profile. How active and in what sorts of things should First Ladies be involved? Do you think a First Gentleman would have similar roles or would our expectations of the President's husband vary from those we have of the President's wife?

national loyalty and patriotism, which together provide solid and crucial support for our governmental system.

Americans also strongly support the idea of equality. Equality is a very complex notion, involving both political and social aspects. There is near-universal support for political equality: The notion of one person, one vote is deeply embedded in our culture. But when we speak of equality in our society (meaning economic equality, educational attainment, social status, and power, for example), the issue becomes more complex. Most of us believe in the idea of equality of opportunity (the belief that everyone should have a chance of success), but many Americans find the idea of **equality of outcome** (using the government to ensure equality) more

▶ How stable is public opinion in the United States?

1. What fundamental values do Americans support? Why do they support these values?

2. How does disagreement about these consensus values develop?

controversial. Examples of policies to grant equal opportunities for success are public schools and public defenders for people accused of crimes who cannot afford to hire their own lawyer. The Equal Pay Act of 1963, which required employers to pay men and women equal wages for equal work, was motivated by a belief in equality of outcome. Today the idea of equal wages for both sexes is not controversial, but other policies to promote equality are. Affirmative action is another example of a public policy that tries to achieve equality of opportunity and equality of outcome, depending on how the policy is designed. Affirmative action in college admissions and scholarships provides equality of opportunity, as many well-qualified students might not otherwise have a chance to attend college. Affirmative action in granting governmental contracts to minority-owned construction firms, for example, is motivated by the goal of equality of outcome, ensuring that these firms are treated equally and without bias in business. But current controversies over affirmative action provide a good example of how, even though many people agree on the basic notion of equality, disagreement occurs when we put these values into action.

1. America is full of diversity, including a diversity of fundamental values.
   a. true   **b.** false

2. The fact that Americans tend to agree on fundamental values tends to
   a. result in universal support or important public policies.
   b. stabilize our political system.
   c. cause noncompetitive elections.
   d. allow newcomers to win more often.

3. That Americans value individualism highly is reflected in
   a. our government's passive stance on health care and poverty, relative to the actions of the governments of Europe.
   b. our commitment to capitalism.
   c. the wording of the U.S. Constitution.
   d. a and b.

4. Affirmative action
   a. is a universally accepted means for correcting past injustices.
   b. provides equality of opportunity to groups historically discriminated against.
   c. has almost nothing to do with equality of outcome.
   d. a, b, and c.

Answers: 1-b, 2-b, 3-d, 4-b.

The Stability of Political Beliefs

▶ **How stable is public opinion in the United States?** Political culture is the set of economic, political, and governmental values and beliefs that support political institutions, processes and practices, and belief systems. Evidence shows that political culture is relatively stable over time, with party identification being the most stable.[8] Opinions can and do change over a lifetime, but major ways of thinking (partisanship, ideology, racial, and attitudes) tend to remain stable once a person reaches adulthood. Evidence also exists that adults often adjust their views to adapt to changing political environments and to changing life circumstances.[9]

One source of stability is the broad consensus on the key values we've just discussed. Because our political elites tend to be better educated, they are even more supportive of democratic ideals than typical individuals. Elites perpetuate the system, aiding in its stability. Although we have experienced conflict, it is more limited than what is seen in other societies. There have been few significant controversies over fundamental issues that have led individuals and groups desiring change to go beyond the established channels to promote their cause. A few exceptions exist: The Civil War is the foremost example of a fundamental conflict, but it ended in the decisive victory of one side, permanently settling the issues of slavery and secession. And a century later, U.S. society faced serious conflicts over the Vietnam War and civil rights. But on the whole, our society has been successful in avoiding violence by using political channels to promote change.

Another reason our system is stable is that in the United States, levels of political distrust, which can be very dangerous and lead to instability, are relatively low. Although trust goes up and down over the years, sufficient levels of trust remain to sustain our system. Well known leaders can play important roles in influencing public opinion and are especially able to influence the less knowledgeable in society.

There have been periods in our history in which large shifts in opinion have occurred; often these shifts have reflected major transformations in American politics. Perhaps the greatest such shift was in the 1760s and 1770s, when overwhelmingly loyal British American subjects turned into republican rebels against the Crown. More recently, there have been large increases in support for civil liberties for communists, socialists, and atheists from the 1950s to the 1970s. From the end of World War II through the early 1970s, a national consensus emerged condemning racial segregation. Since the 1960s, opinion has become much more approving of interracial marriage and of equal employment rights

▶ **What factors or events** can lead to more sudden changes in political opinion?

cohort replacement
natural phenomenon of generational replacement due to death.

for homosexuals. In 1958, only 4 percent of Americans approved of interracial marriages. The number has steadily increased since that time. It went from 20 percent in 1968 to 43 percent in 1983 and reached 73 percent in 2002, the most recent time that the Gallup Organization has asked the question.[10] Support for equal employment opportunities for homosexuals has also risen steadily: 56 percent of American supported equal rights in 1977, 71 percent in 1989, and 87 percent in 2005.[11] Other dimensions of homosexual rights, however, remain hotly debated, including same-sex marriage and the adoption of children by homosexuals. One of the largest changes in public opinion was the 48 percent increase between 1938 and 1975 in the number of people who agreed that it was appropriate for a married woman to work outside the home for wages even if she had a husband who could financially support her.[12]

Most of the significant changes in American public opinion have occurred gradually, over several decades. Rather than sharp changes, what we find more commonly are very slow changes in Americans' beliefs and life circumstances. Attitudes toward abortion, for example, provide a good illustration of the stability of public opinion (see Figure 10.1). Abortion has been a very controversial issue since the 1970s, but overall public opinion has remained consistent over the years. Most gradual change can be explained by **cohort replacement,** which simply means that younger people replace older people; and as each generation has experienced a different world, it is logical that each would have different opinions. It is estimated that 50 percent of the electorate is replaced every twenty years.[13] Demographic changes in society also affect gradual change, and so does changing technology. For example, computer usage clearly affects the way in which people become informed.

▶ **What factors or events can lead to more sudden changes in political opinion?** Sometimes, however, we do see rather abrupt changes in public opinion, particularly in the area of foreign policy. Political scientists Benjamin Page and Robert Shapiro found that shifts in opinions on foreign policy were three times as rapid as changes in domestic preferences, presumably because the landscape of international politics changed more quickly than domestic affairs.[14] Areas that saw abrupt changes were opinions regarding wars (World War II, Korea, Vietnam, the war in Iraq), foreign aid, defense spending, and the Middle East.[15] For example, before the attack on Pearl Harbor, public opinion overwhelmingly favored an isolationist foreign policy; those attitudes shifted with dramatic suddenness after December 7, 1941, the day of the attack and the beginning of U.S. involvement in World War II.

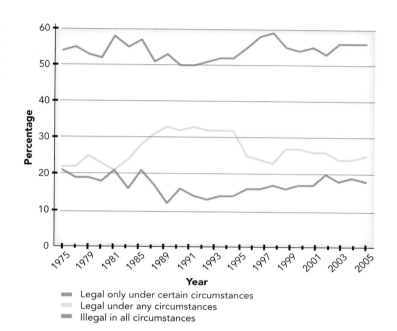

Year

▬ Legal only under certain circumstances
▭ Legal under any circumstances
▬ Illegal in all circumstances

FIGURE 10.1

U.S. Public Opinion on Abortion, 1975–2005

As you can see, opinion on this controversial issue has remained fairly stable. In 1975, 54 percent of Americans thought abortion should be legal under certain circumstances; today, that number is stable at 56 percent. Over the past three decades, the percentage in support of the idea that abortion should be legal under certain circumstances has ranged only between 50 and 59 percent.

SOURCE: "Abortion," Gallup Poll, http://poll.gallup.com/content/default.aspx?ci=1576, January 9, 2006.

pathways past and present

SEXISM RECONSIDERED

E xamining how and why public opinion changes can be fascinating. Consider how public opinion has changed regarding the status of women in our society. Opportunities for women in our society have changed dramatically in recent decades. Because of a concerted effort to improve the position of women in our society, support for women's equality is higher today than ever in our history. Figure 10.2 on page 382 shows the steady increase in the percentage of Americans who believe that women should have a role in society equal to that of men. Before the rise of the modern

▶ **Can pop culture change**
political opinion, or do
changes in political values
influence pop culture?

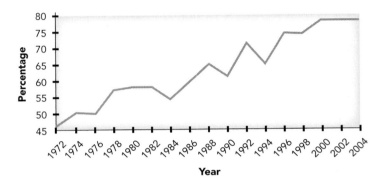

FIGURE 10.2

U.S. Public Opinion on the Proper Role of Women in American Society, 1972–2004

The percentage of Americans who believe that women should have an equal role with men in business, industry, and government has increased steadily from 46 percent in 1972 to 78 percent in 2004. What do you think is responsible for this dramatic increase? What does it mean that 8 percent of the public believes that women's primary role should be in the home? Are you surprised that roughly the same percentage of men and women held both sets of views? Why or why not?

SOURCE: "The NES Guide to Public Opinion and Election Behavior," American National Election Studies, http://www.umich.edu/~nes/nesguide/graphs/g4c_1_1.htm, November 30, 2005, graph 4c.1.1.

women's rights movement in the 1960s, only 46 percent of Americans thought women should be equal with men in business, industry, and government; the numbers had risen to 78 percent in 2004.[16] A number of consequences have emerged from this important cultural change. First, women are seeing a growth in opportunities, most notably in education and business. Today, there are more female-headed businesses than ever before. Nearly half of incoming business graduate students are women; more than half of law students are women. Proportionately more women are now earning associate's and bachelor's degrees (though this is somewhat the result of declining male enrollment, which partly reflects the fact that men can earn high wages without the benefit of a college education in certain industries). Women now earn 42 percent of the doctoral degrees in the United States (though they disproportionately major in the lower-paid and less prestigious fields of education and the humanities).

Although women have made progress, they are still significantly underrepresented in our government: Women make up 15 percent of Congress, 26 percent of statewide elective executive officials, and 23 percent of state legislators.[17] Women run fewer than 2 percent of Fortune 500 companies, and the number of female CEOs of these companies declined from nine to seven in 2005. The Department of Labor examined the "glass ceiling" and found it to be lower than many people thought, often keeping women from top corporate leadership positions. The research also found that the "sticky floor" in corporate America made it difficult for many women to be promoted. Recent class action lawsuits against Wal-Mart and Costco alleging sexual discrimination testify to the problem. The Wal-Mart case (*Dukes* v. *Wal-Mart Stores, Inc.*) is the largest civil rights class action ever certified. Both lawsuits charge that the companies discriminated against female employees in decisions involving pay and promotion. Wal-Mart is a global giant, with approximately 3,566 stores in the United States and more than 1.2 million employees (two-thirds of whom are women). It is doubtful that such lawsuits would ever have been brought in the era before our culture changed to see women as equal participants in our society. Shifts in public opinion can result in tangible cultural change. ■

THE IMPACT OF POPULAR CULTURE ON POLITICAL OPINIONS AND VALUES

▶ **Can pop culture change political opinion, or do changes in political values influence pop culture?** Many people believe that our popular culture can influence our political values and culture.

what YOU can do!

Sports history was made on May 31, 2005, when Danica Patrick became the first woman to lead the Indianapolis 500. With her ultimate fourth-place finish, Patrick became the highest-placed female driver in this prestigious race. Many observers believe that this is evidence that society is changing its views about the proper role of women. What do you think?

Do an Internet search on "Danica Patrick," and examine the press coverage. How does the coverage in official Indy Racing League literature differ from coverage in popular media? Why do you think the coverage differs? Is her gender presented as relevant or irrelevant? Is it used in a way that makes her seem more or less professional and competent?

LEFT: **Pioneers in Sports: Jackie Robinson** broke the color barrier in Major League baseball and RIGHT: Danica Patrick became the fourth woman to race in the Indy 500. In 2005 she became the first woman to lead a lap at the Indy 500, and went on to finish fourth. Since Patrick's accomplishment came after women were competitive, will it have the impact of Robinson's breakthrough? Do you think that these two individuals are role models for others? How important do you think role models are?

Politics and entertainment are increasingly becoming intertwined.[18] Celebrities often make political statements, ranging from open expressions of support for a particular candidate or party to organizing and articulating support for political issues or movements. When discussing the effect of popular culture on political culture, we discover several controversies, most notably focusing on the issue of cause and effect. Does popular culture affect values and beliefs, or do values and beliefs affect popular culture? For example, when in 1997 Ellen DeGeneres "came out" as a gay woman (both personally and as her character Ellen Morgan on the then-popular TV show *Ellen*), did she do so because the climate had changed, making it more acceptable to be gay? Or did her coming out lead to changed attitudes toward homosexuality? Or both? It's difficult to determine what came first. Several theories have been advanced to explain the relationship between popular culture and political culture.

▶ **What are the main differences** between liberal beliefs and conservative beliefs?

catalyst-for-change theory
the assertion that public opinion shapes and alters our political culture, thus allowing for change.

interactive theory
the theory that political culture both shapes and reflects popular opinion.

political ideology
a consistent set of beliefs that form a general philosophy regarding the proper goals, purposes, functions, and size of government.

liberal
a person who generally supports governmental action to promote equality (such as welfare and public education), favors governmental intervention in the economy, and supports environmental issues.

One theory states that popular culture promotes change. According to this **catalyst-for-change theory,** popular culture shapes the independent attitudes and beliefs of the public. One example of the catalyst-for-change theory occurred in 1947, when Jackie Robinson became the first black player in major league baseball. Watching him display remarkable athletic ability as he played for the Brooklyn Dodgers, and his remarkable control and refusal to respond to the hail of racial slurs from fans that he faced in his first year, caused many people to rethink the common racial stereotypes of the time. In the same way, when Vanessa Williams was crowned the first black Miss America in 1983, many people in society began to think differently about issues of race and beauty. A second theory sees popular culture as a barometer of public attitudes, not as the shaper of those attitudes. According to this theory, Ellen Degeneres was able to come out because our culture and beliefs had changed, permitting a more tolerant view of homosexuality. Furthermore, the theory explains the popularity of shows such as *Queer Eye* and *Will and Grace* not because they caused us to see homosexuality differently but rather because our attitudes had already begun to change. Still another explanation, **interactive theory,** asserts that popular culture both changes *and* reflects social values and beliefs. In a highly interactive process, popular culture serves as both a catalyst and as a barometer. This last theory seems most logical and dynamic.[19]

THE POWER OF POPULAR CULTURE

We can and should debate the ways in which popular culture influences our political culture and public opinion, and there are several historical examples that demonstrate ways in which popular culture has had a significant effect. One early example occurred with the abolitionist movement, an antislavery movement that began in the North in the early 1800s but did not get onto the mainstream agenda until after the publication of Harriet Beecher Stowe's novel *Uncle Tom's Cabin* in 1851. The novel personalized the horror of slavery and mobilized people who had previously been unaware of the depth of the problem. The book sold more than 300,000 copies in the first year, and within ten years it had sold more than 2 million copies, becoming the all-time American best-seller in proportion to population. The film *Birth of a Nation* (released in 1916), which glorified the Ku Klux Klan and is arguably one of the most racist movies ever made in the United States, clearly harmed American race relations, especially after it was shown to children in many southern schools as a "history lesson." Betty Freidan's 1963 book *The Feminist Mystique* invigorated the feminist movement in the 1960s. During that same decade, folk and rock music powerfully influenced young people's perceptions of war and peace. Rap and hip-hop music today has both positive and negative aspects. On the one hand, its glorification of violence, its materialism, and its degrading treatment of women can all be socially harmful. On the other hand, the music provides an important outlet through which African Americans can publicize the plight of poor urban residents.

practicequiz

1. Which of the following could be considered a part of U.S. political culture?
   a. belief in the importance of the individual
   b. the assumption that capitalism is a morally just economic system
   c. belief in the legitimacy of the two-party system
   d. a, b, and c

2. Political beliefs have remained relatively stable in this country in part because
   a. common citizens have been invested in keeping it this way.
   b. there has been widespread trust in our political system.
   c. dissent is not easily tolerated in our political system.
   d. a and c.

3. Prevailing attitudes toward interracial marriage over the course of the twentieth century confirm the fact that political beliefs have been quite stable in the United States.
   a. true   b. false

4. What best describes the relationship between popular culture, on the one hand, and political opinions and values in this country, on the other?
   a. Historically, popular culture has reflected public opinions and values.
   b. Historically, popular culture has triggered changes in public opinions and values.
   c. Historically, popular culture has sometimes reflected public opinions and values, sometimes changed those opinions and values, and sometimes done both at the same time.
   d. Historically, popular culture has had only a tangential relation to the country's political opinions and values.

Answers: 1-d, 2-b, 3-b, 4-c.

conservatives
people who believe that government spending should be limited, that traditional patterns of relationships should be preserved, and that a large and powerful government is a threat to personal liberties.

discussionquestions

1. How stable are belief structures? What aspects of society tend to stabilize public opinion?

2. What theories analyze the relationship between popular and political cultures? Give some examples that demonstrate the impact of popular culture on public opinion.

From Values to Ideology

▶ **What are the main differences between liberal beliefs and conservative beliefs? Political ideology** is a consistent set of basic beliefs about the proper purpose and scope of government. Americans tend to fall into two camps: liberals and conservatives. In general terms, **liberals** tend to support social and cultural change (especially in connection with issues of equality) and want an activist government that encourages change. **Conservatives,** by contrast, tend to favor traditional views on social, cultural, and economic matters and demand a more limited role for government in most spheres. Although there is some ideological variation within each party, generally speaking, today's Republican Party is the party of conservatives, whereas most liberals tend to identify with the Democratic Party.

The conservative-liberal distinction holds true when looking at spending on public goods (entities that benefit many people, such as public parks, but are unlikely to emerge naturally in a market economy), but the distinction is less helpful in explaining other issues. Liberals favor government spending on environmental protection, education, public transportation, national parks, and social services. Conservatives want smaller governmental budgets and fewer governmental programs. In theory, liberals favor governmental activism, but they oppose governmental regulation of abortions. In theory, conservatives oppose governmental activism, but they support governmental restrictions on pornography and abortion.

Today, the critical difference between liberals and conservatives concerns not so much the *scope* of governmental activity as the *purpose* of governmental actions. Generally speaking, conservatives approve of using governmental power to promote order, including social order, though there are exceptions to these generalizations. Conservatives typically favor firm police action, swift and severe punishments for criminals, and more laws regulating behavior, such as teen curfews. As you will see in ⓛⓘⓝⓚ *Chapter 12, pages 484–485* such beliefs led many conservatives to support stringent anticommunist domestic and foreign policies in the 1940s and 1950s. Support for the USA PATRIOT Act, initially bipartisan and very popular as an immediate reaction to the September 11, 2001, terrorist attacks, now gets more conservative than liberal support. Conservatives want to preserve traditional patterns of social relations, including the importance of the domestic role of women in family life and the significance of religion in daily life and school. Conservatives today do not oppose equality, but they tend not to view securing equality as a prime objective of governmental action.

TABLE 10.1

Percentage of Americans Identifying with a Particular Political Ideology, 1974–2004

SELF-CHARACTERIZATION	1974	1984	1994	2004
Extremely liberal, liberal, or slightly liberal	21	18	14	23
Moderate or middle-of-the-road	27	23	26	26
Extremely conservative, conservative, or slightly conservative	26	29	36	32
Don't know, haven't thought about it	27	30	24	20

SOURCE: Data from "The ANES Guide to Public Opinion and Electoral Behavior," *American National Election Studies,* http://www.umich.edu/~nes/nesguide/toptable/tab3_1.htm, November 27, 2005, tab. 3.1.

Why do you think the number of liberals declined to a low of 14 percent in 1994 but then returned in 2004 to levels similar to those seen in 1974? Why do you think the percentages identified with conservative ideology saw a steady increase from 1974 until 1994 and then a slight decline? How do the groups of people you come into contact with compare to this distribution?

In general, liberals tend to worry more than conservatives do about the civil liberties implications of the USA PATRIOT Act and government surveillance of potential terrorists. Liberals are less likely to approve the use of governmental power to maintain order, but are more willing to use governmental power to promote equality. Thus they tend to support laws to ensure that homosexuals receive equal treatment in employment, housing, and education. They favor policies that encourage businesses to hire and promote women and minorities, and they want to raise the minimum wage.

Table 10.1 shows how people have identified with ideology in the United States since 1974. There has been an increase in the percent of people who consider themselves conservatives and a slight increase in the percent of people who label themselves liberal. The growth of both groups has come at the expense of the

libertarian
a person who favors little or no regulation of the economy and minimal governmental interference with personal freedoms.

neoconservatism
a political theory that advocates aggressive foreign policy and is more suportive of domestic spending than traditional conservatism.

agents of political socialization
factors that influence how we acquire political facts and knowledge and develop political values.

▶ **What are neoconservatives?**

Members of the College Republicans National Committee dress in Grim Reaper costumes as they march on Capitol Hill in Washington, D.C., to call on the Senate to eliminate the death tax on June 8, 2006. The effort to repeal the tax failed. The death tax is an estate or inheritance tax on the value of a deceased individual's assets before the assets are passed on to heirs. Do you think that theatrics are helpful to a cause or do they tend to marginalize the participants? When and under what circumstances are they likely to be helpful? Harmful?

"undecided" category (reflecting the manner in which society has become more polarized and has been growing more conservative).

In the 1970s and 1980s, the United States saw a revitalization of the conservative movement, as well as the emergence of a new conservative agenda. Several conservative groups came together, greatly increasing their visibility and power. Traditional conservatives, who focused on economic issues, merged with social conservatives, who focused on issues of traditional morality. Traditional conservatives had opposed many of the policies enacted during the civil rights movement of the 1960s, which often created social programs targeted to benefit minorities and the poor. Many of these programs were expensive and materially benefited only a small percentage of people. Many social conservatives resented policies that were designed to promote social change, feeling that they had to bear too much responsibility (including fiscal responsibility) for the change. They opposed the Equal Rights Amendment, busing to promote school integration, gun control, sex education in public schools, government poverty programs, abortion, welfare spending, and immigration. They wanted to preserve traditional cultural values such as prayer in schools and traditional gender roles.[20] The unification of these two groups, fiscal conservatives and social conservatives, greatly expanded the appeal of the Republican Party.

▶ **What are neoconservatives?** We have also seen the growth in numbers and influence of neoconservatives. **Neoconservatism** is a theory that focuses mostly on foreign policy issues but tends to be more supportive of domestic social spending than mainstream conservatives. Neoconservatives advocate aggressive military force to advance what they believe to be in the best interest of the United States. There is a strong neoconservative influence in the administration of George W. Bush (as there was in Ronald Reagan's administration), and neoconservatives are thought to have been key advisers in the decision to invade Iraq in 2003.

pathways profile

NEW COLLEGE CONSERVATIVES

Today's new generation of college activists has attracted a good deal of media attention. Although many Americans associate college activism with the 1960s brand of radical liberalism, recent college activists are decidedly different. College conservatives are making their presence known on campuses throughout the country. Data show that the percentage of first-year college students

What are the main agents
of political socialization?

discussionquestions

1. What is political ideology? How do liberals differ from conservatives? How has the distribution of political ideology changed in recent decades?

2. What do we mean by the *scope* of government? The *purpose* of government? How does each concept relate to political ideology?

who identify themselves as conservatives increased only slightly from 1970 until 2000[21] but that college conservatives have become far more active on campuses across the nation. Liberal organizations on American college campuses are declining in membership and struggling to survive, while conservative groups seem to be thriving. The College Republican National Committee, which had 409 chapters in 1998, increased to 1,148 chapters in 2006. The College Democrats of America have only 903 chapters (20 percent less than the Republicans).[22]

What is perhaps most interesting about college conservatives is the idea that they appear to be different from traditional conservatives, for many focus on more **libertarian** issues (libertarians oppose nearly all interference by government in the private lives of citizens). That is, on the whole they tend to favor traditional Republican issues such as tax cuts and fiscal conservative policies, but they also oppose the USA PATRIOT Act and stricter airport security. They are concerned with the growth in the deficit and are critical of many of President Bush's increases in domestic spending.

Bearing out these trends, a national survey conducted by the American Council on Education found that first-year college students in 2003 were more conservative on a number of issues than students a decade earlier. Students today are less supportive of abortion rights, environmental protection, and affirmative action but tend to be more supportive of women's rights and gay rights. Generally, they want a limited role for government and protection of civil liberties—traditionally libertarian views. In fact, the number of Libertarian Party groups doubled on American college campuses (to 306) between 1997 and 2004.[23] ∎

practicequiz

1. Another term for a coherent set of beliefs about the purpose of government is
   a. a political party.
   b. a political ideology.
   c. popular culture.
   d. public opinion.

2. One clear distinction between liberals and conservatives in the United States is that the former always favor governmental regulation and the latter never do.
   a. true   b. false

3. What explains the revitalization of the conservative movement in the 1970s and 1980s?

a. the unification of social and fiscal conservatives
b. increasing resentment of national policies that promoted social change, such as school desegregation, gun control, and the Equal Rights Amendment
c. Watergate
d. a and b

4. Libertarians now favor some Republican positions, such as
   a. promoting tax cuts, even if it means compromising some social services.
   b. the USA PATRIOT Act.
   c. increased federal investment in public education.
   d. a, b, and c.

Answers: 1-b, 2-b, 3-d, 4-a.

Political Socialization

Political socialization is the conscious and unconscious transmission of political culture and values from one generation to another. It is the process by which people learn political information, organize political knowledge, and develop political values. Socialization is not a onetime event; it occurs continuously. The transmission of knowledge as a part of political socialization is a means of teaching one generation the lessons from its predecessors, leading, ideally, to social stability and better decision making.

▶ **What are the main agents of political socialization?** Research demonstrates that learning during childhood and adolescence affects adult political behavior;[24] we must therefore examine very carefully the process by which people learn about politics. Factors that influence the acquisition of political facts and formation of values are called **agents of political socialization.** Let's examine six such agents: family, school, peers and community, houses of worship, the media, and events.

FAMILY

Children learn a wide range of social, moral, religious, economic, and political values from their family, and what they learn can dramatically shape their opinions. When parents are interested in politics, they tend to influence their children to become more politically interested and informed. Early studies found the family

▶ **Does attending college**
make people more liberal?

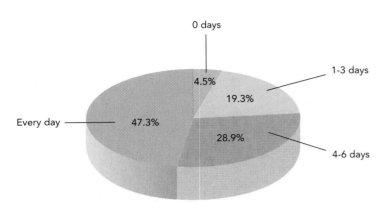

FIGURE 10.3
Family Eating Patterns

Nearly one-half of families eat together daily
while three-fourths eat together at least 4 times
per week. What does your family do?
SOURCE: Data Resource Center on Child and Adolescent
Health, *National Survey of Children's Health*,
http://www.nschdata.org, 2005.

to be a very important agent of socialization, serving as an inter-mediary between children and society. Families are very successful at teaching political values, because children often try to copy the behavior of loved ones.[25] Observing how parents react to different situations can affect values that are learned and beliefs that are developed. For example, how parents react to the police can set the stage for how children will view authority. Parents' views of poverty can affect the attitudes of their children about welfare and social services. Parents are often most influential in transmitting party identification to their children, especially when both parents are of the same political party. If children do not adopt their parents' political party, they are more likely to define themselves as independents than to align with the opposite party.[26]

Researchers have shown that parents are especially influential in teaching gender roles and racial attitudes. Children who are raised by mothers who work outside the home for wages, for example, tend to have more progressive views of gender. Girls who are encouraged by a parent to be more assertive tend to be more independent and to have more independent careers.[27] Families also teach prejudice and racial attitudes. Prejudiced parents are more likely to have prejudiced children. Children learn bigotry directly (from parental attitudes and comments) and indirectly (from watching parental interactions with others). However, once children are exposed to different factors in adolescence, the relationship between parental intolerance and child bigotry diminishes.[28] Parental influence wanes when children mature and other factors increase in importance.

Recent research on the influence of the family on political values is mixed, finding that the actual levels of influence depend on a number of factors. Families with strong relationships and strong mutual ties tend to be the most likely to transmit values. If family ties weaken, so does the family's influence on the development of the children's values.

As the nature of the family changes, we will need to continue examining its influence in shaping the development of children's values. Children today are more likely to be home alone and less likely to spend time with their parents. For example, the number of families eating together has steadily declined. (Figure 10.3 shows the current eating habits of American families with children under 18.) Moreover, the number of children living in single-parent homes has increased. The number of single mothers rose from 3 million in 1970 to 10.3 million in 2004 and the number of single fathers from 393,000 to 2.3 million.[29] It's not hard to see that these changes in family structure and interaction may affect the role families will play in influencing children in the future.

SCHOOL

Schools teach political knowledge, the value of political participation, and the acceptance of democratic principles. However, their effectiveness in doing so is debated. Schools seem to be more effective in transmitting basic political knowledge than in creating politically engaged citizens.

Elementary schools introduce children to authority figures outside the family, such as the teacher, the principal, and police officers, while also teaching about the hierarchical nature of power. In doing so, the schools prepare children to accept social order, to follow rules, and to learn the importance of obedience. Children learn that good citizens obey the laws (just as good children obey the rules of the schools and of their parents). Schools also teach an idealized view of the nation's slogans and symbols (Pledge of Allegiance, national anthem, national heroes, and holidays). School elections for student council and mock presidential elections teach students important democratic principles and procedures, such as the notion of campaigning, voting, and majority rule. Much of the learning in elementary schools is affective, that is, based on feelings. Consequently, most children emerge from elementary school with a strong sense of nationalism and an idealized notion of American government, thus building a general sense of good will for the political system that lays the foundation for future learning.[30] As they mature, children start to see their place in the political community and gain a sense of civic responsibility.

High schools continue building "good citizens" through activities and curriculum. Field trips to the state legislature and classes with explicit political content can result in a greater aware-ness of the political process and the people involved in it. The school curriculum teaches political facts, while the school atmos-phere can affect political values. Students with positive experiences in school, who develop trust in school leaders, faith in the system, and a sense of efficacy, are more likely to show higher levels of sup-port for the national political system. Students who feel that they are fairly treated by school officials tend to have more trust in offi-cials and feel less alienated from their government.[31] Civics classes in high school are potentially a good mechanism for encouraging student engagement in politics. Researchers have found that the simple existence of such classes is not enough to produce civically engaged students; the dynamic of the class is also important. Civics classes that are taught by people who generally like the sub-ject matter and who themselves are politically engaged are far more successful in positively socializing students. Stimulating environments with novel teaching formats help produce better cit-izenship in students. On the whole, however, high school seniors are not very well informed about politics, are not very interested in politics, and have only moderate levels of support for democratic practices.[32]

▶ **Does attending college make people more liberal?** Research consistently demonstrates that a college education has a liberalizing effect on noneconomic issues. Adults with college experience tend to be more liberal on social issues than the less educated. Several theories have attempted to explain this. College tends to make individuals aware of differences between people and allows them to see the complexity of public policy issues. In classes such as the one you're now in, students are exposed to contro-versies in our society and learn that the issues are far more com-plicated than previously thought. Moreover, they learn that intelligent people can disagree. Hence they tend to be more sup-portive of changing opinions and less supportive of the status quo. College students often meet a wider range of people than they had contact with in high school, giving them evidence to reject some social stereotypes and prejudices and to accept more diversity. Meeting people whom you like and respect but who are different from you can provide important opportunities for growth. Also, college faculty are significantly more liberal than their students (and than most people in society). Notwithstanding individual dif-ferences among faculty, those in the liberal arts and the sciences tend to be the most liberal.[33] This leads some conservatives to hypothesize that these liberal college faculty indoctrinate students, causing them to become more liberal. That may be so, but this the-ory would appear to underestimate the ability of college students to think independently and critically. Whatever the explanation, people with a college education are generally more liberal on social issues than those who haven't been to college.

Schools are important agents of socialization, teaching children not only political facts, but also a sense of patriotism and a belief in demo-cratic practices. Children across the country begin their day by pledging allegiance to the American flag and reciting school rules. These practices help create a strong sense of loyalty and nationalism. Do you think that schools focus too much on allegiance, failing to teach students to critically analyze our government, leaders, and policies? When, if at all, should one learn to question authority?

▶ **What political values and information do we get from the media?**

efficacy
the belief that one can influence government. *Internal political efficacy* is the belief that you have the knowledge and ability to influence government. *External political efficacy* refers to the belief that governmental officials will respond to the people.

PEERS AND COMMUNITY

Community and peers are also agents of political socialization. Your community consists of the people of all ages with whom you come in contact through work, school, or your neighborhood. Peers are friends, classmates, and coworkers who tend to be around the same age as you and live in your community. Peer influence tends to be weaker than that of school and family, but our companions do affect us. Differences of opinions and preferences between generations are likely due to peer influence (especially regarding tastes in music, entertainment, clothing, hairstyle, and speech). Peers generally serve to reinforce one another, as people tend to socialize with people like themselves. Research shows that in heterogeneous communities, political participation tends to be higher, with more hotly contested and more competitive elections and more political debate, than in homogeneous environments. People are more likely to participate and pay attention to politics if they believe their vote counts, as is the case when there are a variety of views or disagreements and the election is closely contested.[34] Moreover, the pressure to conform to the dominant view is greater in homogeneous communities than in more diverse settings.

Politically diverse environments are also more likely to provide interesting stimuli and often result in a greater sense that one can have an effect on government.[35] Minorities living in racially diverse environments tend to have higher political **efficacy** than minorities living in segregated environments. Researchers found that African Americans living in predominantly black communities generally did not experience political socialization in a manner that encourages political participation and civic engagement.[36] Racial segregation tends to develop a sense of isolation and disinterest in the political system. Areas with high voter turnout, with politically engaged adult role models, and with racial diversity appear to be the best environments to raise politically aware and knowledgeable children who have a sense that their voice can count.

RELIGION

Religions are important instructors, particularly when it comes to issues of morality, self-sacrifice, and altruism, and they are an important factor in the development of personal identity. Individuals raised in religious households tend to be socialized to contribute to society and to get involved in their communities.[37] Conservative denominations and religions tend to impart conservative attitudes (especially regarding abortion and other issues involving personal morality and sexuality) than more liberal churches. People raised in Reform Judaism more than in any other religious tradition are often socialized to have the greatest involvement in their communities and the highest levels of civic engagement.[38] Those raised in religiously diverse communities are more likely to be engaged in politics and have higher levels of political participation.[39] Religion can act as a reinforcing mechanism of community and family values on a wide array of moral and political issues.

THE MEDIA

▶ **What political values and information do we get from the media?** We will look more closely at the effect of the media in influencing values, politicians, and society in Ⓛ Ⓘ Ⓝ Ⓚ *Chapter 11, pages 429–435.* Here it is appropriate to note that the media are an important agent of political socialization, with varied effects on public opinion. Many authorities believe that the effect of the media on political values and opinions has increased in the past several decades. Today, it is estimated that American children watch approximately twenty-eight hours of TV a week.[40] If we add to that the time spent listening to music, reading magazines, and watching movies and music videos, it's obvious that entertainment may have a big role in influencing values. Entertainment media often present behavior at odds with what is approved in the family, schools, and places of worship. Television and movies often show what appears to be the most pleasurable behavior with few consequences attached. Promiscuous sex, drug use, and materialism are common in contemporary programming, with little attention paid to potential consequences. What can result is a competition for influence between media, parents, schools, and religion. Moreover, because of the drive to get good ratings, the media often focus on negative issues, scandals, and violence. Many analysts worry that this focus on negativity can adversely affect political efficacy and trust in government.[41]

Recent research demonstrates that people do learn valid political information from the media. A poll by CNN found that viewers of late-night television programs were more politically informed than nonviewers. The best informed were the fans of *The Daily Show,* hosted by Jon Stewart on the Comedy Channel. In fact, viewers of this program were more informed than those who read the newspaper regularly. On a test of political knowledge of current affairs, *Daily Show* viewers got 60 percent of the questions

▶ **Did the events of 9/11 have a long-term impact on our political values?**

what YOU can do!

The Web site ReligiousTolerance.org asserts that it examines all topics from multiple positions. What do you think? Examine the site's analysis of the issue of homosexuality **http://www.religioustolerance.org/ homosexu.htm**—does it fairly present the different faith perspectives on the topic? Do you think the site is neutral and objective, or is there a bias?

right, while Leno and Letterman fans answered 49 percent correctly. All of these scores are above the national average, although it should be noted that *Daily Show* viewers are more educated and more affluent than most, explaining some of the variation.[42]

IMPACT OF EVENTS

▶ **Did the events of 9/11 have a long-term impact on our political values?** No event of recent decades has had a more dramatic impact on Americans than the terrorist attacks of September 11, 2001. Not enough time has passed to allow social scientists to assess the long-term effects of those attacks on youth socialization. In the short term, however, these events have altered public opinion in two ways. First, the public is more aware of the danger of terrorism and is consequently more afraid. Before the terrorist attacks, many Americans did not believe that our country was vulnerable to terrorist threats. Americans often viewed terrorism as a problem that occurred in other countries (with the clear exception of the Oklahoma City bombing). Following the 9/11 attacks, the number of Americans who expressed confidence that our government could keep us safe declined significantly. As time passed, concerns over personal safety have diminished, but a general sense of fear remains high.[43] The second observed short-term change has been a surge in patriotism and a sense of uniting in battle. At least for a while after the attacks, we became a unified country standing behind our government.

Long-term consequences are more difficult to ascertain. Research does show that important events can affect the socialization process as significant events focus national attention. By examining other events in our nation's past that were of great political importance (the attack on Pearl Harbor, the Vietnam War, the assassination of President Kennedy, and the Watergate scandal are all examples), we can see how shocking events can alter politics. However, it is too early for researchers to assess with high confidence the long-term impact of this horrific event. The attacks did focus public attention on political events and increased the amount of time and attention that younger people devote to following politics.[44] The attacks neither increased youth hostility toward immigrants nor diminished their support for diversity but rather served to bolster patriotism and national pride. Research that examined students before and after the attacks found that they had higher levels of trust in government after the attacks than before. Once again, it is too soon to determine if this increase in

Jon Stewart, host of the "Daily Show with Jon Stewart" on Comedy Central, often jokes about politics, governmental officials, and current affairs. Watchers of the program tend to be better informed than the general public regarding current affairs. Do you think that they are better informed because of the show or because they tend to be more educated? Do you think Jon Stewart would be a viable candidate for political office? Why or why not?

crosscutting cleavages
divisions in society that separate people
into groups.

1. Why is it important to understand the process of political socialization? What do we mean by *agents of political socialization*?

2. How does each agent that we have discussed affect the socialization process? Which agents can negatively affect socialization? Which agents are reinforcing?

trust will be sustained, but researchers did demonstrate that youth, like most other Americans, did "rally 'round the flag."[45]

Major historical events can influence the socialization of an entire cohort of a nation's people. So it was with the "sixties generation," as young people experienced the Vietnam War and Watergate, yielding a high level of political cynicism and distrust of government. Similarly, the Great Depression fostered among young people who lived through it strong views about fiscal policy and governmental responsibility. Over time, we will see whether a "9/11 generation" similarly emerges.[46]

practicequiz

1. Political socialization refers to
   a. attending social events involving politicians.
   b. the process whereby political systems become socialist in orientation.
   c. the process whereby each generation develops political consciousness, learn political information, organize political knowledge, and form political values.
   d. the process whereby people learn to accept the rules of government—the regulations, laws, and customs of their nation, state, and municipality.

2. Agents of political socialization include
   a. the community and the media.
   b. House of Worship.
   c. both a and b.
   d. peers.

3. Research suggests that children from single-parent homes may be less able and willing to participate actively in the political process because
   a. they have lower feelings of efficacy.
   b. they have less political information.
   c. they are often unemployed.
   d. a and b.

4. Studies have shown that a college education has the effect of making most people less conservative about social issues than they used to be. Why is this so?
   a. Going to college often involves meeting a greater diversity of people, making students more tolerant and understanding of cultural difference.
   b. College prompts students to explore the complexities that often lie behind public policy issues.
   c. Such an education cultivates in students an openness to change—in their own minds and in society itself.
   d. a, b, and c

Answers: 1-c, 2-c, 3-d, 4-d.

Social Groups and Political Values

People with similar backgrounds tend to develop similar political opinions. These group characteristics serve to divide Americans along lines of social class, education, religion, race and ethnicity, and gender. These factors tend to influence public opinion on a variety of domestic and foreign policies and must therefore be examined and understood.

We need to make several important points at the beginning of this section. First, we're going to be generalizing about how various factors influence political opinions, but many exceptions exist. For example, women as a whole tend to be more liberal than men on social issues, but there are many conservative women in our country. Caucasians tend to be more likely than African Americans to be members of the Republican Party, but many African Americans are Republicans. Second, most people are influenced by numerous factors. For some, religion may be the most important factor influencing their values and opinions; for others, it may be race or ethnicity; for yet others, it may be social class or gender. Moreover, the effects of specific factors may vary from issue to issue. Rarely do opinions on issues stem from one source—usually opinions are influenced by many different factors.

We use the term **crosscutting cleavages** to explain how two or more factors work to influence an individual.[47] These cleavages (splits in the population) complicate the work of political scientists, for it is often difficult to say which factors are the most important in shaping particular attitudes. These cleavages work both ways—they also tend to moderate opinions and lend to stability over time. Take income as an example. There are many issues on which the poor agree; there are also many issues on which they disagree. As you will see, income has an important effect on opinions, but it is not the only factor. Race, gender, region, and religion (to name a few) also affect individuals.

ECONOMIC BASES OF PARTISANSHIP AND PUBLIC OPINION

Political socialization does not explain the distribution of party loyalties in the United States. Socialization is helpful in describing *how* rather than *why* an individual acquires party loyalty. One

TABLE 10.2
Percentage of Americans Favoring Particular Public Policies, by Family Income, 2004

PUBLIC POLICY STANCE	FAMILY INCOME			
	UNDER $25,000	*$25,000 TO $50,000*	*$50,000 TO $80,000*	*MORE THAN $80,000*
Oppose capital punishment	57	67	72	73
Favor making it harder to get guns	61	60	52	61
Favor allowing gays in the military	50	54	58	57
Favor allowing gays to adopt	43	45	53	54
Favor never allowing abortion	18	12	13	7
Favor increased spending on the poor	69	58	52	45

SOURCE: Center for Political Studies, *National Election Study* (Ann Arbor: University of Michigan, 2004).

People of higher income tend to be more likely to oppose capital punishment and are more supportive of homosexual rights and reproductive freedoms. They are, however, less supportive of increased spending of tax dollars on the poor. Why do you think this is the case? (Pay attention to subsequent tables, looking at how self-interest affects public opinion. Also look to see if there are instances where self-interest doesn't seem to be as relevant as one might expect.)

important factor in determining why an individual is a Democrat or a Republican is the person's economic standing and that of his or her parents. The principal generalization that you can make about loyalties to the parties in modern times is that they are based primarily on socioeconomic status.

Traditionally, Democrats have been regarded as the "party of the people" and Republicans as the "party of the rich." This characterization goes back to the 1800s, but it became more pronounced in 1930s when Democratic President Franklin D. Roosevelt launched his New Deal programs in the midst of the Great Depression. Labor legislation, Social Security, and minimum wage laws all reinforced the Democratic Party's image as the party of the have-nots. Even African Americans, who ever since the Civil War had aligned with the Republican Party, partly in loyalty to President Abraham Lincoln, in the 1930s abandoned it for the Democratic Party. Ironically, by aligning with the Democrats, African Americans found themselves in the same party with racist white southerners. Beginning in the late 1960s, southern whites who had opposed or remained lukewarm toward racial integration flocked into the Republican ranks.

Even today, many Americans who see themselves as middle- and upper-class tend to be Republicans, while those who identify themselves as working-class tend to be Democrats. However, social class and party loyalties are not as closely linked in the United States as in other Western democracies. Both parties in the United States draw support from upper-, middle-, and lower-status groups. Thus it is difficult for either party to make overt

appeals that reflect sharp class differences. When it comes to purely economic issues, the more affluent tend to be more conservative than the less affluent on fiscal issues such as taxation, *assuming that each group is defining its politics strictly on the basis of self-interest.* But when we add education to the equation, liberal views tend to increase along with rising income. In fact, the higher the level of education a person has received, the more liberal that individual tends to be on social and cultural issues. And because education is highly correlated with income, the relationship is complicated. For example, in 2004, the average annual earnings by highest level of education were

$115,292 for individuals holding advanced professional degrees

$53,581 for recipients of bachelor's degrees

$30,640 for high school graduates

$22,232 for adults with no high school diploma.[48]

People with higher incomes tend to be more supportive of equal rights for women and minorities (including homosexuals) and more supportive of the rights of the criminally accused.[49] These policy stances are related to educational attainment rather than income. As you can see in Table 10.2, the more affluent you are, the more fiscally conservative you'll tend to be on issues relating to spending on the poor but the more liberal on social issues such as gay rights and abortion rights.

► **Which religious denominations are most likely to vote Republican? Democratic?**

TABLE 10.3

Percentage of Americans Favoring Particular Public Policies, by Education, 2004

	LEVEL OF EDUCATION				
PUBLIC POLICY STANCE	DID NOT COMPLETE HIGH SCHOOL	GRADUATED FROM HIGH SCHOOL	ATTENDED COLLEGE	OBTAINED A COLLEGE DEGREE	OBTAINED AN ADVANCED DEGREE
Favor capital punishment	61	70	71	68	53
Favor making it harder to get guns	58	53	51	64	72
Favor allowing gays in the military	47	48	56	58	66
Favor allowing gays to adopt	26	41	45	54	66
Favor never allowing abortion	28	13	12	11	8
Favor increased spending on the poor	66	63	52	48	58

SOURCE: Center for Political Studies, *National Election Study* (Ann Arbor: University of Michigan, 2004).

Do the data presented here surprise you? Why do you think that people with advanced degrees, and presumably high incomes, are more supportive of increased spending on the poor than those who attended or completed college? Considerable differences exist between the more educated and the less educated on issues of reproductive freedom, gun ownership, and homosexual rights. Why do you think this is the case?

EDUCATION

As we've discussed, education tends to increase citizens' awareness and understanding of political issues, often having a liberalizing effect on nonfiscal social issues. For example, a college-educated person will be more likely than a less educated person to choose personal freedom over social order (when they conflict). Thus the more educated groups are more likely to favor gun control and to want limits placed on police authority. There are also differences based on education in issues of foreign policy. The less educated tend to favor isolationist policies that would limit the role of the United States on the world scene, whereas the more educated favor greater U.S. engagement in international affairs.[50]

In Table 10.3, you can see rather significant differences in many areas of public debate. Better-educated people tend to be far more likely than the less educated to support homosexual rights (especially gays' right to adopt children) and far more supportive of abortion rights. However, the more educated (and hence the more affluent) often tend to be more fiscally conservative when it comes to economic issues like spending on the poor. The least economically secure people (as measured by income and education) tend to be the most supportive of increasing governmental spend-

ing on domestic social services such as Social Security and the poor.[51] Whereas college-educated people generally favor governmental spending on social services, many of them are hesitant to support increased social spending, because it will result in higher taxes for them, the more affluent. The less educated overwhelmingly favor increased government spending on social programs. The more educated are also more likely to support gun control and, by a small margin, are less supportive of capital punishment.

RELIGION

► **Which religious denominations are most likely to vote Republican? Democratic?** Religion has always been extremely important in American life. Today, nearly 85 percent of Americans say that they belong to an organized religion; 75 percent say that religion is important to their lives, and 95 percent say that they believe in God.[52] From the beginning of the American republic, there have always been religious differences on issues of public policy and party coalitions. Under the party system inaugurated by the New Deal, Catholics and Jews were among the most loyal supporters of the Democratic Party. Although the Democratic loyalty of Catholics has lessened in recent years, religion remains a significant indicator of political alignment today. Differences in

Jim Wallis, founder of Call to Renewal (an organization devoted to fighting poverty and promoting social justice), traveled around the country by bus during the 2004 presidential campaign to raise the visibility of his organization and its fight against poverty. Evangelical ministers tend to be socially conservative and Republican; Wallis is not. He is critical of both political parties, and he is encouraging the Democratic Party to embrace religion in a manner in which they have traditionally resisted. Do you think he can be successful? Why or why not? Photo: Kenneth Dickerman/The New York Times

ideology and support of political parties have more effect on voting than socioeconomic distinctions. When income, education, and occupation are held constant, Catholics and Jews tend to be more liberal and support the Democratic Party, while nonsouthern Protestants tend to be more conservative and support the Republican Party. Jews have long been disposed to favor the Democratic Party because of their sense of internationalism and support for social and economic justice, central tenets of their faith. Catholics are traditionally tied to the Democratic Party because Catholic immigrants, especially in the Northeast, greatly benefited from the social services provided by urban Democratic Party machines in the late nineteenth and early twentieth centuries. (We'll say more about party machines in Chapter 15.) Like Jews, Catholics also felt themselves victimized by prejudice from Protestants, who were identified (in the North) with the old Republican Party. The three Catholics ever nominated for president (Al Smith in 1928, John F. Kennedy in 1960, and John Kerry in 2004) were all Democrats. But in recent decades, these fairly homogeneous alignments have been growing more complicated. Motivated by issues like abortion and gay rights, "traditional" Roman Catholics today tend to vote Republican, while other Catholics—especially those strongly committed to the reforms of Vatican Council II in the 1960s— have remained in the Democratic column out of concern over social justice and peace issues. Protestants from the so-called mainline denominations (Episcopalians, most Presbyterians, many Methodists, and some Lutherans, for example) tend to be politically more split between the political parties.[53] However, white (but not black) evangelicals, who once were mostly either Democrats or nonpolitical, constituted a record 51 percent of the GOP voters in the 2000 presidential election. Seventy-four percent of evangelical Christians voted in 2000 for George W. Bush, representing the Republican Party's strongest constituency.[54] White evangelical Christians continue to give strong support to the Republican Party.

pathways profile

JIM WALLIS

Today, when most people think of evangelical leaders, they tend to think of them as conservative. While this would be true of most of the contemporary evangelical ministers (such as Jerry Falwell and Pat Robertson), more liberal evangelical leaders are also trying to mobilize voters, register nonvoters, and influence political leaders and party officials. One such leader is Jim Wallis.

Wallis is a founder and editor of the liberal evangelical magazine *Sojourners* and is the author of a number of books, the most recent of which is *God's Politics: Why the Right Is Wrong and the Left Doesn't Get It*. While he is critical of both the left and the right, he believes that the liberals can come together with Christians to correct what he sees as social ills and work for peace. He is frustrated with the Democratic Party, claiming that it is unable or unwilling to speak to the large group of Americans who have liberal ideological leanings but are also very spiritual. He asserts that the Democratic Party has lost the moral battle in politics because it shuns religion and allows the Republicans to define morality. He urges liberals, who traditionally believe in a strong separation of church and state, to avoid portraying themselves as "secular fundamentalists" and encourages them to speak in a manner that appeals to religious people and avoids being disrespectful of faith. He believes that the Democratic Party alienates religious voters because it does not speak their language and is dismissive of religion. He wants to unite liberal causes (fighting poverty, racism, and injustice) with spiritual guidance to improve society.

Jim Wallis has created a faith-based antipoverty organization, Call to Renewal, which is a federation of churches and faith-based organizations. He argues that the Bible demands that we pay more direct attention to poverty and social justice. Challenging the liberal belief in separating faith from politics, he asserts that the church, the religious faithful, and religious communities need to be directly involved in politics, serving as the conscience of the state.

Many people believe that the Democratic Party should listen to Wallis's message. It lost the last two presidential elections, in 2000 and 2004, in which its support declined among many religious communities. However, only time will tell whether Wallis is successful in encouraging liberals to embrace faith—and evangelicals to embrace liberalism. ■

TABLE 10.4

Percentage of Americans Favoring Particular Public Policies, by Religion, 2004

	RELIGION		
PUBLIC POLICY STANCE	PROTESTANTS	CATHOLICS	JEWS
Favor capital punishment	69	65	67
Favor making it harder to get guns	54	64	91
Favor allowing gays in the military	50	64	82
Favor allowing gays to adopt	36	55	78
Favor never allowing abortion	17	14	0
Favor increased spending on the poor	58	52	46

SOURCE: Center for Political Studies, *National Election Study* (Ann Arbor: University of Michigan, 2004).

In most areas we examine, considerable differences exist between people of different religious faiths. Which is the most interesting difference in the table and why? What is the least surprising finding?

TABLE 10.5

Percentage of Americans Identifying with the Major Political Parties, by Religion

PROFESSED RELIGION	1987–1988		2002–2003	
	REPUBLICAN PARTY	DEMOCRATIC PARTY	REPUBLICAN PARTY	DEMOCRATIC PARTY
Total Percentage of Americans affiliated with each political party	**26**	**37**	**29**	**31**
Protestant	29	37	33	32
White evangelical	34	31	44	23
White mainline	33	29	35	26
African American	10	69	5	68
White Catholic	26	39	30	30
Attend regularly	26	41	33	29
Attend rarely or never	26	36	25	31
Jewish	22	47	17	54
No religion	18	32	14	28

SOURCE: Pew Research Center, "2004 Political Landslide," http://people-press.org/reports/display.php3?ReportID =196, November 5, 2003.

Why do you think there was such a dramatic change in party identification between 1987–1988 and 2002–2003 for white evangelical Protestants and white Catholics who attend church regularly? Do you think that these trends will continue? Were you surprised to learn that such a large percentage of Jews and African American Protestants supported the Democratic Party compared with other groups?

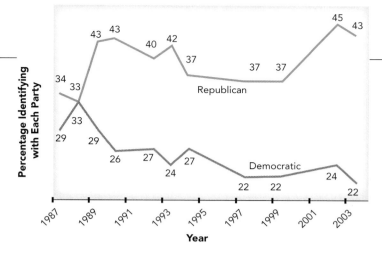

FIGURE 10.4

Party Identification among White Evangelical Protestants

In 1988, white evangelical Protestants were evenly divided in their party identification between Democrats and Republicans. However, the division has since increased dramatically. What consequences do you think this will have for both parties?

SOURCE: The Pew Research Center for the People and the Press. "The 2004 Political Landscape Evenly Divided and Increasingly Polarized."

When we examine the differences between religions on public policy issues, important trends again emerge (see Table 10.4). On every nonfiscal issue (excluding capital punishment, as the differences are not statistically significant), Jews consistently take the most liberal policy stances, while Protestants take the most conservative stance. Catholics typically fall in between. The most significant differences are found regarding gun control, homosexual rights, and abortion.

As you can see in Table 10.5 and Figure 10.4, there are important differences in the distribution of party loyalties based on religion. White Protestants, especially if they describe themselves as evangelicals, are more likely to be Republicans, while black Protestants (who are mostly evangelicals) are far more likely to be Democrats. The more religious Catholics (as measured by the regularity of their church attendance) also became more supportive of the Republican Party, whereas the less observant Catholics voted more heavily Democratic. Jews, on the other hand, became even more supportive of the Democratic Party than previously. Americans who say that they are not members of organized religions are far more likely to be Democrats than Republicans.

RACE AND ETHNICITY

At the beginning of the twentieth century, the major ethnic minorities in America were from Ireland, Germany, Scandinavia, Italy, Poland, and other European countries. They came or descended from those who came to the United States in waves from the 1840s to the early 1900s. These immigrants and their offspring concentrated in urban parts of the Northeast and Midwest. The religious backgrounds of these immigrants (mainly Catholic or Jewish, except for the Scandinavians) differed from the predominant Protestantism of those who had settled colonial America. They were politically energized during the Great Depression, becoming an integral component of the great coalition of Democratic voters that Franklin D. Roosevelt forged in the 1930s. For many years, immigrant groups had political preferences that were consistently different from those of "native" Anglo-Saxons. But as these groups have assimilated into society and risen in economic standing, these differences have been disappearing.

Ever since black people were brought to North America as slaves, they have been at the bottom of the economic, political, and social totem poles. Their disadvantages still exist despite many important social and legal changes in our society.[55] Table 10.6 demonstrates one important discrepancy between the races: differentials in income. African Americans and Hispanics in our society for the most part earn less than Caucasians. The table also illustrates the pay gap between men and women of all races, a factor

TABLE 10.6

Median Annual Earnings, by Race and Sex, 2003

RACE AND SEX	ANNUAL EARNINGS ($)	WAGE RATIO (%)
White men	41,211	100.0
Black men	32,241	78.2
White women	31,169	75.6
Black women	26,965	65.4
Hispanic men	26,083	63.3
Hispanic women	22,363	54.3
All men	40,668	
All women	30,724	
Wage gap		75.5

NOTES: Includes full-time, year-round workers ages 15 and above. "White" and "black" exclude those who reported more than one race category. "Hispanic" includes all those who so identified, regardless of race.

SOURCE: Data from U.S. Census Bureau, *Current Population Survey*, 2004 Annual Social and Economic Supplement (Washington, D.C.: Government Printing Office, 2004), Table 1.

Vast differences in earnings exist between races, and between men and women. For example, half of Hispanic women working full time earned less than $22,363 in 2003 (and half made more than this figure). Compare this to white men, half of whom earn more than $41,211. The difference in median earnings translates into $362 per week—or almost $1,500 per month. Substantial differences of opinion also exist based on race and gender (see Tables 10.7 and 10.8 on pages 399, 400).

▶ **Do the views of African Americans** on civil rights issues differ from those of white Americans?

gender gap
differences in voting and policy preferences between women and men.

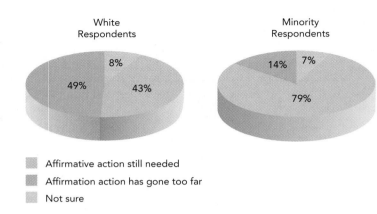

White Respondents

8%

49%   43%

Minority Respondents

14%   7%

79%

▪ Affirmative action still needed

▪ Affirmation action has gone too far

▪ Not sure

FIGURE 10.5
Differences in Views of Affirmative Action, by Race

Dramatic differences exist between minorities and whites in our society. Forty-nine percent of white respondents think that affirmative action has gone too far, while 79 percent of minority respondents think that it is still needed. What are some of the potential consequences of these polarized views?

SOURCE: NBC News and the *Wall Street Journal*. Conducted by Hart and Tester Research Companies, January 16–21, 2003. Data provided by the Roper Center, University of Connecticut.

that will become more relevant when we discuss the effect of gender on opinions and ideology.

Before the civil rights movement of the 1950s and 1960s, black participation in American politics was generally quite limited. It was not always so: African Americans gained not only freedom from slavery but also guarantees of civil rights and (for males) the right to vote after the Civil War, and at that time the Republican Party had been associated with racial equality in the minds of both black and white Americans (largely because of the actions of President Lincoln). By the 1890s, though, blacks in the South (where most still lived) were often denied the right to vote through devious means and were subjected to harsh segregation laws. Blatant discrimination remained largely in place in the South until after World War II. But in the generation between about 1930 and 1960, racial politics began slowly to change direction. In the first place, during these years, many black people moved from the South to northern cities, where they encountered very few obstacles to voting. Second, in the 1950s and 1960s, with the rise of black consciousness and the grassroots civil rights movement led by Martin Luther King Jr. and others, African Americans emerged as a strong national political force. Civil rights and social policies advanced by the Kennedy and Johnson administrations and the Democratic Congress in the 1960s brought most black people to see the national Democratic Party as the advocate of racial equality and integration. Ever since, black Americans have identified overwhelmingly with the Democratic Party.

Activism among other long-oppressed minority groups has also shaped modern political identity. As a result, Chicanos, Puerto Ricans, and Native Americans—but not Cuban Americans—also identify heavily with the Democratic Party.

▶ **Do the views of African Americans on civil rights issues differ from those of white Americans?** Since the 1960s, white people and African Americans have evaluated civil rights issues differently. White people increasingly believe that "a lot" of positive change has occurred with regard to the life circumstances of African Americans, but fewer blacks feel similarly optimistic. Around 60 percent of African Americans say that black poverty is the result of social factors (discrimination, for example), while a plurality of whites (49 percent) attribute black poverty to its victims' personal characteristics, especially laziness.[56] Affirmative action, a policy designed to promote equality of opportunity for most racial and ethnic minorities, elicits considerably different reactions among white and minority respondents. Among whites, 49 percent believe that affirmative action has gone too far; only 14 percent of those belonging to minority groups (including self-identified Asians) feel this way (see Figure 10.5). Seventy-nine

▶ Are there gender differences in political views?

percent of minority Americans say that affirmative action is still needed; only 43 percent of whites agree.

Although they make up only about 13 percent of the general population, in southern states, California, and the Southwest, and in urban areas in northern states, Hispanics represent a sizable and a rapidly growing voting bloc. The Hispanic presence in key border states is very large: 25 percent in Arizona, 32 percent in Texas and California, and 42 percent in New Mexico. But although Hispanics are politically strong in some communities, they lag behind African Americans in organizing across the nation. However, in the last several election cycles, they have mounted important mobilization efforts.

African Americans and members of other minority groups display similar political attitudes, for several reasons. First, all racial minorities (excluding second-generation Asians and some Cuban Americans) tend to have low socioeconomic status—a direct result of racism. Table 10.6 depicts the median income for full-time employees by race and gender. As you can see, substantial differences in earnings continue to exist. Moreover, individuals in all minority groups have been targets of racial prejudice and discrimination. African Americans and other minority members (mostly Hispanics) strongly favor governmental action to equalize incomes and to provide extensive social services. Minorities are often concerned about issues of law and order, for they tend to be more likely to be victims of crime than white people. As you can see in Table 10.7, there are consistent differences on public policy issues between white and black Americans, with a less clear pattern for Hispanic Americans. On many issues, excluding homosexual rights and abortion, Hispanics seem to hold positions very similar to those of whites. Significant differences separate white and black Americans on capital punishment, gun control, gay rights to adopt, and spending on the poor. Given the size of some of these differences, we must be careful to be sensitive to issues of race when evaluating many public policies.

GENDER

▶ **Are there gender differences in political views?** A **gender gap** separates American men and women in their patterns of voting behavior, party identification, ways of evaluating presidents, and attitudes toward various public policies. Some political scientists say that the difference in the way men and women vote first emerged in 1920, when newly enfranchised women registered overwhelmingly as Republicans. However, because women did not tend to vote in rates similar to men, it was not until the 1980 presidential election

TABLE 10.7

Percentage of Americans Favoring Particular Public Policies, by Race, 2004

PUBLIC POLICY STANCE	RACE OF RESPONDENT		
	WHITE	AFRICAN AMERICAN	HISPANIC
Favor capital punishment	73	42	61
Favor making it harder to get guns	54	72	62
Favor allowing gays in the military	54	54	55
Favor allowing gays to adopt	49	35	47
Favor never allowing abortion	13	15	15
Favor more spending on the poor	49	86	69

SOURCE: Center for Political Studies, *National Election Study* (Ann Arbor: University of Michigan, 2004).

When looking at race, we can see substantial differences in opinions on many issues. Were you surprised by some of these differences? Did you know that African Americans are the only major racial group in which a majority does not favor capital punishment? Why do you think this is the case? Why do you think so many African Americans favor gun control? Why do you think that there aren't significant differences between the races regarding allowing gays in the military but there are differences in allowing gays to adopt?

that the gender gap attracted much attention. In that election, when the Republican Ronald Reagan beat the Democratic incumbent Jimmy Carter, he did so with the votes of only 46 percent of the women—but he got the votes of 54 percent of the men. Substantial differences in policy preferences between men and women grew during the 1980s, with women considerably less approving of President Reagan than men were. On many issues, a majority of women embraced the Democratic (or anti-Reagan) position—including a much-publicized movement for declaring a nuclear freeze (a unilateral U.S. cessation of the production and use of nuclear weapons), a demand for spending more on social programs, and criticism of the administration's increased defense spending.

Gaps in public opinion continue to separate men and women. Since both parties are trying to recruit women officials and voters,

attitude hypothesis
the theory that distinctive male and female attitudes and voting preferences arise from gender differences in political perceptions and issue preferences.

salience hypothesis
the theory that the gender gap is largely a function of the fact that men and women put different priorities on different issues, thereby impacting their voting behavior and their political party affiliations.

situational hypothesis
the assertion that the gender gap is largely a function of the differences in living conditions between men and women (most notably differentials in income and living standards).

TABLE 10.8

Percentage of Americans Favoring Particular Public Policies, by Gender, 2004

PUBLIC POLICY STANCE	SEX OF RESPONDENT	
	WOMEN	MEN
Favor capital punishment	62	73
Favor making it harder to get guns	67	48
Favor allowing gays in the military	83	73
Favor allowing gays to adopt	51	43
Favor never allowing abortion	13	13
Favor more spending on the poor	58	53

SOURCE: Center for Political Studies, *National Election Study* (Ann Arbor: University of Michigan, 2004).

In every area of public policy examined but one, there were significant differences between men and women, with a larger percentage of women taking the liberal position (the exception is the issue of abortion, where there is no detectable difference in support between men and women). Given that 8.8 million more women voted in the 2004 presidential election (women had higher turnout rates and more women than men are of voting age), how do you think these trends will affect future elections? What challenges do these figures represent to both political parties and their leaders?

the gender gap will probably continue shaping the political agenda for the foreseeable future. Consistent differences persist between men and women on key issues of public policy, according to research from the Center for American Women in Politics at Rutgers University. In foreign affairs, women continue to oppose U.S. military intervention abroad and are more apt to favor diplomacy in settling foreign disputes. Domestically, women are more likely than men to support programs that protect health care and meet basic human

needs, to support restrictions on the possession and use of firearms, and to favor affirmative action and other governmental efforts to achieve racial equality.[57] Data in Table 10.8 support these findings. Women were more liberal on all social issues, showing lower levels of support for capital punishment and gun ownership and higher levels of support for gay rights and Social Security spending. Perhaps surprisingly, men and women tend to have similar views on abortion.

The gender gap, coupled with the fact that more women than men vote, has changed the national agenda and the political landscape. Issues that were previously considered "women's issues" are now at center stage, except in times of war or international crisis. Thus during the 2000 presidential and congressional campaigns, when foreign tensions were relatively low, issues of education, Social Security, and health care dominated the agenda.

Several theories exist to explain the gender gap. The **attitude hypothesis** states that differences in voting preferences and issue stances between men and women result from the fact that men and women tend to have different opinions on issues of public policy. Women tend to favor more spending on social services and diplomacy, while men tend to want to spend less on social services and favor more aggressive foreign policy stances. Many of these differences can be seen in Table 10.8.

The **salience hypothesis** says that gender differences in party identification and voting result from the relative importance that men and women assign to issues. Abortion is a good example of gender differences in how important issues are perceived to be. Roughly equal percentages of men and women support legal access to abortions. But because women tend to rate the abortion issue as more important than men do, they may assign a higher priority to political decisions involving it. In this way, gender differences can show up even if there are no differences in the underlying attitudes.

A third potential explanation for the gender gap is the **situational hypothesis.** This states that the gender gap reflects different situations that men and women face in our society. According to the theory, women's position in American politics (such as their income, marital and parental status, and employment history) fuels gender differences in policy preferences and issue salience. Economics appears to be the most important issue,

discussionquestions

1. How do people's demographic characteristics affect their political views? Do you think that most people follow the patterns described in the text? Why or why not?

2. If differences in opinions and behavior are partly explained by economics, educational attainment, religion, race or ethnicity, and gender, do you think that we will see more conflict in the future as our county continues to become more diverse? Do you think that the similarities we share as Americans will overcome these differences? Why or why not?

what YOU can do!

Based on what you've just read, it is clear that demographics in a community can dramatically affect public opinion and political behavior. Examine the demographic makeup of your college. How do you think demographics affect the atmosphere and student involvement in your school? Compare the results with a friend attending a different college with different demographic patterns. How relevant do you think demographic patterns are in influencing your environment? Most universities publish this data; if not, you can obtain information for your community at **www.census.gov**

for women and female-headed households are far more likely to live in poverty (see Table 10.6). Given that the Democratic Party is more likely to advocate policies designed to promote economic equality, it is little wonder, according to the situational hypothesis, that women tend to be more supportive of the Democrats.

practicequiz

1. It's fair to say that people with similar backgrounds tend to develop similar political opinions. It's also fair to say that depending on the issue, the specific features that define that background—race, ethnicity, gender, religious affiliation, social class, and so on—can matter in different ways for different people.
   a. true   **b.** false

2. Studies suggest that within the same socioeconomic group,
   a. Catholics and Jews tend to be more conservative than Protestants.
   b. Catholics tend to be more conservative than Protestants.
   c. Jews tend to be more conservative than Catholics.
   d. Jews and Catholics tend to be more liberal than Protestants.

3. The evangelical leader Jim Wallis is trying to
   a. prevent the Democratic Party from alienating religious voters.
   b. increase the already strong relationship between evangelical Christians and the Republican Party.
   c. take religion out of politics.
   d. a and c.

4. Since gaining the right to vote, most African Americans have always voted for Democratic Party candidates.
   a. true   **b.** false

Answers: 1-a, 2-d, 3-a, 4-b.

Measuring Public Opinion

As a wise individual, often said to be Benjamin Disraeli, once tartly observed, "There are three kinds of lies: lies, damned lies, and statistics."

We ensure the accuracy of our measurements of public opinion through the use of polls.

USE OF POLLS

Political scientists and professional pollsters measure public opinion in a variety of ways. Polls are helpful in constructing a sense of what people want and think, but other means also exist to measure public opinion. In addition to polls, people can express themselves politically via protest demonstrations, news (such as people-in-the-street interviews), elections, initiatives or referendums, direct contact with officials, and letters to the editor. And of course, they can vote.

Polls represent an opportunity to view a snapshot of public opinion and allow officials a quick assessment of public policies. People who value citizen participation in a democracy are more likely to see the virtues of polling. Polls allow people to learn the collective preferences of their fellow citizens, but there are both positive and negative consequences of this. On the one hand, polls show people that others in their country may have different opinions, thus enabling citizens to grasp the complexity of many political issues. On the other hand, polls can also silence holders of minority opinions by convincing them that that most people don't agree with them on a particular issue. Feeling isolated, such people may fail to voice their opinion, either abandoning their convictions or becoming deeply isolated. In examining polls' influence on the public and on our leaders, Elizabeth Noelle-Neumann developed the theory of a "spiral of silence."[58] When the public learns about the dominant view on something or someone, dissenters come under pressure to remain silent and accept the majority viewpoint. One common way in which this phenomenon manifests itself is the "bandwagon" effect—the tendency for individuals to agree with the candidate or opinion that polls show to be attracting the most support or that receives the most media attention.

Many observers of contemporary politics are wary about using polls in our democracy. They argue that polls can be misleading, giving a false sense of the democratic process. Some critics assert that polls give the citizenry a false sense of power and

▶ How are opinion polls conducted?

straw poll
an informal, nonscientific survey to measure public opinion; commonly used by political activists to gauge the opinion of a group.

sample
a subset of the population under study; if selected correctly, it represents the population from which it was drawn with reliable and measurable accuracy.

influence because, in the critics' view, ultimately power is exercised by elites who may or may not follow the public's preferences.[59] As we noted at the beginning of this chapter, many believe that officials should not rely on public opinion and other poll data when making decisions but rather should analyze the information presented to them and make informed policy choices. As you will see, polls can be manipulated to advance a political agenda. Thus overreliance on poll data by our officials can be very dangerous.

The political scientist Benjamin Ginsberg thinks that polls weaken the influence of true public opinion.[60] Polls make it easy—perhaps too easy—for people to express their opinions. Often polls give the impression that opinions are more strongly held than they really are and can create the impression that people actually have opinions on specific topics when in fact they may not. Other forms of political expression require more time and energy; people with deeply held opinions are therefore more likely to turn to them, giving a truer sense of public opinion. Polls rely on a passive form of expression (respondents do not volunteer to participate but are solicited), hence you cannot be certain that poll results truly reflect the carefully considered opinion of members of the public who are interested in and care about politics. Polls may simply capture the fleeting thoughts of a group of people who are approached by the pollsters and agree to respond.

Other critics object that polls tend to measure bluntly what is sometimes a very complex entity—the opinions of the people. Reliance on poll data, say these critics, raises many concerns: Suggested opinions, sampling errors, the wording of questions, and the way poll questions are asked can all skew the responses that are obtained.

One thing that is certain, though: Public opinion polling is widespread in our society. Each major TV network has paired with a print media organization to conduct polls—CBS News with the *New York Times*, ABC News with the *Washington Post*, and NBC News with the *Wall Street Journal*. And many newsmagazines—*Newsweek, Time,* and *U.S. News and World Report*, for example—routinely commission polls. Research on these three newsmagazines' cover stories between 1995 and 2003 found that 30 percent of the articles cited polling data.[61] Every year, several million people are called on to participate in polls. Our government alone conducts over a million survey interviews every year.[62] To avoid being manipulated, it is very important for individuals to understand how polls are used, constructed, and interpreted.

HISTORY OF POLLING

People have been interested in getting a sense of the public's opinion in an organized fashion for 180 years in the United States. In 1824, the *Harrisburg Pennsylvanian* conducted the first of what have been called "straw polls" to gauge public opinion in the presidential contest between John Quincy Adams and Henry Clay. A **straw poll** is an unscientific mechanism to estimate public opinion. Straw polls did not become common until the early twentieth century. At the time, polls were often biased methods for individuals to advance their political agendas. One popular way to poll the public was to mail out surveys to registered voters or to magazine or newspaper subscribers; recipients would fill out a survey form and mail it back. One major magazine of the 1930s, the *Literary Digest,* sponsored the best-known and most professional surveys at the time. In general, the reliability rate of straw polls at the time of the 1932 election was low: The average error rate of those conducted by major media outlets was 12 to 17 percent.[63] The *Literary Digest* was not regarded as infallible, but its straw poll did successfully predict the 1932 presidential winner. That successful reputation ended in 1936, when the magazine predicted that Franklin Roosevelt would lose the presidency to Republican Alf Landon; in fact, Roosevelt won 63 percent of the vote, a full 20 percent more than what the *Digest* had predicted FDR would get! Roosevelt had triumphed in one of the greatest electoral landslides in American history. Soon thereafter, the *Literary Digest* ceased publication.

The *Literary Digest*'s 1936 prediction was off target for a number of reasons. First, despite sending out 10 million questionnaires and having 2 million returned, its sampling technique was biased. It sent questionnaires to its subscribers, to registered automobile owners, and to people with telephones—all of whom were more affluent than most people during the Great Depression and substantially more affluent than the average Roosevelt supporter. Also, the *Digest* completed its poll a month before the election, failing to capture the surge in support that went to Roosevelt in the final weeks of the campaign.

The *Digest*'s loss of authority marked the beginning for several young pollsters who, relying on scientific sampling and new technologies that had been developed in market research, successfully predicted Roosevelt's victory. One such upstart who quickly distinguished himself was George Gallup. Although it did take some time to fine-tune sampling theory to ensure the accuracy of these polls, modern public opinion polling began in earnest in the late 1930s.

George Gallup revolutionized public opinion polling by developing a more scientific method of sample selection. His organization, the Gallup Organization, is one of the oldest and most respected polling organizations in the country. How would life be different today without public opinion polls? Do you think politicians should pay attention to public opinion or should they develop a vision and convince us to follow it? In essence, who should be the leaders—our elected officials or us?

pathways profile

GEORGE GALLUP

George Horace Gallup was born on November 18, 1901, in Jefferson, Iowa. Being raised on a farm in America's heartland had a profound impact on young George, instilling in him a firm belief that average people are the heart of our democracy and that politicians need to be aware of their thinking. He believed that by polling the public, he was serving an important role in our republic. Gallup earned a Ph.D. in journalism from the University of Iowa in 1928 and then taught journalism at Drake University, Northwestern University, and Columbia University. While doing research at these institutions, he drew the attention of a prominent New York advertising agency, and in 1932 he left academia to join Young & Rubicam's firm, never regretting the decision. He stayed at Young & Rubicam for sixteen years, researching different methods of increasing the efficiency of advertising with the aim of determining the best mechanisms to promote the recognition and recall of advertisements. His academic research and professional work led him to believe that market research could provide useful tools for studying politics.

Gallup founded the American Institute of Public Opinion, which in 1958 was renamed the Gallup Organization. The first Gallup Poll, "America Speaks," was conducted in September 1935 and released a month later. The poll was popular, but most Americans still relied on the *Literary Digest* to predict the 1936 presidential election.

As we've noted, the method used in the *Literary Digest*'s poll was faulty. Gallup, in contrast, relied on biweekly personal interviews with about 2,000 people. He applied theories from market research, making certain to include in his interviews persons from all classes, races, and regions; thus his sample was far more representative than the *Digest*'s. In the summer of 1936, after having been in business as a pollster for only one year, Gallup made a very risky move: He wrote a newspaper article saying that the *Digest*'s survey would incorrectly project Landon as the winner. His risk-taking paid off when Gallup correctly predicted Roosevelt's 1936 triumph—a success that propelled his polling firm to fame, making it a vital component of American life. The scientific standards that Gallup established in the 1930s still influence survey research. Since 1936, his Gallup Poll has correctly predicted all winning presidential races except Harry Truman's upset victory in 1948. (In that case, Gallup and the other pollsters stopped taking surveys two weeks before the election, missing the last-minute swing of voters to Truman.)

Gallup wrote many articles and several books, including the popular *Public Opinion in a Democracy* (1939) and *The Pulse of Democracy* (with Saul Forbes, 1940). He received a number of honorary degrees and awards and played an important leadership role in market and survey research. Gallup died of a heart attack in 1984 at his summer home in Switzerland. He will be remembered for his pioneering spirit and inquisitive mind and perhaps even more for his valuable contributions to the empirical analysis of social sciences. ∎

MODERN POLLING TECHNIQUES

▶ **How are opinion polls conducted?** One of the major scientific breakthroughs of the twentieth century was the development of statistical sampling theory. This theory made possible scientific public opinion polling and survey research. But because opinion poll results are now reported so widely in the media, you must be knowledgeable about polling methods in order to make appropriate use of poll results. Moreover, you must avoid relying on a single poll as a definitive measure of public opinion; often individual polls provide just a limited "snapshot" view of what the public is thinking. Informed consumers of public opinion polls must learn what can and cannot be correctly learned from them, as being knowledgeable about public opinion data is the best means of protection against being misled or manipulated.

HOW MANY UNITS? SAMPLING   Once the unit of analysis is determined (for example, senior citizens in Florida or 18- to 24-year-olds nationally), the researcher must then decide how many of those units ought to be polled. Researchers almost never question every person in a unit; that would be prohibitively expensive and time-consuming. Instead, they take a **sample**—that is, they

▶ Can certain kinds of survey questions lead to inaccurate data?

probability sample
selection procedure in which each member of the target population has a known or an equal chance of being selected.

accidental sample
a nonprobability sample in which the researcher randomly invites respondents to participate in the survey; Not a statistically valid sampling technique.

simple random sample
a probability sample in which each person in the population under study has an equal chance of being selected.

stratified sample
a probability sample in which the population under study is divided into categories (strata) that are thought to be important in influencing opinions. Then a random sample is drawn from within each stratum.

obtain a portion of the entire population. Sampling theory has grown with the polling industry and survey research since the mid-1930s. The goal of sampling is to be able to make generalizations about a group by examining some of its members. Its basic assumption is that individuals can represent the groups out of which they are selected. Because people in similar situations in life are likely to hold similar opinions, it is not necessary to study all of them. On the other hand, since every person is somewhat different, it is necessary to talk to enough people from each major group so that individual uniqueness can be smoothed out and a typical response obtained.

DUNAGIN'S PEOPLE

"BUT IF YOU <u>HAD</u> TO VOTE, WHO WOULD YOU VOTE FOR?"

SOURCE: © Tribune Media Services, Inc. All rights Reserved. Reprinted with permission.

One of the most important elements in a good sample is how *representative* it is of the major social groups that are apt to hold the opinions being researched. Choosing representative samples requires using the correct sampling technique and an appropriate sample size. The sampling technique most widely used today is the probability technique (discussed in the next paragraph). Good probability techniques should ensure a representative sample if the sample is sufficiently large. Commercial polling agencies such as Gallup or Harris normally use national samples of around 1,200 people. It is hard to imagine that so few could accurately represent the opinions of so many, especially in such a diverse society, but if proper techniques and protocols are followed, reliable data can be achieved.

Drawing a sample is usually a complex process. Several important decisions separate a good sample from a useless one. The first decision that needs to be made is how the sample will be chosen or drawn. Two basic methods of drawing samples are based on probability and nonprobability theories. A **probability sample** is one in which all potential respondents enter the sample with an equal or known probability of being selected. Professional pollsters rely almost exclusively on the probability method; it has been demonstrated to produce better results, with known levels of error and reliability. Nevertheless, nonprobability methods are sometimes used by nonprofessionals or for special situations. One of the most common nonprobability methods is the **accidental sample**, which is drawn by an unsystematic procedure, typically stopping and interviewing a specified number of people encountered in a public place. School newspapers often use this method to poll students. Reporters may go to the cafeteria and ask twenty people at random what they think of the food. One commonplace example is the market research conducted in shopping malls in which interviewers ask people who pass in front of them to participate in the survey. Although this might be interesting, we have no evidence that those twenty people accurately reflect the entire population under study. (For example, students in the cafeteria like the food well enough to be eating it; what about the students who refuse to eat there?) Journalists also use this technique when they solicit opinions by interviewing "people in the street." These types of samples are typically biased, as they depend on where the researcher goes to interview people. For example, you will get a

This drawing of lottery numbers for a draft in World War I is an example of a simple random sample. The blindfolded woman sticks a hand into the container and picks the number; each eligible male has the same chance of being drawn.

different cross section of the public if you stand outside a high-end mall than you would outside a welfare office. Because of concerns over the reliability of nonprobability samples, professionals most often use probability techniques.

One of the simplest probability methods is a **simple random sample.** An easy demonstration of this technique is the way a lottery or raffle winner is selected. Each person who bought a ticket receives a number that corresponds to a numbered ball. All balls are put in a large container, which is mixed thoroughly. Then someone sticks a hand into the container and picks the winner. All potential winners have the same chance of victory. (Men used to be chosen for the military draft in the same way.) Similar procedures are followed in a simple random sample: The researchers keep "picking" until they have selected a predetermined number of respondents. If there is a large population—say, the voters in a state or the entire nation before a presidential election—computers can be used to select respondents randomly. Such a sample is quite easy to draw, and it produces reliable results, but it can be used only when a comprehensive list of all members of the population is available, as well as a means for contacting them. If a list is not available, as is often the case, other techniques must be employed. Another frequently used probability sample is the **stratified sample,** which gets its name from the fact that the target population is broken into subgroups, or *strata* (plural of *stratum*), before the sample is drawn. Each stratum is further broken down until individual respondents can be selected at random, allowing researchers to draw a probability sample even if a comprehensive list of the target population does not exist.

SURVEY RESEARCH

▶ **Can certain kinds of survey questions lead to inaccurate data?** Once the sample has been drawn, the researcher must turn to the art of developing a good questionnaire that accurately elicits respondents' opinions. The proper wording and phrasing of the questions are vitally important to producing reliable, objective data. How questions are worded can dramatically affect the responses people give, so great care must be put into developing questions that obtain true opinions. Several criteria exist to assist

in the development of high-quality questions. First, researchers must use language and vocabulary appropriate for the population under study. For example, different vocabulary would be used in surveying new immigrants to the United States than would be used to poll corporate executives. Questions should also be worded to allow socially acceptable responses, so as to minimize the chance of false replies. If people are not given an acceptable way in which to respond to questions, they may lie.

A good example is voting. People are raised to believe that voting is an important right and responsibility and that a good citizen in our society exercises this right. However, not all people vote. So when asking about whether a respondent has voted, the researcher will obtain more accurate data if the response options include a socially acceptable reason for nonvoting. If the researcher simply asks, "Did you vote in the last election?" a good percentage of nonvoters might lie to avoid looking bad. However, if respondents are asked, "Did you vote in the last election, or because of work or family responsibilities were you too busy?" nonvoters can say that they were too busy without looking bad. Such sensitivity to social acceptance is an important factor in producing superior questions and research.

Also, to get a person's true opinion, questions must be neutrally worded and should never suggest a response. Let's say you were interested in people's opinion of underage drinking. There are a number of ways in which you could phrase your question. You could ask, "What is your opinion of irresponsible underage people who consume alcohol?" You certainly would get an opinion, but would it be an objective one? Probably not, because you characterize the person as irresponsible and are thus leading the respondent to agree with your characterization. A more objectively

closed-ended question
asking a question and providing a list of potential responses from which to choose.

open-ended question
a broad question that requires the respondents to articulate a response.

filter question
a preliminary question used to determine if potential survey respondents are sufficiently knowledgeable about the topic under study.

personal interview
administration of a survey questionnaire verbally, face to face.

telephone survey
administration of a survey questionnaire over the telephone.

mail survey
a public opinion survey conducted by mail. Response rates tend to be low, making the reliability of the results questionable.

worded question would be to simply ask, "What is your opinion of underage people consuming alcohol?" Poll results can vary dramatically, depending on the manner in which the questions are worded and the alternative responses provided. Reliable polling agencies will provide a copy of the survey if asked.

In addition to issues of question wording, important decisions need to be made regarding the way in which questions are asked, as various options exist. There are several approaches for asking questions, each with advantages and disadvantages. The most common type of question is called a **closed-ended question.** The respondent is presented with a set of answers from which to choose. Fixed choices are helpful when a range of likely responses can be predicted. The advantage of such multiple-choice questions is that they are easy and quick to analyze and discover patterns. But if the researcher is unsure of likely responses, errors can arise from forcing respondents into selecting among answers that may not truly represent their opinion. With **open-ended questions,** respondents are asked a question, and they reply in any way they wish. Open-ended questions are very useful if the research is exploratory and are often useful for gaining insight into explanations of the respondent's behavior or

opinions. Surveys of the electorate commissioned by candidates often use open-ended questions to help assess the voters' concerns for use in developing campaign themes and tactics. Such questions have the advantage that respondents can provide their true opinions and aren't forced into the pollster's categories. And because not all people have information or opinions about all issues, **filter questions** are often used. Filter questions separate people who have no opinion or who are unfamiliar with the topic being researched, so that only true opinions are measured, thereby minimizing the inclusion of opinions not based on solid information. It is important to note that open-ended questions provide a lot of information but are more difficult to analyze than closed-ended questions.

Once the sample has been drawn and the questionnaire developed, it's time to administer the survey. Questionnaires can be administered in person, by mail, or by telephone. Each technique has advantages and disadvantages, once again requiring important choices. The researcher must choose the method that is most appropriate for the research and also fits the available budget.

The **personal interview** presents the best opportunity for in-depth questioning. This type of survey is very useful for collecting a large amount of information and exploring the opinions of respondents in detail. Respondents can explain and elaborate on their opinions in personal interviews more than in other formats. Cost and the time required to complete the survey are the major disadvantages.

Telephone surveys, which have been increasing in popularity in recent decades, are attractive because they are quicker and cheaper than personal interviews. The media, for example, have turned to telephone surveys to obtain quick information about public opinion on current events. Researchers were critical of phone surveys in the past, when only fairly wealthy people had telephones, but today nearly everyone has a phone. One thing to note is that women tend to answer the telephone more than men (mainly because they are generally at home more hours per week than men and also because women tend to answer the telephone even if the husband is home). Researchers therefore need to be careful to ensure a representative sample.

The phone survey is most useful when the questions are few and the questionnaire uses simple wording and formats. But if the interview goes on too long or the questions are too complex, respondents are likely to become tired or bored and may hang up.

"I'm undecided, but that doesn't mean I'm apathetic or uninformed."

© The New Yorker Collection 1980 Charles Barsotti from cartoonbank.com. All Rights Reserved.

confidence level
the probability that the results found in the sample represent the true opinion of the entire public under study. The traditional standard confidence level is 95 percent.

Be cautious when consuming public opinion data: Be certain to examine who sponsored the poll, how accurate the poll is, and when it was conducted. Why and when do you think poll data are manipulated? How often do you think this occurs? SOURCE: Rob Rogers: © The Pittsburgh Post Gazette/Dist. by United Feature Syndicate.

Mail surveys are often used when the budget is limited, as they are the cheapest way to survey the public. In this type of survey, questionnaires are mailed to potential respondents, who are asked to fill them out and mail them back to the researcher. Low cost is the principal attraction of this type of survey, but there are several concerns. The main concern is low response rates. To some extent, the response rate depends on the socioeconomic status of the group to be sampled; higher-status groups are more likely to complete and return the questionnaires than lower-status groups, so this misrepresents the overall group being sampled. Mail surveys must also be limited in length since that the respondent can see in advance how long the survey is, and they must have clearly worded questions, because respondents cannot seek clarification the way they can with telephone surveys. Given these limitations, mail surveys are far less desirable than other methods, but they may be the only affordable way for some groups to conduct research.

A few additional points need to be made to ensure that you are an informed consumer of public opinion polls. First, political polls typically try to include only people who are likely to vote. This means that people who state that they are unlikely to vote or are not registered to vote are often screened out and not interviewed. Second, not all polls are released to the general public. Some are conducted to provide politicians with campaign strategies or to determine likely responses to potential stands on an issue. Some groups commission polls but release the results only when they make them appear in a positive light. Hence you must use caution when consuming public opinion data.

Furthermore, it is important that you understand how to interpret the information presented in a poll. Remember that polls rely on a sample of the target population. Even if all the issues identified earlier are accurately addressed, polls still have a chance of being inaccurate. This potential for inaccuracy is an unavoidable cost of using a sample rather than interviewing the entire population (which could never be done even if one had access to unlimited resources). Along with the poll results, the pollster should present two measures of accuracy: the margin of error and the confidence level. Let's provide an example and then explain each.

Say that a hypothetical national poll of likely voters shows that 35 percent of respondents have a favorable opinion of an individual who is considering running for president. How should you

interpret this number? Thirty-five percent of the people who responded to the poll have a favorable view. However, we really aren't interested in the opinion of the poll respondents. We want to use the poll findings to figure out the likely feelings of the general population. To do this, we calculate the margin of error to establish a range in which we think that the actual percentage of favorable ratings will fall. The **confidence level** is the percentage of confidence that we have that the poll truly represents the feelings of everyone in the population.

Going back to the original example, let's say that the margin of error is plus or minus 3 percentage points and the confidence level is 95 percent. This means that we are 95 percent sure that the actual percentage of people in the country who have favorable opinions of the potential candidate is between 32 and 38 percent.

Although the mathematics of calculating these numbers are complex (and not something that you need to understand), to be an informed consumer, it is important that you do understand how to interpret and apply both the margin of error and the confidence level. In many close elections, the numbers fall within the margin of error. When this happens, the media will say that the election is "too close to call."

▶ **Why do some types**
of polling tend to produce
unreliable results?

push polls
a form of telemarketing disguised as a poll in which negative information (often false) is provided with the goal of influencing public opinion.

exit polls
surveys of voters leaving polling places, used by news media to guage how candidates are doing on election day.

CONTROVERSIES SURROUNDING POLLING

▶ **Why do some types of polling tend to produce unreliable results?** Call-in and Internet surveys, often called pseudo-polls, are controversial. That's because the results are often falsely presented to the public as scientific and reliable. Because these are nonprobability samples, we can calculate neither the level of confidence we have in the results nor the likelihood of error. Only individuals watching a particular program on TV or tuning in to a particular radio talk show or visiting certain Internet sites can participate in the poll. In addition, people who call in (especially if there is a cost in time or money) tend to hold more extreme positions than those who do not bother to participate. These surveys may be interesting, but they are statistically unreliable. Research done on the public perception of President George H. W. Bush's 1992 State of the Union address demonstrates how poor these call-in surveys can be. CBS encouraged viewers to call in with their opinion of whether they were better off than they were four years ago. At the same time, CBS conducted a scientific poll to compare the results. In the call-in poll, 54 percent of respondents stated that they were worse off, while in the scientific poll, only 32 percent claimed to be worse off.[64] Additional research demonstrates similar problems with polls conducted on radio talk shows, whose listeners are unrepresentative of the population. They tend to be angrier, more conservative, more Republican, and mostly male.[65] Online surveys suffer many similar problems of self-selected and unrepresentative respondents. **Push polls** are also controversial. Push polls, despite the name, are campaigning tools that are designed to influence public opinion, not to measure it. They are better understood as a form of telemarketing. Push polls are designed to influence public opinion by providing negative (and not always truthful) information about a person. In 1995, the National Council on Public Polls issued a warning about this campaign technique, calling push polls unethical. The American Association of Political Consultants has also condemned push polling.

Contemporary technology has made many people question how representative samples are. Caller ID and call-block have made it increasingly difficult for pollsters to reach many people and to select a random sample of the population. Moreover, refusal rates have been rising, with fewer and fewer of the people reached willing to cooperate with the pollsters. In some surveys, less than 20 percent of calls result in a completed survey, raising the costs of surveys as well as the level of concern about their accuracy. In the 1960s, it was common for two-thirds of contacted people to participate. Today, cooperation rates hover around 38 percent for the national media surveys that take place over a few days, and overnight surveys often have much lower rates.[66] However, research conducted in 2004 indicates that the low response rates are not too troubling, as "missing" respondents were found not to distort results.[67] Those who refused to participate were similar to those who agreed to participate in the survey, so the low response rates did not significantly alter the survey results.

Concerns have also arisen over the number of people who no longer use home phones but rely exclusively on cell phones. It is currently illegal for pollsters to call cell phones, so these people are excluded from samples. Once again, research has found that this may not be as large a problem as some thought: Personal interviews with 2,000 randomly selected adults found that only 2.5 percent had cell phones but no home phones. This might, however, be a larger concern if the survey tries to include a large number of college-age individuals, who are more likely to rely exclusively on cell phones and who tend to move a lot.[68]

One area of public opinion polling that has recently come under much scrutiny is the media's reporting of polling data during campaigns and elections, and especially the use on election day of exit polls to predict outcomes before the votes are counted. **Exit polls** are taken at selected precincts while voting is in progress, with the pollsters typically asking every tenth voter how he or she had voted and why. In the past, exit polls have been helpful for news organizations as they race to be the first to predict the winners of elections. But in 1980, having gotten bad news from exit polls in states in the Eastern and Central time zones, President Jimmy Carter conceded defeat to Ronald Reagan three hours before polls on the West Coast had closed. Democratic officials criticized Carter and the networks, claiming that prematurely publicizing adverse poll data had caused many western Democrats not to vote, affecting many congressional, state, and local elections. As a consequence, the networks agreed not to predict the presidential winner of a state until all polls in that state had closed. In the 2000 presidential election, the exit polls conducted by the Voter News Service (made up of the four major networks, CNN, and the Associated Press) were flawed by sampling errors. Faulty exit poll results in Florida (as well as forgetting that the state's western Panhandle observes Central rather than Eastern time, so that voting there was still going on) led CBS

discussionquestions

1. Why are public opinion polls used? Why are polls controversial? Why do you need to be careful and informed consumers of poll data?

2. Can you think of any objections to exit polling? Does it violate the privacy of the voting booth? Can it affect the outcome of the actual voting? Some critics charge that the main advantage of exit polling is to help news organizations in their race to be the first to predict the outcome on election night. Do you agree or disagree? Why?

what YOU can do!

Do you feel that election season coverage of polling data in the United States needs change? If not, in what ways do you think that current coverage is appropriate and helpful to the public? If you see a need for change, explain why coverage should change and how you would change it.

---

to predict the incorrect winner not just once but twice. (This was not the only problem in the 2000 presidential elections; we discuss other issues in LINK *Chapter 14, pages 538–540*). As a consequence, the networks dropped the Voter News Service and in 2004 used a new service. Exit polls in the 2004 presidential election were also criticized, especially those conducted in Ohio. And in the future, as we see more and more people choosing early voting, the accuracy of exit polls for predicting winners and providing glimpses into the motivations of voters will be even more precarious.

Poll coverage in elections, more generally, is also troubling. The media often take the easy road and focus on "horse race" coverage (who's ahead in the polls, who is gaining, and so forth), to the detriment of discussing issues and other matters of substance. In 2004, several weeks before Canada's national election, the Canadian Broadcasting Corporation abruptly quit preelection polling, stating that constantly reporting poll results deflected public attention from issues and emphasized the superficial. Many critics call for the U.S. networks to follow suit.

Given all the concerns about public opinion polling that have been discussed in this chapter, many critics question the wisdom of the incessant reporting of polling to reflect public opinion and desires for social change. Some argue that we must rely on other forms of political expression to voice the views of the public; others believe that pollsters can adapt to these challenges and continue to provide important information about what the public is thinking.

practicequiz

1. Why are polls sometimes problematic?
   a. When their results are published, they can sometimes have the effect of silencing members of the public who hold minority views.
   b. As another voice of the people, they can sometimes reflect the effectiveness of an elected official or governmental policy.
   c. Some polls aren't really polls at all but campaign devices created to influence public opinion.
   d. a and c

2. The goal of sampling, in the polling process, is to get
   a. as diverse a set of responses as possible.
   b. as random a set of responses as possible.
   c. as representative a set of responses as possible.
   d. as rapid a set of responses as possible.

3. If proper techniques and protocols are used, polls can reliably assess the opinions of the whole nation by gathering the responses of only 1,200 people.
   a. true   b. false

4. Which is an example of an inappropriately worded polling question?
   a. "Do you think abortion under all circumstances should be illegal?"
   b. "Do you think antiabortion groups should be prohibited by law from protesting outside abortion clinics?"
   c. "Have you ever witnessed a fellow student cheating on a test but been prevented by circumstances from reporting the infraction?"
   d. "For whom did you just vote?"

Answers: 1-d, 2-c, 3-a, 4-b.

Conclusion

As you've seen, public opinion influences cultural change, but it can be hard to predict when it will be influential. Examples exist that show how public opinion has influenced government, but also demonstrate that mass opinion is largely ineffective in swaying people in authority (see Pathways Figure on pages 410–411). Politicians often use poll data to build support for policies, and also to avoid making unpopular decisions. Hence there is a reciprocal relationship in which public opinion can influence politicians *and* politicians can use public opinion to influence the people. Public opinion polling is an important device to gauge public sentiment and can influence change in our society. That explains why public opinion polling operations in the White House have become institutionalized. Each modern administration routinely polls the public.[69] Elites often use poll data to claim legitimacy for their positions. When elites disagree, they try to use poll data to claim the high road, thereby minimizing opposition and garnering additional support for their agenda. Polls become strategic tools by which political leaders seek to sell their views and positions to the public.[70] Politicians often act strategically by "rationally anticipating" shifts in public opinion and examining how these changes can affect future elections. In anticipating these changes, leaders can strategically modify their positions. Thus public opinion influences politicians directly, through elections, and also indirectly because they tend to act rationally in anticipating change.[71]

pathways | Environmental Movement

PRO-ENVIRONMENTAL MOVEMENT

 COURTS   CULTURAL CHANGE   ELECTIONS  GRASSROOTS MOBILIZATION  LOBBYING DECISION-MAKERS

1969
National Environmental Policy Act, first major environmental legislation, created the Environmental Protection Agency.

1973
Endangered Species Act passes—powerful tool in protecting the environment

1977
Supreme Court upholds the 1973 Endangered Species Act and stops construction of the Tellico Dam (*Tennessee Valley Authority* v. *Hill et al*). Rules that the extinction of a species is to be prevented no matter the cost (Congress amends law to allow dam construction in 1982).

1969
Santa Barbara oil spill fouls Southern California beaches and arouses public anger against pollution.

1970
April 22
Earth Day! Millions protest for air and water cleanup and the preservation of nature.

1972
Life Magazine publishes a photo essay about the effects of mercury pollution on the children of Minemata, Japan.

1962
Rachel Carson writes *Silent Spring*, a book that alerted the country to the dangers, especially for humans, of pesticides.

1960

1970

ANTI-ENVIRONMENTAL MOVEMENT

The Delicate Balance between Environmental and Economic Concerns?   As scientific evidence shows that there is increased global warming, a reduction in rain forests, and higher levels of pollution, the international community struggles to cope. Governments today must strike a delicate balance between economic growth and development and environmental protections. If there is too much regulation of business to protect the environment, businesses may relocate to other countries or regions, harming the U.S. economy. If there is too little regulation, the environment suffers, because businesses don't want to risk the higher costs that go along with environmentally friendly practices.

When countries go through the complex process of industrialization, concerns for the environment typically take a back seat to concerns for economic growth; countries usually only become concerned with protecting the environment once they are completely industrialized. Environmental protection will enter national consciousness only when the culture of a society changes sufficiently to see this as a priority. Until then, countries usually focus on economic development with little regard for environmental concerns. What do you think? How far should the government go to protect our environment?

1973
July 29
Congress approves the Alaska pipeline.

essayquestions

1. It is often very hard to balance the need to protect the environment and regulate business. Since most regulations to promote clean air and water cost businesses extra money, some believe that they can unduly harm our economy as businesses have less operating funds to expand and invest. Do you think that these concerns are reasonable? Or do you think that environmental protection is worth the costs?

2. Do you think that public opinion ought to influence our environmental policy or should we rely upon the recommendations of the scientific community? How large of a role do you think business leaders ought to play? How should we as a society balance these competing needs?

1980

Congress passes the "Superfund" legislation (CERCLA: The Comprehensive Environmental Response, Compensation and Liability Act), directing the EPA to clean up abandoned toxic waste dumps.

1978

Love Canal scandal—neighborhood finds out that they are living on a major toxic waste dump in Niagara Falls, NY. Alerts the government and society to the dangers of pollution.

1979

Three Mile Island nuclear power facility loses coolant and nearly has a meltdown.

1986

April 26
The worst nuclear disaster to date—Reactor Number Four at Chernobyl suffers a fire and explosion. Raises public awareness of environmental threats.

1989

March 24
Exxon-Valdez disaster. 11 million gallons of oil spilled in Prince William Sound, Alaska. Raises public awareness of destruction of environment.

2006

January 24
Al Gore's documentary on global warming, "An Inconvenient Truth," premieres at the Sundance Film Festival.

July
Newsweek issue on "The Greening of America"

1980 — **1990** — **2000**

James Watt appointed Secretary of the Interior under President Reagan. Proposes many anti-environmental acts and resolutions.

1980

Loggers win fight to resume logging of old-growth forests in the Pacific Northwest despite environmental concerns.

Tom Delay invotes group of 350 lobbyists for the energy industries to draft legislation to dismantle federal health, safety, and environmental laws.

1995

1980s

Joseph Coors organizes the Sagebrush Rebellion and The Heritage Foundation, both anti-environmental groups that attack the rights gained to date by the environmental movement.

1997

Kyoto Protocol (international treaty designed to reduce carbon dioxide and other greenhouse gases) adopted by 121 nations, but not ratified by US. American businesses warn of economic disasters if treaty enforced.

2003

The Bush administration proposes limiting the authority of states to object to offshore-drilling decisions and proposes removing environmental protections for most American wetlands and streams.

YOUR turn!

Design and conduct a poll at your university, formally or informally. Be sure to ensure that the poll is demographically representative, and try to follow the standards discussed for high-quality public opinion polling. Do you see differences in opinion among people from different racial and ethnic, religious, and economic groups? What differences in opinion are there between men and women? Are certain people more or less concerned with national versus campus issues? How knowledgeable are your colleagues regarding current affairs and political facts?

Think about the use of polling in politics today. What do you think are positive uses of polls today? What areas of polling trouble you? Why? What should be done to regulate the polling industry, if anything, and by whom? Remember that polls are often used to manipulate opinion and the behavior of others. Therefore, when looking at poll data, you need to become an informed consumer. Be certain to examine who commissioned the poll to ensure its objectivity, and look for information about the poll's accuracy (including its margin of error and details of how the questions were worded). Don't fall into the trap of believing everything that you read. ◼

Chapter Review

1. Public opinion is a far more complex phenomenon than many people appreciate. It is grounded in political values and tends to be very stable, but it can serve as a mechanism to promote cultural change.

2. Commentators disagree over the role that public opinion ought to play in influencing public officials. Some believe that public opinion ought to have a limited role in American politics, arguing that people are too easily influenced and manipulated and that our elites ought to have the freedom to make the important political decisions. The public can influence politics with the systematic review of elected officials that is permitted with free and competitive elections.

3. Other political commentators believe that it is healthy in a democracy for public officials to track public opinion and act in accordance with it.

4. Americans largely agree on a number of fundamental values, including liberty, individualism, democratic institutions, basic principles, and equality. Disagreements occur when the government translates these rather abstract ideas into specific public policies.

5. Public opinion tends to be stable, though we do see substantial shifts during times of crisis or as a reaction to an important event. As we saw with such issues as gay rights, civil rights, and women's rights, gradual changes in public opinion also occur, reflecting and shaping our political and popular culture.

6. Political ideology is a consistent set of personal values and beliefs about the proper purpose and scope of government.

Once formed, most people's political ideology remains rather stable (barring a critical world or domestic event). The range of political ideologies in the United States is narrower than in other societies; most Americans place themselves fairly close to the center of the political spectrum.

7. People acquire their political knowledge and beliefs through a process called political socialization. Family, schools, community and peers, religious groups, and the media all serve as agents of socialization, introducing individuals into the world of politics and influencing individuals' political values, beliefs, opinions, and ideologies.

8. People with similar life circumstances and experiences tend to develop similar opinions and values. We see many significant differences between groups based on their income, education, religion, race or ethnicity, and gender. Understanding the socialization process and the way in which demographic factors affect public opinion is important in fully appreciating the diversity of our country.

9. Public opinion polls provide data on a plethora of issues of importance to Americans. However, we must be cautious in using poll data to generalize about the population as a whole. Good public opinion polls are very useful for gauging public sentiment, but many factors can adversely affect the quality of the data obtained, including the representativeness of the sample, the wording of questions posed and issues explored, and the manner in which questionnaires are administered. Understanding the issues surrounding public opinion polling is an important part of being an informed consumer of political news and information.

CHAPTER REVIEW TEST

1. Truly great political leaders
   a. never feel obliged to act according to the popular opinions of their constituency.
   b. usually act in accordance with the popular opinions of their constituency.
   c. know when to follow the popular opinions of their constituency and when not to.
   d. look as if they care about popular opinion but really do not.

2. Historically, most Americans believe it's appropriate for the government to ensure that every U.S. citizen has equal opportunities for success but not to ensure equal outcomes.
   a. true   **b.** false

3. Most gradual change in public opinion happens through
   a. cohort replacement.
   b. dramatic events at the national level, such as Pearl Harbor and 9/11.
   c. changes in technology.
   d. a, b, and c.

4. Although public opinion regarding the rights and status of women has become dramatically more favorable in the past thirty years,
   a. women are still in the minority in undergraduate, graduate, and professional schools.
   b. women still hit a "glass ceiling" when trying to gain promotions in the business world.
   c. women discriminated against in the workforce are still reluctant to improve their situation through legal or other means.
   d. a, b, and c.

5. Jackie Robinson, Danica Patrick, and Betty Friedan are all examples of
   a. barometers of public opinion.
   b. catalysts for change.
   c. civil rights activists.
   d. a, b, and c.

6. That popular culture influences our political culture and public opinion has always been a positive feature of our democracy.
   a. true   **b.** false

7. In the past twenty years or so, Americans' political ideology has tended to become
   a. more conservative.
   b. more inconsistent.
   c. more polarized.
   d. a and c.

8. The rise of neoconservatism in the Reagan and George W. Bush administrations has centered around
   a. social issues like abortion and gay marriage.
   b. lowering taxation.
   c. foreign policy.
   d. immigration legislation.

9. Some political scientists study the state of American families because
   a. the nature of family life affects the family's role as an agent of socialization.
   b. family life—how parents and children interact, how much money parents make, and other factors—helps us predict what values children will grow up to embrace.
   c. parents' influence over their children becomes increasingly strong through adolescence.
   d. a and b

10. As agents of socialization, elementary schools have the effect of
   a. training children to value their own contributions to the decision-making process.
   b. training children to think creatively.
   c. training children to accept the hierarchical nature of power.
   d. a, b, and c.

11. Having people live in politically and racially diverse communities is good for our democracy because
   a. such communities cultivate higher political efficacy in individuals than homogeneous or segregated communities do.
   b. such communities are more likely to produce uninformed children than homogeneous or segregated communities are.
   c. living in such communities is the politically correct thing to do.
   d. a and c

12. Consuming popular media, such as late-night television comedy programs, is a good way for people to obtain valid political information.
   a. true   **b.** false

13. For most of the twentieth century, what demographic features characterized Republican party loyalists?
   a. white and well-to-do
   b. ethnic minority and blue-collar
   c. southern
   d. a and c

14. What explains Jewish Americans' loyalty to the Democratic Party?
   a. a concern for social and economic justice in the Jewish tradition
   b. Jews' long-standing focus on international issues
   c. the fact that Jewish American immigrants benefited from social services instituted by Democratic administrations in the early twentieth century
   d. a and b

15. For much of the twentieth century, the political preferences of immigrant groups in the United States were consistently different from those of Americans of Anglo-Saxon origin.

  a. true   **b.** false

16. What is the gender gap?

  a. the inherent differences of ability between men and women

  b. the difference between how women and men have tended to view political issues in this country

  c. the difference between how many men and how few women become elected governmental officials

  d. b and c

17. In 1936, the *Literary Digest* predicted that Republican Alf Landon would defeat Democrat Franklin D. Roosevelt in that year's presidential election, yet Roosevelt won in a landslide. How did the *Digest* reach so erroneous a conclusion?

  a. It was owned and run by Republicans, which made their polling method biased.

  b. It sent its questionnaires to subscribers, car owners, and telephone subscribers—that is, to relatively affluent people.

  c. It had a very high number of non-respondents.

  d. Many questionnaires were never delivered.

18. Professional pollsters almost always use some form of probability sampling in their polling because

  a. it is the most convenient and least expensive method.

  b. its use means that all potential respondents have a known or equal probability of being selected.

  c. it produces more accurate results than other sampling techniques.

  d. b and c

19. Anyone eager to influence American society should understand the nature of both public opinion and political socialization because

  a. both are mechanisms that can bring about social change by influencing elites in our country.

  b. both reinforce conventional thinking and are therefore worth resisting.

  c. both are forces that politicians routinely ignore once they are in office.

  d. a, b, and c

20. The political ideology of most Americans is relatively moderate, compared to those of people from other countries, and it doesn't change much over the course of a lifetime.

  a. true   **b.** false

Answers: 1: c; 2: a; 3: a; 4: b; 5: b; 6: b; 7: d; 8: c; 9: d; 10: c; 11: a; 12: a; 13: a; 14: d; 15: a; 16: b; 17: b; 18: d; 19: a; 20: a.

DISCUSSION QUESTIONS

1. How is public opinion formed? How stable is it? What factors tend to stabilize public opinion, and what factors tend to lead to instability?

2. How do elitist and pluralistic theories differ regarding the importance public officials ought to give public opinion when making decisions? What do you think?

3. Do you think that Americans truly agree on basic issues? Is it important that we should agree?

4. How, if at all, does popular culture influence political culture?

5. What is political ideology? What are the principal differences between liberals and conservatives today?

6. Why is the process of political socialization so important in our society? What factors are the most important, and what role do they play in the process?

7. How does membership in relevant demographic groups affect public opinion? What are some important differences between members of various groups on contemporary issues?

8. How has public opinion polling evolved over the past century? What are straw polls, and why are modern techniques more reliable? Why are many political commentators concerned with the contemporary use of public opinion polling? Do you share their concerns?

INTERNET RESOURCES

American Association for Public Opinion Research (AAPOR): **http://www.aapor.org**

EUROPA – Public Opinion Analysis of Europe, Eurobarometer Surveys: **http://europa.eu.int/comm/public_opinion/index_en.htm**

Gallup Organization: **http://www.gallup.com**

Kinsey Institute for Research on Sex, Gender and Reproduction, University of Indiana: **http://www.indiana.edu/~kinsey/resources/datasets.html**

National Election Study, University of Michigan: **http://www.umich.edu/~nes**

National Gay and Lesbian Task Force: **http://www.ngltf.org**

National Opinion Research Center (NORC), University of Chicago: **http://www.norc.uchicago.edu**

Parents and Friends of Lesbians and Gays: **http://www.pflag.org**

Pew Research Center for the People and the Press: **http://people-press.org**

PollingReport.com: **http://www.pollingreport.com**

Roper Center for Public Opinion Research: **http://www.ropercenter.uconn.edu**

ADDITIONAL READING

Althaus, Scott L. *Collective Preferences in Democratic Politics.* New York: Cambridge University Press, 2003.

Asher, Herbert. *Polling and the Public: What Every Citizen Should Know,* 6th ed. Washington, DC: CQ Press, 2004.

Gimpel, James G., J. Celeste Lay, and Jason E. Schuknecht. *Cultivating Democracy: Civic Environments and Political Socialization in America.* Washington, DC: Brookings Institution Press, 2003.

Jackson, David J. *Entertainment and Politics: The Influence of Pop Culture on Young Adult Political Socialization.* New York: Lang, 2002.

Lewis, Justin. *Constructing Public Opinion: How Political Elites Do What They Like and Why We Seem to Go Along with It.* New York: Columbia University Press, 2001.

Mattson, Kevin. *Engaging Youth: Combating the Apathy of Young Americans toward Politics.* New York: Century Foundation Press, 2003.

Rosenthal, Alan, Burdett A. Loomis, John R. Hibbing and Karl T. Kurtz. *Republic on Trial: The Case for Representative Democracy.* Washington, DC: CQ Press, 2002.

Rusk, Jerrold G. *Statistical History of the American Electorate.* Washington, DC: CQ Press, 2001.

Shea, Daniel. *Mass Politics: The Politics of Popular Culture.* New York: St. Martin's/Worth, 1999.

Stanley, Harold W., and Richard G. Niemi. *Vital Statistics on American Politics, 2003–2004.* Washington, DC: CQ Press, 2003.

Weissberg, Robert. *Polling, Policy, and Public Opinion: The Case against Heeding the "Voice of the People."* New York: Palgrave-Macmillan, 2002.

KEY TERMS

accidental sample   404

agents of political socialization   386

attitude hypothesis   400

catalyst-for-change theory   384

closed-ended question   406

cohort replacement   381

confidence level   407

conservative   385

crosscutting cleavages   392

efficacy   390

elitism   376

equality of outcome   379

exit polls   408

filter question   406

gender gap   398

individualism   379

interactive theory   384

liberal   384

libertarian   386

mail survey   406

neoconservatism   386

open-ended question   406

personal interview   406

political ideology   384

public opinion   376

probability sample   404

push polls   408

salience hypothesis   400

sample   402

simple random sample   404

situational hypothesis   400

stratified sample   404

straw poll   402

telephone survey   406

There is often tension between the desire of the media to present unlimited information to the public, and the government's interest in limiting access to particular facts and details—especially in times of war. Clearly, the government wants to protect our troops and they believe that information needs to be carefully presented and, at times, limited. Others believe that the free flow of information is one key mechanism for the public to hold the government accountable for its actions, especially in times of war. At left is a picture of coffins being returned to the United States from the Iraqi War. The faces and all identifying information of the honor guards were blocked out.

CHAPTER 11

THE POLITICS OF THE MEDIA

Media and Cultural Change   On September 11, 2001, at 8:45 A.M. Eastern Daylight Time, a commercial airplane crashed into one of the World Trade Center twin towers in New York City, forever changing the world. Eighteen minutes later, a second airliner crashed into the other tower. Soon came the equally shocking news that a third airliner had hit the Pentagon and that a fourth hijacked plane, presumably bound for an attack on Washington, D.C., had gone down in a field in Pennsylvania.

The media's live coverage of the Twin Towers collapsing, vividly conveying the horror of the attack, dramatically altered history. Americans had shown relatively little concern over domestic terrorism before this attack. After the attack, terrorism dominated dinner conversations, news programs, the national consciousness, and the government's agenda. President George W. Bush declared

Images of women and their gender roles have changed dramatically in the last fifty years. One of the most popular early television shows (1957–1963) was "*Leave it to Beaver,*" with June Cleaver as the ideal wife and mother. By 1998, the liberated, single women of New York ("*Sex in the City*") are the polar opposites of June Cleaver. How do the fictional characters on television generally reflect changing views of women more in society?

war on terrorism and demanded that other countries stand either with us or against us.

As the experience of 9/11 has so powerfully demonstrated, the contemporary media allow us to see the world beyond our everyday lives, providing the opportunity to share experiences and events. Shocking impressions can change the way people think about themselves, their government, and their world, making the media important actors in shaping and reflecting cultural change. This tremendous power of the media comes with great responsibility.

In Chapter 10, you saw how popular culture changes and at the same time reflects societal values and beliefs—how it serves as both a catalyst and a barometer of social and political change. One of our aims in this chapter is to look at how important the media is in the cultural change pathway.

Consider, for example, the portrayal of women on American television. Over the past fifty years, television has gone from giving very narrow portrayals of women as wives and mothers to *Sex and the City's* sexually assertive and independent women. Analyzing how this dramatic change developed illustrates the dynamic nature of the media, both reflecting and hastening cultural change.

Early TV depictions of women were very limited, most often showing them in traditional roles of wives, mothers, teachers, or housekeepers. On screen, they wore pearls and makeup, cleaned their upscale homes in high heels, and spent their time caring for

and serving their families. In the 1950s and early 1960s, white women characters were shown as happy housewives, while black women were almost entirely shown in servant roles. Stereotypes ran rampant.

Beginning in the late 1960s, the women's movement in the United States actively attempted to break traditional views of women and the gender roles that were enforced in the mass media to reflect these views. In the mid-1960s, powerful women appeared for the first time in television shows, though they often had to use magic to influence others in their lives. (*Bewitched*, first shown in 1964, and *I Dream of Jeannie*, first shown in 1965, are good examples.)

Mary Richards, the main character in *The Mary Tyler Moore Show* (1970), was the first woman on television who was projected as independent, career-oriented, and unmarried. The goals of the women's movement were personified in Mary Richards as she struggled to find her voice, confidence, and inner strength. Diahann Carroll's role as a nurse and mother in *Julia* (1968) was the first show that transcended the racial stereotypes hitherto characterizing African American women in the mass media.

As the women's movement continued to gain support, television began to show even more independent women. In the 1980s, more female characters moved into positions of power. More diverse women were also observed in the programming of the 1980s although television continued to lag behind reality (espe-

cially when it came to images of people of color). Female characters such as *Roseanne* (1988), a working-class woman who was overweight and loud, and *The Golden Girls* (1985), with all older central characters, showed a greater range of women and their activities.

Television shows today have far more diverse roles for women, just as women have come to play more diverse roles in our society. As women became more powerful in society, television responded. The biggest change in television's roles for women, though, is probably the development of 1998's *Sex and the City*. The characters on this program actively reject traditional expectations of female behavior and goals, embracing their sexuality and independence.

It is important not to underestimate the power of the media in stimulating change as well. Selection of programming and character development can steer society in dramatic as well as subtle ways. As women demanded more power in society, more powerful women emerged on television. As Americans saw more powerful women on television, they began to accept women in more diverse roles in society. The reinforcing manner in which the media reflect and shape societal struggles makes them an important component in the cultural change pathway. ▪

419

▶ **How much television does** the typical American watch?

marketplace of ideas
the theory that ideas and theories compete for acceptance among the public.

This chapter discusses the effect of the media on our political system. We will begin with a brief survey of the historical development of the media, paying careful attention to trends and consequences. Next, we will turn to the power of the media and limitations on this influence. Moreover, while assessing the strength of the media, we will also examine the media's responsibilities, as well as governmental regulation of the media. The media are a very influential force in politics and policy for several pathways of action, especially the cultural change pathway and the elections pathway. Consequently, we will consider both the positive and the negative social and political functions of the present-day media. We will conclude by examining many issues surrounding media usage in the United States and the global community.

Key Questions

1. How powerful are the mass media in the United States?

2. Who should control the media? How can we negotiate the delicate balance between the need for governmental regulation and the desire for a vigorous and free press?

3. How do the media shape and reflect our cultural values and struggles? How influential are the media in interpreting and framing news stories?

4. What functions do the media perform in our society? How important are the media in American politics?

5. How effective are the media in influencing the political agenda? How is this changing?

Mass Media

The importance of free media in a democratic society cannot be exaggerated. The success of our democracy depends on our being informed and aware about the policy issues facing our nation, as well as about the action—or inaction—of our government leaders in response to those issues. Your effective involvement as an actor in the country's democratic governing process, whether as a voter, an interest group member, or a political candidate, depends on your knowledge of current events. It is through the media that you see world events beyond those directly observed in your private life. The media show us the "big picture" worlds of politics, entertainment, sports, culture, and economics, as well as the lives of people living in other countries and other cultures.

The media's behavior has undergone intensive scrutiny, for it is widely asserted that the media are very powerful in socializing citizen's attitudes, beliefs, and behaviors. Furthermore, many people believe that the media are very influential in shaping the actions of government officials; some have even called the media the fourth branch of government. However, you should question how influential the mass media actually are. Rather than *shaping* our values and beliefs, do the media simply *reflect* them? Or do they do both—shape as well as reflect our cultural values and struggles? These are questions to keep in mind as you read this chapter.

There is a key link between public opinion, the media, and democracy—an interactive relationship in which each affects the others. All democratic governments must allow for a **marketplace of ideas,** where differing thoughts and beliefs are able to develop and thrive, and the media make possible on a mass scale the vitally important public debate over opposing opinions, ideas, and thoughts. This marketplace, in which ideas and values compete for acceptance, is crucial to a healthy democracy. Public discussions of important and often controversial issues are a fundamental component of a free society. Without free media in which competing ideas can be discussed and debated openly, there can be no effective democratic decision making. The two-way flow of information, from the government to the people and from the people to the government, is fundamental in a representative democracy. Obstructing the two-way information flow is a tactic dictators use to preserve their power. Dictators fear the reaction when their people have access to information about the freedom and prosperity enjoyed under democratic systems of government. In this way, the media play an important role in our democracy, serving as a "communications bridge" between the governed and the governing. The importance of the media in linking government with the people has grown in recent times as the power, influence, and significance of the national government have grown and the clout of other institutions, notably political parties, has diminished.

▶ **How much television does the typical American watch?** Most Americans know that the media are very powerful. The media's news coverage can manipulate public opinion, influence policymaking, and affect elections and even the economy, and the entertainment component can also mold our political, social, and economic values. Today, the average American high school senior has spent more time watching TV than attending school. Even what is learned in school is often influenced by the media's portrayal of events. The average American adult spends

▶ **What would be the** advantages—and disadvantages—of allowing the government to control the news media?

nearly half his or her leisure time watching TV, listening to the radio, and reading newspapers or magazines; the single greatest amount of time is spent watching television. Moreover, TV remains the primary source of news and entertainment in the United States.[1]

Thus TV provides the unique opportunity for millions to share events and experiences, sometimes—as on September 11, 2001—with a dramatic power to alter the political climate and world events. The visual nature of television makes events seem more intimate and intense. It provides almost all of our political knowledge (for we do not observe firsthand most of the things that happen in the world), and thus it mirrors a world much larger than any of us can ever know directly.

For example, Walter Cronkite, the CBS news anchor of the 1960s and 1970s, always ended his broadcast with the words "And that's the way it is." The influence of Cronkite, consistently cited as one of the most trusted men in America, was dramatically shown in 1968. During most of the 1960s, Cronkite had expressed support for the war in Vietnam, but that changed after he visited Southeast Asia in early 1968. Upon returning home, he took the unprecedented step of interjecting a personal opinion at the end of his February 27 broadcast: "For it seems more certain now than ever that the bloody experience of Vietnam is to end in a stalemate." President Johnson, after watching Cronkite's broadcast, is quoted as saying: "That's it. If I've lost Cronkite, I've lost Middle America." A month later, Johnson announced his decision not to seek reelection. Cronkite's words summed up the goal of his news program: his attempt to give Americans a glimpse into the larger world in which they lived.

▶ **What would be the advantages—and disadvantages— of allowing the government to control the news media?** The media's claim to be a mirror to the world raises many questions. Is this mirror an all-inclusive, unbiased, and neutral representation of world events? Or does the mirror reflect selective pictures, ideas, and opinions? Concerns over the objectivity of the media have caused a good deal of disagreement, which we will discuss throughout this chapter.

Given the impact of the media on public opinion and behavior, many people ask who should control the news. Governments? Superficially, it might seem to make sense for public officials to control the news, so that they can use the media to promote images and ideas that could strengthen our democracy. For instance, many people are concerned about the violent nature of

For nearly twenty years, Walter Cronkite served as anchorman of the CBS Evening News (from 1962-1981), becoming one of the most trusted men in the country. His trademark exit line, "And that's the way it is" perfectly characterized his efforts to present fair, accurate and reliable news to his viewers. He is best remembered for his coverage of the Cuban Missile Crisis, the assassination of President Kennedy, and the Vietnam War. Do you think we will once again trust and admire journalists as the country did Cronkite? Why or why not?

mass medium
any channel of communication that reaches a vast audience; examples include newspapers, magazines, television, radio, and the Internet.

party presses
newspapers popular in the early nineteenth century that were highly partisan and often influenced by political party machines.

the news. If the government controlled the news, it could edit stories so that violence is not shown. Showing terrorists decapitating a prisoner certainly is a horrible image that most people would not want to see. Because the evening news is broadcast during "family programming time," perhaps it would be best for the government to determine what is appropriate programming. Or consider another example: The media somehow get a copy of closed-door hearings in the rape trial of a prominent athlete. Can the judge—who is an agent of the government—prohibit the media from publishing the material? What if the material in question is volatile, potentially influencing the jury pool in a manner that would make a fair trial difficult? Should the government have the power to prohibit its publication? Who should make these decisions?

Historically, Americans have opposed censorship, believing that free and vigorous media are necessary to democracy. Authoritarian regimes assume that the government knows what's best for its citizens and thus seek to control all flow of information, thereby molding what their people think about and believe. Authoritarian governments believe that news and entertainment programs should not question government or its policies but rather should build support and loyalty. Conversely, democratic societies assume that government officials can and do make mistakes. This assumption is inherent in the American governing structure, with its checks and balances and its division of power. Democracies therefore insist that the public needs a free press to keep government in line. The citizens of a democracy need to challenge the officials' policies and, through public debate and discussion, build consensus and develop better policies. While it may be frustrating at times, especially when we don't agree with the media's portrayal, a free press is essential for democracy.

practicequiz

1. The media relate to cultural change by both
   a. impeding and influencing it.
   b. reflecting and impeding it.
   c. reflecting and shaping it.
   d. shaping and minimizing it.

2. The media serve as a "communication bridge" primarily between
   a. the governed and the governing.
   b. the advertisers and the consumers.
   c. the United States and other countries.
   d. the cultural present and the cultural future.

3. What prompted Lyndon Johnson to say he had lost the support of Middle America?
   a. the worsening situation for the United States in the Vietnam War
   b. the broadcasting of negative polling data on the nightly news
   c. a string of botched "pseudo-events" in the Chicago area
   d. Walter Cronkite's negative assessment of the Vietnam War on the news one night

4. Inherent in the American governing structure is the assumption that government officials make mistakes and that a free press is therefore needed to monitor them.
   a. true   b. false

Answers: 1-c, 2-a, 3-d, 4-a.

History of Mass Media

Newspapers were the first **mass medium,** intended to communicate information in a timely fashion to a large audience. Magazines and other periodicals (newsletters, journals) also serve as mass media in printed form. The advent of broadcasting gave rise to the electronic media—radio, television, and, most recently, the Internet. Let's see how each began and developed.

PRINT MEDIA

The first newspaper published in what would become the United States was the *Boston News-Letter,* which began appearing in April 1704. The paper was one page long and was published weekly. By 1725, Boston had three newspapers, and Philadelphia and New York City each had one. At the time of the Revolutionary War five decades later, fifty presses were operating in the thirteen colonies.[2] The colonial authorities accepted these early newspapers, partly because they generally tried to avoid controversial issues. Many of these early papers relied on government printing jobs as a key

penny press
cheap newspapers containing sensationalized stories sold to members of the working class in the late nineteenth and early twentieth centuries.

1. Why is a free press vital in a democracy? What is the marketplace of ideas? Why is it important, and how does it develop?

2. What would be the consequences of allowing government officials to control the media? Are there any circumstances under which you believe that such control might at least temporarily be justified?

source to increase their revenue and could not afford to alienate local officials. The Revolutionary War changed all this: Newspapers became important tools in building public support for resistance to British policies and, by 1776, for independence. The historian Arthur Schlesinger Sr. wrote that the war for independence "could hardly have succeeded without an ever alert and dedicated press."[3] By the late 1770s, most presses were actively promoting independence. This activity continued during the war, reporting Patriot successes (often with exaggeration) while downplaying losses.

Newspapers were also used to promote public support for ratifying the Constitution. Compared to the extreme partisanship of the Revolutionary War era, their coverage was more balanced, giving opportunities for opponents to discuss their concerns. Some newspapers of the day allowed for a public debate about the virtues and potential vices of the proposed governmental system. The best examples of the persuasive use of the press to advance a political agenda are the series of newspaper essays written (anonymously) by Alexander Hamilton, James Madison, and John Jay, later published as *The Federalist Papers*. As you saw in LINK *Chapter 2, pages 66–69*, these essays were powerful and persuasive testimonies in support of the Constitution and helped ensure its ratification in the crucial state of New York. To this day, *The Federalist Papers* remain one of the best expressions of the founders' original intent.

Following ratification of the Constitution, political leaders of the time thought it very important to promote newspapers, which informed citizens of major issues facing the new government. Sharing information was vital. Americans worried that the new federal government would prove too powerful and too remote for citizens to control it. Using the press to report the actions of the new government kept people informed and eased their fears. The spread of political information through the press, declared the House of Representatives, is "among the surest means of preventing the degeneracy of a free government."[4] In view of the difficulties and expenses of publishing newspapers at the time, the federal government provided protection for newspapers by granting them special treatment—for example, by charging a reduced rate of postage for papers mailed to subscribers.

The number and circulation of newspapers in the early nineteenth century grew dramatically. For example, by the early 1830s, there were twelve daily newspapers published in Philadelphia and six in New York City. The number of newspapers published across the country soared, from around 200 in 1800 to around 1,200 in the mid-1830s.[5] These early newspapers were almost always created and funded to promote specific political and economic beliefs. For example, parties and political leaders normally encouraged and helped finance newspapers in important cities. These papers are called **party presses** and are best seen as arms of competing political factions. Most newspapers became unabashedly partisan, reaping rewards when their preferred party won an election and suffering when it lost. These papers were targeted to the elite, were relatively expensive, and did not have many subscribers. Ordinary citizens, however, often heard newspapers being read aloud and argued about in public gathering places, including taverns, inns, and coffeehouses.

▶ **When did newspapers become "mass" media, rather than just for the elite?** The year 1833 saw an important change in the nature of journalism in the United States: the advent of the **penny press,** so called because these daily newspapers cost a penny, versus about 6 cents for the established newspapers of the day. These penny papers, the first of which was the *New York Sun*, were marketed to the "common man." (In the sexist thinking of the day, politics, like business, was assumed to be a masculine pursuit, something in which women should not participate.) They offered less political and business coverage but a more diverse range of material—crime and human interest stories, scandals, and sports. These newspapers quickly became very popular, changing the face of journalism by making it a true mass medium. Newspaper publishers covered the costs of publication and made a profit by selling advertising. Unlike earlier newspapers, which had relied on officials or travelers for their political and economic news, the penny presses relied more heavily on reporters who would ferret out stories. These presses were less partisan and were more financially independent of politicians, significantly affecting the way in which politics was covered.[6] Many presses were still partisan, no longer for reasons of economic survival but rather as a reflection of the ideology of the publisher. This change in the nature of journalism encouraged the press to become freer and more vigorous.

By the mid-nineteenth century, newspapers had become somewhat more objective and fact-based. The invention of the telegraph in the 1840s helped this shift. The Associated Press (the world's largest and oldest news agency), created in 1848, inaugurated a new trend in journalism, marked by direct and simple writing designed to appeal to a wide range of readers.

▶ **Why does television have such a unique effect on public opinion?**

yellow journalism
sensationalistic stories featured in the daily press around the turn of the twentieth century.

Growing Locally, Waning Nationally

Newspaper companies that depend on local advertising are doing better than companies that focus on selling national advertising.

	Gannett	Knight Ridder	Tribune	The New York Times	Dow Jones
NEWSPAPER AD REVENUE, FIRST QUARTER	$1,217 mil.	$566 mil.*	$788 mil.	$301 mil.†	$145 mil.§
CHANGE FROM PREVIOUS YEAR	+5.3%	+3.3%*	+1.7%	+0.8%†	−10.8%§

* Total company revenue, which includes Web sites.
† The New York Times, The New York Times Web site and The International Herald Tribune; not the Boston Globe and other local newspapers.
§ Ad revenue for all United States and international print publications, except community newspapers.

Source: Company reports

April 2005, *The New York Times*

FIGURE 11.1
Newspapers Growing Locally, Waning Nationally

The *New York Times* and the *Wall Street Journal* are two of the most respected papers in the country, with worldwide readership. However, they are not as profitable as some local newspapers. Why do you think this is the case? Why is it harder for the *Times* to sell ads than it is for the *Cincinnati Enquirer*?

So-called **yellow journalism,** featuring sensationalism, comics, and scandal to sell papers, became popular at the end of nineteenth century. (The name came from the yellow-tinted newsprint that some of these papers used.) Papers that engaged in yellow journalism competed fiercely with one another and fought desperately to raise circulation. William Randolph Hearst, one of the earliest practitioners of yellow journalism, forthrightly said, "It is the [*New York*] *Journal*'s policy to engage brains as well as to get news, for the public is even more fond of entertainment than it is of information."[7] The stories became increasingly outrageous and shocking. As the newspapers' extreme sensation-mongering generated a public backlash, journalists responded by beginning to develop a code of professional ethics. Many newspapers, oriented toward a more "respectable" readership, rejected sensational journalism and still made profits by selling advertising. (The *New York Times* is a prime example.)

In the early twentieth century, the ownership of newspapers became more centralized, the result of competition that forced many papers to close or merge. We will discuss this centralization of ownership in more detail later in the chapter, but it is important to note the trend toward fewer and fewer independent sources of information (see Figure 11.1). This trend was well under way by the 1930s, when the Hearst chain (consisting of twenty-six daily papers in nineteen cities) controlled 13 percent of the nation's newspaper circulation. In 1933, six newspaper chains owned eighty-one daily papers, representing 26 percent of national circulation.[8] This trend has continued, paralleling a drastic shrinkage in the number of newspapers. In 2003, the Tribune Company owned thirteen daily newspapers and twenty-six TV stations, in twenty-two media markets. When it merged with the *Los Angeles Times* in 2000, the Tribune Company reached nearly 80 percent of U.S. households through one or more media outlets.[9] As we'll discuss later in the chapter, many people are concerned with this trend toward concentration of ownership.

ELECTRONIC MEDIA

The twentieth century witnessed an explosion of new means of mass communication, starting with radio.

RADIO In 1900, a professor of electrical engineering at the University of Pittsburgh named Reginald Fessenden made the first experimental radio transmission. His successful broadcast made radio communication a reality. During World War I, little was done to exploit this technology commercially, but after the war, there was a rush to set up private radio stations. Presidential election returns were broadcast for the first time in 1920. In 1923, the country had 566 radio stations. At first, radio was primarily an activity for hobbyists who built their own sets. But by 1924, some 2.5 million Americans owned radio receivers, and the era of mass radio had begun.[10] When preassembled radios began to be sold in stores, a rapid and dramatic growth of radio audiences occurred. In 1930, for example, radio receivers—14 million of them—were in 45 percent of American households. One decade later, despite the Great Depression, 81 percent of households owned a total of 44 million receivers. By the late 1940s, when television started to become popular, 95 percent of households had radios.[11] Radio had become a source of information and entertainment for practically everyone.

The first radio stations had been strictly local, but the formation of radio networks with syndicated programming began in the late 1920s. This trend was encouraged when Congress passed the Radio Act of 1927, which regulated the rapidly growing industry. The Radio Act established the airwaves as a public good, subject to governmental oversight. Under the new federal policy, radio stations were privately owned, with the government regulating the technical aspects and issuing licenses to broadcast on specific frequencies. Freedom-of-speech concerns kept regulation from extending to content.

Not all liberal democracies have privately owned broadcast media. In the United Kingdom, for example, the government owns and controls the British Broadcasting Corporation, known as the BBC. Private stations do exist in Britain and are regulated by an independent regulatory agency, which is responsible to Parliament, but the BBC is the largest broadcasting corporation in the world, sending out programming on television, radio, and the Internet.

Mirroring the trend in American newspaper publishing, radio broadcasting consolidated as the century wore on. In 1934, one-third of all U.S. radio stations were affiliated with a network, and more than 60 percent were by 1940. Today, radio stations that are not affiliated with networks often have weaker signals and face financial problems. Consolidation helps defer costs, but it also concentrates power.

▶ **Why does television have such a unique effect on public opinion?**

TELEVISION Like radio, once television was perfected, it grew at an astounding rate. Television became technically feasible in the late 1930s, but World War II delayed its commercial development. Commercial TV broadcasting began in the late 1940s. In 1950, there were ninety-eight TV stations in the United States, with 9 percent of American households having TV sets. Four years later, the number of families owning sets had exploded, from less than 4 million to 28 million. By 1958, some 41 million families had TV sets. Today, more than 1,100 broadcast TV stations are licensed in United States, and 98 percent of households have televisions; more than half of all households have two or more sets.[12] Television is unique in two ways—its immediacy (it can show events live) and its visual content, both of which convey a sense of legitimacy to viewers and increase emotional appeal.

Unlike newspapers and radio stations, which were first independently owned and only later were consolidated into chains and networks, high costs dictated that almost from the beginning, TV stations were affiliated with networks, thus centralizing ownership. Today, however, unlike radio and newspapers, where concentration is intensifying, the ownership of television broadcasting is becoming more competitive and diverse. In the last twenty or thirty years, network television's audience has changed dramatically. Cable TV, satellite TV, VCRs, and digital recorders have changed the nature of watching TV, reducing the audience for network programming. Meanwhile, the development of round-the-clock news networks, such as CNN, Fox News, CNBC, and MSNBC, coupled with the dramatic growth of news shows such as *20/20, Dateline,* and *Primetime,* has altered the face of the broadcast media. The arrival of television marked a breakthrough in personalizing communication from officials to the masses, allowing for intimate contact in a diverse and large society.

One of the most respected individuals in the history of broadcast journalism, Edward R. Murrow (1908–1965), is best remembered for devotion to journalistic excellence. *Good Night, and Good Luck* was his signature exit line and is also an Academy Award-nominated film (bottom) directed by George Clooney that portrays the epic struggle between the devoted journalist and Senator Joseph McCarthy during the Red Scare in the 1950s. Murrow's brave challenge of the Senator helped expose the negative aspects of McCarthyism and bring an end to this controversial period in American history.

pathways profile

EDWARD R. MURROW

Of all the newscasters in our history, perhaps the most influential to use this pathway to effect change in American politics was Edward R. Murrow. Born in Greensboro, North Carolina, on April 25, 1908, Murrow led a life of honor and prestige. His example served to alter the profession of newsgathering, leaving a legacy as one of the most distinguished and admired persons in the field of broadcast journalism.

Murrow graduated from Washington State College in 1930. He began his career with the CBS radio network as its director of education in 1935 and was quickly promoted to director of the network's European bureau in London in 1937, where, during World War II, he helped train a very talented group of war correspondents. His dramatic live broadcasts from London during the 1940 "blitz" bombing left an indelible impression on all Americans who heard him. After a brief foray into early television news, he left for a radio series in 1947 but returned to television with his *See It Now* series in 1950.

Murrow is credited with establishing the professionalism of the field of broadcast journalism, and he won nine Emmy Awards during his television career. Guided by his religious upbringing and a solidly defined conscience, Murrow promoted and popularized many democratic ideals such as free speech, civic engagement, and the importance of individual rights and liberties. He also produced a landmark documentary special, *Harvest of Shame*, on the plight of migrant workers that aired on Thanksgiving in 1960. Probably his most notable moment was when he took on Senator Joseph McCarthy on March 9, 1954. He used the senator's own words and pictures to expose the negative side of McCarthyism (which will be discussed in more detail in Ⓛ Ⓘ Ⓝ Ⓚ *Chapter 12, pages 484–485*). At the time, this was a daring challenge of a powerful politician but a good example of Murrow's commitment to tracking down the truth and fighting infringements on civil rights and liberties.

"He set standards of excellence that remain unsurpassed," proclaims a memorial plaque in his honor in the lobby of CBS headquarters in New York City. A constant smoker (he was often photographed with cigarette in hand), Ed Murrow developed lung cancer, to which he succumbed on April 27, 1965. But his legacy of professionalism, his commitment to uncovering the truth, and his devotion to the profession of broadcast journalism live on.

Source: "Murrow, Edward R.," Museum of Broadcast Communications, http://www.museum.tv. ▪

▶ **How has the Internet** changed the way we get news and other political information?

technology gap (digital divide)
the differences in access to and mastery of information and communication technology between segments of the community (typically for socioeconomic, educational, or geographical reasons).

THE INTERNET   The Internet has revolutionized the way we communicate. Developed in the early 1980s, it was originally used to network Department of Defense computers, linking the Pentagon with far-flung military bases and defense contractors. Later it was expanded to include large research universities, and electronic mail (e-mail) communication was its first main use. The growth of the Internet is tied directly to the explosion in the population of personal computers and the development of graphics programming. (Early e-mail appeared on a blank screen, with no cute graphics or icons, and users had to rely on function keys to send messages manually.) As the technology rapidly developed, the public responded avidly. By the late 1980s, the Internet was coming into widespread public use. Recognizing the Internet's economic potential, companies introduced Web pages and developed marketing techniques for the new medium. Public officials also acted strategically, establishing Web sites through which citizens could contact them electronically. (Chapters 12 and 13 discuss the Internet as a tool for the public to mobilize and for groups to communicate.)

▶ **How has the Internet changed the way we get news and other political information?** Richard Davis, a political scientist, has studied the political functions of the Internet. The Internet, he finds, serves as a link between government and the people: Members of Congress, the president, governors, city councils, school boards, and mayors maintain Web pages that provide information and allow citizens to reach officials directly, facilitating communication and political engagement. The Internet can also serve as a forum for the discussion of political issues, and it allows groups and officials to gauge public opinion with immediate (though unscientific and perhaps unreliable) results. Some experts are concerned that the Internet and other new technologies can be used to fragment the public by framing issues very narrowly to appeal to a specialized group of people.[13]

It is important to note that a **technology gap** (also referred to as the **digital divide**) exists in the United States.[14] Class, race, and age all influence a person's access to personal computers and the Internet. The benefits made possible by the Internet are likely to be achieved by people who have basic computer skills and thus are already interested in and informed about politics—that is, the educated, the more affluent, and younger people.[15] Although most public libraries provide free Internet access, not all people are able to take advantage of this opportunity (for example, if they have no access to transportation, lack basic computer skills, or are not literate). Table 11.1 gives details on Internet access. There are clear patterns in terms of who has Internet access and who does not. Least likely to have Internet access are the elderly (who often find

TABLE 11.1

Internet Access by Selected Characteristics: 2003 (in percentages)

AGE	INTERNET ACCESS
15–24 years	47.1%
25–34	60.4
35–44	65.3
45–54	65.1
55–64	56.6
65 years and over	29.4
RACE	
White, non-Hispanic	59.9%
African American	36.0
Asian	66.7
Hispanic	36.0
EDUCATIONAL ATTAINMENT	
Less than high school graduate	20.2%
High school graduate/GED	43.1
Some college or associate's degree	62.6
Bachelor's degree	76.8
Advanced degree	81.1
FAMILY INCOME (ANNUAL)	
Less than $25,000	30.7%
$25,000–$49,999	57.3
$50,000–$74,999	77.9
$75,000–$99,999	85.8
$100,000 or more	92.2

SOURCE: U.S. Census Bureau, Current Population Survey, October 2003.

The Census Bureau regularly conducts surveys of the American public, partly to provide the government information but also to gauge the needs and status of the population (which then can influence public policies and resource allocations). In this survey, the government found that access to the Internet is not evenly divided across important demographic groups. People between the ages of 25 and 64 have more access, as do whites and Asians and those with higher educational attainment and family income. How might the lack of access to the Internet become an issue in the future?

▶ **News is only one** part of what we see on television. Do shows such as sitcoms and crime dramas affect our political views?

TABLE 11.2
Where Americans Learn about Candidates and Campaigns

REGULARLY LEARN INFORMATION FROM:	2000	2004
Local TV news	48%	42%
Cable news networks	34	38
Nightly network news	45	35
News magazines	15	10
Daily newspaper	40	31
Talk radio	15	17
National public radio	12	14
Internet	9	13
News pages from IPOs*	—	10
Comedy TV shows	6	8

* Internet service providers such as AOL and Yahoo

SOURCE: Pew Research Center for the People and the Press, "Cable and Internet Loom Large in Fragmented Political News Universe," January 11, 2004. http://people-press.org/reports/display.php3?ReportID=200

A national survey of over 1500 adults 18 and over, conducted from December 19, 2003 to January 4, 2004, revealed that people were changing their pattern of news consumption compared to a similar survey conducted in 2000. Adults in 2004 are relying less on nightly network news, local television news, and daily newspapers for their information regarding candidates and campaigns than they had in 2000, and are relying more on the Internet and news updates from their Internet service providers. Do you think this is a positive or a negative trend? Does it matter where people get their news from? Why or why not?

it difficult to learn how to use it), African Americans, Hispanics, and the less educated and less affluent. "The digital divide has turned into a 'racial ravine' when one looks at access among households of different races and ethnic origins."[16]

Furthermore, the very nature of the Internet makes it a potentially dangerous place to get *reliable* information. Anyone with the basic computer skills and the interest can create a Web page and a blog (Web log or online journal), and there is no mechanism to differentiate irrelevant, biased, or intentionally manipulative information from reliable and accurate knowledge. You need to be an informed consumer, aware of the trustworthiness of each

online source and careful not to be misled or swayed by imprecise or biased information.

The instantaneous nature of the Internet has dramatically changed news reporting today. For example, Internet users whose Internet service provider offers instantly updated headline news can read the main stories featured in the newspaper many hours before they appear in print. Consequently, the way in which people get their news has changed, with people relying less on local news programs, cable news, nightly network news, newsmagazines, and the daily newspaper for information and more on the Internet and news from their Internet service providers (see Table 11.2). In addition to the issues of race and class with respect to access to the Internet, age also affects the manner in which people consume news. As Table 11.3 on page 429 indicates, those under 30 are far more likely to get their news online than they are from the newspaper or television news, whereas people over 50 are far more likely to rely on television or the newspaper for their news information.

practicequiz

1. From the beginning, the press in colonial America put scandal and controversy on its front page.
   a. true   b. false

2. How did the penny presses improve the quality of journalism in the United States?
   a. They increased competition, since many more such newspapers started up at that time.
   b. More college graduates began to enter the field of journalism at that time.
   c. Their financial independence from politicians made their coverage less constrained.
   d. They expanded the use of photographs and other graphics.

3. When did owning and listening to radio first become popular in this country?
   a. between 1880 and 1890
   b. between 1900 and 1910
   c. between 1920 and 1930
   d. between 1940 and 1950

4. One disadvantage of the Internet as a site for political news and ideas is that
   a. the information on it is not always reliable.
   b. the news items are not covered in great depth there.
   c. only the best-informed individuals can post material on the Web.
   d. most of the people who use the Internet are young and politically disconnected.

Answers: 1-b, 2-c, 3-c, 4-a.

discussionquestions

1. How did the function of newspapers change when they became widely available to the public? Why is private ownership of the media important?

2. How have television and the Internet changed the reporting of news? Why must you be cautious about using the Internet as a source of political information?

Functions of the Media

The media perform a multitude of functions in the United States, which can be summarized as entertaining, informing, and persuading the public. As you have seen, the media provide people with shared political experiences, which can in turn bring people together and affect public opinion. The media model appropriate behavior and reinforce cultural norms, but they also portray behavior that challenges cultural norms and expectations. And sometimes they do both at the same time. Since the media (especially television) are increasingly national in scope, the presentation of some issues in one region to one group will reinforce cultural norms, while the same material challenges cultural norms in another region. Consider same-sex marriage. In some regions, these unions are more accepted as normal expressions of love and commitment, while in other regions, most people consider them immoral and illegal. When the media portray such unions in the news or in sitcoms, the perspective they use can serve to frame the issue.

ENTERTAINMENT

▶ **News is only one part of what we see on television. Do shows such as sitcoms and crime dramas affect our political views?** Even as entertainment, the media can affect the image of officials and institutions. Consider late-night television, where being the frequent butt of jokes can undermine a leader's public image. TV depictions of officials and institutions—the police and the courts, for example—can be either positive or negative, ranging from the humane portrayal of a judge in *Judging Amy* (first aired in 1999) to the corrupt image of a police officer in *The Shield* (2002). The media's negative portrayal of governmental officials, even as entertainment, can have negative effects on public perception and attitudes. Research on media images of public officials from the mid-1950s through the 1990s has demonstrated that the way they were shown was more likely to be negative than positive. The only occupation with worse images was business. Our political system itself was twice as likely before 1975 to be portrayed positively on television than negatively, but by the 1980s, positive portrayals had become uncommon. This shift, the researchers claimed, reflected changes in public opinion in the aftermath of the Vietnam War and the Watergate scandal.[17]

The distinction between entertainment and news has become increasingly blurred, as the news divisions of network media come under pressure to be entertaining in hopes of appealing to a broader audience and generating money for the network. A per-

TABLE 11.3
Patterns of News Use by Age (in percentages)

	TOTAL	<30	30-49	50+
Goes online	54%	74%	62%	33%
Online at least once a week for news	33	46	37	20
Online daily for news	15	17	18	10
Watched TV news yesterday	55	44	51	67
Read newspaper yesterday	46	29	43	58

SOURCE: The Pew Research Center for the People and the Press, "Internet Sapping Broadcast News Audience," http://people-press.org/reports/display.php3?ReportID=36, national survey, June 11, 2000.

A national survey of 3,142 adults 18 and over was conducted from April 20 to May 13, 2000; it found that age affects the manner in which our society consumes its news. Younger people go online for news (going online far more frequently than older Americans), while older Americans rely upon television news and the newspaper. Do you think that these differences will continue as the young people in our society age? Why or why not?

fect example of this occurred with the television show *Murphy Brown* (which aired from 1988 to 1998). Murphy's image was that of a strong, powerful, and intelligent broadcast journalist living a life of success. Murphy sacrificed her personal life to pursue her professional goals, which served her well until she became pregnant. Murphy's pregnancy raised many issues—the challenges of an unplanned pregnancy for a single professional woman, as well as difficulties in balancing family and career. The Murphy character's decision to have the child but not to marry the baby's father generated much criticism from social and cultural conservatives in national politics. In a speech in 1992, Vice President Dan Quayle used *Murphy Brown* as evidence of a national moral decline and of the need to foster "family values." Quayle's remarks sparked as much controversy as the TV program had, mobilizing conservatives and liberals alike. As a result, the public debated what "family" meant, discussed the issue of single-parent families, and pondered issues of morality that ranged from abortion to wedlock and women's sexual desire. In an interesting turn, the Murphy Brown character "addressed" the vice president on her "news show"

▶ **Does the drive for** profits affect the quality of news reporting?

libertarian view
the idea that the media should be allowed to publish information that they deem newsworthy or of interest to the public without regard to the social consequences of doing so.

social responsibility theory (public advocate model)
the idea that the media should consider the overall needs of the society when making decisions about what stories to cover and in what manner.

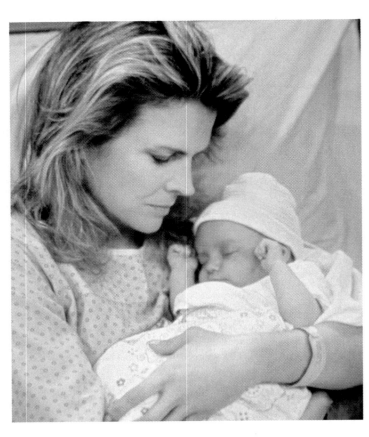

Candice Bergen portrayed the popular professional woman *Murphy Brown* from 1988–1998. This program demonstrates how reality and entertainment can become intertwined. A national conversation about "family values" was started in 1992 when Vice-President Dan Quayle commented upon the unplanned pregnancy of the television character in a national speech. The situation became even more interesting when Murphy responded to the Vice-President on her "news show." Do you think that television programs are increasingly mixing reality and entertainment? What consequences, if any, emerge when fiction and reality mix?

(as a story line in the series), uniquely merging TV entertainment and reality. The incident demonstrates how even the entertainment component of television can have political significance.

pathways past and present
THE ROLE OF PROFITS

The standards used for reporting news are controversial. Many critics attack the media's reliance on exploitative and sensational stories in an obsessive search of profits. The quest for profits, it is said, makes the media bloodthirsty hounds, exploiting the misfortune of others. The central question then becomes, Who should control the media? Some observers argue that they should police themselves, establishing their own standards of decency and ethics. Others argue that the media simply give us, the public, what we want; if we're displeased with what is being shown, we can use the power of the purse, including boycotts, to influence them. There are two theories regarding self-imposed control of the media. The **libertarian view** says that the media should show what they think the public wants, with no worry about the consequences. If viewers want violence, give them violence; if they want sex, give them sex. In contrast, the **social responsibility theory** (also called the **public advocate model** of news coverage) states that the media need to balance what the public wants with what's good for it. In essence, this theory asserts that the media should promote socially desirable behavior by providing information that advances people's ability to be good citizens, conveying information that allows clear and effective popular decision making.[18]

▶ **Does the drive for profits affect the quality of news reporting?** The need to make money often leads newspeople, especially in TV, to determine newsworthiness from the perspective of audience appeal rather than political, educational, or social significance. Historically, the networks did not expect to generate profits from news programs, which they believed were a public good. But in recent years, the networks have decided that news programs must not only cover their costs but also generate profits. Television is dependent on ratings to gauge how much it can charge advertisers. A mere 1 percent increase in the audience can mean millions of dollars in increased advertising revenue. Advertising rates in newspapers are also based on consumption, measured by paid circulation. Changes in programming that reflect profit-driven demands for audience appeal have prompted much criticism. News journalists increasingly believe that the quest for profits is harming coverage (see Table 11.4). For example, newspapers have made a variety of changes to increase circulation and profits: They now use more graphics, feature more but shorter stories, provide more news summaries—for example, bulleted lists of how a story relates directly to readers—and put more emphasis on soft news, such a travel, entertainment, weather, and gossip.[19] Similar changes have occurred on TV news shows, the most notable being the increased use of graphics, especially in reports on the weather.

Some commentators on the state of the media believe that criticism of these developments is unfair and largely elitist. Critics often assert that the "ideal" citizen *should* want hard news—complex, serious, and socially and politically relevant. But in fact, most people want soft news with light entertainment. Given the reality of their world of daily work, who can blame people for wanting to escape and relax in their leisure time? Hard stories and hard entertainment don't allow for diversion or reprieve. In a democracy, the anti-elitist critics argue, people should be free to choose their own entertainment and sources of information without being criticized for being lowbrow or anti-intellectual. Those who don't accept criticism of the media assert that if we want to make news more factual and intellectual, it needs nevertheless to be presented in a way that is appealing and interesting. This, they say, is the true challenge for reformers. ■

SOCIAL EFFECTS OF THE MEDIA

As noted, the distinctive nature of the news media in communicating makes them a unique and potentially powerful political actor. The news media have many functions in our society, with great political and social consequences. Harold Lasswell, a prominent political scientist who pioneered studying the effects of the media on American politics, identified three important societal functions of the media: surveillance, interpretation, and socialization.[20]

SURVEILLANCE TO REPORT WORLD EVENTS According to Lasswell, the media have a watchdog role as the "eyes and ears to the world." That is, the media report what's news, thus keeping us informed of significant events not only in our communities but also in our nation and around the globe. Their surveillance function draws attention to problems that need addressing. For example, news coverage on conditions at a local veterans' hospital could demonstrate the need for more oversight and better patient care. The story could then expand, looking at the quality of care in hospitals across the country, perhaps motivating Congress to examine the care our country provides to veterans, enhancing the quality of their lives. However, it is important to note that not all surveillance reporting is positive. For example, research has shown that

TABLE 11.4
Profits Pressures Hurting Coverage: Effect of Bottom-Line Pressure on News Coverage

	NATIONAL			LOCAL		
	1995	1999	2004	1995	1999	2004
Hurting	41%	49%	66%	33%	46%	57%
Just Changing	38	40	29	50	46	35
Other/Don't Know	21	11	5	17	8	8

SOURCE: The Pew Center for the People and the Press, "Bottom-Line Pressures Now Hurting Coverage, Say Journalists" http://people-press.org/reports/display.php3?ReportID=214

A survey of 547 national and local media reporters, producers, editors, and executives released on May 23, 2004 indicates that journalists believe that the pressure to make a profit is harming both national and local news coverage. This trend goes back at least a decade. Do you agree with the journalists? If they feel this way, why do you think they can't resist that pressure?

crime is often overreported, making people believe that there is more criminal activity in their community than actually exists. Although it can be helpful for the media to probe into scandals and to uncover abuses that need improving, emphasizing negativity can also lead to public cynicism. Negative reporting on the economy has drawn much criticism, with some observers asserting that stories that continually report economic downturns can spread fear among investors, causing them to act in ways that actually do worsen the economy.

pathways profile
DOROTHEA LANGE, PHOTOJOURNALIST

Dorothea Lange was one of America's first women photojournalists. Her work documented the plight of some of the most vulnerable groups in our society and recorded an important era in American history. "Migrant Mother," dating from 1936 and showing the reality of the lives of victims of the Great Depression, is perhaps her most famous photograph. It helped give poverty a

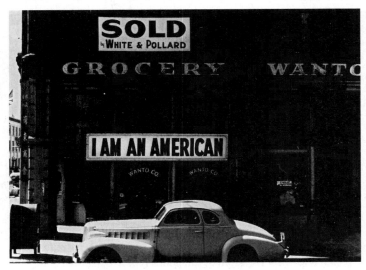

ABOVE: **During the Great Depression,** many were desperately poor and in great need of assistance. The photograph shows migrant workers displaced by the severe drought and the Dust Bowl of the 1930s. The photograph is striking because it so intimately depicts the desperation these people felt.

BELOW: **Following the Japanese attack on Pearl Harbor,** many Japanese Americans were targeted with violence, intimidation, and isolation. In 1942, the U.S. government ordered that Japanese Americans be gathered up and moved away from the west coast of the country. Their internment lasted until 1945, resulting in significant property loss. The photo here is a Japanese-owned grocery store shortly after the attack on Pearl Harbor.

▶ **Can reporters change the** public perception of an event by the way they write about it?

face, personalizing the issue for many who were far removed from the plight of the poor.

Perhaps best known for documenting the terrible distress of migratory workers in California during the Great Depression, Lange later did powerful work recording images of World War II factory workers and of the wartime internment camps for Japanese Americans. In retrospect, those camps were a serious blot on the United States. Beginning shortly after Pearl Harbor, 120,000 Japanese American men, women, and children (more than two-thirds of them native-born U.S. citizens) were ordered relocated from the West Coast to the interior of the continent, though no specific charges of disloyalty were made against any individuals. Lange took more than 700 photographs of Japanese internees as they were evicted from their homes, lost their businesses, and finally were forcibly relocated in what is now acknowledged as a gross violation of their civil rights. Though employed by the federal government, Lange quickly became sympathetic to the ethnic Japanese internees. As a government employee, all pictures she took were the property of the federal government. Not surprisingly, the government censored her photos. Only after her death did the world get access to many of these important images.

Born in 1895, Lange worked hard to break down barriers facing women in American society who chose nontraditional careers. Throughout her life, she won many awards and was the first woman awarded a Guggenheim Fellowship, a prestigious prize given annually to individuals "who have demonstrated exceptional capacity for productive scholarship or exceptional creative ability in the arts." She worked as a photojournalist at *Life* magazine for nearly a decade, traveling extensively throughout the world. She died in 1965.

Lange is remembered for her realistic portrayal of people in their natural setting, for her commitment to documenting the lives of the most vulnerable individuals and groups, and for her pioneering efforts as a woman forging her place in the world. ■

One aspect of surveillance is **investigative reporting,** in which reporters seek out stories and probe into various aspects of an issue in search of serious problems. Some of the earliest forms of investigative journalism, popular around 1900, were called **muckraking**— an expression that President Theodore Roosevelt coined in describing journalists who, he thought, tried to rake up too much sensational social filth. From the 1870s until World War I, there was a good deal of public interest in reforming government, politics, and business (see (L)(I)(N)(K) *Chapter 12, pages 470–472*). To generate support for reform, journalists would investigate areas that they believed needed to be changed and then present their findings to the

investigative reporting
a type of journalism in which reporters thoroughly investigate a subject matter (often involving a scandal) to inform the public, correct an injustice, or expose an abuse.

muckraking
investigating and exposing societal ills such as corruption in politics or abuses in business.

public. One of the most famous examples is Upton Sinclair's examination of the Chicago stockyards. His resulting novel, *The Jungle*, published in 1906, was a scathing exposé of the meatpacking industry. It created a public outcry for reform during Theodore Roosevelt's administration, leading the federal government to regulate the industry and demand more sanitary conditions to make meat production safer. Muckraking lost public support around 1912, sending investigative journalism into a prolonged lull. The Watergate scandal of the early 1970s not only revived modern investigative journalism but also firmly entrenched it in the contemporary media.

Many Americans have welcomed the return of investigative journalism, pointing to the numerous abuses that reporters have recently uncovered. One excellent example is the *Chicago Tribune*'s investigation into the Illinois death penalty in 1999. The *Tribune* exposed serious flaws in the administration of the death penalty in Illinois. Its findings ultimately led Governor George Ryan to impose a moratorium on all executions in the state and to appoint a panel to recommend improving the public defender system, which provides lawyers for indigent persons accused of committing death-penalty offenses. However, some critics believe that investigative journalists often go too far, delving into matters that should be treated confidentially and privately—for example, the extramarital affairs of public officials or the behavior of these officials' children. Some areas, these critics say, should be considered off limits out of respect for individuals' privacy.

INTERPRETATION   According to Lasswell, the second societal role of the media is to interpret the news, putting events into context and helping people to understand the complexities of the world. One example occurred upon the death of former president Ronald Reagan in 2004. Retrospective stories in the newspapers and on television put his presidency into context by focusing on his economic and social policies while typically ignoring the more controversial issues of his administration, such as the Iran-Contra scandal. The media drew historical parallels between Reagan and other presidents and compared his funeral to other presidential funerals. In essence, they put his life and death into context for the nation. The power to set the context, to frame the issue, to interpret the facts, and potentially to provide legitimacy for people, issues, or groups gives the media enormous power. In framing how a story is told—in short, by creating heroes and villains—the media tell us, subtly or otherwise, who is "good" and who is "bad" in a way that is difficult to refute thereafter.

▶ **Can reporters change the public perception of an event by the way they write about it?** Take the civil rights movement as an example. Interpretive stories in the media about prominent

figures and events in the movement have generally been framed to focus on the victims of racism rather than to show that civil rights activists challenged the status quo and broke laws doing it. In 1955, Rosa Parks intentionally and in full awareness broke the law of Montgomery, Alabama, by refusing to give up her seat on a city bus to a white man. Yes, she believed that the law was unjust, but it *was* the law at the time. Media accounts about her at the time of her death in 2005 portrayed her not as a lawbreaker but as a victim and a hero in the struggle for justice. Conversely, the media tended to portray the feminist activists of the late 1960s and early 1970s as extremist, man-hating, lesbian bra burners when they could have been depicted more sympathetically as women fighting gender oppression and patriarchy.

Interpretive journalism is very much in evidence in reporting on the war with Iraq. When the United States invaded Iraq in 2003, the American media framed the war primarily as a defensive measure, to rid the world of Saddam Hussein's weapons of mass destruction, and secondarily as a war to liberate the oppressed Iraqi people. But many Iraqis and others around the world did not share America's announced goal of liberating the Iraqi population. Framing the invasion in terms of waging the post-9/11 war on terrorism, rather than of attacking another nation unprovoked, certainly helped generate public support for the initial invasion. However, events soon caused the war to be framed a bit differently. Neither weapons of mass destruction nor links between Saddam's Iraq and al-Qaeda were discovered, and meanwhile a bitter Iraqi resistance to the American occupation developed. As U.S. military losses mounted and Iraq seemingly lurched toward sectarian civil conflict—and as the media repeatedly reported stories of poor planning for the invasion and of postinvasion chaos—the American public's support for the war and for the president eroded. War critics became more outspoken, many of them preferring to see the war retroactively framed in terms of the United States having invaded a sovereign nation to impose our values and promote our economic self-interest. To what extent investigative journalists will eventually accept—and contribute to—this reframing of the war remains to be seen.

Or consider another example in the United States. Research shows that two-thirds of the poor people shown in the media are black, while in reality two-thirds of the poor are white. The black poor are often portrayed as undeserving of better. (They could escape poverty, runs the underlying assumption, if they really wanted to, but they do not because they don't work hard or are pregnant teenagers or are dependent on drugs.) Conversely, poor white people are generally shown more sympathetically (as old, sick, disabled, or economically disadvantaged). Researchers

▶ **Do the political leanings**
of reporters or editors lead
to bias in news reporting?

contend that such racially defined portrayals affect the public's perception of welfare policies and harden racial stereotypes.[21] Consider also images and controversies that emerged following the coverage of Hurricane Katrina. On August 30, 2005, two news sources—the Associated Press (AP) and Getty Images via Agence France-Presse (AFP)—published two similar pictures with very different captions. In the AP picture, an African American man was shown "looting" a local grocery store, while in the AFP picture, two Caucasian people were depicted "finding" bread and soda at a local grocery store. Critics contended that the characterizations were based on racial stereotypes and were biased.[22] Others claimed that the captions may simply reflect stylistic differences associated with the two news agencies. As consumers, you need to be conscious of this sort of potential bias and to seek numerous sources of news to ensure objectivity.

▶ **Do the political leanings of reporters or editors lead to bias in news reporting?** Many observers of all political stripes are concerned over what they see as bias in news coverage. Some perceive a liberal bias in the news, especially on public radio and television and in such newspapers as the *New York Times;* conservative political commentators such as Rush Limbaugh and Bill O'Reilly, as well as conservative politicians, make much of this alleged bias. Democrats and liberals counter by asserting that Fox News has a conservative bias (a belief echoed in the film *Outfoxed: Rupert Murdoch's War on Journalism*), that the mainstream media actually bend over backward to present conservative views, and that a good deal of reporting is in fact shaded in a conservative direction. Research on this volatile issue is mixed. In 1995, the Media Studies Center and the Roper Center for Public Opinion surveyed Washington-based reporters and national newspaper editors. It found that 50 percent of reporters identified themselves as Democrats, compared with 34 percent of the national public. Editors were more like the national public than reporters, with 31 percent claiming to be Democrats. But only 4 percent of reporters said that they were Republicans, compared to 28 percent of the public and 14 percent of editors.[23] The research also probed political ideology, finding that reporters are far more likely to call themselves liberal than the general population. Editors were more conservative, dividing along the lines found in the population at large. These data, limited to Washington-based journalists and a dozen years out of date, provide some evidence

to bolster assertions that reporters are more likely to be liberals. Other research shows that historically, newspapers have been far more likely to endorse Republican presidential candidates, though the current trend is for papers to remain uncommitted at election time.[24] Research has failed to find empirical evidence that news reporting is biased in favor of either party.[25] So even though reporters may be more liberal, their professional stance on the whole remains neutral. It is difficult to assess whether their neutrality is the result of the influence of editors and owners (both of whom are more conservative), of their ethical commitments, or of competitiveness inherent in the modern journalistic environment.

If we expand the definition of the media to include talk radio, concerns over a liberal bias disappear. Unquestionably, conservative radio personalities and political commentators dominate talk radio, and self-described liberal or left-wing commentators have had difficulty finding a following in this environment. And as for Web sites and blogs, all shades of political opinion seem to have plentiful outlets.

pathways profile

THE TYPICAL JOURNALIST

A national study (Weaver and Wihoit, 1996)[26] of 1,410 randomly selected newspeople working for 574 newspapers, radio and TV stations, and newsmagazines reached the following conclusions (expressed in percentages):

	Journalists	General Population
Caucasian	92	77.1
Male	66	49.1
College graduates	82	24
Democrats	44	34
Republicans	16	33

As you can see, journalists are not a cross-section of the United States' population. They are more likely to be white, male, and politically liberal college graduates. Nonwhite journalists are more likely to be female. The lowest representation of women is in the wire services and television, while their largest presence is on newsmagazines and weekly newspapers.

▶ **Does television play a** major role in children's political socialization?

discussionquestions

1. How do the entertainment media affect politics? What is the difference between the libertarian and social responsibility theories of the media? Which theory seems more persuasive to you, and why?

2. What are the positive and negative aspects of having the media serve as watchdogs? Why is the power of interpretation a powerful tool of the media?

People question whether these disparities are harmful. Research is mixed, encouraging some to conclude that individual demographic characteristics are not important in determining fair news coverage.[27] As you saw in ⓁⒾⓃⓀ *Chapter 10, pages 392–401* people with similar life experiences tend to develop similar opinions. Statistically, college-educated individuals are more liberal on social issues and tend to support constitutional liberties more than people with less education. Whites tend to view the police differently than African Americans and Latinos do. Men and women have different political priorities and often differ on matters of public policy. There is no conclusive answer to the question of the impact of the lack of diversity in news reporting and commentary. If, for example, nonwhite journalists can better present nonwhite perspectives, a lack of diversity would be troubling. However, if people with different demographic characteristics can accurately report the experiences and perspectives of others with different characteristics, there is less reason for concern. Moreover, given the level of competition and peer scrutiny that prevails among journalists, many people believe that media coverage in the United States is generally fair and reasonable. Others, though, strongly disagree. ◼

SOCIALIZATION   The third effect of the media that Lasswell identified is to socialize people. As noted in ⓁⒾⓃⓀ *Chapter 10, pages 390–392*, the media are an agent of socialization, teaching us political facts and opinions that help form our political belief structures and our political culture. Research since the 1970s has shown that the media are a crucial agent of socialization, teaching both facts and values. The media also reinforce economic and social values. Simply looking at MTV provides testimony that the belief in capitalism is alive and well in the United States. Shows such as *The Fabulous Life*, *MTV Cribs*, and *Pimp My Ride*, which dwell on material acquisitions, reinforce the basic tenets of capitalism—the desire for more "bling-bling" drives our economic system.

▶ **Does television play a major role in children's political socialization?**   In winter, young children spend an average of thirty-one hours a week watching TV. Eighty percent of the programming children watch is intended for adults and generally goes far beyond their life experiences, making the potential for molding their minds greater than for adults.[28] Hence the concern in many areas of society is over programming content and over the negative

implications of the high levels of violence, sex, and materialism on television. The media can and do promote positive role models for children, celebrating national holidays and heroes, but there is no denying that negative images in the media far outweigh positive illustrations. For adults whose basic ideology and opinions are already formed, the media provide opportunities for reinforcement, especially with so many options available on TV, cable, the Internet, and the immense variety of print publications. Adults can thus easily find programming to reinforce their ideology and political views; children are more susceptible to what they learn from TV.

practicequiz

1. What explains the increasingly negative portrayal of our political system on television after 1975?
   a. consolidation of the networks
   b. the rise of cable TV
   c. the Vietnam War and the Watergate scandal
   d. the Iran-Contra scandal

2. A series of articles in the *Chicago Tribune* in 1999 about the death penalty in Illinois is an example of investigative journalism that
   a. goes too far, violating the privacy of noncelebrities.
   b. is really more sensationalism than the reporting of hard news.
   c. does not go far enough, leaving social problems intact.
   d. uncovers abuses and leads to real change.

3. Which of these two statements are true?
   1. "Although two-thirds of the poor in the United States are white, two-thirds of the poor people shown in the media are black."
   2. "Newspaper reporters are much more likely to call themselves liberal than the general population."
   a. the first statement
   b. the second statement
   c. neither statement
   d. both statements

4. The personalities and political commentators on talk radio make it clear that this medium
   a. is dominated by liberals.
   b. is dominated by conservatives.
   c. has succeeded in remaining politically neutral.
   d. has shifted from a conservative to liberal bias.

Answers: 1-c, 2-d, 3-d, 4-b.

▶ **How do politicians try** to control news coverage of their activities? Are they successful in this?

earned media coverage
airtime provided free of charge to candidates for political office.

pseudo-events
events that appear spontaneous but are in fact staged and scripted by public relations experts to appeal to the news media or the public.

agenda setting
featuring specific stories in the media to focus attention on particular issues.

gatekeepers
group or individuals who determine which stories will receive attention in the media and from which perspective.

Political Use of Media

▶ **How do politicians try to control news coverage of their activities? Are they successful in this?** Political parties, politicians, interest groups, and individuals use the media to manipulate the public and politics. Political elites have always used communication for political purposes. In 350 B.C., the ancient Greek philosopher Aristotle discussed the role of communication in keeping political communities intact in his *Rhetoric*. Today's modern mass media simply make the process easier. As you'll see, political leaders often directly appeal to the public (with a televised speech, for example) or indirectly (in advertisements designed to sway public opinion). It is important to realize that communication has always been used for political purposes, although today's technology has made it more sophisticated. In light of their exclusive focus on communication, the mass media in the United States should be considered an important political institution.

HOW POLITICIANS MAKE THE NEWS

Politicians try very hard to get positive press coverage free of charge. Many of their actions are designed to increase the likelihood that the media will cover them. This is especially important for elected officials who are up for reelection. As you will see in LINK *Chapter 14, page 540,* people tend to put more credence in what they learn from news programs than in information presented in paid advertisements. Hence, this so-called **earned media coverage** is very important for political officials and political candidates. It raises their visibility and exposes them to the public. Elected officials and other ambitious leaders use various means of getting attention. One popular tactic is to stage **pseudo-events** (a term coined by the historian Daniel J. Boorstin in 1961 to characterize events whose primary purpose is to generate public interest and news coverage).[29] For example, an incumbent may visit a successful drug rehabilitation center, discussing the treatment facility with a former drug addict who is now a productive citizen. The event gives the impression that the politician is sensitive and in control of the issue—but viewers should be aware that the entire event was staged with television and newspaper coverage in mind. The center was carefully selected, as was the "success story." Although the press does not like to cover these staged events, preferring to capture more real-istic news, they will often show them for fear of getting scooped by rivals. Imagine if one network didn't send a crew and something interesting and unexpected happened, such as the "success story" addict's challenging the politician's good intentions! No media executive wants to be the one to make such an error, especially when the official makes a mistake or is put in an embarrassing situation. Politicians try to control the events, but sometimes they are unsuccessful. President Bush was caught on camera once reading a children's book upside down, provoking much media ridicule. When announcing an elementary school spelling bee, Vice President Dan Quayle once misspelled *potato*, dogging him with innumerable jokes about his intelligence for the rest of his political career. Remembering these political goofs, politicians and their aides spend a great deal of time developing mechanisms to garner positive media attention.

There is often an adversarial relationship between public officials and the media. Officials want to control information about themselves and their policies, including the way such information is framed and presented, while the media reject such "spoon-feeding" and try to retain their independence. Government officials want to be seen in a positive light, whereas the media, perpetually seeking to boost ratings or circulation, always find controversies or conflicts more appealing. At the same time, however, reciprocal relationships bind the media, politicians, and the public together. Politicians need the media to communicate with their constituents and advance their agendas, the media need politicians to provide news and entertainment, and the public needs both to make informed voting decisions. The media influence the public with programming—but because the media are driven by the profit motive, the public, their source of revenue, influences them. Similarly, the public influences government through elections and by supporting or rejecting policies, and the government influences the public by making and enforcing policies. Research on the *New York Times*, the *Washington Post*, and the *Chicago Tribune* revealed that fully half of the sources for front-page stories in these papers were government officials.[30]

HOW JOURNALISTS REPORT THE NEWS

Many people believe that the media's ability to select how and what they report is their greatest source of influence. This is called **agenda setting**. It consists of determining which issues will be

Here President George W. Bush talks by video conference to the U.S. National Guard troops from the 42nd Infantry Division in Tikrit, Iraq from the Eisenhower Executive Office Building on the grounds of the White House on October 13, 2005. How effective do you think this new technology is in keeping governmental officials in touch with the people?

covered, in what detail, and in what context—and also of deciding which stories are not newsworthy and therefore are not going to be covered. Agenda setting figures very prominently in the media's capacity to influence the public and politicians. As a consequence, much concern exists about how and by whom stories are decided to be newsworthy. In allowing certain stories to get on the public agenda and by sidelining others, the media are said to be acting as **gatekeepers.** Concern stems from the fact that no one can check the media's selection of news: The media are their own guardians, open to no serious challenge. The media set the political agenda, choose how and when political issues get addressed, and decide when stories draw attention to a problem that is important and needs to be fixed. Thus they create a political climate that can frame subsequent discussions and shape public opinion. For instance, in June 1998, the media publicized the gruesome death of a black man, James Byrd Jr., by racist murderers, who chained him to the back of a pickup truck and dragged him until he was dead, thus focusing public attention on racial tension and bigotry. In doing so, the media illustrated a problem, discussed its roots, and then demonstrated the need for change, helping set the public agenda. The amount of time and space such a story receives can dramatically affect whether it will make it onto the political agenda. These decisions, made by senior media managers, are often deliberative and conscious, leading some analysts to worry about potential media bias. There is only so much room for printing stories and so much time for broadcast, thus the decision of what to cover confers great power.

However, the Internet is changing this process by supplying up-to-the-minute news day and night, as well as almost infinite space for more details and a greater range of stories. Moreover, round-the-clock newscasting by stations such as CNN has also changed the nature of reporting: TV channels need vast quantities of information to fill their continuous broadcasts. Consequently, more stories are reaching a larger audience.

COVERING THE PRESIDENT   Although it may seem that presidents and the press hold each other in mutual contempt, each is dependent on the other. The president needs the press to communicate with the people and to build support for policies. The press needs presidents to provide stories.

However, the nature of the interactions and the type of relationship differs from president to president. Presidents use the media differently, depending on their personal style. President Clinton averaged 550 public talks each year (many very informal),

while President Reagan, dubbed "the Great Communicator," averaged only 320. At the dawn of the television era, President Harry S Truman, who is today remembered for his vigorous and colorful ways of expressing himself in public, averaged a mere 88 talks a year.[31] Clinton's ability to communicate and relate to the public earned him a great deal of flexibility, allowing his candidacy and presidency to survive many scandals and even an impeachment trial. The relationship he was able to develop with the people, via the media, increased his popularity, providing some insulation against the serious charges of personal wrongdoing that he eventually faced.

As noted, there is an interesting dynamic between politicians and the media. Even if the relationship is uneasy, open warfare is rare. On the one hand, the relationship is by definition adversarial, because both sides want to control how information and events are framed. However, as you have seen, they need each other, too. Presidents put great effort into creating photo opportunities ("photo ops") and pseudoevents that are visually appealing and releasing to the press information favorable to the White House. News media with limited resources will often cooperate, but those with more resources can subject the material to greater scrutiny, often presenting information in a manner contrary to what the White House might prefer.

The office of the White House press secretary supplies the White House press corps and the Washington-based media with daily information about the administration. The president's press secretary customarily holds a daily press conference. In addition, each administration has an office of communications, which may be structured differently from administration to administration but is always used to oversee long-term public relations and presidential image making.

press release
a written statement that is given to the
press to circulate information or an
announcement.

news briefing
a public appearance by a governmental
official for the purpose of releasing information to the press.

news conference
a media event, often staged, where
reporters ask questions of politicians or
other celebrities.

▶ How do reporters gather
news from the White House?

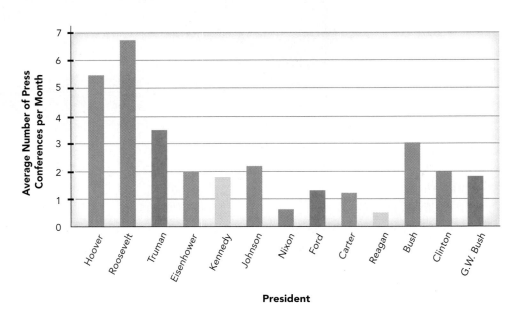

FIGURE 11.2

Presidential Press Conferences

Over the last eighty or so years, the average
number of presidential press conferences
per month has decreased rather dramatically,
from Franklin Roosevelt's high of 6.9 to Ronald
Reagan's low of 0.5. Why do you think this is
the case? Why do you think presidents in
the modern era of television are relying on
other means to communicate with the
country? Do you think this trend isolates
the president too much from the press?

Source: White House Press Office

▶ **How do reporters gather news from the White House?**
Communication from the White House takes three general forms:
press releases, news briefings, and **news conferences.** Press
releases and news briefings are the routine ways to release news.
Press releases are prepared text in which officials present information to reporters, and they are worded in hopes that they will be
used just as they are, without rewriting. To allow the media to ask
direct questions about press releases or current events, the presidential press secretary and other high officials regularly appear for
news briefings. News conferences are direct opportunities for the
president to speak to the press and the public. Theodore Roosevelt
held the first news conference at the White House, but his and all
later presidential news conferences until 1961 were conducted in
private; in that year, John F. Kennedy was the first president to
allow live, televised coverage. Some presidents are wary of conferences, as they can be difficult to control. Others, especially
Kennedy, have been masters of the forum. The number of press
conferences held each year has been in a decline in the age of
investigative reporting, for presidents today try to release information in a more cautious, controlled manner (see Figure 11.2).

Doris Graber has identified four major functions of media
coverage of the executive branch.[32] First, the media serve to
inform chief executives about current events, highlighting issues
that need attention across the nation and world. Second, the
media inform the executive branch about the needs and concerns

of the public, by reporting public opinion polls and by publishing letters to the editor and feature stories. Third, the media also
allow presidents to express their positions and policy proposals
directly to the people and other government officials by means of
press conferences, televised speeches, and staged events, which
always supply the administration in power with ample opportunity to explain its positions and garner support. Finally, the
media keep the president in public view, reporting every scrap of
available information about the first family's daily life. This
reporting is generally framed from a human interest angle but
also includes evaluations of presidential performance. Stories
that show the president golfing, jogging, playing with the White
House dog, or clearing brush show the human side of the person, and keeping tabs on presidential policy initiatives allows the
public to evaluate the chief executive. All four of these functions
allow the public to stay in touch with the actions and life of the
president and allow the president to keep in touch with the
American people. Presidents have used this relationship to their
advantage, knowing that they can command a great amount of
attention and interest in their words and actions. The first
media-conscious president was Theodore Roosevelt, who used
the White House as a platform to influence public opinion and
pursue his political agenda. "I suppose my critics will call that
preaching," Theodore Roosevelt said in 1909, "but I have got
such a bully pulpit!"

President Theodore Roosevelt was one of the first presidents to effectively use the media to forge a link with the public and influence their opinion. Pictured here using his "bully pulpit," Roosevelt was a very effective and persuasive communicator. Do you think that he would be successful using today's technology or is that type of communication style better suited to the days before live broadcast journalism?

pathways of action

THE STRATEGIC USE OF LEAKS

It seems commonplace today to read a story in the newspaper or watch a report on the TV news in which important information is attributed to an unnamed "high-ranking source" or "police insider." When this happens, you should ask yourself why these sources are not named and examine the implications of relying on information that is leaked.

There are many reasons why public officials leak information to the press. One is to gauge the public reaction, sending up a "trial balloon" to see how a potential policy will be received and reported. For example, when Reagan administration officials were considering changing the guidelines for food programs for low-income children to allow ketchup to be considered a vegetable, they leaked this idea to the media. Public outcry was fast and negative, the guidelines remained unchanged, and ketchup was ruled out as a vegetable in federal food programs.[33]

Leaks can also be preemptive. Officials can strategically use leaked information to sway public opinion and pressure other officials. Consider a local school district's decision to eliminate all music classes. Someone on the board who opposes the proposal might leak the material to the press in hopes of generating public pressure on the board to stop the cut. Preemptively leaking material can allow officials to change their minds before making a public vote, as it is often easier to pressure officials before they become publicly committed to a position. Unflattering or bad news can also be leaked a little at a time to lessen the damage that it might cause. It is common knowledge that the best time to leak bad information is on weekends, when many full-time reporters are off and the public is too busy to watch the news. By Monday morning, the initial impact may have faded or be superseded by other news items.

Leaks can also personalize boring stories by adding a human component. Consider a complex tax proposal. It might be boring if there weren't a personal aspect to the story, such as how cutting tax breaks for prescription drug coverage will harm seniors. A story could then be released that focused on the impact of the proposed change on one particular senior citizen; this would get more attention than a more complex and quite dull story about a proposed tax reform. Leaked information can also prompt change. A frustrated congressional committee staff member tipped off the *Philadelphia Inquirer* about bad treatment of kidney dialysis patients. When the *Inquirer* published a story about neglect of patients, immediate action was taken to reform the system.[34]

Leaks are also ways to get information from publicity-shy groups or individuals. People involved with the court system or the police are typically reluctant to release sensitive information. Allowing them a chance to release information without being named could often serve as an important prompt from otherwise silent informants who are hesitant to go on record. It is long-established journalistic practice to grant leakers secrecy so that they are more willing to release information, even if it is illegal to do so. Perhaps the most important leak in modern times was Mark Felt's "Deep Throat" revelations to Bob Woodward and Carl Bernstein of the *Washington Post*. While working as the associate director of the FBI (the second in command) during the early Watergate investigations (1972–1974), Felt leaked important information that ultimately led to the Watergate coverup scandal and Richard Nixon's resignation from office. His identify was kept secret by Woodward until Felt himself went public on May 31, 2005. Although people may question Felt's initial motivations for releasing the classified information, as well as his motives for eventually disclosing his identity, there is no denying the vital importance of the leaked information that he provided.

Let's take a contemporary example (see Figure 11.3). On July 14, 2003, the syndicated columnist Robert Novak published the name of Valerie Plame, a covert CIA officer—such a revelation is a felony if it is knowingly done. A subsequent special prosecutor's investigation into charges that officials in the Bush administration had leaked the name to media sources, including Novak, eventually led to the indictment of Vice President Cheney's chief of staff, I. Lewis "Scooter" Libby, for perjury and obstruction of justice. Plame is married to a former ambassador, Joseph Wilson IV, a strong public critic of the Bush administration's prewar claims about Iraq's developing and possessing weapons of mass destruction. Wilson suggested that the leak, which Novak printed eight days after Wilson had criticized the Bush administration's rationale for the Iraq war in the *New York Times*, was made to discredit his critique and punish him for insubordination.

Chronicle of a Leak

When Vice President Dick Cheney asked the CIA in February 2002 for more information on reports of sales of African uranium to Iraq, he inadvertently set up a chain of events that would lead to controversy over a reference in President Bush's 2003 State of the Union speech, start a criminal investigation of a leak and lead to the scrutiny of the role of Karl Rove, the White House political adviser.

FEBRUARY 2002 At the CIA's request, former Ambassador Joseph C. Wilson IV travels to Niger, where his wife, Valerie, works under cover.

JANUARY 28, 2003 President Bush, in the State of the Union speech, declares: "The British government has learned that Saddam Hussein recently sought significant quantities of uranium from Africa."

JULY 6, 2003 An Op-Ed article by Wilson in The New York Times, "What I Didn't Find in Africa," casts doubt on the uranium reference and claims that the administration "twisted" the intelligence on Iraq.

JULY 8, 2003 Rove discusses Wilson's trip and the role of Wilson's wife with columnist Robert Novak.

JULY 11, 2003 Rove discusses the Wilsons with Time magazine writer Matthew Cooper.

JULY 14, 2003 Novak's column reveals that Wilson's wife works for the CIA as "an agency operative on weapons of mass destruction," citing "two senior administration officials."

SEPTEMBER 29, 2003 Scott McClellan, the White House press secretary, says it is "simply not true" that Rove was involved in the leak and that any official who leaked classified information "would no longer be in this administration."

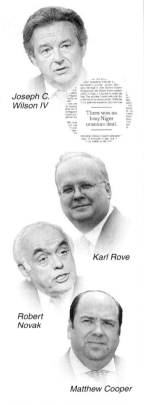

Joseph C. Wilson IV

There was no Iraq-Niger uranium deal.

Karl Rove

Robert Novak

Matthew Cooper

July 2005, The New York Times

FIGURE 11.3
Chronicle of a Leak

Officials leak information to reporters for a number of reasons. Often they want to frame an issue in a manner that augments their self-interest, other times they release information that they feel the public needs to know but are afraid of personal exposure. Important scandals have been revealed by anonymous sources leaking information to journalists, but consumers need to be careful in evaluating this material, as the motivations of the sources may not be pure and may lead to a biased presentation of the material. Do you think that officials who leak information that, while classified, leads to exposure of corruption or abuse ought to be penalized? What penalty, if any, do you think should be imposed when classified information is leaked for personal or political gain?

The Bush administration strongly denied these charges and announced that it would cooperate with the investigation. At least six other journalists also knew Plame's identity before Novak revealed it; one was Judith Miller of the *New York Times*. Miller subsequently spent eighty-five days in jail for refusing to reveal to the special prosecutor's grand jury the name of her confidential source, citing her obligation as a journalist until, apparently, Libby released her from her pledge. Libby's trial is scheduled to begin in early 2007.

Scoops based on leaked information often get more attention than the story would have merited if the material were released through normal channels, prompting other outlets to cover the story, even though they might not have otherwise, out of fear of being "outscooped." When informants are granted secrecy, they are often more willing to reveal information, but the public should be skeptical of leaked information, as it is often released for self-serving reasons. Informants often get to influence how the story is told based on the information they provide, which might not be the full story or the objective truth. Since the name and agenda of the informant are withheld, the political dimensions of the story (and its self-serving motivations) are often hidden, with potentially devastating consequences. That is why reporters must exercise diligence in handling leaks.[35] ∎

COVERING CONGRESS   The media give far less attention to Congress than to the president, for several reasons. People tend to have more interest in the actions of the president, who is the country's highest-ranking official and has a nationwide constituency. No single member of Congress can make that claim or get that recognition. Furthermore, Congress is a much larger institution that requires coalition and consensus building, both of which take time and aren't particularly exciting. By contrast, the president is often seen as working alone, so it becomes easier for the press to focus on his actions. Also, as a deliberative body, Congress works slowly, even tediously, and without drama. Of course, interested people can turn to C-SPAN for gavel-to-gavel congressional coverage—but watching for several hours will reveal just how unexciting such deliberations can be. The local media often cover the actions and votes of members of Congress, with senators typically getting more attention. The preference for coverage of senators versus representatives is especially notable in large metropolitan areas that encompass several congressional districts, making it difficult to cover all members of the local congressional delegation in detail. To get mentioned in the local news or local papers, members of

▶ **Supreme Court decisions can** have a powerful impact on our lives. Why do so few cases get major attention from the media?

Congress often stage pseudoevents and attend local events—even lowly ones like the Watermelon Festival picnic, the Fourth of July parade, or a ribbon-cutting ceremony to celebrate opening a new town library can win visually appealing news coverage.

COVERING THE COURTS   Of the three branches of government, the courts tend to get the least amount of coverage. Why? One reason is that federal judges rarely grant interviews lest their impartiality be questioned. Once appointed, judges normally do not receive much specific personal coverage; rather, attention is focused on their rulings and on the specific cases heard in their courts. The courts, moreover, deliberate and reach their decisions in secret, and very rarely do they allow televised or sound-recorded live coverage of cases as they are being argued.

Exceptions to this pattern are media stories that concern controversial personal information about judges. One recent example occurred in the spring of 2004, when the media learned that Supreme Court Justice Antonin Scalia had gone duck hunting with Vice President Dick Cheney at a time when Cheney had a case pending that would be decided by the Supreme Court. A number of articles and editorials raised concerns over the ethical questions that this seemingly innocuous outing raised. When Scalia decided to remain involved in deciding the case, public outrage grew.

Another area that receives considerable media attention is controversial confirmation hearings. The Senate must confirm all federal court judges, including Supreme Court justices, after the president has nominated them. Perhaps the most prominent example was the 1991 confirmation hearing for Supreme Court nominee Clarence Thomas. Testifying before the Senate Judiciary Committee, Anita Hill, a University of Oklahoma law professor, accused Thomas of sexual harassment when she was an employee at the Equal Employment Opportunity Commission (EEOC), on which he served, in the 1980s. A sharply divided national audience watched the Judiciary Committee's investigation into the charges. The hearings placed the issue of sexual harassment on the national agenda, resulting in many changes in laws, policies, and opinions. They also prompted many women, outraged by the confrontational manner in which Hill was treated by the all-white, all-male Senate Judiciary Committee, to enter politics and seek elected office.[36]

▶ **Supreme Court decisions can have a powerful impact on our lives. Why do so few cases get major attention from the media?** Under most other circumstances, national judges, including Supreme Court justices, rarely generate stories of a personal

While the media tend to focus less time and attention on the coverage of the courts, Supreme Court nominations typically receive a great deal of coverage today. In 1991, when it was revealed that law professor Anita Hill accused Supreme Court nominee Clarence Thomas of sexually harassing her while they both worked at the U.S. Department of Education, a storm of attention ensued. The attention was important for several reasons. Many thought the treatment of Hill by the all-white, all-male Senate Judiciary committee was unfair and disrespectful and may have stimulated some women to run for political office. Moreover, the coverage and analysis of the allegations focused national attention on the matter of sexual harassment, serving to raise awareness of this important issue.

► **How do interest groups** use the mass media to gain attention for their cause?

discussionquestions

1. Why is there an adversarial relationship between public officials and the media? In what ways do they need each other? What positive benefits emerge from this increased scrutiny? Can you think of any negative effects that such scrutiny might have?

2. What do we mean when we say that the media act as gate-keepers? How powerful is this role?

Depicted here are a number of frustrated members of Congress charging up the steps of the Senate building. The women representatives were going to the Senate building to ensure that the charges of sexual harassment brought by Anita Hill against then-Supreme Court nominee Clarence Thomas be taken seriously and investigated. Their diligence was awarded and noted by other women concerned with the lack of female representation in government. These women served as role models for other women who became motivated to enter politics because of their actions. How powerful do you think role modeling is? Can you think of a time that something you saw in the media stimulated you to take action?

nature. However, the press does cover their rulings, especially Supreme Court decisions and controversial federal district and appellate court decisions. The media have been criticized for what some believe is poor coverage of the Supreme Court, but coverage may be improving. Reporting on the Supreme Court is difficult because the court tends to release several rulings at once, forcing reporters to cover numerous often technical and difficult opinions. Typically, the press will select one or two main decisions and discuss them in more detail, while a summary box simply mentions the other Supreme Court decisions released that day. Several key decisions (for example, *Roe* and *Brown*, both of which are discussed in other chapters) attracted enormous press coverage at the time they were released, as well as retrospective stories on their anniversaries, follow-up analyses of their consequences, and even later revelations about how the decisions were reached. However, the media have ignored many important cases and in other instances presented information that had factual errors.[37]

HOW GROUPS USE THE MEDIA

► **How do interest groups use the mass media to gain attention for their cause?** Interest groups and outsiders use the media to promote their agendas, employing a variety of techniques. One popular technique is to stage events similar to politicians' pseudo-events. A child advocacy group might stage a rally to support a proposal for greater funding of a health insurance program for children, hoping that the news media will report it. Appearing on the news is very important, especially to groups that do not have large budgets, for positive coverage gives them exposure and often credibility. A second technique used by groups to get media coverage is to issue press releases and bulletins. The National Organization for Women (NOW), for example, routinely issues press releases on matters of importance to its members. Groups often issue video clips directly to news organizations in hopes that the clips will be aired with no editing to show the group in a positive light. So-called video news releases are designed to make it easy for television stations to use the videos. Groups also provide expert interviews and often have members (who do not necessarily identify themselves as members) write letters to the editors or contribute op-ed articles for local and national newspapers. Groups with sufficient means will also pay for issue advocacy advertising. One example of this is "Pork—the Other White Meat" commercials prompting consumers to consider including pork in a healthy diet. Because the media are such an important means for

► **Can the media affect** the outcome of elections by their coverage of the "horse race"?

what YOU can do!

Each day for one week, select two news stories, and see how they are covered in different sources—the newspaper, radio, television, and the Internet. How does the coverage vary? How is it similar? How does the medium affect the way the story is told? Do you see patterns of differences in content or presentation? Do any sources seem biased?

groups to raise visibility, win support, and influence both the public and officials, interest groups will continue to be creative in developing attention-grabbing tactics.

practicequiz

1. Why are public officials and the media frequently adversarial?
   a. Each wants to control political news stories.
   b. Public officials resent how infrequently they get to use the media to reach voters.
   c. Public officials thrive on policy controversies, whereas the media boosts ratings by emphasizing what's right in the world.
   d. The media need politicians to provide news, yet politicians prefer to avoid the media spotlight.

2. Sometimes government officials intentionally leak news before official announcements in order to
   a. confuse the media.
   b. bypass First Amendment regulations.
   c. measure public reaction to policy changes before they are official.
   d. prove their candor with the public.

3. Who was "Deep Throat"?
   a. Felton Marks
   b. Mark Felt
   c. Bob Woodward
   d. Carl Bernstein

4. Most Supreme Court decisions get substantial media coverage.
   a. true   b. false

Answers: 1-a, 2-c, 3-b, 4-b.

The Media and the Public in the Political Arena

The print media—newspapers, magazines, and other periodicals—tend to cater to an upper-class, better-educated segment of society. Print media are very effective in translating facts, while TV is better at conveying emotion and feelings. Hence better-educated peo-

ple are attracted to the print media, and their readers continue to be better informed about events, reinforcing their advantaged position in society (see Figure 11.4 on page 444). The fact that the more affluent have greater access to information than the general society gives them more opportunities to influence politics. For example, announcements of city council meetings or school redistricting plans are usually made in the local paper. Only individuals who routinely read the local paper will know about proposed changes, public meetings, and scheduled forums. Those who habitually do not read the paper remain uninformed about these events, which may have a significant impact on their lives. A cycle exists: Poorer people pay less attention to the print media because print stories tend to cater to the interests of the more affluent. Since poor people don't subscribe in large numbers, newspapers continue to ignore the needs of the lower class, perpetuating biases in coverage, access to information, and a lack of diverse audiences.

MEDIA IN CAMPAIGNS

► **Can the media affect the outcome of elections by their coverage of the "horse race"?** It is a long-standing belief that the media are very powerful actors in elections in the United States; some people go so far as to claim that the media actually determine the outcomes of elections. Although this is certainly an overstatement, the media do have a great deal of power, especially in anointing the "front-running candidates" long before an election. Marking one or two candidates as front-runners usually has a snowball effect: The media and the public pay more attention to them, making it easier for them to get on the news and raise money. The more money they raise, the more prominent their campaign becomes, and the bigger the campaign, the more attention it gets from the media and the public.

Front-runner status develops its own cycle of success—though certainly there is some liability in being declared the front-runner, too. (Front-runners get heightened media scrutiny, for example, which can be fatally damaging if they make gaffes or if skeletons lurk in their closet.) Many people are concerned about the power of the media in determining the front-runners, as this tends to prematurely narrow the field of candidates, often very early in the nomination cycle. When the media focus on front-runners in polls and stories, lesser-known candidates often encounter many difficulties, especially with fundraising, and are often forced to withdraw early from the race. Moreover, the media often declare winners based not on the absolute vote total but on how well a candidate does

► **How much do candidates spend on TV ads?**

sound bite
a short outtake from a longer film, speech, or interview.

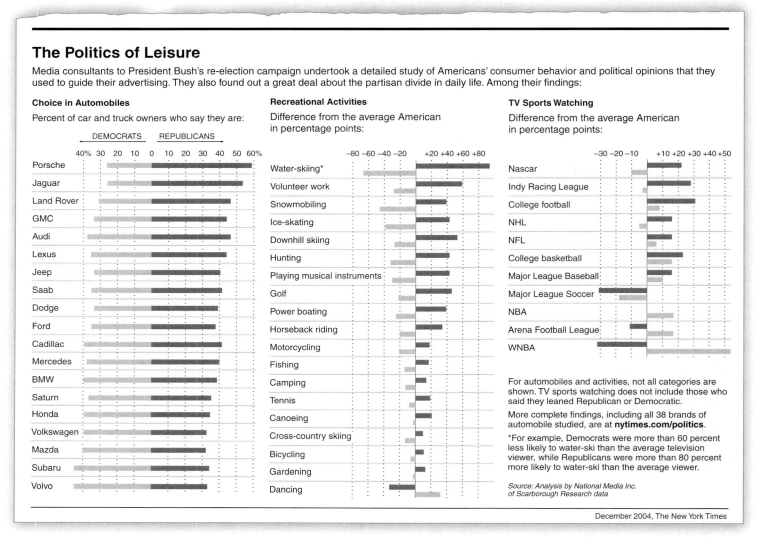

The Politics of Leisure

Media consultants to President Bush's re-election campaign undertook a detailed study of Americans' consumer behavior and political opinions that they used to guide their advertising. They also found out a great deal about the partisan divide in daily life. Among their findings:

Choice in Automobiles

Percent of car and truck owners who say they are:

DEMOCRATS   REPUBLICANS

Porsche
Jaguar
Land Rover
GMC
Audi
Lexus
Jeep
Saab
Dodge
Ford
Cadillac
Mercedes
BMW
Saturn
Honda
Volkswagen
Mazda
Subaru
Volvo

Recreational Activities

Difference from the average American in percentage points:

Water-skiing*
Volunteer work
Snowmobiling
Ice-skating
Downhill skiing
Hunting
Playing musical instruments
Golf
Power boating
Horseback riding
Motorcycling
Fishing
Camping
Tennis
Canoeing
Cross-country skiing
Bicycling
Gardening
Dancing

TV Sports Watching

Difference from the average American in percentage points:

Nascar
Indy Racing League
College football
NHL
NFL
College basketball
Major League Baseball
Major League Soccer
NBA
Arena Football League
WNBA

For automobiles and activities, not all categories are shown. TV sports watching does not include those who said they leaned Republican or Democratic.

More complete findings, including all 38 brands of automobile studied, are at **nytimes.com/politics**.

*For example, Democrats were more than 60 percent less likely to water-ski than the average television viewer, while Republicans were more than 80 percent more likely to water-ski than the average viewer.

Source: Analysis by National Media Inc. of Scarborough Research data

December 2004, The New York Times

FIGURE 11.4
The Politics of Leisure

The data presented above shows the leisure activities of Republicans and Democrats. As you can see, Democrats and Republicans enjoy different activities and tend to own different types of vehicles. Why do you think that this research was conducted? How do you think the media consultants used this data? Do the findings conform with your expectations? How so?

compared to what had been expected. Bill Clinton, at the time governor of Arkansas, serves as a very good example. Massachusetts senator Paul Tsongas won the most votes in the 1992 New Hampshire primary, but simply because he did better than had been expected, Clinton was proclaimed "the winner" by the press. This accolade gave him increased media attention and public support. This "winner" designation sent Clinton's candidacy into high gear, and he went on to win the nomination and the election.

In the 2000 presidential primary cycle, only candidates who were perceived positively in public opinion polls received extensive media coverage. For the Democrats, the only candidate to receive media attention beside Vice President Al Gore (the "front-runner") was former New Jersey senator Bill Bradley, who had been a star basketball player before turning to politics. The other

▶ **Is a candidate's "image"**
more important today than
his or her ideas?

candidates were felt to be uncompetitive and hence unworthy of attention. On the Republican side, Texas governor George W. Bush, the former president's son, received one-third more coverage than all his competitors combined.[38]

After the 2004 campaign season, a study by the Project for Excellence in Journalism, the Pew Research Center, and the University of Missouri School of Journalism, which analyzed newspaper, broadcast, and cable coverage from late March through early June in 2004, found that negative coverage of the two main presidential candidates was quite prevalent. Stories and images of President Bush were negative by more than a 3-to-1 margin. Media assessment of his Democratic opponent, Massachusetts senator John F. Kerry, was found to be more likely to be negative by a 5-to-1 margin. Moreover, the study found that the more people read the print media and watch TV coverage, the more they are likely to support the themes being emphasized by the media. The researchers found that the most common public perception about Bush was that "he is stubborn and arrogant," followed by "he lacks credibility." The most common themes reported about Kerry were that "he flip-flops on issues" and "he is very liberal." Both of these negative "definitions" of Kerry echoed the themes of Bush's campaign advertisements and speeches, and vice versa. It's hard to determine whether it was the press or the Bush campaign that influenced the public against Kerry; most likely it was a combination of two reinforcing messages.[39]

▶ **How much do candidates spend on TV ads?** One key aspect of media usage in campaigns is the need to purchase paid advertising, which is enormously expensive. In the 2000 presidential election, Bush spent $39.2 million on television ads, and Gore spent $27.9 million.[40] Paid advertising is essential because research consistently demonstrates that the news media increasingly portray candidates negatively, with fewer and fewer positive stories. Daniel Hallin found that 5 percent of news stories in the 1968 election were positive and 6 percent were negative. By 1988, however, only 1 percent of stories were positive but 16 percent were negative.[41] TV coverage of campaigns has also shrunk, coming to consist chiefly of tiny, frequently repeated, visual snippets called **sound bites.** And even the length of the sound bites on network evening news programs shriveled, from an average of 42.3 seconds in 1968 to 7.2 seconds in 1996.[42] Given these circumstances, candidates desiring to get their message and vision out to the people must pay heavily for advertising. As you have seen, candidates try to get free earned media coverage by attending events, often staged, to attract the attention of the news media, in an attempt to counter the present-day trend toward negative reporting.

Televised debates can also be important in affecting the public's perception of candidates. The most infamous example of this impact occurred in the very first televised presidential debate in 1960. John F. Kennedy's strong visual performance allayed the public's fears that he was too young and inexperienced compared to his well-known opponent, Vice President Richard M. Nixon. This debate underscored the importance of television's visual nature. TV viewers saw the physically attractive, tanned, and seemingly relaxed Kennedy verbally sparring with a sweaty, earnest, and less photogenic Nixon, and a majority of viewers believed that Kennedy won the debate. However, those listening to the debate on the radio believed that Nixon had won on the substance of what was said. This stark contrast changed the way in which subsequent candidates have viewed the power of television and underscored the importance of cultivating visual images. Ronald Reagan's masterful performance in the 1980 and 1984 presidential debates showed that despite his advanced years, he was mentally alert and able. (His professional training as an actor helped him, too.) More recently, George W. Bush exceeded low initial expectations about his abilities when he used his performance in the 2000 debates against Al Gore to persuade many voters that he was sufficiently knowledgeable and capable to serve as president.[43]

▶ **Is a candidate's "image" more important today than his or her ideas?** The importance of television in campaigns and elections also has a powerful effect on the pool of eligible candidates and the types of people perceived to be electable. Had TV existed in the 1930s, many believe, Franklin D. Roosevelt could not have been elected because, having been crippled by polio, he was confined to a wheelchair. Indeed, Roosevelt worried that his disability would make him seem "weak," and newspaper and newsreel photographers of the day were careful not to show him in his chair or on crutches. Television puts charismatic, telegenic candidates at an advantage; hence candidates for high-profile positions usually hire coaches to teach them how to behave when appearing on television. For example, public opinion polls might show that a candidate is perceived to be "too stuffy." The campaign will then stage outdoor events to make him or her appear more informal, relaxed, and "ordinary." If a candidate is seen as not intellectual enough, events will be staged at a library or university. These coaches work on body language, speech presentations, clothing, and hairstyle. Although this seems superficial, television has made outward appearance crucial. You might wonder if such past presidents as George Washington and Abraham Lincoln could ever be elected today.

GLOBAL ISSUES

CNN reaches every country in the world and has 85 million subscribers. A Russian edition of the *New York Times* is sold in

Breaking News, Por Favor

The number of newspapers aimed at the growing Hispanic population in the United States has surged. In Texas, where Hispanics are estimated to become the state's majority in 20 years, several newspapers have been started in the last several years.

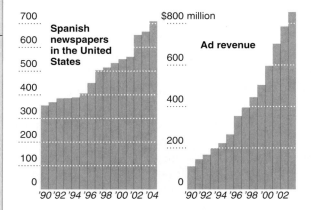

Spanish newspapers in the United States

Ad revenue

Sources: Latino Print Network; Analysis of Census Bureau data by Andrew A. Beveridge, Queens College Department of Sociology

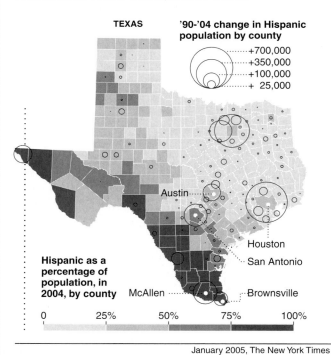

TEXAS

'90-'04 change in Hispanic population by county
- +700,000
- +350,000
- +100,000
- + 25,000

Hispanic as a percentage of population, in 2004, by county

0   25%   50%   75%   100%

January 2005, The New York Times

FIGURE 11.5
Breaking News, Por Favor

As the number of Hispanics in the United States increases, so does their purchasing power and the consumption of news. The last fifteen years has seen dramatic expansion of Spanish newspapers and their profitability. In the ten-year period from 1993 to 2003, the ad revenue from Spanish newspapers increased from $200 million to over $800 million. As the numbers of Hispanics continue to grow, so too will these figures. Today there are over 700 Spanish newspapers in the United States, helping inform these individuals. What other areas do you think will be influenced by this large group and their purchasing power?

▶ **Should we be concerned** about the fact that only a handful of corporations control a large percentage of media sources?

Moscow. MTV is viewed on five continents with an audience of 265 million.[44] Such availability of American culture raises concerns for many people, especially in other countries with very different cultures, who fear "McGlobalization." Foreigners worry that our culture and values, many of which they do not share, are "corrupting" citizens in their countries. This concern is especially significant in the Muslim world, where American and Western values are widely perceived as a mortal threat to Islam. Objections to "excessive" American cultural and political influence are heard around the globe, from Canada and France to China. If you consider the entertainment programs, fears abound over American cultural hegemony (dominance of one culture over others). Foreign programming is available in the United States, but given the fact that much of our programming is years ahead of many countries' (in technology and content alike), the trade is not equal. Because of concerns over American influence in China, for example, the Chinese government has banned all privately owned satellite dishes. Many historians attribute the fall of communism in the Soviet Union and Eastern Europe in part to exposure to Western thought and values on television. Countries proud of their culture, heritage, and values are greatly troubled by the Americanization trend made possible by the global media.

NARROWCASTING

Another area of concern for many is the trend of cable television and the Internet to appeal to narrower audiences. As television and the other mass media have become more specialized, the targeting of specific audiences, known as narrowcasting, has become far more common. Some observers worry that specialized programming may cause groups to become more fragmented, as the media no longer cater to a mass audience. Consider the changes in print media (see Figure 11.5) and in programming for Spanish speakers in the United States. One study found that two-thirds of Hispanic Americans watch Spanish-language programming daily.[45] Telemundo and Univision both have nightly news programs, each with a slightly different focus in their stories than the English-language network news programs. Furthermore, because many Hispanic viewers are not watching national English-language news programs, these "mainstream" networks are less likely to offer programming that appeals to Latinos. As a result, the larger English-speaking audience is not sufficiently exposed to issues of concern primarily to Hispanic viewers, such as immigration. An endless cycle can develop that is troubling

competitive news markets
locales with two or more news organizations that can check each other's accuracy and neutrality of reporting.

news monopoly
a single news firm that controls all the media in a given market.

discussionquestions

1. What do we mean when we say that the media cater to an upscale audience? What are the consequences of this?

2. Why are many people troubled by the concentration of media ownership and the trend toward media cross-ownership? Do they trouble you?

to many analysts, who worry that specialized programming with a narrow appeal will further fragment groups within American society.

CONCENTRATION AND CENTRALIZATION OF OWNERSHIP

▶ **Should we be concerned about the fact that only a handful of corporations control a large percentage of media sources?** Concern also stems from the trend toward more concentrated media ownership, especially of the print media and in radio broadcasting. As media ownership becomes more centralized, a "nationalization" of the news is occurring, which tends to promote a sameness of opinion and experience. This trend has been under way ever since the rise of broadcast networks and of newspaper chains in the 1930s, but today it is accelerating. Competition is generally believed to be healthy, for it makes possible a larger variety of opinions and points of view. There is concern today because much of the news comes from national news services and because there is minimal or no competition between papers in major cities—especially between two or more morning or evening papers. Examine your local paper to see how many stories in the first section come from centralized news sources, such as the Associated Press, the *New York Times,* or the *Washington Post.* You will find that it is not uncommon for the entire first page to be from sources outside your community or state. This trend is evident even in college newspapers, where editorials and stories are often picked up from a news source and do not necessarily reflect the concerns of your particular campus community.

It is widely believed that competition results in the best product, an economic and political belief held by most theorists. Observers of the media enthusiastically approve of **competitive news markets** and regard **news monopolies** as potentially dangerous. Newspaper ownership in recent decades has tended toward monopolies and away from competitive markets. The changes in broadcasting are less clear. The influence of the networks has diminished thanks to the proliferation of cable and satellite alternatives, although ownership has become more centralized. In 1997, the media critic Ben Bagdikian noted that the number of major media corporations had decreased from more than fifty in the early 1980s to only ten by the mid-1990s. By 2001, Bagdikian reported, six huge corporations—Time Warner, Disney, Viacom, News Corp., General Electric, and Bertelsmann—dominated the

mass media.[46] Furthermore, as the media have become deregulated, cross-media ownership is rising, with corporations owning a variety of media outlets, including newspapers, TV and radio stations, newsmagazines, and production companies. In 1995, Capital Cities/ABC owned seven television stations, seven radio networks (with more than 3,000 affiliated stations), eighteen radio stations, and seventy-five weekly newspapers, as well as many magazines and trade publications. When it merged with Disney in 1995, this conglomerate grew even larger.[47]

practicequiz

1. Why are many people concerned about the media's ability to help determine the front-runners in a campaign?
   a. because this determination happens so late in the nomination cycle that voters do not have enough time to assess these front-runners before election day
   b. because the media's criteria for declaring favorites in a campaign bear no resemblance to the voters' criteria
   c. because the media never used to play such a role
   d. because the media declare front-runners so early in the nomination cycle, narrowing the field of candidates prematurely

2. Why has paid political advertising become increasingly important in presidential campaigns?
   a. because voters enjoy and expect it
   b. in order to counteract the largely negative coverage of candidates in the media
   c. in order to comply with new FCC regulations
   d. because media coverage is so thorough and campaigns need to present edited versions of their candidate

3. What is a potential downside to "narrowcasting"?
   a. It may make mainstream networks less diverse culturally.
   b. It may give minority viewers, such as Latinos, less access to Spanish-speaking shows.
   c. It may create fewer choices for television and Internet users.
   d. It may prevent third-party participation in presidential debates.

4. Why does the centralization of newspaper ownership have some people worried?
   a. because it makes news gathering less efficient
   b. because it makes news gathering more expensive
   c. because it gives readers fewer perspectives from which to see and understand the news
   d. because it makes the newspaper business less profitable

Answers: 1-d, 2-b, 3-a, 4-c.

▶ **Freedom of the press**
versus national security—how
do we draw the line?

| **libel** |
| publication of false and malicious material that defames an individual's reputation. |

| **prior censorship** |
| forbidding publication of material thought objectionable. |

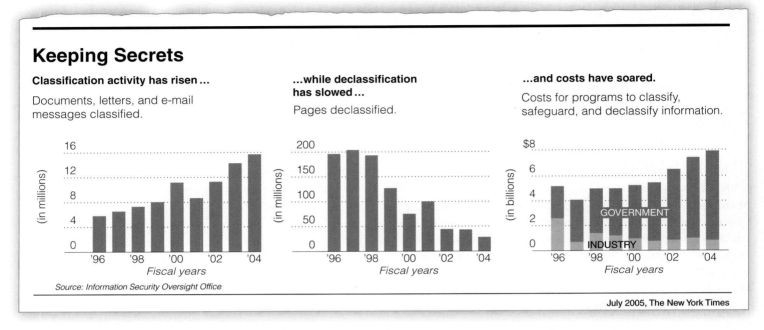

Keeping Secrets

Classification activity has risen ...
Documents, letters, and e-mail messages classified.

...while declassification has slowed ...
Pages declassified.

...and costs have soared.
Costs for programs to classify, safeguard, and declassify information.

Source: Information Security Oversight Office

July 2005, The New York Times

FIGURE 11.6
Keeping Secrets

In the last ten years, the number of classified documents has grown, as has the costs of the classifying and declassifying procedures. Why do you think that declassification has slowed so dramatically since 1998? Who should be the final decision maker when conflict arise?

Governmental Regulations

▶ **Freedom of the press versus national security—how do we draw the line?** All societies have laws regulating the media, most commonly stemming from national security concerns. Laws that define and punish treason and sedition are always necessary to ensure national security; the dilemma is how much regulation is needed before it infringes on personal freedoms. There is a tension between the needs of the government to ensure national security and the desire of a people to be free, as guaranteed by the First Amendment to the Constitution. The 9/11 attacks and President Bush's declaration of a "war on terror," which included enacting the USA PATRIOT Act, threw into high relief these concerns about balancing security and liberty.

This tension is very evident in the relationship between the media and the government. The media want to be allowed to print what they think is newsworthy, while the government wants to limit disclosure in order to promote protection (see Figure 11.6). This tension is most evident in wartime. Many people in government want to limit the amount of information shared, seeking to enhance

national security. Ideally, from the government's perspective, only information it approves for dissemination would be shared with the public. For example, the government successfully structured the sharing of information during the Gulf War of 1991. Information and images passed through a tightly controlled centralized governmental "feed," which released video to all the media; hence there was little variety in the information available. However, with limited information, it is difficult to ensure that the public knows how the war is being fought. Abuses in wartime are not common, but—as events at Abu Ghraib prison in Iraq have shown—they do occur. Many people fear that in the absence of media scrutiny, abuse and cruelty could increase. For instance, does the public have the right to know if the Bush administration or high-ranking military officials approve the use of torture against enemy prisoners in the war on terror? The tension between the public's right to know information to hold officials accountable versus the government's need to conduct war with secrecy to promote victory is very real. Revelations of the abuse of Iraqi prisoners at Abu Ghraib appear to have fanned anti-American militantism throughout the Middle East, putting the lives of American troops in greater danger. However, most citizens agree that the media should have been allowed to share this information to force reforms mandating the humane treatment of prisoners.

Even nonauthoritarian governments have laws to protect government secrets. For example, in the United States laws make top-secret documents unavailable for public scrutiny until many years later, after they have been "declassified" (declared no longer secret). Questions of what is and is not "top secret" are often highly controversial. The government has a perspective very different from that of the press, often forcing the courts into the role of arbiter.

THE RIGHT TO PRIVACY

Democratic societies also have laws that protect individual's privacy and society's morals—for example, bans against obscenity. The need for maintaining a careful balance in a free society continually raises challenges. This becomes evident when we examine privacy issues.

Regarding the right to privacy, two standards apply—those for public figures and those for private individuals. Courts have traditionally allowed a good deal of latitude in publishing personal information about people in the public eye, including celebrities, athletes, and politicians. Public "personalities" are assumed to have lower expectations for privacy and consequently have less protection. Controversy often stems from the right to privacy of *private* citizens, especially as it pertains to the victims of violent crimes. A 1975 rape and murder case in Georgia (*Cox Broadcasting Corporation* v. *Cohn*) provides a good example. The victim's family wanted her name withheld from news reports to protect her right to privacy, especially given the vicious sexual assault that preceded her murder. When newspapers nevertheless published her name and gave the specific details of her rape and murder, her family sued, claiming violation of the victim's privacy right. The court disagreed. Because her name was a matter of public record, newspapers were held to be within their rights to publish it. Papers often have policies not to publish the names of rape victims, but these rules are a matter of decency, not of law. One area where the right to privacy is protected is wherever providing a fair trial is in question. The right to privacy of the accused in order to ensure fair treatment in court is enforced, though less strongly today than in the past. Even in cases involving ordinary citizens—and certainly in cases involving celebrities—media coverage of crimes often reaches a saturation level, impelling some observers to question whether any potential jurors can be impartial. To help ensure a fair trial, gag orders can be issued, ordering all participants to refrain from discussing the case. In extreme circumstances, there can be a change of venue (holding the trial in another city), or the judge might even sequester (put into seclusion) jurors to prevent them from consuming news reports and other media coverage of the trial. In the vast majority of criminal trials, however, these extraordinary measures are neither needed nor employed.

RULES REGARDING CONTENT AND OWNERSHIP

The media are prohibited from publishing material that they know to be incorrect. **Libel** laws are designed to protect the reputations of individuals from negative and false reporting. In *New York*

TABLE 11.5
Public Opinion on Censorship (in percentages)

Agree that the media has too much freedom to publish anything it wants	43%
Believes there is too much government censorship	38
Neither	10
Both	4
Don't know	5

SOURCE: Survey by The Freedom Forum, American Journalism Review.

Methodology: Conducted by Center for Survey Research and Analysis, University of Connecticut, June 3–June 15, 2003 and based on telephone interviews with a national adult sample of 1,000. Data provided by The Roper Center for Public Opinion Research, University of Connecticut. [USCSRA,03AMEND.R22]

A national survey of 1,000 adults 18 and over found that a plurality of Americans believe that the media has too much freedom to publish material. This seems to (at least in the abstract) favor more governmental regulation. However, a large percentage also thinks that there is too much governmental censorship. What do you think? Is there too much or too little governmental regulation of the media? What factors do you think might change public opinion either way?

Times v. *Sullivan* (1964), the Supreme Court ruled that publishing a falsehood about a public official did not constitute libel unless that official could demonstrate "actual malice"—meaning that the medium knew that the published information was false or acted recklessly. The *Sullivan* ruling was extended three years later to cover celebrities and athletes. These rulings made it far more difficult for a public official or celebrity to sue for libel. Still, because libel suits are expensive to defend, the media are careful with what they publish, and sometimes they settle out of court to avoid a trial. It is easier for private citizens to sue for libel, because the standards of proof are lower. Therefore, private individuals are much more successful in bringing lawsuits.

The most controversial issues regarding content are concerns about **prior censorship**—the power of the government to prohibit in advance the publication or broadcast of certain material. Because we believe that a free press is the bedrock of a free society, the American courts are very hesitant to allow prior censorship. Instead, our system of government tends to rely on the threat of punishment after publication in order to keep the press in line. As you saw in L I N K *Chapter 5, pages 170–171,* the courts have ruled that prior censorship is only allowed in the most extreme cases. Table 11.5 shows that while most of the American public believes that the press is too free to publish material it deems appropriate, a large segment of the population also believes that too much governmental regulation currently exists.

Section 315 of the Communications Act of 1934 (and its many subsequent amendments) provides the central rules regarding the censorship of the broadcast media. These rules do not apply to

▶ **What is the role** of the FCC?

equal time rule
FCC rule that requires offering equal air-time in the broadcast media for all major candidates competing for a political office.

fairness doctrine
policy that required television and radio broadcasters to provide time for opposing viewpoints on controversial issues so as to ensure fair and balanced reporting; formally abolished in 1987.

print media or the Internet. The act applied only to the broadcast media because it was believed at the time that these media, perceived to be quasi-monopolies, needed more regulation. When the law was written, the print media seemed to be less monopolistic, and hence more open to ordinary people. Although this is no longer true today, the distinction still applies. Furthermore, as noted earlier, in 1934 the airwaves were considered part of the public domain, to be used for the public good—and hence in need of government regulation. Consequently, the print media do not have to comply with these regulations, whereas the broadcast media do.

▶ **What is the role of the FCC?** Regulation of the broadcast media falls to the Federal Communications Commission (FCC), an independent regulatory agency created by the Communications Act of 1934 to "serve the public interest, convenience, and necessity." The bipartisan FCC consists of five commissioners (there were originally seven, but the number was reduced for budgetary reasons). Appointed by the president and confirmed by the Senate, each commissioner serves for five years (formerly seven). Many observers want the FCC to be stronger and more independent, but the president and Congress continue to exert a good deal of influence on their decisions. Following Janet Jackson's "wardrobe malfunction" in 2004, the FCC has begun issuing large fines for infractions. The brunt of its wrath fell on radio personality Howard Stern, who was fined $495,000 on April 8, 2004, for the content of an April 2003 program. Subsequently, Clear Channel, which broadcast Stern's show on six channels, dropped the program.

In addition to privacy and censorship, three other rules exist with respect to television content issues in politics. If a station makes time available to one candidate running for political office, it must make similar time available under similar circumstances for other candidates running for the same office. This is the **equal time rule.** Thus if the Democratic candidate is allowed to purchase 30 seconds of prime-time television to run an advertisement, the Republican candidate for the same office must also be allowed to purchase 30 seconds of prime time at the same price. The station can refuse to sell time to any candidates from any political party (including minor parties) for particular offices, but if it sells to one, it must sell to the others. A related and controversial issue regarding access is participation of minor party candidates in presidential debates. In 2004, the Presidential Commission on Presidential Debates ruled that for candidates to participate in the nationally televised presidential debates, they must be constitutionally eligible to hold the office of president, must be on enough state ballots to give them a mathematical chance of securing a majority vote in the electoral college, and must have the

support of 15 percent of the national electorate as measured by public opinion polls. Given the difficulty of meeting these tests, third-party and independent candidates are generally excluded from the nationally televised debates. The equal time rule does not apply to airtime talk shows and regular newscasts. Hence David Letterman can invite one candidate on his show without inviting the others, and just because one candidate's speech is carried on the 6 o'clock news does not require the network to carry a rival's speech too.

A similar concept is the **fairness doctrine,** which was in effect from 1949 to 1985. The fairness doctrine was much broader than the equal time rule, which applies only to political candidates. Under the fairness doctrine, the broadcast media were required to allow "reasonable positions" to be presented on controversial issues of public interest. Hence we often see or hear news shows that have one person representing one side of the issue and another person speaking for the other side. Although this is not required any longer (partly at the urging of President Ronald Reagan), it is still a commonplace practice.

The final rule regarding issues of content is the right of rebuttal, which mandates that people who are attacked on the radio or TV in a way that could harm their reputation or standing must have the right to rebut the charges. The idea rests on the notion that people who are criticized on the air have the right to present alternative points of view to the public—in effect, to "face their accusers."

In addition to regulating the content, the government also regulates the ownership of the media. Until recently, attempting to keep airwaves diverse, the federal government limited the number of TV or radio stations that one owner could possess in one market. The Telecommunications Act of 1996 deregulated many previous ownership restrictions in an attempt to make broadcast media more competitive and responsive to audience concerns and interests, but this deregulation has been controversial. Opponents fear that the law eliminated the consumer and diversity protections that were present in the Communications Act of 1934. As a result of this change, we are seeing larger and larger mergers, such as Time Warner's acquisition of Turner Broadcasting Company.[48] Even so, one person or entity is still barred from controlling more than 35 percent of network market share and 30 percent of cable market share.[49]

CHALLENGES RELATED TO THE "NEW MEDIA"

▶ **Do media formats such as talk radio blur the line between entertainment and news?** Many issues have accompanied the creation of the so-called new media, featuring media personalities

► **Do media formats such** as talk radio blur the line between entertainment and news?

1. Why is there tension between governmental regulation of the media and the desire for an independent and rigorous press?

2. How does the right to privacy differ for public officials and private individuals? How is the content of the mass media regulated? By whom?

who are engaged in entertainment-oriented mass communication but also venture into political issues. Examples include "tabloid television," talk radio, and television talk shows. Historically, tabloid newspapers—which featured sensational stories and devoted much of their space to entertainment—had a lower standard of corroboration to verify news stories. Hence they were often willing to cover material that the traditional media shunned, such as stories about celebrities' personal issues and scandals.

Historically, the traditional media held themselves to higher ethical and moral standards. However, standards have been changing as the line between tabloid media and traditional media has blurred. One area of dramatic growth is talk radio. In 1998, there were 1,950 talk radio stations, up from only 200 in 1990.[50] There are both positive and negative aspects to the growth of these new media. More outlets allow more opportunities for individuals to express themselves, but many of these outlets are very narrow in scope, and they can be used to unleash hatred. Even talk stations and talk show hosts focused on comedy raise concerns by presenting as facts things that are not true. The programs can make fun of officials in a manner that is not supportive of our governmental system. For example, David Letterman ran a skit in 2004 that presented President George W. Bush as a "lady's man," clearly mocking and demeaning the president. Certainly, in a free society, we have the right to joke about politicians, but it is hard to argue that the prestige of the Oval Office isn't somewhat diminished by making the president the butt of so many jokes. In 1998, for instance, after the Monica Lewinsky scandal broke, someone tabulated 1,712 late-night jokes about Bill Clinton.[51] Critics could argue that through his personal behavior, Clinton had set himself up to be lampooned, but other presidents and public figures are also made fun of with no restraint. Moreover, reflecting their concerns with profits, the networks are increasingly softening the news and devising programming to compete with these new sources of "news" and entertainment. One example is the increased importance placed on celebrity news compared to twenty years ago.

1. It is against the law for a newspaper to publish the name of a rape victim.
   a. true   b. false

2. Sometimes newspapers do not cover a criminal trial in much detail because
   a. readers are generally not interested in such material.

   b. such coverage violates the First Amendment.
   c. in some cases, gag orders prevent participants from discussing the case.
   d. in some cases, gag orders prohibit journalists from covering a case.

3. The Communications Act of 1934 created
   a. the rules by which newspapers, radio, and television can be censored by the government.
   b. the FCC.
   c. the rules constraining the monopolistic accumulation of radio and television stations.
   d. the FTC.

4. Broadcasting regulations require that third-party candidates be included in nationally televised presidential debates if they are constitutionally eligible to be president, are on enough state ballots to have a chance to win a majority of electoral college votes, and polls show that they have the support of at least
   a. 5 percent of the national electorate.
   b. 10 percent of the national electorate.
   c. 15 percent of the national electorate.
   d. 20 percent of the national electorate.

Answers: 1-b, 2-c, 3-b, 4-c.

Conclusion

Although many researchers have examined the power of the media and their impact, the results are mixed. People certainly believe that the media are a powerful force in American politics. So do politicians. Because politicians believe the media are powerful, they may alter their behavior based on how that behavior might be portrayed in the media and received by the public. This belief is potentially a strong check on our leaders' actions. However, it is very hard to measure this potential impact of the media. Moreover, attempting to isolate how the media's portrayal of a candidate specifically influences voters is nearly impossible. Was it the image portrayed by the media or the candidate's qualifications or demeanor that registered in the minds of voters? The same quandary applies to the issues: Do people support an education bill because it was favorably reported in the news, or was it favorably reported because people support it? In light of these questions, establishing causal links is very hard. The complex task of decision making simply has too many alternative variables. Clearly, the power of the media to influence the political agenda is important, for agenda setting affects what people see, think, and talk about. And, as you saw in ⓁⒾⓃⓀ *Chapter 11, pages 437–438*, the media's powers of agenda-setting and issue-framing also have great potential to influence public opinion.

YOUR turn!

The National Society of Newspaper Editors sponsors an annual survey of journalists, paying particular attention to issues of diversity. It found that in 2004, only 13.4 percent of journalists belonged to racial or ethnic minorities. Only 10.5 percent of supervisors in newsrooms were minorities, and 40 percent of daily newspapers had no minority staffers. Women constitute 37.5 percent of journalists, with the number of minority women remaining low. Findings such as these, as well as a general concern about a lack of diversity in newsrooms across the nation, has led to the creation of several organizations that are working to increase the number of minority journalists and also working to ensure fair and accurate news coverage of people of color. One interesting development is the Parity Project, sponsored by the National Association of Hispanic Journalists. The Parity Project has a five-year plan to increase the number and influence of Latino journalists. Latinos make up only 4 percent of newsroom personnel at English-language newspapers and 6 percent of newsroom staffers at English-language television news outlets, despite constituting 14 percent of the country's population. Other efforts include UNITY: Journalists of Color, Inc., as well as efforts by the National Association of Black Journalists.

Several years ago, the editors of the *Daily Princetonian* became troubled by the lack of minority participation on their school newspaper. After attending a national conference of editors from Ivy League schools, they discovered that the problem was not unique to Princeton. They were concerned that a cyclical effect was occurring—because there weren't many African American or Latino reporters, news important to these students was being underreported, leading to an even greater lack of interest among these students. The editors did more than simply discuss this problem—they acted. Richard Just and several former editors decided to organize a weeklong summer camp for African American and Latino high school students who were editors of their school papers or had related interests. In 2002, the *Daily Princetonian* Class of 2001 Summer Journalism Program began with twenty-one high school students in attendance.[52] If these students can make a difference, so can you.

Look at your own local newscasts, as well as your local newspaper. How many of the faces that you see are of people of color? Look at your school newspaper and other university publications. How many minority reporters, columnists, or featured commentators are present? Do the numbers reflect your student body? Contact the editor-in-chief of your school paper and ask what efforts are being made to include more minorities in the paper. Look in your own field of study—how diverse is it? Look to see what university and community resources exist to perhaps create your own experience to target minority students to participate in your field. ▪

Chapter Review

1. The media are a powerful force in American politics, with the ability to influence what people think about and even what they think.

2. The need to balance a free press with government regulations raises many delicate issues. In times of war, we generally side with allowing more government regulations, but even then tension exists.

3. The intimacy and immediacy of television make it exceptionally influential.

4. As the distinction between news and entertainment has blurred, especially on television, programming has changed, causing concern among many observers.

5. The media perform many important social functions, from monitoring the government to interpreting the news to socializing citizens. These functions all come with the potential for a great degree of power and influence and hence responsibility.

6. Candidates, officials, and groups use many tactics to get positive press coverage, which enhances their legitimacy and visibility and may help garner support.

7. One important aspect of the power of the media is in setting the political agenda by serving as gatekeepers. Round-the-clock news stations and the Internet have made it possible for a greater variety of stories to be explored in greater detail.

8. An uneasy relationship between the press and public officials exists. On the one hand, they need each other. On the other, they both want to control the manner in which the news is reported. Officials want to have the news framed

supportively, while the media often look for controversy to generate audience interest.

9. The media are very important in American elections. Earned media coverage, obtained free of charge, is especially important, as Americans believe it to be more trustworthy and objective than paid advertisements. Paid ads are nevertheless important tools to reach the audience. They can be very effective, as they allow candidates to repeat controlled messages in attempts to sway public opinion.

10. The government exercises some regulation of the content and ownership of the media. The main concerns regarding regulation of the content stem from issues of prior restraint, privacy, and issues related to accurate and fair reporting.

CHAPTER REVIEW TEST

1. The media are a particularly significant force in which two pathways of political action?
   a. the grassroots mobilization and court pathways
   b. the lobbying decision-makers and elections pathways
   c. the court and cultural change pathways
   d. the cultural change and election pathways

2. Free media are crucial for a democratic society because
   a. citizens depend on the publication or broadcasting of polling data to know the majority opinions about policy issues.
   b. free media make possible national public debate on important political issues.
   c. without TV, voters would not know how charismatic their potential political leaders are.
   d. politicians' electoral success depends in part on their savvy use of the media.

3. Which statement best summarizes the functions of the media in the United States?
   a. The media entertain, inform, and persuade the public.
   b. The media divide the public and make reality less vivid.
   c. To reach the widest audience and make as much money as possible, the media strive only to entertain the public.
   d. The media primarily inform the public with little concern for profit-making.

4. If different ideas can be expressed to the public without censorship or constraint, they can in theory compete for public acceptance. This theory is called
   a. the libertarian view.
   b. the gatekeeper model.
   c. the marketplace of ideas.
   d. social responsibility theory.

5. In the early decades of the nineteenth century, newspapers in the United States were usually created to support a specific political party or set of economic beliefs.
   a. true   **b.** false

6. As the American newspaper industry became more centralized, news writing became much more objective.
   a. true   **b.** false

7. What makes televised news so powerful?
   a. the fact that it is not censored
   b. its clear difference from entertainment
   c. its unbiased approach
   d. its intimacy and visual nature

8. The broadcast media in all liberal democracies are privately owned.
   a. true   **b.** false

9. What do Murphy Brown's pregnancy and its political aftermath illustrate?
   a. how realistic the television series was
   b. that single women should not get pregnant, especially if they want to have careers
   c. that the line between news and entertainment can become blurred
   d. how trivial television programs can become

10. What would be an example of the surveillance function that the media can play in the realm of American politics?
   a. a television exposé about the mistreatment of undocumented workers at a handful of Wal-Mart stores
   b. television cameramen hiding outside a candidate's house waiting to document illicit late-night comings and goings
   c. a radio news program that makes use of secretly recorded phone calls between a criminal suspect and his or her lawyer
   d. a long newspaper article putting a politician's career in historical context after she has died

11. Rush Limbaugh is an example of
   a. a political liberal whose popularity suggests the left-leaning tendency of the media.
   b. someone who has been censored by the FCC.
   c. an enormously popular conservative commentator who has emphasized the liberal bias of mainstream media.
   d. someone who has moved from public office to broadcast journalism.

12. Only since about 1950 have politicians in this country used the media for political purposes.
   a. true   **b.** false

13. What best describes the interrelationship of the public, the government, and the media?
- **a.** The government influences the media, which influence the public.
- **b.** The public influences the government, which influences the media.
- **c.** The media influence the government, which influences the public.
- **d.** Each of the three influences the others and is influenced by the others.

14. Who was the first president to discern and make effective use of the power of the media?
- **a.** Abraham Lincoln
- **b.** William McKinley
- **c.** Theodore Roosevelt
- **d.** John Kennedy

15. Why is it wise to approach leaked news stories with some skepticism?
- **a.** because they are usually not true
- **b.** because the leaker sometimes presents the information in an incomplete and self-serving way
- **c.** because leaking information is illegal
- **d.** because most people who leak secrets they are entrusted to keep aren't trustworthy

16. Which branch of government gets covered least by the media?
- **a.** the judicial branch
- **b.** the legislative branch
- **c.** the executive branch
- **d.** All branches are covered about equally.

17. Issue advocacy advertising is an example of
- **a.** how work in the elections pathway uses the media.
- **b.** how interest groups use the media.
- **c.** the fairness doctrine in action.
- **d.** muckraking.

18. How do newspapers in effect worsen the political disengagement of poor people?
- **a.** by routinely endorsing candidates whose agendas disadvantage them
- **b.** by circulation policies that exclude poor neighborhoods, keeping poor residents ignorant about national affairs
- **c.** by using inflated language that only college-educated readers can easily understand
- **d.** by not covering many stories involving the poor because most people with lower incomes cannot afford to subscribe to newspapers

19. What is cross-media ownership?
- **a.** owning one kind of media outlet, such as a radio station; selling it; and then buying another kind of media outlet, such as a newspaper
- **b.** owning all or nearly all of one kind of media outlet
- **c.** owning a variety of media outlets simultaneously
- **d.** the running of a media-owning corporation by a diverse group of individuals

20. Scholarly studies suggest that the effects of the media on American politics are clear and can be described statistically.
- **a.** true
- **b.** false

Answers: 1: d; 2: b; 3: a; 4: c; 5: b; 6: b; 7: d; 8: b; 9: c; 10: a; 11: c; 12: b; 13: d; 14: c; 15: b; 16: a; 17: b; 18: d; 19: c; 20: b.

DISCUSSION QUESTIONS

1. Are the media as powerful as many people believe? What are the functions of the media in our society?

2. A delicate balance exists between the government's need to regulate the media (fueled by the public's desire for regulation) and the ability of the media to remain independent. How have the two been balanced? Do you agree with the balance, or do you think more or less regulation is needed?

3. What do we mean when we say that the media control the public agenda? Why is gatekeeping an important power? How is this changing with advances in technology?

4. Why is the ability to frame issues and images a significant power? How politically influential do you think the media are?

5. Are candidates and groups able to manipulate the press? What is the difference between earned and paid media? What are the uses for each?

6. What does the expression "marketplace of ideas" mean? How is this marketplace potentially affected by the trend toward concentration of media ownership?

7. What are the rules regarding governmental regulation of content and ownership? Do you think these rules go too far or not far enough, and why?

8. Why are there different rules and standards for the broadcast and print media? Should the same rules and standards apply today?

INTERNET RESOURCES

Accuracy in Media: **http://www.aim.org**

American Museum of Image: **http://livingroomcandidate.movingimage.us/index.php**

Black Entertainment Television: **http://www.bet.com**

British Broadcasting Company: **http://www.bbc.co.uk**

CNN: **http://www.cnn.com**

C-SPAN: **http://www.cspan.org/campaign2000/advertising.asp**

Drudge Report: **http://www.drudgereport.com**

Early Radio History: **http://earlyradiohistory.us/index.html**

Fox News: **http://www.foxnews.com**

Freedom Forum: **http://www.freedomforum.org**

New York Times: **http://www.nytimes.com**

Pew Center for Civic Journalism: **http://www.pewcenter.org**

Take Back the Media: **http://www.takebackthemedia.com**

Univision: **http://www.univision.com**

Washington Post: **http://www.washingtonpost.com**

ADDITIONAL READING

Beasley, Maurine Hoffman. *First Ladies and the Press: The Unfinished Partnership of the Media Age.* Evanston, IL: Northwestern University Press, 2005.

Carruthers, Susan L. *The Media at War: Communication and Conflict in the Twentieth Century.* New York: St. Martin's Press, 2000.

Corner, John, and Dick Pels, eds. *Media and the Restyling of Politics: Consumerism, Celebrity, and Cynicism.* Thousand Oaks, CA: Sage, 2003.

Davis, Richard. *The Press and American Politics.* Upper Saddle River, NJ: Prentice Hall, 2001.

Entman, Robert M., and Andrew Rojecki. *The Black Image in the White Mind: Media and Race in America.* Chicago: University of Chicago Press, 2001.

Farnsworth, Stephen, and S. Robert Lichter. *The Mediated Presidency: Television News and Presidential Governance.* Lanham, MD: Rowman & Littlefield, 2006.

Friedman, Thomas. *The Lexus and the Olive Tree: Understanding Globalization.* New York: Anchor Books, 2000.

Gilens, Martin. *Why Americans Hate Welfare: Race, Media, and the Politics of Antipoverty Policy.* Chicago: University of Chicago Press, 1999.

Graber, Doris A. *Mass Media and American Politics* (7th ed.). Washington, DC: CQ Press, 2005.

Leighley, Jan E. *Mass Media and Politics: A Social Science Perspective.* Boston: Houghton Mifflin, 2004.

Paletz, David L. *The Media in American Politics: Contents and Consequences* (2nd ed.). New York: Longman, 2002.

Postman, Neil. *Amusing Ourselves to Death: Public Discourse in the Age of Show Business.* New York: Penguin Books, 1986.

Tumber, Howard. *Media at War: The Iraq Crisis.* Thousand Oaks, CA: Sage, 2004.

KEY TERMS

agenda setting   436

competitive news markets   447

digital divide/technology gap   427

earned media coverage   436

equal time rule   450

fairness doctrine   450

gatekeepers   436

investigative reporting   433

libel   448

libertarian view   430

marketplace of ideas   420

mass medium   422

muckraking   433

news briefing   438

news conference   438

news monopoly   447

party presses   422

penny press   423

press release   438

prior censorship   448

pseudo-events   436

**social responsibility theory/
   public advocate model**   430

sound bite   444

yellow journalism   424

Freedom of speech, press and the right to assemble are precious liberties cherished by Americans. They are fundamentally important for our democratic way of life. Here demonstrators are protesting the World Trade Organization (WTO) Summit in 1999. Marching, protesting, and joining social movements are important ways to express concerns. Our "do something" spirit goes back to the earliest days of our republic.

CHAPTER 12

CIVIC AND POLITICAL ENGAGEMENT

Citizens in Action, Rocking the Vote Rock the Vote seeks to politically motivate young adults. Founded in 1990, this nonpartisan, nonprofit group engages youth in the political process all year round. It encourages voter registration (in many states you can register to vote online from the organization's Web page at http://www.rockthevote.org), get-out-the-vote drives, and voter education campaigns. In 1992, Rock the Vote and its partner organizations registered 350,000 young people and helped motivate more than 2 million new young voters, ending a two-decade decline in voter participation and achieving a 20 percent increase in youth turnout. The next year, it worked aggressively to help enact the National Voter Registration Reform Act, better known as the Motor Voter Law. It developed the first program to register voters by telephone in 1996 and organized the first Web site to provide online voter registration, NetVote '96.

In 2004, Rock the Vote showed up in strength at the Democratic National Convention in Boston to make the point that young people do have a voice and need to make themselves heard by voting. The major focus of the group is getting Americans, young and old to register to vote. In the same year that the group came to the Boston convention, they registered 1.4 million new voters.

That same year, it distributed 200,000 copies of a free nonpartisan voter guide to young people.

Mission: "Rock the Vote is dedicated to protecting freedom of expression and empowering young people to change their world."

In the past few years, Rock the Vote's efforts have broadened to encourage year-round political activism. In 1999, it created a series of public service announcements highlighting youth who are active in their communities, as well as a guide to political activism, "Use Your Power to Rock the Vote Every Day," distributed through music stores and schools. In 2001, Rock the Vote launched a program of "street teams" that work in communities across the country by coordinating get-out-the-vote drives that distribute literature and voter registration cards at concerts, festivals, sporting events, high school graduations, and college orientations. Street teams also serve as a form of peer mentoring, having young people train one another to be activists. In 2001, for example, 120 young people served as street team volunteers, contributing more than 3,000 hours and collecting 31,565 signatures on a hate-crime petition.

Rock the Vote has recently focused on discrimination and intolerance, working with MTV in a campaign called "Fight for Your Rights: Take a Stand against Discrimination." The organization provides grassroots support and is working with the Los Angeles County Commission for Human Relations to develop a public education campaign to fight bigotry. Members help teach

young people interpersonal skills, cultural sensitivity, and peace-keeping skills. Rock the Vote has successfully registered and brought to the polls hundreds of thousands of young people. By coordinating its efforts with a multitude of celebrities, actors, comedians, and musicians; by forging alliances with other groups (even joining forces with AARP for a Rock the Ages campaign); and by working with MTV and other media outlets, Rock the Vote has motivated youth across the country to take advantage of their right to vote and to be heard. In 2004, the group registered 1.4 million new voters (1.2 million online, 200,000 by their Rock the Vote bus tour), marking a large surge in young-voter participation.

In 2006, Rock the Vote continued their efforts to get young people engaged in politics and to vote. They launched a cutting-edge voter registration drive by partnering with Facebook and Young Voter Strategies. Rock the Vote created a highly interactive Facebook group that first focused on registering young people to vote, and then to promote turnout. As of October 31, 2006, there were 14,620 members with 62 different discussion topics—a noteworthy accomplishment in only one month's time. In addition, the Why Vote campaign allows individuals to tell the world why they will vote in the 2006 midterm elections. Interested parties can easily upload a short video clip to the group's web page.

Rock the Vote received funding for these endeavors from Young Voter Strategies, an organization that works to get young people more engaged in politics. They collaborated with 15 orga-nizations and have been able to register 400,000 young voters themselves in 2006.

Over 1 million new members and supporters have joined Rock the Vote to help this generation of young Americans find their voice and influence their world.

As Margaret Mead (right) said, "Never doubt that a small group of thoughtful committed citizens can change the world; indeed it's the only thing that ever has."

▶ **What makes group activity such an important element of a democratic system?**

America is an amazing country. We claim as our birthright some of the most profound liberties and freedoms. Our Bill of Rights establishes some of the most cherished liberties—freedom of speech, religion, press, and assembly, to name only a few. As a result, we have the unrivaled ability to influence our government and our fellow citizens. We have the freedom to speak our minds, to express our most controversial and complex thoughts—thoughts that might be unpopular or even unreasonable, but still ideas that can be presented in public and can compete for acceptance. Furthermore, we have constitutionally guaranteed liberties that allow us to appeal to our government to address our concerns and issues. Many avenues exist to express our freedoms and influence other citizens. Using group action has a distinctive appeal to Americans, for whom the tradition of group activity is deeply ingrained in our national political culture.

Grassroots mobilization and interest group activities are very important for democracy. One key element in the democratic balance is the influence of the masses versus the elites in decision making. For democracy to function and to thrive, there must be a collective sense of community: People must feel tied to each other and united with their government, whether or not they agree with its actions. The linkage of people and government is crucial for democratic rule, and organized groups and citizen engagement forge an important aspect of it.

Organized interests prompt leaders to "do something"—to address pressing problems in society, thus activating the "safety valve" that we discussed in ⓁⓘⓝⓀ *Chapter 1 page 6.* Without organized interests, many issues would be overlooked and problems would grow. Race rioting in the 1960s is clear evidence of anger bred from the frustration of African Americans at being marginalized and disregarded by white society. Years of discrimination and bigotry yielded frustration and rage—which had no structured outlet. By ignoring the racism that was evident in the United States, Americans created a situation that at last exploded violently.[1] Pressure from organized interests serves to hold governing officials accountable by forcing them to pay attention to issues that are important to the people. Involvement also fosters the acquisition of attributes important to democracy—tolerance, political efficacy, and political trust. Groups help teach citizens a sense of social integration and interaction. Joining with others outside our primary relationships (families) is fundamental to political activity. Being civically engaged allows people to develop associations and skills that are essential for healthy democratic communities.

In this chapter and the next, we will examine people and groups working to change our society, our laws, and our culture. We will briefly trace the history of activism, protest, and mass movements in the United States, paying close attention to changes evident today. Next, we will study the role of interest groups in our society and how people are mobilized to participate and the specific tactics organized groups use to persuade others to support their cause and adopt their policy preferences. Later chapters will teach you the rules and the tactics to make a difference—the pathway to change your lives and your community. Grassroots mobilization is an important pathway to influence our society, our government, and our social structures.

Key Questions

1. How do citizens influence our government and our society through organized action?

2. Why is it important that we understand the historical roots of activism and protest? What can the past teach us about the present?

3. What constitutional foundations allow citizens to petition their government?

4. What components of our government help citizens organize, and what factors make organization more difficult?

5. How do organized groups influence democratic developments and practices? What positive and negative functions does civic and political engagement play in our society?

6. How much support exists for allowing people with whom we may politically disagree to have access to the public and to petition the government for action?

▶ **What makes group activity** such an important element of a democratic system?

what YOU can do!

Think about an issue that is important to you. Using the issue as the key topic, do a search on the Web. How many organizations can you find that take a stand, one way or another, on your issue? Is there evidence that Tocqueville's observation that we are a nation of joiners is still apt in describing Americans today?

▶ **Has freedom of association** always been an important part of American political culture?

7. Can we find a balance between pursuing self-interest and promoting the public good? What should we do when the two come into conflict?
8. Is there a crisis in civic engagement?
9. What are the consequences of civic engagement?

Activism and Protest in the United States: A Brief History

While traveling throughout the United States in 1831 and 1832 and studying its society, Alexis de Tocqueville, a young Frenchman, noted that group activities were essential for the development and maintenance of democracy. In his words, "I confess that in America I saw more than America; I sought the image of democracy itself, with its inclinations, its character, its prejudices, and its passions, in order to learn what we have to fear or to hope from its progress."[2] His journey resulted in the book *Democracy in America,* originally published in 1835. Tocqueville's book is still widely read and cited today. Tocqueville was only 25 years old when he came to America to observe our democracy, yet his account of our society is one of the most perceptive ever published.[3]

▶ **Has freedom of association always been an important part of American political culture?** Tocqueville valued personal liberty, and he spent a good deal of time examining Americans' practice of freedom of association and political participation. Compared to Europeans of his time, he noted, Americans had a much stronger tendency to join together to solve problems, to articulate collective interests, and to form social relationships. He asserted that people living in democratic nations must join together to preserve their independence and freedoms. Coming together to help others is one of the binding factors in an otherwise complex and alien environment. Tocqueville noted that the right of association, once recognized, is employed in three vital ways. He observed, in the first place, that Americans used civic engagement to promote certain doctrines or beliefs. By working together in collective organizations to bring about change, people can advance their values. Second, noted Tocqueville, the true power of association is the power of coming together with like-minded people; by coming together, people with little influence individually could act with greater strength. The ability to meet to establish a center of action is also fundamental, for without coordination, the association would not succeed. And third, Tocqueville pointed out, the freedom of association allowed for "partisans of an opinion" to unite in the electoral arena:

DE TOCQUEVILLE.

Alexis Henry de Tocqueville (1805–1859), French writer and commentator, traveled across our country in 1831–1832 to observe our country. His account, *Democracy in America,* is still widely read and cited today. Why do you think this twenty-six year old was so able to characterize the nature of our democracy? Do you think you must be an outsider to best understand a country?

The liberty of association has become a necessary guarantee against the tyranny of the majority. . . . There are no countries in which associations are more needed, to prevent the despotism of faction or the arbitrary power of the prince, than those which are democratically constituted. . . . The most natural privilege of man, next to the right of acting for himself, is that of combining his exertions with those of his fellow-creatures, and of acting in common with them. I am therefore led to conclude that the right of association is almost as inalienable as the right of personal liberty.[4]

As Tocqueville showed, the right to associate and to be active in public affairs is one of the most fundamental rights on which participatory democracy depends. Citizen participation must not simply be limited to voting—though voting is a minimum participatory

▶ **I never knew violent**
protest was so common in
colonial America! Is violence
still a common tactic among
politically motivated groups?

The BLOODY MASSACRE perpetrated in King — Street BOSTON on March 5th 1770 by a party of the 29th REGt.

Engrav'd Printed & Sold by PAUL REVERE BOSTON

Unhappy Boston! see thy Sons deplore,
Thy hallow'd Walks besmear'd with guiltless Gore:
While faithless P—n and his savage Bands,
With murd'rous Rancour stretch their bloody Hands;
Like fierce Barbarians grinning o'er their Prey,
Approve the Carnage and enjoy the Day.

If scalding drops from Rage from Anguish Wrung,
If speechless Sorrows lab'ring for a Tongue,
Or if a weeping World can ought appease
The plaintive Ghosts of Victims such as these:
The Patriot's copious Tears for each are shed,
A glorious Tribute which embalms the Dead

But know Fate summons to that awful Goal.
Where Justice strips the Murd'rer of his Soul:
Should venal C—ts the scandal of the Land.
Snatch the relentless Villain from her Hand,
Keen Execrations on this Plate inscrib'd,
Shall reach a Judge who never can be brib'd.

The unhappy Sufferers were Messrs. Sam. Gray, Sam. Maverick, Jam. Caldwell, Crispus Attucks & Pat. Carr
Killed. Six wounded; two of them (Christr. Monk & John Clark) Mortally

Protests in colonial America were increasingly popular, especially in the years immediately preceding the Revolutionary War. Pictured above is a copy of a print by Paul Revere depicting British troops shooting at a crowd of protesters (coined the Boston Massacre). Five civilians died. The event became a rallying cry to build support for independence. Are you surprised to learn that the colonists turned to protest with such frequency? Do you think the act of protesting itself helped solidify support for the revolution?

requirement. To live in a free society, citizens must have the right of association to petition their government to address their grievances and concerns. Such an understanding of the functioning of collective action in democracies goes back to the infancy of our country. The importance of citizen participation is even greater today because our society has grown far more complex, diverse, and technological, with intimate ties to the global community.

Activism is at the root of our "do something" political culture, and forming groups is essential for political action. Throughout our history, groups have emerged to challenge the status quo—and opposition groups have emerged to fight to preserve the status quo. Our main purpose in the following sections is to illustrate the validity of Tocqueville's observations about the importance of group action in the United States to promote change and enhance liberty, as well as to provide a context for analyzing contemporary group behavior. This pathway is fundamentally important in shaping the very nature and definition of our democracy.

PROTEST IN COLONIAL AMERICA

▶ **I never knew violent protest was so common in colonial America! Is violence still a common tactic among politically motivated groups?** Brutal rioting was fairly common in colonial America. Early rioting often focused on protecting communities against outside intervention and maintaining community morality. A typical eighteenth-century American riot involved fifty to a hundred men armed with clubs. Rioters came from both upper and lower classes, often disguised themselves, and typically focused their anger on the destruction of property—a house or jail, for example. In 1666, people in Brookhaven, New York, assaulted a constable collecting taxes. In 1705, Bostonians rioted when a prominent local man's adulterous affair became public. Because the man belonged to the elite, community complaints were ignored until a crowd rioted outside his lover's house while the offender was "visiting." Two years later, when local soldiers returned home from an abortive invasion of Canada, women rioted in Boston, calling them cowards and throwing chamber pots at them. And 500 people rioted in Boston in 1737, tearing down two regulated markets.[5] The common thread that tied together virtually every riot in America until 1765 was their origin in the defense of some community interest—rescuing a neighbor from a greedy landlord, embarrassing an adulterer, harassing a customs officer, or closing a brothel.

In moving toward revolution in the 1760s, colonial Americans increasingly used violence to express their outrage at British

▶ **Where did the idea** of a "right to revolt" originate?

John Locke, Concerning Civil Government, 1693 second essay, Ch.19	Thomas Jefferson [Plagiarist], Declaration of Independence, 1776
Secondly: I answer, such revolutions happen not upon every little mismanagement in public affairs. Great mistakes in the ruling part, many wrong and inconvenient laws, and all the slips of human frailty will be borne by the people without mutiny or murmur. But if a long train of abuses, prevarications, and artifices, all tending the same way, make the design visible to the people, and they cannot but feel what they lie under, and see whither they are going, it is not to be wondered that they should then rouse themselves, and endeavor to put the rule into such hands which may secure to them the end for which government was at first erected...	Prudence, indeed, will dictate that Governments long established should not be changed for light and transient causes; and accordingly all experience hath shown, that mankind are more disposed to suffer, while evils are sufferable, than to right themselves by abolishing the forms to which they are accustomed. But when a long train of abuses and usurpations, pursuing invariable the same Object evinces a design to reduce them under absolute Despotism, it is their right, it is their duty, to throw off such Government, and to provide new Guards for their future security.

FIGURE 12.1

Two Views of Revolution

Thomas Jefferson and John Locke, both of whom had great impact upon the structure of our constitutional system, argue that the people have the right to revolt against the government after considerable thought and debate—and only when absolutely necessary. How might their arguments change if they were alive today?

SOURCE: www.anesi.com

encroachments on their rights. Before 1765, colonists routinely rioted, but no more frequently than the British themselves. But in 1765, an epidemic of colonial rioting began; over the next four years, there were approximately 150 violent outbreaks in the colonies.[6] Why? One reason is that the colonists were protesting British actions, but the violence also stemmed from social changes. Rapid growth in population and economic strain stressed communities, making for volatile circumstances. In the years immediately preceding the American Revolution, colonists became increasingly radicalized and willing to express their anger with violent mobilization.

One example of this turn toward a violent expression of grievances occurred after Parliament enacted the Stamp Act in 1765. Great Britain introduced the act to provide for internal taxation—what the colonists decried as "taxation without representation." No one anticipated the violent reaction. The first outbreak came when a Massachusetts mob mobilized against a stamp agent named Andrew Oliver. At least sixty riots broke out in more than twenty-five places to protest the Stamp Act between August 1765 and May 1766, when it was repealed.[7] The success of this protest emboldened Americans, inducing them to turn to mass mobilization and violent protest more readily and with greater expectations—for example, in outbreaks that protested the Townshend Act of 1767 and the Tea

Act of 1773. For colonial leaders, tension arose between supporting collective protest actions and trying to rein in the mobs in an effort to augment these leaders' local influence and to ensure public safety.

THE RIGHT TO REVOLT

▶ **Where did the idea of a "right to revolt" originate?** One central idea underlying our political system is our belief in self-government and citizen action. At the end of the seventeenth century, the English philosopher John Locke argued that people have certain God-given, or natural, rights that are inalienable—meaning that they can neither be taken away by nor surrendered to a government (Ⓛ Ⓘ Ⓝ Ⓚ *Chapter 2, pages 45–51*). Locke's social contract theory holds that people set up governments for the very specific purpose of protecting natural rights. All legitimate political authority, said Locke, exists to preserve these natural rights and rests on the consent of the governed. When a ruler acts against the purposes for which government exists, the people have the right to resist and remove the offending ruler. Thomas Jefferson relied on Locke's social contract theory of government when writing the Declaration of Independence (see Fig. 12.1): The central premise of the Declaration is that people have a right to revolt when they

egalitarianism
doctrine of equality that ignores differences in social status, wealth, and privilege.

discussionquestions

1. What is meant by the "right to revolt"? What do you think Jefferson meant when he commented that a little rebellion was necessary from time to time to preserve liberty? Why are the rights of association and petition important in a free society?

2. What is meant by the expression "a nation of joiners"? Do you think we are still a nation of joiners? Why or why not?

Pictured above is the original draft of Thomas Jefferson's Declaration of Independence. The document was not only written to declare independence from England, but was also intended to persuade those who were not convinced that independence was the wise and appropriate path. When Thomas Jefferson wrote, "all men are created equal" he was articulating a very specific view of egalitarianism. However, many think the words ring hollow as he and many of the other founders were slave owners. How can one declare that all men are created equal in a society that allows one human being to own another? Do you think such criticism is fair? Why or why not?

determine that their government has denied them their legitimate rights. The king of England's actions in imposing taxation without representation, according to the Declaration, were evidence of this denial of rights.

One consequence of the Revolution was that faith in mobs and rioting, as well as in self-rule, became entrenched in the new United States. Rioting and mass mobilization had proved an effective tool to resist oppressive government. When Jefferson heard about Shays's Rebellion (LINK *Chapter 2, pages 55–56*), an uprising in Massachusetts against high taxes and severe economic distress in 1786–1787, he remarked that a little rebellion every once in a while was healthy to curb the powers of the government and to ensure that personal liberty would be preserved. The Revolution also helped establish in the United States the sense of **egalitarianism**—the belief that all people are equal. Our republican form of government, in which government rests in the hands of the people, reinforces this egalitarianism. A faith in the legitimacy of collective action, even violent action, in defense of liberty entered into our political culture.

practicequiz

1. According to Tocqueville, civic engagement serves all of the following purposes except
   a. promoting and transferring shared values and beliefs.
   b. strengthening the ability of isolated individuals and groups to come together for collective action.
   c. allowing for like-minded individuals to unite to influence the electoral arena.
   d. allowing for tyranny of the majority to develop and thrive.

2. Eighteenth-century riots were usually aimed toward what end?
   a. to harass minority groups
   b. to redistribute wealth from the rich to the poor
   c. to defend community moral standards or protect local economic interests
   d. to keep foreigners out of the community

3. What is one reason the colonists increasingly turned to violence in the years immediately preceding the Revolution?
   a. to protest unfair housing regulations
   b. to react to strain caused by population growth and economic uncertainty
   c. to protest religious oppression
   d. to react to military draft procedures

4. Rioting in early colonial times was
   a. uncommon and usually unsuccessful.
   b. fairly common and usually futile.
   c. fairly uncommon but often successful, and usually expressed a charismatic individual's desires.
   d. fairly common and often successful, and usually defended a community's interest.

Answers: 1-d, 2-c, 3-b, 4-d.

Influencing the Government through Mobilization and Participation

Perhaps the most significant consequence of the American Revolution, beyond the obvious winning of independence, was the fact that the unleashed American democracy promoted a basic sense of egalitarianism and collective action. This sense of equality, absent from eighteenth-century Europe with its rigid social hierarchies, dramatically shaped attitudes toward participation and public life in the United States.

A second consequence of the Revolution is that our government was designed as a "how-to" system. Our founders were interested in making government function so that the people could control key elements of political power; hence there is an emphasis in our system on bargaining, compromise, and consensus building. We expect our government to listen to our preferences, and we expect to be influential. We acknowledge—or should acknowledge—that we can't always win, but we do expect government to allow us to be heard.

Organized groups provide one mechanism to petition our government. Groups are at the center of our democratic political system—and always have been. Imagine that a developer wanted to build a large factory just outside your neighborhood. You begin to worry about increased traffic, environmental impacts, and decreased property values. What would you do? Most likely you would form an association to address your problem, gathering neighbors who share your concerns and petitioning your city council and zoning commission.

How do we allow citizens to pursue their self-interest while protecting society's interest as well? Balancing these often competing desires is difficult. The example of the neighborhood group organizing to prevent the factory from opening illustrates the dilemma. The neighborhood is probably rational in its concerns. Factories do alter traffic patterns, affect the local ecosystem, and lower property values. But factories also employ people who might desperately need the work, and they pay taxes that can benefit the entire community. How does the community navigate between the needs of local homeowners and the needs of the larger community? Who should win—homeowners or unemployed people in need of jobs? It is a difficult question, underscoring a central dilemma of government.

CONSTITUTIONAL GUARANTEES FOR CITIZEN ACTIVISM AND MOBILIZATION

The United States Constitution provides substantial guarantees that allow for citizen participation, activism, and mass mobilization. For example, the Bill of Rights lists liberties that together ensure our right to petition the government. First Amendment freedoms are fundamental in our democracy because they dramatically determine how we can influence our world, including our fellow citizens and leaders.

In totalitarian systems, lobbying, activism, protest, and other forms of political engagement among citizens are always severely limited—indeed, they are usually forbidden and harshly punished (see Figure 12.2). One vivid illustration of this occurred in June 1989, in Beijing, China, when thousands of pro-democracy students gathered in Tiananmen Square to protest political oppression. The world watched in horror as the Chinese government massacred several thousand young pro-democracy protesters on live television. These students were demonstrating their desire for rights that all Americans enjoy but that many fail to appreciate. In the United States, we generally have vast freedom of expression,

discussion questions

1. What does it mean to say that we have a "how-to" government? How did this mentality develop in the United States? Do you think the perceptions are the same today as they were in colonial times? Why or why not?

2. What are the positive and negative aspects of organized groups in politics? Which do you think better characterizes the current situation in the United States?

FIGURE 12.2

Events in Tiananmen Square

To examine the 1989 crackdown on protestors in Beijing, American and Chinese researchers turned to Google to find images of what happened. They were shown two very different versions, due to the suppression of free speech on the Chinese version of Google.

One Search Subject, Two Results: Tiananmen Square

WHAT CHINESE SEARCHERS SEE The first five results on the Chinese version of Google Images, and dozens after them, largely concern tourism.

WHAT AMERICAN SEARCHERS SEE The first five results on Google Images in the United States show the solitary protester in the path of a tank column during the 1989 crackdown.

June 1989, The New York Times

encompassing the freedoms of speech, religion, assembly, petition, and press. When we discuss freedom of expression (see LINK *Chapter 5, pages 161–168*), we generally mean the broader concept of freedom to communicate. This freedom to communicate is the right of a citizen to convey his or her thoughts—verbally, visually, or in writing—without prior restraint.[8]

practice quiz

1. The belief in egalitarianism and collective action that the Revolution spurred dramatically shaped public life in the new country, making it radically different from European societies.
   a. true   **b.** false

2. What does it mean that our government was designed as a "how-to" system?
   a. The Constitution makes it clear which branch of government should do what and how it should do it.
   b. The Constitution explains how the government should work and how it can be changed if it is not working.
   c. With its emphasis on compromise and consensus building, the Constitution ensures that the people, not the elites, control key elements of political power.
   d. The Constitution operates as a blueprint or owner's manual; any group of people can make our government work.

3. When an individual's self-interest is at odds with society's interest,
   a. the Bill of Rights grants the individual the upper hand.
   b. the interest most effectively lobbied for usually wins out—and should.
   c. society's interest should usually win out, since it represents the greater good.
   d. this conflict always presents a difficult balancing act for our society and government.

4. When we discuss a U.S. citizen's freedom of expression, that freedom includes the freedom of assembly.
   a. true   **b.** false

Answers: 1-a, 2-c, 3-d, 4-a.

Early Social Movements: The First National Groups Emerge, 1830s–1890

The study of American activism is fascinating. By looking into the past, we can learn about the present. An examination of group activity reveals how people viewed the problems of their time, how they

what YOU can do!

Examine the policies at your university regarding the procedures that individuals or groups must follow to plan an organized protest. How difficult or easy would it be to plan a demonstration at your college? What factors do you think lead some universities to limit the ability of students to organize, petition, and protest, while other universities in the same region allow broader access to these same rights?

abolition
the prohibition of slavery.

expected to be heard (or unheard), and how they interacted with their era's social institutions. We will also see how social movements are often interrelated, one leading into the next. As people share experiences in one setting, it often becomes evident that they share experiences and concerns in another. For instance, many of the earliest suffragists first started their political activities in the abolitionist movement. While working to end slavery, women realized that they were being discriminated against because of their gender. They were often prohibited from speaking, and when they were allowed to speak, their words often fell on deaf ears, as many people thought women incapable of rational thought or of making articulate points. As society changes, we often recognize the need for additional change. Moreover, activists in one movement train activists for another by providing the skills to organize, the desire to transform communities and societies, and the self-confidence to get involved.

THE ABOLITIONIST MOVEMENT

The American Anti-Slavery Society was one of the first national political action groups in the United States. Founded by William Lloyd Garrison and Arthur Tappan in 1833, the society became a central organization in the campaign for **abolition**—an end to slavery in America. It sought an immediate, rather than gradual, end to slavery, using state and local auxiliaries. By 1840, there were 2,000 auxiliaries with 150,000 members. The society sponsored meetings, delivered petitions to Congress, published newspapers and other propaganda, and dispatched lecturers into communities. In 1836 alone, seventy lecturers were sent around the northern states.[9] State laws in the South forbade antislavery advocacy, and in the North, the antislavery message was often received with violence and rioting when the society tried to hold meetings. The American Anti-Slavery Society disbanded in 1870 after the formal ratification of the Civil War amendments (the Thirteenth Amendment ending slavery, the Fourteenth Amendment guaranteeing citizenship and civil rights to former slaves, and the Fifteenth Amendment giving freed male slaves the right to vote).

As is the case in most protest movements, disagreements arose regarding appropriate tactics—tension often develops particularly over the choice to advocate violent or nonviolent resistance, and that was true of the abolitionist movement. On the one side were those who advocated nonviolence—most notably the Garrisonians. Garrison was a radical opponent of slavery, but he

stressed nonviolence and passive resistance. In contrast, a small group of abolitionists advocated violent resistance, often viewing the pacifists as cowards. John Brown of Kansas was one of the first white abolitionists to advocate violent resistance. He led others in numerous raids to free slaves forcibly. Reacting to violent acts committed by proslavery forces in Kansas, he led a group of abolitionists to kill five proslavery settlers there in 1856 in what is known as the Pottawatomie Massacre. In 1859, he led a group of men in a raid on a federal armory in Harpers Ferry, Virginia (now West Virginia). He wanted to seize weapons to arm local slaves to start a revolution. He was unsuccessful and was captured by federal troops led by Robert E. Lee. Two months later, he was tried, convicted of treason, and hanged. Although many Americans condemned Brown's tactics, some saw him as a heroic crusader. His example represents one avenue of civic engagement, albeit a controversial one.

pathways profile
FREDERICK DOUGLASS

Frederick Douglass, born Frederick Augustus Washington Bailey in 1818, became one of the most prominent human rights leaders of the nineteenth century. Fathered by a white slave owner, Douglass was separated from his slave mother as an infant, and until he was 8 he lived with his grandmother on a Maryland plantation. Then he was sent to be a house servant in Baltimore. There, the wife of his master defied state law by teaching Frederick to read. But upon the death of his owner, he was sent back to the plantation to work in the fields.

He escaped to freedom in 1838, living in New York and Massachusetts and changing his surname to Douglass to evade fugitive-slave hunters. Shortly he married Anna Murry, with whom he eventually had five children. At an antislavery meeting in 1841 in Nantucket, Massachusetts, Douglass was asked to describe his experiences with slavery. In a remarkably poignant talk, Douglass explained the horror of slavery, thereby launching a career with the abolition movement in which he traveled the country to give speeches and arouse audiences. Despite frequent insults and physical attacks, Douglass worked tirelessly to end slavery. His autobiography, *The Narrative of the Life of Frederick Douglass, an American Slave,* (1845)is one of the most important works of his time.

▶ **What changes did early** feminists work to accomplish?

Underground Railroad
network of people and secret routes prior to the Civil War by which slaves escaped to freedom in Canada, Mexico, and free states in the United States.

feminism
a social and political movement that advocates the belief in the inherent equality of women and men.

Impressive and powerful speaker, Frederick Douglass (1817-1898) was one of the principal leaders in the abolitionist movement. Born into slavery, Douglass traveled the world to speak about the horror and injustice of slavery. During the Civil War, Douglass served as an advisor to President Lincoln. His legacy as a powerful crusader for human rights serves testament to the brilliance of this remarkable man.

After a hugely successful tour of the British Isles that generated international interest in the American abolitionist movement and earned Douglass an impressive international reputation, two English friends raised enough money to buy Douglass's freedom. Although the threat of capture had been a significant concern to Douglass, especially after the publication of his autobiography, in which he revealed his true name, he did not believe that his former master had the right to own him and therefore be paid for his freedom. Several abolitionists criticized Douglass on this point, but the master got his money, whereupon Douglass proclaimed that now that his kidnapper had collected his ransom, Douglass was free to travel the country to vigorously fight slavery without fear of capture. Douglass began to publish an antislavery newspaper, the *North Star,* one of the first black-oriented American publications. While he originally sided with his close friend, William Lloyd Garrison, regarding the need to refuse all compromise and oppose the Constitution and the system it tolerated, he gradually began to see the virtue of working within the system to advocate change. He also began to question Garrison's pacifist approach, wondering if violent resistance was always morally wrong. In 1850, he became active in the **Underground Railroad,** using his own home in Rochester, New York, as a station. Over the years, he and his wife sheltered hundreds of runaway slaves. During the Civil War, Douglass, as a consultant to President Lincoln, argued for granting the freed slaves full civil rights, including the right to vote, once the war ended. Douglass also became a vocal and loyal supporter of women's rights, attending the first women's rights conference and fighting for women's suffrage. To recognize his service, he was appointed the U.S. consul general in Haiti in 1889, making him the first black person to hold this high position in the federal government. Douglass died in 1895, but the legacy of this outspoken, intellectual former slave lives on. ■

The American Anti-Slavery Society was important for many reasons. The most obvious was its actions to end slavery, but its impact goes deeper. The society trained other activists, including leaders of the suffrage and prohibition movements. Moreover, its activities demonstrated to future generations the power of organized action to promote change and modify social values.

THE WOMEN'S RIGHTS MOVEMENT: THE FIRST WAVE

Feminism is the belief in the political, social, and economic equality of men and women. The first feminist movement in the United States was launched on July 20, 1848, with the signing of the

Individuals picketed the White House to pressure President Wilson to support the suffrage movement. Wilson tolerated the suffragists until the U.S. entered World War I. Many saw the suffragists' protests during a time of war to be unpatriotic and irate individuals and mobs often attacked them. In the face of danger, the suffragists continued to demonstrate and were arrested and imprisoned. Despite brutal treatment, the women would not back down. When the situation became public, sentiment changed to support the women and their quest for freedom. Upon their release from prison, these women capitalized upon this newfound support and saw the 19th Amendment ratified into law in 1920, capping a 72-year fight for suffrage.

Declaration of Sentiments at the first women's rights convention in Seneca Falls, New York. Lucretia Mott, a Quaker preacher and activist for social change; her sister, Martha Wright; Mary Ann McClintock; Jane Hunt; and Elizabeth Cady Stanton, the wife of an abolitionist and the only non-Quaker in the group, decided that a meeting must be called to organize a movement to fight the oppression of women. Stanton and Mott were acting out of frustration after being excluded from the 1840 World Anti-Slavery Convention in London. Intelligent and articulate crusaders, the pair had traveled to London only to be refused admission because of their gender.

▶ **What changes did early feminists work to accomplish?** The Seneca Falls convention focused on achieving legal rights for women. The rights demanded ranged from the right to own property and wages (both of which at the time legally belonged not to a woman but to her husband) to access to education, from employment rights and other equal opportunities to the right to vote and to help make the laws under which they were governed. The convention adopted the Declaration of Sentiments, a general plea for equality of rights and opportunities for men and women. The most controversial resolution to emerge from the meeting was the demand for suffrage, the right to vote. From today's viewpoint, it is difficult to imagine how controversial this straightforward demand was, but at the time, the call for women's suffrage was radical.

Feminists continued their political action to win the vote for the next seventy years, times of dramatic economic growth, social change, and political evolution in the United States. The specific goal of obtaining women's right to vote never changed, but the meaning of the vote, as well as the tactics, alliances, and strategies for achieving it, proved to be highly dynamic.

One of the first and most famous arguments for women's rights came as the founders were drafting documents for American independence. Abigail Adams wrote to her husband, John, in the 1770s asking that the delegates "remember the ladies," recognizing that English common law, which was in force in the colonies, led to many legal disabilities for women. "If particular care and attention is

not paid to the ladies, we are determined to foment a rebellion, and will not hold ourselves bound by any laws in which we have no voice or representation."[10] Abigail Adams's request for political rights for women went unheeded, which came as no surprise, since political rights did not yet exist for all men. And it is not clear how seriously she meant what she wrote about fomenting a rebellion. However, her plea demonstrates that calls for equality were being made from the time of the birth of our nation.

The demand for women's suffrage became a mass movement after 1910 as national attention focused on pressuring Congress to amend the Constitution and grant women the vote. Success came when the Nineteenth Amendment was ratified in 1920. The suffragists owed much of this achievement to their willingness to work with other groups, to change tactics and definitions as times dictated, and to respond to the growing complexity of the American social and political environment. It marked the culmination of the hard work of a great many women and men who were committed to allowing women the most fundamental right in a representative democracy—the right to act for themselves and to vote.

pathways profile

ALICE STOKES PAUL

An instrumental actor in the fight for equal rights, Alice Stokes Paul lived to see remarkable changes for women in our society. Born in 1885 to Quaker parents in New Jersey, Paul's worldview was profoundly influenced by the central principle of the Quaker religion, equality of the sexes, and she learned activism

▶ **What conditions led to** the movement to prohibit the sale of alcohol?

Equal Rights Amendment (ERA)
a proposed constitutional amendment that would have guaranteed equal rights for men and women. It was initially suggested following the passage of the Nineteenth Amendment in 1920 but wasn't formally proposed by Congress until 1972, and failed to be ratified by the 1982 deadline.

prohibition
forbidding the manufacture, transportation, and sale of alcoholic beverages; imposed under the Eighteenth Amendment in 1920 and repealed by the Twenty-First Amendment in 1933.

at the side of her mother, Tacie Paul, who brought young Alice with her to suffrage meetings.

Paul was highly educated, earning a bachelor's degree in biology from Swarthmore College in 1905, a master's in sociology from the University of Pennsylvania in 1907, a doctorate in economics from the University of Pennsylvania in 1912, and a law degree from Washington College of Law in 1922. Paul transformed from reserved young woman to militant leader when on a visit to England in 1907, she met the "Pankhurst women," a mother and two daughters who were perhaps the most militant suffragists in England, whose motto was "Deeds, not words." The women took to criminal activities (such as breaking windows) to protest, often resulting in imprisonment. Paul was arrested three times in England (she was later arrested three times in the United States as well). She waged a hunger strike in prison and was brutally force-fed. She returned to the States determined to recharge the U.S. suffrage movement.

To do so, she helped organize a publicity event to gain national attention—the first national suffrage parade in Washington, timed to coincide with Woodrow Wilson's presidential inauguration, on March 3, 1913. Onlookers attacked the women marchers, first verbally and then physically, while the police did little to intervene. In 1916, she founded the National Woman's Party to demand suffrage. The party organized individuals to stand outside the White House to protest the lack of suffrage for women. The protests continued even when the nation entered World War I, angering a large number of people because they thought the women unpatriotic. The suffragists were arrested and sent to the filthy Occoquan Workhouse prison in Virginia, where the women, even the old and the frail, were beaten and brutalized. When the public learned of the prison's unsanitary conditions and the women's mistreatment, opinion toward the suffragists and their cause began to change. As a result, President Wilson reversed his previous opinion and embraced suffrage in 1917. Three years later, the Nineteenth Amendment was ratified, giving women the right to vote.

Paul's courageous behavior was important in changing the tides of opinion and winning women this key democratic right. After winning the vote, Paul continued fighting for equal rights for women, authoring the first **Equal Rights Amendment (ERA)** (which she called the "Lucretia Mott Amendment"). The amendment simply stated, "Men and women shall have equal rights throughout the United States and every place subject to its jurisdiction." Though the Equal Rights Amendment failed to be ratified, the legacy of this courageous woman still affects the rights of women today. Despite many hardships throughout her life, Alice Paul never relented in her pursuit of equality for women and men. When asked about the source of her determination, she quoted an adage her mother taught her as a child: "When you put your hand on the plow, you can't put it down until you get to the end of the row."

SOURCE: Alice Paul Institute, http://www.alicepaul.org.

THE PROHIBITION MOVEMENT

▶ **What conditions led to the movement to prohibit the sale of alcohol? Prohibition** is the legal ban on the manufacture, sale, and distribution of alcoholic beverages. The call for prohibition grew out of the temperance movement, which beginning in the early nineteenth century promoted moderation and abstinence in drinking. (Per capita consumption of hard liquor by 1830 was nearly triple its present-day rate.)[11] Excessive drinking often devastated family life, and it was blamed for all manner of social problems. Churches introduced abstinence pledges in the early 1800s, and the first known temperance organization was founded around 1810 in New York. With church support, the movement grew to approximately 6,000 local societies by 1833.[12] The severe depression called the Panic of 1837, which caused widespread unemployment, helped turn temperance into a mass movement. Many unemployed workingmen (and their wives) attributed their misfortune to drink, joined anti-alcohol "Washingtonian" societies, and took "teetotal" pledges of complete abstinence. In 1851, Maine became the first state to prohibit the manufacture and sale of all intoxicating liquor.

The prohibition movement revived after the Civil War. The most important anti-alcohol group in this period was the Women's Christian Temperance Union (WCTU), founded in 1874. In the beginning, the WCTU focused on individual temperance, encouraging personal pledges of sobriety. However, it later expanded in scope to attack the sale of liquor. By 1892, the WCTU had enrolled 150,000 members, and its newspaper, *Union Signal*, had a circulation of 100,000. Frances Wilson, the most influential president of the WCTU, selected the movement's motto: "Home Protection." The movement was successful because it played on a perceived threat to the female's "sphere." This rationale prompted even the most conservative women to get involved in political action. The argument was that drunkenness was of utmost interest to women because it threatened the sanctity of the home, prompted violence, and wasted family funds. It therefore presented women with a "duty" they could not ignore. In 1884, the WCTU established the World WCTU, which worked for the global suppression of liquor, opium, and prostitution. By 1896, the WCTU had established thirty-nine national subdivisions, all working to purify society, with a special emphasis on the interests of women and children.

The more militant Anti-Saloon League was founded in 1893 and quickly became the driving force in state campaigns for prohibition. The League drew its support largely from evangelical Protestant churches and quickly grew in popularity. The League regularly communicated with a half-million people about the ills of alcohol.[13] Its activities included conducting prayer groups (often outside saloons), lobbying for prohibition legislation, holding marches, and occasionally using violence to destroy taverns and saloons.

By 1919, the efforts of the WCTU, the Anti-Saloon League, and other prohibition groups led thirty-three states to enact prohibition laws, banning the legal purchase of alcoholic beverages by 63 percent of the country's population.[14] In 1919, the Eighteenth Amendment to the Constitution was ratified, under which Congress was empowered to impose Prohibition nationwide. Congress did so, with the Volstead Act, in 1920. The Anti-Saloon League thereafter devoted itself to fighting for stricter enforcement of Prohibition. Despite these efforts, the illegal manufacture and sale of liquor flourished on a large scale during the 1920s, generating much corruption and widespread lawbreaking. The illegal liquor trade created a new breed of crime, bootlegging, and created opportunities for organized criminal gangs. Enforcement of Prohibition varied dramatically, largely depending on the degree of local support or opposition. By the early 1930s, public support for Prohibition was waning, and in 1932, the Democratic Party called for repealing the Eighteenth Amendment. The Twenty-First Amendment, ratified in 1933, repealed national Prohibition. Even today, however, many communities have local laws prohibiting or limiting the sale of alcoholic beverages.

These and other early social movements had an important role in determining who would participate in politics and in what manner. Moving toward mass suffrage promotes political equality and inspires political participation. These early social movements

Temperance crusader Carrie Nation a member of the WCTU, felt herself divinely ordained to forcefully promote temperance. She was arrested 30 times for attacking bars and smashing all the bottles she could reach. She describes herself as a "bulldog running along at the feet of Jesus, barking at what he didn't like."

▶ **What was "progressive" about the Progressive movement? What political and social problems did it seek to resolve?**

discussionquestions

1. What factors explain the emergence of early social movements, such as abolitionism, women's suffrage, and temperance? How did these movements differ from colonial protests?

2. How did early reform movements reinforce one another? What is the legacy of these early successes? What commonalities did each movement have? What were the significant differences?

were also important in cementing average citizens' realization that group action could make them powerful, demonstrating that success is possible when like-minded people unite.

practicequiz

1. The sharpest conflict among U.S. abolitionists arose around the question of
   a. whether the movement should use the court pathway or not.
   b. whether the movement should work for total emancipation or gradual emancipation, state by state.
   c. whether the movement should focus its efforts on lobbying the legislative branch.
   d. whether the movement should use violence as one of its tactics.

2. Frederick Douglass first came to national prominence
   a. through his work in the grassroots mobilization pathway.
   b. through his first autobiography.
   c. through his newspaper, the *North Star*.
   d. by convincing Lincoln to let blacks from the North fight in the Union Army.

3. The first call for the equal treatment of women in the U.S. came in the
   a. 1770s.
   b. 1840s.
   c. 1860s.
   d. 1910s.

4. What pushed temperance into a national movement in this country?
   a. the WCTU
   b. the work of Carrie Nation
   c. the Panic of 1837
   d. the Volstead Act

Answers: 1-d, 2-b, 3-a, 4-c.

Progressive Era Movements, 1890s–1920

▶ **What was "progressive" about the Progressive movement? What political and social problems did it seek to resolve?** The **Progressive movement** is the collective name for the host of

reform programs that flourished in the United States between the 1890s and World War I in response to problems caused by rapid industrialization, immigration, urbanization, and other social change.

Many problems arose in American society during these years—some of the most significant were poverty, crime, exploitation of child labor, unsafe work environments, unsanitary living conditions, political corruption, and discrimination against African Americans and immigrants. Most Progressives were educated, middle-class, native-born Americans who were shocked by the abuses they saw in urban American life. To deal with these abuses, they proposed numerous economic and social reforms and worried about what they saw as rampant political corruption. Reacting against late-nineteenth-century political machines, which controlled the government in many states and cities, Progressives attributed many of the ills of the time to these corrupt and undemocratic organizations. The machines tolerated social abuses, Progressives charged, in return for payoffs and kickbacks. A key Progressive goal was to weaken the political machines by creating direct primaries, civil service reforms, and a secret ballot system. (Before secret ballots were introduced, people voted by publicly declaring their choice in one way or another, making it easier for corrupt bosses to buy their votes.) Progressives strove to change politics by diminishing the power of the parties and increasing the potential for participatory engagement.

Progressives worked for social change as well. The National Child Labor Committee, for example, raised public awareness about the horrific working conditions facing children in the workforce and was influential in getting legislation passed that banned the exploitation of child labor in United States.

THE RISE OF LABOR UNIONS

The post–Civil War decades and the Progressive era marked the beginning of a large-scale labor movement in the United States. The American Federation of Labor (AFL) was born in 1886 when several **labor unions** representing skilled workers consolidated to form a union confederation. It grew rapidly between 1899 and 1904. The AFL focused on "bread and butter" issues: economic advancement (notably wages), working conditions, and fringe benefits. It ignored the interests of factory workers

▶ **Do new groups tend** to emerge as a reaction to groups with competing interests, as business groups did to oppose labor unions?

Progressive movement
a movement calling for reform in government, especially regarding social and moral welfare, political corruption, and governmental reorganization.

labor union
an association of workers formed to promote collective interests such as fair pay and working conditions.

trade association
a professional organization that represents the interests of members of a particular industry.

In the early years of our industrialization employers liked to hire children, because they were a form of cheap labor and were easily controlled. The number of child laborers peaked in the first two decades of the twentieth century, when Congress passed its first attempt to limit the economic exploitation of children in 1916. On the right is a group of child textile workers during a strike in Philadelphia. Do you think that our government should refuse to import merchandise from countries that currently allow the economic exploitation of children?

(many of whom were semiskilled or unskilled immigrants), concentrating on organizing workers in the skilled trades, such as carpenters, plumbers, printers, and railroad employees. The AFL organized and supported local unions that sought to win its objectives through collective bargaining, and hence it lobbied hard for the right of workers to protest and, if necessary, strike. The federation provided strict autonomy to its member unions. It differed from many earlier labor associations in that it was not socialist, generally downplayed class-struggle rhetoric, and seldom strove for workers' political power. Over the years, it showed a remarkable capacity for survival.[15]

Testifying before Congress in 1914, Samuel Gompers, one of the founders of the AFL and one of its most influential presidents, highlighted a few key attributes of the organization. Gompers described the AFL as a *federation* of organizations, not an organization itself. As such, each individual union belonging to the federation had a "right to self-government." The federation's first purpose, he said, was to encourage labor unions to unite so they could aid each other in raising workers' wages and improving their working conditions. The AFL was intended to be a "model of the United States" and had no powers except those that were authorized by its member unions.

The AFL pushed for shortening the workday to eight hours and for establishing maximum hours of work for children and women. Through its actions and the actions of others, it won many of its demands. In 1914, after intense lobbying of Congress, the AFL won one of its greatest victories—passage of the Clayton Act, which recognized a union's right to organize and strike. In reaction, business groups in the United States began to form associations to counter the power of organized labor.

BUSINESS GROUPS AND TRADE ASSOCIATIONS

▶ **Do new groups tend to emerge as a reaction to groups with competing interests, as business groups did to oppose labor unions?** The demands of workers and of businesses are often in direct opposition. Higher wages, safer working conditions, limitations of working hours, and fringe benefits tend to cost businesses more money and thus diminish profits. Consequently, as one side organizes, so does the other.

The National Association of Manufacturers (NAM) was created in 1895, during a severe recession. Many business leaders thought that new markets for their products must be developed abroad. As strong believers in free enterprise, the leaders of the NAM favored "open shop" laws, which outlawed labor unions in workplaces and opposed the right to strike—one of the most effective negotiating tools for organized labor.

The rise of labor unions and of **trade associations** at the end of the nineteenth century illustrates a trend in group formation—the tendency for one group to stimulate the development of an opposing group. It is highly likely that when a certain

discussionquestions

1. What issues were Progressives interested in reforming? Are these issues still important today? Why or why not?

2. Why did labor unions form? Do you think they serve the same purposes today that they did when they were created? Why were business groups and trade associations formed in the late nineteenth and early twentieth centuries? How is the balance between the competing needs of labor and business negotiated?

▶ **What mass movements arose as a result of American involvement in Vietnam?**

group's interests are in opposition to another's, as is the case with business and labor interests, competing organizations will arise too. These two cases also demonstrate that in such circumstances, success or failure will alternate dramatically at different times. In 1914, for instance, labor was successful in lobbying for the right to strike under the Clayton Act, but during the McKinley administration (1897–1901), business had succeeded in getting higher tariffs imposed on imports. This struggle over power and influence between business groups and labor unions, and their alternating levels of success, is an excellent example of how groups compete to promote their interests by using this pathway.

practicequiz

1. What were two of the historical forces to which the Progressive Movement responded?
   a. the Civil War and women's suffrage
   b. the Great Depression and the Cold War
   c. immigration and urbanization
   d. the temperance movement and World War I

2. What were or are political machines?
   a. mechanized voting booths
   b. corrupt organizations that dominated a city's or region's voting patterns for years, controlled government offices in those areas, and made money through this power
   c. politicians who are so remarkably good at winning re-election that the process seems automatic
   d. well-organized political advocacy groups that make effective use of communication technology

3. The American Federation of Labor was
   a. a socialist labor union
   b. a labor union that agitated for workers' political power
   c. a collection of labor unions with socialist tendencies
   d. a collection of labor unions that downplayed class-struggle rhetoric

4. What legislation recognized a labor union's right to organize and strike?
   a. the Clayton Act
   b. the Gompers Act
   c. the Volstead Act
   d. the Twenty-First Amendment

Answers: 1-c, 2-b, 3-d, 4-a.

New Politics: Mass Movements of the Modern Era

The 1960s and 1970s were another era of major social and political change, pervaded by a renewed spirit of reform. Promoting the rights of African Americans, women, the elderly, the poor, and consumers became a high priority. These were years of war abroad and of growing ecological consciousness, impelling those who became dedicated to promoting peace and protecting the environment to become politically active as well.

Nearly every organization that in these years arose to work for equality, peace, or the environment clashed with a counter-organization that bitterly opposed its goals. Just as we have seen in the development of organized labor, individuals and groups use this pathway to promote their self-interests and their values. To illustrate general trends, we will discuss a few of the groups that mobilized during this period, but keep in mind that these years saw a great proliferation of such groups in what has been called the "interest group state."

VIETNAM AND THE ANTIWAR MOVEMENT

The modern American antiwar movement began in the 1950s primarily to express opposition to the nuclear arms race and the intensification of the Cold War. After the United States and the Soviet Union signed a nuclear test-ban treaty in 1963, the older peace coalitions all but disappeared.

▶ **What mass movements arose as a result of American involvement in Vietnam?** The heightened American involvement in the war in Vietnam in 1965 dramatically changed the peace movement. New antiwar groups arose that gradually became more aggressive and confrontational. The peace movement's focus was no longer the Cold War in general but the conflict in Indochina in particular. Numerous groups opposed the war, but there was virtually no centralization among them. From 1967 through 1971, antiwar sentiment shifted markedly to the left and the social turbulence surrounding it increased. As popular dissatisfaction with the Vietnam War mounted, activists within the peace movement made a conscious shift "from protest to resistance." Antiwar activities remained mostly nonviolent and symbolic, including the

The frequency and intensity of public protest grew as the war in Vietnam became increasingly unpopular. Pictured at the right are medals, awards, and discharge papers returned by veterans in 1972 to symbolize their objection to the war. Oftentimes when protests occur during times of war or crisis, the protesters are labeled as unpatriotic. Do you think this label is appropriate and fair? Why or why not?

burning of flags and draft cards. But scattered incidents of violence increased as the fighting in Vietnam escalated and casualties mounted. A few radical activists—a small minority among the large numbers who were deeply involved in the antiwar movement—raised the cry "Bring the war home!" to justify vandalism, attacking the police, and even bombing research laboratories that they associated with the war effort.

The Vietnam era marked the highest point of domestic unrest in the United States since the Civil War, and the antiwar movement of the time reshaped American mass protest. It occurred amid great social turbulence. Most antiwar activists also worked for cultural changes in such areas as religion, race, and gender relations. A broad but generally informal coalition existed between organizations pushing for changes in cultural norms and the antiwar organizations, and their actions often overlapped. The civil rights, women's rights, and peace movements tended to reinforce one other, all working toward their own vision of social justice.[16]

THE CIVIL RIGHTS MOVEMENT

The United States' earliest national civil rights group, the National Association for the Advancement of Colored People, was founded in 1910, the product of a coalition between the Niagara Movement (a group of young black intellectuals led by W. E. B. Du Bois) and sympathetic white Progressives. The NAACP took as its mission improving the lot of African Americans so that they might enjoy their full rights as citizens, including justice in the courts and equal economic, political, and social opportunities. It insisted that black people must be secure in the rights that the Constitution grants, and it demanded the elimination of such racially motivated crimes as lynching. The NAACP has always published a newspaper, *The Crisis*. The organization grew by establishing branches and by adding prominent individuals, especially legal authorities, to its ranks; today it has more than a half-million members and is organized into approximately 2,200 units in all fifty states and the District of Columbia.

The NAACP has been most successful using the court pathway to advance its objectives. For example, it was the NAACP's legal counsel that brought the *Brown* case—the 1954 decision by which the Supreme Court ordered the desegregation of the nation's public schools (see ⓁⒾⓃⓀ *Chapter 6, pages 221–224*). Today, the NAACP believes that "a renewed effort" on behalf of civil rights is necessary "as the forces of racism and retrogression in America are again on the rise" and because "many of the hard-earned civil rights gains of the past three decades are under assault."[17] Committed to protecting the rights of minorities by ensuring that their voices are heard, the NAACP's most important work today is to conduct voter empowerment drives.

Black and white activists founded a second major civil rights organization, the Congress on Racial Equality, in 1942. CORE was initially led by two University of Chicago students, one white (George Houser) and one black (James Farmer). The group was more dedicated to direct action than other groups, pushing for the use of sit-ins and picket lines. CORE cosponsored the 1963 March on Washington and pioneered the sit-in as a protest tactic (and subsequently the "jail-in," in which group members served time in jail rather than pay a fine).[18]

The modern American civil rights movement was born of frustration at the slow pace of integration in the decade after the *Brown* decision. Schools and other public accommodations were slowly desegregated in some states. In the Deep South, however, virtually no integration occurred, and white resistance was fierce. Historians date the start of the modern civil rights movement to Rosa Parks's arrest for refusing to give her seat to a white man on a bus in Montgomery, Alabama, in 1955. As noted in ⓁⒾⓃⓀ *Chapter 6, pages 228–237*, Montgomery's black community, led by Martin Luther King Jr., organized a very effective boycott of the city bus system, ultimately resulting in the desegregation of Montgomery's public busing.

▶ **What protest tactics did the civil rights movement use to draw attention to its cause? Were these tactics effective?**

Equal Pay Act
federal legislation passed in 1963 that made it illegal to pay women lower wages for the same job than men solely because they are women.

Title VII of the Civil Rights Act of 1964
federal civil rights legislation that prohibits discrimination in employment based on race, national origin, religion, sex, or physical condition.

Leaders of the civil rights movement used several pathways to force change, end segregation and discrimination, and promote equality for all Americans. Moreover, they often worked with other groups active at the time (for example peace and women's rights activists). Why do you think that collaboration between these different groups was successful? Do you think that collaboration is always a good tactic to raise awareness and promote change?

▶ **What protest tactics did the civil rights movement use to draw attention to its cause? Were these tactics effective?** Between 1955 and 1960, the movement won moderate successes using nonviolent tactics, including boycotts, sit-ins, and picketing. During this period, new civil rights organizations arose that more directly used the grassroots mobilization pathway. For example, in 1957, Martin Luther King Jr. and other black ministers founded the Southern Christian Leadership Conference (SCLC) to conduct citizen education projects, voter registration drives, and training in leadership throughout the South and in the border states. The SCLC was very active in coordinating the 1963 March on Washington, which mobilized public support for the 1964 Civil Rights Act, and its voter registration campaigns were crucial in demonstrating the need for Congress to pass the Voting Rights Act of 1965. (Today, thanks in part to the NAACP's and SCLC's historic efforts, some 12 million African Americans are registered to vote.)[19] A second key organization that used the grassroots mobilization pathway was the Student Nonviolent Coordinating Committee, or SNCC (usually pronounced "snick"), which was founded in 1960 to use peaceful means to force the integration of department stores, drugstores, and other public accommodations throughout the South. SNCC organized sit-ins and other demonstrations in twenty states to dramatize the injustice of segregation and publicize the horror of racism; some 65,000 students participated in these demonstrations, and 3,600 were arrested. Similarly using nonviolence, in 1961, CORE sent black and white volunteer "freedom riders" into the South to challenge segregation in interstate bus service. CORE wanted to test whether the 1960 Supreme Court ruling in *Boynton* v. *Virginia* (declaring segregation in interstate bus and rail stations unconstitutional) was being upheld. Some freedom riders suffered severe injuries at the hands of racist mobs and local police.

THE WOMEN'S RIGHTS MOVEMENT: THE SECOND WAVE

The first women's rights movement succeeded in 1920 by winning the right to vote for women, and for several decades thereafter, women's rights advocates became less visible. But by the 1950s, it had become apparent that despite winning the right to vote, women still faced discrimination in virtually all other aspects of their lives. Women were discouraged from working in many professions and were barred from certain jobs, some of which paid far more than the occupations that most women in the workforce pursued. Women faced discrimination at all levels of education, and some prestigious colleges and universities as well as the military academies refused to admit women. The police and the court system often ignored domestic violence as "private family matters." Women had no access to reliable contraception or to safe, legal abortion, and many women lacked adequate information about health care issues affecting them.

Social and economic changes after World War II, including increasing numbers of women working outside the home for wages, forced a reexamination of many forms of legal discrimination in the United States (some of which was intended to protect women as the supposedly "weaker sex"). Demands rose for the government to protect gender equality. After 1960, Americans began to shift their view of women away from regarding them as a separate category of citizen requiring special legal treatment (which could be both "protective" and discriminatory) and toward viewing them as worthy of legal equality in all spheres. Many areas of public policy ultimately felt the impact of this shift in focus on gender equality, most notably laws relating to education, work, and the family.

Ensuring equal economic opportunity was one focus of the revived women's movement. In the early 1960s, the movement secured enactment of three equal opportunity provisions: the **Equal Pay Act, Title VII of the Civil Rights Act of 1964,** and *affirmative action*. Congress enacted the Equal Pay Act in 1963 to address discrimination in pay. Although today equal pay for equal work is probably the least controversial of feminist demands, this was not always so. In 1963, women were routinely paid less than men, even for doing the same or more demanding work, because it was assumed that the man was the primary breadwinner and hence needed a larger salary.

Title VII of the Civil Rights Act of 1964 was crucial in prohibiting sex (as well as racial) discrimination in employment, partly by creating the federal Equal Employment Opportunity Commission (EEOC). The EEOC was given responsibility for enforcing antidiscrimination laws and for regulating those employment practices that these laws had declared not permissible. *Affirmative action* is a legal phrase that means taking positive steps to achieve a particular outcome. Affirmative action programs required all businesses and institutions that receive federal contracts or funding to seek out opportunities to correct past discrimination. The rationale of affirmative action is that simply defining past racist or sexist policies as illegal does not by itself achieve equality. The lingering effects of hundreds of years of discrimination are often profound, making societal redress necessary. And because past discrimination was directed against all mem-

bers of a disfavored group—for example, *all* black Americans or *all* American women—the remedy for that oppression must also be group-based.

These three public policies, coupled with reforms in access to higher education, proved fundamentally important for reshaping the status of modern American women. However, legislation itself can only do so much; for real change to occur, effective *enforcement* of the legislation is essential. The EEOC seemed ineffective in enforcing the new civil rights legislation, frustrating some of those who in 1966 attended the Third National Conference of the Commission on the Status of Women; those critics, both women and men, formed the National Organization for Women (NOW) that same year. NOW was formed as a civil rights organization for women with the aim of pressuring the EEOC to take sex discrimination seriously and to work to end it.

Today, NOW is the largest organization of feminist activists in the United States, with 500,000 contributing members and 550 chapters across the nation. NOW declares as its objective to "eliminate discrimination and harassment in the workplace, schools and justice system, and all other sectors of society; secure abortion, birth control and reproductive rights for all women; end all forms of violence against women; eradicate racism, sexism and homophobia; and promote equality and justice in our society."[20]

pathways of action

THE EQUAL RIGHTS AMENDMENT

Section 1. Equality of rights under the law shall not be denied or abridged by the United States or by any state on account of sex.

Section 2. The Congress shall have the power to enforce, by appropriate legislation, the provisions of this article.

Section 3. This amendment shall take effect two years after the date of ratification.

As noted earlier, veteran suffragist Alice Paul and her National Woman's Party first submitted the Equal Rights Amendment (ERA) to Congress in 1923. Congress ignored the proposed amendment, but it was resubmitted to all subsequent Congresses. The Republican Party's convention endorsed the amendment in 1940, and the Democratic Party followed suit in 1944. Nevertheless, putting into the Constitution a declaration that men and women shall have equal rights was a controversial feminist idea at the time it was advanced—and so it remains today. Not until 1972

▶ **You mean after all**
this, it wasn't ratified? Was
there a final vote on it?

When the ERA was formally proposed in 1972, it was initially very popular, however opposition quickly united. One of the most important groups working to defeat the ERA was the Stop ERA Coalition. Pictured above is the group's leader, Phyllis Schlafly, speaking at a rally in the Illinois state capital rotunda. Are you surprised that many of the people opposed to the ERA were women? Why do you think this was the case?

did Congress formally endorse the amendment and submit it to the states for ratification.

Feminists made many legal gains during the 1970s. Supreme Court decisions outlawed obsolete sex classifications, and many states changed criminal and family law to reflect the changing societal definition of gender roles. Blatant forms of employment discrimination were eliminated, and the federal military academies became coeducational. Feminists argued that to ensure that these gains would not subsequently be overturned, a provision calling for gender equality should be added to the Constitution. But as support for the ERA grew in the 1960s and 1970s, so did opposition to it. Many people were concerned that the ERA would eliminate privileges that our society accords to women, such as exemption from the military draft.

When in 1972 Congress endorsed the ERA and sent it to the state legislatures for ratification, the amendment was very popular. Of the thirty-eight state legislatures needed to ratify the amendment (that is, the legislatures of three-fourths of the states), twenty-eight ratified it in the first year. The political momentum was clearly on the side of ratification. But then, even after Congress extended the seven-year deadline for ratification, the ERA stalled, three states short of ratification. Why did what once had been a very popular proposal become controversial and divisive and ultimately fail?

The answer is clear: A group of committed citizens organized grassroots, state-by-state opposition. The STOP-ERA coalition, led by the conservative activist Phyllis Schlafly, endured hardships and long days of work to defeat the ERA. The grassroots coalition included fundamentalist churches and political conservatives who were deeply opposed to what they saw as the evil in the ERA. They believed that it would weaken families, harm homemakers, and promote homosexuality. Opponents—many of whom were women fighting against change—also feared that the ERA would empower federal judges to interpret the Constitution in unforeseen ways, producing unintended consequences. Members of STOP-ERA turned the ERA into a political issue. The 1980 national convention of the Republican Party, which nominated Ronald Reagan for the presidency, rescinded its prior endorsement of the ERA.

▶ **You mean after all this, it wasn't ratified? Was there a final vote on it?** In the end, the ERA lost because it had become too controversial to achieve the supermajority of states that the Constitution requires for amendments. In 1982, the extended time limit for ratification passed, and the ERA, with its clear and simple standard for requiring sexual equality, died. ▪

In the last fifty years, the number of gay rights groups has increased, as has their visibility. Gay rights activists have used several pathways to promote changes in law in such areas as sexual relations, same-sex marriages, and parental rights. To the right is a picture of a large demonstration held on the steps of the Supreme Court in which dozens of activists were arrested. Do you think that protesting is an effective tool to motivate change? Why and when is it most effective? Can all groups successfully use protests?

With the defeat of the Equal Rights Amendment in 1982, the women's movement went through a period of stagnation. Many people of both genders felt that women had now achieved equality and that a feminist movement was no longer really needed. However, the mobilization of conservative Christians to end legalized abortion in the 1980s, as well as realization that many women still suffered job discrimination and earned lower wages, reenergized women's rights advocates. Feminists were further galvanized in 1991 when during Senate hearings for Clarence Thomas's nomination to the Supreme Court, one of his former associates, Anita Hill, alleged that he had sexually harassed her. Following what many thought was unfair treatment of Hill by the all-male senators conducting the hearings, membership in women's organizations grew dramatically.

Currently, women's rights activists are working to achieve a variety of goals important to women and their families, including access to safe and effective health care, reproductive freedom, educational opportunities, the prevention of violence against women, and workplace equality. For decades, too, American women's rights organizations have been working to promote the rights of women worldwide. Over time, organizations come and go and tactics change, but the central goal remains the same: promoting equal rights for men and women, allowing all individuals to reach their full potential.

THE GAY RIGHTS MOVEMENT

The decades since the 1960s have witnessed a dramatic mobilization for homosexual rights in the United States and in other Western countries—followed by a mobilization of the opposition. After World War II, many people migrated to large cities, and by the 1950s, gay communities took shape in some of them. The earliest American organizations to promote homosexual rights were the Mattachine Society, established in 1951 in Los Angeles, and the Daughters of Bilitis (DOB), founded in San Francisco in 1955. These early groups focused on depicting homosexuals as "normal" citizens. They used letters to newspaper editors, picketing, and litigation to call for equal rights. They argued that the First Amendment's guarantees of freedom of expression, assembly, and speech, as well as the Fourteenth Amendment's equal protection clause, should protect homosexuals from discrimination.

As gay people's numbers and visibility grew, so did their frustration and discontent at being treated badly by American society, public officials, and the police. As late as the 1960s, homosexual acts between consenting adults were illegal in most parts of the United States, with sodomy and obscenity laws often applied more strictly to homosexuals than to straight people. Until the early 1970s, the professional association of American psychiatrists officially defined homosexuality as a mental illness, and many gay people were under pressure to be "cured" by psychiatrists. These conditions set the stage for more concerted mobilization efforts. In many American cities, gay and lesbian communities were no longer an invisible subculture; male and female homosexuals were becoming well organized, with businesses, clubs, bars, community centers, and social services of their own.

One watershed event in 1969 catalyzed the demand for "gay power." The New York City police raided the Stonewall Bar, a popular gathering place for gays and lesbians, with the intent of harassing homosexuals, as they had done many times before. The bar patrons resisted arrest, spurring hundreds of homosexuals, frustrated by years of harassment and discrimination, to fight back. The rioting lasted two nights. The Stonewall Riots marked the beginning of a mass movement for homosexual rights, which included the creation of such gay rights groups as the Gay Liberation Front and the Gay Activist Alliance. The first large-scale gay rights march, with 80,000 to 90,000 participants, took place in Washington, D.C., in October 1979. Eight years later, more than 600,000 people marched in Washington in support of homosexual rights.

Today, several organizations use multiple pathways—elections, the courts, and grassroots mobilization—to promote civil rights for homosexuals. Such groups as the Human Rights Campaign Fund and the National Gay and Lesbian Task Force focus on decriminalizing homosexual activity, preventing hate crimes, protecting gays against discrimination, and legalizing same-sex marriage. Gay rights groups have been most successful in using the court pathway to advance their causes, but they have also had success in persuading state legislatures to enact antidiscrimination laws and in obtaining national and state legislation that defines and punishes hate crimes. Gay rights parades and protests are far more common today. But in many communities, they also arouse counterprotests.

ABOVE: **Gary Rice, senior pastor at the Emmanuel Assembly of God Church** in Allentown, Pennsylvania, stands outside his church with election pamphlets. The Republican Party and conservative religious groups used these types of communication pamphlets to rally and mobilize individuals in conservative churches and Christian groups to vote Republican in the 2004 presidential election. Since the mid-1980s, conservative Christians have been marshaling support for Republican candidates and encouraging their members to become more politically active, with great success. Do you think that churches with tax-exempt status should be allowed to promote particular political views and/or candidates? Why or why not?

BELOW: **Dr. James Dobson addresses the congregation** with a nationwide simulcast at Highview Baptist Church in Louisville, Kentucky, in 2005. Dr. Dobson, a conservative Evangelical Christian minister and psychologist, created the nonprofit organization, Focus on the Family, in 1977. His daily radio program is heard by millions.

▶ **Is the recent political** mobilization of the Christian Right largely a sort of backlash to other movements?

CONSERVATIVE CHRISTIAN GROUPS

▶ **Is the recent political mobilization of the Christian Right largely a sort of backlash to other movements?** The decades since 1980 have also seen an important growth in the number and political power of conservative Christian groups, worried about the changing role of women in society, abortion, gay rights, and what they generally perceived as "moral decay." Such concerns have made conservative religious organizations more politically active. Conservative Christian churches have been very effective in mobilizing members—in large part because church members care deeply about the issues advanced by their leaders and are willing to devote considerable time, money, and energy to promote their values. In the late 1970s, many white evangelical Christians became disillusioned with President Jimmy Carter despite his own "born-again" faith, seeing him as too liberal on such issues as women's rights, abortion, and the Supreme Court's rulings banning public school prayer. (Most black evangelicals remained committed to liberal political causes and to the Democratic Party, which they saw as more supportive of civil rights.) Capturing this wave of conservative discontent with liberalism, a Virginia televangelist, Jerry Falwell, in 1979 founded a political movement called the **Moral Majority.** As a leading voice of what is today termed the Christian Right, the Moral Majority demonstrated the effectiveness of conservative churches in mobilizing members by lobbying for a restoration of prayer in the public schools and by actively opposing the ERA, homosexual rights, and abortion. Its tactics, and those of other Christian Right groups, closely resembled those of their liberal opponents, the civil rights, women's rights, and gay rights organizations that we have already discussed

Falwell and the Moral Majority proved their political clout by aiding in Ronald Reagan's 1980 victory over Carter. Falwell dissolved the Moral Majority in 1989 (in large part because the organization's political activism had cost it the tax-exempt status that the IRS had long granted it as an ostensibly religious group), but the **Christian Coalition** took its place, promoting what it calls "traditional family values." By 1994, the Christian Coalition claimed 1.5 million members and 1,100 chapters in all fifty states. Today it is the largest organization of its type in America and is aligned solidly with the Republican Party.

Clergy are key activists on the Christian Right. They are often active in conducting voter registration drives, in compiling and distributing voter guides, and in various Republican Party activities. Conservative church members also volunteer in large numbers for political campaigns. For example, in the 1994

Moral Majority
a religious organization founded in 1979 by Jerry Falwell that advocated outlawing abortion, opposed homosexuality, and upheld what it called "traditional family values."

Christian Coalition
a conservative Christian political advocacy group founded in 1988 by Pat Robertson.

midterm elections, 75,000 volunteers from the Christian Coalition delivered 33 million voter guides across the nation.[21] These guides carefully focused on issues of interest to conservative Christians, portraying key differences between targeted candidates. The Christian Coalition recruits candidates to run for Congress, and it had a hand in formulating the 1994 Republican Party's "Contract with America," the election program widely credited with helping the GOP win control of both houses of Congress that year. The success of the Christian Coalition in 1994 was remarkable. According to research by the political scientist Christopher Soper, 43 percent of the evangelicals who said that they regularly attend church were contacted at least once by a religious group, received information at their church, or were influenced by their pastor.[22]

As a consequence of this effective mobilization, white evangelicals accounted for a record 51 percent of the GOP voters that year and for 27 percent of all voters who went to the polls. In the 2000 national election, evangelical Christians were the Republican Party's strongest constituency: 74 percent of the white evangelicals who voted did so for George W. Bush, and 73 percent voted for Republican candidates for the House of Representatives. Those who were contacted by their church showed an even greater degree of support: 87 percent of white evangelicals who talked to a friend in church about politics voted for Bush, compared to 64 percent support of those who did not discuss politics with other church members. Voter contact also influenced turnout: 71 percent of white evangelicals who talked in church about the election actually voted, compared to a national turnout rate of less than 55 percent. Evangelicals who did not discuss the election in church voted at a far lower rate—only 41 percent.[23] Traditionally, as you will see, evangelical Christians tended to stay clear of politics, considering it self-serving, amoral and "worldly." Many did vote, but often more on economic grounds (concerns for job security, living standards, and health insurance to name a few)—which tended to benefit the Democratic Party. Political scientists believe that the relatively recent influence of evangelical ministers on voting patterns and turnout may be substantial in future elections.

pathways profile

JAMES DOBSON

Trained as a pediatric psychologist, James Dobson is perhaps the most powerful and influential evangelical leader in the country today. Interestingly, this is not a label Dobson sought. For most of his life, he kept his distance from politics, but at the time when his following grew, so did his dissatisfaction with the Republican Party. By the late 1990s, he was concerned with the moral state of our society and thought that the Republican Party needed to be more aggressive in promoting the Christian agenda (opposition to abortion and gay rights). The gay marriage debate troubled him so much that he got involved in the 2004 presidential election. He used his organization, Focus on the Family, to openly campaign for George W. Bush.

Dobson's public career began in 1977 when he published a book, *Dare to Discipline*, which advocated a return to physical punishment of children, rejecting more permissive parenting that was being advocated by many experts at the time. This book became very popular with Christian families and launched his ministry career. That same year, he founded his ministry, Focus on the Family, in Colorado Springs. The ministry has grown dramatically and is the key source of his political influence.

Today his daily radio program reaches nearly 200 million listeners in over 150 nations. His weekly newspaper column is in more than 500 papers nationally. The ministry receives so much mail that it has its own ZIP code. Dobson has written or cowritten thirty-one books, many of them self-help books targeted at Christians. He is deeply committed to fighting gay marriage, a stance that led to his vigorous involvement in the 2004 presidential election. He told his 7 million American radio listeners that it would be a sin if they didn't vote in the election. Many pundits and scholars believe that his campaigning efforts were a significant contributing factor to the Bush victories in Ohio and Florida, both of which were closely contested and pivotal elections in the fight for electoral college votes. Given the fact that his ministry continues to grow and the commitment of his loyal followers is substantial, Dobson will be a powerful political factor for the foreseeable future. ■

Christian Right groups were very active in the 2004 elections, registering and mobilizing record numbers of evangelicals and conservative Roman Catholics. Exit polls showed that Bush won 79 percent of the 26.5 million evangelicals who voted, as well as 52 percent of the 31 million Catholic votes.[24] Moreover, turnout increased significantly in some important battleground states, especially in conservative areas in Ohio, where Bush received significantly more votes than in 2000; his narrow victory provided Bush with his winning electoral college majority.

Besides raising voters' interest and getting them to the polls, Christian groups were also successful in framing the issue agenda in many states—for example, referendums on same-sex marriage were on the ballot in thirteen states. The resulting political debate

▶ **How have grassroots**
movements taken advantage
of changing technology to
advance their causes?

Immigrants, both legal and illegal, have historically been politically marginalized and largely ignored until the time they become citizens. Even as citizens, they are often not specifically targeted by political groups and parties (the clear exception to this was Franklin Roosevelt's New Deal Coalition that relied very heavily upon the support of immigrant groups). This has recently changed as immigrants have become politicized across the country in response to the government's attempt to tackle new immigration legislation. Pictured above are protesters in Los Angeles on May 1, 2006. That day, traditionally known as May Day (International Workers' Day), saw a number of protests and economic boycotts to demonstrate the value immigrants bring to our national economy. Which do you think will be more important in forcing officials to be concerned with the needs of immigrants—protests or boycotts? Why?

Photo: Monica Almeida/The New York Times

in these states inspired social conservatives to turn out in record numbers, greatly boosting the potential vote for the Republican presidential and congressional candidates. Currently, the Christian Coalition claims nearly 2 million members, and its ranks are still growing.[25] These groups, originally organized because they felt that their voices were not being heard, have won an important place in Republican Party and national politics.

OLDER AND NEWER MOBILIZATION TACTICS

The tactics that political groups have used to mobilize supporters and agitate for change have evolved dramatically throughout our history, but many of the oldest tactics remain in place. Activist groups during the Revolutionary era and in nineteenth-century America relied heavily on personal contact to win support, reaching the public through local networks, speeches, and person-to-person contacts. As you saw in the pathway profile earlier in this chapter, antislavery orators like Frederick Douglass traveled throughout much of the nation denouncing slavery and urging its abolition. A lifetime crusader for social justice, Douglass also spoke out on suffrage for women. Susan B. Anthony spent much of her life publicly advocating women's rights by giving speeches, leading petition drives, and challenging unjust laws in the courts, though with little success. Modern groups, especially some environmental groups, use this personal approach, but given the changing technology and demographics of today, they often have greater success by relying on other tactics.

Much of the early activity of American social movements focused on churches, which provided a ready structure to appeal to people and to win financial support. The civil rights movement of the 1950s and 1960s depended heavily on African American churches for organizational, financial, and moral support, and some of the most prominent black freedom leaders (notably Martin Luther King Jr. and Jesse Jackson) were gifted preachers. Liberal white churches and clergy, too, gave valuable support to the civil rights movement and helped arouse white consciences on its behalf across the nation. Today, civil rights groups and the Christian Right also rely heavily on churches to organize supporters. But many modern movements—including women's rights, gay rights, and environmentalist activists—do not.

Early political movements also were more likely to work outside existing party structures. Many of these groups formed third

discussionquestions

1. What elements do many of the twentieth-century movements share? What were some key differences between the movements? What tactics do you think are the most effective at bringing about change, and why?

2. When and why did groups and individuals working to promote civil rights turn to mass mobilization? How has modern technology affected political mobilization and civic engagement? Do you think the changes are for the better? Why or why not?

parties to influence national and local politics. Examples have included the Free Soil Party of the 1840s, which opposed the spread of slavery; the Woman's Party of the early twentieth century, which advocated women's suffrage; the Prohibition Party of the late nineteenth century, which still exists as a tiny fringe group; and the Progressive Party, which split off from one or the other of the major parties in order to run presidential candidates in 1912, 1924, and 1948. American advocates of democratic socialism also organized separate political parties, especially in the early decades of the twentieth century.

On the other hand, most modern political and social movements have worked within the existing party system, rarely forming third parties. The exception is the small, environmentalist Green Party, but we should note that Green Parties exist in many modern industrial states outside the United States—notably in Germany and France. Contemporary groups, beginning with those advocating civil rights, have also been more successful than their predecessors in using the courts in litigation strategies.

▶ **How have grassroots movements taken advantage of changing technology to advance their causes?** Technology has been the most important factor that has changed social and political movements' strategies and tactics. As we will see in (L I N K) *Chapter 13, pages 523–524,* modern technology—especially television, computers, and the Internet—has made possible a wide variety of new tactics to appeal to the public. Television, for example, has made social protests and other political activities far more public. When groups marched in the 1800s, they were visible only locally, although newspapers, and word of mouth could eventually spread word of what had happened. Today, when a political movement holds a march, stages an event, or organizes a protest, it gets immediate public visibility and greatly enhances its opportunities to gain to new followers. Computers allow political and social movements to amass huge databases of supporters' names and contact information, and the Internet has vastly augmented these movements' ability to spread their messages and raise funds.

Most recently, groups have been successful in using text messaging to mobilize individuals and groups for grassroots protests and activities. For example, on March 26, 2006, Gustavo Jimenez, a 16-year-old high school junior in Dallas, Texas, saw a posting on his friend's MySpace.com page that informed him of protests being held nationally objecting to proposed immigration legislation. He was outraged to learn that the proposed legislation would, among

other things, make it a felony, punishable by jail time, to be in the United States illegally. He also objected to the proposal to build a fence on the U.S.-Mexico border. He learned that students in schools in a number of states were staging walkouts to protest. So he proposed a walkout for 10:20 A.M. on March 27, followed by a rally. He posted the information on his MySpace page and also called a few friends. He didn't get much support until he sent a text message to a few people. The message spread like a spider web, allowing hundreds of people to be reached in a very short time. He figured that a turnout of 300 people would be a success; however, his text message mobilized kids throughout the city, and between 3,000 and 4,000 people showed up at the rally. As this example makes clear, using new technology can be an accessible and inexpensive way to reach the masses. The students, using this new technology, launched their own grassroots movement. People in other countries have also used this technology to organize grassroots campaigns. For example, in 2001, the president of the Philippines, Joseph Estrada, was deposed largely due to a text-message campaign. Text-message get-out-the-vote drives in South Korea and Spain also were successful in organizing the masses and influencing electoral outcomes.[26] The full potential impact of new technology on mass mobilization is yet to be fully understood but is certain to be dramatic.

practicequiz

1. The 1960s and 1970s saw the birth of what has been called
   a. entrenched political apathy.
   b. the age of political backlash.
   c. the "Me" generation.
   d. the interest group state.

2. Activities protesting the Vietnam war were mostly non-violent and symbolic.
   a. true   b. false

3. Martin Luther King Jr. helped found what civil rights organization?
   a. The NAACP   b. The SCLC
   c. The SNCC   d. CORE

4. In the 1960s, American psychiatrists officially defined homosexuality as
   a. an inherent, genetic trait.
   b. a mental illness to be "cured."
   c. the product of repressive parenting.
   d. the free expression of a sexual preference.

Answers: 1-d, 2-a, 3-b, 4-b.

▶ **Can the government restrict** an individual's First Amendment freedoms because they might conflict with national security or other public interests?

Espionage Act
law passed by Congress in 1917 that made it a crime to interfere with the United States' military involvement, including troop recruitment, in World War I.

Sedition Act
federal law passed in 1918 that attempted to limit free speech by forbidding criticism of the United States government, the Constitution, or the military; repealed in 1921.

Theory versus Practice

As we have seen, a delicate balance exists between constitutional freedoms and the government's need to regulate human behavior—especially when public security or the interests of the entire society are at stake. For this reason, the federal and state governments impose some restrictions on freedom.

FREE ASSOCIATION AND EXPRESSION VERSUS NATIONAL SECURITY

▶ **Can the government restrict an individual's First Amendment freedoms because they might conflict with national security or other public interests?** One area in which the American government has several times restricted freedom, and today continues to do so, is where personal liberties may conflict with national security. One of the earliest such limitations imposed during the twentieth century was the **Espionage Act,** a World War I federal law enacted on June 15, 1917, with the intent of preventing many antigovernment actions. Congress enacted the law because at the time many Americans saw any effort to oppose wartime government actions as disloyal, even treasonous. The act provided severe punishments for anyone found guilty of "transmitting, communicating, or delivering information regarding defense of the nation." Congress amended the Espionage Act on May 16, 1918, by passing the **Sedition Act,** imposing drastic new punishments on anyone who should "utter, print, write, or publish and distribute profane, scurrilous, or abusive language" directed against the United States government. The vague wording of these laws allowed the federal government to imprison about 2,000 people (largely radicals) who protested the war. Many thousands more were silenced by the threat of prosecution. (The Espionage Act, incidentally, has never been repealed.)

As noted in ⓛⓘⓝⓚ *Chapter 5, pages 167–168,* the most famous case prosecuted under the Espionage Act involved Charles T. Schenck, the general secretary of the Socialist Party. Schenck and fellow party members mailed 15,000 leaflets urging actual and potential draftees to resist the draft. Such behavior was arguably prohibited under the Espionage Act, and Schenck and his colleagues were arrested. Their convictions were eventually upheld by the Supeme Court. Justice Oliver Wendell Holmes established the clear and present danger test: Any action that threatens the government or its soldiers in a time of war can be prohibited in advance to protect national security, provided that the government proves in court that such an act would represent a "clear and present danger."

But can the government limit constitutional rights of speech, assembly, and press when the United States is not in a declared war? Should certain group activities be restricted when the nation faces a perceived threat? (Bear in mind that not since the attack on Pearl Harbor in 1941 has Congress actually declared war.) Such questions were raised during the Cold War era, after 1945, when Americans feared communism and tried aggressively to prohibit its spread to our country. This period in American history is known as the Red Scare. By 1948, anticommunist militancy was running rampant throughout the nation. *Red Channels,* a pamphlet published by *Counterattack: The Newsletter of Facts to Combat Communism,* provided a detailed list of 151 entertainers and organizations that were suspected of being communists, thus creating a blacklist. Fear was so great that the publishers of books, newspapers, magazines, and even comic books, as well the film industry and broadcasters, began regulating what they published and who they employed to avert any suspicion that they might be supporting communism. The anticommunist crusade came to a head in the hearings chaired by Senator Joseph McCarthy in 1953 and 1954. McCarthy's brutal interrogation tactics and wild, unfounded charges have led historians to characterize these hearings as modern "witch hunts." During the Red Scare, opposition to Soviet communism escalated into mass hysteria, allowing politicians and the media to whip up hostility against anything and anyone who seemed "un-American." Even the hint of radical sympathies or "un-Americanism" could get someone branded as a communist sympathizer, which could very well lead to the loss of job and reputation.

The Red Scare fed on fear, even though there was a genuine danger of espionage and of Soviet penetration of certain upper levels of the U.S. government. People feared spies, nuclear war, and even a communist takeover of the United States. Movies, the press, comic books, and conservative politicians exploited intense popular fears of domestic communism and Soviet aggression for their own purposes. The perceived but much exaggerated dread of communism among the American public caused, in many instances, an erosion or violation of civil liberties. The Red Scare did not affect only individuals charged with being sympathetic to communists (often on the basis of things they had said or organizations they had joined years before, especially during the Great Depression). College students found themselves policed by their

USA PATRIOT Act
federal law enacted shortly after the terrorist attacks of September 11, 2001, that grants the federal government broad powers to fight terrorist activities.

universities, lawyers and teachers had to swear loyalty oaths in order to keep their jobs (and could lose their livelihood if someone accused them of disloyalty), and even the printers working at the U.S. Government Printing Office came under suspicion. Eventually, however, the anticommunist fervor went too far, the media exposed McCarthy as a reckless fraud, and the hysteria essentially imploded.

9/11 AND THE USA PATRIOT ACT

Ever since the September 11, 2001, terrorist attacks on the United States, our government has been grappling with the question of how to ensure homeland security. The government's options illustrate the dilemma that democratic governments always face: how to keep citizens safe *and* protect basic civil liberties and civil rights. The balance is delicate and difficult to achieve. For many Americans, the fear of terrorism outweighs concerns for civil liberties (see Fig. 12.3). Others disagree, arguing that personal freedom is the essence of our country. The government must determine how to strike a balance between these often competing choices.

On October 26, 2001, President George W. Bush signed into law sweeping legislation that Congress had just approved—the **USA PATRIOT Act.** The act's stated goal is to "deter and punish terrorist acts in the United States and around the world, to enhance law enforcement investigative tools, and for other purposes." On the whole, the act expands the federal government's authority to conduct surveillance, heightens border protection, removes "obstacles" to investigating terrorist activities, increases aid to the families of public safety officers killed or injured in the line of duty, enhances the sharing of information and intelligence between government agencies, and protects Muslims and Arabs against the abuses of racial profiling. The USA PATRIOT Act also grants the Central Intelligence Agency, the Federal Bureau of Investigation, and the National Security Agency more latitude in electronically collecting data on citizens and resident foreigners. To do so, these agencies were given broad powers to monitor financial transactions, and expedited procedures were provided for granting federal agents subpoenas and warrants to eavesdrop on Internet communications. The law also authorized law enforcement and intelligence agencies to track activity on targeted Web sites, and it required access providers to turn over information on demand about customers' use of Internet services.

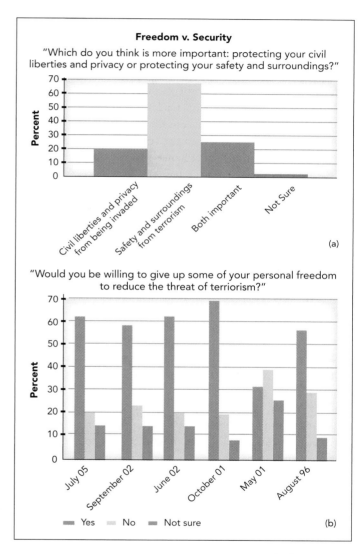

FIGURE 12.3
Freedom versus Security

A Fox News/Opinion Dynamics poll conducted in July 2005 (top figure) shows that most Americans value security over personal freedoms. When people were asked if they would be willing to give up some of their personal freedom in order to reduce the threat of terrorism, a large percentage said yes (bottom figure). Looking at the issue over time, one can see that the terrorist attacks in September 2001 greatly affected our opinions. Do you agree with the majority, or do you think our government should take steps to protect personal freedom as well as ensure our safety? Can we enjoy both at the same time?

SOURCE: FOXNews/Opinion Dynamics Poll, July 29, 2005.

▶ Are Americans becoming less involved in politics or just changing the ways in which they participate?

Many people and organizations have criticized the USA PATRIOT Act, charging that it unduly undermines many fundamental rights and liberties; others—including President George W. Bush and Vice President Dick Cheney—assert that it is needed to fight terrorism and ensure domestic security. Perhaps the most controversial aspect of the act is its loosening of judicial oversight over electronic surveillance—to the point, many people believe, that too much power has been given to the executive branch. These critics fear that the government could abuse this power. Another worrisome concern was the Department of Justice's announcement in 2002 of a new plan to recruit workers, such as mail carriers and utility employees, as informants who are to spot and report "suspicious activity" in what was known as Operation TIPS, for Terrorism Information and Prevention System. (Operation TIPS was subsequently declared illegal and was never implemented.)

While advocates insist that programs of this sort might improve domestic security in the face of terrorist threats, critics see these measures as an infringement on privacy. In a survey conducted in June 2005, an *ABC News* poll revealed that a majority (59 percent) of Americans favored extending the USA PATRIOT Act, but that substantial concerns exist regarding specific components. Fifty-four percent opposed a provision that would require the postal service to let the FBI copy the outside of envelopes and 86 percent opposed allowing the FBI to demand records, such as bank and library records, without a judge's approval.[27] Democrats and Republicans are sharply divided over the USA PATRIOT Act. The majority of Republicans say that they believe such tactics are necessary to fight terrorism, whereas most Democrats feel that they violate individual privacy. In swearing in his new attorney general, Alberto Gonzales, on February 14, 2005, Bush insisted that the act "has been vital to our success in tracking terrorists and disrupting their plans," and Congress voted to extend the act when key aspects of it came up for renewal in 2006.

The controversy surrounding the USA PATRIOT Act illustrates the perpetual need to balance individual liberty and domestic security. These debates are not confined to the United States; all countries must grapple with the dilemma of safeguarding their citizens, ensuring domestic order, and at the same time protecting personal freedom and civil liberties.

TABLE 12.1
What Types of Political Activity are Permissible and by Whom?

STATE OF THE FIRST AMENDMENT 2002 SURVEY

People should be allowed to express unpopular opinions:

67% Strongly Agree

27% Mildly agree

4% Mildly disagree

2% Strongly disagree

SOURCE: Survey by the Freedom Forum, conducted by Center for Survey Research and Analysis, University of Connecticut, June 12–July 5, 2002, and based on telephone interviews with a national adult sample of 1,000.

Data provided by the Roper Center for Public Opinion Research, University of Connecticut.

THE 2004 POLITICAL LANDSCAPE

Freedom of speech should be extended to groups that are sympathetic to terrorists:

29% Strongly agree

21% Mildly agree

24% Strongly disagree

21% Mildly disagree

SOURCE: "The 2004 Political Landscape," Pew Research Center for the People and the Press, Released November 5, 2003, http://people-press.org/reports/print.php3?PageID=762

In two national surveys, people were asked about how supportive they were of allowing people with unpopular opinions to express themselves. In the first survey a solid majority of the people agreed that individuals should be able to express unpopular opinions. However, another survey asked them if groups that were sympathetic to terrorists should be allowed to have free speech. Only 29 percent strongly agreed that the groups should be allowed to exercise free speech. Why do you think that there were discrepancies in the percentages? Do you think that it was because they specifically asked about those supportive of terrorists? Do you think that the polls capture another dynamic—that in the abstract, people support First Amendment freedoms (such a speech and assembly) but when the discussion gets more specific, they hesitate to offer those protections to groups that they do not like?

social capital
networks of relationships among individuals, groups, and institutions that foster trust and cooperation to solve societal problems and establish norms for appropriate behavior in pursuit of mutual benefits and shared interests.

FREEDOM, ACTIVISM, AND PUBLIC OPINION

In theory, the majority of Americans support First Amendment freedoms of speech and assembly. But controversy erupts whenever these broad concepts are put into action. People generally see political participation and activism in positive terms, but they often wonder whether it is good for all groups. Should people be allowed to raise issues with which we disagree or that may offend us? Who should determine what types of activism are permissible and by whom? As you can see in Table 12.1, the public supports free speech when it is vaguely worded (question 1): 67 percent of Americans strongly agree that unpopular positions should be allowed. However, when we examine the issue more specifically, support for free speech is not that strong. After being asked to identify their least liked group, respondents were asked whether this group should be allowed to demonstrate. Seventy-five percent of respondents said that their most disliked group should not have that freedom, showing that a strong majority of Americans' support for activism is quite conditional. As a society, we tend to support rights and privileges for those with whom we agree but oppose the same rights for members of groups that we do not support. As noted in (L I N K) *Chapter 5, pages 169–170,* Americans generally rely on the judiciary to negotiate this fine balance. But if we are to remain a strong participatory democracy, we must as a society come to grips with this controversy. Almost certainly we will never see majority support for obscenity or violence-inducing behavior, but we also need to remember that in a free society, people can and do disagree. The question becomes, how do thoughtful citizens determine the boundaries for legitimate disagreement and allow for reasonable access to free expression? Meanwhile we must also be cautious, as the founders of our country were, to protect the rights of minorities, lest the majority silence their voices and trample their rights.

practicequiz

1. In the context of what "clear and present" national danger did Oliver Wendell Holmes Jr. assert that the Espionage Act curtailing freedom of speech was justified?
   a. World War I
   b. World War II
   c. The Cold War
   d. The Vietnam War

discussionquestions

1. Why is it so difficult for the government to balance personal freedom with homeland security? If the two are in conflict, which do you think is the more important, and why? How much individual freedom should people be required to surrender to ensure their safety?

2. How supportive is the public of civic activism and political mobilization? Do you think people should be more or less supportive? Why?

2. What prompted the lessening of the Red Scare?
   a. the fall of the Soviet Union
   b. grassroots mobilization against Joseph McCarthy
   c. the media's exposure of McCarthy's frauds
   d. anti-McCarthy lobbying in Congress

3. Among other things, the USA PATRIOT ACT
   a. imposes limits on immigration from Middle East countries.
   b. makes it easier for federal agents to keep individuals under surveillance without judicial approval.
   c. suspends the Miranda rights of criminal suspects apprehended at U.S. borders.
   d. limits the sharing of information among federal agencies.

4. Surveys indicate that today the U.S. public's support for activism and free expression
   a. is as strong as ever.
   b. has diminished because of a heightened concern for national security.
   c. has increased.
   d. is quite strong in principle but much weaker when people disagree with the specific position of the activist.

Answers: 1-a, 2-c, 3-b, 4-d.

The Age of Apathy?

▶ **Are Americans becoming less involved in politics or just changing the ways in which they participate?** The level of the American people's engagement with their society and government has caused concern for years and has received even more attention recently. As this book makes clear, to maintain a participatory democracy, it is of fundamental importance that citizens be engaged in politics and community action. Today, many observers of the American scene worry about what appears to be a heightened level of public disengagement from politics, and they dread the consequences in terms of diminished political trust, efficacy, and tolerance.

Nearly a century ago, L. Judson Hanifan became one of the first scholars to raise concerns about political disengagement in the United States. Hanifan is thought to have coined the phrase **social capital,** which he defined as "good will, fellowship, sympathy, and social intercourse among the individuals and families who make up a social unit."[28] He argued that when citizens come

▶ How is technology changing
the way we engage in politics?

together in social and personal interactions, they become accustomed to cooperating with one another and will often use this social capital to work together to improve community well-being.

Many scholars believe that social capital has been steadily declining since World War II and that for several generations Americans have become too focused on their individual wants and needs, at the expense of the collective good. This conclusion, however, is controversial. Some scholars suggest that the level of social engagement has not declined substantially but rather has changed in nature.

To gauge the level of civic engagement in the United States, three political scientists, Sidney Verba, Kay Lehman Schlozman, and Henry Brady, surveyed in 1995 nearly 15,000 people across the country. They found a high level of political participation among young people, especially the college-educated ones.[29] On the other hand, the political scientist Robert Putnam published in 2000 a widely read and discussed book, *Bowling Alone,* in which he contended that the United States is increasingly a nation of nonparticipants.[30] We have groups with no committed activists and citizens with little interest and engagement in civic life and politics. Since the 1950s, Putnam has found membership in traditional organizations—fraternal organizations, the PTA, ethnic-oriented groups, and even bowling leagues (hence his title)—has decreased significantly. Membership in some organizations of these kinds had decreased by 25 percent to 50 percent, and there have been similar levels of decline in the time Americans spend socializing with friends and neighbors. In fact, many Americans don't even know the names of their neighbors.

Putnam's book has aroused much debate and analysis. Many critics acknowledge that indeed there is lower participation in traditional organizations and associations such as the PTA, the Girl Scouts, and bowling leagues, but they argue that other forms of civic participation have increased. Grassroots organizations that focus on local issues appear to be growing, as are local youth sports associations and neighborhood groups—poker clubs, reading clubs, bunko groups, self-help groups, and crime patrols.[31] A prominent social scientist, Theda Skocpol, has found a significant growth in membership in three types of organizations: advocacy groups, public interest groups, and business or professional associations.[32] Advocacy groups—for example, for women, homosexuals, and racial minorities—often start as grassroots organizations but are transformed into professional organizations. In recent decades, there has also been a large increase in public interest advocacy groups working for issues that benefit many—the environment, children, and political reform, for example. Moreover, as

we'll see in (L)(I)(N)(K) *Chapter 13, pages 506–509,* the number of business and professional organizations has grown dramatically.

Researchers' findings on the question of levels of civic participation are mixed. There has been a steady decline in voting and other forms of political participation, but more people today work for political parties or candidates than in the 1950s. Compared to earlier decades, more people discuss politics and try to influence others. Many Americans today call in to talk radio shows, and many still write letters to their members of Congress and city council, as well as to their local newspapers. However, there has also been an increase in the percentage of Americans who do not participate in any political activity—from 50 percent in 1974 to 56 percent in 1994.[33]

By looking at the four aspects of social capital—associations, trust, civic participation, and volunteering—Robert Wuthnow has provided a good structure to analyze the issue of civic engagement.[34] As we have seen, membership levels in traditional organizations are decreasing, but this decline has been almost offset by increasing participation in other organizations. (Overall, there appears to have been a small decrease in associational membership.)

Volunteering has seen a dramatic increase: Wuthnow found that 46 percent of Americans volunteered in the early 1990s, compared to only 26 percent in the early 1970s.[35] As noted, volunteering is more common today than ever, especially among younger Americans. Many high schools require volunteering (often called "community service") for graduation, and many colleges expect to see evidence of volunteering by applicants. Literacy programs are sponsored on many college campuses, and home-building programs such as Habitat for Humanity (in which former President Jimmy Carter became a well-known volunteer) continue to promote civic responsibility. President George H. W. Bush promoted a volunteering program called A Thousand Points of Light, and President Bill Clinton initiated the National Service Proposal. A recent international study found that the United States has the highest levels of volunteerism in the industrial world.[36]

Moreover, concerted student-centered initiatives exist on many college campuses throughout the country to engage students in politics and in their communities. For example, National Basketball Association player Adonal Foyle founded Democracy Matters in 2001 to engage college students in promoting reforms and training them to be lifelong activists. The American Association of State Colleges and Universities partnered with the *New York Times* to create the American Democracy Project, which promotes civic engagement such as voting, advocacy, and grass-

what YOU can do!

Survey your friends to see what kinds of involvement, if any, they have in their community. Are they more likely to be involved in social, religious, or political groups? Are they interested in getting more involved? What sorts of factors prevent them from getting involved? How involved are they in campus politics? Campus life? Based on your findings, prepare a resource guide to help your fellow students get more involved in their community. Web addresses and telephone numbers for local politicians, political parties, and organized interest groups would be handy resources for interested college students. Also provide information about local volunteer opportunities, such as tutoring programs in local public schools, Big Brother and Big Sister programs, local scouting organizations, and similar groups. Helping others get involved is a very rewarding form of political participation in itself.

roots community involvement. Approximately 400 colleges and universities are currently involved with the project.

However, the past decades have witnessed a dramatic drop in levels of trust in government institutions and in one's fellow citizens. In 1964, some 76 percent of Americans said that they could trust officials in Washington to do what was right most or all of the time; by 2004 that number had decreased to 47 percent.[37] Such a dramatic decline in trust is troubling, as the consequences can be vast and dramatic. Moreover the disapproval ratings for the federal government continue to climb (see Figure 12.4).

Thus we have no clear diagnosis of the health of civic engagement in the United States. However, nearly all observers agree that we are at a pivotal moment. As Theda Skocpol has noted, civic engagement is changing dramatically, and further technological changes are likely to continue this process.[38] The growth in advocacy groups raises concerns that political activity is increasingly becoming the sphere of paid professionals, offset by substantially less involvement by "common people." Some believe that this new era of advocacy signals that we are entering an era of more and more leaders and fewer and fewer followers.

▶ **How is technology changing the way we engage in politics?** Contemporary technological advances are dramatically affecting political participation and even politics itself. As noted in LINK *Chapter 11, page 425*, since the early 1950s, television has rapidly developed as an entirely new medium of communication, both positively and negatively affecting civic engagement and political participation. Robert Putnam notes that television pulls people off the streets and into the homes.[39] Gone—probably forever—are the pre–World War II days when people sought most of their entertainment outside their homes: on front porches, at community centers, in movie theaters or music halls, or at local bowling alleys and ballparks. For entertainment, people today tend to stay home and watch television or DVDs, which has isolating effects. Television does have the potential to unite people, as it can arouse deep emotions and engage people through visual appeal, and groups can use television to influence public opinion and recruit supporters. But many critics are concerned that organized groups often use sensationalistic or simplistic television messages to grab viewers' attention at the expense of more substantive communication. In our present era of TV politics, this shift from mass mobilization to attention grabbing has great potential to be exploited by ambitious individuals.

Like television, the Internet can help develop social networks that bridge differences, allowing diverse groups to unite, and it also

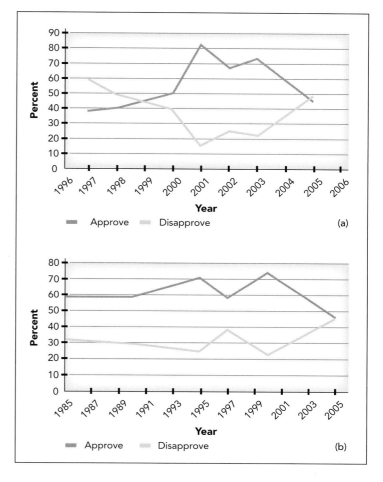

FIGURE 12.4
Public Perception of Government and Business

The data above present the approval rating of the federal government (a) and the approval rating of business corporations (b). Do you see any correlations? What standards do you think were used to rate each?
SOURCE: The Pew Research Center

discussion questions

1. What is social capital? What is the controversy surrounding the civic engagement debate? Is the American population becoming increasingly disengaged and what evidence can be found for and against disengagement? Why is civic engagement important and does it differ for marginalized and privileged groups?

2. How does technology affect political engagement and participation?

what YOU can do!

Mobilize students to resist tobacco use on your campus. For tips about starting a campaign to fight the tobacco industry, check out the "ACT" link on Unfiltered TV's Web page (**http://www.outrageavenue.com**). The Students Working Against Tobacco (SWAT) Web page (**http://www. okswat.com**) has additional tools for activism, giving specific examples— among them health fairs, sit-ins, and youth demonstrations. Take a stand— fight a killer that is directly targeting your age group.

---

helps maintain personal, professional, and family relationships across a distance. But it remains debatable whether the Internet and e-mail help build social capital. If they do, it is a different sort of social capital than we've seen in the past. E-mail is often impersonal, but it does offer great potential for enhancing communication, recruitment, and information sharing. Some analysts believe that technology has made social capital shallower precisely because it is not based on personal and intimate relationships. Only time will prove or disprove the validity of such concerns.

pathways past and present

YOUTH GROUPS

The nature of young people's political activities, like those of other groups, is changing in contemporary America. In the course of this chapter, we have seen that in the era of the Vietnam War (1965–1975), many American young people were active in peace, civil rights, and women's rights groups. Today's youth are contending for different issues. One area in which youth grassroots organizations have been very successful is the fight against the tobacco industry. For example, in 1999, the American Legacy Foundation (ALF) was created as a national, independent public health organization to discourage teenage tobacco use. One of the ALF's initiatives has been the National Truth Campaign, which uses powerful advertising, an interactive Web site (http://www. AmericanLegacy.org), and grassroots events to disseminate facts about the harmful consequences of smoking. To foster statewide *youth-led* efforts against tobacco, the ALF has committed $35 million in grant awards to the states.

State-level grassroots organizations are also launching powerful campaigns to fight smoking among young people. Take, for example, what has been happening in Iowa. The organization JEL (for "Just Eliminate Lies"; http://JELiowa.org) is a grassroots group of Iowa teens, founded with funds that the state received after a major court battle with the tobacco companies. Although the JEL program is administered through a state agency, its board is composed entirely of youth from around the state. On July 25–27, 2005, the Unfiltered JEL Summit, held at Iowa State University, offered a wide variety of classes, from "Tobacco 101" to "Street Marketing." High school students from around Iowa are learning how to oppose Big Tobacco's marketing tactics, get involved in the fight to expose

facts about tobacco use, and resist the misinformation that this industry has been spreading. One example of JEL's activism was to create a dramatic display: a glass case with 1,200 pairs of shoes, representing the number of Americans who die *every day* from tobacco-related causes. Activities like this help young people with fine ideas but little money stand up to a multibillion-dollar industry that they feel seeks to do them harm. ◼

practice quiz

1. What is the central argument of Robert Putnam's book, *Bowling Alone?*
   a. that Americans have become much more independent in their voting patterns and their views on public policy
   b. that since 2001 America has become isolated on the geo-political stage because of its unilateralist tendencies in foreign policy
   c. that Americans lead lives that isolate them socially and make them much less likely to join the civic organizations that people routinely joined forty years ago
   d. that through technology Americans lead lives that are much more interconnected, a fact that underlies the shift to a more globalized economy and social network

2. The scholar Theda Skocpol has found that membership has in fact risen in three kinds of groups:
   a. fraternal orders, unions, and political parties.
   b. public-interest groups, professional organizations, and advocacy groups.
   c. alumni associations, recreational clubs (such as bridge and poker clubs), and religious-based coalitions.
   d. philanthropic societies, internet-based groups, and hobbyists' clubs.

3. Recent studies of the civic engagement patterns of young adults find that they are
   a. volunteering in the community more but trusting people (including the government) less.
   b. caring more about their own contentment and less about the feeling of others (especially the poor).
   c. deepening their engagement in the political system as voters and joining advocacy groups in record numbers.
   d. returning, in increasing numbers, to the activist habits of the young adults of the 1960s and 1970s.

4. It is now clear that the Internet and email help build social capital.
   a. true   b. false

Answers: 1-c, 2-b, 3-a, 4-b.

Conclusion

We have ample evidence that civic engagement is essential to a healthy democracy, but we do not know how much civic disengagement must occur before democracy is threatened. Many observers express concern about the current health of our participatory democracy.

Groups and mass movements develop to help people with problems, reflecting our tradition as a "do something" society (see Pathway Figure on page 493). From the earliest days of our nation, Americans have turned to civic groups both to promote change and to ensure stability. Historically, organized groups have used the grassroots mobilization pathway to advance their objectives, in some cases effectively changing our country. Imagine an America without the civil rights movement, still living with slavery or still legally mandating the separation of people based on race. Imagine an America in which women had no right to vote, own property, resist domestic violence, serve on juries, attend school, or claim custody of their own children in the event of divorce. What would America look like without our constitutional guarantees to come together and petition for change? It would be unrecognizable as America. We so often take these rights for granted, but just contemplating where our country would be without these important social movements puts things into perspective.

It is clear that the grassroots mobilization pathway is not always open to all groups, especially in times of conflict. If we fear for our national security—whether or not the fear is rational—we have reduced the rights of some groups in order to give a sense of safety to the majority. Especially in times of national crisis, we need to be conscious of the temptation to target minority groups, for one of the most basic tenets of our constitutional system is that minority rights must be protected.

Civic activism is one of the greatest freedoms in our participatory democracy. Activism is not a task but a right. Our govern-mental structure and constitutional freedoms allow us the potential to participate directly in the development of our futures. Get involved! As this chapter has amply demonstrated, you *can* make a difference.

YOUR turn!

Are you curious about the views of your fellow students on First Amendment freedoms? Use the information presented in Table 12.1 as a model—starting from the abstract and moving to the specific—in interviewing twenty of your colleagues at random. How many of them support the right of unpopular groups to speak out on campus? First, ask in general terms whether unpopular groups should be allowed to speak on campus. (Most respondents will probably say yes.) Then ask them why they support or oppose this right. Next, ask what group represents the largest terrorist threat to the United States—and finally ask if that group should be allowed to speak on campus, again exploring the reasons for the respondents' support or opposition. Do you agree with them? Why or why not? And then ask ten professors the same questions.

What did you learn from this experiment? Are the attitudes of the faculty similar to those of the students? If not, why do you think they disagree? If so, what does their agreement demonstrate? Who should be allowed to make the final decision to allow a group to speak on campus—students, faculty, or the administration? Examine your school's free-speech policies—how do groups go about getting permission to give a speech or hold a demonstration? Who has final authority to grant permission? Do you agree with the procedure? If not, how might it be changed? Discover what you and others like yourself can do to change university policies that you don't support. Remember, only through action and mobilization can people bring about change. ◼

pathways | Immigration Debate

COURTS   CULTURAL CHANGE   ELECTIONS   GRASSROOTS MOBILIZATION   LOBBYING DECISION-MAKERS

PRO-IMMIGRATION

The Struggle over Immigration Policy   Before 1882, anyone wishing to live in the United States could. Things have changed dramatically since that time. One of the more controversial issues facing our government today is the determination of who should be allowed to immigrate to our country, what we should do to secure our borders, and what should be done with immigrants illegally residing in the country today. Both sides in this debate have taken to the streets to appeal to others to join them and have increasingly turned to mass protest to express their positions. The Pew Hispanic Center estimates the number of illegal immigrants in the United States to be as many as 12 million, or about 1 in 20 workers.

essay questions

1. Many proposals for immigration reform have been debated in recent years. Write an essay in which you critically examine the various proposals presented, being certain to indicate which proposal(s) you think would be most effective in addressing illegal immigration.

2. Why do you think that immigration has become such a hotly contested issue? Why do you think that we are more worried about immigration from Mexico than from other countries? Do you think that Hispanic immigrants are changing our culture? If so, how and in what ways?

1986 1990

Immigration Reform and Control Act allows illegal aliens living in America continuously since January 1, 1982 to apply for legal status; the act also forbids the hiring of illegal aliens, outlines penalties for lack of compliance, and raises annual immigration ceiling to 540,000

Immigration Act sets immigration quotas at 700,000 annually for the next three years and 675,000 for every year thereafter; and eliminates denial of admittance to the U.S. on the basis of individual's beliefs, statements, or associations

1960   **1980**   **2000**

1965

Immigration Act of 1965

Major reform in immigration policy. Sets overall limit of 170,000 immigrants from the Eastern Hemisphere and 120,000 from the Western Hemisphere. Touches off current illegal immigration problem by limiting the number of legal immigrants from neighboring countries.

1977

New act repeals 1965 law; limits immigration to 290,000 worldwide with no more than 20,000 coming from any one country

1978

John H. Tanton founds the Federation for American Immigration Reform, an anti-immigration group

1980

Refugees Act distinguishes refugees from other immigrants and limits the worldwide immigration quota to 270,000

1997

Craig Nelson founds ProjectUSA, an anti-immigration group

1996

Immigration Act doubles Border Patrol to 10,000 agents over five years; also calls for fences to be built at key points on the America-Mexico border; and approves a program to check job applicants' immigration status

1996

President Clinton signs a bill into law cutting numerous social programs for both legal and illegal immigrants in the interest of welfare reform

ANTI-IMMIGRATION

Zadvydas v. Davis
Supreme Court rules that when a detainee's deportation cannot be carried out within a reasonable time period (usually 6 months), the government cannot continue to detain the person

2004
Bush announces new plan allowing 8 million illegal immigrants to obtain temporary worker status

2006
May 1 Boycott Day
About a million immigrants join in a nationwide protest against immigration reform

2001

2004 **2004**

2006

Leocal v. Ashcroft
Supreme Court rules that a drunk driving conviction does not allow for mandatory deportation of legal immigrants

Kerry's campaign spends $1 million on Spanish-language ads, largest amount ever spent by a presidential candidate

March 11
Around 300,000 people march in Chicago to protest the Border Protection, Antiterrorism, and Illegal Immigration Control Act of 2005

2001

INS v. St. Cyr
Supreme Court rules that the government cannot deport aliens without judicial review and cannot apply deportation standards retroactively.

2002
The Homeland Security Act places the Immigration and Naturalization Service under the Department of Homeland Security. Immigration responsibilities are then divided into Citizenship and Immigration Services, Customs and Border Protection, and U.S. Immigration and Customs Enforcement

President Bush unveils a plan for immigraiton reform including sending 6,000 more national guard troops to the Mexican border

2005
The Minuteman Project is launched on the America-Mexico border. Minutemen were civilians who volunteered to monitor 23 miles of the border, claiming that the U.S. Border Patrol was spread too thin to adequately perform its duties

2006

July 9
Anti-Immigration protest held in Los Angeles involving the Minuteman Project and other groups.

2004
Benitez v. Mata
Supreme Court rules that any previously deported immigrant can be prohibited re-entry and can face future deportation

Chapter Review

1. Our constitutional guarantees of speech, religion, press, and assembly permit citizens to unite to petition the government about their concerns. These freedoms allow mass movements to develop, often changing our country and culture.

2. Organized interests allow for a safety valve, especially in times of great social, economic, political, and cultural upheaval and change. In their absence, more violent forms of expression might be employed.

3. The people of our country have a long tradition of coming together in groups to get things done. This tendency for group action has grown in frequency and importance as our society has become more complex and diverse.

4. The success of protests in colonial times left an important mark on our political culture, encouraging ordinary people to participate in civic affairs.

5. Throughout our history, social movements have had much in common, often reinforcing each other, but each movement has also had its unique qualities.

6. In theory, most Americans believe that constitutional guarantees for activism should exist for all, but applying these abstractions to specific cases proves difficult. During war, a delicate balance must be struck between the desire to protect individual rights and the need to promote national security, demonstrating the complexity of the negotiation required.

7. The current scholarly debate over the level of civic engagement in present-day America illustrates the importance of participation on our democracy. So does the development of new civic engagement projects throughout the country and around the world.

CHAPTER REVIEW TEST

1. A citizen's participation in an organized interest group is good for democracy; it cultivates
   a. self-discipline, patience, and partisan fervor.
   b. wisdom, patriotism, and generosity.
   c. political connections, historical perspective, and political endurance.
   d. tolerance, political efficacy, and political trust.

2. One effect of the American Revolution was that faith in mobs and rioting became entrenched in the new nation.
   a. true   **b.** false

3. Nineteenth century activist movements were often mutually supporting; for example,
   a. the prohibition movement helped sow the seeds of the abolition movement.
   b. abolition societies trained leaders of the women's suffrage and prohibition movements.
   c. leaders of the prison reform movement later helped found the Anti-immigration League.
   d. many members of the WCTU later joined the SNCC.

4. Who said "remember the ladies" and what did he or she mean?
   a. Lucretia Mott; she meant that with the Fifteenth Amendment, Congress should grant women, and not just freed black men, the right to vote.
   b. Rutherford B. Hayes; he meant that Congress should remember the delicate sensibilities of women and not thrust them into the sordid world of politics through suffrage.
   c. Abigail Adams; she meant that delegates to the Constitutional Convention should keep in mind how earlier models of representative democracies had created painful legal disadvantages for women by depriving them of any political voice.
   d. Alice Stokes Paul; she meant that when men in American politics complain about women's rights activists, they should recall those who were enduring hunger strikes and force feedings in the cause of political justice.

5. What did W.C.T.U. stand for?
   a. the Worldwide Christian Temperance Union.
   b. the Western Coalition of Trade Unions.
   c. the Women's Christian Temperance Union.
   d. the White Christian Triumphalist Union.

6. Early social movements in this country, such as the abolition, suffrage, and temperance movements, helped make average citizens believe that they could attain political power through group action.
   a. true   **b.** false

7. When was the Progressive Movement?
   a. 1810–1840.   **b.** 1850–1880.
   c. 1890–1920.   **d.** 1960–1970.

8. The rise of the National Association of Manufacturers in 1895 illustrates what historic principle?

a. that factory owners usually have their employees' best interests at heart

b. that the formation of one labor union often spurs the formation of another labor union

c. that the formation of one interest group often spurs the formation of another opposing group

d. that trade unions were on the wane by 1895

9. What era in the twentieth century contained the highest level of domestic unrest in the U.S. since the Civil War?
a. the Great Depression
b. the Red Scare
c. the Vietnam era
d. post-9/11

10. What specifically prompted the modern American civil rights movement of 1955–1965?
a. racism
b. the assassination of Medgar Evers
c. the revitalization of the KKK
d. faltering civil rights progress after the *Brown* decision

11. What historical trend in this country triggered a reconsideration of forms of legal discrimination against women in the twentieth century?
a. women's increased enrollment in universities after WWI
b. the dramatic increase in numbers of women working outside the home after WWII
c. the appointment of Sandra Day O'Connor to the Supreme Court in the 1980s
d. the substantial increase, during the Clinton administration, in the number of women in the federal judiciary

12. Equal pay for equal work
a. was a slogan begun by feminists in the 1980s as part of the ERA initiative.
b. was the principle behind the Equal Pay Act of 1963.
c. has finally been achieved in U.S. employment, no matter the sex of the employee.
d. was a principle declared at the Seneca Falls convention of 1848.

13. NOW was founded in 1966
a. because of the ineffectiveness of the EEOC.
b. because the ERA had failed to be ratified the year before.
c. because Vietnam War protests had that year become popular and powerful enough to trigger activism in other areas, including women's rights.

d. because the charismatic New York congresswoman Bella Abzug had just assumed office and made it her first priority.

14. The once very popular Equal Rights Amendment failed to get ratified because
a. most of the country did not fully subscribe to its principles.
b. Congress would not endorse it.
c. a very well-organized group of activists mobilized effectively against it.
d. it was found to be unconstitutional by the Supreme Court.

15. The Stonewall Riots of 1969
a. marked the unpopularity of the Vietnam War for the majority of Americans.
b. initiated the gay rights movement in this country.
c. demonstrated the lack of a "safety valve" for effective political expression for African Americans at the time.
d. were organized and led by Jerry Falwell, initiating what later became the Moral Majority.

16. What is the largest religiously-affiliated interest group in this country?
a. the Moral Majority
b. the Southern Baptist Leadership Conference
c. Protestants for a Democratic America
d. the Christian Coalition

17. What interest group helped create the Republican Party's "Contract with America" and win both houses of Congress in 1994?
a. the Christian Coalition
b. Protestants for a Democratic America
c. the Southern Baptist Leadership Conference
d. the Moral Majority

18. In the 2000 presidential election, what percentage of white evangelical voters voted for George Bush?
a. About 45 percent   **b.** About 55 percent
c. About 65 percent   **d.** About 75 percent

19. The USA PATRIOT ACT grants the CIA, the FBI, and the National Security Agency increased latitude in conducting electronic surveillance on both resident foreigners and U.S. citizens.
a. true   **b.** false

20. Research indicates that current levels of civic engagement are now at their lowest level in American political history.
a. true   **b.** false

DISCUSSION QUESTIONS

1. What legacy did early American social movements, from colonial times through the Civil War, bequeath to contemporary social movements?

2. How does the social contract theory shape current views of political participation?

3. How does the Constitution guarantee the right of Americans to organize and petition their government?

4. How should the government balance the constitutional guarantees that allow civic organization and mobilization, on the one hand, with the need to protect social and domestic order, on the other?

5. How do social movements influence each other and society? Give some historical and contemporary examples.

6. Why are scholars, politicians, journalists, and citizens concerned about the level of political engagement in the United States and other advanced industrial democracies?

7. How has civic engagement changed in this country, and how do these changes affect American society as a whole? Does technology promote civic engagement or disengagement? Give the evidence for each.

8. What group, movement, or individual do you fear as the greatest danger to the American people? Explain why that group, movement, or individual should or shouldn't be allowed to demonstrate.

INTERNET RESOURCES

AFL-CIO: http://www.aflcio.org

American Civil Liberties Union: http://www.aclu.org

American Democracy Project: http://www.aascu.org/programs/adp/default.htm

Center for Responsive Politics: http://www.opensecrets.org

Christian Coalition of America: http://www.cc.org

Citizenship 2000 Project: http://www.bbc.co.uk/northernireland/schools/11_16/citizenship2000/pdf/pr01.pdf

Democracy Matters: http://www.democracymatters.org

Feminist Majority Foundation: http://www.feminist.org

Heritage Foundation: http://www.heritage.org

Human Rights Campaign: http://www.hrc.org

Internet Nonprofit Center 2000: http://www.nonprofits.org/website.htm

League of Women Voters: http://www.lwv.org

MeetUp—Organizing Local Interest Groups: http://www.meetup.com

National Association for the Advancement of Colored People (NAACP): http://www.naacp.org

National Rifle Association: http://www.nra.org

Peace-Not-War: http://www.peace-not-war.org

Project Vote Smart: http://www.vote-smart.org

Rock the Vote: http://www.rockthevote.org

StreeTheory: http://www.streetheory.org

Truth Organization: http://www.thetruth.com

Youth in Action: http://www.youthlink.org

ADDITIONAL READING

Baumgardner, Jennifer, and Amy Richards. *Grassroots: A Field Guide for Feminist Activism.* New York: Farrar, Straus & Giroux, 2005.

Burns, Nancy, Kay Lehman Schlozman, and Sidney Verba. *The Private Roots of Public Action: Gender, Equality, and Political Participation.* Cambridge, MA: Harvard University Press, 2001.

De Benedetti, Charles, and Charles Chatfield. *An American Ordeal: The Antiwar Movement of the Vietnam Era.* Syracuse, NY: Syracuse University Press, 1999.

Gerston, Larry N. *Public Policy Making in a Democratic Society: A Guide to Civic Engagement.* New York: Sharpe, 2002.

King, Martin Luther, Jr. "Letter from Birmingham Jail." 1963. Available online at http://almaz.com/nobel/peace/MLK-jail.html.

Kryzanek, Michael. *Angry, Bored, Confused: A Citizen Handbook of American Politics.* Boulder, CO: Westview Press, 1999.

Milner, Henry. *Civic Literacy: How Informed Citizens Make Democracy Work.* Hanover, NH: University Press of New England, 2002.

Parenti, Michael. *The Cultural Struggle.* New York: Seven Stories Press, 2006.

Parker, Alison. *Purifying America: Women, Cultural Reform, and Pro-Censorship Activism, 1873–1933.* Chicago: University of Illinois Press, 1997.

Putnam, Robert D. *Bowling Alone: The Collapse and Revival of American Community.* New York: Simon & Schuster, 2000.

Putnam, Robert D., ed. *Democracies in Flux: The Evolution of Social Capital in Contemporary Society.* New York: Oxford University Press, 2002.

Skocpol, Theda, and Morris Fiorina, eds. *Civic Engagement in American Democracy.* Washington, DC: Brookings Institution Press, 1999.

KEY TERMS

abolition   467

Christian Coalition   481

egalitarianism   464

Equal Pay Act   476

Equal Rights Amendment (ERA)   470

Espionage Act   484

feminism   468

labor union   473

Moral Majority   481

Progressive movement   473

Prohibition   470

Sedition Act   484

social capital   487

Title VII of the Civil Rights Act of 1964   476

trade association   473

Underground Railroad   468

USA PATRIOT Act   485

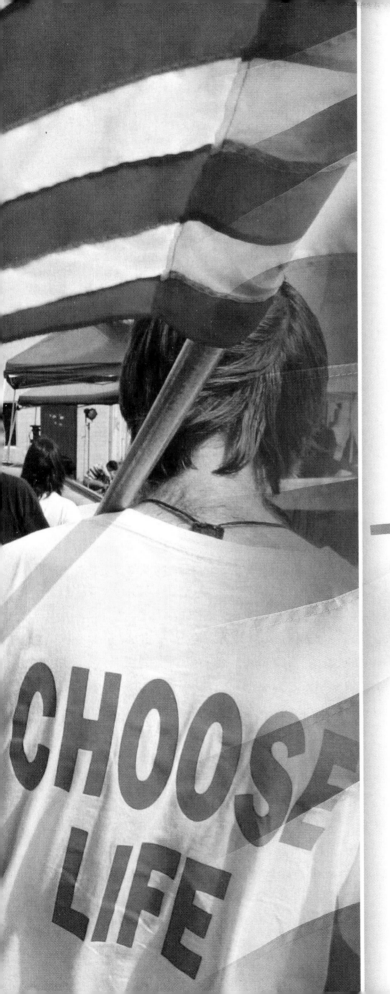

When a Federal District Court judge in Tampa, Florida refused, for a second time, to order the reinsertion of a feeding tube into severely brain-damaged Terri Schaivo, protesters assembled outside her hospice to demonstrate their disagreement over the decision. People often come together—either in protest or celebration—to express their concerns. We have a strong history of "collective action" and it is protected in the Constitution.

CHAPTER 13
INTEREST GROUPS

The Power of the National Rifle Association   On April 20, 1999, twelve students at Columbine High School in Littleton, Colorado, were killed during a murderous rampage by two of their classmates. Twenty-three other students were wounded. It was the worst school shooting ever to occur in the United States. A horrified and outraged American public demanded government action. To many Americans, it seemed clear that although gun control laws would not erase the Columbine tragedy, restricting access to handguns could make society safer. Public opinion solidly favored imposing more restrictions on purchasing and owning guns, and respondents saying that they wanted to see tougher gun laws increased by nearly 10 percent.[1]

During the week following the shootings, gun control measures were discussed and proposed at both state and federal levels. In more than a dozen state legislatures, gun legislation was proposed,

(Photo: James Estrin/The New York Times)

The worst instance of school violence occurred in Columbine High School in 1999. Fifteen people, including one teacher and the gunmen themselves, died. Following this event, people turned to the government to devise security measures to make schools safer. Do you think they have been successful? Are schools more safe today than they were seven years ago?

and—with the tie-breaking vote of Vice President Al Gore—the U.S. Senate passed a bill restricting purchases at gun shows and pawnshops. President Bill Clinton proposed even stronger measures, which would impose a waiting period before purchasing and would hold parents responsible for certain crimes that their children committed with guns. The president pushed very hard to see these proposals become law, even mentioning the need for stricter gun control laws in his State of the Union address in January 2000.

Given intense public pressure, you might expect that major gun control legislation would have passed. Did it? No. The congressional conference committee to which competing Senate and House gun control bills were referred failed to resolve the differences between the Senate's tough measure and the much more lenient bill that, under the guidance of Republican members, passed in the House. This failure was partly the result of intense lobbying by the National Rifle Association. The NRA spent nearly $3 million to fight the Senate bill and advised its members to tell their representatives to vote against the proposal.[2] The amount of money that the NRA spends varies from year to year and is influenced by national events. The clash between the NRA and Clinton helped raise membership in the NRA, which by the end of the year 2000 reached an all-time high of 4.2 million.[3] Founded more than a century ago as an organization representing hunters' interests, the NRA has since evolved into one of the most controversial interest groups in the United States. *Fortune*

magazine in 2001 named it the most powerful lobby in America.[4] It has immense financial resources. It has not wavered from its original purpose, safe gun ownership—nor has it diminished its fierce opposition to any attempt to infringe what its members believe is an unrestricted constitutional right to bear arms under the Second Amendment. ("A well-regulated Militia, being necessary for the security of a free State, . . . the right of the people to keep and bear Arms, shall not be infringed.")

The NRA's financial resources and political clout are enormous. It has about 300 full-time employees at its headquarters outside Washington D.C. and enjoys grassroots support in every congressional district across the nation. It participates in more than 10,000 political campaigns at all levels of government and raises millions of dollars to help support candidates who share its views on gun ownership and its opposition to gun regulation. In 2000, the NRA indirectly spent $6.6 million on behalf of Republican candidates and directly contributed $1.2 million to GOP campaigns while also contributing $472,000 to Democrats who supported its positions.[5]

In elections that the NRA targets, its involvement is impressive. For example, in 2000, it targeted the Virginia Senate race, in which it bought 378 television ads and 155 radio ads; overall, it spent more than $500,000 to support the successful Republican candidate, George Allen.[6] "I don't think that there's any doubt that, in at least five states I can think of, the NRA had a decisive influence," said former president Bill Clinton. "You've got to give it to them; they've done a great job. They probably had more to do than anyone else in the fact that we didn't win the House this time. And they hurt Al Gore," the Democratic presidential candidate who narrowly lost the 2000 election.[7]

The NRA is a good example of the dilemma that interest groups arouse. On the one hand, the National Rifle Association is simply a group of like-minded citizens who strongly believe in the right to bear arms under the Second Amendment and have joined together to petition their government on behalf of their position. On the other hand, because the NRA is so powerful and so successful, many Americans are troubled that the proportionately small number of NRA members are thwarting the will of the majority, which *does* support some forms of gun control. Moreover, because the NRA has extraordinary resources, its lobbying efforts cause concern about the bias in representation that results from well-funded groups' influence on our political system.

The power and sway of the NRA underscore many delicate issues in contemporary American politics. One of these questions is whether people who lack ample private resources or do not join interest groups can nevertheless make their concerns known to the government. Another is what balance should be struck between the public good and the self-interest of powerful groups. As you read this chapter, consider these issues very carefully. ■

▶ **Can an interest group**
use multiple pathways
to achieve its goals?

interest group
a group of like-minded individuals who
band together to influence public policy,
public opinion, or governmental officials.

single-issue interest groups
groups that are interested primarily in one
area of public policy.

multi-issue interest groups
groups interested in pursuing a broad
range of public policy issues.

Interest groups are organizations outside the government that attempt to influence the government's behavior, decision making, and allocation of resources. As you saw in Chapter 12, ever since the nation's founding, Americans have formed groups to address their concerns and to influence their peers, their communities, and their government. To promote their common goals, as you will see in this chapter, people create and join interest groups. We will examine why people join and remain in interest groups, and we will consider the impact that interest groups' actions have in the United States. You will also learn about the tools and tactics that these groups use as they *lobby*—that is, work to gain influence within the government and with the public at large in order to influence officials and win public support.

Many people look skeptically at interest groups and tend to see them in a very negative light. Although extremist members can heavily influence many groups, interest groups perform many valuable functions in our democracy. Often there is tension between what is best for the group and its members and what is best for society, but this tension can be healthy because it focuses attention on issues that otherwise would not receive much notice and can promote constructive public debate. While you are reading this chapter, you should consider the very nature of interest groups—do they give people who are interested in politics an opportunity to turn their energy and activism into action, or do they serve to promote the unhealthy divisions that increasingly characterize American politics?

Key Questions

1. Why are interest groups important in the democratic process? How and why do interest groups form?

2. Why have we seen such a dramatic increase in the number and activity of interest groups in the last forty years? Why are many scholars, politicians, and citizens concerned about this explosion in interest group advocacy?

3. How have the tactics of indirect lobbying changed? What are the consequences of these changes for our governing process?

4. Why do interest groups need money? What tactics do they use to raise funds? How do they attract and maintain membership?

5. How influential are interest groups in American politics?

The Role of Interest Groups in the Policy Process

WHAT ARE INTEREST GROUPS?

In our diverse society, people join interest groups to find a place to belong, to articulate their point of view, and to promote their common goals. Three primary characteristics define interest groups. First, they are voluntary associations of joiners. Some interest groups are formal, including trade groups such as the American Medical Association; others are more informal, such as neighborhood groups that form to fight zoning changes. The second characteristic of all interest groups is that their members share common beliefs. Interest groups are collections of like-minded individuals, drawn together because they have a common set of interests, beliefs, or values. Doctors join groups such as the American Medical Association to promote patient care, to safeguard ethics in the practice of medicine, and to ensure their own economic viability. Hunters join organized groups to uphold their gun ownership rights and to ensure access to public land. Third, interest groups focus on influencing government. People join them because they want government policy to reflect their preferences, and consequently, interest groups spend time, energy, and money trying to influence public officials.

As you will shortly see, interest groups use many different tactics in trying to accomplish their goals. But all interest groups exist for the purpose of influencing others—their own members, other like-minded associations, the general public, and elected and appointed officials. **Single-issue interest groups** focus primarily or exclusively on one issue, such as the environment, peace, or abortion. **Multi-issue interest groups,** by contrast, pursue a broader range of issues grouped around a central theme. One example of a multi-issue group is the National Organization for Women (NOW), which works on a number of issues that members believe advance the rights and status of women—educational equality, sexual harassment, reproductive freedom, and pay issues. Similarly, the Christian Coalition strives to promote its values by fighting same-sex marriage, attempting to stop abortion, and promoting abstinence-only sex education, and in general to give religion a greater role in everyday life. Although these two groups often stand on opposite sides of issues, they have in common many characteristics, ranging from the strength of their members' commitment to the tactics they use in influencing our government and our society. As you'll see, at different times each group may use different strategies to influence others, but they both aggressively try to have their values adopted by our officials and reflected in our public policies.

pathways of action

LULAC

▶ **Can an interest group use multiple pathways to achieve its goals?**

The League of United Latin American Citizens (LULAC) is one of the oldest and most influential organizations representing Latinos in the United States. It was founded in 1929 in Corpus Christi, Texas, when three separate Hispanic groups banded together to demand equal rights and opportunities in education, government, law, business, and health care. Today, LULAC has 115,000 members in the United States and Puerto Rico, organized into 700 councils. LULAC provides its members with a number of important services, ranging from conducting citizenship and voter registration drives to pressuring localities into providing more low-income housing units. It also strives to help Hispanic youth by providing training programs and educational counseling, as well as by offering more than $1 million in scholarships annually.

Through its activism, LULAC has won a number of important successes that have advanced the civil rights and liberties of Hispanic Americans. In 1945, the California LULAC Council successfully sued to integrate the Orange County school system, which had justified segregation with the claim that Mexican children were "more poorly clothed and mentally inferior to white children."[8] LULAC also provided financial support and attorneys to challenge the practice of excluding Hispanics from juries (*Hernandez* v. *Texas*). In 1954, the U.S. Supreme Court ruled that such exclusion was unconstitutional. In 1966, LULAC marched with and financially supported the largely Spanish-speaking United Farm Workers union in its struggle for minimum wages. LULAC National Education Service Centers, Inc., created in 1973, today serves more than 20,000 Hispanic students a year. The LULAC Institute was established in 1996 to provide model volunteer programs for Latino communities, and since 2004, the LULAC Leadership Initiative has been revitalizing Hispanic neighborhoods by creating grassroots programs in 700 Latino communities. ◼

To highlight the impact that immigrants have in America, LULAC helped organize rallies across the country on May 1, 2006. Pictured above are Elba Castro and Saul Torres at the Dallas, Texas rally at City Hall. What challenges do you think LULAC will face when trying to mobilize immigrants? Why do you think that bridging coalitions is important for LULAC?

▶ **How many interest groups**
are there in the United States?

TABLE 13.1
Five Functions of Interest Groups

FUNCTION	DEFINITION
To represent constituents	Government allocates more attention to large groups than to individuals
To provide a means of political participation	Allows an individual to feel a sense of political power
To educate the public	Informs the public about issues through research, congressional testimonies and public relations
To build agendas	Creates awareness of issues
To serve as a government watchdog	Monitors programs and assesses their effectiveness

FUNCTIONS OF INTEREST GROUPS IN A DEMOCRATIC SOCIETY

As you saw in Chapter 12, interest groups play an important role in our representative democracy. They serve as a vehicle for citizens to peacefully express their concerns to government officials—that is, to exercise their First Amendment right to petition their government. Without interest groups, Americans would be overwhelmed by the size of our government and by the fragmentation of our society. This chapter will show how interest groups both advance and hinder democracy.

In the United States, interest groups serve five specific functions (see Table 13.1). First, interest groups represent constituents before the government. Without the organization and strength of interest groups, individual voices might drown in our complex society.

Second, interest groups provide an important means of political participation, often coupled with other forms of political activity. For individuals, voting, writing letters to members of Congress, and donating money to political campaigns are all positive forms of political participation, but so is being active in an interest group. Volunteering time, taking part in a group, and contributing money are all important ways in which people can gain a sense of individual and collective power and thus a voice in our

society. Such feelings of political efficacy promote other forms of political engagement.

A third function of interest groups is to educate the public. By sponsoring research, serving as advocates, testifying before congressional committees, conducting public relations campaigns, and engaging in similar activities, members of the public learn about various issues in more detail. Obviously, interest groups present only their viewpoint on an issue; they are not in the business of arguing their opponent's case. For many Americans, this bias is a concern, and we will discuss it in more detail later in this chapter. It should be noted, however, that on many controversial issues, interest groups emerge on both sides, leading to greater public awareness and knowledge.

Fourth, interest groups influence policymaking by agenda building—that is, simply by bringing an otherwise little-known issue to the forefront. By attempting to educate the public about certain issues or by running public relations campaigns, they focus the attention of the public and of officials on issues that might otherwise be ignored.

Finally, interest groups contribute to the governing process by serving as government watchdogs. They monitor government programs, examining their strengths and weaknesses and thereby assessing the effectiveness of programs that are important to their members. Of course, each individual group's verdict on the programs it monitors may be one-sided, but when we look at interest group activities collectively, we can appreciate that their overall effect is to make our government serve its people more efficiently.

THE INTEREST GROUP EXPLOSION

▶ **How many interest groups are there in the United States?**
Between the 1960s and the 1990s, the United States witnessed an explosion in the number and activity level of interest groups. In 1959, there were 5,843 organizations with a national scope. That number almost doubled by 1970, reaching 10,308; a decade later, 14,726 organizations had registered with the federal government. By the mid-1990s, the level of growth had tapered off to slightly over 22,200 national organizations, and that is about the number that exist today.[9] Since 1960, there has been a dramatic surge in the number of citizen groups advocating civil rights and civil liberties, as well as a sharp rise in the number of public interest groups that seek consumer protection and environmental protection. In the private sector, the number of groups representing businesses and trades has also risen, in part to counter the success of other public interest groups.

Later in this chapter, we will discuss the specific types of groups, but first we need to examine the causes of this explosion of interest groups and some of its consequences.

pathways profile

RALPH NADER

Ralph Nader was born in 1934 in Connecticut to Lebanese immigrants. He excelled in school, graduating from Princeton in 1955 and from Harvard Law School in 1958. After becoming interested in the issue of automobile safety, he became a consultant for the U.S. Department of Labor. In 1965, he published *Unsafe at Any Speed,* a best-selling condemnation of the American auto industry. The book's criticism of unsafe cars prompted Congress to pass the National Traffic and Motor Vehicle Safety Act in 1966. Nader successfully sued General Motors for invasion of privacy after the company aggressively tried to discredit him, going to the extreme of hiring a private detective to follow him.

With the money he won from the lawsuit, Nader founded several advocacy organizations, the most prominent being Public Citizen. The group became involved in various environmental issues, such as land use, pesticides, and nuclear safety. He inspired hundreds of young people ("Nader's Raiders") to become activists, working with him to examine governmental actions and organizations. They scrutinized the practices of the Federal Trade Commission, the Food and Drug Administration, the Interstate Commerce Commission, and the Federal Aviation Administration. Out of this activism, Nader's Raiders published books on such topics as clean air, clean water, nursing homes, and nuclear missiles. Nader himself has written, cowritten, or edited more than twenty books. By focusing their efforts on research, analysis, and lobbying, Nader and his activists dramatically changed how consumer advocacy functions in the United States.

Nader ran for president as the Green Party candidate in 1996 and 2000 and as an independent candidate in 2004. There was a great deal of controversy over his 2000 campaign, causing some observers to assert that he "spoiled" Al Gore's victory because Nader's vote totals far exceeded George W. Bush's margins of victory in New Hampshire and Florida. In fact, if only slightly more than 500 of the 97,488 Nader votes in Florida had instead gone to Gore, Gore would have won the state and the presidency. Nader himself concedes that had he not run, more of his supporters would have voted for Gore than for Bush. Nevertheless, had Gore been able to carry his home state of Tennessee, he would have won the presidency, regardless of what happened in Florida, so not all the responsibility for his loss can be pinned on Nader.

Ralph Nader lives an austere life in a simple apartment and refuses to drive a car. Though he certainly is unorthodox and controversial, there is no denying the significance of his work in changing the way in which we view consumer advocacy. ▪

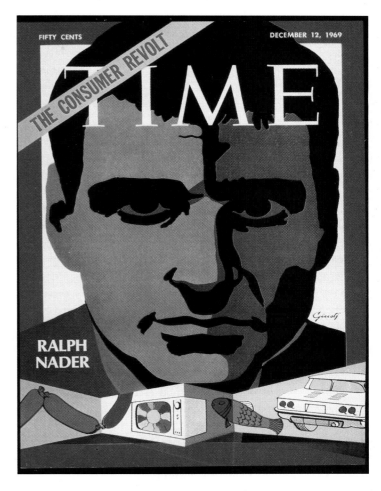

The cover of *Time* magazine from December 12, 1969, shows future presidential candidate Ralph Nader. At the time, Nader was leading what *Time* called the "Consumer Revolt." His actions led to major changes in public policy and made government officials consider consumer safety more directly. How may elections be affected by third party candidates such as Nader?

▶ **Why has the number of** interest groups grown so rapidly since the 1960s?

cleavages
divisions of people based on at least one social characteristic, such as educational attainment or race.

disturbance theory
the idea that interest groups form when resources become scarce to contest the influence of other interest groups.

lobbyists
people who are paid to represent interest groups before governmental officials and institutions.

political action committee (PAC)
a political organization created to raise and spend money to influence electoral outcomes.

▶ **Why has the number of interest groups grown so rapidly since the 1960s?** One of the many reasons why interest groups exist in the United States is to unify subgroups of people in our diverse and complex society. As the country grew in size and began to broaden the range of political power exercised by people of different religions, ethnicities, income levels, genders, and racial makeups, differences deepened to form social divisions or **cleavages.** The presence of these cleavages has been important in the development of various interest groups because many of them strive to gather supporters across social cleavages, serving as a unifying factor in a fragmented society. For example, NOW tries to bring together a diverse coalition of women and men to promote the rights of all women. Other interest groups try to exploit cleavages, often using fear of certain groups to mobilize their supporters.

The nature of our governmental system itself is a second explanation for why interest groups have existed in our society since the earliest days. The American federal system provides many opportunities to influence government at different levels. Groups can appeal to the federal government, to state governments, to county and municipal governments, and to special jurisdictions such as school districts. The division of power among three branches of government, moreover, allows additional opportunities to petition.

Our federal system helps explain why a larger percentage of Americans are involved in interest groups than the citizens of other democracies. People who live in more centralized countries, such as the United Kingdom and France, have fewer opportunities to bring pressure on government. There, a great many issues that would be dealt with locally in the United States are the responsibility of the national legislature. These more unified governments simply do not offer as many points of access as our relatively decentralized system does. Americans therefore tend to be far more active in interest groups than citizens of other nations, as there are more opportunities to influence officials at different levels.

What accounts for the large growth in interest groups in the past forty years? The political scientist David Truman's **disturbance theory** has been well received as an explanation. Truman's theory states that groups form whenever other interests are perceived as threatening or whenever the status quo is disturbed.

Essentially, then, *social change* causes the growth of interest groups. As society becomes more complex, divisions emerge, which then become the basis for new groups. However, not everyone agrees with this theory. Others argue that the development of groups depends crucially on the *quality of leadership* of the group.[10] If we modify the disturbance theory to include the role of leaders in causing social change, we can better explain the growth of groups in recent decades. A hybrid explanation would say that charismatic individuals come forward to lead the new groups that result from social change.

In addition to the fact that American society has been changing rapidly since 1960, the growth of interest groups in the United States can be attributed to the growth of government. As government takes on new responsibilities, interest groups arise to attempt to influence how these responsibilities are carried out. Interest groups also form as people try to get a "piece of the action"—that is, attempt to influence how government allocates resources in exercising its new responsibilities.

A third explanation for the rapid proliferation of interest groups lies in the changing social characteristics of the American population. Americans are more educated and have more disposable income, making it easier for interest groups to target and activate them. As you'll see, the more educated and wealthier citizens become, the more likely they are to participate in politics generally and to join interest groups. Thus interest groups have grown simply because the potential pool of likely members has also grown. Groups have also benefited from new technology, which makes it easier to target potential members and contact interested people.

TYPES OF INTEREST GROUPS

Interest groups span the political spectrum. To make sense of the variety, it's best to divide interest groups into four categories: economic groups, public interest groups, think tanks and universities, and governmental units (see Table 13.2). Each type of group exists to advance its goals, which may or may not be in the nation's best interest. We will discuss the specific tools that interest groups use to advance their cause, but first it is impor-

INTEREST GROUPS CHAPTER THIRTEEN 507

▶ Can a single corporation
have its own interest group?

TABLE 13.2
Types of Interest Groups

Type	Examples	Founded	Members	Issue	PAC	Donations to Federal Candidates in 2004
Economic	U.S. Chamber of Commerce (www.uschamber.com)	1912	3 million businesses	Representation of businesses before the government	Yes	$173,150
	National Association of Realtors (www.realtor.org)	1908	1 million	Increase the profits of realtors	Yes	3.79 million
	American Medical Association (www.ama-assn.org)	1847	13 million	Physician's cooperation on important issues	Yes	2.04 million
	American Federation of Teachers (www.aft.org)	1916	1.3 million	Improve lives of teachers	Yes	1.7 million
Public Interest	AARP (www.aarp.org)	1958	35 million	Quality of life for older citizens	No	
	Human Rights Campaign (www.hrc.org)	1980	600,000	Equal rights for gay, lesbian, bisexual and transgender citizens	Yes	1.17 million
	Sierra Club (www.sierraclub.org)	1892	750,000	Environmental protection	Yes	388,960
	National Rifle Association (www.nra.org)	1871	4.3 million	Promote right to bear arms	Yes	12.8 million
	Public Citizen (www.citizen.org)	1971	150,000	Representation of consumers	No	
	MoveOn.org (www.moveon.org)	1998	3.3 million	Citizen participation in government	Yes	203,422
Think Tanks	Brookings Institution (www.brook.edu)	1916	140 resident/ non resident scholars	Nonprofit research organization	No	
Governmental Units	National Governors Association (www.nga.org)	1908	50	Bipartisan organization of the nation's governors	No	

SOURCE: http://www.fec.gov

tant to understand the variety of groups and their commonalities and differences.

▶ **Can a single corporation have its own interest group?** Economic groups include trade associations, labor unions, and professional associations. Trade associations are organized commercial groups, ranging from industrial corporations to agricultural producers. One of the most prominent trade associations is the U.S. Chamber of Commerce. It presents the interests of member businesses to government officials and institutions.

In their pursuit of profit, many corporations form their own interest groups, hire **lobbyists** (professionals who try to influence governmental officials), create **political action committees (PACs),** and use other techniques to bring their needs to the attention of government and the general public (see Figure 13.1 on page 508).

Hiring Lobbyists, Winning Federal Dollars

More and more public entities like cities, counties, states, utilities and Indian tribes are hiring firms to lobby Congress. One goal of such lobbying is to place earmarks — money directed toward a specific project — into appropriation bills.

The amount spent by public entities on lobbying has climbed steadily over the past eight years ...

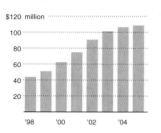

...while at the same time earmarks overall (to both public and private entities) have become much larger.

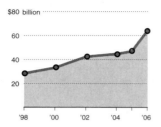

Cities dominate among public clients of lobbyists

Cities account for more than a third of the 1,421 public entities that had lobbyists in 2005.

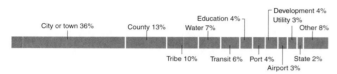

City or town 36% | County 13% | Water 7% | Education 4% | Development 4% | Utility 3% | Other 8%
Tribe 10% | Transit 6% | Port 4% | Airport 3% | State 2%

Cities that lobbied received large earmarks

Between 1998 and 2005, cities large and small spent at least $161 million on lobbying, and received at least $2.57 billion in earmarks. Here are some examples.

CITY	POPULATION (2005, EST.)	LOBBYING SPENDING (1998-2005)	EARMARKS RECEIVED (FISCAL 1999-2006, MILLIONS)
Laredo, TX	193,117	$1,542,500	$44
St. Louis, MO	339,211	1,317,000	45
San Antonio, TX	1,214,725	1,280,000	22
Portland, OR	538,544	1,215,876	94
Sandy City, UT	89,319	1,012,000	12
Pembroke Pines, FL	151,045	180,000	3
Treasure Island, FL	7,514	180,000	51
Homestead, FL	38,396	140,000	2
Cocoa, FL	17,606	60,000	1

How it works

Lobbying paid off for the city of Pharr, Tex. (population 57,000), which spent $340,000 on lobbying over three years and received a $1 million earmark for improvements to the bridge that connects it with Reynosa, Mexico.

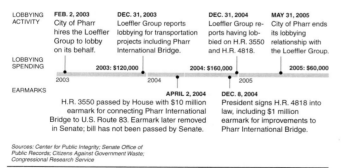

LOBBYING ACTIVITY

FEB. 2, 2003 City of Pharr hires the Loeffler Group to lobby on its behalf.

DEC. 31, 2003 Loeffler Group reports lobbying for transportation projects including Pharr International Bridge.

DEC. 31, 2004 Loeffler Group reports having lobbied on H.R. 3550 and H.R. 4818.

MAY 31, 2005 City of Pharr ends its lobbying relationship with the Loeffler Group.

LOBBYING SPENDING

2003: $120,000 | 2004: $160,000 | 2005: $60,000

2003 | 2004 | 2005

EARMARKS

APRIL 2, 2004 H.R. 3550 passed by House with $10 million earmark for connecting Pharr International Bridge to U.S. Route 83. Earmark later removed in Senate; bill has not been passed by Senate.

DEC. 8, 2004 President signs H.R. 4818 into law, including $1 million earmark for improvements to Pharr International Bridge.

Sources: Center for Public Integrity; Senate Office of Public Records; Citizens Against Government Waste; Congressional Research Service

July 2006, James Bronzan and Aron Pilhofer/The New York Times

FIGURE 13.1

Hiring Lobbyists, Winning Federal Dollars

Public entities, including cities/towns, counties, school districts, transit authorities, tribes, and utility agencies, across the country are increasingly hiring lobbyists to represent their interests before congress in hopes of receiving more federal tax dollars. What are the negative aspects of this widespread use of lobbyists?

▶ **Can opposing groups, such as abortion rights advocates and right-to-life supporters, both claim to be working for the public interest?**

In the same way, individuals involved in agriculture, as well as agribusinesses (large farming operations, sometimes organized as corporations), unite in interest groups that address their economic and political concerns. For example, the American Farm Bureau Federation, which calls itself the "Voice of Agriculture," speaks for farmers and ranchers on a wide range of issues, from biotechnology to migratory workers, immigration, pesticides, and the balance between environmental needs and property rights. Labor unions are groups of workers who have joined together to negotiate collectively with employers and to inform the government and the public of their needs. **Professional associations** represent people—generally well-paid and highly educated ones—in a specific profession. Two prominent examples are the American Medical Association (AMA) for physicians and the American Bar Association (ABA) for attorneys.

▶ **Can opposing groups, such as abortion rights advocates and right-to-life supporters, both claim to be working for the public interest?** Over the past forty years, there has been a dramatic growth in **public interest groups,** which the political scientist Jeffrey Berry defines as groups that form in the pursuit of "a collective good, the achievement of which will not selectively and materially benefit the membership or activists of the organization."[11] One of the earliest modern public interest groups was Common Cause, created in 1970 to advocate governmental reform. There is an enormous variety in the goals of public interest groups, encompassing, for example, people either advocating or opposing gun control, abortion, and environmental protection. The NAACP, the NRA, and the environmentalist Sierra Club are all public interest groups; so are the many right-to-life groups that oppose abortion. Another is AARP, formerly the American Association of Retired Persons, which represents approximately 35 million Americans over age 50. It speaks for its members' concerns on such issues as health care, grandparents' rights, and Social Security.

Think tanks are nonprofit institutions that conduct research on issues of public interest. One of the best-known think tanks is the Brookings Institution, which conducts relatively nonpartisan research on economic questions, foreign policy, and various other issues of governance. Think tanks often advocate a strong ideological viewpoint; examples include the conservative American Enterprise Institute and the Heritage Foundation. Universities also use a variety of techniques to petition the government for resources. You might be surprised to learn that universities hire

professional associations
organizations that represent individuals, largely educated and affluent, in one particular occupational category.

public interest groups
citizen organizations that advocate issues of public good, such as protection of the environment.

think tank
a group of individuals who conduct research on a particular subject or a particular area of public policy.

▶ **Does the fact that** Americans at the lower end of the socioeconomic scale are less likely to join interest groups make a difference in policy outcomes?

lobbyists to appeal to Congress, but in today's tight economic times, institutions of higher education have to be creative in the pursuit of excellence.

Finally, state- and local-level governmental units form interest groups that petition the federal authorities for help and to otherwise voice their concerns. As you saw in Ⓛ Ⓘ Ⓝ Ⓚ *Chapter 3, pages 99–100*, when Congress cuts its financial support to the states and municipalities while at the same time piling more obligations on them, these government entities have to compete for scarce resources. So, naturally, they have formed interest groups, too.

Two excellent examples of such groups are the National Governors' Association (NGA) and the U.S. Conference of Mayors (USCM). The NGA is a bipartisan organization of the nations' governors that helps represent states before our federal government. Their reports share information about effective state programs, provide experts to help states address important issues, and provide networking opportunities for governors and their staff. The USCM is a nonpartisan organization representing cities with populations larger than 300,000. It is an important tool to link national and urban-suburban policy and to strengthen federal and city relationships. The organization also helps mayors develop leadership and managerial skills and serves as an information-sharing forum.

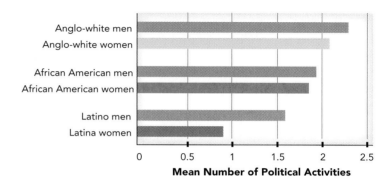

Mean Number of Political Activities

FIGURE 13.2
Mean Number of Political Activities

On the whole, men participate more in politics than do women. Moreover, people of different races are more or less politically engaged. Do you believe that these differences are important? Are you surprised by how few political activities the average person performs?

SOURCE: Reprinted by permission of the publisher from *The Private Roots of Public Action: Gender, Equality, and Political Participation* Nancy Burns, Kay Lehman Schlozman and Sidney Verba p. 80. (Cambridge: Harvard University Press, © 2001 by the President and Fellows of Harvard College.

BIAS IN REPRESENTATION: WHO PARTICIPATES?

At first glance, given the variety of groups, you might think that interest groups represent all Americans equally. But they don't. Activists are not typical Americans—most of them are drawn from the elite strata of society. Activists are more politically sophisticated, more knowledgeable, and more involved in their communities. All Americans have the right to form groups, but the fact is that for many reasons, many categories of Americans do not.[12] Educational attainment, family income, and social class are among the largest factors in predicting participation in organized interest groups and politics more generally. There are many exceptions to this general pattern. The least biased form of political participation is voting; not surprisingly, the most skewed form of participation is in making campaign contributions: People with more education and more income predominate. Participating in interest groups falls roughly between these extremes. Moreover,

Caucasians and high-income people are encouraged by political leaders to participate in politics (from joining interest groups to being persuaded to run for elective office) far more often than people of color and those with low incomes.[13]

▶ **Does the fact that Americans at the lower end of the socioeconomic scale are less likely to join interest groups make a difference in policy outcomes?** Since all American citizens can potentially participate in politics, many observers are not concerned that some Americans choose to remain politically uninvolved. Many other observers, however, are troubled by these patterns of unequal participation and mobilization when they look at the problem from an overall perspective. As Figure 13.2 shows, there is a profound difference among the races, and within races along gender lines, in the level of political participation in the United States. Participation allows voices to be heard, but people do wonder whether all voices are being heard equally effectively. When looking at politics in the aggregate, it is also

► **What factors inhibit** individuals from joining interest groups?

1. Do organized interest groups represent all people? If not, does this matter?

2. Why are there so many interest groups in the United States? What are some of the consequences of the growth that has occurred since 1960?

clear that big business's immense economic resources give it a disproportionate level of political influence. However, as the political scientist James Q. Wilson has noted, "One cannot assume that the disproportionate possession of certain resources leads to the disproportionate exercise of political power. Everything depends on whether a resource can be converted into power, and at what rate and at what price."[14]

Because potential activists (David Truman's name for people outside interest groups) *do* have opportunities to organize in American politics, and because one important counterweight to moneyed interests in politics is the power of united and committed citizens, we must turn our attention to the subject of how interests can be mobilized and organized. But we also need to stress how important for our democracy it is that citizens who have traditionally not participated be encouraged to take part in interest group activity. Individuals who participate in group activity, especially those who participate in a diverse range of groups, more often than not tend to develop political tolerance, trust, and a sense of efficacy—qualities that are very important in maintaining a healthy democracy.[15]

1. Some interest groups in this country bring together individuals from separate population groups (as defined by race, religion, gender, or income level); other interest groups have the effect of reinforcing the divisions among these subgroups.
   a. true   **b.** false

2. Which of the following is a multi-issue interest group?
   a. the NRA
   b. LULAC
   c. the Sierra Club
   d. the UFW

3. Approximately how many interest groups are there in the United States?
   a. 1,500   **b.** 10,000
   c. 20,000   **d.** 250,000

4. Which of the following is *not* a factor that helps explain the rapid proliferation of interest groups since the 1960s?
   a. rapid social change
   b. more people becoming capable of joining interest groups through resources and education
   c. the growth of government itself
   d. the most popular form of participation, voting, being perceived as increasingly inconsequential

Answers: 1-a, 2-b, 3-c, 4-d.

Difficulties in Mobilization

► **What factors inhibit individuals from joining interest groups?**
Before we examine how groups organize, it is important to discuss the barriers that affect organizing—the obstacles that any group must overcome before it can succeed. In this section, we will generalize about the experiences of all groups. But it is important to stress that specific subgroups in the American population may face additional barriers and that some barriers may affect certain groups differently than others.

Take, for example, groups that seek to mobilize Latinos and Latinas. A good percentage of Spanish-heritage people, especially in border states, are not citizens, and many live in the United States illegally. Imagine that you are troubled by the economic exploitation of Latinos in the construction business in your state and want to organize the workers, but you learn that the majority of Spanish-speaking construction workers are not citizens or legal immigrants. You would certainly have trouble organizing them, for they would fear to speak up or even to identify themselves. This would be a major barrier to mobilizing them. Or take another example, perhaps closer to home: Imagine that you are a homosexual student on a conservative college campus where a number of hate-based crimes have been committed in recent months. You want to form a group of other homosexual, bisexual, and transgender students to pressure the university to protect your civil rights. Imagine the problems you would have in encouraging your peers to organize openly. They would be fearful, at worst, of violence against them and, at a minimum, of being ostracized.

In both examples, the pressure would be great to remain silent. Does this mean that neither type of group could be organized? Certainly not, but we must be clear about the barriers that may exist in order to overcome them. Moreover, we must look at barriers that are internalized in individuals and those that reflect the reality of collective action. For example, for you to join a group, you must have confidence in your own abilities to make an important contribution, and you also have to believe that your contribution will make a difference. In smaller, more local organizations, this might be easier to achieve, but in the case of larger groups, it may be more difficult to get a sense that your membership truly matters. As you will see, groups that are successful in recruiting and retaining members are sensitive to each concern and are able to overcome these considerations.

▶ **What benefits do interest** groups offer to attract members?

free-rider problem
the fact that public goods can be enjoyed by everyone, including people who do not pay their fair share of the cost of providing those public goods.

public goods
goods that are used or consumed by all individuals, such as clean air or public roads; also known as **collective goods.**

selective benefits
benefits provided only to members of an organization or group.

The economist Mancur Olson describes some of the key barriers facing people who share concerns and want to create formal problem-resolving organizations.[16] The first barrier is the tendency of individuals to allow others to do work on their behalf. (In essence, why should I spend my time and energy when others will do the work and I will benefit?) This is the **free-rider problem.** Olson notes that free riding is more likely to occur with groups that provide **public** (or **collective**) **goods**—things of value that cannot be given to one group exclusively but instead benefit society as a whole. Clean air is an example. Although one environmentalist group, or more likely a coalition of such groups, works to pass legislation to mandate cleaner automotive emissions, we all benefit from the clean air that the legislation provides. The members of the group who gave their time, money, and energy are not the only beneficiaries— the entire community benefits, even though many members had not contributed to the group effort. Olson examined the incentives for joining groups from a rational perspective. A person will join a group when the benefits outweigh the costs. But if you can reap the benefits without incurring any costs, why join? As you will see, organized groups must be conscious of the free-rider problem so that they can provide other benefits to members to get them to join.

The second barrier that Olson identified in group formation is cost. This is a chief reason why many people who share common concerns do not organize. For one person to form a viable group that attracts many people and can be influential, money must be spent. It takes money to form and to maintain a group, but it also takes a large commitment of time and energy. Some people and groups, of course, are better situated to bear the costs of organizing, most notably the affluent. Less affluent people frequently need to spend their time and energy earning money, including holding second jobs, and simply cannot volunteer or make large contributions to groups that they may support.

The absence of a sense of political efficacy—the belief that one person can make a difference—is the third barrier to interest group formation that Olson identified. Even if you have confidence in your abilities, you might fall into the pessimistic mindset of "What can one person do?" Imagine that you are very concerned about changing the method of trash collection in your city (going from once a week to twice, for example). "But I'm only one person," you might think. "What can I do by myself?" Such pessimism affects not only people thinking of forming new groups but also those who might join or renew their membership in existing groups. Let's say that you're interested in promoting women's rights. You investigate the National Organization for Women and find that it advocates many positions with which you agree. You think about joining but then start to wonder: With 500,000 dues-paying members, what good will my $35 annual dues do? In truth, your dues alone won't do too much for the organization. But you might join once you understand the logic of collective action— that is, when you realize that the dues of 500,000 people come to $17.5 million, a sum that can make a large difference.

OVERCOMING ORGANIZATIONAL BARRIERS

▶ **What benefits do interest groups offer to attract members?** Any group of people who hope to create and maintain an organization must understand these difficulties so that they can work to overcome them. Groups use many means to make membership attractive so that the benefits of membership outweigh the perceived costs. Organizations must also demonstrate to members and potential members that membership is important and that every member helps advance the collective goal. To overcome these barriers, **selective benefits** may be given to members—benefits that only group members receive, even if the collective good for which they strive remains available to everyone. For example, when the National Rifle Association defeats a gun control bill, all citizens who believe in the rights of gun owners benefit, not just dues-paying NRA members. To encourage people to join, the NRA successfully recruits members by providing a variety of benefits. Because the organization works for a collective good— advances in protecting gun ownership do not apply only to the members of the organization but to all citizens—the NRA must fight the free-rider and efficacy problems and recruit dues-paying members to defer its maintenance costs. The following are some of the selective benefits the NRA provides to its members:

- **Material benefits:** Insurance, training and discounts. The group offers $25,000 life insurance policies to police officers who are members if they are killed in the line of duty. It also offers its members gun loss insurance; accidental death insurance at reduced rates; discounts for eye care, car rentals, hotels, and airfares. The group sponsors training programs for the Olympics and funds research on violent crimes.

- **Solidary benefits:** Safety and training classes (including award-winning Eddy Eagle child safety classes) and shooting competitions (including special tournaments for women

▶ **Do some interest groups**
compel members to join?

material benefits
benefits that have concrete value or worth.

solidary benefits
benefits derived from fellowship and
camaraderie with other members.

purposive benefits
intangible rewards people obtain from
joining a group they support and working
to advance an issue in which they believe.

patron
an organization or individual that contributes money to political leaders or
political groups.

and children). Its grassroots groups, Friends of the NRA,
hosts dinners, holds national and state conventions, hosts art
contests, and publishes magazines.

- **Purposive benefits:** The feeling that one is doing something
  to advance one's view of the Second Amendment of the
  Constitution and to preserve access to shooting and hunting.

Sources: Adapted from National Rifle Association,
http://www.nra.org.

The first type of selective benefits is **material benefits**—tangible benefits that have value, such as magazines, discounts, and such
paraphernalia as T-shirts and plaques. One of the first groups to
offer material benefits was the American Farm Bureau. Many people, even nonfarmers, joined the organization in order to receive its
insurance discounts. Today, AARP uses a wider variety of material
benefits to encourage membership, including discounts (on phar-
macy services, airlines, automobiles, computers, vacations, insurance, restaurants, hotels, and cruises), tax information, magazine
subscriptions, legal advice, and credit cards. In addition to material
benefits, which are a major incentive for numerous individuals to
join, many groups also offer **solidary benefits,** which are primarily
social. Solidary benefits focus on providing activity and a sense of
belonging—meetings, dinners, dances, and other such social activities that groups provide to give members a sense of belonging with
other like-minded people. Finally, there are **purposive benefits** of
group membership, "the intangible rewards that derive from the
sense of satisfaction of having contributed to the attainment of a
worthwhile cause."[17] Groups that organize blood drives often try to
convey a purposive benefit. The sense of "helping people" and
"doing good" are important motivators for many who give blood,
encouraging them to endure a modest amount of discomfort and
inconvenience. Many organizations rely on purposive benefits, typically in combination with other benefits, to attract members.

▶ **Do some interest groups *compel* members to join?** Some
organizations do not have to encourage membership; they can
demand it. One prominent example of this is labor unions in many
states. In accordance with the National Labor Relations Act (1935),
in some states, unions can form agreements with employers that
prevent non-union labor from being hired. In other states, "right to
work" laws prohibit such contracts, but in nearly thirty states, people can be required, as a condition of employment, to join a union

and pay dues. Unions, however, also provide many selective benefits
(for example, insurance and employment security) as well as such
solidary benefits as dinners, dances, and holiday parties.[18] Although
these benefits are more important to recruit members in right-to-
work states, they are still used in states that compel membership, to
make the union more attractive and more popular among workers.

Similarly, some corporations use subtle coercion to encourage
"voluntary" donations to their PACs from their executives and
their families. Coercion is also prevalent in some professional associations; thirty-two states, for example, require attorneys to be
members of the state bar association in order to practice law.[19]

The efforts of **patrons**—individuals or organizations that
give money to groups—also help form and sustain interest groups.
Each year, private foundations like the Rockefeller and Ford
Foundations give millions of dollars to citizen groups and think
tanks for purposes ranging from conducting research to founding
new organizations. Corporations also give hundreds of millions of
dollars to interest groups every year. The federal government allocates money to interest groups, generally in the form of a government contract for research or the provision of some other service.
For example, the federal government might hire an environmentalist group to help determine how many snowmobiles should be
allowed into a national park without harming the ecosystem. Of
course, snowmobile companies and the tourist industry may fear
that the estimate by the environmentalist group might be too low
and may consequently lobby Congress to commission additional
research. Few, if any, organizations can rely exclusively on patron
support, but support of this sort is very helpful for some.

THE ROLE OF INTEREST
GROUP LEADERS

In addition to using incentives to mobilize support, interest groups
have used inspirational leadership to build their membership.
Charismatic and devoted leaders can entice potential members to
join an organization. When people believe in the leaders of an
organization, they are more supportive of its goals and more likely
to support it financially. Effective leaders "sell" their issues to the
public, thus attracting media attention and membership.

César Chávez provides perhaps the best example of a leader's
role in winning success for his organization in what appeared to be

what **YOU** can do!

Go to the Sierra Club's Web page **http://www.sierraclub.org** What types of solidary, purposive, and material benefits does this organization provide to its members? Which benefits are likely to appeal to whom? Do you think that any of the benefits would appeal to college students? Are the benefits likely to encourage the "typical" environmentalist to join the club?

César Chávez was a dynamic leader who organized an unlikely group of activists—migrant farm workers (many of whom were not citizens). Pictured are César Chávez (third from the right) and Coretta Scott King (fourth from the right) leading a march in New York City to build support for a lettuce boycott in 1970. Through marches, protests and organized boycotts, Chávez was able to improve the working conditions and compensation for thousands of hard-working laborers. What characteristics do you think are the most important in distinguishing a truly great leader?

hopeless circumstances. Chávez grew up a poor migrant worker farming in states along the U.S.-Mexican border. Throughout his childhood, he was able to attend school only sporadically because he had to move around with his family to work on farms. After serving in the U.S. Navy during World War II, Chávez returned to migratory farm work in Arizona and California. Seeing the desperate circumstances and gross exploitation of farm workers first hand, Chávez dedicated his life to helping them organize and mobilize to demand fair treatment. In 1962, he organized the National Farm Workers Association, a labor union that later merged with other organizations to form the United Farm Workers of America (UFW). Chávez's UFW ultimately led a five-year strike by California grape pickers and inspired a national boycott of California grapes. To draw national attention to the grape pickers' plight, Chávez headed a 340-mile farm workers' march across California in 1966 and went on a much publicized twenty-five-day hunger strike in 1968. The UFW later led successful campaigns against lettuce growers and other agribusinesses (large, corporate farm industries), demanding fair treatment of farm workers. Chávez and his union gained crucial support from middle-class consumers who boycotted grapes and lettuce harvested by non-union labor, ultimately forcing the powerful agribusinesses to capitulate. What is perhaps most remarkable about the success of the groups that Chávez led is their ability to organize the most unlikely people—extremely poor, uneducated immigrants. By the

early 1970s, the UFW had grown to 50,000 dues-paying members and had contracts with 300 growers. It succeeded not only in negotiating collective bargaining agreements but also in forcing the enactment of legislation to change migratory pickers' often deplorable working conditions. Activists and scholars alike agree that the success of the UFW owed much to Chávez's energy, appeal, and dedication to social justice. His charisma enabled Chávez to convince farm workers to unite and work with others—for example, California governor Jerry Brown—to promote their collective interests. As a testimony to his commitment to social justice and nonviolent protest, Chávez was posthumously awarded the Presidential Medal of Freedom in 1994.

The UFW is a good example of a group of low-income people uniting to fight large corporations. By overcoming the barriers to organizing, having solid leadership, and providing benefits to members, groups of all kinds can successfully press for change. The challenges are often large, but the rewards can be profound.

pathways profile

BRUCE S. GORDON

On June 25, 2005, at the organization's national convention, the National Association for the Advancement of Colored People's board of directors unanimously named Bruce S. Gordon its new president and CEO. He succeeded Kweisi Mfume, the

outside lobbying
activities directed at the general public to raise awareness and interest and to pressure officials; also known as *grassroots lobbying*.

inside lobbying
appealing directly to lawmakers and legislative staff either in meetings, by providing research and information, or by testifying at committee hearings.

gaining access
winning the opportunity to communicate directly with a legislator or a legislative staff member to present one's position on an issue of public policy.

Bruce S. Gordon, appointed head of the NAACP in 2005, worked very diligently to oppose the appointment of U.S. Supreme Court nominee John Roberts. Pictured above, Gordon (left) meets with Theodore Shaw (head of the NAACP's Legal Defense Fund), and Marcia Greenberger (co-president of the National Women's Law Center) at a press conference in Washington in August 2005. The three, along with other leading civil and women's rights groups, strongly opposed the nomination of the conservative Roberts. They were unsuccessful in their efforts to deny Roberts a seat on the highest court. Gordon is the first president of this important civil rights organization who was not previously a minister, a politician, or an activist. How will his business experience help the NAACP?

Photo: Doug Mills/The New York Times

past president and former congressman, who had resigned to run for the U.S. Senate.

Gordon's appointment was a departure from tradition. Nearly all past presidents of the NAACP had been ministers or politicians; Gordon is not. Nor is he known as a civil rights leader or activist, although his parents were. Rather, his credentials stem from his success in corporate America, where he was famed for his fundraising skills and strong managerial abilities. His selection by the NAACP was a calculated decision to help an organization that has encountered financial difficulties in recent years. This strategic appointment was clearly designed to invigorate the organization, which has been criticized in recent years for being out of touch with many African Americans (especially urban youth).

A 1968 graduate of Gettysburg College, Gordon started his career as a management trainee. He graduated with a master's degree in management from the prestigious Sloan Fellows Program at MIT's Sloan School of Management in 1988. During his thirty-five years as a business executive, he worked his way up the ladder, finally serving as president of retail markets at Verizon Communications. Gordon earned respect for his hard work ethic, passionate commitment to justice, and strong advocacy for diversity at Verizon and throughout the telecommunications industry. He used his influential position to promote the corporate advancement of African Americans and to mentor young executives. He was named executive of the year by *Black Enterprise* magazine in 1998 and honored as one of America's fifty most powerful black executives by *Fortune* magazine in 2002. ▪

practicequiz

1. One of the strongest barriers to mobilizing individuals in socially vulnerable groups, such as gays or illegal immigrants, is
   a. the free-rider problem.
   b. the inhibiting dangers to such individuals that might come with making their status public.
   c. the unlikelihood of government officials' listening to such individuals.
   d. the fact that their causes are not very strong.

2. You can begin an effective interest group without spending money.
   a. true   b. false

3. If you are attending your labor union's holiday party, you are enjoying what sort of interest group benefit?
   a. material   b. purposive
   c. solidary   d. abstract

discussionquestions

1. What are the barriers to organizing interest groups? How do interest groups overcome these barriers?

2. What factors make some groups more successful and powerful than others? What role do leaders play in the formation, maintenance, and success of interest groups?

4. The unlikely success of the UFW in the early 1970s illustrates
   a. the power of a charismatic leader.
   b. the rising importance of technology in grassroots mobilization.
   c. the effectiveness of large-scale protest demonstrations.
   d. the efficacy of professional lobbyists.

Answers: 1-b, 2-b, 3-c, 4-a.

Inside and Outside Lobbying

Politics is interactive. Successful political actors always pursue multiple ways to enhance their positions. The key to understanding influence in our governmental system is to realize that interest groups and individuals use different pathways, often at the same time, to advance their perspectives and to petition their government. One pathway may prove to be a successful vehicle for a group at one point but fail at another time.

Interest groups use the grassroots mobilization pathway to appeal indirectly to policymakers. **Outside lobbying**, on which we will focus later in this section, aims primarily at influencing citizens rather than public officials.

By contrast, **inside lobbying**, a tool used in the lobbying decision makers' pathway, openly appeals to public officials in the legislature and the executive branch, which includes the bureaucracy. Because inside lobbying is a matter of personal contact with policymakers, it involves some form of direct interaction—often called **gaining access**—between a lobbyist and an agency official, a member of Congress, or a member of the legislator's staff. By having an opportunity to present the group's position directly to lawmakers, staffers, or officials, lobbyists have a greater chance of influencing the decision-making process. To be effective, however, lobbyists must be seen as trustworthy and must develop relationships with individuals who have influence in the relevant policy area. Another inside lobbying tactic is to testify at congressional committee hearings. Such hearings normally occur when Congress is considering a bill for passage, when committees are investigating a problem or monitoring existing programs, or when a nominee for a high executive or judicial position is testifying before a confirmation vote. Testifying allows an interest group to present its views in public and "on the record," potentially raising its visibility and appealing to political actors. Although this is a more visible form of inside lobbying than privately meeting a policymaker in an office or at a restaurant, it is often considered window dressing. Most people who follow politics seriously feel that it is not a very effective tactic. As you can see in Table 13.3, a great

TABLE 13.3
Spending on Inside Lobbying

Category	Representative Interest Group	Amount Group Spent on Lobbying in 2000
Corporations	Microsoft	$8,700,000
Agriculture	American Farm Bureau Federation	7,970,849
Trade associations	U.S. Chamber of Commerce	38,910,000
Labor unions	Teamsters Union	40,000
Professional associations	American Bar Association	1,280,000
Citizen groups	Gun Owners of America	1,306,414
	AARP	27,830,000
Think tanks	National Heritage Foundation	20,000
Universities	University of Texas	240,000
Governmental units	New York City Council	25,000
		120,000

SOURCE: Center for Responsive Politics, http://www.opensecrets.org/lobbyists.

▶ **Doesn't inside lobbying** sometimes become an attempt at private gain, as in the Jack Abramoff scandal? How can we stop it?

The largest lobbying scandal in contemporary times erupted when former high-powered lobbyist Jack Abramoff pled guilty to three felony counts on January 3, 2006. The guilty pleas followed months of intense investigations and will likely result in the indictment of others. Pictured above is Abramoff being sworn in before a U.S. Senate Committee hearing on Indian Affairs in 2004. What do you think needs to be done to prevent this type of corruption?
Photo: Carol T. Powers/The New York Times

deal of money is spent by organizations to lobby the federal government. Such lavish spending, coupled with concern over corruption, has prompted legislation to regulate lobbying—although as you'll see shortly, the legislation was not strict enough to prevent the most distressing lobbying scandal in recent times.

▶ **Doesn't inside lobbying sometimes become an attempt at private gain, as in the Jack Abramoff scandal? How can we stop it?** Two important parts of the Lobbying Disclosure Act of 1995 regulate direct lobbying. The first component of the law tries to provide "transparency" by requiring lobbyists to register with the federal government and report their activities. Many people believe that having full disclosure will raise public confidence in the system by minimizing the potential for abuse and corruption. The second set of provisions in the law bars certain types of informal lobbying activities that have been used in the past, such as giving expensive gifts or purchasing expensive meals and paying for trips for members of Congress. Fees (called *honoraria*) for speaking engagements were outlawed in 1992. Even with this legislation, many people are concerned with the perception of impropriety and potential for corruption; hence watchdog groups are valuable for increasing public trust.

This concern was proved well founded in 2006, when Jack Abramoff, a top political lobbyist, pleaded guilty to three felony accounts of tax evasion, fraud, and conspiracy to bribe a public official. In a deal that requires him to cooperate with a broad investigation into public corruption, Abramoff admitted to corrupting governmental officials and defrauding his clients of $25 million. He spent money lavishly on lawmakers, their staffs, and executive branch officials, paying for luxury trips, expensive meals, entertainment, and tickets to sporting events. Moreover, he hired spouses of officials that he was lobbying in efforts to manipulate their behavior. One charge that he faces is that he arranged for a series of payments adding up to $50,000 to the wife of a congressional staffer, who then helped defeat Internet gambling restrictions that were opposed by one of his clients (see Figure 13.3).

The inquiry into Abramoff's activities began in 2004 when it became public that he and a partner had received $82 million from Indian tribes.[20] Additional investigations are ongoing and will undoubtedly result in more revelations of wrongdoing.

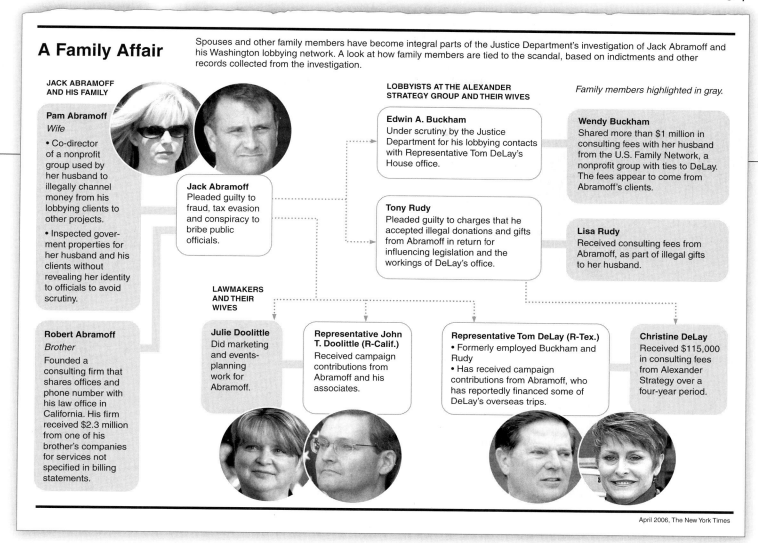

A Family Affair

Spouses and other family members have become integral parts of the Justice Department's investigation of Jack Abramoff and his Washington lobbying network. A look at how family members are tied to the scandal, based on indictments and other records collected from the investigation.

JACK ABRAMOFF AND HIS FAMILY

Pam Abramoff
Wife
• Co-director of a nonprofit group used by her husband to illegally channel money from his lobbying clients to other projects.
• Inspected goverment properties for her husband and his clients without revealing her identity to officials to avoid scrutiny.

Jack Abramoff
Pleaded guilty to fraud, tax evasion and conspiracy to bribe public officials.

Robert Abramoff
Brother
Founded a consulting firm that shares offices and phone number with his law office in California. His firm received $2.3 million from one of his brother's companies for services not specified in billing statements.

LOBBYISTS AT THE ALEXANDER STRATEGY GROUP AND THEIR WIVES

Family members highlighted in gray.

Edwin A. Buckham
Under scrutiny by the Justice Department for his lobbying contacts with Representative Tom DeLay's House office.

Wendy Buckham
Shared more than $1 million in consulting fees with her husband from the U.S. Family Network, a nonprofit group with ties to DeLay. The fees appear to come from Abramoff's clients.

Tony Rudy
Pleaded guilty to charges that he accepted illegal donations and gifts from Abramoff in return for influencing legislation and the workings of DeLay's office.

Lisa Rudy
Received consulting fees from Abramoff, as part of illegal gifts to her husband.

LAWMAKERS AND THEIR WIVES

Julie Doolittle
Did marketing and events-planning work for Abramoff.

Representative John T. Doolittle (R-Calif.)
Received campaign contributions from Abramoff and his associates.

Representative Tom DeLay (R-Tex.)
• Formerly employed Buckham and Rudy
• Has received campaign contributions from Abramoff, who has reportedly financed some of DeLay's overseas trips.

Christine DeLay
Received $115,000 in consulting fees from Alexander Strategy over a four-year period.

April 2006, The New York Times

pathways of action

THE K STREET PROJECT

After many frustrating decades in the minority, Republicans took over both houses of Congress in 1994. In an effort to pressure Washington lobbying companies to hire Republicans for top positions, Republican leaders devised the K Street Project in 1995, named after the street in downtown Washington where many prominent lobbying firms are located. Republican strategist Grover Norquist and then House majority whip Tom DeLay (who later became the House majority leader) told lobbying firms that if they wanted to have influence with the new leaders and majority party, they had to place more Republicans in important positions in their firms.

This project was widely criticized by many Democrats and journalists because they thought it gave too much influence to large corporations and, of course, to the Republican Party. These hiring considerations added to the so-called revolving-door policy of corporations and lobbying firms hiring former governmental officials, making the distinction between lobbyists and politicians

FIGURE 13.3

A Family Affair

The figure above depicts the intimate relationships between the lobbyists, politicians, and their families in the current scandal under investigation by the Justice Department. To most Americans this probably doesn't look "right". Do you think that the lines between lobbyists and politicians need to be more clearly drawn? Do you think it is ethical for a spouse of a member of Congress to work directly for a lobbyist? Should individuals have to sever ties with lobbying firms before becoming married to a public official?

House Majority Leader Tom DeLay (R-TX), then one of the most power-ful Republican leaders in the country and one of the founders of the K-Street Project, places a sparkler on a cake during a $2,000 a plate trib-ute fund-raising dinner in his honor on May 12, 2005. Less than 2 months later DeLay resigned from his post after being indicted on charges of laundering money in Texas elections. Pictured on the cake are plastic hammers, symbolizing his nickname, "The Hammer". He earned the nick-name because of his reputation as a strict enforcer of party loyalty.

extremely blurry. The Republican leadership defended the pro-gram by noting that because of four decades of Democratic con-trol of Congress, most top lobbyists were Democrats (many themselves former members of Congress or Democratic staff). Hence, Republicans argued, the firms needed to increase their ide-ological and partisan balance.

The Republicans' capture of the White House in 2000 and of the Senate in 2002 brought them into full control of the executive and legislative branches of the government. At that point, Repub-lican leaders tried to expand the K Street Project by pressuring lobbying firms to hire *only* Republicans for new and open posts. But since the Abramoff scandal broke, Republican leaders have stated that they will abandon this program.[21] ∎

pathways profile

RECORDING ARTISTS COALITION

The Recording Artists Coalition (RAC), founded in 1998 by Don Henley and Sheryl Crow, is a nonprofit, nonpartisan coalition formed to represent the interests of recording artists in matters of artists' rights and other issues important to the music industry. On June 28, 2005, RAC celebrated a major victory when the United States Supreme Court overturned a circuit court deci-sion in the *Grokster* case, which involved person-to-person (P2P) file sharing. In its unanimous decision, the Court ruled that record labels could sue file-sharing companies to protect the rights of artists. From 1999 to 2004, the recording industry had seen its profits fall by $2.4 billion, which it blamed primarily on the free trading of music first popularized by Napster.

RAC uses multiple pathways to advance its cause. One of its tools was to file an amicus curiae brief in January 2005 support-ing its position in the *Grokster* case using the court pathway. Another of RAC's tools was to plan the Recording Arts Advocacy

Day, held on September 7, 2005, when individual artists and groups appeared on Capitol Hill to publicly support the efforts of the group. Using highly visible artists, such as cochairs Don Henley and Sheryl Crow, the Dixie Chicks, and Bonnie Raitt, to lobby the public directly via the grassroots mobilization path-way, RAC continues working to represent a diverse group of musicians. ∎

OUTSIDE LOBBYING

In appealing directly to the public, interest groups are indirectly lobbying public officials. They are trying to build public sentiment in order to bring pressure to bear on the officials who will actually make the decisions. David Truman, in his classic analysis of inter-est groups, *The Governmental Process*, noted that organized interests engage in "programs of propaganda, though rarely so labeled, designed to affect opinions concerning interests" in hopes that con-cerned citizens will then lobby the government on behalf of what-ever the group is trying to accomplish.[22] As you have already seen, to overcome the barriers to group formulation and maintenance, interest groups must motivate both potential members and the public at large. One important way to do so is to make direct appeals to the public and to other interest groups that share its per-spective on particular issues. Outside or grassroots lobbying, which involves using the grassroots mobilization pathway, is the attempt to influence decision makers indirectly, by influencing the public.

▶ **Why do some interest groups try appealing to the pub-lic rather than pressuring the government directly?** There are several advantages in appealing to the public. First, an interest group can indirectly use the people through the elections pathway to directly affect the selection of officials. Citizens can also pres-sure officials to take action. Moreover, pressure from interest groups can influence which issues the government decides to address, as well as the policies it adopts, modifies, or abandons. Appealing directly to the people can also be advantageous because citizens can take direct actions that can be used to further the group's agenda. By lobbying supporters and the general public, interest groups seek to demonstrate an issue's salience, showing public officials that the issue is important to the people. To suc-ceed, interest groups often have to appeal to an audience beyond their supporters. Sometimes escalating conflict surrounding the issue can be a successful means of attracting public interest, in turn forcing elected officials to get involved.

▶ **Why do some interest groups**
try appealing to the public
rather than pressuring the
government directly?

Examining the activities of more than ninety interest group leaders, the political scientist Ken Kollman found that 90 percent of interest groups engage in some kind of outside lobbying.[23] They do this because it can be very effective. In studying the effect of mobilization in the 1994 debate over President Bill Clinton's health care proposals, Kenneth Goldstein found that citizens in states that were targeted by statewide grassroots campaigns had significantly higher voting rates than citizens in nontargeted states. Moreover, more than one-third of the individuals contacted by organized interest groups communicated with their member of Congress, compared to only 10 percent of those who had not been contacted by a grassroots campaign. Seventy-five percent of those who contacted members of Congress said that they did so at the request of an interest group.[24] Proportionately, more Americans than ever before are communicating—via letters, faxes, phone calls, and e-mails—with members of Congress. But this surge in communication is not spontaneous. Much of it is the direct result of coordinated efforts by organized interests.[25] This communication is intended to demonstrate to public officials that their constituents care about an issue and that the public officials had better act.

LOBBYING OTHER GROUPS AND FORMING ALLIANCES

In addition to directly appealing to the public, interest groups also lobby other groups and try to form alliances with them. It seems odd at first to think about lobbyists petitioning other lobbyists, but it makes perfect sense. Because they understand the notion of collective action, interest groups often work together to advance common interests on a particular issue. The more the groups cooperate, the easier political action often becomes; conversely, conflict and competition tend to diminish success. Coalition building—bringing diverse interests together to advance a cause—is frequently successful. Normally, the coalitions that result are temporary, limited to one specific issue. Once work on that issue is done, the coalition usually dissolves.

Let's look at some examples of coalitions between interest groups. Environmentalist groups often build coalitions with other environmentalist groups or with agricultural groups, even though environmentalist and agricultural groups are on the opposite sides of many issues. But when they do agree, the alliances they forge strengthen their collective voice. Another good example is the

Sheryl Crow, along with Don Henley, formed the Recording Artists Coalition (RAC) in 1998 to represent the interests of recording artists. Pictured above is Crow performing at a RAC benefit concert in 2002. Do you think that musicians have legitimate concerns in trying to limit music sharing? Do you think that individuals have the right to share legally purchased music files with others? Can you think of a reasonable compromise that might be negotiated?

▶ **Isn't outside lobbying more** democratic than inside lobbying?

direct contact
face-to-face meetings or telephone conversations between individuals.

direct mail
information sent by mail to a large number of people to advertise, market concepts, or solicit orders.

tobacco companies. In the late 1990s, realizing that directly appealing to Congress themselves would reduce the impact of their message, tobacco companies persuaded other interest groups to contact Congress on the fiercely debated issue of whether the federal Food and Drug Administration (FDA) should regulate cigarettes as a drug.[26] Tobacco company lobbyists encouraged three diverse groups (smokers, small store owners, and gay rights groups) to contact the federal government on the issue. Each group had different concerns: Smokers wanted the government to "mind its own business," small store owners worried that higher cigarette taxes and more tobacco regulations would cut into their profits, and gay rights groups feared that the FDA's involvement in regulating tobacco would distract the agency from approving new anti-AIDS drugs. But all three groups shared the common goal of preventing the FDA from regulating the production and sale of cigarettes.

GRASSROOTS MOBILIZATION

▶ **Isn't outside lobbying more democratic than inside lobbying?** Interest groups increasingly are relying on grassroots mobilization as a form of outside lobbying to pressure policymakers. A trade association executive interviewed by Kenneth Goldstein gave a very good definition of grassroots mobilization: "The identification, recruitment, and mobilization of constituent-based political strength capable of influencing political decisions."[27]

Grassroots work is very difficult to measure, and its success is perhaps even more difficult to assess. But most experts believe that grassroots mobilization is becoming far more common. Goldstein found that most Fortune 500 companies have full-time grassroots coordinators with solid plans to present their point of view by stirring up citizen interest and that the media cover grassroots lobbying with greater frequency today than they used to. The depth of support on some issues concerns some observers; they note that it is often rather short-lived and superficial. Some refer to such artificially stimulated public interest as "Astroturf" because it gives the *appearance* of widespread popularity but has no real depth. Kollman, however, finds evidence that grassroots lobbying is effective in producing real support and is an important tool for getting groups' messages to officials.[28]

In addition to grassroots mobilizing, some interest groups also use so-called grasstops programs, in which influential people are encouraged to contact legislators directly in the hope that these key people can exert leverage or use their social and professional connections to advance the group's position. However, not all interest groups have access to influential people.

GRASSROOTS LOBBYING TACTICS

Many people believe that indirect lobbying is a new phenomenon. It is not. Indirect lobbying has been going on in our country since the earliest days, although tools and tactics have evolved with the emergence of new technology. Consider, for example, how westward expansion was sold to the American people. Entities with vested interests in expansion, such as the nineteenth-century railroad companies, stressed in their appeals to the public the ease of obtaining property, the lure of frontier adventure, and the chance of finding wealth by moving west. Westward expansion would have occurred without these marketing campaigns, for Americans had long valued property ownership, adventure, and wealth, but the rate of expansion was accelerated by capitalizing commercially on the existing public interest. Would-be settlers in turn put pressure on the government to aid westward migration. Responding to this pressure, in 1862 Congress passed the Transcontinental Railroad Act and the Homestead Act. By making land grants to the companies that built the western railroads, as well as by encouraging western settlement, Congress dramatically increased the value of railroad property.

▶ **What do interest groups do for grassroots mobilization efforts?**

TRADITIONAL TACTICS   One of the earliest forms of grassroots mobilization, going back to the days of the antislavery movement and still used because it is so effective, is **direct contact**. Having committed supporters personally contact fellow citizens is a valuable tool for interest groups. Seeing others who care deeply enough to give of their time and energy can stimulate people to become involved in a cause. The civil rights movement effectively used direct contact to build grassroots support. Today it is popular with environmentalist groups, such as Greenpeace, which targets people in door-to-door campaigns, especially around college campuses.

Direct mail is another way for interest groups to contact potential supporters. Modern technology permits mailings to be personalized in ways that allow a group to frame its message narrowly, so that it appeals to specific types of people. Direct mail is attractive to special-interest groups because recipients can open the mail in the privacy of their home and can confidentially consume the information at their leisure. Such mailings have been shown to be effective in many cases, but they can be very expensive to produce. Knowing a good deal about the individuals targeted in its direct-mail campaign helps an interest group personalize its message and thus make it more efficient. Because modern technology today collects and stores so much personal information, interest groups with substantial financial resources

▶ What do interest groups
do for grassroots mobilization efforts?

can acquire what they want to know about potential recipients, allowing them to exploit this form of propaganda more effectively.

"Getting members is about scaring the hell out of people,"[29] one interest group leader has said of direct mail. By playing on fear and predicting dire consequences if supporters don't unite, the direct mail letter's tone is designed to elicit quick action—especially to raise money and stimulate an outpouring of letters and e-mails to legislators.

In their attempts to influence public opinion, interest groups often directly distribute information—including brochures and reprinted editorials—to potential supporters and policymakers. In fighting President Truman's plan for federal health insurance in the late 1940s, the American Medical Association made one of the earliest and most successful uses of brochures and pamphlets. To bring public opinion to bear on policymakers, the AMA's literature, distributed through doctors' offices, made grim predictions about the potentially dire effects of "socialized medicine." The use of inflammatory language to exploit people's fears became a tactic that interest groups still commonly use today.

Historically, interest groups have also used the court pathway (litigation) to promote or resist change and to shape public opinion. Interest groups that are unsuccessful in bringing about change using other techniques often turn to litigation, the most famous example of which was the NAACP's challenge to school segregation. Realizing that black people in the South were denied access to the elections pathway and were limited in their ability to use the lobbying decision makers pathway to pressure officials, in the 1940s the NAACP decided to rely on the courts to raise consciousness and force change. As discussed in (L)(I)(N)(K) *Chapter 6, page 222,* in 1954 its efforts resulted in the *Brown* v. *Board of Education* decision, which declared school segregation unconstitutional. Women have also been successful in using the court pathway in such areas as sexual harassment, employment discrimination, and domestic violence. So have disabled Americans and other marginalized groups.

Interest groups also use events and activities to influence the public and pressure policymakers. Many of these events are designed to provide members with solidary benefits (discussed earlier in the chapter), but they can also have the advantage of raising the organization's image in the community and demonstrating its importance. Labor unions and public interest groups are most likely to engage in this type of behavior, organizing rallies and marches to promote their cause. Groups that feel that they are being ignored or marginalized often turn to other forms of political expression, including protests (the grassroots mobilizing pathway). Peace groups in the United States and around the world

The "Million Mom March" was a grassroots movement started by Donna Dees Thomases and other mothers upset over gun violence. The first March was held on May 14, 2000, when thousands of supporters came together at the National Mall in Washington, D.C. to demand new gun control laws. The march received a good deal of national media attention. Why do you think that organizations (such as Mothers Against Drunk Driving—MADD and movements led by mothers gain more media attention.

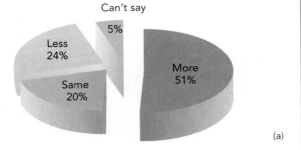

"Do you think politicians in Washington these days are more responsive to special-interest groups, or about as responsive to special-interest groups as was the case twenty years ago?"

(a)

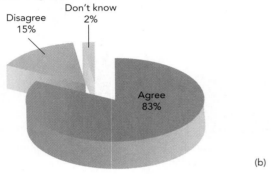

"Do you agree or disagree with the following statement? Special-interest groups have more influence than voters."

(b)

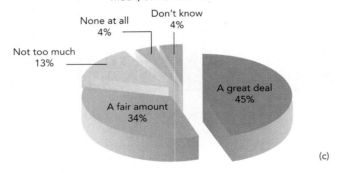

"Generally speaking, when elected and government officials in Washington make decisions about important issues, how much attention do you feel they actually pay to. . . lobbyists and special-interest groups? A great deal, a fair amount, not too much, or none at all?"

(c)

FIGURE 13.4
Americans' Opinions about Interest Groups

Americans overwhelmingly believe that interest groups exert more influence than voters. Moreover, nearly 80% of the public believe that government officials pay at least a fair amount of attention to interest groups when making important decisions. Do you think that these findings are troubling? Do you have similar opinions as depicted above? Why or why not? Do you think that the public has legitimate concerns?

▶ How do interest groups manipulate the media to advance their cause?

have organized rallies to protest American wars from Vietnam to Iraq. Labor unions sometimes rely on marches and rallies to show the strength of their membership and thus remind policymakers of their potential to influence many people. This route doesn't work for everyone: Trade associations, professional associations, and corporations have rarely, if ever, used protest demonstrations.

Feminist and abortion rights groups, as well as the pro-life organizations that oppose them, have long relied on mass demonstrations. In 1989, for example, some 300,000 people, including celebrities, marched in Washington in support of abortion rights and to celebrate the twenty-fifth anniversary of the Supreme Court's *Roe* v. *Wade* decision legalizing abortion. In 1990, tens of thousands of pro-life supporters, especially on January 22 (the anniversary of the *Roe* decision), protested against legalized abortion in Washington and in other cities across the nation. On April 25, 2004, the March for Women's Lives was held to show support for issues important to women, ranging from health care to continued access to contraception and safe abortions. A wide range of women's groups participated in organizing the march, including the Feminist Majority, the Feminist Majority Foundation, NARAL Pro-Choice America, the National Organization for Women, the Planned Parenthood Federation of America, the Black Women's Health Imperative, the American Civil Liberties Union, and the National Latina Institute for Reproductive Health. An estimated 1,110,000 people from diverse backgrounds participated. According to the rally's organizers, over 1,400 organizations and 57 countries were represented, and more than a third of the participants were under 25. Youth leaders from half a dozen organizations addressed the crowd.

To force the pace of change, interest groups have organized boycotts, the organized refusal of large numbers of people to do business with an opponent as a nonviolent expression of disagreement. (see Figure 13.4). Boycotts of imported British manufactured goods, for example, were an important way for American patriots to put pressure on Parliament during the years leading up to the American Revolution. Twentieth-century American civil rights organizations found a combination of boycotts, rallies, marches, and protests to be very effective tools in their fight to end segregation and racism.

Interest groups need to be careful when using protest demonstrations and marches in the lobbying decision makers pathway. Such efforts can backfire if they arouse more public opposition than they generate sympathy. (During the Vietnam War, for example, opinion polls showed that the U.S. public was usually more antiprotest than antiwar.) Decision makers often hesitate to embrace groups that pursue this tactic. Moreover, because protest demonstrations are more common today, they attract less attention

"advertorial"
an advertisement presented as an editorial.

than they once did. Protests can also generate unwelcome police interest and invite infiltration of the organizing groups. As happened in the Vietnam era, protests against the war in Iraq have attracted the attention of the FBI.

NEWER TOOLS OF INDIRECT LOBBYING   The development in recent decades of more sophisticated means of communication has given interest groups far more options than they once had to motivate supporters, recruit new members, and mobilize the public. To sway public opinion, organized interest groups have aggressively and imaginatively used the media. As you can see in Figure 13.5, the public believes that interest groups are very effective in manipulating the media, though it is difficult to gauge how much actual manipulation really occurs.

▶ **How do interest groups manipulate the media to advance their cause?** One way that organized groups try to exploit the media to advance their cause is by manipulating what gets reported. Occasionally they succeed. Pressured by their deadlines, some reporters are willing to use in their stories information presented by interest groups. Careless reporters will often uncritically quote press releases and anonymous off-the-record comments by political insiders, although good journalists know that they must be wary of relying exclusively on such potentially biased material. In this era of heightened expectations for investigative reporting, interest groups often try, sometimes covertly, to advance their views by prompting media exposés of controversial issues. Groups also like to stage visually appealing pseudo-events, such as schoolchildren marching to appeal for higher teacher pay, thus increasing the likelihood that the event will be shown on local TV and maybe even make the national news.

Many Americans believe that there is an antibusiness bias in news coverage. Whether or not such a bias actually exists, citizen groups are often able to invoke sympathy in ways that large corporations cannot. For example, a news story about a local citizens' group fighting some huge, impersonal corporation to protect a beautiful stream from pollution is very attractive. Such "David versus Goliath" stories have a human interest component that is quite appealing to media outlets, which know that people like to see the underdog win. To counter this perception of bias, many corporations and industrial groups spend large sums on public relations campaigns to soften their image.

Well-heeled interest groups advertise in major newspapers and magazines and on TV to increase their visibility and improve their public image. Many of these ads are noncommercial—they aren't trying to sell anything or directly attract members but instead are designed to generate favorable public opinion. Because

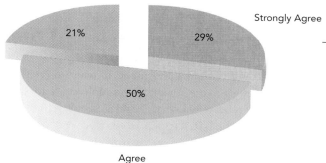

"I believe that it's pretty easy for interest groups to manipulate the press."

Disagree/Strongly Disagree/Don't know

Strongly Agree

21%   29%

50%

Agree

FIGURE 13.5

Public Opinion of Interest Group Manipulation of Media

SOURCE: Survey by American Society of Newspaper Editors. Methodology: Conducted by Urban & Associates during April, 1998 and based on telephone interviews with a national adult sample of 3,000. Data provided by The Roper Center for Public Opinion Research, University of Connecticut.

such ads are frequently designed to resemble editorials, they have sometimes been dubbed **"advertorials."** Thus drug companies run TV ads to show that they care about people's health and not just about making money, and oil companies advertise how they are taking pains to protect the environment in efforts to affect public opinion. Advertorials are often intended not only to persuade the public directly but also to influence people who talk to the public—journalists and other opinion leaders.

There are three general categories of advertorials—image, advocacy, and journalism. With image advertorials, groups are trying to create a positive climate of opinion, largely by focusing on the public good that they claim to provide and the services they perform. Advocacy advertorials more directly advance a group's policy positions and tend to be more ideological and aggressive. Interest groups also directly target journalists by offering awards, grants, and seminars. Clearly, in thus appealing to the press, interest groups are trying to influence how they are portrayed to the public.[30]

Citizen groups also advertise through the media. Their ads try to inform the public of an issue about which the groups are concerned. Imagine a group that opposes an issue on the ballot in an upcoming election, to raise the local sales tax to fund a new professional football stadium. What can it do? Certainly it would want to communicate to the community why it opposes the stadium, because at first public opinion would probably be rather positive toward the idea (most Americans like pro football and want to attract or keep a local team). So if it hoped to succeed in convincing voters to oppose the increase in sales tax, the antistadium group would have to inform citizens about the wider implications of the issue—for example, how a higher sales tax would affect poorer consumers or how a stadium would radically disrupt traffic patterns. Like corporations, citizen groups with plenty of money also advertise to influence the organization's public image. One of the best examples of this technique is the ads that the National Rifle

▶ **Has the Internet led** to new tactics for interest groups?

> **blog**
> a Web log or online journal.

Association runs to impress the public, in which ordinary-looking people who belong to the organization simply say, "I am the NRA." The ads show the public that "regular people," both men and women, support the NRA, lending a more personal image to a vast organization that is often perceived as mainly representing hunters and gun enthusiasts and as tolerating gun violence.

Some interest groups sponsor television shows to influence the public. One example is the televangelist Pat Robertson's *700 Club,* a widely watched cable program that appeals to many supporters and potential supporters in an entertaining and informative way. Groups also try to have their advocates appear as experts on talk shows. Having someone present the group's position on the *Larry King Show* or *Crossfire* raises the group's visibility and credibility in important ways—for, as when using the lobbying decision-makers pathway to influence public officials, groups must appear credible and trustworthy. To further sway public opinion, some groups also try to arrange for their supporters to appear on talk radio. By encouraging supporters to sit in on talk programs or to call in to voice their opinions, the group can get some free publicity and attract new members.

▶ **Has the Internet led to new tactics for interest groups?** Over the past two decades, the Internet has offered interest groups some of the best possibilities for new tactics. Organized groups can use the Internet to advance their cause in many ways, including Web pages, e-mail campaigns, bulletin boards, and chat rooms. The Internet has great potential for mobilizing supporters and raising money. But not everyone can readily use the Internet. Younger people who are more affluent and better educated have home access to the Internet at far greater rates than older, poorer, and less educated people. Interest groups should therefore be aware that certain portions of the public are hard to target with the Internet. Nevertheless, the Internet is a very appealing tool to communicate with the public.

One important new use of the Internet is the use of **blogs,** short for *Web logs,* or online journals. The use of Web journals and electronic newsletters for public consumption has grown dramatically since the 1999 release of software that made the process much more user-friendly. Blogs allow people and groups to post information on Web sites to stimulate interest in particular topics, raise public awareness, and influence public opinion. Groups and individuals often read blogs that are dedicated to particular topics, such as serving as governmental watchdogs, or "investigative" journalists and celebrity gossip (to name only a few). Consumers must use caution, however, when using information posted on the Internet, as nowadays nearly anyone, regardless of level of expertise or knowledge base, can set up and maintain a blog.

Although the Internet has great potential for reaching people quickly, many analysts question whether it has a significant impact on public opinion and behavior. Most people who visit an environmentalist group's Web page, for example, are probably already committed environmentalists and are not necessarily being persuaded by what they read. Political supporters of a particular campaign are more likely to visit the candidate's Web page than people who are undecided or who support an opposing candidate. This does not mean that the Web page is irrelevant. Visiting a Web page may influence some people's opinions, and Web pages can certainly stir interested people to take action—and not just by sending money. Imagine someone who is interested in protecting a local lake that is threatened by pollution. That person might care a great deal about the issue but lack the tools to act. Visiting the Web pages of environmentalist groups might be very helpful to such a person, especially if the groups highlight the actions of individuals in local communities and provide specific organizational tips. The interested environmentalist might learn how to become an activist in the cause.

The Internet has the advantage of offering speed and convenience. Through e-mail campaigns and alerts, groups can communicate to their members instantaneously and virtually free of charge. Web pages communicate information, stimulate supporters to contact their representatives, and raise money for the group or its cause. Cliff Landesman of the Internet Nonprofit Center identifies eight purposes for which interest groups use the Internet: publicity, public education, communication, volunteer recruitment, research, advocacy, service provision, and fundraising.[31] Certainly not all groups pursue all eight of these potential uses; many focus on just one or two. For example, many antigovernment groups use bulletin boards to get out their message and to communicate with others who share their concerns. Project Vote Smart exists to inform citizens about candidates running for federal office, presenting issue stances in a clear and concise format. The Million Mom March against gun violence, held on Mother's Day in 2000, used the Internet quite effectively to mobilize supporters. This march of nearly 750,000 individuals started with a Web site created by one woman, Donna Dees-Thomases, whose idea quickly grew into a national movement. Supporters used Web pages to organize the march, create local chapters, provide logistics, attract media coverage, and raise money.[32]

CAMPAIGN ACTIVITIES

As you will discover in ⓛⓘⓝⓚ *Chapter 14, pages 572–573* in the elections pathway, interest groups play a very active role in local, state, and national election campaigns. Organized groups obviously want to influence elections so that individuals who support their cause will get into office. Groups also want to influence the

> ▶ **Are the tactics that** interest groups use to influence elections legal? Are they fair?

public during elections to influence incumbent policymakers. Groups get involved in elections in many different ways, their central motivation being to advance their own cause.

Most interest groups take part in electoral politics by rating and endorsing candidates. At every point on the political spectrum, special-interest groups rate the candidates to help influence their supporters and sympathizers. A typical example is the Christian Coalition, which provides voter guides (distributed in sympathetic churches across the nation) that examine candidates' voting records and note what percentage of the time they vote "correctly" on what the group considers key issues. In the same way, the AFL-CIO rates members of Congress on their votes on issues important to organized labor, likewise giving its supporters a voting cue. So does the U.S. Chamber of Commerce, from the business perspective.

▶ **Are the tactics that interest groups use to influence elections legal? Are they fair?** Today, many people worry about the influence that special-interest groups have on elections and especially about the impact of interest group money on electoral outcomes and the subsequent actions of elected officials. However, it is important to note that interest groups are simply associations of like-minded people. In a democracy, citizens *should* affect elections, even if they are acting collectively. So while we should certainly scrutinize interest groups' contributions to candidates and political parties, interest group involvement does not necessarily pollute the electoral system. Interest groups can serve as a political cue to their members, other interest groups, voters, and the media. When an interest group donates money to a candidate, it is making a public show of support that can be an important cue for others, either for or against that candidate.

Money has always been important in politics; today's requirement for limited campaign contributions and full disclosure (see ⓛⓘⓝⓚ *Chapter 14, pages 554–555*) makes the system more transparent and honest. In the days when we did not know how much candidates received in contributions and from whom, we might have naively thought that there was less corruption. However, the opposite was probably true. Despite ready access to contributions, greater scrutiny today may in fact ensure that politicians have to be more honest.

pathways past and present
TRADITIONAL VOLUNTEERS VERSUS PAID PROFESSIONALS

Traditionally, interest groups relied on the "people power" of their supporters, from stuffing envelopes to organizing fundraisers and from hanging posters to distributing bumper stickers. Although many small organizations still use volunteers to perform these tasks, nowadays a growing number of interest groups hire paid professionals to communicate with members and potential members, the media, public officials, and the citizenry as a whole. As you can imagine, the services of these professionals are very expensive, but well-funded groups increasingly see the use of professionals as imperative, especially in such areas as the following:

Attorneys (to help comply with federal and state laws)

Direct mail specialists (printing, processing, and strategies)

Fundraising

Grassroots specialists

Initiative and referendum consultants

Internet services and Web site construction

Lobbyists

Mailing and telephone lists

Media buying and consulting

Newsletters and publications

Pollsters

Press relations

Public affairs (events, issue management, and research)

Research (including opposition research)

Voter registration and mobilization ■

practice quiz

1. Testifying before a congressional hearing is an effective form of inside lobbying.
   a. true   b. false

2. In the late 1990s, tobacco company lobbyists cultivated a lobbying coalition of three groups: smokers, small store owners, and
   a. tobacco farmers.
   b. gay rights groups.
   c. the NRA
   d. the Christian Coalition.

3. What's the primary drawback to the tactic of direct-mail lobbying?
   a. It's an indirect approach to legislators and therefore inherently limited in its effect.
   b. "Junk" mail often alienates people.
   c. It appeals to only one person at a time.
   d. It's expensive.

discussionquestions

1. What is the difference between indirect and direct lobbying? Why and how is each used? To which practices do you think the public most objects? Why? What, if anything, should be done to reform lobbying practices?

2. What is grassroots mobilization? How have grassroots tactics changed? Do you think that the more modern techniques are more effective than the tried-and-true methods? Why or why not?

▶ **What evidence shows that** well-funded groups are more successful in reaching their goals?

4. Grassroots mobilization via the Internet is particularly effective with
   a. older people with limited incomes.
   b. people who are not already sympathetic to that particular cause.
   c. young, affluent, and well-educated people.
   d. migrant workers.

Answers: 1-a, 2-b, 3-d, 4-c.

The Importance of Money in Mobilization

As we have noted, cost is one of the key burdens in organizing. It takes a great amount of money to organize and maintain an interest group. Some interests—corporations and professions, for example—are better able to bear these than others, such as ordinary citizens. Despite this, as we have seen, citizen groups have thrived and have brought about great change.

USES OF MONEY

It is difficult to overemphasize the importance of money in mobilization. A significant amount of money is needed just to launch an organization, and continuous funding is needed to maintain it thereafter. Money is needed to recruit members, hire staff, rent offices, pay overhead, and raise additional funds. If the group plans to use many of the tactics discussed in this chapter, substantially more funds will be needed. Advertising on radio or television, and even in newspapers, is very expensive. The ads must be created and effectively placed to maximize their value. Direct mail is also very expensive, so groups need to be careful to use it properly. Money is needed to raise more money. Moreover, given the professionalism that is emerging in interest group activities, money has to be found to hire professionals. Certainly not many groups can afford the full range of professional services, but for those with sufficient resources, a variety of services can be purchased.

▶ **What evidence shows that well-funded groups are more successful in reaching their goals?** Political scientists have found, not surprisingly, that groups with large resources have many advantages and are more successful.[33] Well-funded groups can afford to hire the best lobbyists and workers, make large campaign contributions, hire specialized professionals, and retain attorneys for legal battles. Moreover, affluent groups can use many lobbying techniques with greater success, for they can sustain such activity over longer periods.

In February 2006, South Dakota passed a law that would ban nearly all abortions in virtually all cases (including rape and incest). The law, which would punish doctors who perform abortions with five years in prison and a $5,000 fine, is clearly intended to force the Supreme Court (with its two newest members, Chief Justice John G. Roberts and Justice Samuel A. Alito) to reconsider its 1973 *Roe* v. *Wade* decision legalizing abortion. This is the first challenge to *Roe* since the Supreme Court reaffirmed the right to legalized abortion in 1992 (*Planned Parenthood* v. *Casey*). Legislators concerned with the costs that will stem from legal challenges (Planned Parenthood immediately announced that it will sue to oppose the law) created a fund so that people and groups in favor of the proposal could make contributions to help finance the state's defense of the law. Pro-life groups are working hard to stimulate contributions, too; one anonymous donor contributed $1 million to the fund before the bill was even signed into law by the governor.

Money is often the key predictor of who wins and who loses in American politics. However, money alone does not always win. Public support is equally important, which is why interest groups put so much effort into outside lobbying. The women's rights, civil rights, and farm workers movements are perhaps the best examples of less affluent groups exerting great power for change.

FUNDRAISING TACTICS

Because money is so important to them, interest groups raise it from a variety of sources. Some groups have more difficulty than others raising money, but all spend a great amount of time and energy in fundraising. One important source of funds for groups is donations by members. Though annual dues of $40 don't seem like a lot of money, it adds up: If the group has 400,000 members, dues would yield $16 million yearly. Groups also tap members for

▶ **What is the verdict?**
Are interest groups good
or bad for democracy?

discussionquestions

1. Why do interest groups need money? How do they raise
   money? How is technology changing the patterns and tactics
   of fundraising?

2. How influential are interest groups in the United States? How
   influential does the public *think* interest groups are? What
   are some of the consequences of this public perception?

additional contributions, often through direct mail, direct contact, and personal appeals. Groups also use their Web pages or e-mail to raise money through online solicitations. One of the most successful contemporary groups to use the Internet to solicit donations is the liberal group MoveOn.org. Created in 1998 to promote citizen involvement in politics and born of frustration with the Clinton administration, this group claims a network of 3.3 million online activists, 10,000 of whom donated to the group's PAC. This PAC spent 30 million in 2004, raised largely through online solicitations. For some interest groups, sales of goods and services are another effective fundraising tool. The Sierra Club, for example, sells calendars, T-shirts, and stationery items. The National Organization for Women offers bumper stickers, pins, hats, clothing, and books. Think tanks sell the books, reports, and research articles that they commission and publish. Clearly, not all groups can market their goods, but for those that can, it can be a solid source of fundraising.

Interest Group Influence

▶ **What is the verdict? Are interest groups good or bad for democracy?** As we mentioned in the beginning of this chapter, interest groups play a mixed role in our society. On the one hand, they give people opportunities to band together to increase their power and their ability to influence fellow citizens and government officials. From an early age, we come to appreciate that there is strength in numbers, hence Americans' solid commitment to collective action. But on the other hand, a tension exists: While we believe in collective action as a means for us to influence others, we are often wary of the collective action of groups to which we do not belong or whose views we do not support.

Moreover, it's been asked whether interest groups increase or decrease the influence of individuals: Do interest groups represent ordinary people who would otherwise be powerless? Or do they drown out the voices of ordinary people in favor of special interests?

Participating in groups affects individual citizens in several positive ways. Those who are members of organized interest groups are also more likely to participate in other forms of political activity, at least according to some researchers. Allan Cigler and Mark Joslyn found that people who participated in group activities had higher levels of political tolerance, more trust in elected officials, and a greater sense of political efficacy.[34]

However, other research that focused on the impact of interest groups on social issues paints a different picture. Although participation in interest groups may have positive effects on individuals, the growth of interest groups does correlate with the growth in distrust in government and fellow citizens, voter cynicism, and lower voting rates. Some hypothesize that when interest groups raise the level of conflict surrounding an issue, they simply alienate the public, thus raising the levels of citizen distrust. However, a different interpretation is also possible. Just the reverse may be true: that interest groups are formed because citizens *do* distrust the government, *are* cynical, and *do* have low participation rates. It could be that people join interest groups in order to organize an otherwise chaotic world.

practicequiz

1. What is a crucial ingredient in raising money for interest groups?
   a. social anonymity outside Washington, D.C.
   b. independent wealth
   c. well-qualified legal representation
   d. money

2. What prompted the creation of MoveOn.org?
   a. Democrats' desire to defeat George W. Bush in the 2004 election
   b. Democrats' desire to defeat George W. Bush in the 2000 election
   c. citizens' frustration with the Clinton administration
   d. citizens' frustration with the Supreme Court

3. According to recent research, participating in organized interest groups usually makes people
   a. more inclined to participate in other forms of political activity.
   b. less inclined to participate in other forms of political activity.
   c. less inclined to make financial contributions to a political campaign.
   d. more likely to denigrate the political process in this country.

4. Research suggests that the growth of interest groups in this country correlates with the growth in trust in the government and in fellow citizens.
   a. true   b. false

Answers: 1-d, 2-c, 3-a, 4-b.

Conclusion

We have a "how to" element in our government, focusing on bargaining and compromise that is public-driven. Organized groups are among the most important actors in motivating the public, yet as a society, we have mixed feelings about interest groups.

On the one hand, we acknowledge the need and show our support for organized action. To help influence change, many of us join organized interests and readily form associations that range from parent organizations in schools and neighborhood improvement groups to larger, nationally oriented organizations. In fact, approximately 65 percent of Americans over age 18 belong to at least one politically active organization.[35] Even if we don't join organizations, many of us feel that an existing group is representing our interests. For example, many senior citizens are not dues-paying members of AARP but nevertheless feel that AARP represents them.

However, we also fear organized interests. Polls consistently show that Americans are wary of the influence of "special interests" and believe that the "common person" is not adequately represented. One lobbyist described others' perception of his profession thusly: "Being a lobbyist has long been synonymous in the minds of many Americans with being a glorified pimp."[36] Much of the public believes that interest groups have a great deal of influence with government officials and that their influence has been increasing. Moreover, fully 83 percent of Americans believe that interest groups have more influence than voters. Such feelings were a large reason the public supported the Bipartisan Campaign Reform Act of 2002, which we will discuss in (L)(I)(N)(K) *Chapter 14, pages 559–563.*

Interest groups, as we have emphasized in this chapter, are associations of like-minded people united for a common cause. However, we must be careful not to paint too rosy a picture. Interest groups are primarily concerned with promoting their self-interest. Even groups that seem to be advancing the best interest of the public may not be. Trade-offs are often inevitable. Consider environmentalist groups. They work to protect the environment so that all of us can benefit, but in the process they sometimes create difficulties for a community or certain individuals. Forcing a mining company out of business, for example, might be very important for the local ecosystem but may also throw a large number of people out of work. Hence it is debatable whether the behavior of the interest group is in the best interest of the mining community. In this example, the miners are certainly more interested in pro-

tecting their jobs than the environmentalists, who may live on the other side of the country. Such concerns and debates are important when we examine interest group behavior. To understand fully both the potentially positive and potentially negative impacts of interest group actions, a balanced analysis is essential.

YOUR turn!

Let's reconsider gun control, the example at the beginning of this chapter. Advocates of gun control say that reducing gun ownership and access will reduce gang violence, suicides, and accidental deaths and injuries, making our society safer. Opponents of gun control say that by allowing law-abiding citizens reasonable access to guns, society will be safer because people will be able to protect themselves and their families against criminals. Gun rights supporters also firmly believe that the right to bear arms is guaranteed by our Constitution. Opponents of unrestricted gun rights respond that the eighteenth-century authors of the Second Amendment were thinking about citizen militias armed with flintlocks, not about modern enthusiasts brandishing AK-47s. Each group feels very strongly about the issue and works diligently to articulate its views.

Between 1998 and 2004, gun rights groups have contributed more than $6 million to candidates for federal office and to national political party organizations. Eighty-six percent of these contributions have gone to Republicans. The National Rifle Association is the largest contributor. During this same period, gun control advocates contributed only $700,000 to candidates and political parties, with 99 percent going to Democrats. Most of the contributions came from the Brady Campaign to Prevent Gun Violence (formally known as Handgun Control). Meanwhile, between 1998 and 2004, the NRA spent $11 million in lobbying, and Gun Owners of America spent $18 million. The Brady Campaign spent less than $3 million lobbying, the Coalition to Stop Gun Violence spent $540,000, and Americans for Gun Safety spent $4.8 million. The NRA spent more than $22 million on communication costs to its members and in indirect expenditures from 1989 to 2004.[37]

Let's consider how this dynamic affects our democratic system. Is the fight over gun control fair, with evenly balanced adversaries? Is the fight healthy for our democracy? Consider the figures just quoted as you ponder these questions. Are you troubled that one side has so many more resources than the other? Why or why not? What, if anything, should be done? ∎

Chapter Review

1. Interest groups serve many important purposes in democratic societies, from providing a tool to participate to educating the public and governmental officials to influencing government action.

2. The growth in the number of interest groups has both positive and negative effects. More groups provide additional outlets for participation, but more groups also can produce more conflict. Furthermore, the uneven growth pattern, with some groups increasing at much faster rates than others, has led some people to worry about potential bias in the articulation of some needs over the desires of individuals and groups with less representation.

3. There are many costs associated with forming and maintaining organized groups. Costs include money, time, and overcoming the free-rider and political-efficacy problems. To overcome these barriers, interest groups use many tactics, from offering benefits to providing inducements. Leadership is often a very important factor in group formation, maintenance, and success.

4. Trying to gain access to present their positions, interest groups lobby directly by contacting officials, staff members, and members of the bureaucracy. They also testify at congressional hearings and spend a good deal of time and energy building long-term relationships, thus augmenting their credibility so that they can effectively communicate with policymakers.

5. Indirect lobbying means trying to influence the government by mobilizing public support. Grassroots mobilization is one very effective tactic in indirect lobbying.

6. Traditional tactics of grassroots mobilization include direct contact, direct mail, and the creation of pamphlets to share information with supporters and the public. Newer tools include using the media to reach supporters and the general public. To get their message across, interest groups advertise, sponsor television shows, and appear as experts on news and entertainment programs.

7. Money is very important for interest groups' success; hence they devote a lot of time and energy to fundraising tactics.

8. Debate exists over the actual influence of interest groups in the United States, but the consensus among the public is that interest groups are very powerful—perhaps too powerful—relative to the influence of voters and interested but unorganized citizens.

CHAPTER REVIEW TEST

1. What important idea does the power of the NRA illustrate for students of American government?
   a. Gun enthusiasts willfully misinterpret the Second Amendment.
   b. It is difficult but important to strike a balance between First and Second Amendment rights.
   c. It is difficult but important to strike a balance between the public good and the self-interest of powerful groups.
   d. It can be difficult for interest groups—even those with great resources—to make their concerns known to the government.

2. What is best for a powerful interest group is often at odds with what is best for society—and that conflict is good for our democracy.
   a. true   b. false

3. What's one reason many interest groups need money?
   a. to pay congressional representatives to listen to their lobbyists
   b. to run advertisements that publicize how their lobbyists are influencing governmental officials
   c. to raise additional money
   d. to testify before congressional committees

4. Being active in an interest group constitutes
   a. a shortcut around the democratic process.
   b. a legitimate form of political participation.
   c. a version of grassroots mobilization.
   d. a less effective alternative to voting.

5. Interest groups contribute to the governing process by
   a. overseeing polling places.
   b. monitoring government programs.
   c. representing the concerns of ordinary Americans.
   d. b and c

6. Who were Nader's Raiders?
   a. FBI operatives investigating the activities of Ralph Nader's Green Party campaign committee
   b. interest groups that emerged in opposition to Nader's consumer advocate group Public Citizen
   c. loyal young activists who contributed to Nader's efforts in consumer advocacy and the critique of government's role in consumer safety
   d. George W. Bush campaign workers who secretly promoted Nader's presidential candidacy in 2000

7. Citizens of France and the United Kingdom—countries with more centralized governments than ours—do not join interest groups as often as Americans because their governmental structure affords less political access to its people.
   a. true   b. false

8. Which kind of interest group is the American Bar Association?
   a. a public interest group
   b. a governmental unit
   c. a think tank
   d. an economic group

9. What are think tanks?
   a. research organizations without an ideological bias or agenda
   b. public institutions funded with federal tax dollars
   c. nonprofit public interest groups often operating from a partisan point of view
   d. public interest groups devoted to oceanic issues

10. AARP was formerly known as
   a. the American Association of Regional Policy.
   b. Americans Affiliated for Racial Progress.
   c. the American Association of Retired Persons.
   d. the American Association of Resource Policy.

11. Most leaders of interest groups in this country
   a. come from the ranks of the socioeconomic elite.
   b. are Democrats.
   c. are middle-class.
   d. are lawyers.

12. A friend refuses to join your fledgling interest group working to legalize the medical use of marijuana, saying "The 'War on Drugs' mentality is too powerful in this country." What barrier to interest group formation is in evidence here?
   a. the free-rider problem
   b. the easy-rider problem
   c. the cost problem
   d. the absence of a sense of political efficacy

13. When a lobbyist for the AMA takes a congressional staff member out to an expensive lunch to discusses the limitations of HMOs, that's an example of
   a. outside lobbying
   b. inside lobbying
   c. indirect lobbying
   d. illegal lobbying

14. TV ads funded by interest groups and designed to sway public opinion are often called
   a. infomercials.
   b. paid political announcements.
   c. advertorials.
   d. public service announcements.

15. Interest groups use the Internet to recruit volunteers, raise funds, conduct research, and educate the public.
   a. true   **b.** false

16. One way that the Christian Coalition participates in elections is by
   a. distributing information in churches about the voting records of candidates, noting who voted "correctly" and who did not.
   b. sponsoring debates among candidates for Congress.
   c. organizing get-out-the-vote drives on college campuses across the country.
   d. supporting candidates with a pro–labor union voting record.

17. Money is often the key predictor of who wins and loses in American politics.
   a. true   **b.** false

18. Of Americans over age 18, approximately how many belong to at least one politically active organization?
   a. 15 percent   **b.** 25 percent
   c. 45 percent   **d.** 65 percent

19. In the minds of many Americans, which of the following professions is most analogous to that of the lobbyist?
   a. gambler   **b.** pimp
   c. thief   **d.** forger

20. Gun control advocates in this country
   a. represent a minority viewpoint.
   b. have outspent their political opponents and triumphed legislatively.
   c. represent a majority viewpoint but have spent far less than their opponents.
   d. have no chance of succeeding politically.

Answers: 1: c; 2: a; 3: c; 4: b; 5: d; 6: c; 7: a; 8: d; 9: c; 10: c; 11: a; 12: d; 13: b; 14: c; 15: a; 16: a; 17: a; 18: d; 19: b; 20: c.

DISCUSSION QUESTIONS

1. What is an interest group? What functions do interest groups play in our society? Why do you think that so many people view them negatively? Are these assumptions warranted? Why or why not?

2. Is there a bias in participation? Is the fact that not all types of people participate a matter of concern? Why or why not?

3. How do interest groups mobilize supporters? What specific tactics are used?

4. What is the difference between direct and indirect lobbying? What concerns about each do people have? Do you think that both forms of lobbying are valuable? What are the differences between the traditional and the more contemporary tactics of grassroots mobilization?

5. How has technology affected the options available to organized interest groups for lobbying?

6. Why is money important to interest groups? How do they raise money?

7. How influential are interest groups? How influential do people *think* interest groups are? What are some of the consequences of public opinion on the power of interest groups in American politics?

INTERNET RESOURCES

Blog Search: **http://www.blogsearch.google.com**

Brady Campaign to Prevent Gun Violence: **http://handguncontrol.org**

Center for Responsive Politics: **http://www.opensecrets.org**

Coalition to Stop Gun Violence: **http://www.csgv.org**

Feminist Majority Foundation: **http://www.feminist.org**

Gun Owners of America: **http://www.gunowners.org**

Internet Nonprofit Center, 2000: **http://www.nonprofits.org/website.htm**.

League of United Latin American Citizens: **http://www.lulac.org**

National Association for the Advancement of Colored People: **http://www.naacp.org**

National Organization for Women: **http://www.now.org**

Project Vote Smart: **http://www.vote-smart.org**

Recording Artists Coalition: **http://www.recordingartistscoalition.com**

Rock the Vote: **http://www.rockthevote.org**

U.S. Chamber of Commerce: **http://www.uschamber.com**

ADDITIONAL READING

Barbour, Christine, and Gerald C. Wright, with Matthew J. Steb and Michael R. Wolf. *Keeping the Republic: Power and Citizenship in American Politics.* Washington, DC: CQ Press, 2006.

Berry, Jeffrey M. *The New Liberalism: The Rising Power of Citizen Groups.* Washington, DC: Brookings Institution Press, 1999.

Cigler, Allan J., and Burdett A. Loomis. *Interest Group Politics* (7th ed.). Washington, DC: CQ Press, 2007.

Goldstein, Kenneth. *Interest Groups, Lobbying, and Participation in America.* New York: Cambridge University Press, 1999.

Kamieniecki, Sheldon. *Corporate America and Environmental Policy: How Often Does Business Get Its Way?* Stanford, CA: Stanford University Press, 2006.

Kollman, Ken. *Outside Lobbying: Public Opinion and Interest Group Strategies.* Princeton, NJ: Princeton University Press, 1998.

Kryzanek, Michael. *Angry, Bored, Confused: A Citizen Handbook of American Politics.* Boulder, CO: Westview Press, 1999.

KEY TERMS

"advertorial" 522
blog 524
cleavages 506
direct contact 520
direct mail 520
disturbance theory 506
free-rider problem 511
gaining access 514

inside lobbying 514
interest group 502
lobbyists 506
material benefits 512
multi-issue interest groups 502
outside lobbying 514
patron 512
political action committee (PAC) 506

professional associations 509
public goods 511
public interest groups 509
purposive benefits 512
selective benefits 511
single-issue interest groups 502
solidary benefits 512
think tank 509

Michael Reagan, at podium, during a tribute to his father, former President Ronald Reagan, on the third evening of the Republican National Convention in 2004. Scenes like this give Americans a proud feeling, and have helped define our political system. Yet, if it is true that the electoral process lies at the heart of our system, and it is also true that elections seem rife with problems (as most would agree), does that imply our democracy is in distress? Does it matter that money seems to be a key factor in deciding which candidate wins, and that a shrinking number of Americans are passionate about electoral politics? This chapter will confront these and other important topics.

CHAPTER 14

ELECTIONS AND POLITICAL PARTICIPATION IN AMERICA

How Much for That Senate Seat? When Democrat Jon Corzine announced his bid for the U.S. Senate in September 1999, shockwaves went through New Jersey politics. The field of possible candidates quickly thinned, and even the sitting governor, Christie Todd Whitman, decided not to seek the Republican nomination. It was not his long career of public service, a good reputation, or even a powerful celebrity status that made Corzine a formidable opponent. He was not an ex-governor, a former New Jersey Nets basketball player, or a movie star from Hoboken. Quite the contrary. Corzine had never held elective office, and very few citizens of New Jersey would have recognized his name. What he did bring to the table was more than $400 million in personal resources and an intention to spend as much of it as necessary to win.[1]

Photo: Vincent Laforet/The New York Times

When John Corzine (D-NJ) ran for the United States Senate, it highlighted a telling paradox: On the one hand, our electoral system is open, and anyone wishing to spend their time and resources to run for office can do so. We like candidates who put it on the line and truly "run" for office. On the other hand, not everyone has the same resources, and in Corzine's case that was millions of his own dollars to spend. Has personal wealth become more important than a candidate's policies and character? Is "big money" turning off voters? This chapter will address this issue and many other important topics.

Corzine quickly demonstrated his resolve. His only opponent in the Democratic primary, Jim Florio, had decades of political experience as a former member of Congress and New Jersey's governor. Since both candidates were considered liberal, Florio made Corzine's money the issue, accusing him of trying to buy a Senate seat to bolster his ego. He also attacked Corzine's past as a Wall Street executive. Corzine's response was to spend more money, lavishing massive donations on local Democratic organizations and spending heavily on television. Toward the end of the campaign, Corzine's commercials were especially aggressive, using lines like "Florio lied about Social Security" and "Why would we ever trust him again?"[2] Florio managed to spend $3 million, a lavish sum for a primary election, but Corzine spent more than ten times that much—$33 million. Despite being endorsed by most major New Jersey newspapers, Florio lost the primary by a 16 percent margin.

Corzine's opponent in the general election was Republican Bob Franks. Franks attacked Corzine on a number of fronts, claiming that Corzine was for "the largest expansion of the federal government in American history."[3] The charge seemed to stick; one newspaper editorial called Corzine a "big government liberal" who wanted to spend taxpayer money "like a drunken sailor."[4] Yet Corzine's—not the federal government's—spending seemed to be the defining issue of the race. Franks constantly accused Corzine of trying to buy New Jersey's voters and won-

dered aloud what the nation would think of a state that sold its Senate seat to a Wall Street executive. Corzine attempted to turn his wealth into a virtue, claiming his self-financed status meant that, unlike Franks, he did not have to pander to special interests for donations.[5] In its final days, the race got close, with polls showing Corzine only slightly ahead—but in the end, Franks could not overcome his high-spending opponent. Corzine won by a 3 percent margin. He served in the Senate until 2005, when he was elected governor of New Jersey by a wide margin.

To many people, the story of Jon Corzine's campaign for the United States Senate underscores a serious limitation on the elections pathway: Personal wealth and the ability to raise large sums of money can be more important than a candidate's character and qualifications. As suggested by an organization that watches campaign finances [The Center for Responsive Politics]: "As the costs of running for office have escalated, more and more candidates are jumping into politics using their personal fortune, rather than trying to raise funds from other people." In the 2006 election they found that at least 23 House and Senate candidates were "self-funded," contributing at least $1 million of their own money to

their race. Can personal wealth buy legislative seats? How does money corrupt the system? To other observers, Corzine's success underscores the power of the election pathway to bring about change. He favored universal health care, more government aid to fight poverty, free college education for students with a B average or better—and, if necessary, higher taxes to pay for it all. His stance on many important issues was clear. He was elected because of this stand on these issues, not because of his money. Others would also note that while the number of self-funded candidates has grown in recent years, more often than not these candidates lose.

Even more interesting (and perhaps ironic), candidate Corzine pledged to support stricter campaign finance laws. He argued that the system was seriously askew, because only wealthy individuals like him were able to mount a serious campaign. Once in office, he became a consistent voice for the working poor, and his support of the Bipartisan Campaign Finance Reform Act in 2001, discussed later in this chapter, was critical. Optimistically, we might conclude that although money is a necessary ingredient in modern campaigns, it is not enough; a candidate's positions do matter. ■

▶ **I've heard our government** called a republic *and* a democracy. Which is it?

republican form of government
a system of government in which the general public selects agents to represent it in political decision making.

Plato (427–347 B.C.)
Greek philosopher often considered the first political scientist.

landslide election
an election in which the winners come to power with overwhelming public support.

legitimacy
the sense that the result of a decision-making process is a proper outcome in the minds of the people who must live with that outcome.

Plato was one of the first political theorists.
Among many interesting ideas, he rejected the notion that average citizens should be allowed to select their leaders. Most Americans would disagree, of course, but what are the significant downsides to the use of elections to pick pubic officials?

Precisely how and why government policy turns in one direction and not another can be difficult to understand. The details of policy formation are daunting for even the most seasoned observer. How can an average citizen play a role in this complex process? Many Americans restrict their political involvement to elections—to expressing their preference regarding the personnel of government. It is widely held that what government does is a reflection on the people in charge, so their selection would seem critical. This chapter explores the role of elections in selecting leaders and in some instances directly shaping policy. We begin with a brief look at theoretical issues and then move to legal matters, to the initiative and referendum process, and to some of the most important new dynamics in the election process, including the critical role of money. The chapter closes by taking a close look at levels of political participation in America, with a sharp focus on youth engagement.

By the end of the chapter, you will likely note a stunning irony: Even though the opportunity for Americans to play a role in elections has expanded in recent decades, fewer Americans are interested in doing so. While many citizens believe that elections are a key piece of the democratic process, actual involvement in this pathway, it seems, is out of fashion. Should we care about declining political participation; is it really a big deal? Given the theme of this text, our answer will probably not come as a surprise.

Key Questions

1. What are the theoretical strengths and weaknesses of choosing political leaders through elections?
2. Have changes to the Constitution altered the nature of elections in America?
3. What are some of the most significant changes in state and federal law as they relate to the elections pathway?
4. What forces have driven up the cost of elections in America?
5. Has the mushrooming cost of elections corrupted the process, or is spending money simply part of free speech?
6. What might explain the shrinking number of Americans who participate in the electoral process?
7. How does the level of participation in our nation compare to levels in other democracies?
8. Should we care about shrinking levels of political participation?
9. What changes are in store for the elections pathway, and will these adjustments transform the nature of our political system?

▶ **Do elections just tell** us who's the most popular candidate?

Ross Perot was unsuccessful in his 1992 bid for the presidency, but he did have a significant impact on public policy: He drew attention to mounting federal deficits. How is the "voice of the people" expressed through elections—even when a candidate loses?

Elections and Democratic Theory

We Americans put great faith in elections. We believe that they are a just means of resolving disputes and setting the course of government. Democracy means government by the people, and while there may be other ways of linking citizens to government, elections strike many people as the most efficient and most assured way to achieve this linkage. But is this actually so? Let's explore some theoretical issues regarding elections in a democracy.

REPUBLICANISM AND DIFFERENT WAYS TO SELECT LEADERS

▶ **I've heard our government called a republic *and* a democracy. Which is it?** The United States boasts a **republican form of government.** That is, ours is *not* a direct democracy, in which everyone has a say in what the government does, but is instead a system in which we select individuals—leaders—to work and speak on our behalf. This raises the question of how leaders are best chosen. There are many possibilities. We could randomly select members of the community—literally pick names out of a hat, much as we pick a trial jury. This would not guarantee a government run by experts, but so long as every citizen had the same chance of being selected, you could argue that it would be a fair system. (In fact, just such a system was used in an important city-state in medieval Italy. It didn't work too well because powerful families secretly decided whose names went into the hat!) **Plato** (427–347 B.C.), the first great political theorist, had something a bit different in mind. For Plato, some people are born to rule and some to be ruled. So another possibility would be to give an examination to citizens who are eager to serve and then fill government posts with those receiving the highest scores. Why not give the most qualified and most intelligent citizens the opportunity to serve? Still another option would be to allow public officials to handpick their own successors. Wanting to preserve their standing with the public and to ensure the continuity of their policies, these officials might be careful to choose citizens who would do a good job.

ELECTIONS AS AN EXPRESSION OF POPULAR WILL

▶ **Do elections just tell us who's the most popular candidate?** In short, if choosing public officials were the *only* function of elections, an argument might be made that other options are available. Yet not everyone would agree that the only function of elections is to select leaders.

Another way to think about elections is to realize that they serve as an expression of popular will—as a means of telling government what is on the minds of citizens. This process can work in different ways. A **landslide election** (whereby the winners come to power with overwhelming public support) does more than send a person or group to office: It signals to all the leaders of the system (and in the case of a national election, to the world at large) that the winning candidates' ideas are strongly favored by the voters.

Sometimes the expression of public sentiment in America is voiced through a minor party candidate. In 1992, independent candidate Ross Perot spent most of his time talking about the federal budget deficit. The main party candidates (Arkansas governor Bill Clinton and President George H. W. Bush) were paying little attention to that issue, perhaps because doing so would force difficult choices on the nation and its leaders. Perot's hourlong political "infomercials," filled with graphs, charts, data, and statistics, seemed out of place and rather quirky. But on election day, Perot garnered close to the highest third-party vote in a century. Perot did not win, of course, but a clear message had been sent: The public cares about deficit reduction. And the issue was taken seriously by the administration of the winning candidate, Bill Clinton.

STABILITY AND LEGITIMACY

Although there may be other ways to select government leaders, a core consideration is **legitimacy,** the process of decision making that is perceived to be proper by the people who must live with the

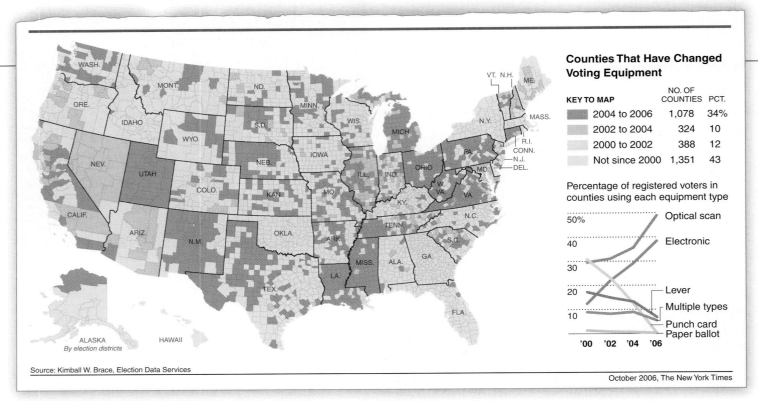

Counties That Have Changed Voting Equipment

KEY TO MAP	NO. OF COUNTIES	PCT.
2004 to 2006	1,078	34%
2002 to 2004	324	10
2000 to 2002	388	12
Not since 2000	1,351	43

Percentage of registered voters in counties using each equipment type

Source: Kimball W. Brace, Election Data Services

October 2006, The New York Times

FIGURE 14.1

The Mechanics of Voting in America

Our faith in the voting process was shaken in the 2000 election, as the recount in Florida revealed numerous hidden problems. Some began to worry about the legitimacy of the process. In response, Congress passed the Help America Vote Act in 2002. Among much else, the measure pushed states to update their voting systems. This figure illustrates where changes in voting equipment have occurred through the 2006 election. What factors might explain why some states have updated their machinery and others have not?

outcome. Legitimacy requires that the mode of selecting leaders be both legal and, in the eyes of citizens, fair. That is why the problem with voting machines in the 2000 election was so troubling (see Figure 14.1). In the American setting, elections serve that end. When citizens accept the need for political representation and feel that the resulting selection of these leaders has been legitimate, they are most likely to accept—though they might not always agree with—the policies that follow.

That is precisely why the outcome of the 2000 presidential election between Democrat Al Gore and Republican George W. Bush was a bit worrisome. What happens when an election ends in a virtual tie, as it did that year? Worse yet, what happens when the candidate who receives fewer votes than the other nevertheless *legally* gets into office? Al Gore received about half a million more votes than George W. Bush in 2000, but because of the way state votes were distributed in the electoral college (discussed in detail later in this chapter), and after the U.S. Supreme Court had ruled on the dispute, Bush wound up with more electoral college votes and became the forty-third president of the United States. This

raised two questions: Would the legitimacy of the federal government suffer?

A similar danger can arise when more than two candidates run for the same office. With only two candidates, the winner, by definition, has the support of a majority of voters (unless, perhaps, that choice has been filtered through a complex prism like the electoral college). But when a third or fourth relatively significant candidate enters the fray, the winner, at least in the American system, often winds up with the most votes (a plurality) but not a majority of the votes cast. For example, because it was a three-person race, Abraham Lincoln was elected with just 39.8 percent of the popular vote in 1860—none of which came from southern states, where he wasn't even on the ballot! Did Lincoln have the legitimacy to lead the nation? Many southern whites thought that he did not, most of the southern states seceded, and the result was four years of civil war. Because minor-party or independent candidates have often joined presidential contests and because the two major parties have been more or less balanced through the years, the United States has had plurality winners rather than majority winners sixteen times since 1824. Bill Clinton won the White House in both 1992 and 1996 with a popular vote of less than 50 percent.

Given snafus of this sort, a question might arise: How does the American system maintain its postelection stability? First, faith in elections runs so deep in Americans that eventual winners are seen as legitimate, regardless of the potholes in the road. The aftermath of the 2000 election was not entirely placid, but very soon the public accepted the outcome of the election as rightful. There was no rioting in the streets—just a few boos from the crowd as George W. Bush's inaugural parade made its way along Pennsylvania Avenue. Second, leaders in our system are bound by a powerful political culture that dictates a code of conduct for losing candidates. Ever since the election of 1800, when Thomas Jefferson and his Democratic-Republican followers defeated John Adams and his Federalist supporters, the losing candidates have accepted election results regardless of how close they were or how few citizens had turned out to vote. Losing candidates are gracious in our system, from the White House to the town council. (Adams, it must be said, did not set a particularly good precedent, sneaking out of Washington at dawn on the day of Jefferson's inauguration!)

It must have been a bitter pill for Al Gore to accept his loss in 2000, but he did so, in the end, with grace and dignity. According to one account, "Gore spelled out his concession so clearly that no pundit could read any doubt into it, or slam him for anything but unconditional surrender."[6] In that speech, Gore stated, "Almost a century and a half ago, Senator Stephen Douglas told Abraham Lincoln, who had just defeated him for the presidency, 'Partisan feeling must yield to patriotism. I'm with you, Mr. President, and God bless you.' Well, in that same spirit, I say to President-elect Bush that what remains of partisan rancor must now be put aside, and may God bless his stewardship of this country. . . . I offer my concession . . . and accept my responsibility, which I will discharge unconditionally, to honor the new president-elect and do everything possible to help him bring Americans together."

In January of 2005 an Iraqi woman flashes the victory sign with a purple finger, indicating she had just voted. Iraqis voted in their first free election in half a century despite a wave of suicide bombings and mortar attacks across the country. Can democracy be brought to a nation simply by instituting elections?

pathways of action

THE POWER OF THE PURPLE FINGER

Just short of two years after the fall of Saddam Hussein's regime, citizens of Iraq took what many hoped would prove a historic step toward creating a democracy in their nation. On January 30, 2005, Iraqi citizens—both men and women—were granted the opportunity to cast a ballot for their leaders. It had been fifty years since the last competitive election in Iraq. Due to threats of violence, many thought that voters would stay home (especially those of a significant Muslim sect of Iraq, the Sunnis). There was grave concern that the government would lack legitimacy.

But those projections proved mostly wrong as massive numbers of Iraqis flooded polling places, forming lines that stretched around blocks. Some stood contentedly for hours, waiting to cast their first vote. "The people of Iraq have spoken to the world," said President George W. Bush, "and the world is hearing the voice of freedom from the center of the Middle East." To ensure that no

▶ **How do elections help**
make us better citizens?

civic participation
citizen involvement in public matters, such as by joining clubs, voting, or attending governmental meetings.

episodic participation
occasional citizen involvement in public matters, such as during elections.

one would be able to cast more than one ballot, each voter's right index finger was dipped in indelible purple ink. For days to follow, Iraqis would proudly raise their ink-stained finger.

Only time would tell whether the election would prove the beginning of a truly open government, but at least for a time, the purple finger seemed to signify the inevitable triumph of democracy in the Middle East. Few claimed that voting alone would be enough to establish a democracy, and in fact the Sunnis actually boycotted the first election. But for many Iraqis, free elections—the chance for average citizens to cast a ballot to select public officials—seemed a turning point. It was a powerful sign that democracy might finally be arriving in their country. ▪

CIVIC EDUCATION

▶ **How do elections help make us better citizens?** In a democracy, citizens must remain aware of the important issues, at least in a broad sense. If the public is unaware of policy options or does not understand alternatives, control of governmental policy can pass to a small group of elites. To counter this possibility, elections serve to educate citizens. As noted in ⓛⓘⓝⓚ *Chapter 10, pages 376–377* Americans pay only a limited amount of attention to public affairs. Things would be much worse were it not for the frequency of elections. Many studies have shown that voters actually learn a good deal from campaigns.[7] One study found that the more campaign ads a citizen sees, the more informed that person is. "The brevity of the advertising message may actually strengthen its informative value," the researchers reported. "The typical person's attention span for political information is notoriously short-lived . . . [and] the great majority of voters bypass or ignore information that entails more than minimal costs . . . Campaign advertising meets the demand for both simplicity and access."[8] In other words, elections serve as a civics refresher course.

FULFILLING ONE'S CIVIC DUTY

Socialization is the means by which new members of society are introduced to the customs and beliefs of a political system. It is how a nation's values are spread from one generation to the next. A core element in our political culture is **civic participation.** It is expected that each citizen occasionally leaves his or her private world to become involved in the affairs of state. Elections serve to introduce many Americans to their role as citizens. *Civic duty*

means at the very least, helping choose who will run the government. It is hoped that by giving citizens this basic opportunity, additional acts of civic participation will follow.

A SAFETY VALVE

Finally, Americans take it for granted that changes in the control of government are always peaceful. We move from one administration to another and from control by one party to the other without violence, without sandbags being loaded into the White House windows or sentries being stationed at the entrance of the Capitol. Losing candidates and their supporters may not like the outcome, but they accept the "will of the voters" peacefully. For voters, elections become the safety valve for discontent; rather than picking up a gun or other weapon, Americans just vow to win the next election.

practicequiz

1. Elections are a process by which political leaders are chosen and
    a. public policies are in effect formulated.
    b. the public in effect indicates where its thoughts about public policy stand.
    c. the preoccupations of a new generation of citizens get clearly articulated.
    d. the principles of the Constitution in effect get reaffirmed.

2. In the 2000 election, George W. Bush won the Electoral College vote
    a. by 23 electoral votes.
    b. but only after a recount of electoral votes.
    c. but lost the popular vote by about 64,000 votes.
    d. but lost the popular vote by about 500,000 votes.

3. Studies indicate that voters learn a lot from campaigns.
    a. true   b. false

4. It's fair to say that elections act as a "safety valve" for public discontent because
    a. if the elected officials are incompetent, there's always another election in the near future to vote them out of office.
    b. people are under the illusion that the authority of elected officials is legitimized by a popular vote.
    c. voting is a safer way to express the desire for change than is armed rebellion.
    d. voting accounts for the policy opinions of nearly every adult in the country.

Answers: 1-b, 2-d, 3-a, 4-c.

discussionquestions

1. As you have read, elections serve many functions beyond selecting leaders. In your opinion, which are the most important functions that elections serve, and why?

2. Are any of the system-wide functions that you have read about not especially well served by elections? That is to say, might other ways of selecting leaders do a better job?

▶ **Is there any downside**
to using elections to
choose leaders?

The Limitations of Elections

▶ **Is there any downside to using elections to choose leaders?**
It is fair to say that some are a bit less optimistic about the role of elections in a democratic system. Perhaps elections have serious limitations, but our habit for them is so great that to suggest dropping them would be like trampling on the flag. Nevertheless, let's offer some criticisms.

ELECTIONS AS A PLACEBO

When we carefully explore the many avenues for changing the course of government—for modifying the outcome of the policy process—elections look like an imperfect choice. Elections do not guarantee that there will be any redirection in policy, only that the *people* running part of the government may change. Many aspects of government are beyond the immediate reach of elected officials, and even when they are not, dramatic change is rare. Some people have even begun to speculate that the distrust many Americans feel toward government is due to the frustration over this disconnect between elections and policy. "He told us that he would change things if he won the election," we might hear a citizen complain. "Well, he won, so why haven't things changed?"

An even bigger concern is that elections lead many citizens to believe that voting is their *only* chance to make a difference. They may be frustrated with the way things are going but feel as though their only course of action is to vote or to help a candidate. This is called **episodic participation.**

A POOR MEASURE OF PUBLIC SENTIMENT

It is often said that elections direct the successful candidates to carry out a particular set of policy alternatives—in other words, the voters send them into office with a clear mandate. But this is not exactly what occurs. Instead, voters select a given candidate for many different reasons, a particular policy choice being just one possibility. Each voter has a slightly different motivation or mix of motivations for favoring one candidate over another. Assuming that the results of an election mean a particular thing can be a mistake. A good example might be the election of 1980, which pitted the incumbent president, Jimmy Carter, against Ronald Reagan. Reagan prevailed over Carter by a large popular margin, suggesting that the electorate had become more conservative. The "Reagan Revolution," as it was called, became the justification for

Many commentators interpreted Ronald Reagan's victory over Jimmy Carter in 1980 as a sign that the pubic backed conservative policies. Yet, polling data suggested that it was more of a rejection of Carter than a shift in attitudes toward policies. Can we really say elections reflect policy preferences—or do they only show which candidates we prefer?

▶ Why do so many good people choose not to run for office?

electoral college
a device for selecting the president and vice president of the United States, defined in Article II of the Constitution, whereby the voters in each state choose electors to attend a gathering where the electors make the final decision.

aggressive policy changes. Many Democrats, too, believed that the election signified a "turn to the right." The only problem was that public opinion polls following the election suggested that much of Reagan's support came from voters displeased with Carter—and much less from those interested in a dramatic policy shift. If anything, they were voting against Carter's failed economic policies. As one presidential scholar noted:

> Studies show that there was not a clear turn to the right by voters in 1980. Reagan beat Carter by 10 percentage points; yet the election was no prospective issue vote or ideological mandate for Reagan. According to polls, the public was more liberal than Reagan on a number of issues. . . . There was no strong shift to the right.[9]

In fact, many potential Carter votes went to a liberal Republican protest candidate, Illinois Congressman John Anderson. The combined Carter and Anderson popular vote was very close to the popular vote for Reagan, making it hard to argue that the 1980 outcome was a sweeping victory for conservatism.

THE ATOMIZATION OF POLITICS

Democracy, in its purest form, is a process that brings citizens together to resolve issues and disputes. This implies face-to-face deliberation, airing one's views, and listening to the concerns of others in an interpersonal brainstorming process. Through discussion and extended deliberation, citizens become better informed not only about their own view on a particular matter but also more sensitive to the opinions of others in the community. Yet an election is in many ways an isolated, individualized act.[10] We *might* discuss candidates and party platform before the election with friends and family, but when it comes to actual voting behavior, that is done in the secrecy of the polling booth. So if an election is in fact an individual act, private interests are more likely to supplant public spirit. That is to say that very often the long-term stability of a system is based on citizens' looking beyond their own short-term interest to the general welfare—something that elections may actually prevent.

CONSTRICTING THE POOL OF PUBLIC OFFICIALS

▶ Why do so many good people choose not to run for office?
The tone and cost of contemporary elections in America limit the pool of candidates to individuals willing to undergo the rigors of

campaigning. These days, campaigning requires a great deal of money and a tremendous amount of time and stamina. Running for statewide positions, and to some extent for congressional seats, has become a full-time job for more than a year before the election. And a trend in the press coverage of candidates is to disclose ever-more intimate information. A mudslinging campaign can subject a candidate and his or her family to stress that might well become unbearable. Who would want to go through this? Many outstanding citizens, eager to serve their community, state, or nation, will never step forward because elections have become so grueling.

A BROKEN PROCESS?

Finally, perhaps the greatest limitation of the election process might be its vulnerability to malfunction. The heart of the election-democracy link is the idea that all citizens should have an equal opportunity to select leaders—that no candidate should have an unfair advantage. But what happens when some candidates have more campaign resources, perhaps on the scale of Jon Corzine's or Ross Perot's immense personal wealth? What if laws limit which adults can vote and which cannot? Does it matter if a shrinking number of voters seem willing to make election decisions? Does it matter that today most incumbent candidates in the House of Representatives—those who already occupy a seat—face no serious opposition? What if legal barriers aid certain political parties and limit the potency of others? Does poor, biased, or limited media coverage of the campaigns distort the process?

*practice*quiz

1. What did Ronald Reagan's large margin of victory over Jimmy Carter in the 1980 presidential election signify?
   a. that a candidate can win in a landslide without a clear ideological mandate
   b. that presidential elections usually follow a cycle of Democratic then Republican dominance
   c. that Carter ran a poor campaign
   d. that the U.S. electorate had become much more conservative in the late 1970s

2. The private, individual experience of voting raises one civic concern:
   a. that people will make irrational choices in the voting booth.
   b. that expensive campaign tactics will not matter when it comes time to vote.

▶ So do elections equal democracy?

discussionquestions

1. Which of the limits of elections seem to you the most significant?

2. Can you suggest some changes that might improve the election process?

   c. that people will vote their personal, short-term interests instead what's good, in the long run, for the community or country.

   d. that people will vote for what's best for the community and country, neglecting their personal, short-term interests.

3. The pool of potential political candidates is limited lately in part because
   a. being a government official is dull, unchallenging work.
   b. running for office is an anonymous process.
   c. fewer people want to serve their community, state, or nation these days.
   d. running for office now often brings unrelenting media attention.

4. What is one reason many people question the truly democratic nature of modern day elections in this country?
   a. it is more difficult than ever for certain people to get registered to vote
   b. some candidates have many more resources to use in an election than others
   c. being an incumbent has become a real disadvantage
   d. in their focus on creating clever "sound bites," candidates often ignore the opinions of the majority of voters

Answers: 1-a, 2-c, 3-d, 4-b.

Elections and the Law

▶ **So do elections equal democracy?** It is commonly said that the framers of the Constitution intended to create a "more democratic system" of government. They did not. Rather, they sought to create a system that would give the new republic long-term stability and safeguard the freedoms achieved through the Revolution. They wanted to preserve the democratic *ideals* launched by the Revolution, but it was *instability* that most worried these men. Under the Articles of Confederation, widespread state-level elections had given rise to political turbulence and bitter factionalism ((L)(I)(N)(K) *Chapter 2, pages 54–56*). One Constitutional Convention delegate forthrightly declared, "The evils we experience flow from the excesses of democracy."[11] A new scheme was needed whereby the democratic character of the new nation could be maintained but widespread, tumultuous participatory politics could be managed.

A number of mechanisms were used to accomplish this goal, including a limited electoral system. Elections would be heavily used at the state level, but for the national government, direct elections would fill only one component—the House of Representatives. The other chamber in Congress, the Senate, would be selected by the state legislatures. And the electoral college, not the voters at large, would select the president. As for the federal judiciary, citizens would have no direct role in filling these posts; judges were to be appointed by the president and confirmed by the Senate.

THE ELECTORAL COLLEGE

One of the most innovative and controversial aspects of American elections is outlined in the Constitution: the use of an **electoral college** to select the president and vice president. The framers of our systems believed that only men of the highest caliber and intellect should become president. Instead of depending on average citizens to make this choice, they decided that a group of elites should have that responsibility. But who should this group be? One proposal, which had significant support at the Constitutional Convention, was to let Congress elect the president. Others suggested that this would blur the important separation between the branches. The compromise, an electoral college, stipulates that each state be allotted the same number of electors as its combined total of House members and senators.

Originally, each elector was assumed to have full independence to name any person he saw fit and would cast two votes; the candidate who got the most votes would become president, and the runner-up would become vice president. During the first decades, only a handful of states allowed voters to pick electors; most were chosen by state legislatures. The electoral college, which this group of electors is called, was supposed to decide, calmly and rationally, who would be the best choice to lead the nation.

This method worked smoothly during the first two elections, when Washington was unanimously selected as president, but it began to unravel as soon as Washington announced that he would not accept a third term. For one, political parties—which the framers had neither foreseen nor wanted—burst onto the scene in the 1790s, leading to partisan electors rather than enlightened statesmen doing the choosing. Second, the original design was to have the top vote getter become president and the second-place finisher become vice president, but this proved completely

Twelfth Amendment (1804)
a change to the Constitution that required a separate vote tally in the electoral college for president and vice president.

unit rule
the practice, employed by forty-eight states, of awarding all of a state's electoral college votes to the candidate for the presidency who receives the greatest number of popular votes in that state.

what YOU can do!

One of the most controversial Supreme Court cases in recent years was *Bush* v. *Gore* (2000), in which it was decided that Florida could not conduct a manual recount, thus giving George W. Bush a narrow victory in the state and enough electoral college votes to win the White House. To learn more about this case—and to actually hear recordings of arguments in the case—visit the Oyez Web site at **http://www.oyez.org/oyez/resource/case/766/audioresources**

unworkable as soon as competing political parties arose. In the 1796 election, this arrangement meant that John Adams got the presidency and his archrival, the leader of the opposing party, Thomas Jefferson, became vice president. For the next four years, each tried to outmaneuver the other.

Finally, in 1800 came an electoral rematch between Adams and Jefferson. This time it seemed that Jefferson had come in first (**LINK** *Chapter 2, pages 69–71*). But in fact Jefferson and his running mate, Aaron Burr, were tied: *All* of Jefferson's supporters in the electoral college had cast their second vote for Burr! The election had to be settled by the House of Representatives. Even though everyone knew that Jefferson was the "top of the ticket," Burr refused to back down, and it took dozens of votes in the House and much wrangling before Jefferson was finally named president and Burr had to settle for the vice presidency. (This account, by the way, greatly simplifies what was an even more complex mess.) As a result, the **Twelfth Amendment** was adopted, which says that in the electoral college, the electors must indicate who they are voting for as president and who for vice president.

There is yet another controversial part of the electoral college: It is quite possible that the candidate who receives the most popular votes will not receive the most electoral votes. This is possible because forty-eight of the fifty states use a winner-take-all model, also called the **unit rule,** under which the candidate who receives the most popular votes in that state gets all of that state's electoral votes. This model makes it *likely* that the most popular candidate (the highest vote getter) will become the president, but it does not *guarantee* it. In fact, the most popular candidate has been denied the presidency four times in American history.

pathways past and present
FOUR WINNERS WHO LOST

In four presidential elections, the candidate who led the popular vote did not win the office.

- In 1824, four candidates were in the running, although one was felled by a stroke just before the election. (Despite being incapacitated, he finished in third place.) The second-place finisher was John Quincy Adams, who got 38,000 fewer pop-

ular votes than the top vote getter, Andrew Jackson. But no candidate won a majority of the electoral college. Adams was awarded the presidency when the election was thrown to the House of Representatives, which under the Constitution had to choose between the *three* top electoral college finishers. The fourth-place finisher, Speaker of the House Henry Clay, threw his support to Adams, who later named Clay secretary of state. Jackson and his supporters howled that a "corrupt bargain" had deprived him of the White House, and he ran again—this time successfully—in 1828.

- In 1876, nearly unanimous support from small states gave Republican Rutherford B. Hayes a one-vote margin in the electoral college, despite the fact that he lost the popular vote to Democrat Samuel J. Tilden by 264,000 votes. There were also credible complaints of crooked vote counting in certain disputed states. The election was decided only when a commission of senators, representatives, and a Supreme Court justice declared Hayes the winner.

- In 1888, Republican candidate Benjamin Harrison lost the popular vote by 95,713 votes to the incumbent Democratic president, Grover Cleveland, but Harrison won by an electoral college margin of 65. In this instance, some say the electoral college worked the way it is designed to work by preventing a candidate from winning an election based on support from one region of the country. The South overwhelmingly supported Cleveland, and he won by more than 425,000 votes in six southern states. However, in the rest of the country, he lost by more than 300,000 votes. (Cleveland won a second term in a rematch election in 1892.)

- In 2000, Vice President Al Gore had over half a million votes more than George W. Bush, 50,992,335 votes to Bush's 50,455,156. But after a recount controversy in Florida and a U.S. Supreme Court ruling in the case of *Bush* v. *Gore*, Bush was awarded the state by 537 popular votes (see Figure 14.2). Like most states, Florida has a winner-takes-all rule, so the candidate who wins the state by popular vote, no matter how thin the margin, gets all of the state's electoral votes. Thus Bush became president with 271 electoral votes—the barest possible majority. ■

Step. 1: The Electoral Formula

The number of electors for each state is determined by the following formula.

(Number of U.S. Senators from the state [always 2])
+
(Number of U.S. Representatives from the state) = Number of electors

Step 2: Parties nominate electors

The political parties (or independent candidates) in each state submit to the state's chief election official a list of individuals pleged to their presidential candidate and equal in number to the state's electoral vote.

• Who can be an elector?
Anyone who is not a member of Congress or an employee of the federal government that is dedicated to the cause of a certain person becoming president.
• Who are electors?
Usually electors are obscure local politicians.

Step 3: Parties nominate candidates

Parties hold national conventions to determine their party's nominations for President and Vice President of the United States.

• When are conventions held?
Usually during the summer preceding the election.
• How do these names get on the ballot?
After the convention, the parties submit the name to the state's chief election official. The chief election official places the name on the ballot.

Step 4: Election Day

On the Tuesday following the first Monday of November in years divisible by four, all those registered to vote are elegible to cast a ballot for their party slate of electors representing their choice for president and vice president.

• Wait, I thought the ballots had the names of the candidates, not the electors?
General election ballots normally say "electors for" each set of candidates rather than list the individual electors.
• If the people vote on electors then how is a president decided?
Whichever party slate wins the most popular votes in the state become that state's electors. In effect, whichever presidential ticket gets the most popular votes in a state wins all the electoral votes of that state.
• Are there any exceptions?
Yes, in Maine and Nebraska two electors are chosen by statewide popular vote and the remainder by the popular vote within each congressional district.

Step 5: Casting Electoral Votes

On the Monday following the second Wednesday of December, each state's electors meet in their respective state capitals and cast their electoral votes. One vote is cast for President and one for Vice-President. The electoral votes are then sealed and transmitted from each state to the President of the Senate. On the following January 6, the President of the Senate opens and reads them before a joint session of Congress.

Step 6: Confirmation

The candidate for president receiving the majority of electoral votes is declared President of the United States. The vice presidential candidate with the absolute majority of electoral votes is declared vice president.

• What if a candidate does not receive an absolute majority of electoral votes?
The House of Representatives shall select the President from among the top three contenders, with each state casting only one vote. An absolute majority of the states is required to elect a President.
• What if there is still no absolute majority?
The U.S. Senate shall elect a Vice-President from among the top two contenders for that office. Presumably, the Vice-President would then exercise the powers of the presidency, though this situation has never arisen.

Step 7: Oath of Office

On January 20, the duly elected President and Vice-President are sworn into office and the President takes up residency at the White House.

FIGURE 14.2
How the Electoral College Works

There are certainly drawbacks to the electoral college—namely that candidates that win more popular votes can be denied the presidency. For some, this alone is enough to jettison the scheme. Yet, are there problems with a direct election process? What is your view on this important part of our political process?

▶ **Don't voters get really**
mad if the person they voted
for won the popular vote but
lost the electoral college vote?

Thirteenth Amendment (1865)
a change to the Constitution that abolished slavery.

Fourteenth Amendment (1868)
a change to the Constitution that defines the meaning of U.S. citizenship and establishes that each state must guarantee equal protection of the laws to its citizens.

Fifteenth Amendment (1870)
a change to the Constitution that guarantees that the right to vote shall not be denied to anyone on the basis of race.

Nineteenth Amendment (1920)
a change to the Constitution that granted the right to vote to women.

Finally, there is the issue of the "faithless elector." The Constitution does not say that electors must vote any particular way once they gather in their respective state capitals (except that the president and vice president cannot come from the same state). Today the political parties of each state name their slate of electors, and if their candidate wins, they will cast that state's electoral votes (see Figure 14.3). On Monday following the second Wednesday of December these groups of electors convene at the fifty different state capitals, and each elector casts one vote for president and another for vice president. But just because the elector was part of a slate put together by party leaders does not legally *guarantee* that he or she has to vote for that party's candidate. True to the intent of the framers, this person can vote for whomever he or she sees fit—including someone who never campaigned for the office. This rarely occurs, but it can happen. In 1988, for example, an elector from West Virginia cast a vote for Senator Bob Dole instead of incumbent President George H. W. Bush, the nominated GOP candidate.

▶ **Don't voters get really mad if the person they voted for won the popular vote but lost the electoral college vote?** Defenders of the electoral college suggest that it adds to the popular support of winners. In other words, somehow we feel that the victor has more legitimacy if the electoral college vote is won by a landslide, even if that candidate has won the popular vote by only a few percentage points. The current system helps promote the legitimacy of the winners, an important part of elections, as discussed earlier. The electoral college also forces candidates to strive for wide geographical appeal, rather than concentrating all their efforts in a few large states. What is more, if small states have a vested interest in keeping the current system, which many would suggest they do, it seems doubtful that a constitutional amendment, where three-fourths of the states are needed for ratification, would pass.

AMENDMENTS TO THE CONSTITUTION AND THE ELECTORAL PROCESS

The first federal constitutional changes that broadened the scope of the electorate were the Fourteenth and Fifteenth Amendments. These changes, plus the **Thirteenth Amendment** abolishing slavery (ratified in 1865), are commonly referred to as the Civil War Amendments because they were enacted in the aftermath of the Civil War. They represented the desire of victorious northerners, who controlled both houses of Congress, both to punish the South

for having caused the Civil War and to confirm the rights of citizenship for black Americans. Although discriminatory state laws blocked the rights these amendments promised from being fully realized for a century, the amendments represented the first attempt to write a broader suffrage (right to vote) into the U.S. Constitution.

The **Fourteenth Amendment,** ratified in 1868, deals with voting rights indirectly. Its first clause guarantees citizenship and the rights of citizenship to all persons born or naturalized in the United States (Ⓛ Ⓘ Ⓝ Ⓚ *Chapter 6, pages 215–219*). While in modern times it might be assumed that this includes voting rights, it should be remembered that at the time, female citizens were denied the right to vote. If gender could be made a condition of suffrage despite citizenship, so could race. In its second clause, the Fourteenth Amendment gave the states an incentive to grant minority citizens the right to vote, essentially basing representation in both Congress and the electoral college not just on population but also on the percentage of its male citizens over age 21 who could vote. If states refused to give African Americans the vote, they would receive fewer seats in Congress and fewer electoral college votes, thus politically marginalizing these states at the national level.[12]

The Fourteenth Amendment did not work as well as its drafters had hoped in giving the vote to former slaves. Therefore, in 1870, the **Fifteenth Amendment** was adopted, stating (in its entirety) that "the right of citizens of the United States to vote shall not be denied or abridged by the United States or by any State on account of race, color, or previous condition of servitude."

The **Nineteenth Amendment,** which gave the vote to women, was the product of a long grassroots movement that began in 1848 but was not enacted until 1920. The feminist movement gained steam throughout the second half of the nineteenth century. (Advocates of woman suffrage had tried but failed to get Congress to add the word *sex* to the Fifteenth Amendment as grounds on which states could not deny the right to vote, but woman suffrage was still considered too radical an idea.) Frontier life, too, helped fuel the movement for women's voting rights; on the frontier, women were considered equal partners in the family's fight for survival. It is not surprising that the first state to grant women the right to vote was Wyoming in 1890, followed by Utah and Idaho in 1896.

Enactment of the Nineteenth Amendment was one of the greatest accomplishments of the Progressive movement at the turn of the twentieth century. Pressure for amending the U.S. Constitution to grant women the vote came mainly from the western states, and opposition was mainly from the South and from

Twenty-Fourth Amendment (1964)
a change to the Constitution that eliminated the poll tax.

poll tax
money that must be paid in order to vote, outlawed by the Twenty-Fourth Amendment to the Constitution (ratified in 1964).

what **YOU** can do!

Go to one of the many online electoral college calculators such as **http://www.grayraven.com/ec**, and explore how this system of choosing our president shapes election strategy.

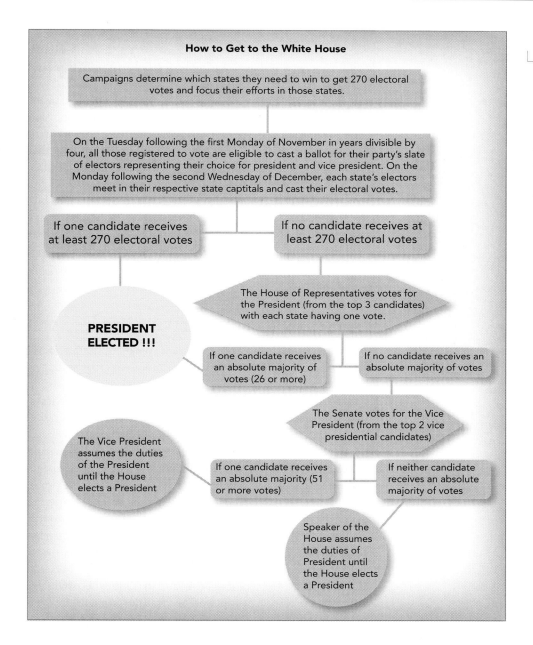

How to Get to the White House

FIGURE 14.3

The Complexities of the Electoral College

The candidate who gets the most votes wins, right? Well if not the most popular votes, than the most Electoral College votes, right? As this figure illustrates, the path to the White House can become complex. Are there any advantages to the process outlined in the figure? Do you think the complexities of the Electoral college plays a role in turning people away from the election process?

eastern conservatives, who feared that women would support further Progressive changes, such as child labor restrictions.[13] Adopted in 1920, more than seventy years after the push for woman suffrage began, the Nineteenth Amendment initiated the largest enlargement of the American electorate in a single act.

The **Twenty-Fourth Amendment** to the Constitution outlawed the **poll tax** in 1964. The poll tax—a fee imposed on voters—had been one of the barriers to African American voting in the South. By 1962, however, when the amendment was proposed, it was used in only five states and generally only amounted to a

▶ **Why didn't the Civil War Amendments make it possible for all African Americans to vote?**

Twenty-Sixth Amendment (1971)
a change to the Constitution that granted 18-year-old citizens the right to vote.

white primary
the system once used primarily in the South that allowed only white citizens to vote in primary elections.

Long lines of African Americans wait to register to vote in a makeshift office in Alabama after the passage of the Voting Rights Act of 1965. Do you believe that all racial barriers to voting in America have been removed?

dollar or two. Nevertheless, enactment of the Twenty-Fourth Amendment struck down one more symbol of the elitism and racism that had disfigured American democracy.

The **Twenty-Sixth Amendment,** giving 18-year-old citizens the right to vote, was the most recent change to the Constitution to extend the franchise. By the late 1960s, a growing proportion of Americans were in their late teens and had proved not only that they could be active in politics, but also that they could be effective in promoting change. Images of young men going off to die in the Vietnam War but not being able to vote gave the movement its biting edge. Initially, Congress attempted to lower the voting age through the Voting Rights Act of 1970. On July 1, 1971, Congress passed the Twenty-Sixth Amendment, giving citizens 18 and older the right to vote in all elections. It passed with little objection, and the state legislatures ratified it in three and a half months.[14]

VOTING AND LEGISLATIVE ACTS

▶ **Why didn't the Civil War Amendments make it possible for all African Americans to vote?** The Constitution says that as long as Congress remains silent, voting regulations and requirements are left to the states. There were many state-level restrictions on voting in the early days of the Republic. For roughly a decade after ratification of the Constitution, some states imposed religious qualifications, and most states had property ownership and taxpaying requirements. By the 1820s, the property owning requirements were generally abolished, and none of the states entering the Union after this time had property requirements for voting. Taxpaying requirements were not fully phased out until the Twenty-Fourth Amendment outlawed the poll tax. However, state laws were generally written so broadly that any citizen who paid a tax of any kind could vote—with the notable exception of the South's poll taxes.[15]

In the late nineteenth century and well into the twentieth, southern states used their power to regulate elections to keep African Americans from the polls. Imposing a variety of restrictions—literacy tests, poll taxes, complicated registration and residency requirements, and the infamous "grandfather clause," which exempted a voter from all these requirements if his (free white) grandfather had voted before 1860—white-ruled southern states managed to disfranchise most blacks. In this they had the tacit approval of Congress and the federal courts, which refused to stop these blatant violations of the Fourteenth and Fifteenth

▶ **Do all states follow**
the same voter registration
and election laws?

residency and registration laws
state laws that stipulate how long a person must reside in a community before being allowed to vote in that community.

motor-voter law
a law passed by Congress in 1993 designed to make it easier for Americans to register to vote.

Help America Vote Act
a measure passed in 2002, in the wake of the controversy surrounding the 2000 election, designed to create a more uniform voting system throughout the fifty states.

Amendments. A favorite exclusionary tool was the **white primary.** Because the Democratic Party dominated the South after the 1870s, the winner of the Democratic nomination was de facto the winner of the election. Southern election laws defined political parties as private organizations with the right to decide their own membership. Thus while blacks might enjoy the right to vote in the general election, as stipulated in the Fifteenth Amendment, they could not vote in the only election that really counted, the Democratic primary.[16] This practice remained in effect until the Supreme Court's decision in *Smith* v. *Allwright* (1944). The Court ruled that primaries were part of the electoral system and therefore the exclusion of blacks from this process violated the Fifteenth Amendment.

The Civil Rights Act of 1957 created the U.S. Civil Rights Commission, an agency empowered to investigate voting rights violations and suggest remedies. In 1964, a second and much more sweeping civil rights act was adopted. The most significant change that directly affected elections came with the Voting Rights Act of 1965. Forcefully challenging the South's discriminatory practices, this law provided that in any congressional district in which fewer then 50 percent of adults went to the polls, a five-year "emergency state" would be triggered. Affected districts could change their election regulations only with the approval of the civil rights division of the Justice Department, and the emergency could be ended only by appeal to a federal court with evidence that no discriminatory devices had been used in the past five years. In addition, the Justice Department could now send election examiners into the states to register voters and observe elections. Although the 1965 Voting Rights Act did not end discrimination, it became the most important tool in protecting the right to vote.[17] Election data reflect the act's importance: Overall, in eleven southern states in 1960, a meager 29.7 percent—and in some states in the region only a negligible number—of adult African Americans were registered to vote. By the end of the decade, this figure had more than doubled, to 63.4 percent.[18]

▶ **Do all states follow the same voter registration and election laws?** Another important area of election regulation deals with signing up to vote. Reforms during the Progressive era (roughly 1900–1917, a period that we'll discuss in greater detail in Chapter 15) were designed to clean up the all-too-common practice of fraudulent voting in general elections. Party bosses, for example, might pay people to travel around the city voting in numerous polling places. To this day, only half jokingly, party

operatives can be heard reminding supporters on election day to "vote early and vote often." Frequently, dead or nonexistent voters were discovered to have cast ballots. **Residency and registration laws** were the solution. Residency laws stipulate that a person can vote in a community only if the person has been a resident for a prescribed period. (The length of time varies from state to state, but the 1970 Voting Rights Act established a maximum of thirty days.) Registration is the process of signing up to vote in advance of an upcoming election. In some states—Maine, Minnesota, New Hampshire, Oregon, Wisconsin, and Washington—a resident can register up to and including election day. But in most other states, there is a stipulated pre–election day cutoff.

The idea behind requiring residency and registration was to reduce corruption. In recent years, however, these laws have become controversial, and some people have even suggested that they are the main reason why many Americans do not vote. In their provocatively titled book *Why Americans Still Don't Vote: And Why Politicians Want It That Way,* Frances Fox Piven and Richard Cloward argue these laws have always been about keeping certain types of voters out of the process.[19] That is, these measures were not about corruption but about control. (And indeed, middle-class Progressive reformers often wanted to keep "ignorant" immigrants away from the polls.) Perhaps trying to find a middle ground, Congress in 1993 required states to allow citizens to register to vote at numerous public facilities used by low-income people, such as state motor vehicle, welfare, and employment offices. This so-called **motor-voter law** also stipulated that states must permit mail-in registration. Interestingly, data suggest that the motor-voter law has increased the number of registered voters but has had a negligible impact on the number of Americans who actually show up at the polls.

In the wake of the confusion surrounding the 2000 presidential election, discussed earlier, in 2002 Congress passed the **Help America Vote Act.** This measure was designed to create a more uniform voting system, replacing with more regularity and consistency the haphazard, state-by-state process that had existed for two centuries. For example, some states were using punch cards and others old-fashioned voting machines, while still others were experimenting with touch-screen machines. Some states kept up-to-date voter lists; others updated them only sporadically. The act set federal standards for all voting systems throughout the United States, provided $325 million to update voting systems, required states to create registered

▶ **Do voters get to vote**
for specific issues rather
than for candidates?

ballot initiative
a system whereby citizens decide policy matters through voting on election day. About one-half of the states allow this process.

referendum
also called a ballot measure, initiative, or proposition; when voters are called upon to accept or reject a proposed piece of legislation (a law).

recall
process whereby voters can remove from office an elected official before the next regularly scheduled election.

voter databases, and called for voter education and poll worker training. The bill inserted the federal government into the mechanics of conducting elections in order to create some consistency and enhance the legitimacy of the electoral process (Figure 14.2, page 538).

practicequiz

1. Which constitutional amendment regulates the behavior of Electoral College electors?
   a. the Eleventh Amendment
   b. the Twelfth Amendment
   c. the Thirteenth Amendment
   d. the Eighteenth Amendment

2. How many electors does each state send to the Electoral College?
   a. the number of U.S. Representatives from that state times 2
   b. the number of U.S. Representatives from that state plus 50
   c. the number of U.S. Representatives from that state plus 2
   d. the population of that state divided by 70,000

3. At the Electoral College electors must vote for the presidential and vice-presidential candidates who won a plurality of votes in their state.
   a. true   **b.** false

4. One advantage of the Electoral College system is that
   a. it mandates that the presidential candidate who wins the popular vote wins the presidency.
   b. the American public has great faith in it.
   c. it finalizes the presidential election within a week of the general election.
   d. it requires candidates to appeal to a broad geographic spectrum of communities and states.

Answers: 1-b, 2-c, 3-b, 4-d.

Referendums, Initiatives, and Recalls

▶ **Do voters get to vote for specific issues rather than for candidates?** Many Americans believe that elections are only used to select public officials. This is not the case, for about half the states

also allow voters to use elections to have a direct say in making policy. (Such a process is not allowed at the federal level.) This is left over from the Progressive era, when reformers were frustrated with the lack of change coming out of state legislatures. Progressive reformers thought up many ways to give voters a direct voice in writing new laws and regulations. These changes stuck, and in states where they are used today, they remain a key mechanism for allowing citizens to make change.

Ballot initiatives allow voters the option of deciding policy matters. To have a question or proposed law listed on the ballot, its advocates must gather a required number of valid voter signatures. Then on election day, all citizens can vote either for or against the measure, and if a majority agrees, it becomes law. A **referendum** is a similar process that asks citizens on election day to reaffirm or reject an existing law. In actual practice, the terms *initiative* and *referendum* tend to be used interchangeably.

Twenty-three states currently allow for referendums or initiatives. The first state to adopt an initiative process was South Dakota, in 1898, and Oregon was the first to use the referendum, in 1902. The movement quickly spread, particularly in the western states, where party machines were less entrenched. California and Oregon have been the biggest users of initiative and referendum, averaging roughly three per year since the turn of the twentieth century. The latest state to adopt such a process was Mississippi, in 1992.

The questions that voters are asked to decide in initiative and referendum elections vary widely. A sampling from recent elections includes many "hot" issues, most of which elected politicians would prefer to ignore out of fear of offending some people: allowing the medical use of marijuana, permitting doctor-assisted suicide, requiring English-only teaching in public schools, giving public school teachers pay raises, protecting wetlands and forests, outlawing the hunting of mountain lions, imposing legislative term limits, prohibiting the trapping of bobcats and bears, legalizing gambling, providing vouchers for students to attend private or parochial schools, and so on. In 2002, Oklahoma voters outlawed cockfighting, and Nevada voters refused to legalize the recreational use of marijuana.

Yet another Progressive era measure designed to give the policy process back to the will of the people is the **recall**. In a recall, citizens can vote an officeholder out of office before the next

discussionquestions

1. What are some of the strengths and limitations of the electoral college? Give reasons for and against abolishing the electoral college and electing presidents by direct popular vote. After considering both sides, what's your opinion?

2. As you now know, many of the changes in state and federal law have opened up the electoral process. But this is not universally true. Which changes, perhaps called "reforms," may have actually constricted the number of election participants?

regularly scheduled election. Petitions are circulated, and if enough signatures are collected, a special election date is set. The politician in office is ordinarily automatically listed on the ballot but goes back to private life if he or she gets fewer votes than another candidate.

Recall elections are rare. Most of the time, even if people become dissatisfied with elected officials, they simply bear with the situation until the next election. After all, it is the voters themselves who elected the person to office, and it has become part of our political culture to accept election outcomes and "wait till next time." Very few recall efforts have been successful in the states that allow them. However, the voters in California shocked the nation in the fall of 2003 when they recalled Democrat Gray Davis, only the second governor ever to be recalled. In his place, they selected Austrian-born Republican film actor and former bodybuilder Arnold Schwarzenegger. The man who once ruled the movie box office stepped to the helm of the largest and in many ways most complex state in the Union.

THE FUTURE OF THE BALLOT INITIATIVE AS A PATHWAY OF CHANGE

To many people, initiatives, referendums, and recall elections represent democracy at its best: average citizens proposing changes in government, working to build support, and allowing the majority of the community to decide its fate. As the *Christian Science Monitor* editorialized, "Such grass-roots efforts can help re-energize voters and preserve an outlet for direct democracy if entrenched interests control the legislature. Research shows that when there's an initiative on the ballot, voter turnout increases 3 to 7 percent."[20] Polls also suggest that roughly two-thirds of Americans believe that they should have some say in policy matters.[21] But direct democracy can be problematic, and the framers of our political system were rather fearful of such a process. (That is why ballot initiatives are permitted only at the state and local levels and not at the federal level.) Even more significant, many critics suggest that the initiative process has changed and no longer represents "democracy in action." For example, wealthy individuals and interest groups can pay workers to collect signatures and can flood the airways with misleading commercials. Poorly

Kevin Cannon's poster, "On the California Recall," shows Arnold Schwarzenegger's triumph in 2003. In that year Gray Davis, shown sitting at a desk, was recalled as governor of California, and Schwarzenegger was selected by voters to replace him. The voters reelected Schwarzenegger in 2006. Does your state allow for recall elections?

funded groups face a tougher struggle both in building support for their measures and in defeating opponents. For example, public interest groups in Oregon sponsored a measure in 2002 to provide comprehensive health care for residents of the state. It was defeated, due in no small measure to the multimillion-dollar campaign waged against it by the medical and pharmaceutical industry lobbies (see Table 14.1 on page 552).

TABLE 14.1

Ballot Initiatives by State: Votes Required, Portion of Population Required, and Total Amount Spent on Initiatives in 2004

State	Votes for Statute	Percent of Population for Statute	Votes for Constitutional Amendment	Percent of Population for Constitutional Amendment	Total Amount Spent on Ballot Initiatives
Alaska	31,451	4.74%	—	—	$950,000
Arizona	122,612	2.06	183,917	3.10%	3,350,000
Arkansas	64,456	2.32	80,570	2.90	340,000
California	373,816	1.03	598,105	1.66	201,720,000
Colorado	67,829	1.45	67,829	1.45	12,920,000
Florida	—	—	611,226	3.44	77,320,000
Idaho	46,000	3.22	—	—	—
Illinois	292,245	2.29	749,949	5.88	—
Maine	50,519	3.82	—	—	3,160,000
Massachusetts	65,653	1.03	65,653	1.03	—
Michigan	251,192	2.48	313,990	3.10	29,010,000
Mississippi	—	—	107,339	3.67	—
Missouri	136,568	2.35	218,509	2.77	1,850,000
Montana	22,308	2.38	44,615	4.77	5,270,000
Nebraska	81,214	4.62	116,020	6.60	3,210,000
Nevada	83,184	3.44	100,840	4.18	13,280,000
North Dakota	12,884	2.02	25,688	4.03	10,000
Ohio	—	—	322,899	2.82	2,140,000
Oklahoma	82,850	2.34	155,343	4.38	—
Oregon	75,630	2.08	100,840	2.77	30,740,000
South Dakota	16,728	2.16	33,456	4.32	120,000
Utah	83,235	3.37	—	—	1,100,000
Washington	224,880	3.58	—	—	11,960,000
Wyoming	38,204	7.50	—	—	—

practicequiz

1. Elections throughout the country can include ballot initiatives, referendums, and recall votes.
   a. true
   b. false

2. Only _____ in our nation's history has a governor been recalled.
   a. twice
   b. five times
   c. seven times
   d. eleven times

3. Ballot initiatives were first conceived
   a. by the framers of the Constitution.
   b. after the Civil War.
   c. in the Progressive Era.
   d. in the aftermath of the Watergate scandal.

4. We know from their writings that the framers of the Constitution
   a. approved of ballot initiatives.
   b. would be leery of ballot initiatives, were they proposed at the time.
   c. prohibited ballot initiatives.
   d. would have little to say on the subject, since examples of direct democracy did not occur to them.

Answers: 1-b, 2-a, 3-c, 4-b.

The Role of Money in Elections

Many people would be surprised to hear that money has not always been central in the election process. In colonial times and during the early days of the Republic, there was simply less to spend money on. Candidates would "treat" voters, meaning that they would sponsor lavish picnics and barbeques. In Virginia, this was called "swilling the planters with bumbo." George Washington, for example, was said to have purchased a quart of rum, wine, beer, and hard cider for every voter in the district when he ran for the Virginia House of Burgesses in 1751 (there were only 391 voters).[22] In 1795, one

discussion**questions**

1. Many people regard ballot initiatives as a good thing, but others suggest that there are significant downsides. Briefly discuss the pluses and minuses of these opportunities.

2. In the years ahead, do you think that more states will create ballot initiative opportunities, or do you think there might be a pulling back on such measures? Explain.

▶ Why is money so important in elections?

FIGURE 14.4
Campaign Expenditures

This figure suggests that the cost of elections has grown dramatically, even when inflation is factored in. What do you think is at the heart of rising elections costs? Does this suggest a serious flaw in the process or a sign of a robust exchange of ideas?

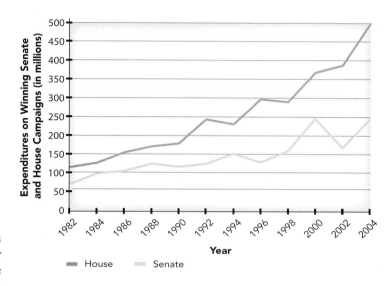

House   Senate

would-be Delaware officeholder roasted a steer and half a dozen sheep for his friends, and another candidate gave a "fish feast." Four decades later, Ferdinand Bayard, a Frenchman traveling in the United States, noticed that "candidates offer drunkenness openly to anyone who is willing to give them his vote."[23] In brief, money was secondary, given that the principal means of connecting with voters was word of mouth, spread by local party activists.

Another common means of spending campaign money during the nineteenth century was to purchase advertisements in newspapers and, more often, to actually purchase a newspaper completely. Some of the most heated campaigns of the century were conducted through "battling newspapers." Often, when a wealthy individual was anxious to aid a particular candidate, he would simply start a newspaper. It has been noted that "even Abraham Lincoln secretly purchased a small newspaper in Illinois in 1860."[24]

▶ **Why is money so important in elections?** As technology changed throughout the twentieth century, so did the cost of elections. Money became critical by the late 1960s, for four main reasons:

1. **Decline of Party Organizations.** Political parties went into decline. **LINK** *Chapter 15, pages 597–599.* Given that party organizations were primarily responsible for connecting with voters, candidates needed new ways of reaching out. Many of these new means were extremely costly.

2. **More Voters Up for Grabs.** In 1790, there were fewer than 4 million Americans, almost a quarter of them slaves. In 1900, there were 75 million Americans, and in 1960, some 180 million. Today the U.S. population is over 300 million. Reaching such a huge number of voters requires enormous amounts of money. As party organizations declined in the late twentieth century, fewer voters maintained steadfast party loyalty. The

number of "independents" grew at a staggering pace in the 1970s and 1980s, causing greater uncertainty at election time. Nervous candidates are willing to spend as much money as necessary to minimize this uncertainty.

3. **Television.** In the early 1950s, only a small percentage of homes boasted a television set; by the 1960s, TV was nearly universal. Television transformed much of American life and certainly changed the way political campaigns were run. And of course buying advertising time requires huge sums of money.

4. **Campaign Consultants.** Coupled with the growing importance of political advertising on television were the professionals hired to create these commercials. Professional campaign consulting burst onto the scene in the 1960s, bringing such sophisticated techniques as direct mail and survey research. These methods proved effective, of course, but they came with a hefty price tag.

One estimate is that in 1952, a presidential election year, *all* campaigns for political office, from president to dogcatcher, added up to $140 million.[25] By 2004, the equivalent figure had swelled to an estimated $4 *billion*, and in 2006, a midterm election year, most estimates were that a similar amount would be spent. In the 1960s, it was common for a successful House candidate to spend less than $100,000, but by 2004, the average cost of winning a seat in the House of Representatives topped $1 million. An "expensive" U.S. Senate race in the 1960s was still under a half-million dollars; in 2004, the *average* Senate race cost nearly $7 million (see Figure 14.4). And as Jon Corzine

▶ **So eventually the system** was reformed?

Federal Election Campaign Act (FECA) law designed to limit the amount of money contributed to campaigns for Congress and the presidency and to broaden donation reporting requirements.

Watergate the "shorthand" name of a scandal that led to the resignation of President Richard M. Nixon in 1974.

showed in New Jersey, some races could be far more expensive than that. In 2006, several Senate races topped the $20 million mark. Elections at all levels have simply gotten very costly.

pathways profile

TWO INNOVATIVE CAMPAIGN OPERATIVES

It's debatable, but many experts agree that the first modern campaign consultant was Mark Hanna.[26] At the end of the nineteenth century, the battle between Democrats and Republicans had grown fierce, and fundamental issues were at stake: Basically, should national economic policy favor agricultural or industrial interests? Looking for any advantage, leaders in the pro-industrial GOP turned to a successful business entrepreneur, Mark Hanna of Cleveland. Hanna took electoral politics in a new direction by showing that money—lots of it—could be decisive in forging a victory. "There are two things that are important in politics—the first is money, and I can't remember what the second one is," he was quoted as saying in 1895.[27] As Republican nominee William McKinley's campaign manager in 1896, Hanna pushed corporate leaders to "pony up," and he soon amassed what for the time was a huge war chest—$7 million. This money was used to sponsor hundreds of speakers, to print and distribute more than 200 million pamphlets, to crank out and paste up hundreds of thousands of posters, to hire hundreds of headquarters employees, and to make heavy investments in newspaper advertising. All this hoopla helped Hanna and the Republicans neutralize the eloquent, rural-oriented oratory of Democratic candidate William Jennings Bryan—for example, by sending out pro-McKinley speakers on trains that preceded and followed Bryan's own whistle-stop barnstorming tours of the country.[28]

A century later, another campaign consultant was pushing the envelope again. Joe Trippi had made his first stab at presidential consulting in 1980. His boss, Senator Edward Kennedy of Massachusetts, was trying to take the Democratic nomination from the sitting president, Jimmy Carter. Kennedy failed, but Trippi caught the consulting bug. After several other races, though, by the early 1990s he had became disgruntled and a bit sour on politics. He turned his attention to high technology start-up companies. But eventually his passion for politics and liberal causes pulled him back into the election world, this time as campaign manager of former Vermont Governor Howard Dean's Democratic nomination bid in 2004. In returning to politics,

Trippi brought a much deeper understanding of the potential of technology and the Web. He pushed Dean to join forces with Meetup.org, an online service that helps people with common interests find one another and plan local gatherings. Dean lost his bid for the Democratic nomination, but he revolutionized campaigning. More than 250,000 people gave Dean money through the Internet (producing an unprecedented $40 million primary campaign treasury), massive e-mail letter-writing campaigns were undertaken, blogs were set up, campaign events were packed by advance word conveyed through e-mail networks, and the candidate himself got instant feedback from rank-and-file supporters. As noted by one observer, "Until Howard Dean and Joe Trippi came along, the only thing I.T. had done was marginally lower the costs of doing the same thing they'd always done. And it wasn't even clear that it did that. But Trippi is doing something radically different. . . . Dean supporters are doing the hard work of organizing *for him*."[29]

It had always been assumed that campaign consultants simply react to their political environment and struggle to develop tactics that get their clients into office. The stories of Mark Hanna and Joe Trippi suggest that campaign consultants can have a hand in shaping the environment of elections. ▪

THE RAGE FOR REFORM

▶ **So eventually the system was reformed?** Efforts to control the flow of money in elections date from the Progressive era, but these measures were largely symbolic. Real reform came in the early 1970s, when members of Congress began to worry about being thrown out of office by a wealthy candidate—perhaps a political novice—who could simply outspend them. The **Federal Election Campaign Act (FECA)** was signed into law by President Richard Nixon in 1971. Three years later, after the **Watergate** scandal revealed a staggering level of corruption in presidential campaigns, a series of amendments made the law even more restrictive. In brief, the legislation limited how much money candidates could spend, how much an individual or group could give, and how much political parties might contribute. It also established voluntary public financing of presidential elections. Presidential candidates who choose to use the system are limited in the amount they can raise and spend.

Few politicians doubted that the provisions were real or that they would have a significant effect on the way elections were conducted. Yet shortly after the amendments took effect, James

Buckley v. Valeo (1976)
perhaps the most significant campaign finance Supreme Court case in American history. The Court ruled that campaign expenditures are akin to free speech and are therefore protected by the First Amendment.

soft money
funds contributed through a loophole in federal campaign finance regulations that allowed individuals and groups to give unlimited sums of money to political parties.

▶ **So the reform efforts**
made things *worse*?

Buckley, a Conservative Party senator from New York, along with a group of politicians from both ends of the political spectrum, challenged the constitutionality of the law. Buckley argued that spending money was akin to free speech and that limiting it would abridge First Amendment protections. The case of **Buckley** v. **Valeo** (1976) was perhaps the most significant election-centered court decision in American history. For the most part, the Supreme Court sided with Buckley. It struck down provisions of the law that put limits on overall spending, on spending by the candidates, and on spending by independent groups. The justices also upheld the public funding of presidential elections so long as it is voluntary. Surprisingly, however, the Court also allowed limits on how much an individual or a group might *give* to a candidate. "The quantity of communication by the contributor," said the Court majority, "does not increase perceptibly with the size of this contribution, since the expression rests solely on the undifferentiated, symbolic act of contributing." In other words, when people give money to a candidate, they are expressing their support regardless of the size of the donation. Some restrictions, designed to level the playing field a bit, are reasonable, the Court concluded. Finally, the decision suggested that political parties are "special," given their role in the democratic process and First Amendment guarantees (freedom of association). Few restrictions should be placed on their activities.

It is hard to overstate the effects of this decision. More than anything else, *Buckley* has shaped the nature of the election process during the last three decades. The decision pushed candidates to raise money from many small sources, rather than rely on a small group of large donors. Although this was the design of the law, and most Americans applauded the change, candidates (including incumbents) soon found themselves spending most of their time chasing donors. An entire industry was born overnight: fundraising consultants.

▶ **So the reform efforts made things *worse*?** Trying to outdo the opposition, candidates thought up new methods of stretching the legal system in each election. The most significant of the loopholes they found is what's called **soft money**. Although individuals and interest groups were limited in the amount they could contribute to a candidate, the law put no restrictions on giving money to a political party. "Fat cats" made immense contributions—often over $1 million—which filtered down to particular candidates. To many Americans, the soft-money loophole had become little more than a scam. "An illness that has plagued previous elections," wrote one observer, "has developed into an epidemic."[30]

ABOVE: **Many would agree that Mark Hanna** (top, right), aide to presidential candidate William McKinley, was one of the first campaign consultants.

BELOW: Consultant Joe Trippi (left) is shown helping Democratic candidate Howard Dean (center) in 2004. Consultants have become an important feature in modern electioneering. One question you might consider is whether they help candidates put their best foot forward, or do they strive to manipulate voters to win the election at all costs? What do you think?

▶ **Can PACs "buy" politicians**
with their contributions?

incumbent advantage
the various factors that favor office holders running for reelection over their challengers.

FIGURE 14.5

Number of Registered Political Action Committees, 1974–2004

This figure shows a dramatic increase in the number of political action committees. What explains this increase, and what effect do you think this change will have on our electoral system?

SOURCE: "PAC Count, 1974 to Present," Federal Election Commission Online, http://www.fec.gov/press/press2006/20060223paccount.html, 2006.

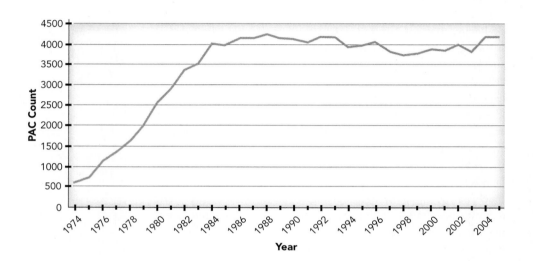

POLITICAL ACTION COMMITTEES

Another spinoff of FECA and *Buckley* has been the proliferation of political action committees (PACs). Earlier acts of Congress had barred labor unions and corporations from giving money to federal candidates. PACs were thought up in the 1940s to get around these restrictions. In PACs, none of the monies used to support a candidate came directly from the union or corporation but instead from these groups' independent political units. Because FECA stipulates limits on how much candidates might raise from an individual, politicians were forced to solicit help from a broad range of sources. The contribution limit for PACs was originally five times higher than for individuals, so the number of groups exploded: In 1974, there were roughly 600 PACs, but by 2004, more than 4,000 were giving out contributions (see Figure 14.5).[31]

▶ **Can PACs "buy" politicians with their contributions?** Political action committees give money to candidates because the interest group that backs them wants a say in public policy. Businesses, for example, want policies that help them make a profit; environmentalist PACs want policies that help protect the natural world; and labor PACs seek policies that help working men and women. But do these groups "buy" policies with their contributions? This is a hotly debated issue. Some analysts suggest that the connection between contributions and policy is direct—that contributors are rational and not inclined to spend their money without a direct payback. The Center for Responsive Politics is a

nonpartisan organization that tracks the flow of money in elections and the development of public policy. Its Web site gives detailed information on who gives and who receives campaign money. On one of its pages, "Tracking the Payback," you can explore possible links between how a member of Congress votes on given policy issues and the source of his or her contributions in previous elections.[32] Their goal is to demonstrate that money may very well "buy" policies.

Precisely what PACs buy with their contribution is unclear, however, and political scientists have been unable to settle the matter. What is clear is that the public perceives a problem. An oft-heard remark is that we have "the best Congress money can buy!" Numerous public opinion polls confirm that regardless of what actually happens between contributors and public officials, average Americans regard the money flowing from PACs to candidates as a threat to the democratic process.

THE INCUMBENT FUNDRAISING ADVANTAGE

Candidates vying for office solicit funds (see Table 14.2) from many sources: individuals (friends, spouses, associates, activists), political parties, PACs, and—believe it or not—other candidates. Figure 14.6, on p. 558, underscores important differences between the three types of candidates. *Incumbents* are candidates already holding the office and up for reelection, *challengers* are those opposing the incumbents, and *open-seat candidates* are

▶ **Why do voters continue** to reelect incumbents, while complaining about "Washington Politics"?

what YOU can do!

The Center for Responsive Politics is a nonpartisan, nonprofit research group based in Washington, D.C. It conducts research on campaign finance issues with the goal of creating a more educated and involved citizenry. Check out its Web site at **http://www.opensecrets.org** and investigate how much money your members of Congress received last election and from what groups.

TABLE 14.2

Top 25 Money Donors to House and Senate Candidates in 2004

RANK	INDUSTRY	TOTAL	DEM PERCENT	GOP PERCENT	TOP RECIPIENT
1	Lawyers/Law Firms	$36,556,078	65%	35%	Hillary Rodham Clinton (D-NY)
2	Retired	22,510,659	44	54	Hillary Rodham Clinton (D-NY)
3	Real Estate	19,873,062	45	55	Hillary Rodham Clinton (D-NY)
4	Health Professionals	17,418,523	35	64	Hillary Rodham Clinton (D-NY)
5	Securities/Invest	15,248,306	50	50	Hillary Rodham Clinton (D-NY)
6	Leadership PACs	13,608,383	19	80	Rick Santorum (R-Pa)
7	Insurance	11,839,421	36	64	Rick Santorum (R-Pa)
8	Lobbyists	10,470,752	42	58	Rick Santorum (R-Pa)
9	Commercial Banks	9,594,990	36	64	Rick Santorum (R-Pa)
10	Misc Finance	8,191,320	43	57	Hillary Rodham Clinton (D-NY)
11	Electric Utilities	7,680,920	34	66	Joe Barton (R-Texas)
12	Pharm/Health Prod	7,434,870	33	67	Rick Santorum (R-Pa)
13	Business Services	7,027,102	51	48	Hillary Rodham Clinton (D-NY)
14	TV/Movies/Music	7,025,824	52	47	Hillary Rodham Clinton (D-NY)
15	Transport Unions	6,894,052	76	24	Bob Filner (D-Calif)
16	Public Sector Unions	6,432,747	82	17	Daniel K. Akaka (D-Hawaii)
17	Bldg Trade Unions	6,369,560	77	22	Robert Menendez (D-NJ)
18	Computers/Internet	5,964,370	43	57	Maria Cantwell (D-Wash)
19	Oil & Gas	5,660,123	17	83	Kay Bailey Hutchison (R-Texas)
20	General Contractors	5,551,203	30	70	Robert Menendez (D-NJ)
21	Air Transport	5,409,050	34	66	Conrad Burns (R-Mont)
22	Hospitals/Nursing Homes	5,237,236	41	59	Rick Santorum (R-Pa)
23	Crop Production	5,217,270	44	56	Saxby Chambliss (R-Ga)
24	Automotive	4,841,773	27	73	James M. Talent (R-Mo)
25	Misc Mfg/Distribution	4,804,302	34	66	James M. Talent (R-Mo)

SOURCE: Based on data released by the FEC on Monday, May 29, 2006. http://www.crp.org/industries/mems.asp?party=A&cycle=2006

running for seats for which no incumbent is seeking reelection. Political action committees hope that their money will somehow produce support for their policies, which means they hope their money will go to the eventual winner. (What can a losing candidate do to shape public policy?) Accordingly, they prefer to send their funds to incumbents, because those already in office have a head start—the so-called **incumbent advantage**—when it comes to reelection. And by sending their money to incumbents, PACs

provide an even greater boost to incumbents' chances of reelection.

▶ **Why do voters continue to reelect incumbents, while complaining about "Washington Politics"?** In some recent elections (see Figure 14.7 on page 558), more than 95 percent of incumbent House candidates won, even though many Americans are frustrated with "business-as-usual politics" and seem anxious to "throw the bums out." Incumbents have always had an advantage, but critics

▶ **Are recent limits on campaign funding more effective than earlier ones?**

term limits laws stipulating the maximum number of terms that an elected official may serve in a particular office.	**Bipartisan Campaign Reform Act (BCRA)** federal law passed in 2002 that outlawed soft money contributions to party organizations.

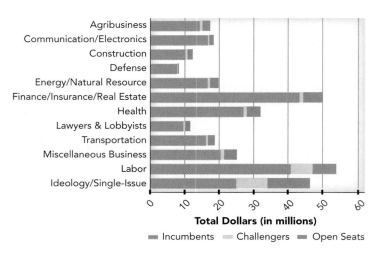

FIGURE 14.6

Contributions to Candidates

There are several factors behind the incumbent advantage, and the ability to raise a great deal of money than their challengers—depicted in the figure—is at the center. But if this is true, what can be done about it? Why would ideological groups be a bit of an exception?

SOURCE: Center for Responsive Politics

point to recent changes that have made matters worse. Yale University scholar David Mayhew was one of the first to draw attention to the problem.[33] In his seminal book *Congress: The Electoral Connection*, Mayhew argues that nearly all legislative activity is now geared toward securing reelection. These efforts fall within three categories: *credit claiming*, which is receiving praise for bringing money and federal projects back to the district; *position taking*, that is, making sure to be on the popular side of issues; and *advertising*, which implies reaching out to constituents in many ways, especially through mailings (when paid for by the government, this is called "franking"). Others have pointed to additional sources of incumbent support, such as ongoing media attention, which challengers rarely get. The growing sophistication of drawing safe district lines for members of Congress following every census (see Ⓛ Ⓘ Ⓝ Ⓚ *Chapter 7, pages 259–263*) has contributed to the problem. Many observers agree that things have gotten out of hand and that the democratic electoral process is threatened.

Many reforms have been suggested to reduce the incumbent advantage. One proposal is **term limits.** If we are worried about an unfair advantage given to politicians already in office, why not create more open-seat contests? Limiting legislative terms, as we do by allowing presidents just two terms, would guarantee turnover—a stream of new faces, energy, and ideas in the legislature. Repre-

sentatives should know the concerns of average citizens; what better way of ensuring that than by forcing entrenched legislators to step aside after a fixed period and make way for fresh blood? Opponents of term limits argue that the legislative process is complex, especially these days, and that it takes time to become familiar with the process. Term limits remove experienced legislators and replace them with green ones. Moreover, term limits deny voters a choice, the chance to reelect a legislator who may actually be doing a good job.

By the early 1990s, roughly half the states had adopted term limits for state legislators and for candidates for federal office. Public opinion polls suggested that a majority of Americans favored these new restrictions. But many legal scholars wondered whether the states had the constitutional power to limit the terms of U.S. House and Senate members. The issue came to a head in the Supreme Court case of *U.S. Term Limits, Inc.* v. *Thornton* (1995). In a 5–4 decision, the Court majority stated that "allowing individual States to craft their own qualifications for Congress would . . . erode the structure envisioned by the Framers, a structure that was designed, in the words of the Preamble to our Constitution, to form a 'more perfect Union.'" With that decision, attempts to limit the terms of members of Congress ended. Many

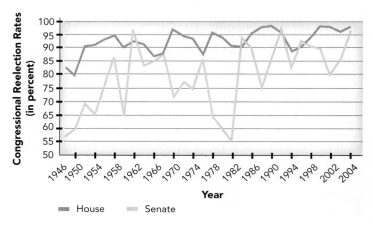

FIGURE 14.7

Congressional Reelection Rates, 1946–2004

Since 1950, reelection rates in the House have fallen below 90 percent only five times. Does this seem right, given the shrinking faith that many Americans have in elected officials? What do you think is driving this trend? In the Senate, reelection rates have risen above 90 percent only five times. Why do you suppose Senate races seem more competitive than House races?

SOURCES: *Vital Statistics on Congress, 1999–2000* (Washington, DC: AEI Press, 2000); *Vital Statistics on American Politics, 2003–2004* (Washington, DC: CQ Press, 2004); *CQ Weekly,* November 6, 2004.

Bipartisanship is rare these days. Senators John McCain (R-AZ) and Russ Feingold (D-WI) were able to work together to push the Bipartisan Campaign Reform Act through Congress in 2002. It remains to be seen, however, if the new law will help Americans feel better about the electoral system. Why might too much money in electoral politics be a big problem? Photo: Paul Hosefros/The New York Times

states do limit the terms of state legislators, but members of Congress are free to run for reelection year after year.

REFORMING THE REFORMS: BCRA

A recent survey found that 75 percent agreed (39 percent "strongly") that "our present system of government is democratic in name only. In fact, special interests run things."[34] Another poll, conducted in 2001, found that 80 percent of Americans felt that politicians often "did special favors for people or groups who gave them campaign contributions."[35] Clearly, the reforms of the early 1970s had done little to halt the flow of big money into elections and, if anything, had made matters worse by *seeming* to limit money. The loopholes were numerous and huge, and the public was ripe for change.

The benefits of new reforms would have to be weighed against other issues related to party advantages. Which party gains an advantage with a more restrictive campaign finance system? Given that the Republicans had finally achieved a majority in Congress by 2000 and their fundraising greatly outpaced the Democrats', it should come as no surprise that many Republicans balked at significant change. Also, many (mostly Republican) legislators once again argued that contributing money is akin to political speech, meaning that further limits would be unconstitutional. While calls for reform echoed across America, reform measures stalled in the legislature.

Two forces emerged to overcome the stalemate. First, leading a bipartisan call for reform were Senators John McCain, a Republican from Arizona, and Russ Feingold, a Democrat from Wisconsin. Both are significant players in national politics, but McCain drew the most attention. He had run for the presidency in 2000, and although he was defeated in the nomination battle by George W. Bush, he had become the darling of the media and of a growing number of reformers across the nation. With McCain speaking out frequently and passionately about a growing corruption in the election process, more and more Americans were drawn into the controversy. And of course, they pushed their legislators to do something. Second, closely related to the attention that McCain focused on it, the campaign finance issue became central in many of the congressional elections in 2000, and most successful candidates pledged to do something about it. After much debate and maneuvering by both parties, the **Bipartisan Campaign Reform Act (BCRA)** was passed and signed into law by President George W. Bush in February 2002.

▶ **Are recent limits on campaign funding more effective than earlier ones?** The new law is sweeping: It outlaws soft money contributions to the national political organizations and bans group-sponsored advertisements thirty days before primary elections and sixty days before general elections. Yet the law also raises the contribution limits to $2,000 for individuals, and it leaves open the ability for wealthy individuals to donate soft money to state and local party organizations (see Table 14.3 on page 560). The ban on soft money does not apply to political action committees, which are still free to raise unlimited cash.

The law took effect the day after the 2002 midterm election and had a controversial beginning. The very same day that the BCRA was signed into law, Republican Senator Mitch McConnell of Kentucky, a strong opponent of campaign finance restrictions, and a host of other legislators, interest groups, and minor parties sought to nullify the measure. They chose the court pathway by filing a federal lawsuit. The core of their argument was that the BCRA represents an assault on free speech. Defenders of the law responded with constitutional arguments that contributions may be regulated without violating the First Amendment because contributions are "indirect" speech. By the end of 2002, all these complaints had been merged into one case, *McConnell v. Federal Election Commission*, argued in the Supreme Court in the fall of 2003. In a 5–4 decision, the Court upheld the law's most important elements. It was, according to a *New York Times* account, a "stunning victory for political reform."[36] The Court reasoned that Congress has a "fully legitimate interest in . . . preventing corruption of the federal electoral process through the means it has chosen." Moreover, the Court majority suggested that the problem with big, unregulated contributions was preferential access and the influence that comes with it. It was, the justices noted, not simply an issue of the "appearance of corruption"; volumes of data strongly suggested real problems.

Another controversial aspect of BCRA has been the growing number of groups not aligned with a political party but quite

527 Organizations
groups organized under Section 527 of the Internal Revenue Code, which allows for the unlimited expenditure of campaign money. These organizations became important after the Bipartisan Campaign Reform Act outlawed soft money in 2002.

TABLE 14.3
Effects of the 2002 Campaign Finance Reforms

	BEFORE 2002 REFORM	AFTER 2002 REFORM
Party contributions to candidates	$5,000 per election or $10,000 per election cycle	National Party committees are limited to $5,000 per election, although there are special limits for Senate candidates. National committees and Senate campaign committees share a contribution limit of $35,000 per campaign.
Party-coordinated expenditures with candidates	*Senate:* State voting age population times 2 cents, multiplied by the cost-of-living adjustment (COLA), or $20,000 multiplied by the COLA, whichever is greater. *House:* $10,000 multiplied by the COLA; if only one representative in the state, same as the Senate limit.	*Senate:* State voting age population times 7,462 cents, multiplied by the COLA, or $74,620 multiplied by the COLA, whichever is greater. *House:* $37,310 multiplied by the COLA; if only one representative in the state, the spending limit for the House nominee is the same as the Senate limit.
Party soft money contributions to the national party committee	Unlimited	Banned
Soft money to national or state and local parties for voter registration and get-out-the-vote drives	Unlimited	Limit of $10,000 per group to each state or local party committee (Levin Amendment)
Contributions to parties for buildings	Unlimited	Banned
Party-independent expenditures	Unlimited	Unlimited, except if ad falls under "electioneering communications definition." Then source of funding is subject to FECA regulations and limits, and the ad may not be broadcast within 30 days of a primary or 60 days of a general election. Parties may choose either independent expenditures or coordinated, but not both.
Individual contributions to candidates per two-year election cycle	$2,000	$4,000
Aggregate individual contribution limit to candidate or parties per two-year election cycle	$50,000	$95,000

www.fed.gov/pages/bcra/bcra_update.htm

TABLE 14.4
Top Twenty-Five 527 Organizations of 2004

COMMITTEE	PARTY LEANINGS	TOTAL RECEIPTS-2004	EXPENDITURES-2004
America Coming Together	Democratic	$79,795,487	$78,040,480
Joint Victory Campaign 2004	Democratic	71,811,666	72,588,053
Media Fund	Democratic	59,414,183	57,694,580
Service Employees International Union	Democratic	48,426,867	47,730,761
Progress for America	Republican	44,929,178	35,631,378
American Fed. of St/Cnty/Municipal Employees	Democratic	25,537,010	26,170,411
Swift Vets & POWs for Truth	Republican	17,008,090	22,565,360
MoveOn.org	Democratic	12,956,215	21,565,803
College Republican National Comm.	Republican	12,780,126	17,260,655
New Democrat Network	Democratic	12,726,158	12,524,063
Citizens for a Strong Senate	Democratic	10,853,730	10,228,515
Club for Growth	Republican	10,645,976	13,074,256
Sierra Club	Democratic	8,727,127	6,261,811
EMILY's List	Democratic	7,739,946	8,100,752
Voices for Working Families	Democratic	7,466,056	7,202,695
AFL-CIO	Democratic	6,585,072	6,541,896
League of Conservation Voters	Democratic	6,049,500	5,078,116
Intl. Brotherhood of Electrical Workers	Democratic	5,457,928	8,182,245
Democratic Victory 2004	Democratic	3,696,869	2,346,179
Laborers Union	Democratic	3,455,921	3,294,785
America Votes	Democratic	3,174,936	2,769,752
November Fund	Republican	3,151,170	3,124,718
Partnership for America's Families	Democratic	3,071,211	2,936,666
National Assn. of Realtors	Democratic	2,979,522	3,002,977
Grassroots Democrats	Democratic	2,819,483	2,592,499

SOURCE: www.opensecrets.org/527s/ Center for Responsive Politics. A project supported by The Pew Charitable Trusts.

interested in certain policies. These groups have been named **527 Organizations** (after Section 527 of the Internal Revenue Code, which regulates their practices). They are allowed to raise unlimited sums of money. Most 527s are advocacy groups that try to influence the outcome of elections through voter mobilization efforts and television advertisements that praise or criticize a candidate's record. A great deal of the funds now flowing to 527s previously went to the parties in the form of soft money.

Two prominent examples of 527s in the 2004 election were the Swift Boat Veterans and POWs for Truth and MoveOn.org.

The Swift Boat Veterans were set up with the intention of portraying Democratic candidate John Kerry's past military service in a negative light. MoveOn.org, by contrast, was created by a group of Americans who were dissatisfied with George W. Bush. Table 14.4 lists the top twenty-five 527 Organizations in the 2004 election. What is most impressive about this list is the massive sums that these organizations were able to raise. As one observer noted, "Although BCRA cracked down on soft money spending by the political parties, it did nothing to constrain spending by outside groups."[37] Indeed, one estimate is that 527 groups spent some $527 million on television ads alone in 2004.[38]

▶ **How do you measure**
voting turnout?

discussionquestions

1. What forces have led to the mushrooming cost of elections in America?

2. As you know, some people suggest that money in elections is simply an expression of public support, while others argue that it's a source of corruption that needs change. Which perspective do you believe, and why?

Are 527s simply the latest loophole in campaign finance law, and do they corrupt the election process? Or are they simply a way for Americans to support candidates and to speak out during elections? If so, perhaps they are protected by the Constitution. The future of 527 Organizations remains unclear. The Federal Election Commission did move forward with rules regulating independent groups, but most observers agree that there remains enough leeway in the law for these units to be key players in the election process for years to come.[39]

THE IRONIES OF MONEY AND POLITICS

In every election, a few candidates run for office on a shoestring budget, overcome the odds, and are sent into public life. We relish such stories: David-like candidates with guts, determination, and grassroots support bringing down overconfident, wealthy Goliaths. Maybe it is not money that wins elections, we think, but ideas and character. Unfortunately, elections of this sort are few and far between. Money plays a powerful role in today's electoral system; as Jesse Unruh, a retired California politician, once accurately but cynically said, "Money is the mother's milk of politics."[40] If we put an optimistic spin on the situation, perhaps we might conclude that fundraising is simply a measure of public sentiment: Some candidates, we would conclude, raise more money than others because they are more popular and thus more likely to win on election day. We might applaud the flow of money into campaigns, seeing it as a form of free speech. In a democracy, we say, the more political speech, the better.

Most Americans are not so optimistic about money in politics and regard the importance of big money in elections as troubling. They believe that it gives some candidates an unfair advantage and spills past the election into the policymaking process. It is one of the many ironies of an open political process: Individuals and interest groups are encouraged to back political candidates vigorously, but in doing so, their efforts distort the playing field. The freedom to participate creates a system with limited participation.

practicequiz

1. One reason for the steep rise in campaign spending in this country is that
   a. campaigns are now federally subsidized, to "even the playing field" for all candidates.
   b. blogs and mass e-mails are enormously expensive.
   c. people are more inclined to vote for a candidate if they know he or she has spent a lot of money campaigning.
   d. there are more potential voters to reach each year, making expensive broadcast advertising a higher priority.

2. In 2004 the average Senate race cost nearly
   a. $1 million.   b. $4 million.
   c. $7 million.   d. $13 million.

3. James Buckley challenged the constitutionality of the Federal Election Campaign Act by arguing that
   a. limiting campaign contributions was a constraint of free speech.
   b. the ability to raise campaign funds was a fair measure of a candidate's popularity.
   c. limiting campaign contributions violated the principles of free market capitalism.
   d. the Twelfth Amendment guaranteed citizens the right to participatory campaigning, which implicitly included monetary contributions.

4. How many states now have term limits for their U.S. representatives and senators?
   a. 0   b. 5
   c. 10   d. 25

Answers: 1-d, 2-c, 3-a, 4-a.

Levels of Political Participation

There are many ways average citizens can shape the course of government. The same is true of participation in the electoral process—there are many ways for citizens to become involved in campaigns and elections. Some people believe that voting is the foundation of all electoral participation, because very few get involved in other political activities without first being a voter. This is incorrect, however. For one thing, it is probably the case that many citizens are politically active but do not vote. For some Americans, nonvoting is either a statement of contentment or a form of political protest. Second, even if there is some sort of ladder of electoral participation, voting is probably not the bottom rung. Simply talking about different candidates with friends and family, for example, or reading news stories or watching TV programs about election happenings are types of electoral participation. Any action that is broadly linked to the conduct or outcome of an election can be considered **electoral behavior.** We might add to the list helping with a campaign; donating money; joining an election-focused interest group; attending election-centered rallies, dinners, or meetings; placing a yard sign in front of your house or a bumper sticker on your car; or even wearing a button. The point is that citizens can become involved in the election process in many ways. Voting is just one of them.

electoral behavior
any activity broadly linked to the outcome of a political campaign.

turnout
the percentage of citizens legally eligible to vote in an election who actually voted in that election.

Another way to think about forms of political participation is to consider the difference between individualistic and collective participation. Individual participation occurs when a citizen engages in activity aimed at changing public policy without interacting with other citizens. Examples include voting, giving money to a candidate or party, watching political news on television, or writing a letter to a candidate or an officeholder. Collective participation occurs when a citizen takes action in collaboration with other like-minded citizens. Examples would be attending a rally, discussing politics with friends and family, working at a party or candidate headquarters, or attending the local meeting of a political party (see Figure 14.8). Although both types of participation can be seen in the American setting, individualistic participation clearly occurs more often. Yet many see our individualistic tendencies as unfortunate and contrary to the ideals of democracy. Many of the most significant changes in public policy, such as worker rights, civil rights, and environmental legislation, stemmed from collective action—but for most Americans, politics is a private matter.

THE SHRINKING ELECTORATE

▶ **How do you measure voting turnout?** In thinking about levels of political participation in any democratic system, we often look at **turnout**. This is the number of citizens who actually vote on election day divided by the total number of citizens legally qualified to vote in that election—an easily quantifiable number. If 1 million residents are allowed to vote but only 600,000 do so, turnout is 0.6, or 60 percent. The number of citizens or residents of a nation does not factor into the turnout ratio; rather, it is the number of those who are legally eligible to vote.

As we have already noted, there was not much interest in federal elections in the early days of our republic. Election turnout for presidential elections, measured by the percentage of eligible (male) voters, reached only into the teens until 1800, when it jumped to 31 percent. It slipped again during the so-called Era of Good Feelings (1816–1824, when there was relatively little partisan strife), falling to roughly 25 percent. After what Andrew Jackson called the "corrupt bargain" in the election of 1824, political participation shot up dramatically: In 1828, some 57 percent of eligible voters went to the polls, and by the 1860s, the voting rate had leveled off very high, hovering around 80 percent for the rest of the nineteenth century. But in the early twentieth century, election day turnouts began to slip. There were a number of likely causes. For one, during this period there was a flood of immigra-

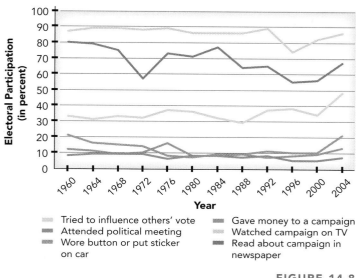

FIGURE 14.8
Forms of Electoral Participation

As this figure suggests, there are many ways individuals can be active in electoral politics. Since the 1960s the trend has been less engagement with the exception being 2004. What do you think has caused this downward trend? What was it about the 2004 election that seemed to bring more Americans into the process?

tion, causing a population boom in urban areas. Although these new citizens would soon be assimilated into the political process, many of them did not immediately vote. Second, registration laws, residency requirements, and other restrictions during the Progressive era made it harder for people in the lower socioeconomic class to participate in elections. Finally, the Nineteenth Amendment to the Constitution in 1920 granted women the right to vote, but at first they were slow to exercise that right. The percentage of women voting improved, pushing the overall turnout up by the middle of the twentieth century.

When Vice President Richard Nixon and an upstart senator from Massachusetts by the name of John F. Kennedy squared off in the presidential election in 1960, some 63 percent of the electorate turned out to vote (see Figure 14.9 on page 564). In the decades since, that figure has dropped more or less steadily. From 1980 until 2000, only about half of eligible voters turned out for presidential elections. Even worse is the participation in midterm congressional elections—the elections between presidential contest years: 1998, 2002, 2006, and so forth. In the 1960s, about 50

▶ Isn't that a contradiction:
Americans complain about
their government, but don't
bother to vote?

FIGURE 14.9
Participation in Presidential Elections

Most Americans believe we are one of the most democratic nations on earth. While that may be true in some respects, our participation in electoral politics is less than stellar. What might explain the various fluctuations in turnout? Do you think 2004 marked a long-term reversal of the downward trend, or was it simply an exception?

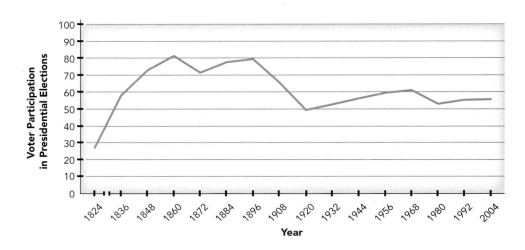

percent of Americans made it to the polls for these elections, but by the 1970s, the proportion had dropped to just over 40 percent—and it has shrunk to just over one-third in recent elections. And the decline in many state and local elections has been even worse. Many cities have seen turnouts for elections to municipal posts, such as mayor and city council, drop into the teens.

One of the most surprising and encouraging bits of elections pathway news in recent years was the upsurge in turnout in the 2004 election. Just over 55 percent of Americans came out to vote for either John Kerry, the Democrat, or George W. Bush, the incumbent Republican. Some observers speculate that the increased turnout was a reaction to the disputed outcome of the 2000 election, in which Al Gore got more popular votes than George W. Bush but fewer electoral college votes. Many Americans were motivated either to defeat the president or to keep him in the Oval Office. Other analysts point to the highly competitive nature of the 2004 election (the race was always close) and to the important issues of the day, not the least of which was terrorism in the wake of 9/11 and wars in Iraq and Afghanistan. Still others think that both campaign teams concentrated on get-out-the-vote efforts as never before. There is also the significant role that young voters played in the 2004 election, which we will discuss in greater detail shortly. But whatever the reason, the 2004 election suggested that Americans might once again be paying greater attention to elections.

WHY HAS TURNOUT DECLINED?

▶ **Isn't that a contradiction: Americans complain about their government, but don't bother to vote?** Most political observers agree that although turnout in 2004 proved encouraging, we are not out of

the woods. One of the great questions of our day is the cause—or causes—of the post-1960 decline in electoral participation. The decline has occurred during a period when we might expect *higher* levels of voting. More Americans than ever attend college, and higher education seems correlated with higher levels of voter turnout, as we will soon discuss. Registration barriers have been all but eliminated, and the civil rights movement has opened the door to far greater involvement by African Americans and other previously oppressed groups of citizens. With so many positive changes, why would levels of electoral participation be sliding? There is no clear answer, but theories abound. One possibility is attitudinal change. Increased cynicism, distrust, alienation, and the like are often identified as the root of the problem. Perhaps Americans are less sure about their own role in changing the course of government. Survey data seem to support the claim that negative attitudes about politics have been on the rise since the 1950s. For instance, in the mid-1950s, about 75 percent of Americans might be described as trusting their government to "do what is right all or at least most of the time." This number plummeted to just over 20 percent by the early 1990s and has since moved back up just a bit, to roughly the 40 percent range. About 22 percent of Americans in the 1950s thought "quite a few" politicians were crooked. That number jumped to 50 percent in the mid-1990s and today stands at about 35 percent. Many other indicators suggest that Americans are less confident about government and politics than in previous times.[41] But can we link these attitudes to lower levels of electoral participation? Most scholars agree that these changes have had an impact on levels of participation, although they debate the degree of its importance.

Closely related to this perspective is what we might call the lifestyle-change theory. According to this hypothesis, life today is

what YOU can do!

Conduct a quick, informal survey of your friends and classmates to find out how many voted in the last election—assuming, of course, that they were 18 years old at the time. What were some of their reasons for not voting?

simply busier than in the past and offers more distractions. According to the sociologist Robert Putnam, author of the widely discussed book *Bowling Alone: The Collapse and Revival of American Community,* "I don't have enough time" and "I'm too busy" are the most often heard excuses for social disengagement.[42] Today, the majority of families have two wage earners, a massive shift from the 1950s, when relatively few women worked outside the home. "And since there are only 24 hours in the day," Putnam concludes, "something had to give," and "it seems plausible that the cutbacks also affected community involvement."[43] The same sort of argument is often made with respect to the shrinking number of Americans' nonworking hours. This argument suggests that we are also more distracted by new technologies, especially television and the Internet, and have to spend too many hours commuting long distances or putting in extra hours at our jobs to be heavily involved in politics (see Table 14.5 on page 566). Above all, television competes for our scarce time: "TV watching comes at the expense of nearly every social activity outside the home," Putnam asserts.[44]

Putnam and others are quick to caution against overstating this argument, however. Although it may be true that more women are spending more time at a workplace and thus have less time to vote, these women also have more opportunity to vote because on election day they are *already* pulled out of the home by work, and we know that gainfully employed women are actually *more* involved in civic life than "stay-at-home" women.[45] As for television, Putnam's best guess is that no more than 15 percent of the decline in civic participation can be attributed to television.[46]

Although changes in attitudes and lifestyles may account for part of the decline, many analysts suggest that the deepest root lies elsewhere. A strong possibility would be changes in local party politics. As you will see in (L I N K) *Chapter 15, pages 591–593,* local-level party organizations—which historically pushed citizens to the polls on election day—seem to be withering. A generation ago, many party workers, nearly always volunteers, kept track of which known party members had voted and which had not yet showed up at the polling place. By dinner time on election day, those who had delayed voting would get a telephone call or even a visit from one of these workers and be "gently" reminded to vote. Political scientists have tested the relationship between local party vitality and levels of turnout, and the data are convincing: Turnout is much higher in communities that still have strong local parties.[47] But fewer and fewer communities have such organizations.

The nature of campaigns is also cited as a reason for voter alienation. Perhaps responding to declining partisanship—or per-haps causing that decline—most candidates in general elections seem eager to position themselves toward the center of the ideological spectrum. (It is often otherwise in the primaries, in which candidates vie for the votes of their party's "true believers.") Some analysts speculate that when voters find it harder to distinguish policy differences between candidates, they simply withdraw from the electoral process. And campaigns, especially for the presidency, have become much longer, conceivably leading to voter burnout. "The long campaign of today runs in spurts, taxes people's attention, and dulls their sensibilities," reports one expert.[48]

Negative campaigning adds to the burnout. There is little question that in recent decades, campaigns have become more negative, and perhaps attack ads simply turn off voters. The first scholarly take on the issue seemed to confirm this theory, but on closer inspection, things seem more complicated. Although some studies have found that negative ads do turn voters off, roughly an equal number of other studies have found that turnout actually increases in these negatively charged races.[49] One impressive study suggests that some voters—the less partisan ones—are turned off when the campaign gets nasty but that negative campaigning activates the most partisan voters.[50] Still another line of research suggests that the effects of negative ads depend on the voter's local political culture.[51] A citizen in Provo, Utah, might respond differently to attack ads than, say, a voter in Brooklyn, New York.

Finally, there is the role of the news media. Some social scientists have suggested that the recent turn toward what one scholar has called "attack journalism" or media "feeding frenzies" has repelled voters.[52] In the past, a politician's personal transgressions were kept out of the news. Journalists and average citizens alike drew a line between a politician's public and private lives. For example, President Franklin D. Roosevelt's long-term relationship with a woman who was not his wife never got into the news, and John F. Kennedy's multiple affairs remained mere rumors until long after his death. Today, presidential transgressions of this sort would not be ignored. Probably due to the highly competitive nature of the news business, anything that draws the public's attention seems fair game to the media nowadays. This often means extensive probing of matters once considered private. The result has been the negative portrayal of politicians—one scandal after the other. Bill Clinton was impeached because he lied to cover up a sexual dalliance about which earlier presidents would never even have been questioned. Scholars have had difficulty directly linking these feeding frenzies with declining turnout, but most would agree that a connection seems likely.

TABLE 14.5

Reasons for Not Voting by Selected Characteristics, 2004

PERCENT DISTRIBUTION OF REASONS FOR NOT VOTING

CHARACTERISTIC	TOO BUSY, CONFLICTING SCHEDULE	ILLNESS OR DISABILITY	OTHER REASON	NOT INTERESTED	DID NOT LIKE CANDIDATES OR ISSUES
SEX					
Male	23%	11%	11%	11%	11%
Female	17	20	11	11	10
RACE					
White alone	19	16	11	11	11
African American	21	17	10	10	6
Hispanic	24	11	12	11	7
Asian	32	6	14	8	4
AGE					
18 to 24	23	3	11	10	6
25 to 44	28	7	12	10	10
45 to 64	17	15	11	11	13
65 and over	3	46	9	12	8
EDUCATION					
Less than High School graduate	14	26	10	12	9
High School graduate or GED	20	15	11	13	11
Some college or associate's degree	23	10	11	9	10
Bachelor's degree or more	22	11	10	6	9

SOURCE: U.S. Census Bureau. http://www.census.gov/prod/2006pubs/p20-556.pdf

One way to read this table is to consider the reasons for not voting, and explore changes that might help. For instance, if "too busy" explains about 20 percent of why people do not vote, perhaps we should consider making elections a national holiday. Another way to explore the data is with a keen eye toward differences in demographic groups. Why would over twice as many respondents with less than a high school degree use "illness and disability" as an excuse for not voting, compared to those with some college? Are Asian Americans really healthier, but busier, than other demographic groups? Why are there so many registration problems for Hispanic Americans?

Percent Distribution of Reasons for Not Voting

Out of Town	Don't Know or Refused	Registration Problems	Forgot to Vote	Inconvenient Polling Place	Transportation Problems	Bad Weather Conditions
SEX						
11%	10%	7%	3%	3%	1%	< 1%
7	7	7	4	3	3	1
RACE						
9	8	6	3	3	2	< 1
6	13	7	4	3	4	< 1
6	10	11	6	2	2	< 1
12	9	6	1	6	1	2
AGE						
13	15	8	6	3	2	< 1
8	8	9	3	3	2	< 1
11	9	6	3	3	2	< 1
5	4	4	2	3	5	1
EDUCATION						
6	7	5	4	2	4	1
7	9	6	3	3	2	< 1
11	10	8	4	3	2	< 1
16	8	11	3	3	< 1	1

pathways profile
MARK SHIELDS—"THIS I BELIEVE"

Mark Shields has worked in politics for more than forty years. He started as an assistant to Wisconsin Senator William Proxmire and then worked on four presidential campaigns and numerous other races. Shields is currently a political analyst for *NewsHour* on PBS. In March 2006, Shields was asked by National Public Radio to comment on American politics and his career. Here is an excerpt from his remarks.

I believe in politics. In addition to being great fun, politics is basically the peaceable resolution of conflict among legiti-mate competing interests. In a continental nation as big and brawling and diverse as ours, I don't know how else—except through politics—we can resolve our differences and live together. Compromise is the best alternative to brute muscle or money or raw numbers. Compromises that are both wise and just [and] are crafted through the dedication, the skill and, yes, the intelligence of our elected politicians.

I like people who run for public office. For most of us, life is a series of quiet successes or setbacks. If you get the big promotion, the hometown paper announces your success. It doesn't add, "Shields was passed over because of unanswered questions about his expense account" or "his erratic behavior at the company picnic."

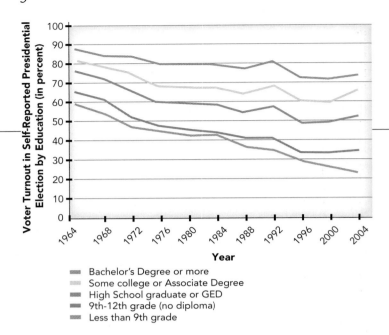

FIGURE 14.10
Presidential Election Voter Turnout by Education

Level of education affects voter turnout, according to the Census Bureau. In 2004, only 40 percent of those without a high school degree voted, compared to the 78 percent with a college degree who voted. Why has the rate of turnout for those with less education decreased faster than for those with higher levels of education? What might be the implications of this trend?

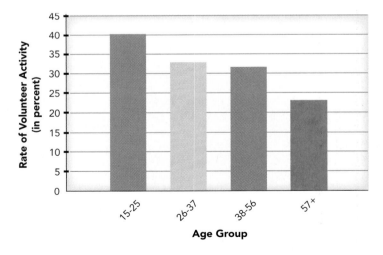

FIGURE 14.11
Volunteerism by Age Group

Many older Americans believe that youngsters are apathetic, indifferent, and lazy. Yet, this is not true. Are you surprised by these figures? Why do you suppose young citizens are so ready to become engaged in numerous community programs and organizations, but at the same time refrain from politics? What can be done to convince younger generations to join the political fray?

SOURCE: Mark Hugo Lopez, "Volunteering among Young People," Center for Information and Research on Civic Learning and Engagement, http://www.civicyouth.org/PopUps/FactSheets/FS_Volunteering2.pdf, 2004.

▶ Why do young people volunteer in their communities but don't vote?

But elections have been rightly described as a one-day sale. If you're a candidate, your fate is front-page news. By 8 o'clock on a Tuesday night, you will experience the ecstasy of victory or you will endure the agony of defeat. Everybody you ever sat next to in study hall, double-dated with or baby-sat for knows whether you won or, much more likely, lost. Politicians boldly risk public rejection of the kind that the rest of us will go to any lengths to avoid.

SOURCE: National Public Radio, March 13, 2006, http://www.npr.org/templates/story/story.php?storyId=5256345.

VOTING AND DEMOGRAPHIC CHARACTERISTICS

Another closely related question is why certain groups of Americans participate less than others. Here too, scholarly findings are inconclusive. One perspective centers on "community connectedness." This theory states that the more you are connected to your community, the more likely you are to vote. Demographic data suggest that poor people, for example, move more often than the affluent do, and they are certainly much less likely to own a home (which creates a strong connection to one's community). Every time you change your permanent address, of course, you also need to change your voter registration. Not surprisingly, the level of political participation for these highly mobile people is quite low. This perspective might explain why younger Americans seem less engaged; many young folks have little true connection to a particular community: Many are in college, and others are floating between jobs. On the other hand, election turnout among elderly voters is quite high. Another perspective centers on the cost-benefit trade-offs of participation. For one thing, there are costs associated with voting. You have to register, make time in your schedule to vote, learn where the polling place is, and know enough about the election to make voting seem worth your while.

Although these costs may seem minor, social scientists suggest that they are enough to keep many voters from participating. Here the deciding characteristic seems to be level of education: The costs of political participation seem to decline as people's level of formal education increases, as noted in Figure 14.10. The Census Bureau has reported that less than 40 percent of registered voters without a high school diploma voted in 2004, as opposed to 78 percent of those with a college degree and 84 percent of those with a graduate degree. Not only does awareness of the mechanics of

what YOU can do!

Some analysts have suggested that part of the voter turnout problem can be explained by felony disfranchisement laws. In about thirty states, felons and ex-felons are not allowed to vote. Is this fair? Does this really affect the turnout picture? To learn more about this issue, visit the Sentencing Project at **http://www.sentencingproject.org**

voting rise with formal education, but so too do the benefits of voting. People's sense of civic duty seems to build through education. As one pair of political behavior scholars have noted, "Length of education is one of the best predictors of an individual's likelihood of voting."[53]

ARE YOUNG VOTERS TUNING OUT?

▶ **Why do young people volunteer in their communities but don't vote?** Finally, there is the issue of age. Age has always been an excellent predictor of who participates in elections. Young Americans appear much less engaged. Beginning in 1972, when 18-year-olds were first granted the right to vote, just over 50 percent of young Americans (defined as those under 26 years old) went to the polls. This figure dropped to roughly 42 percent for almost three decades, some 20 percent less than the voting rate for older Americans. In nonpresidential election years in the past three decades, only one in four young Americans took the time to vote.

Why would younger citizens seem so tuned out? This group clearly has less *completed* education, less affluence, and much less likelihood of owning a home—all factors that seem related to participation, as you have seen. Younger citizens are also much more mobile. Yet this raises the question of why have things gotten *worse.* Perhaps changes in attitudes are the culprit. Have young people become more apathetic and more self-centered, as we often hear? Likely not. In fact, survey data suggest that young Americans are eager to contribute to the betterment of society; their rate of volunteering is higher than for any other age group, as can be seen in Figure 14.11. In many ways, young citizens are the "activist generation."

The irony, of course, is that this willingness to become involved has not spread to political involvement. Scholars have wrestled with this paradox for some time, but no clear answer has emerged as to why youth engagement does not seem to extend to politics. Many believe that younger citizens have become cynical about the political process and often feel that the best way they can make a real difference is to volunteer for a specific project rather than join the political fray. Cleaning up a stream or helping someone learn to read provides immediate, concrete payback for their involvement. The payoff from political involvement, by contrast, does not seem immediate or even certain. Young people increasingly lack a sense of political efficacy, meaning that they doubt that their involvement will make a difference.

ARE THEY GETTING THE MESSAGE? YOUNG VOTERS IN THE 2004 AND 2006 ELECTIONS

What many young citizens forget is that governmental decisions can produce the dirty streams that they clean up as volunteers every spring and the illiteracy that they volunteer to fight. Government and politics are central to our lives, as this book repeatedly argues. Apparently, the message that electoral politics is important *is* spreading among young Americans. Much to the surprise of scholars, pundits, and older Americans, the decline in youth voting made a turnaround in 2004. As you can see in Table 14.6, voter turnout increased among all Americans by about 4 percent, but the increase was greatest among the youngest voters. Whereas just 36 percent of 18- to 24-year-olds voted in 2000, some 47 percent did in 2004. This represented an 11 percent increase—double the rate of increase in any other age group. Young voters still vote less than older Americans, but the 2004 election suggested that the decline among this group may be over and that the difference among age groups may be narrowing.

As to why so many more young voters flocked to the polls in 2004, there are a number of possible explanations. For one thing, the earlier decline in youth participation was so startling that many organizations and programs were initiated to bring young people back to the polls. Such activist groups included MTV's Rock the Vote and Choose or Lose, Justvotenow.org, the New Voters Project,

---

TABLE 14.6
Turnout by Age Groups in 2000 and 2004 Elections

AGE	18-24	25-44	45-64	65 AND OVER	OVERALL TURNOUT
2000	32.3%	49.8%	64.1%	67.6%	51.3%
2004	41.9%	52.2%	66.6%	68.9%	55.3%

SOURCE: U.S. Census Bureau. Current Population Survey. November 2004 and earlier reports. Released 26 May 2005. Accessed: 18 May 2006.

The dramatic increase in young voter turnout in 2004 caught many by surprise. What do you think caused this change? Are young people now "connected" to the political process?

elite democratic model
the view that a democracy is healthy if people acquire positions of power through competitive elections. The level of involvement by citizens in this process is unimportant so long as elections are fair.

popular democratic model
a view of democracy that stresses the ongoing involvement of average citizens in the political process.

Rapper Sean "P. Diddy" Combs kicks off his "Vote or Die" program in 2004. How can popular culture stars help bring young Americans into the political process?

Possibly the intensity of the campaign and the weight of the issues pulled young Americans into the electoral process. Issues such as the war in Iraq, gay marriage, the future of Social Security and stem cell research caught young voters' attention. Whether or not they will remain engaged and perhaps increase their share in the electorate is an open question.

Unfortunately, turnout in the 2006 election among those under 30 did little to resolve the question. While it seems that a slightly larger percentage of this group came to the polls than in previous midterm elections (24 percent, compared to 22 percent in previous years), this amounted to only half the percentage of older voters. Why would more than three-quarters of young Americans choose to sit on the sidelines in such an important election? The young are ready to be involved, and politicians would be foolish to neglect them.

pathways profile

CITIZEN CHANGE: PUFFY GETS POLITICAL

After his efforts in 2004, Sean "P. Diddy" Combs, rap musician-turned-producer/clothing designer/entertainer, can add youth vote advocate to his résumé. Combs founded the national nonpartisan nonprofit organization Citizen Change to educate, motivate, and empower the more than 42 million Americans aged 18 to 30 who are eligible to vote. To sell its message, the group's strategy was to employ the same marketing tools used to promote a CD, clothing item, or other product in the entertainment industry. Ultimately, Citizen Change attempted to sell voting's urgency.

With their in-your-face slogan "Vote or Die!" Combs and his Citizen Change partners fought to convey the importance of voting. He pulled together many celebrities, such as Jay-Z, Ellen Degeneres, 50 Cent, and Leonardo DiCaprio, to ensure that the "Vote or Die!" message was contained in every facet of pop culture. Fashion designers, including Tommy Hilfiger and Phat Farm, were even commissioned to design limited-edition "Vote or Die!" T-shirts, the proceeds of which fueled Citizen Change's registration efforts.

Citizen Change did its best to capitalize on star power and the overriding influence of conformity to convince youth not only that voting is "in" but also that their futures were at stake in the 2004 election. Combs himself appeared at the Republican and Democratic national conventions to spread the message that the outcome

Smack Down Your Vote! and the Youth Vote Coalition. As it became apparent that the presidential election would be close, operatives on both sides sought out new groups of supporters, and young voters were a prime group targeted by both parties' campaigns. Several new elections pathway organizations tried bringing voters to the polls, including Americans Coming Together and MoveOn.org.

discussionquestions

1. What are some of the ways, other than voting, in which citizens can be involved in politics?

2. What demographic characteristics seem to explain which citizens will be more politically active and which will not? What might explain these differences?

of the 2004 race would have serious implications for young Americans. Summing up his goal as he launched the initiative, "For the first time in history, we're going to make voting fashionable."

SOURCE: Daniel M. Shea and John C. Green, *Fountain of Youth: Strategies and Tactics for Mobilizing America's Young Voters* (Lanham. MD: Rowman & Littlefield, 2006). ▪

practicequiz

1. What best describes voter turnout in the first decades of our nation?
   a. paltry
   b. in the 30%–40% range
   c. robust
   d. much higher than at any other time in our history

2. One well respected study indicates that partisan voters are turned off by negative campaigning, but that less partisan voters are activated by it.
   a. true   b. false

3. One reason young people vote less often than their elders is because
   a. young people do not care as much about the world.
   b. young people are less inclined to make efforts to help others.
   c. young people move more often than their elders.
   d. the political views of most young people are not represented by most candidates and ballot initiatives.

4. Who spearheaded the "Vote or Die" young voter turnout campaign?
   a. Britney Spears
   b. Tommy Hilfiger
   c. Ellen DeGeneres
   d. Sean "P. Diddy" Combs

Answers: 1-a, 2-b, 3-c, 4-d.

Conclusion

As you've read, Americans put a great deal of faith in the election process, and over the past two centuries, many changes have opened the system to more involvement. But at the same time, it seems that an ever-smaller number of us are willing to get involved. What difference does it make that fewer Americans seem interested in politics and that Americans on the whole turn out to vote less often than citizens in other democracies? Is this really something to care about?

One way to answer such questions is to take a practical point of view. What policy difference would it make if nonvoters got into

the act? Would the government head in a different direction if turnout were higher? Early studies suggested that on the whole, the policy preferences of nonvoters essentially paralleled those of voters. There would be little policy change if we had full election turnout. More recently, however, studies suggest that who votes *does* matter. The low turnout in the 1994 election allowed the Republicans to capture control of both houses of Congress and helped bring George W. Bush to the White House in 2000. In both cases, public policy shifts that followed these elections reflected a more conservative, a more Republican agenda than overall public opinion would suggest.

Another way to answer such questions is to examine how you define *democracy*. For example, perhaps precise levels of participation are unimportant; so long as enough citizens are involved to make the process competitive, full participation is inconsequential. The people who refrain from involvement in politics are also likely the least well informed. Perhaps we do not want these folks involved in the process; is an uninformed vote really preferable to none at all? Along similar lines, some people speculate that less informed citizens (the nonvoters) are more prone to radical policy shifts, so their absence at the polls actually adds a degree of stability to public policy. The conservative columnist George Will, in a piece titled "In Defense of Nonvoting," argues that good government—not the right to vote—is the fundamental human right. He suggests that high voting rates in Germany's Weimar Republic (1919–1933) enabled the Nazis to take power in 1933.[54] Declining turnout in America, Will asserts, is no cause for worry. This perspective is often called the **elite democratic model.** It insists that so long as fairness and political opportunity are guaranteed, the system is healthy.

The **popular democratic model,** by contrast, suggests that the character of any political system is not simply the outcome of public policy but also the process by which it is reached (see Pathway Figure on page 572–573). This model puts a premium on electoral involvement. When this occurs, citizens develop an affinity for the system because they are convinced that they have a stake in whatever policy results from political decisions. Put a bit differently, this theory says that systems of government designed to reflect the will of the people will do so better, and in the long run will be more prosperous and stable, if average citizens join the electoral process. Echoing this sentiment, the liberal political scientist and journalist E. J. Dionne, in his book *Why Americans Hate Politics,* has written that "a nation that hates politics will not long thrive as a democracy."[55] Which of these well-known commentators, Will or Dionne, in your opinion comes closer to the truth?

pathways | The Struggle over Same-Sex Marriage

 COURTS   **CULTURAL CHANGE**   **ELECTIONS**    **GRASSROOTS MOBILIZATION**    **LOBBYING DECISION-MAKERS**

PRO–SAME-SEX MARRIAGE

2003
Nov. 18
By a 4-3 vote, the Massachusetts Supreme Court rules that there is no "constitutionally adequate reason" to prevent same-sex couples from marrying.

July 14
After much debate and a heated lobbying campaign on both sides of the issue, a constitutional amendment banning same-sex marriages fails in the U.S. Senate.

1999
Dec. 20
A Vermont Supreme Court rules that same-sex partners must be eligible for the same benefits as spouses.

2001
March 2001
Responding to constituents, the Vermont State Legislature legalizes civil unions.

2004
Feb. 12
In San Francisco, city officials respond to pressure from constituents and a strong lobbying effort and perform the first same-sex civil marriage in the United States.

2004

1999 ———— **2001** ———— **2003** — **2004**

2004 **2004**
March 2
Mayor Jason West of New Paltz, NY is charged with 19 counts of solemnizing marriages without a license; these were same-sex marriages.

March 11
California Supreme Court orders San Francisco officials to immediately cease the issuing of marriage licenses to same-sex couples.

2004
Feb. 24
Pressured by conservative organizations, President Bush announces his support for a constitutional amendment banning same-sex marriage. He claims that the "sanctity of marriage" must be protected. He reiterates this stand throughout his reelection campaign in November.

2004
March
Pressure from voters and organized interest groups push the Wisconsin State Legislature to overwhelmingly approve an amendment to the state constitution banning civil unions and same-sex marriages.

ANTI–SAME-SEX MARRIAGE

The Battle Over Gay Marriage and the Election Process   Throughout American history, citizens have turned to the election pathway to express concerns and vent frustrations. Most of this activity is focused on bringing certain politicians into office, but it's also been directed at the ballot initiative process. As we have said, ballot initiatives, also called referendums, are policy issues on which citizens vote. Twenty-three states allow them. Another possibility for using the election pathway to bring about change is to amend state constitutions.

All of these election pathway routes—the selection of certain officials, ballot initiatives, and amendments to state constitutions—have come into play over the issue of same-sex marriage. The trigger for this activity was court cases suggesting that gay marriage was a protected right. The public reacted to these decisions by using elections.

essay questions

1. We sometimes hear that court decisions are the last word in policy disputes; that once the courts speak, the issue is resolved. But the battle over gay marriage in America suggests that in many instances voters can overrule court decisions. First, explain how this can happen. Second, discuss whether or not voters should be able to overturn court decisions in a democracy.

2. Many suggest that the gay marriage issue is rooted in generational differences—that young Americans are more tolerant of homosexual lifestyles and more open to providing gay couples full rights than are older Americans. First, does your experience confirm this perspective? Second, if it were true, how do you think generational differences will shape the gay marriage controversy in the years ahead?

June 7
A proposed constitutional amendment to ban same-sex marriages fails in the U.S. Senate by 11 votes. Once again, groups on both sides push hard through lobbying operations.

July 18
A same-sex marriage amendment is blocked in the House of Representatives.

Feb. 2
A New York Supreme Court judge rules that denying same-sex couples the right to marry violates rights to liberty and privacy and is therefore unconstitutional.

March 14
A California Superior Court judge rules that same-sex marriage bans are unconstitutional.

2005

April 20
Connecticut legislature passes a bill allowing same-sex civil unions. This is the first bill not passed as a direct result of a court case.

2005   **2005**

2005

2006

2006

2006

January
Maryland's legislature passes a bill to allow same-sex civil unions, but it is vetoed by Governor Robert Ehlrich after pressure from conservative groups.

2004
Aug. 3
Missouri voters pass a constitutional amendment specifying marriage to be between a man and a woman.

2004
Sept. 18
A constitutional amendment that bans same-sex marriages is passed by Louisiana voters.

2005
April 5
A constitutional amendment banning same-sex marriages is approved by voters in Kansas.

2005
November
Voters in Texas pass a constitutional amendment banning same-sex marriages.

2006
November
Colorado, South Carolina, South Dakota, Tennessee, Virginia, and Wisconsin all vote to approve a ban on gay marriage.

2004
Nov. 2
Turning to the elections pathway, constitutional amendments banning same-sex marriage are passed by voters in Arkansas, Georgia, Kentucky, Michigan, Mississippi, Montana, North Dakota, Ohio, Oklahoma, Oregon, and Utah.

Nov. 2
George Bush is sent back to the White House, and the Republicans maintain control of both houses of Congress, seemingly due, in part, to their opposition to gay marriage.

YOUR turn!

There are many culprits for declining voting rates in America. Institutional factors, such as residency and registration requirements, inhibit some citizens, mainly the young and the poor, from participation. One way to combat this problem on your own campus is to start a voter registration brigade. Why not team up with a group of students, set up tables, and perhaps also move from dorm room to dorm room signing up new voters? It varies from school to school, but a good estimate is that roughly 30 percent of the students on your campus are not registered to vote. If you attend a school where many of your colleagues are from a different state, it is important to either carry along voter registration forms from each of these states or have ready national voter registration forms, which allow you to register in any state. They can be downloaded from the Federal Election Commission Web site (http://www.fec.gov/votregis/vr.htm). Also, because many students prefer to vote at their home address (as opposed to their campus address), it is also wise to bring along absentee ballot applications from many states. Voter registration can be a hurdle to participation, but by rolling up your sleeves, you and your friends can make a real difference. And can you imagine what a difference similar efforts on every campus across the nation would make! ■

Chapter Review

1. Americans rely on elections as the principal means for selecting political leaders. There are many theoretical advantages to this approach, but there are many downsides as well. That is, elections are an imperfect mechanism for choosing governmental leaders.

2. The framers of our political system worried about "runaway democracy," so they set up a system in which elections would, for the most part, give citizens only an indirect means for expressing their preferences on leaders and public policy.

3. Over time, amendments to the Constitution and changes in state and federal laws have broadened the opportunities for citizens to play a role in the elections pathway.

4. Campaign finance has become a contentious issue in American politics. Some people believe that giving money to a candidate is a form of political participation and should be encouraged, while others suggest that it affords some people and groups a greater say in the process and is therefore undemocratic.

5. Numerous reforms have been implemented to limit "big money" in elections, but few have succeeded. The most recent effort, BCRA, is designed to limit the amount of soft money in the system.

6. Fewer and fewer Americans seem willing to participate in the elections pathway.

7. There are many plausible culprits for the recent decline in political participation. Likely, a confluence of forces is to blame.

8. The great irony of the elections pathway is that while the opportunities to participate have expanded, fewer citizens seem interested in becoming involved.

9. One's perspective on turnout issues depends on one's view of democracy.

CHAPTER REVIEW TEST

1. The electoral success of John Corzine and even Ross Perot suggests that a candidate's character, ideas, and qualifications can sometimes matter less than their
   a. manipulation of the media.
   b. good looks.
   c. personal wealth.
   d. family connections.

2. Ironically, while fewer Americans have participated in elections in recent decades,
   a. more people think they are participating.
   b. more people have the opportunity to participate.
   c. more people run for office.
   d. more Americans vote from overseas.

3. Since 1824 how often have presidents been elected with a plurality but not a majority of votes of the national electorate?
   a. twice
   b. seven times
   c. sixteen times
   d. twenty-six times

4. Regarding elections, the framers of the Constitution had as their first priority
   a. governmental stability.
   b. creating a truly democratic system.
   c. making sure that everyone had equal access to public office and the ballot box.
   d. making sure public policy represented the majority opinion in the land.

5. One original reason for the creation of the electoral college was to ensure that
   a. the will of the majority of voters in each state would be accurately represented in presidential elections.
   b. men of the best character and intellect would be deciding who the next president and vice-president would be.
   c. each state in the new union would have equal representation in the election process.
   d. england would not interfere with the election process.

6. Regarding the role of political parties in elections, the framers of the Constitution
   a. reasoned that electors would rise above partisan preferences and vote for the candidates who would best serve the nation.
   b. assumed that a two-party system would always present the electorate with a clear and fair choice between distinct political philosophies.
   c. worried that partisan politics would compromise the electoral process.
   d. said very little since they never foresaw the emergence of parties in the first place.

7. In the 1960s and 1970s, the 1965 Voting Rights Act, not the Twenty-Fourth or Twenty-Sixth Amendments, was the most important measure in protecting the right to vote.
   a. true   b. false

8. What legislation was enacted in 2002, following the vote-count chaos in the 2000 presidential election?
   a. the 2002 Voting Rights Act
   b. the Motor-Voter Act
   c. the Help America Vote Act
   d. the Butterfly Ballot Abolition Act

9. The "unit rule" in effect means that a presidential candidate
   a. cannot win the presidency if he does not win the popular vote.
   b. can win the presidency even if he does not win the popular vote.
   c. cannot run for reelection if he has been president for two terms.
   d. cannot win the election if he does not win the Electoral College vote.

10. Why did the "motor-voter" law arise?
   a. to help democracy *and* the domestic automobile industry
   b. to confine the pool of registered voters to responsible adults
   c. to counteract state registration laws that may have had the effect of unfairly limiting people's ability to register to vote
   d. to reinforce state registration laws requiring registered voters to be residents of their state and citizens in good legal standing

11. The "motor-voter" law has
   a. increased the number of registered voters and thus the number of people who actually vote.
   b. increased the number of registered voters but not the number of people who actually vote.
   c. in fact reduced the number of registered voters *and* the number of people who actually vote.
   d. disadvantaged people who do not drive to the polls, making them less likely to vote.

12. Which is **NOT** a reason for the mushrooming expense of political campaigns?
   a. an increased dependence on television advertising
   b. an increase in the number of voters that campaign advertising must reach
   c. campaign consultants
   d. the abolition of poll taxes

13. It is fair to say that campaign consultants such as Mark Hanna and Joe Trippi
   a. are now close to obsolete, given campaigns' heavy use of the Internet.
   b. have actually been a part of the electoral process since the eighteenth century.
   c. don't just help their clients win; they can help shape the nature of elections themselves.
   d. invariably compromise the democratic nature of electoral politics.

14. What did the Federal Election Campaign Act and its subsequent amendments prohibit?
   a. limitless campaign spending on the part of candidates, and limitless contributions from individuals, groups, or political parties
   b. warrantless wiretapping
   c. making individual campaign contributions tax deductible
   d. the use of "soft money" in campaigns

15. One result of the Supreme Court case *Buckley* v. *Valeo* was to lift almost all restrictions from the activities of political parties.

a. true **b.** false

16. Incumbency is a powerful advantage in elections. In recent House elections __ % of the incumbents won. One popular argument for why this happens is that _____

a. 65%; incumbents always have more money to spend
b. 75%; incumbents are better, more seasoned leaders
c. 85%; incumbents have earned a greater degree of trust from most voters
d. 95%; nearly all legislative activity is now geared toward securing reelection

17. What does BCRA stand for and what, among other things, does it prohibit?

a. Bicameral Regulation Act; "soft money" campaign contributions from political action committees
b. Bipartisan Campaign Reform Act; "soft money" campaign contributions to national political organizations
c. Better Campaigns Regulation Act; individual campaign contributions over $500

d. Better Congressional Races Act; individual "soft money" donations to state party organizations

18. One explanation for the decline in voter turnout in recent decades is that people's lifestyles have changed.

a. true **b.** false

19. What's paradoxical about the low turnout of young voters?

a. The average age of political candidates themselves has steadily declined.
b. Young people keep up with the news more avidly than do older voters.
c. Young people are more inclined to volunteer to help their community than ever before.
d. Surveys indicate that young people are less disenchanted with the government than are older people.

20. It's fair to say that in recent national elections, low voter turnout has been advantageous to the Democratic party.

a. true **b.** false

Review Test Answers: 1: c; 2: b; 3: c; 4: a; 5: b; 6: d; 7: a; 8: c; 9: b; 10: c; 11: b; 12: d; 13: c; 14: a; 15: a; 16: d; 17: b; 18: a; 19: c; 20: b.

DISCUSSION QUESTIONS

1. What is so great about elections? That is, why would a nation underscore its democratic character by pointing to the elections it holds?

2. What are some of the limits of the electoral process?

3. In what ways has the Constitution been altered to enhance the election process in America?

4. Have statutory changes—laws passed by Congress and state legislatures—followed a path similar to constitutional changes?

5. Why is money so important in contemporary elections? Do financial limitations really put candidates at a disadvantage? What types of candidates receive more money than other types?

6. Why do individuals and groups give money to candidates in the first place?

7. Why was *Buckley* v. *Valeo* so important? What did the Supreme Court say about the relationship between giving money to candidates and First Amendment rights?

8. How would you define political participation? Are some acts more important than others?

9. What has been the trend in political participation in recent years, and what has caused this change?

10. Why do you think electoral participation swelled in the 2004 election?

11. Are young Americans politically a "turned-off generation"? Explain your answer.

12. What do you think caused the dramatic increase in turnout among young citizens in the 2004 election?

13. Should we really care about levels of political participation in America? That is, what difference does it really make if a shrinking number of citizens are involved in politics?

14. What can average citizens do to improve levels of electoral participation?

INTERNET RESOURCES

For information on a range of campaign-related issues, see the Federal Election Commission Web site at **http://www.fec.gov**

For information on ballot initiatives, recalls, and referendums, see the Ballot Initiative Institute's Web site at **http://www.iandrinstitute.org/ballotwatch.htp**

For a host of information on campaign finance, see two sites: the Center for Responsive Politics at **http://www.opensecrets.org** and the Campaign Finance Institute at **http://www.cfinst.org/about/index.html**

For information on professional campaign consulting, see the American Association of Political Consultants' Web page at

http://www.theaapc.org and *Campaigns and Elections* magazine at **http://www.campaignline.com**

For information on levels of political participation in America, see the Committee for the Study of the American Electorate Web page at **http://www.gspm.org/csae**

For information on youth political engagement, see the Center for Information and Research on Civic Learning and Engagement (CIRCLE) at **http://www.civicyouth.org**

ADDITIONAL READING

Johnson, Dennis W. *No Place for Amateurs: How Political Consultants Are Reshaping American Democracy.* New York: Routledge, 2001.

Malbin, Michael J., ed. *Life after Reform: When the Bipartisan Campaign Reform Act Meets Politics.* Lanham, MD: Rowman & Littlefield, 2003.

Patterson, Thomas E. *The Vanishing Voter: Public Involvement in an Age of Uncertainty.* New York: Knopf, 2002.

Piven, Frances Fox, and Richard A. Cloward. *Why Americans Still Don't Vote: And Why Politicians Want It That Way.* Boston: Beacon Press, 2000.

Scher, Richard K. *The Modern Political Campaign: Mudslinging, Bombast, and the Vitality of American Politics.* New York: Sharpe, 1997.

Shea, Daniel M., and Michael J. Burton. *Campaign Craft: The Strategy, Tactics, and Art of Political Campaign Management* (2d ed.). Westport, CT: Praeger, 2001.

Strachan, J. Cherie. *High-Tech Grass Roots: The Professionalization of Local Elections.* Lanham, MD: Rowman & Littlefield, 2003.

KEY TERMS

Not wanting to alienate voters, the two major political parties in the United States seek to be inclusive, "umbrella" organizations. But occasionally an issue will drive a wedge in one or both of the parties. In the summer of 2006, Connecticut Senator Joe Lieberman, far left, sought the Democratic Party nomination even though he had been supportive of George Bush's Iraq war policies. Ned Lamont, (right) received the enthusiastic backing of anti-war Democrats and defeated Lieberman in that primary. The three-term Senator was denied the nomination of his own party! But Lieberman was far from finished. He switched his party registration, ran as an independent in the general election in 2006, and won back his seat.

CHAPTER 15

POLITICAL PARTIES

Religion and Party Politics   James Madison saw so much danger in mixing religion and politics that when he wrote the First Amendment, he placed the establishment clause, which declares the separation of church and state, right next to the free exercise clause. Under the First Amendment, citizens have the right to practice ("exercise") whatever religion they like, but the government must steer clear of officially supporting (that is, "establishing") any religious group. There should be a wall, argued Madison's friend Thomas Jefferson, separating church and state. The founders also worried a great deal about party politics. Any interest group—they used the word *faction*—with a narrow set of interests threatened the whole Republic, they reasoned. They realized, however, that legal barriers to the formation of parties, or "factions," would violate key civic liberties, such as the right to assemble and to petition the government.[1]

Photo: Marko Georgiev/The New York Times

Conservative political adviser and former Christian Coalition executive director, Ralph Reed, at the last night of the Republican National Convention in 2004. The Christian Coalition proved a powerful ally to the Republican Party for nearly two decades. Yet by the 2006 election the relationship seemed to be souring, as the division between social and economic conservatives widened. As we shall see in this chapter, one of the consequences of a two-party system is that each party seeks to build broad coalitions in order to win the next election. Whether these groups can maintain a cozy relationship through the tumultuous policy process is another story.

What, then, about the merging of religion and party politics? The framers would have shuddered at the prospect. In *Federalist No. 10,* in which Madison warns against factions, he also notes that the zeal spawned by different opinions over religion might create opposing factions.

Sure enough, the merging of religion and party politics has been common throughout American history. During the 1980s, groups representing evangelical Christians, called by the media the "Religious Right," were a major force in Ronald Reagan's administration. In 1989, the Christian Coalition (CC) was formed. A vast amount of the Christian Coalition's resources were directed toward the elections pathway—that is, toward filling the ranks of government with fundamentalist Christian politicians. It used massive grassroots networks to support candidates, spent huge sums of money, and distributed tens of millions of voter guides and scorecards. These flyers, which outlined candidates' positions on issues of interest to the CC, were handed out in churches across the nation. By 1994, the Christian Coalition was being called the "800-pound gorilla" of electoral politics, and the Republican Party was happy to forge a close partnership with it.

A prime example of how the Christian Coalition and the Republican Party closed ranks was the candidacy of Ron Freeman in Missouri's Fifth Congressional District in 1994. Freeman, a black Christian fundamentalist, had failed to win the Republican nomination two years earlier. By 1994, he had joined forces with

the CC, and this time the Republicans were eager to back his candidacy; he got 71 percent of the primary vote.

During the early stages of the general election, Freeman unabashedly merged his religious beliefs and his views about public policy. He soon grabbed national media attention. "The possibility of a handsome, articulate black Republican in Congress excited the party regulars," wrote one observer, "so that . . . GOP heavy-hitters all journeyed to Kansas City to raise money for Freeman." Soon Freeman had a legion of volunteers, "drawn heavily from Christian conservatives and citizens who believed in individual empowerment instead of government handouts."[4] His campaign war chest swelled to nearly half a million dollars, a hefty sum for Missouri politics.[5] Freeman had become the darling of the Christian Right and of the Missouri Republican Party.

The only problem was that general-election voters are a bit different from primary-election voters. Because they are not limited to the party faithful and include independents and the other side's supporters, general election voters are more moderate. Freeman decided to tone down his religious beliefs so that he would appear more middle-of-the-road. As one of Freeman's campaign operatives told the *Kansas City Star,* the largest newspaper in the Fifth District, "We're doing everything in the world to distance ourselves from any kind of labeling as a religious anything."[6]

Yet evidence of a close collaboration between the Christian Coalition and Freeman's campaign kept cropping up. For exam-

ple, one of the newspapers in the district reported that members of the Freeman campaign team distributed CC voter guides to churches.[7] By election day, there seemed no doubt that both the Christian Coalition and the Republican National Committee were sponsoring Freeman's candidacy.

Freeman lost the race, capturing just 43 percent of the vote. His opponent, Democrat Karen McCarthy, was also a coalition builder who had eighteen years of experience in the Missouri legislature, a close relationship with Democratic Party leaders, and a large war chest of nearly $800,000.[8] In the end, the decisive factor probably was that Freeman's close collaboration with the Christian Coalition had become unsettling for the typical Fifth District voter.

Nationwide, the CC-Republican bloc caused a massive shakeup in American politics in 1994. Republicans were swept into Congress, into governorships, and into state houses across the nation. It was the first time since 1954 that the GOP controlled both chambers of Congress. Few would dispute the Christian Coalition's central role in that election. The Republicans, it would seem, had found a recipe for victory.

The Republican majority followed through by pushing their agenda, startling many Americans with the depth of their conservative convictions. Once in office, their agenda seemed at odds with the views of most Americans. The Republicans lost seats in Congress in nearly every election after 1994, and their hold on the House lessened. By 2006 the Democrats regained control of the house. ■

▶ **What's the difference**
between a political party
and an interest group?

pragmatic party model
goal of political parties is to win offices
to control the distribution of government
jobs.

responsible party model
assumption that the goal of political
parties is to shape public policy.

In Chapter 14, we noted that Americans place tremendous stock in elections. Most believe that casting a vote for a candidate is the best way to voice their concerns and to change the direction of government. The same chapter also charted the steady progression of expanded voting rights but ended with a paradox: Although most legal barriers to participation have now fallen, the number of Americans willing to vote has also dropped in the past decades.

The extent to which voting actually empowers the average citizen depends on how elections are conducted and who the actors are. Are there mechanisms in the process that accentuate the role of average citizens, or does the system amplify the power of a few—of the elites? As you will see in this chapter, political parties have the *potential* to make elections a more efficient and more democratic pathway for change. Among other things, parties can bring together like-minded groups to form powerful electoral coalitions; the story that opened this chapter illustrated this. At the same time, many factors—especially the decline of local party organizations and the growing sophistication of campaign techniques—seem to be minimizing the average citizen's role in the election process. Today, many critics charge that instead of enhancing citizens' potential to make a difference, parties stand in the way. As you read in this chapter about the past, the present, and the future of party politics in America, keep in mind how various changes might affect your ability to change the system. Surely you will find some elements of this story encouraging—and others a bit less so.

Key Questions

1. What should parties seek to accomplish—to win elections to control the reins of power or to win elections to change public policy?

2. How are political parties different from interest groups and other political organizations?

3. What are some of the most important party functions, and which of these functions empower average citizens to be real players in the governmental process?

4. What were the forces that led to the formation of parties in America?

5. What role did political parties play in American politics more generally during the "heyday period" in the nineteenth century?

6. Why do we have a two-party system in America, and what difference does this make when it comes to citizens' ability to change the outcome of government?

7. Are presidential nomination campaigns more democratic than they used to be?

8. In our political system, do political parties empower the average citizen?

What Is a Political Party?

One of the great ironies of American politics is that precisely the forces that the framers of our Constitution most feared have proved to be the instruments that actually make elections work. We are speaking of political parties. One pair of scholars has called them the "institutions Americans love to hate."[10]

No single definition of political parties satisfies everyone. Any two observers of politics might define parties in different ways. The principal difference focuses on what we might expect from parties—that is, the goals of party activity.

One definition, often called the **pragmatic party model,** is that parties are organizations that sponsor candidates for political office under the organization's name in hopes of controlling the apparatus of government. The ends are the control of government, which has often meant the "perks" of control—patronage jobs, government contracts, and the like. A second definition comes from the other side of the spectrum. It is the **responsible party model.** In this model, parties are organizations that run candidates to shape the outcomes of government—that is, to redirect public policy. Pragmatic parties work to win elections in order to control government, whereas responsible parties work hard during elections in order to shape public policy.

▶ **What's the difference between a political party and an interest group?** Three factors distinguish political parties from other public organizations, such as interest groups, labor unions, trade associations, and political action committees.[11]

1. Political parties run candidates under their own label. Interest groups work hard to win elections; the Christian Coalition and the AFL-CIO both do all they can during each election cycle to win voter support for the candidates they endorse. But they do not nominate candidates to run under their label. Only political parties do this.

2. Political parties have a broad range of concerns, called a **platform.** As umbrella organizations, they develop and put forward positions on an array of policy questions. In contrast, most interest groups limit their efforts to a narrow range of topics. The National Rifle Association, for instance, is concerned with gun regulation, and the Environmental Defense League focuses primarily on issues related to controlling pollution and protecting ecosystems.

platform
the set of issues, principles, and goals that a party supports.

nominees
the individuals selected by a party to run for office under that party's label.

1. Define the "pragmatic" and "responsible" models of political parties. What is the core difference?

2. How would you summarize the key differences between parties and other politically active groups?

3. Finally, ever since the Progressive era, discussed in (L)(I)(N)(K) *Chapter 14, page 549,* political parties have been subject to numerous state and local laws. They are "quasi-public" institutions. Interest groups, on the other hand, are purely private and free of government regulations. Indeed, the extent to which parties are also private organizations has been recently debated in the federal courts.

practicequiz

1. If you walked into a local Green Party headquarters and said, "Sign me up. We need better environmental policy coming out of the state house," you'd be assuming what definition of political parties?
   a. the pragmatic party model
   b. the machine party model
   c. the responsible party model
   d. the long-range party model

2. One feature that distinguishes political parties from other public organizations such as the Christian Coalition and the AFL-CIO is that
   a. parties are private institutions.
   b. you have to pay to join a party.
   c. parties are not bound by federal or state regulation.
   d. parties nominate candidates, other public interest groups do not.

3. What is a party's "platform"?
   a. its positions on a broad range of issues
   b. its mission or founding principle, articulated when the party was first formed (for example, abolition is the platform of the modern Republican party)
   c. the financial base by which a party pays its expenses
   d. the software by which a party connects with its members electronically

4. Unlike other public organizations that support candidates during an election, political parties run candidates under their own label.
   a. true   **b.** false

Answers: 1-c, 2-d, 3-a, 4-a.

Party Functions

Just as there is disagreement over the precise definition of *party,* there are differences regarding what parties contribute to a democratic system. The following is a list of party functions that most

observers would agree on. It contains numerous *overt* functions (activities that we can see and clearly measure) and also mentions many *latent* functions (theoretical activities that we hope parties provide).

1. **Organizing the Election Process.** Devising a system of elections to pick governmental leaders is much tougher than it sounds. Imagine dozens, perhaps even hundreds, of citizens vying for a single office. Parties serve an important organizing function, because they narrow the pool of office seekers to party **nominees** and establish a platform of issues for their candidates. Both these functions help organize the process for voters.

2. **Facilitating Voter Choice.** Psychologists tell us that humans are cognitive misers: We wish to make rational decisions with the least amount of information necessary. Given that we as voters need not know everything or even very much about a candidate other than his or her party affiliation, parties help us cast an informed, rational vote. If, for example, a voter prefers Republican policies and an election pits a Republican against a Democrat, the voter can make an informed choice with no additional information. (Notice that we're not saying that the voter is making the *best* choice—merely that knowing that a candidate is supported by this or that party gives a voter who knows something about the parties *enough* information to make an *informed* choice among candidates.) Without party labels, the voter would have to study each candidate's positions in detail. Forced to undertake such a chore, many would simply sit on the sidelines or vote at random.

3. **Recruiting Candidates.** Anxious to win elections, parties often try to recruit good, qualified citizens to run for office. Of course, they don't always succeed. But when they do, they give voters excellent choices and a winner who is qualified to govern.

4. **Screening Candidates.** Parties also try to screen out unqualified or corrupt candidates. Receiving a party's nomination is a crucial step in winning a post in government. Parties deny endorsements to weak office seekers, not wishing to be tarnished by their shortcomings. (Unfortunately, most people would agree, this screening mechanism is far from perfect!)

5. **Helping Candidates.** Parties help candidates put their best foot forward to voters. In the past, assistance was primarily labor. Party workers would spread the word about their candidates and work on their behalf leading up to election day.

constitutional obstruction
the various ways that the U.S. Constitution slows down the policy process, such as the necessity for legislation to pass both houses of Congress and to be signed by the president before becoming law.

unified party control
when the executive and a majority of members in both houses of the legislature are of the same political party.

divided party control
when one party controls the White House and another party controls one or both branches of Congress.

Vice-presidential candidate John Edwards receives a warm welcome from Democrats at the party's national convention on July 28, 2004. Edwards and his running mate, John Kerry, lost the 2004 national election, of course, but most experts believe that Edwards will give it another try in 2008.

More recently, parties have begun providing many high-technology campaign services, such as polling, computerized targeting, radio and television productions, and direct mail. Of course, fundraising has also become a huge part of how parties lend a hand.

6. **Organizing a Complex Government.** The complexity of our government can seem overwhelming. There are three branches of the federal government, two houses in one of those branches, a massive bureaucracy, and a state and local sphere that repeats this intricate system. This complexity was by design, part of the checks and balances envisioned by the framers. But the outcome has been what some observers call **constitutional obstruction**—the many ways in which the Constitution deliberately makes swift action difficult. Parties counteract this effect by helping bring the many pieces of our system into united action. For example, throughout American history, political parties have helped bridge the gap between executives (presidents, governors, or mayors) and legislatures, as well as to

bring two houses of the legislature into united action. (Strong parties are no guarantee of overcoming constitutional obstruction, as we have seen throughout American history, but you can imagine how much worse things would be without them.)

7. **Aggregating Interests.** In their efforts to win elections, parties try to build coalitions of groups. Just as our government is complex, so is our society. Parties want to win elections, and interest groups want a say in the policy process. The outcome of this mutually beneficial relationship is that individual and group interests are melded into a broad philosophy of governing.

8. **Educating Citizens.** As each party works to build support for its candidates, the byproduct is voter education. Not only do the voters learn more about the candidates because of party activities, but they also learn more about government policies and the workings of our system.

9. **Ensuring Accountability.** Because our political system is so complex, it is difficult for voters to make accountability judgments. Whom should we blame if the economy turns sour or medical costs skyrocket? Who should get credit if crime rates fall or inflation stays in check? Voters use parties to make these assessments. If the party in power has done a good job, its members tend to be voted back into office. If things get worse, voters often give the other party a chance. This process works best when one party controls all parts of the government, called **unified party control. Divided party control** exists when each party controls at least one branch of the government but neither controls all three branches. During much of our nation's history, control has been unified, but during the past thirty years, the norm has been a divided system (see Figure 15.1), which make accountability judgments more difficult.

10. **Organizing Social Functions.** Although less so today than in the past, parties provide many Americans with civic and social opportunities. Party-sponsored potluck dinners, ice-cream socials, and barbecues have been a common feature in many communities throughout the United States.

11. **Promoting Civic Participation.** Either as part of their mission to build a more fully democratic system or simply in an effort to win the current election, parties promote political participation. This has included the cultivation of candidates, donors, volunteers, and voters on election day through get-out-the-vote efforts. Many studies have found that communities with strong political parties have higher levels of voting and other modes of political participation.[12]

discussionquestions

1. Which of the party functions that have been noted make our system of government more democratic?

2. Which of these functions give individuals more say in the public policy process?

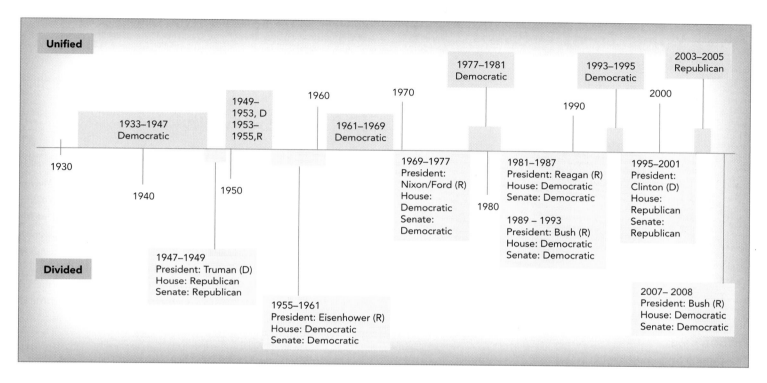

FIGURE 15.1

Party Control of Government 1933–2005

As this figure suggests, our government has been divided most of the time since 1968. What do you believe is the root of divided government? Why would voters split their vote between candidates of different parties? Perhaps most importantly, what are the differences between unified and divided governments? Do the pathways of change work the same when government is divided?

SOURCE: www.laits.utexas.edu

practicequiz

1. How do political parties help organize the election process for voters?
   a. by forcefully encouraging them to vote a certain way
   b. by helping to get multiple candidates on the various ballots during an election, so voters have plenty of options from which to choose
   c. by diminishing the number of nominees on a ballot, so voters do not have to choose from among dozens of candidates
   d. by telling voters in which elections they should or should not participate

2. Parties make voting efficient. By encouraging voting for the candidate nominated by the party with which they are themselves affiliated, voters can quite easily, and without further research, make the best choice in an election.
   a. true   b. false

3. Among other functions, political parties now provide which high tech service?
   a. touch-screen voting
   b. computer voting
   c. polling for candidates
   d. cell-phone electioneering

4. Let's say Republican Party organizers call a meeting with Christian Coalition members and pro-Israel lobbyists to organize their support of a congressional candidate who strongly supports pro-Israel U.S. foreign policy. Such a meeting would illustrate a political party's ability to
   a. organize a complex government.
   b. educate citizens.
   c. ensure accountability.
   d. work with aggregate interests.

Answers: 1-c, 2-a, 3-c, 4-d.

▶ **When we say "the Republican Party,"** who are we talking about—the people who vote for Republicans, the Republican members of Congress, the people who raise money and work for the Republican Party, or all of these?

tripartite view of parties
a model based on the theory that parties have three related elements: party-in-government, party-in-the-electorate, and party-as-organization.

party unity score
various ways to measure the extent to which legislators of the same party vote together on policy matters.

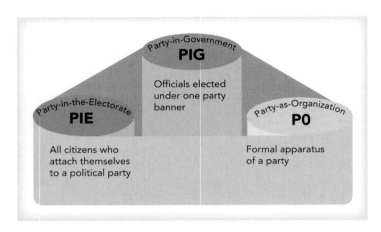

FIGURE 15.2
The Three Interrelated Elements of Political Parties

This figure shows the three core pieces of American political parties: party-in-government (PIG), party-in-the-electorate (PIE), and party-as-organization (PO). While few would doubt that each exists, some believe that they should be seen as distinct elements rather than linked together. When you think of "political party," which element comes to mind?

The Components of Political Parties

▶ **When we say "the Republican Party," who are we talking about—the people who vote for Republicans, the Republican members of Congress, the people who raise money and work for the Republican Party, or all of these?** One of the most confusing aspects of political parties is precisely what the term *party* implies. By the 1950s, political scientists developed what is called the **tripartite view of parties.** According to this model, political parties have three interrelated elements: party-in-government (PIG), party-in-the-electorate (PIE), and party-as-organization (PO) (see Figure 15.2).

PARTY-IN-GOVERNMENT

Party-in-government refers to the officials who were elected under a party banner. All the Republicans in the House of Representatives, for example, make up one piece of the GOP party-in-government (GOP means "Grand Old Party," which is the nickname for Republicans). They call themselves the Republican Conference, and if they have a majority in the chamber, their leader is the speaker of the House; if not, he or she is the minority leader L I N K *Chapter 7, page 264.* Other segments of the Republican party-in-government include the Republicans in the Senate and the president when a member of the GOP. There are also subbranches of the national party-in-government, such as governors, state-level elected officials, municipal officials, and so on. They, too, often form their own institution, such as the Republican Governors Association. Similarly, the House Democrats call themselves the Democratic Caucus, and all the Democrats in the Buffalo City Council consider themselves part of the same team.

▶ **Do members of Congress always vote with their party?** The American system is rather unique in that party-in-government structures are weak. In other democracies, it is expected that elected officials will vote with their party on most or all matters. Dissenters who vote with the opposition party are rare. If

what YOU can do!

Each party in each house in Congress has its own organization. To find out more about these units, check their Web pages. For the House Republicans, go to **http://www.gop.gov/defaulthb.asp**; for the Senate Republicans, visit **http://src.senate.gov/public**; for the House Democrats, type in **http://dems.house.gov**; and for the Senate Democrats, go to **http://democrats.senate.gov**

▶ Do members of Congress always vote with their party?

necessary, enormous pressure is exerted to force officials to "stay in line." In our system, however, party leaders *hope* that members will vote with the party, but the tradition is that elected officials can stray without serious repercussions. In fact, most voters in America look down on "party politics" and applaud their elected officials' independence. Still, you should keep in mind that the single best predictor of how legislators will vote on any given bill is their party affiliation. Most elected officials vote with their party most of the time, but in our political system, a degree of independence is both expected and accepted, as discussed in greater detail in ⓁⒾⓃⓀ *Chapter 7, pages 270–272.*

One way to assess the extent to which legislators vote with their fellow partisans is through what are called **party unity scores.** There are different ways to measure party unity, but the concept is the same: a gauge of how often members of the same party stick together. Since 1954 there is a clear pattern of greater unity, echoing what many see as an increasingly polarized Congress. Whether or not this is a good thing for our political system has been the source of debate. Some analysts believe this polarization hinders the legislative process and makes moderate policies less likely, while others believe that sharp differences are good for the electorate, allowing voters a clear and meaningful choice on election day.

pathways of action
THE CONTRACT WITH AMERICA

By the early 1990s, Republicans had likely grown accustomed to being in the minority in the House of Representatives, a spot they had held since 1954. But a light appeared at the end of the tunnel. Their ranks in both the House and the Senate had been growing in previous elections, and across the country, Republicans were winning more and more state legislative and gubernatorial contests. The South, in particular, had become fertile ground for GOP candidates. By 1994, Democratic president Bill Clinton's approval ratings were in the 40 percent range, and the president's party historically loses seats in midterm elections.

Rep. Nancy Pelosi of California, and Senators Harry Reid of Nevada and Charles Schumer of New York on election night in 2006. There were reasons for them to celebrate, as their party, the Democrats, recaptured the majority in both chambers—a position that they had not held since 1994. Pelosi and Reid would become the leaders of their respective chambers. What makes majority party control so important? Don't all legislators have an equal say in the legislative process?

▶ **Did the Contract with** America make Republicans more accountable to voters?

party identification
a belief that one belongs to a certain party.

straight-ticket voters
voters who cast ballots only for candidates of the same party in a given election year.

split-ticket voters (swing voters)
voters who cast ballots for candidates of different parties in a given election year or for candidates of different parties in different election years.

independent
a voter who is not registered or affiliated with any political party.

In the fall of 1994, Republicans, lead by House Minority Whip Newt Gingrich (GA), spelled-out their policy agenda in the Contract with America. Most scholars saw the move as a positive step in helping voters understand clear differences between the parties. Do you think similar pledges would help restore confidence in the electoral process or do you believe less partisanship and more compromise would help?

Republican operatives, however, were still not convinced that these forces would be enough to bring them to power. So they devised a plan: They would ask all GOP congressional candidates to sign a platform of popular positions and then announced, with great fanfare, that if the voters gave them the chance, they would vote on all of these items within the first hundred days of a new Congress. They called their platform the Contract with America. The principal architect of the strategy, Minority Whip Newt Gingrich of Georgia, reasoned that the Contract would nationalize local elections. That is, by suggesting to voters that all Republican candidates who had signed the agreement would vote as a group once in office, national policy could be change dramatically and quickly. They also reasoned that Republican candidates would benefit from the plan, given that they would have something specific to offer voters.

The scheme worked. The Republican sweep in 1994 was hailed as a watershed event, a titanic shift in the political landscape. There was no shortage of metaphors; the media called election an "earthquake," a "tidal wave," and a "meteor strike." Not only did the GOP take control of both chambers of Congress, but many prominent Democrats were sent packing—including the sitting speaker, an upset that had not happened for 130 years.[13] Control in state legislatures across the country shifted to the Republicans, and Republican challengers defeated five sitting Democratic governors. It was a big event indeed.

▶ **Did the Contract with America make Republicans more accountable to voters?** The platform offered to voters in the Contract with America contained ten popular policies, such as giving the president a line-item veto, a balanced-budget constitutional amendment, the death penalty for certain federal crimes, tax incentives for families wanting to adopt a child, and term limits on members of both the House and the Senate. True to the Contract's word, the House voted on each of these proposals in less than a hundred days (actually, ninety-two days), and all but the term limit amendment were passed. Gingrich and his followers proudly boasted of "promises made, promises kept." Only two of the bills got through the Republican-controlled Senate and were finally signed into law by President Clinton. Nevertheless, the Contract with America changed political dynamics in America, and perhaps more important, it changed the policy agenda. As one observer noted, "The Republicans had managed a sweeping change in the political agenda that would shape law and policy into the new century."[14] Gingrich and his colleagues made

▶ **What does it mean**
to vote a "split ticket"?

party enrollment
official or legal designation of one's membership in a political party.

primaries
elections held by political parties to select their nominees.

it clear that elections and party politics can merge on the pathway of change. ■

PARTY-IN-THE-ELECTORATE

The party-in-the-electorate refers to every citizen who attaches him or herself to that political party. An average citizen who says "I am a Democrat" or "a Republican" or "a Green" or "a Libertarian" is acknowledging membership in a party-in-the-electorate.[15] Another way of thinking about it is that the party consists of all the voters that consider themselves members of that party.

In many other countries, belonging to a political party can be a big deal. In dictatorships such as China, Cuba, or the old Soviet Union, being a member of the Communist Party—the only legal party—means joining the country's ruling class and gaining valuable career opportunities. It also requires proving political reliability and coming under strict discipline. In democratic countries such as Great Britain, citizens can choose among many parties and can change their affiliation any time they want, but they still have to join up officially, sign a membership card, pay dues, and attend local party meetings—and they get to vote directly for party leaders and the party platform. Identifying a British party-in-the-electorate is thus relatively straightforward.

Belonging to a party in the United States is very different. In this country, party-in-the-electorate is an ambiguous concept and the source of much scholarly debate. Some suggest that a person's attitude, or **party identification,** is enough to consider him or her a partisan. Party ID is the deep-seated feeling that a particular party best represents one's interests and outlook toward government and society. If a citizen tells a pollster, for example, that he thinks of himself as a "strong Republican," he would be considered part of the party-in-the-electorate.

As suggested in Table 15.1 on page 590, the percentage of Democratic and Republican identifiers has remained more or less constant during the last two decades—and it is about the same as those who do not align themselves with either—that is, the "independents."

▶ **What does it mean to vote a "split ticket"?** Other social scientists suggest that an American's behavior is more important than attitude when it comes to determining partisanship. If a person votes for Democrats most of the time, then perhaps this person should be tagged a Democrat regardless of what he or she

might tell a pollster. **Straight-ticket voters** are those who support candidates of the same party in every election. Voters who choose candidates from both parties on election day or who switch from one party to the other from election to election are called **split-ticket** or **swing voters.** They might vote for the Republican gubernatorial candidate, the Democratic House candidate, and the Green Party candidate for mayor. Voting behavior of this sort would suggest that the citizen is a nonpartisan, or what we often call an **independent.** (There are many independents in the United States but no actual Independent Party.) As noted in Figure 15.3 on page 591, the number of split-ticket voters has declined in recent years.

For people who consider themselves true partisans, the impact of this allegiance on their vote choice is significant. People who see themselves as "strong Republicans" or "strong Democrats" nearly always vote with their party on election day. Very few true partisans defect, and when they do, it is usually for a compelling but temporary reason—a war, economic turmoil, or their party's nomination of a totally unacceptable candidate. Generally, they return to their old party in the next election.

Another possibility to measure party-in-the-electorate would be to rely on official voter registration lists. **Party enrollment,** a legalistic approach to measuring PIE, makes some sense—except that many people register with a party when they reach voting age, only to change their attitudes and voting habits over time. Some change their official registration; but many others do not bother. Still another possibility is to consider that true PIE membership comes from an active involvement with a party. There are two possibilities here: first, voting in primary elections, and second, helping in party activities. **Primaries** are elections in which voters select party nominees. Each of the candidates on a primary election ballot is vying for the party's nomination, the privilege of representing the party in the general election in November. There are many ways to conduct primary elections, which we will discuss in more detail later in this chapter, but the point here is that it offers still another concrete way of deciding who is a member of a party. Not surprisingly, the number of citizens participating in primary elections has also shrunk over the years. Americans can also be active with a party by helping undertake party activities. This would be the most selective way of deciding which citizens are in PIE, as only about 5 percent of Americans either give money to a party organization or otherwise help it with grassroots functions.

▶ **What if voters don't** return to their party in the next election?

partisan realignment
historic shifts of public opinion and voter concerns that generally lead to a different party's control of government and a new set of policies.

dealignment
the loss of affinity for party politics among voters who no longer consider themselves partisans.

REALIGNMENT THEORY

▶ **What if voters don't return to their party in the next election?** **Partisan realignment** is a concept first advanced by the political scientist V. O. Key; it explains events in which the overall partisan balance of the electorate is transformed rapidly, often by a major event or crisis, resulting in a new party's taking control of government for a significant length of time. In other words, occasionally there are "earthquakelike" elections that shift the partisan balance of the country and the policy agenda for a period. Most analysts regard the election of 1932 as "realigning," given that it occurred during the Great Depression and the Democrats took over the reins of government from the Republicans for the next several decades. Other commonly cited realigning elections are those of 1828, 1860, and 1896. Some experts have suggested that the elections of 1980, 1994, and perhaps 2006 (L I N K *Chapter 14, page 537*) were realigning as well.

The idea of realignments and realigning periods is an attractive model for students of the electoral process. First, it does seem that some elections are more important, bigger, and more consequential than other elections. This label helps distinguish the truly big elections from others. Second, realignments seem to explain a number of interrelated phenomena. Before realignments, for instance, minor-party activity is especially pronounced, and during these events, turnout seems to rise and voter loyalties switch. Most young voters favor the dominant party. Immediately after these events, public policy moves in new directions, and the number of nonpartisan voters (independents) shrinks. Third, realignment theory helps break U.S. history into neat periods, which is handy for

studying the past. We can talk of the "second" or "third party era," and most will understand what we are referring to.

But realignment theory has its problems. For example, although the theory holds that these events mark a prolonged period of one-party control, seldom has this been the case. For example, the decades following the 1896 election were considered part of a "Republican period," but Woodrow Wilson, a Democrat, served two terms as president during this time. Dwight Eisenhower, a Republican, was elected president during a "Democratic period." Realignment advocates will point to the reasons for these exceptions, but others suggest that with so many exceptions, the theory loses its power. Perhaps most important, elections in recent decades seem to confuse our understanding of realignment theory. When was our last true realignment? Some political scientists suggest 1968, given that Richard Nixon, a Republican, took control of the White House in that election and, except for Jimmy Carter from 1976 to 1980, other Republicans lived there until Bill Clinton in 1992. Yet Democrats maintained control of one or both houses of Congress during this period—and realignment implies comprehensive change, not simply a change in which party captures the presidency. Some experts point to 1994 as the last realigning election, given that the GOP swamped the Democrats and took control of both houses of Congress. Yet Bill Clinton was reelected just two years later, and although the Republicans controlled Congress for years thereafter, they lost seats in the next several elections. Moreover, until the 2004 election, it seemed that the system was undergoing a **dealignment**—meaning a movement away from party politics altogether—rather than any sort of realignment.

TABLE 15.1
Trends in Party Identification

	1988	1989	1991	1992	1993	1994	1996	1998	2001	2004	2005
Republicans	27%	33%	31%	28%	27%	29%	28%	28%	29%	30%	31%
Democrats	30	33	32	34	34	33	39	38	34	33	34
Independents	38	34	33	34	34	35	33	34	37	37	35

SOURCE: "Beyond Red vs. Blue," Pew Research Center for the People and Press, http://people-press.org/commentary/display.php37.analysis0ID=95. May 10, 2005; Times Mirror Center for the People and the Press, *The New Political Landscape*, October 1994, p. 43; *American National Election Studies*, Center for Political Studies, University of Michigan, and Gallup Poll Election Survey, 1998.

As this table suggests, the division between the two parties and among those not allied with a party is about even. Why do you suppose one third of the electorate would consider themselves non-partisan? Do you think there are generational issues at work; that is, are young Americans more or less likely to be a partisan?

what YOU can do!
Recent studies reveal that all state party committees and about 75 percent of county party organizations now have a Web site. Do an online search for local party committees in your area. What do these sites suggest about party politics in your area?

So where do scholars stand on realignment? Some continue to believe in the theory, some have never bought into it, and still others have sought to modify the model to explain some of its inconsistencies. Others have suggested that while the theory may have explained big elections in our past, realignments are no longer possible in American politics. One of your authors, Daniel M. Shea, argues that local parties were key players in past realignments, drawing average voters into the process. But as local party structures became less viable (a topic to be discussed shortly), the system has lost its base. Realignments, he argues, are a thing of the past.[16] Only time will tell if Shea is correct.

PARTY-AS-ORGANIZATION

Party-as-organization means the formal apparatus of the party, including party headquarters, offices, and leaders. It is the official bureaucracy of the party, and it is found in the form of committees in every state and nearly every community in the nation. If you go to the telephone book and look up "Republican Party" or "Democratic Party," a phone number and address will be listed in most larger communities.

Party organizations exist at each layer of our political system (see Figure 15.4). At the national level are the Democratic National Committee (DNC) and the Republican National Committee (RNC). Each state has both a Republican and Democratic party—the Indiana Democratic Party, the New York State Democratic Committee, the Arizona Democratic Party, the Republican Party of Texas, the California Republican Party, and so on. Much the same

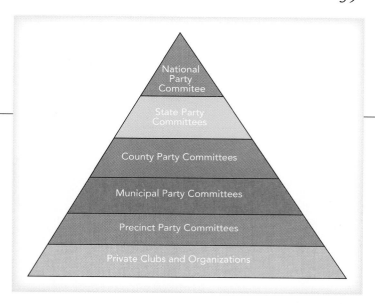

FIGURE 15.4

Layers of the Party System

One should be careful in interpreting this figure. It is true that there are layers in the party system—that in some ways the national committee is "above" the state committees. But there is a strong tradition of autonomy in party politics in America, and many organizations would balk at the suggestion that a "higher" unit could send any sort of commands down the line. There is a hierarchy, but is also a good deal of independence.

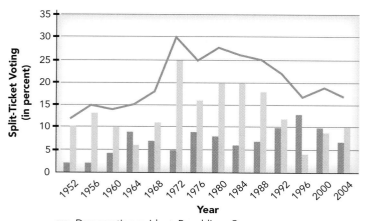

Democratic president, Republican Congress
Republican president, Democratic Congress
Split-ticket total

FIGURE 15.3

Trends in Party Identification

This figure suggests that split-ticket-voting is clearly on the decline. Why do you suppose this is true? What would cause a voter to split her vote in the first place? Do you think divided governments will fade with the decline in split-ticket-voting?

SOURCE: The American National Election Studies (www.electionstudies.org).

▶ **Why are local party organizations becoming weaker? Is this bad?**

party machines
local party organizations in major cities which influenced elections and operated on the basis of patronage and behind-the-scenes control.

Richard Daly, Jr. is the current mayor of Chicago, and his father, pictured behind, was a powerful party boss in Cook County for decades. Most agree that party machines have mostly faded from the political landscape. But is this someting we should applaud or bemoan? What type of benefits did strong local party organizations provide?
Photo: Peter Thompson/ The New York Times

can be found at the county and municipal levels; there is a Crawford County Republican Committee in western Pennsylvania and a Farmington Democratic Town Committee in Massachusetts. At the very bottom of the structure you can still occasionally find ward or precinct organizations. The Chicago Democratic Committee, for example, is made up of a mass of different precinct organizations.

Many casual observers of party politics believe that a formal hierarchy connects the layers, with the national parties controlling the state parties and the state organizations dictating orders to the county or municipal committees. This is not the case. A somewhat unique aspect of the American parties is that while there is a good bit of interaction between layers of the system, most of it involving the sharing of resources, few commands find their way down to lower-level committees. For the most part, party organizations at all levels of the system operate as semi-independent units. The same is true with regard to horizontal linkages: County organizations in a state might touch base occasionally, but for the most part they go it alone.

Party activities and functions are conducted by the party organizations through activists. In most cases, these are volunteers, giving their time and efforts because they believe in the party's mission (its approach to government) or because they see their efforts as somehow helping them down the line (perhaps with a job or a chance to run for office) or else simply because they enjoy the social aspects of involvement. The national parties—and a growing number of the state party committees—use a mix of volunteers and paid staffers. Some of the larger county and city committees do much the same, but at the municipal level, most activists are amateur—that is, unpaid.

Throughout much of our history, local party organizations had a rather distinctive, even aggressive face. These units, called **party machines,** were especially strong around the turn of the twentieth century in large cities such as New York City, Boston, Chicago, Philadelphia, and Kansas City. The leader of a machine was known as "the boss." Party machines wielded a double-edged sword: On the one hand, their strong desire to win elections and thereby control patronage jobs, city contracts, and the enforcement of municipal regulations, as well as their efficient "machinelike" organization, brought otherwise disfranchised citizens (those who could not vote) into the political process. This was particularly important for newly arrived immigrants, most of them poor, who flooded the cities in the second half of the nineteenth century. In exchange for their help on election day, party bosses and their machines provided poor people with a kind of social safety net. (This, remember, was long before Social Security, welfare, and unemployment insurance existed.) If a man needed a job, if a family was evicted from its apartment and

discussionquestions

1. Define each of the three pieces of political parties. Does any of these constitute the core of parties in America, or are they all necessary components?

2. Some observers suggest that the tripartite view of parties no longer makes sense. Why might that be the case?

needed another place to live, if a widow needed a loan to pay for a funeral or some cash to post bond for her wayward son—the party machine would lend a hand. In exchange, voters would support the party's slate of candidates on election day. There was also an accountability mechanism: If the machine failed to take care of the citizens of the community, it could be voted out of office and a new group given a chance. But few machines were ever voted out of office.

On the other hand, a great deal of corruption was thrown into the mix of machine politics. Election fraud was rampant. One of the last of the real big-city bosses, Chicago's Richard Daley (the father of today's Chicago mayor of the same name), would urge his workers on election day, with only a hint of a smile, to "vote early and vote often." (Daley is widely believed to have helped give John F. Kennedy his winning margin in the 1960 election by producing enough phony ballots in Chicago to carry the state of Illinois.) Because the machines controlled the reins of government, they also rigged the workings of the government (including the enforcement or nonenforcement of local ordinances) to suit their political needs and to line their own pockets. For example, in many cities, public employees were required to kick back a portion of their pay to the machine, which had gotten them their job—generally about 2 or 3 percent. The machines' humanitarian efforts extended only to supporters and potential voters. Some racial minorities, especially African Americans, did not get machine assistance because they were of no use, given that most either could not vote or did not vote "correctly." (In northern cities, where blacks faced few barriers to voting, they tended, until the 1930s, to vote overwhelmingly for the Republicans, "the party of Lincoln," thus alienating them from the Democratic bosses who ran most of the urban machines.)

For these reasons and others, a series of reforms were passed at the end of the nineteenth century, collectively called the Progressive movement (discussed in greater detail in (LINK) *Chapter 14, pages 550–551*). Change sometimes took decades to have a real effect, but gradually big changes occurred in the workings of party machines. Civil service reforms deprived the machines of some of their power over patronage (jobs handed out to loyal supporters), the secret ballot lessened the machines' control of people's votes on election day, and the direct primary undermined their ability to control nominations. Local party organizations survived these changes, but the machines faced overwhelming challenges and slowly faded away.

▶ **Why are local party organizations becoming weaker? Is this bad?** The fate of party organizations at the dawn of the twenty-

first century is unclear. State and national party organizations seem to be doing well; they have benefited from a massive influx of campaign contributions and have more equipment and staff and better facilities than at any point in American history. But the picture is much different at the local level. Local party organizations—what have been called the "mom and pop shops of the party system"[17]—are finding it difficult to survive. This is mostly because they rely on volunteers. Whereas a few decades ago many local committees were vibrant, dynamic organizations, today this would be the exception. We have entered a "baseless" party system—an era of parties that are strong at the national and state levels but weak at the community level.[18] Do you suspect that this change has altered the relationship between parties and average citizens?

practicequiz

1. What is the Democratic Caucus?
   a. all the Democrats in the House of Representatives
   b. a select group of Congressional (House and Senate) Democrats who meet regularly to strategize about legislation and elections
   c. a select group of Democrats in the House who meet regularly to strategize about legislation and elections
   d. a subgroup of the Democratic National Committee who meet regularly to strategize about elections

2. What best describes the political consequences of "The Contract with America"?
   a. ten conservative policies quickly became law and the policy agenda in Washington was dramatically changed
   b. the Republican party soon secured both houses of Congress and the White House
   c. although few of the policies advocated in the "Contract" became law, the policy agenda in Washington was dramatically changed
   d. its consequences were much more minimal and fleeting than people at first believed

3. According to the theory of partisan realignment, which of the following historical events has provoked such a phenomenon?
   a. World War I
   b. The Great Depression
   c. World War II
   d. the Cold War

4. What was one factor in the demise of political machines?
   a. civil service reforms
   b. the dominance of the Democratic party in the middle decades of the 20th century
   c. the presidency of Dwight D. Eisenhower
   d. the Great Depression

Answers: 1-a, 2-c, 3-b, 4-a.

▶ **What did the founders** think might happen if parties developed?

Whiskey Rebellion
an insurrection in 1794 by settlers in western Pennsylvania who fought against the Whiskey Tax, a federal tax on distilled drinks to provide money for national projects.

Democratic-Republicans
the first American political party, formed by believers in states' rights and followers of Thomas Jefferson.

Party Eras in American History

Like nearly every other aspect of American government, the nature of the party system has changed over time. In reviewing the history of American political parties,[19] two points emerge: First, from nearly the beginning, political parties have been at the center of the American electoral process. Second, the story of parties in the United States continues to unfold. In the years ahead, what they look like, what functions they serve, and how they fit in the elections pathway will probably be much different from today.

PHASE I: THE EMERGENCE OF PARTIES IN AMERICA (1790s–1828)

James Madison warned his fellow Americans about the dangers of partylike organizations, which he called "factions," in *Federalist No. 10*. "The friend of popular government," wrote Madison, "never finds himself so much alarmed for [its] character and fate as when he contemplates [its] propensity of this dangerous vice." A few years later, George Washington said that too. In his famous Farewell Address, published (not spoken) on the occasion of his departure from the presidency, Washington admonished the citizenry: "Let me . . . warn you in the most solemn manner against the baneful effects of the spirit of party . . . . It is truly [our] worst enemy." Many other statesmen and early political thinkers uttered similar words of caution: Political parties were the bane of democratic systems.

▶ **What did the founders think might happen if parties developed?** What drove these apprehensions? Before this, political systems that allowed ordinary citizens the opportunity to speak up and organize invariably degenerated into rival groups, each vying for its own interests. Consideration of the whole came second to consideration of the self. This was particularly likely in the early Republic, given that a national identity—and indeed a national citizenship—would not develop until much later. (Many historians have suggested that this national identity was forged only by the Civil War.) The freedom to speak out and join up with like-minded citizens made it even more likely that factions, or parties, would emerge.

FEDERALISTS AND JEFFERSONIANS Within a decade after the adoption of the Constitution, parties had burst onto the scene. Wishing to fill his cabinet with the best and the brightest minds of the day, President Washington selected Thomas Jefferson for

secretary of state and Alexander Hamilton for secretary of the treasury. Both men were distinguished and intelligent, and each had impressive Revolutionary War credentials (important for the legitimacy of the new government). The problem was that Hamilton and Jefferson passionately disagreed about the future of the nation. Jefferson believed that America's hope lay in small, agriculture-based communities. The United States was at that time overwhelmingly rural, and Jefferson, who disliked cities and worried about urban mobs, put his faith in the ordinary citizen-farmer: "Those who labour in the earth are the chosen people of God, if ever He had a chosen people."[20] Jefferson also distrusted a strong national government.

Hamilton, on the other hand, believed that the future of the nation lay in the development of vibrant cities, based on a strong manufacturing sector. He was a capitalist through and through and was convinced that a strong central government was the best mechanism to ensure long-term economic growth. Unlike Jefferson, Hamilton distrusted the ability of the average citizen to govern and believed that it would be best for elites to run the government.

The two got along in Washington's cabinet for a while, but soon their differing philosophies spilled over into heated debate. The spark was a plan that Hamilton put forward to spur the nation's economy. Among other things, Hamilton called for the federal government to invest in infrastructure improvements—in roads, bridges, ports, and canals. To pay for these projects, Hamilton proposed a tax on distilled spirits.

Opposition to Hamilton's plans grew, his leading critics being none other than Thomas Jefferson and James Madison. They, like most southern landowners, hated banks and were aghast at the idea of enriching wealthy city speculators at the expense of honest farmers and debtors—like themselves. They saw Hamilton's plans as bringing back the very corruption that had driven Americans to rebel against British rule. Hamilton and Jefferson squared off daily, leading Washington to complain that the two went at it "like two cocks in a pen" during cabinet meetings. Soon the battle extended beyond Washington's inner circle to the halls of Congress and to newspapers across the nation. Lines were drawn, sides were taken, and the public was quickly becoming partisan, favoring one side or the other.

Hamilton's plans passed through Congress. In a surprise move, Madison actually endorsed the plan in exchange for Hamilton's support for moving the nation's capital from Philadelphia to a small piece of land on the Potomac River, which separates

Federalist Party
party founded by Alexander Hamilton whose members believed in a strong, centralized government and were supporters of the Washington and Adams administrations.

Corrupt Bargain of 1824
the alleged secret agreement in the disputed election of 1824 that led the House of Representatives to select John Quincy Adams, who had come in second in the popular vote, as president if he would make House Speaker Henry Clay his secretary of state.

As distant as this event seems in American history, in some ways the core issues of the *Whiskey Rebellion* continue to shape politics: How should government best collect necessary resources and to what extent should public policy help shape our economy? While violent uprisings are rare, few issues stir public sentiment these days as does tax policy.

Maryland and Virginia. (Southerners thought that having the capital in the South would lessen the danger of northern domination.) But the controversy surrounding Hamilton's financial plans continued to simmer in the hinterland. In 1794, shortly after the plan's approval, a group of farmers in western Pennsylvania refused to pay the tax on distilled spirits. Federal troops were sent to collect it but met armed resistance. This **Whiskey Rebellion** was one of the first tests of the rule of national law in the states. President Washington decided to confront the farmers head on. In September 1794, he issued a proclamation ordering the militia to assemble and march against the insurgents. More than 150 prisoners were taken by federal troops, but Washington later pardoned all, and the uprising eventually fizzled. The essential point had been made: Federal law was supreme and would be enforced.

A second issue that helped solidify the partisans behind Jefferson and Hamilton was the French Revolution, which had begun in 1789 and had turned very radical by 1793. Many Americans, including Jefferson, felt that the United States government should back the French revolutionaries in the war that had broken out with Great Britain. The French, after all, had helped America in its Revolution and were struggling for self-rule and against domination by aristocracies and kings—theoretically the same struggle that had been fought on American soil a few years earlier. But to Hamilton and his supporters, the French Revolution meant "anarchy" and mob rule. Washington sought to keep America out of the conflict—to remain neutral.

Partisan animosity got even worse during Adams's presidency. Opponents of the administration (led by Jefferson and his "antiparty" friend James Madison) called themselves **Democratic-Republicans.** Supporters of Adams and Hamilton organized the **Federalist Party.** (The Federalist Party was unrelated to the supporters of the Constitution in 1787–1788, who also called themselves Federalists.) One prominent historian described this period as the "great consolidation," when parties finally emerged in America.[21]

The dispute over the legitimacy of political parties was mostly settled with the election of 1800. Even James Madison, who had attacked factions in *The Federalist Papers,* had been an ardent Democratic-Republican (he was elected president as Jefferson's successor in 1808) and in his old age embraced the party system.[22] The Federalists, lacking a large base of support outside New England, gradually faded from the scene—although they revived during the War of 1812, to which New Englanders were bitterly opposed. In the presidential elections held between 1804 and 1820, the Democratic-Republicans (who became known as the Republicans and then as the National Republicans, not to be confused with today's Republican Party) won between 53 and 92 percent of the electoral college votes.[23]

COLLAPSE OF THE FIRST PARTY SYSTEM AND THE ERA OF GOOD FEELINGS   After the War of 1812, the nation moved into a period of one-party politics. The years 1815–1824 were at the time called the Era of Good Feelings. The name was deceptive, because instead of Federalist-Republican battles, politics degenerated into feuds between National Republican factions, waged mainly in Washington, D.C. At that time, the federal government had relatively little impact on local affairs, and average citizens took little interest in national politics. Rates of voter participation in federal elections reached an all-time low, and the National Republican Party had few local organizations. The disintegration of the Federalist Party after 1815 and the degeneration of the National Republicans into feuding factions marked the end of what historian Richard Hofstadter called the first party system.

Then came the so-called **Corrupt Bargain of 1824.** As we saw in L I N K *Chapter 2, pages 71–72,,* the complicated election

► **What was "democratic"**
about Jacksonian democracy?

Whig Party
party formed in 1834 in opposition to the Democratic Party and President Andrew Jackson. It advocated a loose interpretation of the Constitution and high protective tariffs.

Democratic Party
one of the two major political parties in the United States. It generally draws support from working class people, women, and minorities; and has traditionally supported expanding the role of government in society and the economy.

of 1824 ended in an electoral college deadlock between candidates representing clashing National Republican factions. Following the constitutional procedure for resolving such situations, the House of Representatives selected as president John Quincy Adams, who had come in second in popular votes, rather than the popular-vote leader, Andrew Jackson. Because another candidate, House Speaker Henry Clay, threw his support to Adams, who named Clay secretary of state, Jackson and his supporters charged that a "corrupt bargain" had been struck.

PHASE 2: THE HEYDAY OF PARTIES (1828–1900)

THE SECOND PARTY SYSTEM   A backlash against this insiders' deal was felt across America, which showed itself in two ways. First, the National Republican Party was torn apart, and by the mid-1830s, another major party had arisen, the **Whig Party.** Although (like all successful American parties) it was a coalition of diverse interests, its program emphasized industrial development and personal morality. Second, what was left of the National Republicans regrouped as the **Democratic Party.** Like their Whig rivals, the Democrats also represented many different interests, from urban workers and immigrants to southern slave owners, but in the main the Democrats were the party of small government, states' rights, and personal freedom (except for slaves, of course). The Democrats' leaders were Andrew Jackson (the colorful general who at the Battle of New Orleans in 1815 had brought the War of 1812 to a victorious conclusion) and a wily New York politician named Martin Van Buren. Jackson, on Van Buren's advice, used local party organizations to rally opposition to Adams. These organizations helped Jackson unseat Adams in 1828, to reelect Jackson in 1832, and to elect Van Buren as his successor in 1836. By that time, Van Buren faced the organized opposition of the Whig Party.

► **What was "democratic" about Jacksonian democracy?**
It was a rebirth of party politics, this time down at the community level. Party operatives spread the word that unless average citizens became involved, the nation would be ruled through elite deals like the Corrupt Bargain. Both of the new national parties called on the average citizen to stand up and exert his role in the political process. (Politics at this time was supposed to be for men— white men—only.) This emphasis on individual involvement

ushered in a new era in electoral politics, which historians have called Jacksonian democracy (see Ⓛ Ⓘ Ⓝ Ⓚ *Chapter 2, pages 71–73*). Simply put, this was a move toward egalitarian politics and a more democratic social life. Politics *was* for the average person, not just for the economic and social elite. Not surprisingly, the percentage of adult males participating in 1828, when Jackson was first elected president, was nearly four times higher than in 1824. Political participation reached its all-time high in the election of 1840.[24] In that famous campaign, the Whig candidate, William Henry Harrison, was elected after his managers loudly boasted of his love of hard cider and his contentment with living in a log cabin. This was the first example of "selling" a consciously manufactured image in presidential electioneering. It would not be the last.

CIVIL WAR AND THE RECONSTRUCTION OF THE PARTY SYSTEM
Although local party politics was cemented in American political and social life, the lines of division between the parties shifted in the mid-nineteenth century. Slavery caused the most significant disruption. Both the Whigs and the Democrats were desperate to avoid the slavery question. Competition between the two was fierce, and neither party wanted to alienate its southern or northern supporters. It was better to dodge the slavery question altogether. "Northern abolitionists were often uncomfortably seated next to slave holders in presidential cabinets and in the halls of Congress."[25] But as new states sought admission to the Union, the slave question was thrust to the fore, and the delicate sectional balance was tested. A third party, the Free Soil Party, was organized in 1848 to oppose the westward expansion of slavery. The Whig Party collapsed after 1852 over the slavery issue, and the Democrats split into northern and southern factions. Democratic senator Stephen Douglas from Illinois in 1854 offered the **Kansas-Nebraska Bill** in an attempt to strike a sectional compromise. Under what Douglas called popular sovereignty, the voters in proposed new states would decide for themselves whether or not to allow slavery. But far from satisfying each side, opening up the West to even the *possibility* of slavery poured fuel on the fire. By 1854, a group of antislavery politicians from all the major parties met in Ripon, Wisconsin, to create a new political party, the modern **Republican Party.** One participant observed, "We came into the little meeting held in a schoolhouse Whigs, Free Soilers, and Democrats. We came out of it Republicans."[26]

The sectional split only worsened in the late 1850s. In the election of 1856, the Republicans failed to win the presidency by

Kansas-Nebraska Bill
an act of Congress in 1854 that allowed residents of the new territories in the West to decide whether slavery would be permitted in their state. Its passage exacerbated the rift between northern and southern states.

Republican Party
one of the two major parties of the United States, organized in 1854 to oppose the expansion of slavery.

Industrial Revolution
a period of economic and technological development in the late 1800s and early 1900s that resulted in the creation of factories and the extensive use of machinery.

a slim margin, and clashes between northerners and southerners grew increasingly violent. Things came to a head in the election of 1860. Abraham Lincoln, the Republican nominee, won an electoral college victory with a majority of votes in the more populous Northeast and the Midwest. But he was not even on the ballot in the South. His nationwide popular vote total fell well short of a majority. His election was the last straw for many white southerners. Between December 1860 and April 1861, most of the slave states seceded from the Union and organized a new nation, the Confederate States of America. When Lincoln sent federal troops to suppress the "insurrection," the Civil War began. It would last until 1865, cost nearly 1 million lives (3 percent of the population), and consume most of the South's wealth. But when the North won and reabsorbed the Confederacy, it had also preserved the Union and put an end to slavery.

The Civil War, the North's victory, and the postwar Reconstruction period reordered the party system. By 1877, when the last federal troops were withdrawn from the old Confederacy and all the southern states resumed self-government, the system had once again settled into two camps. The Republican Party was essentially the party supported by industrial interests in the Northeast. The Democratic Party was the party of the white South. The two parties battled it out for the votes of the agricultural Midwest and West. During the so-called Gilded Age, from 1877 through 1896, the two parties were very closely matched. Elections were always hard-fought and close, and the battling parties mobilized the average (male) citizens in huge numbers to vote. Most Americans took their party allegiances very seriously because such allegiances reflected a mixture of religious affiliation, economic interest, social class, ethnic heritage, and regional loyalties forged in the Civil War.

Many wonder how progressive reforms were successful, given that party machines and large corporations controlled public policy. The key was muckraking journalists, such as Ida Tarbell, who brought the depth of the corruption to light for average Americans. In the end, it was middle class citizens who demanded change. The Progressive Movement underscores the power of different pathways of change in a democratic political system. Do you think a similar reform movement is possible in the years ahead?

PHASE 3: PARTY DECLINE (1900–1970s)

GRAFT AND BOSSES The **Industrial Revolution** was an important phase in our nation's economic and technological development. Although it laid the foundation of modern America's power and wealth, industrialization also caused much suffering for the American working class. Colossal fortunes were being made, but most urban citizens found themselves working long hours and earning small wages in unsafe, unsanitary factories and sweatshops. Farmers—still the majority of the American people—

merit system (civil service)
introduced in 1883, an approach to managing the bureaucracy whereby people are appointed to government positions on the basis of either competitive examinations or special qualifications, such as professional training.

Australian ballot
the secret ballot, which keeps voters' choices confidential.

muckrakers
investigative journalists and novelists who uncovered corruption in business and government in the early 1900s.

candidate-centered era
after 1960, a period when candidates began to portray themselves as independent from party politics, even though they often ran under a party banner.

struggled with high interest rates, falling crop prices, and the extremely high cost of having the railroads haul their crops to market. By the 1880s, a growing number of citizens—mainly middle-class Americans—set to work cleaning up the political and economic system. Around 1900, various reform impulses joined to become the Progressive movement, which we have already encountered.

Politics in the post–Civil War era were notoriously corrupt. Graft—the bribes, kickbacks, and other "perks" that politicians took in—was rampant. Responding to public outrage, a number of important changes were gradually made. To strip political machines of their ability to use the patronage jobs by which they controlled government, the **merit system** (also called the **civil service**) was introduced in 1883 and later expanded, making many officeholders career bureaucrats rather than temporary political appointees. To reduce the ability of bosses to control what happened in polling places, the **Australian ballot** (or "secret ballot") was instituted; now voters no longer had to either orally announce their vote or publicly deposit their ballot in the box of one party or the other. And to reduce the chance that bosses would simply handpick nominees who faithfully toed the party line, the direct primary was established. In this system, the rank-and-file would choose the party nominee by casting a secret ballot on primary-election day. All told, these and many other reforms greatly reduced the power of party machines.

Another blow to party bosses was disclosure of corruption in the popular press. As you saw in Ⓛ Ⓘ Ⓝ Ⓚ *Chapter 11, pages 432–433*, around 1900, **muckrakers**—investigative journalists, we would call them today—were busy uncovering both political and economic misdeeds. "Newspapers, magazines, and books exposed evidence of abuse—from entire police departments in partnership with gangsters, to churches owning whole blocks of foul-smelling slums, to an entire U.S. Senate 'on the take.'"[27]

FROM THE PROGRESSIVES TO THE NEW DEAL These new laws and the flurry of media coverage did away with most party machines. So did the prosecutions of corrupt political bosses that district attorneys were empowered to launch after 1900—anti-corruption crusades that on occasion brought a triumphant prosecutor into a governor's chair or a Senate seat. The reins of government were slipping from machine hands, and the public's trust in party politics was shaken. The Progressive era marked a sea change in the place of party organizations in American politics. They were still important institutions and would remain so as late as the 1960s, especially for candidates who needed party volunteers to reach out to voters. But the heyday period was over.

The Great Depression dealt another blow, although sometimes a slow-moving one, to machine politics. The economic crisis of the 1930s tore to shreds the "safety net" that political machines had provided to help out-of-luck citizens get through tough times. To replace these tattered safety nets, President Franklin D. Roosevelt's New Deal established federal Social Security, unemployment insurance, public works projects, and social welfare programs. Roosevelt, a Democrat, often cooperated with urban political machines, which were almost always Democratic. Urban machines were an important part of the New Deal political coalition, turning out Democratic voters. But in the long run, the coming of the welfare state undermined ordinary people's dependence on political bosses. So did the surge in post–World War II prosperity and the decline of central cities, which generally lost population to the suburbs.

THE RISE OF CANDIDATE-CENTERED POLITICS By the 1960s, public attitudes about political parties had grown especially sour. Young people felt no reverence for traditional politics, and their parents were often prosperous enough to think that they could afford to abandon old partisan loyalties. During this turbulent period in American history, many Americans felt that parties were part of the problem. The number of Americans considering themselves partisan took a nosedive, and it seemed that we were headed toward a partyless age. David Broder's 1971 book *The Party's Over* seemed to capture the mood of the times.[28]

On top of this—and perhaps partly fueling this change—candidates came to realize that parties were no longer necessary or even desirable. Historically, party workers were needed to bring the candidate's message to the voter, but by the 1960s, television and direct mail could reach more voters in a single day than party operatives could contact in weeks. Party assistance also came with a price tag, as it suggested that the candidate was not "independent minded." It became advantageous to run your own show and be seen as "independent-minded." Moreover, new-style campaign consultants burst on the scene in the 1960s. These professionals could be hired (for a lot of money), and their allegiance would be solely to the candidate.

discussionquestions

1. Some people have suggested that regardless of the framers' concerns, parties were inevitable. Why would that be the case? How does the rise of first one and then another party system demonstrate the inevitability of parties?

2. What are some of the forces that have led to the decline of party politics in modern America?

what YOU can do!

Conduct an informal poll of your classmates, friends, and family about their attitudes toward minor parties. Do they wish for additional choices on election day—for a vibrant multiparty system—but refrain from voting for third-party candidates because of the wasted-vote syndrome?

What we might call the post-1960 **candidate-centered era** sent repercussions throughout the political system. As candidates pitched themselves as independent, voters saw little reason to hold to any notion of partisanship. Party organizations lost even more sway. As more citizens became independent, voting cues were lost, leading to lower election day turnouts. Once in office, elected officials saw little reason to stick to the party caucus, leading to less policy coherence and a less efficient legislative process.

PHASE 4: ORGANIZATIONAL RESURGENCE (1970s–PRESENT)

By the 1970s, many observers came to believe that parties were fading from the scene permanently. But if anything is true about political parties, it is that they are adaptive creatures, eager to adjust whenever confronted with adverse conditions. National party operatives, at first mostly at the Republican National Committee, realized that they were quickly becoming irrelevant and that changes were essential. Instead of improving their relations with voters, however, the parties chose to expand their services to candidates. Parties became service-oriented, meaning that they broadened their activities to include a host of high-tech services to candidates. They developed, for example, computerized direct-mail operations, in-house television and radio production studios, and sophisticated polling operations. This also meant hiring new professionals—their own new-style campaign consultants—and greatly expanding their facilities. Of course, all this cost a great deal of money.

This change has had significant ramifications. For one thing, the parties have seemed to get back on their feet in recent years, again becoming central players in elections. Books such as *The Party Goes On*, *The Party's Just Begun*, and *The Parties Respond* The Tell Tale of adaptation and rebirth.[29] It's as if "the phoenix has risen from the ashes."[30] A quick tour of either party's national headquarters today would suggest that parties are doing quite well.

But there have been negative effects, too. Sophisticated services require ever more resources. In their never-ending efforts to get around campaign finance laws, politicians and their consultants discover new loopholes each year, breeding voter cynicism. At precisely the same time that party organizations are regaining their footing, a growing number of Americans see parties as cor-

rupt, and while the national parties have done well during this period, revitalization has not yet reached the grass roots (that is, local party committees). Finally, while many candidates appreciate the help they get, the parties know that they can get more mileage out of targeting only a handful of races. In short, the revitalization of the national party *committees* has been significant, but it has also transformed the nature of the party *system*.

---

practicequiz

1. What best characterizes the disagreement between Thomas Jefferson and Alexander Hamilton that led to the creation of separate political parties?
   a. Jefferson called for the creation of a national bank and Hamilton abhorred the idea.
   b. Jefferson called for a national investment in the infrastructure (roads, bridges, canals, etc.), and Hamilton distrusted big government and the raising of taxes.
   c. Hamilton thought the basis of American democracy was in level-headed landowners, but Jefferson thought cities and city dwellers should dictate policy.
   d. Jefferson trusted the average (usually land-owning) citizen to dictate policy in the Republic, but Hamilton believed in a more centralized government run by elites.

2. Who were the leaders who first inspired the Federalist Party?
   a. George Washington and Thomas Jefferson
   b. John Adams and Alexander Hamilton
   c. John Burr and James Madison
   d. James Madison and Thomas Jefferson

3. What characterized the political philosophy of Democrats in the 1830s was:
   a. that the federal government should help the less fortunate and avoid entanglements abroad.
   b. that the federal government should be small, states' rights robust, and personal freedom (for whites) forever preserved.
   c. that the government should help nurture industrial development and individual morality.
   d. that slavery is evil and the union of states sacred.

4. What were elections like in the Gilded Age:
   a. Corrupt.
   b. One-sided, with low voter turnout.
   c. Close, with high voter turnout.
   d. Close, with little party allegiance on the part of voters.

Answers: 1-d, 2-b, 3-b, 4-c.

▶ **Why do states make** it hard for minor parties to get their candidates on the ballot?

two-party model
a system in which two major political parties compete for control of the government.

institutional barriers
legal impediments, such as laws, court decisions, and constitutional provisions, that limit the possibilities of minor parties in the United States.

single-member district
a legislative district that elects only one representative.

first-past-the-post system
awarding an elected post to the candidate who receives the most votes for that position.

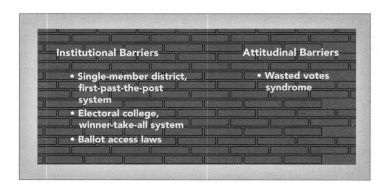

FIGURE 15.5
Barriers to Minor Party Success

It is clearly difficult for minor parties in American politics. But do we really want a viable multi-party system, especially given the structure of our government (federalism, separation of poweres, etc)? What is your take on this issue?

Minor Parties in American Politics

For most Americans, parties come in two brands—Democratic or Republican. This **two-party model** seems deeply rooted in the American political system—indeed, in the public's psyche. As we will see, the sheer power of momentum is one of the explanations for the two-party model's durability. Ours is a two-party system because it has almost always been a two-party system. At the same time, a growing number of Americans seems to want more choices on election day.

BARRIERS TO MINOR PARTY SUCCESS

The barriers to minor-party success in the United States can be divided into two categories (see Figure 15.5). Let's consider first the **institutional barriers**—the legal impediments created by statutes, by court decisions, or by the Constitution itself. The most significant of these is the **single-member district** or **first-past-the-post system** that is used in legislative elections. In the American model, legislative districts have only one legislator who gets

into office by simply getting more votes than any other candidate. The single-member district model alone propels a two-party model. Imagine that candidates from *three* parties are competing for a congressional seat. One candidate winds up with 45 percent of the vote, and the others get about 27 percent each. Because the first candidate received more votes than the others—was "the first past the post"—and because only one person can represent the district, that candidate is sent to Washington. The losing parties get nothing for their efforts. This might continue for a few elections, but eventually operatives of the two losing parties will consider joining forces if they are not ideologically too far apart. After all, their combined strength is mightier than the winning party's. An ideologically pure party might refuse to merge with another, but eventually its supporters get tired of losing, and the inclination to join forces with the party closest to them becomes irresistible. The outcome is a two-party system.

Another institutional barrier to third parties is the electoral college. The Constitution allows the states to allocate their electoral votes as they see fit, but forty-eight states have decided to cast their electoral votes as a block in a winner-take-all system. This is often referred to as the unit rule. (Two states have another rule: Maine and Nebraska select presidential electors at the congressional-district level, and the winner of the statewide contest gets an extra two electors.) To have a chance at winning the presidency, a candidate has to win states outright; he or she gains nothing by running a strong second.

▶ **Why do states make it hard for minor parties to get their candidates on the ballot?** Many states have **ballot access laws,** which help sustain the two-party system. States have an interest in limiting the number of candidates on a general-election ballot. Would we really wish to choose among forty or fifty or perhaps even a hundred candidates? Probably not—but if not, what grounds should be used in restricting ballot access? Beginning at the turn of the twentieth century, states created schemes to limit the number of candidates and at the same time make things easy for the major parties. (After all, members of the two major parties were writing the regulations!) Generally speaking, parties whose candidates received 25 percent in the previous election automatically get a place on the next election's ballot. Other parties have to gather a lot of signatures on petitions to be allowed a spot on the ballot.

wasted-vote syndrome
the feeling that a vote for a minor-party candidate will be wasted because the candidate stands little chance of winning.

Anti-Masonic Party
party founded in 1825 in opposition to Freemasonry in public affairs.

American Party (Know-Nothings)
party in the 1850s that hoped to keep power out of the hands of immigrants and Roman Catholics.

ballot access laws
laws in each state that determine how a third-party candidate can get on the general election ballot.

attitudinal barriers
those perceptions and beliefs that help maintain the two-party system in America.

▶ Who were the
Know-Nothings?

The second category of barriers to minor party success is **attitudinal barriers.** Perhaps the greatest attitudinal hurdle is the **wasted-vote syndrome.** Americans seem anxious to have their vote count—to help make a difference in selecting who will serve in office. Because minor-party candidates usually stand little chance of victory most Americans are reluctant to support such candidates on election day, "wasting" (they say) their vote. It is revealing that support for minor-party candidates often peaks several weeks before the election. But as election day approaches, voters abandon the minor-party candidate, hoping to add their voice to the contest between the "real" candidates, one of whom everyone knows is going to win. This would also explain why so many Americans tell pollsters that they want more parties in the election process but at the same time minor-party candidates languish on election day.

Minor parties confront a hostile environment in the American setting. There are many laws and regulations that limit their chance for success, as well as deep-seated attitudinal factors that make matters worse. Democracies around the globe flourish with multiparty systems, but the chances of one emerging here are slim—though perhaps improving. If voter support for additional choices remains high, it is conceivable that significant changes may occur. In the short term, however, the pathway of electoral politics will be paved by two-party bricklayers.

MINOR PARTIES IN AMERICAN HISTORY

This is not to suggest that minor parties play *no* role in the system. Quite the contrary. Minor parties have sprouted up throughout American political history and have changed the political landscape. They fall into two categories. First have been the fledgling parties that appeared on the rare occasions when one or both of the major parties were actually collapsing. Second have been the true third parties that periodically challenged the established two-party system and provoked changes in both parties. Examining both categories tells us much about the forces that enable our two-party system to survive.

WOULD-BE SECOND PARTIES The Corrupt Bargain of 1824 delivered the presidency to John Quincy Adams, popular disgust with government through political deals among the elite spread widely among the citizenry. This disgust mainly fueled enthusiasm

for electing Andrew Jackson president, but it also inspired the **Anti-Masonic Party.** Anti-Masonry momentarily filled a void in American politics that the disintegration of the National Republicans was opening. The Anti-Masonic presidential candidate (Jefferson's former attorney general William Wirt) got 8 percent of the popular vote and Vermont's 8 electoral votes in the 1832 election, though of course he lost to Jackson. Anti-Masonry, though, proved to be too weak a pillar on which to build a major political party, and its followers dispersed into one of the other parties—Democratic or Whig—that took shape during Jackson's presidency.

▶ **Who were the Know-Nothings?** The **American Party,** popularly known as the **Know-Nothings,** proved the same point in the 1850s. Large numbers of immigrants, many of them Catholics from Ireland or Germany, were pouring into American cities. Many old-stock Americans' Protestant fears and prejudices awakened at the sight of beer- and whiskey-drinking Roman Catholics gaining a major foothold in the Republic and playing a pivotal role in the politics of major northern cities. The fact that the Democrats welcomed these immigrants and usually got their votes disturbed former Whigs profoundly. The anti-immigrant and anti-Catholic American Party movement was the result, filling the void left by the collapse of the Whigs. In 1854, the American Party racked up huge votes in Massachusetts and other northeastern states, and in 1856, it nominated ex-President Millard Fillmore, a former Whig, for the White House. Fillmore got a whopping 21.6 percent of the popular vote but only 8 electoral votes. Almost immediately afterward, the American Party collapsed. Like Anti-Masonry, anti-Catholic and anti-immigrant "nativism" was too narrow a base on which to assemble a coalition opposed to Democratic rule. The candidates elected under the American Party banner, moreover, were inexperienced political outsiders; once in office, they were inept in dealing with the issues. Thus as the 1850s sectional crisis rooted in slavery deepened, the new Republican Party became a far more promising home for northern Whigs and antislavery northern Democrats. The Republicans, organized by veteran politicians at about the same time that the American Party formed, came much closer to winning the 1856 presidential election. (Their nominee, John C. Frémont, got 33 percent of the popular vote and 114 electoral votes.) After the American Party collapsed, most of its supporters joined the Republicans.

▶ **Why do minor parties often "disappear" into one of the major parties?**

Bryan did not win the presidency in 1896, but he came exceedingly close. He benefited from the fusion of the Populist Party with the Democratic Party, and by the fact that he was a gifted orator. Yet his opponent in that race, William McKinley, proved that massive campaign spending can be a critical factor in the election process.

▶ **Why do minor parties often "disappear" into one of the major parties?**

TRUE THIRD PARTIES All the other minor parties in American history have been unsuccessful challengers to the powerful two-party system, and all of them failed. In the 1840s, there were two minor antislavery parties, the **Liberty Party,** which ran a presidential candidate in 1840 and 1844, and the **Free-Soil Party,** which nominated former President Martin Van Buren in 1848. After the Civil War, the various third-party movements that rose and fell expressed the economic distress of farmers in the Midwest and, briefly, also the South. These included the **Greenback Party** of 1876–1884, which urged that paper money ("greenbacks") be printed to inflate the currency in hopes of raising farm prices, and the **People's** (or **Populist**) **Party** of 1892, which put forward a sweeping reform program demanding not only an inflated currency but also many constructive proposals: railroad regulation, an income tax, curbs on monopolies, the initiative and referendum, the direct election of U.S. senators, and other measures to empower ordinary Americans. In 1896, the Populists disappeared when the Democratic candidate, William Jennings Bryan, endorsed one of their major issues, the coinage of silver as well as gold. The Populists also nominated Bryan, but they went down with him to defeat at the hands of William McKinley's Republicans. Populism, a rural and small-town movement, was displaced by urban-oriented Progressivism as the vehicle for Americans' reform impulses after 1900.

Have socialist or communist parties ever run for office in the United States? There have been various socialist parties in American history, all appealing primarily to urban workers and intellectuals, but none has been powerful enough to challenge the two-party system and the capitalist organization of the American economy. The most formidable of these movements was the **American Socialist Party,** launched in the 1890s. At its height, in the elections of 1912 and 1920, its candidate, Eugene Debs, twice won more than 900,000 votes (representing as much as 3.4 percent of the total)—but these votes were scattered so widely that Debs took no electoral votes. The Socialists were strongly democratic, dedicated to winning power through the ballot box, and they did succeed in electing mayors and congressmen in cities such as

American Socialist Party
party created in the 1890s that advocated government control of certain elements of business and society.

Communist Party USA
party founded in 1920 by radical Marxists who broke away from the American Socialist Party.

Socialist Labor Party
party formed in 1874 to advocate the peaceful introduction of socialism. It is the oldest socialist party in the United States and the second oldest in the world.

States' Rights Democratic ("Dixiecrat") Party
party formed in 1948 by Democrats in the South who opposed desegregation.

Milwaukee, Wisconsin, and Schenectady, New York. In 1920, radical Marxists who admired the Bolshevik Revolution in Russia broke away from the Socialists to form the **Communist Party USA,** which never attracted more than a handful of votes and fell completely under the control of the Kremlin. Various other splinter socialist and communist movements, such as the **Socialist Labor Party,** also maintain a tenuous place on the ballot and still garner a few votes.

The question of why socialism never became a major force in American politics—comparable to, say, the Labour Party in Great Britain or the socialist and Marxist parties in continental Europe—has caused much scholarly debate. The full answer depends on a complex historical analysis of American society and economics, including the American people's reluctance to define their politics primarily in terms of class war. But one important part of the reason for socialism's failure in the United States has simply been the inability of socialist parties to break the institutional grip of the two-party system.

Defenders of racial segregation have several times tried to take the third-party path, always in the hope of denying either of the major-party candidates an electoral college majority and throwing the election into the House of Representatives. There, remembering the deadlocks of 1800 and 1824, they hoped to be able to bargain with the major-party candidates to stop civil rights programs. Southern Democrats tried this strategy first in 1948, angrily reacting to President Truman's steps to begin desegregating American life by integrating the armed forces and enforcing fair-employment laws. They walked out of the 1948 Democratic convention and created the **States' Rights Democratic** (or **"Dixiecrat"**) **Party,** which nominated South Carolina's governor, Strom Thurmond, for president. All through the summer and fall, polls predicted that Truman's unpopularity, coupled with the Progressive and Dixiecrat splits in the Democrats' ranks, would send the president down to defeat. But the pollsters were wrong—largely because they stopped polling too early. As election day approached, potential Democratic voters found themselves pulled by the logic of not wanting to waste their vote, and most wound up sticking with Truman. Thurmond got 1.1 million popular votes, but the 39 Deep South electoral votes he netted

Strom Thurmond (left) was a States Rights Democratic candidate for the presidency in 1948. The core of Thurmond's platform was the continuation of racial segregation. Racial issues have been wrapped up in party politics since well before the Civil War. Are we over this—or do you think racial issues continue to shape electoral politics?

▶ **So will the major** parties adopt some of the Libertarian or Green Party platforms to avoid losing voters to those groups?

American Independent Party
party established in 1968 by Alabama Governor George Wallace that opposed the Civil Rights Act of 1964 and federal government welfare programs.

Libertarian Party
party established in 1971 that opposes laws that limit human behavior, advocates a free-market economy without government regulation or assistance, and opposes government spending on welfare.

were not enough to deny Harry Truman an electoral college victory. Segregationist Democrats tried anew in 1960, running slates of "uncommitted electors" that picked up 15 electoral votes, but once again this failed to block the election of the Democratic candidate, John F. Kennedy.

These two segregationist efforts were confined to the South, but in 1968—with many whites in the North also expressing their fear of ghetto rioting—white supremacists tried to "go national." Alabama's Governor George Wallace, who had gained notoriety for trying to halt integration at the University of Alabama, launched the **American Independent Party** and sought votes in all parts of the country. By choosing as his running mate retired Air Force General Curtis LeMay, an advocate of all-out war in Vietnam, Wallace hoped to capitalize not only on white racism but also on public frustration with Lyndon Johnson's military failure in Southeast Asia and on the backlash against "hippie" antiwar protestors. Like Thurmond, Wallace aimed not to win the election but to force the decision into the House, where he planned to bargain for what he wanted. His strategy failed, but Wallace did net 9.9 million votes.

When Americans realized that the two-party system obliged them to choose between the major-party nominees, Republican Richard Nixon and Democrat Hubert Humphrey. Nixon edged out Humphrey in popular votes, and Wallace got no electoral college votes. However, the combined "law-and-order" majority of popular votes for Nixon (31.7 million, or 43.4 percent of the total) and Wallace (9.9 million, or 13.5 percent) signaled the public's rejection of the liberal domestic policies of presidents Kennedy and Johnson. Thereafter, "liberal" was a negative label that Democratic presidential candidates learned to shun. When in 1972 a gunman inflicted a paralyzing wound on Wallace (while he was campaigning in a Democratic presidential primary), his career as a national politician was over.

There have been three significant third-party movements in recent years. On the right, the **Libertarian Party** regularly runs candidates for president (and occasionally for other offices too) who advocate very conservative economic polices but also demand maximum personal freedom in such areas as drugs, guns, and gay rights. They usually get about 1 percent of the popular vote in presidential contests. On the left stands the **Green Party,** the

American version of an environmentalist party that is very important in Germany and other European countries. As we have noted, in 2000, the Greens' nominee, Ralph Nader, who got 3 percent of the nationwide popular vote, may have tipped the balance against Al Gore in several states, allowing George W. Bush to win in the electoral college. But by far the biggest vote-getter among recent American third parties has been the **Reform Party,** formed by H. Ross Perot.

In 1992, many Americans seemed unsure about the two major-party candidates: incumbent President George H. W. Bush and Governor Bill Clinton of Arkansas. Rumors began to spread of a third potential candidate, Texas billionaire H. Ross Perot. Excitement grew, and Perot soon announced that he would enter the race if volunteers would do the difficult job of getting his name on the ballot in all fifty states. This was soon done, and Perot entered the fray. Although polls showed the Texan doing well, and in fact leading the pack at points throughout the early summer, Perot withdrew his candidacy by August. Then, in another surprise move, he reentered the race in September. By then, Perot's popularity was waning and he was getting a reputation as something of a crank. Still, on election day he netted a huge 19 percent of the popular vote, which did not translate into a single electoral college vote. Most analysts agree that the Perot vote had little effect on the outcome of the race. But it certainly proved that an immensely wealthy amateur candidate could have a major impact on presidential election politics by lavishly financing his own campaign.

Perot's political star kept a bit of its luster after the 1992 election. He tried to mobilize the public against NAFTA, the free trade agreement with Mexico, but failed. He also decided to put his efforts into creating the Reform Party. Its platform focused on two issues: cleaning up the electoral system by removing big money from the process and cutting the soaring national deficit. Emphasizing these issues, Perot entered the 1996 presidential contest and of course received his own party's nomination. This time he got a still respectable 12 percent of the popular vote but, again, not a single electoral vote.

The Reform Party struggled after the 1996 election, due in large measure to the absorption of its issues by the two major parties—a common fate of third parties. In 1998, Jesse Ventura, a retired professional wrestler, shocked the political establishment

Green Party
party active since the 1980s that supports environmentalist issues and other progressive social measures.

Reform Party
party founded by Ross Perot in 1995 in the belief that Americans were disillusioned with the state of politics at the time.

discussionquestions

1. Why does American politics rest on a two-party model when most other democracies around the globe have multiparty systems?

2. Would our system be more democratic if additional parties competed for power? Is our system undemocratic because usually only two parties have a chance of victory?

by winning a run for governor of Minnesota as a Reform Party candidate, but he broke his ties with the party shortly thereafter and in the end left politics, bored and disillusioned. The Reform Party has since withered away.

MINOR PARTIES IN THE TWENTY-FIRST CENTURY

▶ **So will the major parties adopt some of the Libertarian or Green Party platforms to avoid losing voters to those groups?** Given the challenges that minor parties face in the American system as well as their limited success at the polls throughout our history, you might be tempted to conclude that they are a waste of time—that they play no role in changing the course of government. Nothing could be further from the truth. First, notice how minor parties have played a significant role in shaping public policy by drawing attention to particular issues and by threatening to drain support from the major parties. In fact, it has often been the initial success of minor parties that has led to their downfall: Once a new party dramatizes an issue and shows that there are votes at stake, one (or even both) of the major parties will pick up the issue, and the voters will fall back in line. The minor party falters, but the issue has new life and perhaps gets attended to. As noted by one observer, "Established parties rarely develop ideas or present new issues on their own."[31] The major parties are reinvigorated precisely because minor parties nip at the edges of the process.

Second, history shows that minor parties have played a significant role in bringing more citizens into the political process. Voters often begin to feel distrustful of the major parties—or at the very least not represented by them. They slowly withdraw, only to be drawn back into the process by the energy and excitement of minor-party activity. When minor parties are most active, the number of people heading to the polls increases.

Support for minor parties appears to be on the rise. Survey after survey suggests that Americans are ready for more alternatives on election day, and other data tell us that the number of minor party candidates is also on the rise. It might be some time before we move into a genuine multiparty system—for which many institutional adjustments would have to be made—but a shift does seem to be under way. Minor parties have always been

an avenue for change, and perhaps in the years ahead, they will prove to be an even more potent force in American politics.

practicequiz

1. How do single member districts discourage the continuation of minor parties?
   a. because such districts require a particularly high number of petitions for any third-party candidate to get on the ballot
   b. because such districts usually bar third-party candidates
   c. because parties whose candidates repeatedly place in second or third place (and therefore lose elections in such districts) usually dissolve from discouragement or combine forces to win—as one party
   d. because one of the two dominant parties usually adopts the policy position that spurred the third party into existence in the first place

2. What is the wasted-vote syndrome?
   a. voters' tendency to vote for candidates they know will lose—just to "send a message"
   b. voters' tendency not to vote for a minor-party candidate, even if they significantly prefer him or her, because they are sure that the candidate will not win
   c. legislators' tendency to vote for a measure they know will be defeated or vetoed—just to demonstrate their own commitment to a certain policy
   d. votes that, because of some technical malfunction, cannot be read and tabulated by election officials and so must be literally discarded

3. On what principle was the American Party founded?
   a. the desire to limit or curtail immigration and the presence of Catholics in positions of authority
   b. a return to the gold and silver standard for U.S. currency
   c. the desire to thwart monopolies and corporate corruption
   d. abolition

4. Which of the following third parties received the largest percentage of votes in a twentieth-century presidential election?
   a. Liberty   b. American
   c. Reform   d. Free Soil

Answers: 1-c, 2-b, 3-a, 4-c.

TABLE 15.2
Party Platforms in 2004

DEMOCRATIC	ISSUE	REPUBLICAN
Stem-cell research Right to Choose	Abortion	Adoption & Abstinence Human Life Amendment to Constitution
Cut deficit in half in 4 years Cut barriers to international Free Trade	Budget & Economy	
Reform USA Patriot Act Support Affirmative Action No Federal bans on marriage	Civil Rights	Enhance USA Patriot Act Ban on Gay Marriage Amendment to Constitution Support women in military
Crack down on gangs & drugs	Crime	Support death penalty
Fund No Child Left Behind Support Distance Learning Allow Charter Schools Disallow Vouchers	Education	Support school choice & home schools Support prayer in schools
Energy independence Develop renewable energy sources	Energy & Oil	No to Kyoto No on Carbon Emissions Controls
More conservation lands Promote healthy environment	Environment	Private property laws Market-based pollution reductions
Humanitarian leadership in Africa "One China" policy but support Taiwan Enhance Asian relations Improve US–Latin America relations Continue work with Russia End Castro Regime in Cuba	Foreign Policy	Fight WMD proliferations Spread democracy to other Middle East nations Help poor nations Make Iraq example of reform
Promote Line-item Veto Reform Voting system	Government Reform	Stop activist judges
Assault Weapons Ban	Gun Control	Open more land to hunting No gun licensing

This table outlines policy differences between the Democratic and Republican platforms, established at the 2004 presidential national conventions. In some areas there are significant differences, but in many the gap seems insignificant. On the whole, would you agree "There's not a dimes worth of difference between the parties?" If so, what would lead parties to agree on so many issues?

Political Parties and Ideology

When Alabama Governor George Wallace threw his hat into the ring for the presidency in 1968 as an American Independent, he summed up his rationale for not running as a Democrat—or as a Republican, for that matter: "There isn't a dime's worth of difference between the two parties." In other words, Wallace claimed that voters deserved a true choice, something not provided by the two major parties.

But is this true? Are the two major parties in the United State really two sides of the same coin? On one hand, there would seem to be a bit of truth to this contention, especially from a comparative perspective. Major political parties in America tend to be centrist, meaning that they adhere to policies at the middle of the

TABLE 15.2 (continued)
Party Platforms in 2004

DEMOCRATIC	ISSUE	REPUBLICAN
Expand coverage & cut costs	Healthcare	No euthanasia
		No cloning
		No stem-cell research
		Only ethical research
		Abstinence for AIDS
Reform Intelligence community	Homeland Security	Minimum safety requirements at chemical plants
Enhance border security		Increase bioterrorism budget
Challenges: War on Terror, WMD's, stable world		Enlarge Coast Guard
		Establish National Counterterrorism Center
		Increase funding for VA healthcare
		Improve living conditions for Armed Forces
Create means for undocumented aliens to earn citizenship	Immigration	No illegal immigration
		Tight border control
		Biometric tracking system for international travellers
Discourage outsourcing jobs	Jobs/Welfare	Move welfare receivers off rolls
Raise EITC	and Poverty	Faith-based welfare grants
Raise minimum wage to $7		
Cut taxes for middle class	Tax Reform	
Small Business Tax Credit		
End Corporate Welfare		
Promote scientific research	Technology	Support do-not-call and do-not-email lists
Reform highway & transportation policy		
Fight terrorism through education	War & Peace	Crack down on terrorism
Commit to Israel but support Palestinian state		
Secure peace in Iraq		
Internationalize Iraqi military		

SOURCE: *The Democratic Platform for America: Strong at Home, Respected in the World*, the Party Platform of the Democratic National Committee, approved July 2004. http://www.issues2000.org/Dem_Platform_2004.htm. Released 10 Jul 2004. Viewed 11 May 2006. 2004 Republican Party Platform: A Safer World and a More Hopeful America. http://www.issues2000.org/2004_GOP_Platform.htm Viewed 11 May 2006.

political spectrum and seek incremental change rather than sweeping reform (see Table 15.2). In most democracies, numerous parties are viable, each representing different points on the ideological spectrum. In the American setting, Republicans are thought to be "conservative" and Democrats "liberal." We covered this topic in greater detail in (L I N K) *Chapter 10, pages 385–387,* but we should reiterate here that in general, conserva-tives believe in the least possible government (except in national security matters) and in "traditional family values." They tend to favor, for instance, state over federal action, fiscal responsibility, limited government spending, following a supply-side economic strategy, restricting or outlawing abortion, ensuring more efficient crime control, eliminating gun control, defending traditional marriage structures, and cutting taxes.[32] Liberals, who sometimes

▶ **Do the parties soften**
their positions to try to
attract the large group
of "in-between" voters?

1. What forces likely push the two major parties in America toward the middle of the ideological spectrum?
2. Is our democracy well served by centrist political parties?

prefer to call themselves progressives, believe that government can be used to help cure some of society's ills—especially economic inequality. They back policies designed to ensure a healthy environment; are tolerant toward different lifestyle choices; want to protect women's reproductive rights; advocate wider access to health care, education, and housing; demand caution about using the military and want to cut military spending; hope to increase the minimum wage; and propose paying for all these "positive" government programs with higher taxes on the wealthiest Americans.

It is true that many of the most involved members of the two major parties in the United States, the party activists, are quite ideological. Most Republican activists are very conservative, and most Democratic activists are quite liberal. The problem with relying on this information to suggest that parties in America are ideological is the relatively small size of the activist wing in both parties. It is likely that they constitute less than 20 percent of the overall population. A solid majority of Americans are far less ideological. That is, they are much more centrist, as we noted in Chapter 10.

This does not mean that Wallace was right—that "there's not a dime's worth of difference" between the parties. Table 15.2 compares the platforms of the Democratic and Republican Parties at the time of the 2004 presidential elections.

▶ **Do the parties soften their positions to try to attract the large group of "in-between" voters?** Both major parties approve platforms at their presidential nominating conventions, held every four years. These statements do not formally bind the parties to any specific positions, nor do they require that every member of the party must hold the same outlook. But they do lay out in general terms the principles and policies that appeal to most members of the party. If you read the "planks"—the specific provisions—in the Democratic and Republican platforms over the years, you'll be struck by elements of consistency and difference. (For a complete list of the platforms for the two major parties since 1840, visit the American Presidency Project at http://www.presidency.ucsb.edu/platforms.php.) Both parties firmly endorse our approach to governance and our capitalist economic system, as well as the many elements of the democratic creed summarized in the Introduction to this book. But with regard to specific polices, the two parties differ dramatically, especially when it comes to such contemporary issues as reproductive rights, stem-cell research, gun control, private school vouchers, the legal rights of gay couples, and the war in Iraq.

So is there really a "dime's worth of difference between the parties"? The answer probably depends on your perspective. Visitors from other nations have a difficult time seeing big differences between the major American parties. Nor can hard-core activists in this nation at either end of the political spectrum. Many academics also complain of the centrist policies advanced by the two major parties.[33] But for average Americans, who themselves are rather centrist, these middle-of-the-road parties suit them very well. Most citizens do see differences between the parties. They see a big difference in policies when the Republicans control Congress or when the Democrats run city hall. And they tend to feel strongly about whatever they see.

1. Which of the following policy positions does **NOT** typically get advocated by current members of the Republican Party?
   a. cutting taxes
   b. state action over federal action
   c. more efficient crime control
   d. gun control

2. Which of the following policy positions does **NOT** typically get advocated by current members of the Democratic Party?
   a. using government to compensate for the consequences of economic inequality
   b. environmental-friendly legislation
   c. lowering taxes on the wealthiest Americans
   d. advocating wider access to health care

3. Experts estimate that true Democrats and Republicans constitute _____% of the population.
   a. 5%   b. 20%
   c. 30%   d. 70%

4. Why do visitors from other countries have a difficult time discerning genuine political differences between the Republican and Democratic parties?
   a. because of the centrist political tendencies in the American electorate and, thus, in our two major parties
   b. because people from other countries do not really understand how our electoral process works
   c. because, during most of the presidential election season (when foreigners are most interested in American politics) the two major parties appear quite similar; it's when the primaries are over that the differences emerge
   d. because what used to be the Republican Party's platform in the nineteenth century has become the Democrats', and vice versa

Answers: 1-d, 2-c, 3-b, 4-a.

► **What's the difference**
between an open primary
and a closed primary?

what YOU can do!
Where do you fall on the ideological spectrum? One way to find out
is to take a "political personality test." Visit Harvard University's Institute of
Politics Web page, and answer a series of questions to know more about
your political character. The site is located at **http://www.iop.harvard.edu/
research_political_personality_test.php**

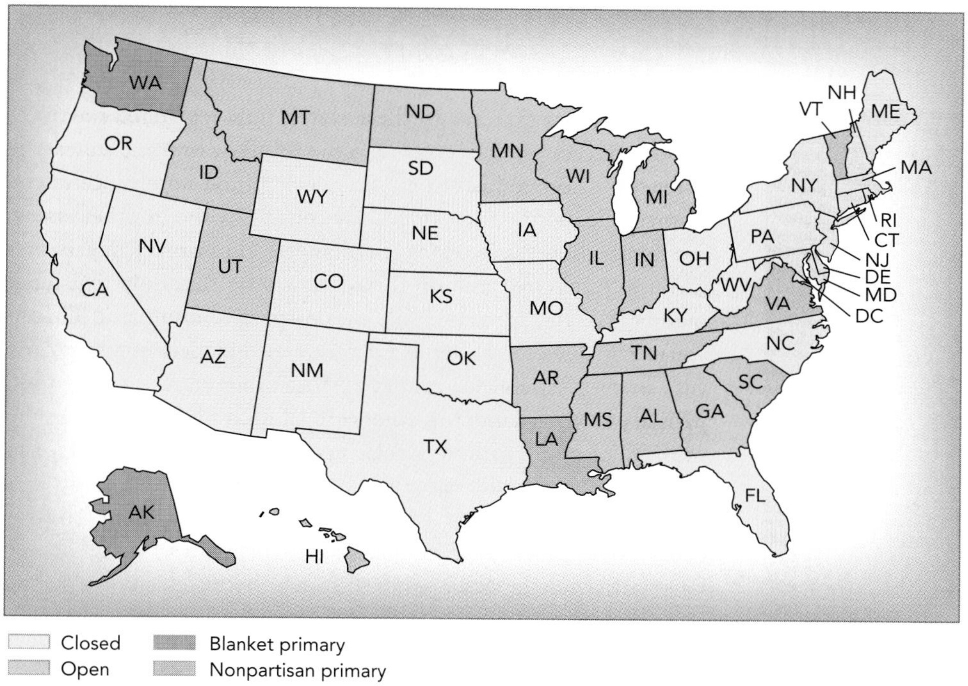

FIGURE 15.6
Primary Systems in the United States

As this figure suggests, the split between
open and closed primary states is about even.
But this does not mean that they are randomly
distributed across the United States. Can you
see any geographic patterns? If so, what might
explain the configuration?
SOURCE: www.csulb.edu

Closed   Blanket primary
Open   Nonpartisan primary

The Nomination Process

As you have seen in this chapter, political parties serve many functions. Here we'll outline one of the most important: the process of
choosing candidates to appear on the general-election ballot under
the party's banner—a procedure called nomination. The way the
major parties select (nominate) presidential candidates for the
general election has varied over time and is today one of the most
controversial aspects of elections.

For voters, nominations limit their choices on election day.
On the one hand, we might applaud this process, given that without nominations we might find dozens or even hundreds of candidates on each ballot. But on the other hand, perhaps voters want
more choices than they usually get, and the winnowing down by
the parties limits the types of candidates on the ballot. Write-in
candidates, allowed to run but without party backing, stand very
little chance of winning.

Even if we accept the usefulness of party nomination, how
might the parties go about this process? In the early years, a handful of party leaders did the choosing. The party was a private organization, they argued, and nominating was simply their own

business. At first few people objected; if the voters did not like the
candidates they chose, they could simply vote for someone else.

The nomination process changed during the Progressive era.
By controlling the choice of nominee, nineteenth-century party
bosses could limit voters' options, often shutting out reformers
who might otherwise be popular with the public. Reformers
could—and did—run without the blessing of a major party, often
as write-in candidates, but their chances of victory on election day
were almost nil. The solution for reformers was therefore to pass
laws mandating that the parties get widespread voter input in
selecting nominees. Today we call this process direct primary elections. Today, both major parties choose their candidates by letting
rank-and-file members (average citizens) vote.

We begin with a discussion of the primary system more generally but will quickly turn our attention to presidential nominations.

DIFFERENT PRIMARY SYSTEMS

► **What's the difference between an open primary and a
closed primary?** Not every state uses the same primary system
(see Figure 15.6). Roughly half the states have what is called a

▶ **What used to happen**
at the early conventions?

closed primary system
primary election process in which only registered members of the party are allowed to cast ballots. Roughly half the states use this system.

open primary system
primary election process in which voters are allowed to cast ballots in the primary election without declaring which party they are voting for.

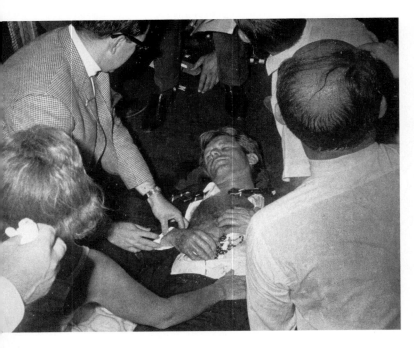

Many agree that 1968 was one of the most turbulent years in American history. Here Robert Kennedy lies dying after being shot on the evening of the California Democratic presidential primary, which he had won. Hubert Humphrey was later given the nomination, even though many "regulars" in the party wanted a true anti-Vietnam War candidate. Four years later, the party had transformed its nomination rules—leading to binding primaries and caucuses. But have these changes made the system truly more democratic?

closed primary system. In these states, only registered members of the party are allowed to vote in the primary. In some states, the voter must declare his or her party registration in advance of the primary election—often thirty days or so—while in other states, the registration can be done (or changed) on primary day. Either way, the states that rely on this system state that only registered members of the party can vote on prospective nominees. Thus if you're registered as a Democrat or are an independent, you can't vote in the Republican primary. Most other states use an **open primary system.** Under it, voters are allowed to participate in the primary election without declaring membership in a party. On primary day, the voter can choose to vote in the Republican primary or the Democratic primary, and no record is kept. (But of course, one cannot vote in both parties' primaries.) Some people have criticized the open primary system because activists in one party can vote for the *weaker* candidates in the other party's primary election. Others suggest that this sort of "strategic primary voting" is quite rare.

PRESIDENTIAL NOMINATIONS

Our political system began without political parties and amid great hopes that parties ("factions") would not arise. Thus the framers of the Constitution saw no reason to specify a procedure for nominating presidential candidates. They assumed that the local notables who would gather in each state to cast its electoral college votes would select the most qualified men they could think of. That was how George Washington was unanimously chosen as the first president. When the early party system of Democratic-Republicans and Federalists nevertheless emerged, each party's representatives in Congress named its presidential (and, beginning in 1804, its vice presidential) candidates. The caucus-based nomination system became so important in selecting the eventual president that it became known as King Caucus. But the Corrupt Bargain of 1824 suggested that the reign of King Caucus should end and that something less elitist—something that better reflected the will of average voters—should be substituted. The outcome was the **national nominating convention,** which was first used by the Anti-Masonic Party. The idea was that delegates should be sent from communities across the nation to discuss the strengths and weaknesses of potential

national nominating convention
a meeting of delegates from communities across the nation to discuss candidates' qualifications, choose their party's nominee, and adopt a party platform.

McGovern-Fraser Commission
a reform panel established in 1968 by the Democrats to make the presidential nomination process more democratic.

binding primaries
process established in most states whereby voters in primary elections choose delegates who have pledged their support to a particular presidential candidate. The delegates then vote for this candidate at the nominating convention.

nomination caucus
a meeting of party activists to choose delegates to support candidates at their party's presidential nominating convention.

candidates and thus produce the best choice. The convention would also be an opportunity to hammer together a party platform, as well as rules for conducting party business. It would be a gathering of local party representatives every four years. The major parties held their first national conventions in 1832 and have done so every four years since.

One of the sticking points in the convention system was how delegates would be chosen from their communities and what role they might play at the convention. A few states developed mechanisms to allow rank-and-file party members to select delegates, but most simply allowed state and local party bosses to handpick who went to the national convention. Once there, these delegates were obliged to follow the orders of their party leader. This often led to high drama at party conventions. Party bosses used their delegates as negotiating chips, looking to play a key role in nominating the candidate—for what could be better than to be perceived as the party's "kingmaker"?

▶ **What used to happen at the early conventions?** Conventions were about selecting the presidential nominee and about cutting deals in "smoke-filled rooms." There were florid speeches, tumultuous floor fights, protracted voting (the Democratic convention of 1924 took 103 ballots before nominating a colorless compromise candidate). This system lasted nearly 140 years, through the 1960s.

The strain between party bosses and average party followers came to a head in a fight over the 1968 Democratic presidential nomination. As 1968 began, everyone assumed that President Lyndon B. Johnson would accept his party's renomination. But there arose a groundswell of opposition to Johnson within the Democratic Party over his waging of the Vietnam War. When Johnson failed to win decisively in the March New Hampshire primary, he announced that he was withdrawing from the race. A sharp division emerged between the party leaders, who backed Vice President Hubert Humphrey, and the "antiwar Democrats," who supported either Minnesota Senator Eugene McCarthy (not to be confused with Senator Joseph McCarthy of Wisconsin, the anticommunist demagogue of the 1950s) and New York Senator Robert F. Kennedy (the late President John F. Kennedy's younger brother and his former attorney general). Kennedy gradually outpaced McCarthy in the primary elections, yet the party bosses continued to back Humphrey, who was staying out of the pri-

maries. (At that time, many states did not have presidential primaries.) Robert Kennedy's assassination in 1968 on the night he won the California primary created a crisis for the antiwar Democrats. Faithful to their bosses, the majority of delegates at the Democratic National Convention in Chicago nominated Humphrey, while thousands of antiwar young people filled the streets in protest outside the convention hall and were beaten and bloodied by Mayor Daley's police. Humphrey went on to lose the general election to Richard Nixon. The Democratic Party seemed in shambles.

After this disastrous election, Democrats established a reform panel, called the **McGovern-Fraser Commission,** after the men who chaired the group, Senator George McGovern of South Dakota and Congressman Donald Fraser of Minnesota. Their report, *Mandate for Reform,* forever changed the way presidential nominations would be conducted. It argued that the Democratic Party's nomination process must be "open, timely, and representative." A number of mechanisms were devised to achieve these goals, the most important pertaining to the process of selecting delegates. **Binding primaries** were established in most states. Similar to direct primaries, in binding primaries voters head to the polls to pick delegates who have pledged their support for a particular presidential candidate. The winners in each state are sent to the convention, where they vote to nominate that candidate. Another way to pick delegates, used in about fifteen states, is a **nomination caucus.** Here, rank-and-file party members attend a neighborhood meeting, share ideas and concerns about particular candidates, and cast a ballot for pledged delegates to attend a statewide meeting. There, the same process takes place, and the delegates who win at the state level go to the national party convention. The key difference between primaries and caucuses is that the former is an election and the latter a series of "town-hall-like" meetings. As for ensuring a "representative process," rules were installed to mandate specific proportions of women, minority, young, and old delegates. For example, 50 percent of each state's delegates must be women.

The Republican Party was not bound by the new Democratic Party rules. But as the notion of binding primaries and caucuses spread, they felt compelled to abandon the boss-centered model. Put a bit differently, as the Democrats moved to what was perceived to be a more open system, the older model lost legitimacy,

▶ **Didn't Howard Dean raise** a lot of support over the Internet in 2004?

invisible primary
raising money and attracting media attention early in the election process, usually before the primary election year.

and the Republicans were obliged to make similar changes. The GOP does not mandate certain quotas for demographic groups as the Democrats do, but they now rely on caucuses and primaries to nominate their candidates.

pathways of action
HOWARD DEAN'S INNOVATIVE INTERNET CAMPAIGN

▶ **Didn't Howard Dean raise a lot of support over the Internet in 2004?**

We live in an age when computers and the Internet are part of nearly every aspect of our lives. Recognizing this, Howard Dean, the former governor of Vermont, took things to a new level by using the Internet to raise funds, mobilize supporters, and get publicity in his bid for the Democratic Party's 2004 presidential nomination. First, Dean raised a whopping $14.8 million online in just two months. What was even more incredible was that most of this money came in small donations; the average donor gave just $77.[34] Second, Dean's campaign built a massive volunteer base by joining Meetup.com, a site designed to help would-be activists organize into a political or social group. By the middle of November 2003, Dean's Meetup.com team had more than 140,000 members.[35] Third, the campaign used another Web tool, blogs, to get feedback from his supporters. Because it can be difficult for people to be heard in the midst of a hectic campaign, Dean created a dialogue with constituents through online surveys, polls, and petitions. Commenting on his foray into the new world of Internet campaigning, Dean noted:

> The Internet community is wondering what its place in world of politics is. Along comes this campaign to take back the country for ordinary human beings, and the best way you can do this is through the Net. We listen. We pay attention. If I give a speech and the blog people don't like it, next time I change the speech.[36]

In the future, we are likely to see a whole new campaign style in which the Internet will be the central player. Dean was unsuccessful in his bid for the White House, but all observers seem to agree that he effectively revolutionized electoral politics. ◼

Howard Dean is credited as being one of the first candidates to capitalize on the power of the Internet. While he did not win the 2004 Democratic presidential nomination, he changed the nature of electoral politics. After the election he became the Chair of the Democratic National Committee. Do you think the Internet will continue to transform politics?

▶ **Does the new primary** system produce better candidates than the old party boss approach?

discussionquestions

1. What is the purpose behind primary elections?
2. What are some of the real downsides to the current process of nominating candidates to run for the presidency? What are some of the upsides?

A MORE DEMOCRATIC PROCESS?

The nomination reforms of the early 1970s dramatically transformed the way Americans select presidents. It is hard to overstate the importance of the shift from party boss to party voter control. Many have applauded the change; the process, they argue, better reflects the will of the electorate and is therefore more democratic. Perhaps more important, it is a process that most Americans believe is fair. It conveys legitimacy, which is essential for any political system. But critics point to a number of problems with the new process. For one, the nomination process may *not* reflect the will of the average party member, let alone the average American, because relatively few people participate in the primaries and caucuses—and the ones who do are much more ideological, more "extremist," than the typical citizen. Turnout in primaries is generally about 15 percent of eligible voters, and attendance at caucuses rarely gets beyond 5 percent. This might not be a problem if those who come out are more or less like everyone else. But they are not. Only the most committed—which usually means the most ideological—voters generally participate in primaries and caucuses.

A second broad area of concern relates to the host of issues that arise when candidates appeal directly to voters. Because candidates win or lose based on how citizens feel about them, the nomination process has become very expensive, time-consuming, and often negative. Candidates who can raise the most money—and raise it the fastest—have every advantage. This money can be used to attack the other candidates, who are all part of the same party. Some of the hardest attacks against presidential candidates come during the primaries, not the general election. The bitterness of the primaries leaves many Americans distrustful about the electoral process.

Those candidates who are able to grab media attention before and during the primary and caucus season do much better, which gives an unfair advantage to the best-known and best-funded candidates. Together, the ability to raise early money and to draw media attention has been called the **invisible primary.** The process is drawn out, but at the same time, it puts a premium on winning early primary and caucus contests—and winning there, of course, helps raise more money and draw more media hype. Many critics have argued that small and perhaps atypical New Hampshire and Iowa, which hold their events at the very start of the process, exert grossly disproportionate weight in selecting the eventual nominee.

▶ **Does the new primary system produce better candidates than the old party boss approach?** The current system gives every qualified citizen the opportunity to run for the presidency. Although this may sound like a good idea, critics suggest that some sort of screening mechanism should filter out unworthy candidates. It can be argued that in today's system, anyone with a huge bank account and a good team of campaign consultants can try to become president. And such a candidate can do quite well regardless of his or her knowledge, experience, background, or character. In the past, political bosses did the screening, and although they occasionally came up with some very bad choices (a few of whom got elected), they also managed to see winners in such men as Abraham Lincoln, Woodrow Wilson, Franklin Roosevelt, Dwight Eisenhower, and John Kennedy.

Should we bring back the bosses in smoke-filled rooms? Most people would balk at this, but at the same time they acknowledge that the pathway to the presidential nomination is rife with problems. Changes designed to make the system more open, timely, and representative have moved things in the right direction but have also created a new set of issues. We have to wonder, would some of our greatest presidents, all of them masters of back-room deal-cutting as well as inspiring public oratory—Lincoln, for example, with his odd appearance and his melancholic demeanor, or Franklin Roosevelt, wheelchair-bound at a time when people with disabilities were shunned—have gotten their party's nomination in today's process?

Finally, we might consider whether the new approach truly engages the interest of most Americans, especially young Americans. Old-time conventions were often flamboyant, dramatic events, full of unexpected twists that riveted the country's attention. There was much wheeling and dealing behind the scenes, but they were never like the totally scripted, made-for-media events that modern political conventions have become, which are now so boring and predicable that they get less airtime from the networks and attract fewer television viewers with each successive election. And the extreme importance of money and big media in the presidential nomination process virtually ensures that the nomination is going to be sewn up months before the convention even meets. The only suspense nowadays involves the nominee's choice of running mate. Perhaps this is yet another reason why voters are increasingly tuning out, as discussed in Ⓛ Ⓘ Ⓝ Ⓚ *Chapter 14, pages 562–568.*

practicequiz

1. In the first years of the country, a small group of congressional leaders nominated presidential candidates.
   a. true
   b. false

2. When did direct primary elections first get instituted?
   a. during the "Era of Good Feelings"
   b. after the "Corrupt Bargain" of 1824
   c. in the first election after the Civil War
   d. in the Progressive era

3. At national conventions, party bosses negotiated the presidential nomination (in "smoke-filled rooms") until what year?
   a. 1948
   b. 1960
   c. 1972
   d. 1980

4. What replaced national conventions as the actual mechanisms for establishing presidential nominees?
   a. binding primaries and nomination caucuses
   b. national primary elections
   c. indirect primaries
   d. national polls

Answers: 1-a, 2-d, 3-c, 4-a.

they will aid average citizens in their struggle to keep government responsive by using the elections pathway in the twenty-first century is, however, anyone's guess.

A related issue is what role political parties play in shaping public policy. Do parties help the average American use the elections pathways to mold the outcomes of the policy process? Or do parties perhaps get in the way, distorting the will of the people? Many of the functions discussed in this chapter imply that parties have made a big difference in the past—that they have been a key link in our democratic system. Yet a transformation is under way—a dramatic change in the party system. Local parties seem to be on the endangered species list, while state and national organizations, flush with cash, technology, and expertise, are filling the void. Many people applaud this "renewal," but it is also fair to ask whether the role of citizens will be enhanced or reduced in the years ahead. Historically, local party organizations have been the access point into the electoral process. If these structures disappear, will the elections pathways continue to be a viable route for change? And if so, for whom?

Conclusion

At the dawn of the American experiment, the founders assumed that any organization designed to capture control of government would be adverse to the public interest. But what these great men—and many others—failed to recognize is that political parties, or similar electoral organizations, are inevitable in a free society. Whether they emerge in response to a desire to change public policy or simply to grab control of the reins of office is unclear. What seems elementary, nevertheless, is that they will emerge. They can also enhance the democratic process: parties can educate voters, aggregate interests, check the ambitions and abuses of those in power, mobilize opposition, and, in short, turn private citizens into public actors. There is more to party politics than mere "partisan wrangling."

There is not a modern democracy that does not have political parties. A prominent political scientist is very emphatic: "It should be flatly stated that political parties created democracy and that modern democracy is unthinkable save in terms of political parties."[37] This might be an overstatement, but few people would dispute that parties have been and will continue to be an integral part of the election process for years to come. What these structures will look like, what they will seek to accomplish, and how

YOUR turn!

Many young Americans are frustrated by the current party system. But there is also a realization that the two major parties are not going anywhere and that party politics can prove a useful tool in changing the course of government. Indeed, recent data suggest that a growing number of young Americans are becoming involved in party activities. How about you—are you interested in becoming a party activist? If so, you might consider joining up with a local party committee. As we have seen, nearly every community in the United States has a local Democratic and Republican committee. Check the phone book or the Internet for contact information, and plan to attend a function. You might also consider joining a campus party organization. College Republicans and Young Democrats of America have chapters on most campuses. Find out when they meet, and get involved. If there is no party committee on your campus, why not start your own? Lots of help is available. For information on the College Republicans, visit **http://crnc.org**, and for material on the Young Democrats of America, go to **http://www.yda.org**. Many colleges and universities also have minor-party organizations, such as the Campus Greens (**http://www.campusgreens.org**). Opportunities abound, so why not roll up your sleeves and become a twenty-first-century party hack! ■

Chapter Review

1. Political parties differ from other political organizations in that they nominate candidates to run under their label, take positions on a range of issues, and are subject to state and local regulations.

2. Parties undertake a host of functions that aid the electoral system as a whole as well as individual voters.

3. There are three components to a political party. The *party-in-government* consists of the elected officials of the party, the *party-in-the-electorate* encompasses average citizens who identify with the party, and *party organizations* are the official apparatus of the party, such as the national and state committees.

4. Although party structures in government and party organizations seem to be growing, fewer Americans consider themselves partisan, and the number of independent voters is growing.

5. Local political party organizations have not experienced the revival that has occurred at the state and national levels.

6. Many forces push our system toward a two-party model. The most significant are institutional, such as single-member legislative districts and first-past-the-post elections.

7. Although minor-party candidates rarely win elections in America, they have played an important role in our political system. Minor parties often raise important issues that are later picked up by the one or both of the major parties.

8. Although the major parties in America find themselves under pressure to be ideologically centrist, most Americans see important differences between them.

9. Nominations are an important party function, and the direct primary has become a tool for concerned citizens to make a change from within their party.

10. Presidential nominations have changed a great deal over the past two hundred years. Originally, candidates were selected in caucuses of party leaders, then conventions did the nominating. Today, direct primaries and caucuses select delegates to attend a nominating convention. Many people are satisfied that the current process is open and fair, but others are quick to point out the numerous downsides, including the amount of time and money it takes to win a party's nomination.

11. Parties can be an important tool for average Americans interested in changing the course of government, but the transformation away from local party structures will likely have a profound impact on the party system.

CHAPTER REVIEW TEST

1. Political parties educate voters, aggregate interests, and help turn private citizens into public actors.
   a. true
   b. false

2. What would the framers of our Constitution have thought of the political successes of the Christian Coalition?
   a. They would have applauded it.
   b. They would have predicted its success—as spelled out in *The Federalist Papers*.
   c. They would have been outraged by its combination of religion and party politics.
   d. It is impossible to tell, since they never addressed the idea of political parties or religion in politics.

3. What strategic change in campaigning do both major parties often make when the election season shifts from the primaries to the general election?
   a. They use much more negative campaigning.
   b. They become less centrist in their appeals.
   c. They become more centrist in their appeals.
   d. They abandon negative campaigning.

4. In what year did the Christian Coalition cause an enormous change in American politics?
   a. 1968
   b. 1980
   c. 1994
   d. 2000

5. What phenomenon seems to be a key reason for the decline of the average citizen's participation in the election process?
   a. how unimportant the issues seem these days
   b. how uninspiring or incompetent most candidates seem to be these days
   c. the decline in the parties' attempts to communicate with average citizens
   d. the decline of local party organizations

6. Studies indicate that communities with vital political party operations
   a. have higher levels of voting
   b. have more negative campaigning
   c. have lower levels of voting
   d. are becoming more common

7. Members of the Washtenaw County Democratic Committee, in Ann Arbor, Michigan, are part of the:
   a. PIG.
   b. PO.
   c. PIE.
   d. SHMO.

8. In the United States legislators vote along party lines
   a. all of the time.
   b. almost all of the time.
   c. just a little more than half the time—party loyalty is not really expected.
   d. most of the time.

9. A somewhat formal hierarchy or "chain of command" exists among national, state, and local party committees, in descending order of authority.
   a. true
   b. false

10. Which political party dominated national politics in the early ninteenth century?
    a. The Federalist Party
    b. The Whig Party
    c. The Democratic-Republican Party
    d. The Liberty Party

11. What was one characteristic of Jacksonian Democracy?
    a. an anti-elite sentiment
    b. a dependence in campaigns on special interests
    c. low voter turnout
    d. a rejection of advertising presidential candidates in a certain image

12. What prompted the creation of the modern Republican Party in 1854?
    a. the Gold Rush
    b. slavery
    c. prohibition
    d. anti-immigration sentiment

13. In recent years, at the same time that party organizations are regaining their footing nationally, a growing number of Americans see parties as corrupt.
    a. true
    b. false

14. Regarding minor parties it's fair to say that
    a. they have all come and gone and made little difference in how electoral politics and governing have unfolded in this two-party country.
    b. there have been a handful of cases in which minor parties have triumphed, but these cases are the exception.
    c. they have all come and gone but a number of them have significantly affected the political landscape of their time.

d. in a few instances, minor parties have become major parties, evolving into the two parties that now dominate the political landscape.

15. Which of the following was **NOT** a third party in ninteenth-century America?
    a. the People's Party
    b. the Greenback Party
    c. the Free-Soil Party
    d. the Confederate Party

16. Among other causes, the Populist Party, and its 1896 presidential nominee, William Jennings Bryan, advocated
    a. the abolition of income tax.
    b. the institution of income tax.
    c. the deregulation of corporations.
    d. increased federal funding to urban centers.

17. Recent surveys indicate that Americans would view the emergence of a third party with:
    a. increasing skepticism.
    b. approval.
    c. disapproval.
    d. outrage.

18. How is an open primary different from a closed primary?
    a. In an open primary, voters from one party can vote in the primary election of the other party.
    b. In an open primary, candidates in one party can run in the primary election of the other party.
    c. In an open primary, voters from either party can cast one vote in *both* parties' primary elections.
    d. In an open primary, a third-party candidate can be on the ballot of either of the two main parties.

19. According to some, one problem with the voter-controlled primary system is that
    a. it has made the nomination a popularity contest.
    b. it has made the nomination process too short.
    c. it grants a disproportionate significance to voters and caucus members in two small regions, New Hampshire and Iowa.
    d. it has exaggerated candidates' need to appeal to big city voters.

20. Does the withering of local party organizations mean that the role of citizens in the electoral process has been reduced?
    a. Definitely so.
    b. Definitely not.
    c. There's a good chance it will be, but we don't know yet.
    d. It's unlikely, but it's too soon to tell.

DISCUSSION QUESTIONS

1. Name some key functions of political parties. Is democracy well served by these structures, or are they a hindrance?

2. What is the tripartite view of political parties? Has this model become outdated? Explain why or why not.

3. How did parties become such an important part of American politics, especially given the fear of parties on the part of framers of our system?

4. In which party period would you say the link between average citizens and government was closest?

5. Do you suspect that in the United States we are moving toward a viable multiparty system? If so, how soon do you suspect it will arrive?

6. What are some of the downsides to multiparty systems, especially given the structure of our system of governance, including the separation of powers?

7. Name some of the downsides to the current method of nominating candidates to run for the presidency. Evaluate whether these are really negatives.

8. Many people suggest that parties are inevitable in a democratic system and that they actually enhance the system. After having read this chapter, what is your take—are parties inescapable, and do they make things better?

INTERNET RESOURCES

Democratic National Committee: **http://www.democrats.org**

Republican National Committee: **http://www.rnc.org**

America First Party: **http://www.americafirstparty.org**

American Conservative Party: **http://dir.yahoo.com/Government/U_S_Government/Politics/Parties/American_Conservative_Party**

American Reform Party: **http://www.americanreform.org**

Centrist Party: **http://centrist.meetup.com**

Communist Party USA: **http://www.cpusa.org**

Confederate Party of America: **http://www.confederateparty.org**

Constitution Party: **http://www.constitutionparty.com**

Constitutionalist Party: **http://home.earthlink.net/~jmarkels/cp.html**

Creator's Rights Party: **http://www.christiangallery.com/creator.html**

Democratic Party: **http://www.democrats.org**

Green Party of North America: **http://www.greens.org/na.html**

Jeffersonian Party: **http://www.jeffersonianparty.com**

Labor Party: **http://www.thelaborparty.org**

Libertarian Party: **http://www.lp.org**

Natural Law Party: **http://www.natural-law.org**

New Party: **http://www.newparty.org**

New Union Party: **http://www1.minn.net/~nup**

Pot Party 2002: **http://www.pot-party.com**

Reform Party: **http://www.reformparty.org/cgi-bin/hcgmain.cgi**

Republican Party: **http://www.rnc.org**

Social Democrats: **http://www.socialdemocrats.org**

Socialist Labor Party of America: **http://www.slp.org**

Socialist Party USA: **http://sp-usa.org**

States Taxpayers Party: **http://www.ustaxpayers.org/do/Home**

Timesizing Party of Massachusetts: **http://www.timesizing.com**

United States Independent American Party: **http://www.usiap.org**

Workers Party USA: **http://www.workersparty.org**

Workers World Party: **http://www.workers.org**

Working Families Party: **http://www.workingfamiliesparty.org**

Young Democratic Socialists: **http://www.ydsusa.org**

National Election Studies: **http://www.umich.edu/~nes/nesguide/nesguide.htm**

Ballot Access News: **http://www.mega.nu:8080/revolution/by_name/B/BAN.html**

ADDITIONAL READING

Bibby, John F., and L. Sandy Maisel. *Two Parties or More? The American Party System* (2d ed.). Boulder, CO: Westview Press, 2003.

Reichley, A. James. *The Life of the Parties: A History of American Political Parties.* Lanham, MD: Rowman & Littlefield, 2000.

Riordon, William L. *Plunkett of Tammany Hall.* New York: Signet, 1995.

White, John K., and Daniel M. Shea. *New Party Politics: From Jefferson and Hamilton to the Information Age* (2d ed.). Belmont, CA: Wadsworth, 2004.

KEY TERMS

Heading back to school from City Hall, a student holds a sign out of the school bus window March 27, 2006 as part of an organized protest of the immigration reform bill being considered by Congress that spring. The United States is a nation of immigrants, but the rapid pace of change in recent years—due to the burgeoning number of residents of Hispanic descent—has caught many off guard and has shaken the political landscape. Most agree that the immigration issue will become even more contentious in the years ahead.

CHAPTER 16

PUBLIC POLICY IN THE UNITED STATES

Hooters and Polluters: The Politics of Public Policy In the fall of 2003, President Bush asked for congressional action on the nation's energy policy, and the U.S. House of Representatives responded by introducing a bill that provided tax incentives for companies involved in energy production, conservation incentives for consumers, and changes in energy regulation. The bill was controversial because it contained what some people saw as unwise rollbacks of federal regulations on the energy industry that could potentially damage air and water quality. Environmentalists and their champions in the House—mostly Democrats—blasted the bill as a gift to the energy industry and a threat to the environment.[1]

One other small detail caught the attention of Congress watchers. Some members of the House had inserted language into the bill that would allow localities to issue tax-free bonds to fund

A sign warns of chemical danger July 11, 2001 in a former junkyard where General Electric Company had been dumping PCB-filled capacitors for decades in Queensbury, New York. General Electric is also fighting efforts by the federal government to dredge areas of the Hudson River to rid it of PCB contamination in the riverbed silt.

local development projects. One of the businesses that stood to benefit from this part of the bill was Hooters, a chain of eateries in which minimally dressed young women wait on customers. Democrats and their allies jumped at this poetic opportunity to claim that the bill was a legislative giveaway to "Hooters and polluters."

There were other controversial aspects to the bill. For one, Bush was the top recipient of campaign contributions in the 2000 presidential election from the oil and gas, electric utility, coal, and nuclear power industries. In the 2000 election, oil and gas industries (and their executives) gave over $35 million to federal office candidates, of which nearly 80 percent was given to Republicans. Many saw this bill as payback for this support.

Vice President Dick Cheney was clearly close to the oil and gas industry, given that he was the Chief Executive Officer of Halliburton Energy Services from 1995 to 2000. Halliburton is a multinational corporation with operations in over 120 countries. Cheney also directed what was called the Energy Task Force, a group of representatives of the energy industry pulled together to create policy recommendations for the new administration. Needless to say, critics argued that this was improper—not unlike asking a fox to watch the chicken coop.

Because the Senate did not pass the version of the bill containing the "Hooters" provision, this legislative effort never became law. However, the attempt gave many people, inside and

outside of government, the feeling that the nation's policies were at the mercy of special interests who used their influence—in the form of campaign contributions and other possible rewards—to get more than their fair share.

This cynicism has more than a grain of truth in it. But just how does our government make policy? So far, you have learned how a bill becomes a law (in Chapter 7) and how the laws get administered (in Chapter 9), but public policy is more than simply passing and enforcing laws. As the political scientist Harold Lasswell noted, politics is the study of who gets what, when, and how.[2] If we apply this deceptively simple formula of questions to public policy, a rich picture emerges of a complex government with many sources of influence over what it does and does not do.

In essence, public policy is the action or inaction of the government on a problem or issue of concern to the public. However, this definition does not accurately show the complexity of the concept. Who, for example, gets to determine whether something really is a problem and not just an unfortunate circumstance? Decades ago, PCBs, chemicals used to cool electrical transformers, were routinely dumped into New York's Hudson River by General Electric Corporation, a global manufacturer of everything from light bulbs to jet engines. When PCBs were linked to cancer in humans, GE spent large amounts of money for a media campaign claiming that it was safer to leave the chemicals at the bottom of the river than to try to remove them. In response, many people who lived near the river notified the Environmental Protection Agency (EPA), the federal agency charged with carrying out environmental policy, that they were opposed to dredging the PCB-laced sediment from the river bottom. Although members of New York's congressional delegation also doubted the need for dredging, the EPA did not agree, and the dredging continues to move forward.[3] ■

▶ **What's the difference**
between *politics* and *policy?*

policy process model
a way of thinking about how policy is
made in terms of steps in a progression.

freedom
a core value, usually expressed as either
"freedom from" (positive) or "freedom
to" (negative).

The very existence of a problem often creates a highly
charged political atmosphere even before discussion of
potential solutions. Take global warming, for example.
Opponents have had many heated debates over whether the earth
is really heating up and what role, if any, human activity may play
in this process. The Bush administration has gone to great lengths
to argue that global climate change, the administration's preferred
term for global warming, is not the result of what we humans do
or do not do here on earth. Each part of the process of policy formation has the potential to be influenced by and, in turn, to influence the multiple pathways we have discussed throughout this
text. Think about public policy as what comes after the equal sign
in a mathematical equation. The structure of the government plus
the political process form the elements on the left side of the equation. The sum of these interactions equals the policies that affect
each citizen. Any change caused by the effects of the policies (the
right side of the equation) influences the structure of the government and the political process (the left side of the equation), and
vice versa.

You probably see the point by now: Public policy is more than
just a law, the action of an agency, or a court decision. For a complete understanding of public policy, you must know why these
tangible outputs of government exist in the first place and anticipate how they may change in the future.

Key Questions

1. How is it possible to see public policy as both an outcome of
    governmental action (or inaction) and a political process?

2. Are some parts of the policy process more easily influenced by
    one pathway, or are all of the parts equally open to influence by
    all the pathways?

3. How do liberals and conservatives differ in their views of what
    government ought to do in setting public policy?

4. How do political considerations shape how people identify
    problems?

5. Which types of problems are likely to stay on the decision-making
    agenda? Which types are likely to fall off? Explain the difference.

6. How has the modern presidency transformed the policymaking
    process in Washington, D.C.?

7. What are the advantages and disadvantages of incremental
    policymaking?

The Nature of Public Policy

▶ **What's the difference between *politics* and *policy?***
Politicians, members of the media, and everyday citizens often
draw a distinction between politics and policy. This difference

rests on the notion that politics is like a game or even a war, in
which strategies are used to gain advantages over opponents and
win battles. (The very word *campaign* is borrowed from the vocabulary of warfare.)

Policy is the output of politics and, to some people, not political in itself. You may have heard commentators praising presidential debates as a time for "setting politics aside," forcing the
candidates to deal with *policy* issues. But this common notion of
an either-or relationship is an artificial way of thinking about these
two concepts.

As defined, public policy is what you get after the equal sign
in the equation of politics plus government. Elections, social movements, interest group activity, and the actions of political institutions such as Congress or the federal courts all go into the equation
before this equal sign. Using this metaphor, public policy is inherently political. It reflects the exercise of power in our system of government, our economic system, and our society in general.

Very often, however, social scientists and other policy specialists think about public policy as a collection of phases in a
process, as though the intricacies of the process were somehow
disconnected from the political world. There is a well-worn
approach to the study of the process of policy formation, usually
called the **policy process model,** which begins with the identification of a problem and concludes with the analysis of the effectiveness of the solutions applied to that problem.[4] This model
forms the core of this chapter, but we will also help you see the
pathways that connect politics with public policy and the effect of
these variables on the public as well as other segments of our society and political world.

As you read this chapter, keep in mind that theories about
policy and the process of public policymaking are not just abstract
stabs at ideas motivated by academic curiosity. Rather, the need to
theorize comes from the desire to make sense of what seems, at
first, like a tangled mess of motivations, actors, and actions.

Ideas and Values in Public Policy

The policy process model describes policymaking in five or six
steps: identifying the policy problem, setting an agenda, formulating a solution, legitimizing the solution, implementing the solution, and (in some versions) evaluating the solution. Deborah
Stone is one of several political scientists trying to get us to think
beyond the limits of the policy process model. In Stone's view, the
policy process model lacks connections to the ways that real people and their governments make decisions about policy. She uses
slightly different terms to describe a major shortcoming of this
model, but her point is clear:

▶ So what went wrong
in the policy process?

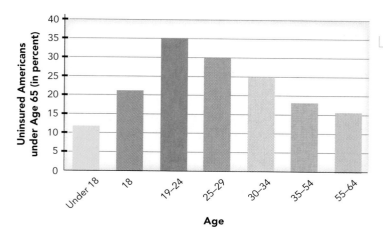

FIGURE 16.1

Uninsured Americans under Age 65

Does the percentage of uninsured Americans surprise you? Why is the highest percentage indicated for the 19 to 24 age group? How would you resolve this dilemma?

SOURCE: Jeffrey A. Rhoades. *The Uninsured in America, 2004: Estimates for the U.S. Civilian Noninstitutionalized Population under 65*, Agency for Healthcare Research and Quality, http://www.meps.ahrq.gov/papers/st83/stat83.pdf, June 2005.

The production [process] model fails to capture what I see as the essence of policy making in political communities: the struggle over ideas. Ideas are a medium of exchange and a mode of influence even more powerful than money and votes and guns . . . . Ideas are at the center of all political conflict. Policy making, in turn, is a constant struggle over the criteria for classification, the boundaries of categories, and the definition of ideals that guide the way people behave.[5]

For Stone, the heart of policymaking is how people interpret values such as equity, efficiency, security, and liberty and how they use these values in the identification of problems and possible solutions. For example, most people would agree that equality is a highly desirable goal for our society. Should we therefore guarantee an equal level of health care for all citizens? Or should the government simply offer the *opportunity* for health care through policies that help businesses hire more workers, who might then receive some health care coverage through their employers? Our answers to such questions reflect our preferences about the role of government in our lives. They also reflect the influence exerted on us by the government, the media, and other organized interests.

In the early 1990s, debate about health care coverage for the roughly 40 million Americans who lacked insurance (today's numbers are even higher; see Figure 16.1) took center stage. President Clinton presented a plan to provide health care coverage that mobilized both supporting and opposing forces. Some critics charged that the bill was done in by an oppressive and misleading lobbying campaign, led by the nation's health care and health insurance industries. The lobbying campaign featured TV ads voicing opposition to an overly complex policy that would ultimately hurt the average health care consumer and urging people to

contact their government representatives. The ads worked wonderfully, and public support for Clinton's plan slipped drastically. Opinion polls taken at the time still showed strong support for the basic idea of insuring those who lacked coverage, but the Clinton plan was dead in the water.[6] Ultimately, Clinton's health care policy proposal died at the congressional committee stage.

▶ **So what went wrong in the policy process?** This issue is difficult to fit into the policy process model. Using this model, we might say that the president put health care onto the nation's agenda but that it then failed to move successfully through the other phases of the process. This is a fairly accurate statement, but it tells us very little about the pathways of politics or what actually happened along the way. This is where ideas about how people view what's good and desirable in government and politics become important.

Let's look at two terms that are often found at the bull's-eye of debates about public policy: **freedom** versus equality. Consider this familiar portion of the Declaration of Independence: "We hold these truths to be self-evident, that all men are created equal, that they are endowed by their Creator with certain unalienable Rights, that among these are Life, Liberty and the pursuit of Happiness." This often-cited excerpt is the profession of a set of values that, presumably, makes us one people sharing core beliefs in equality and liberty. There is some truth in this statement: Not many people in this country would openly denounce the ideas of freedom or equality.

These two values frame many of the policies proposed by our representatives or by those seeking governmental action. For example, President George W. Bush signed a bill into law that made it harder for people to declare bankruptcy and thus avoid repaying their debts. He praised the policy as an opportunity for lower-income Americans to get access to loans and other credit, indicating

what YOU can do!

The terms *liberal* and *conservative* are sometimes a bit difficult to use when describing how a person looks at politics, government, and policy. Challenge a few friends to answer the questions "What does freedom mean to you?" and "What does equality mean to you?" Discuss how the values of freedom and equality match up with liberal and conservative ideologies and see whether your friends agree with the liberal or conservative labels attached to their answers.

Economic freedom index

The index of economic freedom is based on 21 criteria, including freedom of personal choice, protection of private property and freedom of exchange.

Political freedom ratings

- Free
- Partially free
- Not free

The top-ranked countries:	Index number	Quality of life rank
1. Hong Kong	9.4	24
2. Singapore	9.3	22
3. New Zealand	8.9	18
4. Britain	8.8	10
5. United States	8.7	3
6. Australia	8.5	7
7. Ireland	8.5	20
8. Switzerland	8.5	12
9. Luxembourg	8.4	17
10. Netherlands	8.4	8
11. Argentina	8.3	39
12. Bolivia	8.3	112
13. Canada	8.2	1
14. Finland	8.1	13

0 1 2 3 4 5 6 7 8 9 10

Other selected countries:	Index number	Quality of life rank
20. Japan	7.9	4
62. Mexico	6.5	50
72. Indonesia	6.2	105
81. China	5.8	98
92. India	5.3	132
Some of the lowest-ranked countries:		
110. Rwanda	4.4	164
114. Gabon	4.3	124
114. Syria	4.3	111
117. Russia	3.9	71
118. Romania	3.8	68
119. Sierra Leone	3.5	174
121. Congo	3.0	141
122. Algeria	2.6	109
123. Myanmar	1.9	128

0 1 2 3 4 5 6 7 8 9 10

FIGURE 16.2
Freedom and Prosperity

Political freedom rankings are based on *Freedom House's* Freedom in the World survey, which provides an annual evaluation of political rights and civil liberties. Quality of life ranking is based on the Human Development Index, which ranks nations based on criteria including health, life expectancy, education and economic data. For economic ranking, best score is high (10); for quality of life ranking, best score is low (1). Political freedom is indicated by color.

Source: Cato Institute, Freedom House, U.N. Development Program.

that banks and lenders would approve more loans because of the decreased possibility of failure to repay them. In other words, the president was praising the new policy as a way to equalize access to credit for all citizens. Critics of the bill charged that this change in the law would increase profits and reduce risks for the already powerful banks and other financial institutions by decreasing the freedom of those not in power, the down-on-their-luck defaulters, to get out of paying back what they owed. *Both* the president and his opponents spoke the language of freedom and equality.

Think about how the word *freedom* is used. President Bush used it twenty-seven times in his second inaugural address—in connection with proposals as different as his vision for a free Iraq and a plan he called the "ownership society," which would give each U.S. citizen more control over his or her personal finances

and economic future. (It probably doesn't come as a surprise to you that "economic freedom" is a core value in our system. Figure 16.2 underscores this fact.) Bush zeroed in on reform of the nation's Social Security system as the centerpiece for domestic policy in his second term in office. Social Security is the most important strand in the so-called safety net—created in the 1930s by FDR's New Deal and extended in the 1960s by LBJ's Great Society—which protects workers in their retirement years. Bush proposed that workers divert some of their Social Security taxes, which currently pay benefits to existing retirees, into individual investment accounts. Those accounts would earn or lose money like other private investments, such as stocks. According to the president, this change in policy would give workers the freedom to exercise more control over their finances in preparation for retirement.

Not everyone agrees with the president's use of the terms *equality* and *freedom* in conjunction with bankruptcy reform and the "ownership society." Critics of the bankruptcy bill said that ensuring equal access to credit is not really an issue, since banks are happy to give credit even to people with poor financial histories so that the banks can make money on late fees, high credit card interest rates, and other penalties that snare people who become financially overextended. (Watch out—young people are especially vulnerable to these traps!) These critics charge that the real purpose of the new law is to bar debtors from seeking bankruptcy so

U.S. President George W. Bush speaks with retiree Helen Lyons about Social Security reform in Shreveport, Louisiana, March 11, 2005. Under Bush's proposed reforms, which were representative of negative freedom, younger workers would shift part of their payroll taxes into private stock and bond accounts.

that creditors can keep making profits from them.[7] Bush's detractors see the "ownership society" not as an advancement of personal freedom but as a way for the government to decrease its responsibilities to honest, hardworking citizens who have contributed to Social Security and count on it to ensure a comfortable retirement.

So who is right? How can people on one side see an advancement of equality or freedom when those on the other view the same actions as a retreat from these cherished values? One persuasive answer is that each side defines *freedom* and *equality* in different ways. A number of political thinkers have pondered this solution, and their ideas have much to say about the nature of public policy.

FREEDOM

In the "land of the free," we assume that we share the same meaning of liberty or freedom. If this is true, we should pursue policies that promote freedom, right? However, freedom is a complex idea, and not everyone defines it in the same way. Is freedom the ability to think, travel, and speak freely and to associate with whomever you want? Or is it the limitation of other people's meddling in your life? Of course, you can only think, travel, speak, and associate to the degree that you are limited by other people and outside forces. However, as Americans, we tend to group ourselves into two camps. Some say that freedom exists to the extent that we can do what we wish; others see freedom only in the absence of someone or some force limiting what we can do. The British political theorist Sir Isaiah Berlin called the first version *positive* liberty or freedom because people tend to express it as the ability to do something. Berlin labeled the second version *negative* liberty or freedom because the measure of freedom, usually expressed as the freedom from some outside force, is based on how few limits there are on its enjoyment.[8]

These two versions of freedom are connected closely to people's views of the role of government. If freedom is measured and defined by what you can do (positive freedom), whatever helps you extend this enjoyment of liberty must be a good thing. Students in a public university or college may see that government can create opportunities for a high-quality education that would otherwise not be available to them. Students in both private and public colleges and universities can experience the extension of freedom through the federal and some state governments' student loan programs, such as Pell Grants. Without this support, your freedom to learn and gain an advantage in the competition for good jobs and careers would be decreased. From this viewpoint, government creates freedom by expanding opportunity. However, a reasonable person could look at the same example and make the case that to provide a lower-cost, high-quality education to a wider segment of the population at a public college or university, the public must pay higher taxes. This person might view these increased taxes as an intrusion into his or her private life and a limitation on the freedom to use the money as he or she sees fit. If we look at it this way, government activity such as sponsorship of grants, loans, and funding of public colleges and universities causes a loss of personal freedom.

Let's revisit the example of President Bush's "ownership society." The president stresses individual freedom in a way that touches largely on negative freedom, increasing personal freedom by limiting government action. If the federal government controls the Social Security taxes used to fund the benefit system, this limits your enjoyment of personal freedom. A policy that frees up your earnings by diverting them away from the existing Social Security program and allowing you to choose how to invest that money creates more freedom for you.

People who see freedom in its positive form would likely take the perspective that the federal government's Social Security program does something that private accounts may not be able to do: provide retirement benefits that are resistant, if not immune, to the ups and downs of the financial markets. In this way, government lifts the burden of worry about the performance of stocks and other investments, freeing individuals to concentrate on other matters, which may include additional ways to save and invest for retirement.

EQUALITY

Like freedom, equality is highly valued by Americans. And like freedom, equality is divisible into two meanings that have powerful effects on public policy. The ideas of Alexis de Tocqueville, the French aristocrat and political thinker who traveled through the United States in the 1830s to study our version of democracy,

▶ What about the other pathways, do they affect policy too?

classical liberalism
a political philosophy based on the desire for limited government.

conservatism
a modern update of classical liberalism.

modern liberalism
a political philosophy based on a belief in the beneficial nature of the power of government.

progressivism
a political philosophy based on the belief that government is the best actor to solve social, economic, and political problems.

persist today. He argued that Americans often hold conflicting interpretations of equality, especially if it means political equality or something broader, such as social or economic equality.[9] Later political thinkers have elaborated on Tocqueville's insights by asserting that there are two forms of this value, one based on the *equality of process* and the other based on the *equality of outcomes*.[10]

Deborah Stone illustrates the difference between these two concepts by asking us to do a mental exercise: dividing a cake among a group of people. How, she asks, might we go about this task in a way that would ensure equality? One sure way to do this would be to do what happens at most birthday parties: You count the number of people who want cake and then divide the whole cake by that number. What matters here is that the final result is fair, as measured by who gets what. But there's an equally logical way to approach divvying up the cake that reflects another way of thinking about equality. What if the cake were placed in the center of a room and all who wanted some sat in a circle at an equal distance from it? Now everyone has an equal opportunity to get what they want—a messy proposition, especially if you're talking about kids, especially if some want more than others. And of course, some may be faster or more ruthless in their pursuit of the cake. (Think again of the kids.) It's safe to assume that some party guests will get more cake than others. Stone calls the opportunity-based version of equality the *equality of process*.[11] But is this equality? If it is, it's not the same kind of equality as an equal division based on the number who say that they want cake would be.

The cake example is likely to stick in your mind because of the absurdity of the exercise. We can easily imagine the slapstick results of an all-out mad dash for cake at a child's birthday party. But what if the desired object is not cake but health care, a well-paying job, or a sound education? Should we strive for the equality of outcomes and redistribute those outcomes from the haves to the have-nots? Or should we seek out and support solutions that provide opportunities to equalize competition? The answers to these questions rest on your view of equality. As with the concept of freedom, this view is closely connected to how you perceive the role of government. If you champion equality of outcomes, you will likely see the need for government action to create equal outcomes, because you see human beings as generally self-interested and unwilling to share their resources. Our nation's founders stated this eloquently in their writings, notably *Federalist No. 10*. Ⓛ Ⓘ Ⓝ Ⓚ *Appendix 3*. People who believe that equality prevails

TABLE 16.1
Summarizing Notions of "Freedom" and "Equality"

	POSITIVE FREEDOM ("FREEDOM TO . . .")	NEGATIVE FREEDOM ("FREEDOM FROM . . .")
Equality of Process	Mixed ideology	Conservative ideology
Equality of Outcomes	Liberal ideology	Mixed ideology

when the rules of the game are fair and open for participation (the equality of process) will view active governmental involvement less favorably: To them, government's role should be limited to setting and enforcing basic standards of fair play and access.

POLITICAL IDEOLOGY

These ideas about freedom and equality may sound more familiar when they are linked to political ideology. Table 16.1 shows that the ideas of someone who holds the *process* view of equality and the *negative* view of freedom have a strong resemblance to **classical liberalism,** an ideology of the eighteenth and nineteenth centuries that today we call **conservatism.** In many ways, modern conservatism is a view of politics built on faith in the free market to regulate the economics of a society; modern conservatives see government's main role as setting basic policies to see that people have equal *opportunities*, but government's activity must stop there so that it does not limit personal liberty. In opposition to this present-day conservative ideology stands **modern liberalism,** or what is now often called **progressivism.** Liberals or progressives, who tend to favor equal *outcomes* and share faith in the *positive* version of freedom, favor a more activist government. They see government as a powerful force needed to overcome inequality and expand the amount of freedom available to all citizens.[12] Of course, these are models of pure ideologies, and most Americans have more mixed ideological orientations. Some analysts argue that the pragmatism of America's political culture comes from a mainstream, blended ideology that uses its views of these key values in different ways in different situations.

Rachel Carson working with a microscope at home. She was a committed policy entrepreneur whose actions directly impacted government regulations on air and water quality and the creation of the Federal EPA.

The underlying beliefs that shape what people want and expect from public policy have clear links to the five pathways of political action. Both liberals and conservatives can and do use any of the pathways to influence the making of public policy. Elections influence public policy indirectly: We assume, for example, that if we elect different representatives to Congress, they will approach what needs to be done in new ways because of their different skills, talents, and views. The idea of elections in a democracy is to have choices among different approaches to governing and policy. Courts can also be a means for citizens and other political actors to influence public policy. As we saw in ⓁⒾⓃⓀ *Chapters 13, pages 520–521* the landmark 1954 *Brown* case, which declared legally mandated public school segregation unconstitutional, marked a sharp turn along the path of the nation's race relations policies.

▶ **What about the other pathways, do they affect policy too?** The grassroots mobilization and cultural change pathways are other avenues along which citizens can make their mark on government actions. The social movements of the 1960s and 1970s fundamentally changed major policy areas in this country. In ways both large and small, these citizen actions resulted in concrete policy changes and in changes in the attitudes of the public. For example, in the 1970s, the environmentalist movement scored major legislative victories with the passage of laws such as the Clean Air Act and the Clean Water Act. This movement also helped mold the mind-set of today's more ecologically aware public, which takes for granted the recycling of glass and plastic bottles and many other formerly discarded items. (Once upon a time, not long ago, everyone automatically threw away aluminum cans, glass bottles, newspapers, and cardboard as trash, buried in the massive landfills we live with today. The changes we have seen since that time are a powerful use of the cultural change pathway.)

The most potent pathway for influencing public policy involves lobbying decision makers. The public often thinks of lobbying as negative because it implies that a "special interest" is using undue influence to get more than its "fair share." When people disagree with the goals of someone lobbying the government for a favored policy, the person or group doing the lobbying usually gets labeled as a "special interest," complete with all the negative connotations that come with that phrase. But when people agree with or share the goals of those doing the lobbying, "special interest"

takes on a more positive meaning. Ultimately, the lobbying pathway is a major thoroughfare available to everyone, and we will return to this pathway later in the chapter.

pathways profile

RACHEL CARSON

Rachel Carson (1907–1964) was notable for many reasons. She was a woman who became a leading voice in the male-dominated scientific community of the 1950s and 1960s and won renown as the author of *Silent Spring,* a 1962 book laying out the science behind species destruction that became a best-seller among the general public. She was also a highly articulate and committed policy entrepreneur whose actions had a direct role in the founding of the modern environmental movement, in formulating major parts of government policy regulating air and water quality, and in the creation of the federal Environmental Protection Agency (EPA).

A marine biologist, Carson first achieved public recognition with her beautifully written book on the ocean and sea life, *The Sea Around Us,* published in 1951. In the late 1950s, she became aware of the deaths of large populations of songbirds and began researching possible causes. At the time, the federal government regulated pesticides and other potentially hazardous chemicals only casually, and pesticides were often misused and overused. Carson's findings pointed out that one chemical in particular, DDT, a highly effective pesticide and disinfecting agent, was responsible for a sizable decline in the songbird population. She argued that if the use of DDT continued to be unregulated, it would cause a massive decrease in, or even the extinction of, many bird species. The consequence would be unthinkable—a springtime without the sound of bird songs. When the nation's chemical companies, determined to head off federal regulation, attacked her findings and tried to discredit her ideas, Carson fought back. Shortly before her death in 1964, she testified before Congress as an expert on the effects of regulatory policy on the environment.

distribution
government providing things of value to specific groups.

regulation
government prohibiting or requiring certain actions of organizations and businesses.

redistribution
government providing a broad segment of the society with something of value.

discussionquestions

1. How do equality of process and equality of outcome differ? How are they similar?

2. What is the difference between positive freedom and negative freedom? How are they related to the opposing ideologies of modern conservatism and modern liberalism?

Rachel Carson's ability to shape public opinion and to mobilize legislative and administrative action make her a prime example of someone who mastered key aspects of the pathways of political action. ■

practicequiz

1. For the political scientist Deborah Stone, the key to how public policy is formed is
   a. the sequence that begins with political actors identifying a problem and ends with the implementation and assessment of a solution.
   b. how people interpret principles such as liberty, equality, and efficiency.
   c. who has political power and what their relation to the perceived problem is.
   d. when, in a policy process cycle, political actors converge to address the perceived problem.

2. Why is the policy process model an incomplete description of the Clinton administration's attempt at health care policy in the early 1990s?
   a. It does not account for the complications created by an array of political actors who assume different ideas about what is good and desirable in government.
   b. It does not account for the formulation of public policy and Congress's large role in that part of the process.
   c. It does not account for the implementation and assessment of public policy and the Executive branch's large role in that part of the process.
   d. It does not account for the huge number of Americans who are uninsured.

3. Recall two opposing views of publicly-funded higher education: that the taxes needed to support it are an unfair intrusion on taxpayers; and that such taxes are worth it since state schools greatly broaden citizens' access to higher education and its rewards. What do these views illustrate?
   a. Democratic and Republican ideology, respectively
   b. the conflict between private and public views of freedom
   c. the conflict between positive and negative views of freedom
   d. the conflict between short-term and long-term views of freedom

4. Classical liberalism is roughly synonymous with what we call conservative ideology.
   a. true   b. false

Answers: 1-b, 2-a, 3-c, 4-a.

Types of Public Policy

So far, we've discussed public policy as a process that is influenced by many factors, especially the basic underlying beliefs people hold about politics and government. We've also seen where each of the five pathways can lead in both the substance and the process of public policy. Moving beyond these rather theoretical and somewhat philosophical ideas, how can we study public policy in order to compare one policy choice with another in a meaningful way? How can we find better solutions to ongoing problems?

For answers, we can look at all the attempts to solve problems in a particular issue area, a broad category, such as the environment, which contains the problems of preserving old-growth forests and of reducing air pollution. Organizing policies by issue areas helps us make sense of the broad contours of both the problems and their possible solutions. But it is a rather blunt instrument for studying existing policies and figuring out how to devise new ones.

A more sophisticated approach to studying public policy involves creating categories that classify what policies do and how they do it. To do this, political scientists break down the basic functions of government into **distribution, regulation,** and **redistribution.**[13] A government *distributes* a society's resources, such as wealth, services, or other things of value, when it gives benefits to specific groups in that society. (When undertaken by a legislature, such distribution is often given the negative label "pork barrel" spending, since it seems designed to bring credit to the congressperson who proposed it.)

Regulation takes place when a government uses legislative, military, or judicial power to stop an action by a person, organization, or group or when it mandates other behaviors or actions. For example, because of the actions of citizens like Rachel Carson, today's energy producers must meet federal regulations designed to limit air pollution. If an electric plant does not meet these requirements, its owners can be fined or punished in other ways.

Redistribution resembles distribution in many ways, but instead of a specific group benefiting from the actions of government, a much larger segment of society receives goods or services. Of course, redistributive policies mean that resources are taken from one part of society and given to another. An example of a redistributive policy is taxing workers to fund social welfare programs for the poor. Because

what **YOU** can do!

Are you interested in becoming involved in the policy process but feel that it's for "someone else" to do? The Study Circle Movement in the United States and other nations is an effort to get everyday people involved in understanding a wide range of policy issues, from racism to foreign policy, and to use their brain power to formulate solutions.

Government is often necessary to carry out policy, but citizen study circles can be a way for you to learn more and influence the policymaking process in a unique way. For more information, visit **http://www.studycircles. org/pages/who.html**

Water and ice being distributed in Saucier, Mississippi following Hurricane Katrina in 2005. Do you think tangible benefits are the responsibility of federal, state or local government? Why?

redistributive policies usually pit one social class against another, they are generally the most difficult policies to enact and implement.

Because all government policies can be placed in one of these three categories, this approach allows us to see the way governments operate and, with a bit more thought, how each of the pathways of political action can influence each of these government functions.

Categorizing policies by the nature of their benefits is also useful. Policies themselves can either produce tangible benefits for the public or merely symbolic benefits.[14] A tangible benefit, like the federal government's policy of assistance for victims of hurricanes and other natural disasters, is something that the recipients will experience in a material way—say, truckloads of clean drinking water and dry ice to preserve food. A symbolic benefit does not offer concrete, material results; it provides a theoretical solution to a problem. For example, the independent commission that investigated the intelligence failures leading up to the 9/11 terrorist attacks could not directly change the U.S. government's antiterrorism policy, nor could it restore life to the almost 3,000 people who perished in the attacks, and a number of its suggestions have not been adopted by the federal government. Still, the actions of the commission did communicate to the public that the government was working to solve this very difficult problem. The benefit—the feeling of security we may get from knowing that intelligent and dedicated people are trying to make us safer—may not help put food on the table, but it is still a benefit.

4. A proposed Constitutional Amendment outlawing the burning of the American flag means to grant what sort of benefit to U.S. citizens?
   a. patriotic   **b.** tangible
   c. symbolic   **d.** incremental

Answers: 1-d, 2-b, 3-a, 4-c.

practicequiz

1. What's an example of an issue area?
   a. gun control
   b. wetlands conservation
   c. the minimum wage
   d. civil rights

2. Studying issue areas is a particularly sophisticated way to learn how current policies came into existence and how future ones can be enacted, too.
   a. true   **b.** false

3. A transportation bill that appropriates millions of dollars to build a bridge in Alaska is an example of what kind of policy?
   a. distributive   **b.** regulatory
   c. redistributive   **d.** deregulatory

The Public Policy Process

Much of what we know about public policy and how it is made can be related to the policy process model, which we discussed earlier in the chapter. Like all models, it is a generalization—a simplified representation of reality. It must exclude some complexities in order to make a very intricate process easier to understand.

As mentioned earlier, although scholars in the field of public policy disagree over some details, the major parts of the policy process model are generally thought to consist of the following

Problem Identification
Publicize a problem and demand government action.

PARTICIPANTS
Media
Interest Groups
Citizen Initiatives
Public Opinion

Agenda Setting
Decide what issues will be resolved and what matters government will address.

PARTICIPANTS
Elites
President
Congress

Policy Formulation
Develop policy proposals to resolve issues and ameliorate problems.

PARTICIPANTS
Think Tanks
Presidents and Executive Office
Congressional Committees
Interest Groups

Policy Legitimation
Select a proposal, generate political support for it, enact it into law, and rule on its Constitutionality.

PARTICIPANTS
Interest Groups
President
Congress
Courts

Policy Implementation
Organize departments and agencies, provide payments or services, and levy taxes.

PARTICIPANTS
President and White House
Executive Departments and Agencies

Policy Evaluation
Report outputs of government programs, evaluate policy impact on target and non-target groups, and propose changes and "reforms."

PARTICIPANTS
Executive Departments and Agencies
Congressional Oversight Committees
Mass Media
Think Tanks
Interest Groups

▶ **Is it the group** that shouts the loudest that gets its way?

steps (see Figure 16.3): identifying the problem, setting an agenda, formulating policy, legitimizing policy, and implementing policy. (Some versions of this model also include evaluating policy—analyzing how well a policy works to solve the problem it was intended to solve. Other versions of the model omit policy evaluation, regarding it as an administrative or academic pursuit and therefore too disconnected from politics to have a place in the model.)

Process implies separate actions that lead to a final goal. The process of making dinner might consist of peeling and chopping vegetables and slicing meat for a main course and then cooking the raw ingredients so that they come together in a way that produces a pleasing meal. The order of the steps is important in cooking, and doing things out of order may produce disastrous results. The process model offers a recipe for creating public policy. This analogy between cooking and policymaking is faulty, however, because in many cases, the steps in the process do not directly flow one from the other. (Because of this, we can say that the policy process model is not truly *linear*, with all parts flowing in one direction. Nor is it truly *cyclical*, with each part necessarily following from the preceding part.) Imagine, for example, a chef cooking the vegetables for a stew and then peeling them. In the policy process, such disjunctures are not necessarily the disasters they are in the kitchen; they may not be the best way to make policy, but what the policy process model does well is to tell us how policy was made—well, poorly, or indifferently. The fact that making public policy is a highly political endeavor—open to and resulting from the activity of political actors moving along the pathways of politics—helps explain why the model does not always reveal a nice, neat set of predictable steps. Political actors can affect the process at every stage, and sometimes they cause an unexpected progression of phases or the elimination of phases. This is a point worth keeping in mind as you read about each of the five major parts of the policy process model.

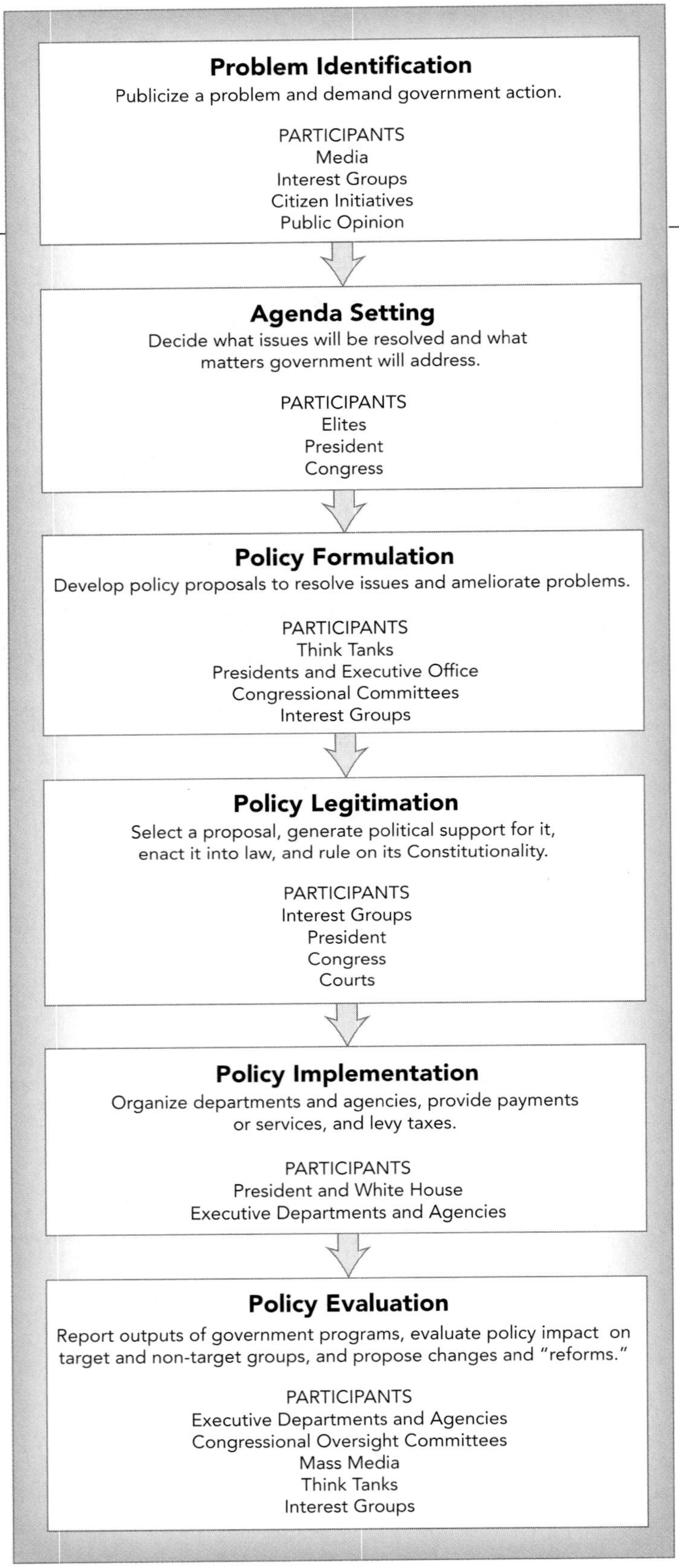

FIGURE 16.3
The Policy Making Process

pluralists
people who believe that power is widely distributed in a society.

focusing events
moments that capture attention and high-light the existence of a problem.

trigger mechanism
the means, often tied to focusing events, to push a recognized problem further along in the policy cycle.

IDENTIFYING THE PROBLEM

Let's go back to the story at the beginning of the chapter about General Electric and the contamination of the Hudson River with PCBs. In response to the Environmental Protection Agency's plan to dredge the river bottom to remove the cancer-causing PCBs from the river, two opposing camps sprang up. GE, some local governments, and citizens living along the river did not want dredging. This camp believed GE's position: that the river was cleaning itself and that dredging would increase the presence of PCBs in the water. These people did not doubt the presence of PCBs in the river; after all, GE itself had documented their presence. Nor were there many who argued about the cancer-causing potential of PCBs. But rather than seeing a problem requiring action, this camp saw a circumstance in which inaction was the best choice.

In the opposite camp were people who saw the presence of PCBs as a problem that needed to be acted on. Think about the dilemma that this situation poses for a government official in charge. Do you side with the local governments, with a huge multinational corporation that employs thousands of people in the area of the contaminated river, and with the residents who live along its banks and see only a condition or a circumstance, not a problem? Or do you side with the residents, local governments, and environmental interest groups that are equally adamant that a problem exists, requiring action for resolution?

▶ **Is it the group that shouts the loudest that gets its way?** There is no easy answer, which is true of many of the issues that confront policymakers. Scholars of public policy have supplied few guidelines for identifying problems. Whether an issue is a problem depends for the most part on who is advocating each position. Well-organized groups with the resources of money, larger memberships, and connections are more likely to gain access to decision makers to persuade them to see things their way. Disorganized collections of people, even those representing very large segments of the population, may not sway decision makers simply because their message is not as well focused. There's a major debate within the social sciences about this question: Whom do the policymakers listen to? Social scientists calling themselves **pluralists** argue that our system of open government, with its multiple points of access to policymakers, allows people without resources like money and connections to still have their voices heard.[15] Others argue that policymaking is really driven by elitism—that only people with power and money will get access to the decision makers.[16]

President Reagan signs legislation that forced states to either impose a 21-year-old drinking age or lose federal aid. Why do you agree or disagree with this legislation?

Without a doubt, some problems simply cry out for action. Terrorism on American soil crystallized in an unforgettable display of violence and brutality on September 11, 2001. Such events, including many of far lower magnitude, are known as **focusing events** because they bring a problem to the attention of both the public and policymakers. At least at first, there is no debate about the existence of a problem, and the event serves as a **trigger mechanism**—a means of propelling an established problem on to the next stage of the policy process, setting an agenda.[17]

pathways of action
MOTHERS AGAINST DRUNK DRIVING

Two mothers whose children had been killed by drunk drivers came together in 1980 to form an organization that would change public policy and alter the ways in which Americans view

▶ **Are some of these pathways** more effective at changing policy than others?

institutional agenda
the set of problems that governmental decision makers are actively working to solve.

issue-attention cycle
the pattern of certain problems' quickly garnering attention but then failing to remain in the spotlight.

themselves and their fellow citizens. In 1980, Candace Lightner and Cindi Lamb cofounded Mothers Against Drunk Driving (MADD) in Sacramento, California, and encouraged others to form chapters of the group in other states. Soon the organization was flourishing throughout the country. The group had a major early success when it raised public awareness about pending federal legislation to increase the drinking age to 21 in all states. Television movies were made about the start of the organization. Its founders were interviewed by news organizations, and it became a well-known player in the policymaking world. MADD now has chapters in all fifty states and credits in part the policies it has promoted for the drop in alcohol-related deaths and injuries on the nation's highways. ∎

SETTING AN AGENDA

At some point in your life, you have probably attended at least one meeting of a school club, a town planning board, or some other formal gathering. To make good use of time and to provide structure, well-organized meetings are always planned around an *agenda,* a list of issues and ideas up for discussion or actions to be undertaken. Of course, this is probably old news to you. But what you may not have thought about is the power available to the individuals who set the agenda. Many groups and organizations use rules that exclude or severely limit any action on—or even discussion of—items not listed on the agenda. The ability to exclude an item from the agenda, for whatever reason, is a powerful way to control what government does.[18]

Let's take an example from American politics. In the 1950s and 1960s, one of the Senate's most powerful members, Georgia's Richard Russell, was instrumental in keeping civil rights policy off the nation's agenda by declaring that there was no problem with racial segregation because segregation worked![19]

The process of crafting a solution even to shockingly obvious problems, such as the racial segregation of the 1950s, cannot begin until formal decision makers, generally those who hold positions of governmental authority, actually place the problem on the nation's formal or **institutional agenda.**[20] For example, the flood of legislation introduced in Congress after 9/11 gave tangible proof that our national legislators now believed the problem of terrorism to be urgent enough to require an immediate solution. There had been terrorism on U.S. soil before 9/11. The underground parking garage of the World Trade Center had been bombed in 1993 (luckily with little loss of life). Yet awareness and concern do not always transport a problem onto the institutional agenda. Often a focusing event is needed to provide this push. Think of the issue of global warming today. Many scientists and

citizens are deeply concerned about it, yet no focusing event seems to have occurred—so far. (Although it's too early to know for sure, some suspect that Al Gore's book and movie, *An Inconvenient Truth,* may prove to be a focusing event.)

Citizens' actions can also propel problems onto the formal agenda. In ⓛⓘⓝⓚ *Chapter 6, pages 228–235* we traced some of the actions of the people involved in the struggle over civil rights in the 1950s and 1960s. Their efforts forced decision makers to face the problems associated with our racially segregated society.

Like problem identification, in the absence of a major crisis, agenda setting is largely determined by the organization and resources of individuals and coordinated interests. People and groups who can best articulate their position or who have what it takes to gain access to policymakers (such as money for reelection campaigns, the support of group members, or well-connected lobbyists) will usually succeed in getting their problem on the agenda.

Once a problem is on the agenda, how do you keep it there? There is no guarantee that policymakers will consistently treat an issue as a high priority, year in and year out. Anthony Downs has created a valuable way of thinking about the nature of agenda items that he calls the **issue-attention cycle.**[21] Downs argues that some issues are more likely to remain on the formal agenda, just as others are doomed to fade away. Even issues that affect small slices of the population, that lack political, economic, or social clout, or that are difficult to address may first grab lots of attention. But they usually fall off the agenda because of the cost and inconvenience associated with solving them or the inability of the affected parties to keep the decision makers' attention. For example, a series of highly publicized events in the 1960s, including a badly polluted river actually catching fire, propelled the state of our environment onto the nation's policy agenda. Although pollution and other environmental issues have not completely disappeared from that agenda, they got bumped down the list of priorities once people learned of the difficulties associated with the proposed solutions to the overconsumption of fossil fuels—such as giving up their big gas-guzzling cars. Downs's thoughts about agenda setting remind us that multiple pathways shape this and all phases of the policy process.

FORMULATING AND LEGITIMIZING POLICY

Clearly, many actors both inside and outside government can affect the agenda-setting process. But once a problem makes it onto the agenda, the political pathways haven't reached their end. In fact, the next phase of the policymaking process, formulation, is as politically driven as agenda setting—if not more so.

| **laws** rules created or recognized by government. | **decisions** court rulings that interpret the meaning of policy. | **rule-making authority** lawmaking power delegated to executive branch agencies or departments. |

Formulating policy means crafting solutions to identified problems. Of course, how you define the problem will frame the acceptable solutions. Was the terrorist attack on 9/11 a crime against U.S. citizens and property, or was it an act of war? If your answer, like that of the Bush administration, is "war," then legal actions (such as capturing those who planned and funded the attacks, trying them in court, and possibly sentencing them to death) won't do. If your answer is "crime," the solution is simply to track down the "bad guys" and bring them to justice.

Solutions can come in many forms. Clearly, the **laws** passed by legislatures, like those passed by Congress, are attempts to solve problems. (The legislative process itself, including the introduction of bills, hearings, and floor debates, are all parts of formulating public policy: At each of these stages, the solution can change and evolve.) When presidents issue executive orders directing the federal government to do—or to stop doing—various things, they are also engaging in problem solving.

For example, after George W. Bush was sworn in as president in 2001, one of his first executive orders cut off federal funding to organizations that work overseas to promote family planning, including abortion services (thereby reversing many policies that the U.S. government had been following during the Clinton administration). The **decisions** made by courts, especially the U.S. Supreme Court, are policies, since other branches of government and the nation's citizens are bound by these decisions as though they were laws passed by Congress. When Congress passes legislation that delegates congressional lawmaking authority for specific problem-solving purposes, the actions of the federal government's departments and agencies are also considered laws. Such **rule-making authority** allows a department or an agency to pass rules and regulations that affect a wide range of our lives, such as imposing standards on the food we eat and the cars we drive. Because thorny problems often require highly skilled and specialized officials to design exceedingly technical solutions—and sometimes because Congress may want to simply pass off a tough, politically charged problem to someone else—the delegation of rule-making authority has become a fact of modern policymaking life.

▶ **Are some of these pathways more effective at changing policy than others?** In today's federal government, each access point—Congress, the president, the Supreme Court, and the federal bureaucracy—is connected to us by one or more of the pathways of political action. Not all pathways offer an equally open journey to one of these centers of policy formulation. Of the four access points, Congress is the most accessible. Elections can change congressional membership. Lobbying, along with interest group and social movement activism, can influence the nature of solutions. Congress, and

Senator Richard P. Russell (left) and Senator Lister Hill in discussion with southern senators prior to the filibuster fight to exclude civil rights policy from agenda.

ABOVE: **U.S. President George W. Bush** (left) shakes hands with former President Bill Clinton after Bush was sworn in as the forty-third president of the United States, January 20, 2001. Bush would soon issue an executive order to eliminate federal funding to organizations that supported family planning and abortion, undoing many of Clinton's policies.

BELOW: **President Franklin D. Roosevelt** broke the voluntary two-term limit by winning a third term in 1940, and then election to a fourth term in 1944. However, he died in 1945, just a few months into that term. Could presidents be more effective in shaping public policy if there were no limits on how many terms they could serve in office?

lame duck
an elected official in the final months or years of his or her term of office, often assumed to be a position of weakened power.

in particular the House of Representatives, "the people's house," was designed by the founders to be the most open of the policymaking institutions of the federal government. This may still be true today. (However, the fact that dislodging incumbents from their seats is now very difficult has, in many critics' eyes, made the House more immune to pressure from dissatisfied constituents.) Although most of the opportunities for policymaking (and the greatest opportunity for citizen influence) still lie with Congress, the presidency and the federal courts have grown in power in ways far beyond what our country's founders imagined.

The power of the presidency to not only formulate policy by executive order but also to shape the policymaking by Congress deserves special attention. Routinely, modern presidents have been able to influence policy formulation by exercising a set of informal powers that have grown since the administration of Franklin D. Roosevelt. As you saw in (L)(I)(N)(K) *Chapter 8, page 316*, the opportunities for going public, meaning to speak directly to the American people and ask them to pressure their own members of Congress, has given presidents of the twentieth and twenty-first centuries the power to augment the actions of Congress in both agenda setting and policymaking.[22]

Although the presidency is receptive to each of the pathways of political action, it is still not as responsive to our needs as Congress because of the structure of the office and other institutional factors. Presidents serve longer terms than members of the House of Representatives, but they are limited to two full four-year terms in office. Although prospects for reelection do not worry a second-term president, presidential power usually erodes rapidly once Congress and the public begin to regard a second-term occupant of the Oval Office as a **lame duck** (someone who can't do much because everyone is waiting for the next president to take office).

Originally, the Constitution placed no restriction on the number of terms a president could serve. But beginning with George Washington, presidents voluntarily observed a two-term limit. (Theodore Roosevelt tried but failed to win a third term in 1912.) Democratic President Franklin Roosevelt broke the tradition by winning a third term in 1940, on the eve of U.S. involvement in World War II, and while the war was still raging, he was elected to a fourth term in 1944, though he died in 1945, just a few months into that term. In 1951, the Republican-dominated Congress reacted to FDR's success by passing the Twenty-Second Amendment, mandating the two-term limit, and the states quickly ratified it. Ironically, the amendment would bar the popular Republican Presidents Eisenhower and Reagan from running for third terms to which they probably would have been elected. The two-term limit may also have contributed to the perception of second-term presidents as lame ducks.

coercion
using force or punishment to make someone do something the person does not want to do.

The power of the presidency has been increased by another aspect of the Constitution: the winner-take-all setup of the electoral college. This means that presidential candidates can essentially ignore large segments of the nation and still win election. The restrictions of the electoral pathway on presidential power are, oddly enough, related to the limitations created by the existence of other pathways. For example, the pathways that can powerfully stir public opinion—mass political action and cultural change—are most likely to limit presidents to solutions that are more or less in step with the wishes of the nation and Congress. Because modern presidents owe much of their leadership powers to their abilities to gain and retain the public's support, these pathways do check the power of presidents in formulating public policy.

A government's policymaking actions can confer legitimacy on the policies it makes. Legitimacy implies fairness; formal rules and the ability to see the process in action help ensure fairness. When legitimacy is established, people are willing to accept policies, even if they dislike them. Legitimacy is different from **coercion,** which is the threat or actual use of force or punishment to secure compliance with a policy. The most vivid example of such coercion in American history was the action of President Lincoln and Congress in raising armies to crush the South's attempted secession. The seceding states in the South had viewed Lincoln's election, by northern votes alone, as illegitimate. Massive coercion is necessary to obtain compliance with policies that are widely seen as illegitimate, but policies viewed by the public as being fair generally require very little, if any, such action. The fair and open nature of the policymaking process helps ensure that solutions are not favoring one part of society as a payoff or a special favor. If Congress did all its work behind closed doors or if the process by which the Supreme Court renders decisions were to change from case to case, we might justifiably wonder about the legitimacy of the decisions made by these institutions.

Florence Owens Thompson, a poverty-stricken migrant mother with three children, gazes off into the distance during the Great Depression of the 1930s. The Aid to Families with Dependent Children (AFDC) originated in 1935 as an effort to defeat childhood poverty. What would American society be like if the government had no programs aimed at alleviating poverty?

pathways past and present

THE WELFARE DEBATE

The Great Depression of the 1930s, a stunning economic collapse throughout the industrialized world, sent U.S. unemployment rates as high as 25 percent. (For African Americans, unemployment sometimes hit 50 percent during this era.) Associated with this bleak picture was a sharp rise in childhood poverty, especially in families that lacked a father. Congress created a federal program called *Aid to Families with Dependent Children* (AFDC) and included it in the Social Security Act of 1935. The

▶ **So who checks to**
see that laws are well
written and carried out?

discretion
the power to apply policy in ways that fit
particular circumstances.

AFDC program allowed states to participate in a system of assistance to needy children on a voluntary basis. The federal government reimbursed each state for a portion of the money it spent on the program. Later, the federal government mandated that each state participate in the program and that adults, as well as dependent children, be eligible for benefits.

Originally, AFDC was described as an emergency response to the Great Depression. But except for wartime measures, few "temporary" government programs ever get phased out. In its first decades, AFDC and its revisions did much to achieve the original program's major goal of curtailing childhood poverty. But by the 1960s, critics were charging that AFDC was part of a failing national welfare policy. According to these critics, AFDC now served so many people beyond its intended target of poor, fatherless children that it had created a "culture of poverty." They argued that when children grow up in an environment dominated by government assistance rather than employment, they become adults who continue to depend on such assistance. Indeed, by the late twentieth century, four or more generations of parents and children owed their economic survival to welfare. Critics also pointed out that the federal government had too much control over matters such as eligibility for the program and level of benefits. For these critics, the states were better positioned to know what their citizens required, and they could be more inventive about lowering the costs of administering the program.

The congressional elections of 1994 swept the Republican Party back into power in both houses of Congress for the first time in forty years. Part of the Republicans' victory rested on a promise of fundamental change to the nation's welfare system. The supposed failure of the welfare system in the United States served as a shorthand means of attacking the performance of the Democrats, who were responsible for the system's creation and growth. Bills were introduced to undo much of what had been in place since AFDC's formation. A coalition including the Catholic church, the National Council of Churches, and antihunger and antipoverty groups formed to oppose these changes.

As the 1996 election approached, President Bill Clinton, possibly seeing an advantage in co-opting a powerful Republican issue, decided to support calls for welfare reform. In August 1996, he signed the Personal Responsibility and Work Opportunity Reconciliation Act (PRWORA), more commonly known as "welfare reform."

As a result, AFDC is now history. A new program has been created, called Temporary Assistance for Needy Families (TANF). The new program gives states a far greater degree of control over social welfare policy. TANF's advocates hoped to "end welfare as

we know it." The benefit of this reform to the poor is still not clear, but the process of welfare reform illustrates the effectiveness of the pathways of political action. ▪

As noted in the introduction to this chapter, citizens' ability to affect the formulation of policy is also crucial to the legitimacy and stability of any system of government. Openness and rules may be meaningless if the public does not believe that it can influence the solutions that are being crafted to solve problems. If the public beats its fists on the doors of the Congress, lobbying and mobilizing grassroots public relations campaigns, only to have the House and Senate ignore these concerns, the final result will likely be a law that is mocked as illegitimate. This is why most policymakers take great pains to follow the rules of their institutions and, where practical, make room for public involvement. Back in the late seventeenth century, the great political thinker John Locke, who had great influence on the framers of our Constitution, argued that the people enter into a contract with government by giving their consent to be governed. Locke's argument is still valid: On that consent rests our belief in the legitimacy of the entire process of governing, including the formulation of policy.

IMPLEMENTING POLICY

Once policies have been created, someone has to actually do something with them. As its name implies, the executive branch of government is charged with executing or implementing the policies made by a legislature, the courts, or the executive branch itself—as you saw in our earlier discussion of executive orders issued by presidents and rules crafted by departments and agencies. The founders divided up the functions of government in order to lessen the chance that it might take away the people's liberty. The result is that policy implementation is largely done by the executive branch. However, the other two branches also influence how the policies they make are carried out. Add to this the openness of the government to citizen activity, and a picture emerges of implementation as a highly political process.

This may seem like simple common sense, but for a long time, political scientists and other scholars of public policy did not see the links between politics and implementation. In fact, one branch of political science focuses on *public administration* as distinct from *public policy*. This view of a policy-administration divide may have been based on a desire to separate the executers of policy from outside pressure, so that good policy would not be subverted by biased implementation. This sounds like a reasonable goal, and if we take this idea to a more everyday level, its worth becomes even more apparent.

Many of us, driving above the speed limit, have passed a police officer and yet received no ticket. Clearly the law, a policy setting a maximum speed limit, was broken. What explains the lack of a ticket in this case is the **discretion** given to the individuals who implement policy. Perhaps going a few miles over the speed limit is acceptable for that stretch of road at that time of the day with that level of traffic and that weather. A change in one of these circumstances might mean getting a ticket. Since formulating a law for each stretch of highway, while factoring in things such as road conditions and weather, would be nearly impossible, legislatures often write laws with the presumption that the executive branch will use reasonable discretion in applying them. The key word in this presumption is *reasonable*. What if a police officer pulled over all drivers exceeding the speed limit by *any* amount, but only if they sported a "Bush-Cheney" bumper sticker? Or what if this officer gave speeding tickets only to African Americans? We would, rightfully, argue that this kind of law enforcement was unjust and an unreasonable exercise of discretion. These are dramatic examples of prejudice (which, unfortunately, sometimes do occur), but there are other, more subtle ways in which discretion is used that are out of step with the intent of policy and demonstrate the political aspect of implementation. Knowing this, legislators must be especially attuned to the implementation process.

Since all democratic legislatures, including the U.S. Congress, are bodies where majorities are needed to pass laws, legislation is often written in ways designed to attract wide support among the diverse membership. One way to do this is to write a vaguely worded policy that allows legislators to read their own interests and the interests of their constituents into the proposal. Another reason for the lack of specificity in legislative proposals is the highly scientific and technical expertise required. Members of Congress are often generalists, knowing a little about many things but lacking deep knowledge about most things. It therefore makes a lot of sense for Congress to give general directions to an executive agency or department and not go into specific details.

▶ **So who checks to see that laws are well written and carried out?** Because of the need for vaguely worded policy and the need to rely on the executive branch for expert formulation of the details and implementation, legislators cannot simply walk away from a policy once it is in the implementation phase. Legislatures typically review policy implementation through oversight. Legislative oversight takes two forms, reauthorization and investigation.

Let's look first at reauthorization. Consider a program that gives federal subsidies to farmers to grow or not grow various crops or one that pays benefits to veterans for certain medical conditions.

Both of these programs require funding. Since Congress controls the government's purse strings, each program must be reauthorized at regular intervals in order for the necessary funds to be appropriated. What better time to determine the effectiveness of implementation than at a reauthorization hearing? Members of Congress use these opportunities to get feedback about how (and how effectively) the policy is being carried out. If the results are unsatisfactory, Congress can influence the executive branch to implement the policy more effectively by threatening to cut off or reduce funding.

Investigation is another form of oversight. Congress has the authority to call officials of the executive branch before its committees to answer questions about alleged problems with implementation. Investigations can be launched based on information gleaned during the reauthorization process, from other hearings, from contacts with constituents, from media reports, from court proceedings, or from many other sources. Like reauthorization, investigations can result in measures designed to change the executive branch's implementation of policy. Sometimes, as Table 16.2 on page 640 demonstrates, congressional investigations can be dramatic and far-reaching.

The courts also exercise a form of oversight. Unlike legislatures, courts do not control the funding of programs directly, but the cases that come before them, either at the trial level or on appeal, can have a major impact on implementation. For example, Congress may pass a bill that becomes law and is implemented by an executive department or agency. If an individual, a group, or a local or state government believes that the implementation of the bill is problematic, even causing some kind of injury, it may bring the matter before the court. In such cases, a court ruling pertains more to the implementation of the law by the executive branch than to the policy itself. This form of judicial oversight asks a court to delve into the intent of Congress when it passed legislation and to determine whether the implementation has been faulty, biased, or otherwise defective. If so, the decision rendered by a court can direct the agency or department to change its administration of a policy.

What are the chances that a citizen can influence the implementation of social policy? The main institutions of government exerting oversight over the implementation of policy are legislatures and courts, and each of these institutions is wired in a different way to the various pathways we have discussed throughout this book. Legislatures are populated by elections—so, clearly the electoral pathway is crucial. Grassroots mobilization and cultural change can also influence the willingness of legislatures to respond. We have already introduced the influence of the courts on the implementation of policy, and they in turn can be affected by some of the other pathways. In ⓛⓘⓝⓚ *Chapter 4, pages 132–134,* you learned that some state and local judges are elected rather than appointed (this

▶ **You mean that making** policy is more difficult than your model says?

discussionquestions

1. Discuss why it is so important to have citizen involvement in making public policy.

2. How does the oversight process play an important role after legislation has been passed?

TABLE 16.2
Major Senate Investigations in Recent Decades

1973–1974: Select Committee on Presidential Campaign Activities (Watergate Committee)
Investigation of possible corruption in the 1972 presidential election campaign

1987–1989: Select Committee on Secret Military Assistance to Iran and the Nicaraguan Opposition (Iran-Contra Hearings)
Investigation into alleged covert sales of military equipment to Iran and diversion of the proceeds to aid the Nicaraguan Contra rebels

1991–1993: Select Committee on POW/MIA Affairs
Investigation into the possibility that some unaccounted-for American servicemen might have survived in captivity even after POW repatriations at the conclusion of World War II, the Korean War, Cold War incidents, and particularly the war in Vietnam

1995–1996: Special Committee to Investigate Whitewater Development Corporation and Related Matters (Whitewater Committee)
Investigation into the way White House officials handled documents in the office of White House Deputy Counsel Vincent Foster after his death; matters related to actions by the White House or the Resolution Trust Corporation in handling the Madison Guarantee Savings and Loan Association or Whitewater Development Corporation; and other related matters

1997–1998: Committee on Governmental Affairs Investigation of 1996 Election Campaign
Investigation into illegal or improper activities in connection with the 1996 federal election campaign

2002: Joint Inquiry into Intelligence Community Activities before and after the Terrorist Attacks of September 11, 2001
Investigation into the intelligence community's activities before and after the terrorist attacks of September 11, 2001, by the U.S. Senate Select Committee on Intelligence and U.S. House Permanent Select Committee on Intelligence

SOURCE: http://www.senate.gov/reference_index_subjects/investigations_vrd.htm

occurs below the federal court system, where all judges are appointed by the president and confirmed by the Senate). Furthermore, courts, even the U.S. Supreme Court, may be swayed by citizen and group activism through channels such as amicus curiae briefs filed by interested parties to pass along their suggestions concerning specific cases.

practicequiz

1. The policy process model is
   a. linear
   b. not always linear
   c. cyclical
   d. never cyclical

2. Which of the following would be the most likely example of a focusing event?
   a. finding illegal immigrants working in a restaurant in California
   b. a 5 percent increase in handgun fatalities in this country in 2007
   c. the federal response to Hurricane Katrina
   d. 100 degree weather for one day in all 48 states in the continental U.S.

3. Which of the following is **NOT** a policy formulation?
   a. the independent, bipartisan "9/11" commission
   b. the "No Child Left Behind" law
   c. any executive order
   d. *Roe v. Wade*

4. The courts exercise a form of oversight of policy implementation.
   a. true
   b. false

Answers: 1-b, 2-c, 3-a, 4-b.

Alternative Views of the Policy Process

▶ **You mean that making policy is more difficult than your model says?** In this chapter, we have traced the policy process model from identifying the problem to setting the agenda to

garbage can model
a way of thinking about policymaking as an unordered mix of problems and solutions.

policy entrepreneurs
advocates of particular solutions to problems.

discussion questions

1. Are any of the phases of the policy process model more open to political influence than others? Explain your answer.

2. Why do legislatures, such as Congress, give rule-making authority to executive branch agencies and departments?

formulating and implementing the policy designed to fix the problem. At the outset of this discussion, we noted that the model did some things quite well and fell short in other ways. The model is valuable as a way to map out the typical progression of policy making, especially the tried-and-true formula of "how a bill becomes a law."

Yet people who study public policy have documented considerable variations that offer a level of detail missing from the process model we have outlined so far. Augmented versions of the process model ask us to realize that, like real life, the making of policy is messy. Some scholars think of policymaking by using the so-called **garbage can model,** which depicts problems, solutions, actors, and other parts of the policymaking universe jumbled together, much as trash builds up in a garbage can.[23] In this model, no clear order of steps dictates what happens first or next. Solutions can exist without problems, just as easily as problems can exist without solutions.

For example, in the 1990s, when the nation seemed flush with oil and gasoline prices were low, there were people (whom some called **policy entrepreneurs**)[24] pushing for policies that would support the development of hybrid cars. The entrepreneurs were advocating a solution to a problem that did not yet exist or could only be glimpsed on the horizon. In the garbage can model, all the elements of public policy float together, and the solving of problems, if it happens at all, is often based on the unintended mix of ideas and players, not on a set of linear steps.

A refinement of the garbage can approach involves what the political scientist John Kingdon describes as policy windows and streams. He envisions problems, solutions, and political factors (such as elections and interest group campaigns) as three separate streams that flow at the same time but often do not merge with one another. Like the garbage can model, these streams are not linear steps or cyclical phases but rather factors that exist at the same time. When the three streams can be brought together in the proper combination, the policy process goes to work. But to bring the streams together, an opportunity or "policy window" must open.[25] A national crisis is one such policy window. The 2001 terrorist attacks opened the window for Congress to pass a sweeping set of measures, known as the USA PATRIOT Act, which raised the permissible level of government surveillance of the public considerably. Without the events of 9/11, it is highly

unlikely that Congress would have considered such a dramatic policy shift.

These alternative approaches do not attempt to supplant the process model and its phases. Rather, they offer a way to use the process model more realistically and give us a better sense of how the pathways of political action link up with real-world policymaking.

practice quiz

1. What is the "garbage can model"?
   a. A theory that explains how temporary or "disposable" public policy is in this country.
   b. A theory that explains why no one really wants to do the dirty work of public policy formation in this country.
   c. A theory that explains what can go wrong if it takes too long for public policy initiatives to get formulated, approved, and implemented.
   d. A theory that explains how "messy" or unmethodical the process really is that produces public policy in this country.

2. Another theory, asserting that policy gets successfully formed when certain problems, solutions, and political factors converge, describes this process by comparing it to
   a. tributary convergence.
   b. windows and streams.
   c. the perfect storm.
   d. the alignment of the planets.

3. The closest equivalent stage in the conventional policy process to John Kingdom's idea of an open "policy window" is
   a. agenda-setting.
   b. implementation.
   c. a focusing event.
   d. policy formulation.

4. What is the study circle movement?
   a. a government project to gather public opinion on specific policy issues
   b. a grassroots effort in which citizens study policy problems and try to influence their solutions
   c. the cyclical pattern that certain policy processes follow
   d. a grassroots mobilization effort, initiated by the interest group Common Cause, to counteract the influence corporations have on policy formation

Answers: 1-d, 2-b, 3-c, 4-b.

Conclusion

Now that you have learned more about public policy, let's go back to the discussion at the beginning of the chapter of what people want from the American version of democracy. Should any government be able to swiftly change public policy on a grand scale? You might assume that modern liberals, with their greater faith in the positive power of government, would answer yes to this question but that modern conservatives might give a no response based on their desire for a reduced role of government.

Comprehensive policy change is unusual in the United States, for a number of reasons. Our fragmented branches of government, the existence of political parties, the power of interest groups and social movements that are often in competition with one another—these are a few of the main factors that fulfill what James Madison sought in his plan for the Constitution. No single interest or faction, even one comprising a majority of the population, can easily take control of such a system and use it to its own advantage. This plan for society and government often sounds strange to Americans because of our deep belief in the fairness of majority rule. The low popularity of Congress today (and in the past) offers a good example. The negative view of Congress arises, in part, because of the assumption that there is one public good, or general set of values, that most of us share. It's widely felt that if only Congress would stop catering to the needs of special interests and follow the will of the people, we would have much better government and much better public policy![26]

No one disputes the influence of so-called special interests. But congressional policymaking is often a reflection of an increasing diversity of interests in our nation of 300 million people. For many if not most policy issues, there is no one public good but rather a wide range of solutions for the many different people in a single congressional district or state.

Because of the structure of our government and the diversity of our wants and needs, much of our policymaking is best described as incremental in its impact.[27] These small modifications to existing policy make sense in a government as open to the pathways of political action as ours, in which citizens, groups, corporations, the mass media, and other actors have multiple ways to influence outcomes. The pathways can be used to hinder or block the actions of others as well as to open access to the policy process. Large, comprehensive policy changes are often hard to come by unless there is a crisis such as 9/11 or an unusual political change such as a dramatic realigning election.

In their plan for our government and society, the founders sought stability, not flexibility. If the incremental policymaking that we see in the contemporary United States is any indication,

they succeeded. Small changes keep political, economic, and social arrangements in relatively the same relationship to one another. People who are happy with the status quo may applaud our incremental policymaking system; others might be willing to trade a degree of stability for a more responsive and responsible policymaking system. How do you feel? In either case, the pathways of political action offer you opportunities to participate in the policymaking process.

YOUR turn!

The federal government's executive branch departments and agencies often have mandated periods for the public to comment on proposed rules and regulations before they are enacted. State departments and agencies also have comment periods. These policymakers are required to listen to us about the policies they are formulating. But they can't listen if no one is speaking. Is there an issue that you care about? Recall the example of the PCB dredging plan for New York's Hudson River. There may not be an issue that touches you in a direct way as this one did many New Yorkers, but one very enlightening result of looking into the actions of state and federal policymakers is to see just how wide a range of issues and problems comes before them for consideration.

Check out **http://www.loc.gov/rr/news/fedgov.html** for a listing of federal executive branch agencies and departments. Search the Web pages for the agencies or departments that cover an issue that interests you, and take note of the public comment periods for proposed rules and regulations. At the state level, look up your state's executive branch agencies and departments on the Web and seek out the ones that are likely actors on your policy issue. Through these sources, you can find the date, time, and location of public meetings concerning policy issues. You have every right to present your point of view in person to the individuals who will make policies that have the potential to change your life!

Don't forget that a major component of public policymaking is oversight of existing policies. All citizens can play a role in the process of oversight by doing the following:

- **Contact your members of the U.S. House and Senate.** Congressional offices receive vast quantities of letters, e-mails, phone calls, faxes, and personal visits from people interested in improving existing policy. Since we, as the public, experience policy implementation directly, we are uniquely qualified to critique the effectiveness of many policies. Members of Congress listen to us because they take their duties of representation seriously and because they know that if they do not, the electoral pathway gives us the ability to find someone who will.

- **Contact your state and local elected representatives.** Getting in touch with state or local government officials is sometimes an even more effective means of citizen policy oversight, since these representatives often know more about a regional or local issue than members of Congress. State and local representatives also make great advocates for influencing policymakers higher up in our federal system.

- **Help shape opinion.** Edmund Burke, the great orator and political thinker of eighteenth-century Britain, once said,

"All that is necessary for the triumph of evil is that good men do nothing." Making your opinion heard contributes to the oversight of public policy. Writing letters to the editor of your local paper, speaking up at town or city council meetings, and attending meetings sponsored by local citizen groups are some ways that you can let people with oversight power know that the public is interested in reworking policy to correct a problem more effectively. ■

Chapter Review

1. Public policy can be thought of as what comes after the "equal sign" in the equation of the structure of government plus the political process. Public policy is both what the government does and what it does not do.

2. The nature of public policy rests on the values of the public and of policy decision makers. Freedom and equality are values that are especially important in determining what government ought to do and the way it should go about it. These two concepts are the basis for a model of political ideology that contrasts the liberal and conservative approaches to politics and government.

3. Public policies can be categorized by issue area (such as the environment, education, and agriculture) or by the functions of government necessary to carry out the policy. The three basic policy functions are distribution, regulation, and redistribution. It is also possible to categorize policy outputs as either tangible or symbolic.

4. The policy process model shapes much of our thinking about public policy. The advantages of the model are that it allows us to think about a very complex series of events in a fairly simple way and seems to explain much of what happens in the traditional "how a bill becomes a law" format for studying policymaking. The model's limitations are that policymaking is not always a linear or cyclical process and that policymaking is more than the functioning of formal political institutions.

5. Problems are not always obvious. Politics plays a major role in framing circumstances, enabling them to be seen as problems in need of solutions.

6. Decision makers determine which problems receive attention by controlling their agendas. Not all problems are recognized as being worthy of a place on the agenda.

7. Policies come in many forms, including bills passed by legislatures such as Congress, executive orders from presidents or governors, and decisions rendered by courts. The executive branch can also create policy by way of the rule-making power delegated to it by a legislature.

8. It is important that the public and other political actors see the process of policy formulation as legitimate rather than coercive. Rules and procedures help give legitimacy to the policy process and its outcomes.

9. Implementation was once thought of as the apolitical administration of law. However, the more contemporary view of implementation is that it is highly political because of the discretion of the parties who carry out policy.

10. Oversight of public policy is done by many actors and helps ensure that a policy and its implementation are solving the problem as intended.

11. In the United States, the scope of change resulting from policymaking is usually rather small because our Constitution and competition among different interest groups makes sweeping change all but impossible except during times of crisis.

CHAPTER REVIEW TEST

1. What is public policy?
   a. another word for the laws that Congress creates and the President signs
   b. laws and policies pertaining to public spaces, such as highways, parks, and public schools
   c. the action or inaction of the government on an issue of concern to the public
   d. governmental decisions that come from public input

2. While policy is the product of political processes, some consider it to be not political in itself.
   a. true   b. false

3. Many political theorists assert that Americans revere the principle of equality but assume two conflicting versions of that idea:
   a. equality of opportunity and equality of process.
   b. equality of process and equality of outcomes.
   c. equality of outcomes and equality of incomes.
   d. equality of resources and equality of outcomes.

4. What political camp would a citizen occupy if he or she defined freedom negatively and believed in an equality of process, not outcome?
   a. progressive
   b. liberal
   c. centrist
   d. conservative

5. For influencing public policy, what it the most powerful pathway?
   a. grassroots
   b. court
   c. lobbying
   d. elections

6. What are all the phases and their chronological order in the classic policy process model?
   a. a focusing event, setting an agenda, formulating policy, and implementing policy
   b. identification of the problem, setting an agenda, legitimizing policy, formulating policy, and implementing policy
   c. identification of the problem, setting an agenda, formulating policy, legitimizing policy, and implementing policy
   d. a focusing event, setting an agenda, identifying the problem, formulating policy, implementing and assessing policy

7. Why isn't the policy formation process neat?
   a. because policies are always complicated
   b. because of all the different political actors who participate in that process
   c. because the Constitution mandates that policy formation itself be "checked and balanced" by all three branches of the government
   d. because "neat" policy would be much less easy to enforce

8. What are the competing models political scientists use to describe who does and does not get access to the policy-making process?
   a. the elite and pluralist models
   b. the populist and hierarchical models
   c. the short-term and long-term models
   d. the left-wing and right-wing models

9. What is one common reason certain issues on the country's "institutional agenda" slip off and are never acted on?
   a. The issue only serves one geographic segment of the country.
   b. The would-be policy only possesses symbolic value.
   c. The would-be policy is clamored for by the public and legislators resist such a coercive context.
   d. The would-be policy would be too costly or inconvenient to enact and enforce.

10. In the absence of a major crisis, what is a force crucial to keeping certain problems on the institutional agenda?
    a. the continuation of the problem
    b. effective lobbyists
    c. elections
    d. legislators' patience

11. Where can average citizens most easily enter into the policy formation process?
    a. through the executive branch
    b. through the judicial branch
    c. through the U. S. Senate
    d. through the U.S. House of Representatives

12. How does public policy acquire legitimacy in this country?
    a. through Americans' traditional faith in political authorities
    b. through the law enforcement firepower that often backs up such policy
    c. through the transparent (fair and open) policymaking process and citizens' own input into that process
    d. by how long it is implemented and enforced

13. What was one difference created by the 1996 "welfare reform" legislation?
    a. a clear, long-term improvement in the quality of life for impoverished Americans
    b. individual states attained greater control over welfare policy
    c. all welfare benefits were discontinued in all 50 states
    d. president Clinton's chances for reelection were greatly diminished

14. Why is discretion so commonly an ingredient in the implementation of a law or policy?

a. Policies are sometimes worded vaguely enough to attract wide support in Congress, so those doing the practical implementing of the policies must decide on details.

b. The ambiguous nature of language itself always leaves a lot of room for interpreting policy.

c. Legislators are often quite proficient in technical matters but executive agencies or departments that implement policy usually are not, so laws are written in general terms that the implementers can understand.

d. Article II of the Constitution grants agencies or departments implementing policy the authority to shift the emphasis or focus of any law or policy, provided they do not violate the "spirit of the law."

15. What is congressional oversight?

a. when high-ranking members of the executive branch monitor the actions of Congress during the policy formation

b. when Congress monitors what is and is not on its two-year policy agenda

c. when Congress makes sure that the policies it helped create are being carried out appropriately

d. when the House or Senate neglects some segments of legislation the other legislative body has included in a bill

16. What prompts Congress to exercise oversight through the reauthorization process?

a. The wording in all legislation includes a reauthorization clause.

b. Partisan politics usually compels members of the minority party to check up on the policies initiated by their majority colleagues.

c. Tradition.

d. Congress's responsibilities as keeper of the government's purse-strings.

17. One reason Congress holds formal investigations into the implementation of policy is that media reports convince them of a problem in that area.

a. true   b. false

18. Unlike Congress, the courts do exercise oversight of policy implementation.

a. true   b. false

19. What is one reason that substantial shifts in public policy are rare in the U.S.?

a. Politicians tend to feel less passionate about policy in this country than in some others.

b. Most Americans do not want such policy shifts, even if they would help create a more just and effective government and society.

c. Powerful interest groups have developed on the opposite sides of many big issues, in effect countering the political influence of each other.

d. There are fewer problems that demand policy attention in this country than in some others.

20. The negative view that many people hold of Congress's policymaking is probably unfair because

a. people do not realize that Congress usually *does* create policies that serve the public good.

b. the media routinely distorts what Congress does and does not report the problematic policies it almost always rejects.

c. people forget that there is not one public good; Congress's policymaking often reflects the vast diversity of interests in this country.

d. people do not realize that the Constitution prevents Congress from making policy on a great many issues.

Answers: 1: c; 2: a; 3: b; 4: d; 5: c; 6: c; 7: b; 8: a; 9: d; 10: b; 11: d; 12: c; 13: b; 14: a; 15: c; 16: d; 17: a; 18: b; 19: c; 20: c.

DISCUSSION QUESTIONS

1. Americans are said to greatly prize the values of freedom and equality. If this is true, why do we seem to have so much disagreement over policy in this country?

2. The presidency has taken on a much larger role in all phases of the policymaking process, far greater than that envisioned by most of the Constitution's framers. Is this a positive or negative development for our democracy? Explain your answer.

3. The process model of policymaking says a great deal about how the institutions of government function but not much about our role as citizens in any of the phases of the process. At which phases in the process does citizen action have an impact on the final result? Why?

4. Explain how oversight works. Is oversight a necessary part of policymaking? Why or why not?

5. Why are models such as the garbage can model and John Kingdon's policy streams model said to be more realistic portraits of the process of public policymaking than that depicted by the process model?

6. The argument has been made that one of the best things about our system of government is its stable and incremental policymaking. What are the upsides and downsides to incremental policymaking? What problems in our history would incremental policy change not have been able to address?

INTERNET RESOURCES

Learn about policy issues from the liberal or progressive viewpoint: **http://www.movingideas.org**

Learn about policy issues from the conservative viewpoint: **http://www.heritage.org**

The House of Representatives is a policymaker with oversight functions. Find out what it is doing in both these areas: **http://www.house.gov**

The Senate is also a policymaker with oversight functions: **http://www.senate.gov**

Presidents are powerful policy players. See what issues President Bush supports: **http://www.whitehouse.gov/infocus/index.html**

Learn about the roles of the departments and agencies of the federal government in formulating public policy: **http://www.firstgov.gov/Agencies/Federal/Executive.shtml**

Learn about the federal courts and their roles as policymakers: **http://www.firstgov.gov/Agencies/Federal/Judicial.shtml**

Study circles offer citizen involvement in public policy: **http://www.studycircles.org/pages/who.html**

Watch a slideshow describing the problem of PCBs in the Hudson River: **http://www.clearwater.org/pcbs/slideshow/slide1.html**

ADDITIONAL READING

Derthick, Martha A. *Up in Smoke.* Washington, DC: CQ Press, 2002.

Kingdon, John W. *Agendas, Alternatives, and Public Policies.* New York: Harper & Row, 1984.

Lindblom, Charles E., and Edward J. Woodhouse. *The Policy-Making Process* (3d ed.). Englewood Cliffs, NJ: Prentice Hall, 1993.

Spitzer, Robert J. *The Politics of Gun Control.* Washington, DC: CQ Press, 2004.

Stone, Deborah. *Policy Paradox: The Art of Political Decision Making.* New York: Norton, 1997.

Theodoulou, Stella Z., and Chris Kofinis. *The Art of the Game: Understanding American Public Policy Making.* Belmont, CA: Wadsworth, 2004.

KEY TERMS

classical liberalism   628

coercion   637

conservatism   628

decisions   635

discretion   639

distribution   630

focusing events   633

freedom   624

garbage can model   641

institutional agenda   634

issue-attention cycle   634

lame duck   636

laws   635

modern liberalism   628

policy entrepreneurs   641

pluralists   633

policy process model   624

progressivism   628

redistribution   630

regulation   630

rule-making authority   635

trigger mechanism   633

Worker John Abidelli mans a crane beneath the National Debt Clock after it was restarted July 11, 2002 in New York City. The digital sign shows the U.S. National Debt and was turned off two years earlier when the federal government had a budget surplus. Now that the federal debt is again increasing, owner Douglas Durst decided to turn the clock on again.

CHAPTER 17

MAKING ECONOMIC POLICY

Bridge Too Far It had, in a way, the feel of a 1940s Hollywood epic. Eighty-two-year-old Senator Ted Stevens, an Alaska Republican, stood on the floor of the United States Senate, threatening to resign if the proposed amendment passed. His impassioned appeal was riveting and dramatic. Was Stevens speaking out against corruption, in support of a civil rights bill, or against an extension of the USA Patriot Act? Was he fighting to open more of his state to lucrative oil production? What could bring a man, clearly approaching the twilight of his political career, to make such a bold declaration?

One of Stevens's pet projects had come under attack. Called "the bridge to nowhere" by its numerous critics, the appropriation called for $223 million in federal expenditures by the Department of Transportation to connect an island with fifty residents to the Alaskan mainland (a topic discussed briefly in Chapter 7). That's a

U.S. Sen. Ted Stevens (R-AK), 82, talks to the news media after a meeting of the Senate Republican Policy Committee at the Capitol on December 20, 2005 in Washington, DC. A bipartisan group of senators were filibustering the conference report that reauthorizes the sun-setting provisions of the Patriot Act.

project cost of more than $4 million a person. The target of Stevens's wrath was a fellow Republican senator, Tom Coburn of Oklahoma, who had the audacity to suggest that the funds be transferred to the Hurricane Katrina relief effort. With rising deficits, Coburn believed that the national government needed to prioritize its spending and that hundreds of thousands of displaced victims on the Gulf Coast were a higher priority than fifty people in Alaska who had always lived without a bridge.

"Pork," federal government funding earmarked for a special project in a congressional member's district, is a long-standing tradition. But something about this bridge just went too far. Getting national media attention in the wake of Katrina and in the midst of rising national debt, Stevens's pet project became an easy target and a visible symbol of pork-barrel spending. Citizens were upset and vocal about it. Taxpayer groups opposed to the project generated enough of a public outcry to make it an issue. Although Stevens's threat to resign saved the bridge on the floor of the Senate, the grant was ultimately doomed. But the money wasn't. In the kind of compromise crafted in congressional conference committees, the bridge disappeared, but the funding remained. Instead of receiving a specific grant to build the bridge, the Alaska Department of Transportation received the $223 million as part of its federal highways allocation.

could still do his constituents a favor. Coburn, although failing to achieve his goal of redistributing the appropriation, had at

least brought national attention to the practice of earmarking funds for such projects and touched off a debate over whether such grants should be specific to each project or broader in nature. Realistically, Coburn must know that such a change will be difficult to achieve. Pork wins votes, and members of Congress like to "bring home the bacon" by pointing to specific projects and reminding their constituents that they are responsible for the capital improvements, the jobs, and the money that came along with them. With some incumbents writing the budget and others trying to protect their jobs, it is no wonder that pork finds its way into most appropriation bills. Political scientists call the underlying process logrolling—"you vote for my special project, and I'll vote for yours."

As illustrated by the "bridge to nowhere," elected officials may steer government money and attendant economic benefits to their constituents. However, this does not mean that government officials can readily control the overall nature of economic conditions locally, state-wide, or nationally.

Economic conditions, especially unemployment, inflation, and energy prices, often become important issues in election campaigns. Political incumbents and their challengers make claims about what they will do to build the economy, but it is difficult for them to produce exactly the results that they desire. In the 2006 governor's race in Michigan, a state with a high unemployment rate, both candidates talked about how they would work to create

jobs. Yet, neither candidate had any realistic possibility of preventing American automobile manufacturers, Michigan's primary industry, from suffering further financial and job losses in the face of foreign competition.

The overall economy is affected by a variety of forces, including factors that are beyond the control of government officials. Clearly, elected officials in the United States cannot control the decisions of corporate leaders who may make mistakes, such as switching to an emphasis on building gas-guzzling SUVs just before rising oil prices made American consumers more interested in smaller, fuel efficient cars. Similarly, elected officials cannot control the decisions of foreign governments and corporations or prevent the economic consequences of natural disasters, such as hurricanes, earthquakes, and floods. As you will see in this chapter, government officials use a variety of strategies involving taxing, spending, setting interest rates, and controlling the money supply in an effort to influence the economy. Despite often being blamed by voters for economic conditions, government officials cannot control all aspects unemployment rates, prices, product availability, and other matters of keen interest to consumers. ▪

▶ **Was Adam Smith**
proven wrong?

macroeconomics
the study of national economies as a whole.

Keynesians
economists who believe that government should take an active role in correcting economic inefficiencies.

By writing the book *The Wealth of Nations* in 1776, Adam Smith helped to explain and justify the free enterprise system that has been central to the shared values and stability in the democratic governing system of the United States. Are you surprised that an eighteenth-century economist's ideas are still influential in our modern, technologically-advanced society?

Often we tend to see politics as a big game. We keep score of who is winning or losing based not only on the results of the last election but also on the success or failure of the efforts of various factions to get Congress to enact their policies. When we look at economic policy—and that includes more than just the federal government's taxing and spending decisions—we are talking about *your money*. These decisions affect *you*, whether in the form of benefits flowing to you from the federal government or of your hard-earned income flowing, as taxes, to the federal government. The economic actions of government will affect your life, your livelihood, and your financial well-being both now and far into the future. The economic course set today will have a dramatic influence on your standard of living ten, thirty, or even fifty years from now. That's why you will see the phrase *long-term* used more than once in this chapter. Becoming involved in the process will take a little time. The pathways of participation in economic policy formation are not as clear as in other areas, because economics is complicated and points of access to the system are often obscured. But since it is your money, you should make the extra effort. The cost of doing nothing could be staggering.

Key Questions

1. Is economic liberty a basic freedom? Why or why not?
2. What are the basic differences between fiscal policy and monetary policy?
3. Who are the major actors in creating economic policy?
4. What are the major sources of U.S. government revenue?
5. What are the major areas of expenditure for the government? Do the levels of expenditure in those areas seem reasonable?
6. What long-term fiscal problems does the United States face? What steps should be taken to address these challenges?
7. What are the major instruments of monetary policy?
8. How does trade policy affect the economy?

Economic Basics

When we think about freedom, we generally think in terms of voting rights and civil liberties—freedom of religion, speech, and press. It is easy to forget the vital role that economic security and stability play in ensuring our other freedoms. When Thomas Jefferson wrote of our "inalienable rights" to "life, liberty and the pursuit of happiness" in the Declaration of Independence, he was subtly editing John Locke's argument, advanced almost a century earlier, that government's legitimacy rests on its protection of "life, liberty and property." There was little doubt, however, that Jefferson's "pursuit of happiness" incorporated the right to own property and reap the benefit from doing so. The Declaration of

Independence was written the same year as *The Wealth of Nations*, by the Scottish economist and moral philosopher Adam Smith (1723–1790). Describing the underpinnings of our capitalistic society, Smith's book discussed property, trade, and the accumulation of wealth. The acquisition, ownership, and manipulation of property, Smith believed, allowed individuals to acquire wealth and thus pursue happiness. The scope of a nation's private enterprise system, not the size of the king's treasury, becomes the true measure of a nation's wealth. When each person pursues his or her self-interest, an "invisible hand," in the form of the laws of supply and demand, acts as a self-correcting force for the overall economy.[1] In a real sense, we participate in the economic process every time we make a purchase and each day that we go to work.

As men of the Enlightenment, the framers of our Constitution were profoundly influenced by the idea that society was best served when citizens had the right to follow their self-interest. In fact, many political scientists on both the right and the left consider the Constitution to be primarily an economic document and believe that its intention was to solidify the foundation of our capitalistic society and protect the rights of property owners. Smith was a founder of what is now called the "classical" school of economic theory. Classicists hold that prices are established by a combination of output, technology, and wages. In the long run, Smith believed, the economic system would be self-correcting.

▶ **Was Adam Smith proven wrong?** In the twentieth century, the British economist John Maynard Keynes (pronounced "Caynz") (1883–1946) emerged as the leading critic of the classical school. To explain why the Great Depression of the 1930s occurred, to map out a policy for overcoming this profound economic crisis, and to prevent its recurrence, Keynes developed a new field of economic analysis, **macroeconomics**—the study not of individual markets (microeconomics), in which the classical rules continue to hold true, but of national economies as a whole. Classical economists accept the natural ups and downs of business cycles. **Keynesians** (CAYN-zee-enz) find that notion irresponsible and believe that the government must play an active role in smoothing out natural business cycles through taxation and spending policies. For example, increased government spending during periods of excessive savings can avert economic recession and keep the economy from stagnating. Conversely, according to Keynesians, the government should raise taxes during times of economic prosperity to keep the economy from overheating—a strategy that is easier said than done. (What politician wants to advocate higher taxes and reduced government services?) Keynesian macroeconomic policies were aimed primarily at the *demand* side of the economic equation, seeking to effect change through economic stimulation and regulation. (We will return to the politics of regulation toward the end of this chapter.)

John Maynard Keynes influenced the thinking of subsequent generations of economists by advocating a greater role for government in shaping a nation's economy. Do government actions help protect people from economic downturns, or do such actions interfere with natural patterns of economic growth?

▶ **How will lowering taxes**
improve the economy?

supply-side economists
economists who believe that high taxes burden the economy and can reduce government revenue.

monetarists
economists who believe that government economic actions should focus on targeting the supply of money in circulation.

inflation
an increase in prices over time.

Consumer Price Index (CPI)
figure representing the cost of a specific set of goods and services tracked at regular intervals by the Department of Labor.

▶ **How will lowering taxes improve the economy?** By the early 1980s, a third school had emerged. The **supply-side economists** believe that the level of taxation has the greatest impact on economic health. Higher taxes curtail efficiency, but lower taxes encourage productivity and specialization, thereby improving the performance of the overall economy. Many supply-siders believe that lower tax rates will increase government revenues because of overall economic growth. The emergence of this school was part of a conservative backlash against the perceived failures of Keynesian economics.

Although supply-siders share many of the same post-Keynesian views as another modern school, the **monetarists,** they differ on one key point. Monetarists believe that the nation's central bank should focus on maintaining a targeted money supply, but supply-side economists believe that the bank should focus on the price of money, not its overall supply. (We will discuss the government's monetary policy more broadly later in this chapter.)

An important factor in the strength of the American economy is the status of the dollar as the world's most important currency. A stable monetary system is vital for a modern economy. "The history of money is the history of civilization or, more exactly, of some important civilizing values," said former Federal Reserve Board Chairman Alan Greenspan. "Its form at any particular period of history reflects the degree of confidence, or the degree of trust, that market participants have in the institutions that govern every market system, whether centrally planned or free."[2] (A *Pathways Profile* of Alan Greenspan can be found on page 675.) Throughout the post–World War II era, the long-standing stability of the dollar has helped sustain confidence in the American economic system.

In the United States today, we take for granted that we can own property, start our own businesses, keep most of what we earn, and work at jobs created by the private sector. If you don't like your job, you quit and find another one. Of course, the free-enterprise system also means that there is no government guarantee that another job will be waiting for you. Critics of our system argue that employment is too precarious, that American jobs often flow to lower-paid workers overseas, and that wealth is concentrated in the hands of a relative few. Disparities between salaries of chief executive officers and low-paid workers have widened in recent years. Wal-Mart in particular has been the target of intense media criticism for its alleged low pay and limited benefits for entry-level positions. Although the United States has

seen tremendous economic growth over the past decade, real earnings—wages that factor in the impact of inflation—have decreased for the lowest-paid fifth of American workers. At the same time, real earnings have skyrocketed for the wealthiest Americans.

▶ **How do changes in economic policy affect us?** It can be argued that government economic policy has a more profound impact on our freedom than any other type of government action. Collectively, it affects our take-home pay, the benefits we collect from our employers and our government, and the health of the overall economy. Every promise made by Congress represents a liability that will need to be addressed eventually. By voting, speaking up, and joining with others who share your views—particularly interest groups—you can help carve out your own future.

There are two primary types of economic policy: fiscal and monetary. Fiscal policy is the taxing and spending decisions enacted by Congress in cooperation with the president. Monetary policy concerns the money supply and is managed by the independent Federal Reserve Board ("the Fed"). Both fiscal and monetary policy can affect growth, employment, and inflation. Often the goals of fiscal and monetary policy clash because the Fed, the president, and Congress don't always share the same objectives.

THE BIG FIVE: MEASURING ECONOMIC PERFORMANCE

When economists gauge the economy's performance, they usually focus on five figures: inflation, unemployment, gross domestic product, the balance of trade, and the budget deficit or surplus. These measures matter to politicians as well. A healthy economy helps incumbents stay in office. In fact, politicians are often more willing to make potentially painful economic decisions early in the political cycle—right after an election—in hopes that the actions will produce long-term benefits that will show up before the next election. (But, as the first President Bush and President Carter will tell you, your timing has to be right.) The first two measures in particular seem to resonate with the voting public. Let's examine all of them in turn.

Inflation measures the rate at which prices increase. The classic definition of inflation is "too many dollars chasing too few goods." Inflation is bad. High inflation rates can undermine and distort all other aspects of the economy. When inflation is out of control, it can wipe out the middle class's savings, devalue the

▶ How do changes in
economic policy affect us?

deflation
a decrease in prices over time.

unemployment rate
the percentage of Americans who are currently not working but are seeking jobs.

gross domestic product (GDP)
the value of all goods and services produced in a nation.

balance of trade
the net difference between a nation's imports and its exports.

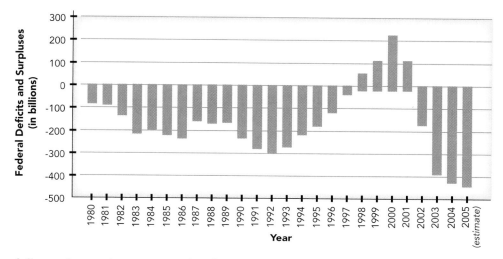

FIGURE 17.1

Federal Deficits and Surpluses

The federal government has operated with budget deficits for most of the past 25 years. The few years of budget surpluses were caused by a thriving economy in the late 1990s. The return to budget deficits came after 9/11, when the federal government cut taxes and then soon initiated expensive military actions in Afghanistan and Iraq and also experienced rising costs in entitlement programs.

SOURCE: 2006 Statistical Abstract of the U.S. http://www.census.gov/compendia/statab/tables/0650459

dollar, and cause immense social and political unrest. When we look at monetary policy later in this chapter, we will see that inflation has been the major area of concern for the Fed since the mid-1970s. At that time, inflation ran at more than 10 percent annually, topping out at 13.5 percent in 1980. Since that period, it has dropped back toward its historic norm of between 2 and 3 percent per year. The inflation rate is measured by the **Consumer Price Index (CPI),** a figure computed by the Department of Labor. The CPI is calculated at regular intervals, based on the changing costs of a specified "market basket" of goods and services. The Fed must also guard against **deflation**—dropping prices. Deflation might sound good, but falling prices discourage spending: If prices are going down, consumers refuse to spend today in hopes of paying less tomorrow. Consumers who sit on their wallets are not engaging in the kind of economic activity that creates jobs and a vibrant economy. Eroding prices mean eroding jobs. The last significant episode of deflation in American history occurred during the Great Depression.

The **unemployment rate** measures the percentage of Americans who are out of work. It is not a perfect measure, for it accounts only for people who identify themselves as actively seeking work, and sampling techniques are used in calculating it. Those who have given up looking for jobs are not counted, either as employed or unemployed—they are regarded as simply outside the workforce. The several million "undocumented" workers and the people involved in the illegal or "underground" economy are also left out. Unemployment is therefore often understated in particular geographic areas or during periods of great poverty. A "good" unemployment rate is around 5

percent. (One hundred percent employment would be impossible, for a certain number of people are always between jobs or just entering the workforce.) In the 1980s, many economists considered 5 percent to be full employment, only to have unemployment drop below that figure in the late 1990s and again in 2005 and 2006.

Sometimes a slight uptick in unemployment can be a sign of a vibrant economy—people are more willing to leave a job they don't like when they are confident that they can find better work elsewhere, and those who hadn't previously sought work become active job seekers. Employment rates that are too low, on the other hand, can make Wall Street wary of wage-driven inflation; when employers have trouble finding people to fill all available jobs, they have to pay their workers more. That's why the stock market often drops in response to "good" employment news.

Gross domestic product (GDP) is the value of all of the goods and services produced in the United States. GDP measures the size of the American economy. Generally, economic growth is good, but overly rapid economic growth can be harmful, as it can feed inflation. Here's where the Fed steps in to try to curb runaway growth before inflation can gain a foothold. A good growth target for GDP is between 3 and 4 percent. The growth rate commonly reported in the media is the "real GDP" rate—GDP adjusted to account for the effects of the CPI so that actual economic growth does not falsely include the rate of inflation.

The **balance of trade** measures the difference between imports and exports. A positive balance means that a nation has a trade surplus—it exports more goods than it imports. A negative balance of trade means a trade deficit—the country imports more

▶ **What do the Democrats**
think about deficits?

budget deficit
the amount by which a government's
expenditures exceed its revenues.

budget surplus
the amount by which a government's revenues exceed its expenditures.

national debt
a nation's cumulative deficits.

fiscal policy
taxation and spending decisions made by
the government.

Congressional Budget Office (CBO)
the research arm of Congress, a major
player in budget creation.

goods than it exports. The United States has been running a significant trade deficit for years. The same American consumers
who express their concerns about the outsourcing of American
jobs also love to buy cheap imported goods. We'll talk more about
trade later, as it is a complex political and economic issue.

A major concern for the U.S. economy has been the budget
deficit and the rising national debt. The **budget deficit** is the
amount by which, in a given year, government spending exceeds
government revenue. (The rare circumstance when revenue out-
strips expenditures is called a **budget surplus;** see Figure 17.1 on
page 655.) The net sum of the budget deficit minus the surplus is
the **national debt,** or the amount that the government owes. With
the exception of the four years between 1998 and 2001, the United
States has run a budget deficit every year since 1970. That's added
up to a national debt of about $8.6 trillion, forcing Congress to
raise the nation's authorized borrowing limit past the $9 trillion
mark. (The current debt averages out to more than $28,525 for
every man, woman, and child in the United States.) The national
debt must be financed through money that is borrowed—with
interest—both at home and abroad, which makes balancing the
budget that much harder with each passing year. With Republicans controlling both Congress and the White House, the politics
of deficit financing have taken an interesting turn. With the
budget shortfalls of recent years, many Republicans, long-time
deficit hawks (opponents of increasing the deficit), have turned
into deficit doves (supporters of increasing the deficit), even as
an increasingly vocal faction of the Republican Party has sounded
the alarm.

▶ **What do the Democrats think about deficits?**
Meanwhile many Democrats, longtime advocates of more generous government spending, especially on social programs, have
become hard-line deficit opponents. Democrats claim that the
debt—and the deficits rung up by George W. Bush's administration—has been hitting all-time highs. Many Republicans claim
that the numbers, from a historical perspective, aren't all that
bad. Who is telling the truth? Both or neither, depending on
your perspective. In raw numbers, the national debt is at an all-
time high. The 2004 budget deficit of $413 billion was the
nation's largest. It beat out the 2003 deficit to claim that mark.
Expressed as a percentage of GDP, though, both the debt and

deficit are far below historic records set during World War II.
The economy is much larger than it was then. What is more
important, raw debt and deficit numbers or the size of the economy? Can we grow our way out of the debt? Is a debt approaching $9 trillion too much under any circumstances? And shouldn't
we be doing something about the debt now when we know that
we have larger problems down the road? We'll revisit these questions later in the chapter.

practicequiz

1. What did Adam Smith mean by the "invisible hand" of a
   nation's economy?
   a. God's divine will directing the nature of economic reality
   b. the natural forces of supply and demand that, through
      people's pursuit of their self interest, keep a market
      economy healthy
   c. the forces of nature which, in largely unnoticed ways, dic-
      tate the cycles of an agricultural economy
   d. stealthy, often illegal acts undertaken by merchants,
      which compromised the health of England's economy in
      the eighteenth-century

2. According to many political scientists, the Constitution's primary intent was to reinforce the foundation of our capitalistic
   economy and protect the rights of property owners.
   a. true   b. false

3. In recent years the disparities between salaries of chief executive officers and low-paid workers have
   a. narrowed considerably.
   b. widened.
   c. remained the same.
   d. narrowed but only slightly.

4. Why does the stock market often go down after good economic news?
   a. Bad economic news always follows good.
   b. When the good news is a lowering of inflation, that alerts
      investors to the likelihood of higher employment rates—
      which can in turn trigger higher taxes.
   c. When the good news is a higher employment rate, that
      alerts investors to the likelihood of higher inflation—and
      a downturn in the economy.
   d. When the economic picture brightens, people are more
      inclined to buy consumer goods; to do this they sell
      stock (which lowers the stock's value).

Answers: 1-b, 2-a, 3-b, 4-c.

▶ **How many committees get** involved in the budget process?

discussionquestions

1. What are the differences among the Keynesian view, the classical view, the monetarist view, and the supply-side view of the economy?

2. What is the difference between the deficit and the national debt?

3. How is inflation measured?

Fiscal Policy

The game of politics is all about deciding who gets what. Part of the answer to that question involves deciding who pays for what. That is what **fiscal policy**—the politics of taxing and spending—is all about. With the federal budget now at $2.5 trillion, there is a lot of money up for grabs. As you learned in the preceding section, the federal government is currently spending more money than it is collecting in taxes, creating a budget deficit. Collectively, our deficits add up to a national debt of about $8.6 trillion. The stage is set for the national debt to become much larger.

Technically, the United States has two budgets. One is "on budget"; it includes general revenue from income tax and corporate taxes and pays for things such as defense, NASA, and poverty prevention programs. The other is "off budget" because it includes money from the Social Security and Medicare payroll taxes and trust funds. In reality, this separation is a legalistic fiction. For our purposes, we are going to view the budget as a unified, integrated whole, except when we specifically discuss on-budget and off-budget aspects.

MAJOR ACTORS

Budgets are created through interactions between Congress and the president. There are several other major actors in the realm of fiscal policy, the most significant of which is the **Congressional Budget Office (CBO).** A research arm of Congress, the CBO was created by the Budget and Impoundment Act of 1974. The act was for all practical purposes two separate pieces of legislation. The impoundment portion dealt with reining in a power exercised excessively during the administration of President Richard Nixon. If Nixon opposed a program that had been passed and funded by Congress, the president would simply order his secretary of the treasury to "impound" the funds—in other words, to not spend them. By cutting off the money, Nixon could effectively kill a program even if he didn't have the votes to have his veto sustained. The 1974 law required House and Senate approval of presidential impoundment; otherwise the funds would automatically be spent. Since then, impoundment has been rare.

The budget portion of the 1974 act was more significant. It fundamentally changed how the budget of the United States is crafted. Before this, the White House Office of Management and Budget (OMB) had the primary responsibility for drawing up the budget. The president would present the basic document, and Congress would make adjustments. Since 1975, the CBO has created long-term budget outlooks, analyses of the president's proposed budget, and fiscal impact statements for every bill that comes out of a congressional committee. As a result, Congress has become the primary player in creating the budget. The OMB still draws up a budget, and although that budget sometimes has some influence, it is often "dead on arrival" when it gets to Congress.

The OMB still provides the president with information and guidance. The power of the veto gives the president an important role in determining the final budget, which is always a compromise. Of course, the OMB carries a little more weight when the presidency and Congress are both controlled by the same party. Since 1946, the president has also had the "help" of the Council of Economic Advisers (CEA). The CEA was created by Congress back when the initial budget document was primarily the chief executive's responsibility, in order to help the White House make budget decisions. The CEA's three members are usually leading academic economists, appointed by the president. Some presidents, notably John F. Kennedy, have relied heavily on the CEA; others, such as Ronald Reagan, have all but ignored it.

KEY CONGRESSIONAL PLAYERS

▶ **How many committees get involved in the budget process?**
As you saw earlier (**LINK** *Ch. 7, pages 265–266*), committees do the real work of Congress. Although the Constitution requires that all revenue bills originate in the House, the 435 House members sitting together could never write a budget. Instead, appropriations and tax bills are products of committees in the Senate and the House. Each chamber has an appropriations committee, which has primary responsibility for deciding where federal money should be spent. The House Ways and Means Committee is responsible for tax bills. The Senate Finance Committee serves as its counterpart. The House and Senate also each have budget committees, which review the fiscal process.

discussionquestions

1. How does the Congressional Budget Office exercise budgetary power?

2. What were the major provisions of the Budget and Impoundment Act of 1974?

practicequiz

1. Which of the following areas of governmental expense is "off budget"?
   a. defense
   b. education
   c. medicare
   d. unemployment insurance

2. What triggered the impoundment portion of the Budget and Impoundment Act, which also created the CBO?
   a. Jimmy Carter's budgetary miscalculations
   b. the Iran-Contra scandal
   c. the Watergate scandal
   d. Richard Nixon's fiscal undermining of the legislature

3. What is the significance to the budget process in the Budget and Impoundment Act?
   a. Its long-term budget forecasting and assessment of the president's proposed budget has made the CBO the central factor in creating the budget.
   b. As an extension of the GOP, the CBO has made congressional fiscal policy much more conservative.
   c. As an extension of the minority party, the CBO has made congressional fiscal policy much more contentious than it used to be.
   d. As a part of executive branch's Treasury department, the CBO's effective budget forecasting has made the president a much more powerful player in the budget process.

4. Members of the president's Council of Economic Advisers are usually
   a. party loyalists.
   b. nationally known leaders of business.
   c. academic economists.
   d. members of the Federal Reserve Board.

Answers: 1-c, 2-d, 3-a, 4-c.

Revenue

Before discussing the nation's fiscal policy, let's see where the money comes from. In 2005, the United States government collected $2.15 trillion in revenue. The largest portion of that total came from taxes on individual income, bringing in $929 billion, or almost half the revenue. Taxes to fund the Social Security program, referred to as Social Security taxes or **payroll taxes,** produced another $793 bil-

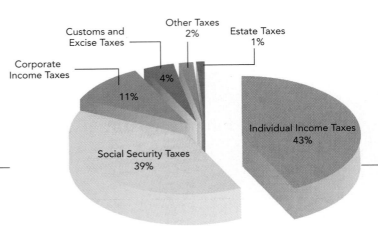

FIGURE 17.2
The Federal Revenue Budget

Federal government revenue comes primarily from individual income tax and payroll taxes for Social Security and Medicare. How can an increase in the unemployment rate affect tax revenues?

lion. Revenue from corporate taxes amounted to $279 billion. Other assorted taxes produced $153 billion (see Figure 17.2).

The tax burden for the majority of Americans comes in the form of income tax and Social Security tax. Income tax is a **progressive tax**—the more money you make, the higher the percentage you pay in taxes up to a top rate of 35 percent. The Social Security tax, on the other hand, is a **regressive tax.** If you make enough money, your Social Security tax burden drops. At first glance, payroll taxes seem flat—everyone pays the same rate. However, this tax is collected only on the first $90,000 of income, indexed to 2005 dollars; earnings (from salaries and self-employment) above that level are not subject to the Social Security tax. So the tax burden for higher-income earners is felt more heavily through income taxes, while those with lower incomes are hit harder by payroll taxes.

INCOME TAXES

Taxes on income make up just over 7.5 percent of GDP. Currently there are six different income taxation levels in the United States (see Table 17.1). For comparison, we show the rates for a single person and for a married couple filing jointly. As you earn more money in a given year, you move into a higher **marginal tax bracket**—*marginal* meaning the tax rate you pay on the last dollar you earn that year. Everyone pays 10 percent on the first dollar of taxable income. But not all dollars are taxed: In addition to the taxpayer's personal deduction, there is an additional deduction for each dependent, and the taxpayer either gets a standard deduction or itemizes deductions and subtracts them from gross earnings. Currently, a family of four pays no taxes on approximately its first $22,800 of gross income. The tax brackets in Table 17.1 cover net

payroll tax
a tax on earnings that funds Social Security and Medicare.

progressive tax
a tax structured such that higher-income individuals pay a larger percentage of their income in taxes.

regressive tax
a tax structured such that higher-income individuals pay a lower percentage of their income in taxes.

marginal tax bracket
the tax rate you pay on the last dollar that you earn in a given year.

TABLE 17.1
Tax Brackets, 2005

SCHEDULE X: SINGLE TAXPAYER

IF TAXABLE INCOME IS OVER	BUT NOT OVER	THE TAX IS
$0	$7,550	10% of the amount over $0
$7,550	$30,650	$755 plus 15% of the amount over $7,550
$30,650	$74,200	$4,220.00 plus 25% of the amount over $30,650
$74,200	$154,800	$15,107.50 plus 28% of the amount over $74,200
$154,800	$336,550	$37,675.50 plus 33% of the amount over $154,800
$336,550	no limit	$97,653.00 plus 35% of the amount over $336,550

SCHEDULE Y-1: MARRIED TAXPAYERS FILING JOINTLY OR QUALIFYING WIDOW OR WIDOWER

IF TAXABLE INCOME IS OVER	BUT NOT OVER	THE TAX IS
$0	$15,100	10% of the amount over $0
$15,100	$61,300	$1,510.00 plus 15% of the amount over $15,100
$61,300	$123,700	$8,440.00 plus 25% of the amount over $61,300
$123,700	$188,450	$24,040.00 plus 28% of the amount over $123,700
$188,450	$336,550	$42,170.00 plus 33% of the amount over $188,450
$336,550	no limit	$91,043.00 plus 35% of the amount over $336,550

SOURCE: Internal Revenue Service.

income after all these deductions—known as *taxable income.* The average tax rate is always less than the marginal tax rate. Some low-income workers even "pay" a negative income tax when they file because they receive an earned income credit. The tax codes are so complicated and deductions are so difficult to understand that it is almost impossible for many taxpayers to calculate their own taxes. Each year, more and more Americans hire outside experts or accountants to prepare their tax returns. Even the Internal Revenue Service's own telephone help line often gives out erroneous answers and advice. Unfortunately, the necessity of hiring accounting help adds to the overall costs of our system of taxation.

PAYROLL TAXES

Social Security taxes make up 6.5 percent of GDP. They take the form of a payroll tax, a tax split so that employees pay half and their employers pay the other half. Each pays 6.2 percent into the

Social Security Trust Fund and 1.45 percent into the Medicare trust fund. (We'll describe these trust funds later.) In effect, this tax split obscures the full impact of its burden—half is hidden in your employee benefits. (Of course, this is money that your employer might otherwise have been willing to pay to you directly as wages or fringe benefits.) If you are self-employed, however, you carry the full burden: 15.3 percent of the first $90,000 of the net income from your business or profession.

THE TAX BURDEN

So who pays what? Analysis of household income and tax burden by the CBO show that the top 10 percent of earners pay almost 50 percent of taxes. The bottom 20 percent pay only about 1 percent. Those numbers are a little skewed, however, as they only include the employee's portion of the payroll tax. The top 1 percent of

▶ **Do corporations pay their**
share in takes?

The floor of the New York Stock Exchange in New York City is where stock transactions affect the ownership and value of corporations. The decisions of corporate leaders that expand their businesses or, alternatively, lay off employees also affect government tax revenues. If you were the president or a member of Congress, how would you react if a major corporation announced that it was going to lay off 20,000 workers?

earners pay 21 percent of federal taxes. The bottom line is this: Most American workers pay more per year in payroll taxes than they do in income taxes.

Critics argue that the CBO analysis is flawed because it measures income, not wealth. Capital gains, such as the increase in the value of stock someone owns, are taxed at a lower rate than earned income. Profits from stock and real estate transactions are taxed only when they are sold, so capital gains can accumulate for years without generating any government revenue. As a result, the wealthy—especially the nonworking wealthy—escape taxation on the vast majority of their assets. Critics contend that the poor have little opportunity to accumulate wealth.

CORPORATE TAXES

▶ **Do corporations pay their share in taxes?** Taxes on corporations generate about 15 percent of the federal government's revenue. The United States has one of the highest effective corporate tax rates in the industrialized world, with a top tax rate of 35 percent. Taking into account state corporate taxes as well, the average U.S. corporation has an effective marginal tax rate of almost 40 percent on its net income. At the same time, corporate tax collection amounts to only about 2 percent of GDP, well below the international average of about 3.4 percent. The disparity between the tax rate and the taxes actually collected is explained by the numerous deductions and credits that federal and state laws provide. Even though the corporate tax rate is relatively high, the U.S. government depends less on business taxes as a source of revenue than most other nations.

Corporate income tax revenues depend, of course, on whether companies make a profit. During a recession, corporate profits can plummet or even vanish completely. Recession was one reason for the decline in corporate revenue in the first years of this century. It also explains the rapid expansion of corporate tax revenues in 2005 as the economy recovered. The U.S. corporate tax system also has numerous write-offs, often targeted to specific industries and resulting from successful lobbying, which are intended to elicit certain corporate behavior. Tax reforms implemented in 2003, for example, allowed many businesses to write off their expenses faster. One provision, called the SUV loophole, allowed businesses to deduct luxury sports utility vehicles from their income, provided that the vehicles were used for business purposes. Many critics of business tax policy brand such incentives "corporate welfare."

The consensus among most business experts is that worldwide, corporate tax revenues are in a period of decline. This trend began at the end of the Cold War and the breakup of the Soviet Union in the early 1990s. As nations try to remain competitive,

▶ **How can government seek**
increased revenues if it can't
keep raising tax rates forever?

this downward trend is likely to continue, keeping pressure on the
United States to lower its corporate tax rates

OTHER TAXES

Other taxes include excise taxes, customs duties, inheritance taxes,
and miscellaneous receipts. Excise taxes levied on fuel, alcohol,
and tobacco are paid by the producer and are folded into the price
of the product. Customs duties are taxes on foreign-made goods
imported into the United States and, like excise taxes, are part of
the consumer's final price. Inheritance taxes are on the asset value
of a person's estate; opponents have recently taken to calling this
the "death tax." Miscellaneous receipts include income earned by
the Federal Reserve in its day-to-day operations.

The federal portion of the gasoline tax is 18.4 cents per gallon.
States add up to 33 cents per gallon on top of the federal rate (the
average state adds a little over 20 cents). Federal cigarette taxes range
from 39 to 82 cents a pack. The federal tax on beer is a nickel a can.
On wine, it varies from 21 to 67 cents for a standard 750-ml bottle.
(Imported wine also carries a hefty customs duty.) The tax rises with
alcohol content. Eighty-proof liquor is taxed at $2.14 for a 750-ml
bottle. There are also taxes on cigars, smokeless tobacco, and loose
tobacco. Critics of our tax system maintain that the "sin taxes" on
alcohol and tobacco add to the regressivity of the overall system.
Because today the poor are more likely to smoke than the wealthy
and because their income is smaller, tobacco taxes eat up a larger
percentage of a poor person's income than a richer person's income.

Despite increased imports, customs duty income has
remained relatively stable, due in large part to our expansion of
free-trade zones and worldwide limits on tariffs. The inheritance
tax is due to be phased out by 2010; however, unless further legislation is passed, it will reappear in 2011.

TAX ANALYSIS

Finding the optimum tax rate is a difficult job for the government
to perform. At first glance, you might think that generating more
revenue is a simple matter of raising tax rates. But as we shall see,
it is not that simple.

▶ **How can government seek increased revenues if it can't
keep raising tax rates forever?** In the mid-1970s, Professor Arthur
Laffer of the University of Southern California sketched out an
interesting theory on a cocktail napkin. (Figure 17.3) (He happened
to be conversing with a *Wall Street Journal* columnist, who did not
allow the theory to remain confined to the cocktail napkin.) Laffer
reasoned that if the tax rate is zero, government revenue is zero.
That's pretty obvious. Zero times anything is zero. But Laffer

Critics complain that taxes on tobacco
and alcoholic beverages hit the poor harder
than the wealthy. Why are tobacco and
alcoholic beverages taxed more heavily
than other consumer products?

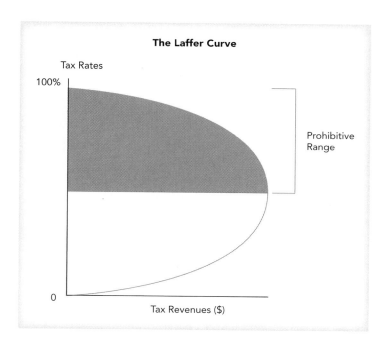

FIGURE 17.3
The Laffer Curve

**The Laffer Curve represents an economist's the-
ory** about how to design tax rates in a manner
that will help the government and the economy. It
argues that setting tax rates too high will actually
reduce the amount of revenue collected by government. Are there any specific assumptions that
underlie this theory? Should the theory be proven
before it is adopted by government officials?

SOURCE: investopedia.com

▶ **How fair is the** tax system to the poor? the wealthy? the middle class?

Laffer curve
an economic model that maintains that a higher rate of taxation can result in lower government revenues.

dynamic modeling
tax analysis that takes into account how an increase or decrease in one tax rate can affect government revenue from other sources.

Arthur Laffer advanced the controversial theory that government revenues can increase by cutting taxes. His views were influential during Ronald Reagan's presidency. What are the risks from using Laffer's theory as the basis for tax policy?

maintained that government revenue will also be zero if the tax rate is 100 percent. Why? Because if the government takes all their earnings, no one will go to work! Zero times everything is still zero. Laffer sketched out a graph, now known as the **Laffer curve,** to demonstrate that there exists some rate of taxation above which government revenue drops. A sufficiently high tax rate, Laffer concluded, discourages productivity.

Laffer was one of the chief proponents of supply-side economics, the theory that cutting taxes would increase the economy, thereby ultimately increasing government revenues. The supplysiders were the major theoretical force behind President Reagan's tax cut policies of the early 1980s. Although opponents argue that the tax cuts were a failure because the deficit exploded during the Reagan years, revenues did increase dramatically. From 1980 to 1990, government revenues almost doubled, from $517 billion to over $1 trillion. Spending, however, skyrocketed from $591 billion to $1.25 trillion. A yearly deficit that had been about $70 billion at the beginning of the decade had ballooned to over $220 billion by the end. Congress and the president spent all the new revenue, plus an additional $1.7 trillion that had to be raised by borrowing.

The bottom line on tax revenue seems to be this:

1. Over a period of several years, revenues increase.
2. If the government raises marginal tax rates, revenue goes up. (Overall economic growth might slow a bit, but tax revenue rises.)
3. If the government cuts marginal tax rates, revenue goes up. (It might dip at first during a transitional period, but that decline won't last for long as the overall economy grows; a smaller percentage of a larger pie can still lead to a larger piece of pie.)

▶ **How fair is the tax system to the poor? the wealthy? the middle class?** A second big question that arises when we analyze the tax system is equity. Is it fair? No one likes paying taxes, but the government needs a source of revenue to fund even the most minimal services. Should the wealthy be taxed at a higher rate—a more progressive rate—in order to provide more services for the poor? Critics argue that the current economic system is unfair. They say that the disparity between rich and poor is too wide. Despite significant gains in real GDP (GDP after factoring out inflation), most real-wage increases have gone to the wealthiest Americans. Would a more progressive tax system help reverse that trend? Or would it discourage the wealthy from putting forth the extra effort and productive investments that lead to gains in productivity? A related question is this:

▶ **Are there any better**
ways to collect taxes?

flat tax
a tax structured such that all income, after limited exemptions, is subject to the same tax rate.

national sales tax
a flat tax collected on all purchases.

Does fairness matter as much as efficiency? Should the government try to foster an economic system that generates revenue while boosting the overall economy, or is it preferable to sacrifice growth for equity? Many Americans disagree about the answers.

INTENDED AND UNINTENDED CONSEQUENCES: DYNAMIC MODELING

Tax policies have consequences. If we raise cigarette taxes significantly, we will certainly raise per-pack revenue, but that may not raise government revenue. If we raise taxes high enough, people will smoke less or fewer people will smoke. That might be the goal that we are trying to achieve. Many health experts believe that reducing smoking rates will reduce long-term health care costs. But then we might end up with huge organized crime–dominated enterprises illegally smuggling cigarettes, cutting off revenue and forcing increased government spending as we try to battle this new tobacco cartel. Sound familiar? That was what happened with alcohol when the United States conducted its "noble experiment" of Prohibition between 1920 and 1933.

Barring the organized crime scenario, our tax increase will have other consequences. The less people smoke, the less they drink. (You might think that is a good thing as well. But let's just stick with the tax consequences here.) When people drink less, the government ends up with less alcoholic-beverage tax revenue. **Dynamic modeling** tries to take such effects into account by asking, How will a tax increase in one area affect revenue in another area? Our example is a small, relatively isolated situation. It is important to understand that all taxation decisions have similar unintended effects, can be difficult to predict, and can have significant consequences that may not be revealed until years later. Any responsible policymaker must consider both the short-term and long-term effects of a proposed tax.

▶ **Are there any better ways to collect taxes?** The IRS tax code is long, complicated, and not particularly efficient. Its evolution over the years has turned it into a mishmash of special-interest tax breaks and exemptions. Many of those exemptions—such as the home mortgage interest exemption—benefit such a wide range of taxpayers that any attempt to revise the code stirs up wide-ranging opposition. Nonetheless, numerous reforms have been offered in recent years. Some would tinker with the existing system. One common suggestion, often promoted by liberals, is to raise rates on the highest earners. Others would reform and simplify the entire system.

Major reform initiatives fall under one of two basic concepts, a flat tax or a national sales tax. The most common variant of the **flat tax** is one offered by former U.S. Congressman Dick Armey, a Republican from Texas (and a former economics professor). Under his proposal, married couples would receive a $26,000 standard exemption plus a personal exemption of just over $5,000 for each family member. There would be no other deductions. All income over the exempted amount would be taxed at 17 percent. Net business income would be likewise taxed at 17 percent. This flat tax would generate a little less revenue than the present system, and the large standard deduction would make this tax modestly progressive. Many lower-income families would pay no income tax at all, and most taxpayers would not need to hire accountants to do their taxes.

Under a proposed **national sales tax,** the federal government would collect a surcharge of about 23 percent on purchases of all goods and services. Since such a sales tax would, by its nature, be regressive (low-income people typically have to spend everything they earn; higher-income people can save part of their income), each household would receive a rebate check at the beginning of each month, equal to 23 percent of poverty-level income based on family size. Although the tax rate might seem high, the sales tax would replace both income and payroll taxes. Many economists believe that under this plan, retail prices for many goods would drop: they argue that a significant portion of the cost of goods comes from embedded taxes. One aim of the national sales tax would be to bring illegal business activities under the tax umbrella. No one is suggesting that drug dealers would collect and pay taxes on their sales, but when they spend their profits, they would make a greater contribution to the legitimate economy.

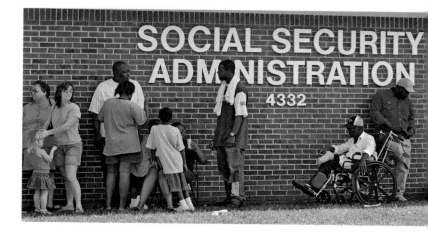

Social Security provides modest income support for the elderly, disabled, widows and widowers, and children who have had a parent die. Do you think this expensive government program will still exist when you retire? What might cause the program to end?

discussionquestions

1. What differentiates a progressive tax from a regressive tax? Which tax has the biggest impact on the average American?

2. Do you think that corporations pay their fair share of taxes? Why or why not? What are the consequences of raising corporate taxes?

▶ **What do we spend**
most of our tax money on?

practicequiz

1. What are progressive income taxes?
  a. when taxation rates get higher and higher each year, usually because the rates are tied to the Consumer Price Index
  b. when taxation gets progressively lower, year after year
  c. when income is taxed at a higher percentage the more income one makes
  d. when income is taxed at a lower percentage the more income one makes

2. How is revenue generated for the Social Security trust fund?
  a. federal income tax
  b. the employee portion of the payroll tax
  c. the employer portion of the payroll tax
  d. half and half from employee payroll tax and employer payroll tax

3. What's "corporate welfare"?
  a. government assistance for high-income business people who file fraudulent welfare claims
  b. various tax write-offs and loopholes for corporations that are meant to induce certain behavior (such as keeping a company's main factory in the U.S.)
  c. governmental subsidies granted to certain businesses for their compliance with environmental regulations
  d. corporations' voluntary donations to governmental welfare programs

4. How are "sin taxes" regressive?
  a. because people who buy "sin taxed" goods, like caviar and imported champagne, are more likely to be rich
  b. because the people who consume "sin taxed" goods, such as cigarettes and 80-proof liquor, are more likely to be poor
  c. because notions of taxing goods because they are "sinful" is believed to be politically regressive by some
  d. because the people who consume things such as cigarettes and high-proof alcohol are usually well off

Answers: 1-c, 2-d, 3-b, 4-b.

Expenditures

▶ **What do we spend most of our tax money on?** In 2005, the United States government's largest expenditure was Social Security benefits, with an outlay of $522 billion. Defense spending came in second, at $495 billion. Income security, which you will learn about shortly, came in third at $346 billion. Medicare absorbed $298 billion, and other health care programs accounted for $250 billion in spending. Interest on the national debt ate up $183 billion. All other major spending programs, including education, science, transportation, veterans' benefits, and justice, came in at well under $100 billion each.[3]

Government expenditures continually expand. One reason for this is that levels of "current services" have become the baseline for most government programs. That means that the starting point for next year's budget is this year's budget, plus increases needed because of increased population and inflation. When politicians talk about balancing "the budget," they are generally referring to the current services budget. So even if spending increases from one year to the next, government officials can claim that they have cut the budget as long as the rate of increase is below the current services projection.

SOCIAL SECURITY

The U.S. government's Social Security program was established in 1935, during the Great Depression. At that time, more than half of the elderly lived in poverty, and the program's goal was to provide a minimal pension for older Americans. In many ways, Social Security was a conservative response to the far more radical demands during the 1930s for guaranteed levels of income and more substantive aid to the poor. The initial payroll tax rate was 1 percent, paid by both employee and employer. It was levied on only the first $3,000 of annual income. At first, monthly benefits were not indexed to inflation—what you received was what you expected to receive for life. Not until the 1950s did Congress authorize a cost-of-living-adjustment (COLA). And not until 1975 did these COLA increases become annual and automatic. Originally, Social Security covered only employees of industrial and commercial firms, excluding farm workers and domestic servants. Since then, it has been expanded to include not only those workers but also retirement-age surviving spouses, dependents, and disabled working-age people.

Technically, Social Security is an independent, off-budget program. It was originally intended to be self-financing. As long as there were several workers for each retiree, that concept worked fairly well. In the 1970s, however, Social Security started running a slight deficit. It was evident that the problem would worsen over

▶ **Does that mean that**
Social Security will go broke?!

Social Security Trust Fund
a fund to pay future Social Security bene-fits supposedly being built through today's payroll tax.

the long term. Americans were getting older. There were fewer workers per retiree, and retirees were living longer. Anyone examining the demographics could see more substantial problems on the horizon. When baby boomers started to retire and the smaller Generation X took their place in the workforce, an even greater burden would fall on the remaining workers.

In 1983, a special commission headed by the economist Alan Greenspan generated a number of reform measures that were enacted by Congress. The central purpose of the reforms was to create a surplus, known as the **Social Security Trust Fund,** that would save money over the years to help bridge the gap created as the boomers retired. It did this primarily in two ways. First, the retirement age was raised: Over several years, the age for drawing full retirement benefits increased from 65 to 67. Second, the reform significantly increased payroll taxes—again, over a period of years—to the relatively high rate that now prevails. It also introduced several other changes, including raising the tax rate on the self-employed so that it now equals the combined rate paid by employers and employees. As a result, Social Security immediately began running a surplus, surpassing $50 billion a year by 1989 and $100 billion by 1999. In 2005, the surplus was $173 billion, and it is projected to continue to grow through 2015. But shortly thereafter, the picture will change dramatically: as ever more baby boomers retire, Social Security payments will start to outstrip payroll taxes.

By the time we get to 2018, when Social Security is expected to start paying out more than it is bringing in, the fund will be worth more than $4 trillion. The problem is that the trust fund money isn't sitting in a vault somewhere. It's already been spent. One reason that the nation has been able to run such large deficits over the past couple of decades is that the Treasury has borrowed money from the Social Security Trust Fund, depositing an electronic IOU in its place. Although, as we have said, Social Security is supposed to be off-budget, deficit figures subtract the Social Security surplus. In fact, a closer look at the alleged surpluses from 1998 through 2001 shows mainly smoke and mirrors. On-budget surpluses occurred in only two of the four years, and in one of those years, the surplus was less than $1 billion. The reported cumulative surplus of $559 billion amounted to an on-budget surplus of only $23 billion!

▶ **Does that mean that Social Security will go broke?!** So if the $4 trillion has already been spent, does that mean that it is gone? Not really. The government owes itself electronic IOUs,

which have also accrued interest payments. Does it mean that the federal government will default on its Social Security obligations—that when *you* retire, there will be no Social Security for you? Almost certainly not. The strength of the American dollar, and the confidence that it engenders, depends on the United States' meeting its financial obligations. The United States has never defaulted on its debt—even to itself—and it would be financial suicide if it were to start now. But the long-term consequences of rising Social Security obligations and decreasing surpluses will have significant implications for future U.S. budgets. We'll talk about the long-range forecast for Social Security later in this chapter.

DEFENSE

The nation's largest on-budget appropriations are for defense. Since the dawn of history, war and defense have been expensive propositions. Many factors lead to the high costs of maintaining the armed forces. Of course, military personnel need to be paid. Salary and retirement benefits comprise a large portion of the U.S. military budget. In addition, the armed services provide housing and medical care for soldiers and their families, and the military employs a large number of civilian personnel. Throw in administrative costs, base construction and upkeep, training, and logistics, and more than half of the military budget goes for operations and support.

The second large defense spending area includes the development, testing, and procurement of weapons systems. Weapons development and procurement are always controversial, especially in a world in which the United States is clearly the dominant superpower. The Air Force, for example, has to decide whether to proceed with the purchase of more sophisticated F-22 fighters or whether it would be better served with the cheaper but newer Joint Strike Fighter. The Marines have to decide whether their long-term interests are best served by buying more conventional heavy-lift helicopters or by transitioning to the more expensive but faster tilt-rotor aircraft. The Army has to decide whether it needs more reconnaissance helicopters or whether it should transition to unmanned drones. The Navy has to decide whether to keep all eleven of its nuclear-powered aircraft carriers and their support groups or to build smaller, nonnuclear carriers to allow it to spread its presence over a greater area. All these decisions must be made within the context of what is best for national security and for military personnel and within the scope of the overall budget. It also

▶ What's the difference between Medicare and Medicaid?

income security
the notion that the government should establish programs that provide a safety net for society's poorest members.

Medicare
health care coverage for senior citizens.

Medicaid
health care coverage for the poor.

This Nimitz-class aircraft carrier is on its way to aid in disaster relief after a tsunami hit Southeast Asia in late 2004. Each such vessel costs about $4.5 billion to build and $160 million a year to operate. Are such expensive ships necessary for our nation's defense?

requires military leaders and members of Congress to make certain assumptions about future threat levels that are difficult to predict and that may well change over time. Will China emerge as a major threat? If so, will the Chinese match us technologically or just try to offset our power with a larger military? Will we remain the sole global superpower? How can we fashion rapid-response units that can take the field in several global hotspots at one time? What should be our worst-case scenario for planning troop and asset deployment? Uncertainty makes each of these decisions difficult and potentially costly in terms of both dollars and security.

These decisions are also influenced by the lobbying decision makers pathway because companies that supply planes, ships, and other equipment will pressure their congressmen and Defense Department officials to choose to buy their products.

Despite the fact that defense spending, in dollars, is at record levels, it is much lower as a percentage of both GDP and the overall budget than it was during the latter stages of the Cold War and

far below comparable levels during World War II. At the height of World War II, in 1944, military spending accounted for more than 80 percent of the federal budget and 38 percent of GDP. Cold War defense spending peaked in the late 1980s at 27 percent of the federal budget and 6 percent of GDP. Today, defense absorbs 20 percent of the budget, but this percentage could increase, depending on developments in the Iraq war, military action in Afghanistan, and the defense against terrorism.

INCOME SECURITY

The idea behind **income security** is that the government should provide a safety net for the most vulnerable members of society. The largest components of the income security program are the earned-income credit, the child tax credit, supplemental security income, unemployment compensation, and food stamps. Together, these programs comprise almost three-fourths of total federal income security spending. Unemployment payments tend to rise and fall, depending on the state of the economy; they have fallen over the past several years as the economy has recovered from its post-9/11 slump. The food stamp program is administered by the Department of Agriculture and provides aid to about 24 million families. Smaller income security programs include Temporary Assistance to Needy Families (TANF), the Women, Infants and Children (WIC) program, and federal child support enforcement measures. Even smaller amounts go to foster care and adoption assistance. The number of families receiving TANF has been cut in half in the past decade as a result of the Welfare Reform Act of 1996. TANF, the cash portion of income assistance, is often referred to generically as "welfare."

GOVERNMENT MEDICAL CARE

▶ **What's the difference between Medicare and Medicaid?**
Medicare and Medicaid are two separate, often-confused programs with common origins. Both were established in the mid-1960s as part of President Lyndon Johnson's Great Society. Since then, exploding medical costs have been one of the largest contributors to increased government spending. Over the past forty years, health care costs have outstripped the general rate of inflation. Part of this is due to improvements in treatment procedures, most of which are very expensive. Improvements in the quality of health care lead to longer life expectancy—which means that the average senior citizen spends more years receiv-

▶ **Why does so much** go to pay off the interest on the debt rather than the debt itself?

what **YOU** can do!

Go to the Web site at the Congressional Budget Office at **www.cbo.gov** and read the projected costs of specific programs. Can you identify any wasteful or unnecessary expenditures? If so, write a letter to your representative and senator.

ing Medicare coverage and that coverage costs far more than it did in earlier times.

Medicare provides health insurance coverage for retired people (beginning at age 65), as well as for disabled younger people. Part A, which covers hospitalization, is funded through the Medicare payroll tax. Part B, which covers doctor visits, is funded through general revenues and premiums paid by recipients. The new Part D, which took effect in 2006, provides prescription drug coverage to seniors, who will pay a little less than a quarter of the costs of the program through premiums. Parts B and D are optional, although almost all seniors enroll in Part B and most will likely enroll in Part D. In 1974, Medicare spending accounted for 0.7 percent of GDP; today, it is over 2.6 percent. By 2050, if no reforms are enacted, Medicare spending alone will account for between 8 and 9 percent of the *total* U.S. economy. About 30 percent of this cost will result from the new prescription drug benefit. As the investment expert Warren Buffett once said, "When you find yourself in a hole, the first thing to do is stop digging."[4] When faced with long-term Medicare financing questions, Congress did not follow Buffett's advice and added an expensive new benefit before addressing stability issues. Later in this chapter, we'll discuss these long-term issues in the context of total federal debt.

Medicare is for the general over-65 population and for the disabled; the economically disadvantaged receive health services through **Medicaid.** Under this joint program between the federal government and the states, the federal government provides an average of 57 percent of Medicaid's financing. Because some states provide more services than others, matching percentages vary. Most of the 57 million Medicaid enrollees are children and pregnant women. But the overwhelming amount of Medicaid funding goes to the elderly and disabled. Much of that money is spent on nursing homes, home health care, and social services for retired people who have exhausted their life savings.

Five years after it was established in 1965, Medicaid spending comprised 0.3 percent of GDP; today, it accounts for 1.7 percent. If increases continue at current levels, total spending could hit 4 percent of GDP by 2050.

INTEREST AND OTHER SPENDING

As government debt rises, interest payments also rise. In 2005, interest on the debt totaled $182 billion. Almost 7 percent of the total budget goes to pay interest on the debt. More than half of the 2005 federal budget deficit consisted of interest payments.

▶ **Why does so much go to pay off the interest on the debt rather than the debt itself?** But that's only part of the story. Notes held by the Social Security and Medicare trust funds also receive interest payments. Using smoke-and-mirrors accounting again, the federal government considers this interest to be income, offsetting total interest payments. Since the trust fund interest technically accrues, a truer mark of interest costs in 2005 is $352 billion. That's because the debt held by government trust funds is about two-thirds the size of the trust fund held by the public.

The size of the debt is only one factor when it comes to interest payments. Because interest rates are set by the open market, an issue we'll discuss when we cover monetary policy later in the chapter, the cost of financing the debt can rise or fall independently of the size of the debt. If interest rates were to rise from 4 percent to 5 percent, debt-financing costs would rise by 25 percent. Of course, the government has its debt instruments spread over several years, with varying lengths of maturity, so a temporary rate change would have little overall impact. However, an extended period of rising rates could force the government to issue more of its notes at a higher cost, thereby driving up the long-term cost of borrowing. Unfortunately, interest rates have been on a slow, steady climb for the past few years, paralleling both the reviving economy and continual increases in government borrowing.

Spending for all other programs falls significantly below those that we have discussed in detail. For example, the entire Department of Education budget for 2005 was about $71 billion. This includes a significant increase in federal education spending over the past decade as a result of the No Child Left Behind Act (see **LINK** *Chapter 3, pages 79–80*). NASA's budget was $16 billion; the National Science Foundation accounted for $5.5 billion. The Department of Energy received about $24 billion. The Department of Transportation—mentioned in the introduction to this chapter—spent $58 billion. The Agriculture Department's budget was about $95 billion, but $33 billion of that included the food stamps program. (Subsidies to farmers, also a part of the Agriculture Department's budget, accounted for about $15 billion.) The Environmental Protection Agency (EPA) receives less than $8 billion annually. With its $21 billion budget, the Department of Justice runs the federal prisons, the Federal Bureau of Investigation (FBI), the Drug Enforcement Agency (DEA), and the Bureau of Alcohol, Tobacco, Firearms, and Explosives (ATF), as well as the U.S. Attorney's Office.

▶ **Everyone talks about** the crisis that is coming in Social Security and Medicare—is it real?

discussionquestions

1. What government program accounts for the greatest percentage of government spending?

2. How have medical care costs affected government spending? What are entitlements, and how are they created?

One of the difficulties of creating the budget at the federal level is caused by the pervasiveness of **entitlements**—mandatory spending required by law that is not subject to the budgetary process. Entitlements account for three out of every five dollars that the federal government spends. Almost all of the spending on Social Security and Medicare is mandatory, as are large percentages of income security and Medicaid. Federal law requires that all who meet certain specifications are entitled to certain benefits. Since discretionary spending accounts for less than half of the total budget, Congress's hands are somewhat tied as legislators attempt to constrain spending. Of course, since Congress wrote the laws enacting the entitlements in the first place, it can rework legislation to alleviate this complication. As you might suspect, that would tend to anger the people benefiting from the current system. (See the *Pathways of Action* feature on AARP on page 671.) All of these spending discussions lead back to one central point: It's still *your* money. The only way you can influence how it is spent is to let federal officials know what you think about their priorities.

practicequiz

1. When politicians talk about balancing the budget they are usually referring to
   a. the current services budget
   b. the "big five" areas of the budget: Social Security, Defense, Medicare, national debt interest, and Homeland Security
   c. all major expenditures, minus Social Security
   d. all major expenditures, minus the Social Security Trust Fund

2. Cost of Living Allowance (COLA) increases were a part of the Social Security program from the start, though they did not become annual and automatic until the 1950s.
   a. true   **b.** false

3. What's one reason defense spending involves difficult decisions for the government?
   a. because spending billions on destructive weaponry is morally problematic to many people in government
   b. because it's not always clear if national defense is more important to our government than other areas such as education and the environment
   c. because specific choices—regarding weaponry, for instance—are always based on future geo-political circumstances that are sometimes hard to predict
   d. because the public scrutinizes these choices and, given the expense, can be outraged if unwise decisions are made

4. As a percentage of the GDP, current defense spending is
   a. much higher than it was during the end of the Cold War.
   b. somewhat higher than it was during the end of the Cold War.
   c. about the same as it was during the end of the Cold War.
   d. much lower than it was during the end of the Cold War.

Answers: 1-a, 2-b, 3-c, 4-d.

Long-Term Budget Challenges: The Coming Storm

For most of the past thirty-five years, the United States government has run deficits. For the last twenty years, the impact of those deficits has been lessened by surpluses pouring into the Social Security and Medicare trust funds. But fifteen years from now, if changes aren't made, the surpluses will disappear. Over the long term, commitments to Social Security, Medicare, and Medicaid will become such a large part of the overall economy that they will become unsustainable.

▶ **Everyone talks about the crisis that is coming in Social Security and Medicare—is it real?** Left unchecked, spending for Social Security will account for 6.4 percent of GDP in 2050, and Medicare and Medicaid will use a combined 21.9 percent, for a total of 27.3 percent.[5] Over the past fifty years, total government spending has averaged 18.5 percent of GDP. What this means is that by 2050, these three programs will absorb 150 percent of average government spending without appropriating a penny for food stamps, defense, science, space exploration, or anything else—including interest on the federal debt, which is projected to average 2 percent of GDP in coming years.

Something's got to give. You can't run an annual deficit equal to 18 percent of GDP without wrecking the economy. Solving this problem will require either huge tax increases or huge benefit cuts—or some combination of the two. With our aging workforce, this seems to foreshadow some sort of generational conflict, a conflict that might be eased in part if the immigration of working-age foreign-born people continues to surge and more of them become legal, Social Security–paying workers. Boston University economist Laurence Kotlikoff and financial columnist Scott Burns have

▶ **Would it help to**
raise the retirement age?

entitlements
government expenditures required by law.

Treasury bills (T-bills)
interest-bearing IOUs issued by the Treasury Department.

crowding-out effect
the fact that interest rates are forced higher as the government borrows a larger portion of available money.

called this confluence of more retirees and fewer workers "the coming generational storm."[6]

For two decades, trust fund surpluses have masked the true size of the nation's debt. The actual trust fund money has already been spent on budgeted appropriations, and in its place the Treasury holds interest-bearing notes, called **Treasury bills (T-bills).** When the social insurance programs go into deficit, they will call in these IOUs. At that time, the U.S. government will have to replace the portion of the deficit that has been hidden by trust fund borrowing and start repaying, with interest, the money that it initially borrowed from the trust funds. The notes that represent the trust fund surplus will come due around 2042. After that, the rising social insurance deficit will have to be financed from other taxes or by borrowing.

This generational storm is still decades down the road and may break just when *you* are ready to retire. Some analysts think that the trust fund might be solvent as late as 2050. At present, the trust fund will continue to grow for another ten years, so there is little public sense of urgency or alarm. Meaningful reform will require hard choices, some of which we'll outline. But keep this in mind: House members are elected to two-year terms, senators come up for reelection every six years, and presidents are elected every four years, for a maximum of two terms. This means that our political system tends to focus on immediacy. Not many politicians want to run on a campaign platform of cutting future benefits and raising present taxes to solve a problem that will come to a head long after they have cleaned out their desks and moved on.

No matter what long-term measures the United States takes in addressing these revenue shortfalls, it is almost certain that part of the equation will include higher debt. If the debt rises as a percentage of GDP, not just in absolute terms, we risk driving up interest rates. If the government borrows an increasing share of the money supply, rates will go up for everyone. This is called the **crowding-out effect.** As rates rise, many potential borrowers find themselves priced out of the market, with negative long-term effects on employment and the overall economy. Higher rates also mean that the government's debt is financed at a greater cost. Not only will government interest payments be higher because the debt has increased, but the problem will be compounded because the rate that the government pays on T-bills and savings bonds will be higher.

ADDRESSING THE PROBLEM

The problem is simple, but the solution must be multifaceted. Simply put, there is not enough money to meet the government's long-term obligations. However, the problem is so large that no single adjustment can bring the budget into balance.

▶ **Would it help to raise the retirement age?** Let's start with Medicare. Since 1970, Medicare costs have increased from 0.7 percent to 2.5 percent of GDP. So far, the overwhelming majority of this increase—more than 80 percent of it—has been due to health care cost increases, not the aging of the population. But the rapid aging of the population over the next two decades will compound this problem even if medical costs cease to grow faster than inflation, which is unlikely. One simple step toward alleviating this problem would be to raise the age of eligibility for Medicare. Although the full retirement age for Social Security rises over time, people are still eligible for Medicare coverage at age 65. At the very least, it would make sense to tie Medicare coverage to the retirement age, thus reducing the total number of coverage years. Other changes, such as increasing premiums and capping payments, would be more painful for recipients but would result in greater savings.

The federal government has several options for Medicaid. Since it is a matching-fund cooperative program administered jointly by the federal and state governments, the federal government could reduce its matching rate. Alternately, it could require copayments from program recipients. This would both increase government revenue and likely reduce the use of services, because recipients would probably be more selective about the number of trips to their doctor if they were responsible for part of the cost. The federal government gives the states great latitude in the types of services they offer under Medicaid. By eliminating matching funds for all but select programs, the federal government could significantly reduce its obligations.

Savings from the Social Security programs could come from a reduction of benefits, a decidedly unpopular option. Cuts could be achieved in a number of ways other than across-the-board reductions. The Congressional Budget Office has suggested that Congress consider one or more of the following: reduction in initial benefits, reduction in the cost of living allowances, or a higher retirement age.

One way to reduce costs would be to tie future initial benefits to the consumer price index. Historically, wages have risen faster than prices. Initial benefits are currently linked to wages. By instead

1. If no adjustments are made, how much of GDP will mandatory government spending require by 2050? How much will be left for discretionary spending?

2. What area will account for the largest increase in spending between today and 2050? How can this increase be lessened? Why does the debt problem present a potential generational crisis?

linking benefits to prices, future beneficiaries would receive benefits equivalent to those of today's retirees but less than they would under the wage method. The long-term savings would be tremendous, reducing Social Security outlays by more than 25 percent in 2050. Program payments would be about 4.7 percent of GDP. That's still a significant increase from today, but it represents considerable savings over current projections. Since savings become more significant as time passes, the people most affected by the change—that is, *you*—would have decades to make adjustments.

Some economists believe that the CPI overstates the actual rate of inflation for most Americans. Individuals make lifestyle choices by substituting lower-priced items. Advocates of such a change argue that COLA increases could be safely set below CPI so that program costs would be lowered without affecting real purchasing power. Opponents counter that the CPI may actually understate inflation for the elderly, since health care costs are rising faster than overall inflation. Without question, cutting the COLA rate would save the government money.

Raising the retirement age would also cut future government spending. One way to counter rising life expectancies would be to push back the age at which a person can draw full retirement benefits. When Social Security paid its first monthly payment, in 1940, a 65-year-old person could expect to live another thirteen years. Now such a person can look forward to an average of eighteen more years. (You should also realize that when the Social Security program began, life expectancy at birth was less than 65 for white males and just a little over 65 for white females—and significantly lower for African Americans of both genders. The average person could not expect to live until retirement age.) Twenty years from now, life expectancy will most likely be even higher. By slowly raising the retirement age to account for longer lives, costs could be contained. One plan under consideration would raise the age incrementally until it reaches 70 in 2032. After that, it would continually increase one month every two years. That would decrease outlays for Social Security by 0.8 percent of GDP by 2050 and by a greater amount from that point forward. Additional savings would be realized if the Medicare eligibility age were tied to this increasing retirement age.

Of course, boosting the payroll tax remains an option. Even a small increase now would help add to the trust fund and extend the life of the systems. Some analysts contend, however, that payroll taxes are a detriment to employment. Businesses have to consider the increased tax cost when adding new jobs, and the higher the payroll tax goes, the more hesitant they will be to take on more workers. Furthermore, a payroll tax increase would shift a larger burden to younger workers, often as they are starting out in entry-level jobs with limited benefits and incurring the heavy costs of setting up households, buying homes, and starting families.

There are options beyond the CBO recommendations, of course. Means testing could be established for both Medicare and Social Security, eliminating or drastically reducing benefits for wealthier Americans. To do that, however, Congress would face an angry response from motivated retirees with time on their hands and resources at their disposal to use the elections, lobbying decision makers, and grassroots mobilization pathways.

1. What, according to some economists, is "the coming generational storm"?
   a. when a new generation of Americans realizes that they will have to pay for the inroads into our infrastructure caused by global warming
   b. when a new generation of Americans will confront the problem of the government's galloping expenses and shrinking revenues precipitated, in part, when the baby boom generation starts receiving Social Security benefits
   c. when a new generation of Americans will have to confront the economic problems created by an underqualified national workforce—a product of today's neglect of public education
   d. when a new generation of Americans realizes that the money set aside for social assistance programs is drying up, yet neither poor Americans nor the private sector is equipped to help

2. In what way is our political system designed to avoid confronting long-range economic challenges?
   a. It is run by elites who do not personally feel the pressure of future economic disadvantage.
   b. Most politicians are lawyers, not economists.
   c. Because of brief election cycles, politicians can get away with avoiding the painful decisions that long-term solutions require; indeed they are rewarded politically for such avoidance.
   d. With its check and balances, and its layered structure, the government isn't designed to make any one figure or branch of government responsible for tough solutions.

what YOU can do!

As we have discussed, with congressional attention focused on the next election cycle, long-term issues often get pushed onto the back burner. You can help bring public attention to the grave challenges faced by our budgetary system over the next few decades by writing an editorial or composing a letter to the editor for your local newspaper. As a voice for tomorrow, you can help avert a crisis that could affect your entire generation.

---

3. Why would tying future Social Security benefits to the consumer price index improve the future of Social Security?
   a. because businesses would be encouraged to keep costs down, making the social security dollars that seniors spend go a lot farther
   b. because now Social Security benefits are determined by the cost of living allowance (COLA), which rises more quickly than the CPI
   c. because Social Security benefits are now determined by a set percentage of the GDP that is higher than the CPI
   d. because Social Security benefits are now linked to wages, which are higher than prices

4. When Social Security began, the average person could not expect to live until the legal retirement age of 65.
   a. true   b. false

Answers: 1-b, 2-c, 3-d, 4-a.

pathways of action

AARP

As it approaches its fiftieth anniversary, AARP, formerly known as the American Association of Retired Persons, ranks as one of the nation's most powerful interest groups. Claiming more than 35 million members, AARP has an additional advantage: Its members vote. Americans older than 50—the minimum age to join AARP—are the demographic group most likely to vote. Add in the fact that interest group members are more likely to vote than average citizens, and the organization's power becomes even more formidable.

Advocating for Social Security and Medicare, AARP played a key role in pushing through prescription drug coverage for seniors. It considers Part D only a first step toward making medical care more affordable and believes that patients should be able to purchase prescription medicine from other countries (for example, Canada) if that option is less expensive. Although AARP supports maintaining current Social Security benefits for the already retired, it recognizes that the system faces long-term problems. AARP's leaders believe that the sooner incremental changes are made, the better. Although they opposed President George W. Bush's proposal to put a portion of the payroll tax into private accounts—they were instrumental in defeating this idea before it ever got out of the

AARP is a powerful interest group with millions of members. If young adults are not organized and active, is there a risk that the interests of older Americans will receive extra protection in government policies?

▶ **Does the Federal Reserve change with elections?**

monetary policy
money supply management conducted by the Federal Reserve.

Federal Reserve System (the Fed)
the independent central bank of the United States.

Federal Open Market Committee (FOMC)
the policymaking arm of the Federal Reserve Board of Governors.

FIGURE 17.4
Regional Federal Reserve System

The Federal Reserve System contains twelve regional banks, each operating in a distinct economic district of the country. Each district is known by the name of the city where the federal reserve bank for that district is located.

SOURCE: http://www.federalreserve.gov/ communityaffairs/national/reservebanks.com

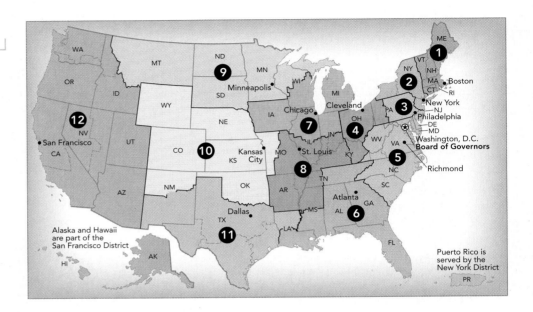

starting gate—they do advocate the creation of separate private accounts as a supplement to Social Security. AARP also works at both the state and national levels for laws that protect senior citizens from predatory lending practices and financial scams.

AARP is nonpartisan. It does not endorse particular candidates. Because more than half of all seniors belong to AARP, many of them attracted by the peripheral benefits that this group offers (LINK Ch. 13, pages 511–512), membership crosses demographic and political lines. As a result, its members do not vote as a bloc, which reduces its political power to some degree. However, politicians throughout the country realize the danger in taking positions contrary to policies supported by this powerful organization. ▨

Monetary Policy

In the simplest terms, **monetary policy** involves managing the supply of money in circulation within the United States. It is essential to strike a balance. Too much money coursing through the economy will be inflationary—remember the definition of inflation as "too much money chasing too few goods." But too little money will stifle economic growth. Keeping the balance right by managing monetary policy is the job of the Federal Reserve Board of Governors and its Federal Open Market Committee.

THE FEDERAL RESERVE BOARD

▶ **Does the Federal Reserve change with elections?** Created in 1913 by an act of Congress, the **Federal Reserve System (the Fed)** is our nation's independent central bank. (In most other Western nations, the central bank is controlled by the national government.) Although it is accountable to Congress, the Fed is free from political pressure because of the way it is structured. The seven members of its Board of Governors are appointed by the president of the United States, but they hold staggered fourteen-year terms. That makes it difficult for any president or for Congress to exert too much influence over its policies. Moreover, there are twelve regional federal reserve banks within the system (see Figure 17.4), each of which selects its own president, subject to approval by the Board of Governors. Although the presidents' terms are five years, most are reappointed. This further shields the Fed from political pressure.

The **Federal Open Market Committee (FOMC),** the Fed's policymaking arm, consists of the seven governors, the president of the New York Federal Reserve Board (who has a permanent seat), and four of the remaining eleven regional presidents, who serve on a rotating basis. The other seven presidents offer input.

Maximizing GDP and employment while minimizing inflation, which has been compared to walking a tightrope while

reserve ratios
minimum percentage of deposits that a financial institution must keep on hand.

federal funds rate
the interest rate that banks charge each other for overnight loans.

open-market operations
the buying and selling of securities by the Federal Reserve Board to manipulate the money supply.

discount rate
the rate the Fed charges member banks for short-term loans.

prime rate
interest rate that a bank charges its best customers.

stagflation
the combination of stagnant GDP, rising unemployment, and rapid inflation.

---

carrying a chainsaw, has been a formal part of the Fed's job description since 1977. When GDP is high and employment is full, the risk of inflation is ever present. A tight job market can drive up wages (which sounds good), but that can drive up prices (which is bad). Over the long term, inflation will undercut employment. A stagnant or declining GDP, mounting unemployment, or rapid inflation, whether they occur simultaneously or separately, will all trigger domestic and international demands that the Fed "do something."

The FOMC has five main tools to manipulate monetary policy. The first is bank **reserve ratios.** The Fed sets the amount of cash that member banks must keep on hand in order to insure against a run on deposits. (Such runs last occurred, on a major scale, during the Great Depression.) By raising the reserve ratio—in effect, lowering the amount of money that banks can loan out—the Fed can reduce the money supply. This is not a particularly effective Fed instrument, as most banks keep more cash than they are required to.

The second tool is the **federal funds rate**—a market-driven interest rate that banks charge one another for short-term (often overnight) loans. Rates drop when there is excess money in the system; they rise when available loan money is restricted. In fact, interest rates are essentially the "price" of money. Like any other commodity, its price goes up when there is more demand than supply, and its price drops when there is more supply than demand. Because the funds rate is market-driven—member banks negotiate interest rates, each participant looking for the best deal possible—the Fed has no direct control over this rate. But it does greatly influence the rate through the third tool, its **open-market operations,** by which it manipulates the total amount of money available in the market.

Most open-market operations today are carried out electronically, but consider the following simple example. Picture a huge safe with a divider down the middle. On the left side are piles of money. On the right side are piles of treasury bills (T-bills) and savings bonds—the federal government's IOUs. This hypothetical safe belongs to the Fed. Now, let's suppose that the Fed wants the federal funds rate to rise. Because the Fed cannot set this rate directly, it needs to make money scarcer so that interest rates rise. It takes some of its T-bills and savings bonds from the right side of the safe and sells them on the open market. It takes the cash that it receives from these sales and puts it in the left side of the safe, removing those funds from the circulating money supply. With less money available, the federal funds rate will rise. Higher interest rates will put the brakes on the economic engine. Because

the member banks immediately pass higher rates on to their customers, businesses and consumers are less likely to borrow, which slows business expansion and spending. If, by contrast, the Fed wants federal funds rates to fall, it takes money from the left side of the safe and puts it into circulation to buy securities from the open market, thus increasing the supply (and lowering the price) of money.

The fourth way that the Fed can intervene is though the **discount rate.** This is the interest rate that the Fed charges its member banks for loans. The discount rate is generally about 0.1 percent above the federal funds rate. Although the discount rate does not directly set the **prime rate,** the rate that banks charge their best customers, there is significant correlation between the two.

Finally, the Fed can buy and sell foreign currencies in an effort to stabilize world financial markets and currency exchange rates. Although this instrument is generally not used to affect the U.S. money supply, it is sometimes used to adjust the value of the dollar relative to other currencies.

The most significant of these tools are open-market operations and the discount rate. True monetarists favor creating a target money supply and manipulating policy to achieve that goal. Other economists, with less strictly monetarist views, choose different targets to keep inflation under control.

THE FED IN ACTION

When Paul Volcker was appointed chairman of the Fed Board of Governors in 1979, the economy was teetering on the edge of disaster. Skyrocketing energy prices, declining productivity, huge budget deficits, and a malignant condition that the media dubbed **stagflation** (the combination of a stagnant GDP, rising unemployment, and rapid inflation) had thrown the U.S. economy into its worst shape since the Great Depression. Volcker had to make a hard decision. If the Fed cut the money supply, interest rates would rise. That made sense. Less of a commodity drives up the price. But if the money supply went up, interest rates would rise as well. That seemed to violate the rule of supply and demand, but there was another culprit here: inflationary expectations. Inflation erodes the value of money. One dollar today will purchase more than one dollar will buy five years from now because prices will have increased. Banks and other lending institutions figured out where they thought inflation was headed and only lent at rates high enough to compensate for the devaluing effects of the expected inflation. That particular set of circumstances also violated

▶ **How are interest rates** and unemployment rates related to each other?

Phillips curve
an economic model that assumes an inverse relationship between unemployment and inflation.

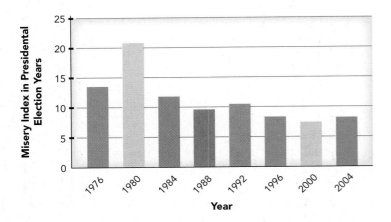

FIGURE 17.5
The Misery Index

The misery index shows the sum of the unemployment and inflation rates.

SOURCE: www.miseryindex.us

the **Phillips curve**—an economic model that assumes an inverse relationship between unemployment and inflation.

By tightening the money supply, Volcker's Fed could hold down inflation, but according to the Phillips curve, this would drive up unemployment. Phillips curve advocates argued that a certain level of inflation was acceptable as long as employment was maximized, but surprisingly, both inflation and unemployment shot up in the 1970s. For some economists, the validity of Keynesian macroeconomics—the pillar of post–World War II economic policy—seemed to have been cast in doubt. Headed into the 1976 presidential elections, Democrats had coined the term "misery index" to denote the sum of the unemployment and inflation rates (see Figure 17.5). This phrase would come back to haunt them in 1980.

From Volcker's perspective, the economy's problem was "loose money." The "accommodating" policy that the Fed pursued during the 1970s, along with generous federal spending on domestic and Cold War defense programs, had produced inflationary expectations. As banks forced interest rates up, unemployment rose. Volcker understood that the first order of business was to kill those inflationary expectations—"to wring inflation out of the economy," as it was said at the time. He put a stranglehold on the money supply.

▶ **How are interest rates and unemployment rates related to each other?** Volcker knew that his prescription would be painful. Tight money drove up interest rates and unemployment. But it killed inflation. After inflation had been brought under con-

trol, in the early 1980s, Volcker allowed the money supply to expand, but not fast enough to reignite inflationary expectations. More money in circulation lowered its price, meaning that interest rates fell. With lower interest rates, unemployment rates began to ease. In 1983, President Ronald Reagan appointed Volcker to a second four-year term as chairman, during which he continued to maintain a relatively tight money supply.

During Volcker's reign, the Fed focused on fighting inflation by controlling the actual amount of money in circulation. The problem with this approach is that money is hard to define and even harder to measure. The narrowest definition of money is cash in circulation. A broader definition includes checking accounts, savings accounts, and certificates of deposit. Even this broader definition is perhaps inadequate in a society where credit is relatively easy to obtain and people can spend money they don't actually have. That's one reason that Volcker's successor, Alan Greenspan (appointed in 1987), focused more on inflationary risk and interest rates—particularly the discount rate—and less on targeting a certain supply of money. Greenspan's successor, Ben Bernanke (appointed in 2006), hopes to hit a specific inflation target.

One of the problems the Fed faces in enacting monetary policy is that there is a significant lag time between Fed action and economic results. Efforts to slow the economy and control inflation—such as raising the discount rate—won't affect inflation and unemployment until months later. So the Fed has to be right twice: First, it needs to know where the economy is headed, and second, after making the correct initial determination, it needs to conjure up the correct response to the circumstances that it believes are emerging. To make things even more difficult, it has to be right every time, or its actions can make things worse. (Many economists and economic historians blame the length and severity of the Great Depression, to a significant degree, on the Fed's bad policy choices.)

MONETARY POLICY AND FISCAL POLICY

Monetary and fiscal policies don't always work together. Fiscal actions, taken by politicians, tend to inflate the economy. Elected officials are continually trying to serve their constituents and get through the next election cycle; their goal is to keep the economy going until their jobs are secured. The monetary policies of the Fed, by contrast, are focused on long-term economic interests. Former Fed Chairman Greenspan voiced concerns about rising budget deficits that we have noted in this chapter more than once. Congress, for its part, has often criticized the Fed for keeping too tight

discussion questions

1. What is the Federal Open Market Committee? How can it influence monetary policy?

2. From 1979 to 1987, what actions did Paul Volcker take to get the economy back on track? Did they work?

a rein on the money supply. Some members of Congress have occasionally gone so far as to threaten the Fed's independence.

When push comes to shove, though, the Fed has more weapons in its arsenal than Congress. By tightening the money supply sufficiently, it can significantly reduce the inflationary aspects of tax cuts or increased government spending. A concerted effort by the Fed could even put pressure on Congress to bring the debt problem under control. By tightening the money supply and driving up interest rates, the Fed could make deficit financing so expensive that it becomes a big issue sooner rather than later.

practice quiz

1. It's fair to say that, in terms of partisan politics, the Federal Reserve Board is
a. liberal
b. independent
c. conservative
d. aligned with the sitting president's politics

2. What's the FOMC?
a. the Federal Open Market Committee
b. the Financial Operation Monitoring Committee
c. the First Order Monetary Council
d. the Federal Organization of Monetary Concerns

3. The most significant tools by which the Fed manipulates the country's money supply are
a. congressional testimony by the Fed chair and FOMC directives.
b. open-market operations and the discount rate.
c. federal treasury directives and the prime lending rate.
d. closed-market operations and the federal funds rate.

4. Congress has more power to influence fiscal and monetary realities in the U.S. than does the Fed.
a. true   **b.** false

Answers: 1-b, 2-a, 3-b, 4-b.

ABOVE: **Federal Reserve Bank Chairman Ben Bernanke** will be highly influential with respect to interest rates and policies concerning inflation. In a democracy, is it wise to give unelected officials significant power over economic policy and other matters?

BELOW: **Former Federal Reserve Chairman Alan Greenspan** was very effective in communicating with the business community in ways that generally helped to avoid inflation and other problems. Thus he was appointed and reappointed by both Republican and Democratic presidents. Are there aspects of or goals concerning economic policy that attract agreement from both Democrats and Republicans?

pathways profile

ALAN GREENSPAN

When Alan Greenspan retired as the chairman of the Federal Reserve Board of Governors in January 2006, he brought the curtain down on a fascinating public career. An aspiring musician, Greenspan attended the prestigious Juilliard School of Music in the 1940s and became a professional jazz saxophonist before pursuing bachelor's and master's degrees in economics at New York

▶ **Why does it cost** business
so much to comply with
government regulations?

University. After college, he founded a successful economic consulting firm in New York City. He was a friend of the philosopher and novelist Ayn Rand, an "objectivist" writer who believed passionately in capitalism, free markets, and self-determination and tolerated little dissent among her loyal disciples. Greenspan was one of the few in her inner circle who would stand up to her when he thought she was wrong. His contrariness seemed to make her admire him more.

His consulting success brought Greenspan to the attention of Republican Party leaders. He became chair of the Council of Economic Advisers under Gerald Ford in 1974. From 1981 to 1983, Greenspan chaired President Ronald Reagan's National Commission on Social Security Reform. Although the commission did not solve all of the system's long-term problems, Greenspan and his colleagues tweaked the Social Security system enough to ensure its solvency for several decades. Reagan named Greenspan chair of the Federal Reserve Board of Governors in late 1987.

Replacing the legendary Paul Volcker, Greenspan faced an immediate crisis when the stock market crashed less than two months into his term. Greenspan received high marks for working with financial institutions to free up liquidity and helping the market regain stability. The stock market crash of 1929 had ushered in the Great Depression; by contrast, the almost equally severe crash of 1987 proved to be a passing blip, thanks largely to the Fed's skillful action.

If one word characterized the Greenspan era, it was stability. A vigilant inflation fighter, the chair worked to keep prices under control by manipulating interest rates. He was so successful that he was reappointed by Presidents George H. W. Bush, Bill Clinton (twice), and George W. Bush (twice).

Many people thought that Greenspan's true talent was his obliqueness. Testifying before Congress or otherwise making public pronouncements in economic policy, he could talk circles around a problem to the point that different people took different meanings from the same words. One of the most famous examples of "Greenspeak" was his reference to "irrational exuberance" in world stock markets during a speech to the American Enterprise Institute in 1996. The Tokyo stock exchange immediately lost 3 percent of its value.

Another typical example of Greenspeak came in a 2005 address:

"If the currently disturbing drift toward protectionism is contained and markets remain sufficiently flexible," said the inscrutable chairman, "changing terms of trade, interest rates, asset prices, and exchange rates will cause U.S. saving to rise,

reducing the need for foreign finance and reversing the trend of the past decade toward increasing reliance on it. If, however, the pernicious drift toward fiscal instability in the United States and elsewhere is not arrested and is compounded by a protectionist reversal of globalization, the adjustment process could be quite painful for the world economy."[7]

In other words, free trade is good, and protectionism is bad.

Greenspan didn't seem much concerned with how his actions were read, once telling a congressional committee, "Since I have become a central banker, I have learned to mumble with great incoherence. If I seem unduly clear to you, you must have misunderstood what I said."[8] *He* knew what he believed. ■

Regulatory Policy

Regulatory policy plays an important role in shaping the American economy. The rise of Keynesianism—the idea that government should take a role in shaping economic policy—roughly coincided with a period of increasing business regulation by the federal government due to the influence of the progressives in the early twentieth century. Progressives were elected by voters who believed that businesses needed limits and followed through with regulatory policies aimed at stopping predatory business practices and breaking up monopolies. President Franklin Roosevelt's New Deal helped government regulation become more widely accepted as the federal government became more involved in farming and other industries and helped the banking industry find its way out of the Depression. By the time of President Lyndon Johnson's Great Society, regulation of businesses had expanded to cover workplace issues such as overtime, fair hiring, and working conditions. Even President Richard Nixon, considered a conservative, proclaimed in 1971, "We are all Keynesians now." It was under Nixon that government entities like the Environmental Protection Agency and Occupational Safety and Health Administration began imposing even greater restrictions on business activities.

▶ **Why does it cost business so much to comply with government regulations?** Regulatory policy is more than just acts of Congress and proposals of the president. Most such policy is created by executive departments and agencies, like OSHA and the EPA. Congress creates general guidelines; the agencies carve out the regulatory details. Today, the estimated cost of complying with these regulations is close to $1 trillion a year. Much of this cost comes in the form of the paperwork required of businesses to prove that they are

discussionquestions

1. What are the trade-offs between environmental and energy policy?

2. What has been the net effect of deregulation over the past thirty or so years?

what YOU can do!

Go to the Information and Regulatory Affairs link at the Web page of the Office of Management and Budget at **www.omb.gov**. Can you identify any unnecessary proposed regulations that will hurt the economy? If so, make your views known to the appropriate agency.

---

meeting government standards and tax laws. This burden falls disproportionately on small businesses, where per-employee compliance costs are 60 percent higher than for large businesses. The government maintains, with much justification, that the costs are more than offset by the benefits of a cleaner environment, safer working conditions, and protection against monopolies. Nonetheless, conforming to these regulations is an obstacle for start-up companies and small businesses, which may fail to add jobs or to grow because of regulatory costs. When we as Americans ask, "Why doesn't the government do something"? about a certain issue, we must consider the costs of government intervention. How much government are you willing to pay for? What regulations are worthwhile? What are the trade-offs?

By the 1970s, there was general agreement that regulation had become too oppressive. The move toward deregulation began during the Carter administration. Ironically, after almost three decades of deregulation in many industries, compliance costs are higher than ever today. Additional regulation in other, less visible industries has driven up the overall cost of doing business. The victims of deregulation are not always the environment or consumers. One of the first industries to experience large-scale deregulation—the airlines—has seen many of its largest firms go bankrupt. The reality of business regulation in America today is that many companies support government restriction because it helps them retain the market share they have carved out for themselves.

Economic regulation has political as well as economic costs. Most newly proposed industry regulations are going to face opposition from interest groups representing the affected industry. On the other side are interest groups in favor of regulation. These groups bring their resources—both economic and political—into the fray. One way that you can influence proposed regulations is by joining and working with an interest group in the lobbying and elections pathways.

Environmental policy and energy policy are intrinsically intertwined. Anyone visiting a gas station in the summer of 2006 longed for the good old days of $2 gas. Energy supplies are stretched thin, and not just for transportation. Home heating and cooling costs are up substantially. As industry demands increase, environmentalists fight to protect our air and water. What are the alternatives to the use of increasingly scarce fossil fuels? Coal is a cheaper source of energy, but it produces greenhouse gases and dangerous byproducts such as mercury. Although new technology can make the process cleaner, "clean coal" plants are more expensive to build and operate. Nuclear energy is only marginally more expensive than coal, but critics contend that the potential for an

accident is too high to justify going nuclear at any cost. Solar and wind technologies are not yet cost-effective. The battle for workable energy sources is being waged by the energy industry on one side and environmental groups on the other. Consumers are stuck in the middle, hoping for reliable, affordable energy that doesn't destroy the air we breathe or the water we drink.

One battlefield is the Arctic National Wildlife Refuge (ANWR) in Alaska, where oil companies want to drill because of known oil reserves. Environmentalists want to preserve the ANWR, one of the last pristine areas on the globe in its natural state. In a closely divided Congress, the fate of the ANWR hangs on the votes of only a few members. If your representative is one of those on the fence, your personal contact could help shape an important government decision.

practicequiz

1. The rise of Keynesianism coincided with
   a. the Gilded Age.
   b. the Rise of the Progressive Party.
   c. the New Deal.
   d. Johnson's Great Society.

2. The move toward deregulation began during which administration?
   a. Nixon's
   b. Carter's
   c. Reagan's
   d. George H.W. Bush's

3. Today many companies in this country support government regulation.
   a. true   b. false

4. What most accurately describes the current situation with environmental and energy policy?
   a. Global warming has meant that environmental concerns are beginning to overshadow short-term energy needs in the minds of governmental policy-makers.
   b. Global warming and other long-term environmental concerns are still abstract enough that short-term energy needs are the first priority for the government and the American people.
   c. The energy industry and environmental groups battle over which energy sources are best for the country and world, while consumers hope for energy that's affordable *and* earth-friendly.
   d. Americans are now clearly ready to reduce their consumption of energy but the government's energy policy remains committed to expanding fossil fuel-based sources.

Answers: 1-b, 2-b, 3-a, 4-c.

▶ **What are the different**
viewpoints on U.S. trade policy?

protectionists
people who believe in protecting American jobs and businesses from foreign competition.

free traders
people who believe that the nation's economic interests are best served through open markets.

Trade Policy and Globalization

As noted earlier, the United States has a negative balance of trade, or a trade deficit—we import far more than we export. The cause of this imbalance, its significance, and its long-term consequences are all subject to interpretation. U.S. trade policy has emerged as one of today's hottest political topics.

▶ **What are the different viewpoints on U.S. trade policy?** From a policy perspective, there are two divergent viewpoints on how trade relations should be structured. **Protectionists** believe that the main goal of trade policy should be to protect domestic producers and workers from foreign competition. **Free traders** believe that trade barriers should be dismantled—that the flow of goods, capital, and labor should be as unrestricted as possible. Protectionists believe that "unfair" foreign competition costs domestic jobs. Free traders believe that open exchange allows different parts of the world to specialize in what they do best, thereby promoting global efficiency and productivity. Most nations have trade policies that fall somewhere between the two extremes.

The trade debate has an interesting history in the United States. In the period immediately following the Civil War, most business interests and the Republican Party tended to be protectionist. Like many emerging economies, the American manufacturing sector sought to shield itself from competition, a position supported by probusiness Republicans. Democrats generally opposed protectionism, both in the nineteenth century, when they represented southern agrarians, and throughout most of the twentieth century, as the party moved in an "internationalist" direction. With a few exceptions, businesses today favor free trade. Although there is a sizable protectionist faction among Republicans and a sizable free-trade faction among Democrats, today's Democrats tend to be more protectionist, and Republicans in general favor free trade. Why did business change its stance? Ever since World War II, the established business sector has wanted to gain reciprocal access to foreign markets and the ability to purchase raw materials and component parts from cheaper foreign sources.

The worldwide trend over the past few decades has been toward freer trade. It has not been a straight-line progression—some periods were more protectionist than others—but the overall trend is clear. It is also clear that free trade causes some transitional discomfort. A major objection in the United States is the outsourcing of American jobs. Many U.S.-based companies have shipped manufacturing jobs, call centers, and even accounting support services overseas. Whole sectors, such as textile man-ufacturing, have all but disappeared. Even newer developments in American business such as programming and computer hardware production are moving overseas.

▶ **How can a large trade deficit be positive?!** Nonetheless, the U.S. economy has proved to be amazingly resilient. Most major innovations of the past one hundred years, from airplanes to televisions to computers and the Internet, were first developed in the United States. New industries arise from new technologies just as fast as old jobs are outsourced or disappear. Although the trade deficit has increased, employment and productivity have remained strong. Part of the reason for the increase in the trade deficit is the increasing productivity of the U.S. economy. It takes money to buy imports. If the American economy is growing faster than those of our trading partners, it should not be surprising that our imports are growing faster than our exports. From that perspective, a trade deficit can be seen as a sign of economic strength rather than weakness. Cheaper imports can also be an incentive for greater American production. Workers are likely to put in extra hours if they know their efforts can be converted to bargain-priced tangible goods.

Another big factor in the trade deficit has been the rising price of crude oil. The first major jump came in 1973, when the Organization of Petroleum Exporting Countries (OPEC), an international cartel of oil-rich nations, forced the industrialized countries of the world to accept major price increases. The Iranian Revolution of 1979 produced a second "oil shock." Subsequent discoveries of new sources of oil and significant gains in energy efficiency, along with competition among oil producers, caused prices to drop in the 1980s and 1990s. However, since the United States is the largest single user of oil in the world, and since most of that oil is imported, the significant increase in oil prices over the past five years has had a negative impact on the trade balance. If U.S. usage and energy prices both continue to rise, the deficit will worsen.

Even with a global shift toward freer trade, concerns remain over fair trade and reciprocity. Free trade is more than just customs and tariffs. A big issue between the United States and the European Union has been agricultural subsidies—payments made to farmers to ensure a price floor; that is, the government guarantees that producers will be paid a minimum price for a product. Both the United States and the EU pay significant subsidies to their farmers. While both consider their own efforts to be assistance to a vital industry, they each brand the other's policies as unjustified protectionism.

International trade liberalization has been a U.S. foreign policy goal since World War II. The United States led the way in

▶ **How can a large** trade deficit be positive?!

discussionquestions

1. What is outsourcing? Why is it controversial?
2. What factors have been most significant in the rising U.S. trade deficit?

insisting that the post–World War II "new world order" include such institutions as the World Bank, the International Monetary Fund (IMF), and the General Agreement on Tariffs and Trade (GATT)—now known as the World Trade Organization (WTO). The WTO's policy is to promote freer global trade by sponsoring multilateral tariff reduction negotiations and mediating global trade disputes. In recent years, WTO meetings have often touched off vehement and sometimes violent protests from antiglobalization activists who believe that free trade hurts poor nations.

The United States is also a member of the North American Free Trade Association (NAFTA), which in 1993 established a free-trade zone among the United States, Canada, and Mexico, promoting the free flow of goods. NAFTA immediately ended many tariffs among the three countries while gradually phasing out others. NAFTA has a larger combined GDP than the twenty-five nations of the European Union. Not without controversy, NAFTA was—and is—opposed by many protectionists throughout the region. Opposition in the United States by unions who feared that high-paying jobs would flow to Mexico made passage of the founding legislation difficult. Although Republicans generally supported the agreement, many from agrarian areas opposed NAFTA. Democrats were almost evenly split on the issue. Unlike the European Union, we have no "international court" to judge NAFTA disputes. Instead, bilateral panels work to resolve differences.

The World Trade Organization faces protests in many countries from people who believe that poor countries do not gain sufficient benefits from the decisions of international economic organizations. How much of a risk is there that wealthy, powerful countries will join together in order to make economic decisions that increase advantages already enjoyed by affluent nations?

practicequiz

1. Regarding trade policy, where have the two major parties stood?
   a. Both used to be more protectionist than they are today.
   b. Democrats used to be more protectionist than Republicans, but now the roles are reversed.
   c. Republicans used to be more protectionist than Democrats, but now the roles are reversed.
   d. Both used to be less protectionist than they are today.

2. Sometimes it is fair to see a national trade deficit as a sign of economic strength.
   a. true   b. false

3. National farm subsidies are a big issue in U.S./EU trade relations because
   a. Europe grants their farmers large subsidies, which, as U.S. officials and farmers complain, constitute unjustified protectionism.
   b. The U.S. grants its farmers large subsidies, which, as EU officials and farmers complain, constitute unjustified protectionism.

   c. Neither the U.S. nor the EU currently subsidize their agricultural industry at significant levels, but both sides worry about increases across the Atlantic and the trade consequences that would follow.
   d. Both the U.S. and the EU subsidize their farmers at significant levels, yet both label the other's policies unjustified protectionism.

4. Why has NAFTA been controversial?
   a. because it has undermined free trade among the U.S., Canada, and Mexico
   b. because many believe that the trade arrangement disadvantages Mexico, the least developed country of the three
   c. because the trade arrangement makes it more likely that U.S. companies will take their operations and high-paying jobs to Mexico, where wages are lower
   d. because the trade arrangement has helped the U.S. and Mexican economies but has hindered Canada's

Answers: 1-c, 2-a, 3-d, 4-c.

Conclusion

The American economic system is based on the concepts of individuals' property rights and the free enterprise system, yet the government is deeply involved in shaping economic policy. Through the operation of the elections and lobbying decision makers pathways, government officials affect the economic health of the nation by pursuing their ideas about proper policies concerning taxes, government spending, and the regulation of businesses.

These policies have helped most Americans enjoy notable economic prosperity since the 1950s. The citizens in relatively few other countries can compare to middle-class and affluent Americans with respect to disposable income, vacation travel, and ownership of computers, DVD players, automobiles, and other consumer goods. Despite this relative affluence, several significant issues pose challenges to government decision makers and potentially threaten the level of prosperity enjoyed by most Americans. Government officials must make decisions about a series of vexing questions: How will we pay the expanding costs of entitlement programs such as Social Security and Medicare? Will we take action against the nation's growing budget and trade deficits? How will we react to the rising cost of foreign oil without sacrificing our own economic growth and environmental quality? Because the policy decisions to address these issues will require difficult choices and will affect all Americans, it is especially important for active and engaged citizens to use the elections, lobbying, and other pathways to communicate their preferences and concerns to government leaders.

YOUR turn!

Creating economic policy is one of the most difficult jobs the government performs. To have an impact, you need to contact the right people. As you've learned in this chapter, the key players in setting fiscal policy are the Appropriations Committee in both the House and the Senate, the Ways and Means Committee in the House, and the Finance Committee in the Senate. Members of those committees have the greatest influence over fiscal policy. In addition to your own representatives, the committees would be a good place to start if you want to have an impact on the budget.

The following links will connect you directly with the Web pages of the pertinent committees. These sites allow you to contact committee members; each also contains information on subcommittees, hearings, and current proposed legislation.

> http://appropriations.house.gov
>
> http://waysandmeans.house.gov
>
> http://appropriations.senate.gov
>
> http://finance.senate.gov

Because the Federal Reserve Board of Governors is an independent entity, the Fed is less susceptible to public pressure than members of Congress or the White House. Nonetheless, it is worth your time as a citizen to be aware of what the Fed is doing, especially if you plan to invest in the stock market. In addition to news and press releases, the Fed's Web site (http://www.federalreserve.gov) also contains a significant amount of practical information for consumers, including tips on managing your money, understanding credit reports, and protecting yourself from identity theft. ■

Chapter Review

1. Property rights and capitalism are at the heart of the American economic system. Americans have a greater degree of economic freedom than most of the world's population.

2. The most important measures of the health of the U.S. economy are inflation, employment, gross domestic product, the budget deficit or surplus, and the balance of trade.

3. Fiscal policy is the policy of taxing and spending. The Congressional Budget Office is an important source of budgetary analysis and planning. Congress and its relevant committees shape the budget.

4. Under a progressive taxation system, higher-income people pay a larger percentage of their income in taxes. Under a regressive system, lower-income people pay a higher percentage of their income in taxes.

5. The largest source of revenue for the U.S. government is the income tax. The payroll tax is second. Corporate taxes are third.

6. Taxation decisions affect both economic performance and the perception of equity.

7. The largest area of expenditure for the United States is Social Security. Defense is second; income security is third.

8. Because of debt and long-term commitments for Social Security and medical care, the United States faces significant budgetary challenges in the future.

9. Monetary policy involves managing the nation's money supply in order to stabilize inflation, interest rates, and employment. The Federal Reserve Board's Federal Open Market Committee has primary responsibility for setting monetary policy.

10. The primary instruments of the FOMC are the discount rate and open-market operations.

11. Government regulation has had a significant impact on American businesses. Compliance costs run close to $1 trillion a year.

12. Trade policy is controversial because of disagreements between protectionists and free traders.

CHAPTER REVIEW TEST

1. What is the difference between fiscal and monetary policy?
   a. Fiscal policy concerns the national money supply, monetary policy is focused on taxing and spending decisions.
   b. Monetary policy is focused on deficits and surpluses, fiscal policy is concerned with interest rates and employment rates.
   c. Fiscal policy concerns taxing and spending decisions, monetary policy focuses on the national money supply.
   d. Fiscal policy is economic policy formulated by the Federal Reserve Board, monetary policy is economic policy formulated by the Congress and the president.

2. Who are among the major actors in creating U.S. economic policy?
   a. the president, the House Ways and Means Committee, the Senate Finance Committee, the CBO, and the Fed Chair
   b. the president, the Council of Economic Advisors, the Treasury Secretary, the Fed Chair, and the Secretary of Commerce
   c. AARP, the FOMC, the COLA, the CEA, and the NAACP
   d. the president, the Fed Chair, the president of the AFL-CIO, the president of the AMA, and the CBO

3. The key feature of Keynesian economics is that
   a. free-market capitalism must remain unfettered by government intervention.
   b. the economic fortunes of nations naturally wax and wane; government's job is to assist victims during the lean years and stay out of the way when times are good.
   c. taxation should be kept to a minimum, since the main engine of an economy is corporate investment and consumer spending.
   d. government should help flatten the ups and downs of an economy through taxation and spending policies.

4. Supply-side economists assert that
   a. the prime interest rate should be raised during periods of inflation and lowered during "stagflation."
   b. lower taxes have the effect of improving the economy.
   c. higher taxes have the effect of improving the economy.
   d. a higher supply of money in the economy is detrimental.

5. When measuring the health of the nation's economy, economists usually focus on
   a. the gross domestic product.
   b. the gross domestic product and the budget deficit or surplus.
   c. the gross domestic product, the budget deficit or surplus, and unemployment.
   d. inflation, unemployment, the gross domestic product, the balance of trade, and the budget surplus or deficit.

6. What exactly is the national debt?
   a. how much the U.S. government owes private investors and other countries in a given year
   b. the budget deficit plus the trade deficit in a given year
   c. the net sum of the budget deficit, minus the surplus
   d. the budget deficit plus the trade deficit, minus the Social Security trust fund

7. Most American workers pay less per year in payroll taxes than they do in income taxes.
   a. true   **b.** false

8. Wealthy, non-working Americans escape taxation on the vast majority of their assets.
   a. true   **b.** false

9. The major theoretical force behind Reagan's economic policies were
   a. monetarists.   **b.** Keynesians.
   c. deficit hawks.   **d.** supply-siders.

10. America's Gross Domestic Product continues to grow
   a. yet, when you factor in inflation, the GDP has actually shrunk.
   b. yet most real-wage increases have gone to the wealthiest Americans.
   c. and middle-class Americans have prospered the most.
   d. and everyone has enjoyed proportionally equivalent real-wage increase (a rising tide raises all boats).

11. The government spends at least five times as much on defense as it does on
    a. Social Security benefits.
    b. Medicare.
    c. science.
    d. all of the above.

12. How will the Social Security trust fund be used when the baby boom generation starts retiring?
    a. to bridge the gap between inadequate Generation X Social Security payments and the enormous retirement needs of their elders
    b. it's not clear, since the government has been borrowing heavily from the trust fund already
    c. to supplement private investment portfolios that are being phased in to replace Social Security as we know it
    d. to supplement national subsidies that make the new prescription drug plan (Plan D) possible

13. If no changes are implemented, it is possible that, by the time current college students retire, Social Security will have gone into bankruptcy.
    a. true   b. false

14. More than half of the 2005 federal budget deficit consisted of interest payments.
    a. true   b. false

15. The United States government has run budget deficits for about how long?
    a. five years
    b. fifteen years
    c. twenty-five years
    d. thirty-five years

16. Why do most people not know the true size of the national debt?
    a. Given how many sources contribute to both the revenue and expenditure sides of the budget, it is actually impossible to know the national debt at any given time.
    b. For political reasons governmental officials are quite invested in keeping that figure obscure.

c. Because national debt figures, for the past twenty years, have included the whole Social Security trust fund, as if it were not already deeply eroded by further governmental borrowing.
    d. Because Americans, like most people, do not want to know dangerous news.

17. The primary aim of the Federal Reserve Board is to
    a. make sure the president's economic policy is working well.
    b. make sure Congress's economic policy is working well.
    c. regulate the national banking system.
    d. try to control inflation and keep the economy stable and growing.

18. The Phillips Curve theorizes that inflation and unemployment cannot both go up at the same time. When this in fact happened in the 1970s, Democrats measured the results with something they called
    a. the misery index
    b. the stagflation index.
    c. the hardship curve.
    d. the inflament index.

19. How does the Fed have to be "right twice"?
    a. by creating the correct response to an economic problem, and then knowing when to stop the corrective action
    b. by knowing where the economy is headed, and then by making the correct response to the anticipated circumstances
    c. by knowing when to stop digging one economic hole (the national debt) and when to start digging another (into unemployment)
    d. by knowing where the economy is headed, and then by giving key economic policymakers the right advice about staving off future problems

20. Which of the following is **NOT** an international trade organization or treaty in which the U.S. government has ever participated?
    a. GATT   b. IMF
    c. OSHA   d. WTO

Answers: 1: c; 2: a; 3: d; 4: b; 5: d; 6: c; 7: b; 8: a; 9: d; 10: b; 11: c; 12: b; 13: a; 14: a; 15: d; 16: c; 17: d; 18: a; 19: b; 20: c.

DISCUSSION QUESTIONS

1. What do the five major economic measures tell us about the health of the economy?

2. How much of the federal government's revenue comes from the income tax?

3. In what way is the payroll tax burden higher than it appears?

4. What are the major areas of expenditure for the federal government?

5. How does the debt affect the deficit?

6. What are the major factors in the long-term debt problems facing the government?

7. Why is it important for the Fed to be independent? Is the operation of the Fed consistent with the principles of democracy?

8. How do inflation and deflation affect the overall economy?

9. Describe the debate between protectionists and free traders. Who do you think is right?

INTERNET RESOURCES

AARP: http://www.aarp.org

Concord Coalition, a nonpartisan group lobbying for sound fiscal policy: http://www.concordcoalition.org

Congressional Budget Office: http://www.cbo.gov

Government Accountability Office: http://www.gao.gov

National Center for Policy Analysis: http://www.ncpa.org/newdpd/index.php

Office of Management and Budget: http://www.whitehouse.gov/omb

Progressive Policy Institute's link to fiscal and economic policy issues: http://www.ppionline.org/ppi_ka.cfm?knlgAreaID=125

ADDITIONAL READING

Friedman, Milton, and Rose Friedman. *Free to Choose.* New York: Harcourt Brace, 1979.

Greider, William. *Secrets of the Temple: How the Federal Reserve Runs the Country.* New York: Touchstone, 1987.

Woodward, Bob. *Maestro: Greenspan's Fed and the American Boom.* New York: Simon & Schuster, 2000.

KEY TERMS

balance of trade   655
budget deficit   656
budget surplus   656
Congressional Budget Office (CBO)   656
Consumer Price Index (CPI)   654
crowding-out effect   669
deflation   655
discount rate   673
dynamic modeling   662
entitlements   669
federal funds rate   673
Federal Open Market Committee (FOMC)   672
Federal Reserve System (the Fed)   672
fiscal policy   656

flat tax   663
free traders   678
gross domestic product (GDP)   655
income security   666
inflation   654
Keynesians   652
Laffer curve   662
macroeconomics   652
marginal tax bracket   659
Medicaid   666
Medicare   666
monetarists   654
monetary policy   672
national debt   656

national sales tax   663
open-market operations   673
payroll tax   659
Phillips curve   674
prime rate   673
progressive tax   659
protectionists   678
regressive tax   659
reserve ratio   673
Social Security Trust Fund   665
stagflation   673
supply-side economists   654
Treasury bills (T-bills)   669
unemployment rate   655

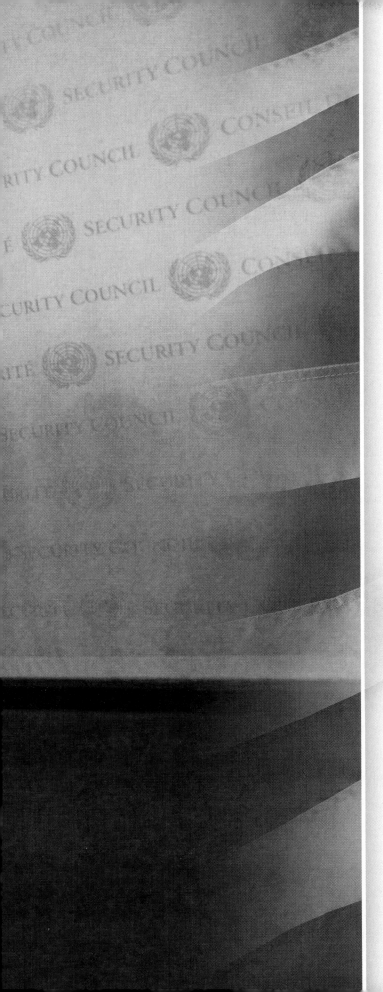

Statement on foreign affairs—in words and images. John Bolton, the Bush administration's controversial and outspoken representative to the United Nations, answers questions during the Iraq War. Visible over his shoulder is a reproduction of Pablo Picasso's painting "Guernica," the famous artist's protest against the horrors of war. At this very spot in 2003, when then-U.S. Secretary of State Colin Powell spoke at the U.N. about the need to launch military action against Iraq, a large drape had covered Picasso's jarring representation of Spanish civilians killed by German air force bombers. Foreign policy is shaped by communicating messages. Apparently, there were fears that Picasso's message would detract from American announcements about its foreign policy plans in Iraq.

CHAPTER 18

FOREIGN AND NATIONAL SECURITY POLICY

September 11, 2001   As the workday began, there was no hint among Washington foreign policy officials that September 11, 2001, would be different from any other day. President George W. Bush, accompanied by Chief of Staff Andrew Cord and senior political adviser Karl Rove, was to visit an elementary school class in Sarasota, Florida, where he would read students a book and talk about the importance of education. As usual, he began his day with an early morning run. Secretary of State Colin Powell was in Peru attending a meeting of the Organization of American States. National security adviser Condoleezza Rice was in Washington; later in September, she was scheduled to give a major foreign policy speech that had nothing to do with terrorist threats to the United States.

Along the East Coast of the United States, events were quickly moving in a direction that was anything but normal.[1] Word

At 9:03 a.m. on Sept. 11th, terrorists hijacked United Airlines Flight 175 and flew it into the South Tower of the World Trade Center in New York City. The events of 9/11 forced a change in foreign policy and national security goals.

of the hijacking of American Airlines Flight 11, bound from Boston to Los Angeles, was first transmitted from flight attendants onboard to American Airlines at 8:19 A.M. Four minutes later, the Boston Center Air Traffic Control was made aware that a hijacking was in progress. At 8:32, having lost significant contact with American Airlines Flight 11 and observing it making a sharp turn to the south, the Boston Center contacted the Federal Aviation Administration (FAA) about a possible hijacking. Air traffic controllers also went out of the normal chain of command, and at 8:37, they directly contacted the North American Aerospace Defense Command's Northeast Air Defense Sector (NEADS) with word of a hijacking. Assured that this was real and not an exercise, NEADS ordered two F-15 alert aircraft stationed at Otis Air Force Base in Falmouth, Massachusetts, to battle stations. Scrambled without any idea of their destination or direction, the jet fighters were airborne for only forty seconds before Flight 11 crashed into the North Tower of the World Trade Center in New York City at 8:46—and they were still trying to locate that flight at 8:50, when word reached NEADS of the crash.

The first notification the military received about the hijacking of United Airlines Flight 175, also scheduled to fly from Boston to Los Angeles, came at 9:03 A.M., the exact time it flew into the South Tower of the World Trade Center. The F-15 fighters from Otis Air Force Base activated to intercept Flight

175 did not arrive over New York City until 9:15, twelve minutes after the crash.

American Airlines Flight 77, scheduled to fly from Washington, D.C., to Los Angeles, began to veer off its flight path at 8:54 A.M. At first, air traffic controllers in Indianapolis thought it had crashed and at 9:08 they asked for a search and rescue operation. By 9:20, Indianapolis officials had learned of the other hijackings, and five minutes later, they informed the FAA that Flight 77 was missing. At 9:34, almost by accident, NEADS found out about the missing Flight 77. Only minutes before, at 9:23, NEADS had ordered fighters based at Langley Air Force Base in Hampton, Virginia, to go airborne because it had received an erroneous report that Flight 11 was still in the air and heading for Washington, D.C. After confirming that Flight 11 had gone down and that another plane was a few miles from the White House, NEADS sought to redirect the fighters from Baltimore to Washington, only to find that they were now heading east over the Atlantic Ocean. The Langley-based fighters were 150 miles away when Flight 77 crashed into the Pentagon Building; a government building that serves as the headquarters of the United States Military outside Washington, at 9:37. At 10:03, United Airlines Flight 93, heading from Newark to San Francisco, went down in a field in Shanksville, Pennsylvania, even before NEADS was made aware of the hijacking. It is believed that the fourth plane was headed for the White House or the Capitol before passengers, alerted by their cell phones to the other events, overwhelmed the hijackers. A "shoot-down" order for Flight 93 to prevent it from reaching Washington was authorized by President Bush at 10:20 A.M. but only received by NEADS at 10:31, more than twenty-six minutes after the flight came crashing down in the Pennsylvania countryside. ▪

▶ How was American foreign policy affected by the downfall of the Soviet Union?

terrorism
violence for the purpose of political intimidation.

TABLE 18.1

Changing Foreign Policy Goals before and after September 11, 2001

	BEFORE	AFTER	NET CHANGE
Reduce the spread of AIDS	73%	59%	−14%
Deal with world hunger	47%	43%	−13%
Combat drug trafficking	64%	55%	−9%
Promote American business interests	37%	30%	−7%
Ensure adequate energy supplies	74%	69%	−5%
Promote democracy	29%	24%	−5%
Reduce world poverty	25%	20%	−5%

SOURCE: Pew Research Center for the People and the Press, *Public Opinion in a Year for the Books* (Pew Research Center, 2002), p. 12.

September 11th forced reprioritization of foreign policy goals. As shown in public opinion polls, issues such as these suddenly were not as important as homeland security and terrorism prevention for people and politicians alike. Do you think this shift of priorities has benefited the country and its international standing? How or how not?

Like the domestic policy issues we discussed in Chapter 17, American foreign policy is about choices, the goals and values of the American people, and the types of threats they wish to deter. American foreign policy is also about costs—how much the American people are willing to pay to achieve their goals and what types of sacrifices they are willing to make.

▶ **How was American foreign policy affected by the downfall of the Soviet Union?** For more than four decades after World War II ended in 1945, questions of values, threats, costs, and sacrifice were framed with reference to one overriding problem: the Soviet menace. The challenge from the Soviet Union and the international communist movement that the USSR spearheaded was global and all-encompassing. It took many forms, from the nuclear arms race to domestic espionage, from diplomatic confrontations at the United Nations to economic rivalry, from Third World guerrilla warfare and the subversion of pro-American governments to more conventional wars in Korea and Vietnam. Suddenly, in the late 1980s, all that changed. American foreign policy lost its "magnetic north pole." In 1989, the Berlin Wall, which had long symbolized the division of Europe into two competing alliances, came down, and the band of Soviet satellite states in Eastern Europe won their freedom. The next year, the Soviet Union itself turned its back on the ideology of communism, and in 1991 the Soviet Union passed into history, giving way to the Russian Federation and fourteen other post-Soviet republics.

Having lost its point of reference, American foreign policy drifted through the 1990s. While the international system still seemed full of "poisonous snakes" that threatened American interests (in the words of President Bill Clinton's head of the Central Intelligence Agency, R. James Woolsey), for the most part, neither American leaders nor the American public showed much enthusiasm for a sustained effort to eliminate these perceived dangers.

Clarity and focus returned suddenly to American foreign policy on September 11, 2001. For a short time, the war against **terrorism** overrode all other foreign policy problems (see Table 18.1). American leaders and the public were united regarding the severity of the threat posed by terrorism and of the need for prompt action. The first battle in the war against terrorism was in Afghanistan, where the United States drove the Taliban government from power and pursued but failed to capture Osama bin Laden, the al-Qaeda leader who has masterminded the attacks on America. However, success in Afghanistan did not lead to a consensus on America's role in the world. In fact, it helped spawn three major debates about the conduct and content of American foreign policy in an age of terrorism. First, what strategic principles should guide

neoconservatives
people who believe that the United States
has a special role to play in world politics;
they advocate the unilateral use of force
and the pursuit of a value-based foreign
policy.

American foreign policy? Second, what is the proper relationship between foreign policy and domestic policy, particularly civil rights and liberties? And third, who should make American foreign policy? As we take up each of these questions in this chapter, it will become clear that these issues are not new. They have appeared continuously throughout the history of American diplomacy.

Key Questions

1. What key divisions separate Americans in their thinking about foreign policy?
2. To what extent is American thinking about foreign policy rooted in American history?
3. In what ways are American foreign and domestic policy linked?
4. How can the public express itself on foreign policy issues?
5. What political institutions compete for influence in making American foreign policy?
6. What major issues confront the United States today?

Competing Principles for American Foreign Policy

Today there are two major approaches to U.S. interaction with the rest of the world. Both perspectives view the United States as the unchallenged sole remaining superpower in world politics. They differ on what the United States should try to accomplish from this position of strength. A group we'll call the "transformers" believes that the United States should try to transform the international system in a way that will not just protect American goals and values but allow them to prosper and become universally accepted. According to the "maintainers," the United States should consolidate its gains and not try to impose itself or its values on others. Within each perspective, we can identify two major competing camps, for a total of four different stances on American foreign policy (see Table 18.2 on page 690). Transformers are divided into neoconservatives and neoliberals. Maintainers have conservative and isolationist wings. After describing the beliefs of these four groups, we will bring them into sharper focus by examining the position of each on the Iraq War.

Let's begin with the **neoconservatives,** a group that has occupied prominent foreign policy positions in both George W. Bush administrations. Neoconservative thinking has guided foreign policy since 9/11.[2] Four common themes tend to unite neoconservatives in their views on American foreign policy. First, because the United States is the unchallenged sole superpower, it

ABOVE: **People from East Berlin** and West Berlin, separated for four decades by armed guards and the Berlin Wall, reached across to greet one another as the collapse of communist governments in Eastern Europe permitted them to dismantle the wall in 1989. How did American foreign policy change after the collapse of communism in the Soviet Union and Eastern Europe?

BELOW: **Vice President Dick Cheney** (left) and Secretary of Defense Donald Rumsfeld (right) are regarded as the primary architects of foreign policy for the administration of President George W. Bush. From your understanding of the causes and consequences of the Iraq War, do you think Cheney and Rumsfeld can accurately be labeled as neoconservative transformers?

▶ **What are the central** beliefs of conservatives on American foreign policy?

North Atlantic Treaty Organization (NATO)
the Cold War alliance of the United States, Canada, and Western European states against the Soviet Union. It continues to exist but no longer has a clear-cut role in world politics.

TABLE 18.2
Four Perspectives on Foreign Policy

PERSPECTIVES AND BELIEFS

NEOCONSERVATIVE TRANSFORMER
- The United States must enforce the rules on other countries (although not necessarily abide by them) because it is the sole unchallenged superpower.
- Military power is the most important factor in foreign policy.
- The United States must be able to act as its leaders see fit; international organizations may come between the United States and its best interests.
- Spreading democracy to other nations is in the best interests of the United States.

CONSERVATIVE MAINTAINER
- The United States must be prepared to use military force.
- Global interests may be different from U.S. interests.
- Power is an important asset and must be maintained and used carefully.
- Power is more effective if it is viewed as legitimate.

NEOLIBERAL TRANSFORMER
- Spreading democracy is in the American national interest.
- Nonmilitary means are preferred over military action.
- Support from international organizations and agreements can be important to future endeavors.

ISOLATIONIST MAINTAINER
- Military power should be used as a shield to protect U.S. interests.
- The United States is minimally accountable to its allies and the international community.
- Foreign policy should consist mostly of cultural, commercial, and diplomatic interactions.

---

plays a fundamentally different role in world politics than other states do. This means that the United States is in a position to force others to follow rules of proper behavior, but it does not have to abide by those rules itself. In a very real sense, according to neoconservatives, the United States stands above and apart from other states. Second, the ever-present military power of the United States is the central instrument of American foreign policy, and the United States should not be apologetic or timid about using it. Third, neoconservatives believe that unilateralism is the proper approach for dealing with foreign policy problems. Instead of helping the United States achieve its goals, alliances such as the **North Atlantic Treaty Organization (NATO)** and international institutions like the United Nations more often than not place roadblocks in its way. Rather than be hamstrung by these bodies, neoconservatives insist that America must always be free to act in response to the wishes of American leaders. Fourth, neoconservatives believe that it is in the American national interest to spread democracy around the world.

Neoconservative transformers think about world politics in terms of conflict and struggle. This is not the case for **neoliberals,** who see in place in the world much of the shared identity and potential for cooperation that neoconservatives seek.[3] Along with conservatives and isolationists, to whom we shall turn shortly, neoliberals fear that neoconservative principles will provoke a global backlash that will increase American insecurity and lead to a world that is less supportive of American values.

Neoliberal transformers share three common objectives. The first is one they share with neoconservatives: spreading democracy to further American national interests. However, neoliberals disagree with neoconservatives about how to go about this. Where neoconservatives stress the ability of the United States to come into a society and build democracy, neoliberals maintain that democracy is best built from within, by local political forces. Second, neoliberals tend to stress nonmilitary means for achieving foreign policy ends. They favor foreign aid and economic assistance programs, especially when such aid is made dependent on conditions such as respect for human rights. But neoliberals do not reject the use of military force outright. During the 1990s, they routinely advocated using force as part of humanitarian peacekeeping operations in chaotic areas of the world such as Bosnia, Haiti, and Somalia. Third, in contrast to the neoconservative embrace of unilateralism, neoliberals stress the importance of

▶ **How do conservatives differ** from isolationists?

neoliberals
people who strongly support international law and organizations and are skeptical about the use of military force because they attribute many of the world's problems to economic, political, and social conditions.

weapons of mass destruction
weapons capable of inflicting widespread devastation on civilian populations.

international institutions and agreements as ways of accomplishing foreign policy objectives. In their view, unilateral exercise of power puts the United States in direct conflict with other states, which are forced to make one of two choices: support the United States or be regarded by Washington as an enemy. In the neoliberal view, it is in the United States' best interests to limit its freedom of action and to play by the rules of the game, thus giving legitimacy to other states' concerns and gaining their long-term cooperation and support.

Whereas both the neoconservative and neoliberal transformers are optimists, the conservative and isolationist maintainers are pessimists. Maintainers do not see the current international system as one in which the United States stands unchallenged and in a position to bring about fundamental changes in other states. They see the international system as a threat to American interests. Caution, not opportunism, is the order of the day for both maintainer camps.

▶ **What are the central beliefs of conservatives on American foreign policy?** Conservatives believe that an effective American foreign policy must be built around four themes. First is the realization that to protect its interests, the United States must be prepared to act militarily. Diplomacy and economic aid are no substitutes for military power. Second, American national interests are limited and not identical to global interests. When the two are in conflict, national interests must always take precedence. Global crusades, whether to build democracy or defeat terrorism, are dangerous because they divert the United States from real and more immediate dangers. Third, power, especially military power, as the key measure that countries use to compare one another, must be refreshed constantly and used carefully. It is better to take action through alliances and coalitions than it is to act alone, so the costs and risks of military action can be shared. Fourth, the exercise of American power is most effective when others view it as legitimate. Power robbed of legitimacy is reduced to brute force, and brute force, which tries to achieve its objectives through fear and intimidation, is self-defeating in the long run because it will cause others to form coalitions against the oppressor.[4]

▶ **How do conservatives differ from isolationists?** Isolationist maintainers have little doubt about the importance of military power and the need to defend American national interests. Where they part company from the conservative maintainers is in the number and range of events abroad that call for military action on America's part. For isolationists, the major

threats to U.S. security come from an overactive foreign policy and responses that threaten to undermine core American values.[5] Three themes guide isolationist foreign policy thinking. First, American foreign policy must concentrate on protecting American lives and property, the territory of the United States, and the integrity of the American political system. To do so, American military power must become less a lance to strike out at others and more a shield to defend our homeland. Second, American responsibility to allies and the international community is minimal. Other states must learn to become responsible for their own defense. Third, the proper way for the United States to be active in the world is through cultural, commercial, and diplomatic interactions. Foreign aid should be reduced and American troops brought home.

CONFLICTING EVALUATIONS OF THE IRAQ WAR

On March 19, 2003, following much public debate in the United States, political maneuvering at the United Nations, and the presentation of a forty-eight-hour ultimatum to Iraq's dictator, Saddam Hussein, the Iraq War began. President George W. Bush had branded Iraq part of an "axis of evil," along with North Korea and Iran, in his 2002 State of the Union address. The Bush administration argued that Iraq's possession of **weapons of mass destruction** required preemptive military action on the part of the United States. (That claim was later recognized as incorrect.) The military operation was a spectacular success. On April 9, Baghdad fell, and on May 1, President Bush declared an end to major combat operations.

However, violent opposition continued throughout the region, and the American occupation of Iraq has proved to be far more difficult than expected. In July 2003, deaths among U.S. combat forces in Iraq reached the level of the 1991 Persian Gulf War; in September 2004, they passed the 1,000 mark, and in October 2005, they surpassed 2,000.

Political and economic setbacks, unforeseen by the war's planners, have also been numerous. Iraq's oil production has been slow to recover, and U.S. funds aimed at economic recovery have had to be diverted to improve security. Amid seemingly endless sectarian and ethnic strife, including a major insurgency supported by the once-dominant Sunni Arab minority, Iraqi political leaders repeatedly failed to meet reestablished deadlines to lay the foundation for a new democratic political order. And the American

▶ How do each of the four foreign policy perspectives view the Iraq War?

Monroe Doctrine
Policy advocated by President James Monroe in 1823 that called for European non-intervention in North and South America in exchange for the neutrality of the United States in European matters.

Hamiltonians
supporters of Alexander Hamilton who argued that United States foreign policy should be designed to act in the best economic interests of the country as a whole and should promote the economic good of the nation at home and abroad.

After the government of Saddam Hussein collapsed, U.S. soldiers in Iraq found themselves in a drawn-out conflict. They fought insurgents who resisted the American invasion and attempted to control violence between the Sunni and Shiite segments of Iraqi society that have long-standing grievances against each other. Which of the four foreign policy perspectives, if any, seems to best describe what has occurred in the Iraq War?

security presence in Iraq became the source of added controversy when, in April 2004, photos were published around the world graphically depicting the torture and mistreatment of Iraqi prisoners by U.S. personnel at Abu Ghraib prison.

▶ **How do each of the four foreign policy perspectives view the Iraq War?** Let's evaluate the Iraq War from the four foreign policy perspectives we have introduced. We will consider the judgments of each camp in turn, beginning with the neoconservatives, who dominated the Bush administration's decision making.

Neoconservatives view the Iraq War as essential to the future security of the United States. It is the second military operation in the war against terrorism (the invasion of Afghanistan was the first). Removing Saddam Hussein from power was necessary even if he did not have weapons of mass destruction, because his was a dangerous and aggressive government that had once tried to obtain these weapons and if permitted would do so again. Removing him from power was also necessary in order to build democracy in Iraq and set the stage for the democratization of the Middle East. In the neoconservative view, the United States cannot leave Iraq until democracy and economic recovery are assured, just as they were in post–World War II West Germany and Japan.

Neoliberals shed no tears over Saddam Hussein's downfall, recognizing that he was a ruthless dictator with a record of foreign aggression and domestic genocide. Before the war, however, neoliberals had asserted that nonmilitary means, such as economic sanctions, were a preferable line of action for removing Saddam from power. They had also cautioned that occupying and reconstructing Iraq would be difficult and that democracy could not be imposed from outside. Neoliberals also maintain that if the reconstruction of Iraq is to succeed, the United Nations must play a larger role, so that the stigma of a largely American occupation is removed and so that concern for respecting human rights, meeting basic human needs, and establishing the rule of law will replace the emphasis on counterterrorism.

Conservatives make two general points about the Iraq War. First, to wage it, they would have favored creating a true international alliance to reduce the political and economic costs to the United States, both in the actual fighting of the war and during the subsequent occupation. Second, conservatives see the Iraq War as having distracted the United States from pursuing the true enemy: Osama bin Laden and his terrorists. In fact, the Iraq War gave anti-American terrorism new life, and Iraq has become a magnet for international terrorist groups. Related to this is the conservatives' concern that by acting unilaterally, the United States disrupted the balance of global politics, in the end leaving our country less secure. Conservatives believe that other countries—especially those we defined as enemies—drew the conclusion that unchecked American power is dangerous and must be countered.

Finally, the isolationists mostly supported the war in Afghanistan because it was a direct response to the 9/11 terrorist attack. They saw little value added in the Iraq War and regard attempts at building democracy in Iraq and the Middle East as a "fool's errand." Isolationists would prefer to focus on more rigorous efforts to promote homeland security.

▶ **Why have we always**
tried to keep other countries
away from Latin America?

pathways past and present

THE UNITED STATES AND LATIN AMERICA

▶ **Why have we always tried to keep other countries away from Latin America?**

Latin America has always been of special concern in American foreign policy. Generations of American presidents, from Theodore Roosevelt to John F. Kennedy and Ronald Reagan, pursued policies designed to keep "foreign" influences out of the Western Hemisphere. The policy statement supporting this is the **Monroe Doctrine** of 1823. In a message sent to Congress by President James Monroe (largely formulated by Monroe's secretary of state, John Quincy Adams), the European powers were warned to stay out of the Western Hemisphere because it was a special area of interest to the United States. (At the time, the leading powers of continental Europe were considering intervening to help Spain recover its rebellious Latin American colonies.) In return, Monroe declared, the United States would stay out of European affairs. This position on foreign policy was already so much a part of American thinking that it was not viewed as anything remarkable. It was not even referred to as the Monroe Doctrine until the 1850s.

Consistent with the Monroe Doctrine, on numerous occasions through the late 1920s, the United States sent military forces into Mexico, Central America, Cuba, Haiti, and the Dominican Republic. Their usual mission, as the United States proclaimed it, was to restore peace and order, protect American lives and property, and keep out hostile foreign influences. Under Franklin D. Roosevelt's administration, this policy of "gunboat diplomacy" was replaced by the self-proclaimed Good Neighbor policy. But underneath it all, the goals remained the same. The key difference was that diplomacy, rather than military force, was to be the foreign policy instrument of choice.

With the onset of the Cold War between the United States (as the leader of the Western "free world") and Soviet-sponsored international communism in the late 1940s, fears grew in Washington that communist governments would be set up in Latin America. These worries drove American presidents starting with Eisenhower to authorize covert actions aimed at removing suspected communists or other anti-U.S. leftist reformers from power in favor of pro-U.S. regimes. In 1954, the CIA overthrew the mildly leftist Arbenz government in Guatemala, and in 1965, Marines were sent into the Dominican Republic to support a pro-

U.S. president against his rival. The United States sponsored various attempts to overthrow or assassinate Fidel Castro, the anti-U.S. rebel who in 1959 came to power in Cuba and soon established a communist dictatorship that still exists today. Washington supported the overthrow of leftist presidents Salvadore Allende in Chile (1973) and Maurice Bishop in Grenada (1983). Under Ronald Reagan, the United States opposed, both overtly and covertly, left-wing revolutionary movements in El Salvador, Nicaragua, and Guatemala. In recent years, Washington has become concerned about anti-U.S. influences in Colombia and in Venezuela, whose president, Hugo Chavez, has been openly critical of American foreign policy.

In light of this history of aggression, critics have expressed concern about U.S. foreign policy toward Latin America. They note that in practice, the United States almost always acts unilaterally, without consulting other states in the region. These actions may have protected U.S. security interests, but human rights, economic development, and democracy in the region of interest have often suffered. Defenders of American foreign policy toward Latin America argue that depictions of aggression have been far too negative. They justify their actions in Latin America as mutually beneficial policy initiatives, citing the North American Free Trade Agreement, the Alliance for Progress under Kennedy, and the Caribbean Basin Initiative under Reagan. ◼

ECHOES FROM THE PAST

Americans have almost always disagreed about the proper way to interact with the rest of the world. A convenient way to organize these different approaches, or schools of thought, is to identify them with key figures from America's past. Four such schools stand out.[6] No one individual's perspectives on American foreign policy are likely to match up perfectly with those of any one of these historical figures. But the shadow that their thinking and actions cast over American foreign policy thinking is very much in evidence today.

The first school is identified with Alexander Hamilton, President Washington's first secretary of the treasury. **Hamiltonians** are the most "European" of the four schools of thought about foreign policy in that they are most comfortable thinking in terms of strictly defined national interests and the pursuit of national power in a world of shifting global balances. They are not interested in global crusades. For them, the primary purpose of American foreign policy is the promotion of American economic strength at home and abroad.

▶ **Did America choose to** isolate itself in the early years of our history?

Wilsonians
supporters of President Wilson who believed that United States foreign policy should be designed to spread U.S. ideals, values, and morals throughout the world, promoting free trade to strengthen our economy. He believed that intervention in foreign countries was appropriate to create peace and to spread freedom and democracy to protect the interests of the United States.

Jeffersonians
followers of Thomas Jefferson and his belief that foreign policy, including military spending, ought to be narrow and limited to protecting democracy at home. Jefferson believed that democracy should be promoted abroad but without broad military engagement.

Alexander Hamilton's name is associated with a view of foreign policy that emphasizes promoting the strength of American economic interests at home and abroad. Can you think of examples of foreign policy actions that could be characterized as Hamiltonian?

The second school is identified with Woodrow Wilson, although Wilson was not the first to take this position. **Wilsonians** see the central purpose of American foreign policy as the spread of American ideals, values, and morals throughout the world. In their view, this is not imperialism but rather an honorable duty reflecting the superiority of American ideas and the shared desire of people everywhere for democracy. Wilsonians also see a practical benefit in such a foreign policy. A world in which American ideas are triumphant will be a world in which American economic interests will be protected and secure. The Wilsonian emphasis on spreading democracy has been joined with an emphasis on liberalizing trade and promoting free-market economics.

The third school is identified with Thomas Jefferson. Like Wilsonians, **Jeffersonians** are committed to promoting democracy abroad. They differ on how to go about this. Whereas Wilsonians wish to remake the world in America's image in order to protect American democracy, Jeffersonians see foreign entanglements as a great threat to the success of American democracy. Neo-Jeffersonians fear that the strong governmental powers and large military establishment necessary to conduct an interventionist foreign policy will result in threats to American democracy and civil liberties at home. Today, this is the stance most typically assumed by libertarians.

The fourth and final school is identified with Andrew Jackson. His actions provide a foundation for those who admire the populist principles of the American frontier—courage, honor, and self-reliance—and want to apply them to the conduct of American foreign policy. Suspicious of outsiders and their values, **Jacksonians** champion a foreign policy of constant vigilance, backed by overwhelming might that should be employed with few if any constraints.

▶ **Did America choose to isolate itself in the early years of our history?** It is important to also recall that the United States has not always been so powerful or so deeply involved militarily and economically in the affairs of the rest of the world. During the American Revolution, Congress sent diplomats to Europe pleading for crucial military and financial help to defeat the British. Upon leaving office in 1796, President George Washington recommended a foreign policy of isolation and noninvolvement. Succeeding presidents did not always follow this advice, but on the

Jacksonians
populists who saw President Andrew Jackson as a man of the people. Characterized as very patriotic and nationalistic, Jackson strongly supported aggressive defense of United States interests, including geographic expansion.

ABOVE: **Woodrow Wilson championed a foreign policy** vision that advocated the spread of American ideals, values, and morals. This approach involves spreading democracy and the idea of a free market economy. ABOVE (RIGHT): **Thomas Jefferson** is associated with caution about risks of a large military establishment and strong governmental powers. This perspective expresses concern about the potential domestic impact that can follow from building the institutional components for an aggressive foreign policy. BELOW: **Andrew Jackson** is associated with nationalism that aims to use the country's full might in being vigilant against enemies and rivals. Which of these perspectives is closest to your views on appropriate foreign policy?

▶ **Do our views on human rights abroad reflect our views of civil liberties and freedom at home?**

discussionquestions

1. What are the differences among the views of the neoliberals, neoconservatives, conservatives, and isolationists regarding the Iraq War?
2. In what ways did American foreign policy undergo fundamental changes after the attack on Pearl Harbor?

whole, the United States concentrated on continental expansion. Engagement with other countries was generally close to home in the Western Hemisphere.

Only on the eve of the twentieth century, with the Spanish-American War (1898), did the United States became a major player on the world stage. By defeating Spain, the United States acquired an overseas colony, the Philippines. Under the first twentieth-century presidents, Theodore Roosevelt, William Howard Taft, and Woodrow Wilson, the United States carved out a sphere of influence in Mexico, Central America, and the Caribbean. In 1917, Wilson took the United States into World War I, and American forces contributed significantly to defeating Germany in 1918. Wilson took an active role in negotiating the peace treaty (the Treaty of Versailles) and the creation of the League of Nations. But then the United States returned to its pre–World War I policy of neutrality. The Senate rejected joining the League of Nations, and American foreign policy in the 1920s was largely confined to bolstering U.S. domination in Latin America—and to insisting that Britain and France repay their World War I debts to us. During the 1930s, the United States gave little support to the democratic nations of Britain and France after Adolf Hitler came to power in Germany.

Japan's attack on Pearl Harbor on December 7, 1941, changed forever how Americans saw the outside world. The "Fortress America" strategy of relying on the protection of the oceans no longer seemed realistic. The nation mobilized its military might and achieved victory in Europe and Asia. With World War II over and the onset of the Cold War, the United States had no choice but to play a major and sustained role in world affairs. The United States helped create the United Nations, international economic organizations such as the World Bank and the International Monetary Fund, and alliances such as NATO. The struggle against the Soviet Union and communism became global, especially after communist revolutionaries triumphed in China in 1949. The image of dominoes, standing precariously on edge and tumbling one after the other, was frequently invoked to represent this conflict. No country, in this metaphor, could be allowed to fall to communism, for that would set off a chain reaction in which one country after another would "go communist."

practicequiz

1. Which of the following is a key principle to neoconservative foreign policy?
   a. Global crusades, such as building democracies abroad, divert the U.S. from real and more immediate dangers.
   b. The United States' unparalleled military power in the world is the central instrument of American foreign policy.
   c. It is better to take military action through alliances and coalitions than to act alone.
   d. The major threats to U.S. security come from an overactive foreign policy.

2. Whose foreign policy makes them "maintainers," not "transformers"?
   a. neoliberals
   b. neoconservatives
   c. conservatives
   d. liberals

3. Which foreign policy perspective asserts that American military force should become less like a lance and more like a shield?
   a. isolationists
   b. conservatives
   c. both isolationists and conservatives
   d. neoliberals

4. During the 1930s, the U.S. gave little support to Britain and France (two democratic nations) after Adolf Hitler came to power in Germany.
   a. true   b. false

Answers: 1-b, 2-c, 3-a, 4-a.

Foreign and Domestic Policy

We commonly talk of American foreign policy and domestic policy as two separate areas. We have even placed these topics in different chapters of this book, primarily to keep them from becoming too long and thus discouraging to read. But it is important to realize that the boundary separating domestic and foreign policy is not and never has been watertight. In this section, we will examine three different links between American foreign and domestic policy. First, American foreign policy is linked to domestic policy because foreign policy is often based on ideas that guide domestic policy. Second, American foreign and domestic policies are

Kyoto Protocol
an international agreement to address the problem of global warming. The United States was involved in its negotiation but has refused to ratify the agreement, citing excessive economic costs.

connected because of the presence and activity of international factors in the political decision-making process. Finally, and perhaps most important, American foreign policy and domestic policy are related because our country's foreign policy can affect the distribution of costs and benefits among different groups here at home.

LINKS BETWEEN FOREIGN AND DOMESTIC POLICY

▶ **Do our views on human rights abroad reflect our views of civil liberties and freedom at home?** First, let's consider the impact of domestic policies on American foreign policy by looking at how the United States approaches human rights and environmental issues at the global level.[7] Three guiding principles lie at the heart of our country's human rights foreign policy. First, American policy, both domestic and foreign, emphasizes individual legal rights and civil liberties; it pays less attention to economic and social rights. Second, Washington usually regards hostile, overly strong governments as the primary threat to human rights; rarely does American policy see a need to strengthen foreign governments in order to promote human rights. Third, American foreign policy generally rejects violence as a means for promoting human rights. Attempts to advance workers' rights or civil rights through violence have never been received favorably in the United States; instead, we generally look to legal and electoral means of promoting rights. Because this historical experience is not shared by many other countries, American calls for rejecting violence as a means of change are often met with skepticism.

The influence of American domestic policy on its foreign policy is also evident in U.S. environmental policy. By and large, international environmental proposals put forward by the United States have not imposed new costs on Americans; they have instead sought to persuade other countries to adopt American standards. For example, the United States was one of the strongest advocates of a ten-year ban on commercial whaling, an area in which the United States has few economic interests but many citizens who worry about the fate of the world's whale population. But the United States has also vigorously opposed efforts to establish an international register of toxic chemicals, and it has refused to ratify the 1993 **Kyoto Protocol** on reducing greenhouse gases—in both cases citing the costs to American firms and the threat to American living standards.

Nelson Mandela, the revered former president of South Africa (1994–1999), visits President Bush at the White House. Mandela served nearly three decades in prison for seeking to overthrow the previous white-supremacist government of South Africa. When Mandela was released from prison in 1990, he lobbied American officials to impose sanctions on his country as part of the effort that eventually led to the creation of a multiracial democracy in 1994. How do foreigners use the lobbying pathway in an effort to influence American policy?

INTERNATIONAL INFLUENCE ON U.S. POLITICAL ACTIVITY

Foreign lobbying has become big business in Washington. In 1988 alone, 152 Japanese firms and government agencies contracted with 113 Washington lobbying firms. Between 1998 and 2004, companies with headquarters in seventy-eight foreign nations spent more than $620 million lobbying the U.S. government. These companies employed 550 lobbying firms and a total of 3,800 lobbyists, more than 100 of them former members of Congress. In 1990, with his capital city under attack by rebel forces, Liberian President Samuel Doe paid a Washington lobbyist $800,000 to improve his image and increase lukewarm U.S.

▶ **So the United States** allows foreign governments and businesses to lobby *our* government in support of *their* interests?

globalization
the expansion of economic interactions between countries.

Corporate executives from Toyota chose to build a new plant in Canada rather than in the United States. Domestic policies, especially the national health care coverage in Canada, helped to sway the decision. How do you feel about foreign corporations lobbying American governments to change tax policies and other laws in order to help them operate more profitably in the United States?

support. (It didn't help—Doe was later overthrown and executed by the rebels.) That same year, former South African political prisoner Nelson Mandela traveled to Washington, in part to lobby Congress to keep economic sanctions in place against the white-supremacist government that ruled his country. And in 2003, Bob Livingstone, a former Republican representative from Louisiana and the onetime chair of the House Appropriations Committee, helped Turkey defeat an attempt by the Republican-controlled Congress to take away $1 billion worth of foreign aid because of its failure to help the United States in the Iraq War.

Many foreign governments are deeply concerned about American foreign aid legislation and arms sales. To secure their objectives in these areas, they pursue a two-step lobbying campaign. They first try to gain leverage by lobbying the executive branch, usually the White House, the State Department, and the Defense Department. As already noted, they also lobby Congress.

The primary concern of foreign firms that operate in the United States is the ability of their affiliates to conduct business profitably and without hindrance. Between 1998 and 2004, for example, twenty-two foreign companies operating in the United States actively lobbied the Environmental Protection Agency over issues connected with the agency's Superfund cleanup policies. At the state and local levels, taxation, zoning, education, and labor laws and policies are all of considerable concern to foreign firms. In one well-known case, Sony threatened to stop planned construction of new plants in California or Florida unless those states repealed portions of their tax codes that would have taxed Sony on its worldwide sales rather than on sales of items produced in that particular state. After both states changed their tax laws, Sony went ahead and built the new plants. In 2005, Toyota was planning the location of a new automotive plant, in either the United States or Canada. Although several U.S. states offered more lucrative tax packages, both the national government and several provincial governments in Canada offered money for worker training; in addition, the Canadian system of universal health care would allow Toyota to save on the cost of health care benefits. Canada ended up getting the plant.

One of the most intense national lobbying campaigns occurred in 1987–1988. On that occasion, the Senate, angered by news that the Japanese electronics giant Toshiba had sold sensitive technology to the Soviet Union, voted to ban the corporation from the U.S. market. In response, Toshiba began a $9 million lobbying campaign focusing on the idea that such a ban would cost 100,000 Americans

▶ **Who really benefits**
from foreign aid?

their jobs. In the end, the legislation that passed merely barred Toshiba from obtaining U.S. government contracts for three years.

▶ **So the United States allows foreign governments and businesses to lobby *our* government in support of *their* interests?** The scale of foreign political activity in the United States has repeatedly raised two concerns. The first is that the more our representatives listen to foreign lobbyists, the less they will hear from the American public. The second concern is that foreign interests and American interests are not compatible. By listening to and responding to foreign voices, policymakers may ignore or, worse, harm American national interests. This concern is reinforced by periodic revelations of foreign attempts at bribery and espionage. For example, in 2002, it was revealed that Taiwan kept a secret $100 million fund to buy influence in this country, and in 2005, two former employees of a pro-Israeli lobbying firm were indicted for disclosing U.S. defense information.

The ever-increasing pace of **globalization** has added a third concern. Foreign governments and firms might not stop at seeking to influence American political decisions; they might also seek to influence American economic decisions in ways that harm the United States. In 2005, it was announced that CNOOC Ltd., a Chinese government-controlled oil company, was attempting to buy Unocal Corporation, the third-largest U.S. oil company. When the news broke, many American lawmakers raised economic and security issues and threatened to block the takeover. In their view, China was a major competitor with the United States for global influence and power. Faced with this opposition, CNOOC withdrew its $18.4 billion offer—clearing the way for Chevron, the second-largest American oil company, to acquire Unocal, even though its offer was $700 million less. In 2006, domestic and foreign policy again collided in the controversy over the turnover of the operation of American ports to a company with ties to the government of the United Arab Emirates. Would this be a national security risk or a prudent economic move?

INTERNATIONAL AND DOMESTIC GAINS AND LOSSES

▶ **Who really benefits from foreign aid?** One obvious answer to this question might be the country receiving the assistance. But there are other answers. For example, one of the best-known and best-supported foreign aid programs is Food for Peace. It allows countries to buy American farm products in local currency. This is

ABOVE: **A farmer surveys** his field of grains planted by assistance from the Food for Peace program.

BELOW: **Analysts debate whether food assistance** provided to foreign countries actually promotes the interests of American farmers and the U.S. government more than it helps impoverished people in foreign lands. Should the United States be more generous in providing assistance to foreign countries?

▶ What else affects Americans' support of foreign policy?

important because it means that they can reserve their limited amounts of "hard currency," such as dollars, euros, and pounds sterling, to buy other products from countries (including the U.S.) that will not accept their local currencies as payment. But where does this food come from? U.S. government warehouses, filled with American farm products purchased under price support programs. Without these programs, many farm products would sell at such low prices that farmers would be driven out of business. (Agricultural price supports were introduced in the New Deal era and have been maintained ever since.) The peasant farmers in the countries buying the food are undersold by relatively cheap American imports, which depresses local markets. Some critics argue that the Food for Peace program really amounts to foreign aid for American farmers. One of the major stumbling blocks to reaching a new international trade agreement today is the insistence of Third World countries on an end to U.S. price support programs for agricultural products. But prospects for ending these subsidies—which today go mainly to agribusinesses and the wealthiest farmers—are very small because of the power of agricultural lobbies in the U.S. Congress.

As the cost of foreign policy increases, requiring that domestic programs be canceled, cut back, or delayed because of economic pressures, support for foreign policy decreases.[8] The Democrats used to be the low-tariff party, going back to its days as an agrarian party based in the South and West; the GOP has always been more protectionist because it appealed to manufacturers and (often) workers who feared "cheap foreign competition." But protectionism was widely, and rightly, blamed for intensifying the Great Depression, so in the post–World War II world, U.S. foreign policy favored trade liberalization and the expansion of American exports. However, globalization has complicated matters. Today, the Democrats are becoming increasingly protectionist to appeal to workers threatened with job loss and to environmentalists worried about the environmental impact of industrializing the Third World. The Republicans have become the party of free trade because they represent the interests of export-oriented American business and emphasize the benefits of international trade to American consumers.

▶ **What else affects Americans' support of foreign policy?** Although the evidence is not as clear-cut as once thought, Americans also weigh the cost of foreign policy by counting the number of battlefield deaths. This grim equation first contributed to the erosion of the American public's support of the Vietnam War—which ultimately cost the lives of more than 55,000 U.S.

troops—in the late 1960s and early 1970s. The conventional wisdom is that the greater the number of American deaths in a foreign war, the less support Americans give to the president who is waging that war. To some extent, this is now happening to President George W. Bush. In 2006, as casualties mounted and Iraq showed little sign of ending its insurgency and establishing a viable government, Bush's standing in public opinion polls (overall job rating, handling of the war, and honesty) plummeted to record lows. A decline in presidential popularity does not appear to be automatic, however. Even as battlefield deaths mount, solidarity among political elites and a widely accepted military mission may keep a president's standing in the opinion polls high.[9] But the U.S. experience in Vietnam suggests that such public support cannot be maintained indefinitely in the absence of visible military success.

Public concerns about the benefits and costs of American foreign policy today run high in two areas: international trade policy and protection of civil liberties. In 2005, the Bush administration battled in the House of Representatives for passage of the Central American Free Trade Agreement (CAFTA), which passed by a vote of 217–215. Supporters argued that CAFTA was vital to the overall economic health of the U.S. economy in an era of globalization, because it fostered competition from abroad and provided consumers with more choices at competitive prices. They argued that CAFTA would also help long-impoverished countries develop and diversify their economies. Opponents cited the potential loss of American jobs as firms moved overseas to produce goods and then sell them in the American market. The U.S. sugar lobby also fought CAFTA because it slightly increases the amount of sugar that Central American countries may export to the United States, cutting into the profits of wealthy American sugar producers.

The second area of public concern is how to safeguard civil liberties while fighting the war against terrorism. Particularly worrisome to some are provisions of the USA PATRIOT Act, which was passed after the 9/11 bombings and renewed in 2006. These provisions give law enforcement officials access to an individual's private information without his or her knowledge. New federal laws also curtail the rights of foreigners who are detained on suspicion of being or aiding terrorists. Suspects can be detained for indefinite periods without being charged with a crime or having access to legal representation. Revelations that the Bush administration, on its own authority, approved electronic eavesdropping inside the United States were equally controversial.

▶ **How strong a role** does public opinion play in foreign policy?

discussionquestions

1. How does American domestic policy influence American foreign policy and does it affect participation in politics here at home?

2. In what ways does American foreign policy create winners and losers in domestic politics?

practicequiz

1. Historically, how has U.S. foreign policy responded to the violation of human rights abroad?
   a. through military intervention
   b. through clandestine attempts to foster revolt
   c. through legal and electoral means to promote rights
   d. through inaction

2. Recall the 1987–1988 episode involving Toshiba and the U.S. Senate, which was outraged at the electronics giant's earlier sale of sensitive technology to the Soviet Union. The results of Toshiba's aggressive, expensive lobbying to reverse Congress's outrage suggest that
   a. in the U.S. Senate, some principles are above the reach of foreign money.
   b. Congress takes a dim view of foreign businesses meddling in domestic U.S. policy.
   c. the U.S. domestic electronics business is robust enough to employ plenty of Americans and satisfy American consumer needs.
   d. in the U.S., the economic leverage of corporations like Toshiba is enormous.

3. Why have some argued that the Food for Peace program constitutes foreign aid for American agribusinesses?
   a. because in this program American farmers sell their products to foreign governments at inflated prices
   b. because the food shipped to foreign countries is first purchased from American farmers, at above-market rates, by the U.S. government through federal subsidies
   c. because foreign countries pay American farmers to travel to their countries and develop crops there, for which they are paid above-market rates
   d. because the U.S. government gives U.S. farmers substantial tax breaks to contribute to this program

4. Invariably a president's popularity drops during a high-casualty war.
   a. true   **b.** false

Answers: 1-c, 2-d, 3-b, 4-b.

Making American Foreign Policy

Perhaps more than any other aspect of policy in the United States, the making and carrying out of foreign policy seems distant and remote to most Americans. It can be argued that Americans'

reluctance to find pathways for expression of their views on American foreign policy, whether supportive or critical, is a major weakness. After all, successful foreign policy must combine a well-crafted response to international challenges and opportunities with public support. Others argue that the public should leave foreign policy to the experts. The question then becomes, who are the experts? The president and his advisers? Professional military and diplomatic officials? Congress? The seemingly knowledgeable journalists and academics who voice their support for or criticism of American foreign policy?

To answer these questions, we will examine public opinion, elections, interest group activity, and political protest in search of pathways for citizen participation in the making of American foreign policy. We will then turn to the national-level political institutions that deal with foreign policy.[10]

THE DOMESTIC CONTEXT

Keep in mind that some individuals are better positioned than others to influence public policy. Who are they? They come from varied backgrounds, but what sets them apart is the knowledge they possess and, even more important, the access they have to policymakers. Some are former government officials now at a think tank or university. Others are major contributors to a political party or leaders in organizations on whose support political parties depend to win elections. Still others are opinion leaders who write columns for major newspapers or present commentaries on television.

PUBLIC OPINION   Public opinion provides a first pathway for most citizens to express their views about American foreign policy. Although they may claim not to be influenced by opinion polls in their decision making, every president since Richard Nixon has employed pollsters to find out what the public thinks.

The influence of public opinion on American foreign policy can be seen in two ways. First, public opinion can serve as a source of public policy innovation, as when it pressured the Bush administration to create the Department of Homeland Security and the position of director of national intelligence after the 9/11 terrorist attacks. Alternatively, public opinion can restrain innovation or serve as a policymaking resource to preserve the status quo.

▶ **How strong a role does public opinion play in foreign policy?** One of the major obstacles President Franklin D. Roosevelt faced in the 1930s, despite being well aware of the growing

▶ **Are Americans familiar enough with these issues to give informed opinions to policymakers?**

Vietnam syndrome
the belief, attributed to the American experience in Vietnam, that the public will not support the use of military force if it results in significant American casualties.

"rally 'round the flag" effect
the expectation that Americans will unite behind the nation's leaders in times of crisis.

President George W. Bush used "rally 'round the flag" themes in his successful reelection campaign against Democratic challenger Senator John Kerry in 2004. Only after the election did public opinion turn strongly away from support for the Iraq War as American casualties mounted and there was little evidence of progress in establishing a stable democracy in Iraq. What, if anything, would prevent a president from using military action abroad as a means to gain a short-term boost in political support at home?

danger of Nazi Germany, was the American public's strongly isolationist mood. In fact, FDR's efforts to aid Great Britain and the Soviet Union in their resistance to German aggression in the years leading up to World War II were severely constrained by domestic isolationism; only the attack on Pearl Harbor removed this obstacle. American policymakers in the 1970s and 1980s worried about the so-called **Vietnam syndrome,** the belief that the public was no longer willing to support a prolonged military presence abroad that caused appreciable losses of American soldier's lives if it looked like it might become an unwinnable "quagmire." Concern about the Vietnam syndrome compelled President Reagan to withdraw American forces from Lebanon in 1983 and President Clinton to beat a hasty retreat from Somalia ten years later—in

both cases, these actions were taken after it became apparent that American military casualties were rising.

Policymakers tend to regard public opinion as a resource to be mobilized in international conflicts. They want to show foreign leaders that the American public is united behind the president. This happens almost reflexively when crises erupt that are perceived as threatening American security or when American troops are sent into combat. This **"rally 'round the flag" effect** was very noticeable at the start of the Iraq War. President George W. Bush's rating in the polls jumped 13 points the moment the war began. He had experienced an even bigger leap—39 percentage points—right after the 9/11 terrorist attacks.

But what conditions are necessary for policymakers to hear the public's voice? Research seems to confirm that at least 50 percent of the American public must be in agreement on a foreign policy issue before their opinion has any influence.[11] Public opinion is likely to be heard most clearly in the agenda-building and ratification stages of foreign policy decision making. Between those two stages, the institutional forces in the executive branch and Congress are the focus of attention.

ELECTIONS   The winning candidate in modern presidential elections claims that the results provide a mandate for that candidate's program, and foreign policy is no exception. But do elections really serve as a pathway for influencing foreign policy decisions? The evidence is mixed at best. Both major-party candidates tend to be on the same side of the issue. In 1980, both incumbent President Jimmy Carter and challenger Ronald Reagan favored increasing U.S. military capabilities. In 2004, both George W. Bush and his opponent, John Kerry, favored standing firm in Iraq and defeating terrorism. Presidential elections turn out to be less a debate over foreign policy and more a contest about whom the public trusts to achieve those goals.

▶ **Are Americans familiar enough with these issues to give informed opinions to policymakers?** Part of the problem is that the American public tends not to be well informed about foreign policy issues. In 1964, at the height of the Cold War, only 38 percent of Americans knew that the Soviet Union was not a member of the North Atlantic Treaty Organization (NATO). In 1979, only 23 percent knew which two countries were participating in the **Strategic Arms Limitation Talks (SALT)** (it was the United States and the Soviet Union, who were negotiating limits on the size of their respective nuclear forces). In 1993, fully 43 percent of Americans could not identify the continent on which Somalia was located, where American peacekeeping forces were

▶ **Which interest groups are** most involved in lobbying on foreign policy issues? Is this an effective pathway?

Strategic Arms Limitation Talks (SALT)
negotiations between the United States and the Soviet Union during the Cold War that produced two major agreements on limiting the size of each country's nuclear forces.

apartheid
the system of strict racial segregation and white supremacy in South Africa.

facing significant local opposition. And in 2003, an amazing 68 percent of Americans believed—incorrectly—that Iraq had played a major role in the 9/11 terrorist attacks. Some members of Congress believe that the low level of their constituents' information makes incumbents dangerously vulnerable. Challengers can and have won elections by taking foreign policy and national defense votes out of context and misrepresenting them in a negative light.

There is one way in which presidential elections clearly have influenced American foreign policy. Foreign governments rarely try to do serious business with the United States during presidential elections. Foreign policy measures initiated at that time have always run the risk of failure. During the Cold War, every political candidate dreaded being attacked as "soft on communism"; fear of that accusation was one factor that pulled Lyndon Johnson into the Vietnam War and kept him from cutting his losses. In anticipation of an upcoming election, a president often tries to tie up the loose ends of major foreign policy initiatives—such as trade agreements, treaties, and military activity—in order to keep them from becoming electoral issues.[12]

▶ **Which interest groups are most involved in lobbying on foreign policy issues? Is this an effective pathway?**
INTEREST GROUPS   The third avenue down which the public can travel to express its outlook on foreign policy issues is interest group activity. A wide variety of groups use this pathway to influence American foreign policy. A representative list of interest groups active in trying to influence U.S. policy toward China, for example, would include the AFL-CIO, Amnesty International, the Christian Coalition of America, the Committee of 100 for Tibet, the Emergency Committee for American Trade, the Family Research Council, and the National Endowment for Democracy.

Among the most influential interest groups are ethnic-identity groups. Most observers regard the American-Israeli Public Affairs Committee (AIPAC) and the Cuban-American National Foundation (CANF) as the two most successful such groups. African American groups have had a mixed record. They were active in opposing **apartheid** in South Africa and in pressing for humanitarian intervention in Haiti. But they were slow to speak out against the genocide in Rwanda (see *Pathways of Action* on this page). Hispanic Americans have also been slow to find their foreign policy voice. Although most Latinos take a deep interest in immigration issues, they are more likely to focus on issues related to their countries of origin. When it comes to American foreign policy, Mexican Americans, Cuban Americans, and people from

Randall Robinson (second from left) was joined by U.S. Senator Gary Hart (fourth from left) while leading a protest against apartheid, the system of white-supremacy that governed South Africa until 1994. Robinson founded TransAfrica, an organization that used lobbying and grassroots mobilization to influence American foreign policy toward Africa and the Caribbean. Which issues do you feel strongly enough about to contribute to lobbying and public protests?

the various countries in Central America and the Caribbean all have their own country-specific priorities and interests, and sometimes these lead to antagonisms among them.

pathways of action

RANDALL ROBINSON AND TRANSAFRICA

Randall Robinson was president of TransAfrica (1977–2001, a lobbying organization that focuses on foreign policy issues of particular interest to African Americans. Founded in 1977 with a budget of $70,000, it later had 15,000 members and an annual operating budget in excess of $1 million. Robinson was born in Richmond, Virginia, at a time when legally mandated segregation

▶ **Who helps the president**
set the foreign policy agenda?

what YOU can do!

Test your knowledge of foreign affairs. Read the foreign policy and international affairs section of a major newspaper, online or in hard copy. Using a map of the world that outlines countries but does not show their names, see how many of the countries you read about you can locate correctly on the map (Free Map Tests are available at **http://worldatlas.com/ webimage/testmaps/maps.htm**

was in place and dominated the political, social, and economic landscape of the South. He attended an all-black secondary school and went on to attend a black college, Norfolk State College, for three years before dropping out and being drafted into the U.S. Army. After leaving the Army, Robinson received a sociology degree from Virginia Union University and a law degree from Harvard Law School. After graduating from Harvard, he went to Tanzania on a Ford Foundation fellowship. Upon returning to the United States, he worked in public assistance and community development programs in Boston, during which time he organized protests against Gulf Oil Corporation for its operations in Portugal's African colonies.

From Boston, Robinson went to Washington, where he served briefly as foreign policy adviser to Congressman William Clay (D-MO) and then as an aide to Congressman Charles Diggs Jr. (D-MI). He accompanied Diggs on a trip to South Africa, where he witnessed at first hand the policy of apartheid, the strict segregation of races. This trip led to a meeting of the Congressional Black Caucus at which establishment of a lobbying campaign for an increased U.S. presence in Africa and the Caribbean was discussed. The result of these discussions was the formation of TransAfrica.

Ending apartheid was TransAfrica's first major goal. To bring this about, Robinson organized the Free South Africa Movement, which produced demonstrations in twenty-six cities that led to 4,000 arrests. The twenty members of Congress who participated in these demonstrations ultimately played a major role in pushing Congress to pass the Comprehensive Anti-Apartheid Act in 1986. President Reagan vetoed the bill, but Congress passed it over his veto.

From South Africa TransAfrica turned its attention to Rhodesia (today known as Zimbabwe), where a white minority government ruled over a black majority population. TransAfrica sought economic sanctions to force the white minority government out of power. Robinson also opposed American involvement in Angola's civil war and spoke out against the military dictatorship in Nigeria.

TransAfrica's most recent success came in the mid-1990s, when it lobbied the Clinton administration to intervene in Haiti, where the democratically elected government of Jean-Bertrand Aristide had been overthrown by a military coup, prompting thousands of Haitians to flee as refugees to the United States on

tiny, makeshift rafts. Virtually all who survived the perilous open-sea crossing were turned away and sent back to Haiti. To dramatize his position, Robinson began a hunger strike. On the twenty-seventh day of his fast, President Clinton announced a change in U.S. policy.

Most recently, TransAfrica has focused on increasing U.S. foreign aid to Africa and on expanding foreign markets for Caribbean countries' agricultural exports. ▪

Today, religion-based interest groups are becoming increasingly active on foreign policy issues. Among the most prominent are those on the "religious right." Primarily identified as supporting the Republican Party, these groups were firm opponents of communism during the later part of the Cold War. Today, they actively lobby on family planning and population control policies and in support of Christians persecuted abroad, particularly in China, Russia, and Sudan. But the religious right by no means has a monopoly on religiously motivated interest group activity. During the period leading up to the Iraq War, religious groups were active both for and against. Evangelicals tended to support the war, while the Catholic church, the Religious Society of Friends (Quakers), the World Council of Churches, and the Muslim Peace Fellowship all spoke out against it.

POLITICAL PROTEST Globalization has aroused much debate among Americans, particularly on college campuses. Images in the media of protesters clashing with police in Seattle in December 1999 at a meeting of the World Trade Organization (WTO) brought back for many vivid memories of political protests against the war in Vietnam—a prominent feature on the American political landscape in the late 1960s and early 1970s. Globalization as a political issue has succeeded in mobilizing protesters largely because it taps into two important contemporary issues: quality of life and civil rights and liberties.

Images of demonstrators in the streets are an important reminder that the public voice is expressed through both officially sanctioned and unofficial pathways. Not unexpectedly, administrations tend to dismiss protest activity as unimportant. But political protests on the scale of the peace movement and the antiglobalization movement can alter the political agenda, forcing policymakers to confront issues they otherwise would ignore. Recall the protests at Bush's Crawford, Texas, ranch involving

The World Trade Organization (WTO), composed of representatives from 149 countries, meets in cities throughout the world to discuss international trade issues. Since the 1990s, large-scale protests have been staged outside many of these meetings by people concerned about exploitation of Third World workers, environmental issues, and the spread of corporations' economic and political power. These protests have gained significant attention from the news media, largely because they have often led to property damage, violent resistance to police control, and many arrests. How effective are such methods of grassroots mobilization for shaping foreign policy?

Cindy Sheehan, which mobilized the previously silent antiwar faction. Protests can also bring new voices into the political process and reenergize long-established political forces, such as labor unions.

POLITICAL INSTITUTIONS

As in other policy areas, the Constitution allocates political power among the president, Congress, and the courts in the formation of foreign policy. Because three constitutionally defined powers are especially important in foreign affairs, they are all controversial. The first is treaty-making power. The Constitution states that the president, by and with the consent of the Senate, has the power to make treaties. Confirmation by two-thirds of the Senate is required for ratification of a treaty. Presidents can get around this requirement by signing an executive agreement with another country, which does not require any congressional action.

The second constitutionally defined power is appointment. Presidents nominate ambassadors and other key foreign policy officials to their posts, who must then be confirmed by the Senate. Once again, a president may get around Congress by using personal representatives to conduct negotiations or by making recess appointments—nominations that are automatically approved because Congress is not in session. (However, recess appointees do not hold office with the same permanent tenure as confirmed appointees, so this is used as a stopgap measure.)

Finally, there are the war powers. The Constitution gives to Congress the power to declare war and the power to raise and maintain military forces. The president is constitutionally designated as commander in chief. A major issue here is that since World War II, no American war has been formally declared by Congress. (For more discussion of this thorny issue, see LINK *Chapter 8, page 325.*)

▶ **Who helps the president set the foreign policy agenda?**
THE PRESIDENCY   In today's public eye, the president makes American foreign policy. It is the president who announces decisions on war and peace; meets foreign leaders at the White House, at international summit conferences, or in foreign capitals; and signs treaties and international agreements. However, presidents do not make foreign policy decisions in isolation. We have already noted that through public opinion polling, they are kept well aware of the domestic political consequences of their foreign policy decisions.

CHIEF OF STAFF   The White House Chief of Staff (COS) plays an increasing role in foreign policy matters.[13] Andrew Card, then President George W. Bush's COS, advocated immigration reform as a means of attracting Hispanic voters to the Republican Party, and after 9/11, he was put in charge of the Homeland Security Council. Howard Baker Jr., formerly an influential Republican senator, served as COS in the last years of President Ronald Reagan's administration. During that time, he played an important part in controlling the backlash from Reagan's possible involvement in the Iran-Contra scandal (see LINK *Chapter 8, page 324*) and influenced Reagan to hold frequent summit conferences with Soviet leader Mikhail Gorbachev with the goal of ending the Cold War.

THE VICE PRESIDENCY   A relatively new foreign policy voice from within the White House comes from the vice president.[14] Dick Cheney, George W. Bush's vice president, once served as COS to President Gerald Ford and as secretary of defense to President George H. W. Bush. Within George W. Bush's administration, Cheney was a powerful advocate of the Iraq War, and some observers considered him the architect of the president's foreign policy, at least during Bush's first administration. Although Cheney's role in foreign policy far exceeds that of many vice presidents, he was following in the footsteps of his two immediate predecessors, Dan Quayle and Al Gore. Quayle, the vice president under George H. W. Bush, was active in designing Latin American policy, and Gore established himself as an expert on Russia and some of the bordering countries, which became independent upon the collapse of the Soviet Union. However, keep in mind that the influence of both the COS and the vice president has increased only because presidents have allocated significant authority to these officials.

NATIONAL SECURITY COUNCIL   A modern president's most important source of advice about foreign policy problems inside

▶ **How heavily does the president rely on the NSC for advice, compared with other agencies such as the State Department?**

At a meeting of the National Security Council during the first term of President George W. Bush, the President is flanked by then-Secretary of State Colin Powell and Vice President Dick Cheney. Because presidents determine the organization and composition of the National Security Council, what are the risks that its members will simply tell the president what he wants to hear?

the White House is the National Security Council (NSC).[15] The NSC was created in 1947, at the beginning of the Cold War. At the same time, the Central Intelligence Agency (CIA) was established and the old War and Navy Departments were consolidated to form the Department of Defense. These changes represented a wide-ranging reorganization of the foreign affairs bureaucracy under the 1947 National Security Act. The term *foreign affairs bureaucracy* is used to describe those bureaucratic units most deeply involved in shaping foreign policy, which commonly include the State Department, the Defense Department, and the CIA. One of the major lessons learned from the attack on Pearl Harbor and World War II was that to protect the United States, much greater coordination and communication was needed among the foreign affairs and domestic bureaucracies.

The NSC has evolved over time. Its focus has shifted from the council itself to smaller subgroups, the NSC staff, and the national security adviser. Finding the NSC too large and unmanageable in times of crisis, presidents have routinely relied for advice on smaller groups, such as Lyndon Johnson's "Tuesday Lunch Group" during the Vietnam War and Jimmy Carter's "Friday Breakfast Group" during the Soviet Union's 1979 invasion of Afghanistan and the Iranian hostage crisis. Similarly, George W. Bush established the "War Cabinet" to help with the planning and conduct of the Afghanistan and Iraq wars.

Since its inception, the NSC has grown from a small presidential staff of ten people to a bureaucratic body that at times has employed more than 200, including 100 professional national security analysts. The NSC staff is charged with making policy recommendations and overseeing the implementation of foreign policy decisions. The president sets up the organizational structure for the NSC. George W. Bush organized his NSC into two committees: The Principals Committee debates policy and makes recommendations to the president, and the Deputies Committee focuses on implementing the NSC's decisions. President Nixon created the most elaborate NSC organization, with separate committees for Vietnam, crisis management, covert action, arms control, intelligence, and other policy areas.

▶ **How heavily does the president rely on the NSC for advice, compared with other agencies such as the State Department?** Presidents have turned to the NSC staff for advice out of frustration with the advice they have received from the State Department, the Defense Department, and the CIA. Too often presidents have felt that these foreign policy bureaucracies have not been sensitive enough to presidential perspectives in making foreign policy. The big issue is time frame. Foreign policy professionals are sensitive to how foreign governments will respond over the long term. Presidents, on the other hand, think in terms of four-year electoral cycles and are of course vitally concerned with how the American public will judge their immediate response to events.

NATIONAL SECURITY ADVISER   The national security adviser was initially intended to be a kind of neutral referee, managing the NSC and reporting to the president. This changed during the Kennedy and Johnson administrations, when national security advisers began openly to advocate policy solutions and paid less attention to their managerial role. Henry Kissinger (under Nixon),

Zbigniew Brzezinski (under Carter), Colin Powell (under Reagan), and Condoleezza Rice (under George W. Bush) are among the most visible and most powerful recent national security advisers. Today, the national security adviser plays a central role in formulating American foreign policy. But that role is frequently challenged by other high officials, most notably the secretary of state and the secretary of defense.

STATE DEPARTMENT   According to historical tradition, the president looks first to the State Department in making foreign policy. The State Department is the formal channel of information between the United States and foreign governments and serves as a resource for senior policymakers. Each year, the State Department represents the United States at meetings of more than fifty major international organizations and at more than 800 international conferences. From day to day, the State Department also plays a central role in managing American foreign policy through U.S. embassies abroad, where the ambassador serves as chief of mission and heads the country team. The country team is made up of all U.S. personnel assigned to an embassy. In 1994, only 38 percent of these people worked for the State Department; 36 percent worked for the Defense Department, 5 percent for the Justice Department, 3 percent for the Transportation Department, and 18 percent for the Treasury, Commerce, and Agriculture Departments. CIA officials (who often operate covertly) are left out of the official accounting. Complicating the difficulty of asserting control over such a diverse set of government agencies is the fact that ambassadors are frequently not career foreign service officers. Many—especially in glamorous European capital cities—are political appointees who were made ambassadors as a reward for campaign contributions or as consolation after an election loss or retirement. Under Reagan, only 60 percent of ambassadors were career diplomats, but under Clinton, 70 percent came up through the ranks of the foreign service.

pathways profile

MADELEINE ALBRIGHT

Madeleine Albright was born in Czechoslovakia on May 15, 1937. Her father, Josef Korbel, was an important Czech diplomat. In 1948, when Madeleine was 11, the government of postwar Czechoslovakia was taken over by the communists in a coup d'état. Her father, who held strong prodemocracy views,

ABOVE: **The United States maintains embassies** in countries throughout the world. At these embassies, the politically appointed ambassador and a professional staff represent American interests and seek to maintain good relationships with the governments of each host country. These embassies are part of the State Department, which is directed by the Secretary of State.

BELOW: **Madeleine Albright was the first woman** appointed to be Secretary of State. She served in that capacity during the second administration of President Bill Clinton. How would American foreign policy be better represented abroad if all ambassadors were career-diplomats from the State Department rather than politically-connected associates of the president, as is true of ambassadors sent to many European capitals?

▶ **Who decides when we should use military force?**

Powell Doctrine
a view that cautions against the use of military force, especially where public support is limited, but states that once the decision to use force has been made, military power should be applied quickly and decisively.

McNamara Doctrine
a view that military power can be applied to situations in controlled and limited amounts that rise over time and that public support should not be a major factor governing its use.

feared for the safety and security of his family. Along with her mother, brother, and sister, she fled to London. Shortly after that, they left for the United States, where the family was granted political asylum.

Madeleine—whose birth name was Marie Jana Korbelová—moved with her family to Colorado, where her father obtained a teaching position at the University of Denver. In 1959, she earned her undergraduate degree in political science at Wellesley College in Massachusetts. While there, she became active in Democratic Party politics, campaigning for Adlai Stevenson in 1956. She married Joseph Albright shortly after graduating from college and began to raise a family while her husband pursued a career in journalism. During this time, she began to take graduate courses at Columbia University and studied under Zbigniew Brzezinski, a Polish-born expert on Soviet bloc affairs who would become national security adviser in the Carter administration. Albright went on to receive her Ph.D.

In 1968, when her husband's job took him to Washington, D.C., Albright became active in fundraising for Senator Edmund Muskie's failed 1972 attempt to win the Democratic presidential nomination. She went on to work in Muskie's Senate office and in 1978 joined Brzezinski's NSC staff, where she concentrated on congressional relations. After leaving the NSC, Albright took a position at Georgetown University and continued to be active in Democratic politics, serving as a foreign policy adviser to Walter Mondale and Michael Dukakis in their presidential races. Her next professional position was as president of the Center for National Policy, a Washington think tank aligned with the Democratic Party.

Albright helped write much of the Democratic Party's foreign policy position statement in its 1992 platform and was selected by newly elected President Bill Clinton to become the U.S. ambassador to the United Nations. She held this position throughout Clinton's first term. On December 5, 1996, Clinton selected Albright as the first female secretary of state upon the retirement of Warren Christopher. Both at the United Nations and as secretary of state, Albright was a strong advocate of American internationalism and the use of military force to promote democracy and bring an end to ethnic violence, particularly in civil war–torn Bosnia. ▪

Once the centerpiece of the foreign affairs bureaucracy, the State Department has seen its power and influence decline steadily. It has gone from the leading force behind such policies as the Marshall Plan, which promoted Western European economic recovery after World War II, and the establishment of NATO, the primary American alliance system against the Soviet Union, to largely playing the role of foreign policy critic.

Two complaints are frequently voiced about the State Department's performance. First, its recommendations are too predictable. The State Department prefers risk-free solutions that follow a safe course of action and focus on the long run. Second, as we noted before in discussing the NSC, the recommendations of the State Department can often be insensitive to the president's political perspective.

Nowhere is its decline in influence as obvious as in international economic policy. It has lost out in this area to the Office of the U.S. Trade Representative, which was created by Congress in 1963 and is located in the White House. The U.S. trade representative is responsible for U.S. negotiations at international trade conferences, such as those organized by the WTO and those that led to the creation of CAFTA. Congress established the office because it felt that the State Department was not acting vigorously enough to protect American economic interests in international trade negotiations.

DEPARTMENT OF DEFENSE   For most of its history, the military security of the United States was provided by forces under the direction of the War Department and the Department of the Navy. These two departments coordinated the activity of the armed forces under the sole direction of the president. This changed dramatically with the passage of the National Security Act in 1947, which established the offices of the secretary of defense and chairman of the Joint Chiefs of Staff and created the National Military Establishment. In 1949, the National Military Establishment was renamed the Department of Defense.

Secretaries of defense have generally adopted one of two approaches. Generalists will defer to military know-how and see themselves as the military's representatives in policy deliberations with the president and other foreign affairs bureaucracies. Secretaries who see themselves as experts in defense matters seek to shape and control the Defense Department in accordance with their views. Donald Rumsfeld, George W. Bush's former secretary of defense, quickly established himself as a controversial military authority whose ideas about how to fight the war on terror, drive Saddam Hussein from power, and occupy Iraq after the war often clashed with those of the professional military officers.

covert action
efforts to secretly influence affairs in another state, which may include propaganda, disinformation campaigns, bribery, fomenting political and economic unrest, and in the extreme, assassination.

intelligence
gathering and analyzing information and communications, often secret, about potential enemies and other national security matters.

As Secretary of Defense, Donald Rumsfeld was a controversial figure, identified with an Iraq policy that had lost favor with the general public and caught in struggles with the military leadership over the size and make-up of the armed services. Rumsfeld saw himself as an expert on military matters and, as part of the civilian leadership, a counter-balance to life-long members of the armed services.

These disagreements became public in 2006 when six retired generals with combat experience in Iraq voiced their opposition to Rumsfeld and called for his resignation. He stepped down in Novermber of that year.

A major point of debate among civilian and military officials in the Pentagon is the future size and shape of the military. How much emphasis should be given to information technologies in planning for and fighting future wars? For what type of conflicts should the military be trained? The type of military operation that defeated the Iraqi army in 2003 is very different from counterinsurgency operations against terrorists or humanitarian interventions to halt genocide. One consequence of an increased emphasis on technology is a reduction in the size of the military, at home and abroad. This means reliance on National Guard units for combat missions and the closure of many military bases—both of which can be very disruptive to and unpopular with local communities in the United States.

▶ **Who decides when we should use military force?** Another long-standing issue involves the conditions under which American military forces should be sent into combat. There are two poles in this debate: the Powell Doctrine and the McNamara Doctrine. The **Powell Doctrine,** named for Colin Powell, calls for the decisive use of American military only when there is clear public support for the use of force and an exit strategy in place. According to the **McNamara Doctrine,** named for Robert McNamara, secretary of defense during much of the Vietnam War, limited and graduated use of military force is permissible when there is a recognized problem demanding a military response, with or without public support. The professional military tends to favor the Powell Doctrine, and Defense Department civilians are more likely to advocate a position in line with the McNamara Doctrine.

Regardless of the prevailing view concerning the use of military force, the military does not have the final say. Under the Constitution, the president is commander in chief, and in the United States, the military has traditionally deferred to civilian authority.

CENTRAL INTELLIGENCE AGENCY   We often associate the Central Intelligence Agency with **covert action,** but one of the agency's primary functions is the gathering of intelligence. Intelligence is *evaluated* information, not simply news snippets or rumors. Ideally, intelligence should provide policymakers with enough warning and insight to allow policymakers to act in the face of a challenge to American security interests. This is not easy, because surprise is a constant element of global politics.[16]

The CIA's ability to undermine surprise, or at least reduce its negative consequences, is determined largely by two factors. The first is the relationship between the CIA and the president. The second is the relationship between the CIA and the other intelligence agencies.

There are several points of friction in the relationship between the CIA and the president. First, the logic of intelligence clashes with the logic of policymaking. Good intelligence limits policy options by clarifying the assumptions behind and consequences of various policy options, but good policymaking often requires keeping as many options open for as long as possible. Second, how close should intelligence be to policy? The traditional answer is that intelligence and policy must be kept separate so the intelligence is not infected by policy considerations and can provide neutral information. Also, intelligence that is kept separate from policy is likely to be useless, since intelligence cannot inform policymaking if it is not aware of policy. Third, there is often a difference between the type of information the president wants to receive and the type of information the CIA is inclined to collect. Policymakers are most eager to obtain information that will help them convince Congress and the American public about the merits of their favored policy. They are frustrated by intelligence that is impossible to use because it is tentative, secretive, or not easily understood. Finally, the CIA is not the president's only source of intelligence. It is in competition for the president's attention with interest groups, lobbyists, the media, and well-placed individuals.

The CIA has a unique relationship with other members of what is known as the "intelligence community." Besides the CIA,

▶ **Are the roles of the CIA**
and other agencies well
defined, or are there turf
wars over power and policy?

> **containment**
> a Cold War strategy that sought to control
> and encircle the Soviet Union rather than
> defeat it militarily.

the most prominent members of that community are the intelligence units of each branch of the military, the State Department, the FBI, the National Security Agency (in charge of protecting America's secret communication codes as well as breaking the codes of others), the Defense Intelligence Agency (whose director is the primary adviser to the secretary of defense on military intelligence matters), and the National Reconnaissance Office (charged with developing American information-gathering technology).

▶ **Are the roles of the CIA and other agencies well defined, or are there turf wars over power and policy?** Turf wars between these organizations are not uncommon as each seeks to protect its mission from being encroached on by others. Today, one of the most serious disputes is between the CIA, the State Department, and the Pentagon over covert (secret) action. Covert action has traditionally been carried out by the CIA, but since 9/11, the military has played an increasing role, and it does not need the approval of the ambassador to a country to carry out such operations.

The various members of the intelligence community often have different approaches to foreign policy problems. Consider the issue of spies. The FBI takes a law enforcement perspective, indicating that people suspected of engaging in espionage for foreign governments should be arrested and prosecuted for breaking the law. The CIA prefers to let spies continue to operate so that it can watch them, discover their contacts, and feed them misinformation. Nor does the CIA want its own operations revealed in a public trial.

Until 2006, when the position of director of national intelligence was created, the head of the CIA and the head of the rest of the intelligence community were one and the same, an individual who held the title of director of central intelligence (DCI). Today, these positions are held by two different officials. During the time that the CIA and the intelligence community were both led by the DCI, the DCI had budget authority only over the CIA. So an estimated 80 to 90 percent of the intelligence community's budget was beyond DCI control, falling under the control of the Pentagon. In the federal government, budget control gives powerful bureaucratic leverage. One of the many unresolved problems facing the first national intelligence director, John Negroponte, is that so far he lacks effective budget control over members of the intelligence community.

DEPARTMENT OF HOMELAND SECURITY The Department of Homeland Security (DHS) is the newest part of the intelligence community. More than any other government unit, the DHS occupies a gray area between domestic and foreign policy bureaucracies.[17] The DHS came into existence in November 2002 in response to the terrorist attacks of September 11, 2001. Its creation was the largest bureaucratic transformation in American history, affecting 170,000 employees and combining twenty-two different agencies from eight different departments. The DHS swallowed up the Federal Emergency Management Agency (FEMA), the Coast Guard, the Secret Service, the Customs Service, the Immigration and Naturalization Service (INS), and the recently created Transportation Security Administration. Formation of the DHS did not affect the FBI and the CIA directly, but the new DHS does have an intelligence and threat analysis unit that makes it a challenger to these traditional intelligence-gathering agencies in the policymaking process.

The newness of the Department of Homeland Security makes it difficult to judge the role it will play in foreign policy decision making. Its first major venture into policymaking, devising a color-coded nationwide terrorist threat alert system, was not well received. Tom Ridge, its first secretary, left office amid criticism for failing to navigate the shoals of bureaucratic warfare. His successor, Michael Chertoff, quickly proposed a wide range of organizational reforms intended to improve the glaring inadequacies of its organizational performance, which became apparent in the government's response to Hurricane Katrina in September 2005. These proposed reforms include faster funding for first responders, tighter security in American ports, and improved cooperation with intelligence agencies.

▶ **How often does Congress challenge the president's foreign policy decisions—and on what issues?**
CONGRESS If you go by newspaper and television accounts, it would seem that the president and Congress are always in conflict over the conduct of American foreign policy. This is not the case. Viewed over time, presidential-congressional relations in foreign policy have alternated between long stretches of presidential dominance and moments when Congress emerged as an important force, fully capable of frustrating presidential initiatives. These swings depend on two factors: the level of congressional *activity* and the level of congressional *assertiveness*.[18]

A supportive Congress is actively engaged in foreign policy issues but does not try to assert control over them. From the onset of the Cold War around 1947 until the late 1950s, Congress was largely supportive. Relations between the president and Congress

► **How often does Congress** challenge the president's foreign policy decisions— and on what issues?

The creation of the Department of Homeland Security included the federal government's takeover of security functions and screening passengers at the nation's airports. Have there been indications that the Department of Homeland Security loses effectiveness by being responsible for too many different agencies and government functions?

were positive. These were the years of "bipartisan" foreign policy, when "politics stopped at the water's edge," meaning that differences between Republicans and Democrats hardly surfaced in foreign policy decision making. A broad consensus existed that the Soviet Union and communism were the enemy and **containment** was the proper strategy for meeting the threat. Congress saw its role as supporting the president and providing him with the means to carry out his foreign policy. Exceptions to this rule involved a good dose of domestic politics. One such case was the McCarthy hearings, primarily conducted by Republicans, into charges that communists had infiltrated the State Department (controlled by Democrats) and the Defense Department and were responsible for such key foreign policy setbacks as the triumph of communism in China, described at the time as the "loss of China." Similarly, congressional-presidential relations were inflamed by Democratic President Truman's firing of General Douglas MacArthur, a would-be Republican presidential candidate who was in charge of American and UN military forces in Korea during the Korean War and who had openly disagreed with Truman over how to conduct the war effort.

From roughly 1958 through 1968, a "strategic" Congress emerged. This meant that Congress was not particularly active but was willing to be assertive on selected issues. Resolutions of support for presidential foreign policy initiatives were still the rule. Notable examples occurred in 1961, after the failed Bay of Pigs invasion of Cuba to remove Fidel Castro from power; during the 1962 Cuban Missile Crisis, when the world reached the brink of a Soviet-American nuclear confrontation; and in 1964, when Congress passed almost unanimously and with little debate the Gulf of Tonkin Resolution, which gave President Lyndon Johnson a virtual free hand to confront North Vietnam militarily. However, key members of Congress such as Senator J. William Fulbright, who chaired the Senate Foreign Relations Committee, clashed with President Johnson as the Vietnam War escalated with little evidence of success. The second issue on which Congress was active during this period was military strength. The biggest military issue of the time was the "missile gap," the idea that the Soviet Union was ahead of the United States in missile production and that the president had not done enough to protect American national security. In the 1960 presidential campaign, which pitted Democratic candidate John Kennedy against Republican Richard Nixon, the Democrats used the "missile gap" very effectively. Once in office, however, Kennedy discovered that no such gap existed.

From 1969 into the mid-1980s, Congress was *competitive*— both active and assertive. During that time, Congress challenged presidents on both the content and the conduct of American foreign policy. For example, in 1974, the Jackson-Vanik Amendment, which made improved economic relations with the Soviet Union

▶ **How does Congress**
have its say on foreign policy?

détente
reduction of tension or strained relations
between previously hostile nations.

At a congressional hearing on intelligence issues, members of Congress can ask questions of the officials appointed by the president to handle national security and intelligence matters. Such hearings also provide an opportunity for members of Congress to express their disagreement with the president about the conduct of foreign policy. Do members of Congress possess enough information to understand and criticize the operations of secretive intelligence agencies?

contingent on allowing persecuted Jews to emigrate more freely, openly challenged President Richard Nixon's policies toward the USSR. Since better economic relations were a key aspect of Nixon's foreign policy of **détente,** which was designed to improve relations with the Soviet Union and lessen international tensions, this amendment became a major problem in Nixon's negotiations with the Kremlin. At the end of the 1970s, President Jimmy Carter faced a congressional challenge over the Panama Canal Treaty, which restored the Panama Canal to Panamanian control, removing a key irritant from U.S.–Latin American relations. Carter managed to get the treaty approved by the Senate, but only after making concessions to senators who had raised strong objec-

tions. In the 1980s, congressional-presidential struggles focused largely on President Reagan's policy of staunch support for the Contra rebels in Nicaragua despite congressional prohibitions on funding rebel activity. A complex arms sales program to Iran was engineered behind the scenes to help accomplish the fall of the Sandinista government in Nicaragua as well as the release of Americans held captive in Lebanon; when revealed, it became known as the Iran-Contra scandal.

The most important challenge to the president's ability to conduct foreign policy has been the War Powers Resolution, which Congress passed over Nixon's veto in 1973. As you learned in LINK *Chapter 7, page 324,* this law sought to limit the president's ability to use military force by requiring that Congress receive formal notification of troop deployment abroad into combat situations and issue its approval. If congressional approval is not granted, the forces must be withdrawn within sixty days. Although all presidents since 1973 have objected to this law on the grounds that it is unconstitutional, they have all observed it when committing American forces abroad. President George H.W. Bush was careful to obtain a supportive congressional vote before launching the Gulf War in 1991, and Bill Clinton did likewise before he committed American forces to the brief war that NATO waged against Serbia over Kosovo in 1999. So far, Congress has never exercised its power to withdraw military forces.

A strategic Congress slowly began to reemerge in the mid-1980s, a pattern that was the norm until September 11, 2001. During this period, Congress pulled back from broad-based challenges to the president's conduct of foreign policy and concentrated on a smaller set of highly visible issues. Foremost among these was the annual vote granting China "most favored nation" status; the Comprehensive Nuclear Test Ban Treaty (rejected in 1999); and the North American Free Trade Agreement (passed in 1993).

The 9/11 terrorist attacks brought back a disengaged Congress. In the immediate aftermath of 9/11, Congress ceded much of its authority and initiative in making crucial foreign policy decisions to the president, including mobilization of resources for the war on terror. But it seems clear that Congress is again becoming more strategic. Concern is more frequently voiced by members of both parties regarding the Bush administration's postwar policies in Iraq, the use of torture on suspected terrorists in American custody, and the claim of inherent presidential authority to order electronic wiretaps on Americans in order

what YOU can do!

Make a list of the major foreign policy votes in the last Congress. How did your state's senators and your House representative vote on these issues? Do you agree or disagree with these votes? If you disagree with them, what are your options?

to prosecute the war on terrorism. The centerpiece of Bush's post-9/11 national security legislation, the USA PATRIOT Act, was renewed in 2006, but only after strongly debated changes were made.

The mounting congressional challenges are not limited to Iraq-related issues. In 2006, Bush won congressional support for the Central American Free Trade Agreement only by the narrowest of margins after much lobbying and arm-twisting. The Bush administration had to use its recess appointment power to send John Bolton to the United Nations as ambassador after opposition by some Democrats and Republicans blocked a vote on his nomination. And members of both parties openly disagreed with the president over allowing management of American ports by a firm with close connections to the government of Dubai.

▶ **How does Congress have its say on foreign policy?** Congress most frequently uses three tools to influence foreign policy: legislation, funding, and oversight. Congress often seeks to assert its influence by attaching amendments to foreign policy legislation that place conditions on the president's actions. Congress may target foreign aid and military assistance money for certain countries, as it has done repeatedly for Israel and Egypt. It may make foreign aid conditional on annual reports that give passing grades on such matters as human rights, antidrug and antiterrorism efforts, and nuclear weapons control. Presidents can ignore these limitations, however, by certifying that assistance is in the "national interests" of the United States. Presidents have used this power to continue foreign aid to Mexico and Panama despite those countries' poor records in the war on drugs and to Pakistan after 9/11 in spite of its questionable record in opposing terrorism and in enforcing nuclear nonproliferation.

Congress's budgetary powers are equally blunt and hard to use with finesse, partly because of the committee structure within Congress. There is also a problem with presidential impoundment of funds resulting from congressional budgetary decisions. During the Vietnam War, the Defense Department transferred to Taiwan several million dollars appropriated by Congress for the war effort and then went back to ask for replacement funds for Vietnam. President Nixon refused to spend money appropriated for a new manned bomber because he opposed the program. In 2003, the Bush administration asked Congress for funds to help rebuild Iraq, yet delays resulting from the insurgency and bureaucratic battles prevented much of this money from being spent. Perhaps

the biggest obstacle to using its budgetary powers to control American foreign policy is that whereas programs require funding, presidential policy announcements do not. Congress often finds itself reluctant to undercut a president once the White House has publicly committed the United States to a course of action with important international implications.

Several factors limit the impact of congressional oversight. One is the small political payoff for a great investment of time. Constituent work and shaping of domestic legislation is much more valuable for reelection purposes. A second limiting factor is organization: More than eighty committees have some kind of jurisdiction over the sprawling Department of Homeland Security. Third, most congressional oversight of foreign policy tends to be after the fact. For example, the 9/11 hearings were highly visible undertakings, fraught with emotion and geared toward establishing blame. Routine oversight of foreign policy programs involves far less effort and minimal media attention.

Presidents and critics of Congress tend to see the legislature as an obstacle course that must be run in order to formulate and carry out a coherent foreign policy. Defenders see congressional input as vital to keeping the government in touch with the national mood and ensuring long-term public support for American foreign policy.

THE SUPREME COURT The Supreme Court seldom voices an opinion regarding American foreign policy. However, over the course of its history, the Court has produced three types of rulings regarding foreign policy. First, when there is a conflict between state laws and treaties on a subject involving American foreign policy, the Court has ruled consistently that treaties take precedence over state laws. Second, it has consistently supported the president in conflicts with Congress. For example, it has ruled that executive agreements (which do not require congressional approval) have the same validity as treaties (which do require such approval). Finally, the Supreme Court has been very reluctant to grant the government broad powers that may restrict American civil liberties and constitutionally guaranteed freedoms. With pending cases such as the treatment of accused terrorists detained in Guantanamo Bay and elsewhere and the administration's program of warrantless surveillance in the United States, the Court will certainly be watched closely to see if historical precedents retain their influence in an age when the war on terrorism is the defining feature of American foreign policy.

discussionquestions

1. Which institutions are most involved in making foreign and national security policy?

2. What choices does a president have in seeking advice on foreign policy decisions, and in what ways might the advice from various sources differ?

▶ **How has the nature of terrorism changed since 9/11?**

practicequiz

1. What is the "Vietnam Syndrome"?
   a. Americans' reluctance to support a U.S. military operation which produces significant U.S. casualties and does not appear to be winnable.
   b. Americans' distaste for military adventures that are motivated by ideological, not moral or economic, reasons.
   c. Americans' reluctance to support U.S. military operations in Asia.
   d. Americans' reluctance to support U.S. military's participation in guerrilla warfare.

2. How effective are elections as a pathway for public input about foreign policy?
   a. Extremely effective: Presidents often claim foreign policy mandates after they win elections.
   b. Effective: Presidential candidates can count on voters to be well informed about foreign affairs and so respect the foreign policy implications of their voting.
   c. Not very effective: Often, as in the presidential election of 2004, the candidates' positions on most foreign policy issues were nearly the same.
   d. Completely ineffective: Foreign policy is the domain of well-qualified elites and the popularity of their decisions with voters is politically irrelevant.

3. Which of the following interest groups is the most influential in American foreign policy making?
   a. TransAfrica
   b. The Committee of 100 for Tibet
   c. The United Auto Workers
   d. The Cuban-American National Foundation

4. In the last decade, the president's most important source of foreign policy information has been
   a. The CIA
   b. The NSC
   c. The Secretary of State
   d. The president's Chief of Staff

Answers: 1-a, 2-c, 3-d, 4-b.

Foreign Policy and National Security Issues

The United States faces many current foreign policy problems and challenges. We will examine three categories of foreign policy problems: military security, economic, and human welfare.

Although we will discuss them separately, in many cases these problems are intimately connected.

These connections come through quite clearly if we look at the problem presented by the spread of infectious diseases such as the acquired immune deficiency syndrome (AIDS). Because there is no cure, it is tempting to treat AIDS as a health problem, which would put it in the human welfare category. But consider that according to the World Bank, the spread of the human immunodeficiency virus (HIV) and AIDS is in part responsible for decreased economic growth rate in sub-Saharan African countries. In Africa, the HIV/AIDS pandemic also raises complex military security issues: The presence of large numbers of infected people can be seen as a threat that needs to be contained by neighboring countries, and the presence of a large number of infected individuals within a country's armed forces can drastically reduce its ability to carry out military missions or defend itself from foreign invasion.

MILITARY SECURITY ISSUES

Combating terrorism and stopping the proliferation of weapons of mass destruction (nuclear weapons, chemical and biological weapons, and ballistic missile delivery systems) top everyone's list of pressing military security issues. Responding to them is a challenge not only because of the elevated level of danger but also because the nature of the problem changes constantly.

In the early 1990s, the intelligence community's dominant view was that Middle Eastern terrorists were controlled, or at least heavily influenced, by hostile regional powers, such as Iran, Syria, and Libya. When President Clinton signed an executive order imposing sanctions on twelve Middle Eastern terrorist groups in 1995, al-Qaeda was not even on the list. The United States was aware of Osama bin Laden but regarded him as a financier of international terrorism, not as a terrorist himself. Our understanding of terrorism changed slowly during the 1990s, and portions of the intelligence community began to speak of a new breed of radical Islamic terrorism that operated independently of government control. Gradually, bin Laden's activities came under closer watch, and in 1996, the CIA Counterterrorist Center set up a special office to deal with him alone. Still, few experts in either the Clinton or the George W. Bush administration placed this new terrorist threat above all others, despite strong evidence of al-Qaeda's

jihadists
participants in a crusade or holy war, especially in defense of Islam.

preemption
a military strategy based on striking first in self-defense.

complicity in the 1998 bombings of American embassies in Kenya and Tanzania and the attack on the USS *Cole* in Aden in 2000.

▶ **How has the nature of terrorism changed since 9/11?** After 9/11, the United States moved quickly to destroy al-Qaeda's sanctuary in Afghanistan, and to a large extent, it succeeded. However, the July 2005 bomb attacks on the London mass transit system made it painfully clear that terrorism on Western soil had not been brought to an end. Most experts now argue that we are seeing the emergence of yet another form of terrorism.[19] Instead of being highly centralized and directed by a single leader, such as bin Laden, or a single source, such as al-Qaeda, terrorist groups now operate as independent **jihadist** (Islamic holy war) agents, linked by an anti-Western ideology and the Internet. The number of jihadist-related Web sites, which has grown from dozens in 2001 to thousands today, provide training information and manuals on how to build and deploy biological and chemical weapons.

A fundamental reality of the nuclear age is that the knowledge needed to build nuclear, chemical, and biological weapons is readily available. Of even greater concern is that security at many facilities in the former Soviet Union where weapons of mass destruction were once built or stored still leaves much to be desired. Until recently, the U.S. position was that the spread of weapons of mass destruction needed to be stopped because they were dangerous weapons in their own right. Today, the Bush administration's position is that it is not so much the proliferation of such weapons as the identity of the recipients. American policymakers therefore do not view Israeli or Indian nuclear weapons in the same light as Iranian and North Korean nuclear weapons projects. The ultimate nightmare scenario involves theft and use of one of these weapons of mass destruction by a terrorist group.

In its *2002 National Security Strategy for the United States*, the Bush administration advanced a new strategic doctrine of **preemption** in dealing with terrorism and the proliferation of weapons of mass destruction. Preemption simply means striking first in self-defense. The Iraq War is an example of preemption in action. The administration argued that preemption is necessary because the strategies of containment and "mutually assured destruction" (sardonically referred to as MAD), which were used successfully during the Cold War, do not work against these shadowy and often stateless enemies. Containment controls hostile states by blocking and countering expansion of their sphere of

It took time for the United States to recognize that Osama bin Laden and his associates posed a serious threat. Now it is well understood that independent terrorist groups around the world are capable of inflicting great harm if given the opportunity. However, it is difficult to identify and stop small cells of terrorists who operate independently. If the United States captures or kills bin Laden, will Americans be safer than they are now?

▶ **What economic issues are most important in foreign policy today?**

deterrence
a military strategy associated with the Cold War that sought to prevent an unwanted military action from taking place by raising the prospect of large-scale retaliation.

Marshall Plan
the massive post–World War II foreign aid program of the United States that helped speed Western Europe's economic recovery and block the spread of communism.

WalMart built 66 stores in China before announcing in 2006 that it would purchase 100 additional stores from a Chinese retail chain. Like other American corporations, WalMart seeks to expand its profits by becoming deeply involved in overseas markets. As a result, American businesses are keenly interested in foreign policy and the development of good relationships with countries around the world. What is the impact of such global economic activities on workers and consumers in the United States?

influence or territorial control. **Deterrence** threatens a state-based enemy with swift and overwhelming retaliation for actions such as nuclear attacks or acts of aggression.

Preemption is controversial for several reasons. First, in some cases, containment and deterrence may be effective against some enemies. If this is true, then preemption might be a policy of last resort rather than the first choice. Second, preemption cannot be carried out very often. The human and economic costs of invading Afghanistan and Iraq have shown that it would be difficult to respond effectively to threatening activity by North Korea or Iran. Also, if the United States justifies preemption, other states might adopt the same policy. This would be especially troubling in the event of an escalation in the conflicts that now simmer between India and Pakistan, China and Taiwan, and Israel and its Arab neighbors. A third concern is morality. Going first in self-defense is an age-old principle of world politics, but the price for being wrong is also very high, including being seen as the aggressor and becoming the object of global condemnation and a potential target for retaliation.

A second element of the Bush administration's strategy for countering terrorist threats is to build a national ballistic missile defense system. It would function as a shield protecting the United States from weapons of mass destruction delivered by intercontinental ballistic missiles.[20] The idea for such a system, which goes back to the 1950s, was actively pursued in the 1980s by the Reagan administration. One of the major roadblocks, then as now, is the technological challenge of building and operating such a system. The system would have to work flawlessly the first time and every time—yet simulating a threat or testing the system would be almost impossible. The expense of the system is also a concern because of the fact that terrorists could strike devastatingly at the United States, even with nuclear weapons, without using ballistic missiles. Only against a "rogue state," such as Iran or North Korea, might a missile shield offer any potential protection.

ECONOMIC AND FOREIGN TRADE ISSUES

▶ **What economic issues are most important in foreign policy today?** The most fundamental economic issue in American foreign policy is how to respond to the growing pace of globalization. Goods, people, ideas, and money now move across national borders more frequently and with greater speed than ever before. Consider that from about 1996 to 2004, Europeans invested more capital in the state of Texas than Americans invested in the entire nation of Japan, and that large American technology firms such as Microsoft earn about half of their total revenues from their European operations. Although there are tremendous economic benefits from this heightened economic activity (including many relatively cheap imported consumer goods), there are also significant costs. Jobs are lost to foreign countries, and national policies in areas such as workers' rights and environmental regulation must give way to international standards. For example, the Byrd Amendment was enacted by Congress to provide the aging American steel industry with $710 million worth of financial aid to offset losses suffered as a result of steel imports from Europe, Canada, South Korea, and Japan. The World Trade Organization—the international organization that oversees international trade—ruled in 2003 that the Byrd Amendment constitutes an unfair trading practice and must end. The WTO ruling also gave other countries the right to impose penalties on U.S. exports until the United States complies with the ruling.

How should the United States respond to the growing economic power of other nations? In 2004, China was the world's largest recipient of foreign direct investment and the world's third-

Millennium Challenge Account
a major U.S. foreign policy initiative that seeks to tie foreign aid to improved government performance in the areas of democratization and economic development.

largest trader. It is the largest trading partner for Japan, the second-largest for Europe and Russia, and the fourth-largest for the United States. China also holds the world's second-largest currency reserves. Because many technologies being traded globally today can be used for both commercial and military applications, the stronger China grows economically, the more powerful it is likely to become militarily. As it grows economically and militarily, the political influence of this Communist country will increase in Asia and around the world. In addition, China's industrial growth and its growing love affair with automobiles are placing an immense strain on the global environment, with grave implications for climate change and fossil fuel depletion. Yet globalization makes it expensive, if not impossible, to isolate China and curb its growth without causing serious harm to the American economy and to the competitive position of U.S. firms abroad.

A second, related question deals with the future of foreign aid. How much aid should be given? For what purposes should aid be rendered?[21] The popular impression of foreign aid is that large amounts of American money are being sent overseas, which is why it is usually the first item to go in budget battles. In truth, foreign aid usually makes up less than 1 percent of the U.S. budget. A breakdown of George W. Bush's 2003 budget request shows that 0.9 percent was targeted for foreign aid, 19.7 percent for national defense, and 24.7 percent for Social Security. When one examines foreign aid comparatively, we can see that while the United States contributes the most foreign aid in absolute dollars of any other advanced industrial country; our contribution, relative to our Gross National Income (GNI), is the lowest of the group (see Table 18.3). American foreign aid funds are not evenly distributed around the world but are concentrated in a few countries. When food aid is excluded, the six largest recipients of American military and economic aid in 2002, in order, were Israel, Egypt, Pakistan, Colombia, Afghanistan, and Jordan. All play vital roles in American foreign policy, either in the war on terror or the war on drug trafficking. In all, 54 percent of all U.S. foreign aid goes to the Middle East.

One reason why the American public looks suspiciously on foreign aid is our frustration over the failure of such aid to produce meaningful economic results. No contemporary economic development program has duplicated the success of the **Marshall Plan,** which in the late 1940s spurred Western Europe's economic recovery from the devastation of World War II. The difference is that Marshall Plan aid went to rebuild war-ravaged industrial economies, not to modernize traditional, low-income societies. The most important foreign aid initiative under way today is the **Millennium Challenge Account.** Announced by President

TABLE 18.3
Foreign Aid Spending, 2005

NATION	TOTAL SPENDING (IN BILLIONS OF U.S. DOLLARS)	PERCENT OF GROSS NATIONAL INCOME (GNI)
Norway	$2.76	0.93
Sweden	3.28	0.92
Netherlands	5.13	0.82
Denmark	2.11	0.81
United Kingdom	10.75	0.48
France	10.06	0.47
Switzerland	1.77	0.44
Germany	9.92	0.35
Canada	3.73	0.34
Spain	3.12	0.29
Italy	5.05	0.29
Japan	13.10	0.28
United States	27.48	0.22

SOURCE: 2005 Rankings from the Center for Global Development, Washington, at http://www.cgdev.org Based on data from the OCED.

Though the United States contributes the most foreign aid by far in dollar terms, it is at the bottom of the pack of developed nations in terms of the portion of GNI spent in aid. The United Nations agreed on a target goal of 0.7 percent of GNI. Most nations fall short of this goal. Do you think the United States has a moral obligation to be more generous, or is our substantially larger contribution sufficient?

▶ **Is the decision not**
to respond to genocide
inconsistent with American
values on human rights?

genocide
the deliberate and systematic extinction
of an ethnic or cultural group.

George W. Bush in 2002, this narrowly focused new foreign aid program, which supports economic growth and reduction of poverty, is directed at low-income countries that have demonstrated a commitment to democracy and good government. Because results often take years of effort, the success of the Millennium Challenge Account has yet to be seen.

HUMAN WELFARE ISSUES

Human welfare issues focus on improving the lives of people around the world. For some Americans, addressing such challenges is an act of unselfishness and a statement about the shared humanity of people around the world. Others, who take a more pragmatic approach, believe that human rights abuses are a prime contributor to the domestic and international tensions that threaten U.S. interests.

▶ **Is the decision not to respond to genocide inconsistent with American values on human rights?**

GENOCIDE   Defined by the United Nations as "the intent to destroy, in whole or in part, a national ethnic, racial, or religious group," **genocide** is the most extreme category of human rights violation. The number of victims of genocide in the twentieth century is staggering. Six million Jews, as well as millions more Gypsies (Roma) and various other European minorities, perished in the most notorious instance of modern genocide, the Nazi Holocaust. More than a million Armenians in the Ottoman Empire were killed in genocidal attacks, and in the wars in Southeast Asia in 1975, well over a million Cambodians were massacred by communist guerrillas in the Cambodian "killing fields." Large-scale genocide also occurred in the 1990s in the central African country of Rwanda and in Bosnia and other parts of the former Yugoslavia in Eastern Europe. Between 1992 and 1995, about 200,000 predominantly Muslim Bosnians were killed by Serbs and Croats. An estimated 800,000 Rwandans were slaughtered in just a few months during 1994. Most recently, genocide has raged in Sudan, a vast country in northeastern Africa with mixed Arab and black populations. From early July 2003 through 2004, an estimated 50,000 people were killed in Sudan and another 2 million, desperately short of medicine and food, were driven into the desert region called Darfur.[22]

In spite of these horrific numbers, no clear-cut policy toward genocide has been enunciated in the United States, the United Nations, or anywhere else in the world. Rwandan genocide was met with global inaction. Genocide in the former Yugoslavia brought only a tardy and reluctant military response from the Western powers.

Two dilemmas face any attempt to formulate policies against genocide. The first is that the pace of killing is much faster than the ability of states to respond. In Rwanda, at least half of the 500,000 Tutsi victims were killed by their Hutu neighbors in three weeks. In 1995, Bosnian Serbs murdered 7,000 Muslims in one day in the town of Srebenica. Second, there is what is known as the "moral hazard": Knowing that the United States and others will respond to genocide may actually encourage some to provoke violence against their people in hopes of involving outside forces.

LAND MINES   One of the greatest tragedies of modern warfare is that the killing and maiming of people often continues after the fighting ends. The culprit? Land mines. It is estimated that about 120 million land mines are still concealed in more than eighty countries today. Annually, they kill or seriously injure 26,000 people, an average of one every twenty-six minutes. Each year, some 100,000 land mines are deactivated, but another 2 million are placed in the ground. The United States has played an ambiguous role in the land mine issue. It was a leader in the initial global effort to do away with them and actively fund and support demining efforts around the world. On the other hand, the United States has refused to sign the 1997 Ottawa Treaty banning the use of land mines in war, maintaining that continued research and development efforts are necessary to preserve military capabilities in potential combat zones such as the Korean peninsula. In place of the Ottawa Treaty, the United States proposes a worldwide ban on land mines that do not deactivate themselves after a given period of time.

HUMAN TRAFFICKING   It is important to keep in mind that human welfare issues are not solely a result of civil wars or international conflicts. Consider the plight of women and children who are transported across borders as sex workers. The global trafficking of people is now a $12 billion-a-year industry, involving 800,000 to 900,000 individuals.[23] Human trafficking is now the third-largest illegal business on earth, following drug and weapons trafficking. The United States is not immune from this problem. Up to 20,000 people are transported into the United States each year for the sex trade or other forms of economic exploitation, and as many as 750,000 people may have been illegally smuggled into the United States in the 1990s. Since the passage of the little-noticed Trafficking Victims Protection Act by Congress in 2000, the United States is required to cut off most nonhumanitarian foreign aid to countries not making an effort to eliminate this problem. In 2003, only twenty-five countries were judged to be actively fighting human trafficking.

discussionquestions

1. What is the impact of globalization on American foreign policy?

2. What do you think are the three most pressing human welfare issues facing American foreign policy today?

what YOU can do!

People really can make a difference in foreign policy problems. Go to **http://www.landmines.org**, and look at the Adopt-a-Minefield program as an example of what can be accomplished.

This short account hardly does justice to the full range of human welfare issues that the United States must face. If you, like many people, are concerned about high gasoline prices, perhaps you consider the price of oil and America's dependence on foreign oil the most important foreign policy issue. Or your primary focus may be the issue of religious freedom; many nations around the world do not permit individuals to practice their religious beliefs freely or to convert from one religion to another. Other important issues include child labor, the status of women, poverty, and access to health care. Almost 3 billion people, almost half the world's population, live on less than $2 a day. There are 400 million children in the world today who have no access to safe water, and 270 million have no access to health services. Environmental problems, such as global warming, insufficient clean water supplies, and the loss of species, are also of concern to all of us. A key symbol of the failure of American foreign policy on environmental issues is our withdrawal from the 1993 Kyoto Protocol, which seeks to reduce global warming.

Land mines continue to cause thousands of deaths and injuries each year around the world, even after military conflict in a specific country has ended. Here a soldier from Thailand uses a trained dog to identify the location of land mines as part of the effort to safely remove these dangerous explosives. The United States has failed to reach an agreement with other countries about whether landmines should be completely banned under international law. What position do you think that the United States should adopt on this issue?

practicequiz

1. Which of the following is currently the top military-security concern for the U.S. government?
   a. the threat of totalitarian regimes to global stability
   b. the spread of communism
   c. the proliferation of nuclear weapons
   d. AIDS

2. What is one reason preemption is a risky strategy in the United States' "war on terror"?
   a. because history tells us it almost never works
   b. because the U.S. armed forces might be insufficiently powerful to succeed
   c. because, given the defense budget, the U.S. cannot afford such a strategy
   d. because, as the aggressor, the U.S. risks becoming the object of international condemnation and a target for retaliation

3. From 1996 to 2004, Europeans invested more money in the state of Texas than Americans invested in the entire nation of Japan.
   a. true
   b. false

4. U.S foreign aid usually makes up _____% of the U.S. budget.
   a. less than 1%
   b. around 4%
   c. around 6%
   d. around 8%

Answers: 1-c, 2-d, 3-a, 4-a.

Conclusion

The terrorist attacks on the World Trade Center and the Pentagon on September 11, 2001, marked a turning point in American foreign policy. For more than a decade, foreign policy had seemed adrift and the American public seemed uninterested in world affairs.

Despite this apathy, American foreign policy has never really been separate from domestic policy. Ideas used to guide American foreign policy have their roots in domestic policy, and American foreign policy provides an avenue for foreign governments and firms to participate in the American political process. Most important, American foreign policy has created winners and losers among domestic groups. The terrorist attacks of 9/11 represent a turning point, not as America's reentry into world affairs but because they provide a new point of reference for an ongoing debate over the content and conduct of American foreign policy.

In this chapter, we have looked at the broad outlines of that debate as they are framed by neoconservatives, neoliberals, conservatives, and isolationists. These competing ideas draw on and bring together long-established ways of thinking about American foreign policy, dating back to the founding of the United States.

The making of American foreign policy is the product of interaction between people and institutions. The American public expresses its voice through public opinion, elections, interest group activity, and political protest. Policymakers often have difficulty understanding what they hear from the public. They also have a desire to use the American public to help achieve their goals, which often reduces their willingness to listen. Presidents face a similar dilemma in reaching out for advice, whether it is to their White House staff or to the foreign policy bureaucracies. They want and need information but often hear unwelcome news. Competition among offices in the White House and within the foreign affairs bureaucracy provides the president with many choices of information sources and sets the stage for controversy. This controversy is often played out in public, especially when it involves conflict between the president and Congress.

Finally, it is important to remember that terrorism is not the only foreign policy issue facing the United States today. A wide range of military security, economic, and human welfare issues are on the national agenda. Failure to address them adequately today may hold dire consequences for the future.

YOUR turn!

Many young people interested in foreign affairs think about careers as diplomats. To become a diplomat, you must pass the Foreign Service Officer Test. The first part of the test contains objective multiple-choice questions and an essay question. If you score high enough on this part of the test, you get invited for a group interview. Should you pass this stage, you are eligible to be appointed to the Foreign Service for the next year. The test, which is free and usually given once a year throughout the United States, is very competitive, but you can take it as many times as you wish. People from all walks of life pass the test. You can contact the State Department through its Web site (http://careers.state.gov/office/index.htm) to obtain a practice exam and learn more about a career in the Foreign Service.

Even if you are not interested in a diplomatic career, there are plenty of opportunities in your community and college to learn more about the world and help address global problems. These opportunities range from participating in clubs to volunteering your time to help local civic and church groups provide funds and materials for people overseas or to programs that help immigrants adjust to life in the United States. ▪

Chapter Review

1. Two groups of "transformers" (neoliberals and neoconservatives) and two groups of "maintainers" (conservatives and isolationists) differ in their view of the proper content and conduct of American foreign policy.

2. These four different schools of thought have existed throughout American history and continue to influence today's thinking on foreign policy.

3. Three different types of linkages exist between American foreign policy and domestic policy. First, American policy, both domestic and foreign, emphasizes individual legal rights and civil liberties. Second, Washington usually sees hostile, overly strong governments as the primary threat to human rights. Third, American foreign policy generally rejects violence as a means for promoting human rights.

4. Public opinion, elections, interest group activity, and political protest are four different means by which the public can use pathways to influence foreign policy decisions.

5. The president does not make foreign policy decisions alone but relies heavily on advisers and staff within the White House.

6. The key foreign affairs bureaucracies, which compete for influence in making foreign policy, are the State Department, the Defense Department, the CIA, and the Department of Homeland Security.

7. The relationship between the president and Congress is dynamic and varies from strategic to competitive. Regardless of how they interact, Congress has a fixed number of tools at its disposal to influence foreign policy.

8. The Supreme Court intervenes only rarely in foreign policy matters, but occasionally it reviews a case important to national security and foreign policy issues.

9. A complex set of military security, economic, and human welfare issues confront the United States today.

CHAPTER REVIEW TEST

1. The United States' war in Afghanistan reignited three central and long-standing questions about American foreign policy, now considered in the age of terrorism. One of those questions is
   a. should the U.S. return to an isolationist approach or try to be "policeman" to the world?
   b. what should be the proper relationship between U.S. foreign policy and domestic policy?
   c. should the U.S. maintain its considerable military superiority in the world or scale back that budgetary commitment in the face of other pressing needs?
   d. should the U.S. acknowledge the limitations of diplomacy and curtail the authority of the State Department?

2. Which of the following approaches dominates the foreign policy of the George W. Bush's administration?
   a. neoliberal   b. isolationist
   c. conservative   d. neoconservative

3. Although there are important differences between neoliberal and neoconservative approaches to foreign policy, one belief they share is that
   a. the U.S. should never hesitate to use its military force to achieve foreign policy ends.
   b. the U.S. should routinely solicit the support of coalition governments and international institutions, such as the U.N., to help achieve its foreign policy ends.
   c. the U.S. should include in its foreign policy objectives the spreading of democracy throughout the world.
   d. world politics is a realm defined by conflict and struggle.

4. Neoliberals probably would have handled Saddam Hussein and regime change in Iraq
   a. by extending the economic sanctions against Iraq and, if fighting broke out, by trying to enable Iraqis to create a democratic government from within.
   b. by defeating Hussein militarily and installing an interim, U.S.-controlled Iraqi government.
   c. by not doing anything—such regime change would not be a foreign policy priority.
   d. by extending the economic sanctions against Iraq and, if that did not work, by bombing all the Iraqi locations where weapons of mass destruction were thought to exist.

5. The United States' longstanding commitment to keeping "foreign" influences out of the Western Hemisphere is called
   a. the Marshall Plan.
   b. the "Good Neighbor" policy.
   c. the Monroe Doctrine.
   d. the Powell Doctrine.

6. What is or was "gunboat diplomacy"?
   a. terrorist attacks by sea, like the attack on the USS *Cole*
   b. U.S. military incursions into Central American and the Caribbean in the 1920s to protect American interests and lives
   c. a key U.S. tactic in the Pacific during World War II
   d. Cuba's response to U.S. attempts at establishing better relations between the two countries in the early 1960s

7. Which contemporary U.S. foreign policy perspective most closely adheres to the Wilsonian view?
   a. liberal
   b. isolationist
   c. conservative
   d. neoconservative

8. American policy—both domestic and foreign—pays much more attention to individual legal rights and civil liberties than it does to economic and social rights.
   a. true   b. false

9. What best characterizes current U.S. global environmental policy?
   a. more environmentally progressive than almost any other country
   b. not environmentally progressive at all
   c. environmentally progressive when such progress does not come at the expense of American economic interests
   d. forward thinking about global climate change but not in some other areas

10. What is CAFTA and who was one of its opponents?
    a. a trade agreement ratified during the Clinton administration; Ross Perot strongly opposed it, citing the loss of U.S. jobs as its result
    b. a trade agreement ratified during the George W. Bush administration; wealthy U.S. sugar producers opposed it because it would cut into their profits
    c. a trade agreement ratified during the Reagan administration; the airline industry opposed it because it would tighten competition for them
    d. an organization within the U.N. created during the Carter administration; American libertarians opposed it because it required funding from industrialized countries, such as the U.S. taxpayers' money, as libertarians reminded Congress

11. How well informed is the American public regarding foreign affairs?
    a. Usually quite well informed: For example, at the height of the Cold War, in 1964, 90 percent of Americans knew that the Soviet Union was not part of NATO.
    b. Not very: For example, in 1979, 23 percent of Americans knew that the U.S. and the Soviet Union were the two countries involved in the Strategic Arms Limitation Talks.
    c. Moderately well informed: For example, in 1993 only 13 percent of Americans could not identify the continent on which Somalia is located.
    d. Very well indeed: For example, in 2003, 94 percent of Americans knew that Iraq did not play a major role in 9/11.

12. Religious groups that try to influence U.S. foreign policy are almost always from the "religious right."
   a. true
   b. false

13. Of the following powers, which does the Constitution deny the president?
   a. the making of treaties
   b. the appointment of ambassadors
   c. the commanding of the armed forces
   d. the declaring of war

14. The Constitution grants the vice president significant responsibilities in the formation of foreign policy.
   a. true
   b. false

15. Which institution is the formal channel through which the U.S. and foreign countries pass information?
   a. the State Department
   b. the NSC
   c. the CIA
   d. the Department of Defense

16. In the early 1960s, what responsibility did Congress shift from the State Department to a newly created office in the White House?
   a. treaty negotiations
   b. arms negotiation
   c. trade policy and negotiation
   d. global environmental policy and negotiation

17. Who has the final say regarding the use of U.S. military force overseas?
   a. Congress
   b. the Joint Chiefs of Staff
   c. the American People
   d. the president

18. The Powell Doctrine asserts that military force should be used overseas
   a. provided that such a force can be of minimal size, maximum speed and maneuverability, and enjoys a technological advantage over the adversary.
   b. provided that the American public clearly supports the cause, overwhelming force can be brought to bear in the conflict, and a clear exit strategy is already in place.
   c. provided that an expansion of democracy is a predictable result of the conflict and America's economic interests are not compromised.
   d. provided that such intervention has the support of the international community: the U.N., NATO, and the so-called "court of public opinion."

19. In attempting to have their intelligence influence U.S. foreign policy, the CIA is now competing with what other intelligence office?
   a. the Pentagon's
   b. Homeland Security's
   c. the ambassador to the U.N.'s
   d. the FBI's

20. Between 1958 and 2004, what has been the pattern of Congress's working relationship to the President regarding foreign policy?
   a. 1958–1968: supportive and disengaged; 1969–1980: strategic; 1981–2001: competitive; 2001–2004: strategic.
   b. 1958–1968: competitive; 1969–1980: supportive and disengaged; 1981–2001: strategic; 2001–2004: competitive.
   c. 1958–1968: strategic; 1969–1980: competitive; 1981–2001: strategic; 2001–2004: supportive and disengaged.
   d. 1958–1968: competitive; 1969–1980: strategic; 1981–2001: supportive and disengaged; 2001–2004: strategic.

Answers: 1: b; 2: d; 3: c; 4: a; 5: c; 6: b; 7: d; 8: a; 9: c; 10: b; 11: b; 12: b; 13: d; 14: b; 15: a; 16: c; 17: d; 18: b; 19: a; 20: c.

DISCUSSION QUESTIONS

1. How do the foreign policy views of the neoconservatives and the neoliberals differ?

2. What are the differences between "transformers" and "maintainers"?

3. Describe the differences between the four guiding principles of U.S. foreign policy in how they approach the Iraq War.

4. How do Wilsonians, Hamiltonians, Jeffersonians, and Jacksonians differ regarding the use of force abroad and building democracy around the globe?

5. How do ideas from American domestic policy influence American foreign policy on human rights?

6. In what ways does American foreign policy create winners and losers in American domestic politics?

7. How and why do foreign governments and firms seek to influence American politics?

8. How does public opinion influence foreign policy?

9. Who in the White House is available to the president for foreign policy advice?

10. Describe the four patterns of congressional-presidential relations in foreign policy.

11. In what ways has the relationship between the president and Congress changed over time with regard to making foreign policy?

12. Who belongs to the foreign affairs bureaucracies?

13. What are the pros and cons of preemption as a military security strategy?

INTERNET RESOURCES

Americans and the World, a source of comprehensive information on U.S. public opinion on international issues:
http://www.americans-world.org

Central Intelligence Agency, "The Global Infectious Disease Threat and Its Implications for the United States":
http://www.odci.gov/cia/reports/nie/report/nie99-17d.html

Foreign Service Dispatches and Periodic Reports on United States Foreign Policy: **http://www.unc.edu/depts/diplomat**

"National Security Strategy of the United States of America":
http://www.whitehouse.gov/nsc/nss.html

ADDITIONAL READING

Hook, Steven, and John Spanier. *American Foreign Policy since World War II* (16th ed.). Washington, DC: CQ Press, 2004.

Ikenberry, G. John. *American Foreign Policy: Theoretical Essays* (5th ed.). Upper Saddle River, NJ: Prentice Hall, 2005.

Johnson, Loch, and Karl Inderfurth, eds. *Fateful Decisions: Inside the National Security Council.* New York: Oxford University Press, 2004.

Sobel, Richard. *The Impact of Public Opinion on U.S. Foreign Policy since Vietnam.* New York: Oxford University Press, 2001.

Woodward, Bob. *Plan of Attack.* New York: Simon & Schuster, 2004.

KEY TERMS

apartheid   703

containment   710

covert action   709

détente   712

deterrence   716

genocide   718

globalization   698

Hamiltonians   692

Jacksonians   695

Jeffersonians   694

jihadists   715

Kyoto Protocol   697

Marshall Plan   716

McNamara Doctrine   708

Millennium Challenge Account   717

Monroe Doctrine   692

neoconservatives   689

neoliberals   691

North Atlantic Treaty Organization (NATO)   690

Powell Doctrine   708

preemption   715

"rally 'round the flag" effect   702

Strategic Arms Limitation Talks (SALT)   703

terrorism   688

Vietnam syndrome   702

weapons of mass destruction   691

Wilsonians   694

By the early 1770s, relations between Great Britain and thirteen colonies in North American had become strained. Actual hostilities broke out in 1775 at Lexington and Concord, marking the beginning of the Revolutionary War.   But the "patriot cause" was not universally accepted thoughout the colonies. A second Continental Congress was called, and on May 10, 1775, representatives appointed by state legislatures from all of the colonies except Georgia convened in Philadelphia. A committee consisting of John Adams, Benjamin Franklin, Robert R. Livingston, Roger Sherman, and a slim, quiet delegate from Virginia named Thomas Jefferson (the "Committee of Five") was formed to draft a statement that would justify a war for independence. Adams suggested that Jefferson take the first stab at writing a draft document. With a few minor edits from Adams and Franklin, Jefferson presented his "Declaration" to the Continental Congress on June 28, 1776. Many agree that it is one of the most eloquent political statements ever written.

The Preamble of the Declaration is influenced by Enlightenment philosophy, a 17th century European intellectual movement that held that all questions of math, science, and government could be solved through clear logic and careful experimentation. As such, it rejected superstition and religious "truths."

These words also clearly reflect the writings of English philosopher John Locke (1632-1704), particularly his *Second Treatise on Government*. Jefferson also seemed to be "borrowing" from the Virginia Declaration of Rights, which had been adopted about a month earlier.

Jefferson presents a notion of natural rights. That is, individuals possess certain privileges—certain guarantees by virtue of being human. These rights are *not* granted by government, but instead by God, or what Jefferson calls the Creator. They cannot be given, nor can they be taken away.

Here Jefferson introduces the social contract theory, drawn in large measure from the writings of John Locke. Humans have the option of living alone in what he called "the state of nature." According to this theory, humans originally lived without government or laws, enjoying complete personal freedom. Yet the state of nature meant "a war of all against all," in which—in the words of another philosopher, Thomas Hobbes—life was "solitary, poor, nasty, brutish, and short." To end this perpetual conflict and insecurity, people created governments, thereby giving up some of their freedoms in order to protect their lives and their property.

Jefferson also agreed with Locke that governments, having been created by the people to protect their rights, are limited; they get their powers from the will of the people and no one else. (In arguing this, Locke was attacking the traditional claim that kings ruled by the will of God.)

When a government fails to respect the will of the people—that is, when it appears no longer to be limited—it becomes the right, indeed the obligation, of citizens to change the government. This passage is Jefferson's call for revolution.

APPENDIX I

The Declaration of Independence of the Thirteen Colonies

In CONGRESS, July 4, 1776

THE UNANIMOUS DECLARATION OF THE THIRTEEN UNITED STATES OF AMERICA,

When in the Course of human events, it becomes necessary for one people to dissolve the political bands which have connected them with another, and to assume among the powers of the earth, the separate and equal station to which the Laws of Nature and of Nature's God entitle them, a decent respect to the opinions of mankind requires that they should declare the causes which impel them to the separation.

We hold these truths to be self-evident, that all men are created equal, that they are endowed by their Creator with certain unalienable Rights, that among these are Life, Liberty and the pursuit of Happiness.

That to secure these rights, Governments are instituted among Men, deriving their just powers from the consent of the governed, that whenever any Form of Government becomes destructive of these ends, it is the Right of the People to alter or to abolish it, and to institute new Government, laying its foundation on such principles and organizing its powers in such form, as to them shall seem most likely to effect their Safety and Happiness.

Prudence, indeed, will dictate that Governments long established should not be changed for light and transient causes; and accordingly all experience hath shewn, that mankind are more disposed to suffer, while evils are sufferable, than to right themselves by abolishing the forms to which they are accustomed. But when a long train of abuses and usurpations, pursuing invariably the same Object evinces a design to reduce them under absolute Despotism, it is their right, it is their duty, to throw off such Government, and to provide new Guards for their future security. —Such has been the patient sufferance of these Colonies; and such is now the necessity which constrains them to alter their former Systems of Government. The history of the present King of Great Britain [George III] is a history of repeated injuries and usurpations, all having in direct object the establishment of an absolute Tyranny over these States. To prove this, let Facts be submitted to a candid world.

He has refused his Assent to Laws, the most wholesome and necessary for the public good. He has forbidden his Governors to pass Laws of immediate and pressing importance, unless suspended in their operation till his Assent should be obtained; and when so suspended, he has utterly neglected to attend to them.

He has refused to pass other Laws for the accommodation of large districts of people, unless those people would relinquish the right of Representation in the Legislature, a right inestimable to them and formidable to tyrants only.

He has called together legislative bodies at places unusual, uncomfortable, and distant from the depository of their public Records, for the sole purpose of fatiguing them into compliance with his measures.

He has dissolved Representative Houses repeatedly, for opposing with manly firmness his invasions on the rights of the people.

He has refused for a long time, after such dissolutions, to cause others to be elected; whereby the Legislative powers, incapable of Annihilation, have returned to the People at large for their exercise; the State remaining in the mean time exposed to all the dangers of invasion from without, and convulsions within.

Here Jefferson seems to provide a caution: Governments should be responsive to the will of the people, but just because the public is upset with government does not imply the need for revolution. Yes, governments can be changed, but not for "light and transient causes."

This next section is called the List of Grievances, which is essentially a laundry list of all the bad things that the British Government has done to the colonies. The idea here was to create such a long and powerful list that few would disagree with the need for a change.

In all these passages, "He" refers to King George III.

Precisely what defined a "government by the people" was still a bit vague at this time, but many suspected that representative assemblies were a necessary ingredient. So when the King dissolved these legislatures it seemed that he was striking a direct blow against self-rule.

An independent judiciary was also an element deemed essential for democratic governance, and the King's control of the courts seems a clear illustration of tryany.

While most countries keep "standing armies" these days, in the eighteenth century armies were assembled only when war was at hand. Many colonists saw the King's army as an instrument of aggression and control.

What is interesting about the list of grievances is that many of the items refer to more theoretical matters pertaining to just governance and the rights of citizens. But other items point to pragmatic issues, such as improperly taking money from colonists. Make no mistake, the Revolution was about creating a democratic system of government, a government responsive to "the people," but it was also about creating a system where average citizens could prosper financially.

Many colonists were anxious to pursue independence because they believed in self-rule, but many others were mostly interested in commercial issues (economic gain). So the "open trade" issue was critical for building broad public support for independence.

He has endeavoured to prevent the population of these States; for that purpose obstructing the Laws for Naturalization of Foreigners; refusing to pass others to encourage their migrations hither, and raising the conditions of new Appropriations of Lands.

He has obstructed the Administration of Justice, by refusing his Assent to Laws for establishing Judiciary powers.

He has made Judges dependent on his Will alone, for the tenure of their offices, and the amount and payment of their salaries.

He has erected a multitude of New Offices, and sent hither swarms of Officers to harass our people, and eat out their substance.

He has kept among us, in times of peace, Standing Armies without the consent of our legislatures.

He has affected to render the Military independent of and superior to the Civil power.

He has combined with others to subject us to a jurisdiction foreign to our constitution and unacknowledged by our laws; giving his Assent to their Acts of pretended Legislation:

For Quartering large bodies of armed troops among us:

For protecting them, by a mock Trial, from punishment for any Murders which they should commit on the Inhabitants of these States:

For cutting off our Trade with all parts of the world:

For imposing Taxes on us without our Consent:

For depriving us, in many cases, of the benefits of Trial by Jury:

For transporting us beyond Seas to be tried for pretended offences:

For abolishing the free System of English Laws in a neighbouring Province, establishing therein an Arbitrary government, and enlarging its Boundaries so as to render it at once an example and fit instrument for introducing the same absolute rule into these Colonies:

For taking away our Charters, abolishing our most valuable Laws, and altering fundamentally the Forms of our Governments:

For suspending our own Legislatures, and declaring themselves invested with power to legislate for us in all cases whatsoever.

He has abdicated Government here, by declaring us out of his Protection and waging War against us.

He has plundered our seas, ravaged our Coasts, burnt our towns, and destroyed the lives of our people.

He is at this time transporting large Armies of foreign Mercenaries to compleat the works of death, desolation and tyranny, already begun with circumstances of Cruelty and perfidy scarcely paralleled in the most barbarous ages, and totally unworthy the Head of a civilized nation.

He has constrained our fellow Citizens taken Captive on the high Seas to bear Arms against their Country, to become the executioners of their friends and Brethren, or to fall themselves by their Hands.

He has excited domestic insurrections amongst us, and has endeavoured to bring on the inhabitants of our frontiers, the merciless Indian Savages, whose known rule of warfare, is an undistinguished destruction of all ages, sexes and conditions.

In every stage of these Oppressions We have Petitioned for Redress in the most humble terms: Our repeated Petitions have been answered only by repeated injury. A Prince whose character is thus marked by every act which may define a Tyrant, is unfit to be the ruler of a free people.

Nor have We been wanting in attentions to our British brethren. We have warned them from time to time of attempts by their legislature to extend an unwarrantable jurisdiction over us. We have reminded them of the circumstances of our emigration and settlement here. We have appealed to their native justice and magnanimity, and we have conjured them by the ties of our common kindred to disavow these usurpations, which, would inevitably interrupt our connections and correspondence. They too have been deaf to the voice of justice and of consanguinity. We must, therefore, acquiesce in the necessity, which denounces our Separation, and hold them, as we hold the rest of mankind, Enemies in War, in Peace Friends.

Again, many saw colonial assemblies as the foundation of a free society, so the King's suspension of their laws suggested tyrannical rule.

With the French and Indian War only a few years distant, many of the colonists continued to have grave fears about hostilities with Native Americans. So to suggest that the King was in flaming conflict was no small matter.

This was perceived as especially harsh language. To call the King a Tyrant was considered an act of treason.

Was the Declaration of Independence effective in rallying support behind the revolutionary cause? We do know that many New Yorkers were so inspired upon hearing these words that they toppled a statute of King George and had it melted down to make 42,000 bullets for war. Still, many balked at joining the revolution and even enlisted in the British Army. We also know that public support for the Continental Army, headed by George Washington, lagged considerably throughout the Revolution.

We, therefore, the Representatives of the united States of America, in General Congress, Assembled, appealing to the Supreme Judge of the world for the rectitude of our intentions, do, in the Name, and by the Authority of the good People of these Colonies, solemnly publish and declare, That these United Colonies are, and of Right ought to be Free and Independent States; that they are Absolved from all Allegiance to the British Crown, and that all political connection between them and the State of Great Britain, is and ought to be totally dissolved; and that as Free and Independent States, they have full Power to levy War, conclude Peace, contract Alliances, establish Commerce, and to do all other Acts and Things which Independent States may of right do. And for the support of this Declaration, with a firm reliance on the protection of divine Providence, we mutually pledge to each other our Lives, our Fortunes and our sacred Honor.

The signers of the Declaration represented the new states as follows:

NEW HAMPSHIRE
Josiah Bartlett, William Whipple,
Matthew Thornton

MASSACHUSETTS
John Hancock, Samuel Adams, John Adams,
Robert Treat Paine, Elbridge Gerry

RHODE ISLAND
Stephen Hopkins, William Ellery

CONNECTICUT
Roger Sherman, Samuel Huntington,
William Williams, Oliver Wolcott

All the signers assumed that they were, in effect, signing their own death warrant if indeed the Revolution were to fail. The above paragraph, about absolving allegiances to the British Crown and creating independent states, would surely be interpreted as treason in England. Signing the Declaration was an act of true courage.

On July 19, 1776, Congress ordered a copy be handwritten for the delegates to sign, which most did on August 2, 1776. Two delegates never signed at all. As new delegates joined the Congress, they were also allowed to sign. A total of 56 delegates eventually signed

The first and most famous signature on the embossed copy was that of John Hancock, President of the Continental Congress.

NEW YORK
William Floyd, Philip Livingston, Francis Lewis, Lewis Morris

NEW JERSEY
Richard Stockton, John Witherspoon, Francis Hopkinson, John Hart, Abraham Clark

PENNSYLVANIA
Robert Morris, Benjamin Rush, Benjamin Franklin, John Morton, George Clymer, James Smith, George Taylor, James Wilson, George Ross

> Franklin was the oldest signer, at 70.

DELAWARE
Caesar Rodney, George Read, Thomas McKean

MARYLAND
Samuel Chase, William Paca, Thomas Stone, Charles Carroll of Carrollton

VIRGINIA
George Wythe, Richard Henry Lee, Thomas Jefferson, Benjamin Harrison, Thomas Nelson, Jr., Francis Lightfoot Lee, Carter Braxton

> Two future presidents signed the Declaration— Thomas Jefferson and John Adams.

NORTH CAROLINA
William Hooper, Joseph Hewes, John Penn

SOUTH CAROLINA
Edward Rutledge, Thomas Heyward, Jr., Thomas Lynch, Jr., Arthur Middleton

> Edward Rutledge, at age 26, was the youngest signer of the Declaration.

GEORGIA
Button Gwinnett, Lyman Hall, George Walton

After its adoption by the Congress, a handwritten draft was then sent a few blocks away to the printing shop of John Dunlap. Through the night between 150 and 200 copies were made, now known as "Dunlap broadsides." One was sent to George Washington on July 6, who had it read to his troops in New York on July 9. The 25 Dunlap broadsides still known to exist are the oldest surviving copies of the document. The original handwritten copy has not survived.

The signed copy of the Declaration of Independence is on display at the National Archives.

"We, the people." Three simple words are of profound importance and contentious origin. Every government in the world at the time of the Constitutional Convention was some type of monarchy, wherein sovereign power flowed from the top. The Founders of our new country rejected monarchy as a form of government and proposed instead a republic, which would draw its sovereignty from the people.

It is this very sense of empowerment that allows the "people" to influence our government and shape the world in which we live. We are amongst the freest people in the world largely because of this document. We are presented with multiple pathways to influence our government and better our lives.

Article I. The very first article in the Constitution established the legislative branch of the new national government. Why did the framers start with the legislative power instead of the executive branch? The framers truly believed it was the most important component of the new government.

It was also something that calmed the anxieties of average citizens. That is, they had experience with "legislative-centered governance" under the Articles and even during the colonial period. It was not perfect, but the legislative process seems to work.

Section 1. Section 1 established a bicameral (two-chamber) legislature, or an upper (Senate) and lower (House of Representatives) organization of the legislative branch.

A bicameral legislature offers more opportunities to influence the policy process, as you can appeal to both your Senators and your representatives through the lobbying decision-makers pathway, or indirectly through the elections pathway, the grassroots mobilization pathway, or the cultural change pathway. If you do not like a law passed by Congress, you can appeal to the courts to invalidate it or to change its meaning.

Section 2 Clause 1. This section sets the term of office for House members (2 years) and indicates that those voting for Congress will have the same qualifications as those voting for the state legislatures. Originally, states limited voters to white property owners. Some states even had religious disqualifications, such as Catholic or Jewish.

There was a great deal of discussion about how long a legislator should sit in office before appealing to constituents for reelection. Short terms of office, such as the two years used in the House of Representatives, help force members to pay attention to the needs of their constituents.

Clause 2. This section sets forth the basic qualifications of a representative: at least 25 years of age, a U.S. citizen for at least 7 years, and a resident of the state in which the district is located. Note that the Constitution does not require a person to be a resident of the district he or she represents.

Clause 2 does not specify how many terms a representative can serve in Congress, but some critics support limiting the number of terms members can serve in order to make Congress more in touch with the citizenry—and to overcome some of the advantages incumbents have created to help win elections. Currently the average length of service in the House is 9 years (4.6 terms).

APPENDIX 2
The Constitution of the United States

THE PREAMBLE

We the People of the United States, in Order to form a more perfect Union, establish Justice, insure domestic Tranquility, provide for the common defence, promote the general Welfare, and secure the Blessings of Liberty to ourselves and our Posterity, do ordain and establish this Constitution for the United States of America.

Article I
THE LEGISLATIVE ARTICLE

Legislative Power

SECTION 1. All legislative Powers herein granted shall be vested in a Congress of the United States, which shall consist of a Senate and House of Representatives.

House of Representatives: Composition; Qualifications; Apportionment; Impeachment Power

SECTION 2 CLAUSE 1. The House of Representatives shall be composed of Members chosen every second Year by the People of the several States, and the Electors in each State shall have the Qualifications requisite for Electors of the most numerous Branch of the State Legislature.

CLAUSE 2. No Person shall be a Representative who shall not have attained to the Age of twenty five Years, and been seven Years a Citizen of the United States, and who shall not, when elected, be an Inhabitant of that State in which he shall be chosen.

CLAUSE 3. Representatives and direct Taxes[1] shall be apportioned among the several States which may be included within this Union, according to their respective Numbers, which shall be determined by adding to the whole Number of free Persons, including those bound to Service for a Term of Years, and excluding Indians not taxed, three fifths of all other Persons.[2] The actual Enumeration shall be made within three Years after the first Meeting of the Congress of the United States, and within every subsequent Term of ten Years, in such Manner as they shall by Law direct. The Number of Representatives shall not exceed one for every thirty Thousand, but each State shall have at Least one Representative; and until such enumeration shall be made, the State of New Hampshire shall be entitled to chuse three, Massachusetts eight, Rhode-Island and Providence Plantations one, Connecticut five, New-York six, New Jersey four, Pennsylvania eight, Delaware one, Maryland six, Virginia ten, North Carolina five, South Carolina five, and Georgia three.

CLAUSE 4. When vacancies happen in the Representation from any State, the Executive Authority thereof shall issue Writs of Election to fill such Vacancies.

CLAUSE 5. The House of Representatives shall chuse their Speaker and other Officers; and shall have the sole Power of Impeachment.

**Senate Composition:
Qualifications, Impeachment Trials**

SECTION 3 CLAUSE 1. The Senate of the United States shall be composed of two Senators from each State, chosen by the Legislature thereof,[3] for six Years; and each Senator shall have one Vote.

CLAUSE 2. Immediately after they shall be assembled in Consequence of the first Election, they shall be divided as equally as may be into three Classes. The Seats of the Senators of the first Class shall be vacated at the Expiration of the second Year, of the second Class at the Expiration of the fourth Year, and of the third Class at the Expiration of the sixth Year, so that one third may be chosen every second Year; and if Vacancies happen by Resignation, or otherwise, during the Recess of the Legislature of any State, the Executive thereof may make temporary Appointments until the next Meeting of the Legislature, which shall then fill such Vacancies.[4]

CLAUSE 3. No Person shall be a Senator who shall not have attained to the Age of thirty Years, and been nine Years a Citizen of the United States, and who shall not, when elected, be an Inhabitant of that State for which he shall be chosen.

Clause 3. This clause contains the Three-Fifths Compromise, in which American Indians and blacks were only counted as 3/5 of a person for congressional representation purposes. This clause also addresses the question of congressional reapportionment every 10 years, which requires a census. Since the 1911 Reapportionment Act, the size of the House of Representatives has been set at 435. This is the designated size that is reapportioned every 10 years. Based on changes of population, some states gain and some states lose representatives.

While the Constitution never directly addresses the issue of slavery, this clause and others clearly condone its existence. It ultimately took the Civil War (1861-1865) to resolve the issue of slavery.

Clause 4. This clause provides a procedure for replacing a U.S. representative in the case of death, resignation, or expulsion from the House. Essentially, the governor of the representative's state will determine the selection of a successor. Generally, if less than half a term is left, the governor will appoint a successor. If more than half a term is remaining, most states require a special election to fill the vacancy.

Clause 5. Only one officer of the House is specified, the Speaker. The House decides all other officers. This clause also gives the House authority for impeachments—the determination of formal charges—against officials of the executive and judicial branches.

Interestingly, this clause does not stipulate that the Speaker be a member of Congress. The House might choose an outsider to run their chamber, but this has never happened—and will likely not happen in the future.

Section 3 Clause 1. This clause treats each state equally—all have two senators. Originally, state legislators chose senators, but since passage and ratification of the 17th Amendment, they are now elected by popular vote. This clause also establishes the term of a senator—6 years—three times that of a House member.

This clause is very important when thinking about pathways of change. For one, it creates a mechanism by which the minority, through their Senators, can thwart the will of the majority. Each state has the same number of Senators. A majority of Senators, representing states with small populations, have the ability to control the process—or at least stall things. In our system "majority will" does not always prevail.

Also, six-year terms give Senators the chance to worry only periodically about an approaching reelection. Unlike members of the House, who come up for reelection so frequently that their actions may be constantly guided by a concern for pleasing the voters, this extended term in office offers Senators some leeway to do what they think is best for their state and the nation, rather than what might be seen as popular.

Clause 2. To prevent a wholesale replacement of senators every six years, this clause provides that one-third of the Senate will be elected every two years. In other words, in order to remove at least one-half of the Senators from office, two elections are needed.

Senate vacancies are filled in the same way as the House—either appointment by the governor or by special election. Currently the average length of service in the Senate is 11.3 years (slightly less than two terms).

Clause 3. This clause sets forth the qualifications for U.S. senator: at least 30 years old, a U.S. citizen for at least nine years, and a citizen of a state. The equivalent age of 30 today would be 54 years old. The average age of a U.S. senator at present is 59.5 years.

A-8

Clause 4. The only constitutional duty of the vice president is specified in this clause—president of the Senate. This official only has a vote if there is a tie vote in the Senate; then the vice president's vote breaks the tie.

The split between Democrats and Republicans in Congress has been tiny in recent years. Not surprisingly, the Vice President has been called upon to cast several deciding votes.

Clause 5. One official office in the U.S. Senate is specified—temporary president, who fills in during the vice president's absence (which is normally the case). All other Senate officers are designated and selected by the Senate.

Clause 6, 7. The Senate acts as a trial court for impeached federal officials. If the accused is the president, the Chief Justice of the U.S. Supreme Court presides. Otherwise, the vice president normally presides. Conviction of the charges requires a 2/3 majority vote of those senators present at the time of the vote. Conviction results in the federal official's removal from office and disqualification to hold any other federal appointed office.

Section 4 Clause 1. Through the years this clause has proven to be a critical aspect of the elections pathway. By allowing states to regulate elections procedures (that is, until Congress acts), the types of citizens able to participate in the process have been limited. First, religions and property qualifications were common, and many southern states used this provision to discriminate against black voters until the 1960s. Many states barred women from voting in election until the ratification of the 19th Amendment, and still others kept 18-year olds out until the 25th Amendment.

Lingering issues include residency and registration requirements. In some states citizens can register to vote on Election Day, but in many others they have to take this step 30 days in advance. Indeed, many argue that residency and registration requirements unnecessarily inhibit voting, especially for young folks who tend to be more mobile. Others argue that such laws help to reduce voter fraud.

Clause 2. The states determine the place and manner of electing representatives and senators, but Congress has the right to make or change these laws or regulations, except for the election sites. Congress is required to meet annually, and now, by law, annual meetings begin in January.

Section 5 Clause 1. This clause enables each legislative branch to essentially make its own rules. Normally, to take a vote, a quorum is necessary. But if no votes are scheduled, fewer than a quorum can convene a session.

CLAUSE 4. The Vice President of the United States shall be President of the Senate, but shall have no Vote, unless they be equally divided.

CLAUSE 5. The Senate shall chuse their other Officers, and also a President pro tempore, in the Absence of the Vice President, or when he shall exercise the Office of President of the United States.

CLAUSE 6. The Senate shall have the sole Power to try all Impeachments. When sitting for that Purpose, they shall be on Oath or Affirmation. When the President of the United States is tried, the Chief Justice shall preside: And no Person shall be convicted without the Concurrence of two thirds of the Members present.

CLAUSE 7. Judgment in Cases of Impeachment shall not extend further than to removal from Office, and disqualification to hold and enjoy any Office of honor, Trust or Profit under the United States: but the Party convicted shall nevertheless be liable and subject to Indictment, Trial, Judgment and Punishment, according to Law.

Congressional Elections: Times, Places, Manner

SECTION 4 CLAUSE 1. The Times, Places and Manner of holding Elections for Senators and Representatives, shall be prescribed in each State by the Legislature thereof; but the Congress may at any time by Law make or alter such Regulations, except as to the Places of chusing Senators.

CLAUSE 2. The Congress shall assemble at least once in every Year, and such Meeting shall be on the first Monday in December, unless they shall by Law appoint a different Day.[5]

Powers and Duties of the Houses

SECTION 5 CLAUSE 1. Each House shall be the Judge of the Elections, Returns and Qualifications of its own Members, and a Majority of each shall constitute a Quorum to do Business; but a smaller Number may adjourn from day to day, and may be authorized to compel the Attendance of absent Members, in such Manner, and under the Penalties as each House may provide.

CLAUSE 2.   Each House may determine the Rules of its Proceedings, punish its Members for disorderly Behaviour, and, with the Concurrence of two thirds, expel a Member.

CLAUSE 3.   Each House shall keep a Journal of its Proceedings, and from time to time publish the same, excepting such Parts as may in their Judgment require Secrecy; and the Yeas and Nays of the Members of either House on any question shall, at the Desire of one fifth of those Present, be entered on the Journal.

CLAUSE 4.   Neither House, during the Session of Congress, shall, without the Consent of the other, adjourn for more than three days, nor to any other Place than that in which the two Houses shall be sitting.

Rights of Members

SECTION 6 CLAUSE 1.   The Senators and Representatives shall receive a Compensation for their Services, to be ascertained by Law, and paid out of the Treasury of the United States. They shall in all Cases, except Treason, Felony and Breach of the Peace, be privileged from Arrest during their Attendance at the Session of their respective Houses, and in going to and returning from the same; and for any Speech or Debate in either House, they shall not be questioned in any other Place.

CLAUSE 2.   No Senator or Representative shall, during the Time for which he was elected, be appointed to any civil Office under the Authority of the United States, which shall have been created, or the Emoluments whereof shall have been encreased during such time; and no Person holding any Office under the United States, shall be a Member of either House during his Continuance in Office.

Legislative Powers: Bills and Resolutions

SECTION 7 CLAUSE 1.   All Bills for raising Revenue shall originate in the House of Representatives; but the Senate may propose or concur with Amendments as on other Bills.

Clause 2.   Essentially, each branch promulgates its own rules and punishes its own members. Knowing exactly how each chamber of the legislature conducts its proceedings is essential for political activists. The lobbying decision-makers pathway can be a potent means of shifting public policy, but only when internal rules are well understood. Perhaps this is one of the reasons why former members of Congress make such good lobbyists.

Clause 3.   An official record called the Congressional Record, House Journal, etc., is kept for all sessions. It is a daily account of House and Senate floor debates, votes, and members' remarks. However, a record is not printed if a proceeding is closed to the public for security reasons. Many votes are by voice vote, and if at least 1/5 of the members request, a recorded vote of Yeas and Nays will be conducted and documented. This procedure permits analysis of congressional role-call votes.

Clause 4.   This clause prevents one house from adjourning for a long period of time or to some other location without the consent of the other house.

Section 6 Clause 1.   This section refers to a salary paid to senators and members of the House from the U.S. Treasury. This clearly states that federal legislators work for the entire nation, and not for their respective states.

Currently, the salary for members of congress is $165,200; Some leadership positions, like Speaker of the House, receive a higher salary. The Speaker receives a salary of $212,100. Members of Congress receive many other benefits: free health care, fully funded retirement system, free round trips to their home state or district, etc. This section also provides immunity from arrest or prosecution for congressional actions on the floor or in travel to and from the Congress. For example, few members of Congress have ever been charged with drunk driving.

Clause 2.   This section prevents the U.S. from adopting a parliamentary democracy, since congressional members cannot hold executive offices and members of the executive branch cannot be members of Congress.

Section 7 Clause 1.   This clause specifies one of the few powers specific to the U.S. House—revenue bills. Since the House was intended to be more closely tied to the people (since members are elected more frequently and they represent fewer people than the Senate), the founders wanted to grant them the power of the purse.

Given that much of politics centers on the allocation of scarce resources (the distribution of money), this provision is a key piece of information for would-be political activists.

Clause 2. The heart of the checks and balances system is contained in this clause. Both the House and Senate must pass an identical bill and present it to the president. If the president fails to act on the bill within 10 days (not including Sundays), the bill will automatically become law if Congress is in session. If the president signs the bill, it becomes law. If the president vetoes the bill and sends it back to Congress, this body may override the veto by a 2/3 vote in each branch. This vote must be a recorded vote.

The systems of checks and balances, as well as a division of power at the federal level, allow many ways to pursue change by a variety of pathways.

Clause 3. This clause covers every other type of legislative action other than a bill. Essentially, the same procedures apply in most cases. There are a few exceptions. For example, a joint resolution proposing a new congressional amendment is not subject to presidential veto.

Section 8 Clause 1, Clause 2. This power allows the federal government to deficit-spend (which most states are not allowed to do). Thus, when times of economic difficulty arise, individuals and groups can petition government for financial aid and relief with job shortages.

Clause 3. This is one of the most sweeping powers granted Congress, because so much can be linked to interstate "commerce." Since the early twentieth century, the U.S. Supreme Court has defined interstate commerce broadly and thereby enabled Congress to use this power to pass antidiscrimination laws, criminal justice laws, and other statutes.

Clause 4. This provision helps us understand why Congress, rather than state legislatures, has been at the center of the recent immigration reform debate.

CLAUSE 2. Every Bill which shall have passed the House of Representatives and the Senate, shall, before it becomes a Law, be presented to the President of the United States; If he approve he shall sign it, but if not he shall return it, with his Objections to that House in which it shall have originated, who shall enter the Objections at large on their Journal, and proceed to reconsider it. If after such Reconsideration two thirds of that House shall agree to pass the Bill, it shall be sent, together with the Objections, to the other House, by which it shall likewise be reconsidered, and if approved by two thirds of that House, it shall become a Law. But in all such Cases the Votes of both Houses shall be determined by yeas and Nays, and the Names of the Persons voting for and against the Bill shall be entered on the Journal of each House respectively. If any Bill shall not be returned by the President within ten Days (Sundays excepted) after it shall have been presented to him, the Same shall be a Law, in like Manner as if he had signed it, unless the Congress by their Adjournment prevent its Return, in which Case it shall not be a Law.

CLAUSE 3. Every Order, Resolution, or Vote to which the Concurrence of the Senate and House of Representatives may be necessary (except on a question of Adjournment) shall be presented to the President of the United States; and before the Same shall take Effect, shall be approved by him, or being disapproved by him, shall be repassed by two thirds of the Senate and House of Representatives, according to the Rules and Limitations prescribed in the Case of a Bill.

Powers of Congress

SECTION 8 CLAUSE 1. The Congress shall have Power To lay and collect Taxes, Duties, Imposts and Excises, to pay the Debts and provide for the common Defence and general Welfare of the United States; but all Duties, Imposts and Excises shall be uniform throughout the United States.

CLAUSE 2. To borrow Money on the credit of the United States;

CLAUSE 3. To regulate Commerce with foreign Nations, and among the several States, and with the Indian Tribes;

CLAUSE 4. To establish an uniform Rule of Naturalization, and uniform Laws on the subject of Bankruptcies throughout the United States;

CLAUSE 5. To coin Money, regulate the Value thereof, and of foreign Coin, and fix the Standard of Weights and Measures;

CLAUSE 6. To provide for the Punishment of counterfeiting the Securities and current Coin of the United States;

CLAUSE 7. To establish Post Offices and post Roads;

CLAUSE 8. To promote the Progress of Science and useful Arts, by securing for limited Times to Authors and Inventors the exclusive Right to their respective Writings and Discoveries;

CLAUSE 9. To constitute Tribunals inferior to the supreme Court;

CLAUSE 10. To define and punish Piracies and Felonies committed on the high Seas, and Offences against the Law of Nations;

CLAUSE 11. To declare War, grant Letters of Marque and Reprisal, and make Rules concerning Captures on Land and Water;

CLAUSE 12. To raise and support Armies, but no Appropriation of Money to that Use shall be for a longer Term than two Years;

CLAUSE 13. To provide and maintain a Navy;

CLAUSE 14. To make Rules for the Government and Regulation of the land and naval Forces;

CLAUSE 15. To provide for calling forth the Militia to execute the Laws of the Union, suppress Insurrections and repel Invasions;

CLAUSE 16. To provide for organizing, arming, and disciplining, the Militia, and for governing such Part of them as may be employed in the Service of the United States, reserving to the States respectively, the Appointment of the Officers, and the Authority of training the Militia according to the discipline prescribed by Congress;

CLAUSE 17. To exercise exclusive Legislation in all Cases whatsoever, over such District (not exceeding ten Miles square) as may, by Cession of particular States, and the Acceptance of Congress, become the Seat of the Government of the United States, and to exercise like Authority over all Places purchased by the Consent of the Legislature of the State in which the Same shall be, for the Erection of Forts, Magazines, Arsenals, dock-Yards, and other needful Buildings;

Clause 5, 6, 7. Congressional power over coining money, counterfeiting, and post offices provides the justification for the creation of many criminal laws that are handled by federal law enforcement agencies such as the Federal Bureau of Investigation (FBI) and Secret Service. Because these matters are specified as under federal authority in the Constitution, it is a federal crime—rather than a state crime—to counterfeit money and engage in mail fraud. Most other kinds of crimes, such as murders, robberies, and burglaries victimizing ordinary citizens, are governed by state law.

Clause 9. Congress is responsible for the design of and procedures used in the federal court system. The U.S. Supreme Court is the only court created by the Constitution (see Article III). The lower federal courts are created by—and can be changed by—laws enacted by Congress. When there are changes in the design of the federal court system, such as the creation of a new court, these matters are under the power of Congress rather than under the control of the Supreme Court.

Clause 10, Clause 11. Although Congress possesses the exclusive authority to declare war, presidents use their powers as commander-in-chief (see Article II) to initiate military actions even when there is no formal congressional declaration of war. There have been periodic disputes about whether presidents have exceeded their authority and ignored the Constitution's explicit grant of war-declaring power to Congress.

Clause 11, 12, 13. These three clauses, clauses 11, 12, and 13, ensure that Congress is involved in foreign policy decisions; thus citizens and groups can appeal to Congress if they do not like the president's foreign policy decisions or actions. Giving Congress the power to make appropriations to fund the military is potentially a significant power they have in rivaling the president for influence.

Clause 14, 15, 16. These clauses establish what are known as the "expressed" or "specified" powers of Congress.

Clause 17. This clause establishes the seat of the federal government, which was first located in New York. It eventually was moved to Washington, D.C., when both Maryland and Virginia ceded land to the new national government, which then established the District of Columbia.

Clause 18. This clause, known as the "Elastic Clause," provides the basis for the doctrine of "implied" congressional powers, which was first introduced in the U.S. Supreme Court case of *McCulloch* v. *Maryland,* 1819. It greatly expanded the power of Congress to pass legislation and make regulations.

The "necessary and proper" clause increases the powers of Congress, granting the legislature a great deal more authority and influence in our system of government. It has proven essential in creating a stong national government and in placing Congress at the center of the policy process.

Section 9 Clause 1. This clause was part of the Three-Fifths Compromise. Essentially, the new Congress was prohibited from stopping the importation of slaves until 1808, but it could impose a head tax not to exceed ten dollars for each slave.

Condoning slavery, from today's perspective, clearly clashed with the Declaration of Independence's assertion that all men are created equal. It is hard to understand the hypocrisy of a free society with slaves. Without this provision, however, southern delegates would have left the Constitutional Convention, and southern states would not have voted to ratify the new Constitution.

Clause 2. Habeas Corpus is a judicial order forcing law enforcement authorities to produce a prisoner they are holding, and to justify the prisoner's continued confinement. Congress cannot suspend the writ of habeas corpus except in cases of rebellion or invasion. The writ of habeas corpus permits a judge to inquire about the legality of detention or deprivation of liberty of any citizen. This is one of the few legal protections for individuals enshrined in the Constitution before the Bill of Rights.

Clause 3. This provision prohibits Congress from passing either bills of attainder (an act of legislature declaring a person or group of persons guilty of some crime, and punishing them, without benefit of a trial) or ex post facto laws (retroactive crimes after passage of legislation). Similar restrictions were put in many state constitutions. These protections were among the few specifically provided for individuals in the body of the Constitution before the creation of amendments.

Clause 4. This clause was interpreted to prevent Congress from passing an income tax. When the Supreme Court struck down congressional efforts to impose an income tax, passage of the 16th Amendment in 1913 counteracted the Supreme Court decision and gave Congress this power.

Clause 5. This section establishes free trade within the U.S. That is, one state cannot tax the importation of domestic goods, and the federal government cannot tax state exports.

Clause 6. This clause also applies to free trade within the U.S. The national government cannot show any preference to any state or maritime movements among the states.

Clause 7. This clause prevents any expenditure unless it has been provided for in an appropriations bill enacted by Congress. At the beginning of most fiscal years, Congress has not completed the budget. Technically, the government cannot then spend any money, and would have to shut down. So Congress usually passes a Continuing Resolution Authority providing temporary authority to continue to spend money until the final budget is approved and signed into law.

CLAUSE 18. To make all Laws which shall be necessary and proper for carrying into Execution the foregoing Powers, and all other Powers vested by this Constitution in the Government of the United States, or in any Department or Officer thereof.

Powers Denied to Congress

SECTION 9 CLAUSE 1. The Migration or Importation of such Persons as any of the States now existing shall think proper to admit, shall not be prohibited by the Congress prior to the Year one thousand eight hundred and eight, but a Tax or duty may be imposed on such Importation, not exceeding ten dollars for each Person.

CLAUSE 2. The Privilege of the Writ of Habeas Corpus shall not be suspended, unless when in Cases of Rebellion or Invasion the public Safety may require it.

CLAUSE 3. No Bill of Attainder or ex post facto Law shall be passed.

CLAUSE 4. No Capitation, or other direct, Tax shall be laid, unless in Proportion to the Census or Enumeration herein before directed to be taken.[6]

CLAUSE 5. No Tax or Duty shall be laid on Articles exported from any State.

CLAUSE 6. No Preference shall be given by any Regulation of Commerce or Revenue to the Ports of one State over those of another; nor shall Vessels bound to, or from, one State, be obliged to enter, clear, or pay Duties in another.

CLAUSE 7. No Money shall be drawn from the Treasury, but in Consequence of Appropriations made by Law; and a regular Statement and Account of the Receipts and Expenditures of all public Money shall be published from time to time.

CLAUSE 8. No Title of Nobility shall be granted by the United States: And no Person holding any Office of Profit or Trust under them, shall, without the Consent of Congress, accept of any present, Emolument, Office, or Title, of any kind whatever, from any King, Prince, or foreign State.

> **Clause 8.** Feudalism would not be established in the new country. We would have no nobles. No federal official can accept a title of nobility (even honorary) without permission of Congress.

Powers Denied to the States

> This section sets out the prohibitions on state actions.

SECTION 10 CLAUSE 1. No State shall enter into any Treaty, Alliance, or Confederation; grant Letters of Marque and Reprisal; coin Money; emit Bills of Credit; make any Thing but gold and silver; Coin a Tender in Payment of Debts; pass any Bill of Attainder, ex post facto Law, or Law impairing the Obligation of Contracts, or grant any Title of Nobility.

> **Section 10 Clause 1.** This clause is a laundry list of denied powers. These restrictions cannot be waived by Congress. States cannot engage in foreign relations or acts of war. Letters of marque and reprisal were used to provide legal cover for privateers. The federal government's currency monopoly is established. The sanctity of contracts is specified, and similar state prohibitions are specified for bills of attainder, ex post facto, etc.

CLAUSE 2. No State shall, without the Consent of the Congress, lay any Imposts or Duties on Imports or Exports, except what may be absolutely necessary for executing its inspection Laws: and the net Produce of all Duties and Imposts, laid by any State on Imports or Exports, shall be for the Use of the Treasury of the United States; and all such Laws shall be subject to the Revision and Controul of the Congress.

> **Clause 2.** This section establishes the monopoly control of the national government in matters of both national and international trade. The only concession to states is health and safety inspections.

> **Clause 3.** This final section of the Legislative article establishes the war monopoly power of the national government. The only exception to state action is actual invasion or threat of imminent danger.

CLAUSE 3. No State shall, without the Consent of Congress, lay any Duty of Tonnage, keep Troops, or Ships of War in time of Peace, enter into any Agreement or Compact with another State, or with a foreign Power, or engage in War, unless actually invaded, or in such imminent Danger as will not admit of delay.

> **Article II.** This article establishes an entirely new concept in government—an elected executive power. This was a touchy topic in 1787. On one hand, there was great worry about executive power—it was seen as the root of tyranny. On the other hand, many believed that a powerful executive was necessary for long-term stability for the new nation. The right balance was a system with a strong executive, where the executive's power could be limited.

Article II
THE EXECUTIVE ARTICLE

Nature and Scope of Presidential Power

SECTION 1 CLAUSE 1. The executive Power shall be vested in a President of the United States of America. He shall hold his Office during the Term of four Years, and, together with the Vice President, chosen for the same Term, be elected as follows:

> **Section 1 Clause 1.** This clause establishes the executive power in the office of the president of the United States of America. It also establishes a second office—vice president. A four-year term was established, but not a limit on the number of terms. A limit was later established by the 22nd Amendment.

CLAUSE 2. Each State shall appoint, in such Manner as the Legislature thereof may direct, a Number of Electors, equal to the whole Number of Senators and Representatives to which the State may be entitled in the Congress: but no Senator or Representative, or Person holding an Office of Trust or Profit under the United States, shall be appointed an Elector.

> **Clause 2.** This paragraph establishes the electoral college to choose the president and vice president. Each state can determine how electors will be allotted to different candidates. For instance, today 48 states give the candidate who receives the most votes from citizens all of its electoral votes. This "winner take all" system puts an important twist on presidential election strategy. The trick for the candidates is to amass 270 electoral votes from different combinations of states.
>
> Another implication of this system of choosing an executive is that it is possible for one candidate to receive more votes from citizens than other candidates, but still not become president. This has occurred four times in American history, most recently in 2000, when Al Gore received roughly 500,000 votes more than George W. Bush but fewer Electoral College votes.

Clause 3. This paragraph has been superseded by the 12th Amendment. The original language provided for a House election in the case of no majority vote or a tie vote among the top five candidates. Now the number of candidates is three. The Senate is to select the vice president if a candidate does not have an electoral majority or in the case of a tie vote. The Senate considers only the top two candidates. The amendment also clarifies that the qualifications of the vice president are the same as those for president.

Clause 4. Congress is given the power to establish a uniform day and time for the state selection of electors.

Clause 5. The qualifications for the offices of president and vice president are specified here—at least 35 years old, 14 years' resident in the U.S., and a natural-born citizen. The 14th Amendment clarified who is a citizen of the U.S., a person born or naturalized in the U.S. and subject to its jurisdiction. But the term "natural-born citizen" is unclear and has never been further defined by the judicial branch. Does it mean born in the U.S. or born of U.S. citizens in the U.S. or somewhere else in the world? Unfortunately, there is no definitive answer.

Clause 6. This clause concerns presidential succession and has been modified by the 25th Amendment. Upon the death, resignation, or impeachment conviction of the president, the vice president becomes president. The new president nominates a new vice president, who assumes the office if approved by a majority vote in both congressional branches. The president is also now able to notify the Congress of his or her inability to perform the duties of office.

CLAUSE 3. The Electors shall meet in their respective States, and vote by Ballot for two Persons, of whom one at least shall not be an Inhabitant of the same State with themselves. And they shall make a List of all the Persons voted for, and of the Number of Votes for each; which List they shall sign and certify, and transmit sealed to the Seat of the Government of the United States, directed to the President of the Senate. The President of the Senate shall, in the Presence of the Senate and House of Representatives, open all the Certificates, and the Votes shall then be counted. The Person having the greatest Number of Votes shall be the President, if such Number be a Majority of the whole Number of Electors appointed; and if there be more than one who have such Majority and have an equal Number of Votes, then the House of Representatives shall immediately chuse by Ballot one of them for President; and if no Person have a Majority, then from the five highest on the List the said House shall in like Manner chuse the President. But in chusing the President, the Votes shall be taken by States, the Representation from each State having one Vote; A quorum for this Purpose shall consist of a Member or Members from two thirds of the States, and a Majority of all the States shall be necessary to a Choice. In every Case, after the Choice of the President, the Person having the greatest Number of Votes of the Electors shall be the Vice President. But if there should remain two or more who have equal Votes, the Senate shall chuse from them by Ballot the Vice President.[7]

CLAUSE 4. The Congress may determine the Time of chusing the Electors, and the Day on which they shall give their Votes; which Day shall be the same throughout the United States.

CLAUSE 5. No Person except a natural born Citizen, or a Citizen of the United States, at the time of the Adoption of this Constitution, shall be eligible to the Office of President; neither shall any Person be eligible to that Office who shall not have attained to the Age of thirty five Years, and been fourteen Years a Resident within the United States.

CLAUSE 6. In Case of the Removal of the President from Office, or of his Death, Resignation, or Inability to discharge the Powers and Duties of the said Office, the Same shall devolve on the Vice President, and the Congress may by Law provide for the Case of Removal, Death, Resignation or Inability, both of the President and Vice President, declaring what Officer shall then act as President, and such Officer shall act accordingly, until the Disability be removed, or a President shall be elected.[8]

CLAUSE 7. The President shall, at stated Times, receive for his Services, a Compensation, which shall neither be encreased nor diminished during the Period for which he shall have been elected, and he shall not receive within that Period any other Emolument from the United States, or any of them.

CLAUSE 8. Before he enter on the Execution of his Office, he shall take the following Oath or Affirmation:—"I do solemnly swear (or affirm) that I will faithfully execute the Office of President of the United States, and will to the best of my Ability, preserve, protect and defend the Constitution of the United States."

Powers and Duties of the President

SECTION 2 CLAUSE 1. The President shall be Commander in Chief of the Army and Navy of the United States, and of the Militia of the several States, when called into the actual Service of the United States; he may require the Opinion, in writing, of the principal Officer in each of the executive Departments, upon any Subject relating to the Duties of their respective Offices, and he shall have Power to grant Reprieves and Pardons for Offences against the United States, except in Cases of Impeachment.

CLAUSE 2. He shall have Power, by and with the Advice and Consent of the Senate, to make Treaties, provided two thirds of the Senators present concur; and he shall nominate, and by and with the Advice and Consent of the Senate, shall appoint Ambassadors, other public Ministers and Consuls, Judges of the supreme Court, and all other Officers of the United States, whose Appointments are not herein otherwise provided for, and which shall be established by Law: but the Congress may by Law vest the Appointment of such inferior Officers, as they think proper, in the President alone, in the Courts of Law, or in the Heads of Departments.

CLAUSE 3. The President shall have Power to fill up all Vacancies that may happen during the Recess of the Senate, by granting Commissions which shall expire at the End of their next Session.

Clause 7. This section covers the compensation of the president, which cannot be increased or decreased during his/her office. The current salary is $400,000/year. The prohibition against decreasing the president's salary was considered an important part of the separation of powers. If Congress were at odds with the president and also able to decrease his pay, then it could drive him from office or punish him by reducing his salary.

Clause 8. This final clause in Section 1 is the oath of office administered to the new president. Interestingly, the phrase "so help me God," is not part of this oath, but has become customary in recent years.

Section 2 Clause 1. This clause establishes the president as Commander-in-Chief of the U.S. armed forces. George Washington was the only U.S. president to actually lead U.S. armed forces, during the Whiskey Rebellion.

The second provision is the basis for cabinet meetings that are used to hear the opinions of executive department heads. The last provision grants an absolute pardon or reprieve power for the president.

Since the president is Commander-in-Chief, citizens and groups concerned with U.S. foreign policy (especially armed military conflicts) can hold the president accountable for policy decisions. Litigation, protests, marches, and electoral battles have all been used by citizens dissatisfied with presidential foreign policy decisions.

Clause 2. This clause covers two important presidential powers: treaty making and appointments. The president (through the State Department) can negotiate treaties with other nations, but these do not become official until ratified by a 2/3 vote of the U.S. Senate.

The president is empowered to appoint judges, ambassadors, and other U.S. officials (cabinet officers, military officers, agency heads, etc.) subject to Senate approval.

These powers are important to ensure the division of power between the three branches of our national government as well as the system of checks and balances. Sharing these powers allows for input by the people and organized groups. The Senate approves most treaties and most presidential appointments, especially if it is controlled by members of the same party as the president. But this is not always true; many treaties and appointments have been rejected, often because the Senate was responding to strong public opinion.

Clause 3. This allows recess appointments of the officials listed in Clause 2 above. These commissions automatically expire unless approved by the Senate by the end of the next session. Presidents have used this provision to fill jobs when the nomination process is stalled.

Section 3. This section provides for the annual State of the Union address to a joint session of Congress. Presidents have learned that the ability to reach out to the public can be the source of tremendous power. The State of the Union address is thus an important opportunity to speak directly to the American public, build support for initiatives, and shape the policy agenda. The president is also authorized to call special meetings of either the House or Senate. If there is disagreement between the House and Senate regarding adjournment, the president may adjourn them. This would be extremely rare. The next-to-last provision, to faithfully execute laws, provides the basis for the whole administrative apparatus of the executive branch.

Section 4. This section provides the constitutional authority for the impeachment and trial of the president, vice president, and all civil officers of the U.S. for treason, bribery, or other high crimes and misdemeanors (the exact meaning of this phrase is unclear and is often more political than judicial). Impeachment proceedings have been undertaken against two presidents in American history: Andrew Johnson, in 1868, and Bill Clinton in 1998. In both cases the Senate failed to convict the president, and both were allowed to stay in office. Richard Nixon would have also confronted impeachment proceedings in 1974 for his involvement in the Watergate scandal, but he resigned from office and avoided the process.

Article III Section 1. This section establishes the judicial branch in very general terms. It only for the Supreme Court; Congress must create the court system. It first did so in the Judiciary Act of 1789, when it established 13 district courts (one for each state) and 3 appellate courts. All federal judges hold their offices for life and can only be removed for breaches of good behavior—a very ambiguous term. Federal judges have been removed for drunkenness, accepting bribes, and other misdemeanors. To date, no justice of the U.S. Supreme Court has ever been removed.

The tenure of judges in office, which can be for life, is meant to give judges the ability to make decisions according to their best judgments without facing the prospect of removal from office for issuing an unpopular judgment. While this protected tenure is an undemocratic aspect of the Constitution in the sense that it removes federal judges from direct electoral accountability, it has been an important aspect of the judiciary's ability to enforce civil rights and liberties on behalf of minority groups and unpopular individuals.

This protected tenure is one aspect of government that makes the court pathway especially attractive to individuals, small groups, and others who lack political power. For example, federal judges acted against racial discrimination in the 1950s at a time when most white Americans accepted the existence of such discrimination when applied to African Americans. The salary of federal judges is set by congressional act but can never be reduced.

Section 2 Clause 1, 2, 3. This section establishes the original and appellate jurisdiction of the U.S. Supreme Court. Original jurisdiction cases are essentially limited to disputes between states. The Eleventh Amendment limited the ability of individuals to sue states. Even in these cases involving states, the Supreme Court now typically appoints a special judge to hear the evidence and make a recommendation to the justices rather than hold an actual trial at the Supreme Court. Since 1925, the Supreme Court no longer hears every case on appeal but can select which cases it will accept, which is now only about 75-85 cases per year. Although this provision mentions trial by jury in all cases, the Supreme Court's interpretations of the jury trial right, also contained in the Sixth Amendment, limits the right to criminal cases involving serious crimes with punishments of six months of more of imprisonment.

SECTION 3 He shall from time to time give to the Congress Information of the State of the Union, and recommend to their Consideration such Measures as he shall judge necessary and expedient; he may, on extraordinary Occasions, convene both Houses, or either of them, and in Case of Disagreement between them, with Respect to the Time of Adjournment, he may adjourn them to such Time as he shall think proper; he shall receive Ambassadors and other public Ministers; he shall take Care that the Laws be faithfully executed, and shall Commission all the Officers of the United States.

SECTION 4 The President, Vice President and all civil Officers of the United States, shall be removed from Office on Impeachment for, and Conviction of, Treason, Bribery, or other high Crimes and Misdemeanors.

Article III
THE JUDICIAL ARTICLE

Judicial Power, Courts, Judges

SECTION 1 The judicial Power of the United States, shall be vested in one supreme Court, and in such inferior Courts as the Congress may from time to time ordain and establish. The Judges, both of the supreme and inferior Courts, shall hold their Offices during good Behaviour, and shall, at stated Times, receive for their Services, a Compensation, which shall not be diminished during their Continuance in Office.

Jurisdiction

SECTION 2 CLAUSE 1. The judicial Power shall extend to all Cases, in Law and Equity, arising under this Constitution, the Laws of the United States, and Treaties made, or which shall be made, under their Authority;—to all Cases affecting Ambassadors, other public Ministers and Consuls;—to all Cases of admiralty and maritime Jurisdiction;—to Controversies to which the United States shall be a Party;—to Controversies between two or more States—between a State and Citizens of another State;[9]—between Citizens of different States;—between Citizens of the same State claiming Lands under Grants of different States, and between a State, or the Citizens thereof, and foreign States, Citizens, or Subjects.

CLAUSE 2. In all Cases affecting Ambassadors, other public Ministers and Consuls, and those in which a State shall be Party, the supreme Court shall have original Jurisdiction. In all the other Cases before mentioned, the supreme Court shall have appellate Jurisdiction, both as to Law and Fact, with such Exceptions, and under such Regulations as Congress shall make.

CLAUSE 3. The Trial of all Crimes, except in Cases of Impeachment, shall be by Jury; and such Trial shall be held in the State where the said Crimes shall have been committed; but when not committed within any State, the Trial shall be at such Place or Places as the Congress may by Law have directed.

Treason

SECTION 3 CLAUSE 1. Treason against the United States, shall consist only in levying War against them, or in adhering to their Enemies, giving them Aid and Comfort. No Person shall be convicted of Treason unless on the Testimony of two Witnesses to the same overt Act, or on Confession in open Court.

CLAUSE 2. The Congress shall have Power to declare the Punishment of Treason, but no Attainder of Treason shall work Corruption of Blood, or Forfeiture except during the Life of the Person attainted.

Article IV
INTERSTATE RELATIONS

Full Faith and Credit Clause

SECTION 1 Full Faith and Credit shall be given in each State to the public Acts, Records, and judicial Proceedings of every other State. And the Congress may by general Laws prescribe the Manner in which such Acts, Records and Proceedings shall be proved, and the Effect thereof.

Privileges and Immunities; Interstate Extradition

SECTION 2 CLAUSE 1. The Citizens of each State shall be entitled to all Privileges and Immunities of Citizens in the several States.

CLAUSE 2. A person charged in any State with Treason, Felony or other Crime, who shall flee from Justice, and be found in another State, shall on Demand of the executive Authority of the State from which he fled, be delivered up, to be removed to the State having Jurisdiction of the Crime.

Clauses 1, 2, 3. This section establishes the original and appellate jurisdiction of the U.S. Supreme Court. Original jurisdiction cases are essentially limited to disputes between states. The Eleventh Amendment limited the ability of individuals to sue states. Even in these cases involving states, the Supreme Court now typically appoints a special judge to hear the evidence and make a recommendation to the justices rather than hold an actual trial at the Supreme Court. Since 1925, the Supreme Court no longer hears every case on appeal but can select which cases it will accept, which is now only about 75-85 cases per year. Although this provision mentions trial by jury in all cases, the Supreme Court's interpretations of the jury trial right, also contained in the Sixth Amendment, limits the right to criminal cases involving serious crimes with punishments of six months of more of imprisonment.

Section 3 Clauses 1, 2 Treason is the only crime defined in the U.S. Constitution. Congress established the penalty of death for treason convictions. Note that two witnesses are required to convict anyone of treason.

Article IV Section 1. This section provides that the official acts and records (for example, marriages and divorces) of one state will be recognized and given credence by other states. It is one of several clauses that were designed to create a strong national government. Concerns about this clause have taken on new importance in recent years, as the gay marriage issue has heated up in most state legislatures.

Section 2 Clause 1 This clause requires states to treat citizens of other states equally. For example, when driving in another state, a driver's license is recognized.

Clause 2. *Extradition* is the name of this clause. A criminal fleeing to another state, if captured, can be returned to the state where the crime was committed. But this is not an absolute. A state's governor can refuse, for good reason, to extradite someone to another state.

Clause 3. This clause was included to cover runaway slaves. It has been made inoperable by the 13th Amendment, which abolished slavery.

CLAUSE 3. No person held to Service or Labour in one State, under the Laws thereof, escaping into another, shall, in Consequence of any Law or Regulation therein, be discharged from such Service or Labour, but shall be delivered up on Claim of the Party to whom such Service or Labour may be due.[10]

Admission of States

SECTION 3 CLAUSE 1. New States may be admitted by the Congress into this Union; but no new State shall be formed or erected within the Jurisdiction of any other State; nor any State be formed by the Junction of two or more States, or Parts of States, without the Consent of the Legislatures of the States concerned as well as of the Congress.

Section 3 Clauses 1, 2. This section concerns the admission of new states to the Union. In theory, no state can be created from part of another state without permission of the state legislature. But West Virginia was formed from Virginia during the Civil War without the permission of Virginia, which was part of the Confederacy. With fifty states now part of the Union, this section has not been used for many decades. The only foreseeable future use may be in the case of Puerto Rico or perhaps Washington, D.C.

CLAUSE 2. The Congress shall have Power to dispose of and make all needful Rules and Regulations respecting the Territory or other Property belonging to the United States; and nothing in this Constitution shall be so construed as to Prejudice any Claims of the United States, or of any particular State.

Republican Form of Government

SECTION 4 The United States shall guarantee to every State in this Union a Republican Form of Government, and shall protect each of them against Invasion; and on Application of the Legislature, or of the Executive (when the Legislature cannot be convened) against domestic Violence.

Section 4. This section commits the federal government to guarantee a republican form of government to each state and to protect the states against foreign invasion or domestic insurrection.

By mandating a republican form of government, the Constitution guarantees that power rests in the hands of the citizens and is exercised by their elected representatives. As such, citizens are able to appeal directly to their governing officials through several pathways, such as through the courts, via elections, or by lobbying.

Article V

THE AMENDING POWER

The Congress, whenever two thirds of both Houses shall deem it necessary, shall propose Amendments to this Constitution, or, on the Application of the Legislatures of two thirds of the several States, shall call a Convention for proposing Amendments, which, in either Case, shall be valid to all Intents and Purposes, as Part of this Constitution, when ratified by the Legislatures of three fourths of the several States, or by Conventions in three fourths thereof, as the one or the other Mode of Ratification may be proposed by the Congress; Provided that no Amendment which may be made prior to the Year One thousand eight hundred and eight shall in any Manner affect the first and fourth Clauses in the Ninth Section of the first Article; and that no State, without its Consent, shall be deprived of its equal Suffrage in the Senate.

Article V. Amendments to the U.S. Constitution can be originated by a 2/3 vote in both the U.S. House and Senate or by 2/3 of the state legislatures asking for a convention to propose amendments. Proposed amendments, by either route, must be approved by 3/4 of state legislatures or by 3/4 of conventions convened in the states for purposes of ratification. Only one amendment has been ratified by the convention method—Amendment 21 to repeal the 18th Amendment establishing Prohibition.

Thousands of amendments have been proposed; few have been passed by 2/3 vote in each branch of Congress. The Equal Rights Amendment was one such case, but it was not ratified by 3/4 of state legislatures. There have only been 27 successful amendments to the U.S. Constitution.

Since both the federal and state levels of government are involved in amending the Constitution, interested parties have several strategies to pursue to increase the likelihood that a proposed amendment is successful or is defeated.

Article VI

THE SUPREMACY ACT

CLAUSE 1. All Debts contracted and Engagements entered into, before the Adoption of this Constitution, shall be as valid against the United States under this Constitution, as under the Confederation.

CLAUSE 2. This Constitution, and the Laws of the United States which shall be made in Pursuance thereof; and all Treaties made, or which shall be made, under the Authority of the United States, shall be the supreme Law of the Land; and the Judges in every State shall be bound thereby, any Thing in the Constitution or Laws of any State to the Contrary notwithstanding.

CLAUSE 3. The Senators and Representatives before mentioned, and the Members of the several State Legislatures, and all executive and judicial Officers, both of the United States and of the several States, shall be bound by Oath or Affirmation, to support this Constitution; but no religious Test shall ever be required as a Qualification to any Office or public Trust under the United States.

Article VII

RATIFICATION

The Ratification of the Conventions of nine States, shall be sufficient for the Establishment of this Constitution between the States so ratifying the Same.

Done in Convention by the Unanimous Consent of the States present the Seventeenth Day of September in the Year of our Lord one thousand seven hundred and Eighty seven and of the Independence of the United States of America the Twelfth. In Witness whereof We have hereunto subscribed our Names.

Amendments

The Bill of Rights

AMENDMENT 1
RELIGION, SPEECH, ASSEMBLY, AND PETITION

Congress shall make no law respecting an establishment of religion, or prohibiting the free exercise thereof; or abridging the freedom of speech, or of the press; or the right of the people peaceably to assemble, and to petition the Government for a redress of grievances.

Clause 1. This clause made the new national government responsible for all debts incurred during the Revolutionary War. This was very important to banking and commercial interests.

Clause 2. This is the National Supremacy Clause, which provides the basis for the supremacy of the national government. This seems to be a rather straightforward issue these days, but until the conclusion of the Civil War, "national supremacy" was not a settled concept.

Clause 3. This clause requires essentially all federal and state officials to swear or affirm their allegiance to and support of the U.S. Constitution. Note that a religious test was prohibited for federal office. However, some states used religious tests for voting and office qualification until the 1830s.

Article VII. In the end, all 13 states ratified the Constitution. But it was a close call in several states.

Realizing the unanimous ratification of the new Constitution by the 13 states might never have occurred, the framers wisely specified that only 9 states would be needed for ratification. Even this proved to be a test of wills between Federalists and Anti-Federalists, leading to publication of the great political work *The Federalist Papers*.

[The first ten amendments were ratified on December 15, 1791, and form what is known as the "Bill of Rights."]

The Bill of Rights applied at first only to the federal government and not to state or local governments. Beginning in 1925 in the case of *Gitlow* v. *New York*, the U.S. Supreme Court began to selectively incorporate the Bill of Rights, making its provisions applicable to state and local governments, with some exceptions, which will be discussed at the appropriate amendment.

Until the Supreme Court incorporated the Bill of Rights to include protections from state governments, citizens had to look to state constitutions for protections of civil liberties.

Amendment 1. This amendment protects five fundamental freedoms: religion, speech, press, assembly, and petition. The press is the only business that is specifically protected by the U.S. Constitution. Freedom of religion and speech are two of the most contentious issues and generate a multitude of Supreme Court cases.

These freedoms are crucial for nearly every pathway of change; without each fundamental right, individuals and groups could not pursue change without fear of reprisal. This amendment is perhaps the most crucial to guarantee a free society.

Amendment 2. Those who favor gun ownership, either for protection, hunting or sport, cite this amendment. This amendment has not been incorporated for state/local governments; that is, state and local governments are free to regulate arms, provided such regulation is not barred by their own state constitutions.

There is controversy as to the meaning of this amendment. Some believe that it specifically refers to citizen militias, which were common at the time of the Constitution but now have been replaced by permanent armed forces (state national guard units), thereby allowing the federal government to regulate gun ownership. Others believe that the amendment refers to individuals directly, therefore guaranteeing private citizens the right to own guns. The Supreme Court's decisions have never declared that this amendment guarantees to individuals the right to own or carry firearms.

Amendment 3. It was the practice of the British government to insist that colonists provide room or board to British troops. This amendment was designed to prohibit this practice. Today, military and naval bases provide the necessary quarters and this issue does not arise. This amendment has not been incorporated and applies only against the federal government.

Amendment 4. This extremely important amendment is designed to prevent the abuse of police powers. Essentially, unreasonable searches or seizures of homes, persons, or property cannot be undertaken without probable cause or a warrant that specifically describes the place to be searched, the person involved, and the suspicious things to be seized.

People who believe that these rights have been violated have successfully used the court-centered pathway for protection, either by seeking to have improperly obtained evidence excluded from use in court or by seeking money damages from police officials to compensate for the invasion of a home or an improper search of an individual's body.

Many people feel that the rights of the accused are often given more precedence than the rights of victims. The Constitution does not contain rights for victims, but a constitutional amendment has been proposed to protect victims' rights. This does not mean that victims are unprotected by the law. States and the federal government have statutes that provide protections and services for crime victims.

Amendment 5. Only a grand jury can indict a person for a federal crime. (This provision does not apply to state/local governments because it has not been incorporated by the Supreme Court.) This amendment also covers double jeopardy, or being tried twice for the same crime in the same jurisdiction. This amendment also covers the prohibition of compelled self-incrimination. The deprivation of life, liberty, or property is prohibited unless due process of law is applied. This provision applies to the federal government, and there is a parallel provision that applies to state and local governments in the Fourteenth Amendment. Finally, private property may not be taken under the doctrine of "eminent domain" unless the government provides just compensation.

AMENDMENT 2
MILITIA AND THE RIGHT TO BEAR ARMS

A well-regulated Militia, being necessary to the security of a free State, the right of the people to keep and bear Arms, shall not be infringed.

AMENDMENT 3
QUARTERING OF SOLDIERS

No Soldier shall, in time of peace be quartered in any house, without the consent of the Owner, nor in time of war, but in manner to be prescribed by law.

AMENDMENT 4
SEARCHES AND SEIZURES

The right of the people to be secure in their persons, houses, papers, and effects, against unreasonable searches and seizures, shall not be violated, and no Warrants shall issue, but upon probable cause, supported by Oath or affirmation, and particularly describing the place to be searched, and the persons or things to be seized.

AMENDMENT 5
GRAND JURIES, SELF-INCRIMINATION, DOUBLE JEOPARDY, DUE PROCESS, AND EMINENT DOMAIN

No person shall be held to answer for a capital, or otherwise infamous crime, unless on a presentment or indictment of a Grand jury, except in cases arising in the land or naval forces, or in the Militia, when in actual service in time of War or public danger; nor shall any person be subject for the same offence to be twice put in jeopardy of life or limb; nor shall be compelled in any criminal case to be a witness against himself, nor be deprived of life, liberty, or property, without due process of law; nor shall private property be taken for public use, without just compensation.

AMENDMENT 6
CRIMINAL COURT PROCEDURES

In all criminal prosecutions, the accused shall enjoy the right to a speedy and public trial, by an impartial jury of the State and district wherein the crime shall have been committed, which district shall have been previously ascertained by law, and to be informed of the nature and cause of the accusation; to be confronted with the witnesses against him; to have compulsory process for obtaining witnesses in his favor, and to have the Assistance of Counsel for his defence.

AMENDMENT 7
TRIAL BY JURY IN COMMON LAW CASES

In Suits at common law, where the value in controversy shall exceed twenty dollars, the right of trial by jury shall be preserved, and no fact tried by a jury shall be otherwise reexamined in any Court of the United States, than according to the rules of the common law.

AMENDMENT 8
BAIL, CRUEL AND UNUSUAL PUNISHMENT

Excessive bail shall not be required, nor excessive fines imposed, nor cruel and unusual punishments inflicted.

AMENDMENT 9
RIGHTS RETAINED BY THE PEOPLE

The enumeration in the Constitution, of certain rights, shall not be construed to deny or disparage others retained by the people.

AMENDMENT 10
RESERVED POWERS OF THE STATES

The powers not delegated to the United States by the Constitution, nor prohibited by it to the States, are reserved to the States respectively, or to the people.

Amendment 6. This amendment requires public trials by jury for criminal prosecutions. However, the Supreme Court only applies the right to trial by jury to serious offenses, not petty offenses. Anyone accused of a crime is guaranteed the rights to be informed of the charges; to confront witnesses; to subpoena witnesses for their defense; and to have a lawyer for their defense. The government must provide a lawyer for a defendant unable to afford one for any case in which the defendant faces the possibility of a jail or prison sentence.

There are serious questions about the adequacy of attorney performance and resources for criminal defense. In some jurisdictions, there are not enough defense attorneys for poor defendants, so that the attorneys spend little time on each case. In addition, the Supreme Court does not have strict standards for attorney performance, so some defendants have been represented by attorneys who know very little about criminal law.

Amendment 7. The right to trial by jury in civil cases will never be incorporated by the Supreme Court for application against state and local governments, because it would impose a huge financial burden (jury trials are very expensive).

Amendment 8. The Supreme Court has not clearly defined the limits imposed by prohibition of excessive bail or excessive fines. Thus these rights rarely arise in legal cases, and bail amounts in excessive of $1 million will periodically be imposed for serious crimes or wealthy defendants. The prohibition on cruel and unusual punishments focuses on criminal punishments, not other contexts (such as the punishment of children in public schools or civil fines against businesses). Cruel and unusual punishments are defined according to current societal values and thus the definition of what is "cruel and unusual" can change over time. This provision bars punishments that are either excessive or torturous.

Capital punishment is covered by this amendment, as well as the treatment of prisoners inside prisons. Court cases challenging the constitutionality of capital punishment cite this amendment's language prohibiting cruel and unusual punishment. For a period of 4 years (1973-1976), the Supreme Court banned capital punishment as it was then being applied by the states. When states modified their statutes to provide a two-part judicial process of guilt determination and punishment, the Supreme Court allowed the reinstitution of capital punishment by the states.

Amendment 9. This amendment implies that there may be other rights of the people not specified by the previous amendments, but the wording gives no guidance about what those rights might be. Instead, when the Supreme Court has identified rights not specifically mentioned in the Bill of Rights, it has tended to claim that these rights, such as privacy and the right to travel between states, are connected to the right to "due process" found in the Fifth and Fourteenth Amendments.

Amendment 10. The 10th Amendment was seen as the reservoir of reserved powers for state governments. But the doctrine of implied national government powers, which was established by the U.S. Supreme Court in *McCulloch* v. *Maryland* in 1819, undercut the words and apparent intent of this amendment. With the exception of a few decisions, the Supreme Court has generally deferred to assertions of federal power since the 1930s.

Amendment 11. Article 3 of the U.S. Constitution originally allowed federal jurisdiction in cases of one state citizen against another state citizen or state. This amendment removes federal jurisdiction in this area. In essence, states may not be sued in federal court by citizens of another state or country.

Amendment 12. This was a necessary amendment to correct a flaw in the Constitution covering operations of the Electoral College. In the election of 1800, Thomas Jefferson and Aaron Burr, both of the same Democratic-Republican Party, received the same number of electoral votes, 73, for president. Article II of the original Constitution specified that each elector would cast two ballots. It did not specify for whom. This amendment clarifies that the electoral vote must be specific for president and vice president. The original Constitution provided that if no candidate received a majority of electoral votes, the House would decide from the candidates with the top five vote totals. This amendment reduces the candidate field to the top three vote totals. If the House delays in this selection past the fourth day of March, the elected vice president will act as president until the House selects the president. The original Constitution provided that the candidate with the second highest number of electoral votes would become vice president.

This amendment, which requires a separate vote tally for vice president, provides for selection by the U.S. Senate if no vice presidential candidate receives an electoral vote majority.

AMENDMENT 11
SUITS AGAINST THE STATES
[Ratified February 7, 1795]

The Judicial power of the United States shall not be construed to extend to any suit in law or equity, commenced or prosecuted against one of the United States by Citizens of another State, or by Citizens or Subjects of any Foreign State.

AMENDMENT 12
ELECTION OF THE PRESIDENT
[Ratified June 15, 1804]

The Electors shall meet in their respective states, and vote by ballot for President and Vice-President, one of whom, at least, shall not be an inhabitant of the same state with themselves; they shall name in their ballots the person voted for as President, and in distinct ballots the person voted for as Vice-President, and they shall make distinct lists of all persons voted for as President, and of all persons voted for as Vice-President, and of the number of votes for each, which lists they shall sign and certify, and transmit sealed to the seat of the government of the United States, directed to the President of the Senate;—The President of the Senate shall, in the presence of the Senate and House of Representatives, open all the certificates and the votes shall then be counted;—The person having the greatest number of votes for President, shall be the President, if such number be a majority of the whole number of Electors appointed; and if no person have such majority, then from the persons having the highest numbers not exceeding three on the list of those voted for as President, the House of Representatives shall choose immediately, by ballot, the President. But in choosing the President, the votes shall be taken by states, the representation from each state having one vote; a quorum for this purpose shall consist of a member or members from two-thirds of the states, and a majority of all the states shall be necessary to a choice. And if the House of Representatives shall not choose a President whenever the right of choice shall devolve upon them, before the fourth day of March next following, then the Vice-President shall act as President, as in the case of the death or other constitutional disability of the President.[11] The person having the greatest number of votes as Vice-President, shall be the Vice-President, if such a number be a majority of the whole numbers of Electors appointed, and if no person have a majority, then from the two highest numbers on the list, the Senate shall choose the Vice-President; a quorum for the purpose shall consist of two-thirds of the whole number of Senators, and a majority of the whole number shall be necessary to a choice. But no person constitutionally ineligible to the office of President shall be eligible to that of Vice-President of the United States.

AMENDMENT 13
PROHIBITION OF SLAVERY

[Ratified December 6, 1865]

SECTION 1 Neither slavery nor involuntary servitude, except as a punishment for crime whereof the party shall have been duly convicted, shall exist within the United States, or any place subject to their jurisdiction.

SECTION 2 Congress shall have power to enforce this article by appropriate legislation.

AMENDMENT 14
CITIZENSHIP, DUE PROCESS, AND EQUAL PROTECTION OF THE LAWS

[Ratified July 9, 1868]

SECTION 1 All persons born or naturalized in the United States, and subject to the jurisdiction thereof, are citizens of the United States and of the State wherein they reside. No State shall make or enforce any law which shall abridge the privileges or immunities of citizens of the United States; nor shall any State deprive any person of life, liberty, or property, without due process of law; nor deny to any person within its jurisdiction the equal protection of the laws.

SECTION 2 Representatives shall be apportioned among the several States according to their respective numbers, counting the whole number of persons in each State, excluding Indians not taxed. But when the right to vote at any election for the choice of electors for President and Vice President of the United States, Representatives in Congress, the Executive and Judicial officers of a State, or the members of the Legislature thereof, is denied to any of the male inhabitants of such State, being twenty-one years of age, and citizens of the United States, or in any way abridged, except for participation in rebellion, or other crime, the basis of representation therein shall be reduced in the proportion which the number of such male citizens shall bear to the whole number of male citizens twenty-one years of age in such State.

Amendment 13. This is the first of the three Civil War amendments. Slavery is prohibited under all circumstances. Involuntary servitude is also prohibited unless it is a punishment for a convicted crime.

Amendment 14 Section 1. This section defines the meaning of U.S. citizenship and protection of these citizenship rights. It also establishes the Equal Protection Clause, meaning that each state must guarantee fundamental rights and liberties to all of its citizens. It extended the provisions of the 5th Amendment of due process and protection of life, liberty, and property and made these applicable to the states. The due process clause has been especially important for the expansion of civil rights and liberties as the Supreme Court interpreted it in a flexible manner to recognize new rights (e.g., privacy, right of choice for abortion, etc.) and to apply the Bill of Rights against the states.

Section 2. This section changed the Three-Fifths Clause of the original Constitution. At the time of ratification of this amendment, all male citizens, 21 or older, were used to calculate representation in the House of Representatives. If a state denied the right to vote to any male 21 or older, the number of denied citizens would be deducted from the overall state total to determine representation.

This is the first time that gender was entered into the Constitution. It was not until 50 years later (in 1920 with the 19th Amendment) that women were granted the right to vote.

Section 3. This section disqualifies from federal office or elector for president or vice president anyone who rebelled or participated in an insurrection (that is, the Confederate Army after the Civil War) against the Constitution. This was specifically directed against citizens of Southern states. Congress by a 2/3 vote could override this provision.

Sections 4, 5. Section 4 covers the Civil War debts; Section 5 grants to Congress the very specific authority to create legislation that will implement and enforce the provisions of the Fourteenth Amendment.

Unlike the Bill of Rights, which is intended to protect individuals by limiting the power of the federal government, including Congress, Section 5 intends to empower Congress to create laws that will protect individuals from actions by states that violate their rights.

Although the 13th and 14th amendments were designed to end slavery, and provide citizenship, due process, and equal protection rights for freed slaves and their offspring, they were interpreted very narrowly until the 1960s. Civil rights activists had to use the court-centered, cultural change, and grassroots mobilization pathways to force legal, political, and social change to allow all individuals, regardless of color or race, to enjoy full civil rights.

Amendment 15 Sections 1, 2. This final Civil War amendment states that voting rights could not be denied by any states on account of race, color, or previous servitude. It did not mention gender. Accordingly, only male citizens 21 or over were guaranteed the right to vote by this amendment. Some states sought to defeat the intent of the amendment by adopting additional restrictions to voting rights (such as poll taxes, whites-only primaries and literacy tests) in order to block the participation of African American voters. These restrictions were eliminated in the 1960s as civil rights activists effectively used several pathways for change: court, lobbying decision-makers, and grassroots mobilization.

Amendment 16. Article I, Section 9 of the original Constitution prohibited Congress from enacting a direct tax unless in proportion to a census. Congress in 1894 passed an income tax law, levying a 2 percent tax on incomes over $4,000. In 1895, the U.S. Supreme Court in a split decision (5–4) found that the income tax was a direct tax not apportioned among the states and was thus unconstitutional. Thus, Congress proposed an amendment allowing it to enact an income tax. Once this amendment was ratified, the flow of tax money to Washington increased tremendously.

SECTION 3 No person shall be a Senator or Representative in Congress, or elector of President and Vice President, or hold any office, civil or military, under the United States, or under any State, who, having previously taken an oath, as a member of Congress, or as an officer of the United States, or as a member of any State legislature, or as an executive or judicial officer of any State, to support the Constitution of the United States, shall have engaged in insurrection or rebellion against the same, or given aid or comfort to the enemies thereof. But Congress may by a vote of two-thirds of each House, remove such disability.

SECTION 4 The validity of the public debt of the United States, authorized by law, including debts incurred for payment of pensions and bounties for services in suppressing insurrection or rebellion, shall not be questioned. But neither the United States nor any State shall assume or pay any debt or obligation incurred in aid of insurrection or rebellion against the United States, or any claim for the loss or emancipation of any slave; but all such debts, obligations and claims shall be held illegal and void.

SECTION 5 The Congress shall have power to enforce, by appropriate legislation, the provisions of this article.

AMENDMENT 15
THE RIGHT TO VOTE
[Ratified February 3, 1870]

SECTION 1 The right of citizens of the United States to vote shall not be denied or abridged by the United States or by any State on account of race, color, or previous condition of servitude.

SECTION 2 The Congress shall have power to enforce this article by appropriate legislation.

AMENDMENT 16
INCOME TAXES
[Ratified February 3, 1913]

The Congress shall have power to lay and collect taxes on incomes, from whatever source derived, without apportionment among the several States, and without regard to any census or enumeration.

AMENDMENT 17
DIRECT ELECTION OF SENATORS

[Ratified April 8, 1913]

The Senate of the United States shall be composed of two Senators from each State, elected by the people thereof, for six years; and each Senator shall have one vote. The electors in each State shall have the qualifications requisite for electors of the most numerous branch of the State legislatures.

When vacancies happen in the representation of any State in the Senate, the executive authority of such State shall issue writs of election to fill such vacancies: Provided, That the legislature of any State may empower the executive thereof to make temporary appointments until the people fill the vacancies by election as the legislature may direct.

This amendment shall not be so construed as to affect the election or term of any Senator chosen before it becomes valid as part of the Constitution.

AMENDMENT 18
PROHIBITION

[Ratified January 16, 1919. Repealed December 5, 1933 by Amendment 21]

SECTION 1   After one year from the ratification of this article the manufacture, sale, or transportation of intoxicating liquors within, the importation thereof into, or the exportation thereof from the United States and all territory subject to the jurisdiction thereof for beverage purposes is hereby prohibited.

SECTION 2   The Congress and the several States shall have concurrent power to enforce this article by appropriate legislation.

SECTION 3   This article shall be inoperative unless it shall have been ratified as an amendment to the Constitution by the legislatures of the several States, as provided in the Constitution, within seven years from the date of the submission hereof to the States by the Congress.[13]

AMENDMENT 19
FOR WOMEN'S SUFFRAGE

[Ratified August 18, 1920]

The right of the citizens of the United States to vote shall not be denied or abridged by the United States or by any State on account of sex.

Congress shall have power to enforce this article.

Amendment 17. Before this amendment, U.S. senators were selected by state legislatures. Now U.S. senators would be selected by popular vote in each state. Further, the governor of each state may fill vacancies, subject to state laws.

Amendment 18. This amendment was largely the work of the Women's Christian Temperance Union and essentially banned the manufacture, sale, or transportation of alcoholic beverages. Unintended consequences of this attempt to legislate morality were the brewing of "bathtub gin" and moonshine liquor and the involvement of organized crime in importing liquor from Canada. The 21st Amendment repealed this provision. This is also the first amendment where Congress fixed a period for ratification—7 years.

Amendment 19. Women achieved voting parity with men. It took enormous efforts by a large number of women and men to win this right, spanning over seventy years (from the call for the right to vote at the first women's rights convention in Seneca Falls, New York in 1848). Suffragists protested, sued, marched, lobbied, and were imprisoned in their battle to win equal voting rights for men and women.

Amendment 20. Called the Lame Duck amendment, this amendment fixes the dates for the end of presidential and legislative terms. A new president is elected in November, but the current president remains in office until January 20 of the following year, thus the term "lame duck." Legislative terms begin earlier, on January 3.

AMENDMENT 20
THE LAME DUCK AMENDMENT
[Ratified January 23, 1933]

SECTION 1 The terms of the President and Vice President shall end at noon on the 20th day of January, and the terms of the Senators and Representatives at noon on the 3d day of January, of the years in which such terms would have ended if this article had not been ratified; and the terms of their successors shall then begin.

SECTION 2 The Congress shall assemble at least once in every year, and such meeting shall begin at noon on the 3d day of January, unless they shall by law appoint a different day.

SECTION 3 If, at the time fixed for the beginning of the term of the President, the President elect shall have died, the Vice President elect shall become President. If a President shall not have been chosen before the time fixed for the beginning of his term, or if the President elect shall have failed to qualify, then the Vice President elect shall act as President until a President shall have qualified; and the Congress may by law provide for the case wherein neither a President elect nor a Vice President elect shall have qualified, declaring who shall then act as President, or the manner in which one who is to act shall be selected, and such person shall act accordingly until a President or Vice President shall have qualified.

SECTION 4 The Congress may by law provide for the case of the death of any of the persons from whom the House of Representatives may choose a President whenever the right of choice shall have devolved upon them, and for the case of the death of any of the persons from whom the Senate may choose a Vice President whenever the right of choice shall have devolved upon them.

SECTION 5 Sections 1 and 2 shall take effect on the 15th day of October following the ratification of this article.

SECTION 6 This article shall be inoperative unless it shall have been ratified as an amendment to the Constitution by the legislatures of three-fourths of the several States within seven years from the date of its submission.

AMENDMENT 21
REPEAL OF PROHIBITION

[Ratified December 5, 1933]

SECTION 1 The eighteenth article of amendment to the Constitution of the United States is hereby repealed.

SECTION 2 The transportation or importation into any State, Territory, or possession of the United States for delivery or use therein of intoxicating liquors, in violation of the laws thereof, is hereby prohibited.

SECTION 3 This article shall be inoperative unless it shall have been ratified as an amendment to the Constitution by conventions in the several States, as provided in the Constitution, within seven years from the date of the submission hereof to the States by the Congress.

AMENDMENT 22
NUMBER OF PRESIDENTIAL TERMS

[Ratified February 27, 1951]

SECTION 1 No person shall be elected to the office of the President more than twice, and no person who has held the office of President, or acted as President, for more than two years of a term to which some other person was elected President shall be elected to the office of the President more than once. But this article shall not apply to any person holding the office of President when this article was proposed by the Congress, and shall not prevent any person who may be holding the office of President, or acting as President, during the term within which this article becomes operative from holding the office of President or acting as President during the remainder of such term.

SECTION 2 This article shall be inoperative unless it shall have been ratified as an amendment to the Constitution by the legislatures of three-fourths of the several states within seven years from the date of its submission to the states by the Congress.

AMENDMENT 23
PRESIDENTIAL ELECTORS FOR THE DISTRICT OF COLUMBIA

[Ratified March 29, 1961]

SECTION 1 The District constituting the seat of government of the United States shall appoint in such manner as the Congress may direct:

A number of electors of President and Vice President equal to the whole number of Senators and Representatives in Congress to which the District would

Amendment 21. This unusual amendment nullified the 18th Amendment. The amendment called for the end of Prohibition unless prohibited by state laws.

This is the only instance of one amendment nullifying another. Here, governmental actions reflected the will of the majority. Initially, there was concern that the production and consumption of alcohol was detrimental to society, but as time passed, public opinion shifted. The public became less concerned about consumption and more worried about the illegal manufacture of alcohol and the subsequent growth of illegal markets and urban violence.

Amendment 22. This amendment could be called the Franklin D. Roosevelt amendment. It was FDR who broke the previously unwritten rule, established by George Washington, of serving no more than two terms as president. Democrat Roosevelt won election to an unprecedented four terms as president (although he died before completing his fourth term). When the Republicans took control of the Congress in 1948, they pushed through the 22nd Amendment, limiting the U.S. president to a lifetime of two full four-year terms of office.

Amendment 23. This amendment gave electoral votes to the residents of Washington, D.C., which is not a state and thus not included in the original scheme of state electoral votes. Currently, Washington, D.C., has 3 electoral votes, bringing the total of presidential electoral votes to 538. Residents of Washington, D.C. do not, however, have voting representation in Congress. Puerto Ricans are citizens of the U.S. but have no electoral votes. Both Washington, D.C. and Puerto Rico are represented in Congress by non-voting delegates.

Amendment 24. The poll tax was a procedure used mostly in southern states to discourage poor white and black voters from registering to vote. Essentially, one would have to pay a tax to register to vote. The tax was around $34/year (sometimes retroactive), which amounted to a great deal of money to the poor, serving to disenfranchise a great proportion of the poor. As part of the fight for universal voting rights for all, the poll tax was abolished. Literacy tests, another device to disqualify voters, were abolished by the Voting Rights Act of 1965.

By banning this tax (coupled with other civil rights reforms), the United States delivered what the civil rights amendments promised – full voting rights for all citizens regardless of race.

Amendment 25. President Woodrow Wilson's final year in office was marked by serious illness. It is rumored that his wife acted as president. There was no constitutional provision to cover an incapacitating illness of a president. This amendment provides a procedure for this eventuality. The president can inform congressional leaders of his/her incapacitation, and the vice president then takes over. When the president recovers, he/she can inform congressional leaders and resume office.

The amendment also recognizes that the president may not be able or wish to indicate this lack of capacity. In this case, the vice president and a majority of cabinet members can inform congressional leaders, and the vice president takes over. When the president informs congressional leadership that he/she is back in form, he/she resumes the presidency unless the vice president and a majority of the cabinet members disagree. Then Congress must decide who is to be president. The likelihood that this procedure will ever be used is relatively small.

The most immediate importance of this amendment concerns the office of vice president. The original Constitution did not address the issue of a vacancy in this office. This amendment was ratified in 1967, only a few years before it was needed. In 1973, the sitting vice president, Spiro Agnew, resigned his office. Under the provisions of this amendment, President Nixon nominated Gerald Ford as vice president. As a former member of the House, Ford was quickly approved by the Congress. But a year later, President Nixon also resigned. Now Vice President Ford became President Ford, and he in turn appointed Nelson Rockefeller as the new vice president. For the first time in our history, neither the president nor the vice president were selected by the electoral college after a national election.

be entitled if it were a state, but in no event more than the least populous state; they shall be in addition to those appointed by the states, but they shall be considered, for the purposes of the election of President and Vice President, to be electors appointed by a state; and they shall meet in the District and perform such duties as provided by the twelfth article of amendment.

SECTION 2   The Congress shall have power to enforce this article by appropriate legislation.

AMENDMENT 24
THE ANTI-POLL TAX AMENDMENT
[Ratified January 23, 1964]

SECTION 1   The right of citizens of the United States to vote in any primary or other election for President or Vice President, for electors for President or Vice President, or for Senator or Representative in Congress, shall not be denied or abridged by the United States or any state by reason of failure to pay any poll tax or other tax.

SECTION 2   The Congress shall have power to enforce this article by appropriate legislation.

AMENDMENT 25
PRESIDENTIAL DISABILITY, VICE PRESIDENTIAL VACANCIES
[Ratified February 10, 1967]

SECTION 1   In case of the removal of the President from office or of his death or resignation, the Vice President shall become President.

SECTION 2   Whenever there is a vacancy in the office of the Vice President, the President shall nominate a Vice President who shall take the office upon confirmation by a majority vote of both Houses of Congress.

SECTION 3   Whenever the President transmits to the President pro tempore of the Senate and the Speaker of the House of Representatives his written declaration that he is unable to discharge the powers and duties of his office, and until he transmits to them a written declaration to the contrary, such powers and duties shall be discharged by the Vice President as Acting President.

SECTION 4   Whenever the Vice President and a majority of either the principal officers of the executive departments, or of such other body as Congress may by law provide, transmit to the President pro tempore of the Senate and the Speaker of the House of Representatives their written declaration that the President is unable to discharge the powers and duties of his office, the Vice President shall immediately assume the powers and duties of the office as Acting President.

Thereafter, when the President transmits to the President pro tempore of the Senate and the Speaker of the House of Representatives his written declaration that no inability exists, he shall resume the powers and duties of his office unless the Vice President and a majority of either the principal officers of the executive department, or of such other body as Congress may by law provide, transmit within four days to the President pro tempore of the Senate and the Speaker of the House of Representatives their written declaration that the President is unable to discharge the powers and duties of his office. Thereupon Congress shall decide the issue, assembling within forty-eight hours for that purpose if not in session. If the Congress, within twenty-one days after receipt of the latter written declaration, or, if Congress is not in session, within twenty-one days after Congress is required to assemble, determines by two-thirds vote of both Houses that the President is unable to discharge the powers and duties of his office, the Vice President shall continue to discharge the same as Acting President; otherwise, the President shall resume the powers and duties of his office.

AMENDMENT 26
EIGHTEEN-YEAR-OLD VOTE
[Ratified July 1, 1971]

SECTION 1   The right of citizens of the United States, who are 18 years of age or older, to vote, shall not be denied or abridged by the United States or by any state on account of age.

SECTION 2   The Congress shall have power to enforce this article by appropriate legislation.

AMENDMENT 27
CONGRESSIONAL SALARIES
[Ratified May 7, 1992]

No law varying the compensation for the services of the Senators and Representatives shall take effect until an election of Representatives shall have intervened.

Amendment 26 Sections 1, 2. During the Vietnam War, 18 year olds were being drafted and sent out to possibly die in the service of their country. Yet they did not even have the right to vote. This incongruity led to the 26th Amendment, which lowered the legal voting age from 21 to 18.

Before the passage of this amendment, young people, being denied the ability to express themselves peacefully with the vote, often felt frustrated with their inability to express their concerns and influence public policy. With the passage of this amendment, those citizens over the age of 18 could pursue the election-centered pathway (and others) to instigate change.

Amendment 27. This is a "sleeper" amendment that was part of 12 amendments originally submitted by the first Congress to the states for ratification. The states only ratified 10 of the 12, which collectively became known as the Bill of Rights. But since Congress did not set a time limit for ratification, the other two amendments remained on the table. Much to the shock of the body politic, in 1992, 3/4 of the states ratified original amendment 12 of 12. This reflected the disgust of seeing Congress continuing to increase its salary and benefits. The amendment delays any increase of compensation for at least one election cycle.

1 Modified by the 16th Amendment	6 Modified by the 16th Amendment	11 Changed by the 20th Amendment
2 Replaced by Section 2, 14th Amendment	7 Changed by the 12th and 20th Amendments	12 Changed by the 26th Amendment
3 Repealed by the 17th Amendment	8 Modified by the 25th Amendment	13 Repealed by the 21st Amendment
4 Modified by the 17th Amendment	9 Modified by the 11th Amendment	
5 Changed by the 20th Amendment	10 Repealed by the 13th Amendment	

APPENDIX 3

The Federalist, No. 10, James Madison

To the People of the State of New York: Among the numerous advantages promised by a well-constructed union, none deserves to be more accurately developed than its tendency to break and control the violence of faction. The friend of popular governments, never finds himself so much alarmed for their character and fate, as when he contemplates their propensity of this dangerous vice. He will not fail, therefore, to set a due value on any plan which, without violating the principles to which he is attached, provides a proper cure for it. The instability, injustice, and confusion introduced into the public councils, have, in truth, been the mortal diseases under which popular governments have everywhere perished; as they continue to be the favorite and fruitful topics from which the adversaries to liberty derive their most specious declamations. The valuable improvements made by the American constitutions on the popular models, both ancient and modern, cannot certainly be too much admired; but it would be an unwarrantable partiality, to contend that they have as effectually obviated the danger on this side, as was wished and expected. Complaints are everywhere heard from our most considerate and virtuous citizens, equally the friends of public and private faith, and of public and personal liberty, that our governments are too unstable; that the public good is disregarded in the conflicts of rival parties; and that measures are too often decided, not according to the rules of justice, and the rights of the minor party, but by the superior force of an interested and overbearing majority. However anxiously we may wish that these complaints had no foundation, the evidence of known facts will not permit us to deny that they are in some degree true. It will be found, indeed, on a candid review of our situation, that some of the distresses under which we labor have been erroneously charged on the operations of our governments; but it will be found, at the same time, that other causes will not alone account for many of our heaviest misfortunes; and, particularly, for that prevailing and increasing distrust of public engagements, and alarm for private rights, which are echoed from one end of the continent to the other. These must be chiefly, if not wholly, effects of the unsteadiness and injustice, with which a factious spirit has tainted our public administrations.

By a faction, I understand a number of citizens, whether amounting to a majority of the whole, who are united and actuated by some common impulse of passion, or of interest, adverse to the rights of other citizens, or to the permanent and aggregate interests of the community.

There are two methods of curing the mischiefs of faction: the one, by removing its causes; the other, by controlling its effects.

There are again two methods of removing the causes of faction: the one, by destroying the liberty which is essential to its existence; the other, by giving to every citizen the same opinions, the same passions, and the same interests.

It could never be more truly said, than of the first remedy, that it was worse than the disease. Liberty is to faction what air is to fire, an aliment without which it instantly expires. But it could not be a less folly to abolish liberty, which is essential to political life, because it nourishes faction, than it would be to wish the annihilation of air, which is essential to animal life, because it imparts to fire its destructive agency.

The second expedient is as impracticable, as the first would be unwise. As long as the reason of man continues fallible, and he is at liberty to exercise it, different opinions will be formed. As long as the connection subsists between his reason and his self-love, his opinions and his passions will have a reciprocal influence on each other; and the former will be objects to which the latter will attach themselves. The diversity in the faculties of men, from which the rights of property originate, is not less an insuperable obstacle to an uniformity of interests. The protection of these faculties is the first object of government. From the protection of different and unequal faculties of acquiring property, the possession of different degrees and kinds of property immediately results; and from the influence of these on the sentiments and views of the respective proprietors, ensues a division of the society into different interests and parties.

The latent causes of faction are thus sown in the nature of man; and we see them everywhere brought into different degrees of activity, according to the different circumstances of civil society. A zeal for different opinions concerning religion, concerning government, and many other points, as well of speculation as of practice; an attachment to different leaders ambitiously contending for preeminence and power; or to persons of other descriptions whose fortunes have been interesting to the human passions, have, in turn, divided mankind into parties, inflamed them with mutual animosity, and rendered them much more disposed to vex and oppress each other, than to cooperate for their common good. So strong is this propensity of mankind, to fall into mutual animosities, that where no substantial occasion presents itself, the most frivolous and fanciful distinctions have been sufficient to kindle their unfriendly passions and excite their most violent conflicts. But the most common and durable source of factions, has been the various and unequal distribution of property. Those who hold, and those who are without property, have ever formed distinct interests in society. Those who are creditors, and those who are debtors, fall under a like discrimination. A landed interest, a manufacturing interest, a mercantile interest, a moneyed interest, with many lesser interests, grow up of necessity in civilized nations, and divide them into different classes, actuated by different sentiments and views. The regulation of these various and interfering interests forms the principal task of modern legislation, and involves the spirit of the party and faction in the necessary and ordinary operations of the government.

No man is allowed to be a judge in his own cause; because his interest will certainly bias his judgment, and, not improbably, corrupt his integrity. With equal, nay, with greater reason, a body of men are unfit to be both judges and parties at the same time; yet what are many of the most important acts of legislation, but so many judicial determinations, not indeed concerning the right of single persons, but concerning the rights of large bodies of citizens? And what are the different classes of legislators, but advocates and parties to the causes which they determine? Is a law proposed concerning private debts? It is a question to which the creditors are parties on one side, and the debtors on the other. Justice ought to hold the balance between them. Yet the parties are, and must be, themselves the judges; and the most numerous party, or, in other words, the most powerful faction, must be expected to prevail. Shall domestic manufacturers be encouraged, and in what degree, by restrictions on foreign manufacturers? Are questions which would be differently decided by the landed and the manufacturing classes; and probably by neither with a sole regard to justice and the public good. The apportionment of taxes, on the various descriptions of property, is an act which seems to require the most exact impartiality; yet there is, perhaps, no legislative act, in which greater opportunity and temptation are given to a predominant party to trample on the rules of justice. Every shilling, with which they overburden the inferior number, is a shilling saved to their own pockets.

It is in vain to say, that enlightened statesmen will be able to adjust these clashing interests, and render them all subservient to the public good. Enlightened statesmen will not always be at the helm, nor, in many cases, can such an adjustment be made at all, without taking into view indirect and remote considerations, which will rarely prevail over the immediate interest which one party may find in disregarding the rights of another, or the good of the whole.

The inference to which we are brought is, that the causes of faction cannot be removed; and that relief is only to be sought in the means of controlling its effects.

If a faction consists of less than a majority, relief is supplied by the republican principle, which enables the majority to defeat its sinister views, by regular vote. It may clog the administration, it may convulse the society; but it will be unable to execute and mask its violence under the forms of the Constitution. When a majority is included in a faction, the form of popular government, on the other hand, enables it to sacrifice to its ruling passion or interest, both the public good and the rights of other citizens. To secure the public good, and private rights, against the danger of such a faction, and at the same time to preserve the spirit and the form of popular government, is then the great object to which our inquiries are directed. Let me add, that it is the great desideratum, by which alone this form of government can be rescued from the opprobrium under which it has so long laboured, and be recommended to the esteem and adoption of mankind.

By what means is this object attainable? Evidently by one of two only. Either the existence of the same passion or interest in a majority, at the same time, must be prevented; or the majority, having such coexistent passion or interest, must be rendered, by their number and local situation, unable to concert and carry into effect schemes of oppression. If the impulse and the opportunity be suffered to coincide, we well know that neither moral nor religious motives can be relied on as an adequate control. They are not found to be such on the injustice and violence of individuals, and lose their efficacy in proportion to the number combined together; that is, in proportion as their efficacy becomes needful.

From this view of the subject, it may be concluded, that a pure democracy, by which I mean a society consisting of a small number of citizens, who assemble and administer the government in person, can admit of no cure for the mischiefs of faction. A common passion or interest will, in almost every case, be felt by a majority of the whole; a communication and concert, results from the form of government itself; and there is nothing to check the inducements to sacrifice the weaker party, or an obnoxious individual. Hence, it is, that such democracies have ever been spectacles of turbulence and contention; have ever been found incompatible with personal security, or the rights of property; and have in general been as short in their lives, as they have been violent in their deaths. Theoretic politicians, who have patronized this species of government, have erroneously supposed, that by reducing mankind to a perfect equality in their political rights, they would, at the same time be perfectly equalized and assimilated in their possessions, their opinions, and their passions.

A republic, by which I mean a government in which the scheme of representation takes place, opens a different prospect, and promises the cure for which we are seeking. Let us examine the points in which it varies from pure democracy, and we shall comprehend both the nature of the cure and the efficacy which it must derive from the union.

The two great points of difference, between a democracy and a republic, are, first, the delegation of the government, in the latter, to a small number of citizens, elected by the rest; secondly, the greater number of citizens, and greater sphere of country, over which the latter may be extended.

The effect of the first difference is, on the one hand, to refine and enlarge the public views, by passing them through the medium of a chosen body of citizens, whose wisdom may best discern the true interest of their country, and whose patriotism and love of justice, will be least likely to sacrifice it to temporary or partial considerations. Under such a regulation, it may well happen, that the public voice, pronounced by the representatives of the people, will be more consonant to the public good, than if pronounced by the people themselves, convened for the purpose. On the other hand the effect may be inverted. Men of factious tempers, of local prejudices, or of sinister designs, may by intrigue, by corruption, or by other means, first obtain the suffrages, and then betray the interest of the people. The question resulting is, whether small or extensive republics are most favourable to the election of proper guardians of the public weal; and it is clearly decided in favour of the latter by two obvious considerations.

In the first place, it is to be remarked that, however small the republic may be, the representatives must be raised to a certain number, in order to guard against the cabals of a few; and that however large it may be, they must be limited to a certain number, in order to guard against the confusion of a multitude. Hence, the number of representatives in the two cases not being in proportion to that of the constituents, and being proportionally greatest in the small republic, it follows, that if the proportion of fit characters be not less in the large than in the small republic, the former will present a greater option, and consequently a greater probability of a fit choice.

In the next place, as each representative will be chosen by a greater number of citizens in the large than in the small republic, it will be more difficult for unworthy candidates to practice with success the vicious arts, by which elections are too often carried; and the suffrages of the people being more free, will be more likely to centre in men who possess the most attractive merit, and the most diffusive and established characters.

It must be confessed, that in this, as in most other cases, there is a mean, on both sides of which inconveniences will be found to lie. By enlarging too much the number of electors, you render the representatives too little acquainted with all their local circumstances and lesser interests; as by reducing it too much, you render him unduly attached to these, and too little fit to comprehend and pursue great and national objects. The federal constitution forms a happy combination in this respect; the great and aggregate interests being referred to the national, the local and particular to the state legislatures.

The other point of difference is, the greater number of citizens, and extent of territory, which may be brought within the compass of republican, than of democratic government; and it is this circumstance principally which renders factious combinations less to be dreaded in the former, than in the latter. The smaller the society, the fewer probably will be the distinct parties and interests composing it; the fewer the distinct parties and interests, the more frequently will a majority be found of the same party; and the smaller the number of individuals composing a majority, and the smaller the compass within which they are placed, the more easily will they concert and execute their plans of oppression. Extend the sphere, and you take in a greater variety of parties and interests; you make it less probable that a majority of the whole will have a common motive to invade the rights of other citizens; or if such a common motive exists, it will be more difficult for all who feel it to discover their own strength, and to act in unison with each other. Besides other impediments, it may be remarked, that where there is a consciousness of unjust or dishonourable purposes, communication is always checked by distrust, in proportion to the number whose concurrence is necessary.

Hence, it clearly appears, that the same advantage, which a republic has over a democracy, in controlling the effects of faction, is enjoyed by a large over a small republic—is enjoyed by the union over the states composing it. Does this advantage consist in the substitution of representatives, whose enlightened views and virtuous sentiments render them superior to local prejudices, and to schemes of injustice? It will not be denied that the representation of the union will be most likely to possess these requisite endowments. Does it consist in the greater security afforded by a greater variety of parties, against the event of any one party being able to outnumber and oppress the rest? In an equal degree does the increased variety of parties, comprised within the union, increase the security? Does it, in fine, consist in the greater obstacles opposed to the concert and accomplishment of the secret wishes of an unjust and interested majority? Here, again, the extent of the union gives it the most palpable advantage.

The influence of factious leaders may kindle a flame within their particular states, but will be unable to spread a general conflagration through the other states; a religious sect may degenerate into a political faction in a part of the confederacy; but the variety of sects dispersed over the entire face of it, must secure the national councils against any danger from that source: a rage for paper money, for an abolition of debts, for an equal division of property, or for any other improper or wicked project, will be less apt to pervade the whole body of the union than a particular member of it; in the same proportion as such a malady is more likely to taint a particular county or district, than an entire state.

In the extent and proper structure of the union, therefore, we behold a republican remedy for the diseases most incident to republican government. And according to the degree of pleasure and pride we feel in being republicans, ought to be our zeal in cherishing the spirit, and supporting the character of federalists. ∎

APPENDIX 4

The Federalist, No. 51, James Madison

To what expedient, then, shall we finally resort, for maintaining in practice the necessary partition of power among the several departments as laid down in the Constitution? The only answer that can be given is that as all these exterior provisions are found to be inadequate the defect must be supplied, by so contriving the interior structure of the government as that its several constituent parts may, by their mutual relations, be the means of keeping each other in their proper places. Without presuming to undertake a full development of this important idea I will hazard a few general observations which may perhaps place it in a clearer light, and enable us to form a more correct judgment of the principles and structure of the government planned by the convention.

In order to lay a due foundation for that separate and distinct exercise of the different powers of government, which to a certain extent is admitted on all hands to be essential to the preservation of liberty, it is evident that each department should have a will of its own; and consequently should be so constituted that the members of each should have as little agency as possible in the appointment of the members of the others. Were this principle rigorously adhered to, it would require that all the appointments for the supreme executive, legislative, and judiciary magistracies should be drawn from the same fountain of authority, the people, through channels having no communication whatever with one another. Perhaps such a plan of constructing the several departments would be less difficult in practice than it may in contemplation appear. Some difficulties, however, and some additional expense would attend the execution of it. Some deviations, therefore, from the principle must be admitted. In the constitution of the judiciary department in particular, it might be inexpedient to insist rigorously on the principle: first, because peculiar qualifications being essential in the members, the primary consideration ought to be to select that mode of choice which best secures these qualifications; second, because the permanent tenure by which the appointments are held in that department must soon destroy all sense of dependence on the authority conferring them.

It is equally evident that the members of each department should be as little dependent as possible on those of the others for the emoluments annexed to their offices. Were the executive magistrate, or the judges, not independent of the legislature in this particular, their independence in every other would be merely nominal.

But the great security against a gradual concentration of the several powers in the same department consists in giving to those who administer each department the necessary constitutional means and personal motives to resist encroachments of the others. The provision for defense must in this, as in all other cases, be made commensurate to the danger of attack. Ambition must be made to counteract ambition. The interest of the man must be connected with the constitutional rights of the place. It may be a reflection on human nature that such devices should be necessary to control the abuses of government. But what is government itself but the greatest of all reflections on human nature? If men were angels, no government would be necessary. If angels were to govern men, neither external nor internal controls on government would be necessary. In framing a government which is to be administered by men over men, the great difficulty lies in this: you must first enable the government to control the governed; and in the next place oblige it to control itself. A dependence on the people is, no doubt, the primary control on the government; but experience has taught mankind the necessity of auxiliary precautions.

This policy of supplying, by opposite and rival interests, the defect of better motives, might be traced through the whole system of human affairs, private as well as public. We see it particularly displayed in all the subordinate distributions of power, where the constant aim is to divide and arrange the several offices in such a manner as that each may be a check on the other—that the private interest of every individual may be a sentinel over the public rights. These inventions of prudence cannot be less requisite in the distribution of the supreme powers of the State.

But it is not possible to give to each department an equal power of self-defense. In republican government, the legislative authority necessarily predominates. The remedy for this inconveniency is to divide the legislature into different branches; and to render them, by modes of election and different principles of action, as little connected with each other as the nature of their common functions and their common dependence on the society will admit. It may even be necessary to guard against dangerous encroachments by still further precautions. As the weight of the legislative authority requires that it should be thus divided, the weakness of the executive may require, on the other hand, that it should be fortified. An absolute negative on the legislature appears, at first view, to be the natural defense with which the executive magistrate should be armed. But perhaps it would be neither altogether safe nor alone sufficient. On ordinary occasions it might not be exerted with the requisite firmness, and on extraordinary occasions it might be perfidiously abused. May not this defect of an absolute negative be supplied by some qualified connection between this weaker department and the weaker branch of the stronger department, by which the latter may be led to support the constitutional rights of the former, without being too much detached from the rights of its own department?

If the principles on which these observations are founded be just, as I persuade myself they are, and they be applied as a criterion to the several State constitutions, and to the federal Constitution, it will be found that if the latter does not perfectly correspond with them, the former are infinitely less able to bear such a test.

There are, moreover, two considerations particularly applicable to the federal system of America, which place that system in a very interesting point of view.

First. In a single republic, all the power surrendered by the people is submitted to the administration of a single government; and the usurpations are guarded against by a division of the government into distinct and separate departments. In the compound republic of America, the power surrendered by the people is first divided between two distinct governments, and then the portion allotted to each subdivided among distinct and separate departments. Hence a double security arises to the rights of the people. The different governments will control each other, at the same time that each will be controlled by itself.

Second. It is of great importance in a republic not only to guard the society against the oppression of its rulers, but to guard one part of the society against the injustice of the other part. Different interests necessarily exist in different classes of citizens. If a majority be united by a common interest, the rights of the minority will be insecure. There are but two methods of providing against this evil: the one by creating a will in the community independent of the majority—that is, of the society itself; the other, by comprehending in the society so many separate descriptions of citizens as will render an unjust combination of a majority of the whole very improbable, if not impracticable. The first method prevails in all governments possessing an hereditary or self-appointed authority. This, at best, is but a precarious security; because a power independent of the society may as well espouse the unjust views of the major as the rightful interests of the minor party, and may possibly be turned against both parties. The second method will be exemplified in the federal republic of the United States. Whilst all authority in it will be derived from and dependent on the society, the society itself will be broken into so many parts, interests and classes of citizens, that the rights of individuals, or of the minority, will be in little danger from interested combinations of the majority. In a free government the security for civil rights must be the same as that for religious rights. It consists in the one case in the multiplicity of interests, and in the other in the multiplicity of sects. The degree of security

in both cases will depend on the number of interests and sects; and this may be presumed to depend on the extent of country and number of people comprehended under the same government. This view of the subject must particularly recommend a proper federal system to all the sincere and considerate friends of republican government, since it shows that in exact proportion as the territory of the Union may be formed into more circumscribed Confederacies, or States, oppressive combinations of a majority will be facilitated; the best security, under the republican forms, for the rights of every class of citizen, will be diminished; and consequently the stability and independence of some member of the government, the only other security, must be proportionally increased. Justice is the end of government. It is the end of civil society. It ever has been and ever will be pursued until it be obtained, or until liberty be lost in the pursuit. In a society under the forms of which the stronger faction can readily unite and oppress the weaker, anarchy may as truly be said to reign as in a state of nature, where the weaker individual is not secured against the violence of the stronger; and as, in the latter state, even the stronger individuals are prompted, by the uncertainty of their condition, to submit to a government which may protect the weak as well as themselves; so, in the former state, will the more powerful factions or parties be gradually induced, by a like motive, to wish for a government which will protect all parties, the weaker as well as the more powerful. It can be little doubted that if the State of Rhode Island was separated from the Confederacy and left to itself, the insecurity of rights under the popular form of government within such narrow limits would be displayed by such reiterated oppressions of factious majorities that some power altogether independent of the people would soon be called for by the voice of the very factions whose misrule had proved the necessity to it. In the extended republic of the United States, and among the great variety of interests, parties, and sects which it embraces, a coalition of a majority of the whole society could seldom take place on any other principles than those of justice and the general good; whilst there being thus less danger to a minor from the will of a major party, there must be less pretext, also, to provide for the security of the former, by introducing into the government a will not dependent on the latter, or, in other words, a will independent of the society itself. It is no less certain that it is important, notwithstanding the contrary opinions which have been entertained that the larger the society, provided it lie within a practicable sphere, the more duly capable it will be of self-government. And happily for the republican cause, the practicable sphere may be carried to a very great extent by a judicious modification and mixture of the federal principle. ■

APPENDIX 5

The Gettysburg Address, Abraham Lincoln

Gettysburg, Pennsylvania
November 19, 1863

Four score and seven years ago our fathers brought forth on this continent, a new nation, conceived in Liberty, and dedicated to the proposition that all men are created equal.

Now we are engaged in a great civil war, testing whether that nation, or any nation so conceived and so dedicated, can long endure. We are met on a great battle-field of that war. We have come to dedicate a portion of that field, as a final resting place for those who here gave their lives that that nation might live. It is altogether fitting and proper that we should do this.

But, in a larger sense, we can not dedicate—we can not consecrate—we can not hallow—this ground. The brave men, living and dead, who struggled here, have consecrated it, far above our poor power to add or detract. The world will little note, nor long remember what we say here, but it can never forget what they did here. It is for us the living, rather, to be dedicated here to the unfinished work which they who fought here have thus far so nobly advanced. It is rather for us to be here dedicated to the great task remaining before us—that from these honored dead we take increased devotion to that cause for which they gave the last full measure of devotion—that we here highly resolve that these dead shall not have died in vain—that this nation, under God, shall have a new birth of freedom—and that government of the people, by the people, for the people, shall not perish from the earth. ▮

SOURCE: *Collected Works of Abraham Lincoln*, edited by Roy P. Basler. The text above is from the so-called "Bliss Copy," one of several versions which Lincoln wrote, and believed to be the final version. For additional versions, you may search *The Collected Works of Abraham Lincoln* through the courtesy of the Abraham Lincoln Association.

Related Links

Battlefield Map (Library of Congress)
Civil War Institute (Gettysburg College)
Gettysburg Address Essay Contest (Lincoln Fellowship of Pennsylvania)
Gettysburg Address Exhibit (Library of Congress)
Gettysburg Address Eyewitness (National Public Radio)
Gettysburg Address News Article (New York Times)
Gettysburg Address Teacher Resource (C-SPAN)
Gettysburg Civil War Photographs (Library of Congress)
Gettysburg Discussion Group (Bob & Dennis Lawrence)
Gettysburg Events (NPS)
Gettysburg National Military Park (NPS)
Letter of Invitation to Lincoln (Library of Congress)
Lincoln at Gettysburg
Lincoln at Gettysburg Photo Tour
Lincoln Fellowship of Pennsylvania
Lincoln's Invitation to Stay Overnight (Library of Congress)
Lincoln's Letter from Edward Everett (Library of Congress)
Photograph of Lincoln at Gettysburg (Library of Congress)
Reading of the Gettysburg Address (NPR)
Recollections of Lincoln at Gettysburg (Bob Cooke)
Response to a Serenade
Seminary Ridge Historic Preservation Foundation
The Gettysburg Powerpoint Presentation (Peter Norvig)
Wills House

Related Books

Graham, Kent. *November: Lincoln's Elegy at Gettysburg.* Indiana University Press, 2001.

Hoch, Bradley R. and Boritt, Gabor S. *The Lincoln Trail in Pennsylvania.* Pennsylvania State University Press, 2001.

Kunhardt, Philip B., Jr. *A New Birth of Freedom—Lincoln at Gettysburg.* Boston: Little, Brown, 1983.

Wills, Garry. *Lincoln at Gettysburg: The Words That Remade America.* Touchstone Books, 1993.

APPENDIX 6

I Have a Dream, Martin Luther King

In 1950's America, the equality of man envisioned by the Declaration of Independence was far from a reality. People of color, blacks, Hispanics, Orientals, were discriminated against in many ways, both overt and covert. The 1950's were a turbulent time in America, when racial barriers began to come down due to Supreme Court decisions, like *Brown* v. *Board of Education*; and due to an increase in the activism of blacks, fighting for equal rights.

Martin Luther King, Jr., a Baptist minister, was a driving force in the push for racial equality in the 1950's and the 1960's. In 1963, King and his staff focused on Birmingham, Alabama. They marched and protested non-violently, raising the ire of local officials who sicced water cannon and police dogs on the marchers, whose ranks included teenagers and children. The bad publicity and break-down of business forced the white leaders of Birmingham to concede to some anti-segregation demands.

Thrust into the national spotlight in Birmingham, where he was arrested and jailed, King organized a massive march on Washington, DC, on August 28, 1963. On the steps of the Lincoln Memorial, he evoked the name of Lincoln in his "I Have a Dream" speech, which is credited with mobilizing supporters of desegregation and prompted the 1964 Civil Rights Act. The next year, King was awarded the Nobel Peace Prize.

The following is the exact text of the spoken speech, transcribed from recordings.

I am happy to join with you today in what will go down in history as the greatest demonstration for freedom in the history of our nation.

Five score years ago, a great American, in whose symbolic shadow we stand today, signed the Emancipation Proclamation. This momentous decree came as a great beacon light of hope to millions of Negro slaves who had been seared in the flames of withering injustice. It came as a joyous daybreak to end the long night of their captivity.

But one hundred years later, the Negro still is not free. One hundred years later, the life of the Negro is still sadly crippled by the manacles of segregation and the chains of discrimination. One hundred years later, the Negro lives on a lonely island of poverty in the midst of a vast ocean of material prosperity. One hundred years later, the Negro is still languishing in the corners of American society and finds himself an exile in his own land. So we have come here today to dramatize a shameful condition.

In a sense we have come to our nation's capital to cash a check. When the architects of our republic wrote the magnificent words of the Constitution and the Declaration of Independence, they were signing a promissory note to which every American was to fall heir. This note was a promise that all men, yes, black men as well as white men, would be guaranteed the unalienable rights of life, liberty, and the pursuit of happiness.

It is obvious today that America has defaulted on this promissory note insofar as her citizens of color are concerned. Instead of honoring this sacred obligation, America has given the Negro people a bad check, a check which has come back marked "insufficient funds." But we refuse to believe that the bank of justice is bankrupt. We refuse to believe that there are insufficient funds in the great vaults of opportunity of this nation. So we have come to cash this check — a check that will give us upon demand the riches of freedom and the security of justice. We have also come to this hallowed spot to remind America of the fierce urgency of now. This is no time to engage in the luxury of cooling off or to take the tranquilizing drug of gradualism. Now is the time to make real the promises of democracy. Now is the time to rise from the dark and desolate valley of segregation to the sunlit path of racial justice. Now is the time to lift our nation from the quicksands of racial injustice to the solid rock of brotherhood. Now is the time to make justice a reality for all of God's children.

It would be fatal for the nation to overlook the urgency of the moment. This sweltering summer of the Negro's legitimate discontent will not pass until there is an invigorating autumn of freedom and equality. Nineteen sixty-three is not an end, but a beginning. Those who hope that the Negro needed to blow off steam and will now be content will have a rude awakening if the nation returns to business as usual. There will be neither rest nor tranquility in America until the Negro is granted his citizenship rights. The whirlwinds of revolt will continue to shake the foundations of our nation until the bright day of justice emerges.

But there is something that I must say to my people who stand on the warm threshold which leads into the palace of justice. In the process of gaining our rightful place we must not be guilty of wrongful deeds. Let us not seek to satisfy our thirst for freedom by drinking from the cup of bitterness and hatred.

We must forever conduct our struggle on the high plane of dignity and discipline. We must not allow our creative protest to degenerate into physical violence. Again and again we must rise to the majestic heights of meeting physical force with soul force.

The marvelous new militancy which has engulfed the Negro community must not lead us to distrust of all white people, for many of our white brothers, as evidenced by their presence here today, have come to realize that their destiny is tied up with our destiny and their freedom is inextricably bound to our freedom. We cannot walk alone.

As we walk, we must make the pledge that we shall march ahead. We cannot turn back. There are those who are asking the devotees of civil rights, "When will you be satisfied?" We can never be satisfied as long as the Negro is the victim of the unspeakable horrors of police brutality. We can never be satisfied, as long as our bodies, heavy with the fatigue of travel, cannot gain lodging in the motels of the highways and the hotels of the cities. We can never be satisfied as long as a Negro in Mississippi cannot vote and a Negro in New York believes he has nothing for which to vote. No, no, we are not satisfied, and we will not be satisfied until justice rolls down like waters and righteousness like a mighty stream.

I am not unmindful that some of you have come here out of great trials and tribulations. Some of you have come fresh from narrow jail cells. Some of you have come from areas where your quest for freedom left you battered by the storms of persecution and staggered by the winds of police brutality. You have been the veterans of creative suffering. Continue to work with the faith that unearned suffering is redemptive.

Go back to Mississippi, go back to Alabama, go back to South Carolina, go back to Georgia, go back to Louisiana, go back to the slums and ghettos of our northern cities, knowing that somehow this situation can and will be changed. Let us not wallow in the valley of despair.

I say to you today, my friends, even though we face the difficulties of today and tomorrow, I still have a dream. It is a dream deeply rooted in the American dream.

I have a dream that one day this nation will rise up and live out the true meaning of its creed: "We hold these truths to be self-evident: that all men are created equal."

I have a dream that one day on the red hills of Georgia the sons of former slaves and the sons of former slave owners will be able to sit down together at the table of brotherhood.

I have a dream that one day even the state of Mississippi, a state sweltering with the heat of injustice, sweltering with the heat of oppression, will be transformed into an oasis of freedom and justice.

I have a dream that my four little children will one day live in a nation where they will not be judged by the color of their skin but by the content of their character.

I have a dream today.

I have a dream that one day, down in Alabama, with its vicious racists, with its governor having his lips dripping with the words of interposition and nullification; one day right there in Alabama, little black boys and black girls will be able to join hands with little white boys and white girls as sisters and brothers.

I have a dream today.

I have a dream that one day every valley shall be exalted, every hill and mountain shall be made low, the rough places will be made plain, and the crooked places will be made straight, and the glory of the Lord shall be revealed, and all flesh shall see it together.

This is our hope. This is the faith that I go back to the South with. With this faith we will be able to hew out of the mountain of despair a stone of hope. With this faith we will be able to transform the jangling discords of our nation into a beautiful symphony of brotherhood. With this faith we will be able to work together, to pray together, to struggle together, to go to jail together, to stand up for freedom together, knowing that we will be free one day.

This will be the day when all of God's children will be able to sing with a new meaning, "My country, 'tis of thee, sweet land of liberty, of thee I sing. Land where my fathers died, land of the pilgrim's pride, from every mountainside, let freedom ring."

And if America is to be a great nation this must become true. So let freedom ring from the prodigious hilltops of New Hampshire. Let freedom ring from the mighty mountains of New York. Let freedom ring from the heightening Alleghenies of Pennsylvania!

Let freedom ring from the snowcapped Rockies of Colorado!

Let freedom ring from the curvaceous slopes of California!

But not only that; let freedom ring from Stone Mountain of Georgia!

Let freedom ring from Lookout Mountain of Tennessee!

Let freedom ring from every hill and molehill of Mississippi. From every mountainside, let freedom ring.

And when this happens, when we allow freedom to ring, when we let it ring from every village and every hamlet, from every state and every city, we will be able to speed up that day when all of God's children, black men and white men, Jews and Gentiles, Protestants and Catholics, will be able to join hands and sing in the words of the old Negro spiritual, "Free at last! free at last! thank God Almighty, we are free at last!"

APPENDIX 7 Presidents and Congresses, 1789–2006

TERM	PRESIDENT AND VICE PRESIDENT	PARTY OF PRESDIENT	CONGRESS	MAJORITY PARTY HOUSE	MAJORITY PARTY SENATE
1789–97	**George Washington** John Adams	None	1st 2d 3d 4th	N/A N/A N/A N/A	N/A N/A N/A N/A
1797–1801	**John Adams** Thomas Jefferson	Fed	5th 6th	N/A Fed	N/A Fed
1801–09	**Thomas Jefferson** Aaron Burr (1801–5) George Clinton (1805–9)	Dem Rep	7th 8th 9th 10th	Dem Rep Dem Rep Dem Rep Dem Rep	Dem Rep Dem Rep Dem Rep Dem Rep
1809–17	**James Madison** George Clinton (1809–12)[1] Elbridge Gerry (1813–14)[1]	Dem Rep	11th 12th 13th 14th	Dem Rep Dem Rep Dem Rep Dem Rep	Dem Rep Dem Rep Dem Rep Dem Rep
1817–25	**James Monroe** Daniel D. Tompkins	Dem Rep	15th 16th 17th 18th	Dem Rep Dem Rep Dem Rep Dem Rep	Dem Rep Dem Rep Dem Rep Dem Rep
1825–29	**John Quincy Adams** John C. Calhoun	Nat'l Rep	19th 20th	Nat'l Rep Dem	Nat'l Rep Dem
1829–37	**Andrew Jackson** John C. Calhoun (1829–32)[2] Martin Van Buren (1833–37)	Dem	21st 22d 23d 24th	Dem Dem Dem Dem	Dem Dem Dem Dem
1837–41	**Martin Van Buren** Richard M. Johnson	Dem	25th 26th	Dem Dem	Dem Dem
1841	**William H. Harrison**[1] John Tyler (1841)	Whig			
1841–45	**John Tyler** (VP vacant)	Whig	27th 28th	Whig Dem	Whig Whig
1845–49	**James K. Polk** George M. Dallas	Dem	29th 30th	Dem Whig	Dem Dem
1849–50	**Zachary Taylor**[1] Millard Fillmore	Whig	31st	Dem	Dem
1850–53	**Millard Fillmore** (VP vacant)	Whig	32d	Dem	Dem
1853–57	**Franklin Pierce** William R. D. King (1853)[1]	Dem	33d 34th	Dem Rep	Dem Dem
1857–61	**James Buchanan** John C. Breckinridge	Dem	35th 36th	Dem Rep	Dem Dem
1861–65	**Abraham Lincoln**[1] Hannibal Hamlin (1861–65) Andrew Johnson (1865)	Rep	37th 38th 38th	Rep Rep Rep	Rep Rep Rep
1865–69	**Andrew Johnson** (VP vacant)	Rep	39th 40th	Union Rep	Union Rep
1869–77	**Ulysses S. Grant** Schuyler Colfax (1869–73) Henry Wilson (1873–75)[1]	Rep	41st 42d 43d 44th	Rep Rep Rep Dem	Rep Rep Rep Rep
1877–81	**Rutherford B. Hayes** William A. Wheeler	Rep	45th 46th	Dem Dem	Rep Dem
1881	**James A. Garfield**[1] Chester A. Arthur	Rep	47th	Rep	Rep
1881–85	**Chester A. Arthur** (VP vacant)	Rep	48th	Dem	Rep
1885–89	**Grover Cleveland** Thomas A. Hendricks (1885)[1]	Dem	49th 50th	Dem Dem	Rep Rep
1889–93	**Benjamin Harrison** Levi P. Morton	Rep	51st 52d	Rep Dem	Rep Rep
1893–97	**Grover Cleveland** Adlai E. Stevenson	Dem	53d 54th	Dem Rep	Dem Rep

Term	President and Vice President	Party of Presdient	Congress	Majority Party	
				House	Senate
1897–1901	**William McKinley**[1] Garret A. Hobart (1897–99)[1] Theodore Roosevelt (1901)	Rep	55th 56th	Rep Rep	Rep Rep
1901–09	**Theodore Roosevelt** (VP vacant, 1901–05) Charles W. Fairbanks (1905–09)	Rep	57th 58th 59th 60th	Rep Rep Rep Rep	Rep Rep Rep Rep
1909–13	**William Howard Taft** James S. Sherman (1909–12)1	Rep	61st 62d	Rep Dem	Rep Rep
1913–21	**Woodrow Wilson** Thomas R. Marshall	Dem	63d 64th 65th 66th	Dem Dem Dem Rep	Dem Dem Dem Rep
1921–23	**Warren G. Harding**[1] Calvin Coolidge	Rep	67th	Rep	Rep
1923–29	**Calvin Coolidge** (VP vacant, 1923–25) Charles G. Dawes (1925–29)	Rep	68th 69th 70th	Rep Rep Rep	Rep Rep Rep
1929–33	**Herbert Hoover** Charles Curtis	Rep	71st 72d	Rep Dem	Rep Rep
1933–45	**Franklin D. Roosevelt**[1] John N. Garner (1933–41) Henry A. Wallace (1941–45) Harry S. Truman (1945)	Dem	73d 74th 75th 76th 77th 78th	Dem Dem Dem Dem Dem Dem	Dem Dem Dem Dem Dem Dem
1945–53	**Harry S Truman** (VP vacant, 1945–49) Alben W. Barkley (1949–53)	Dem	79th 80th 81st 82d	Dem Rep Dem Dem	Dem Rep Dem Dem
1953–61	**Dwight D. Eisenhower** Richard M. Nixon	Rep	83d 84th 85th 86th	Rep Dem Dem Dem	Rep Dem Dem Dem
1961–63	**John F. Kennedy**[1] Lyndon B. Johnson (1961–63)	Dem	87th	Dem	Dem
1963–69	**Lyndon B. Johnson** (VP vacant, 1963–65) Hubert H. Humphrey (1965–69)	Dem	88th 89th 90th	Dem Dem Dem	Dem Dem Dem
1969–74	Richard M. Nixon[3] Spiro T. Agnew (1969–73)[2] Gerald R. Ford (1973–74)[4]	Rep	91st 92d	Dem Dem	Dem Dem
1974–77	**Gerald R. Ford** Nelson A. Rockefeller[4]	Rep	93d 94th	Dem Dem	Dem Dem
1977–81	**Jimmy Carter** Walter Mondale	Dem	95th 96th	Dem Dem	Dem Dem
1981–89	Ronald Reagan George Bush	Rep	97th 98th 99th 100th	Dem Dem Dem Dem	Rep Rep Rep Dem
1989–93	**George Bush** J. Danforth Quayle	Rep	101st 102d	Dem Dem	Dem Dem
1993–2001	**William J. Clinton** Albert Gore, Jr.	Dem	103d 104th 105th 106th	Dem Rep Rep Rep	Dem Rep Rep Rep
2001–2004, 2005–2006	George W. Bush Richard Cheney	Rep	107th 108th 109th	Rep Rep Rep	Dem Rep Rep

[1] Died in office. [2] Resigned from the vice presidency.. [3] Resigned from the presidency.. [4] Appointed vice president.

APPENDIX 8 Supreme Court Justices

Name[1]	Years on Court	Appointing President	Name[1]	Years on Court	Appointing President
JOHN JAY	1789–1795	Washington	SALMON P. CHASE	1864–1873	Lincoln
James Wilson	1789–1798	Washington	William Strong	1870–1880	Grant
John Rutledge	1790–1791	Washington	Joseph P. Bradley	1870–1892	Grant
William Cushing	1790–1810	Washington	Ward Hunt	1873–1882	Grant
John Blair	1790–1796	Washington	MORRISON R. WAITE	1874–1888	Grant
James Iredell	1790–1799	Washington	John M. Harlan	1877–1911	Hayes
Thomas Johnson	1792–1793	Washington	William B. Woods	1881–1887	Hayes
William Paterson	1793–1806	Washington	Stanley Matthews	1881–1889	Garfield
JOHN RUTLEDGE[2]	1795	Washington	Horace Gray	1882–1902	Arthur
Samuel Chase	1796–1811	Washington	Samuel Blatchford	1882–1893	Arthur
OLIVER ELLSWORTH	1796–1800	Washington	Lucious Q. C. Lamar	1888–1893	Cleveland
Bushrod Washington	1799–1829	J. Adams	MELVILLE W. FULLER	1888–1910	Cleveland
Alfred Moore	1800–1804	J. Adams	David J. Brewer	1890–1910	B. Harrison
JOHN MARSHALL	1801–1835	J. Adams	Henry B. Brown	1891–1906	B. Harrison
William Johnson	1804–1834	Jefferson	George Shiras, Jr.	1892–1903	B. Harrison
Brockholst Livingston	1807–1823	Jefferson	Howel E. Jackson	1893–1895	B. Harrison
Thomas Todd	1807–1826	Jefferson	Edward D. White	1894–1910	Cleveland
Gabriel Duvall	1811–1835	Madison	Rufus W. Peckman	1896–1909	Cleveland
Joseph Story	1812–1845	Madison	Joseph McKenna	1898–1925	McKinley
Smith Thompson	1823–1843	Monroe	Oliver W. Holmes	1902–1932	T. Roosevelt
Robert Trimble	1826–1828	J. Q. Adams	William R. Day	1903–1922	T. Roosevelt
John McLean	1830–1861	Jackson	William H. Moody	1906–1910	T. Roosevelt
Henry Baldwin	1830–1844	Jackson	Horace H. Lurton	1910–1914	Taft
James M. Wayne	1835–1867	Jackson	Charles E. Hughes	1910–1916	Taft
ROGER B. TANEY	1836–1864	Jackson	**EDWARD D. WHITE**	1910–1921	Taft
Philip P. Barbour	1836–1841	Jackson	Willis Van Devanter	1911–1937	Taft
John Cartron	1837–1865	Van Buren	Joseph R. Lamar	1911–1916	Taft
John McKinley	1838–1852	Van Buren	Mahlon Pitney	1912–1922	Taft
Peter V. Daniel	1842–1860	Van Buren	James C. McReynolds	1914–1941	Wilson
Samuel Nelson	1845–1872	Tyler	Louis D. Brandeis	1916–1939	Wilson
Levi Woodbury	1845–1851	Polk	John H. Clarke	1916–1922	Wilson
Robert C. Grier	1846–1870	Polk	**WILLIAM H. TAFT**	1921–1930	Harding
Benjamin R. Curtis	1851–1857	Fillmore	George Sutherland	1922–1938	Harding
John A. Campbell	1853–1861	Pierce	Pierce Butler	1923–1939	Harding
Nathan Clifford	1858–1881	Buchanan	Edward T. Sanford	1923–1930	Harding
Noah H. Swayne	1862–1881	Lincoln	Harlan F. Stone	1925–1941	Coolidge
Samuel F. Miller	1862–1890	Lincoln	**CHARLES E. HUGHES**	1930–1941	Hoover
David Davis	1862–1877	Lincoln	Owen J. Roberts	1930–1945	Hoover
Stephen J. Field	1863–1897	Lincoln	Benjamin N. Cardozo	1932–1938	Hoover

Name[1]	Years on Court	Appointing President
Hugo L. Black	1937–1971	F. Roosevelt
Stanley F. Reed	1938–1957	F. Roosevelt
Felix Frankfurter	1939–1962	F. Roosevelt
William O. Douglas	1939–1975	F. Roosevelt
Frank Murphy	1940–1949	F. Roosevelt
HARLAN F. STONE	1941–1946	F. Roosevelt
James F. Brynes	1941–1942	F. Roosevelt
Robert H. Jackson	1941–1954	F. Roosevelt
Wiley B. Rutledge	1943–1949	F. Roosevelt
Harold H. Burton	1945–1958	Truman
FREDERICK M. VINSON	1946–1953	Truman
Tom C. Clark	1949–1967	Truman
Sherman Minton	1949–1956	Truman
EARL WARREN	1953–1969	Eisenhower
John Marshall Harlan	1955–1971	Eisenhower
William J. Brennan, Jr.	1956–1990	Eisenhower
Charles E. Whittaker	1957–1962	Eisenhower
Potter Stewart	1958–1981	Eisenhower
Byron R. White	1962–1993	Kennedy
Arthur J. Goldberg	1962–1965	Kennedy
Abe Fortas	1965–1970	L. Johnson
Thurgood Marshall	1967–1991	L. Johnson
WARREN E. BURGER	1969–1986	Nixon
Harry A. Blackmun	1970–1994	Nixon
Lewis F. Powell, Jr.	1971–1987	Nixon
William H. Rehnquist	1971–1986	Nixon
John Paul Stevens	1975–	Ford
Sandra Day O'Connor	1981–2006	Reagan
WILLIAM H. REHNQUIST	1986–2005	Reagan
Antonin Scalia	1986–	Reagan
Anthony Kennedy	1988–	Reagan
David Souter	1990–	Bush
Clarence Thomas	1991–	Bush
Ruth Bader Ginsburg	1993–	Clinton
Stephen Brever	1994–	Clinton
John G. Roberts, Jr.	2005–	Bush
Samuel A. Alito, Jr.	2006–	Bush

[1]Capital letters designate Chief Justices

[2]Never confirmed by the Senate as Chief Justice

APPENDIX 9

Student Guide

ABCNEWS PRENTICE HALL VIDEO LIBRARY: AMERICAN GOVERNMENT

DVD 1

FEDERALISM

MOMENT OF CRISIS—SYSTEM FAILURE

Originally Aired: 9/15/05
Program: *Primetime*
Running Time: 29:12

Katrina ranks as the country's most expensive natural disaster and one of the deadliest in U.S. history. It has killed more than 700 people, uprooted tens of thousands of families, destroyed countless homes, and forced the evacuation of a major American city. Two and a half weeks after the hurricane roared ashore, just east of New Orleans, the country is trying to make sense of the resulting failures of local, state, and federal government. On this program, ABC News will piece together what we know and where the breakdowns occurred.

Born as a garden-variety tropical depression, Katrina grew into a tropical storm and officially earned hurricane status on August 24, 2005. It initially made landfall north of Miami, causing serious flooding and eleven deaths. But only when it marched across the Florida peninsula and hit the warm waters of the Gulf of Mexico did Katrina rapidly intensify and unleash its full fury. And as it evolved into a monster storm, the National Hurricane Center issued pointed warnings to the target communities along the Gulf Coast. The director made phone calls to key officials, including the mayor of New Orleans, saying Katrina could be "the big one" officials had long feared. Simultaneously, weather service bulletins were issued with unusually apocalyptic language. One predicted a storm of "unprecedented strength," "the area will be uninhabitable for weeks," and went on to predict human suffering "incredible by modern standards."

Given the dire warnings, should the deaths and suffering throughout the Gulf region have been as great? Were the recommendations issued by the 9/11 Commission put into practice?

Ted Koppel hosts a *Primetime* special edition, "Moment of Crisis: System Failure," a moment-by-moment chronology of what went so terribly wrong in the horrific days following Katrina's strike on the Gulf Coast. This was America's first major test of emergency response since 9/11, a test that has received failing grades.

questions for review

1. In "Moment of Crisis—System Failure," state and local officials blame federal officials for the grossly inadequate response to this natural disaster and federal officials blame state and local officials. What are the responsibilities of the federal government, particularly agencies such as FEMA and the Department of Homeland Security, in regard to both natural and man-made disasters? What are the responsibilities of state and local governments?

2. How much of a role did poverty play in the tragic aftermath of Hurricane Katrina? Do you get the impression from viewing the program that race had any impact on the way the federal government responded to the crisis?

3. Could this disaster have been averted simply by reinforcing New Orleans' levee system years ago as a preventive measure? Does the federal government have an obligation to maintain and update the infrastructure in places such as New Orleans or is this the responsibility of state and local governments?

4. Does the Constitution provide any guidance on whether the response to disasters such as Hurricane Katrina should be orchestrated at the federal level or at the state and local levels?

5. In light of the response to Hurricane Katrina, what can be said about American federalism both in theory and in practice? Would a stronger federal government have been better equipped to deal with the crisis, or was the inadequate response an isolated case of mismanagement that does not reflect upon the basic structure of the U.S. government?

REPORT CARD

Originally Aired: 10/8/03
Program: *Nightline*
Running Time: 17:24

Public education is one of the great promises of this country. But is America keeping that promise? This ABC News program offers a timely report card on the nation's public education system. Hard hit by state budget cuts in recent years, the system is also under immense pressure from the No Child Left Behind initiative—legislation that demands much of schools but, say critics, provides little funding to help them meet the mandated goals. Visits to a school in Arlington, Massachusetts, and The University of Texas at Austin amply illustrate the hard realities of faculties being slashed and class sizes swelling . . . and the promise of public education steadily fading.

questions **for review**

1. What is an unfunded mandate? Give examples of unfunded mandates in the No Child Left Behind Act discussed in "Report Card."

2. In "Report Card," author Jonathan Kozol says the "way we finance education in the United States is archaic, chaotic, and utterly undemocratic." What about our education financing leads him to say this?

3. States have raised a number of objections to federal education standards. Briefly discuss two objections that states might have.

INTEREST GROUPS

GOD AND COUNTRY

Originally Aired: 11/26/02
Program: *Nightline*
Running Time: 12:41

Over the last couple of years, what has come to be called the Christian Right has become more and more active in supporting the Sharon government in its war with the Palestinians. And their political clout with the Bush administration is considerable. They are opposed to giving the Palestinians any land, taking a much harder line than many Americans. The reason? Prophecy. Many believe that what is playing out now in the Middle East is all part of the process leading toward the Second Coming. The existence of the state of Israel is crucial to that process and many believe that Israel must cover all of the land, including the occupied territories, in order for this process to move forward. So they send money, take trips to Israel, meet regularly with Israeli officials, including Sharon, and at the same time, seem to be breaking what was a strong alliance between American Jews and the Democratic Party. That would certainly change the political landscape in this country as well. Israel needs friends now, facing serious criticism from much of the world over its tactics in the current conflict.

And so both sides are sort of glossing over a theological issue. According to the prophecies that many Christians believe, as part of the Second Coming, Jews will have the opportunity to either convert to Christianity, or perish. In other words, they will disappear as a people, or religion, one way or the other. You might think that this would be a point of contention between the

two religions but it doesn't appear to be. Ted Koppel interviews Pat Robertson, founder and chairman of the Christian Broadcasting Network. He is a former presidential candidate and arguably one of the most recognized leaders of the evangelical Christian community.

questions **for review**

1. In "God and Country," conservative Christians explain their strong support for Israel, especially their support of Jewish occupation of the West Bank. Briefly discuss the reasons they give for this support.

2. Not all Jews welcome the support of conservative American Christians. What implications of that support concern them?

3. As a general rule, interest groups rarely have a decisive role in the formulation of foreign policy. How might conservative Christian support for Israel be an exception to that rule?

PUBLIC OPINION, PARTICIPATION, AND VOTING

AIR WARS

Originally Aired: 8/25/04
Program: *Nightline*
Running Time: 9:07

The group known as the "Swift Boat Veterans for Truth" continues to stir the 2004 presidential election. One of President Bush's election lawyers, Benjamin Ginsberg, stepped down from his role in the Bush campaign after admitting ties with the group that has been attacking John Kerry's war record. Mr. Ginsberg resigned after voluntarily disclosing his role as an advisor to both the Bush campaign and the "Swift Boat Veterans for Truth." Is this dual role a violation of federal election laws? Technically it isn't, but the appearance of a "connection" could still have political consequences. Ginsberg's admission of ties with the so-called "527 group" comes after the president has categorically denied that a connection exists between his campaign and the television ads in question. Chris Bury talks to Benjamin Ginsberg about his connection with the "Swift Boat Veterans for Truth," his decision to resign from his position as National Counsel to the Bush campaign, and what this means for the Republicans.

Both sides of the political spectrum have 527 groups—for example, you may have heard of the liberal Moveon.org or conservative Club for Growth. What's important to note is that a significant amount more—$136 million more—has been raised by Democratic-tied groups over the Republican-tied groups.

On this program, ABC's Jake Tapper will help us understand these groups and their impact on the 2004 election. He'll also explain the political connections on both sides to these groups.

questions **for review**

1. The Bipartisan Campaign Reform Act (BCRA) bans most forms of soft money. According to "Air Wars," a loophole in BCRA has allowed outside groups to raise and spend unlimited amounts of money supporting or attacking candidates as long as the candidate's campaign doesn't "coordinate the messages." What does this mean? Use examples from the video.

2. What is a 527 group? What are 527 groups allowed to do? What aren't they allowed to do?

3. In "Air Wars," political scientist Ken Goldstein gives reasons why negative ads are so successful. Briefly discuss at least three of these reasons.

4. Are there any important campaign finance-related issues that BCRA does not address? Briefly discuss one or two of these issues and any efforts to address them independently of BCRA.

Mass Media

Q & A

Originally Aired: 4/28/05
Program: *Nightline*
Running Time:

Every year, at more or less the same time, the president gets to address the nation—and the world—on his vision for the coming term. Where we are and where we're going. What he intends to do. How does he take all the issues—from social security to gay marriage, from Iraq to Iran, from the nuclear threat to terrorism—and figure out what gets priority? On this program, we talk to some people who have worked closely with presidents and who have actually written many of the State of the Union speeches. We'll see what goes into the address and what the president is actually trying to say. One of our panelists is a consultant on the popular TV show *West Wing*. Over the years, they've tried to give the audience a behind-the-scenes look at the frenzied jockeying and preparation that goes into this yearly address. We hope our panel will tell us whether the television show comes close.

A veteran of hard-nosed politics, Mary Matalin has most recently served as an assistant to President Bush and as counselor to Vice President Cheney. Michael Waldman was President Bill

Clinton's chief speechwriter from 1995 to 1999. He cranked out 2,000 speeches for the president, including many of the State of the Union Addresses. Ken Duberstein was President Ronald Reagan's chief of staff from 1988 to 1989. He's also a consultant to *West Wing*. Ted Koppel joins this panel prior to the 2005 State of the Union address to try to pick apart what the president does. They'll view a few scenes from previous *West Wing* episodes to see how close their storylines come to reality. Who does he hear from? What are the issues that get into the speech? How important is every adjective and every adverb? There are fights, literally, over every single word and issue that goes into the speech. It's a statement of intent for the year. And this one is particularly important during a volatile period in this country's history. It will be interesting to see what President Bush sets out to do on the heels of his victory in November.

After we record the first part of the conversation, we'll review the speech, and then come back to our panelists to see how President Bush did. What were the surprises? How was the tone? What did he focus on? Was it a wide-ranging and all-encompassing speech or a narrowly focused one?

questions **for review**

1. Briefly compare press conferences with the U.S. president and press conferences with the British prime minister.

2. Why do the reporters in "Q&A" believe U.S. presidents are not questioned as aggressively as are the leaders of other countries?

3. While the number of presidential addresses and appearances has grown dramatically in the last 50 years, the number of presidential press conferences has dropped just as dramatically. Why might this be so?

AMERICA IN BLACK & WHITE

Originally Aired: 9/24/96
Program: *Nightline*
Running Time: 14:54

Discusses racial issues concerning local television news reporting.

questions **for review**

1. After studying local television stations in Philadelphia, what conclusions did an Annenberg study draw about coverage based on race?

2. What guidelines did an Austin TV station put into place to avoid negative racial stereotypes in its reporting?

3. While most experts agree the media have the power to shape public opinion, there are some factors that limit media influence. Briefly discuss a few of these factors that might apply to local TV coverage of race.

CONGRESS

PRICE OF VICTORY

Originally Aired: 3/25/04
Program: *Nightline*
Running Time: 14:34

It was meant to be a victory that could be savored all the way through the 2004 election. When the president signed the Medicare bill into law last December, it was a landmark event. This bill had managed to achieve what seniors had been demanding for years—prescription drug coverage. That's definitely something to celebrate. Well, a funny thing happened on the way to the bill becoming law: accusations of bribery, lying, intimidation, political shenanigans—it has become quite a Washington drama. A bureaucrat who you probably wouldn't normally hear about testified on Capitol Hill. Richard Foster is the chief actuary of the Medicare program and he says that his boss threatened to fire him if he publicized his estimates of how much the Medicare bill would actually cost. His boss happens to be a political appointee. The bill that passed had a cost estimate of around $400 billion. Foster's estimate—$534 billion—became public a month after the signing of the bill. Needless to say, people are furious, including Republicans who now say if they knew then what they know now, they would not have voted for the bill.

Then there is that story of the endless vote in the House—a fifteen-minute roll call that stayed open for 3 hours. A lot of arm-twisting occurred that night, including allegations that retiring Congressman Nick Smith (R-MI) was told that if he voted for the bill his son would get $100,000 worth of help for his upcoming congressional race. Smith voted against the bill, but there is another investigation of this allegation.

There are some people who roll their eyes at the very thought of the congressional process. But this is a dramatic one. People are really emotional about it, as you will see in this program.

questions **for review**

1. In "Price of Victory," of what does Medicare actuary Richard Foster accuse the administration?
2. In the process of passing the 2003 Medicare bill, what was unusual in regard to the timing of the vote?

3. In "Price of Victory," of what does Representative Nick Smith accuse the House leadership?
4. Your text describes the process by which bills become laws. How does the process in the text differ from the process in the video?

DVD 2

CIVIL LIBERTIES

LIFE OR DEATH DECISION, PART 2

Originally Aired: 3/22/05
Program: *Nightline*
Running Time: 16:25

The Terri Schiavo case is the ultimate "on the one hand, on the other hand" debate. Each aspect of this debate—legal, medical, political, even the moral and ethical—has a deep rift of opinions. And all sides were watching the 11th Circuit Court of Appeals in Atlanta for the next step in this case.

A federal judge denied a request for an emergency order to restore Terri Schiavo's feeding tube. The judge took the position that the lawyers representing her parents were unlikely to succeed in a resulting federal trial. Her parents immediately appealed the case to the 11th Circuit. If the Schindlers, Schiavo's parents, lose there, it will almost certainly be taken quickly to the U.S. Supreme Court, which has already declined to hear the case three times.

But in the meantime, Terri Schiavo is in her fourth day without nutrition. Doctors say she could live another week or more without food or water.

And so the debate rages on, with all sides staking out firm positions. In the medical debate, there are those that point to the evidence that her brain function is irreversibly damaged. But on the other hand, there is the loving care that her parents have shown for their profoundly disabled daughter.

The intervention of Congress turned this into a major political battle. On the one hand, there are right-to-life advocates who see this as another test of the sanctity of life. On the other hand, there are those who are offended at Congress for inserting itself into a family tragedy.

And finally, there are the ethical issues that are at the heart of so many of these factors—the medical, the legal, and the political. If you believe it is wrong, simply wrong, to remove a feeding tube in order to expedite death, how can you ever accept any of the other arguments? And on the other side, if you believe Michael

Schiavo is holding strong for his wife's stated intentions, how can you ever accept any of the other arguments?

On this program, George Stephanopoulos discusses all of these matters—medical, legal, political, and ethical—with a panel of guests.

questions for review

1. Given that the Terry Schiavo case had spent years in state court, on what grounds was the case sent to federal court?

2. The experts in "Life or Death Decision, Part 2" differentiate between the right to die and the right to refuse unwanted medical intervention. Describe the differences between these two concepts.

3. Those who supported keeping Terri Schiavo alive often referred to her right to due process under the Fourteenth Amendment. To what do you think they were referring? Would procedural due process apply to this case? Would substantive due process apply to this case?

CRIME & PUNISHMENT

Originally Aired: 12/1/04
Program: *Nightline*
Running Time: 13:57

Voting to have a man or woman put to death has to be one of the hardest decisions facing any American juror. How do we ever know for sure if the person convicted of the crime actually committed it? One death row prisoner in Texas served 17 years for a crime he didn't commit, and Ernest Willis's case was built entirely on circumstantial evidence. At one point, he was days away from being executed, but now he is a free man.

Ernest Willis, who on four different dates was scheduled for execution, learned in October 2004 that he would be exonerated and released from prison. After years of appeals, litigation, and the drive of a young lawyer in a large law firm, Willis was completely exonerated of the murder charges that put him on death row. ABC correspondent Mike von Fremd was at the prison when he was released after 17 years. They sat down for a conversation about how he ended up on death row, his feelings on facing execution, his surprising release, and what it was like to finally meet the woman he had married while he was in prison.

Texas puts more prisoners to death than any other state.

questions for review

1. One reason appeals courts often overturn a death sentence is due to the incompetence of the defendant's attorney. As an example of this, describe the problems with Ernest Willis's attorney in "Crime & Punishment."

2. In "Crime & Punishment," Ori White, the Pecos County, Texas, district attorney, says prosecutors often feel that "the ends justify the means." What do you think he meant by this?

3. More than two-thirds of all death sentences are overturned on appeal. On what grounds are they overturned?

ILLEGAL IMMIGRANT WORKERS

Originally Aired: 12/14/04
Program: *Nightline*
Running Time: 15:22

When Bernard Kerik, President Bush's first choice to run the Department of Homeland Security, withdrew his nomination because of a nanny who was an undocumented worker that he hired and failed to pay taxes on, it was a story that probably sounded familiar. Cabinet nominees have been tripped up on this issue before in both the Clinton and Bush administrations. So the question is, why does this keep happening?

One of the reasons it keeps happening is that it is pretty easy to get by hiring undocumented workers. It seems that the only way to get tripped up is if you undergo a background check for an important government post. You would be hard pressed to find any aspect of the nation's economy where undocumented workers are not making a contribution. It could be in the service industry or the construction business. You will eat something today that has been brought to you as a result of the labor of illegal immigrants working here. A conservative estimate is that at least 50 percent of agricultural laborers are undocumented workers. So is this a result of American employers being cheap or is it a result of the efficiency of market forces? Many employers say it is not easy to find Americans willing to do a lot of the low-paying, menial, and tedious tasks that immigrants are willing to do. Labor advocates say that illegal immigrants depress the wage market so Americans are shut out of these jobs. Everyone can find statistics to back their argument.

So what is the solution? When the president announced a proposal earlier this year to grant legal status to millions of undocumented workers in the United States, it wasn't greeted with unanimous enthusiasm. "Out of common sense and fairness, our laws should allow willing workers to enter our country and fill jobs that Americans are not filling," the president said. He wasn't calling for amnesty but a temporary guest worker program. But will that satisfy both sides? Michel Martin examines the arguments advanced on something that has always been a hot-button issue. We also speak with Senator John McCain of Arizona. His state has addressed the illegal immigration issue by voting for a sweeping proposition that bans all government services to illegal immigrants. He says that this is an issue that the nation has to wake up to and start dealing with as a high priority.

questions **for review**

1. Why aren't immigration laws more strictly enforced?
2. Explain the "geographic" component to immigration law enforcement.
3. The inability to bar illegal aliens from entering the country is not a question of power. Rather, the problems are political and practical. Briefly explain what this means.

CHURCH & STATE, AND PLEDGE OF ALLEGIANCE

Originally Aired: 7/8/02
Program: *Nightline*
Running Time: 14:44

Where does religion fit into American politics? In light of the furor over the decision by a federal appeals court on the 'Pledge of Allegiance,' what about 'In God We Trust'? Does this country treat religion differently than other countries? *Nightline* looks at the connection between church and state.

questions **for review**

1. Why are voters so interested in a candidate's religion, according to "Church & State, and Pledge of Allegiance"?
2. Under what circumstances was the phrase "under God" made part of the Pledge of Allegiance?
3. Justice Sandra Day O'Connor's "endorsement test" has been the basis of several Supreme Court decisions. What is it and how might it apply to the Pledge of Allegiance?

VOICES OF DISSENT

Program: *Nightline*
Originally Aired: 11/2/01
Running Time: 12:10

Disagreement is an essential component of one of America's most cherished freedoms: the right to free speech. On this program, *Nightline* makes room for voices representing opinions that are likely to be less popular or less mainstream than what is normally heard in the media.

questions **for review**

1. In "Voices of Dissent," author Arundhati Roy says, "Operation Enduring Freedom is ostensibly being fought to uphold

the American way of life. It'll probably end up undermining it entirely." What does she mean by this?
2. In "Voices of Dissent," cartoonist Aaron McGroder says that "in the six days after the bombing, America became the most intensely stupid place on the planet." Why does McGroder believe this to be true?
3. Although Americans overwhelmingly support the principle of free speech, many do not support the freedom to say things with which they disagree. Why might it be even more important to protect free speech in times of crisis than in normal times?

MUSLIMS IN AMERICA

Originally Aired: 5/4/95
Program: *Nightline*
Running Time: 13:41

Nightline looks at one of the fastest-growing groups in America: Muslims. Members of the oldest Muslim community in Cedar Rapids, Iowa, speak to Ted Koppel about their beliefs and customs.

questions **for review**

1. Differentiate between Arabs and Muslims.
2. The video "Muslims in America" gives several possible explanations why, even before 9/11, Americans were quick to blame Muslims for every terrorist act. Briefly discuss two explanations.
3. If the equal protection clause applies only to the actions of governments, how may we limit the discriminatory actions of private individuals?

SOCIAL POLICY

ON THE EDGE

Originally Aired: 4/15/04
Program: *Nightline*
Running Time: 16:16

When we say "poor" or "poverty-stricken Americans," what image comes to mind? The homeless man sleeping on the grate? The unemployed person standing in line at the unemployment or welfare office? What about someone who has a full-time job making $9 an hour? That sounds like a decent wage, right? Well, that actually comes out to just above $18,000 a year, and for a family with one adult and three children, that means poverty. We've decided to launch a new, occasional series that looks at the working poor: the millions of Americans who live on the edge of poverty.

The genesis of tonight's show was a new book by former *New York Times* reporter and Pulitzer Prize-winner, David Shipler. "The Working Poor" takes a comprehensive look at the lives of people set to plunge into the abyss of financial ruin if just one payment isn't met, if their car breaks down, or if they call in sick at work. Such seemingly minor events can have catastrophic effects on this segment of the population, and Mr. Shipler has documented many of their lives, weaving economic analysis into the story of what these people face trying to survive from day to day. Ted Koppel sat down with Mr. Shipler for an extensive interview on his findings.

questions **for review**

1. How does author David Shipler define "working poor"?

2. How does the video's title, "On the Edge," apply to the working poor?

3. The underlying problem of the working poor seems to be their vulnerability in every area of life. Explain how the working poor are vulnerable in ways not experienced by other economic groups.

4. Author David Shipler disagrees with the concept of a "culture of poverty." Instead, he speaks of an "ecological system of interactions." What does he mean?

5. What is the difference between an entitlement and a means-tested entitlement?

abolition The prohibition of slavery.

accidental sample A nonprobability sample in which the researcher randomly invites respondents to participate in the survey; not a statistically valid sampling technique.

accommodationist Interpretive approach to the establishment clause of the First Amendment that would permit the government to provide financial support for certain religious institutions and programs or sponsor specific religious practices, such as prayer in public schools.

Acts for Trade A series of moves by Parliament to channel money from the American colonies back to the commercial class in Great Britain during the mid-1700s.

Adams, John (1735–1826) One of the founders of the American political system. He served as vice president under George Washington and as president from 1797 to 1801.

administrative law judge (ALJ) Official who presides over quasi-judicial proceedings within government agencies and renders decisions about disputes governed by statutes, such as appeals from denials of Social Security disability benefits.

adversarial system Legal system (used by the United States and other countries that draw their legal traditions from England) in which a judge plays a relatively passive role as attorneys provide zealous advocacy to protect each side's interests.

"advertorial" An advertisement presented as an editorial.

affirmative action Measures taken in hiring, recruitment, employment, and education to remedy past and present discrimination against specific groups.

agenda List of issues that legislative leaders wish to address during a session of Congress.

agenda setting Featuring specific stories in the media to focus attention on particular issues.

agents of political socialization Factors that influence how we acquire political facts and knowledge and develop political values.

American Independent Party Party established in 1968 by Alabama governor George Wallace that opposed the Civil Rights Act of 1964 and federal government welfare programs.

American Party (Know-Nothings) Party in the 1850s that hoped to keep power out of the hands of immigrants and Roman Catholics.

American Socialist Party Party created in the 1890s that advocated government control of certain elements of business and society.

amicus briefs Written arguments submitted to an appellate court by lawyers who are interested in the issue being examined in a case but are not representing either party in the case; often submitted by interest groups' lawyers to advance a specific policy position.

Amtrak The government corporation, officially titled the National Railroad Passenger Corporation, that manages passenger rail travel in the United States.

Anti-Federalists Opponents of the ratification of the U.S. Constitution in 1787 and 1788.

Anti-Masonic Party Party founded in 1825 in opposition to Freemasonry in public affairs.

apartheid The system of strict racial segregation and white supremacy in South Africa.

appellate briefs Written arguments submitted by lawyers in appellate court cases.

appellate jurisdiction Authority of specific courts to hear appeals concerning allegations of specific errors in cases previously decided in trial courts.

apprenticeship The norm that new members of Congress are expected to work hard and quietly learn the legislative process.

at-large districts Districts encompassing an entire state or large parts of a state in which House members are elected to represent the entire state.

attitude hypothesis The theory that distinctive male and female attitudes and voting preferences arise from gender differences in political perceptions and issue preferences.

attitudinal barriers Those perceptions and beliefs that help maintain the two-party system in America.

attitudinal model An approach to analyzing judicial decision making that looks at individual judges' decision patterns to identify the values and attitudes that guide their decisions.

Australian ballot The secret ballot, which keeps voters' choices confidential.

authoritarian regime A system of government in which leaders face few formal or legal restrictions but are checked by noninstitutional forces such as political parties, religious groups, and business leaders.

authority The recognized right of a particular individual, group, or institution to make binding decisions, and compel others to obey them.

***Baker* v. *Carr* (1961)** Supreme Court case that set the standard that House districts must contain equal numbers of constituents, thus establishing the principle of "one person, one vote."

balance of trade The net difference between a nation's imports and its exports.

ballot access laws Laws in each state that determine how a third-party candidate can get on the general election ballot.

ballot initiative A system whereby citizens decide policy matters through voting on election day. About one-half of the states allow this process.

***Barron* v. *Baltimore* (1833)** Early Supreme Court interpretation of the Fifth Amendment declaring that the Bill of Rights provided legal protections only against actions by the federal government.

bench trials Trials in which a judge presides and makes determinations of fact and law, including decisions about guilt, without a jury.

bicameral legislature A legislature composed of two houses.

bifurcated proceedings The division of capital punishment trials into two separate parts: an initial trial to determine guilt followed by a separate hearing focused entirely on the question of whether the convicted individual will be sent to prison or executed.

Bill of Rights The first ten amendments to the U.S. Constitution, ratified in 1791, protecting civil liberties.

bill sponsor The member of Congress who introduces a bill.

binding primaries Process established in most states whereby voters in primary elections choose delegates who have pledged their support to a particular presidential candidate. The delegates then vote for this candidate at the nominating convention.

Bipartisan Campaign Reform Act (BCRA) A federal law passed in 2002 that outlawed soft money contributions to party organizations.

block grants Grants of money to states, which are given substantial discretion to spend the money with minimal federal restrictions (sometimes called revenue sharing grants).

blog A Web log or online journal.

boycott A coordinated action by many people who agree not to buy a specific product, use a specific service, or shop at a specific store until a policy is changed.

***Brandenburg* v. *Ohio* (1969)** U.S. Supreme Court decision that articulated a test for permissible speech by allowing the government to regulate expressions that incite a danger of imminent lawless action, such as a riot or other violent event.

***Brown* v. *Board of Education of Topeka* (1954)** U.S. Supreme Court decision that overturned *Plessy* v. *Ferguson* (1896) and declared that government-mandated racial segregation in schools and other facilities and programs violates the equal protection clause of the Fourteenth Amendment.

***Buckley* v. *Valeo* (1976)** Perhaps the most significant campaign finance Supreme Court case in American history. The Court ruled that campaign expenditures are akin to free speech and are therefore protected by the First Amendment.

budget deficit The amount by which a government's expenditures exceed its revenues.

budget surplus The amount by which a government's revenues exceed its expenditures.

bully pulpit The public platform from which the president can urge people to support certain causes and "preach to the national congregation."

bureaucracy An organization with a hierarchical structure and specific responsibilities that operates on management principles intended to enhance efficiency and effectiveness. In government, it refers to departments and agencies in the executive branch.

Burke, Edmund (1729–1797) A British writer and politician who was a member of Great Britain's House of Commons during America's pre-Revolutionary period.

cabinet A group of presidential advisers, primarily the secretaries of federal departments.

candidate-centered era After 1960, a period when candidates began to portray themselves as independent from party politics, even though they often ran under a party banner.

capitalism An economic system in which the means of production and distribution are privately owned and there is little governmental interference.

capitalist system An economic system in which the means of production and distribution are privately owned and there is little governmental interference. Also known as an *open-market* or *free-market system*.

capital punishment A criminal punishment, otherwise known as the *death penalty*, in which a person is subject to execution after conviction, reserved for the most serious offenses.

case precedent A legal rule established by a judicial decision that guides subsequent judicial decisions. The use of case precedent is drawn from the common law system brought from Great Britain to the United States.

catalyst for change The assertion that public opinion shapes and alters our political culture, thus allowing for change.

categorical grants Grants of money from the federal government to state or local governments for very specific purposes. The grants often require that funds be matched by the receiving entity.

census A precise count of the population.

Chávez, César Latino civil rights leader who founded the United Farm Workers and used grassroots mobilization to seek civil rights for Latinos and improved working conditions for agricultural workers.

checks and balances A principle of the American governmental system whereby each branch of government (legislative, executive, and judicial) has the power to limit the actions of the others. For example, Congress can pass laws, but the president can veto these measures.

chief of staff The highest-ranking member of the Executive Office of the President and hence the most important of the president's advisers.

Christian Coalition A conservative Christian political advocacy group founded in 1988 by Pat Robertson.

civic participation Citizen involvement in public matters, such as by joining clubs, voting, or attending governmental meetings.

civility The congressional norm that members show respect for all other members despite personal, partisan, or ideological differences.

civil law A body of law that applies to private rights, such as the ownership of property or the ability to enter into contracts.

civil lawsuits Legal actions filed by individuals, corporations, or governments seeking remedies from private parties for contract violations, personal injuries, or other noncriminal matters.

civil liberties Individuals' freedoms and legal protections guaranteed by the Bill of Rights that cannot be denied or hindered by government.

civil rights Public policies and legal protections concerning equal status and treatment in American society to advance the goals of equal opportunity, fair and open political participation, and equal treatment under law without regard to race, gender, disability status, and other demographic characteristics.

Civil Rights Act of 1964 Federal statutes that prohibit racial discrimination in public accommodations (hotels, restaurants, theaters).

civil service See *merit system*.

civil service system Government employment system in which employees are hired on the basis of their qualifications and cannot be fired merely for belonging to the wrong political party; originated with the federal Pendleton Act in 1883 and expanded at other levels of government in the half-century that followed.

classical liberalism A political philosophy based on the desire for limited government.

clear and present danger test A test for permissible speech articulated by Justice Oliver Wendell Holmes in *Schenck* v. *United States* (1919); allows government regulation of some expressions.

cleavages Divisions of people based on at least one social characteristic, such as educational attainment or race.

closed rule Prohibiting a bill from being amended on the floor of the House of Representatives.

closed-ended questions Asking a question and providing a list of potential responses from which to choose.

closed primary system Primary election process in which only registered members of the party are allowed to cast ballots. Roughly half the states use this system.

closed process Prohibiting a bill from being amended on the floor of the House of Representatives.

cloture Rule declaring the end of a debate in the Senate.

coercion Using force or punishment to make someone to do something the person does not want to do.

Coercive Acts/Intolerable Acts A series of laws passed by the British Parliament in 1774 in response to growing unrest in the American colonies. Enforcement of these laws played a major role in precipitating the outbreak of the American Revolutionary War. The colonists called them the **Intolerable Acts.**

cohort replacement Natural phenomenon of generational replacement due to death.

collective participation Citizens taking action with others to alter the course of governmental policy.

colonial assemblies An early form of self-governance in colonial America. Members of colonial assemblies were elected by the citizens of the towns or counties annually. Their role was to counsel the governor.

commercial speech Texts such as advertising, promoting business ventures. Such speech is subject to government regulation to ensure truthfulness and to protect the public from unsafe products.

committee appointment process Party leaders' assignment of party members to committees.

communism A political and economic system in which all property is owned by the community and each person contributes and receives according to his or her ability and needs.

Communist Party USA Party founded in 1920 by radical Marxists who broke away from the American Socialist Party.

compelled self-incrimination Being forced through physical abuse or other coercion to provide testimony against oneself in a criminal case, a practice that is prohibited by the Fifth Amendment.

compelling government interest The demonstration of necessity that the government must provide to justify interference with fundamental rights—the central element of a strict scrutiny standard for examining the existence of rights violations.

competitive news markets Locales with two or more news organizations that can check one another's accuracy and neutrality of reporting.

compulsory process A right contained in the Sixth Amendment to enable criminal defendants to use court orders to require witnesses to appear and to require the production of documents and other evidence.

concurring opinion Appellate court opinion by judge who endorses the outcome decided by the majority of judges, but wants to express different reasons to justify that outcome.

conference committee A committee of members of the House and Senate that irons out differences in measures that have passed both houses to create a single bill.

confidence level The probability that the results found in the sample represent the true opinion of the entire public under study. The traditional standard confidence level is 95 percent.

confrontation Right contained in the Sixth Amendment for criminal defendants to see their accusers in court and hear at first hand the accusations and evidence being presented.

Congressional Budget Office (CBO) The research arm of Congress, a major player in budget creation.

Connecticut Compromise See *Great Compromise.*

conscience model of representation The philosophy that legislators should follow the will of the people (that is, act like a delegate) until they truly believe that it is in the best interests of the nation to act differently.

conservatism A modern update of classical liberalism.

conservatives People who believes that government spending should be limited, that traditional patterns of relationships should be preserved, and that a large and powerful government is a threat to personal liberties.

constituent service A legislator's responsiveness to the questions and concerns of the people he or she represents.

Constitutional Convention A meeting in Philadelphia in 1787 in which delegates from the colonies drew up a new system of government. The finished product was the Constitution of the United States.

constitutional government A political system in which leaders are subject to both procedural checks and institutional limits. The United States has a constitutional government.

constitutional monarchy A political system in which the king or queen performs ceremonial duties but plays little or no role in actually governing the country.

constitutional obstruction The various ways that the U.S. Constitution slows down the policy process, such as the necessity for legislation to pass both houses of Congress and to be signed by the president before becoming law.

Consumer Price Index (CPI) Figure representing the cost of a specific set of goods and services tracked at regular intervals by the Department of Labor.

containment A Cold War strategy that sought to control and encircle the Soviet Union rather than defeat it militarily.

contempt of court A finding made by a judge concerning an individual's disobedience of court rules or a judicial order. This can be a basis for sending individuals to jail without trial, as in the case of news reporters who refuse to provide information about criminal investigations.

cooperative federalism The powers of the federal and state government are intertwined and shared. Each level of government shares overlapping power, authority, and responsibility.

Corrupt Bargain of 1824 The alleged secret agreement in the disputed election of 1824 that led the House of Representatives to select John Quincy Adams, who had come in second in the popular vote, as president if he would make House Speaker Henry Clay his secretary of state.

Council of Economic Advisers (CEA) A group of economists within the Executive Office of the President, appointed by the president to provide advice on economic policy.

court-packing plan Proposal by Franklin D. Roosevelt in 1937 to appoint an additional Supreme Court justice for every sitting justice over age 70, in hopes of changing the composition of the court to make it more supportive of his New Deal proposals.

courts of last resort The highest courts in each American court system, typically called supreme courts, that hear selected appeals from the lower courts.

covert action Efforts to secretly influence affairs in another state, which may include propaganda, disinformation campaigns, bribery, fomenting political and economic unrest, and, in the extreme, assassination.

cracking Drawing district lines such that they divide voters of particular groups into many districts, thereby reducing their influence and their likelihood of winning an election.

criminal law A body of law that applies to violations against rules and regulations defined by the government.

criminal prosecutions Legal processes in which the government seeks to prove that an individual is guilty of a crime and deserving of punishment for it.

crosscutting cleavages Divisions in society that separate people into groups.

crowding-out effect The fact that interest rates are forced higher as the government borrows a larger portion of available money.

cultural hegemony The overwhelming of traditional cultures by aspects of American culture (including movies, television shows, food, music, and products) exported to other countries.

cultural relativism The concept that ethical and moral standards are relative to what a particular society believes to be good or bad, right or wrong, at a particular time.

dealignment The loss of affinity for party politics among voters who no longer consider themselves partisans.

decentralization Proposed reform for government agencies intended to increase efficiency in administration and create closer contacts with the local public; permits regional and local offices to manage their own performances without close supervision from headquarters.

decisions Court rulings that interpret the meaning of policy.

de facto segregation Racial segregation in housing and schools that was presumed to occur through people's voluntary choices about where they wanted to live but was actually facilitated by the discriminatory actions of landlords, real estate agents, and banks.

deflation A decrease in prices over time.

de jure segregation Racial segregation mandated by laws and policies created by government officials.

delegate model of representation The philosophy that legislators should adhere to the will of their constituents.

democracy A political system in which all citizens have a right to play a role in shaping government action and are afforded basic rights and liberties.

Democratic Party One of the two major political parties in the United States. It generally draws support from working class people, women, and minorities, and has traditionally supported expanding the role of government in society and the economy.

Democratic-Republicans The first American political party, formed by believers in states' rights and followers of Thomas Jefferson.

department Any of the fifteen major government agencies responsible for specific policy areas, whose heads are usually called secretaries and serve in the president's cabinet.

détente Reduction of tension or strained relations between previously hostile nations.

deterrence A military strategy associated with the Cold War that sought to prevent an unwanted military action from taking place by raising the prospect of large-scale retaliation.

devolution Transfer of jurisdiction and fiscal responsibility for particular programs from the federal government to state or local governments.

dictator The sole ruler of a political system with the power to control most or all actions of government.

digital divide See *technology gap*.

Dillon's rule Iowa state court decision in 1868 that narrowly defined the power of local governments and established the supremacy of state governments when conflict exists with localities. Subsequently upheld by the Supreme Court.

direct contact Face-to-face meetings or telephone conversations between individuals.

direct democracy A governing system in which decisions are made by all the members of the community rather than elected representatives. Also known as *pure democracy*.

direct mail Information sent by mail to a large number of people to advertise, market concepts, or solicit orders.

direct primary elections Elections in which citizens vote to nominate their parties' candidates.

discount rate The rate the Fed charges member banks for short-term loans.

discovery Pretrial stage in the litigation process in which the lawyers for each side gather information, interview potential witnesses, and request documents and information from their opponents.

discretion The power to apply policy in ways that fit particular circumstances.

dissenting opinion Appellate court explaining the views of one or more judges who disagree with the outcome of the case as decided by the majority of judges.

distribution Government providing things of value to specific groups.

disturbance theory The idea that interest groups form when resources become scarce to contest the influence of other interest groups.

divided party control The situation that exists when one party controls the White House and another party controls one or both branches of Congress.

Dixiecrat Party See *States' Rights Democratic Party*.

doctrine of nullification Theory that state governments had a right to rule any federal law unconstitutional and therefore null and void in that state. The doctrine was ruled unconstitutional but served as a source of southern rebellion, contributing to the secession of southern states from the Union and ultimately the Civil War.

doctrine of secession Theory that state governments had a right to declare their independence and create their own form of government. Eleven southern states seceded from the Union in 1860-61, created their own form of government (the Confederate States of America), and thereby precipitated the Civil War.

double jeopardy Being tried twice for the same crime, a practice prohibited by the Fifth Amendment.

dual court system Separate systems of state and federal courts throughout the United States, each with responsibilities for its own laws and constitutions.

dual federalism The powers of the federal and state governments are strictly separate, with interaction often marked by tension rather than cooperation.

due process clause A statement of rights in the Fifth Amendment (aimed at the federal government) and the Fourteenth Amendment (aimed at state and local governments) that protects against arbitrary deprivations of life, liberty, or property. The Fourteenth Amendment phrase is also interpreted flexibly by the Supreme Court to expand a variety of rights.

Duncan v. *Louisiana* **(1968)** The case in which the U.S. Supreme Court incorporated the Sixth Amendment right to trial by jury and applied it to the states under the due process clause of the Fourteenth Amendment.

dynamic modeling Tax analysis that takes into account how an increase or decrease in one tax rate can affect government revenue from other sources.

earmarks/pork-barrel legislation Legislation that benefits one state or district; also called *particularized legislation.*

earned media coverage Airtime provided free of charge to candidates for political office.

efficacy The belief that one can influence government. *Internal political efficacy* is the belief that you have the knowledge and ability to influence government. *External political efficacy* refers to the belief that governmental officials will respond to the people.

egalitarianism Doctrine of equality that ignores differences in social status, wealth, and privilege.

egalitarian principles The belief in political, economic, social, and civil equality—in other words, that all people in a political system should be treated the same.

elastic clause/necessary and proper clause A statement in Article I, Section 8, of the U.S. Constitution that grants Congress the power to pass all laws "necessary and proper" for carrying out the list of expressed powers.

electoral behavior Any activity broadly linked to the outcome of a political campaign.

electoral college A device for selecting the president and vice president of the United States, defined in Article II of the Constitution, whereby the voters in each state choose electors to attend a gathering where the electors make the final decision.

elite democratic model The view that a democracy is healthy if people acquire positions of power through competitive elections. The level of involvement by citizens in this process is unimportant so long as elections are fair.

elites People with political connections, status, or expertise who are positioned to influence public policy through the individual decision-making authority they possess as agency administrators or legislators or through their connections to decision makers.

elitism The theory that a select few—better-educated, more informed, and more interested—should have more influence than others in our governmental process.

Engel v. *Vitale* **(1962)** U.S. Supreme Court decision that prohibited sponsored prayer in public schools as a violation of the establishment clause of the First Amendment.

entitlements Government expenditures required by law.

episodic participation Occasional citizen involvement in public matters, such as during elections.

equality A core value, usually expressed as either a desired outcome or fairness in the "rules of the game."

equality of condition Conception of equality that exists in some countries that value equal economic status as well as equal access to housing, health care, education, and government services.

equality of opportunity Conception of equality that seeks to provide all citizens with opportunities for participation in the economic system and public life but accepts unequal results in income, political power, and property ownership.

equality of outcome Egalitarian belief that government must work to diminish differences between individuals in society so that everyone is equal in status and value.

Equal Pay Act Federal legislation passed in 1963 that made it illegal to pay women lower wages for the same job than men solely because they are women.

Equal Rights Amendment (ERA) A proposed constitutional amendment that would have guaranteed equal rights for men and women. It was initially suggested following the passage of the Nineteenth Amendment in 1920 but wasn't formally proposed by Congress until 1972, and failed to be ratified by the 1982 deadline.

equal time rule FCC rule that requires offering equal airtime in the broadcast media for all major candidates competing for a political office.

Era of Good Feelings The period in American history from about 1815 to 1824 when the ruling political party, the Democratic-Republicans, faced no opposition.

Espionage Act Law passed by Congress in 1917 that made it a crime to interfere with the United States' military involvement, including troop recruitment in World War I.

establishment clause Clause in the First Amendment guaranteeing freedom from religion; provided the basis for Supreme Court decisions limiting government support for and endorsement of particular religions.

exclusionary rule General principle that evidence obtained illegally, including through the violation of Fourth Amendment rights, cannot be used against a defendant in a criminal prosecution. The Supreme Court has allowed certain exceptions to the rule that permit the use of improperly obtained evidence in particular circumstances.

executive agreement Binding commitment between the United States and other countries agreed to by the president but, unlike treaties, not requiring approval by the Senate.

Executive Office of the President (EOP) A group of presidential staff agencies, created in 1939, that provides the president with help and advice.

executive order Rule made by a president that has the force of law.

exit polls Surveys of voters leaving polling places, used by news media to gauge how candidates are doing on election day.

expressed powers The powers explicitly granted to the national government in the U.S. Constitution.

fairness doctrine Policy that required television and radio broadcasters to provide time for opposing viewpoints on controversial issues so as to ensure fair and balanced reporting; formally abolished in 1987.

fast-track trade authority The right of the president to negotiate trade agreements with other nations, which are then submitted to Congress for approval or rejection within a specified time.

Federal Election Campaign Act (FECA) Law designed to limit the amount of money contributed to campaigns for Congress and the presidency and to broaden the donation reporting requirements.

federal funds rate The interest rate that banks charge each other for overnight loans.

The *Federalist Papers* A series of eighty-five essays in support of the ratification of the U.S. Constitution, written by James Madison, Alexander Hamilton, and John Jay and published under the byline "Publius" in New York City newspapers between October 27, 1787, and May 28, 1788.

Federalist Party Party founded by Alexander Hamilton whose members believed in a strong, centralized government and were supporters of the Washington and Adams administrations.

Federalists Supporters of the ratification of the U.S. Constitution.

Federal Open Market Committee (FOMC) The policymaking arm of the Federal Reserve Board of Governors.

Federal Reserve System (the Fed) The independent central bank of the United States.

federal system A system of government in which power and authority are divided between a central government and regional sub-units.

feminism A social and political movement that advocates the belief in the inherent equality of women and men.

Fifteenth Amendment (1870) A change to the Constitution that guarantees that the right to vote shall not be denied to anyone on the basis of race.

fighting words doctrine The U.S. Supreme Court's formulation of a justification for government regulation of expressions, such as personal insults, that are likely to provoke a fistfight or other immediate breach of the peace.

filibuster Process in the United States Senate used to block or delay voting on proposed legislation or on the appointment of a judge or other official by talking continuously. Sixty senators must vote to end a filibuster.

filter question A preliminary question used to determine if potential survey respondents are sufficiently knowledgeable about the topic under study.

first-past-the-post system Awarding an elected post to the candidate who receives the most votes for that position.

fiscal policy Taxation and spending decisions made by the government.

527 organizations Groups organized under Section 527 of the Internal Revenue Code, which allows for the unlimited expenditure of campaign money. These organizations became important after the Bipartisan Campaign Reform Act outlawed soft money in 2002.

flat tax A tax structured such that all income, after limited exemptions, is subject to the same tax rate.

flexible interpretation Approach to interpreting the U.S. Constitution that permits the meaning of the document to change with evolving values, social conditions, and problems.

focusing events Moments that capture attention and highlight the existence of a problem.

formula grants Specific type of categorical grant in which money is allocated and distributed based upon a prescribed formula.

Fourteenth Amendment (1868) A change to the Constitution that defines the meaning of U.S. citizenship and establishes that each state must guarantee equal protection of the laws to its citizens.

freedom A core value, usually expressed as either "freedom from" (negative) or "freedom to" (positive).

freedom of expression The right to speak, publish statements, assemble, and petition government freely without fear of punishment, guaranteed by the First Amendment.

free exercise clause Clause in the First Amendment guaranteeing freedom to practice one's religion without government interference as long as those practices do not harm other individuals or society.

free media Independent media disseminating information that allows citizens to make responsible and informed decisions and serves as a check on governmental officials.

free-rider problem The fact that public goods can be enjoyed by everyone, including people who do not pay their fair share of the cost of providing those public goods.

Free-Soil Party Party organized in 1848 to oppose the extension of slavery into the territories and to advocate the abolition of slavery itself.

free traders People who believe that the nation's economic interests are best served through open markets.

French and Indian War The nine-year conflict (1754–1763) in North America that pitted Great Britain and its North American colonies against France. France lost, and the British maintained control of much of North America.

gaining access Winning the opportunity to communicate directly with a legislator or a legislative staff member to present one's position on an issue of public policy.

garbage can model A way of thinking about policymaking as an unordered mix of problems and solutions.

gatekeepers Group or individuals who determine which stories will receive attention in the media and from which perspective.

gender gap Differences in voting and policy preferences between women and men.

genocide The deliberate and systematic extinction of an ethnic or cultural group.

geographic representation   The idea that a legislator should represent the interests of the people living in a specific geographic location.

gerrymandering   Drawing legislative district boundaries in such a way as to gain political advantage.

Gitlow v. New York **(1925)**   The case in which the U.S. Supreme Court applied the First Amendment right of free speech against the states. It was the first case to incorporate a personal right from the Bill of Rights into the due process clause of the Fourteenth Amendment.

globalization   The expansion of economic interactions between countries.

going public   Appealing directly to the people to gain support for presidential initiatives.

government   The formal structures and institutions through which binding decisions are made for citizens of a particular area.

government corporations   Agencies with independent boards and the means to generate revenue through sales of products and services, fees, or insurance premiums, and which are intended to run like private corporations.

grants-in-aid   Funds given from one governmental unit to another governmental unit for specific purposes.

grassroots mobilization   Actively involving common citizens at the local level.

Great Compromise/Connecticut Compromise   An agreement at the Constitutional Convention that the new national government would have a House, where the number of members would be based on each state's population, and a Senate, where each state would have the same number of representatives. This was a compromise between two competing proposals, the Virginia Plan and the New Jersey Plan. Also known as the Connecticut Compromise.

Great Squeeze   The British Parliament's passage of a series of measures to raise additional revenue from colonists in order to recoup some of the costs of the French and Indian War.

Greenback Party   Party organized in 1874 that opposed any reduction in the amount of paper money in circulation.

Green Party   Party active since the 1980s that supports environmentalist issues and other progressive social measures.

gross domestic product (GDP)   The value of all goods and services produced in a nation.

Hamilton, Alexander (1755–1804)   One of the framers of the Constitution and secretary of the treasury in George Washington's administration.

Hamiltonians   Supporters of Alexander Hamilton who argued that the United States foreign policy should be designed to act in the best economic interests of the country as a whole and should promote the economic good of the nation at home and abroad.

Hatch Act   Federal law that limits the participation of federal government employees in political campaigns to protect them from feeling obligated to donate money or work for political candidates.

hate speech   Expressions that direct animosity toward individuals based on their race, gender, national origin, religion, sexual orientation, or other characteristic. Certain forms of hate speech may be regulated through the use of criminal laws.

hearings   Committee sessions for taking testimony from witnesses and for collecting information on legislation under consideration or for the development of new legislation.

Help America Vote Act   A measure passed in 2002, in the wake of the controversy surrounding the 2000 election, designed to create a more uniform voting system throughout the fifty states.

Hobbes, Thomas (1588–1679)   An English philosopher who argued that humans are selfish by nature and live lives that are "nasty, brutish, and short." For safety, people form governments but give up certain rights. His most influential book was *Leviathan,* published in 1651.

hold   Rule that allows a senator to announce the intention to use delaying tactics if a particular piece of legislation moves to a vote.

home rule   In contrast to Dillon's Rule, this view asserts that local governments should be granted greater authority. According to this view, local government may exercise all authority not specifically denied to it by state constitution or state law.

horizontal powers   The powers distributed among the three branches of the U.S. national government, as outlined in the Constitution. See also *sharing of powers.*

Hundred Days   The first hundred days of Franklin Roosevelt's administration, when landmark legislation was passed to cope with the Great Depression.

ideology   The core beliefs that guide an individual's thinking.

impeachment   Process in Congress for removal of the president, federal judges, and other high officials.

impoundment   Action by the executive branch to curtail the spending of authorized funds.

income security   The notion that the government should establish programs that provide a safety net for society's poorest members.

incorporation   Process used by the Supreme Court to protect individuals from actions by state and local governments by interpreting the due process clause of the Fourteenth Amendment as containing selected provisions of the Bill of Rights.

incumbent advantage   The various factors that favor officeholders running for reelection over their challengers.

independent   A voter who is not registered or affiliated with any political party.

independent agencies   Federal agencies with narrow responsibilities for a specific policy issue, such as the environment, not covered by one of the fifteen departments.

independent regulatory commissions   Organizational entities in the federal government that are not under the control of the president or a department.

individualism   A social theory that stresses the importance of guaranteeing freedoms, rights, self-expression, and independent actions of human beings.

Industrial Revolution   A period of economic and technological development in the late 1800s and early 1900s that resulted in the creation of factories and the extensive use of machinery.

inflation   An increase in prices over time.

inner cabinet   The advisers considered most important to the president—usually the secretaries of the departments of State, Defense, Treasury, and Justice.

inquisitorial system   Legal system in most of Europe in which a judge takes an active role in questioning witnesses and seeking to discover the truth.

inside lobbying   Appealing directly to lawmakers and legislative staff, either in meetings, by providing research and information, or by testifying at committee hearings.

institutional agenda   The set of problems that governmental decision makers are actively working to solve.

institutional barriers   Legal impediments, such as laws, court decisions, and constitutional provisions, that limit the possibilities of minor parties in the United States.

institutional presidency   The conception of the presidency as a working collectivity, a massive network of staff, analysts, and advisers with the president as its head.

intelligence   Gathering and analyzing information and communications, often secret, about potential enemies and other national security matters.

interactive theory   The theory that political culture both shapes and reflects popular opinion.

interest group   A group of like-minded individuals who band together to influence public policy, public opinion, or governmental officials.

intermediate appellate courts   Courts that examine allegations concerning uncorrected errors that occurred during trials; such courts exist in the federal court system (circuit courts of appeals) and in most state court systems (usually called courts of appeals).

Intolerable Acts   See *Coercive Acts.*

investigative reporting   A type of journalism in which reporters thoroughly investigate a subject matter (often involving a scandal) to inform the public, correct an injustice, or expose an abuse.

invisible primary   Raising money and attracting media attention early in the election process, usually before the primary election year.

Iran-Contra affair   The Reagan administration's unauthorized diversion of funds from the sale of arms to Iran to support the Contras, rebels fighting to overthrow the leftist government of Nicaragua.

iron triangle   The tight relationships between employees in government agencies, interest groups, and legislators and their staff members, all of whom share an interest in specific policy issues and work together behind the scenes to shape laws and public policy.

isolationists   People who feel that the United States is overly involved in world affairs and believe that military power should be used only for self-defense.

issue attention cycle   The pattern of problems' quickly gathering attention but then failing to remain in the spotlight.

issue networks   Interest groups, scholars, and other experts that communicate about, debate, and interact regarding issues of interest and thus influence public policy when the legislature acts on those issues; also known as **policy communities.**

Jacksonian democracy   A political and social egalitarian movement that rejected political aristocracy and emphasized the role of the average citizen in public life. It began in 1828 with the election of Andrew Jackson to the presidency and lasted several decades.

Jacksonians   Populists who saw President Andrew Jackson as a man of the people. Characterized as very patriotic and nationalistic, he strongly supported aggressive defense of United States interests, including geographic expansion.

Jeffersonians   Followers of Thomas Jefferson and his belief that foreign policy, including military spending, ought to be narrow and limited to protect democracy at home. Jefferson believed that democracy should be promoted abroad but without broad military engagement.

jihadists   Participants in a crusade or holy war, especially in defense of Islam.

Jim Crow laws   Laws enacted by southern state legislatures after the Civil War that mandated rigid racial segregation. The laws were named after a minstrel song that ridiculed African Americans.

joint committee   Units that conduct oversight or issue research, but do not have legislative powers.

judicial review   The power possessed by American judges to nullify decisions and actions by other branches of government if the judges decide that those actions violate the U.S. Constitution or the state constitution.

Judiciary Act of 1789   Early statute in which Congress provided the initial design of the federal court system.

jury trials   Trials in which factual determinations, decisions about guilt (criminal cases), and imposition of liability (civil cases) are made by a body of citizens drawn from the community.

Kansas-Nebraska Bill   An act of Congress in 1854 that allowed residents of the new territories in the west to decide whether slavery would be permitted in their state. Its passage exacerbated the rift between Northern and Southern states.

Keynesians   Economists who believe that government should take an active role in correcting economic inefficiencies.

King, Martin Luther Jr. (1929–1968)   Civil rights leader who emerged from the Montgomery bus boycott to become a national leader of the civil rights movement and a recipient of the Nobel Peace Prize.

King Caucus   The caucus-based nomination system used to select the president in the early party system of Democratic-Republicans and Federalists. Each party's representatives in Congress would decide their party's nominee.

Know-Nothings   See *American Party.*

Kyoto Protocol   An international agreement to address the problem of global warming. The United States was involved in its negotiation but has refused to ratify the agreement, citing excessive economic costs.

labor union   An association of workers formed to promote collective interests such as fair pay and working conditions.

Laffer curve   An economic model that maintains that a higher rate of taxation can result in lower government revenues.

lame duck   An elected official in the final months or years of his or her term of office, often assumed to be a position of weakened power.

landslide election   An election in which the winners come to power with overwhelming public support.

***Lawrence* v. *Texas* (2003)**   U.S. Supreme Court decision invalidating state laws regulating consenting noncommercial, private sexual conduct between adults as violations of the constitutional right to privacy. Many such laws had been enforced against gays and lesbians.

laws Rules created or recognized by government.

legal model An approach to analyzing judicial decision making that focuses on the analysis of case precedent and theories of interpretation.

legitimacy The sense that the result of a decision-making process is a proper outcome in the minds of the people who must live with that outcome.

***Lemon* test** A three-part test for establishment clause violations deriving from the U.S. Supreme Court's decision in *Lemon* v. *Kurtzman* (1971), which examines whether government policies or practices provide support for religion or cause an excessive entanglement between government and religion.

libel Publication of false and malicious material that defames an individual's reputation.

liberal A person who generally supports governmental action to promote equality (such as welfare and public education), favors governmental intervention in the economy, and supports environmental issues.

libertarian A person who favors little or no regulation of the economy, and minimal governmental interference with personal freedoms.

Libertarian Party Party established in 1971 that opposes laws that limit human behavior, advocates a free-market economy without government regulation or assistance, and opposes government spending on welfare.

libertarian view The idea that the media should be allowed to publish information that they deem newsworthy or of interest to the public without regard to the social consequences of doing so.

liberty Freedom from government interference in private actions.

Liberty Party Party formed around the abolitionist cause; merged with the Free-Soil Party in 1848.

litigation Act of carrying on a lawsuit.

lobbyists People who are paid to represent interest groups before governmental officials and institutions.

Locke, John (1632–1704) An English political theorist who introduced the notion of a "social contract" under which all just governments derive their powers from the consent of the governed. Locke's writings provided the theoretical framework of Thomas Jefferson's Declaration of Independence and the entire Revolutionary movement in America.

logrolling See *reciprocity*.

macroeconomics The study of national economies as a whole.

mail survey A public opinion survey conducted by mail. Response rates tend to be low, making the reliability of the results questionable.

majority leader The head of the majority party in the Senate; the second-highest-ranking member of the majority party in the House.

majority-minority districts Voting districts in which members of a minority group make up the majority of the population.

majority opinion Appellate court opinion that explains the reasons for the case outcome as determined by a majority of judges and that establishes any rules of law produced by that judicial decision.

mandates An authoritative instruction that is required.

***Mapp* v. *Ohio* (1961)** U.S. Supreme Court decision that applied the exclusionary rule to state criminal justice cases.

***Marbury* v. *Madison* (1803)** Case in which the U.S. Supreme Court asserted the power of judicial review, despite the fact that this is not explicitly mentioned in the U.S. Constitution.

marginal tax bracket The tax rate you pay on the last dollar that you earn in a given year.

margin of error The range in which we reasonably believe the true opinion of the entire population under study falls.

marketplace of ideas The theory that ideas and theories compete for acceptance among the public.

markup The section-by-section review and revision of a bill by committee members; the actual writing of a piece of legislation.

Marshall, John (1755-1835) Important chief justice of the early U.S. Supreme Court (1801–1835) who wrote many opinions establishing the power of the federal government and the authority of the Court.

Marshall Plan The massive post–World War II foreign aid program of the United States that helped speed Western Europe's economic recovery and block the spread of communism.

mass media Any channel of communication that reaches a vast audience; examples include newspapers, magazines, television, radio, and the Internet.

material benefits Benefits that have concrete value or worth.

Mayflower Compact An agreement made by the male pilgrims aboard the Mayflower in 1620 that provided for the temporary government of the Plymouth Colony. The document created a government that was designed to promote the general good of the colony.

McGovern-Fraser Commission A reform panel established in 1968 by the Democrats to make the presidential nomination process more democratic.

McNamara Doctrine A view that military power can be applied to situations in controlled and limited amounts that rise over time and that public support should not be a major factor governing its use.

Medicaid Health care coverage for the poor.

Medicare Health care coverage for senior citizens.

merit selection A method for selecting judges used in some states that seek to reduce the role of politics by having the governor select new judges from lists of candidates presented by a selection committee.

merit system (civil service) Introduced in 1883, an approach to managing the bureaucracy whereby people are appointed to government positions on the basis of either competitive examinations or special qualifications, such as professional training.

Millennium Challenge Account A major U.S. foreign policy initiative that seeks to tie foreign aid to improved government performance in the areas of democratization and economic development.

***Miller* v. *California* (1973)** U.S. Supreme Court decision that provided the primary test for obscenity to determine what materials, especially pornography, can be regulated as outside of the protection of the First Amendment.

minority leader The leading spokesperson and legislative strategist for the minority party in either the House or the Senate.

***Miranda* v. *Arizona* (1966)** U.S. Supreme Court decision that requires police officers, prior to questioning a suspect in custody, to inform that suspect about the right to remain silent and the right to have a lawyer present during custodial questioning.

modern liberalism   A political philosophy based on a belief in the beneficial nature of the power of government.

modern presidency   A political system in which the president is the central figure and participates actively in both foreign and domestic policy.

modified process   Allowing certain amendments to a bill on the floor of the House of Representatives.

monarchy   A system of hereditary rule in which one person, a king or queen, has absolute authority over the government.

monetarists   Economists who believe that government economic actions should focus on targeting the supply of money in circulation.

monetary policy   Money supply management conducted by the Federal Reserve.

Monopoly   Exclusive control by one group or individual over specified services or commodities.

Monroe Doctrine   Policy advocated by President James Monroe in 1823 that called for European non-intervention in North and South America in exchange for the neutrality of the United States in European matters.

Montesquieu, Charles-Louis de Secondat   A French political thinker who was famous for his writings on the importance of separation of power with a balance of power and authority.

Moral Majority   A religious organization founded in 1979 by Jerry Falwell that advocated outlawing abortion, opposed homosexuality, and upheld what it called "traditional family values."

Motor-Voter Law   A law passed by Congress in 1993 designed to make it easier for Americans to register to vote.

muckrakers   Investigative journalists and novelists who uncovered corruption in business and government in the early 1900s.

muckraking   Investigating and exposing societal ills such as corruption in politics or abuses in business.

multi-issue interest groups   Groups interested in pursuing a broad range of public policy issues.

multiple referrals   The forwarding of a piece of legislation to more than one committee for consideration.

narrowcasting   Creating and broadcasting highly specialized programming that is designed to appeal to a specified subgroup rather than to the general population.

National Association for the Advancement of Colored People (NAACP)   Civil rights advocacy group founded by African Americans and their white supporters in 1909; used the court pathway to fight racial discrimination in the 1930s through the 1950s and later emphasized the election and lobbying pathways.

national debt   A nation's cumulative deficits.

national nominating convention   A meeting of delegates from communities across the nation to discuss candidates' qualifications, choose their party's nominee, and adopt a party platform.

national sales tax   A flat tax collected on all purchases.

national security adviser   The chief adviser to the president on national security matters; a lead member of the National Security Council.

National Security Council (NSC)   An organization within the Executive Office of the President to advise the president on foreign and domestic military policies related to national security.

natural rights   Basic rights that no government can deny.

***Near v. Minnesota* (1931)**   U.S. Supreme Court decision that incorporated the First Amendment right to freedom of the press and applied that right against the states.

necessary and proper clause   See *elastic clause.*

neoconservatives   People who believe that the United States has a special role to play in world politics; they advocate the unilateral use of force and the pursuit of a value-based foreign policy.

neoconservativism   A political theory that advocates aggressive foreign policy and is more supportive of domestic spending than traditional conservativism.

neoliberals   People who strongly support international law and organizations and are skeptical about the use of military force because they attribute many of the world's problems to economic, political, and social conditions.

New Deal   Programs designed by Franklin D. Roosevelt to bring economic recovery from the Great Depression by expanding the role of the federal government in providing employment opportunities and social services; advanced social reforms to serve the needs of the people, greatly expanding the budget and activity of the federal government.

new institutionalism   An approach to understanding judicial decision making that emphasizes the importance of courts' structures and processes as well as courts' roles within the governing system.

New Jersey Plan   A scheme for government advanced at the Constitutional Convention that was supported by delegates from smaller states. It called for equal representation of states in a one-house legislature.

new media   Recently developed radio and television outlets that blend mass-oriented entertainment with commentary on political issues.

news briefing   A public appearance by a governmental official for the purpose of releasing information to the press.

news conference   A media event, often staged, where reporters ask questions of politicians or other celebrities.

news monopoly   A single news firm that controls all the media in a given market.

***New York Times Company v. United States* (1971)**   U.S. Supreme Court decision prohibiting prior restraint of the Pentagon Papers, thus permitting major newspapers to publish information on the Vietnam War that the government had sought to keep secret.

Nineteenth Amendment (1920)   A change to the Constitution that granted the right to vote to women.

nomination   The process of choosing candidates to appear on the election ballot under their party's banner.

nomination caucus   A meeting of party activists to choose delegates to support candidates at their party's presidential nominating convention.

nominees   The individuals selected by a party to run for office under that party's label.

North Atlantic Treaty Organization (NATO)   The Cold War alliance of the United States, Canada, and Western European states against the

Soviet Union. It continues to exist but no longer has a clear-cut role in world politics.

Office of Management and Budget (OMB) The office that controls the financial operation of the government.

oligarchy A government run by a small group of people.

one-house bill A bill that is passed in only one house of Congress.

open process Allowing a bill to be amended on the floor of the House of Representatives.

open-ended questions A broad question that requires respondents to articulate a response.

open-market operations The buying and selling of securities by the Federal Reserve Board to manipulate the money supply.

open primary system Primary election process in which voters are allowed to cast ballots in the primary election without declaring which party they are voting for.

orientation function The job of familiarizing a new member of Congress with the procedures, norms, and customs of the chamber.

original intent An approach to constitutional interpretation that emphasizes following the meanings intended by the individuals who wrote or ratified specific constitutional provisions.

original jurisdiction A court's authority to hear a case in the first instance; authority typically possessed by trial courts but also to a limited extent by the U.S. Supreme Court in certain cases, primarily lawsuits filed by one state against another.

outside lobbying Activities directed at the general public to raise awareness and interest and to pressure officials; also known as *grassroots lobbying*.

oversight Congress's responsibility to keep an eye on agencies in the federal bureaucracy to ensure that their behavior conforms to its wishes.

packing Consolidating specific groups of voters into a small number of districts, thus reducing their electoral influence in surrounding districts.

Paine, Thomas (1737–1809) An American Revolutionary writer and democratic philosopher whose pamphlet *Common Sense* (1776) argued for complete independence from Britain. Later pamphlets inspired colonists to join the Patriot cause.

partisan realignment Historic shifts of public opinion and voter concerns that generally lead to a different party's control of government and a new set of policies.

party enrollment Official or legal designation of one's membership in a political party.

party identification A belief that one belongs to a certain party.

party machines Local party organizations in major cities who influenced elections and operated on the basis of patronage and behind-the-scenes control.

party presses Newspapers popular in the early nineteenth century that were highly partisan and often influenced by political party machines.

party unity Voting along party lines, often used as a measure of legislators' loyalty.

party unity score Various ways to measure the extent to which legislators of the same party vote together on policy matters.

pathways of action The various activities, institutions, and decision points in American politics and government that affect the creation, alteration, and preservation of laws and public policies.

patron An organization or individual that contributes money to political leaders or political groups.

patronage system Successful political candidates' and parties' rewarding their supporters with government jobs and firing supporters of the opposing party. Also known as **spoils system.**

payroll tax A tax on earnings that funds Social Security and Medicare.

penny press Cheap newspapers containing sensationalized stories sold to members of the working class in the late nineteenth and early twentieth centuries.

People's Party (Populist Party) Party formed in 1891 to advocate currency expansion and state control of the railroads.

personal interview Administration of a survey questionnaire verbally, face to face.

Phillips curve An economic model that assumes an inverse relationship between unemployment and inflation.

platform The set of issues, principles, and goals that a party supports.

Plato (427–347 B.C.) Greek philosopher often considered the first political scientist.

plea bargain Negotiated resolution of a criminal case in which the defendant enters a guilty plea in exchange for a reduction in the nature or number of charges or for a less-than-maximum sentence.

***Plessy* v. *Ferguson* (1896)** U.S. Supreme Court decision that endorsed the legality of racial segregation laws by permitting "separate but equal" services and facilities for African Americans, although the services and facilities were actually inferior. This case was later overturned by the Supreme Court's decision in *Brown* v. *Board of Education of Topeka* (1954).

pluralism A system of government in which multiple competing and responsive groups vie for power.

pluralists People who believe that power is widely distributed in a society.

pocket veto The president's killing of a bill that has been passed by both houses of Congress, simply by not signing it; occurs only if Congress has adjourned within ten days of the bill's passage.

police powers The powers reserved to state governments related to the health, safety, and well-being of citizens.

policy communities See *issue networks.*

policy entrepreneurs Advocates of particular solutions to problems.

policy process model A way of thinking about how policy is made in terms of steps in a progression.

political action committee (PAC) A political organization created to raise and spend money to influence electoral outcomes.

political culture The norms, customs, and beliefs that help citizens understand appropriate ways to act in a political system; also, the shared attitudes about how government should operate.

political equality Fundamental value underlying the governing system of the United States that emphasizes all citizens' opportunities to vote, run for public office, own property, and enjoy civil liberties protections under the Constitution.

political ideology   A consistent set of beliefs that forms a general philosophy regarding the proper goals, purposes, functions, and size of government.

political socialization   The process through which we acquire our political facts and knowledge and develop our political values.

political speech   Expressions concerning politics, government, public figures, and issues of public concern—the form of expression that contemporary commentators view as most deserving of First Amendment protection.

politico model of representation   The philosophy that legislators should follow their own judgment (that is, act like a trustee) until the public becomes vocal about a particular matter, at which point they should follow the dictates of constituents.

politics   The process by which the character, membership, and actions of a government are defined. It is the means by which the will of a community is determined and implemented.

poll tax   Money that must be paid in order to vote, outlawed by the Twenty-Fouth Amendment to the Constitution (ratified in 1964).

popular culture   Shared practices and beliefs of ordinary people in their day-to-day lives.

popular democratic model   A view of democracy that stresses the ongoing involvement of average citizens in the political process.

popular sovereignty   The notion that political and legislative power resides with all citizens rather than a select few. See also *democracy.* The principle of allowing new states to decide for themselves whether or not to allow slavery within their borders.

Populist Party   See *People's Party.*

pork-barrel legislation   See *earmarks.*

Powell Doctrine   A view that cautions against the use of military force, especially where public support is limited, but states that once the decision to use force has been made, military power should be applied quickly and decisively.

power   The ability to exercise control over others and get individuals, groups, or institutions to comply.

pragmatic party model   The assumption that the goal of political parties is to capture control of offices so as to control the distribution of government jobs.

pragmatism   The consideration of practical issues when assessing situations and solving problems.

preemption   A military strategy based on striking first in self-defense.

preferred freedoms   The rights contained in the First Amendment that judges have viewed as especially important in the eyes of the country's founders and essential for a society based on personal liberty and a democratic governing system.

prerogative power   Extraordinary powers the president may use under certain conditions.

president pro tempore   The chief presiding officer of the Senate in the absence of the vice president.

press release   A written statement that is given to the press to circulate information or an announcement.

press shield law   A statute establishing reporter's privilege. Such statutes exist in some states and have been proposed in Congress.

primaries   Elections held by political parties to select their nominees.

prime rate   Interest rate that a bank charges its best customers.

prime sponsor   The member of Congress responsible for the language of legislation.

prior censorship   Forbidding publication of material considered objectionable.

prior restraint   Government prohibition or prevention of the publication of information or viewpoints. Since its decision in *Near* v. *Minnesota* (1931), the U.S. Supreme Court has generally forbidden prior restraint as a violation of the First Amendment freedom of the press.

privatization   Turning portions of the government responsibilities over to private organizations on the assumption that they can administer and deliver services more effectively and inexpensively.

privileges and immunities clause   Article IV, Section 2 of the U.S. Constitution, which mandates that out-of-state citizens shall have the same legal rights as citizens of that state.

probability sample   Selection procedure in which each member of the target population has a known or an equal chance of being selected.

pro bono   Short for the Latin phrase *pro bono publico,* meaning "for the benefit of the public" and describing lawyers' representing clients without compensation as a service to society.

professional associations   Organizations that represent individuals, largely educated and affluent, in one particular occupational category.

Progressive movement   A movement calling for reform in government, especially regarding social and moral welfare, political corruption, and governmental reorganization.

Progressive Party   Party founded by Theodore Roosevelt during the presidential campaign of 1912, when the Republican Party refused to support him; also known as the *Bull Moose Party.*

progressive tax   A tax structured such that higher-income individuals pay a larger percentage of their income in taxes.

Progressivism   A political philosophy based on the belief that government is the best actor to solve social, economic, and political problems.

Prohibition   Forbidding the manufacture, transportation, and sale of alcoholic beverages; imposed under the Eighteenth Amendment in 1920 and repealed by the Twenty-First Amendment in 1933.

project grants   A type of categorical grant in which a competitive application process is required for a specific project (often scientific or technical research or social services).

Protectionists   People who believe in protecting American jobs and businesses from foreign competition.

pseudo-events   Events that appear spontaneous but are in fact staged and scripted by public relations experts to appeal to the news media or the public.

public advocate model   See *social responsibility theory.*

public goods   Goods that are used or consumed by all individuals, such as clean air or public roads; also known as **collective goods.**

public interest groups   Citizen organizations that advocate issues of public good, such as protection of the environment.

public opinion   The attitudes of individuals toward their political leaders and institutions as well as on political and social issues.

public policy   What government decides to do or not do; governmental laws, rules, or expenditures that express the government's goals.

purposive benefits   Intangible rewards people obtain from joining a group they support and working to advance an issue in which they believe.

push polls   A form of telemarketing disguised as a poll in which negative information (often false) is provided with the goal of influencing public opinion.

quorum   The minimum number of members that must be present at a meeting to make proceedings valid.

"rally 'round the flag" effect   The expectation that Americans will unite behind the nation's leaders in times of crisis.

rational choice model   An approach to analyzing judicial decision making that identifies strategic decisions by judges in order to advance their preferred case outcomes.

reapportionment   The process by which seats in the House of Representatives are reassigned among the states to reflect population changes following the census (every 10 years).

reasonable time, place, and manner restrictions   Permissible government regulations on freedom of speech that seek to prevent disruptions or threats to public safety in the manner in which expressions are presented. Such regulations cannot be used to control the content of political speech.

recall   Process whereby voters can remove from office an elected official before the next regularly scheduled election.

reciprocity/logrolling   Supporting a legislator's bill in exchange for support of one's own bill.

redistribution   Government providing a broad segment of the society with something of value.

redistricting   The process of redrawing legislative district boundaries within a state to reflect population changes.

Red Scare   A period of intense anticommunism in the United States.

referendum   Also called a ballot measure, initiative, or proposition; when voters are called upon to accept or reject a proposed piece of legislation (a law).

Reform Party   Party founded by Ross Perot in 1995 in the belief that Americans were disillusioned with the state of politics at the time.

regressive tax   A tax structured such that higher-income individuals pay a lower percentage of their income in taxes.

regulation   Government prohibiting or requiring certain actions of organizations and businesses.

regulations   Legal rules created by government agencies based on authority delegated by the legislature.

reporter's privilege   The asserted right of news reporters to promise confidentiality to their sources and to keep information obtained from sources, including evidence of criminal activity, secret. The U.S. Supreme Court has held that reporter's privilege does *not* fall within the First Amendment right to freedom of the press.

representational style   A legislator's priorities—for example, the ratio of time devoted to constituent issues versus time spent on the development of public policy.

representative democracy   A republic in which the selection of elected officials is conducted through a free and open process.

republic   A system of government in which members of the general public select agents to represent them in political decision making.

republican form of government   A system of government in which the general public selects agents to represent it in political decision making.

Republican Party   One of the two major parties of the United States, organized in 1854 to oppose the expansion of slavery.

reserve ratios   Minimum percentage of deposits that a financial institution must keep on hand.

residency and registration laws   State laws that stipulate how long a person must reside in a community before being allowed to vote in that community.

responsible party model   The assumption that the goal of political parties is to shape public policy and that ideology is more important than material gain.

restrictive covenant   A clause added to a deed restricting real estate sales for a reason.

retention elections   Elections held in merit selection systems in which voters choose whether to keep a particular judge on the bench after that judge has completed a term in office.

right to privacy   A constitutional right created and expanded in U.S. Supreme Court decisions concerning access to contraceptives, abortion, private sexual behavior, and other matters, although the word privacy itself does not appear in the Constitution.

***Roe* v. *Wade* (1973)**   Controversial U.S. Supreme Court decision that declared that women have a constitutional right to choose to terminate a pregnancy in the first six months following conception.

rotation   The staggering of senatorial terms such that one-third of the Senate comes up for election every two years.

rule-making authority   Lawmaking power delegated to executive branch agencies or departments.

salience hypothesis   The theory that the gender gap is largely a function of the fact that men and women put different priorities on different issues, thereby impacting their voting behavior and their political party affiliations.

sample   A subset of the population under study; if selected correctly, it represents the population from which it was drawn with reliable and measurable accuracy.

Sedition Act   Federal law passed in 1918 that attempted to limit free speech by forbidding criticism of the United States government, the Constitution, or the military; repealed in 1921.

select committee   A temporary committee created to deal with a specific issue.

selective benefits   Benefits provided only to members of an organization or group.

senatorial courtesy   Traditional deference by U.S. senators to the wishes of their colleagues representing a state concerning the appointment of specific individuals to federal judgeships in that state.

Senior Executive Service (SES)   Program within the federal executive branch, established by Congress in 1978 to enable senior administrators with outstanding leadership and management skills to be moved between jobs in different agencies to enhance the performance of the bureaucracy.

seniority   length of time served in a chamber of the legislature. Members with greater seniority have traditionally been granted greater power.

seniority system   Giving leadership positions to the legislators who have served in Congress the longest.

separationist   Interpretive approach to the establishment clause of the First Amendment that requires the clause saying a "wall of separation" between church and state.

settlements   Negotiated resolutions of civil lawsuits prior to trial.

Seventeenth Amendment   Change to the U.S. Constitution, ratified in 1913, that provides for the direct election of senators.

sharing of powers   The U.S. Constitution's granting of specific powers to each branch of government while making each branch partly dependent on the others for carrying out its duties.

Shays's Rebellion   An armed uprising in western Massachusetts in 1786 and 1787 by small farmers angered by high debt and tax burdens.

signing statements   Written proclamations issued by presidents regarding how they intend to interpret a new law.

simple random sample   A probability sample in which each person in the population under study has an equal chance of being selected.

single-issue interest groups   Groups that are interested primarily in one area of public policy.

single-member district   A legislative district that elects only one representative.

situational hypothesis   The assertion that the gender gap is largely a function of the differences in living conditions between men and women (most notably differentials in income and living standards).

Smith, Adam (1723–1790)   A Scottish political and economic philosopher whose views on free trade and capitalism were admired in colonial America.

social capital   Networks of relationships among individuals, groups, and institutions that foster trust and cooperation to solve societal problems and establish norms for appropriate behavior in pursuit of mutual benefits and shared interests.

social contract theory   A political theory that holds that individuals give up certain rights in return for securing certain freedoms. If the government breaks the social contract, grounds for revolution exist. This notion was as at the core of the Declaration of Independence.

socialism   An economic system in which the government owns and controls most factories and much or all of the nation's land.

Socialist Labor Party   Party formed in 1874 to advocate the peaceful introduction of socialism. It is the oldest socialist party in the United States and the second oldest in the world.

social responsibility theory/public advocate model   The idea that the media should consider the overall needs of society when making decisions about what stories to cover and in what manner.

Social Security   A federal program started in 1935 that taxes wages and salaries to pay for retirement benefits, disability insurance, and hospital insurance.

Social Security Trust Fund   A fund to pay future Social Security benefits, supposedly being built through today's payroll tax.

soft money   Funds contributed through a loophole in federal campaign finance regulations that allowed individuals and groups to give unlimited sums of money to political parties.

solidary benefits   Benefits derived from fellowship and camaraderie with other members.

sound bite   A short outtake from a longer film, speech, or interview.

sovereignty   The exclusive right of an independent state to reign supreme and base absolute power over a geographic region and its people.

speaker   The presiding officer of the House of Representatives, who is also the leader of the majority party in the House.

special governments   Local governmental units established for very specific purposes such as the regulation of water and school districts, airports, and transportation services.

specialization   Extensive knowledge in a particular policy area.

speedy and public trial   A right contained in the Sixth Amendment to prevent indefinite pretrial detention and secret trials.

split-ticket voters (swing voters)   Voters who cast ballots for candidates of different parties in a given election year or for candidates of different parties in different election years.

spoils system   See *patronage system*.

stagflation   The combination of stagnant GDP, rising unemployment, and rapid inflation.

Stamp Act Congress   A meeting in October 1765 of delegates from Britain's American colonies to discuss the recently passed Stamp Act. The Congress adopted a declaration of rights and wrote letters to the King and both houses of Parliament. Many historians view this gathering as a precursor of the American Revolution.

States' Rights Democratic ("Dixiecrat") Party   Party formed in 1948 by Democrats in the South who opposed desegregation.

statutes   Laws written by state legislatures and by Congress.

straight-ticket voters   Voters who cast ballots only for candidates of the same party in a given election year.

Strategic Arms Limitation Talks (SALT)   Negotiations between the United States and Soviet Union during the Cold War that produced two major agreements on limiting the size of each country's nuclear forces.

stratified sample   A probability sample in which the population under study is divided into categories (strata) that are thought to be important in influencing opinions. Then a random sample is drawn from each stratum.

straw poll   An informal, nonscientific survey to measure public opinion; commonly used by political activists to gauge the opinion of a group.

strict scrutiny   An exacting test for violations of fundamental rights by requiring the government to demonstrate a compelling interest when policies and practices clash with certain constitutional rights.

subcommittees   Specialized groups within standing committees.

supply-side economists   Economists who believe that high taxes burden the economy and can reduce government revenue.

swing voters   See *split-ticket voters*.

symbolic representation   The assumption that a legislator will represent or favor his or her own ethnic group or gender among the constituency, as opposed to the entire population; also known as *descriptive representation*.

symbolic speech The expression of an idea or viewpoint through an action, such as wearing an armband or burning an object. Symbolic speech can enjoy First Amendment protection.

technology gap/digital divide The differences in access to and mastery of information and communication technology between segments of the community (typically for socioeconomic, educational, or geographical reasons).

telephone survey Administration of a survey questionnaire over the telephone.

term limits Laws stipulating the maximum number of terms that an elected official may serve in a particular office.

terrorism Violence for the purpose of political intimidation.

test case A case sponsored or presented by an interest group in the court pathway with the intention of influencing public policy.

Texas v. Johnson (1989) Controversial U.S. Supreme Court decision providing First Amendment protection for flag burning as symbolic speech.

think tank A group of individuals who conduct research in a particular subject or a particular area of public policy.

Thirteenth Amendment (1865) A change to the Constitution that abolished slavery.

time-structured rule Allowing amendments to a bill being discussed in the House of Representatives only within a certain time frame.

Title VII of the Civil Rights Act of 1964 Federal civil rights legislation that prohibits discrimination in employment based on race, national origin, religion, sex, or physical condition.

Tocqueville, Alexis de A French scholar who traveled throughout the United States in the early 1830s. He published his notes on the trip as _Democracy in America,_ a book that is still widely read.

totalitarian regime A system of government in which the ruling elite holds all power and controls all aspects of society.

trade association A professional organization that represents the interests of members of a particular industry.

Treasury Bills (T-bills) Interest-bearing IOUs issued by the Treasury Department.

treaty A formal agreement between governments.

trial by jury A right contained in the Sixth Amendment to have criminal guilt decided by a body of citizens drawn from the community.

trigger mechanism The means, often tied to focusing events, to push a recognized problem further along in the policy cycle.

tripartite view of parties A model based on the theory that parties have three related elements: party-in-government, party-in-the-electorate, and party-as-organization.

trustee model of representation The philosophy that legislators should consider the will of the people but act in ways that they believe best for the long-term interests of the nation.

turnout The percentage of citizens legally eligible to vote in an election who actually voted in that election.

Twelfth Amendment (1804) A change to the Constitution that required a separate vote tally in the electoral college for president and vice president.

Twenty-Fourth Amendment (1964) A change to the Constitution that eliminated the poll tax.

Twenty-Sixth Amendment (1971) A change to the Constitution that granted 18-year-old citizens the right to vote.

two-party model A system in which two major political parties compete for control of the government.

unanimous consent Agreement of all senators on the terms of debate, required before a bill goes to the floor.

Underground Railroad Network of people and secret routes prior to the Civil War by which slaves escaped to freedom in Canada, Mexico, and free states the United Stataes.

unemployment rate The percentage of Americans who are currently not working but are seeking jobs.

unified party control The situation that exists when the executive and a majority of members in both houses of the legislature are of the same political party.

unitary system A system of government in which political power and authority are located in one central government that runs the country and may or may not share power with regional sub-units.

unit rule The practice, employed by forty-eight states, of awarding all of a state's electoral college votes to the candidate for the presidency who receives the greatest number of popular votes in that state.

USA PATRIOT Act Federal law enacted shortly after the terrorist attacks of September 11, 2001, that grants the federal government broad powers to fight terrorist activities.

U.S. Commission on Civil Rights Federal commission created in 1957 to study issues of discrimination and inequality in order for the federal government to consider whether additional laws and policies are needed to address civil rights matters.

U.S. district courts Trial courts in the federal court system located in each state.

U.S. Equal Employment Opportunity Commission Federal commission created in 1964 to handle complaints about employment discrimination and file lawsuits on behalf of employment discrimination victims.

universal suffrage The right to vote for all adult citizens.

veto Disapproval of a bill or resolution by the president.

veto message A document appended to a veto that outlines the rationale for the president's rejection of the measure.

Vietnam syndrome The belief, attributed to the American experience in Vietnam, that the public will not support the use of military force if it results in significant American casualties.

Virginia Plan A plan made by delegates to the Constitutional Convention from several of the larger states, a bicameral legislature, a national executive, a national judiciary, and legislative representation based on population. Much of this plan found its way into the Constitution.

voting cues Summaries encapsulating the informed judgment of others in the legislature on which members of Congress rely to streamline the decision-making process.

Voting Rights Act of 1965 Federal statute that effectively attacked literacy tests and other techniques used to prevent African Americans from voting.

War Powers Resolution A measure passed by Congress in 1973 designed to limit presidential deployment of troops unless Congress grants approval for a longer period.

warrant A judicial order authorizing a search or arrest. Under the Fourth Amendment, police and prosecutors must present sufficient evidence to constitute "probable cause" in order to obtain a warrant from a judge.

Warren, Earl (1891-1974) Chief justice of the United States (1953–1969) who led the Supreme Court to its unanimous decision in *Brown* v. *Board of Education of Topeka* (1954) and also took a leading role in many decisions expanding civil liberties and promoting civil rights.

wasted-vote syndrome The feeling that a vote for a minor-party candidate will be wasted because the candidate stands little chance of winning.

Watergate The "shorthand" name of a scandal that led to the resignation of President Richard M. Nixon in 1974.

weapons of mass destruction Weapons capable of inflicting widespread devastation on civilian populations.

***West Virginia* v. *Barnette* (1943)** U.S. Supreme Court decision protecting First Amendment free exercise rights by prohibiting schools from punishing children who, for religious reasons, decline to recite the Pledge of Allegiance.

Whig Party Party formed in 1834 in opposition to the Democratic Party and President Andrew Jackson. It advocated a loose interpretation of the Constitution and high protective tariffs.

whips Assistants to House and Senate leaders, responsible for drumming up support for legislation and for keeping count of how members plan to vote on different pieces of legislation.

Whiskey Rebellion An insurrection in 1794 by settlers in western Pennsylvania who fought against the Whiskey Tax, a federal tax on distilled drinks to provide money for national projects.

whistleblower An employee who reports or reveals misconduct by government officials or others.

Whistleblower Protection Act A federal law intended to prevent employees in the bureaucracy from being punished for reporting or revealing governmental misconduct.

white primary The system once used primarily in the South that allowed only white citizens to vote in primary elections.

Wilsonians Supporters of President Wilson who believed that the United States foreign policy should be designed to spread U.S. ideals, values, and morals throughout the world, promoting free trade to strengthen our economy. Wilson believed that intervention in foreign countries was appropriate to create peace, and to spread freedom and democracy to protect the interests of the United States.

writ of certiorari A legal action that asks a higher court to call up a case from a lower court; the legal action used to ask the U.S. Supreme Court to accept a case for hearing.

writ of mandamus A legal action that asks a judge to order a government official to take a specific action.

yellow journalism Sensationalistic stories featured in the daily press around the turn of the twentieth century.

CHAPTER 1

1. Virginia Gray and David Lowery, "Where Do Policy Ideas Come From? A Study of Minnesota Legislators and Staffers," *Journal of Public Administration Research and Theory 10* (2000): 573–595.
2. Stephanie Dunlap, "Pollution Is a Crime: Activists Find a Creative and Frugal Way to Protect Air Quality," *Cincinnati CityBeat*, May 12, 2004, http://www.citybeat.com; Kevin Aldridge, "City's Clean Air Act Targets Polluters, " *Cincinnati Enquirer*, May 6, 2005, http://www.enquirer.com
3. George F. Cole and Christopher E. Smith, *The American System of Criminal Justice*, 9th ed. (Belmont, CA: Wadsworth, 2001), pp. 83–84.
4. Quoted in John K. White and Daniel M. Shea, *New Party Politics: From Jefferson and Hamilton to the Information Age*, 2d ed. (Belmont, CA: Wadsworth, 2004), p.13.
5. Thomas Dye, *Politics in America*, 4th ed. (Upper Saddle River, NJ: Prentice Hall, 2001), p. 25.
6. For an interesting discussion of the link between political culture and system stability, see Oliver H. Woshinsky, *Culture and Politics* (Upper Saddle River, NJ: Prentice Hall, 1995).
7. Alexis de Tocqueville, *Democracy in America*, ed. Richard Heffner (New York: New American Library, 1956), vol. 1, ch. 14. (Originally published 1835.)
8. Ibid., pp. 117–118.
9. Gunnar Myrdal, *An American Dilemma: The Negro Problem and Modern Democracy* (New York: Harper Bros., 1944), p. 27.
10. Ibid.
11. Arthur M. Schlesinger Jr., *The Disuniting of America: Reflections on a Multicultural Society* (New York: Norton, 1992), p. 27.
12. Robert A. Dahl, *Who Governs? Democracy and Power in an American City* (New Haven, CT: Yale University Press, 1961), pp. 316–317.

CHAPTER 2

1. David McCullough, *John Adams* (New York: Simon & Schuster, 2001), p. 26.
2. Joseph J. Ellis, *Founding Brothers: The Revolutionary Generation* (New York: Vintage Books, 2002), p. 89.
3. Ibid., pp. 88–89.
4. James Madison, Constitutional Convention, June 28, 1787; *The Records of the Constitutional Convention of 1787*, ed. Max Farrand (New Haven, CT: Yale University Press, 1937), pp. 486–487.
5. Ellis, *Founding Brothers*, p. 92.
6. Ibid., p. 93.
7. Max Weber, "Politics as a Vocation" (1918), in *From Max Weber: Essays in Sociology*, ed. H. H. Gerth and C. Wright Mills (New York: Oxford University Press, 1946), p. 128.
8. Theodore J. Lowi and Benjamin Ginsberg, *American Government: Freedom and Power*, 2d ed. (New York: Norton, 1992), p. 10.
9. Ibid.
10. McCullough, *John Adams*, p. 60.
11. McCullough, *John Adams*.
12. Audrey Williamson, *Thomas Paine: His Life, Work and Times* (London: Allen & Unwin, 1973), p. 122.
13. Ibid., pp. 60–61.
14. Howard Bement, ed., *Burke's Speech on Conciliation with America* (Norwood, MA: Ambrose, 1922), pp. 45, 54–55, 61.
15. Barbara Ehrenreich, "Their George and Ours," *New York Times*, July 4, 2004, sec. 4, p. 9.
16. Ibid.
17. "Thomas Paine: Life in America," Encyclopaedia Britannica Online, http://search.eb.com, 2004.
18. Ehrenreich, "Their George and Ours," sec. 4, p. 9.
19. Thomas Jefferson, letter to William Stephens Smith, November 13, 1787.
20. "Articles of Confederation," Encyclopaedia Britannica Online, http://search.eb.com, 2004.
21. See Robert A. Feer, *Shays's Rebellion* (New York: Garland, 1988), pp. 504–529, cited in Larry Berman and Bruce Allen Murphy, *Approaching Democracy*, 3d ed. (Upper Saddle River, NJ: Prentice Hall, 2001), pp. 38–39.
22. George Washington, quoted in Samuel E. Morrison, Henry Steele Commager, and William Leuchtenberg, *The Growth of the American Republic*, vol. 1 (New York: Oxford University Press, 1969), p. 244.
23. Bruce Miroff, Raymond Seidelman, and Todd Swanstrom, *The Democratic Debate: An Introduction to American Politics*, 4th ed. (Boston: Houghton Mifflin, 2007), p. 26.
24. James Madison, *Federalist No. 10*.
25. Theodore J. Lowi and Benjamin Ginsberg, *American Government: Freedom and Power* (New York: Norton, 1990), p. 41.
26. Ibid., p. 42.
27. Ellis, *Founding Brothers*, p. 94.
28. Ibid., p. 91.
29. Alexander Hamilton, James Madison, and John Jay, *Federalist No. 57*.
30. "Essays of Brutus, No. 1," in *The Complete Anti-Federalist*, ed. Herbert Storing (Chicago: University of Chicago Press, 1981).
31. George Mason, quoted in Berman and Murphy, *Approaching Democracy*, p. 67.
32. Marcus Burton, quoted in Alan Taylor, *William Cooper's Town: Power and Persuasion on the Frontier of the Early American Republic* (New York: Vintage Books, 1996), p. 266.
33. Ibid.
34. Ibid.

CHAPTER 3

1. Andrew Rudalevige, "The Politics of No Child Left Behind," Education Next Online, http://www.educationnext.org, January 2004.
2. Terri Duggan Schwartzbek, "The Federalism Debate," *School Administrator 61* (2004): http://www.aasa.org/publications/saarchive.cfm ?snItemNumber=950tnItemNumber=1995 (September, 2004 edition).
3. Marty Solomon, "The Problems with No Child Left Behind," EducationNews.org, http://www.educationnews.org, January 2005.
4. George F. Will, "Utah Brushes Off Federal Education Controls," *Albany Times Union*, November 10, 2005, p. A15.
5. Morris P. Fiorina, Paul E. Peterson, Bertram Johnson, and D. Stephen Voss, *The New American Democracy*, 4th ed. (Upper Saddle River, NJ: Prentice Hall, 2005), p. 57.
6. "Era of Colonization," Encyclopaedia Britannica Online, http://search.eb.com, 2006.
7. M. Judd Harmon, *Political Thought: From Plato to the Present* (New York: McGraw-Hill, 1964), p. 289.
8. Charles F. Hobson, *The Great Chief Justice: John Marshall and the Rule of Law* (Lawrence: University Press of Kansas, 1996), p. 206.
9. James W. Loewen, *Lies My Teacher Told Me: Everything Your American History Textbook Got Wrong* (New York: Simon & Schuster, 1995), p. 141.
10. See Howard Gillman, *The Constitution Besieged: The Rise and Demise of Lochner Era Police Powers Jurisprudence* (Durham, NC: Duke University Press, 1993).
11. Gerald Gunther, *Constitutional Law*, 11th ed. (Mineola, NY: Foundation Press, 1985), p. 129.
12. Morton Grozdins, *The American System*, ed. Daniel J. Elazar (Chicago: Rand McNally, 1966).
13. U.S. Office of Management and Budget, 2005.
14. See David Osborne and Peter Hutchinson, *The Price of Government* (New York: Basic Books, 2004), for a succinct discussion of the crises faced across the nation.

CHAPTER 4

1. Lea Brilmayer, "Same-Sex Marriage Raises Legal Questions," *Washington Post,* February 15, 2004.
2. "Same-Sex Couples Exchange Vows in Massachusetts," CNN.com, May 17, 2004, http://www.cnn.com
3. Henry J. Abraham, *The Judicial Process,* 6th ed. (New York: Oxford University Press, 1993), pp. 96–97.
4. Ibid., pp. 97–100.
5. Christopher E. Smith, *Courts, Politics, and the Judicial Process,* 2d ed. (Chicago: Nelson-Hall, 1997), p. 37.
6. Stephen L. Wasby, *The Supreme Court in the Federal Judicial System,* 4th ed. (Chicago: Nelson-Hall, 1993), pp. 56–57, 238–244.
7. *Mistretta* v. *United States,* 109 S.Ct. 647, 672–673 (1989).
8. Smith, *Courts, Politics,* pp. 4–7.
9. Laurence H. Tribe and Michael C. Dorf, *On Reading the Constitution* (Cambridge, MA.: Harvard University Press, 1991), pp. 1–5.
10. See Doris Marie Provine, "Courts in the Political Process in France," in Herbert Jacob et al., *Courts, Law, and Politics in Comparative Perspective* (New Haven, CT: Yale University Press, 1996), pp. 181–185.
11. Abraham, *Judicial Process,* p. 270.
12. Daniel A. Farber, William N. Eskridge Jr., and Philip P. Frickey, *Constitutional Law* (St. Paul, MN: West, 1993), pp. 10–27.
13. Lee Epstein, Jack Knight, and Olga Shvetsova, "Selecting Selection Systems," in *Judicial Independence at the Crossroads: An Interdisciplinary Approach,* ed. Stephen B. Burbank and Barry Friedman (Thousand Oaks, CA: Sage, 2002), p. 191.
14. Jeffrey A. Segal and Harold J. Spaeth, *The Supreme Court and the Attitudinal Model* (New York: Cambridge University Press, 1993), pp. 64–73.
15. Lawrence Baum, *The Puzzle of Judicial Behavior* (Ann Arbor: University of Michigan Press, 1997), pp. 89–124.
16. Herbert Kritzer, "Martin Shapio: Anticipating the New Institutionalism," in *The Pioneers of Judicial Behavior,* ed. Nancy Maveety (Ann Arbor: University of Michigan Press, 2003), p. 387.
17. See, for example, Samuel Walker, *In Defense of American Liberties: A History of the ACLU* (New York: Oxford University Press, 1990).
18. Wasby, *Supreme Court,* p. 155.
19. Joseph D. Kearney and Thomas W. Merrill, "The Influence of Amicus Curiae Briefs on the Supreme Court," *University of Pennsylvania Law Review 148* (2000): 753.
20. Jeff Yates, *Popular Justice: Presidential Prestige and Executive Success in the Supreme Court* (Albany: State University of New York Press, 2002), p. 2.
21. Gerald Rosenberg, *The Hollow Hope: Can Courts Bring About Social Change?* (Chicago: University of Chicago Press, 1991).
22. Bradley C. Canon, "The Supreme Court and Policy Reform: The Hollow Hope Revisited," in *Leveraging the Law: Using the Courts to Achieve Social Change,* ed. David A. Schultz (New York: Lang, 1998), pp. 215–249.
23. See Richard E. Morgan, *Disabling America: The "Rights Industry" in Our Time* (New York: Basic Books, 1984); Jeremy Rabkin, *Judicial Compulsions: How Public Law Distorts Public Policy* (New York: Basic Books, 1989).
24. Gallup Poll, "Civil Liberties," national opinion poll conducted September 14–15, 2001, www.galluppoll.com

CHAPTER 5

1. This account is based on Mike Anderson, "Crawford Authorities Arrest Five in Bush Protest," *Waco Tribune,* May 4, 2003; "Anti-War Protesters Convicted for Demonstrating Near Bush's Ranch," Reporters' Committee for Freedom of the Press, http://www.rcfp.org/news; and Nikki Buskey, "Arrested Protesters File Lawsuit," *Daily Texan,* January 21, 2005, p. 1.
2. See Texas Civil Rights Project, http://www.texascivilrightsproject.org
3. *The Supreme Court at Work* (Washington, DC: CQ Press, 1990), p. 129.
4. Henry J. Abraham, *Freedom and the Court: Civil Rights and Liberties in the United States,* 5th ed. (New York: Oxford University Press, 1988), p. 41.
5. Ibid., p. 206.
6. Mary Beth Tinker, "I'm Going to Kill You!" quoted in Peter H. Irons, *The Courage of Their Convictions: Sixteen Americans Who Fought Their Way to the Supreme Court* (New York: Free Press, 1988), p. 251.
7. "Student Pleads Guilty to Harassment Incident," *Lansing State Journal,* March 1, 2003, p. 3B.
8. Thomas R. Hensley, Christopher E. Smith, and Joyce A. Baugh, *The Changing Supreme Court: Constitutional Rights and Liberties* (St. Paul, MN: West, 1997), p. 329.
9. Christopher E. Smith, *Justice Antonin Scalia and the Supreme Court's Conservative Moment* (Westport, CT: Praeger Publishers, 1993), pp. 42–45.
10. Joshua Lipton, "Vanessa Leggett: Why She Wouldn't Give Up Her Notes," *Columbia Journalism Review,* March-April 2002, http://www.cjr.org/issues/2002/2/qa-leggett.asp
11. Hensley, Smith, and Baugh, *Changing Supreme Court,* p. 130.
12. Ibid., p. 131.
13. Linda Greenhouse, "Documents Reveal the Evolution of a Justice," *New York Times,* March 4, 2004, p. A16.
14. Craig Uchida and Timothy Bynum, "Search Warrants, Motions to Suppress, and 'Lost Cases': The Effects of the Exclusionary Rule in Seven Jurisdictions," *Journal of Criminal Law and Criminology 81* (1991): 1034–1066.
15. Christopher E. Smith, *Constitutional Rights: Myths and Realities* (Belmont, CA: Wadsworth, 2004), pp. 115–128.
16. George F. Cole and Christopher E. Smith, *Criminal Justice in America,* 4th ed. (Belmont, CA: Wadsworth, 2004), p. 10.
17. See Lee Epstein and Joseph Kobylka, *The Supreme Court and Legal Change* (Chapel Hill: University of North Carolina Press, 1992).
18. Mark Costanza, *Just Revenge: Costs and Consequences of the Death Penalty* (New York: St. Martin's Press, 1997), pp. 95–111.
19. Stanley Cohen, *The Wrong Men* (New York: Carroll & Graf, 2003), pp. 298–322; Death Penalty Information Center, http://www.deathpenaltyinfo.org
20. Christopher E. Smith, *Courts and the Poor* (Chicago: Nelson-Hall, 1991), p. 118.

CHAPTER 6

1. "Desegregation of the Armed Forces," Harry S Truman Presidential Library, http://www.trumanlibrary.org
2. Jack N. Rakove, *Original Meanings: Politics and Ideas in the Making of the Constitution* (New York: Knopf, 1996), p. 215.
3. See, for example, Peter Kolchin, *American Slavery, 1619–1877* (New York: Hill & Wang, 1993); Walter Johnson, *Soul by Soul: Life inside the Antebellum Slave Market* (Cambridge, MA: Harvard University Press, 1999); Ira Berlin, Marc Favreau, and Steven F. Miller, eds., *Remembering Slavery* (New York: New Press, 1998); John Hope Franklin and Loren Schweninger, *Runaway Slaves: Rebels on the Plantation* (New York: Oxford University Press, 1999).
4. See, for example, Andrew Hacker, *Two Nations: Black and White, Separate, Hostile, Unequal* (New York: Scribner, 1992); Tom Wicker, *Tragic Failure: Racial Integration in America* (New York: Morrow, 1996).
5. Eric Foner, *The Story of American Freedom* (New York: Norton, 1998), p. 104.
6. Kolchin, *American Slavery,* p. 215.
7. Ibid., pp. 220–224.
8. David E. Kyvig, *Explicit and Authentic Acts: Amending the U.S. Constitution, 1776–1995* (Lawrence: University Press of Kansas, 1996), pp. 182–183.

9. Foner, *Story of American Freedom*, p. 105.

10. William Gillette, *Retreat from Reconstruction, 1869–1879* (Baton Rouge: Louisiana State University Press, 1979), pp. 335–347.

11. Leon F. Litwack, *Trouble in Mind: Black Southerners in the Age of Jim Crow* (New York: Knopf, 1998), pp. 150–151.

12. Ronald Takaki, *A Different Mirror: A History of Multicultural America* (Boston: Little, Brown, 1993), pp. 191–221.

13. Tony Mauro, "Life during Wartime," *Legal Times*, January 8, 2004.

14. Loewen, *Lies My Teacher Told Me*, p. 165.

15. Ibid., pp. 164–166.

16. See Richard Kluger, *Simple Justice* (New York: Random House, 1975), pp. 657–747.

17. Summary drawn from Irons, *Courage of Their Convictions*, pp. 65–79.

18. "An Interview with Congressman Charles Diggs," in Juan Williams, *Eyes on the Prize: America's Civil Rights Years* (New York: Viking, 1987), p. 49.

19. Ibid., p. 52.

20. See Myrdal, *American Dilemma*.

21. Taylor Branch, *Parting the Waters: America in the King Years, 1954–1963* (New York: Simon & Schuster, 1988), pp. 128–205.

22. Williams, *Eyes on the Prize*, pp. 59–89.

23. Ibid., pp. 99–113.

24. Branch, *Parting the Waters*, p. 891.

25. Williams, *Eyes on the Prize*, p. 197–200.

26. Ibid., pp. 276–277.

27. Gerald Gunther, *Constitutional Law*, 11th ed. (Mineola, NY: Foundation Press, 1985), p. 932.

28. Eleanor Flexner, *Century of Struggle: The Women's Rights Movement in the United States*, rev. ed. (Cambridge, MA: Harvard University Press, 1975), pp. 154–158.

29. Ibid., pp. 167–171, 295.

30. Ibid., p. 228.

31. Ibid., p. 300.

32. Kyvig, *Explicit and Authentic Acts*, p. 364.

33. Oscar J. Martinez, "A History of Chicanos/Mexicanos along the U.S.-Mexico Border," in *Handbook of Hispanic Cultures in the United States: History*, ed. Alfredo Jimenez (Houston, TX: Arte Publico Press, 1994), pp. 261–280.

34. Pedro Caban, Jose Carrasco, Barbara Cruz, and Juan Garcia, *The Latino Experience in U.S. History* (Paramus, NJ: Globe Fearon, 1994), pp. 208–220.

35. Ibid., pp. 282–287.

36. See, for example, Matthew R. Durose, Erica L. Schmitt, and Patrick Langan, *Contacts between Police and the Public: Findings from the 2002 National Survey* (Washington, DC: U.S. Bureau of Justice Statistics, 2005); Robin Shepard Engel and Jennifer M. Calnon, "Examining the Influence of Drivers' Characteristics during Traffic Stops with Police: Results from a National Survey," *Justice Quarterly* 21 (2004): 49–90.

37. "How Long Would They Lock Up Your Killer?" *Legal Affairs*, July-August 2004, p. 25.

38. Statement of Senator John McCain, chair of the Senate Committee on Indian Affairs, hearing on S.1439, July 26, 2005, http://www.itmatrustfunds.org

39. Marvin Wingfield and Bushra Karaman, "Arab Stereotypes and American Educators," *ADC and Education*, March 1995.

40. "Muslim Girl Suspended for Head Scarf," CNN.com, October 11, 2003, http://www.cnn.com

41. Darcia Harris Bowman, "High School Students Stay Silent to Protest Mistreatment of Gays," *Education Week*, April 17, 2002.

42. Bill Pennington, "Title IX Trickles Down to Girls in Generation Z," *New York Times*, June 29, 2004.

CHAPTER 7

1. Tiahrt Provision Requires Destruction of Gun Purchase Records. *Wichita Eagle*, January 27, 2004.

2. Brady Campaign to Prevent Gun Violence, press release February 1, 2004. Statement of Sarah Brady on Passage of the Omnibus Appropriation Bill.

3. "The Power of the Gun Lobby" [editorial], *New York Times*, January 22, 2004, p. A26.

4. Kelly D. Patterson and Daniel M. Shea, eds., *Contemplating the People's Branch* (Upper Saddle River, NJ: Prentice Hall, 2000), p. 6.

5. Tom Hamburger, "Senators Debate Role of Public Will as Polls Call for Trial to End," *Minneapolis Star Tribune*, February 1, 1999, p. A1.

6. Patterson and Shea, *Contemplating the People's Branch*, p. 7

7. Roger H. Davidson and Walter Oleszek, *Congress and Its Members*, 10th ed. (Washington, DC: CQ Press, 2004), p. 122.

8. Gary W. Cox and Jonathan N. Katz, *Elbridge Gerry's Salamander* (Cambridge: Cambridge University Press, 2002), p. 3.

9. See, for example, Ralph Blumenthal, "GOP Is Victorious in Remapping," *New York Times*, January 7, 2004, p. A12.

10. Adam Clymer. "Why Iowa Has So Many Hot Seats," *New York Times*, October 27, 2002, p. A-22.

11. L. Sandy Maisel, *Parties and Elections in America: The Electoral Process*, 3d ed (Lanham, MD: Rowman & Littlefield, 1999), p. 207.

12. Cox and Katz, *Elbridge Gerry's Salamander*, pp. 12–13.

13. Ibid., pp. 25–28.

14. Davidson and Oleszek, *Congress and Its Members*, 10th ed., 2004, pp. 193–194.

15. Ibid., p. 199.

16. Ibid., p. 213.

17. Opening remarks of Senator Arlen Spector before the Senate Subcommittee on Labor, Health and Human Services, Education, and Related Agencies, Committee on Appropriations, June, 5, 1997.

18. Davidson and Oleszek, *Congress and Its Members*, 10th edition, p. 242.

19. Ibid., p. 337.

20. David J. Vogler, *The Politics of Congress* (Madison, WI: Brown & Benchmark, 1993), p. 76.

21. Michael J. Malbin, *Unelected Representatives: Congressional Staff and the Future of Representative Government* (New York: Basic Books, 1979).

22. Charles Peters, *How Washington Really Works* (Reading, MA: Addison-Wesley, 1992), p.133; Fred Harris, *In Defense of Congress* (New York: St. Martin's Press, 1995), pp. 40–41.

23. Patterson and Shea, *Contemplating the People's Branch*, pp. 133–134.

24. Ibid., p. 136.

25. Norman Ornstein of the American Enterprise Institute, quoted on Nancy Pelosi's Web site, http://www.democraticleader.house.gov/about/personal_story.cfm, March 30, 2004.

26. *National Review*, February 22, 2003, cited on ibid.

27. Steven S. Smith, "The Senate in the Postreform Era," in *The Postreform Congress*, ed. Roger H. Davidson (New York: St. Martin's Press, 1992), pp. 173, 185.

28. Donald R. Matthews, *U.S. Senators and Their World* (New York: Vintage Books, 1960).

29. Ibid., p. 97.

30. Ibid., p. 99.

31. Davidson and Oleszek, *Congress and Its Members*, p. 234.

32. Congressional Black Caucus http://www.congressionalblackcaucus.net accessed February 2004.

33. Ibid.

34. Stephen J. Wayne, *Is This Any Way to Run a Democratic Election?* 2d ed. (Boston: Houghton Mifflin, 2003), p. 54.

35. Sean Loughlin and Robert Yoon, "Millionaires Populate U.S. Senate," CNN.com/Inside Politics, June 13, 2003, http://www.cnn.com

36. "Income," U.S. Census Bureau, http://www.census.gov/hhes/www/income.html, February 2004.

37. Roger H. Davidson and Walter Oleszek, *Congress and Its Members,* 7th ed. (Washington, DC: CQ Press, 2000), pp. 128–129.

38. Roger H. Davidson and Walter Oleszek, *Congress and Its Members,* 10th ed. (Washington, DC: CQ Press, 2006), p. 479.

39. Harris, *In Defense of Congress,* p. 59.

40. Norman J. Ornstein, "Prosecutors Must Stop Their Big Game Hunt of Politicians," *Roll Call,* April 26, 1993, p. 6.

41. Larry J. Sabato, *Feeding Frenzy: How Attack Journalism Has Transformed American Politics* (New York: Free Press, 1993), p. 1.

42. Katherine Isaac, *Ralph Nader's Practicing Democracy 1997: A Guide to Student Action* (New York: St. Martin's Press, 1997).

CHAPTER 8

1. William Langley, "Revealed: What Really Went On during Bush's 'Missing Hours,'" *Daily Telegraph,* December 16, 2001, http://www.telegraph.co.uk

2. Lowi and Ginsberg, *American Government,* 1st ed., p. 241.

3. John Locke, *The Second Treatise on Government,* cited in ibid., p. 241.

4. James P. Pfiffner and Roger Davidson, eds., *Understanding the Presidency* (New York: Longman, 1996), p. 2.

5. Sidney M. Milkis and Michael Nelson, *The American Presidency: Origins and Development, 1776–1998* (Washington, DC: CQ Press, 1999), p. 26.

6. Marcus Cunliffe, *George Washington: Man and Monument* (New York: New American Library, 1958), p. 15.

7. Milkis and Nelson, *American Presidency, 1776–1998,* p. 28.

8. David Mervin, *The President of the United States* (New York: Harvester Press, 1993), p. 22.

9. Michael Nelson, ed., *The Evolving Presidency,* 2d ed. (Washington, DC: CQ Press, 2004), p. 10.

10. Robert Dallek, *Hail to the Chief: The Making and Unmaking of American Presidents* (New York: Hyperion, 1996), p. 14.

11. William K. Muir Jr., *The Bully Pulpit: The Presidential Leadership of Ronald Reagan* (San Francisco: ICS Press, 1992), p. 44.

12. Theodore Roosevelt, "The Stewardship Doctrine," in *Classics of the American Presidency,* ed. Harry Bailey (Oak Park, IL: Moore, 1980), pp. 35–36.

13. Dallek, *Hail to the Chief,* p. 18.

14. Michael A. Genovese, *The Power of the American Presidency, 1789–2000* (New York: Oxford University Press, 2001), p. 132.

15. Ibid, p. 143.

16. Joseph A. Pika and John Anthony Maltese, *The Politics of the Presidency,* 6th ed. (Washington, DC: CQ Press, 2004), p. 243.

17. Sidney M. Milkis and Michael Nelson, *The American Presidency: Origins and Development, 1776–2002* (Washington, DC: CQ Press, 2003), p. 424.

18. Ibid.

19. Ibid., p. 428.

20. Nathan Miller, *FDR: An Intimate History* (Lanham, MD: Madison Books, 1983), p. 276.

21. Edward S. Greenberg and Benjamin I. Page, *The Struggle for Democracy,* 5th ed. (New York: Longman, 2002), p. 361.

21. Ibid., p. 434.

22. Milkis and Nelson, *American Presidency, 1776–2002,* p. 438.

23. Ibid., p. 440.

24. Ibid., p. 193.

25. "Poll: Bush Ratings Hit New Low," CBS News.com, October 6, 2005. http://www.cbsnews.com/stories/2005/106/opinion/polls/main924485

26. Gary King and Lyn Ragsdale, *The Elusive Executive: Discovering Statistical Patterns in the Presidency* (Washington, DC: CQ Press, 1988), p. 35.

27. The Supreme Court case was *United States* v. *Curtis Wright Corp.,* 299 U.S. 304 (1936).

28. U.S. Department of State, "Trade Protection Authority Fact Sheet," http://www.state.gov/g/oes/rls/fs/2002/12953.htm, December 10, 2004.

29. Louis Fisher, "Invitation to Struggle: The President, Congress, and National Security," in Pfiffner and Davidson, *Understanding the Presidency,* p. 269.

30. Abraham Lincoln, "A Special Session Message, July 4, 1861," cited in Genovese, *Power of the American Presidency,* p. 81.

31. Theodore J. Lowi, *The Personal President: Power Invested, Promise Unfulfilled* (Ithaca, NY: Cornell University Press, 1985), p. xii.

32. Ray Price, an aide to Richard Nixon during his 1968 presidential campaign, cited in Pika and Maltese, *Politics of the Presidency,* p. 25.

33. Ibid., p. 1.

34. Dallek, *Hail to the Chief,* p. xx.

35. These points are made by political scientist Fred I. Greenstein, "A Change and Continuity in Modern Presidency," in *The New American Political System,* ed. Anthony King (Washington, DC: American Enterprise Institute, 1978), pp. 45–46.

36. Arthur M. Schlesinger Jr., *The Imperial Presidency,* 2d ed. (Boston: Houghton Mifflin, 1989).

CHAPTER 9

1. Eric Lipton and Scott Shane, "Leader of Federal Effort Feels the Heat," *New York Times,* September 3, 2005; Daren Fonda and Rita Healy, "How Reliable Is Brown's Résumé?" *Time,* September 8, 2005.

2. "Arsenic in Drinking Water," Environmental Protection Agency, http://www.epa.gov/safewater/arsenic, April 19, 2006; "Bush Administration's Belated Arsenic Decision Doesn't Imply Insensitivity, Expert Says," Alabama Cooperative Extension Service, http://www.aces.edu, November 8, 2001; "EPA Delays Lower Arsenic Standards for Water," CNN.com, www.cnn.com, March 21, 2001.

3. Pew Research Center for the People and the Press, "Performance and Purpose: Constituents Rate Government Agencies," http://people-press.org/reports, April 12, 2000.

4. Peter D. Hart Research Associates, *Partisanship Up, Confidence Down: Americans Want Compromise and Competition* (Washington, DC: Council for Excellence in Government, 2006), p. 2.

5. Charles T. Goodsell, *The Case for Bureaucracy* (Chatham, NJ: Chatham House, 1983), p. 15.

6. Steve Hoffman, "Clerk Hits Political Roadblocks," *Akron (OH) Beacon Journal,* February 13, 1991, p. D1.

7. Diana Jean Schemo, "Problems Seen for More Testing of U.S. Students," *New York Times,* October 5, 2004, www.nytimes.com

8. "TSA Takes Heat for Background Check Miscues," Government Security, http://govtsecurity.securitysolutions.com, February 11, 2004.

9. Jeff Johnson, "TSA Screeners Claim They're 'Being Used for Cannon Fodder,'" CNSNews.com, http://www.cnsnews.com, March 4, 2003.

10. B. Guy Peters, *American Public Policy: Promise and Performance,* 5th ed. (Chatham, NJ: Chatham House, 1999), p. 33.

11. Elizabeth Gettelman, "The K(a-ching!) Street Congressman," *Mother Jones,* November-December 2004, p. 24.

12. "Biographies of Key Officials: Jeffrey N. Shane," U.S. Department of Transportation, http://www.dot.gov

13. Tony Pugh, "Medicare Cost Estimates Concealed, Expert Says," *San Diego Union-Tribune,* March 12, 2004.

14. "General: Army Leaned on Whistleblower," CBSNews.com, http://www.cbsnews.com, November 1, 2004.

15. "Whistleblower Protection Act Information," U.S. Securities and Exchange Commission, http://www.sec.gov/eeoinfo/whistleblowers.htm

16. Neely Tucker, "A Web of Truth," *Washington Post,* October 19, 2005, p. C1.

17. Robert A. Katzmann, *Regulatory Bureaucracy* (Cambridge, MA: MIT Press, 1980), p. 180.

18. Stephen Labaton, "Agencies Postpone Issuing New Rules until after Election," *New York Times,* September 27, 2004.

19. Ibid.

20. Joel Brinkley, "Out of Spotlight, Bush Overhauls U.S. Regulations," *New York Times,* August 14, 2004.

21. Laura Meckler, "$1.2 Million Fine for Fox's 'Married by America' Show," *Chicago Sun-Times,* October 13, 2004.

22. See Donna Price Cofer, *Judges, Bureaucrats, and the Question of Independence* (Westport, CT: Greenwood Press, 1985).

23. Christopher H. Foreman Jr., *Signals from the Hill: Congressional Oversight and the Challenge of Social Regulation* New Haven, CT: Yale University Press, 1988), p. 13.

24. See Lawrence C. Dodd and Richard L. Schott, *Congress and the Administrative State* (New York: Wiley, 1979).

CHAPTER 10

1. Robert S. Erikson and Kent L. Tedin, *American Public Opinion,* 5th ed. (Boston: Allyn & Bacon, 1995), p. 152.

2. See, for instance, the seminal work by Angus Campbell, Philip Converse, Warren Miller, and Donald Stokes, *The American Voter* (Chicago: University of Chicago Press, 1960).

3. See, for instance, V. O. Key Jr., *The Responsible Electorate* (Cambridge, MA: Belknap Press, 1966); see also Warren E. Miller and J. Merrill Shanks, *The New American Voter* (Cambridge, MA: Harvard University Press, 1996).

4. Walter Lippmann, *Public Opinion* (New York: Macmillan, 1922).

5. Robert Weissberg, *Polling, Policy, and Public Opinion: The Case against Heeding the "Voice of the People"* (New York: Palgrave-Macmillan, 2002).

6. Sidney Verba, *Participation in America: Political Democracy and Social Equality* (Chicago: University of Chicago Press, 1972).

7. Herbert Asher, *Polling and the Public: What Every Citizen Should Know,* 6th ed. (Washington, DC: CQ Press, 2004), p. 195.

8. Starting with the seminal research of Philip E. Converse, "The Nature of Belief Systems in Mass Publics," in *Ideology and Discontent,* ed. David E. Apter (New York: Free Press, 1964).

9. Erikson and Tedin, *American Public Opinion,* p. 144.

10. Jack Ludwig, "Acceptance of Interracial Marriage at Record High," Gallup Poll, http://poll.gallup.com/content/default.aspx?ci=11836&pg=1, June 1, 2004.

11. "Homosexual Relations," Gallup Poll, http://poll.gallup.com/content/default.aspx?ci=1651, 2006.

12. Ibid.

13. Paul Abramson, *Political Attitudes in America* (San Francisco: Freeman, 1983).

14. Benjamin I. Page and Robert Y. Shapiro, *The Rational Public* (Chicago: University of Chicago Press, 1992), p. 178.

15. Ibid., 179.

16. "The NES Guide to Public Opinion and Electoral Behavior," *American National Election Studies,* http://www.umich.edu/~nes/nesguide/graphs/g4c_1_1.htm, November 30, 2005, graph 4C.1.1.

17. "Women in Elective Office, 2006," Center for American Women in Politics, http://www.rci.rutgers.edu/~cawp/Facts/Officeholders/elective.pdf, 2006.

18. See David J. Jackson, *Entertainment and Politics: The Influence of Pop Culture on Young Adult Political Socialization* (New York: Lang, 2002), ch. 1.

19. See Daniel Shea, "Introduction: Popular Culture—the Trojan Horse of American Politics?" in *Mass Politics: The Politics of Popular Culture,* ed. Daniel Shea (New York: St. Martin's/Worth, 1999).

20. David F. Walsh, "American Politics in Transition: The 1980s and 1990s," in *America in the 21st Century: Challenges and Opportunities in Domestic Politics,* ed. Kul B. Rai, David F. Walsh, and Paul J. Best (Upper Saddle River, NJ: Prentice Hall, 1998).

21. Harold W. Stanley and Richard G. Niemi, *Vital Statistics on American Politics, 2003–2004* (Washington, DC: CQ Press, 2003).

22. John Cloud, "The Right's New Wing," *Time,* August 30, 2004, p. 25

23. Paul Allen Beck and M. Kent Jennings, "Pathways to Participation," *American Political Science Review* 76 (1982): 94–108; Eric Plutzer, "Becoming a Habitual Voter: Inertia, Resources, and Growth in Young Adulthood," *American Political Science Review* 96 (2002): 57–74.

24. Jackson, *Entertainment and Politics,* p. 9.

25. M. Kent Jennings and Richard G. Niemi, *Generations and Politics: A Panel Study of Young Adults and Their Parents* (Princeton, NJ: Princeton University Press, 1981).

26. Stuart Oskamp, *Attitudes and Opinions,* 2d ed. (Englewood Cliffs, NJ: Prentice Hall, 1991), p. 160.

27. Ibid., ch. 15.

28. U.S. Census Bureau, *America's Families and Living Arrangements, 2004* (Washington, DC: Government Printing Office, 2004).

29. David Easton, *A Systems Analysis of Political Life* (New York: Wiley, 1965).

30. James G. Gimpel, J. Celeste Lay, and Jason E. Schuknecht, *Cultivating Democracy: Civic Environments and Political Socialization in America* (Washington, DC: Brookings Institution Press, 2003), p. 147.

31. Lee Anderson, *The Civics Report Card* (Princeton, NJ: Educational Testing Service, 1990).

32. U.S. Census Bureau, *Educational Attainment in the United States, 2003* (Washington, DC: Government Printing Office, 2003).

33. Earnest Boyer and Mary Jean Whitelaw, *The Condition of the Professorate* (New York: Harper & Row, 1989).

34. Gimpel, Lay, and Schuknecht, *Cultivating Democracy,* p. 63.

35. Ibid.

36. Ibid., p. 92.

37. See, for instance, Penny Edgell Becker and Pawan H. Dhingra, "Religious Involvement and Volunteering: Implications for Civil Society," *Sociology of Religion* 62 (2001): 315–335; Corwin Smidt, "Religion and Civic Engagement: A Comparative Analysis," *Annals of the American Academy of Political and Social Sciences* 565 (1999): 176–192.

38. Gimpel, Lay, and Schuknecht, *Cultivating Democracy,* p. 142.

39. Ibid., p. 143.

40. Landrea Wells, "Viewing," Children and Television, http://iml.jou.ufl.edu/projects/Spring03/Wells/viewing.htm, 2003.

41. See, for instance, Gimpel, Lay, and Schuknecht, *Cultivating Democracy,* p. 35.

42. CNN.com, http://www.cnn.com, September 29, 2004."Daily Show Viewers Ace Political Quiz", by Brian Long, http://www.cnn.com/2004/SHOWBIZ/TV/09/28/comedy.politics/index.html

43. Gimpel, Lay, and Schuknecht, *Cultivating Democracy,* ch. 7.

44. Ibid., p. 182.

45. Ibid., p. 191.

46. See Erikson and Tedin, *American Public Opinion,* ch. 5, for a good discussion of generational theories.

47. Paul Lazarfeld, Bernard Berelson, and Hazel Gaudet, *The People's Choice* (New York: Columbia University Press, 1944).

48. U.S. Census Bureau, *Current Population Survey, 2005: Annual Social and Economic Supplement* (Washington, DC: Government Printing Office, 2005).

49. Erikson and Tedin, *American Public Opinion,* p. 181.

50. Ibid., p. 183.

51. William H. Flanigan and Nancy H. Zingle, *Political Behavior of the American Electorate,* 11th ed. (Washington, DC: CQ Press, 2006), p. 132.

52. Pew Research Center for the People and the Press, "Religion in American Life," http://people-press.org, April 10, 2001.
53. Flanigan and Zingle, *Political Behavior,* p. 106.
54. James L. Guth, Lyman A. Delestedt, John C. Green, and Corwin E. Smidt, "A Distant Thunder? Religious Mobilization in the 2000 Elections," in *Interest Group Politics,* 6th ed., ed. Allen J. Cigler and Burdett A. Loomis (Washington, DC: CQ Press, 2002).
55. Oskamp, *Attitudes and Opinions,* p. 390.
56. Ibid., p. 391.
57. Center for American Women and Politics, *The Gender Gap: Attitudes on Public Policy Issues* (New Brunswick, NJ: Eagleton Institute of Politics, Rutgers University, 1997); Susan J. Carroll and Richard F. Fox, eds., *Gender and Elections* (New York: Cambridge University Press, 2006).
58. Reported in Justin Lewis, *Constructing Public Opinion: How Political Elites Do What They Like and Why We Seem to Go Along with It* (New York: Columbia University Press, 2001), p. 34.
59. Asher, *Polling and the Public,* p. 23.
60. Benjamin Ginsberg, *The Captive Public: How Mass Opinion Promotes State Power* (New York: Basic Books, 1986).
61. Asher, *Polling and the Public,* p. 3.
62. Lewis, *Constructing Public Opinion,* p. 41.
63. Erikson and Tedin, *American Public Opinion,* p. 9.
64. Asher, *Polling and the Public,* p. 10.
65. Andrew Kohut, "The Vocal Minority in American Politics," Times Mirror Center for the People and the Press, Washington, DC, July 16, 1993.
66. Richard Morin, "Don't Ask Me: As Fewer Cooperate on Polls, Criticism and Questions Mount," *Washington Post,* October 25, 2004, p. C1.
67. Ibid.
68. Ibid.
69. Ibid., p. 25.
70. See, for, instance Lewis, *Constructing Public Opinion,* p. 37.
71. James A. Stimson, *Public Opinion in America,* 2d ed. (Boulder, CO: Westview Press, 1999), p. 122.

CHAPTER II
1. W. Lance Bennett, *News: The Politics of Illusion* 6th edition (Longman: New York, 2005, p. 6.
2. Alfred McClung Lee, *The Daily Newspaper in America,* (Macmillian: New York, 1937), p. 21.
3. Quoted in Philip Davidson, *Propaganda and the American Revolution, 1763–1783* (University of North Carolina Press: Chapel Hill, NC, 1941), p. 285.
4. *Messages and Papers of the Presidents 1789–1908,* vol.1 (Bureau of National Literature and Art: Washington, D.C., 1909), p. 132.
5. Lee, *The Daily Newspaper in America,* p. 716–717.
6. See Jan E. Leighley, *Mass Media and Politics: A Social Science Perspective* (Boston: Houghton Mifflin Company, 2004) chapter 1.
7. Quoted in W.W. Swanberg, *Citizen Hurst* (Scribner: New York, 1961), p. 90.
8. Lee, p. 215–216.
9. Doris A. Graber, *Mass Media & American Politics,* 7th edition (CQ Press: Washington, D.C., 2006) p. 38.
10. Edwin Emery and Michael Emery, *The Press and America* (Prentice Hall: Englewood Cliffs, NJ, 1984) p. 372–379.
11. Frank Luther Mott, *American Journalism, a History: 1690–1960* (Macmillian: New York, 1962) p. 679.
12. Richard Davis, *The Press and American Politics* (Upper Saddle River, NJ: Prentice-Hall, 2001) p. 2.
13. See for instance, W. Lance Bennet, *News: The Politics of Illusion,* 6th edition (New York: Longman).
14. See for instance, Christopher P. Latimer, "The Digital Divide: Understanding and Addressing" http://www.nysfirm.org/documents/html/whitepapers/nysfirm_digital_divide.htm
15. Kathy Koch, "The Digital Divide," in *The CQ Researcher Online* 10.3 (2000). 10 July 2004 <http://libnt2.lib.tcu.edu:2426/cqresearcher/cqresrre2000012800>. Document ID: cqresrre2000012800.
16. "Falling Through the Net, III: Defining the Digital Divide," National Telecommunications and Information Administration, July 1999, 8.
17. Robert S. Lichter, Linda S. Lichter and Daniel Amundson, "Government Goes Down the Tube: Images of Government in TV Entertainment, 1955–1998," *The Harvard International Journal of Press/Politics 5* (2000): 96–103.
18. Graber, *Mass Media & American Politics,* 19 -21.
19. Leighley, *Mass Media and Politics,* 80.
20. Harold D. Lasswell, "The Structure and Function of Communication in Society," in Wilbur Schramm, ed., *Mass Communications* (Urbana: University of Illinois Press, 1969): 103.
21. Martin Gilens, *Why Americans Hate Welfare: Race, Media, and the Politics of Antipoverty Policy* (Chicago: University of Chicago Press, 1999) 112.
22. For a good analysis of the issue of race and media coverage, see Robert M. Entman and Andrew Rojecki's *The Black Image in the White Mind: Media and Race in America* (Chicago: University of Chicago Press, 2001).
23. Reported in Jerry L. Yeric, *Mass Media and the Politics of Change* (Itasca, Illinois: Peacock Publishers, 2001), chapter 6.
24. Harold W. Stanley and Richard G. Niemi, *Vital Statistics on American Politics, 2003–2004,* 6th edition (Washington, D.C.: CQ Press, 2003).
25. See Yeric, *Mass Media and the Politics of Change,* and Graber, *Mass Media & American Politics.*
26. David H. Weaver and G. Cleveland Wilhoit, *The American Journalist in the 1990s* (Mahwah, N.J.: Erlbaum, 1996).
27. See for instance Wolfram Peiser, "Setting the Journalist Agenda: Influences from Journalists' Individual Characteristics and from Media Factors," *Journalism and Mass Communication Quarterly* 77 (summer 2000): 243–257.
28. Graber, *Mass Media & American Politics,* 198.
29. Daniel Boorstin, *The Image: A Guide to Pseudo-Events in America* (New York: Vintage, 1961).
30. Ibid., 102.
31. Ibid., 271.
32. Leighley, *Mass Media and Politics,* 112.
33. David L. Protess, Fay Lomax Cook, Jack C. Doppelt, James S. Ettema, Margaret T. Gordon, Donna R. Leff, and Peter Miller, *The Journalism of Outrage: Investigative Reporting and Agenda Setting* (New York: Builford Press, 1919), p. 180.
34. See for instance Bennett, *News.*
35. Ibid.
36. See Linda Witt, Karen M. Paget, Glenna Matthews, *Running as a Woman: Gender and Power in American Politics* (New York: Free Press, 1994) for a good discussion of the impact the Thomas hearings had in mobilizing women voters and candidates.
37. See for instance Graber, *Mass Media & American Politics,* 311; see also Vincent James Strickler and Richard Davis, "The Supreme Court and the Press," in Mark J. Roxell, ed, *Media Power, Media Politics* (Lanham, MD: Rowman & Littlefield), 2003.
38. Graber, Ibid.
39. Howard Kurtz, "Paint by Numbers: How Repeated Reportage Colors Perceptions," *Washington Post,* Monday, July 12, 2004; Page C01.
40. Leighley, *Mass Media and Politics,* 4.
41. Daniel C. Hallin, "Sound Bite News: Television Coverage of Elections, 1968–1988," *Journal of Communication* 42 (1992) 15.
42. Robert S. Lichter and Richard E. Noyes, "There They Go Again: Media Coverage of Campaign '96," in Robert E. DeClerico ed., *Political*

Parties, Campaigns and Elections (Upper Saddle River, NJ: Prentice Hall, 2000): 98.

43. See Graber, *Mass Media & American Politics,* chapter 8 for a good discussion of debates.
44. Davis, *The Press and American Politics,* 93.
45. Ana Vecina-Suarez, *Hispanic Media USA: A Narrative Guide to Print and Electronic Media in the United States* (Washington, D.C.: Media Institute, 1987).
46. Ben H. Bagdikian, *The Media Monopoloy,* 5th edition (Boston: Beacon Press), p. x.
47. Graber, *Mass Media & American Politics,* 41. See also Yeric, *Mass Media and the Politics of Change,* chapter 1.
48. See Leighley, *Mass Media and Politics,* chapter 2 for a good discussion of deregulation.
49. Graber, *Mass Media & American Politics,* 49.
50. Davis, *The Press and American Politics,* 124.
51. Ibid., 127.
52. Reported at http://www.diversityweb.org/digest/sm02/changing.html

CHAPTER 12

1. See Jane Mansbridge, "A Deliberative Theory of Interest Representation," in *The Politics of Interests: Interest Groups Transformed,* ed. Mark P. Petracca (Boulder, CO: Westview Press, 1992), for a good discussion of the importance of organized groups in democratic theory.
2. Tocqueville, *Democracy in America,* vol. 1, p. 16.
3. His actual charge was to examine our penal system, but his true interest was to examine our democracy so that he could take lessons back to France.
4. Term originally coined by Arthur Schelsinger Sr., "Biography of a Nation of Joiners," *American Historical Review 50* (1944): 1–25.
5. Tocqueville, *Democracy in America,* vol. 1, pp. 220, 222–225.
6. Paul A. Gilje, *Rioting in America* (Bloomington: Indiana University Press, 1996), p. 25.
7. Ibid., p. 37.
8. Ibid., p. 38.
9. Henry J. Abraham and Barbara A. Perry, *Freedom and the Court: Civil Rights and Liberties in the United States,* 8th ed. (Lawrence: University Press of Kansas, 2003), p. 188.
10. "American Anti-Slavery Society," Encyclopaedia Britannica Online, http://search.eb.com, 2004.
11. Letter from Abigail Adams to John Adams on March 31, 1776.
12. The annual consumption of hard liquor in 1830 has been estimated at seven gallons for every man, woman, and child; Paul S. Boyer et al, *The Enduring Vision: A History of the American People,* 2d ed. (Boston: Heath, 1993), p. 334.
13. "Temperance Movement," Encyclopaedia Britannica Online, http://search.eb.com, 2004.
14. Peter Odegard, *Pressure Politics: The Story of the Anti-Saloon League* (New York: Columbia University Press, 1928).
15. "Prohibition," Encyclopaedia Britannica Online, http://search.eb.com, 2004.
16. For a good discussion of the early years of the AFL, see Lewis Loewin, *The American Federation of Labor: History, Policies, and Prospects* (New York: AMS Press, 1970). (Originally published 1933.)
17. Charles De Benedetti and Charles Chatfield, *An American Ordeal: The Antiwar Movement of the Vietnam Era* (Syracuse, NY: Syracuse University Press, 1999).
18. Quoted on http://www.naacp.org
19. For more information about the history of CORE, visit http://www.core-online.org/history/history.htm
20. NAACP, http://www.NAACP.org
21. National Organization for Women, http://www.now.org

22. John C. Green, "The Christian Right and the 1994 Elections," in Mark Rozell and Clyde Wilcox, *God at the Grass Roots: The Christian Right in the 1994 Elections* (Lanham, MD: Rowman & Littlefield, 1995), p. 16.
23. Christopher J. Soper, "The Politics of Pragmatism: The Christian Right and the 1994 Elections," in Philip A. Klinker, *Midterm: The Elections of 1994 in Context* (Bolder, CO: Westview Press, 1996).
24. James L. Guth, Lyman A. Delestedt, John C. Green, and Corwin E. Smidt, "A Distant Thunder? Religious Mobilization in the 2000 Elections," in Cigler and Loomis, *Interest Group Politics,* p. 175.
25. Alan Cooperman and Thomas B. Edsall, "Evangelicals Say They Led Charge for the GOP," *Washington Post,* November 8, 2004, p. A1.
26. Weaver, David H. and Wilhoit, G. Cleveland (1996). *The American Journalist in the 1990s,* (Mahwah, NJ: Lawrence Erlbaum Associates, Publishers) p. 8–11, 18 and 29.
27. Heather Svokos, "Texting Is Taking It to the Streets," *Fort Worth Star Telegram,* April 20, 2006, p. E1; see also Howard Rheingold, *Smart Mobs: The Next Social Revolution* (Cambridge, MA: Perseus, 2002).
28. *Los Angeles Times* Poll, December 12–15, 2002.
29. Quoted in Robert D. Putnam and Kristin A. Gross, "Introduction," in Robert D. Putnam, *Democracies in Flux* (New York: Oxford University Press, 2002), pp. 5–6.
30. Sidney Verba, Kay Lehman Schlozman, and Henry E. Brady, *Voice of Equality: Civic Voluntarism in American Politics* (Cambridge, MA: Harvard University Press, 1995).
31. Robert D. Putnam, *Bowling Alone: The Collapse and Revival of American Community* (New York: Simon & Schuster, 2000).
32. See Theda Skocpol and Morris P. Fiorina, *Civic Engagement in American Democracy* (Washington, DC: Brookings Institution Press, 1999), for a good discussion of the alternative methods used to examine civic engagement.
33. Theda Skocpol, "United States: From Membership to Advocacy," in Putnam, *Democracies in Flux,* pp. 103–136.
34. Robert Wuthnow, "United States: Bridging the Privileged and the Marginalized," in Putnam, *Democracies in Flux,* p. 74.
35. Ibid.
36. Ibid., p. 88.
37. Michael Kryzanek, *Angry, Bored, Confused: A Citizen Handbook of American Politics* (Boulder, CO: Westview Press, 1999), p. 60.
38. Wuthnow, "United States," p. 71, The American National Election Study (Table generated 27Nov05), http://www.umich.edu/-nes/nesguide/toptable/tab5a_1htm, accessed 7/7/06.
39. Theda Skocpol, "United States: From Membership to Advocacy," in Putnam's *Democracies in Flux.*
40. Robert D. Putnam, *Bowling Alone* (New York: Simon & Schuster, 2000).

CHAPTER 13

1. Kelly D. Patterson and Matthew M. Singer, "The National Rifle Association in the Face of the Clinton Challenge," in Cigler and Loomis, *Interest Group Politics,* p. 61.
2. Ibid.
3. Ibid., p. 62.
4. Jeffrey H. Birnbaum. "Fat and Happy in D.C.," *Fortune,* May 25, 2001, pp. 94–103.
5. Patterson and Singer, "National Rifle Association," pp. 70–71.
6. Ibid., p. 70.
7. Quoted in ibid., p. 72.
8. League of United Latin American Citizens, http://www.lulac.org
9. Frank R. Baumgartner and Beth L. Leech, *Basic Interests: The Importance of Groups in Politics and in Political Science* (Princeton, NJ: Princeton University Press, 1998), p. 103.

10. Robert Salisbury et al.
11. Jeffrey M. Berry, *Lobbying for the People: The Political Behavior of Public Interest Groups* (Princeton, NJ: Princeton University Press, 1977), p. 7.
12. David B. Truman, *The Governmental Process: Political Interests and Public Opinion*, 2d ed. (New York: Knopf, 1971).
13. Verba, Schlozman, and Brady, *Voice of Equality*, pp. 150–154.
14. James Q. Wilson, "Democracy and the Corporation," in Ronald Hessen, *Does Big Business Rule America?* (Washington, DC: Ethics and Public Policy Center, 1981), p. 37.
15. Allan J. Cigler and Mark Joslyn, "Group Involvement and Social Capital Development," in *Interest Group Politics*, ed. Allan J. Cigler and Burdett A. Loomis, 6th edition, 2002, Chapter 2.
16. Mancur Olson, *The Logic of Collective Action* (Cambridge, MA: Harvard University Press, 1971).
17. James Q. Wilson, *Political Organizations* (New York: Basic Books, 1974), p. 34.
18. Anthony Nownes, *Pressure and Power: Organized Interests in American Politics* (Boston: Houghton Mifflin, 2001), p. 50.
19. Ibid., 51.
20. Susan Schmidt and James V. Brimald, "Abramoff Pleads Guilty to 3 Counts," *Washington Post*, January 4, 2006, p. A1.
21. Jeffrey H. Birnbaum and Dan Balz, "Case Bringing New Scrutiny to a System and a Profession," *Washington Post*, January 4, 2006, p. A1.
22. Truman, *Governmental Process*, p. 213.
23. Ken Kollman, *Outside Lobbying: Public Opinion and Interest Group Strategies* (Princeton, NJ: Princeton University Press, 1998), p. 58.
24. Kenneth M. Goldstein, *Interest Groups, Lobbying, and Participation in America* (Cambridge: Cambridge University Press, 1999), p. 111.
25. Ibid., p. 125; see also Nownes, *Pressure and Power*.
26. Goldstein, *Interest Groups*, p. 65.
27. Ibid., p. 3.
28. Kollman, *Outside Lobbying*.
29. William P. Browne, *Groups, Interests, and U.S. Public Policy* (Washington, DC: Georgetown University Press, 1998), p. 23.
30. Clyde Brown and Herbert Waltzer, "Lobbying the Press: 'Talk to the People Who Talk to America,'" in Cigler and Loomis, *Interest Group Politics*, pp. 251–252.
31. Cliff Landesman, "Nonprofits and the World Wide Web," Internet Nonprofit Center, http://www.nonprofits.org/website.htm, 2000.
32. Christopher J. Bosso and Michael Thomas Collins, "Just Another Tool? How Environmental Groups Use the Internet," in Cigler and Loomis, *Interest Group Politics*, p. 101.
33. Darrell W. West and Burdett A. Loomis, *The Sound of Money* (New York: Norton, 1998).
34. Cigler and Joslyn, "Groups, Social Capital."
35. Verba, Schlozman, and Brady, *Voice of Equality*, pp. 81–82.
36. Jeffrey H. Birnbaum, *The Lobbyists* (New York: Times Books, 1992), p. 7.
37. "Gun Control vs. Gun Rights," Center for Responsive Politics, http://www.opensecrets.org/news/guns, October 6, 2004.

CHAPTER 14
1. "Corzine Prevails on $62 Million Senate Bid," *Bergen County (NJ) Record*, November 8, 2000, p. A1.
2. David M. Halbfinger, "The Ad Campaign: Florio's Words Used vs. Florio," *New York Times*, May 24, 2000, p. B6.
3. Quoted in Jeff Pillets, "Spending on Campaign and Country," *Bergen County (NJ) Record*, October 13, 2000, p. A3.
4. "For New Jersey, Bob Franks," *New York Post*, October 30, 2000, p. O48.
5. Halbfinger, "Ad Campaign," p. B6.

6. "Vice President Gore's Concession Speech," December 13, 2000. The American Presidency Project Web Site: http://www.presidency.ecsb.edu/showtransition2001.php?fileid=gore_concession 12–13, accessed July 19, 2006.
7. See, for example, Stephen Ansolabehere and Shanto Iyengar, *Going Negative: How Political Advertisements Shrink and Polarize the Electorate* (New York: Free Press, 1997), ch. 3.
8. Ibid., p. 60.
9. Myron A. Levin, *Presidential Campaigns and Elections*, 2d ed. (Itasca, IL: Peacock, 1995), p. 184; see also Kathleen A. Frankovic, "Public Opinion," in *The Election of 1980*, ed. Gerald Pomper (Chatham, NJ: Chatham House, 1981), pp. 97–102.
10. Howard L. Reiter, *Parties and Elections in Corporate America* (New York: St. Martin's Press, 1987), p. 4.
11. Quoted in James MacGregor Burns, *Cobblestone Leadership: Majority Rule, Minority Power* (Norman: University of Oklahoma Press, 1990), p. 5.
12. Alan P. Grimes, *Democracy and the Amendments to the Constitution* (Lexington, MA: Lexington Books, 1978), pp. 44, 45.
13. Ibid., pp. 94, 95.
14. Ibid., pp. 131, 142–147.
15. Alexsander Keyssar, *The Right to Vote: The Contested History of Democracy in the United States* (New York: Basic Books, 2000).
16. Ibid., p. 111.
17. Ibid., pp. 264–265.
18. Maisel, *Parties and Elections in America*, p. 97.
19. Frances Fox Piven and Richard A. Cloward, *Why Americans Still Don't Vote: And Why Politicians Want It That Way* (Boston, Beacon Press, 2000).
20. "Bubble-Up Democracy" [editorial], *Christian Science Monitor*, November 8, 2002, p. 10.
21. Jack Citrin, "Who's the Boss? Direct Democracy and Popular Control of Government," in *Broken Contract?* ed. Stephen C. Craig (Boulder, CO: Westview Press, 1996), p. 271.
22. John K. White and Daniel M. Shea, *New Party Politics: From Jefferson and Hamilton to the Information Age* (New York: Bedford St. Martin's, 2000), p. 210.
23. Quoted in Robert Dinkin, *Campaigning in America: A History of Election Practices* (Westport, CT: Greenwood Press, 1989), p. 8.
24. White and Shea, *New Party Politics*, 1st ed., p. 210.
25. Reiter, *Parties and Elections*, p. 171.
26. White and Shea, *New Party Politics*, 2d ed., p. 241.
27. The Center for Responsive Politics, http://www.opensecrets.org/pubs/history/history2.html
28. "Mark Hanna," Encyclopaedia Britannica Online, http://search.eb.com, 2004.
29. Norm Scheiber, "Organization Man," *New Republic Online*, http://www.tnr.com, March 22, 2004.
30. Anthony Corrado, "Financing the 1996 Elections," in *The Election of 1996: Reports and Interpretations*, ed. Gerald M. Pomper (Chatham, NJ: Chatham House, 1997), p. 151.
31. White and Shea, *New Party Politics*, 1st ed., p. 220.
32. "Tracking the Payback," Center for Responsive Politics, http://www.opensecrets.org/payback/index.asp, April 23, 2003.
33. David Mayhew, *Congress: The Electoral Connection* (New Haven, CT: Yale University Press, 1974).
34. Roper Center for Public Opinion Research, 1994, cited in Center for Responsive Politics, *The Myths about Money in Politics* (Washington, DC: Center for Responsive Politics, 1995), p. 19.
35. Bloomberg News Poll, conducted by Princeton Survey Research Associates, July 31–August 5, 2001.
36. "A Campaign Finance Triumph" [editorial], *New York Times*, December 11, 2003, p. 42.

37. Marian Currinder, "Campaign Finance: Funding the Presidential and Congressional Elections," in *The Election of 2004,* ed. Michael Nelson (Washington, DC: CQ Press, 2005), p. 122.
38. Ibid.
39. Daniel M. Shea and Michael John Burton, *Campaign Craft: The Strategies, Tactics, and Art of Political Campaign Management,* 3d ed. (Westport, CT: Praeger, 2006), p. 141.
40. This remark was made by California State Treasurer Jesse Unruh. See White and Shea, *New Party Politics,* 2000, p. 95.
41. These data, and much else, can be found at the National Election Study Cumulative Data File, 1952–2000, at http://www.umich.edu/~nes/nesguide/nesguide.htm
42. Putnam, *Bowling Alone,* p. 189.
43. Ibid., p. 194.
44. Ibid., p. 237.
45. Ibid., p. 196.
46. Ibid., p. 284.
47. John P. Frendreis, James L. Gibson, and Laura L. Vertz, "Electoral Relevance of Local Party Organizations," *American Political Science Review 84* (1990): 225–235; Stephen Brooks, Rick Farmer, and Kyriakos Pagonis, "The Effects of Grassroots Campaigning on Political Participation," paper presented at the annual meeting of the Southern Political Science Association, November 8–10, 2001, Atlanta.
48. Ibid., p. 127.
49. For details of these studies, see Richard Lau, Lee Sigelman, Caroline Heldman, and Paul Babbit, "The Effects of Negative Political Advertising: A Meta-Analytic Assessment," *American Political Science Review 93* (1999): 851–875.
50. Ansolabehere and Iyenger, *Going Negative,* ch. 5.
51. Kelly D. Patterson and Daniel M. Shea, "Local Political Context and Negative Campaigns: A Test of Negative Effects across State Party Systems," *Journal of Political Marketing 3* (2004): 1–20.
52. Larry J. Sabato, *Feeding Frenzy: How Attack Journalism Has Transformed American Politics* (New York: Free Press, 1993).
53. William H. Flanigan and Nancy H. Zingal, *Political Behavior and the American Electorate,* (Washington, DC: CQ Press, 1998), p. 40.
54. Steven J. Rosenstone and John Mark Hansen, *Mobilization, Participation, and Democracy in America* (New York: Macmillan, 1993), p. 247.
55. George F. Will, "In Defense of Nonvoting," *Newsweek,* October 10, 1983, p. 96.
56. E. J. Dionne, *Why Americans Hate Politics* (New York: Simon & Schuster, 1991), p. 355.

CHAPTER 15

1. Much of this tale is adapted from John M. Swomley, "Anatomy of a Stealth Candidate," *Humanist,* May-June 1995, pp. 32–34.
2. Immanuel Ness, *The Encyclopedia of Interest Groups and Lobbyists,* vol. 2 (New York: Sharpe, 2002), p. 481.
3. Ibid.
4. Swomley, "Anatomy of a Stealth Candidate," p. 33.
5. Michael Barone and Grant Ujifusa, *The Almanac of American Politics, 1996* (Washington, DC: National Journal, 1997), p. 783.
6. Swomley, "Anatomy of a Stealth Candidate," p. 33.
7. Ibid.
8. Barone and Ujifusa, *Almanac of American Politics,* p. 783.
9. Walter Dean Burnham, "Realignment Lives: The 1994 Earthquake and Its Implications," in *The Clinton Presidency: First Appraisals,* ed. Colin Campbell and Bert A. Rockman (Chatham, NJ: Chatham House, 1996), p. 363.
10. Colin Campbell and Bert A. Rockman, "Introduction," in ibid., p. 14.
11. White and Shea, *New Party Politics,* 1st ed, p. 19.

12. See, for example, John P. Frendreis, James L. Gibson, and Laura L. Vertz, "Electoral Relevance of Local Party Organizations," *American Political Science Review 84* (1990):225–235.
13. Clyde Wilcox, *The Latest American Revolution: The 1994 Elections and Their Implications for Governance* (New York: St. Martin's Press, 1995), p. 1.
14. James G. Gimple, *Fulfilling the Contract: The First 100 Days* (Needham Heights, MA: Allan & Bacon, 1996), p. 95.
15. White and Shea, *New Party Politics,* 1st ed., p. 20.
16. Daniel M. Shea, "The Passing of Realignment and the Advent of the 'Base-Less' Party System," *American Politics Quarterly 27* (1999): 33–57.
17. White and Shea, *New Party Politics,* 1st ed., p. 174.
18. Ibid., pp. 302–311.
19. This examination of party periods parallels the approach used in White and Shea, *New Party Politics,* 1st ed.
20. Thomas Jefferson, *Notes on the State of Virginia,* 1787, ch. 19.
21. William Nisbet Chambers, *Political Parties in a New Nation: The American Experience, 1776–1809* (New York: Oxford University Press, 1963).
22. E. E. Schattschneider, *Party Government* (New York: Rinehart, 1942), p. 1.
23. White and Shea, *New Party Politics,* 1st ed., p. 41.
24. George C. Edwards III and Stephen J. Wayne, *Presidential Leadership: Politics and Policy Making* (New York: St. Martin's Press, 1999), p. 61.
25. White and Shea, *New Party Politics,* 1st ed., p. 45.
26. George H. Mayer, *The Republican Party, 1954–1964.* (New York: Oxford University Press, 1964), p. 26.
27. White and Shea, *New Party Politics,* 1st ed., p. 66.
28. David S. Broder, *The Party's Over: The Failure of Politics in America* (New York: Harper & Row, 1972).
29. Xandra Kayden and Eddie Mahe Jr., *The Party Goes On: The Persistence of the Two-Party System in the United States* (New York: Basic Books, 1985); Larry J. Sabato, *The Party's Just Begun* (Glenview, IL: Scott, Foresman, 1988); L. Sandy Maisel, ed., *The Parties Respond: Changes in the American Party System* (Boulder, CO: Westview Press, 1990).
30. Kayden and Mahe, *The Party Goes On,* p. 3.
31. Theodore J. Lowi, "Toward a Responsible Three-Party system," in Daniel M. Shea and John C. Green, eds.,*The State of the Parties: The Changing Role of Contemporary American Parties* (Lanham, MD: Rowman and Littlefield, 1994), p. 50.
32. Jack Plan and Milton Greenbert, *The American Political Dictionary,* 10th ed. (Orlando, FL: Harcourt Brace, 1997), p. 7.
33. Theodore J. Lowi, "Toward a Responsible Three-Party System: Plan or Obituary?" in *The State of the Parties,* 3d ed., ed. John C. Green and Daniel M. Shea (Lanham, MD: Rowman & Littlefield, 1999), pp. 171–189.
34. Felix Schein, "Howard Dean," *Hardball,* MSNBC, http://msnbc.msn.com/id/3607157, December 1, 2003.
35. Gary Wolf, "How the Internet Invented Howard Dean," *Wired,* http://www.wired.com/wired/archive/12.01/dean.html, January 2004.
36. Ibid.
37. Schattschneider, *Party Government,* p. 1.

CHAPTER 16

1. "Congratulations" [editorial], *Washington Post,* November 23, 2003, p. B6.
2. Harole Lasswell, *Politics: Who Gets What, When, and How* (New York: Smith, 1950).
3. Matt Pacenza, "GE: Bill Adds to Knowledge," *Albany (NY) Times Union,* May 13, 2005, p. A1.
4. For a well-known example, see Charles E. Lindblom and Edward J. Woodhouse, *The Policy-Making Process,* 3d ed. (Englewood Cliffs, NJ: Prentice Hall, 1993).
5. Deborah Stone, *Policy Paradox: The Art of Political Decision Making* (New York: Norton, 1997), p. 11.

6. Theda Skocpol, *Boomerang: Health Care Reform and the Turn against Government* (New York: Norton, 1997).

7. Jennifer Brooks, "Senate Passes Bankruptcy Bill Making It Harder to Shed Debts," *USA Today,* March 10, 2005, p. 1.

8. Isaiah Berlin, *Four Essays on Liberty* (Oxford: Oxford University Press, 1969).

9. Tocqueville, *Democracy in America.*

10. Robert Nozick, *Anarchy, State, and Utopia* (New York: Basic Books, 1974).

11. Stone, *Policy Paradox,* p. 53.

12. This is an iteration of Milton Rokeach's "two-value" model of political ideology; see Milton Rokeach, *The Nature of Human Values* (New York: Free Press, 1973).

13. Theodore J. Lowi, "American Business, Public Policy Case Studies, and Political Theory," *World Politics 16* (1965): 677–715.

14. Murray Edelman, *The Symbolic Uses of Politics* (Urbana: University of Illinois Press, 1967), ch. 2.

15. See Robert A. Dahl, *Who Governs? Democracy and Power in an American City* (New Haven, CT: Yale University Press, 1961).

16. See C. Wright Mills, *The Power Elite* (Oxford: Oxford University Press, 1956).

17. Roger W. Cobb and Charles D. Elder, *Participation in American Politics: The Dynamics of Agenda Building* (Baltimore: Johns Hopkins University Press, 1983), pp. 82–93.

18. For a fascinating discussion of how power is exercised by controlling the agenda, see Peter Bachrach and Morton S. Baratz, "Two Faces of Power," *American Political Science Review 56* (1962): 947–952.

19. Robert A. Caro, *Master of the Senate: The Years of Lyndon Johnson* (New York: Knopf, 2002), ch. 7.

20. Cobb and Elder, *Participation in American Politics,* p. 86.

21. Anthony Downs, "Up and Down with Ecology: The 'Issue-Attention Cycle,'" *Public Interest,* Summer 1972, pp. 38–50.

22. See Samuel Kernell, *Going Public: New Strategies of Presidential Leadership* (Washington, DC: CQ Press, 1986).

23. Michael D. Cohen, James G. March, and Johan P. Olsen, "A Garbage Can Model of Organizational Choice," *Administrative Science Quarterly 17* (1972): 1–25.

24. John W. Kingdon, *Agendas, Alternatives, and Public Policies* (New York: Harper & Row, 1984), pp. 129–130.

25. Ibid., ch. 8.

26. John R. Hibbing and Elizabeth Theiss-Morse, *Congress as Public Enemy* (New York: Cambridge University Press, 1995).

27. For a through discussion of the incremental approach, see Charles E. Lindblom, "The Science of Muddling Through," *Public Administration Review 19* (1959): 79–88.

CHAPTER 17

1. Adam Smith, *Wealth of Nations,* bk. 4, ch. 2.

2. Remarks by Federal Reserve Board Chairman Alan Greenspan at the Opening of an American Numismatic Society Exhibition, Federal Reserve Bank of New York, New York, January 16, 2002.

3. Budget at the United States Government, Fiscal Year 2007, Table 3.2—outlays by Function and Subfunction, 1962–2011 www.whitehouse.gov/omb/budget/for2007/hist.html

4. Warren Buffett, letter to Berkshire Hathaway shareholders, December 1990.

5. Unless otherwise indicated, all figures in this section are from Congressional Budget Office, *Long-Term Budget Outlook* (Washington, DC: Congressional Budget Office, 2005).

6. Laurence J. Kotlikoff and Scott Burns, *The Coming Generational Storm: What You Need to Know about America's Economic Future* (Cambridge, MA: MIT Press, 2005).

7. Remarks by Alan Greenspan at the Advancing Enterprise Conference, London, December 2, 2005.

8. Matthew Benjamin, "Huh? Greenspan Left Many Guessing," *Dallas Morning News,* January 29, 2006, p. 6D.

CHAPTER 18

1. The details of this account are drawn from *The 9/11 Commission Report* (New York: Norton, 2004).

2. Charles Krauthammer, "The Unipolar Moment Revisited," *National Interest,* Winter 2002–2003, pp. 5–18; Max Boot, *The Savage Wars of Peace* (New York: Basic Books, 2002).

3. G. John Ikenberry, *After Victory: Institutions, Strategic Restraint, and the Rebuilding of Order after Major Wars* (Princeton, NJ: Princeton University Press, 2001).

4. Robert Tucker and David Hendrickson, "The Sources of American Legitimacy," *Foreign Affairs 83* (2004): 18–32; Henry Nau, "No Enemies on the Right," *National Interest,* (Winter 2004–2005), pp. 19–28.

5. Gary Dempsey with Roger Fontaine, *Fool's Errands: America's Recent Encounters with Nation Building* (Washington, DC: Cato Press, 2001).

6. Walter Russell Mead, *Special Providence* (New York: Routledge, 2002).

7. Glenn Hastedt, ed., *One World, Many Voices* (Englewood Cliffs, NJ: Prentice Hall, 1995), pp. 240–250, 288–300.

8. Peter Trubowitz, *Defining the National Interest* (Chicago: University of Chicago Press, 1998).

9. Miroslav Nincic, "Domestic Costs, the U.S. Public and the Isolationist Calculus," *International Studies Quarterly 41* (1997): 593–610; Bruce Jentleson, "The Pretty Prudent Public: Post-Vietnam American Opinion on the Use of Force," *International Studies Quarterly 36* (1990): 49–74.

10. For a more extensive discussion, see Glenn Hastedt, *American Foreign Policy: Past, Present, Future,* 6th ed. (Upper Saddle River, NJ: Prentice Hall, 2006).

11. Thomas Graham, "Public Opinion and U.S. Foreign Policy," in *The New Politics of American Foreign Policy,* ed. David Deese (New York: St. Martin's Press, 1994), pp. 190–215.

12. William Quandt, "The Electoral Cycle and the Conduct of American Foreign Policy," *Political Science Quarterly 101* (1986): 825–837.

13. David Cohen, Chris Dolan, and Jerel Rosati, "A Place at the Table," *Congress and the Presidency 29* (2002): 119–149.

14. Paul Kengor, "The Vice President, the Secretary of State, and Foreign Policy," *Political Science Quarterly 115* (2000): 175–190.

15. Amy Zegart, *Flawed by Design: The Evolution of the CIA, JCS, and NSC* (Stanford, CA: Stanford University Press, 2000).

16. Loch Johnson and James Wirtz, eds., *Strategic Intelligence: Windows into a Secret World* (Los Angeles: Roxbury, 2004).

17. Glenn Hastedt, "The Department of Homeland Security: Politics of Creation," in Ralph Carter, *Contemporary Cases in American Foreign Policy* (Washington, DC: CQ Press, 2004).

18. James Scott and Ralph Carter, "Acting on the Hill," *Congress and the Presidency 29* (2002): 151–169.

19. Audrey Kurth Cronin and James Ludes, eds., *Attacking Terrorism* (Washington, DC: Georgetown University Press, 2004).

20. Ashton Carter, "How to Counter WMD," *Foreign Affairs,* September 2004, pp. 72–85.

21. Lael Brainard, "Compassionate Conservatism Confronts Global Poverty," *Washington Quarterly,* Spring 2003, pp. 149–169.

22. Scott Straus, "Darfur and the Genocide Debate," *Foreign Affairs,* January-February 2005, pp. 123–133.

23. David Masci, "Human Trafficking and Slavery," *CQ Researcher 14* (2004): 273–296.

COVER: Scott Bookman and Katvan Studios/Workbookstock

CHAPTER 1: *2* (CO) Chris Hondros/Reportage/Getty Images, Inc.; *4* © Tom Stewart/CORBIS/All Rights Reserved; *10* (left) © Rebecca Cook/CORBIS/All Rights Reserved; (right) Arthur Tsang/Corbis/Reuters America LLC; *14* (above) Corbis RF; (center) Barrie Fanton/Omni-Photo Communications, Inc.; (below) Dirck Halstead/Getty Images/Time Life Pictures; *15* (above) Stephen Ferry/Getty Images, Inc.; (below) Michael Smith/Getty Images, Inc.; *18* (above) Rex Hardy Jr./Getty Images/Time Life Pictures; (below) Tyler Hicks/The New York Times; *21* (above) Carol T. Powers/The New York Times; (below) Carmel Zucker/The New York Times; *25* (above) © Joseph Sohm/Visions of America/CORBIS/All Rights Reserved; (below) © Joseph Sohm/Visions of America/CORBIS/All Rights Reserved; *27* Doug Mills/New York Times

CHAPTER 2: *33* (CO) North Wind Picture Archives; *42* Courtesy of the Pilgrim Society, Plymouth, Massachusetts; *43* Salvatore DiMarco, Jr./The New York Times; *44* The Granger Collection; *47* Jonathan Player/The New York Times; *49* © CORBIS/All Rights Reserved; *50* (above) John C. McRae/The Granger Collection; (below) Craig Nelson/Cox Newspapers, Inc.; *52* (above) © Greg Smith/CORBIS/All Rights Reserved; (below) Jim Bourg/The Getty Images Inc.; *53* CORBIS/Reuters America LLC; *55* CORBIS/All Rights Reserved; *59* © Martin H. Simon/CORBIS/All Rights Reserved; *64* (left) Kenneth Garrett/National; (right) ; *70* The Granger Collection, New York

CHAPTER 3: *78* (CO) © Michael Mulvey/Dallas Morning News/CORBIS/All Rights Reserved; *80* Max Whittaker/The New York Times; *83* Greg Gibson/AP Wide World Photos; *86* Architect of the Capital; *89* (above) © Alexander Gardner/CORBIS/All Rights Reserved; (below) © Bettmann/CORBIS/All Rights Reserved; *90* © Ron Edmonds/Bettmann/CORBIS/All Rights Reserved; *91* Lewis Hine (American, 1874–1940), "A Carolina Spinner," 1908. Gelatin silver print, 4 3/4 x 7in. Milwaukee Art Museum, Gift of the Sheldon M. Barnett Family. M1973.83; *99* © Frank Wolfe/CORBIS/All Rights Reserved; *100* © Greg Smith/CORBIS/All Rights Reserved; *103* David Burnett/Contact Press Images, Inc.; *104* Larry Downing/CORBIS/Reuters America LLC

CHAPTER 4: *110* (CO) Yuri Gripas/Corbis/Reuters America LLC; *112* © Philip James Corwin/CORBIS/All Rights Reserved; *115* Ben Curtis/Pool/ Corbis/Reuters America LLC; *120* (left) Paul J. Richards/Agence France Presse/Getty Images; (center) Mark Willson/Getty Images, Inc.; (right) © Matthew Cavanaugh/epa/CORBIS/All Rights Reserved; *121* (left) Mark Wilson/Getty Images, Inc.; (center) Mark Wilson/Getty Images, Inc; (right) Mark Wilson/Getty Images, Inc.; *122* The Granger Collection, New York; *127* John Marshall by Chester Harding (1792–1886), Oil on Canvas, 1830. U.R. 106.1830. Collection of the Boston Athenaeum; *129* Stock Montage/Getty Images, Inc.; *132* Doug Mills/The New York Times; *140* Stephen Crowley/The New York Times; *142* Ed Clark/Getty Images/Time Life Pictures; *143* Robert Lindneux, American. Trail of Tears. Woolaroc Museum, Bartlesville, Oklahoma; *144* Doug Mills/The New York Times

CHAPTER 5: *152* (CO) CORBIS/All Rights Reserved; *154* (below) Corbis/Reuters America LLC; *156* Joe Raedle/Getty Images, Inc.; *157* Copyright © North Wind/North Wind Picture Archives—All Rights Reserved; *158* John Nordell/The Christian Science Monitor/Getty Images, Inc.; *159* CORBIS/All Rights Reserved; *160* Franklin D. Roosevelt Library; *162* Getty Images, Inc.–Hulton Archive Photos; *163* (above) David Leeson/Getty Images/Time Life Pictures; *166* (above) Anne Fishbein; (right) Stefan Zaklin/Getty Images, Inc.; (below) Kevin Moloney/Getty Images, Inc.; *167* CORBIS/All Rights Reserved; *168* Corbis/Bettmann;

169 David J. Phillip/AP Wide World Photos; *173* Scott Gries/Getty Images, Inc.; *174* (left) Alex Wong/Getty Images, Inc.; (right) Dave Martin/AP Wide World Photos; *175* (left) Cover of "The War on Christmas" by John Gibson. Jacket design by Joseph Perez. Jacket illustration by Mirko LLic. Published by Sentinel HC, a division of Penguin Books, USA; (right) Chip Somodevilla/Getty Images, Inc.; *176* Corbis/Bettmann; *178* Kevin Wolf/AP Wide World Photos; *179* (above) Joe Raedle/Getty Images, Inc.; (below) DeMoss News Pond; *181* Oleg Volk/Volk Studio; *183* (above) John Marshall Mantel/AP Wide World Photos; (below) Chip Somodevilla/Getty Images, Inc.; *185* © Judith Miller/Dorling Kindersley/Posteritati; *187* Robert Gailbraith/REUTERS/CORBIS–NY; *188* (left) Don Ryan/AP Wide World Photos; (right) Courtesy of Florida Department of Corrections, Central Records; *189* Getty Image/Time Life Pictures; *191* AP Wide World Photos; *192* Corbis/Bettmann; *194* (above) Chip Somodevilla/Getty Images, Inc.; (below) Robert Kusel/Getty Images, Inc.–Stone Allstock; *196* (right) CORBIS/All Rights Reserved; *197* (right) Jim Wilson/The New York Times

CHAPTER 6: *204* Corbis/Bettmann; *206* Bregg/AP Wide World Photos; *208* Doug Mills/The New York Times; *209* Corbis/Bettmann; *210* William Thomas Cain/Getty Images, Inc.; *213* (above) Steve Cole/Getty Images, Inc.–Photodisc; (middle) Scott Cohen/AP Wide World Photos; (below) Getty Images, Inc.–Hulton Archive Photos and AP Wide World Photos; *214* Karen Kasmauski/CORBIS/All Rights Reserved; *216* Katherine Wetzel/The Museum of the Confederacy, Richmond, Virginia; *217* Otis Noel Pruitt/Corbis/Bettmann; *218* (above) Corbis/Bettmann; (below) Bettman/Corbis, All Rights Reserved; *219* © Flip Schulke/CORBIS-NY/All Rights Reserved; *220* Paul J. Richards/Agence France Presse/Getty Images, Inc.; *221* © CORBIS/All Rights Reserved; *223* © Bettmann/CORBIS All Rights Reserved; *228* (above) Joe Migon © Bettmann/CORBIS/All Rights Reserved; (below) © Bettmann/CORBIS/All Rights Reserved; *229* Corbis/Bettmann; *230* MPI/Getty Images, Inc.; *231* Lori Waselchuk/The New York Times; *232* Bob Gomel/Getty Images/Time Life Pictures; *235* © Underwood & Underwood/CORBIS/All Rights Reserved] *237* © Steve Schapiro/CORBIS/All Rights Reserved; *238* (above) © Bettmann/CORBIS/All Rights Reserved; (below) Monica Almeda/The New York Times; *242* Stephen Crowley/The New York Times

CHAPTER 7: *248* (CO) Jamie Rose/The New York Times; *250* Eddie Adams/Corbis/Sygma; *254* The Marblehead Museum & Historical Society; Kevin Rivoli/AP Wide World Photos; © Bettmann/CORBIS/All Rights Reserved; Reuters Limited; *260* (right) Rick Scibelli, Jr./The New York Times; © Bettmann/CORBIS/All Rights Reserved; *269* CORBIS/All Rights Reserved; *271* Paul Hosefros/The New York Times; *273* Stephen Crowley/The New York Times; *276* Mannie Garcia/Corbis/Reuters America LLC; *279* (above) Karen Bleier/Agence France Presse/Getty Images; (below) Shaun Heasley/Getty Images, Inc.; *284* © Bettmann/CORBIS/All Rights Reserved

CHAPTER 8: *296* (CO) AP Wide World Photos; *298* Paul J. Richards/Agence France Presse/Getty Images; *301* Shawn Thew/Agence France Presse/Getty Images; Stefan Zaklin/Getty Images, Inc.; Larry Downing/Corbis/Reuters America LLC; Paul J. Richards/Agence France Presse/Getty Images; Freddie Lee/Fox News/Getty Images, Inc.; Mark Wilson/Getty Images, Inc.; *302* Courtesy of the Library of Congress; *307* © Bettmann/CORBIS/All Rights Reserved; *311* Getty Images, Inc./Hulton Archive; *312* Corbis/Bettmann; *313* (above) Alex Wong/Getty Images, Inc.; (below) Pablo Martinez Monsivais/AP Wide World Photos; *314* Stephan Crowley/The New York Times; *315* AP Wide World Photos; *316* Larry Downing/Corbis/Reuters America LLC; *321* North Wind Archive; *324* © Attila Kisbenedek/epa/CORBIS/All Rights

Reserved; *325* Pfc. L. Paul Epley/AP Wide World Photos; *327* AP Wide World Photos

CHAPTER 9: *336* (CO) Dan Levine/Agence France Presse/Getty Images; *338* Tyler Hicks/The New York Times; *340* CORBIS/All Rights Reserved; *345* © Cecil Stoughton/CORBIS/All Rights Reserved; *346* © Frank Wolfe/CORBIS/All Rights Reserved; *349* Doug Mills/The New York Times; *350* Mike Temchine/Agence France Presse/Getty Images; *351* Bill Ingalls/NASA/Getty Images, Inc.; *352* Mario Tama/Getty Images, Inc.; *361* Omni-Photo Communications, Inc.; *367* Joe Raedle/Getty Images, Inc.

CHAPTER 10: *372* (CO) Corbis/Bettmann; *374* © epa/CORBIS/All Rights Reserved; *379* Focus on Sport/Getty Images, Inc.; *383* (left) Photo by Time Life Pictures/Time Magazine. Copyright Time Inc./Time Life Pictures/Getty Images, Inc.; (right) Chad Buchanan/Getty Images, Inc.; *386* Alex Wong/Getty Images, Inc.; *389* Robyn Beck/Agence France Presse/Getty Images; *391* Scott Gries/Getty Images, Inc.; *395* Kenneth Dickerman/The New York Times; *403* AP Wide World Photos; *404* © Tribune Media Services, Inc. All Rights Reserved. Reprinted with Permission; *405* Culver Pictures, Inc.; *406* © The New Yorker Collection 1980 Charles Borsotti from Cartoonbank.com. All Rights Reserved; *407* Rob Rogers: © The Pittsburgh Post-Gazette/Dist. by United Features Syndicate, Inc.

CHAPTER 11: *416* (CO) The National Security Archive; *418* (above) © Bettmann/CORBIS/All Rights Reserved; (below) © Steve Sands/New York Newswire/CORBIS/All Rights Reserved; *421* © Bettmann/COR-BIS/All Rights Reserved; *426* (above) © Bettmann/CORBIS/All Rights Reserved; (below) Warner Independent Pictures/Warner Bros.; *430* © Bettmann/ CORBIS/All Rights Reserved; *432* (above) © Dorothea Lange/CORBIS/All Rights Reserved; (below) © Dorothea Lange/COR-BIS/All Rights Reserved; *437* © Shawn Thew/CNP/CORBIS/All Rights Reserved; *439* CORBIS/Bettmann; *441* (above) Greg Gibson/AP Wide World Photos; (below) Rick Wilkins/Reuters/Corbis/Bettmann; *442* Paul Hosefros/The New York Times

CHAPTER 12: *456* (CO) Sion Touhig/Corbis/Sygma; *458* Courtesy of Rock the Vote; *460* Corbis/Bettmann; *461* © Bettmann/CORBIS/All Rights Reserved; *462* Corbis/Bettmann; *464* Francis Miller/ Getty Images/Time Life Pictures; *468* © Bettmann/CORBIS/All Rights Reserved; *469* © Hulton-Deutsch Collection/Bettmann/CORBIS/All Rights Reserved; *471* UPI/Corbis/Bettmann; *473* Bettmann/CORBIS/All Rights Reserved; *475* Steven Clevenger/CORBIS/All Rights Reserved; *476* © Bettmann/CORBIS/All Rights Reserved; *478* © Bettmann/CORBIS/All Rights Reserved; *479* Joe Marquette/© Bettmann/CORBIS/All Rights Reserved; *480* (above) Jane Therese/The New York Times; (below) Mike Simons/Getty Images, Inc.; *482* Monica Almeida/The New York Times

CHAPTER 13: *498* (CO) James Estrin/The New York Times; *500* Corbis/Reuters America LLC; *503* © Brandon Thibodeaux/Dallas Morning News/CORBIS/All Rights Reserved; *505* Time Life Pictures/Time Magazine/Getty Images; *513* Bob Parent/Hulton Archive/Getty Images; *514* Doug Mills/The New York Times; *516* Carol T. Powers/The New York Times; *518* Brendan Smialowski/Getty Images, Inc.; *519* Tim Mosenfelder/Getty Images/ImageDirect; *521* Larry Downing/Corbis/Reuters America LLC

CHAPTER 14: *532* (CO) Vincent Laforet/The New York Times; *534* Laura Pedrick/Corbis/Sygma; *536* Alfredo Dagli Orti/The Art Archive/

CORBIS/All Rights Reserved; *537* James Glen/Corbis/Sygma; *539* Andrew Parsons/Agence France Presse/Getty Images, Inc.; *541* Cristian Pena/Courtesy of Thoseshirts.com; *548* Flip Schulke/Corbis/Bettmann; *551* Kevin Cannon; *555* (above) © CORBIS/All Rights Reserved; (below) Corbis/Reuters American LLC; *559* Paul Hosefros/The New York Times; *570* William Thomas Cain/Getty Images, Inc.

CHAPTER 15: *578* (CO) Mark Georgiev/The New York Times Agency; *580* © Andrew Lichtenstein/CORBIS/All Rights Reserved; *584* Stan Honda/Agence France Presse/Getty Images; *587* Doug Mills/ The New York Times; *588* © Erik Freeland/CORBIS/All Rights Reserved; *592* Peter Thompson/The New York Times; *595* © Bettmann/CORBIS/All Rights Reserved; *597* © Bettmann/CORBIS/All Rights Reserved; *602* Hulton Archive/Getty Images; *603* © Bettmann/CORBIS/All Rights Reserved; *610* © Bettmann/CORBIS/All Rights Reserved; *612* Nancy Kaszerman/ZUMA/CORBIS/All Rights Reserved

CHAPTER 16: *620* (CO) © Daron Dean/Dallas Morning News/COR-BIS/All Rights Reserved; *627* Kevin Lamarque/Corbis/Reuters America LLC; *629* Alfred Eisenstaedt/Getty Images/Time Life Pictures; *631* Robert Sullivan/Agence France Presse/Getty Images; *633* © Bettmann/ CORBIS/All Rights Reserved; *635* Paul Schutzer/Getty Images/Time Life Pictures; *636* (above) Kevin Lamarque/Corbis/Reuters America LLC; (below) George Skadding/Getty Images/Time Life Pictures; *637* © Dorothea Lange/CORBIS/All Rights Reserved

CHAPTER 17: *648* (CO) Mario Tama/Getty Images, Inc.; *650* Chip Somodevilla/Getty Images, Inc.; page: *652* Time Magazine/Getty Images/Time Life Pictures; *653* Time Magazine/Getty Images/Time Life Pictures; *660* © Stephen Chernin/Getty Images, Inc.; *661* Ian Waldie/ Getty Images, Inc.; *662* Walter Bennett/Getty Images/Time Life Pictures; *663* Paul J. Richards/Agence France Presse/Getty Images, Inc.; *666* Patrick M. Bonafede/U.S. Navy/Getty Images, Inc.; *671* Ralph Notaro/ Getty Images, Inc.; *675* (above) Chip Somodevilla/Getty Images, Inc.; (below) Mark Wilson/Getty Images, Inc.; *679* Raveendran/Agence France Presse/Getty Images

CHAPTER 18: *684* (CO) Spencer Platt/Getty Images, Inc.; *686* © Rob Howard/CORBIS/All Rights Reserved; *689* (above) Robert Maass/ CORBIS/All Rights Reserved; (below) Jason Reed/Corbis/Reuters America LLC; *692* Caren Firouz/Corbis/Reuters America LLC; *694* © Lee Snider/Photo Images/CORBIS/All Rights Reserved; *695* (above, left) © Bettmann/CORBIS/All Rights Reserved; (above, right) Tim Rights/ CORBIS/All Rights Reserved; (below) © Archivo Iconografico, S.A./ CORBIS/All Rights Reserved; *697* © Brooks Kraft/CORBIS/All Rights Reserved; *698* J.P. Moczulski/Corbis/Reuters America LLC; *699* (above) Jim Gipe/CORBIS/All Rights Reserved; (below) Howard Burditt/Corbis/ Reuters America LLC; *702* James A. Finley/Pool/Corbis/Reuters America LLC; *703* Jim Hubbard/© Bettmann/CORBIS/All Rights Reserved; *705* © David Butow/ Corbis/SABA Press Photos, Inc.; *706* Kevin Lamarque/ Corbis/Reuters America LLC; *707* (above) Bob Strong/Corbis/Reuters America LLC; (below) © Wally Mcnamee/CORBIS/ All Rights Reserved; *711* © Ramin Talaie/CORBIS/All Rights Reserved; *712* Hyungwon Kang/Corbis/Reuters America LLC; *715* U.S. Navy/Corbis/Reuters America LLC; *716* © Adraian Bradshaw/epa/CORBIS/All Rights Reserved; *719* Adrees Latif/Corbis/Reuters America LLC